INDEX OF

DEATH, MARRIAGE, AND MISCELLANEOUS

NOTICES APPEARING IN THE

LIBERTY HALL AND CINCINNATI GAZETTE

1804 – 1857

INDEX OF

DEATH, MARRIAGE, AND MISCELLANEOUS

NOTICES APPEARING IN THE

LIBERTY HALL AND CINCINNATI GAZETTE

1804 – 1857

Indexed by

Jeffrey G. Herbert

HAMILTON COUNTY CHAPTER OF
THE OHIO GENEALOGICAL SOCIETY

Cincinnati, Ohio
2014

Published by the
Hamilton County Chapter, OGS
P.O. Box 15865
Cincinnati, OH 45215-0865
513-956-7078
http://hcgsohio.org

Printed in the United States of America.
ISBN-13: 978-0615998046

Table of Contents

Introduction

This index is intended to give the researcher another means of discovering information about their early Hamilton County, Ohio ancestors who lived in the greater Cincinnati area between 1804 and 1857. Many families, while not settling here permanently lived in the area for a time, and had spouses and children who were married or died here while they were passing through this region. Traces of these early pioneer families are hard to find through cemetery or court records during the first half of the nineteenth century. This index is intended to serve as another tool in the family history researcher's toolbox.

The scope of this index covers death, marriage, and other miscellaneous notices that were published during this time period in the early Cincinnati newspaper named *Liberty Hall and Cincinnati Gazette*. This index contains over 15,750 deaths, over 4200 marriages, and over 3000 miscellaneous notices which were reported and published in this early Cincinnati newspaper. It should be noted that the names in this index are not only from the Cincinnati and Hamilton County area, but for much of the former Northwest Territory during the early years, and as far north as Dayton, as far east as Columbus and Chillicothe, south to Lexington and Shelbyville, Kentucky, and west as far as Indianapolis and Richmond, Indiana during the later years.

The information in this index was compiled using the most complete set of collections from both the Public Library of Cincinnati and Hamilton County (PLCH) and the Cincinnati History Library and Archives in the Cincinnati Museum Center (CHLA), and using both the microfilm collection as well as the original hardbound paper copies when the microfilm copies were not available. This provides the most comprehensive and complete index using all the available existing sources. Researchers should first request the microfilm copies in order to avoid wear on the hardbound paper copies.

On December 4, 1804 Reverend John W. Browne started the *Liberty Hall* newspaper under the title *Liberty Hall and Cincinnati Mercury* as a weekly publication. During its long history in the first part of the 19th century, it had various names, but all began with the Liberty Hall title. John Browne died on January 3, 1813, and James H. Looker took over publication, merged with other partners, and eventually sold his interest in the newspaper. In December 1815, the Cincinnati Gazette was consolidated with this paper, and the name was changed to *Liberty Hall and Cincinnati Gazette*. At this point the newspaper had over 1400 subscribers at a time when the population of the Township of Cincinnati was only 6000 inhabitants. This early newspaper continued under many names, and is one of the most important newspapers in the early part of the 19th century for genealogists. It contained lists of deaths reported by the Cincinnati Board of Health on a weekly basis during the 1820s and 1830s. It should also be noted that the *Liberty Hall* is currently the only known newspaper to list the cholera deaths on a daily basis during the height of the epidemic in Cincinnati in July and early August of 1849, and could serve as a valuable resource in finding missing ancestors who perished in this massive epidemic which gripped the city during the summer months of 1849. This index runs through December 1857.

The page number codes L1 – L8 correspond to the numeric page number in the particular issue of the newspaper. For example, L3 means to look for the item on page three. During the earlier time periods, the newspaper was published in a four page format.

The gaps in the collection are as follows:
  June 1818 – July 1818
  January, March, April, and June 1834
  October 1855
  May – July 1856

The alternate names for this newspaper are listed below and the time period.

Liberty Hall and Cincinnati Mercury	Dec. 1804 – Apr. 1809
Liberty Hall	Apr. 1809 – Dec. 1815
Liberty Hall and Cincinnati Gazette	Jan. 1816 – Dec. 1857

Section 1 – Death notices and obituaries

This section contains over 15,750 deaths, which were reported and published before December 1857 in Hamilton County and surrounding counties. If the birthplace of the person is listed in the death notice, an " * " is placed before the page number in the index to alert the researcher to additional vital information.

During the early periods of this index, it was not very common to take out a death notice or an obituary, but in some cases there were administrator and executor notices or estate sales listed when someone who owned property died, and their estate was being sold off. These notices were published so that creditors and debtors of the deceased could file a claim against the estate. These notices were recorded in this index, and instead of the age of the person, the word "**estate**" is listed in that column so that the researcher will know to look in the original papers for an estate notice or sale vs. a death notice. While a death notice will most likely give the date of death and age, the administrator or estate notice will give the name of the deceased, where they owned property (i.e. the township), and the name of the administrator or executor. In many cases this will be the name of the surviving spouse or the name of one of the sons. This can be an important clue before 1850 when only the head of the household was listed in the census data.

If the word "executor" (man) or "executrix" (woman) was listed, then it means that the deceased left a will and this person was named as the executor of the will to dispose of the property in the estate. This was usually the surviving spouse or a son, or son-in-law of the deceased person, or some other close relative that was trusted. The researcher should check Hamilton County wills to see if a will is still available and would most likely contain additional family information.

If the word "administrator" (man) or "administratrix" (woman) was listed, this person was formally appointed at a quarterly session of the Common Pleas Court (before 1852) or Probate Court (after 1852). The surviving court records should be searched for additional information. The appointment of an administrat(or/rix) could mean that the deceased died intestate or without a will, or the requested execut(or/rix) declined to serve, or in the court's opinion was not capable of serving. This could just be that the person didn't feel capable because of age or infirmity or they now lived out of Hamilton County, or because of the size of the estate, could not post an adequate bond. If the widow declined, perhaps she felt uncomfortable dealing with the management and/or sale of property left to her. In some cases, multiple administrators were named, like brother and son, or two brothers for example. If the administratrix was a woman, she was most likely the widow of the deceased. If her last name is different than the deceased, there are a number of examples in the Probate Court account records where she had remarried while the estate was still being settled. These may provide many additional clues to follow up on.

In a similar manner, sometimes the Probate Court published in this newspaper a list of recent cases brought before the court. These have also been included in the index and listed as "**probate**" in the age column. The actual date of death would not be listed in the notice, but it would provide the latest possible date when a death would have occurred, and that they owned property or owed debts in Hamilton County that needed to go before the Probate Court for disposition. In the earlier years, the Probate Court met in quarterly sessions and typically handled 25 to 30 cases a quarter. This may lead the researcher to other court documents for additional information since there was a case filed in Probate Court on that date. These notices will typically be listed on the page of the newspaper as "Probate Notice" or "Probate Court".

There may be a great deal of variation in the information recorded in these early notices. In some cases there is only the name of the deceased, the date of death, their age, and when and where the funeral will take place. In other cases, the surviving spouse might be listed, especially in the case where the wife died, and occasionally more information about their life and where they were born or when they migrated to the area. For almost all the cases, where the person was a small child, the names of the parents are listed in the notice.

During the cholera outbreaks of 1832, 1833, and 1849, there were many deaths in the city on a daily basis, and at the height of these epidemics, this issue consumed the city, and was the topic of many articles in the newspaper each day. During these times of epidemic, a list of deaths on a daily basis was gathered and published by the Board of Health for three of these major outbreaks. The deaths in the summer months of 1849 that were printed in the *Liberty Hall* included the name of the person, their age, address, date of death, and in some cases their marital status and place of birth.

Section 2 – Marriage notices

This section contains over 4,200 marriages, which were reported and published before December 1857 in Hamilton County and surrounding counties. It should be noted that the marriage notices listed are not only from the Cincinnati and Hamilton County area. In most of the cases, the date and place of the marriage was listed along with the name of the minister or justice of the peace that performed the marriage. In many cases, the name of the father of the bride or both of her parents was listed. The notice date in the index is the date of the publication in the newspaper, not the date of the marriage.

Section 3 – Miscellaneous notices

This section contains over 3000 notices of divorce cases, bankruptcy lists, guardianships, and other valuable notices that were reported and published before December 1857 in Hamilton County as notice to the public. These notices include guardianships, where a minor child inherited property and an adult guardian was appointed by the court to administer and protect this property until the child reached adulthood. Another important set of notices published was debt relief notices. This was the equivalent of our modern bankruptcy laws, where the individual could not pay his expenses and filed for protection under the insolvent debtor laws in existence at the time. This would provide notice to the individuals that he owed money to, and they could plead their case before the judge to recover some of their investments. In the case of the early 1830s when a financial panic occurred, these lists were quite extensive.

Along with many other useful notices that appear in these early issues of Cincinnati newspapers, there were notices of divorce or abandonment by one spouse or another, and later in the 1850s the Common Pleas Court notices that appear in the newspaper started listing hearings for divorce. During the 1850s and later, these notices frequently gave the detailed reasons for the petition for divorce, when the couple was originally married, how many children were involved in the settlement, any alimony that was requested, and in some contested cases, there were actual transcripts of the hearings printed in the papers. When a divorce hearing was requested, there needed to be a notice given in the local newspapers to the public, and in many cases these listed both names and a short reason for the divorce petition. In the earlier newspapers before the 1850s, these notices were more common when one spouse abandoned the other one or just disappeared (e.g. went west but was never heard from again and did not return). These notices were to protect the other person from being responsible for the debts incurred by the other spouse, and for permission for the spouse left behind to legally remarry. In other cases where the domestic environment was intolerable due to mistreatment or habitual drunkenness, a wife might simply flee the marriage, since there was little legal alternative available at the time. An example of an early notice appearing the newspaper where the wife left is as follows.

"I do hereby notify the public that my wife <*Wife's name*> has voluntarily left my bed and board, and that debts contracted by her will not be paid by me." <*Husband's name*>

This can be especially useful information since before 1850 only the head of household was listed in the census. These kinds of early notices would give the name of the wife, and that a marriage had existed before the date of the notice.

Name	Notice Date	Death Date	Age		Page	Maiden Name
----, Charles	5, July 1849	June	30		L3	
----, Joseph	28, Oct. 1847	Oct.			L3	
----, Peter	13, Aug. 1857	12, Aug.	29		L3	
----, Robert	18, July 1850	July			L3	
Abbot, Mary B.	21, Sept 1843	15, Sept	82	*	L3	
Abbot, Robert S.	8, May 1828	May	34		L1	
Abbott, (Mr)	18, Oct. 1832	15, Oct.			L2	
Abbott, James	12, Sept 1833		estate		L3	
Abbott, James	1, Nov. 1832	23, Oct.			L4	
Abercromby, Martha J.	31, Oct. 1833	Oct.	6		L4	
Ablamowicz, Rudolph Nicholas	14, Dec. 1848	9, Dec.	5		L2	
Abraham, Kate	30, Sept 1852	23, Sept	2- 9m		L3	
Abrams, James	15, Sept 1817		estate		L3	
Abrams, Louisa H.	28, July 1842	26, July			L3	
Ackerman, Vallentine	31, Oct. 1839	Oct.	24		L3	
Ackley, Alphonzo	14, June 1849	June	36		L3	
Acree, Benjamin	23, May 1850	May	23		L3	
Acton, Mary Elizabeth	6, Aug. 1857	31, July			L3	
Acton, William Woodnutt	3, July 1851	25, June	16m		L3	
Adalair, Mary	11, Sept 1834	Aug.	8m		L1	
Adams, (child of Charles)	9, Jan. 1851	4, Jan.	14		L3	
Adams, (child of Harriet)	31, Oct. 1850	Oct.	1d		L3	
Adams, (son of Th. J.)	24, Feb. 1842	5, Feb.	infant		L3	
Adams, Abijah	5, June 1816	18, May	62		L3	
Adams, Alexander	4, Aug. 1842	Aug.	30		L3	
Adams, Bridget	25, Aug. 1807		estate		L1	
Adams, Eliza	7, Oct. 1847	26, Sept			L3	
Adams, Ellen	16, July 1857	9, July	31	*	L3	Pace
Adams, Frank Corwin	17, Aug. 1854	13, Aug.	6m-27d		L3	
Adams, George	13, Sept 1849				L2	
Adams, Harry	11, July 1833		probate		L3	
Adams, Henry W.	26, Nov. 1829		estate		L3	
Adams, Isabella	12, 19, Feb. 1857	7, Feb.	55		L3	
Adams, Jane	12, Apr. 1849	Apr.	85		L3	
Adams, John	21, July 1826	4, July	90		L3	
Adams, John W.	7, Aug. 1834	July	8		L3	
Adams, Joseph	21, July 1853	16, July			L3	
Adams, Mary	26, Mar. 1846	Mar.	3m		L3	
Adams, Mary Jane	26, Aug. 1847	13, Aug.	33		L3	
Adams, N.F.	14, Aug. 1815		estate		L3	
Adams, N.F. (Capt)	22, May 1815				L3	
Adams, Rosalind Baltimore	28, Aug. 1856	24, Aug.	2-16m		L5	
Adams, Samuel (Dr)	6, Mar. 1845	27, Feb.	78	*	L3	
Adams, Sarah	9, Mar. 1854	5, Mar.	96		L3	
Adams, William	22, Apr. 1852	20, Apr.	62		L3	
Adamson, Susanna	21, Sept 1812	20, Sept		*	L3	
Addams, A.A.	27, Mar. 1851	19, Mar.			L3	
Addis, John	13, Dec. 1832	Dec.	59		L1	
Addison, (child of Mary Ann)	6, June 1839	May	3w		L2	
Addison, Cyrus	25, July 1850	July	48		L3	
Addison, Ruben	19, Sept 1833	Sept	25		L4	
Addison, William	30, May 1839	May	12d		L2	
Adle, Samuel	15, Nov. 1832	Nov.	53		L1	
Agan, John	1, June 1854	27, May			L3	

Name	Notice Date	Death Date	Age	Page	Maiden Name
Agan, Thomas	2, Apr. 1846	Mar.	26		L3	
Agar, J. VanRansellaer (Mrs)	4, Mar. 1847	27, Feb.	37		L3	
Agar, William W.	11, Jan. 1849	Jan.	29		L3	
Agen, Robert	22, Mar. 1855	17, Mar.	15		L3	
Agna, George	28, Sept 1848	Sept	34		L3	
Agnes, William	23, Dec. 1805		estate		L3	
Agnew, Ann E.	10, Dec. 1857		probate		L3	
Agnew, Ann Elizabeth	6, Sept 1855		probate		L3	
Ahearn, Dennis	19, July 1849	July	35		L3	
Aickens, John	25, Oct. 1832	21, Oct.			L2	
Aiken, Giles	14, Mar. 1839	Mar.	24		L3	
Aiken, John	24, Feb. 1807		estate		L1	
Aikins, Thomas	22, Aug. 1833	Aug.	22		L4	
Aimes, (man)	25, Aug. 1853	22, Aug.			L3	
Aitcheson, George	8, Aug. 1833	July	2- 5m		L1	
Akins, Ruth	28, Sept 1837	Sept	1d		L4	
Akoetter, Anton	10, Dec. 1857		probate		L3	
Albright, Elizabeth	18, Jan. 1855	3, Jan.	30		L3	
Albright, Matthias	1, Feb. 1849	Jan.	70		L3	
Alcoke, James B.	28, June 1849	21, June	39		L3	
Aldevolt, Joseph	10, Sept 1857		probate		L3	
Aldred, George	7, May 1840		probate		L3	
Aldrich, Elias T.	8, Nov. 1849	13, Oct.			L3	
Alexandar, Charles	26, Sept 1833	Sept	15		L4	
Alexander, (child of John)	12, Sept 1833	Sept	stillborn		L1	
Alexander, Agnes	29, Sept 1807	24, Sept			L3	
Alexander, Amanda Duffield	28, Aug. 1856	27, Aug.	52		L5	
Alexander, Andrew	10, Oct. 1844	Oct.	56		L3	
Alexander, Horace	17, June 1835		estate		L3	
Alexander, Horace	15, Sept 1836		probate		L3	
Alexander, Joseph	30, Mar. 1854	25, Mar.	73		L3	
Alexander, Joshua	4, July 1850	June	25		L3	
Alexander, Mary Ann	12, Sept 1833	Sept	23		L1	
Alexander, Robert	5, Nov. 1846		estate		L3	
Alexander, Thomas	1, Nov. 1832	28, Oct.			L2	
Alexander, William	27, Feb. 1851	20, Feb.	22- 3m	*	L3	
Alexander, William Hamilton	6, Aug. 1857	26, July		*	L3	
Alfred, (child of Bonnel)	14, Feb. 1828	Feb.	1d		L1	
Allan, Martha	26, Apr. 1855	23, Apr.	22		L3	
Allcorn, James (Capt)	3, June 1847	29, May	74	*	L3	
Alled, Marcus	20, Mar. 1851	Mar.	48		L3	
Allen, (child of A.H.)	10, Jan. 1828	Jan.	infant		L4	
Allen, (child of Charles)	2, Aug. 1832	July	1d		L1	
Allen, (son)	1, Nov. 1832	24, Oct.	7		L1	
Allen, A.W.	26, July 1849	July			L3	
Allen, C.	7, Nov. 1844	3, Nov.	72	*	L3	
Allen, Caleb	10, Dec. 1857		probate		L3	
Allen, Charles	5, Oct. 1848	Sept			L3	
Allen, Charlotte	14, Nov. 1839	4, Nov.			L3	
Allen, Edwin C.	17, Jan. 1850	9, Jan.	26	*	L3	
Allen, Eliza	13, May 1847	May	50		L3	
Allen, George M.	22, Feb. 1855	19, Feb.			L3	
Allen, James	9, May 1850	Apr.	38		L3	
Allen, Jane	27, Nov. 1834	Nov.	30		L1	

Name	Notice Date	Death Date	Age		Page	Maiden Name
Allen, John L.	6, Aug. 1835		estate		L3	
Allen, John L.	28, Sept 1843		estate		L3	
Allen, John L.	11, Jan. 1844		estate		L3	
Allen, John L.	11, June 1840		estate		L4	
Allen, Joseph S.	25, June 1857		estate		L3	
Allen, Joseph W.	24, Mar. 1842		estate		L3	
Allen, Mary Ann	23, Oct. 1834	Oct.	20		L2	
Allen, Nathaniel	30, Apr. 1840		estate		L3	
Allen, Nelson M.	1, June 1843	27, May	27		L3	
Allen, Oscar D.	5, Oct. 1848	Sept	27		L3	
Allen, Rebecca A.	24, Oct. 1844	18, Oct.			L3	
Allen, Samuel	15, Feb. 1820	14, Feb.	30	*	L3	
Allen, Samuel	21, Dec. 1848	Dec.	48		L3	
Allen, Samuel R.	20, Sept 1832	3, Sept			L1	
Allen, Samuel R.	11, Oct. 1832		estate		L3	
Allen, Samuel S.	26, Sept 1839	10, Sept	42	*	L3	
Allen, Samuel W.	14, Dec. 1824		probate		L3	
Allen, Sarah	26, Jan. 1854	16, Jan.	71		L3	
Allen, Sarah E.	15, Aug. 1833	Aug.	5-11m		L1	
Allen, Stephen P.	6, Nov. 1839		estate		L3	
Allen, Thomas	4, Jan. 1849				L2	
Allen, Virginia D.	20, June 1833	June	4m- 9d		L1	
Allen, W.H.	12, Nov. 1846		estate		L3	
Allen, William	9, Oct. 1845	4, Oct.	24		L3	
Allen, William	20, Apr. 1854	15, Apr.	31		L3	
Allen, William	15, July 1841		37	*	L3	
Allen, William	26, July 1849	July	2- 6m		L3	
Allen, William	26, Sept 1833	Sept	42		L4	
Allen, William	1, Nov. 1832	24, Oct.			L4	
Alley, David S.H.	29, Dec. 1842	19, Dec.	52		L3	
Alley, Lydia	19, Sept 1833	Sept	27- 8m- 5d		L4	
Alley, Sarah Jane	15, Aug. 1844	22, July	13m		L3	
Alliback, James	18, Oct. 1832	13, Oct.			L2	
Alling, Sarah Ann	19, July 1849	8, July	30- 7m		L3	Sibley
Allis, Joseph	20, May 1852	19, May			L3	
Allison, Adam	26, Aug. 1847	Aug.	39		L3	
Allison, Catharine Ann	29, June 1854	27, June	19		L3	
Allison, Isaac	14, Dec. 1854				L2	
Allison, Isaac	20, Dec. 1855	26, June			L3	
Allison, Isaac H.	29, June 1854	27, June	31		L3	
Allison, James	26, June 1845	June	23		L3	
Allison, Maria Louisa	30, Nov. 1837	Nov.	6		L3	
Allison, Richard	3, Nov. 1818		estate		L3	
Allison, Richard (Dr)	25, Mar. 1816	22, Mar.	59	*	L3	
Allison, Richard (Dr)	23, Sept 1816		estate		L3	
Allman, Dirk	14, June 1838		probate		L4	
Alloway, Archelaus	1, Dec. 1808		estate		L3	
Allsop, Henry	6, Aug. 1840	July	11		L3	
Alpionalys, Peter	11, July 1833	July	6m		L1	
Alsbaugh, Frederick	12, Sept 1844	Sept	65		L3	
Alsop, Richard	9, June 1842	19, May	53		L3	
Alter, Frederick	7, July 1853		estate		L3	
Alter, Frederick	14, Dec. 1824		probate		L3	
Alter, John	29, June 1837		estate		L3	

Name	Notice Date	Death Date	Age		Page	Maiden Name
Alter, John	2, Aug. 1838		estate		L3	
Alter, John	3, Sept 1840		probate		L3	
Altheimer, Amelia	5, Oct. 1848	Sept	31		L3	
Althoreseren, Mary	5, July 1849	June	40		L3	
Altinge, William	20, Feb. 1851	Feb.	3m		L3	
Altman, Dirk	17, Dec. 1835		estate		L3	
Amberg, John	14, June 1849	June	70		L3	
Amberg, Lewis	22, Mar. 1855		estate		L3	
Amberg, Louis	4, June 1857		probate		L3	
Ames, Benjamin	15, Oct. 1835	28, Sept	58		L3	
Ames, Daniel	28, Aug. 1856	26, Aug.	74		L5	
Ames, Henry P. (Capt)	17, Sept 1846	18, July	33	*	L3	
Ames, James	17, Sept 1846	Sept	27		L3	
Ammen, David	10, Dec. 1846		estate		L3	
Ammon, Sarah	30, Sept 1852	24, Sept	71		L3	
Ancker, Adolph	4, July 1850	22, June	78	*	L3	
Ancker, Elias M.	15, Apr. 1852	8, Apr.	28		L3	
Anderson, (child of Cynthia)	13, Nov. 1834	Nov.			L1	
Anderson, (child of Malinda)	13, Sept 1832	Sept	stillborn		L1	
Anderson, (child)	18, Oct. 1832	Oct.	18d		L4	
Anderson, Alex.	11, Apr. 1850		estate		L3	
Anderson, Alexander	30, Aug. 1849	23, Aug.	47	*	L3	
Anderson, Charles G.	30, Mar. 1849	21, Mar.	12		L3	
Anderson, Charles Winton	8, Feb. 1849	7, Feb.	3- 6m- 5d		L3	
Anderson, Crayton	19, May 1842	May	2		L3	
Anderson, Diana	8, Aug. 1833	July	60		L1	
Anderson, Elizabeth	9, Feb. 1854	5, Jan.	25		L3	
Anderson, Elizabeth	14, Mar. 1839	Mar.	32		L3	
Anderson, Elizabeth	27, Oct. 1842	14, Oct.			L3	Corry
Anderson, Elizabeth Ann	4, Nov. 1841	Oct.	3m		L3	
Anderson, Enoch	7, Feb. 1856		probate		L3	
Anderson, James	20, June 1833	June	12- 9m		L1	
Anderson, James	28, June 1849	26, June	20		L3	
Anderson, Jane	4, July 1833	June	12- 3m		L2	
Anderson, John	29, Sept 1818	25, Sept	55	*	L2	
Anderson, John	18, Mar. 1847	Mar.			L3	
Anderson, John G.	23, Sept 1830		estate		L4	
Anderson, Julia	6, Sept 1827	Sept	20m		L1	
Anderson, Julia A.	22, Aug. 1833	Aug.	9m-15d		L4	
Anderson, Lewis	4, Sept 1845	Aug.	26		L3	
Anderson, Maria J.	14, Oct. 1852	29, Sept			L3	Gano
Anderson, Mary	8, May 1845	Apr.	3d		L3	
Anderson, Matilda	24, May 1849	May	40		L3	
Anderson, Paul	10, May 1849	8, May	infant		L3	
Anderson, Porter Dobyns	25, Dec. 1856	20, Dec.	1-10m- 8d		L3	
Anderson, Rachel V.	11, Aug. 1812	5, Aug.	24		L3	
Anderson, Richard Clough	4, July 1850	26, June	12		L3	
Anderson, S.	1, Nov. 1832	Oct.	46		L2	
Anderson, Sally	25, Oct. 1832	18, Oct.	45		L3	
Anderson, Sally	31, Aug. 1854	25, Aug.	77		L3	
Anderson, Sarah	8, Aug. 1850	July	20		L3	
Anderson, Susan	5, Mar. 1857		probate		L3	
Anderson, Thomas	2, Oct. 1811	18, Aug.	25		L3	
Anderson, Thomas	7, Sept 1848	Aug.	29		L3	

Name	Notice Date	Death Date	Age		Page	Maiden Name
Anderson, Thomas B.	19, Apr. 1855	15, Apr.	64		L3	
Anderson, William	26, May 1853	18, May	45	*	L3	
Andress, Gabriel	2, Sept 1852	Aug.	30		L3	
Andress, Laura W.	2, Aug. 1855	24, July	1- 5m		L3	
Andress, Mary	2, Aug. 1855	26, July	2- 5m- 8d		L3	
Andrews, (child of Eliza)	6, Apr. 1843	Mar.			L3	
Andrews, (girl)	9, Mar. 1848	8, Mar.	child		L1	
Andrews, A.B.	29, Jan. 1846	28, Jan.	24		L3	
Andrews, Anne	30, Mar. 1843	22, Mar.	24- 3m		L3	
Andrews, Cornelia Jane	22, Apr. 1852	14, Apr.	15		L3	
Andrews, David	5, Aug. 1852	July	32		L3	
Andrews, Dudley	20, Sept 1832		estate		L3	
Andrews, Eliza Anne	24, Mar. 1842	10, Mar.	27		L3	
Andrews, Elizabeth	4, July 1850	27, June			L3	
Andrews, George	8, May 1845	15, Apr.	62	*	L3	
Andrews, Isaac	14, June 1849	June	45		L3	
Andrews, J.	7, June 1849	May	45		L3	
Andrews, J.W.	4, Apr. 1833	Mar.	51	*	L1	
Andrews, James	11, Mar. 1852	3, Mar.			L4	
Andrews, John	19, July 1849	11, July			L3	
Andrews, Lavina	4, July 1850	June	37		L3	
Andrews, Maria	13, Dec. 1832	Dec.	29		L1	
Andrews, Martin	30, Aug. 1849	22, Aug.	71	*	L3	
Andrews, Mary	27, Aug. 1857	20, Aug.	32		L3	McCormick
Andrews, Mary Elizabeth	10, May 1849	3, May	1- 4m- 9d		L3	
Andrews, S.H.	27, Aug. 1840	11, Aug.			L3	
Andrews, Samuel	13, Sept 1855	11, Sept	21m-14d		L3	
Andrews, Samuel	9, Sept 1852	8, Sept			L3	
Andrews, Sarah	19, July 1832	July	1- 5m		L1	
Andrews, Sarah	13, Feb. 1840	10, Feb.	14m		L3	
Andrews, Thomas W.	11, July 1833		probate		L3	
Andries, Baptist	13, Dec. 1849	Dec.	45		L3	
Andro, Adam	15, Nov. 1832	Nov.	20		L1	
Annier, John	20, Mar. 1851	Mar.	52		L3	
Anselm, Joseph	6, Sept 1855		probate		L3	
Ansett, John	30, Aug. 1832	Aug.	37		L1	
Ansmann, Theodore	18, Mar. 1852	12, Mar.			L4	
Antes, Henry (Major)	13, Aug. 1805	5, Aug.			L3	
Anthony, Christopher	6, 13, Nov. 1815	28, Oct.	71	*	L3	
Anthony, Christopher	17, Oct. 1826		estate		L3	
Anthony, Joseph	31, July 1845	July	63		L3	
Anthony, Joseph Bowen	10, Nov. 1836	9, Nov.	3		L2	
Anthony, Sarah Aborn	27, July 1854	11, July		*	L3	Rhodes
Anton, Alexander	26, June 1851	June	30		L3	
Antonhebel, (man)	13, Mar. 1851	9, Mar.			L3	
Antony, Edward G.	21, Mar. 1850	16, Jan.	18	*	L3	
Antram, Rebecca	12, Mar. 1857	27, Feb.			L3	
Antrim, Aaron	18, June 1829		estate		L2	
Apperson, Lizzie C.	25, Dec. 1856	15, Dec.			L3	Chenoweth
Apple, Henry	28, Aug. 1851	21, Aug.			L3	
Applegate, Eleanor	19, Aug. 1852	10, Aug.	43- 7m-28d		L3	
Applegate, George	27, Oct. 1831		probate		L1	
Applegate, H.S.	4, June 1857		probate		L3	
Applegate, Henry	8, Apr. 1847		estate		L3	

Name	Notice Date	Death Date	Age		Page	Maiden Name
Applegate, Henry S.	6, Jan. 1853	30, Dec.	33- 4m-23d		L3	
Applegate, John Williams	21, Apr. 1853	19, Apr.	8m-25d		L3	
Applegate, Lewis	4, Oct. 1849		estate		L3	
Applegate, Lewis	12, Dec. 1850		estate		L3	
Appleton, William W.	22, Nov. 1838	17, Nov.	32	*	L3	
Aprends, Charles	23, Mar. 1854	22, Mar.			L3	
April, Catharine	29, Aug. 1833	Aug.	6m		L1	
Arbegust, Benjamin	6, Dec. 1849				L3	
Arbegust, George	22, Mar. 1838		probate		L3	
Arbegust, George	14, Jan. 1836		estate		L4	
Arbegust, William	31, Dec. 1835		estate		L3	
Arbegust, William	14, Feb. 1839		probate		L3	
Arbegust, William	15, Sept 1836		estate		L4	
Arcamble, Elizabeth	6, Apr. 1837	4, Apr.	75	*	L3	
Archer, George	30, Nov. 1843		25		L3	
Archibald, Robert	10, June 1820		estate		L3	
Archibald, Thomas	15, June 1837	June	55		L4	
Archibald, William	18, June 1846	June	38		L3	
Archibald, William A.	29, May 1834		probate		L3	
Archibald, William A.	12, Jan. 1837		probate		L3	
Ardener, Andrew	14, June 1849	June	3		L3	
Argabritt, John F.	23, Dec. 1852	15, Dec.			L3	
Armitege, Joseph	2, May 1833	Apr.	40		L1	
Armor, F.W.	13, Sept 1832	Sept	1- 2m-24d		L1	
Armstreet, Richard	25, Oct. 1832	20, Oct.			L2	
Armstrong, (son of Robert)	26, July 1849	20, July	4		L2	
Armstrong, Caroline	26, June 1851	24, June	29		L3	
Armstrong, Cornelia	31, July 1845	July	11m		L3	
Armstrong, Edith Greenleaf	22, Oct. 1857	14, Oct.	1- 9m		L3	
Armstrong, James	24, May 1855	23, May	29		L3	
Armstrong, James	4, Mar. 1841	24, Feb.	57		L3	
Armstrong, James	4, June 1808				L4	
Armstrong, Jane	24, Jan. 1839	Jan.	71		L3	
Armstrong, Jane	12, July 1838	2, July			L3	
Armstrong, John	16, Dec. 1816		estate		L3	
Armstrong, John	7, Nov. 1844	31, Oct.			L3	
Armstrong, John	23, May 1833	May	26		L4	
Armstrong, John	21, May 1825		estate		L4	
Armstrong, John (Gen)	13, Apr. 1843	1, Apr.	85		L3	
Armstrong, John H.	6, June 1810	31, May	28		L2	
Armstrong, John H.	11, July 1810		estate		L3	
Armstrong, Nathaniel S.	16, July 1840	4, July	91		L3	
Armstrong, R.G.	4, June 1857		probate		L3	
Armstrong, Reuben	26, Apr. 1849	Apr.	20		L3	
Armstrong, Robert	3, Jan. 1839	Dec.	81		L1	
Armstrong, Robert G.	12, July 1855	9, July			L3	
Armstrong, Samuel	29, Nov. 1849	Nov.	54		L3	
Armstrong, Thomas	8, Aug. 1833	July			L1	
Armstrong, William	22, Aug. 1833	Aug.	25		L4	
Arnet, John	13, Aug. 1857		90	*	L3	
Arnold, Benjamin	4, Jan. 1844	3, Jan.	32		L3	
Arnold, Henry	7, Aug. 1834	July	30		L3	
Arnold, John R.	12, Oct. 1854	9, Oct.	63		L3	
Arnold, Magdalena	18, Sept 1851	14, Sept			L3	

Name	Notice Date	Death Date	Age	Page	Maiden Name
Arnold, Mary Frances	22, Aug. 1833	Aug.		L4	
Arnold, William	12, Dec. 1810		estate	L2	
Arnold, William	22, June 1837		probate	L3	
Arnot, John	9, Dec. 1847	4, Dec.	54	L3	
Arones, Alexander	8, Aug. 1833	July	51	L1	
Arons, J.J. (Dr)	21, Dec. 1854	17, Dec.	24	L3	
Arrison, Thomas	20, Jan. 1842	7, Jan.		* L3	
Arthouse, Henry	25, July 1850	July	25	L3	
Arthur, B.H. (Capt)	20, Mar. 1856	11, Mar.		L3	
Arthur, Henry	11, Mar. 1852	2, Mar.		L4	
Arthur, Oscar D.	12, Dec. 1833	Dec.	7	L4	
Arthur, William	6, Nov. 1834		estate	L3	
Arthurs, G.J.V.	11, Sept 1834	Aug.	1	L1	
Arthurs, Jeremiah	1, Apr. 1852	27, Mar.		L3	
Arthurs, Jesse	1, Apr. 1852	27, Mar.		L3	
Arthurs, John	29, Aug. 1833	Aug.	34	L1	
Arthurs, William	1, Apr. 1852	27, Mar.		L3	
Artrup, Andrew	30, June 1842	June	18	L3	
Artrup, William H.	23, June 1842	June	1	L3	
Arwood, Thomas R.	31, May 1849	May	45	L3	
Asbury, Francis (Rev)	29, Apr. 1816	31, Mar.	72	L3	
Ash, James	3, Apr. 1845	Mar.	50	L3	
Ashley, (child of Stephen)	1, Aug. 1833	July	1- 6m	L1	
Ashley, John	24, May 1849	May	40	L3	
Ashton, Lucy	6, July 1843	June	4m	L3	
Askeen, Joseph M.	12, Aug. 1852	26, July		L3	
Aspel, Mary	13, Mar. 1851	Mar.	2	L3	
Aspy, William	13, Feb. 1840		probate	L3	
Asselineau, Edward Felix	6, Mar. 1845	27, Feb.	2- 1m	L3	
Asser, Catharine	1, Jan. 1846	Dec.	68	L3	
Atchinson, Isabella	18, Oct. 1827	Oct.	13m	L3	
Atden, (child of Mary)	25, July 1850	July	2d	L3	
Atdridge, Richard	15, Aug. 1850	Aug.	9m	L3	
Athearn, Isaac M.	23, Apr. 1857	15, Apr.	18	L3	
Athearn, Jacob Strader	11, Jan. 1849	5, Jan.		L3	
Atherton, David	10, Mar. 1842		estate	L4	
Atkeson, Mary	9, Feb. 1854	8, Jan.	76	L3	
Atkin, (child of Polly)	24, Feb. 1842	Feb.	3	L3	
Atkins, Elizabeth	2, June 1842	May	11m	L3	
Atkins, George W.	3, Dec. 1840		probate	L3	
Atkins, Hannah	30, May 1850	25, May		L3	
Atkins, William	27, July 1843	July	7	L3	
Atkinson, (child of Jane)	3, May 1849	Apr.		L3	
Atkinson, Andrew	3, May 1849	Apr.	38	L3	
Atkinson, Clayton G.	10, Aug. 1848	30, July	1- 6m- 9d	L3	
Atkinson, Henry	26, July 1849	17, July		L2	
Atkinson, James	10, May 1849	May	3	L3	
Atkinson, James	21, June 1849	June	45	L3	
Atkinson, Jane	24, May 1849	May	21	L3	
Atkinson, Mary	31, May 1849	May	34	L3	
Atkinson, Thomas	3, May 1849	Apr.	4	L3	
Atkinson, Thomas E.	21, June 1849	June	5	L3	
Atlee, Ann Mackintosh	21, June 1838	30, May	23	* L3	Edwards
Atlee, James	5, Sept 1833	Aug.	75	L1	

Name	Notice Date	Death Date	Age		Page	Maiden Name
Atret, Joseph	20, Sept 1827	Sept	64		L1	
Attee, William	14, Oct. 1841	9, Oct.		*	L3	
Atterbury, William	17, Nov. 1842	16, Nov.	52		L6	
Atwater, Alfred	28, June 1849	20, June	6m		L3	
Atwater, Anna Clarissa	4, Nov. 1847	31, Oct.	5m- 6d		L3	
Aubrey, Sarah	2, Mar. 1843	22, Feb.	17m-10d		L3	
Aucutt, Richard	22, Nov. 1832		estate		L3	
Audett, Richard	15, Nov. 1832	Nov.	63		L1	
Auer, Xavier	26, Feb. 1852	Feb.	48		L4	
Augustu, (child of R.)	6, Nov. 1834	Oct.	3m		L1	
Augustus, George	3, Oct. 1850	2, Oct.			L3	
Augustus, Joseph	1, Aug. 1850	July	7m		L3	
Auld, Michael	6, Apr. 1819	3, Apr.			L2	
Aulton, Jesse	26, July 1849	July	50		L3	
Austact, Adam	2, May 1833	Apr.	49-11m		L1	
Austin, Benjamin	24, May 1820		68		L3	
Austin, Benjamin	29, Feb. 1844	14, Feb.	86		L3	
Austin, Charles Vincent	28, Sept 1843	22, Sept	infant		L3	
Austin, Gertrude	3, Feb. 1853	25, Jan.	8-11m		L3	
Austin, Henry	1, Jan. 1846	Dec.	35		L3	
Austin, Horace	8, Nov. 1832	Nov.	1- 5m		L1	
Austin, Lydia	3, Feb. 1853	21, Jan.	51		L3	
Austin, Mary	31, Dec. 1846	30, Dec.	18		L3	
Austin, Warren Burgess	31, May 1832		estate		L4	
Austin, William W.	5, Feb. 1852	28, Jan.	62		L3	
Avery, Charles	9, June 1807		estate		L2	
Avery, Charles	6, Sept 1809		estate		L2	
Avery, Ebenezer	7, Feb. 1828	10, Jan.	82		L1	
Avery, Howard B.	12, July 1849	29, June	13m		L3	
Avery, James B.	1, Apr. 1847	Mar.	28		L3	
Avery, John C.	25, Apr. 1850		estate		L3	
Avery, John C.	4, June 1857		probate		L3	
Avery, John C. (Col)	7, Feb. 1850	1, Feb.	58		L3	
Avery, John Leake	28, Feb. 1828	Feb.	4- 9m		L1	
Avery, Martha	27, Mar. 1856	22, Mar.			L3	
Avery, Nancy	11, Sept 1828	10, Sept			L3	
Avery, Simeon F.	3, July 1845	7, June	30		L3	
Avey, Franklin S.	24, Sept 1857	23, Sept	6		L3	
Avey, William T.	7, Aug. 1834	July	1- -13d		L3	
Avis, Henry	26, Oct. 1837	Oct.	34		L4	
Avis, Joseph J.	10, Nov. 1853	5, Nov.	24- 3m		L3	
Avis, Susan	9, Oct. 1851	7, Oct.	54		L3	
Avis, William	11, July 1850	7, July	36	*	L3	
Avis, William	7, Sept 1837	Aug.	11m		L3	
Aydelott, Caroline	20, Aug. 1840	15, July			L3	
Aydelotte, Caroline	23, July 1840	15, July			L3	
Aydelotte, David Brainerd	17, Dec. 1840	12, Dec.	15		L3	
Ayer, Ebenezer	6, Oct. 1818		estate		L3	
Ayer, Richard	7, Aug. 1828		estate		L3	
Aylor, (man)	28, Apr. 1853	27, Apr.			L3	
Ayre, John	9, Sept 1825		probate		L3	
Ayres, Edith	1, Aug. 1839	July	8m		L3	
Ayres, Eli	2, Mar. 1848	Feb.	24		L3	
Ayres, John B.	11, Jan. 1849	Jan.	29		L3	

Name	Notice Date	Death Date	Age	Page	Maiden Name
Ayres, Mark	26, Feb. 1829		estate	L3	
Ayres, Mary	8, Nov. 1849	Oct.	43	L3	
Ayres, Richard	16, June 1842	10, June	56	L3	
Ayres, Samuel, Sen.	20, Feb. 1845	9, Feb.	68	L3	
Babb, Daniel	3, July 1851	June	21	L3	
Babbitt, Calvin	13, Jan. 1848	9, Jan.	2- 6m	L3	
Babcock, David	9, July 1857		probate	L3	
Babcock, Gideon	11, Nov. 1816	2, Nov.		L3	
Babinger, (Mrs)	18, Oct. 1832	14, Oct.		L2	
Babinger, Valentine	3, Sept 1840		probate	L3	
Babinger, Valentine	7, Mar. 1839		estate	L4	
Babtiste, John	18, Oct. 1849	Oct.	28	L3	
Bacchus, Joshua	3, Feb. 1807		estate	L4	
Bachelor, Daniel	16, May 1833	May	69	L1	
Backer, Jasper	1, Oct. 1846	Sept	54	L3	
Backover, Benedict	2, Sept 1852	Aug.	40	L3	
Bacon, Catharine Eberle	7, Oct. 1841	28, Sept	28	L3	
Bacon, Maria	18, Apr. 1844	16, Apr.		* L3	Lewis
Bacon, S.C.	11, Jan. 1855	9, Jan.		L3	
Badger, Frances	6, Nov. 1845	2, Nov.		L3	
Badger, Francis	26, Nov. 1846	23, Nov.		L3	
Badgley, William	16, Aug. 1814		estate	L3	
Badin, (Rev)	28, Apr. 1853		98	L3	
Bagget, Alice	24, Apr. l845	Apr.	2	L3	
Bagley, Catharine A.	21, Feb. 1839	15, Feb.		L3	
Bagley, Isaac	15, Oct. 1846	Oct.	9- 8m	L3	
Bagot, Charles	9, Mar. 1843	9, Feb.		L3	
Bailey, (child of Linda)	20, Feb. 1845	Feb.	3w	L3	
Bailey, (child of Martha)	1, Aug. 1833	July		L1	
Bailey, Amos	6, Mar. 1851		estate	L3	
Bailey, Amos	1, Jan. 1852		estate	L3	
Bailey, Andrew M.	24, Mar. 1831	17, Mar.		L3	
Bailey, Ann	20, Dec. 1825	22, Nov.	115	L3	
Bailey, Caroline Victoria	17, July 1845	9, July	7-10m	L3	
Bailey, Charles	10, June 1847	June	56	L3	
Bailey, Charles S.	10, Aug. 1837	7, Aug.		L3	
Bailey, Daniel	27, Sept 1855	24, Sept		L3	
Bailey, Henry A.	16, Apr. 1846	10, Apr.	12m-22d	L3	
Bailey, James K.	30, Dec. 1816	26, Dec.		L3	
Bailey, John	23, Aug. 1849	Aug.	15m	L3	
Bailey, John	10, Apr. 1856		probate	L3	
Bailey, John Rankin	6, Mar. 1845	1, Mar.	15m	L3	
Bailey, L.A.	19, Jan. 1843	12, Jan.	26	L3	
Bailey, Mary L.	21, Sept 1854	13, Sept	21	L3	
Bailey, Reuben	4, Sept 1856	2, Sept	43	L5	
Bailey, Sarah	28, May 1846	May	5	L3	
Bailhache, Elizabeth Harwood	19, July 1849	1, July	52	* L3	Heath
Bailie, Sarah Burgin	11, Sept 1851	3, Sept		L3	
Bails, Thomas	4, Oct. 1833	Sept	35	L1	
Baily, (child of John)	5, July 1849	June	1	L3	
Baily, Amos W.	4, Oct. 1849		estate	L3	
Baily, Ann	5, July 1849	June	34	L3	
Baily, Edward	18, Apr. 1850	Apr.	17	L3	

Name	Notice Date	Death Date	Age		Page	Maiden Name
Baily, Thomas	3, Jan. 1850	Dec.			L3	
Bain, Simeon (Mrs)	19, Apr. 1855	17, Apr.			L3	
Baird, Harriet Augusta	24, July 1845	17, July	14	*	L3	
Baird, John	19, Apr. 1832		estate		L3	
Baird, John B.	26, May 1836	10, May			L3	
Baird, John B.	22, Sept 1836		estate		L4	
Baird, Nancy	22, Feb. 1844	1, Feb.	70		L3	
Baird, William (Capt)	16, Oct. 1851	14, Oct.			L3	
Baites, David	8, Aug. 1833	July	23		L1	
Baker, (Mrs)	1, Nov. 1832	29, Oct.			L3	
Baker, Adeline	9, July 1846	June	6		L3	
Baker, Albert R.	18, Dec. 1856	12, Dec.	29		L3	
Baker, Ann	18, Sept 1834	Sept	40		L1	
Baker, Barbary	31, Dec. 1846	Dec.	9w		L3	
Baker, Benjamin F.	5, July 1849	4, July	21		L2	
Baker, Chloe	15, July 1847	19, June	28		L3	
Baker, Felise	18, Oct. 1832	Oct.	24		L4	
Baker, Florentine	4, Mar. 1847	Feb.	19		L3	
Baker, George	16, July 1846	July	3		L3	
Baker, Henry	14, June 1849	June	67		L3	
Baker, Henry F. (Col)	26, Feb. 1857	26, Jan.		*	L3	
Baker, Isaac	8, Nov. 1838		probate		L3	
Baker, James H.	27, Nov. 1828	20, Nov.	42		L1	
Baker, Jane	23, Feb. 1854	3, Feb.	44		L3	
Baker, John	5, Feb. 1857	1, Feb.	65		L3	
Baker, John	19, Feb. 1857		estate		L3	
Baker, John	28, Sept 1854	27, Sept		*	L3	
Baker, Lavina P.	26, Oct. 1854	18, Oct.		*	L3	
Baker, Lucinda	16, Oct. 1845	Oct.	50		L3	
Baker, Margaret	6, Apr. 1837	2, Apr.	36		L3	
Baker, Mary	21, Apr. 1853	13, Apr.			L3	
Baker, Nathan	21, Oct. 1841	18, Oct.			L3	
Baker, Phebe	29, Sept 1842	Sept	2- 6m		L3	
Baker, Timothy L.	26, Aug. 1852	21, Aug.	54		L3	
Baker, Valentine	24, Sept 1829		estate		L4	
Baker, William	8, Apr. 1847	Mar.	58		L3	
Baker, William	23, Nov. 1843	Nov.	81		L3	
Bakewell, Benjamin	29, Feb. 1844	20, Feb.	78	*	L3	
Bakewell, Charles	3, Apr. 1851	Mar.	28		L3	
Bakewell, Franklin	20, Feb. 1840	19, Feb.	9		L3	
Bakewell, Howard	12, Apr. 1849	Mar.	23		L3	
Bakewell, John Palmer	1, Dec. 1842	25, Nov.	43		L3	
Bakewell, Thomas R.	12, Mar. 1840	8, Mar.	infant		L3	
Bakewell, William W.	19, Dec. 1850	28, Nov.			L3	
Bakler, (child of Mary)	18, Oct. 1838	Oct.	1m		L3	
Balback, Sebastian	9, Jan. 1851	Dec.	31		L3	
Balders, Mary	19, Apr. 1849	Apr.	3		L3	
Balding, James	25, Sept 1815		estate		L1	
Baldock, (Mrs)	1, Nov. 1832	26, Oct.			L1	
Baldridge, Caroline	30, Mar. 1854	23, Mar.	22		L3	
Baldridge, William	14, Feb. 1833		estate		L3	
Baldwin, (Mrs)	25, Oct. 1832	18, Oct.			L1	
Baldwin, Adolphus Edwin	5, June 1845	30, May	infant		L3	
Baldwin, Arden W.	29, Apr. 1847	20, Apr.	34		L3	

Name	Notice Date	Death Date	Age	Page	Maiden Name
Baldwin, Cyrus B.	30, Aug. 1855	15, Aug.	73	L3	
Baldwin, George Holmes	26, July 1855	23, July	16m	L3	
Baldwin, Joel G.	6, Sept 1838	Aug.	21	L3	
Baldwin, John	7, Mar. 1850	Feb.	3w	L3	
Baldwin, Joseph Ashland	15, June 1843	9, June	11m-20d	L3	
Baldwin, Michael	14, Mar. 1810	9, Mar.		L3	
Baldwin, Samuel	27, Aug. 1840	23, Aug.	63	L3	
Baldwin, Samuel	4, Mar. 1841		estate	L3	
Baldwin, William	23, June 1842	June	26	L3	
Balgenart, Francis	10, Dec. 1857		probate	L3	
Ball, (child of William)	19, July 1849	July	stillborn	L3	
Ball, Alice Deveraux	19, Aug. 1852	14, Aug.	9m	L3	
Ball, Amanda	18, Oct. 1832	13, Oct.		L2	
Ball, Barney	4, July 1850	June	28	L3	
Ball, Charles Henry	16, Nov. 1843	11, Nov.	2- 2m	L3	
Ball, Davis	6, Apr. 1819	3, Apr.		L2	
Ball, John	12, Aug. 1852	Aug.	31	L3	
Ball, Joshua	10, Feb. 1817			L3	
Ball, Mary	30, Apr. 1824	26, Apr.	25	L3	
Ball, Samuel Candler	21, July 1836	17, July	1- 5m- 7d	L2	
Ballance, Charles Howard	28, June 1849	21, June	5- 6m-10d	L3	
Ballance, John Howard	6, Feb. 1845	1, Feb.	22m	L3	
Ballance, Mary Ann	13, Jan. 1848	8, Jan.	21m	L3	
Ballard, Charles	13, Sept 1849	Sept	26	L3	
Ballards, Thomas	12, Aug. 1852	Aug.	7	L3	
Balser, Henry	17, Mar. 1826		probate	L3	
Balster, Hannah	13, June 1844	8, June	75	L3	
Balthald, John	9, Oct. 1845	Sept	44	L3	
Baltzell, Charles	15, Nov. 1832	Nov.		L1	
Baltzell, Charles, Jr.	8, Nov. 1832	5, Nov.		* L3	
Bamberger, Charles	7, May 1857		probate	L3	
Bane, Charles	12, June 1845	June	3m	L3	
Bane, Lydia	30, May 1839	May	38	L2	
Banflier, Augustus	28, Mar. 1850	Mar.	49	L3	
Bangs, Louisa	7, June 1849	2, June	39	L3	
Banister, John P.	23, Oct. 1834	Oct.	31	L2	
Bankes, Martha	4, July 1833	June	72	L2	
Banks, George	8, Feb. 1849	Jan.	35	L3	
Banks, Hiram	22, Nov. 1849	15, Nov.		L3	
Banks, Lucretia	6, Apr. 1843	Mar.		L3	
Banks, Martha L.	6, May 1847	Apr.	3	L3	
Banks, Rebecca R.	29, Apr. 1847	Apr.	2	L3 ·	
Banks, Symmes Harrison	12, Aug. 1847	8, Aug.	20m	L3	
Banks, Thomas	19, Dec. 1826		probate	L3	
Banks, Tomlin M. (Dr)	6, June 1850	2, June		L3	
Banks, Tomlin Pike	9, May 1850	7, May	infant	L3	
Banks, William	29, Apr. 1847	Apr.	6	L3	
Bannaker, Murphy	22, Jan. 1852	Jan.	25	L3	
Bannan, Judith	30, May 1850	May	40	L3	
Bannister, John P.	6, Aug. 1835		estate	L3	
Bannister, John P.	12, July 1838		estate	L3	
Banshaub, Matthias	9, Apr. 1857		probate	L3	
Banta, James	8, Feb. 1849	Jan.	25	L3	
Bantrom, Mary	4, July 1833	June	3m	L2	

Name	Notice Date	Death Date	Age		Page	Maiden Name
Bantz, Clara Elizabeth	2, Nov. 1848	8, Oct.	1- 4m-23d		L3	
Barber, Hannah	25, Jan. 1855	26, Dec.			L3	
Barber, Lucretia	23, July 1846	July	3		L3	
Barber, Noyes	25, Jan. 1844	3, Jan.	62		L3	
Barber, Uriah (Major)	9, July 1846	27, June	92	*	L3	
Barbour, C.V. (Dr)	12, Apr. 1832	10, Apr.	35		L3	
Barbour, Charles V.	29, May 1834		probate		L3	
Bard, John	4, Feb. 1830		estate		L3	
Bard, Joseph H.	15, May 1851	9, May	27		L3	
Bard, Joseph H.	14, Aug. 1851		estate		L3	
Bard, Kitty	18, July 1833	July	5		L2	
Barge, William	19, Sept 1833	Sept	52		L4	
Barkalo, Lydia	23, Sept 1852	18, Sept	14- - 9d		L3	
Barkalow, Kate	20, Aug. 1857	11, Aug.	19		L3	
Barke, Elisha	27, Oct. 1831		probate		L1	
Barker, (Mrs)	18, Oct. 1832	9, Oct.			L4	
Barker, Archibald	18, Oct. 1832	Oct.			L4	
Barker, Fanny F.	21, Feb. 1850	15, Feb.	5- 2m		L3	
Barker, Franklin	23, Jan. 1851	Jan.	2d		L3	
Barker, Franklin D.	4, Sept 1856	28, Aug.	2- 1m-22d		L5	
Barker, Joseph	1, Nov. 1832	30, Oct.			L3	
Barker, Martha	9, June 1853		28		L3	
Barker, Peter	26, Dec. 1833	Dec.	53		L4	
Barker, Thomas C. (Dr)	12, June 1815	7, June			L3	
Barker, W.B.	12, Mar. 1840		estate		L4	
Barker, William	4, July 1850	June	24		L3	
Barker, William	14, Aug. 1851		40	*	L3	
Barkley, Elizabeth C.	6, Jan. 1853	24, Dec.			L3	Best
Barlow, Asa F.	13, Nov. 1822	7, Nov.	16m		L3	
Barlow, Eli	25, Aug. 1853	13, Aug.			L3	
Barlow, Joseph	25, Aug. 1853	13, Aug.			L3	
Barlow, Mary	17, June 1852	15, June	66		L3	
Barlow, T.S.	29, Jan. 1846	20, Jan.	28	*	L3	
Barminsker, Martin	25, Oct. 1832	Oct.	60		L1	
Barnan, Edward	11, July 1850	6, July	45		L3	
Barnard, (child of Charles)	21, Feb. 1828	Feb.	infant		L1	
Barnard, (Mr)	6, June 1826	4, June			L3	
Barnard, Charles W.	26, June 1851	18, June	24		L3	
Barnard, Charles W.	24, May 1855		estate		L3	
Barnard, Zaccheus	14, Mar. 1833	Mar.	50		L1	
Barnes, Abraham	22, Dec. 1817		estate		L3	
Barnes, Euphemia	4, Aug. 1831	23, July	36		L3	
Barnes, George	1, Nov. 1849	Oct.	23		L3	
Barnes, James	23, Mar. 1843	16, Mar.	70		L3	
Barnes, Oswald	15, Apr. 1847	12, Apr.			L3	
Barnes, Thomas	26, July 1849	24, July			L3	
Barnes, William	4, Mar. 1841		estate		L3	
Barnes, William (Dr)	11, May 1837	23, Apr.			L3	
Barnet, Elizabeth	13, Aug. 1808	11, Aug.	67		L3	
Barnett, Zeph	21, Apr. 1853	17, Apr.			L3	
Barney, Dewitt C.	15, Aug. 1833	Aug.	8		L1	
Barney, Electa C.	30, May 1844	21, May		*	L3	Crane
Barnkill, Robert	18, Sept 1834	Sept	29		L1	
Barnville, Jacob	1, Sept 1842	Aug.	56		L3	

Name	Notice Date	Death Date	Age		Page	Maiden Name
Barnwell, Charles F.	23, Oct. 1834	Oct.	25		L2	
Barr, Charles	8, July 1841	June	3		L3	
Barr, Enos	28, June 1849	June	48		L3	
Barr, John	3, Jan. 1828	Jan.	32		L1	
Barr, William	23, Mar. 1837	18, Mar.	60		L3	
Barr, William	20, May 1816	15, May	74		L3	
Barr, William	22, Sept 1842		estate		L3	
Barr, William	16, May 1844		estate		L3	
Barr, William	2, Apr. 1846		estate		L3	
Barr, William	8, Nov. 1838		probate		L3	
Barr, William	5, Sept 1839		probate		L3	
Barret, Ann	15, July 1847	12, July	42		L3	DeGolyer
Barret, Nancy	26, Dec. 1844	Dec.	25		L3	
Barrett, John Pratt	16, Nov. 1843	31, Oct.	22		L3	
Barrett, Thomas	4, July 1844	22, June	35	*	L3	
Barrey, (child)	1, Aug. 1833	July			L1	
Barrow, John	30, Jan. 1840		estate		L3	
Barry, (boy)	12, July 1849	9, July	8		L2	
Barry, A.M.	15, May 1845	13, May			L3	
Barry, H.	8, Aug. 1833	July	1- 6m		L1	
Barry, James	31, Jan. 1850	Jan.	40		L3	
Barry, Thomas	5, Nov. 1857	30, Oct.	75		L3	
Bartholomew, Daniel	21, June 1849	13, June			L3	
Bartholomew, David D.	9, Mar. 1848	Mar.	36		L3	
Bartle, John	26, Dec. 1839	12, Dec.	94	*	L1	
Bartler, James	7, Aug. 1834	July	1- 3m		L3	
Bartlett, Caroline	26, Dec. 1833	Dec.	21-10m		L4	
Bartlett, Elizabeth Yeatman	16, Oct. 1856	14, Oct.	11- 8m- 8d		L5	
Bartlett, Henry	3, Oct. 1850		80	*	L3	
Bartlett, Jonathan	15, Nov. 1849	7, Nov.	62	*	L3	
Bartlett, Joseph M.	8, Aug. 1833	July	1- 8m		L1	
Bartlett, Joseph R.	1, Aug. 1833	July	27		L1	
Bartlett, Mary Elizabeth	9, June 1842	4, June	11m		L3	
Bartlett, Roswell	2, July 1805		estate		L3	
Bartlett, Samuel	1, Aug. 1833	July	15		L1	
Bartlett, William	7, May 1840	Apr.	49		L3	
Bartlett, William Henry	21, July 1842	18, July			L3	
Bartlette, J. Yates	7, July 1842	21, June	28	*	L3	
Bartley, Elizabeth	18, Sept 1851	27, Aug.	62		L3	
Bartley, Joesph	24, May 1849	May	27		L3	
Bartley, Julia M.	18, Mar. 1847	1, Mar.			L3	
Bartley, Samuel	14, Aug. 1845	Aug.	22		L3	
Barton, (Mr)	18, Oct. 1832	13, Oct.	74		L2	
Barton, Benjamin Smith (Dr)	8, Jan. 1816	19, Dec.	49		L3	
Barton, George (Mrs)	25, Nov. 1852	24, Nov.			L3	
Bascoe, Thomas F.	13, Mar. 1856		estate		L3	
Bascos, Andrew	17, Aug. 1837	Aug.	35		L3	
Bascum, Richard Robertson	7, Sept 1843	23, Aug.	6m		L3	
Baser, Carl	5, Dec. 1850	30, Nov.			L3	
Baskerville, Mary	10, Apr. 1856	6, Apr.	75	*	L3	
Basly, Martin	18, Jan. 1849	Jan.	30		L3	
Bass, Moses T.	6, Apr. 1837	3, Apr.	26	*	L3	
Bass, Moses T.	3, Sept 1840		probate		L3	
Bassenger, Henry	7, June 1849	May	34		L3	

Name	Notice Date	Death Date	Age		Page	Maiden Name
Bassett, (Mrs)	25, Oct. 1832	20, Oct.			L2	
Bassett, Benjamin	31, Mar. 1830		estate		L3	
Bassett, Benjamin	4, Sept 1856		probate		L5	
Bassett, David B.	18, Oct. 1838		estate		L3	
Bassett, David B.	5, Sept 1839		probate		L3	
Bassett, Elisha	25, Mar. 1815		estate		L3	
Bassett, Joseph F.	28, May 1846	23, May	27	*	L3	
Baswicker, Samuel	14, Dec. 1848	Dec.	33		L2	
Batchelder, John (Capt)	23, Jan. 1845	11, Jan.			L3	
Batchelor, Elizabeth	8, Feb. 1844	4, Feb.	20	*	L3	Pemberton
Bateman, John M.	13, Nov. 1834	Nov.	1- 6m		L1	
Baterlolet, Frederick	11, Sept 1834	Aug.	8m		L1	
Bates, Alice	23, May 1844	15, May			L3	
Bates, Alvin	14, July 1821	11, July			L3	
Bates, Arabella	6, Apr. 1848	31, Mar.	3- 2m		L3	
Bates, Caleb	14, July 1853	13, July			L3	
Bates, Clark Vandine	2, Feb. 1843	15, Jan.	16m		L3	
Bates, Elizabeth Rachel	8, July 1847	5, July	3- 6m		L3	
Bates, George H.	15, Aug. 1850		estate		L3	
Bates, Hannah	4, May 1854	3, May	56		L3	
Bates, Isaac	12, July 1838		estate		L3	
Bates, James P.	8, Oct. 1857		probate		L3	
Bates, James W.	24, Feb. 1853				L3	
Bates, John	19, May 1842	18, May			L3	
Bates, Jonathan	30, Apr. 1846	29, Apr.	49		L3	
Bates, Joseph S.	21, Apr. 1853	17, Apr.	41		L3	
Bates, Joseph S.	6, Dec. 1855		probate		L3	
Bates, Joseph Trotter	14, Mar. 1850	12, Mar.			L3	
Bates, Mary Perry	1, Aug. 1850	24, July	2- 4m		L3	
Bates, Matilda Ellen	31, Oct. 1839	25, Oct.	20m		L3	
Bates, Timothy G.	21, Jan. 1847	5, Jan.			L3	
Bates, William Grandin	16, Feb. 1843	11, Feb.	infant		L3	
Batti, (child of Archibald)	11, July 1833	July	5m		L1	
Bauer, George C.	19, Apr. 1849	Apr.	50		L3	
Bauer, O. Ella	3, July 1851	30, June	2- 6m		L3	
Baum, (son of Martin)	24, Feb. 1807	19, Feb.	infant		L3	
Baum, Caroline	8, Nov. 1832	Nov.	43		L1	
Baum, David C.	20, June 1839	8, June			L3	
Baum, Jacob	11, Nov. 1841	6, Nov.	34		L3	
Baum, Kershner	27, Sept 1838	10, Sept			L3	
Baum, Martin	29, May 1834		probate		L3	
Baum, Martin	15, Sept 1836		probate		L3	
Baum, Martin	22, Dec. 1831	14, Dec.			L4	
Bauman, Henry S.	1, Oct. 1846	14, Sept	32		L3	
Baumgardner, Francis	24, Feb. 1853	21, Feb.	10m- 4d		L3	
Baumgartinger, Jacob	6, Apr. 1843	Mar.	29		L3	
Bawles, John	16, May 1839		estate		L3	
Baxter, Archibald	15, Nov. 1855				L3	
Baxter, Christopher Marshall	9, Jan. 1845	6, Jan.	18m		L3	
Baxter, Francis M.	31, July 1845	July	25		L3	
Baxter, James	3, Sept 1840		probate		L3	
Baxter, James	3, Oct. 1821		estate		L4	
Baxter, James (Dr)	11, Oct. 1838			*	L3	
Baxter, John	14, Apr. 1842	Apr.	4		L3	

Name	Notice Date	Death Date	Age	Page	Maiden Name
Baxter, Marshall	28, Jan. 1847	21, Jan.		L3	
Baxter, Polly	29, May 1845	May	25	L3	
Baxter, Robert	25, Sept 1856		estate	L8	
Baxter, Schuyler	7, 14, Dec. 1843	5, Dec.	83	* L3	
Bayly, James K.	6, Jan. 1817		estate	L3	
Baymiller, Anna T.	8, Dec. 1817	2, Dec.		L3	
Baymiller, Jacob	16, July 1824	9, July	42	L2	
Baymiller, Jacob	23, July 1824		estate	L3	
Baymiller, Jacob	2, May 1826		estate	L3	
Bazzel, Charles	15, Apr. 1847	Apr.	56	L3	
Beach,	18, Nov. 1847	12, Nov.		L2	
Beach, John G.	8, Jan. 1846		estate	L3	
Beach, Solomon (Dr)	22, Aug. 1850	12, Aug.	67	* L3	
Beach, Solomon (Dr)	29, Aug. 1850		estate	L3	
Beacham, Sarah Jane	26, Jan. 1854	13, Jan.	17	L3	
Beagle, Christian	5, July 1832		estate	L3	
Beagle, William	26, Feb. 1816		estate	L3	
Beal, Franklin	25, July 1833	July	11	L1	
Beal, Nathaniel G.	25, Oct. 1827	Oct.	18	L2	
Beale, Sarah	2, Jan. 1851	28, Dec.	25	L3	
Bealer, John B.	12, Sept 1850	5, Sept		L3	
Beall, Hannah H.	7, Feb. 1828	Feb.	6m	L1	
Beall, Mary	25, Mar. 1812	21, Mar.		L3	
Beall, Reasin (Gen)	9, Mar. 1843	20, Feb.	73	L3	
Bealor, Ruth A.	7, Sept 1854	3, Sept	27	L3	
Beament, William	3, Jan. 1850	Dec.	28	L3	
Bean, Nehemiah	27, June 1839	June	5m	L3	
Bean, Thomas	18, Apr. 1844	Apr.	34	L3	
Beans, Sarah	14, May 1846	May	18	L3	
Beard, William	12, Nov. 1805	9, Nov.		L3	
Bearmont, Mary	29, Feb. 1844	Feb.	2	L3	
Beasley, Mary E.	5, Dec. 1850	Nov.	17	L3	
Beatty, (child of S.)	19, Sept 1833	Sept	5m	L4	
Beatty, William	22, Jan. 1852	Jan.	32	L3	
Beaty, Arthur	12, Nov. 1835		estate	L3	
Beaty, Arthur	22, June 1837		probate	L3	
Beauchamp, Hiram	26, Aug. 1831		estate	L3	
Bebb, Margaret	11, Dec. 1851	2, Dec.	78	* L3	
Beck, John	31, July 1851	July	38	L3	
Beck, Mary	21, Nov. 1833		estate	L3	
Becking, Rebecca J.	12, Sept 1850	10, Sept	20	L3	Warden
Beckler, Matthias	29, Nov. 1838	Nov.	30	L3	
Beckman, Gasper	9, Dec. 1847	Dec.	27	L3	
Beckman, Lewis	3, Oct. 1850	Sept		L3	
Bedient, Zalmon	13, Feb. 1851	12, Feb.	36	L3	
Bedinger, George	19, Sept 1833	Sept		L4	
Bedinger, Henry	23, Aug. 1838	17, Aug.	infant	L3	
Bedinger, Lavinia	5, June 1822	25, May	25	* L3	Drake
Bedon, Elizabeth	2, Oct. 1834	Sept	12	L4	
Bee, James	25, July 1844	July	1	L3	
Bee, Sarah Ann	28, Aug. 1834	Aug.	1- 5m	L1	
Beecher, (child of Harriet)	11, Nov. 1852	Oct.	infant	L3	
Beeman, David	8, Nov. 1838		probate	L3	
Beerhaust, (man)	26, Feb. 1852	25, Feb.		L4	

Name	Notice Date	Death Date	Age		Page	Maiden Name
Beesfield, John	12, Dec. 1833	Dec.			L4	
Beesley, Sarah	29, Aug. 1850	19, Aug.	30		L3	
Beesom, A.	28, Sept 1848		estate		L3	
Beeson, Amos	22, Nov. 1838		estate		L3	
Beeson, Amos	19, Oct. 1837	18, Sept			L3	
Beezan, Patrick	23, Oct. 1845	Oct.	35		L3	
Beezley, John	25, Aug. 1818		estate		L4	
Beggs, Eliza B.	25, June 1846	21, June			L3	
Begley, Christina	2, Aug. 1832	July	14		L1	
Behil, John	3, Aug. 1848	July	17		L3	
Behm, John	16, Mar. 1849	Mar.	28		L3	
Behm, Simon (Mrs)	26, July 1855				L3	
Beker, Bernard	16, June 1842	June			L3	
Bela, (child of A.)	25, July 1833	July	stillborn		L1	
Belcher, Elizabeth	14, Sept 1837	Sept	31		L4	
Belcher, George	12, July 1849	July	27		L3	
Belcher, John	12, Oct. 1837	Oct.	7m		L4	
Belcher, Samuel	2, Nov. 1837	Oct.	2		L4	
Beler, (child of H.)	16, Oct. 1834	Oct.			L1	
Bell, Adeline	10, Aug. 1854	7, Aug.			L3	
Bell, Catharine F.	13, Feb. 1851	8, Feb.	37	*	L3	
Bell, Elizabeth	23, Mar. 1843	Mar.	1d		L3	
Bell, Frederick	20, Aug. 1846	Aug.	30		L3	
Bell, George	13, Feb. 1840		probate		L3	
Bell, George	7, Feb. 1839		estate		L4	
Bell, James	8, Aug. 1833	July	11m		L1	
Bell, James	13, Apr. 1843	Apr.	29		L3	
Bell, James	13, Aug. 1846	Aug.	30		L3	
Bell, James M. (Gen)	19, Apr. 1849		53		L3	
Bell, John	22, Oct. 1846	Oct.	36		L3	
Bell, John	13, May 1816		estate		L3	
Bell, John	3, June 1852	23, May			L3	
Bell, John	22, May 1834	May	14d		L4	
Bell, Louisa	2, July 1846	June	1- 6m		L3	
Bell, Margaret	17, Sept 1846	14, Sept	78		L3	
Bell, Margaret	7, Aug. 1845	4, Aug.	79		L3	
Bell, Margaret Anna	25, Mar. 1847	20, Mar.	2- 1m-18d		L3	
Bell, Monroe	22, June 1843				L3	
Bell, Peter	27, Oct. 1831		probate		L1	
Bell, Peter	13, May 1830	9, May			L3	
Bell, Rebecca C.	11, Jan. 1855	7, Jan.		*	L3	
Bell, Reuben	12, July 1849	July	48		L3	
Bell, Robert	25, Oct. 1832	Oct.	29		L1	
Bell, Samuel	6, Apr. 1843	20, Mar.			L3	
Bellamy, Mary	11, Mar. 1847	Mar.	4		L3	
Belle, John	14, Mar. 1850	2, Mar.	45	*	L3	
Bellia, Isabella	9, Feb. 1854	14, Jan.	20		L3	
Bellue, Augustus	16, May 1850	May	39		L3	
Belman, Clarissa	14, Oct. 1852	8, Oct.	26		L3	
Belman, Gertrude Amelia	12, Jan. 1854	30, Dec.	2- 3m		L3	
Belman, Mary C.	14, Sept 1854	6, Sept	17		L3	
Belser, William C.	14, Aug. 1856		probate		L6	
Belt, Levin	20, Oct. 1842		77	*	L3	
Belt, Wolf	18, June 1846	June	30		L3	

Name	Notice Date	Death Date	Age	Page	Maiden Name
Beltz, Frederick	10, Apr. 1856		probate	L3	
Beman, Elizabeth	20, Mar. 1845	16, Mar.	60	L3	
Benbridge, Henry	3, Jan. 1823	1, Jan.		L3	
Benbridge, Richard M.	17, Oct. 1823	13, Sept	16	L3	
Benbridge, Virginia	18, Sept 1822	12, Sept		L3	
Bendell, Ann	27, May 1847	May	45	L3	
Bender, Adam	1, Sept 1842	Aug.	60	L3	
Benedict, Isaac	8, July 1847	June	27	L3	
Benefield, Joseph	13, Jan. 1806	31, Dec.	18	L3	
Benford, Thomas	15, June 1848	June	20	L3	
Benghinstrough, Adam	1, Aug. 1833	July		L1	
Benham, Courtlandt (Lt)	10, Feb. 1853	30, Oct.		L3	
Benham, Isabella G.	7, Nov. 1828	6, Nov.		L4	
Benham, Joseph S.	23, July 1840	22, July	43	L3	
Benham, L.S.	1, Nov. 1832	26, Oct.	6	L3	
Benham, Nancy	12, July 1849	2, July	63	L3	
Benjamin, Jonathan	4, Nov. 1841	26, Aug.	103	*	L3	
Benner, Albert	1, Nov. 1838	Oct.	27	L3	
Bennet, (child of Sarah)	16, June 1842	June	2w	L3	
Bennet, Lewis	11, July 1833		probate	L3	
Bennet, Louisa	15, June 1837	June	6	L4	
Bennet, Patrick	17, May 1849	May	40	L3	
Bennet, Samuel	10, June 1816		estate	L4	
Bennet, Susan F.	2, May 1833	Apr.	7m- 6d	L1	
Bennet, William	19, July 1832	July	70	L1	
Bennett, (Mr)	19, Mar. 1857	15, Mar.		L3	
Bennett, A.D.	28, June 1849	June	23	L3	
Bennett, Anna	29, Jan. 1852	22, Jan.	3- 2m	L3	
Bennett, Charles	27, June 1850	June	40	L3	
Bennett, Charlotte R.	17, Aug. 1854	10, Aug.	33	L3	
Bennett, George	15, Oct. 1846	Oct.	17	L3	
Bennett, Harriet	1, June 1848	25, May		L3	
Bennett, J.K.	26, Dec. 1850	25, Dec.		L3	
Bennett, James	25, May 1848	May		L3	
Bennett, Jane	5, Oct. 1854	28, Sept	47	L3	
Bennett, John	12, Jan. 1837	Jan.	28	L3	
Bennett, Mary A.	28, Feb. 1850	25, Feb.		L3	
Bennett, Milo	27, Dec. 1832	Dec.	34	L1	
Bennett, Samuel	5, Jan. 1813		estate	L3	
Bennett, William	26, June 1845	June	3	L3	
Benninger, Martin	22, Nov. 1838		estate	L3	
Benninghaus, Francis	25, June 1846	6, June	26	L3	
Benson, Amelia Jane	27, Mar. 1856	20, Mar.	2m	L3	
Benson, Benjamin W.	4, June 1857	1, June	23m	L3	
Benson, Blackley	9, Aug. 1855		probate	L3	
Benson, Charles Edwin	17, Aug. 1854	9, Aug.	11m	L3	
Benson, David T.	11, Apr. 1839	22, Mar.		L3	
Benson, Gabriel L.	7, Jan. 1825	6, Jan.		*	L3	
Benson, Lizzie Fulton	5, Aug. 1852	1, Aug.	infant	L3	
Benson, Mary Jane	11, Oct. 1838	23, Sept	20m	L3	
Benson, Mathew	31, May 1832		estate	L4	
Benson, Matthew	12, Jan. 1837		probate	L3	
Benson, Peter	23, Feb. 1843	14, Feb.		L3	
Benson, Peter	2, Mar. 1843	14, Feb.		L3	

Name	Notice Date	Death Date	Age	Page	Maiden Name
Bentley, Thomas S. (Dr)	10, Sept 1857	2, Sept	28	L3	
Benton, (child of F.R.)	9, Oct. 1834	Sept	stillborn	L1	
Benzky, Michael	25, Apr. 1850	Apr.	30	L3	
Berach, Maria	26, July 1849	July	36	L3	
Beresford, Elizabeth	8, May 1845	1, May	81	L3	
Beresford, Jeptha D.G.	19, July 1849	16, July	13- 4m	L3	
Beresford, Richard	9, Oct. 1828		estate	L2	
Beresford, Susanna Isabelle	15, Nov. 1855	14, Nov.	5- 5m	L3	
Beresford, William	3, Apr. 1845	31, Mar.	27	L3	
Berg, Henry	26, July 1849	July	4- 6m	L3	
Berg, John	4, Jan. 1849	Dec.	27	L3	
Berg, John K.	12, Apr. 1855	3, Apr.	21	L3	
Bergen, Daniel	10, May 1849	May	37	L3	
Bergen, Judith	3, May 1849	Apr.	28	L3	
Bergen, Margaret	21, June 1849	June	3	L3	
Bergen, Mary	28, June 1849	June	9w	L3	
Berger, Henry	17, June 1847	June	60	L3	
Berger, Jacob	25, July 1850	July	33	L3	
Berger, John	11, July 1850	July	45	L4	
Berhard, John G.	1, Aug. 1833	July	31	L1	
Berngarten, Jacob	7, Aug. 1834	July	1	L3	
Berrien, John (Major)	11, Dec. 1815	5, Nov.	55	L3	
Berrman, John	25, Apr. 1850	Apr.	21	L3	
Berry, James	25, Mar. 1847	17, Mar.	89	L3	
Berry, Joseph R.	18, Nov. 1852		estate	L3	
Berry, Mary Ann	2, Mar. 1848	Feb.	48	L3	
Berry, Mary Ann	12, Aug. 1847	4, Aug.		L3	
Berry, Mary Stentinius	10, Apr. 1856	4, Apr.	16	L3	
Berry, Polly	2, Oct. 1851		estate	L3	
Berry, Rachel	28, May 1857		90- 2m-25d	L3	
Berry, Washington	14, Sept 1813		estate	L3	
Berry, William	2, July 1857	19, June	16	L3	
Berry, William	7, Sept 1837		estate	L3	
Berryman, Margaret	14, Aug. 1845	Aug.	60	L3	
Berstein, J.	12, May 1853	6, May		L3	
Besbarth, Daniel	4, Dec. 1845	Nov.	32	L3	
Bessom, R.D.	29, July 1841	21, July	43	L3	
Best, Clarissa	18, Mar. 1823	17, Mar.		L3	
Best, Emma	28, Apr. 1842	19, Apr.		L3	
Bestow, Laura H.	23, Feb. 1854	2, Feb.		L3	
Betshols, George	16, May 1833	May	33	L1	
Better, Agness	5, July 1849	June	36	L3	
Betts, (child of David)	28, Feb. 1828	Feb.	1d	L1	
Betts, Eliza Ann	7, Sept 1843	1, Sept		L3	
Betts, Eugene Aubrey	9, Feb. 1854	7, Feb.	4- 4m- 7d	L3	
Betts, Frederick G. (Rev)	23, Jan. 1845	22, Jan.		L3	
Betts, Joseph	25, Apr. 1850	Apr.	49	L3	
Betts, Oliver C.	1, Mar. 1855	24, Feb.	51	L3	
Betts, Phebe	25, Jan. 1844	24, Jan.	75	L3	
Betts, Phebe	1, Feb. 1844	23, Jan.	75	L3	
Betts, Samuel	12, Oct. 1837		estate	L3	
Betzner, John	25, July 1839	July	27	L3	
Beverly, James	1, Mar. 1849	Feb.	18	L3	
Bevis, Anna	21, Sept 1837		probate	L4	

Name	Notice Date	Death Date	Age	Page	Maiden Name
Bevor, William	9, Aug. 1838		probate	L3	
Beyer, F.R.	14, Oct. 1841	24, Sept		L3	
Beyer, Theodore	25, Oct. 1832	Oct.	40	L1	
Biber, Debolt	14, Mar. 1850	Mar.	45	L3	
Bickham, Jefferson H.	7, Feb. 1833	Feb.	3- 2m- 2d	L1	
Bickham, Thomas D.	3, May 1855		probate	L3	
Bickham, William	23, Oct. 1845		estate	L3	
Bickham, William	22, July 1847		estate	L3	
Bickham, William	2, Mar. 1848		estate	L3	
Bidaker, (Mr)	18, Oct. 1832	13, Oct.		L2	
Biddle, Andrew	14, June 1838	June	23	L3	
Biddle, Hiram	27, June 1810	17, June	10	L3	
Biddle, W.H.	5, Mar. 1857		probate	L3	
Bierle, John	28, Aug. 1834	Aug.	2m- 3d	L1	
Bigelow, Abijah	2, Nov. 1854	25, Oct.		L3	
Bigelow, Edward	19, Dec. 1850	1, Dec.	24	L3	
Bigelow, John	5, 12, Sept 1833	30, Aug.	58	L1	
Biggar, George D.	10, June 1847	29, May	33	L3	
Biggar, James	4, May 1848	2, May	5- 3m	L3	
Biggin, Ann	14, June 1849	June	27	L3	
Biggs, Benjamin	22, June 1848	22, May	35	L3	
Biggs, Catherine	19, July 1849	15, July	25	L3	Miller
Biggs, Joseph	7, Aug. 1834	July	3	L3	
Biggs, Maria	14, Aug. 1845	11, Aug.	65	L3	
Biggs, Samuel R.	31, Oct. 1833	Oct.	1- 1m-21d	L4	
Biggs, Thomas	30, Oct. 1845	Oct.	3m	L3	
Biggs, William	1, Aug. 1839	28, July		L3	
Biggs, Zaccheus	10, Oct. 1826		estate	L3	
Biggs, Zaceheus	29, May 1828		estate	L3	
Biggs, Zacheus	7, July 1836		estate	L3	
Biggs, Zacheus	8, Sept 1826	4, Sept		L3	
Bigham, Benjamin	25, Oct. 1827	Oct.	25	L2	
Bigler, John H.	10, Sept 1857	8, Sept	68	L3	
Bilbey, James	14, Sept 1837	Sept	28	L4	
Biliomly, Mary A.	19, July 1849	July	37	L3	
Billerbeck, Mary	28, Jan. 1847	20, Jan.		L3	
Billington, Thomas	17, Aug. 1837	13, Aug.		* L3	
Billins, Sarah	1, Jan. 1852	26, Dec.		L3	
Bills, James	13, Apr. 1813		estate	L2	
Bills, James	30, Mar. 1813	26, Mar.		L3	
Billwood, Ralph	25, Sept 1845	Sept	55	L3	
Billy, Scotch	8, Jan. 1846	Dec.	54	L3	
Binder, George	8, Jan. 1816	6, Dec.	43	L3	
Bingham, Amos	4, Feb. 1841	Jan.	43	L3	
Bingham, R. (Mrs)	25, Oct. 1832	21, Oct.		L3	
Bingham, Rebecca	15, July 1841	July	43	L3	
Bird, Jefferson	28, May 1840		estate	L3	
Bird, Norman	13, Feb. 1840		probate	L3	
Birden, Adomi	18, Oct. 1827	Oct.		L3	
Birkel, Michael	28, June 1849	June	19	L3	
Birkel, Nicholas	30, Oct. 1851	16, Oct.	6	L4	
Birmingham, Daniel	2, Jan. 1845	Dec.	32	L3	
Birmingham, William	9, Apr. 1846	Mar.	57	L3	
Birne, Henry	28, June 1849	June	39	L3	

Name	Notice Date	Death Date	Age		Page	Maiden Name
Birrell, William	11, June 1840		estate		L3	
Bishop, Alexander	3, Nov. 1836		2w		L3	
Bishop, Daniel L.	6, Apr. 1848	26, Mar.	72		L3	
Bishop, Deborah	2, May 1839		estate		L3	
Bishop, George B.	28, Dec. 1837	14, Dec.	25		L3	
Bishop, George Nathaniel	18, Feb. 1847	16, Feb.	4- 4m		L3	
Bishop, James Flagg	11, Mar. 1847	8, Mar.	2		L3	
Bishop, John Hoge	8, Jan. 1846	2, Jan.	22m-20d		L3	
Bishop, Josephine Maria	25, Jan. 1855	8, Jan.	19		L3	
Bishop, Lucy Perkins	8, Mar. 1855	27, Feb.	5- 3m		L3	
Bishop, Mary	3, Aug. 1854	28, July	72		L3	
Bishop, Mary	25, May 1848	19, May			L3	
Bishop, Robert H. (Rev)	3, May 1855	29, Apr.	77	*	L3	
Bishop, Samuel	21, June 1855	14, June	5m- 9d		L3	
Bishop, Thomas	7, Sept 1824		probate		L3	
Bishop, Truman (Dr)	15, Jan. 1829				L3	
Bissell, Edward M.	5, Mar. 1840	29, Feb.	16m		L3	
Bissell, Elizabeth Martha	30, Jan. 1845	10, Jan.			L3	
Bissell, Simon B.	30, Mar. 1843	13, Mar.			L3	
Bittner, George	10, Feb. 1848	Feb.	40		L3	
Bixbee, George	2, May 1844	Apr.	16		L3	
Bixler, Edward I.	30, Aug. 1838	23, Aug.	22	*	L3	
Blachley, Oliver B.	15, Sept 1836	12, Sept			L3	
Blachly, Caroline W.	11, July 1823	6, July			L3	
Blachly, Elizabeth Spencer	18, Apr. 1839	15, Apr.	78		L3	
Black, (child of Dayton)	18, Apr. 1839	Apr.	3m		L3	
Black, Catharine	24, July 1851	2, July			L3	
Black, Daniel	27, June 1850	June	22		L3	
Black, David	24, Sept 1846		estate		L3	
Black, David	24, Feb. 1848		estate		L3	
Black, David	9, Dec. 1847				L3	
Black, Diana	21, Apr. 1842	20, Apr.	54		L3	
Black, Harriet	21, Oct. 1841	10, Oct.			L3	Jones
Black, James	27, Feb. 1845	24, Feb.	66		L3	
Black, James	25, Oct. 1832	23, Oct.			L3	
Black, James	5, Oct. 1837	Sept	11m		L4	
Black, John	11, July 1850	5, July	35		L3	
Black, John	7, Feb. 1839		estate		L3	
Black, John	13, Feb. 1840		probate		L3	
Black, John B.	30, Mar. 1848		estate		L4	
Black, John L. (Capt)	25, Aug. 1853	17, Aug.	42		L3	
Black, Joseph	22, July 1847	July	27		L3	
Black, Peter	13, Jan. 1848	Jan.	40		L3	
Black, William	18, July 1833	July	2		L2	
Black, William	6, Aug. 1846	30, July			L3	
Black, William	19, Feb. 1852	13, Feb.			L3	
Blackburn, Alexander	31, Jan. 1850	Jan.	35		L3	
Blackburn, Edward	18, Sept 1851	11, Sept	70	*	L3	
Blackeman, Elizabeth	8, Aug. 1833	July	23- 6m		L1	
Blacken, Mary	15, Oct. 1857	Oct.			L3	
Blackman, David	11, Jan. 1838		estate		L3	
Blackwell, Jacob	5, Nov. 1819		estate		L4	
Blades, Benjamin	9, June 1836		probate		L3	
Blair, (child of Granville)	12, Sept 1839	Sept	1- 5m		L3	

Name	Notice Date	Death Date	Age	Page	Maiden Name
Blair, Ann Eliza	23, Mar. 1843	20, Mar.	11	L3	
Blair, Dascum Allen	14, Feb. 1850	10, Feb.	2- 4m-14d	L3	
Blair, David	15, Feb. 1838	Feb.	71	L3	
Blair, Elizabeth	16, May 1833	May	1- 3m	L1	
Blair, Frank	3, Dec. 1857	30, Nov.	21m	L3	
Blair, Greenville	26, Aug. 1847	Aug.	40	L3	
Blair, John	17, June 1847	June	39	L3	
Blair, Letitia	12, July 1849	July	16	L3	
Blair, Lucinda	6, Sept 1849	Aug.	44	L3	
Blair, Mary Ann	26, Sept 1839	Sept	10	L3	
Blake, Charles	13, July 1843	July	46	L3	
Blake, George	21, Oct. 1841	6, Oct.	73	L3	
Blake, John Brooke	27, June 1850	21, June	2- 4m	L3	
Blakely, William	8, Nov. 1832	30, Oct.		L4	
Blanchard, Abieb	29, Jan. 1816		estate	L3	
Blanchard, Lorenzo	5, Oct. 1848	Sept	26	L3	
Blanchard, Thomas	6, Feb. 1851		estate	L3	
Blanchard, William	29, May 1845	May	49	L3	
Bland, Charlotte	4, July 1833	June	34	L2	
Bland, Henry	15, Aug. 1833	Aug.	31	L1	
Bland, Mary	15, Aug. 1833	Aug.	1- 5m	L1	
Bland, Robert	8, Nov. 1832	Nov.	1- 1m	L1	
Bland, Robert	29, May 1845		estate	L3	
Blank, Martin	7, Sept 1848	Aug.	25	L3	
Blanke, John	25, May 1848	May		L3	
Blatchford, John (Rev)	19, Apr. 1855	8, Apr.	56	L3	
Blatzee, John	31, May 1849	May	40	L3	
Blaud, Mary	1, Aug. 1833	July	3m	L1	
Bledsoe, Polly	8, Apr. 1847	Mar.	84	L3	
Blermer, Bernard	19, Mar. 1846	Mar.	29	L3	
Blessington, John	28, Sept 1848	Sept	40	L3	
Blew, John	29, Aug. 1850	Aug.	9m	L3	
Blinn, Mercy	28, Oct. 1841	19, Oct.	101	L3	
Bliss, Caroline Ellen	12, June 1845	6, June	7m-14d	L3	
Bliss, Elvira	4, Sept 1856	27, Aug.	25	L5	Ketchum
Bliss, Francis	1, Oct. 1846	24, Sept	1- -24d	L3	
Bliss, Harriet Louisa	2, July 1846	24, June	1- 8m	L3	
Bliss, Lucinda	11, July 1833	July	4-11m	L1	
Bliss, Pliny (Capt)	9, Mar. 1854	3, Mar.	78	L3	
Bliss, Samuel	13, Apr. 1854	7, Apr.	50	L3	
Bliven, David	2, Aug. 1855	25, July	62	L3	
Block, Simon	18, Oct. 1832	13, Oct.		L2	
Blodget, Nathan	4, May 1848	Apr.	52	L3	
Blodget, William H.	7, Apr. 1842	24, Mar.		L3	
Blodgett, Darius	17, Nov. 1842	12, Nov.	40	L6	
Bloemer, Joseph	24, Sept 1846	Sept	29	L3	
Bloeth, George	10, Jan. 1850	Jan.	22	L3	
Blong, Joseph	6, Mar. 1856	1, Mar.	38	L3	
Blood, Hosea (Dr)	28, Oct. 1816	12, Sept		L2	
Blood, William	25, July 1810			L3	
Bloom, (child of Ellen)	30, Mar. 1849	Mar.	1d	L3	
Bloom, Mary Ann	14, May 1857	6, May	42	L3	
Bloomfield, Joseph	23, Mar. 1843		estate	L3	
Blue, (Mr)	25, Oct. 1832	17, Oct.		L1	

Name	Notice Date	Death Date	Age		Page	Maiden Name
Blue, Ezekiel	1, Nov. 1832	Oct.	54		L2	
Blue, John	8, Aug. 1833	July	24		L1	
Blundell, Charles Percival	3, Mar. 1853	25, Feb.	3- 6m-13d		L3	
Blunt, Amelia	22, June 1848	20, June			L3	
Boadman, Mary	4, Apr. 1833	Mar.	5- 6m		L1	
Boal, Catharine	4, May 1848	Apr.	17		L3	
Boal, James	21, Sept 1837		probate		L4	
Boal, Robert	13, Mar. 1856	9, Mar.	66	*	L3	
Boal, Thomas	8, Feb. 1820		estate		L3	
Boal, Thomas	27, Dec. 1814	25, Dec.			L3	
Boals, W.	7, Feb. 1839		estate		L4	
Board, George	8, Nov. 1832	Nov.	3- 8m		L1	
Boardman, (Mrs)	1, Nov. 1832	27, Oct.			L2	
Boardman, Charles	24, July 1834	13, July	33	*	L4	
Boardman, Elizabeth	10, Dec. 1840	9, Dec.	64	*	L3	
Boatman, Samuel Lee	12, Oct. 1843	Oct.	35		L3	
Bocknower, Mary M.	22, Aug. 1833	Aug.	1- 2m		L4	
Bodine, Joseph S.	11, Apr. 1833	Apr.	3		L1	
Bodman, Adelaide A.	16, Dec. 1847	10, Dec.			L3	
Bodman, Mary Louvinia	5, Jan. 1837	27, Dec.	2		L3	
Boef, Jacob	13, Dec. 1832	Dec.	73		L1	
Boehinger, Paul H.	4, Sept 1856		probate		L5	
Boehringer, Paul Herman	13, Nov. 1850		estate		L3	
Boelling, Frederick	9, Dec. 1847	Dec.	40		L3	
Boeske, Frederick	9, July 1857		probate		L3	
Bogart, Helmus	9, Apr. 1857		probate		L3	
Bogart, Helmus	14, Aug. 1856		probate		L6	
Bogart, Peter	5, Mar. 1857		probate		L3	
Bogen, Margaretta	15, Nov. 1832	Nov.	1		L1	
Boggins, Michael	5, Dec. 1850	Nov.	27		L3	
Boggs, D. (Mrs)	25, Jan. 1849	19, Jan.	29		L3	
Boggs, James	18, June 1846		estate		L3	
Bogie, Janet	26, Mar. 1840	25, Mar.	80	*	L3	
Bogie, John	15, Nov. 1832		estate		L3	
Bogie, William	18, Oct. 1832	15, Oct.			L2	
Bogie, William	15, Nov. 1832		estate		L4	
Bohle, John Gerhard	10, July 1851		estate		L3	
Bohlman, Margaret E.	5, July 1849	June	79		L3	
Bohmer, G.H.	5, Feb. 1857		probate		L3	
Bohnen, John	11, Mar. 1852	2, Mar.			L4	
Bohsomman, Ann S.	22, Aug. 1833	Aug.	11m		L4	
Bolander, Adam	11, June 1846	June	26		L3	
Bolden, (child)	22, Aug. 1833	Aug.	4m		L4	
Boles, James	18, Jan. 1849	Jan.	14		L3	
Bolsel, George	27, Oct. 1831		estate		L3	
Bolsel, George	11, July 1833		probate		L3	
Bolser, Jane	1, Aug. 1833	July	26		L1	
Bolser, Reason	22, Mar. 1838		probate		L3	
Bolte, Henry	6, Mar. 1856		probate		L3	
Bolton, (child of J.)	15, Aug. 1833	Aug.	1		L1	
Bomgardner, Robert	29, Nov. 1849	Nov.	7w		L3	
Bomgartner, Jacob	9, Mar. 1848	Mar.	56		L3	
Bonati, Catharine	19, Mar. 1846	Mar.	33		L3	
Bond, Catharine	29, Jan. 1846	Jan.	64		L3	

Name	Notice Date	Death Date	Age	Page	Maiden Name
Bond, Forster	5, Oct. 1854	22, Sept	20m	L3	
Bonnel, Benjamin C.	16, Apr. 1846	4, Apr.	48	L3	
Bonnell, Edith	18, July 1844	11, July	15m	L3	
Bonnell, Moses	18, Aug. 1842	16, Aug.	68	L3	
Bonner, Ann	20, Apr. 1809	2, Apr.		L3	Pelham
Bonner, Hugh (Dr)	2, Mar. 1837	27, Feb.	37	L3	
Bonsall, Joseph	16, Nov. 1843		estate	L3	
Bonsall, Joseph	16, May 1844	14, May	infant	L3	
Bonsall, Martha Newbold	17, Mar. 1842	19, Feb.	10- - 7d	L3	
Bonte, Julia Ellen	5, Dec. 1850	3, Dec.	8	L3	
Bonte, Mary Aurelia	28, June 1849	24, June	2- -16d	L3	
Bonte, O.B.	11, Sept 1834	Aug.	6-11m	L1	
Bonte, P.J.	12, Jan. 1843		estate	L3	
Bonte, Peter J.	29, Dec. 1842	20, Dec.	56	L3	
Bontell, George William	20, Mar. 1845	16, Mar.	2-10m-20d	L3	
Bonton, (Lt)	4, Dec. 1815	9, Oct.		L1	
Bonwell, William B.	16, Nov. 1848		estate	L3	
Boofee, Eliza	19, July 1849	July	40	L3	
Boome, Lucy	19, Jan. 1854	19, Nov.	70	L3	
Boon, Rachel	15, Oct. 1857	6, Oct.	91	L3	
Boon, Ratliff (Col)	5, Dec. 1844	20, Nov.	64	* L3	
Boon, William	12, Apr. 1814		estate	L2	
Boon, William	17, Mar. 1826		probate	L3	
Boon, William	26, Sept 1826		probate	L3	
Boon, William	16, Feb. 1827		probate	L3	
Boossey, Grace	13, June 1833	June	29	L1	
Booth, Abraham (Rev)	2, June 1806		73	L3	
Booth, Benjamin	7, Sept 1824		probate	L3	
Booth, James	18, Sept 1845	Sept	34	L3	
Booth, Joseph	7, Oct. 1841	30, Aug.		* L3	
Booth, Ralph Waldron	30, July 1857	22, July	2- 1m- 2d	L3	
Boothe, Edward (Capt)	5, Nov. 1840	20, Oct.		L2	
Boothe, Thomas	11, Oct. 1849	Oct.	41	L3	
Boots, Benjamin	25, Jan. 1838	Jan.	54	L3	
Boots, Hezekiah	1, Aug. 1833	July	80	L1	
Boram, Aaron	10, Jan. 1856		probate	L3	
Borden, Joseph	22, Aug. 1833	Aug.	3m	L4	
Borden, Louisa	13, Jan. 1848	4, Jan.	12	L3	
Borden, Samuel	15, Sept 1836		probate	L3	
Borden, Samuel (Gen)	6, Nov. 1834	Oct.	52	L1	
Borden, Samuel (Gen)	30, Oct. 1834	22, Oct.	53	L2	
Borden, Samuel (Gen)	16, Apr. 1835		estate	L3	
Borden, Sarah	13, Mar. 1851	5, Mar.	68	L3	
Borgman, Herman L.	26, July 1849		estate	L3	
Borland, Sarah	1, Aug. 1833	July	51	L1	
Borton, Jacob (Dr)	7, June 1855	11, May	49	L3	
Borton, Rebecca Ann	19, Jan. 1854	17, Jan.	12- 4m	L3	
Bos, Yant J.	1, July 1847	June	59	L3	
Boss, John	1, Nov. 1832	Oct.	7	L2	
Bosse, Henry	29, Aug. 1850	Aug.	27	L3	
Bosson, Charles M.	27, June 1850	11, May		L3	
Bosson, J.S. (Dr)	8, Apr. 1818	4, Apr.		L3	
Bosson, Joseph	1, Nov. 1838	23, Oct.		* L3	
Bosson, Mary H.	30, July 1819	26, July		L3	

Name	Notice Date	Death Date	Age		Page	Maiden Name
Bosson, Susannah	10, Feb. 1826	10, Feb.	67		L3	
Bosson, William	12, Aug. 1823	11, Aug.	72		L3	
Boswell, John	11, Sept 1828		estate		L3	
Boswell, Mary	12, July 1849	July	40		L3	
Boswick, T.B.	15, Sept 1853	8, Sept	51		L3	
Botsford, Russell	16, Dec. 1829		estate		L3	
Bott, Isabella	1, July 1847		93- 6m		L3	
Bott, Jacob	6, June 1850	May	24		L3	
Botts, Martin	22, Aug. 1833	Aug.	9m		L4	
Botts, Thomas	1, Aug. 1850	July	7		L3	
Boucher, Henry	18, July 1850	July	28		L3	
Boudinot, Elias	22, Sept 1836		estate		L4	
Boughman, Richard D.	18, July 1833	July	3m		L2	
Boulton, Charles	1, June 1848	26, May	5- 6m		L3	
Bourn, George	29, Nov. 1832	Nov.			L1	
Bourne, Jason	5, July 1849	29, June	14m		L3	
Bourne, Theodore	6, Nov. 1834	Oct.	9m		L1	
Bovert, Ennis	8, May 1828	May	30		L1	
Bowdle, Daniel (Mrs)	29, June 1837	26, June			L3	
Bowen, Bridget	28, Nov. 1850	Nov.	14		L3	
Bowen, Clark S.	28, Aug. 1856	2, Aug.	42- -5d	*	L5	
Bowen, G.G.	25, Nov. 1847	18, Nov.	39		L3	
Bowen, George A.	31, Dec. 1857	24, Dec.	1		L3	
Bowen, George G.	7, June 1855		probate		L3	
Bowen, H.R.	30, Aug. 1832	Aug.	25		L1	
Bowen, James	21, Sept 1837		probate		L4	
Bowen, John D.	22, Aug. 1850	19, Aug.	40		L3	
Bowen, Margaret	14, May 1846	May	11		L3	
Bowen, Mary R.	18, 25, Sept 1856	15, Sept	15		L5	
Bowen, Samuel	15, Nov. 1832	Nov.	48		L1	
Bowen, Samuel	6, Dec. 1832		estate		L3	
Bowens, Francis S.	10, Dec. 1857		probate		L3	
Bower, Adam	3, Apr. 1845	Mar.	3m		L3	
Bower, Catharine	21, May 1846	May	7		L3	
Bower, Mary	28, May 1846	May	4		L3	
Bowerger, John C.	15, Aug. 1833	Aug.	1		L1	
Bowers, Adeline Eliza	14, June 1855	13, June	58- 9m		L3	
Bowers, John George	19, Sept 1850	Sept			L3	
Bowers, Samuel	25, Oct. 1832	13, Oct.			L1	
Bowet, William J.	7, Nov. 1844	Oct.	24		L3	
Bowie, Donald	5, July 1855	27, June	64	*	L3	
Bowler, Jane Hunt	10, Apr. 1856	2, Apr.	16m		L3	
Bowler, Jesse Hunt	6, June 1850	28, May	22m		L3	
Bowler, Nathaniel Pendleton	24, July 1845	15, July	22m		L3	
Bowles, Morrean	25, May 1848	May	3		L3	
Bowles, William	23, Oct. 1834	Oct.	34		L2	
Bowlin, Addison	5, Feb. 1852	3, Feb.	24		L3	
Bowlin, Elizabeth	24, Dec. 1840	22, Dec.	56		L3	
Bowlin, George W.P.	2, Mar. 1843	22, Feb.	23		L3	
Bowlin, Robert	10, Dec. 1840	3, Dec.	22		L3	
Bowlin, Rose	16, Mar. 1848	Mar.	20		L3	
Bowlin, William	3, July 1851	June	12		L3	
Bowman, (child of William)	10, Jan. 1828	Jan.	infant		L4	
Bowman, Albert	20, Feb. 1845	Feb.	6m		L3	

Name	Notice Date	Death Date	Age		Page	Maiden Name
Bowman, Betsy	11, July 1839	June	37		L3	
Bowman, Richard	27, Oct. 1831		probate		L1	
Bowman, Richard	25, Jan. 1849	Jan.	20		L3	
Bowmar, Emeline	18, May 1848	12, May	38		L3	Tunis
Bowring, John	5, July 1849	June	48		L3	
Bowvas, John	22, Aug. 1833	Aug.	2		L4	
Boyce, Cornelius	28, Mar. 1839	Mar.	68		L3	
Boyd, (child of Henry)	12, Sept 1833	Sept	7m		L1	
Boyd, Agnes	26, Feb. 1852		20	*	L4	George
Boyd, Alexander	29, Aug. 1844	Aug.	44		L3	
Boyd, Allen	31, Jan. 1850		estate		L3	
Boyd, Allen	24, Mar. 1853		estate		L3	
Boyd, Daniel	3, July 1845	25, June	62		L3	
Boyd, Henry	4, July 1850	June	28		L3	
Boyd, James	28, Mar. 1839	Mar.	22		L3	
Boyd, John	26, Oct. 1837	19, Sept	23		L3	
Boyd, John	9, Oct. 1845	26, Sept	48		L3	
Boyd, John	14, Nov. 1833		estate		L3	
Boyd, John	15, Sept 1836		probate		L3	
Boyd, John	5, Sept 1839		probate		L3	
Boyd, John	15, Nov. 1832		estate		L4	
Boyd, John (Rev)	25, Oct. 1832	22, Oct.			L3	
Boyd, Joseph	9, Feb. 1854	30, Jan.	73		L3	
Boyd, Marshall	21, Mar. 1850		estate		L3	
Boyd, Mary	26, Aug. 1852	19, Aug.	65	*	L3	
Boyd, Nelson	6, Feb. 1840	Jan.	32		L3	
Boyd, Robert	18, July 1850	July	29		L3	
Boyd, William	14, Sept 1848	Sept	27		L3	
Boyd, William	13, Jan. 1842	Jan.	28		L3	
Boyd, William H.	7, Aug. 1845	July	3m		L3	
Boyer, G.A.	28, June 1849	24, June	29		L3	
Boylan, Benjamin	4, Sept 1856	29, Aug.	46		L1,5	
Boylan, Charlotte	30, Nov. 1843	Nov.	5m		L3	
Boylan, James	4, Sept 1851	1, Sept	6m		L3	
Boylan, Kate	14, Jan. 1847	8, Jan.	infant		L3	
Boyle, George Jackson	17, Sept 1846	8, Sept	5		L3	
Boyle, James	16, Mar. 1849	Mar.	24		L3	
Boyle, James	24, Mar. 1842	Mar.	30		L3	
Boyle, William	25, Dec. 1845	Dec.	48		L3	
Bozel, Elizabeth	22, Jan. 1852	Jan.	21		L3	
Brackenridge, Henry Hugh	22, July 1816	25, June	67		L2	
Bradburn, (son of John)	31, Mar. 1806	25, Mar.	7		L3	
Bradbury, Edward A.	11, Dec. 1851	20, Oct.	24		L3	
Bradbury, George W. (Col)	4, Nov. 1847	1, Nov.	31		L3	
Bradbury, M.T.C.	18, Sept 1845	7, May	65	*	L3	
Braddock, James	24, Jan. 1850	Jan.	52		L3	
Braden, Epenetus	26, May 1842		estate		L3	
Braden, Jeremiah	7, May 1840		probate		L3	
Brades, G.S.	1, Aug. 1833	July	1m		L1	
Bradfish, (child of Godfrey)	30, June 1842	June	stillborn		L3	
Bradford, George	11, Jan. 1849	Jan.	40		L3	
Bradford, John	31, July 1845	July	32		L3	
Bradford, Louisa S.	31, Mar. 1836	29, Mar.	21		L3	Palmer
Bradford, Susan M.	17, Feb. 1848	11, Feb.	24		L3	

Name	Notice Date	Death Date	Age	Page	Maiden Name
Bradford, Thomas Alonzo	12, June 1851	6, June	4	L3	
Bradford, William	23, Jan. 1851	14, Jan.	9	L3	
Bradley, Caroline	23, Dec. 1847	Dec.	7w	L3	
Bradley, Charles	4, Oct. 1838	Sept		L3	
Bradley, Samuel	13, Feb. 1840		probate	L3	
Bradling, Jeremiah (Dr)	14, June 1838		probate	L4	
Bradshan, Alexander	25, Oct. 1849	Oct.	27	L3	
Bradshaw, David M.	23, Mar. 1854	19, Mar.	38	L3	
Bradshaw, Elizabeth	1, Nov. 1832	Oct.	49	L2	
Bradshaw, George	26, July 1849	July	28	L3	
Bradshaw, Jacob T.	30, Nov. 1848	Nov.	14m	L3	
Bradshaw, Nancy	1, Nov. 1832	Oct.	49	L2	
Bradshaw, Richard	16, July 1846	July	33	L3	
Brady, Barny	10, July 1851	1, July		L4	
Brady, Benjamin	1, Nov. 1832	24, Oct.		L4	
Brady, Hugh	7, Oct. 1847	Sept	29	L3	
Brady, James	13, May 1847	May	46	L3	
Brady, John	11, July 1850	July	26	L3	
Braim, Louis	6, Mar. 1851	Feb.	38	L3	
Brainerd, Charles	31, Aug. 1837	28, Aug.		L3	
Bram, Elon	26, Sept 1826		probate	L3	
Bramble, Elon	27, June 1823		estate	L3	
Brammer, S.	7, June 1849	May	25	L3	
Bramon, (child of George)	16, May 1833	May	3	L1	
Bramsche, G.H.	10, Apr. 1856		probate	L3	
Brand, (child of H.)	14, Mar. 1833	Mar.	9m	L1	
Brand, (child of William)	16, Sept 1841	Sept	2d	L3	
Brand, David	13, Feb. 1840		probate	L3	
Branden, (child of Mary)	13, Feb. 1840	Feb.	4d	L3	
Branderiff, J.	23, Apr. 1846	Apr.	33	L3	
Brandiver, Henry	15, May 1834	May	6m	L4	
Brandon, Maria E.B.	20, Dec. 1838	17, Dec.		L3	Dorman
Brandon, Sarah Jane	30, May 1839	May	9m	L2	
Brandriff, Timothy	20, Sept 1827	Sept	43	L1	
Brandriff, Timothy	4, Oct. 1827		estate	L2	
Brandruff, Timothy	27, Oct. 1831		probate	L1	
Brands, William	29, Aug. 1833	Aug.	31	L1	
Brandt, F.L.	6, Dec. 1855		probate	L3	
Brandt, Francisco	2, Sept 1852	Aug.	4w	L3	
Branin, Richard	12, Oct. 1848	Oct.	34	L3	
Brannagan, Edward D.	2, Mar. 1854	22, Feb.	38	L3	
Brannagan, William	21, Sept 1848	Sept	40	L3	
Brannan, James	5, Sept 1850	Aug.	23	L3	
Brannan, Mary E.	9, Apr. 1857	3, Apr.		L3	Doddridge
Brannan, Mary Louisa	13, Dec. 1849	5, Dec.	infant	L3	
Brannan, Susan	22, Nov. 1849	Nov.	32	L3	
Brannon, Andrew	18, Feb. 1818		estate	L3	
Brannon, Andrew	3, Nov. 1817	31, Oct.		L3	
Brannon, Matthew	18, Mar. 1852	5, Mar.	35	L4	
Brant, Thomas	20, Nov. 1845	Nov.	48	L3	
Brashear, John	9, May 1850			L3	
Brashears, Francis James	3, Aug. 1854	30, July	16- 9m	L3	
Brashears, Samuel	18, Jan. 1849	14, Jan.	4-10m	L3	
Brasher, Caroline Ann	7, Oct. 1841	6, Oct.	6m- 3d	L3	

Name	Notice Date	Death Date	Age		Page	Maiden Name
Brasher, Caroline Penn	10, Dec. 1857	9, Dec.	39		L3	
Brasher, Granville	21, Aug. 1856	15, Aug.	8- 7m-15d		L5	
Brasher, Helen F.	20, Aug. 1840	18, Aug.	infant		L3	
Brat, Lucinda	5, July 1849	June	35		L3	
Bratton, James	2, Oct. 1828		estate		L3	
Bratton, James	24, Sept 1846		estate		L3	
Bratty, Alexander	7, Oct. 1841	28, Sept	102		L3	
Bray, Henry	30, Jan. 1840		estate		L3	
Bray, Peter	25, Apr. 1839		estate		L2	
Bray, Peter	3, Sept 1840		probate		L3	
Bray, Peter	10, Apr. 1856		probate		L3	
Bray, Peter	22, Nov. 1838		estate		L4	
Brayton, Charles D. (Dr)	20, Mar. 1851	10, Mar.	47		L3	
Brazel, Ann	11, Nov. 1852	Oct.	33		L3	
Brazell, John	6, Apr. 1848	Mar.	55		L3	
Bread, Adarina	25, Jan. 1844	Jan.	1m		L3	
Bread, Adarina	1, Feb. 1844	Jan.	1m		L3	
Bread, George	25, Jan. 1844	Jan.	30		L3	
Bread, George	1, Feb. 1844	Jan.	30		L3	
Breakenridge, Mary	16, Feb. 1854	30, Jan.			L3	
Breall, James	23, Dec. 1841	11, Dec.			L1	
Brearley, Charles	26, Nov. 1846	22, Nov.	70		L3	
Breeze, (Mrs)	1, Nov. 1832	23, Oct.			L4	
Breeze, James	25, Oct. 1832	17, Oct.			L1	
Breeze, Lewis	9, June 1853		estate		L3	
Bregen, Otta H.	6, May 1847	Apr.	27		L3	
Bremer, Otto	27, May 1847	May	27		L3	
Brenlend, Augustus	25, July 1850	20, July	22	*	L3	
Brenton, John	26, Aug. 1847	Aug.	53		L3	
Brenton, John	26, Aug. 1847		estate		L3	
Breslan, Bridget	24, May 1849	May	2		L3	
Breslan, Mary	24, May 1849	May	11		L3	
Breslan, Rosa	14, June 1849	June	28		L3	
Breslan, Timothy	24, May 1849	May	37		L3	
Breslin, Edward	6, Jan. 1853	5, Jan.			L3	
Brevit, John F.	21, Feb. 1850	Feb.	29		L3	
Brewer, Jonathan	7, Aug. 1834	July	1- 3m-10d		L3	
Brewster, Deborah K.	2, Nov. 1843	28, Oct.	36		L3	
Brewster, Diadama	23, Oct. 1834	Oct.	36		L2	
Brewster, Lot E.	28, June 1849	June			L3	
Brewster, Thomas	18, Feb. 1836	6, Feb.		*	L3	
Brewster, Thomas	25, Feb. 1836		estate		L4	
Briant, Charles	21, June 1832		estate		L3	
Briant, Charles	24, July 1834		estate		L3	
Briant, Cornelius	21, Aug. 1815		estate		L2	
Brick, John	12, Feb. 1846	Feb.	29		L3	
Brickell, Edwin W.	22, Sept 1853		3- 9m		L3	
Brickell, Margaret	9, Nov. 1848	8, Nov.	5		L3	
Bricker, Catharine	1, Nov. 1832	26, Oct.	13		L1	
Brickman, Joseph	21, June 1838	June	28		L3	
Bridges, William	8, July 1847	June	1		L3	
Bridgman, Samuel W.	7, Jan. 1841	28, Dec.			L3	
Bridle, Catharine	8, Dec. 1842	Dec.	33		L3	
Brigadier, Samuel	18, Apr. 1839	Apr.	35		L3	

Name	Notice Date	Death Date	Age		Page	Maiden Name
Brigden, William	29, June 1848	June	40		L3	
Briges, Melissa	21, Apr. 1842	Apr.	22		L3	
Brigger, Narcissa	18, Oct. 1849	Oct.	37		L3	
Briggs, Henry	18, Apr. 1850	Apr.	62		L3	
Brigham, (Mrs)	9, July 1857	8, July			L1	
Brigham, Elisha	25, June 1846	22, June	66		L3	
Brigham, John	25, Oct. 1827	Oct.	35		L2	
Brigham, Marcus Marcellus	9, July 1840	1, July			L3	
Brigham, Stanley T.	29, Jan. 1852	21, Jan.	2m		L3	
Bright, Elizabeth	7, Aug. 1834	July	73		L3	
Briney, Zara	17, Jan. 1850	Jan.	45		L3	
Brinker, Henry	19, July 1849	July	30		L3	
Brinkerhoff, Cornelius	29, Dec. 1812	17, Dec.	38	*	L3	
Brinkman, John	2, Aug. 1849		estate		L3	
Brinkmann, Matthew	6, Aug. 1857		probate		L3	
Brinnin, William	11, Apr. 1850	Apr.	8m		L3	
Brinton, Samuel	2, Aug. 1814		estate		L3	
Brisbane, Bentley H.	26, Mar. 1846	22, Mar.	16- 6m		L3	
Brisher, William	26, July 1849	July	25		L3	
Briston, Henry	19, Aug. 1847	10, Aug.	52	*	L3	
Bristow, Henry	23, Sept 1847		estate		L3	
Briton, Martha	23, Nov. 1848	Nov.	20		L3	
Britt, Frances	26, Mar. 1857	20, Mar.	74	*	L3	Stevens
Britten, Margaret	1, Feb. 1849	Jan.	5w		L3	
Britting, Margaret	25, Jan. 1849	Jan.	21		L3	
Britton, Nathan	21, Apr. 1853	20, Apr.			L3	
Britton, Priscilla J.	15, May 1834	May	7d		L4	
Broadel, Leonard	12, Dec. 1850	Dec.	22		L3	
Broadmeadow, Simeon	31, May 1849	May	65		L3	
Broadwell, Caroline	18, July 1850	7, July			L3	
Broadwell, Ella Maria	21, May 1857	13, May	34-10m		L3	Cutter
Broadwell, Jacob	24, Dec. 1835		estate		L3	
Broadwell, Jacob	9, Aug. 1838		probate		L3	
Broadwell, Jane	16, June 1842		estate		L3	
Broadwell, Jerome	24, Dec. 1840	22, Dec.	3- 4m-15d		L3	
Broadwell, Lewis	8, Nov. 1855		estate		L3	
Broadwell, Lewis	16, Apr. 1857		estate		L3	
Broadwell, Lewis	3, Sept 1857		estate		L3	
Broadwell, Lewis	7, May 1857		probate		L3	
Broadwell, Mahlon L.	9, June 1836		probate		L3	
Broadwell, Maria	26, Nov. 1840	15, Nov.	15		L3	
Broadwell, Samuel	12, Jan. 1837		probate		L3	
Broadwell, Samuel	7, May 1840		probate		L3	
Brocaw, Ferdinand	1, Oct. 1808		estate		L3	
Brock, Casper	6, Mar. 1856		probate		L3	
Brockell, John	22, Nov. 1832		estate		L3	
Brockoff, John	14, June 1849	June	56		L3	
Brocks, Lydia	16, May 1833	May	41		L1	
Brocon, Ann	25, Oct. 1832	Oct.	19		L1	
Broderick, Sarah	14, Mar. 1850	Mar.	4m		L3	
Broders, Mary	21, Aug. 1856	20, Aug.	14		L1	
Brodie, Ann	3, Oct. 1844	18, Sept	7m		L3	
Brogan, Michael	12, Apr. 1849	Apr.	57		L3	
Brokaw, Ferdinand	30, June 1812		estate		L3	

Name	Notice Date	Death Date	Age		Page	Maiden Name
Brokell, John	29, May 1834		probate		L3	
Brokenshire, Richard	3, Aug. 1848	27, July	56		L3	
Bromell, George	6, June 1833	May	3		L2	
Bromwell, Alice	27, Feb. 1851	19, Feb.	infant		L3	
Bromwell, Jacob	29, Mar. 1855	22, Mar.	45		L3	
Bromwell, Jacob	19, Apr. 1855		estate		L3	
Bronson, Charles H.	1, Aug. 1850	22, July	35	*	L3	
Bronson, Emma Kate	31, Mar. 1853	22, Mar.	3- 9m		L3	
Bronson, Norman S.	7, Oct. 1823	3, Oct.		*	L3	
Bronson, Sarah M.	20, Nov. 1851	15, Nov.	28		L3	
Brooke, (child of Mrs)	21, Nov. 1833	Nov.	1		L3	
Brooke, John Thomson	26, Jan. 1843	21, Jan.	6		L3	
Brooke, Louisa	14, Oct. 1841	9, Oct.	18m		L3	
Brooke, R.S.	8, Aug. 1833	July	28		L1	
Brooke, Richard	1, Nov. 1838	24, Oct.	10		L3	
Brookman, William	2, June 1842	May	24		L3	
Brooks, (daughter of A.W.)	5, Feb. 1852	31, Jan.	infant		L3	
Brooks, Frances Adelaide	8, Jan. 1857	3, Jan.	20		L3	
Brooks, George W.	8, Dec. 1853	3, Dec.			L3	
Brooks, George W.	21, Aug. 1856		estate		L8	
Brooks, John	13, Feb. 1840	7, Feb.	38	*	L3	
Brooks, John	13, Oct. 1842	5, Oct.	81		L3	
Brooks, John	14, Dec. 1824		probate		L3	
Brooks, John, Jr.	26, Sept 1826		probate		L3	
Brooks, Lizzie	27, June 1850	22, June	infant		L3	
Brooks, Lydia	9, May 1833	5, May			L3	
Brooks, Rachael	11, Sept 1834	Aug.	37		L1	
Broome, John (Lt)	5, Sept 1810	4, Sept	72		L3	
Brophy, Joseph	25, Jan. 1849	Jan.	37		L3	
Brose, T.	7, Feb. 1833	Feb.	40		L1	
Brosius, Daniel	1, Feb. 1814		estate		L3	
Brosius, Daniel	25, Jan. 1813		estate		L4	
Brotherton, Richard	27, Oct. 1821		estate		L3	
Brough, William P.	4, Nov. 1841	26, Oct.	21		L3	
Brousiff, James	1, Aug. 1833	July	11		L1	
Brower, Hannah H.	12, Dec. 1833	25, Nov.	36		L4	
Brower, Susan Dunn	30, Aug. 1849	24, Aug.	2- 6m		L3	
Brown, (child of Ellen)	13, Apr. 1843	Apr.	stillborn		L3	
Brown, (child of Hester)	25, May 1848	May	1w		L3	
Brown, (child of William)	7, Feb. 1828	Feb.	3m		L1	
Brown, (child of William)	25, Oct. 1849	Oct.	stillborn		L3	
Brown, (Mr)	1, Aug. 1833	July			L1	
Brown, (Mr)	18, Oct. 1832	13, Oct.			L2	
Brown, (Mrs)	7, Mar. 1850	5, Mar.			L2	
Brown, Abigail	6, June 1833	May	1- 4m		L2	
Brown, Adam	1, Jan. 1846	21, Dec.	44		L3	
Brown, Almira	12, Sept 1850	3, Sept	46		L3	
Brown, Ann	18, Oct. 1827	Oct.	27		L3	
Brown, Ann	7, Nov. 1844	6, Nov.	88		L3	
Brown, Anna	3, Sept 1846	Aug.	1- 6m		L3	
Brown, Antonette Lodevine	12, May 1836	9, May			L2	
Brown, Archibald	5, Nov. 1857		probate		L3	
Brown, Barbara	29, Aug. 1850	23, Aug.	79		L3	
Brown, Benjamin	3, Jan. 1850	28, Dec.			L2	

Name	Notice Date	Death Date	Age	Page	Maiden Name
Brown, Catharine Albina	2, Jan. 1840	26, Dec.		L2	
Brown, Charles	3, Mar. 1807		estate	L3	
Brown, Charles E.	17, Dec. 1857	12, Dec.	25	L3	
Brown, D.M.	18, Oct. 1832	13, Oct.		L2	
Brown, David	8, Nov. 1855		probate	L3	
Brown, David L.	4, Jan. 1855	30, Dec.	45	L3	
Brown, Ebenezer	29, Nov. 1832	Nov.	23	L1	
Brown, Edward	1, Aug. 1833	July	33	L1	
Brown, Edward	10, Jan. 1839		estate	L3	
Brown, Eliza Coffin	24, May 1838	18, May		* L3	
Brown, Emily Graham	20, Mar. 1851	12, Mar.	infant	L3	
Brown, Emma Jane	28, Nov. 1844	Nov.	2	L3	
Brown, Ephraim	30, Aug. 1835		estate	L3	
Brown, Ephraim	22, June 1837		probate	L3	
Brown, Ethan A.	6, Dec. 1855		probate	L3	
Brown, Frances	11, Sept 1834	Aug.	8m	L1	
Brown, Frances	1, Aug. 1850	July	22	L3	
Brown, Frances Mary	26, Feb. 1852	20, Feb.		L3	Young
Brown, George	25, Apr. 1850	Apr.	60	L3	
Brown, Harriet	19, Sept 1833	Sept	22	L4	
Brown, Henry	25, Oct. 1832	20, Oct.		L2	
Brown, Henry Walstein	11, July 1850	4, July	13m	L3	
Brown, Huston	25, Oct. 1832	17, Oct.		L1	
Brown, Isabella	25, July 1850	17, July	65	L3	
Brown, Jackson	23, Jan. 1851	Jan.	24	L3	
Brown, Jacob	21, Nov. 1833		estate	L3	
Brown, Jacob	31, Oct. 1833	Oct.	39	L4	
Brown, Jacob	28, Sept 1837		estate	L4	
Brown, James	26, Jan. 1854	29, Dec.	74	L3	
Brown, James	5, Feb. 1857		probate	L3	
Brown, Jeremiah W.	14, Feb. 1850	Feb.	24	L3	
Brown, John	23, Dec. 1847	Dec.	27	L3	
Brown, John	28, Dec. 1843	19, Dec.	28	L3	
Brown, John	28, Mar. 1844	Mar.	36	L3	
Brown, John	28, Jan. 1825		estate	L3	
Brown, John	13, Feb. 1840		probate	L3	
Brown, John	15, May 1834	May	30	L4	
Brown, John	2, Oct. 1834	Sept		L4	
Brown, John Francis	3, Oct. 1844	29, Sept	infant	L3	
Brown, Joseph	19, July 1832	July	1-11m	L1	
Brown, Joseph	4, Nov. 1841	Oct.	4	L3	
Brown, Malinda	12, Dec. 1850	Dec.	50	L3	
Brown, Mary	4, Jan. 1849	Dec.	21	L3	
Brown, Mary	18, July 1850	July	22	L3	
Brown, Mary	26, Dec. 1844	Dec.	25	L3	
Brown, Mary	22, Oct. 1840	Oct.	45	L3	
Brown, Mary Agnes	27, Mar. 1851	24, Mar.	5- 6m	L3	
Brown, Nancy N.	16, Feb. 1843	14, Feb.	24	L3	
Brown, Polly	30, Apr. 1808	22, Apr.		L3	
Brown, Rachael	12, July 1849	July	40	L3	
Brown, Rachel	11, Oct. 1832	4, Oct.		L2	
Brown, Rachel	5, Aug. 1852	27, July	84	L3	
Brown, Rachel	8, Nov. 1855		probate	L3	
Brown, Ralph	25, Nov. 1847	18, Nov.	43	L3	

Name	Notice Date	Death Date	Age		Page	Maiden Name
Brown, Rosetta	6, Sept 1827	Sept	6		L1	
Brown, Rowland	19, Feb. 1852	12, Feb.			L4	
Brown, Samuel	6, Sept 1849	Aug.	26		L3	
Brown, Samuel	17, Dec. 1846	Dec.	54		L3	
Brown, Sarah	2, Jan. 1845	Dec.	62		L3	
Brown, Stephen G.	7, Aug. 1851	3, Aug.	65		L3	
Brown, Stephen G.	6, Nov. 1851		estate		L3	
Brown, Sterling M.	14, Oct. 1847	12, Oct.		*	L1	
Brown, Susan	26, July 1855	18, July			L3	
Brown, Thomas	30, Dec. 1805		estate		L3	
Brown, Thomas	16, Apr. 1840		estate		L3	
Brown, Thomas	19, Mar. 1846		estate		L3	
Brown, Thomas	9, Apr. 1846		estate		L3	
Brown, Thomas	29, Oct. 1805	23, Oct.			L3	
Brown, Vincent	8, Dec. 1836		estate		L3	
Brown, Vincent	14, June 1838		probate		L4	
Brown, Washington	17, Mar. 1853	15, Mar.			L3	
Brown, William	30, May 1850	May	30		L3	
Brown, William	4, Mar. 1852	27, Feb.	35		L3	
Brown, William	18, Apr. 1850	Apr.	42		L3	
Brown, William	29, June 1848	June	45		L3	
Brown, William	7, Jan. 1847	Dec.	10w		L3	
Brown, William	4, May 1854	28, Apr.			L3	
Brown, William	11, Mar. 1852	Mar.	35		L4	
Brown, William	20, Dec. 1825		probate		L4	
Brown, William James	8, Nov. 1838		probate		L3	
Brown, Zadock	19, July 1849	14, June			L3	
Browne, Eliza Emma	24, May 1838	17, May	8		L3	
Browne, Frances	25, Jan. 1838	17, Jan.			L3	
Browne, John W.	4, Jan. 1814		estate		L2	
Browne, John W.	13, Apr. 1813		estate		L3	
Browne, John W. (Rev)	5, Jan. 1813	3, Jan.	58	*	L3	
Browne, Katharine	11, May 1854	10, May	86		L3	
Browne, Susan T.	15, Feb. 1855	9, Feb.	33	*	L3	
Browning, Charles S.	24, Aug. 1848	20, Aug.	10m		L3	
Browning, Elizabeth	22, Apr. 1847	19, Apr.	75	*	L3	
Browning, Ellen	29, Oct. 1857	27, Oct.			L3	
Browning, Martha Ann	14, Oct. 1847	11, Oct.	23		L3	Holmes
Brownrigg, Amyas D.	1, Apr. 1852	27, Mar.	33		L3	
Brua, Henry	24, June 1841	June	30		L3	
Bruce, Andrew	26, July 1838	20, July	60	*	L3	
Bruce, Ann	3, 10, July 1845	June	14m		L3	
Bruce, Catharine W.	16, Dec. 1852	8, Dec.	27- 3m-15d		L3	
Bruce, Charles	26, Apr. 1849	Apr.	35		L3	
Bruce, Charles David	25, July 1850	21, July	17m- 2d		L3	
Bruce, David	6, July 1837		estate		L3	
Bruce, David	25, Jan. 1838		estate		L3	
Bruce, David	3, Sept 1840		probate		L3	
Bruce, James T.	30, May 1839	May	34		L2	
Bruce, Mary Jemima	23, Nov. 1854	21, Nov.	5-11m-15d		L3	
Bruck, William (Rev)	29, Aug. 1850	27, Aug.	71- 3m		L3	
Bruekmeyer, Frederick	15, July 1847	July	26		L3	
Bruen, David H.	27, Jan. 1853	19, Jan.	42		L3	
Bruen, Mary	16, Dec. 1852	9, Dec.	67		L3	

Name	Notice Date	Death Date	Age	Page	Maiden Name
Brunson, John	22, June 1822		estate	L3	
Brunton, William H.	6, Apr. 1837	Apr.	2	L4	
Brush, C.D.L.	15, Aug. 1844			L3	
Brush, Charles D.	8, May 1845		estate	L3	
Bruska, Gerhard	5, Dec. 1850	Nov.	34	L3	
Brussell, Moses	24, Apr. 1856		estate	L3	
Bryan, Julia	31, May 1849	May	18	L3	
Bryan, Michael	7, Feb. 1850	Jan.	40	L3	
Bryan, William J.	20, May 1847	5, May		L3	
Bryant, Benjamin	4, Jan. 1844	Dec.	33	L3	
Bryant, Charles	10, Mar. 1836		estate	L3	
Bryant, Charles	7, Dec. 1837		probate	L3	
Bryant, Dennis	25, Oct. 1832	17, Oct.		L1	
Bryant, Elizabeth	7, Oct. 1847	Sept	18	L3	
Bryant, James	27, Oct. 1831		probate	L1	
Bryant, James	14, May 1829		estate	L3	
Bryant, Julia	8, Mar. 1838	7, Mar.		L3	
Bryarly, George Murray	31, July 1845	27, July		L3	
Bryden, Elizabeth	20, Sept 1838	Sept	9	L3	
Bryson, Elizabeth Sellman	19, June 1815	15, June	19m	L3	
Bryson, Robert S.	12, Aug. 1847			L3	
Bryson, William Walker	17, Aug. 1843	8, Aug.	20m	L3	
Buchanan, Claudius (Rev)	5, June 1815	19, Feb.		L3	
Buchanan, Elizabeth	2, Apr. 1840	1, Apr.		L3	
Buchanan, George W.	29, Nov. 1849	Nov.	13m	L3	
Buchanan, James	10, June 1841	9, June		L3	
Buchanan, John, Jr.	4, Apr. 1844	28, Mar.	21	L3	
Buchanan, Lillian	26, July 1855	20, June		L3	
Buchanan, Susan	19, Oct. 1822	11, Oct.	31	L3	
Buck, Bernard H.	6, June 1833	May	32	L2	
Buck, Thomas	12, July 1849	July	2	L3	
Buckhart, Peter	25, July 1850	July	40	L3	
Buckholtz, Conrad	5, Nov. 1857		probate	L3	
Buckingham, Margaret G.	11, Apr. 1850	8, Apr.	26	L3	Gest
Buckingham, Maria	4, June 1857		probate	L3	
Buckingham, William	5, Feb. 1857		probate	L3	
Buckley, (child of Joseph)	25, Oct. 1832	17, Oct.		L1	
Buckley, (Mrs)	18, Oct. 1832	13, Oct.		L2	
Buckley, Henry	7, Mar. 1839	Feb.	28	L3	
Buckley, Joseph	18, Oct. 1832	12, Oct.		L2	
Buckley, Joseph	11, Apr. 1833		estate	L3	
Buckley, Joseph	17, Dec. 1835		estate	L3	
Buckley, Joseph	27, Sept 1838		estate	L3	
Buckley, Joseph	22, Mar. 1838		probate	L3	
Buckley, Josephine	1, Nov. 1832	Oct.	1- 6m	L2	
Buckley, Sarah	3, May 1855		probate	L3	
Bucklies, William	6, Dec. 1849	Nov.	26	L3	
Buckman, (child of Henry)	6, June 1833	May	1m	L2	
Buckner, Mina	25, Oct. 1832	21, Oct.		L3	
Buckner, P.J. (Dr)	25, Aug. 1853	24, Aug.	53	L3	
Buckner, Robert	8, Oct. 1846	21, Sept	45	L3	
Budd, Charlotte	13, Nov. 1834	Nov.	1m- 8d	L1	
Budd, Jane	19, Sept 1833	Sept	1	L4	
Budlong, Benjamin	18, July 1844	2, July	56	L3	

Name	Notice Date	Death Date	Age	Page	Maiden Name
Budlong, Samuel	23, May 1844	24, Apr.		* L3	
Buell, Leonard	15, Oct. 1835	31, Aug.	31	L3	
Buell, Salmon	2, Oct. 1828		estate	L3	
Buffum, John	10, June 1820		estate	L3	
Buffum, John	24, May 1820			L3	
Buhner, Rudolph	26, July 1849		estate	L3	
Bull, Asaph	15, June 1813		estate	L2	
Bullard, Mary	16, Oct. 1845	Oct.	14m	L3	
Bullington, Lemuel	27, July 1843	July	74	L3	
Bullock, Robert M.	20, July 1848	13, July	21	* L3	
Bumgardner, John	12, July 1849	July	38	L3	
Bumgardner, Mary	12, July 1849	July	40	L3	
Bunda, Josephine	24, Oct. 1844	Oct.	7m	L3	
Bunker, Frank W.	2, May 1850	Apr.	30	L3	
Bunker, Henrietta	31, Apr. 1845	28, Apr.	18m- 8d	L3	
Bunnar, Ballanfer	1, Nov. 1832	Oct.	1m	L2	
Bunnell, Calvin	16, July 1805	July		L3	
Burby, Jane	14, Feb. 1828	Feb.	26	L1	
Burch, Charles	2, Sept 1816		estate	L3	
Burch, Oliver	24, Dec. 1846	Dec.	18	L3	
Burck, Elizabeth	22, Dec. 1836	Dec.	2	L3	
Burdel, (Dr)	19, Feb. 1857			L3	
Burdin, James	2, Oct. 1834	Sept		L4	
Burdin, Louisa	2, Oct. 1834	Sept		L4	
Burdsal, Aaron W.	26, Jan. 1854	21, Jan.	20	L3	
Burdsal, Charles E.	6, Jan. 1853	3, Jan.	22m- 9d	L3	
Burdsal, Eliza	19, July 1849	5, July		L3	
Burdsal, George Wetherill	21, Aug. 1851	14, Aug.		L3	
Burdsal, Mary K.	10, May 1855	6, May	35	L3	
Burdsal, Nancy S.	15, Jan. 1846	14, Jan.	34	L3	
Burdsal, William S. (Dr)	19, July 1849	5, July	29	L3	
Burdsall, James	4, Sept 1834		estate	L3	
Buret, Thomas	12, Oct. 1848	Oct.	3	L3	
Burgess,	12, Aug. 1852	Aug.	7	L3	
Burgess, (child of Mary)	5, Aug. 1852	July	3	L3	
Burgess, (child of Stephen)	18, Oct. 1832	Oct.	stillborn	L4	
Burgess, Isabella	21, Nov. 1839	3, Nov.		L1	
Burgess, John	27, Jan. 1817		estate	L3	
Burgesson, William	6, June 1833	May		L2	
Burgett, Silas	25, Aug. 1842	Aug.	32	L3	
Burgos, (child of Daniel)	26, Dec. 1833	Dec.	2d	L4	
Burgot, (girl)	3, June 1847	29, May	12	L2	
Burgoyne, Jane M.	30, Jan. 1851	22, Jan.		L3	
Burgoyne, Mary Ann	18, Nov. 1847	16, Nov.	14m	L3	
Burgoyne, Sarah Ann	6, Sept 1838	30, Aug.		L3	
Burgoyne, Susan	21, July 1836	12, July		L3	
Burgoyne, William	27, Nov. 1845	23, Nov.	6	L3	
Burham, (child of Mr)	7, Aug. 1834	July		L3	
Burk, Alexander	18, Sept 1845	Sept	36	L3	
Burk, Andrew	12, July 1849	July	36	L3	
Burk, Edward	12, July 1849	July	6	L3	
Burk, Elisha	27, July 1819		estate	L3	
Burk, Henry	16, July 1846	July	6	L3	
Burk, Mary C.	15, Feb. 1844	Feb.	18	L3	

Name	Notice Date	Death Date	Age		Page	Maiden Name
Burk, Michael	25, Sept 1845	Sept	31		L3	
Burk, Michael K.	28, Oct. 1847	Oct.			L3	
Burk, Peter	13, Dec. 1849	Dec.	26		L3	
Burk, Theodore	26, Aug. 1847	Aug.	42		L3	
Burk, William	14, Apr. 1842	Apr.	35		L3	
Burke, Anthony	22, July 1847	July	30		L3	
Burke, Betsy	1, Nov. 1832	26, Oct.			L1	
Burke, George	5, Mar. 1840	Feb.	46		L3	
Burke, Hugh	3, Sept 1846	Aug.	25		L3	
Burke, Sallie	15, Aug. 1850	11, Aug.			L3	Carneal
Burke, Stephen S.	22, Feb. 1849	Feb.	38		L3	
Burke, William Wesley	20, July 1843	14, July			L3	
Burkham, Mary	10, Apr. 1856	5, Apr.			L3	
Burkhard, Mary Ann	19, Oct. 1848	Oct.	12d		L3	
Burkhart, Conrad	26, July 1849	July	29		L3	
Burkhart, George	21, June 1849	June	40		L3	
Burkhart, Margaret	26, July 1849	July	27		L3	
Burks, Serilda	23, July 1846	July	7		L3	
Burland, John H.	13, Sept 1849		estate		L3	
Burland, W.H. (Dr)	12, July 1849	5, July	40	*	L3	
Burley, Frances	7, June 1849	2, June	88	*	L3	
Burley, Michael	18, July 1833	July	48		L2	
Burne, Thomas	23, May 1850	May	30		L3	
Burnes, Dixon	26, Sept 1850	Sept	26		L3	
Burnes, Phebe	15, Feb. 1838	Feb.	24		L3	
Burnet, (Mr)	25, Oct. 1832	18, Oct.			L1	
Burnet, Anna	12, May 1853	3, May	30	*	L3	VanValkenburgh
Burnet, Louisa	4, Jan. 1849	16, Dec.			L3	
Burnet, Margaret	28, Jan. 1836	26, Dec.		*	L4	Curry
Burnet, Maria Gregory	12, Feb. 1852	2, Feb.	17m		L3	
Burnet, States	30, Jan. 1822	20, Jan.	7		L3	
Burnet, Susan M.	15, Dec. 1853	2, Dec.	33		L3	Clark
Burnet, Thomas	19, Sept 1844	Sept	48		L3	
Burnett, Isaac G.	13, Mar. 1856	11, Mar.	72		L3	
Burnett, Isaac G.	27, Mar. 1856		estate		L3	
Burnham, William A.	4, Sept 1834		estate		L3	
Burnham, William A.	9, June 1836		estate		L3	
Burnham, William A.	15, Sept 1836		probate		L3	
Burns, (child of Robert)	25, Oct. 1832	Oct.	3m		L1	
Burns, Adam	18, Aug. 1842	Aug.	20		L3	
Burns, Barney	27, Mar. 1851	Mar.	13		L3	
Burns, Catharine	22, Nov. 1825		estate		L3	
Burns, David	19, July 1832		22		L1	
Burns, Elizabeth	6, June 1844	May	2		L3	
Burns, George	7, Sept 1848	Aug.	30		L3	
Burns, Hugh	25, Apr. 1850	Apr.	27		L3	
Burns, John	8, Aug. 1850	July	5		L3	
Burns, John	9, Jan. 1851	Dec.	25		L3	
Burns, John G.	13, Apr. 1848	Apr.			L3	
Burns, Mary	27, Feb. 1851	Feb.			L3	
Burns, Michael	14, Oct. 1847	Oct.	38		L3	
Burns, Michael	9, Sept 1847	Aug.	51		L3	
Burns, Richard	31, Oct. 1839	Oct.	23		L3	
Burns, S.L. (Capt)	19, Feb. 1846	1, Feb.	34		L3	

Name	Notice Date	Death Date	Age		Page	Maiden Name
Burns, William H.	16, May 1850	May	21		L3	
Burnscooney, Charles	17, Aug. 1843	Aug.	44		L3	
Burnside, Daniel	13, June 1839		estate		L3	
Burr, Aaron	29, Sept 1836	14, Sept	81		L2	
Burrett, Thomas	13, Apr. 1843	Apr.	60		L3	
Burris, (child of Jesse)	14, Feb. 1833	Feb.			L1	
Burrison, John	7, June 1855	Sept			L3	
Burritt, Moses	21, Sept 1837	Sept	22		L4	
Burrough, Cornelia Augusta	16, Oct. 1845	9, Oct.		*	L3	
Burroughs, Benjamin	28, Dec. 1837		estate		L3	
Burroughs, Benjamin	21, Nov. 1839		probate		L3	
Burroughts, Benjamin	30, Apr. 1835		estate		L4	
Burrowes, Ambrose Dudley	5, July 1849	1, July	13m		L3	
Burrowes, Indiana	27, Dec. 1855	21, Dec.			L3	
Burrowes, Joseph H.	23, Aug. 1855	16, Aug.	42		L3	
Burrows, Ferdinand	25, Oct. 1832	17, Oct.			L1	
Burrows, John A.C.	5, Sept 1850	29, Aug.	39		L3	
Burrows, John A.D.	24, Oct. 1850		estate		L3	
Burrows, John A.D.	6, Mar. 1851		estate		L3	
Burrows, Joseph H.	13, Sept 1855		estate		L3	
Burrows, Sarah M.	30, Oct. 1845	25, Oct.	67		L3	
Burrows, Stephen	2, Aug. 1849		estate		L3	
Burrows, Stephen	8, Nov. 1855		probate		L3	
Burrows, Stephen R.	13, May 1841	29, Apr.		*	L3	
Burrows, Theodore H.	10, Apr. 1856	7, Apr.			L3	
Burson, Edward (Dr)	2, Sept 1852	24, Aug.	73		L3	
Burt, Cora	18, Dec. 1851	11, Dec.			L3	
Burton, Andrew J.	15, Feb. 1844	Feb.	26		L3	
Burton, Elizabeth	27, Mar. 1845	Mar.	44		L3	
Burton, George L.	14, 21, Sept 1854	8, Sept			L3	
Burton, Isaac	8, June 1848	4, June	78		L3	
Burton, John	20, June 1844	June	35		L3	
Burton, John H.	2, May 1826		estate		L2	
Burton, Mary Ann	25, July 1850	17, July	6- 7m- 8d		L3	
Burts, Robert	2, Jan. 1840	22, Dec.	24		L3	
Burts, Thomas	11, Dec. 1856	8, Dec.	32		L3	
Burtz, Robert	26, Dec. 1839	22, Dec.	24		L3	
Buscher, (man)	23, Dec. 1852	22, Dec.			L3	
Buschman, Henry	17, May 1849	May	45		L3	
Bush, Amos T.	11, June 1846	June	43		L3	
Bush, Augustus	1, June 1848	May	4		L3	
Bush, Francis	29, June 1848	June	40		L3	
Bush, Garret	21, Jan. 1847	Jan.	4d		L3	
Bush, J.E.	10, Jan. 1833		estate		L3	
Bush, John E.	9, June 1836		probate		L3	
Bush, John E. (Dr)	18, Oct. 1832	15, Oct.			L3	
Bush, John S.	20, Nov. 1850	15, Nov.			L3	
Bush, Julia	11, Mar. 1852	Mar.			L4	
Bush, Juliana	4, Mar. 1852	26, Feb.			L4	
Bushe, (child of Mrs)	15, Aug. 1833	Aug.			L1	
Bushnell, A.L. (Dr)	29, July 1852	22, July			L3	
Bushnell, Andrew L. (Dr)	29, July 1852		estate		L3	
Bushnell, Sarah P.	13, Mar. 1851	5, Mar.			L3	
Buskirk, Jane	21, Oct. 1847	Oct.	24		L3	

Name	Notice Date	Death Date	Age		Page	Maiden Name
Buskirk, John	8, Aug. 1833	July	4- -16d		L1	
Buskirk, John	1, Nov. 1832	26, Oct.			L3	
Busler, Henry	28, Nov. 1833	Nov.	5m		L4	
Buss, Jacob	6, Mar. 1851	Feb.	35		L3	
Bussman, Bernhard Henry	5, Jan. 1843		estate		L3	
Bussuy, Henry	8, Aug. 1833	July			L1	
Bustrand, Charles	20, Sept 1849	Sept	30		L3	
Busugny, Louis	11, Jan. 1844	Jan.	30		L3	
Butcher, George	9, Apr. 1857		probate		L3	
Butcher, John	21, June 1849	June	35		L3	
Butcher, Samuel G.	25, June 1846	June	25		L3	
Butcher, Thomas	9, Apr. 1857		probate		L3	
Butler, (Miss)	25, Oct. 1832	Oct.			L1	
Butler, Alex (Judge)	9, Mar. 1854	3, Mar.			L3	
Butler, Ann	28, Mar. 1844	27, Feb.	64		L3	
Butler, Beale	30, June 1842	12, June	76		L3	
Butler, Caroline	5, Dec. 1850	Nov.	18		L3	
Butler, Charles Duncan	22, Jan. 1857	16, Jan.	4		L3	
Butler, Cornelia Rutgers	26, July 1849	17, July	31	*	L3	Bayard
Butler, David T.	21, Sept 1843	4, Sept	22		L3	
Butler, Ellen	13, Mar. 1851	Mar.	33		L3	
Butler, Frederick Tomlin	5, Nov. 1840	24, Oct.	2		L2	
Butler, Henrietta	13, Nov. 1850	Nov.	22		L3	
Butler, Henry	31, May 1849	May	20		L3	
Butler, Henry	25, Oct. 1832	22, Oct.			L3	
Butler, Jane Ann	20, Nov. 1851	16, Nov.	56		L3	
Butler, Jeremiah	18, July 1850	July			L3	
Butler, John	28, Aug. 1834	Aug.			L1	
Butler, John	27, Dec. 1849	Dec.	32		L3	
Butler, John	22, July 1847	July	60		L3	
Butler, Joseph	27, July 1848	July	25		L3	
Butler, Julia Bayard	21, Oct. 1852	13, Oct.	4- 8m		L3	
Butler, Kate Una	6, Mar. 1851	1, Mar.	2- 8m		L3	
Butler, Lewis	18, Oct. 1832	13, Oct.			L2	
Butler, Lucretia	3, May 1849	28, Mar.	17		L3	
Butler, Lucy	3, Jan. 1833	Dec.	10		L4	
Butler, Margaret	25, July 1839	24, July			L3	
Butler, Martha	25, July 1833	July	14m		L1	
Butler, Matthias	20, Jan. 1848	Jan.	32		L3	
Butler, O.P.	1, Oct. 1840	23, Sept	49		L3	
Butler, R.E.	17, Feb. 1853	13, Feb.	45		L3	
Butler, Robert W.	12, Dec. 1850	8, Dec.	37		L3	
Butler, Seaborn Jones	20, Sept 1849	11, Sept	18m- 7d		L3	
Butler, Thomas	10, Mar. 1853	Feb.	34		L3	
Butler, Thomas	13, Aug. 1857	9, Aug.			L3	
Butler, Thomas (Col)	12, Nov. 1805	9, Nov.			L3	
Butler, William	14, Feb. 1833	Feb.	23		L1	
Butler, William	11, June 1840		estate		L3	
Butler, William	8, Nov. 1855		probate		L3	
Butler, William (Capt)	20, Sept 1827	12, Sept	71		L1	
Butterfield, James	29, May 1828	May	60		L2	
Butterfield, John	29, Apr. 1823		estate		L3	
Buttermiller, George	9, Apr. 1857		probate		L3	
Butterwick, Amos	19, Sept 1844	Sept	34		L3	

Name	Notice Date	Death Date	Age		Page	Maiden Name
Butts, Sarah A.	14, May 1846	3, May	41		L3	
Buxton, Edmund	28, July 1806	26, July	38		L3	
Byam, Mary Ann	2, Aug. 1838	July	21		L3	
Byers, Mary	6, Nov. 1834	Oct.	45		L1	
Byington, Charles A.	28, Dec. 1843	23, Dec.	33		L3	
Byington, Edward	1, Oct. 1846				L2	
Byington, Lucy Frances	18, Jan. 1844	13, Jan.	10m		L3	
Byington, Sarah M.	14, July 1836		estate		L4	
Byington, Zebulin	4, Aug. 1836		estate		L4	
Bynaker, William	14, Feb. 1850	Feb.	8		L3	
Byram, (Mrs)	22, Aug. 1833	Aug.			L4	
Byrn, Emily	20, Nov. 1834	Nov.	7- 8m- 6d		L1	
Byrn, Philip B.	22, Dec. 1831		estate		L3	
Byrne, (Dr)	4, Mar. 1852		30		L4	
Byrne, Catharine	13, Sept 1855	10, Sept	15		L3	
Byrne, Thomas	25, Mar. 1847	Mar.	23		L3	
Byrnes, (Mrs)	18, Oct. 1832	11, Oct.			L1	
Byrnes, Nicholas	19, Apr. 1849	Apr.	27		L3	
Byrnes, Owen	15, Feb. 1849	Feb.	46		L3	
Byrnes, Patrick	25, Oct. 1832	Oct.			L4	
Byron, John	9, Oct. 1834	Sept	42		L1	
Bywaters, H.R.	7, Oct. 1852	29, Sept	68		L3	
Cable, George	19, July 1849	July	3		L3	
Cadwallader, Catharine R.P.	2, Oct. 1856	22, Sept			L5	
Cadwallader, Inez	9, Sept 1852	30, Aug.			L3	
Cadwallader, Thomas (Gen)	4, Nov. 1841	26, Oct.	61		L3	
Cady, John C.	12, July 1849	7, July	51		L3	
Cafferty, (man)	9, Sept 1847				L2	
Cafferty, Michael	3, Mar. 1853				L3	
Caffery, Mary	22, June 1848	June	22		L3	
Caffery, Rose	31, July 1851	July	51		L3	
Cahel, Michael	29, July 1847	July	35		L3	
Cahmbers, James Francis	4, May 1848	30, Apr.	1- 4m		L3	
Cahoan, Anthony	20, June 1833	June	30		L1	
Cahoone, Daniel K.	14, Oct. 1841	13, Oct.	37		L3	
Cain, (Mrs)	15, Aug. 1833	Aug.	39		L1	
Cain, Susan	27, Dec. 1849	Dec.	40		L3	
Caknife, James L.	6, June 1839	May	20		L2	
Caldbrook, William	28, June 1849	June	38		L3	
Caldwell,	10, Feb. 1848	Feb.	infant		L3	
Caldwell,	1, Oct. 1808				L3	
Caldwell, Angeline	1, Aug. 1850	July	39		L3	
Caldwell, Ann	24, July 1811		infant		L3	
Caldwell, Anne	5, July 1849	27, June	49		L3	
Caldwell, David	29, Oct. 1846	Oct.	37		L3	
Caldwell, Eliza	7, Oct. 1841	Sept	31		L3	
Caldwell, Elizabeth	20, Aug. 1846	Aug.	67		L3	
Caldwell, Helen Estelle	7, Oct. 1841	5, Aug.	7m-20d		L3	
Caldwell, Hiram	8, Aug. 1850	July	7		L3	
Caldwell, John (Gen)	4, Dec. 1804	Dec.			L1	
Caldwell, John Milton	21, July 1842	1, July	24		L3	
Caldwell, Margaretta D.H.	19, Jan. 1837	17, Jan.	20	*	L3	
Caldwell, Richard	13, Nov. 1834	Nov.	55		L1	

Name	Notice Date	Death Date	Age		Page	Maiden Name
Caldwell, Robert	4, Mar. 1847	23, Feb.	46		L3	
Caldwell, Robert C. (Gen)	30, Dec. 1852	18, Nov.	42	*	L3	
Caldwell, Roxana	10, Feb. 1848	Feb.	27		L3	
Caldwell, William	10, Sept 1846	Sept	77		L3	
Caldwell, William	30, Mar. 1849	11, Mar.	86	*	L3	
Calhoun, Hamilton	6, Dec. 1855	29, Nov.			L3	
Calhoun, John Lord	12, Sept 1850	10, Sept	13m-15d		L3	
Calice, Sarah J.	21, Sept 1848	Sept	18m		L3	
Callagan, James	31, Jan. 1850	Jan.	28		L3	
Callaghan, Dennis	14, Dec. 1824		estate		L3	
Callaghan, James	16, May 1850	May	18		L3	
Callahan, Edward	20, Jan. 1848	Jan.	29		L3	
Callahan, James	16, Sept 1852	12, Sept			L3	
Callahan, John	6, May 1841	Apr.	19		L3	
Callahan, Michael	7, Aug. 1851	3, Aug.			L3	
Callender, Ann Matilda	15, July 1847	13, July			L3	
Calligan, James	16, Aug. 1849	Aug.	35		L3	
Calvert, George	10, Mar. 1853	Feb.	78		L3	
Calvin, James	9, June 1836		probate		L3	
Calvin, John	28, Sept 1848	Sept	26		L3	
Cambles, Frederick	2, June 1842	May	22		L3	
Camel, John	1, Aug. 1833	July	37		L1	
Camel, Mary	1, Aug. 1833	July	38		L1	
Cameron, Daniel	12, Feb. 1816		estate		L3	
Cameron, Eliza	4, Apr. 1839	3, Apr.			L3	
Cameron, Hugh	20, Jan. 1848	Jan.	51		L3	
Cameron, James B.	14, Sept 1843	3, Sept	46		L3	
Cameron, John	1, Aug. 1839		estate		L3	
Cameron, Romanza	19, June 1845	10, June	2-11m		L3	
Cameron, Sarah	27, Feb. 1845	20, Feb.			L3	
Cameron, William	2, Sept 1852	1, Sept	5- 4m		L3	
Cammack, Hugh	16, Apr. 1846	6, Apr.		*	L3	
Cammack, Laura M.	22, Aug. 1844	16, Aug.	10m-14d		L3	
Camp, John	8, Nov. 1849	Oct.	28		L3	
Camp, Mary Esther	7, Jan. 1847	1, Jan.	7w		L3	
Campbell, (child of William)	15, Aug. 1833	Aug.	4m		L1	
Campbell, Alexander W.	6, Aug. 1840	July	34		L3	
Campbell, Caroline S.	6, Apr. 1854	19, Mar.			L3	
Campbell, Charles	21, June 1849	13, June	infant		L3	
Campbell, Edward	20, Mar. 1851	Mar.	20		L3	
Campbell, Edward	29, Dec. 1842	Dec.	30		L3	
Campbell, Eleanor	19, July 1832	July	44- 9m		L1	
Campbell, Emma Jane	26, July 1849	9, July	12		L3	
Campbell, Harriet	26, July 1849	17, July	61	*	L3	Stoddert
Campbell, Isabella	29, June 1848	June	16		L3	
Campbell, James P.	23, Aug. 1849	17, July	43	*	L3	
Campbell, James P.	3, Apr. 1851		estate		L3	
Campbell, James P.	19, 26, July 1849	17, July		*	L3	
Campbell, John	11, Apr. 1839		estate		L4	
Campbell, John B. (Col)	20, Sept 1814	28, Aug.			L3	
Campbell, John P. (Rev)	15, 22, Nov. 1814	5, Nov.	46		L3	
Campbell, John W.	26, Sept 1833	Sept			L1	
Campbell, Joseph	25, Oct. 1832	Oct.	8		L1	
Campbell, Joseph	15, Jan. 1846	Jan.	35		L3	

Name	Notice Date	Death Date	Age	Page	Maiden Name
Campbell, Katy	2, Oct. 1851	28, Sept	13m	L3	
Campbell, Lane	18, Sept 1845	Sept	1- 6m	L3	
Campbell, Margaret B.	18, Oct. 1832	Oct.	39	L4	
Campbell, Robert	10, May 1814		estate	L1	
Campbell, Samuel	6, Aug. 1846		95	* L3	
Campbell, Sarah J.	16, July 1857	10, July	28	L3	
Campbell, Thomas	2, Mar. 1854	4, Jan.	94	L3	
Campbell, Thomas	15, Feb. 1844	Feb.		L3	
Campbell, Virginia Dickinson	7, Oct. 1841	14, Sept	1-11m	L3	
Campbell, William	23, July 1846	July	3	L3	
Campfield, Robert M.	1, Apr. 1852	20, Mar.		* L3	
Candler, Cecilia Ball	9, Mar. 1837	7, Mar.	2- 1m-12d	L3	
Canfield, Charles Edward	21, Jan. 1847	14, Jan.	6-10m	L3	
Canfield, Ella Daisey	30, Aug. 1855	7, Aug.	8m	L3	
Canfield, George	17, June 1841	June	56	L3	
Canfield, Ida Maria	18, Nov. 1852	14, Nov.	5w	L3	
Canfield, John P.	2, Sept 1825	28, Aug.		* L3	
Canfield, Mary Jane	30, Aug. 1855	25, Aug.	39	L3	
Canfield, Urand	15, Mar. 1855	10, Mar.	79	* L3	
Cannon, James	8, Aug. 1833	July		L1	
Cannon, Michael	3, Oct. 1850	Sept	26	L3	
Cannon, Newton	7, Oct. 1841	16, Sept		L3	
Cannon, Robert	29, Aug. 1833	Aug.	47- 4m-12d	L1	
Cannon, Theophilus	16, Mar. 1843	9, Mar.	28	L3	
Canovan, Patrick	14, Sept 1848	Sept	23	L3	
Cantwell, Francis	18, Aug. 1842	Aug.	2	L3	
Capsey, John	11, July 1844	July	23	L3	
Careg, Nancy	18, July 1833	July	7m- 6d	L2	
Carey, Abraham	3, Feb. 1817		estate	L4	
Carey, Catharine	6, Feb. 1840	Jan.	38	L3	
Carey, Charles	22, Sept 1853	20, Sept	21- -16d	L3	
Carey, David P.	22, Aug. 1833	Aug.	3	L4	
Carey, Hannah	12, Sept 1850		estate	L3	
Carey, Lewis	19, Sept 1850		estate	L3	
Carey, Lou Allen	8, July 1847	4, July	infant	L3	
Carey, Matthew	26, Sept 1839			L2	
Carl, (child of Gilbert S.)	18, Oct. 1827	Oct.	27d	L3	
Carl, James	17, Jan. 1850	Jan.	29	L3	
Carle, Thomas	18, Oct. 1832	13, Oct.		L2	
Carlen, Jane	12, Dec. 1833	Dec.	47	L4	
Carley, (Mr)	11, Oct. 1832	5, Oct.		L2	
Carley, Eliza F.	15, May 1851	10, May	10	L3	
Carlin, John	20, Apr. 1819		estate	L3	
Carll, C.K.	25, Nov. 1847	22, Nov.		L3	
Carll, M.M. (Rev)	2, Oct. 1856	25, Sept		L5	
Carly, Stephen V.	8, May 1851	12, Apr.		L3	
Carmack, Catharine	30, June 1806	23, June		L3	
Carmack, Daniel (Major)	9, Dec. 1816	5, Nov.		L3	
Carman, Mary A.	18, July 1833	July	2- 1m	L2	
Carmical, James	9, Oct. 1834	Sept	23	L1	
Carmichael, (Mrs)	18, Oct. 1832	12, Oct.	35	L1	
Carmichael, Thomas J.	18, Apr. 1839		estate	L4	
Carnahan, Patrick	12, July 1849	July		L3	
Carneal, Thomas	18, Nov. 1852	10, Nov.		L3	

Name	Notice Date	Death Date	Age	Page	Maiden Name
Carnes, Caroline	13, Dec. 1832	Dec.	9m	L1	
Carnes, Charlotte	1, Sept 1853	26, Aug.		L3	
Carnes, Francis I.	30, Apr. 1846	14, Mar.	29	L3	
Carnes, John	19, July 1849	July	30	L3	
Carnes, Mary	14, Mar. 1850	5, Mar.	50	L3	
Carney, David L.	14, Aug. 1856	1, Aug.	77	L5	
Carney, Mary	27, June 1850	June	12	L3	
Carney, Mary Montgomery	3, Sept 1857	21, Aug.	9m- 6d	L3	
Carney, Matthew	13, Feb. 1851	Feb.	23	L3	
Carney, Nicholas	23, July 1846	July	60	L3	
Carney, Thomas	23, Nov. 1848	Nov.	17	L3	
Carney, Thomas	12, Apr. 1849	Apr.	27	L3	
Carpenter, Calvin	14, May 1846	13, May	39	L3	
Carpenter, Clifford H.	30, Aug. 1849		12	L3	
Carpenter, Eliza A.	16, Oct. 1834	Oct.	27	L1	
Carpenter, Ind.	20, Nov. 1834	Nov.	27	L1	
Carpenter, Ira	8, Jan. 1835		estate	L3	
Carpenter, Ira	3, Sept 1857		estate	L3	
Carpenter, Ira	12, Jan. 1837		probate	L3	
Carpenter, John	2, Aug. 1832	July	1- 2m	L1	
Carpenter, John	18, Oct. 1832	Oct.	30	L4	
Carpenter, Joseph	24, July 1834		estate	L3	
Carpenter, Joseph	29, Jan. 1835		estate	L3	
Carpenter, Joseph	15, Feb. 1808	Feb.		L3	
Carpenter, Joseph	25, Oct. 1832	22, Oct.		L3	
Carpenter, Joseph	15, Nov. 1832		estate	L4	
Carpenter, Joseph (Capt)	22, Mar. 1814	10, Mar.		L3	
Carpenter, Joseph Percy	28, Dec. 1848	24, Dec.	3- 5m	L3	
Carpenter, Joshua	1, Jan. 1835		estate	L4	
Carpenter, Mary Stevens	26, Oct. 1848	22, Oct.	15m- 7d	L3	
Carpenter, Nathan	29, May 1834		probate	L3	
Carr, (child of Eliza)	27, Nov. 1845	Nov.	1d	L3	
Carr, Arthur	1, Aug. 1833	July	50	L1	
Carr, Arthur	25, July 1833	23, July		L4	
Carr, Catharine	26, Dec. 1833	Dec.	64	L4	
Carr, Francis	28, Mar. 1839		estate	L3	
Carr, Francis	4, Apr. 1844		estate	L3	
Carr, Francis	13, Mar. 1845		estate	L3	
Carr, Francis	12, Jan. 1837		probate	L3	
Carr, Francis	8, Nov. 1838		probate	L3	
Carr, Francis	3, Sept 1840		probate	L3	
Carr, Francis	13, Nov. 1834		estate	L4	
Carr, Francis	17, Mar. 1836		estate	L4	
Carr, Francis (Col)	1, 8, Aug. 1833	30, July	60	L1	
Carr, Hugh	15, Aug. 1844		estate	L3	
Carr, James	1, Aug. 1833	July	1m-14d	L1	
Carr, James	14, Dec. 1848	Dec.	62	L2	
Carr, James	31, Dec. 1846	Dec.	67	L3	
Carr, John	6, Jan. 1853	5, Jan.		L3	
Carr, John L.	28, Aug. 1834	Aug.	11m	L1	
Carr, Owen	27, Mar. 1851	Mar.	39	L3	
Carr, Rose Ann	25, July 1833	July	19	L1	
Carr, Sarah	17, Nov. 1821	14, Nov.	38	L3	
Carr, William	10, Oct. 1821		estate	L2	

Name	Notice Date	Death Date	Age	Page	Maiden Name
Carr, William	19, Aug. 1841		estate	L3	
Carrel, Mary	17, Jan. 1850	11, Jan.		L3	
Carrel, Rachel H.	15, Apr. 1847	3, Apr.	22	L3	
Carrell, William A.	11, July 1833		probate	L3	
Carrick, Cunningham	8, Aug. 1833	July	37	L1	
Carrick, Cunningham	22, June 1837		probate	L3	
Carrick, Edward Lawless	19, Feb. 1857	16, Feb.	5m- 7d	L3	
Carrigan, Ann Lucy	28, Apr. 1853	26, Apr.	22	L3	
Carrigan, William	11, July 1833		probate	L3	
Carrington, Abijah	3, Apr. 1851	15, Mar.	73	L3	
Carrington, Licester	13, Jan. 1831		estate	L3	
Carrol, (Mr)	1, Sept 1842	31, Aug.		L1	
Carroll, Cornelius	3, July 1851	June	21	L3	
Carroll, Foster (Dr)	17, 24, July 1851	14, July	28	L3	
Carroll, John (Rev Dr)	8, Jan. 1816	3, Dec.	80	L3	
Carroll, Lydia B.	22, Jan. 1857	19, Jan.		L3	
Carroll, Mary	8, May 1851	1, May		L3	
Carroll, Patrick	5, Apr. 1849	Mar.	63	L3	
Carroll, Thomas	4, Oct. 1838	Sept	30	L3	
Carroll, William	21, Mar. 1850	Mar.	30	L3	
Carson, Alexina	20, Sept 1855	16, Sept	21	L3	Mayo
Carson, Enoch	28, Apr. 1817	14, Apr.	53	L3	
Carson, Enoch	11, Aug. 1817		estate	L3	
Carson, Isaac D.	4, Sept 1851	31, Aug.	26	L3	
Carson, James V.	22, Dec. 1812	15, Dec.	19	L3	
Carson, Mary Frances	19, July 1855	13, July	9	L3	
Carson, Ruth Ann	26, Aug. 1847	24, Aug.		L3	
Carson, William J.	5, Nov. 1846	28, Oct.	58	L3	
Cartelo, Thomas	5, Dec. 1850	Nov.	45	L3	
Carter, Ada A.M.	14, July 1842	11, July	18- 6m	L3	
Carter, Alex.	8, Nov. 1832	Nov.	1m-15d	L1	
Carter, Anna E.	9, Feb. 1843	30, Jan.	21- 6m	L3	Hamilton
Carter, Catharine	27, May 1847	May	65	L3	
Carter, Charles	7, Aug. 1856	29, July	13- 4m-20d	L5	
Carter, Daniel	16, Mar. 1854	25, Feb.		L3	
Carter, Daniel C.	6, Nov. 1834		estate	L3	
Carter, Ephraim	27, Apr. 1848	22, Apr.	67	L3	
Carter, Hannah	10, Dec. 1857		probate	L3	
Carter, James	9, Sept 1847	Aug.	67	L3	
Carter, James C.	4, Apr. 1844		estate	L3	
Carter, Jewell D.	8, Nov. 1838		probate	L3	
Carter, John	9, Oct. 1834	Sept	26	L1	
Carter, John S.	9, Feb. 1854	5, Sept		L3	
Carter, Lewis	30, Dec. 1847	Dec.	29	L3	
Carter, Lydia B.	24, Nov. 1842	22, Nov.		L6	
Carter, Martha Wishart	9, Oct. 1845	3, Oct.	infant	L3	
Carter, Nelson	10, Mar. 1853	Feb.	52	L3	
Carter, Richard	23, Aug. 1838	4, Aug.	69	L3	
Carter, Thomas	20, Aug. 1846	13, Aug.	61	L3	
Carter, Thomas	3, Sept 1846	13, Aug.	61	*	L3
Carter, Warren	14, Feb. 1856		estate	L3	
Carter, Warren	10, May 1849	3, May		L3	
Carteree, (Mrs)	25, Oct. 1832	18, Oct.		L1	
Cartny, William	23, Oct. 1834	Oct.	42	L2	

Name	Notice Date	Death Date	Age		Page	Maiden Name
Cartwright, Elizabeth	15, Aug. 1833	Aug.	35		L1	
Carver, Caroline Elizabeth	7, Dec. 1848	4, Dec.	8		L3	
Carver, Henry Augustus	5, Jan. 1837	3, Jan.			L3	
Carver, James Mason	5, Jan. 1837	31, Dec.			L3	
Cary, (child of Ellen)	26, Jan. 1843	Jan.			L3	
Cary, Christopher	16, Feb. 1837	6, Feb.	74	*	L3	
Cary, Christopher	6, Aug. 1808	3, Aug.			L3	
Cary, H.E.	6, Aug. 1857		probate		L3	
Cary, Hannah Ellen	9, Nov. 1854	30, Oct.	40		L3	
Cary, Helen Mar	9, Nov. 1854	25, Oct.	18		L3	
Cary, L. (Rev)	29, Jan. 1857	24, Jan.	42		L3	
Cary, Maria Louisa	30, Sept 1847	26, Sept			L3	
Cary, Mary Evangeline	18, Aug. 1853	11, Aug.	9m-27d		L3	
Cary, Olive	23, Sept 1852	19, Sept	14m		L3	
Cary, William W.	27, July 1848	18, July	36		L3	
Cary, William W.	9, Nov. 1848		estate		L3	
Caryl, Levi	26, Jan. 1854	2, Jan.	91	*	L3	
Casay, John	27, July 1843	10, July	106	*	L1	
Case, Esther	11, Dec. 1815		92		L3	
Case, George W.	23, Mar. 1849	Mar.	34		L3	
Case, Henry	2, Aug. 1814		estate		L3	
Case, James	11, July 1850	July	45		L3	
Casey, Addison	28, Nov. 1833	Nov.	13		L4	
Casey, Humphrey	1, Aug. 1833	July	63		L1	
Casey, James	21, June 1849	June	25		L3	
Casey, Patrick	27, Sept 1838	Sept	40		L3	
Casey, Patrick	15, Oct. 1857	Oct.			L3	
Casey, Thomas	30, Apr. 1846	Apr.			L3	
Casey, William	4, June 1857		probate		L3	
Casey, William	6, July 1854	29, June			L3	
Cashay, Archibald	8, Jan. 1857		probate		L3	
Casner, Frederick	25, Oct. 1832	15, Oct.			L4	
Casner, Jacob	18, Oct. 1832	Oct.	42		L4	
Caspar, John	10, Apr. 1856		probate		L3	
Cass, Charles Lee (Capt)	13, Jan. 1842	4, Jan.	55		L3	
Cass, Elizabeth	14, Apr. 1853	31, Mar.	64	*	L3	Spencer
Cass, William	26, July 1849	July	29		L3	
Casse, (Mr)	25, Oct. 1832	20, Oct.			L2	
Casse, Herman H.	5, Nov. 1857		probate		L3	
Casseday, Eliza	28, June 1849	20, June			L3	
Casserty, Barney	12, July 1849	July	20		L3	
Cassilly, Kate	5, May 1853	28, Apr.			L3	
Cassilly, Michael	31, Jan. 1856		estate		L3	
Cassily, M.P.	9, Mar. 1854	6, Mar.	80		L3	
Castello, Patrick	11, Feb. 1847	Feb.	45		L3	
Castner, (Mrs)	25, Oct. 1832	16, Oct.			L4	
Caststeel, (child of Jeremiah)	29, Oct. 1846	Oct.	stillborn		L3	
Caswell, Henry	3, Jan. 1833	Dec.	5		L4	
Cater, Jewell D.	23, Dec. 1830		estate		L3	
Cathcart, Samuel	24, Oct. 1844	16, Oct.	18		L3	
Cathell, Emily	29, Nov. 1832	Nov.	4		L1	
Cathull, Tryphend (Mrs)	23, Oct. 1834	Oct.	27- 9m		L2	
Cating, William	26, July 1849	July	22		L3	
Catlin, Abel (Dr)	31, Jan. 1856	13, Jan.	86		L3	

Name	Notice Date	Death Date	Age		Page	Maiden Name
Catlin, Clara B.	28, Aug. 1845	25, July		*	L3	Gregory
Catlin, Peter	7, Apr. 1842	7, Mar.	77		L3	
Cato, Carle	12, July 1849	July	32		L3	
Catoo, Jacob	26, Jan. 1854	3, Jan.	64		L3	
Catt, George B.	29, Aug. 1833	Aug.	11m-14d		L1	
Catt, Isaac	27, Dec. 1849	Dec.	20		L3	
Cattenhorn, Ortges	7, Dec. 1837		estate		L3	
Cattenhorn, Ortigeous	5, Sept 1839		probate		L3	
Caufman, William	18, Jan. 1849	Jan.	20		L3	
Caughliss, Michael	5, Apr. 1849	Mar.	40		L3	
Caulfield, Thomas	22, Apr. 1815	22, Apr.			L3	
Cavalier, Walter	13, June 1850	June	24		L3	
Cavana, Anna	18, July 1850	July	3		L3	
Cavana, John	6, Dec. 1849	Nov.	45		L3	
Cavana, Maria	5, June 1845	May	2		L3	
Cavanaugh, John Hubbard	1, Feb. 1849	30, Jan.			L3	
Cavano, Peter B.	25, Apr. 1850	Apr.	35		L3	
Cave, Daniel	1, July 1841	June	24		L3	
Cavin, Bridget	28, Nov. 1850	Nov.	30		L3	
Cawley, Thomas	1, Mar. 1849	Feb.	26		L3	
Ceale, (child of John)	19, Sept 1833	Sept	stillborn		L4	
Celia, James N.	6, Nov. 1851				L4	
Cerroll, John M.	3, June 1847	May	31		L3	
Chace, Ira H.	14, Feb. 1856	26, Jan.			L3	
Chace, John Holland	21, Feb. 1850	13, Feb.	27- 9m	*	L3	
Chadwick, Alice	2, Jan. 1851	28, Dec.	5-11m- 2d		L3	
Chalfant, Henry Clay Motier	9, Sept 1841	8, Sept			L3	
Chalfant, Lafayette W.	29, July 1847	7, July	23		L3	
Chalfant, Lafayette W.	12, Aug. 1847	7, July	23		L3	
Chalkley, Jacob	5, July 1849	June	18		L3	
Challen, Joseph	20, June 1833	12, June			L2	
Challis, Lydia B.	12, Mar. 1846	11, Mar.			L3	
Chamberlain, Ann	6, Feb. 1811				L3	
Chamberlain, E.K. (Dr)	10, Feb. 1853	26, Jan.			L3	
Chamberlain, Elijah	2, Nov. 1837	10, Oct.	67		L4	
Chamberlain, George W.	19, Aug. 1847		estate		L3	
Chamberlain, Reuben	9, Jan. 1845		estate		L3	
Chamberlain, Richard	12, Jan. 1837		probate		L3	
Chamberlain, T.G.	11, Apr. 1844	5, Apr.		*	L3	
Chamberlin, J.L.	9, Apr. 1857		probate		L3	
Chamberlin, Reuben	17, Feb. 1842		estate		L4	
Chamberlin, Susan	20, Sept 1849	Sept	25		L3	
Chamberlin, William	23, Mar. 1837		estate		L3	
Chamberlin, William	14, Feb. 1839		probate		L3	
Chamberlin, William	21, Mar. 1839		estate		L4	
Chamberling, Joseph	29, Aug. 1833	Aug.	45		L1	
Chambers, (child of Benjamin)	6, June 1810	24, May	infant		L2	
Chambers, Benjamin	28, May 1805		estate		L3	
Chambers, Catharine	1, Aug. 1850	25, July	4		L3	
Chambers, Clara Frances	4, Nov. 1847	31, Oct.	6m		L3	
Chambers, Henry	20, July 1843	13, July	70	*	L3	
Chambers, James	8, Nov. 1855		probate		L3	
Chambers, James	5, Nov. 1857		probate		L3	
Chambers, John	29, Aug. 1833	Aug.	7		L1	

Name	Notice Date	Death Date	Age	Page	Maiden Name
Chambers, John	18, Oct. 1832	Oct.	44	L4	
Chambers, John H.	16, Sept 1847	Sept	17	L3	
Chambers, John T.	10, Dec. 1857		probate	L3	
Chambers, Laura M.	3, July 1851	25, June	6m	L3	
Chambers, Susannah	4, July 1850	27, June		L3	
Chambers, Theodore Finley	25, July 1850	21, July	2- - 2d	L3	
Chambers, W.C.	22, Aug. 1839			L3	
Champlin, Amelia A.	31, Oct. 1844	23, Oct.		L3	
Champlin, Richard Henry	4, Sept 1851	26, Aug.	8	L3	
Chana, George C.	25, Oct. 1832	21, Oct.		L3	
Chandler, Charles	4, Feb. 1847	Jan.	45	L3	
Chandler, Daniel (Capt)	1, July 1847	16, June	59	L3	
Chandler, Jeremiah	16, June 1812		estate	L3	
Chandler, John (Gen)	21, Oct. 1841	25, Sept	81	L3	
Chandler, W.H.	14, Sept 1854	3, Sept	22	L3	
Channing, William (Dr)	1, Mar. 1855	11, Feb.		L3	
Chanton, Dudley	8, Feb. 1838	Feb.	24	L3	
Chapin, Calvin (Rev)	3, Apr. 1851	16, Mar.	88	L3	
Chapin, Manley	5, July 1849	19, June	36	L3	
Chapline, Moses W. (Gen)	5, Nov. 1840	21, Oct.		L2	
Chapman, Aaron	10, Dec. 1846	Dec.	69	L3	
Chapman, Charley Stillman	5, Nov. 1857	1, Nov.	2- 5m	L3	
Chapman, George A.	23, Feb. 1854	3, Feb.	6	L3	
Chapman, Hanlon (Rev)	27, July 1854	23, July		L3	
Chapman, Hannah E.	26, Feb. 1852	Feb.	27	L4	
Chapman, Joseph B.	9, Sept 1847	31, Aug.	48	L3	
Chapman, Mary A.	8, Aug. 1833	July	6m	L1	
Chapman, Robert	18, July 1833	July	38	L2	
Chapman, William Daniel	28, Oct. 1841	14, Oct.	14m-17d	L3	
Chappel, Morris	8, July 1847	June	22	L3	
Chappell, John George	2, Sept 1852	30, Aug.	7m-17d	L3	
Charity, Louisa	12, Mar. 1840	Mar.	1w	L3	
Charnock, George	16, Oct. 1856		probate	L6	
Charter, Elizabeth	1, Nov. 1832	Oct.	22	L2	
Charters, George	26, Mar. 1846	1, Mar.	71	L3	
Charters, James	21, Sept 1837		probate	L4	
Chase, Abraham	8, Nov. 1832		estate	L4	
Chase, Abram L.	9, June 1836		probate	L3	
Chase, Alexander R.	1, Apr. 1847	23, Mar.	49	L3	
Chase, Catharine Jane	13, Feb. 1840	6, Feb.	4- 3m	L3	
Chase, Dudley	19, Aug. 1852	31, July	30	L3	
Chase, Eliza Ann	2, Oct. 1845	29, Sept	23-10m	L3	
Chase, Isaac	9, June 1836		probate	L3	
Chase, John	15, Aug. 1844	Aug.		L3	
Chase, Josephine	15, Aug. 1850	27, July	1- -22d	L3	
Chase, Lizzie	8, Sept 1842	30, Aug.	3m	L3	
Chase, Sarah Bella D.L.	22, Jan. 1852	13, Jan.	32	L3	Ludlow
Chavers, (Mr)	25, Oct. 1832	18, Oct.		L1	
Checkley, Sarah	13, July 1854		estate	L3	
Checks, Nathan	2, Oct. 1834	Sept	44	L4	
Cheeseborough, Robert J.	18, July 1850			L3	
Cheesebrough, Joseph	27, Nov. 1834	Nov.	1- 3m	L1	
Cheeseman, Richard W.	22, Mar. 1838		probate	L3	
Cheesman, R.W.	11, Feb. 1836	25, Jan.	52	L1	

Name	Notice Date	Death Date	Age		Page	Maiden Name
Cheesman, Richard W.	11, Feb. 1836		estate		L3	
Cheetham, James	10, Oct. 1810	19, Sept	38		L3	
Cheever, Margaret L.	1, June 1848	23, May	26		L3	Beecher
Cheney, Anna Woodbridge	26, Aug. 1841	16, Aug.	13m		L3	
Cheney, Mary Howell	26, May 1836	18, May	22m		L3	
Cheney, Mary Howell	7, July 1836	18, May	22m		L4	
Cheney, Sarah Shaw	7, July 1836	20, June	9m		L4	
Cheney, Waitstiel Dexter	15, Apr. 1841	6, Apr.	31		L3	
Chenoweth, Eliza Arthur	1, Mar. 1855	26, Feb.	1- 9m-24d		L3	
Chenoweth, Frank G. (Capt)	23, Dec. 1847	19, Dec.			L3	
Chenoweth, James	15, Jan. 1852	10, Jan.	75		L3	
Chenoweth, James (Mrs)	3, Apr. 1851	31, Mar.			L3	
Chenoweth, Julia	30, Jan. 1851	28, Jan.		*	L3	Rogers
Chenoweth, Ross	23, Aug. 1855	19, Aug.			L3	
Cheseldine, Margaret Ann	12, Oct. 1848	10, Oct.	6- 1m		L3	
Cheseldine, Martha G.	1, Nov. 1855	30, Oct.		*	L3	Phelps
Chesney, William R.	23, Sept 1847	16, Sept			L3	
Chester, Franklin	28, June 1849	June	59		L3	
Chester, John K.	9, Jan. 1851				L3	
Chester, Mary Elizabeth	26, Aug. 1841	15, Aug.	1		L3	
Chew, Delia A.	23, Feb. 1854	18, Feb.			L3	
Child, David	1, July 1841	25, June	40	*	L3	
Child, John R.	5, Nov. 1857		probate		L3	
Child, John R.	16, Oct. 1856	11, Oct.	33		L5	
Child, Margaret	18, Mar. 1847	14, Mar.			L3	
Child, Richard E.	2, July 1840	28, June	22m		L3	
Childers, Lewis N.	5, Sept 1850	Aug.	3- 6m		L3	
Childress, Rebecca	20, Jan. 1848	16, Jan.	30	*	L3	Jennings
Childs, Amos	17, May 1849	May	26		L3	
Childs, Stanley	5, Mar. 1840		estate		L3	
Chiles, Elizabeth	16, Nov. 1848	10, Nov.			L3	Morgan
Chilton, Thomas	9, Aug. 1838	July	35		L3	
Chlera, James	15, Nov. 1832	Nov.			L1	
Choat, Rufus King	28, Mar. 1839	23, Mar.	infant		L3	
Chresty, (child of Elizabeth)	2, July 1840	June	2w		L3	
Chrisman, Elias	12, Feb. 1835		estate		L3	
Chrisman, Elizabeth	29, Jan. 1835		estate		L3	
Chrisman, Elizabeth	9, June 1836		probate		L3	
Christian, David	4, Jan. 1844	Dec.	70		L3	
Christian, Henry	20, Oct. 1818		estate		L3	
Christian, Priscella	18, May 1843	May	55		L3	
Christie, George	24, Sept 1846	4, Sept			L3	
Christie, Jannett	14, Feb. 1839	11, Feb.	41		L3	
Christman, Jacob (Rev)	21, Mar. 1810	11, Mar.	64		L3	
Christopher, Salome Ohley	19, Oct. 1848	12, Oct.	4- 2m-21d		L3	
Church, Joseph N.	9, May 1839	26, Apr.		*	L3	
Church, Kerener	25, Oct. 1832	Oct.	11		L1	
Churchill, Caroline H.	22, June 1854	17, June	59		L3	
Churchill, Charles Milton	23, Mar. 1848	20, Mar.	1-11m		L3	
Churchill, Emma	25, Apr. 1844	17, Apr.	2- 8m		L3	
Churchill, Frederick Augustus	29, July 1841	24, July	11m		L3	
Churchill, Mary A.J.	29, May 1845	23, May	3- 6m- 6d		L3	
Churchin, Mary	17, Oct. 1839	Oct.	45		L3	
Churhill, Mary M.	2, June 1853	28, May	40		L3	

Name	Notice Date	Death Date	Age		Page	Maiden Name
Ciegelnyer, Elias	29, Feb. 1844	Feb.			L3	
Cilley, Benjamin	7, May 1857		probate		L3	
Cilley, Benjamin	9, July 1857		probate		L3	
Cilley, Caroline Louisa	4, Mar. 1847	25, Feb.			L3	
Cilley, Henry	19, Apr. 1845		estate		L3	
Cilley, Jonathan	5, May 1807		estate		L3	
Cilley, Jonathan	24, Mar. 1807	Mar.			L3	
Cinckner, Harvey	27, Sept 1827		18m		L1	
Cisco, Andrew S.	7, Aug. 1834	July	1- 4m		L3	
Ciser, Casper	14, June 1849	June	22		L3	
Cist, Anna T.	21, Nov. 1844	17, Nov.	24-10m		L3	
Cist, Edward	4, Jan. 1844	3, Jan.	2- 1m		L3	
Cist, Jane Martha	26, Nov. 1840	22, Nov.	17		L3	
Cist, Mary	1, June 1837	26, May	3		L3	
Cist, William	1, June 1837	25, May	5		L3	
Claiborne, William Chas. Cole	22, Dec. 1817	23, Nov.			L2	
Clancy, Michael	17, Feb. 1848				L3	
Clapp, John	17, May 1814		estate		L2	
Clark, (child of John M.)	8, Aug. 1833	July			L1	
Clark, (child of Nancy)	18, Mar. 1847	Mar.	stillborn		L3	
Clark, (child of William)	7, Aug. 1834	July			L3	
Clark, Alexander	7, Oct. 1852	29, Sept	56		L3	
Clark, Alexander	6, Dec. 1855		probate		L3	
Clark, Alexander	8, Jan. 1857		probate		L3	
Clark, Andrew	17, May 1849	May	30		L3	
Clark, Ann E.	25, July 1833	July	19		L1	
Clark, Catharine W.	9, Aug. 1855	2, Aug.	48		L3	
Clark, Charlotte	6, Feb. 1851		estate		L3	
Clark, Daniel	12, Oct. 1813	16, Aug.	45		L3	
Clark, David	28, July 1842	July	40		L3	
Clark, Edward	22, May 1845	20, May	2- 4m		L3	
Clark, Edward Taylor	26, July 1849	20, July	1- 7m-16d		L3	
Clark, Eliza	20, Sept 1825	19, Sept	26		L3	
Clark, Elizabeth	1, July 1852	22, June	64		L3	
Clark, Elizabeth	15, July 1847	July	8m		L3	
Clark, Elizabeth S.	26, Nov. 1835	22, Nov.	2- 5m		L3	
Clark, George	26, July 1849	July	4		L3	
Clark, George	7, Sept 1854	2, Sept		*	L3	
Clark, George Rackett	10, Jan. 1850	6, Jan.	3- 5m		L3	
Clark, Georgette Louise	13, Sept 1849	12, Sept	2- 8m		L3	
Clark, Grace A.C.	14, Mar. 1850	8, Mar.	23- 8m		L3	Taylor
Clark, Hannah	25, Nov. 1852	23, Nov.	65		L3	
Clark, Hiram O. (Dr)	17, Mar. 1853	17, Mar.	30		L3	
Clark, Isabella	26, July 1849	July	35		L3	
Clark, James	20, May 1816		estate		L3	
Clark, Jean	27, Sept 1849	21, Sept	69	*	L3	
Clark, Jennett	21, Dec. 1848	Dec.	1w		L3	
Clark, John	9, Oct. 1834	Sept	45		L1	
Clark, John	20, Sept 1849	17, Sept	71	*	L3	
Clark, John	8, Jan. 1857		probate		L3	
Clark, John (Rev)	23, Feb. 1854	6, Jan.	55		L3	
Clark, John M. (Capt)	3, Aug. 1848	30, July	41		L3	
Clark, John Martin	31, Mar. 1853	27, Mar.	33		L3	
Clark, Jonathan	4, Oct. 1820		estate		L3	

Name	Notice Date	Death Date	Age		Page	Maiden Name
Clark, Joseph	2, Oct. 1834	Sept	35	*	L4	
Clark, Joseph L.	10, Dec. 1857	probate			L3	
Clark, Josephine S.	4, May 1843	6, May	15		L3	
Clark, Landy	15, Nov. 1849	Nov.	38		L3	
Clark, Mary	5, Sept 1833	Aug.	56		L1	
Clark, Mary	17, 24, July 1845	10, July	32	*	L3	
Clark, Mary	21, June 1838	16, June	48		L3	
Clark, Mary	27, Feb. 1851	Feb.	50		L3	
Clark, Mary	26, June 1851	June	55		L3	
Clark, Mary Ann K.	24, May 1855	17, May	43		L3	
Clark, Mary S.	4, Sept 1851	14, Aug.	1- 7m		L3	
Clark, Nancy	25, Dec. 1851	17, Dec.	21		L3	
Clark, Nicholas	14, Nov. 1844	Nov.	22		L3	
Clark, Patrick	29, June 1848	June	14		L3	
Clark, Robert	1, June 1848	May	2		L3	
Clark, Samuel	6, Apr. 1848	Mar.	28		L3	
Clark, Sarah A.	7, Aug. 1834	July	1		L3	
Clark, Sarah Turner	12, Feb. 1846	8, Feb.	7		L3	
Clark, Thomas	26, Mar. 1835	estate			L4	
Clark, Thompson	17, Mar. 1826	probate			L3	
Clark, Timothy	19, Mar. 1835	estate			L3	
Clark, Willey	31, May 1855	24, May	10m		L3	
Clark, William	23, Feb. 1843	Feb.	33		L3	
Clark, William	6, Sept 1832	estate			L4	
Clark, Willie	7, May 1857	30, Apr.	4m-11d		L3	
Clark, Zenas	3, Nov. 1842	Oct.	43		L3	
Clarke, Augustus	5, Mar. 1840	14, Feb.	23		L3	
Clarke, Dolly	13, June 1833	June	1m		L1	
Clarke, John B.	3, Sept 1846	2, Sept	46		L3	
Clarke, Margaret	27, May 1841	17, May	26		L3	
Clarke, Nathaniel	11, July 1833	July	35		L1	
Clarke, Richard R.	22, Jan. 1852	18, Jan.	7m-12d		L3	
Clarkson, Christiana	9, Aug. 1855	probate			L3	
Clarkson, Christiana	7, May 1857	probate			L3	
Clarkson, David	20, June 1833	15, June	44		L1	
Clarkson, Margaret D.	25, Mar. 1852	23, Mar.	16		L3	
Clary, Benjamin	19, May 1806	27, Mar.			L3	
Clary, Bridget	28, Mar. 1850	Mar.	19		L3	
Clary, James	26, Apr. 1849	Apr.	30		L3	
Clary, Michael	7, Mar. 1850	Feb.	20		L3	
Clasky, Ann	20, June 1850	June	9		L3	
Classon, Smith	23, Feb. 1832	estate			L3	
Clatback, Adolphus	18, July 1850	July	26		L3	
Clausing, William	2, Dec. 1852	estate			L3	
Clawson, Elizabeth	1, Nov. 1832	Oct.	1- 6m		L2	
Clawson, Frank	26, Aug. 1852	19, Aug.	18m		L3	
Clawson, George	9, May 1850	Apr.	14		L3	
Clawson, William	2, May 1833	Apr.			L1	
Claxton, James	7, Sept 1824	probate			L3	
Clay, Ann	5, Sept 1833	Aug.	64		L1	
Clay, Eliza H.	19, Aug. 1825	12, Aug.			L3	
Clay, Samuel	1, Sept 1842	Aug.	34		L3	
Clay, William	5, Apr. 1849	1- 4m			L3	
Claypoole, Joseph	31, Jan. 1856	22, Jan.	45		L3	

Name	Notice Date	Death Date	Age	Page	Maiden Name
Claypoole, Joseph	7, Feb. 1856		estate	L3	
Clayton, James	26, June 1851		estate	L3	
Clayton, Jane	22, June 1843	15, June		L3	
Clayton, Joseph	1, Aug. 1833	July	9m	L1	
Clayton, Mary Ann	14, June 1849	8, June	22	L3	
Clayton, Robert	24, Sept 1846	Sept	29	L3	
Cleary, Thomas	8, May 1845	Apr.	32	L3	
Cleary, Thomas	12, Aug. 1841	Aug.	35	L3	
Cleavland, Elizabeth	18, Mar. 1847	Mar.	67	L3	
Clemens, Harriet	5, Aug. 1852	July	11	L3	
Clement, Elizabeth	11, July 1850	6, July	28	L3	
Clement, Elizabeth Steiner	29, May 1851	18, May	1- - 3d	L3	
Clement, Ephraim	27, Apr. 1827	26, Apr.	42	L3	
Clement, J.P. (Major)	8, May 1851			* L3	
Clement, Jessie Letford	12, Nov. 1857	9, Nov.	6m- 5d	L3	
Clement, John B.	29, June 1848	24, June	25	L3	
Clement, Joseph	10, May 1855		estate	L3	
Clement, Thomas	7, Feb. 1833	Feb.	40	L1	
Clement, William Morrow	21, June 1849	19, June	5	L3	
Clemmens, John	9, Oct. 1834	Sept	28	L1	
Clemmer, Jacob Henry	12, July 1855	8, July	19m	L3	
Clendenen, David	23, Mar. 1843	13, Mar.	70	L3	
Clendening, Sarah	2, May 1839	Apr.	19	L3	
Cleneay, John	11, Nov. 1852	8, Nov.	39- 9m	L3	
Cleveland, Francis A.	20, 27, July 1822	17, July	25	* L3	
Cleveland, Levi	5, Apr. 1814		estate	L3	
Cleveland, Stephen Blythe (Dr)	12, Jan. 1837	1, Jan.	45	L3	
Clift, Elisha	26, July 1814		estate	L4	
Clind, William	3, Jan. 1833	Dec.	39	L4	
Cline, Adam	9, Mar. 1854	2, Feb.	63- 4m-21d	L3	
Cline, Mary Margaret	9, Mar. 1854	27, Feb.	19- 4m- 5d	L3	
Clingman, John	13, June 1850	7, June	76	L3	
Clingman, John	4, Feb. 1825		estate	L3	
Clingman, John R.	8, Feb. 1849	Jan.	43	L3	
Clinkenbeard, Alexander	29, Dec. 1836		estate	L3	
Clinkenbeard, Clarissa	6, June 1833	May	29	L2	
Clinkenbeard, Russ	6, June 1833	May	6	L2	
Clinkinbeard, John R.	25, Sept 1845	16, Sept	39	* L3	
Clinton, George	4, Oct. 1809			L3	
Clinton, James	12, Jan. 1813	22, Dec.	76	L3	
Cloon, Delia Pease	3, Apr. 1851	27, Mar.	2	L3	
Clopper, Andrew M.	20, Oct. 1853	Sept	63	L3	
Clopper, Anna Rebecca	9, Aug. 1838	2, Aug.	10m	L3	
Clopper, Nicholas	21, July 1842		estate	L3	
Clopper, Rachael Ruhanah	7, Aug. 1845	30, July		L3	
Clopper, Rebecca C.	26, June 1845	17, June		L3	
Clopton, John	30, Sept 1816	11, Sept		L3	
Close, David P. (Capt)	24, Aug. 1837	21, Aug.	39	L3	
Clospole, Albert	29, Aug. 1833	Aug.		L1	
Clough, Ebenezer	13, July 1848	4, July	81	L3	
Clough, James	27, Jan. 1848	Jan.	55	L3	
Clouser, John (Mrs)	23, Sept 1852	17, Sept		L3	
Clutter, William	13, June 1810	8, June		L3	
Clyde, Louisa C.	31, Oct. 1850	30, Oct.	26	L3	

Name	Notice Date	Death Date	Age	Page	Maiden Name
Coates, James	12, Nov. 1840		estate	L3	
Coats, Jacob	31, Jan. 1850	Jan.	42	L3	
Cobaugh, William	30, Aug. 1838	Aug.	19	L3	
Cobb, James	1, Aug. 1833	July		L1	
Cobb, James	25, July 1833		53	* L3	
Cobb, James	6, Nov. 1834		estate	L3	
Cobb, James	7, May 1840		probate	L3	
Cobb, James	5, Sept 1833		estate	L4	
Cobb, James	14, June 1838		probate	L4	
Cobb, James Hayden	6, Mar. 1845	25, Feb.	11m-25d	L3	
Cobb, John B.	2, Aug. 1849	29, July	31	L3	
Cobb, John P. Harrison	6, Dec. 1849	3, Dec.	infant	L3	
Cobb, Joseph	14, Mar. 1839	6, Mar.	48	L3	
Coburn, Hannah	9, July 1846	June	1- 6m	L3	
Coburn, James A.	3, June 1847	31, May	42	* L3	
Cocheny, Mary	15, July 1847	July	5	L3	
Cocheny, Patrick	29, July 1847	July	4	L3	
Cochlin, (Mrs)	21, June 1849	June	40	L3	
Cochlin, Daniel	21, June 1849	June	45	L3	
Cochnaces, Margaret	8, Aug. 1833	July	34	L1	
Cochnower, Edward B.	13, July 1854	6, July		L3	
Cochnower, Luticias	22, Jan. 1852	18, Jan.		L3	
Cochran, John	9, Aug. 1838		probate	L3	
Cochran, Mary	18, Jan. 1849	Jan.	28	L3	
Cochran, Mary	6, Mar. 1851	Feb.	55	L3	
Cochran, Peter	25, Apr. 1850	Apr.	37	L3	
Cochran, Richard	9, Aug. 1838		probate	L3	
Cochran, Sarah A.	25, Apr. 1850	Apr.	50	L3	
Cochran, William	27, Oct. 1831		probate	L1	
Cochrin, John	28, Aug. 1834	Aug.	1- 3m	L1	
Coddington, James	9, Sept 1841		estate	L3	
Coddington, Stephen	14, Feb. 1839		probate	L3	
Cody, John	5, Oct. 1854	24, Aug.	45	L3	
Coe, George Stanley	27, Sept 1849	19, Sept	8m-19d	L3	
Coe, Lucy Anna	21, Oct. 1847	10, Oct.	3- 1m-18d	L3	
Coen, Michael	27, Sept 1849	Sept	19	L3	
Coen, Thomas	25, Dec. 1815		estate	L3	
Coey, John	10, Aug. 1843	Aug.	35	L3	
Coffee, Charity	15, Feb. 1844	Feb.	65	L3	
Coffeen, E.W.	4, Sept 1856		probate	L5	
Coffeen, Edwin W.	23, Nov. 1854		estate	L3	
Coffin, Benjamin F.	23, Apr. 1819		estate	L3	
Coffin, Edward	2, Oct. 1834	Sept	1- 3m	L4	
Coffin, Eliza Ann	16, Oct. 1834	Oct.	3- 8m	L1	
Coffin, Henry B.	29, July 1841	18, July	36	L3	
Coffin, Margaret	15, Aug. 1833	Aug.	69- 1m	L1	
Coffin, Phebe Starbuck	3, Mar. 1817	27, Feb.	infant	L3	
Coffin, Walter	20, Nov. 1850	15, Nov.	3m- 9d	L3	
Coffinan, Mary	11, July 1833	July	9m- 5d	L1	
Coffman, Andrew	26, Mar. 1846		estate	L3	
Coffman, Andrew	9, Jan. 1845	1, Jan.		L3	
Coghill, Angeletta	12, July 1849	July	16	L3	
Cogswell, Osmond	25, Mar. 1841	9, Mar.		L3	
Cogy, James	23, Apr. 1840		estate	L3	

Name	Notice Date	Death Date	Age	Page	Maiden Name
Cogy, Joseph	3, Mar. 1831		estate	L4	
Cohen, Benhart H.	29, Aug. 1844	18, Aug.		L3	
Cohoon, Albert F.	1, July 1841	25, June	8m	L3	
Cohoon, Robert	1, Nov. 1855	29, Oct.	53	L3	
Cohoon, Robert	22, Nov. 1855		estate	L3	
Cohoon, Robert	8, Jan. 1857		probate	L3	
Coil, Michael	25, Apr. 1833	Apr.	50	L1	
Coin, Thomas	27, Sept 1849	Sept	27	L3	
Coit, Elizabeth J.	12, 19, Feb. 1857	3, Feb.		L3	
Coit, Roger	21, Aug. 1856	9, Aug.	70	L5	
Colama, (boy)	27, June 1850		12	L3	
Colburn, Jesse	11, July 1833		probate	L3	
Colburn, Josiah	8, Mar. 1855	6, Mar.	76	L3	
Colby, A.C. (Mrs)	25, Jan. 1838	19, Jan.	38	L3	
Colby, Abraham	21, Apr. 1806	17, Apr.	23	L3	
Colby, Z.	10, Mar. 1826	26, Feb.		L3	
Cole,	25, July 1839	July	infant	L3	
Cole, Abby	27, June 1850	June	25	L3	
Cole, Helen A.	15, Aug. 1850	7, Aug.	24	L3	
Cole, Isaac	2, July 1840	June	46	L3	
Cole, John H.	20, Apr. 1843	Apr.	21	L3	
Cole, N.L.	27, Mar. 1845	22, Mar.		L3	
Cole, William R.	17, June 1847	10, June	66	L3	
Coleborn, Rebecca	22, Aug. 1833	Aug.	45	L4	
Coleburn, Charles	28, Mar. 1839	Mar.	20	L3	
Coleman, (child of Jane)	12, Dec. 1850	Dec.	1d	L3	
Coleman, Adbeel (Rev)	19, Nov. 1824	16, Nov.	42	L3	
Coleman, Alfred	9, Sept 1847	14, Aug.		* L3	
Coleman, Alice Carneal	20, Aug. 1840	18, Aug.	16m- 1d	L3	
Coleman, Benjamin	18, Jan. 1808		estate	L3	
Coleman, Catherine	26, June 1851	June	19	L3	
Coleman, Charles W.	1, July 1820		22	L3	
Coleman, Charles W.	2, Dec. 1820		estate	L3	
Coleman, David	28, Apr. 1853	27, Apr.		L3	
Coleman, Edward M.	7, Sept 1843	Aug.	6w	L3	
Coleman, Elizabeth	30, Aug. 1849	Aug.	75	L3	
Coleman, Emily	22, Aug. 1833	Aug.	10	L4	
Coleman, Esther	19, Oct. 1813	17, Oct.		L3	
Coleman, Francis	2, June 1812		estate	L1	
Coleman, Jacob	3, Sept 1840		probate	L3	
Coleman, James	19, Apr. 1849	Apr.	53	L3	
Coleman, Mary Emma	5, Feb. 1852	31, Jan.		* L3	Wood
Coleman, Milton R.	15, May 1851	5, May	25	* L3	
Coleman, Randall	6, Sept 1849	Aug.	2w	L3	
Coleman, Susan	28, Aug. 1834	Aug.	9m	L1	
Coleman, Susanna	8, Jan. 1852	24, Dec.	84	* L3	
Colemire, Frederick	9, Nov. 1837	Oct.		L4	
Colerick, Charles (Capt)	15, Feb. 1838	7, Feb.		* L3	
Coles, Anna Frances	27, Nov. 1845	22, Nov.	2- 8m-16d	L3	
Coles, Henry	4, Mar. 1841	Feb.	20	L3	
Coley, Joseph	26, Apr. 1849	Apr.	21	L3	
Colgan, John	20, June 1833	June	25	L1	
Colin, Catharine	26, June 1851	June	12	L3	
Colin, Mary	26, June 1851	June	18	L3	

Name	Notice Date	Death Date	Age		Page	Maiden Name
Collier, (son of Henry)	2, Oct. 1834	Sept			L4	
Collier, Joseph	1, Feb. 1849	Jan.	45		L3	
Collier, Lydia Frances	29, July 1852	22, July			L3	
Collier, Thomas	31, Mar. 1842	11, Mar.	82	*	L3	
Collins, Ephraim	2, July 1846		estate		L3	
Collins, Harriet A.	6, Sept 1855	20, Aug.			L3	
Collins, Henry	4, Apr. 1839	Mar.	55		L3	
Collins, Isaac	28, Apr. 1817	21, Mar.			L3	
Collins, James	28, June 1849	June	29		L3	
Collins, John	2, July 1808	29, June			L3	
Collins, John	14, June 1855				L3	
Collins, John J.	16, Sept 1847	14, Sept			L3	
Collins, Luther	5, July 1855		probate		L3	
Collins, Lydia	21, Jan. 1847	19, Dec.		*	L3	
Collins, Martin	25, Oct. 1832	21, Oct.			L2	
Collins, Mary	11, Oct. 1832	6, Oct.			L2	
Collins, Mary	18, Oct. 1832	Oct.	35		L4	
Collins, Norman	28, Aug. 1834	Aug.	63		L1	
Collins, Susan	8, Nov. 1849		65		L3	
Collins, Timothy	2, Nov. 1843	Oct.	27		L3	
Collison, Charlotte	5, Nov. 1840		estate		L2	
Collord, Rebecca	7, Aug. 1856	4, Aug.			L5	
Colton, Francis Fellowes	2, June 1842	26, May	10m		L3	
Colvert, (child of John)	9, Jan. 1845	Dec.	3m		L3	
Colvin, James	25, Oct. 1832	21, Oct.			L2	
Colvin, James	13, July 1854	26, June	77		L3	
Colvin, Martha	19, Mar. 1840	14, Mar.			L3	
Colvin, Rosalie	14, Sept 1854	7, Sept	10m		L3	
Combs, Fielding A.	13, Apr. 1854		63		L3	
Comfort, Patrick	21, June 1849	June	25		L3	
Comley, Reney	1, June 1819	26, May			L3	
Comley, Sarah	1, June 1819	23, May			L3	
Comly, James	4, Sept 1834		estate		L3	
Comly, James D.	14, Feb. 1850	6, Feb.	34		L3	
Comly, Joseph Mason	30, June 1826	25, June			L3	
Comly, Sarah R.	11, Jan. 1849	9, Jan.			L3	Judkins
Commerford, James	1, Aug. 1850	July	56		L3	
Commins, (child of H.)	13, Sept 1832	Sept	1		L1	
Compton, Elizabeth	16, June 1842	2, June			L3	
Compton, Jacob R.	17, Mar. 1826		probate		L3	
Compton, Rachel A.	22, Aug. 1850	Aug.	8		L3	
Compton, Richard	20, Sept 1809		estate		L3	
Comstock, Ann	8, Aug. 1833	July	55		L1	
Comstock, Mary	4, Oct. 1849	1, Oct.			L3	
Comstock, Susan	7, Nov. 1844	30, Oct.			L3	
Conahan, Sarah	7, Apr. 1853	31, Mar.			L3	
Conan, John	14, Dec. 1848	Dec.	50		L2	
Conchleton, Mary Ann	18, Oct. 1827	Oct.	11m		L3	
Concklin, Halstead	5, Sept 1823	1, Sept	22		L3	
Concklin, Halstead	5, Sept 1823		estate		L3	
Conckling, William M.	20, June 1833	June	4- 2m		L1	
Conclin, George	18, May 1854	9, May	53		L3	
Conclin, George	8, Nov. 1855		estate		L3	
Conclin, George	9, Apr. 1857		probate		L3	

Name	Notice Date	Death Date	Age	Page	Maiden Name
Conclin, Robert	12, Sept 1833	Sept	1- 3m	L1	
Conclin, Sarah Ann	24, Sept 1846	21, Sept	36	L3	
Cone, Charles	9, June 1853		estate	L3	
Cone, Charles (Major)	28, Apr. 1853	26, Apr.	81	L3	
Cones, Margaret C.	19, Apr. 1849	14, Apr.	24	L3	
Coney, Benjamin	25, Oct. 1832	19, Oct.		L1	
Coney, Peggy	5, Mar. 1846	Feb.	80	L3	
Conger, Horace	25, Dec. 1845	Dec.	33	L3	
Conger, John	5, Dec. 1833		estate	L4	
Conger, Moses	13, Sept 1814		estate	L3	
Congor, John	21, Sept 1837		probate	L4	
Conkiln, Halstead	14, Dec. 1824		probate	L3	
Conkle, Charles	17, Aug. 1848	Aug.	19	L3	
Conkleton, (child of James)	2, May 1833	Apr.	stillborn	L1	
Conklin, (child)	15, Oct. 1840	Oct.	stillborn	L3	
Conklin, David	1, Dec. 1826		estate	L3	
Conklin, David	15, Apr. 1841		estate	L3	
Conklin, Freelove	6, May 1841	5, May		L3	
Conklin, George	5, Nov. 1857		probate	L3	
Conklin, Isaac	6, Mar. 1828		estate	L3	
Conklin, Josiah	6, Oct. 1821		estate	L3	
Conklin, Miller	13, Sept 1838	Sept	40	L3	
Conkling, G.W. Lafayette	20, Oct. 1853	11, Oct.	6	L3	
Conkling, Joseph	15, Mar. 1814		estate	L3	
Conkling, Joseph	8, Apr. 1816		estate	L3	
Conkling, Margaret	17, July 1845	15, July	44	L3	
Conkling, Margaret	13, Mar. 1856	4, Mar.		L3	
Conley, Owen	3, Apr. 1851	Mar.	30	L3	
Conly, (child of James)	8, Aug. 1833	July		L1	
Conn, (daughter of Charles)	23, July 1808	15, July	6	L3	
Conn, (heirs of Joseph)	14, Dec. 1824		probate	L3	
Conn, James M.	13, Sept 1825	12, Sept		L3	
Conn, Joseph	27, Oct. 1831		probate	L1	
Conn, Joseph	15, Sept 1836		probate	L3	
Connable, Henry	22, Apr. 1852	17, Apr.	infant	L3	
Connell, Patrick	23, June 1853	21, June		L3	
Connelly, James	23, Dec. 1847	Dec.	32	L3	
Connelly, James	8, Oct. 1846	Sept	50	L3	
Connelly, John	6, Aug. 1846	July	28	L3	
Connelly, Michael	11, May 1843	May	46	L3	
Connelly, Patrick	6, Dec. 1849	Nov.	53	L3	
Connelly, Peter	1, Aug. 1844	July	28	L3	
Conner, Charles T.	4, Jan. 1849	17, Dec.	29	L3	
Conner, Jacob	28, June 1849	June	40	L3	
Conner, Margaret	2, Aug. 1832	July	9m	L1	
Conner, Mary	14, Feb. 1850	Feb.	3	L3	
Conner, P.S. (Dr)	5, Oct. 1854	27, Sept	41	L3	
Conner, Stevens S.	21, Mar. 1850	25, Feb.	38	L3	
Conner, Thomas	21, Aug. 1845	Aug.	31	L3	
Conover, (child of Harriet K.)	4, July 1833	June	8m	L2	
Conover, Henry Shreve	4, Feb. 1836	30, Jan.	9m-15d	L3	
Conover, Julia Ann E.	31, Mar. 1836	24, Mar.	24- 3m	L1	Sellman
Conrad, Daniel	30, June 1807		estate	L3	
Conrad, Daniel	19, May 1807	13, May		L3	

Name	Notice Date	Death Date	Age		Page	Maiden Name
Conrad, James M.	15, Aug. 1833	Aug.	2- 3m		L1	
Conrey, John	25, Oct. 1832	22, Oct.			L3	
Conrey, Jonathan	5, Feb. 1857	probate			L3	
Conroy, Peter	2, Sept 1852	Aug.	32		L3	
Conshear, (child of Febert)	18, Oct. 1832	Oct.	21d		L4	
Const, (child of Joseph B.)	8, Aug. 1833	July	2- 6m		L1	
Constable, George	14, Feb. 1839	probate			L3	
Contee, Benjamin (Rev Dr)	8, Jan. 1816	23, Nov.	61		L3	
Convers, Rebecca	17, Oct. 1850	15, Oct.			L3	VanBuren
Conway, Catharine	19, July 1849	16, July	50		L3	
Conway, James R.	24, July 1845	19, July	15		L3	
Conway, John	1, Nov. 1849	Oct.	1w		L3	
Conway, Oney	2, Sept 1852	Aug.	7		L3	
Conway, Thomas	20, Mar. 1851	Mar.	23		L3	
Conway, William	27, Jan. 1853		45		L3	
Conway, William	13, Feb. 1851	Feb.	60		L3	
Conwell, Lillie	25, Dec. 1856	19, Dec.	10m- 3d		L3	
Cook, (heirs of)	12, Jan. 1837	probate			L3	
Cook, (Mrs)	1, Nov. 1832	29, Oct.			L3	
Cook, Anstenia	23, Aug. 1838	Aug.	13m		L3	
Cook, Benoni	21, Dec. 1854	17, Dec.		*	L3	
Cook, Charles	25, Dec. 1845	Dec.	7d		L3	
Cook, Francis	21, Nov. 1844	Nov.	4w		L3	
Cook, Henry	16, Sept 1841	Sept	45		L3	
Cook, Jacob	25, Jan. 1855	23, Jan.	74		L3	
Cook, Jesse D.	21, Nov. 1839	probate			L3	
Cook, Jesse S.	27, Mar. 1828	Mar.	34		L1	
Cook, Jesse S.	15, Jan. 1829	estate			L3	
Cook, Leander	25, Oct. 1832	19, Oct.			L1	
Cook, Leander	22, Nov. 1832	estate			L3	
Cook, Mary	15, Feb. 1844	6, Feb.	52	*	L3	
Cook, Mary F.	24, July 1851	20, July	33		L3	
Cook, Nancy	28, May 1846	May	38		L3	
Cook, Robert Fulton	27, Nov. 1845	20, Nov.	61		L3	
Cook, Samuel	22, May 1851	14, May	43- 2m		L3	
Cook, Sarah	25, Jan. 1855	15, Jan.	67		L3	
Cook, Shubael P.	14, Oct. 1816	9, Oct.	27		L3	
Cook, Theodore M. (Dr)	14, June 1849	22, May			L3	
Cook, William	23, May 1850	estate			L3	
Cooke, Elizabeth W.	19, Apr. 1849	12, Apr.			L3	
Cooke, Thomas S.	25, June 1857	23, June	15m		L3	
Cookholse, John	27, Sept 1838	Sept	50		L3	
Cookson, John T.	8, June 1854	1, June			L3	
Cooley, John	26, June 1851	June	55		L3	
Coolidge, Anna	24, Apr. 1851	15, Apr.	9m-20d		L3	
Coolidge, Henry Farnsworth	2, Aug. 1849	31, July	6		L3	
Coolidge, Henry W.	7, Aug. 1845	29, July	9m		L3	
Coolidge, John K.	27, Apr. 1837	20, Apr.	58	*	L3	
Coolidge, Josephine	2, Oct. 1834	Sept	22		L4	
Coolidge, Joshua H.	18, Feb. 1841	6, Feb.			L3	
Coolidge, Joshua H.	18, Mar. 1841	estate			L4	
Coolidge, Timothy W.	9, Mar. 1843	12, Feb.			L3	
Coombs, Albert Russell	1, Mar. 1855	27, Feb.	infant		L3	
Coombs, Alfred	11, Oct. 1838	5, Oct.	15m		L3	

Name	Notice Date	Death Date	Age	Page	Maiden Name
Coombs, Annie D.	8, July 1841	2, July		L3	
Coombs, Atlee	7, Aug. 1834	July	1- 6m-25d	L3	
Coombs, Hannah	1, Aug. 1833	July	63	L1	
Coombs, James G.	23, Aug. 1855		estate	L3	
Coombs, John	30, Aug. 1827		estate	L3	
Coombs, John (Capt)	2, Aug. 1827	1, Aug.		L1	
Coombs, Margaret D.	6, Sept 1855	2, Sept	67	L3	
Coombs, Samuel A.	23, Oct. 1834	Oct.	25	L2	
Coombs, Samuel A.	9, June 1836		probate	L3	
Coombs, Samuel A.	6, Nov. 1834		estate	L4	
Coombs, Sarah	8, Dec. 1842	27, Nov.		L3	Smith
Coon, Aaron	1, Aug. 1850	27, July	52	L3	
Coonse, John	11, Oct. 1832	30, Sept		L2	
Cooper, (child of Emily)	9, Nov. 1837	Oct.	1d	L4	
Cooper, (Mr)	18, Oct. 1832	16, Oct.		L3	
Cooper, Betsy	19, July 1849	July	40	L3	
Cooper, Delphi	10, Mar. 1853	Feb.	35	L3	
Cooper, Frances E.	10, June 1847	1, June	33	L3	
Cooper, Harriet	20, Sept 1832	Sept	60	L1	
Cooper, Hiram	25, May 1837	May	22	L2	
Cooper, Isaac	27, Oct. 1831		probate	L1	
Cooper, Isaac	27, Oct. 1826		estate	L3	
Cooper, Isaac	26, Sept 1826		probate	L3	
Cooper, James	8, Oct. 1857		probate	L3	
Cooper, James	29, Dec. 1836	7, Sept		L3	
Cooper, Jesse	19, Oct. 1848	16, Oct.	65	L1	
Cooper, John W.	5, Aug. 1847		estate	L3	
Cooper, John W.	3, June 1847	29, May		L3	
Cooper, Peter	5, July 1849	June	35	L3	
Cooper, Thomas	8, Oct. 1857		probate	L3	
Cooper, Titus	16, Aug. 1849	Aug.	35	L3	
Cooper, William	16, May 1833	May	27	L1	
Cooper, William	5, Aug. 1847	29, July	*	L3	
Cooper, William W.	1, Aug. 1850		estate	L3	
Cooter, John	8, Aug. 1850	July	23	L3	
Cope, (child)	29, Aug. 1833	Aug.	11m	L1	
Cope, George	22, July 1847	15, July		L2	
Cope, Jacob	18, Oct. 1832	13, Oct.	50	L2	
Cope, Jason	13, Mar. 1845		estate	L3	
Cope, Jason	6, Feb. 1845	30, Jan.		L3	
Copelen, Ruth	28, Dec. 1848	20, Dec.	59	L3	
Copes, William M.	8, Nov. 1832	Nov.	39	L1	
Coplin, A.G.	6, Dec. 1832	Dec.	2- 3m	L1	
Coram, John R.	19, 26, Sept 1850	17, Sept	60	L3	
Coram, John R.	24, Oct. 1850		estate	L3	
Coram, Rhoda	22, Feb. 1849	17, Feb.	81	L3	
Coray, Cordelia E.	16, Nov. 1854		30	L3	Baker
Corbin, (woman)	26, June 1851	June	32	L3	
Corbin, John	4, Oct. 1833	Sept	1	L1	
Corbin, William F.	21, Aug. 1856	12, Aug.	20	L5	
Corbitt, James	4, Nov. 1847	Oct.	35	L3	
Corbly, George Washington	5, July 1849	3, June		L3	
Corbly, John	4, Oct. 1814		estate	L3	
Corcunnel, Moses	25, Oct. 1832	Oct.	1-10m	L1	

Name	Notice Date	Death Date	Age	Page	Maiden Name
Cord, Lewis	27, Feb. 1851	Feb.		L3	
Cordes, Albert	6, Oct. 1842	Sept	54	L3	
Cordey, (child of Abel)	19, July 1832	July	1d	L1	
Corentee, (child)	7, Feb. 1833	Feb.		L1	
Corey, Elizabeth Ann	30, Aug. 1832	Aug.	24d	L1	
Corey, Josephine	9, Jan. 1845	Dec.	11m	L3	
Corey, Lebia Smith	18, Aug. 1836	13, Aug.	3m-15d	L3	
Corfin, Sergus	11, Nov. 1852	Oct.	38	L3	
Corliss, Carrie E.	23, Oct. 1856	20, Oct.		L5	
Corliss, Ella	23, Oct. 1856	17, Oct.	3d	L5	
Corliss, Ellen	28, Aug. 1856	24, Aug.	60	L1	
Cormack, Nancy	11, Sept 1845	Sept	61	L3	
Corneau, John A.	23, Aug. 1855	17, Aug.	41	L3	
Cornell, (child of James)	16, Sept 1847	Sept	1w	L3	
Cornell, John P.	28, Aug. 1851		estate	L3	
Corney, John	11, Apr. 1850	Apr.	17	L3	
Cornick, David	9, June 1836		probate	L3	
Corning, Leonard	19, Dec. 1844	23, Nov.		L3	
Cornish, Robert	7, Feb. 1850		estate	L3	
Cornwall, E.M.	28, Sept 1843	Sept	21	L3	
Corr, David	28, Feb. 1850		estate	L3	
Corr, David	14, Feb. 1850	9, Feb.		L3	
Corr, John	4, June 1857		probate	L3	
Corrogan, Barney	4, July 1844	June	34	L3	
Corry, Alice	28, Oct. 1847	22, Oct.		L3	
Corry, Alice	18, Nov. 1847			L3	
Corry, John Arburthnot (Dr)	27, Oct. 1842	16, Oct.		L3	
Corry, Mary A.	27, Mar. 1845	26, Mar.		L3	
Corry, William	4, June 1835		estate	L3	
Corry, William	23, Mar. 1837		estate	L3	
Corson, Abel	13, July 1813		estate	L3	
Cortes, Ferdinand	16, Oct. 1856		probate	L6	
Corwin, Eddie	12, May 1853	11, May	2- 5m	L3	
Corwin, Eliza P.	8, Aug. 1833	July	32- 5m	L1	
Corwin, Ichabod	12, Oct. 1843	9, Oct.	36	L3	
Corwin, Sarah L.	27, July 1843	14, June	19	L3	Sinard
Corwin, Willie	8, Aug. 1839	1, Aug.	infant	L3	
Corwine, Joab H.	16, Mar. 1848	12, Mar.	20- 9m	L3	
Corwine, Lucas	18, July 1850	14, July	1- 1m	L3	
Corwine, Mary Elizabeth	6, Jan. 1848	31, Dec.	3- 2m	L3	
Corwine, Mollie	11, Sept 1856	4, Sept	5	L5	
Corwine, Mortimer Hall	26, Dec. 1850	23, Dec.	4- -23d	L3	
Corwine, Richard	8, Jan. 1816	12, Dec.		L3	
Cory, Jeremiah	31, Mar. 1806		estate	L4	
Coseu, (child of Mr.)	2, Aug. 1832	July	1d	L1	
Cosger, Michael	27, Mar. 1851	Mar.	50	L3	
Cosgrove, Eliza	13, Aug. 1846	Aug.	43	L3	
Cosgrove, Harriet Thurber	29, Apr. 1852	23, Apr.	6- 5m- 7d	L3	
Cosgrove, Nicholas	15, July 1847	July	2	L3	
Cosgrove, Patrick	7, Oct. 1847	Sept	3	L3	
Cosgrove, Peter	5, Aug. 1852	3, Aug.		L3	
Cosgrove, Thomas	17, June 1847	June	47	L3	
Cosler, Lewis	14, Jan. 1818		estate	L2	
Costler, Elizabeth	16, Mar. 1849	10, Mar.	38	L3	

Name	Notice Date	Death Date	Age		Page	Maiden Name
Cottem, Bruce	8, Aug. 1833	July	32		L1	
Cottenhead, Janett	4, May 1848	Apr.	20		L3	
Cotter, James	18, Jan. 1849	Jan.	30		L3	
Cotterall, William H.	17, Dec. 1857	12, Dec.	6m		L3	
Cottle, (man)	12, July 1849	July			L3	
Cotton, Elizabeth	28, Aug. 1834	Aug.	47		L1	
Cotton, John (Dr)	15, Apr. 1847	2, Apr.	55		L3	
Cotton, Rachael	28, Aug. 1834	Aug.	31		L1	
Cottrell, Gorham	9, Feb. 1854	22, Dec.	74		L3	
Cottrell, Leonard	18, Jan. 1849	Jan.	20		L3	
Couch, Ellen	23, Nov. 1837	Nov.	16		L3	
Coughlin, Rebecca	1, Aug. 1850	27, July	73		L3	
Coughlin, Sabina	28, Mar. 1850	Mar.	19		L3	
Coughlin, William	4, Oct. 1838	29, Sept	70	*	L3	
Coughlin, William	18, Oct. 1838		estate		L3	
Couland, Dorothy	26, July 1849	July	45		L3	
Couland, William	26, July 1849	July	16		L3	
Coulter, Susan	23, Mar. 1849	19, Mar.	29		L3	
Coulter, Thomas B.	3, Sept 1857		48	*	L3	
Counce, (child of Samuel)	29, Aug. 1833	Aug.	stillborn		L1	
Councellor, Jerome	14, June 1849	June	5m		L3	
Countee, (child of Tobias)	2, Oct. 1834	Sept	stillborn		L4	
Courtis, Francis	21, Sept 1848	Sept	46		L3	
Courtmeyere, Louisa	3, Aug. 1848	July	20		L3	
Covalt, Isaac	18, Oct. 1832	12, Oct.			L2	
Covalt, Isaac	15, Nov. 1832		estate		L3	
Covalt, Isaac	9, June 1836		probate		L3	
Covalt, Isaac	18, Apr. 1839		probate		L3	
Covert, (Mrs)	1, Nov. 1832	28, Oct.			L3	
Covert, John T.	12, Nov. 1835		estate		L3	
Cowan, Mary	2, Jan. 1845	Dec.	2		L3	
Cowden, Edith	3, July 1851	29, June	15		L3	
Cowdin, Charlotte M.	27, May 1823	20, May	26		L3	
Cowdrey, Cornelia Maria	6, Apr. 1837	5, Apr.		*	L3	
Cowley, Patrick	18, July 1850	July	60		L3	
Cox, (Capt)	2, Jan. 1851	31, Dec.			L3	
Cox, Amanda	30, Sept 1852	26, Sept			L3	
Cox, Garret	12, Jan. 1827		estate		L3	
Cox, James H.	29, Nov. 1849				L3	
Cox, John	6, Dec. 1832	Dec.	24- 7m		L1	
Cox, John (Sgt)	23, Feb. 1813	14, Feb.		*	L3	
Cox, John M.	13, Feb. 1840		probate		L3	
Cox, John, Sen.	24, Mar. 1817		estate		L3	
Cox, Joseph	24, Feb. 1842	29, Jan.	96		L3	
Cox, Lewis	25, May 1843	16, May	32		L3	
Cox, Mary E.	13, June 1833	June	1m- 5d		L1	
Cox, Rebecca	7, Aug. 1834	July	63		L3	
Cox, William	18, Sept 1834	Sept	1		L1	
Coxe, Margaret	27, Sept 1855	14, Sept	52		L3	
Coyl, Alexander	30, May 1850	May	2m		L3	
Coyl, Jane	4, July 1850	June	26		L3	
Coyl, Morris	30, Oct. 1851	16, Oct.	6		L4	
Coyle, James	20, July 1848	July	30		L3	
Cozyes, (child of Mary)	31, Oct. 1850	Oct.	2		L3	

Name	Notice Date	Death Date	Age		Page	Maiden Name
Crabb, Alexander	29, July 1852	27, July	10m		L3	
Crabb, Georgiana	11, Mar. 1852	4, Mar.	27	*	L3	
Craffort, Henry	27, Oct. 1831		probate		L1	
Craft, Ellen	10, July 1851	7, July			L3	
Crage, John H.	20, June 1833	June	5m		L1	
Craig, (man)	7, Aug. 1851	3, Aug.		*	L3	
Craig, Charles	16, May 1850	May	27		L3	
Craig, Daniel	6, Apr. 1819	3, Apr.			L2	
Craig, Emilly H.	22, Jan. 1852	6, Jan.	14- 2m-18d		L3	
Craig, Frances	12, Feb. 1846	Feb.	22		L3	
Craig, Frederick	18, Aug. 1842	Aug.	53		L3	
Craig, John	24, Sept 1846	10, Sept	77	*	L3	
Craig, John C.	2, Aug. 1838		estate		L3	
Craig, W.	20, May 1847				L2	
Craig, William	6, Apr. 1819	3, Apr.			L2	
Craige, Archibald	24, May 1814	20, May			L3	
Craige, Thomas	24, May 1814				L3	
Craigh, Mary	8, Aug. 1850	July	40		L3	
Crail, (child of Milton)	27, Dec. 1832	Dec.	1d		L1	
Crain, Abigail	9, Aug. 1838		probate		L3	
Crain, Daniel	28, June 1849	June	22		L3	
Crain, Oliver	26, July 1832	July	59		L1	
Crain, William	15, Nov. 1832	Nov.	29		L1	
Crainbert, John	10, May 1849	May	42		L3	
Crainner, Mahard	30, Aug. 1832	Aug.	2- 9m		L1	
Cramer, John	21, Aug. 1845	Aug.	67		L3	
Cramer, Sarah	14, Apr. 1806	22, Mar.			L3	
Cranch, Nancy	28, Sept 1843	16, Sept	71		L3	Greenleaf
Crane, Ann	28, June 1849	22, June			L3	
Crane, Ebenezer	26, July 1838		estate		L3	
Crane, Ebenezer	21, Nov. 1839		probate		L3	
Crane, Elizabeth D.	16, May 1844	10, May	18		L3	
Crane, Hager	14, Nov. 1833		estate		L3	
Crane, Hager	13, Feb. 1840		probate		L3	
Crane, Henry Barney	4, Dec. 1845	26, Nov.	2- 3m		L3	
Crane, Henry Francis	26, Aug. 1852	22, Aug.	infant		L3	
Crane, Lydia	12, Nov. 1846	31, Oct.	51		L3	
Crane, Noah, Jr.	29, Aug. 1810	22, Aug.	28		L5	
Crane, Robert	22, Aug. 1839		estate		L3	
Crane, Samuel	25, Oct. 1832	20, Oct.			L2	
Crane, Samuel	29, Nov. 1832		estate		L3	
Crane, Sears	18, Oct. 1832	Oct.	24		L4	
Cranmer, John (Dr)	15, Nov. 1832	Nov.	54		L1	
Cranmer, Rachel	3, Apr. 1811	27, Mar.			L3	
Crary, Mary Jane	17, Jan. 1850	14, Jan.	1-11m		L3	
Craven, Henry	5, Mar. 1857	2, Mar.	70		L3	
Craven, Martha	25, July 1850	16, July	79		L3	
Craven, Mary	23, May 1833	May	80		L4	
Craven, William H.	26, Sept 1833	Sept	8- 6m		L4	
Crawford, (child of Sarah)	8, July 1841	June	stillborn		L3	
Crawford, (Mrs)	2, Aug. 1855	27, July			L3	
Crawford, Amanda	7, Mar. 1850	Feb.	3		L3	
Crawford, Charles Hamilton	16, May 1850	4, May	3m-13d		L3	
Crawford, Clinton	16, May 1833	May	2- 6m		L1	

Name	Notice Date	Death Date	Age		Page	Maiden Name
Crawford, Emily Armstrong	22, June 1854	15, June	infant		L3	
Crawford, George	25, May 1854	19, May			L3	
Crawford, James C.	16, Feb. 1843	15, Feb.	28	*	L3	
Crawford, John N.	12, Feb. 1846	1, Dec.	23		L3	
Crawford, Mary Jane	31, Apr. 1845	30, Apr.	21		L3	
Crawford, Robert	24, June 1847	June	52		L3	
Crawley, William	6, Aug. 1846	July	24		L3	
Crawly, Patrick	3, May 1855	4, July			L3	
Creaghead, Joseph H.	26, June 1851	14, June	36	*	L3	
Creain, Nancy	17, Nov. 1842	11, Nov.	16		L6	
Creain, Robert	8, Jan. 1846	31, Dec.	30		L3	
Creaven, Michael	10, May 1849	May	28		L3	
Creed, John	11, May 1843	27, Apr.	64	*	L3	
Cregar, Hannah	12, Sept 1833	Sept	27- 6m		L1	
Crien, Charlotte E.	16, Oct. 1834	Oct.	5m- 4d		L1	
Crifield, Arthur	9, Aug. 1855		probate		L3	
Cringman, Joseph	24, Jan. 1850	Jan.	25		L3	
Crippen, George	23, Feb. 1843	Feb.	10		L3	
Crisman, Elias	27, Oct. 1831		probate		L1	
Crispe, John	1, Jan. 1835		estate		L4	
Crissey, Sarah Ann	5, Nov. 1857		probate		L3	
Crist, Elias	25, Mar. 1847		estate		L3	
Crist, Joseph	5, Jan. 1819		estate		L3	
Croft, Peter	21, Jan. 1847	Jan.			L3	
Croker, James H.	28, July 1842	20, July	36	*	L3	
Crompton, Thomas	23, Nov. 1848	Nov.	20		L3	
Cromwell, George	8, Aug. 1833	July	5m		L1	
Cromwell, John William	1, June 1837	25, May	6		L3	
Cromwell, Margaret	25, May 1848	19, May	52		L3	
Cronan, Catharine	5, July 1849	June	6		L3	
Cronan, Catharine	12, July 1849	July	3w		L3	
Cronge, Solomon	11, Dec. 1815				L3	
Cronimus, John	11, Sept 1834	Aug.	2-11m		L1	
Cronk, Charles	18, Apr. 1844	Apr.	34		L3	
Crooks, Benjamin	8, Mar. 1849	Feb.	46		L3	
Crooks, Elizabeth Ann	7, May 1846	30, Apr.	3m		L3	
Crookshank, Nathaniel (Dr)	15, Apr. 1847	1, Apr.	76		L3	
Crosby, Josiah	11, July 1833		probate		L3	
Crosley, Abel	13, Feb. 1840		probate		L3	
Cross, Gideon O.	29, Sept 1842		estate		L3	
Cross, J.C.	3, June 1852		12		L3	
Cross, James H.S.	23, Aug. 1855	15, Aug.			L3	
Cross, James S.	20, Sept 1855		estate		L3	
Cross, James S.	7, May 1857		probate		L3	
Cross, John J.	7, Oct. 1852	29, Sept	76		L3	
Cross, Thomas	2, May 1833	Apr.	33		L1	
Crossley, (son of John)	16, May 1850				L3	
Crossman, Sarah W.	15, Jan. 1835	13, Jan.			L3	
Crossman, Susannah	8, Aug. 1833	July	6- 5m		L1	
Crossman, W.A.	22, Mar. 1838	14, Mar.			L3	
Crosson, Maria	20, Sept 1825	14, Sept			L3	
Crosson, Phoebe	5, Mar. 1857	26, Feb.	20		L1	
Crosson, William H.	19, 26, July 1832	July	2- 3m		L1	
Croteau, Louis	19, Aug. 1816	16, July	25		L3	

Name	Notice Date	Death Date	Age	Page	Maiden Name
Crothers, Martha	18, July 1833	July	36	L2	
Croton, (child of Margaret)	5, Aug. 1852	July	16m	L3	
Croul, John	10, May 1849	May		L3	
Crouse, Charles F.M.	8, Mar. 1849		18	L3	
Crouse, George	29, Aug. 1833	Aug.	2- 5m	L1	
Crouse, Lucy M.	29, Aug. 1833	Aug.	5	L1	
Crow, Henry	23, Jan. 1851	Jan.	1d	L3	
Crowel, John	25, Dec. 1815		estate	L3	
Crowell, (child of Peter)	26, July 1832	July	stillborn	L1	
Crowell, Abner	22, Feb. 1849	Feb.	47	L3	
Crowell, Royal	5, Oct. 1843	Sept	40	L3	
Crowell, Royal Shelton	22, June 1843	June	7m	L3	
Crowell, Sarah	10, Aug. 1843	Aug.	4	L3	
Crowing, Mary	12, July 1849	July	6w	L3	
Crowley, Daniel	16, Aug. 1849	Aug.	35	L3	
Crowley, Johannah	2, Oct. 1834	Sept	57	L4	
Crozier, Kannady	25, Feb. 1823		estate	L4	
Crozier, Kennady	28, May 1824		estate	L3	
Crozier, Kennedy	26, Sept 1826		probate	L3	
Crumb, John	12, July 1809			L3	
Crumbauch, Peter	7, July 1812		estate	L2	
Crump, (child of Mrs)	6, June 1833	May	3	L2	
Crutchfield, (child of Mary)	5, Aug. 1847	July	stillborn	L3	
Culbertson, Charles	26, July 1855	23, July	infant	L3	
Culbertson, Henry Duncan	28, Apr. 1842	22, Apr.	5m-28d	L3	
Culbertson, William H.	15, Jan. 1835	12, Jan.	infant	L3	
Culbreth, Thomas	8, June 1843		57	L3	
Cullom, George, Sen.	6, Feb. 1822		estate	L3	
Cullom, William T.	19, Oct. 1843	10, Oct.	73	L3	
Cullum, James	19, Sept 1833	Sept	7m	L4	
Cullum, Margaret	8, June 1837	31, May		L2	
Cullum, William A.	29, Aug. 1833	Aug.	1m- 7d	L1	
Culver, Adam	21, Dec. 1819		estate	L3	
Culver, George	1, Oct. 1846	Sept	8m	L3	
Cummings, Alexander	14, Feb. 1826		estate	L3	
Cummings, Jeremiah	12, July 1849	July	23	L3	
Cummings, Joseph	7, June 1855		probate	L3	
Cummings, William	27, Apr. 1843		*	L3	
Cummins, (child of A.)	13, Sept 1832	Sept	stillborn	L1	
Cummins, David	23, Jan. 1811		estate	L3	
Cummins, Jennett	27, Mar. 1845		estate	L3	
Cummins, John	22, Aug. 1844		estate	L3	
Cummins, John	20, Mar. 1845		estate	L3	
Cummins, Peter	23, Feb. 1837		probate	L3	
Cummins, William	3, Nov. 1812	29, Oct.		L3	
Cunningham, Charles H.	28, Aug. 1851	26, Aug.	15m	L3	
Cunningham, Francis	14, June 1849	June	35	L3	
Cunningham, Hiram	16, July 1846	July	37	L3	
Cunningham, James	30, May 1844	19, May	23	L3	
Cunningham, James	7, Aug. 1834	July	30	L3	
Cunningham, James	15, Mar. 1813		estate	L4	
Cunningham, Jane	22, Apr. 1852	14, Apr.	45	L3	
Cunningham, Janet	7, Dec. 1837		probate	L3	
Cunningham, Jenet	22, June 1837		probate	L3	

Name	Notice Date	Death Date	Age		Page	Maiden Name
Cunningham, John	15, July 1830		estate		L3	
Cunningham, John	5, Nov. 1857		probate		L3	
Cunningham, Mary E.	29, Nov. 1832	Nov.	3- 1m		L1	
Cunningham, Richard	5, Sept 1850	Aug.	40		L3	
Cunningham, Ruth	4, Sept 1856		probate		L5	
Cunningham, Sarah	1, Nov. 1849	Oct.	27		L3	
Cuny, William	26, July 1838	20, July	8- 6m		L3	
Curie, Catharine R.	2, May 1833	Apr.	42		L1	
Curles, John	30, Mar. 1813	29, Mar.	20		L3	
Curran, (child of Ann)	20, Apr. 1843	Apr.	4d		L3	
Curran, John	3, May 1855		probate		L3	
Curree, Thomas	11, Mar. 1852	8, Mar.			L3	
Curren, James	4, Nov. 1847	Oct.	42		L3	
Currie, Sarah S.	29, Apr. 1847	22, Apr.	22	*	L3	Lockett
Currier, Oscar	3, Apr. 1851	1, Apr.			L3	
Curry, Betsy	20, Aug. 1840	Aug.	69		L3	
Curry, Hannah	24, Sept 1846	20, Sept	19		L3	
Curry, James	11, Mar. 1852	Mar.			L4	
Curry, Mary A.P.	8, Mar. 1849	5, Mar.	13- 1m		L3	
Curry, Moses	21, Mar. 1839	Mar.	1		L3	
Curry, Zebulon	23, Dec. 1852	5, Nov.	28	*	L3	
Curtice, Percy	2, Sept 1823	27, Aug.		*	L3	
Curtis, Benjamin R.	14, Mar. 1850	Dec.	55	*	L3	
Curtis, Clarissa	2, Aug. 1849	27, July	40		L3	
Curtis, George	27, July 1843	July	2m		L3	
Curtis, Henry J.	29, Apr. 1852	3, Apr.			L3	
Curtis, Hudson B.	9, July 1857		probate		L3	
Curtis, James	13, Dec. 1849	Dec.	40		L3	
Curtis, Sarah Ann	18, May 1843	May	41		L3	
Curtis, Sebina	8, Sept 1842	Aug.	67		L3	
Curtis, Vesta A.	16, 23, Aug. 1855	14, Aug.	20		L3	
Cusan, Sarah A.	27, Dec. 1832	Dec.	5		L1	
Cushing, Ellen	24, May 1849	May	27		L3	
Cushion, Philip	29, Aug. 1850	Aug.	37		L3	
Custin, Nicholas	27, Sept 1849	Sept	58		L3	
Cutler, Jervis (Major)	11, July 1844	25, June	76	*	L3	
Cutler, Sarah	9, Aug. 1849	July	40		L3	
Cutter, Andrew	15, Sept 1826	13, Sept	36	*	L3	
Cutter, Andrew	25, Mar. 1852		estate		L3	
Cutter, Effy	8, Aug. 1833	July	21		L1	
Cutter, Harriet	4, July 1844	27, June	8m-14d		L3	
Cutter, Hurdus	26, Sept 1833	Sept	1m		L4	
Cutter, James	15, Sept 1836	9, Sept	49	*	L3	
Cutter, James	26, Jan. 1837		estate		L3	
Cutter, Joseph M.	14, Aug. 1851		estate		L3	
Cutter, Seth	9, May 1810		estate		L3	
Cutter, Seth	7, Sept 1824		probate		L3	
Cypress, Catharine	2, Nov. 1854	31, Oct.			L3	
Daab, Henry	1, Nov. 1855		estate		L3	
Daab, Henry	4, Sept 1856		probate		L5	
Dacher, Conrad	23, Mar. 1849	Mar.	62		L3	
Dachtler, John	8, Aug. 1839	July	20		L3	
Dagan, Andrew	14, Feb. 1850	Feb.	26		L3	

Name	Notice Date	Death Date	Age		Page	Maiden Name
Dagneaux, Gregory	2, Apr. 1835		estate		L3	
Dagneaux, Mary	5, Sept 1833		estate		L3	
Dagnell, Martha	5, July 1849	June	58		L3	
Dailey, Eveline	26, July 1849	July	10		L3	
Dailey, Matthew	9, Oct. 1845	Sept			L3	
Dailey, Michael	5, Oct. 1848	Sept	24		L3	
Daily, (child of Mary)	29, Aug. 1850	Aug.	stillborn		L3	
Daily, Mary	5, Sept 1850	Aug.	35		L3	
Daily, Patrick	28, June 1849	June	30		L3	
Dair, Luman Reed	9, Apr. 1840	3, Apr.	3- 9m		L3	
Dair, Mary Alice	24, June 1841	23, June			L3	
Dair, Robert (Capt)	21, Dec. 1854	13, Dec.	74		L3	
Dakey, Sarah	14, Feb. 1839		probate		L3	
Dakins, (Mrs)	1, Nov. 1832	24, Oct.			L1	
Dale, Andrew J.	8, Oct. 1857	4, Oct.	23- -14d		L3	
Dale, Thomas	9, May 1839	Apr.	32		L3	
Dalie, Abigail	11, July 1844			*	L3	Fowler
Dalton, Richard	21, June 1849	June	24		L3	
Dalton, Sarah A.	20, Mar. 1856	12, Mar.	19- 7m		L3	
Damager, Frederick	13, July 1848	July	37		L3	
Damery, Malchiah	6, Jan. 1848	Dec.	20		L3	
Damon, David (Rev)	6, July 1843	25, June			L3	
Damon, Ester	9, Mar. 1854	25, Feb.	81		L3	
Damrad, (child of Michael)	20, June 1833	June	1m-14d		L1	
Danahy, Jeremiah	29, July 1847	July	29		L3	
Danaw, (Mrs)	29, Aug. 1833	Aug.			L1	
Danby,	24, May 1820				L3	
Dandridge, Sarah K.	16, Aug. 1849	13, Aug.	infant		L3	
Danforth, Asa	13, Dec. 1838		estate		L2	
Daniel, Michael	10, Sept 1857		probate		L3	
Danields, Barbara	26, Nov. 1846	Nov.	42		L3	
Daniels, Isaac	27, Oct. 1831		probate		L1	
Daniels, Nicholas	20, Dec. 1855		estate		L3	
Daniels, Nicholas	7, May 1857		probate		L3	
Daniels, Rebecca	6, Aug. 1829	24, July	53		L4	
Danke, Hellen	2, July 1846	June	1		L3	
Dannenhold, Julia Ann	5, Mar. 1857	3, Mar.	1		L3	
Dannettell, Lucy Dorothea	26, Oct. 1848	21, Oct.	34		L3	
Dans, John	5, July 1855		probate		L3	
Darby, (child of Mary)	5, Aug. 1852	July	5w		L3	
Darby, Henry	10, Apr. 1856		probate		L3	
Darby, Jane	10, Jan. 1828	Jan.	9		L4	
Darens, Joseph	8, Aug. 1833	July	80		L1	
Darey, Baylea C.	16, Oct. 1834	Oct.	7m-19d		L1	
Darling, Horace	7, Sept 1824	1, Sept	25	*	L3	
Darling, Horace	17, Mar. 1826		probate		L3	
Darling, Horace	22, Oct. 1824		estate		L4	
Darns, Alexander	10, Aug. 1837		estate		L3	
Darr, Abraham	1, Apr. 1852	30, Mar.	75		L3	
Darr, Harry Robert	5, Mar. 1857	27, Feb.	20m-27d		L3	
Darrow, Julia E.	12, Dec. 1833	Dec.	23		L4	
Darst, Jacob	24, Aug. 1854	16, Aug.			L3	
Dart, Levi	28, Feb. 1828	Feb.	20d		L1	
D'Arusmont, W.P.	5, Mar. 1857		probate		L3	

Name	Notice Date	Death Date	Age		Page	Maiden Name
D'Arusmont, William P.	4, Sept 1856		probate		L5	
D'Arutmont, Frances Wright	16, Dec. 1852	13, Dec.	57		L3	
Dashy, (Mrs)	25, Oct. 1832	22, Oct.			L3	
Daubenheyer, Peter	18, Feb. 1818		estate		L3	
Daugherty, George	11, May 1848	May	30		L3	
Daugherty, John	15, Sept 1842	Sept			L3	
Daugherty, Patrick	6, Sept 1849	Aug.	30		L3	
Daugherty, Sarah	30, Aug. 1849	Aug.	58		L3	
Daughters, Turpin	25, July 1844	10, July	7		L3	
Daulton, Naomi	2, Feb. 1827		estate		L3	
Davenport, Carrie Elizabeth	14, Aug. 1856	8, Aug.	infant		L5	
Davenport, D.	7, Feb. 1856		probate		L3	
Davenport, Darius	15, Dec. 1853	9, Dec.	64		L3	
Davenport, Darius	5, July 1855		probate		L3	
Davenport, Mary	20, Aug. 1857	17, Aug.		*	L3	
Davenport, Ruth	26, June 1845	16, June	40	*	L3	Doan
Davenport, Sarah	10, Sept 1846	5, Sept	42		L3	
Davey, Isaac	24, Apr. 1851		estate		L3	
Davids, Phineas	10, Dec. 1840	30, Nov.	60	*	L3	
Davids, Phineas	11, Feb. 1841		estate		L3	
Davidson, Carlos	18, July 1833	July	22- 5m- 5d		L2	
Davidson, James D.	20, Dec. 1825		probate		L4	
Davidson, James S.	25, Dec. 1856	20, Dec.		*	L3	
Davies, Charles M.	2, Apr. 1846	1, Apr.			L3	
Davies, Daniel	5, July 1849	June	35		L3	
Davies, David (Deacon)	5, July 1855	24, June	62	*	L3	
Davies, Edward C.	15, Oct. 1846	10, Oct.	34		L3	
Davies, John	22, Apr. 1852		estate		L3	
Davies, John	1, Oct. 1829		estate		L4	
Davies, John M.	1, Apr. 1852		estate		L3	
Davies, John M.	6, Aug. 1857		probate		L3	
Davies, S. Hiley	21, Sept 1848	14, Sept	39		L3	
Davies, Samuel W.	28, Dec. 1843	21, Dec.	67		L3	
Davis, (child of William)	15, May 1834	May	stillborn		L4	
Davis, A. Fanny S.	8, Aug. 1850	6, Aug.	26		L3	
Davis, Adaline	20, June 1844	June	1		L3	
Davis, Amelia L.	26, Mar. 1857	22, Mar.			L3	Temple
Davis, Ann	1, Aug. 1833	July	1- 6m		L1	
Davis, Ann W.	7, Aug. 1834	July	20		L3	
Davis, Asa	18, Oct. 1832	11, Oct.			L1	
Davis, Charles	4, June 1857		probate		L3	
Davis, Charles (Capt)	19, Jan. 1854	9, Jan.	32		L3	
Davis, Cincinnatus	19, Sept 1833	Sept	2- 9m- 7d		L4	
Davis, Daniel	17, May 1849	May	22		L3	
Davis, Daniel	16, July 1805	9, July			L3	
Davis, Edward	5, Mar. 1846	Feb.	40		L3	
Davis, Edward	9, Mar. 1843	5, Mar.	64		L3	
Davis, Edward P.	21, Mar. 1850		35		L3	
Davis, Edward P.	13, June 1850		estate		L3	
Davis, Edward Tilton	29, Oct. 1857	24, Oct.	4		L3	
Davis, Edward Wilson	13, Dec. 1849	9, Dec.	2-10m-10d		L3	
Davis, Elenor	21, Sept 1843	14, Sept			L3	
Davis, Elmira	3, May 1855	28, Apr.	33		L3	
Davis, Ezekiel	6, Dec. 1849	Nov.	3		L3	

Name	Notice Date	Death Date	Age	Page	Maiden Name
Davis, George	23, Nov. 1848	Nov.	2	L3	
Davis, George	21, Sept 1843	Sept	19	L3	
Davis, George C.	5, Sept 1850		62	L3	
Davis, George C.	24, Oct. 1850		estate	L3	
Davis, George M.	27, Sept 1827	4, Sept	29	L1	
Davis, George S.	13, Dec. 1849	9, Dec.	22	L3	
Davis, Henry	4, Dec. 1815	9, Oct.		L1	
Davis, Herman	23, May 1850	May	26	L3	
Davis, Isaac	25, Oct. 1832	20, Oct.		L2	
Davis, Isabella Marsh	6, Oct. 1853	3, Oct.	2- 1m	L3	
Davis, J.N.	10, Jan. 1856		probate	L3	
Davis, J.N.	5, Feb. 1857		probate	L3	
Davis, Jane	25, Oct. 1832	Oct.	1m-11d	L1	
Davis, Jemima	26, Oct. 1854	18, Sept	92	L3	
Davis, John	18, Sept 1845	Sept	10m	L3	
Davis, John (Rev)	1, Dec. 1807	23, Nov.	32	L3	
Davis, John Sloan	27, July 1854	23, July	19	L3	
Davis, John, Jr.	25, Oct. 1832	19, Oct.		L3	
Davis, Joseph	17, May 1849	May	23	L3	
Davis, Lydia	27, Sept 1849	25, Sept	48	L3	
Davis, Lydia	14, Aug. 1856	11, Aug.	32	L5	
Davis, Martha	6, Nov. 1834	Oct.	45	L1	
Davis, Martha Glover	15, Feb. 1855	12, Feb.	53	L3	
Davis, Mary Weir	3, Feb. 1848	1, Feb.	11	L3	
Davis, Matilda J.	24, Feb. 1848	Feb.	3	L3	
Davis, Rebecca	7, Feb. 1833	Feb.	1m- 8d	L1	
Davis, Rebecca E.	28, Feb. 1850	25, Feb.		L3	
Davis, Rebecca Mary	3, Feb. 1853	31, Jan.		L3	
Davis, Samuel	28, June 1809		estate	L2	
Davis, Sarah	20, Dec. 1825		probate	L4	
Davis, Seytha	10, Oct. 1844	Oct.	14m	L3	
Davis, Solomon (Rev)	27, Oct. 1853	28, Aug.	53	L3	
Davis, Thomas	21, June 1849	June	25	L3	
Davis, William	14, Feb. 1833	Feb.	75	L1	
Davis, William	18, Oct. 1832	12, Oct.		L2	
Davis, William	4, May 1837	30, Apr.	22	L3	
Davis, William	1, Nov. 1849	Oct.	25	L3	
Davis, William	24, Jan. 1850	Jan.	45	L3	
Davis, William	26, June 1845	June	50	L3	
Davis, William	9, Aug. 1849	July	8m	L3	
Davis, William	11, May 1837	30, Apr.	22	L4	
Davis, William H.	9, July 1857	5, July		L3	
Davis, Willis	2, Mar. 1837		estate	L3	
Davis, Zadock	16, Oct. 1834		estate	L3	
Davis, Zadock	15, Sept 1836		probate	L3	
Davison, (child of Margaret)	17, June 1847	June		L3	
Davison, Elizabeth	19, July 1849	July	70	L3	
Davison, Peter	27, June 1850	25, June		L3	
Davison, Peter	4, Mar. 1852	2, Mar.		L4	
Davisson, John	22, Nov. 1832		estate	L3	
Davy, Godfrey	1, Mar. 1849	Feb.	80	L3	
Dawson, James	7, Dec. 1843	Dec.	30	L3	
Dawson, Jane	8, Nov. 1832	Nov.	33	L1	
Dawson, Jane	6, Nov. 1834	Oct.	76	L1	

Name	Notice Date	Death Date	Age		Page	Maiden Name
Dawson, John	6, May 1841	Apr.	46		L3	
Dawson, Martha	9, Dec. 1847	Dec.	20		L3	
Dawson, Moses	5, Dec. 1844			*	L3	
Dawson, Thomas	25, Aug. 1842	Aug.	1m		L3	
Dawson, William L.	6, Dec. 1832	Dec.	50		L1	
Day, Albert G.	20, Sept 1849	11, Sept	35		L3	
Day, Anna	11, July 1850	July	25		L3	
Day, Elias	2, Oct. 1856	26, Sept	64		L5	
Day, Elias Harvey	2, Jan. 1851	29, Dec.	22		L3	
Day, Eliza	18, Oct. 1832	14, Oct.			L2	
Day, Henrietta C.	4, Nov. 1847	26, Oct.	23		L3	
Day, Jesse	29, May 1845	May	45		L3	
Day, Mary Ann	6, Dec. 1832	Dec.	18		L1	
Day, Mary Ann	1, Aug. 1833	July	11m		L1	
Day, Nicolaus	28, Oct. 1847	Oct.			L3	
Day, Samuel	5, Sept 1833		estate		L3	
Day, William	22, June 1837		probate		L3	
Days, Sarah	11, Nov. 1847	Nov.	35		L3	
Dayton, Jonathan	6, Jan. 1831		estate		L3	
Dayton, Jonathan	16, Feb. 1827		probate		L3	
Dayton, Jonathan (Gen)	11, July 1839		estate		L3	
Dayton, Julia T.	13, July 1837	5, July			L3	Burrows
Deal, Joseph	14, Oct. 1847	Oct.	21		L3	
Dean, Amelia A.	18, July 1833	July	9m- 2d		L2	
Dean, James E.	3, Aug. 1854		estate		L3	
Dean, Joshua	10, Aug. 1837		estate		L3	
Dean, Lewis Judson	22, July 1852	15, July	10m		L3	
Dean, Mary J.	29, Sept 1853	17, Sept	23	*	L3	Baltzell
Dearling, William	25, Jan. 1849	Jan.	34		L3	
Death, Absalom	18, 25, Sept 1856	15, Sept	52		L5	
DeBarr, Clara Julia	3, May 1849	23, Apr.	19- 9m-17d		L3	Levassor
Debolt, George	9, June 1836		probate		L3	
Debolt, Henry	24, Mar. 1807		estate		L2	
Debolt, John	9, July 1857		probate		L3	
Debolt, Michael	2, Dec. 1816		estate		L3	
Dec, George	12, Sept 1833	Sept	1- 6m		L1	
DeCamp, Elizabeth C.	8, June 1854	1, June	28		L3	
DeCamp, Ellen	3, Feb. 1853	29, Jan.	4-10m		L3	
DeCamp, Frank	9, Nov. 1848	3, Nov.	4		L3	
DeCamp, George	2, Aug. 1855	30, July	22m		L3	
DeCamp, Harriet	22, Mar. 1855	10, Mar.	5-11m- 3d		L3	
DeCamp, Henry	10, Feb. 1853	3, Feb.	41		L3	
DeCamp, James	19, Sept 1850	Sept	41		L3	
Decamp, John Wesley	23, Mar. 1848	16, Mar.	infant		L3	
Decamp, John Wesley	6, June 1850	4, June	infant		L3	
DeCamp, Martha L.	23, Oct. 1851	20, Oct.	4		L3	
DeCamp, Robert Osborn	17, Dec. 1857	14, Dec.			L3	
Decker, Elizabeth	18, Jan. 1849	Jan.	63		L3	
Decker, Josiah	30, Sept 1823		estate		L2	
Deckers, Mary	18, Oct. 1849	Oct.	27		L3	
Dee, Christiana	18, July 1833	July			L2	
Dee, Jane	25, Sept 1845	17, Sept	75		L3	
Deeds, John	23, Nov. 1848	Nov.	45		L3	
Deer, Samuel	9, June 1842	May	36		L3	

Name	Notice Date	Death Date	Age	Page	Maiden Name
Deeser, Andrew	8, Oct. 1846	Sept	24	L3	
Deevvl, Molin	4, July 1833	June	2m-20d	L2	
DeForest, George S.	23, Apr. 1857	11, Apr.	6m	L3	
DeForest, Jacob P. (Major)	9, Mar. 1854	18, Feb.		L3	
DeForest, Lucy Stephenson	12, Mar. 1846	10, Mar.	4- 9m	L3	
DeForest, Mary	23, Oct. 1856	16, Oct.	42	L5	Stephenson
Degler, Leopold	19, July 1849	July	26	L3	
DeGolyer, Joseph	19, June 1851	1, June	44	L3	
DeGolyer, Joseph	16, Dec. 1847	23, Nov.	85	* L3	
DeGraw, Henry Farmer	13, Jan. 1853	4, Jan.	20m	L3	
DeGraw, John Howard	27, Jan. 1853	24, Jan.	4- 4m	L3	
DeGroff, Oliver G.	12, July 1849	1, July	50	L3	
Delamater, Chandler P.	6, Aug. 1857		probate	L3	
Delamp, Mattie	14, Aug. 1856	8, Aug.	20	L5	
DeLanatter, Chandler	6, Mar. 1856	27, Feb.	40	L3	
Delanie, Aristides	1, Nov. 1832	27, Oct.		L2	
Delano, Amasa, Jr.	21, Feb. 1826	15, Feb.	15	L3	
Delany, Joseph	22, Nov. 1849	Nov.		L3	
Delany, Mary	11, Mar. 1852	10, Mar.		L4	
Delaplain, Nehemiah	21, Jan. 1841		estate	L3	
DeLean, Emanuel G.	3, May 1849	Apr.	21	L3	
Dellaman, Richard	13, June 1844	June	32	L3	
Dellinger, A.F.	19, Oct. 1843	11, Oct.		L3	
Dellinger, Adolphus F.	14, Dec. 1843		estate	L3	
Delvin, Joseph	28, Sept 1848	Sept	35	L3	
Delzell, Amanda	11, May 1848	3, May	22	L3	
Dement, Richard	18, Oct. 1832	Oct.	44	L4	
Demery, William	13, May 1847	May	30	L3	
Demmeier, Henry	9, Aug. 1855		probate	L3	
Demming, Henry	12, Aug. 1852			L3	
Dempsey, Bridget	26, Sept 1850	Sept	64	L3	
Dempsey, Hannah	20, June 1833	June	3- 3m	L1	
Dempsey, James	9, Nov. 1848	Oct.	35	L3	
Denberger, Frederick	7, June 1849	May		L3	
Deneen, Washington P.	19, Oct. 1854		estate	L3	
Denham, Sarah	6, Sept 1827	Sept	36	L1	
Denier, Jacob	8, Oct. 1857		probate	L3	
Denis, J.L. (Col)	25, Oct. 1832	20, Oct.		L2	
Denison, Carrie Howard	16, July 1857	8, July	3m-18d	L3	
Denison, William W.	22, Apr. 1847	19, Apr.	35	L3	
Denisot, Simon	17, Feb. 1807		estate	L2	
Denler, Jacob	8, Oct. 1857		probate	L3	
Denman, David	16, June 1807		estate	L3	
Denman, David	5, June 1816		estate	L4	
Denman, Mary E.	16, Oct. 1834	Oct.	2- 3m- 8d	L1	
Denman, William	5, Sept 1839		probate	L3	
Dennes, Sarah	13, Sept 1832	Sept	2d	L1	
Denney, Eliza Jane	4, Oct. 1833	Sept	17	L1	
Denney, William	6, Apr. 1837	Apr.	65	L4	
Denning, John D.	23, Mar. 1854	24, Feb.	46	L3	
Dennis, Elizabeth	12, June 1845	8, June		L3	
Dennis, Frances C.	20, June 1833	June	6m	L1	
Dennis, Jacob	8, Aug. 1850	24, July	63	L3	
Dennis, Jacob	6, Mar. 1851		estate	L3	

Name	Notice Date	Death Date	Age	Page	Maiden Name
Dennis, Jacob J.	8, Nov. 1855		probate	L3	
Dennis, John Francis	27, Mar. 1828	Mar.	6d	L1	
Dennis, Nancy	17, Sept 1857	Sept		L3	
Dennis, Samuel B.	20, June 1833	June	10m	L1	
Dennis, Samuel Cloon	29, June 1843	27, June	22m	L3	
Dennison, Edward S.	17, Aug. 1843	15, Aug.		L3	
Dennison, James	7, Nov. 1810		estate	L2	
Dennison, Polly	27, Jan. 1853	21, Jan.	63-10m-13d	L3	
Dennison, William	28, Jan. 1841	6, Jan.		L3	
Denniston, Alexander (Rev)	8, Jan. 1857	1, Jan.	77	L3	
Denniston, Ann	23, July 1857	22, July	80	L3	
Denniston, James J.	26, July 1855		estate	L3	
Denny, Henry Hall	6, June 1844	13, May	23	* L3	
Denny, James (Gen)	11, Dec. 1815	23, Nov.		L3	
Dent, Jesse McGowan	5, May 1853	28, Apr.	8m- 4d	L3	
Dent, William	14, Sept 1848	Sept	21	L3	
Dentler, William G.	23, Dec. 1852	16, Dec.	29	L3	
Dentsch, Mary	6, July 1843	June	14m	L3	
Derby, Charles	28, Oct. 1852	23, Oct.	4m- 8d	L3	
Deres, John Henry	5, Mar. 1857		probate	L3	
Dermot, Mary M.	1, Nov. 1832	20, Oct.	6	L4	
Derrett, (Mrs)	25, Oct. 1832	20, Oct.		L2	
Dervas, James	30, Oct. 1851		23	L3	
DeSalis, J.F.	20, Dec. 1825		probate	L4	
DeSalis, Julius Ferdinand	4, Sept 1822	3, Sept		L3	
Desmon, Humphrey	22, Jan. 1852	Jan.	21	L3	
Desmond, Catharine	31, Aug. 1854	27, Aug.		L3	
Detert, August	30, Mar. 1848	Mar.	35	L3	
Deuber, Jacob	10, Jan. 1856		probate	L3	
Deurling, Henry	25, July 1839	July	34	L3	
Deuson, Matthew	18, Oct. 1827	Oct.	66	L3	
Deutsch, George	24, May 1849	May	46	L3	
Deutschle, Helena	5, July 1855		probate	L3	
Devenport, Emmel	1, Aug. 1833	July	33	L1	
Deveraeux, Joseph	4, Nov. 1841	18, Aug.	70	L3	
Devere, Aaron	5, Mar. 1857		probate	L3	
Deviney, Richard	31, Aug. 1848	Aug.	22	L3	
Devinney, J.M. (Capt)	12, Aug. 1841	14, July		L3	
Devinny, Mary Ann	7, Oct. 1841	2, Oct.		L3	
Devire, Philip	14, June 1855			L3	
Devos, Samuel	9, Aug. 1855		probate	L3	
Devou, Amelia Eliza	7, Apr. 1842	4, Apr.		L3	
Devou, Demetrius P.	18, Sept 1834	Sept	19	L1	
Devou, Samuel (Col)	3, Mar. 1853	25, Feb.	61	L3	
Dewey, Mary Elizabeth	7, Aug. 1845	26, July	27	L3	
Dewson, Frederick	9, Oct. 1834	Sept	62	L1	
Dexter, Ann	24, July 1845	17, July	76	L3	
Dexter, Caroline A.	7, Aug. 1834	July	18	L3	
Dexter, Samuel	20, May 1816	3, May		L3	
DeYoung, Hannah	23, Oct. 1834	Oct.	34	L2	
DeYoung, Michael	18, May 1854	25, Apr.	63- 6m	L3	
DeYoung, Moses J.	9, Aug. 1855		probate	L3	
Diamond, Patrick	22, Aug. 1850	15, Aug.	25	L3	
Dibble, Eunice	9, Aug. 1855	4, Aug.	57	L3	

Name	Notice Date	Death Date	Age	Page	Maiden Name
Dick, Louis	8, June 1854		estate	L3	
Dickel, Barnhart	23, July 1846	July	39	L3	
Dickens, Archibald	25, Oct. 1832	21, Oct.		L2	
Dickens, Stephen	8, Aug. 1833	July	1- 7m	L1	
Dickerson, Samuel	26, Sept 1850	Sept	73	L3	
Dickey, (Mrs)	1, Nov. 1832	27, Oct.		L2	
Dickey, Patrick	19, Feb. 1816		estate	L3	
Dickhaus, C.	6, Mar. 1856		probate	L3	
Dickinson, Arthur	3, July 1845	25, June	18m	L3	
Dickinson, Charles G.	23, Jan. 1845		estate	L3	
Dickinson, Charles G.	26, Mar. 1846		estate	L3	
Dickinson, S.H.	28, Dec. 1848	16, Dec.	47	L3	
Dickinson, Samuel S.	24, Aug. 1837	16, Aug.	31	L3	
Dickinson, Samuel S.	26, Oct. 1837		estate	L3	
Dickison, Edmund	20, May 1847	19, May	80	L3	
Dickman, Henry	24, May 1849	May	30	L3	
Dicks, Edward	6, June 1833	May	4- 4m	L2	
Dicks, William	10, Sept 1835		estate	L3	
Dickson, D.	8, Aug. 1833	July		L1	
Dickson, Jane	14, Feb. 1839	Feb.	3	L3	
Dickson, Joshua G. (Capt)	8, Jan. 1852	1, Jan.	61	* L3	
Dickson, Mary Ann	11, Dec. 1856	7, Dec.	11	L3	
Dickson, Robert Johnston	9, Aug. 1855	4, Aug.	13	L3	
Dickson, William	29, May 1851		estate	L3	
Dickson, William	3, Nov. 1853	2, Nov.		L3	
Dickson, William Alfred	5, Oct. 1854	26, Sept	25	L3	
Didon, Hagerty	31, Oct. 1833	Oct.	25	L4	
Dietrich, Mathias	17, Jan. 1850	10, Jan.	30	L2	
Dietz, George	18, Mar. 1852	14, Mar.		L3	
Digman, James	31, Aug. 1843	Aug.	31	L3	
Dike, Robert B.	2, Aug. 1832	July	8m-12d	L1	
Dilges, William	1, Nov. 1849	Oct.	1	L3	
Dilks, Arthur	28, Nov. 1850	Nov.	43	L3	
Dill, (child of Margaret)	24, Mar. 1842	Mar.		L3	
Dill, Elizabeth	4, Jan. 1849	28, Dec.		L3	
Dill, Isaac	17, June 1841	June	48	L3	
Dill, James (Gen)	30, Aug. 1838	18, Aug.		L3	
Dill, Martha Ann	23, July 1840	July	3	L3	
Dill, Patience	9, Sept 1841	Aug.	11	L3	
Dillihunt, William	17, Aug. 1843	Aug.	64	L3	
Dillman, Adam	7, Feb. 1856		probate	L3	
Dillon, James	7, June 1849	May	39	L3	
Dillon, Samuel	5, July 1849	June	50	L3	
Dimmitt, David	17, Oct. 1821		estate	L4	
Dimmitt, Moses (Capt)	26, Jan. 1854	14, Jan.	78	L3	
Dimmock, Henry Bunker	14, Aug. 1856	2, Aug.	9	L5	
Dinsmoor, Mary Gordon	23, Nov. 1854	10, Nov.	78	L3	
Dinsmore, Silas (Col)	1, July 1847	17, June	81	L3	
Dinsmore, Silas G.	5, July 1849	28, June	40	L3	
Dinsmore, Susan Bell	28, Aug. 1851	19, Aug.	15	L3	
Dinton, John	20, July 1848	July	22	L3	
Dirkman, William	13, Oct. 1842	Oct.		L1	
Diserens, Florence Ann	17, Aug. 1848	8, Aug.	2- 8m-14d	L3	
Diserens, Francis	1, June 1848	26, May		L3	

Name	Notice Date	Death Date	Age		Page	Maiden Name
Diserens, John Louis	24, May 1849	22, May	1- 7m-12d		L3	
Disney, Ann	9, Aug. 1838	3, Aug.	80	*	L3	
Disney, Anna	22, Feb. 1844	21, Feb.	8		L3	
Disney, Anna	5, May 1836	3, May			L3	Metcalf
Disney, Charles (Dr)	7, Sept 1854	3, Sept			L3	
Disney, Ellen	4, Apr. 1833	Mar.	23		L1	
Disney, Mary Ann	15, Nov. 1855	12, Nov.			L3	
Disney, Wiliam, Sen.	11, July 1850		estate		L3	
Disney, William	4, July 1850	1, July	69		L3	
Disney, William, Jr.	8, Nov. 1849	5, Nov.	43		L3	
Disselwast, Vineheart	25, July 1833	July	50		L1	
Distin, Edward H.	1, Apr. 1847	25, Mar.	20		L3	
Distin, Florence	5, Sept 1850	2, Sept	20m		L3	
Ditch, Samuel	6, Mar. 1851	Feb.	31		L3	
Ditman, Robert	1, Feb. 1849	Jan.	27		L3	
Ditwiler, Christian	23, Feb. 1854	11, Jan.	51		L3	
Dix, Mary J.	17, Sept 1846	Sept	20		L3	
Dixon, George M.	31, Dec. 1857	24, Dec.	11m		L3	
Dixon, George W.	2, Oct. 1845	Sept	10w		L3	
Dixon, John	13, Dec. 1849	Dec.	25		L3	
Dixon, Joshua	2, Dec. 1841		estate		L3	
Dixon, Joshua	7, Feb. 1856		probate		L3	
Dixon, Sarah	20, Aug. 1857	18, Aug.	38		L3	
Dixon, Stephen	15, Mar. 1813		estate		L1	
Dobbins, Thomas Henry	7, May 1857	29, Apr.	19		L3	
Dobbs, T.	24, Sept 1857				L3	
Dobson, Matthew	23, Apr. 1835		estate		L4	
Dochterman, Charles	21, May 1835		estate		L3	
Dockwilder, Peter	19, July 1849	July	40		L3	
Dodd, H.S. (Mrs)	21, Dec. 1854	14, Dec.	74	*	L3	
Dodge, Charles Frederick	9, Aug. 1849	5, Aug.	infant		L3	
Dodge, Edward Dana	23, Apr. 1857	14, Apr.	8m		L3	
Dodge, George Henry	9, Feb. 1854	5, Feb.	19m		L3	
Dods, T.J.	9, Feb. 1854	17, Oct.			L3	
Dodson, Edward	12, Jan. 1854	6, Jan.	71		L3	
Dodson, Edward	7, June 1855		probate		L3	
Dodson, John R.	25, Nov. 1847	21, Nov.	39		L3	
Dodson, Pamelia	31, Dec. 1846	23, Dec.	58		L3	
Dodson, Samuel	28, June 1849		estate		L4	
Dodsworth, Ann	18, Sept 1834	Sept	38		L1	
Dodwell, John C.	22, Mar. 1855		estate		L3	
Dodworth, Henrietta	15, Oct. 1857	13, Oct.			L3	
Doelker, Adam	11, Apr. 1850	Apr.	25		L3	
Doepker, John D.	4, July 1850	June	26		L3	
Doherty, William	8, May 1845	Apr.	48		L3	
Doherty, William (Gen)	12, Mar. 1840		50	*	L3	
Doherty, William A. (Dr)	28, June 1849	22, June			L3	
Doisy, Augustus	12, Dec. 1850	9, Dec.	20		L3	
Dolan, (child of William)	4, Feb. 1847	Jan.	stillborn		L3	
Dolan, John	22, Jan. 1846	Jan.	24		L3	
Dolan, Patrick	11, July 1850	July	36		L3	
Dolan, Peter	25, Oct. 1849	Oct.	40		L3	
Dolan, Rebecca	28, June 1849	June	10m		L3	
Dolan, Thomas	28, June 1849	June	3		L3	

Name	Notice Date	Death Date	Age		Page	Maiden Name
Dole, (child of Joshua)	7, Aug. 1834	July	stillborn		L3	
Dole, Mary	2, May 1833	Apr.	27		L1	
Dolen, Patrick	15, Oct. 1846	Oct.	23		L3	
Dolen, Sarah	13, Apr. 1848	Apr.	16		L3	
Dolis, Rebecca A.	13, Sept 1832	Sept	1		L1	
Dolker, Frederick W.	4, June 1857		probate		L3	
Doll, Henry	5, July 1849	June	24		L3	
Doll, John Conrad	4, Nov. 1847	Oct.	27		L3	
Doll, Matthew	7, June 1855		probate		L3	
Doll, William	24, Oct. 1850	Oct.	24		L3	
Dollson, Archibald	8, Dec. 1842	Dec.	23		L3	
Dolweber, Anthony	16, Aug. 1849		estate		L3	
Donagan, Barney	31, July 1845	July	35		L3	
Donagan, Patrick	2, Mar. 1848	Feb.	32		L3	
Donaher, Mary	3, July 1851	June	34		L3	
Donahue, Patrick	2, Oct. 1845	Sept	40		L3	
Donahue, Thomas	14, June 1849	June	21		L3	
Donaldson, Anna Margaretta	9, May 1844	30, Apr.	77	*	L3	
Donaldson, Charles P.	8, Mar. 1849	1, Mar.	20		L3	
Donaldson, Francis, Sen.	16, Jan. 1824	5, Feb.	61	*	L3	
Donaldson, George	22, June 1848	18, June	25		L3	
Donaldson, James M.	24, May 1855	24, Apr.	22- 6m		L3	
Donaldson, Jessy	27, Dec. 1825	18, Dec.		*	L3	
Donaldson, Mary	26, July 1849	12, June			L3	
Donaldson, Rebecca	9, Jan. 1845	2, Jan.	20		L3	
Donavan, Sarah S.	5, June 1845	May	2m		L3	
Donbar, Seth	27, Oct. 1831		probate		L1	
Doner, Henry	5, July 1855		estate		L3	
Donig, Madaline	18, May 1843	May	16		L3	
Donivan, Michael	10, May 1849	9, May			L2	
Donivan, Michael	13, Nov. 1850	Nov.	65		L3	
Donlay, Francis	28, Mar. 1839	Mar.	17		L3	
Donlon, James	29, July 1847	July	54		L3	
Donnahue, Catharine	28, June 1849	June	43		L3	
Donogh, Elizabeth	23, June 1853	1, June			L3	
Donogh, Esther Mahard	12, Nov. 1846	7, Nov.			L3	
Donogh, Mary Eliza	20, Apr. 1848		estate		L3	
Donohue, Ellie J.	14, Aug. 1856	12, Aug.	6- 7m-19d		L5	
Donohugh, John	12, July 1849	July	35		L3	
Donough, Mary E.	13, Apr. 1848	9, Apr.	32		L3	
Donough, Mary E.	19, Dec. 1850		estate		L3	
Doolan, Henry	13, July 1854	4, July			L3	
Dooley, Susan	25, Oct. 1832	20, Oct.			L2	
Doolittle, Curtis M.	10, Apr. 1856		probate		L3	
Doolittle, Curtis Miller	21, June 1849	1, June	50	*	L3	
Doolittle, Louis H.	4, Oct. 1833	Sept	9m- 8d		L1	
Doolittle, Robert	9, Oct. 1834	Sept	28		L1	
Dooner, (child of William)	26, Dec. 1833	Dec.	stillborn		L4	
Door, David	17, May 1855				L3	
Dopke, C.	5, Mar. 1857		probate		L3	
Dopke, Christopher	8, Nov. 1855		probate		L3	
Dopke, John H.	9, Apr. 1857		probate		L3	
Dora, (Mrs)	25, Oct. 1832	22, Oct.			L3	
Doran, Michael	26, July 1849	July	2- 6m		L3	

Name	Notice Date	Death Date	Age		Page	Maiden Name
Doran, Simon	8, Oct. 1857	5, Oct.			L3	
Doren, John (Mrs)	24, May 1849	May			L3	
Doris, Peter	3, Jan. 1833	Dec.			L4	
Dorman, Ann	15, Aug. 1833	Aug.	28		L1	
Dorman, Caroline Augusta	26, Nov. 1846	22, Nov.	5- 6m		L3	
Dorman, H.	25, July 1833	July			L1	
Dorman, Jesse Byrd	15, July 1852	11, July	69		L3	
Dorman, Leah Gale	5, June 1851	3, June	73		L3	
Dorne, (child of James)	25, Aug. 1853	22, Aug.	1		L3	
Dorney, John	25, June 1846	June			L3	
Dornin, Bernard	2, Mar. 1837	24, Feb.		*	L3	
Dorr, Samuel W.	14, Aug. 1856	6, Aug.	4- 5m- 5d		L5	
Dorsay, William	24, Sept 1857	Sept			L3	
Dorset, Nancy	19, Oct. 1848	Oct.	46		L3	
Dorsey, J.L. (Dr)	8, Aug. 1833	July	25		L1	
Dorsey, John L. (Dr)	18, Sept 1834		estate		L3	
Dorsey, Mary Anne	1, May 1828		27		L1	
Dougan, William	1, Nov. 1832		estate		L3	
Dougan, William	29, May 1834		probate		L3	
Dougan, William	22, Mar. 1838		probate		L3	
Dougart, Lewis	5, Aug. 1847	July	36		L3	
Dougherty, (man)	9, Oct. 1851	3, Oct.	42		L3	
Dougherty, Alexander	15, Aug. 1850	Aug.	37		L3	
Dougherty, Cornelius	4, July 1850	June	40		L3	
Dougherty, Samuel	5, Jan. 1854	29, Dec.	28		L3	
Dougherty, Samuel	9, Aug. 1855		probate		L3	
Dougherty, Thomas	19, Apr. 1849	Apr.	20		L3	
Doughty, John D.	29, Mar. 1855	24, Mar.	46		L3	
Doughty, Mary	23, Aug. 1849	16, Aug.	54		L3	
Doughty, Mary Isabella	29, July 1852	25, July	2- 9m		L3	
Douglas, James P.	16, Apr. 1840			*	L3	
Douglass, James	23, Apr. 1840		estate		L3	
Douglass, James W.	5, Sept 1850	28, Aug.	43		L3	
Douglass, Luke (Dr)	20, Sept 1820	4, Sept		*	L3	
Douglass, Montgomery Hunt	7, Oct. 1841	22, Sept	2- 1m-14d		L3	
Douthwaite, James	14, May 1824		estate		L3	
Dove, Richard	1, June 1848	May	36		L3	
Dover, James	21, Aug. 1815		estate		L3	
Dover, James	12, June 1815	11, June		*	L3	
Dover, Joseph	26, July 1849	July	22		L3	
Dover, Michael	29, July 1847	July	45		L3	
Doverner, Peter	24, May 1849	May	28		L3	
Dowd, Patrick	18, Oct. 1849	Oct.	40		L3	
Dowell, John	13, Nov. 1850	Nov.	20		L3	
Downes, Alexander H.	11, Sept 1845	Sept	50		L3	
Downes, Charles	11, Dec. 1815	13, Sept			L3	
Downes, Henry	12, Aug. 1841	Aug.	20		L3	
Downes, William P.	16, Oct. 1822		estate		L3	
Downey, James	2, July 1846	June	31		L3	
Downey, Richard	16, Nov. 1843	Nov.	68		L3	
Downing, John	7, Sept 1837	Aug.	50		L3	
Downing, William	16, Sept 1847	Sept	47		L3	
Doyle, Christopher	31, Apr. 1845	Apr.	33		L3	
Doyle, Eliza	8, Aug. 1850	July	31		L3	

Name	Notice Date	Death Date	Age	Page	Maiden Name
Doyle, Henry	19, Aug. 1852	Aug.	1- 6m	L3	
Doyle, James	11, Sept 1834	Aug.		L1	
Doyle, James	6, Nov. 1834	Oct.		L1	
Doyle, James	27, Dec. 1849	Dec.	18	L3	
Doyle, James	14, Oct. 1847	Oct.	36	L3	
Doyle, James W.	27, Dec. 1849	15, Dec.	18- 5m-26d	L3	
Doyle, Margaret	10, Mar. 1806	4, Mar.		L3	
Doyle, Michael	5, July 1849	June	43	L3	
Doyle, Thomas	26, Mar. 1805		estate	L1	
Doyle, Thomas (Major)	19, Feb. 1805	15, Feb.		L3	
Doyle, Thomas H.	21, May 1846	May	53	L3	
Doyle, W.	29, Nov. 1832		estate	L3	
Doyle, William	25, Oct. 1832	19, Oct.		L2	
Dozier, Evans (Dr)	6, Oct. 1821	29, Sept	30	L3	
Drachbach, Frederick	16, Aug. 1849	Aug.	30	L3	
Drake, (Dr)	11, Nov. 1852			L3	
Drake, Archibald	19, Jan. 1854		77	L3	
Drake, Benjamin	23, Mar. 1849		estate	L3	
Drake, Benjamin	8, Apr. 1841	7, Apr.		L3	
Drake, Harriet	4, Oct. 1825	1, Oct.		L3	
Drake, Hervey	3, July 1845	1, July	25	L3	
Drake, Isaac	18, Oct. 1832	14, Oct.		L2	
Drake, James Foster	15, Aug. 1850	5, Aug.		L3	
Drake, John Mansfield	12, Feb. 1816	4, Feb.	2	L3	
Drake, Joseph Charles	19, July 1849	11, July	13	L3	
Drake, Lewis	12, Jan. 1837		probate	L3	
Drake, Mary	28, Sept 1848	Sept	49	L3	
Drake, William Henry	8, May 1845	4, May	3-11m- 7d	L3	
Draper, Cornelia	6, Mar. 1845	Feb.		L3	
Draper, William	26, July 1832	July	64	L1	
Drefz, J.G.	6, June 1839	May	22	L2	
Drenan, William	29, Nov. 1832	Nov.	44	L1	
Drennan, William	27, Dec. 1832		estate	L3	
Drennan, William	21, Nov. 1839		probate	L3	
Drennen, Margaret	18, Jan. 1849	13, Jan.	64	L3	
Drenning, Alexander	9, June 1836		probate	L3	
Dresbach, Jacob	4, Sept 1845	3, Sept	41	L3	
Dresbach, Jacob	15, Apr. 1847		estate	L3	
Drese, William	19, July 1849	July	27	L3	
Dresher, Casper	18, May 1854	10, May		L3	
Dreskel, Dennes	25, July 1850	July	26	L3	
Drinker, Frances	5, Dec. 1833	Nov.	4- 6m	L3	
Drinker, Frances	21, Nov. 1833	18, Nov.		L3	
Drinker, T.B.	30, Mar. 1848	21, Mar.		L3	
Driver, James	3, Aug. 1843	July	30	L3	
Driver, Lucien	8, Jan. 1852	5, Jan.	2	L3	
Driver, Lucien	26, July 1849	20, July		L3	
Drost, Michael	14, Dec. 1848	Dec.	28	L2	
Drover, Joseph	19, July 1849	18, July		L2	
Drown, Charlotte V.	25, Feb. 1847	20, Feb.	25	L3	
Drown, Philip (Capt)	5, Oct. 1843	3, Oct.	37	L3	
Droyer, John	18, July 1850	July	26	L3	
Druge, Diedrich	13, July 1843	July	33	L3	
Druir, Benjamin	3, Nov. 1853	30, Oct.		L3	

Name	Notice Date	Death Date	Age	Page	Maiden Name
Drummond, Mary	1, Aug. 1850	26, July		L3	
Drury, Mary E.	19, July 1838	15, July	27	L3	
Drury, Patrick	3, May 1855	3, Apr.		L3	
Dryden, William	25, July 1833	July	100	L1	
Dryden, William Franklin	6, Mar. 1851	3, Mar.	21m	L3	
Dryer, Georgette	29, July 1841	July	2m	L3	
Drynan, Dennis	14, June 1855			L3	
Dubliose, William H.	15, Feb. 1838	16, Jan.		L3	
Dubois, Andrew	25, Oct. 1832	19, Oct.		L2	
DuBois, Charles McIlvaine	31, Aug. 1854	29, Aug.	8m	L3	
Dubois, Isaac L.	11, Dec. 1815	19, Nov.		L3	
Dubois, John	27, Nov. 1834	Nov.	59	L1	
DuBois, Mary C.	16, Apr. 1857	10, Apr.		L3	Orr
Dubolt, Mary E.	5, Sept 1833	Aug.	4m	L1	
Dubuque, John	16, Aug. 1849	Aug.	35	L3	
Duckworth, Nancy	4, Apr. 1844	Mar.	19	L3	
Dudley, (child of A.)	1, Nov. 1832	Oct.	stillborn	L2	
Dudley, Elias	14, June 1855		estate	L3	
Dudley, George	9, Oct. 1834	Sept	34	L1	
Dudley, George	18, Oct. 1832	Oct.	1	L4	
Dudley, Martha C.	23, Oct. 1834	Oct.	38	L2	
Duer, Alfred H.	10, Apr. 1845	6, Apr.		* L3	
Duer, Henry	5, Oct. 1848	29, Sept	9- 3m	L3	
Duer, Robert	30, Sept 1847	28, Sept	21	L3	
Duff, (Mrs)	1, Nov. 1832	26, Oct.		L3	
Duff, George	22, Jan. 1846	Jan.	26	L3	
Duff, James	17, Nov. 1842	Nov.	26	L6	
Duff, John R.	15, Aug. 1839	Aug.	24	L3	
Duff, Robert	14, Dec. 1848	Dec.	33	L2	
Duff, Thomas	2, Jan. 1840	Dec.	40	L2	
Duffee, George	15, Aug. 1839	Aug.	20m	L3	
Duffey, Patrick	26, June 1851	June	88	L3	
Duffie, Benjamin	15, July 1841	July	50	L3	
Duffie, Matilda	25, Oct. 1832	23, Oct.		L3	
Duffield, Catharine	7, Oct. 1841	6, Oct.	6	L3	
Duffield, Edward	7, Aug. 1834	July	17	L3	
Duffield, Margaret	24, Dec. 1840	20, Dec.	26	L3	
Duffield, Margaret	17, June 1841	16, June		L3	
Duffield, Saunders B.	9, Apr. 1846	25, Feb.	3- 6m	L3	
Duffy, James	11, Aug. 1842	Aug.	54	L3	
Dugan, Edith	16, May 1833	May	34	L1	
Dugan, Frances	28, Apr. 1853	26, Apr.	77	L3	
Dugan, Margaretta H.	23, Mar. 1854	4, Mar.	23	L3	
Dugan, Mary	18, Dec. 1845	Dec.	35	L3	
Dugan, William	25, Oct. 1832	19, Oct.		L1	
Dugan, William	28, Mar. 1850	Mar.	31	L3	
Dugan, William	9, June 1836		probate	L3	
Dugan, William	2, May 1833		estate	L4	
Dugane, (Mrs)	16, Dec. 1852	10, Dec.		L3	
Duggin, Daniel	19, Aug. 1847	Aug.	17	L3	
Duhme, John H.	28, July 1853	24, July	37	L3	
Duhrman, Henry	28, June 1849	June	28	L3	
Dull, Sarah D.	10, July 1845	6, July	19	L3	Fithian
Dulweber, Anthony	2, Aug. 1849		estate	L3	

Name	Notice Date	Death Date	Age	Page	Maiden Name
Dummiels, Catharine	29, Aug. 1833	Aug.	1	L1	
Dunbar, Charles	2, July 1846	June	4	L3	
Dunbar, Sarah	16, July 1846	July	6	L3	
Dunbar, Seth	14, June 1838		probate	L4	
Duncan, (man)	6, Mar. 1851	28, Feb.		L3	
Duncan, Alexander (Dr)	31, Mar. 1853	23, Mar.		L3	
Duncan, James	9, Oct. 1845	Sept	36	L3	
Duncan, Jesse S.	28, Feb. 1835		estate	L3	
Duncan, John	24, May 1849	May	57	L3	
Duncan, Matilda	16, Aug. 1838	Aug.	70	L3	
Duncan, Thomas	11, Mar. 1852	2, Mar.		L4	
Duncan, Thomas T.	11, Mar. 1852	2, Mar.		L3	
Duncan, William	7, Jan. 1847	Dec.	27	L3	
Duncan, Yanard	26, Aug. 1847		estate	L3	
Dundy, Mary	13, July 1843	July	2w	L3	
Dunham, Asa	8, Sept 1817		estate	L3	
Dunham, George W.	30, June 1842	June	3	L3	
Dunham, Martha W.	8, Feb. 1855	22, Jan.	73	L3	
Dunham, William E.	16, Apr. 1846		estate	L3	
Dunican, Edward	12, Sept 1850	Sept	40	L3	
Dunlap, Mary	8, Aug. 1833	July	9- 3m	L1	
Dunlap, Patrick	28, Aug. 1845	Aug.	39	L3	
Dunlap, Robert	25, Oct. 1832	19, Oct.		L2	
Dunlap, Robert	6, Nov. 1834		estate	L3	
Dunlap, Robert	17, Mar. 1836		estate	L3	
Dunlap, Robert	15, Sept 1836		probate	L3	
Dunlap, Robert James	2, June 1842	31, May	2- 1m	L3	
Dunlap, William	25, Oct. 1832	20, Oct.		L2	
Dunlap, William	15, Sept 1836		probate	L3	
Dunlop, Robert	20, Aug. 1857	17, Aug.	43 *	L3	
Dunn, Dennis	3, Feb. 1848	2, Feb.		L3	
Dunn, Denton	6, Mar. 1845	4, Mar.	49	L3	
Dunn, Israel W.	27, Oct. 1826	18, Oct.	12	L3	
Dunn, James	5, July 1849	June	20	L3	
Dunn, James	13, June 1850	June	37	L3	
Dunn, James	26, Aug. 1847	Aug.	49	L3	
Dunn, John G.	18, June 1857	9, June	34	L3	
Dunn, John L.	31, July 1845	July	1m	L3	
Dunn, Lawrence	2, Aug. 1838	July	21	L3	
Dunn, Martha A.	24, Dec. 1840	1, Dec.	20	L3	
Dunn, Mary	9, Aug. 1849	July	3w	L3	
Dunnaven, John R.	25, Oct. 1832	19, Oct.		L1	
Dunnigan, Michael	24, Oct. 1850	Oct.	3- 6m	L3	
Dunseth, David	8, Feb. 1820		estate	L3	
Dunseth, Mary	22, Aug. 1844	17, Aug.	64	L3	
Dunseth, Mary	9, Feb. 1854	1, Feb.	12-11m-11d	L3	
Dunseth, Stephen	6, May 1847	2, May	29	L3	
Dupust, Elizabeth A.	26, July 1832	July	10m	L1	
Duralde, Martin (Mrs)	18, Oct. 1825	18, Sept		L3	Clay
Durant, John	30, Aug. 1849			L2	
Durenzenk, Henry	4, Apr. 1844	Mar.	57	L3	
Durfee, James (Mrs)	4, July 1850	27, June		L3	
Durham, Daniel	12, Feb. 1846	1, Feb.	85	L3	
Durham, Frank	14, Dec. 1854	6, Dec.		L3	

Name	Notice Date	Death Date	Age		Page	Maiden Name
Durigan, Peter	18, July 1850	15, July			L3	
Durka, John	4, Sept 1845	Aug.			L3	
Durner, Joseph	6, Sept 1849	Aug.	35		L3	
Dury, Henry	15, July 1847	11, July	33		L3	
Dushuk, Edward	30, Jan. 1851	Jan.	3d		L3	
Dusmons, Adeline A.	25, Oct. 1832	22, Oct.			L3	
Dutchman, Philip	24, Aug. 1854	19, Aug.			L3	
Dutton, Algeron S.	13, Jan. 1831		estate		L3	
Duval, (child of John)	1, Nov. 1832	Oct.	2		L1	
Duval, Adeline M.	9, Aug. 1855	4, Aug.	55		L3	
Duvall, Ann (Mrs)	1, Nov. 1832	25, Oct.			L1	
Duvall, William (Gov)	30, Mar. 1854	16, Mar.	70	*	L3	
Dwire, William	10, Apr. 1851	3, Apr.			L3	
Dwyer, James	5, Apr. 1849	Mar.	40		L3	
Dwyer, Jeremiah	7, May 1840	25, Apr.	60	*	L3	
Dwyer, John	1, Feb. 1849	Jan.	26		L3	
Dwyer, Owen	7, Oct. 1847	Sept	30		L3	
Dye, James	15, June 1854	27, May			L3	
Dye, Samuel	5, July 1814		estate		L1	
Dyer, Daniel (Dr)	23, Jan. 1827	16, Nov.	46	*	L3	
Dyer, Noah	24, Aug. 1848	Aug.	39		L3	
Dykeman, Margaret	25, Oct. 1832	19, Oct.			L1	
Dyson, John	8, Sept 1842	Aug.	57		L3	
Eagan, Frank	1, Dec. 1853				L1	
Eagan, James	10, Apr. 1845	5, Apr.			L3	
Eagen, Julia	11, Nov. 1852	Oct.	25		L3	
Eames, John	9, Aug. 1855		probate		L3	
Eames, John	5, Mar. 1857		probate		L3	
Earhart, George	9, June 1836		probate		L3	
Earheart, Martin W.	20, Jan. 1848				L3	
Early, Amanda L.	1, Mar. 1849	16, Feb.	20		L3	
Earnest, George W.	26, Oct. 1843	Oct.	7		L3	
Easternbrook, Julia	7, Sept 1854	6, Sept	84		L3	
Eastman, Lydia B.	16, June 1853		54		L3	Knowlton
Easton, Charlotte	14, Nov. 1839	2, Nov.	30		L3	
Easton, Eliphalet	5, Nov. 1857	26, Oct.			L3	
Easton, Elizabeth	5, Nov. 1857	26, Oct.			L3	
Easton, Fanny	10, Jan. 1850	Jan.	26		L3	
Easton, Samuel	4, Dec. 1845	Nov.	40		L3	
Eastres, Oliver	21, June 1849	June	1		L3	
Eaton, Asa Brooks	12, Oct. 1848	8, Oct.	21		L3	
Eaton, Elkanah C.	23, Mar. 1854		74		L3	
Eaton, Jeremiah A.	31, Oct. 1850	Oct.	45		L3	
Eaton, John	24, Feb. 1848	Feb.	17		L3	
Eaton, John	17, Feb. 1853		estate		L3	
Eaton, Mary	20, July 1843	13, July	59		L3	
Eaton, Mary P.	12, Oct. 1848	7, Oct.	43		L3	
Eaton, Mercy	15, Aug. 1833	Aug.	38		L1	
Eaton, William	17, Apr. 1827	14, Apr.			L3	
Eaton, William (Gen)	3, July 1811	1, June			L3	
Eberle, John	7, Dec. 1837	Nov.	2		L3	
Eberle, John, Jr.	14, Mar. 1839	8, Mar.	28		L3	
Eberle, Lucretia	14, Mar. 1850	21, Feb.	25		L3	

Name	Notice Date	Death Date	Age		Page	Maiden Name
Eberle, Richard	10, Aug. 1843	5, Aug.	8m-24d		L3	
Eberlee, John	18, May 1837	May	35		L4	
Eberns, John	9, May 1850	Apr.	76		L3	
Ebersole, Lydia Ann	18, Mar. 1847	4, Mar.	23	*	L3	Rogers
Eby, John	19, Jan. 1854	5, Jan.	55		L3	
Eccles, Jane	30, May 1850	27, May	28		L3	
Echar, Mary Jane	24, Jan. 1839	Jan.	27		L3	
Eckart, Samuel	28, Jan. 1818		estate		L3	
Eckert, Michael	10, Aug. 1854				L3	
Eckert, William	12, Sept 1850		estate		L3	
Eckerts, John G.	16, Mar. 1849	Mar.	30		L3	
Eckhart, Alexander	9, May 1850	Apr.	47		L3	
Eckstein, Frederick	12, Feb. 1852	10, Feb.	77		L3	
Eddy, Charles	1, June 1843	26, May	3		L3	
Eddy, Emma Caroline	11, Dec. 1851	2, Dec.	6- 2m		L3	
Edel, Tobias	14, Oct. 1847	Oct.	72		L3	
Edens, Abraham	22, May 1845	May	45		L3	
Edgeworth, Robert	12, Jan. 1827		estate		L4	
Edginton, John	5, Sept 1850	Aug.	31		L3	
Edington, Edmund	7, Aug. 1834	July	58		L3	
Edington, Nancy	13, June 1833	June	4- 6m		L1	
Edmands, Horace S.	2, Mar. 1843	25, Feb.			L3	
Edmeston, Robert	14, Feb. 1839		probate		L3	
Edmeston, Robert	2, July 1835		estate		L4	
Edmunds, John D. (Capt)	4, Feb. 1841	26, Jan.	35		L3	
Edmunson, (child)	22, Aug. 1833	Aug.	7		L4	
Edoux, Francis	20, Sept 1849		estate		L3	
Edson, Harriet	8, May 1828	May	19		L1	
Edwards, Alexander	5, Apr. 1849	Mar.			L3	
Edwards, Andrew J.	1, July 1847	June	29		L3	
Edwards, Charles	18, July 1833	July	17		L2	
Edwards, Eliza Ann	17, Oct. 1850	Oct.	21		L3	
Edwards, Emma	13, July 1854	9, July			L3	
Edwards, Henry Holcomb	14, July 1806	7, July	16		L3	
Edwards, J.D. (Col)	8, July 1847	1, July			L1	
Edwards, James	26, Sept 1833	Sept	4- 2m- 4d		L4	
Edwards, John C.	30, Aug. 1855	21, Aug.	63		L3	
Edwards, John F.	20, May 1841	19, May			L3	
Edwards, Lucy	28, Jan. 1841	Jan.	49		L3	
Edwards, Michael	8, Aug. 1839	July	64		L3	
Edwards, Sallie C.	5, Feb. 1857	21, Jan.			L3	
Edwards, W.P.	25, Aug. 1853	13, Aug.	20- 2m- 2d		L3	
Edwards, Wiley	7, Aug. 1834	July	2		L3	
Eells, Samuel	17, Mar. 1842	13, Mar.			L3	
Effray, Susan Ann	24, May 1855	17, May	37- 6m		L3	
Egarson, Arthur	1, Nov. 1832	27, Oct.			L3	
Egbert, Eliza	16, Aug. 1849	3, Aug.			L3	
Ege, Stephen	30, Jan. 1840		estate		L3	
Egerlin, Charles	5, Jan. 1854	4, Jan.			L2	
Eggbert, Andrew	22, Aug. 1850	Aug.	3		L3	
Eggbert, Edward	15, Aug. 1850	Aug.	7		L3	
Eggbert, Harriet	15, Aug. 1850	Aug.	4		L3	
Eggers, Elizabeth	25, Oct. 1832	18, Oct.			L1	
Egghert, Anna	22, Aug. 1850	Aug.	5		L3	

Name	Notice Date	Death Date	Age	Page	Maiden Name
Eggleston, (dau. of Benjamin)	20, Sept 1849	13, Sept	infant	L3	
Eggleston, Elizabeth Mariah	26, June 1851	19, June	9m	L3	
Eggleston, Hurbert Palmer	12, Nov. 1857	7, Nov.	7- 6m-29d	L3	
Eggleston, William Henry	17, Aug. 1848	12, Aug.	4- 4m	L3	
Egner, Martha	28, Aug. 1834	Aug.	24	L1	
Egner, Samuel	11, Sept 1834	Aug.	26	L1	
Eibel, Martha	6, Jan. 1848	Dec.		L3	
Eichelberger, Margaret	15, Apr. 1816	27, Mar.	109	L3	
Eichelberger, Rudolph	24, July 1851	20, July	22	L3	
Eichholz, Solomon	13, Dec. 1849	Dec.	25	L3	
Eichler, John	19, July 1849	July	36	L3	
Eichsteller, Catharine	7, Dec. 1848	Nov.	26	L3	
Eickhoff, Charles L.	14, Oct. 1841	Oct.	38	L3	
Eidgenoss, Bitha	19, July 1849	July	6m	L3	
Eigleheimer, Mary	18, July 1850	July	56	L3	
Eiler, (child of Mary)	5, Aug. 1852	July	11m	L3	
Eipel, John	1, Apr. 1841	Mar.	25	L3	
Eirich, Elizabeth	6, Dec. 1855		probate	L3	
Elcock, Mary	10, Jan. 1828	Jan.	90	L4	
Elder, Ely	15, Aug. 1833	Aug.		L1	
Elder, Louise Frances	14, Feb. 1850	7, Feb.	29	L3	
Elder, Mary P.	28, July 1842	25, July	27	L3	
Eldridge, Thomas	14, May 1846	May	36	L3	
Elias, Betsy	14, Mar. 1844	Mar.	42	L3	
Elias, Sarah	4, Apr. 1833	Mar.	3	L1	
Elithop, Martha	1, Apr. 1841	Mar.	10d	L3	
Elkin, (Mr)	18, Oct. 1832	12, Oct.		L2	
Elliot, George C.	25, July 1833	July	3	L1	
Elliot, Henry M.	6, Jan. 1848	10, Dec.	29	L3	
Elliot, John Newton	20, Mar. 1845	15, Mar.	19	* L3	
Elliot, William H., Jr.	6, Jan. 1853	8, Dec.		L3	
Elliott, Caroline A.	2, Apr. 1857	1, Apr.	19	L3	
Elliott, Eleanor	25, Apr. 1833	Apr.	39	L1	
Elliott, Elizabeth Gertrude	30, Mar. 1849	19, Mar.	4- 6m	L3	
Elliott, Jabez	28, Nov. 1844	27, Nov.	39	L3	
Elliott, Martha	2, Apr. 1857	29, Mar.	23	L3	
Elliott, William	20, Feb. 1840		estate	L3	
Ellis, Abel (Capt)	29, Aug. 1844	21, Aug.		L3	
Ellis, Catherine	7, May 1857		probate	L3	
Ellis, Charlotte Lewis	24, Aug. 1837	22, Aug.	11m	L4	
Ellis, Cora A.E.	23, Oct. 1856	15, Oct.		L5	
Ellis, Cordelia	6, Apr. 1843	5, Apr.	4- 6m	L3	
Ellis, David	9, June 1836		probate	L3	
Ellis, George W.	15, July 1841	4, July		L3	
Ellis, Jane	7, June 1855	3, June	66	* L3	
Ellis, John Wilder	17, July 1851	10, July	18m	L3	
Ellis, Mary	24, Apr. 1856	19, Mar.	27	L3	
Ellis, Mary	3, July 1851	June	5m	L3	
Ellis, Mary Caroline	21, Apr. 1853	14, Apr.	43	L3	
Ellis, Sarah	27, Feb. 1851	Feb.	20	L3	
Ellis, Thomas	30, Aug. 1827		estate	L4	
Ellis, William Charles	6, Apr. 1843	3, Apr.	3- 4m	L3	
Ellmaker, Horace	16, Sept 1847	29, Aug.		* L3	
Elmor, Anne	13, Dec. 1832	Dec.	17	L1	

Name	Notice Date	Death Date	Age		Page	Maiden Name
Elmore, Jesse	13, Nov. 1850	Nov.	42		L3	
Elstner, Casper	30, Apr. 1829		estate		L3	
Elstner, Elizabeth	28, Dec. 1843	23, Dec.	20		L3	
Elstner, John	22, Oct. 1857	16, Oct.	59	*	L3	
Elstner, John	5, Nov. 1857		estate		L3	
Elvidge, Jonathan	15, Nov. 1832		estate		L4	
Elvidge, Jonathan	1, Nov. 1832	24, Oct.			L4	
Elvidge, Mary	15, May 1834	May	73		L4	
Ely, Elisha (Capt)	16, Nov. 1854	3, Nov.	70	*	L3	
Ely, Florence	30, Nov. 1848	29, Nov.	5- 2m		L3	
Ely, Jacob W.	29, Nov. 1849	25, Nov.	39		L3	
Ely, Jesse	3, July 1851	June	43		L3	
Ely, Jonathan	17, June 1847	8, June	50		L3	
Emans, John	12, Jan. 1837		probate		L3	
Embich, Matilda M.	19, Jan. 1854	13, Jan.	31		L3	
Embs, Henry	31, July 1851	July	48		L3	
Emerson,	1, Aug. 1844	28, July	53	*	L3	
Emerson, Mary M.	31, Oct. 1833	Oct.	2- 6m		L4	
Emerson, Vincent	30, Apr. 1835		estate		L3	
Emery, Charles	20, Oct. 1836	10, Oct.	42		L3	
Emery, Charles	9, Aug. 1838		probate		L3	
Emery, Mary	12, Sept 1839		estate		L3	
Emmett, Elizabeth	28, Feb. 1850	21, Feb.	70	*	L3	
Emmons, Ellen & child	2, Aug. 1832	July			L1	
Emmons, Job	2, Aug. 1832	July			L1	
Emmons, Nathaniel	27, July 1843	18, July	84		L3	
Emory, Abigail	19, Jan. 1854	26, Nov.			L3	
Emory, George W.	19, Jan. 1854	26, Oct.	20- -21d		L3	
Emory, Newton J.	19, Jan. 1854	20, Oct.			L3	
Empson, Daniel	18, June 1857	10, June	23		L3	
Empson, John H.	21, June 1855	18, June	46		L3	
Empson, Thomas	15, May 1834		estate		L3	
Emrick, Michael D.	8, Jan. 1857	23, Dec.			L3	
Emuel, Elizabeth	9, Aug. 1849	July	28		L3	
Enderlin, Theobald	6, Sept 1855		probate		L3	
Engelharer, Peter	7, Sept 1848	Aug.	43		L3	
Englemenke, Maria	11, July 1850	July	24		L3	
Enness, Susan	6, June 1826	4, June			L3	
Enneszer, Jacob	30, Sept 1847	Sept	40		L3	
Enoch, Ann	23, Sept 1847	Sept	34		L3	
Enos, Benjamin	17, Aug. 1848	14, Aug.	2- 1m-14d		L3	
Entwisle, (child of Mary)	8, Dec. 1842	Dec.	stillborn		L3	
Enyart, Elizabeth C.	12, Dec. 1850	18, Nov.			L3	
Enyart, Samuel	5, Sept 1839		probate		L3	
Enyart, V.D.	19, Oct. 1848	13, Oct.	49		L3	
Enyart, Vincent D.	2, Nov. 1848	14, Oct.	49		L3	
Enyart, William	27, Oct. 1831		probate		L1	
Enyart, William	2, Sept 1830		estate		L4	
Epicy, Joseph	6, Mar. 1856		probate		L3	
Epley, Joseph	21, Sept 1837		probate		L4	
Epply, Francis Burke	10, Aug. 1843	5, Aug.	6m		L3	
Epply, William Wesley	24, Feb. 1848	18, Feb.	6m		L3	
Erant, John	23, Oct. 1834	Oct.	11m		L2	
Erbert, Margaret	19, July 1849	July	75		L3	

Name	Notice Date	Death Date	Age		Page	Maiden Name
Ernst, Dorothy Maria	28, Oct. 1841	25, Oct.	71		L3	
Ernst, Eliza M.	31, Apr. 1845	25, Apr.	33		L3	
Ernst, Emily Jane	18, 25, Nov. 1847	16, Nov.	23		L3	
Erok, Margaret T.	18, Oct. 1838	Oct.	63		L3	
Ervingham, Enoch	2, Sept 1820		estate		L3	
Erwin, Anna Louisa	10, Aug. 1854	7, Aug.	6- 7m-18d		L3	
Erwin, Ellen Ceclia	1, June 1854	28, May	3- 5m-28d		L3	
Escarax, Henry	26, Jan. 1837	Jan.	22		L3	
Eshelby, George Jethro	25, July 1850	23, July	2m-14d		L3	
Eshelby, Isabella	31, Dec. 1840	21, Dec.	3- 9m		L3	
Eshelby, James Alexander	31, Dec. 1840	23, Dec.	5- 3m		L3	
Eshelby, Margaret Jane	25, July 1850	24, July	1- 9m-14d		L3	
Eshelby, Sarah Emily	1, July 1847	26, June	8m- 4d		L3	
Espy, Josiah M.	4, Nov. 1847	29, Oct.	76	*	L3	
Espy, Mary Jane	14, Oct. 1841	1, Oct.			L3	
Este, David K.	5, June 1845		estate		L3	
Este, John	25, Aug. 1842	17, Aug.	2		L3	
Estel, Tobias (Mrs)	26, July 1849	July			L3	
Estell, Nancy	13, Feb. 1840		probate		L3	
Estell, Susan	25, Oct. 1832	20, Oct.	4		L2	
Estell, William	22, May 1834	May	25		L4	
Estep, (son of Henry)	26, Feb. 1852	12, Feb.	9		L3	
Esther, Sarah A.	31, May 1849	May	10		L3	
Estin, John	18, Oct. 1832	13, Oct.			L2	
Etheridge, T.	4, Nov. 1816	30, Oct.			L3	
Eubank, John J.	9, Sept 1852	1, Sept	29- 6m		L3	
Eugene, William	1, Oct. 1840	Sept	1- 6m		L3	
Evans, (Mr)	18, Oct. 1832	11, Oct.			L1	
Evans, (Mr)	18, Oct. 1832	16, Oct.			L3	
Evans, Abraham	7, Sept 1837		estate		L3	
Evans, Abraham	11, July 1839		estate		L3	
Evans, Abraham	13, Feb. 1840		probate		L3	
Evans, Catharine	31, May 1849	May	47		L3	
Evans, Daniel T. (Dr)	25, Mar. 1841	16, Jan.	44- 7m		L3	
Evans, Elizabeth	27, July 1854	19, July	49		L3	Sellman
Evans, George	6, Dec. 1849	Nov.	21		L3	
Evans, George W.	24, July 1851	2, July			L3	
Evans, Griffen	17, May 1849	14, May	24		L3	
Evans, Isaac	28, Nov. 1850		estate		L3	
Evans, Isaac	18, Oct. 1832	15, Oct.			L3	
Evans, Lucy A.	20, June 1844	12, June			L3	
Evans, Nicholas	24, Aug. 1854				L3	
Evans, Richard	6, Sept 1838	Aug.	38		L3	
Evans, Samuel R.	31, Aug. 1854	25, Aug.	54		L3	
Evans, Thomas	30, Aug. 1832	Aug.	20		L1	
Evans, Watson	7, Oct. 1852	5, Oct.			L3	
Evans, William	28, Feb. 1839	Feb.	21		L3	
Evanshire, Jacob	6, Apr. 1848	Mar.	42		L3	
Eveleth, Isaac Newton	23, Feb. 1837	19, Feb.	7- 5m		L3	
Eveleth, William Price	16, Mar. 1837	11, Mar.	3		L3	
Everet, William	1, Nov. 1832	27, Oct.			L3	
Everets, Charles Carrol	19, Jan. 1854	28, Dec.	25		L3	
Everett, Amanda M.	22, Oct. 1840	15, Oct.	23		L3	Broadwell
Everett, William H.	2, Dec. 1841	29, Nov.	28		L3	

Name	Notice Date	Death Date	Age	Page	Maiden Name
Everett, William H.	9, Dec. 1841		estate	L3	
Everett, William H.	26, Sept 1833	Sept	4- 2m	L4	
Everingham, Enoch	17, Mar. 1826		probate	L3	
Everingham, Enoch	20, Dec. 1825		probate	L4	
Evers, (child of Henry)	12, Sept 1833	Sept	9m	L1	
Eversall, Isaac	4, May 1848	30, Apr.		L3	
Eversfield, Michael	14, Oct. 1847	Oct.	64	L3	
Eversole, Christian	3, Aug. 1837		estate	L3	
Eversull, Catharine	5, Feb. 1857		probate	L3	
Evert, Frederick	19, July 1849	July	28	L3	
Every, Anna S.	22, Jan. 1852	14, Jan.	18	L3	Worcester
Ewan, Caroline J.	9, May 1850	1, May	19-10m	L3	
Ewan, James Verner	23, June 1853	15, June	24	L3	
Ewan, Sarah	3, Aug. 1848	1, Aug.	36	L3	
Ewing, (Mrs)	12, Feb. 1835	11, Oct.		L1	Sullivan
Ewing, (Mrs)	23, Oct. 1834	Oct.		L2	
Ewing, Charlotte	16, Aug. 1838	11, Aug.	56	L3	
Ewing, Edith Wallace	16, Jan. 1845	10, Jan.		L3	
Ewing, Isabella	7, Sept 1854	31, Aug.		L3	
Ewing, James	30, Aug. 1838	22, Aug.	36	L3	
Ewing, James	2, Jan. 1851		estate	L3	
Ewing, James H.	16, Aug. 1849	12, Aug.		L3	
Ewing, Mary	26, Jan. 1843	17, Jan.	infant	L3	
Ewing, Mary Ann	3, Apr. 1845	29, Mar.	36	L3	
Ewing, Morgan	15, Jan. 1852	9, Jan.	35	L3	
Ewing, Morgan	6, Nov. 1851	3, Nov.	5-11m-24d	L3	
Ewing, Morgan	29, Jan. 1852		estate	L3	
Ewing, Morgan	10, Mar. 1853		estate	L3	
Ewing, Morgan	3, May 1855		probate	L3	
Ewing, William Griffith	7, Sept 1854	18, July		L3	
Exener, John	1, Aug. 1850	July	1- 6m	L3	
Eyl, Christina	17, Jan. 1850	Jan.	54	L3	
Ezel, Leonard	18, July 1850	July	38	L3	
Faber, J.W.	5, Nov. 1857		probate	L3	
Facon, Daniel F.	3, Sept 1840		probate	L3	
Fagerty, Edward	22, Aug. 1850	Aug.	19	L3	
Fagin, Charles	24, Apr. 1851		estate	L3	
Fagin, Joseph	1, Nov. 1855		estate	L3	
Faha, Michael	26, July 1849	July	26	L3	
Fahay, Jane	16, Aug. 1849	Aug.	40	L3	
Fahey, Martin	18, Jan. 1849	Jan.	28	L3	
Fahrenbach, Christian	25, Oct. 1849	Oct.	13	L3	
Fahs, Casper	24, Mar. 1836		estate	L3	
Fahy, Martin	12, July 1849	July	14m	L3	
Fairbanks, Ephraim W.	1, May 1828		24	L1	
Fairchild, (Mrs)	25, Oct. 1832	23, Oct.		L3	
Fairchild, Oliver (Dr)	20, Aug. 1840			L3	
Fairchild, Olivia	30, Sept 1841		estate	L3	
Fairchild, Samuel	11, Oct. 1809	7, Oct.	48	L3	
Fairchild, Samuel	13, Feb. 1811		estate	L3	
Fairchild, Samuel	13, May 1818		estate	L3	
Falchett, James	13, Nov. 1851	12, Nov.		L3	
Fales, R. Stephen	10, Apr. 1856		probate	L3	

Name	Notice Date	Death Date	Age		Page	Maiden Name
Fales, Stephen	7, Sept 1854				L3	
Falkner, Joseph	9, Jan. 1845	Dec.	24		L3	
Falkner, William H.	1, Nov. 1832	25, Oct.			L1	
Fallis, Joseph B.	16, Apr. 1857	8, Apr.	8		L3	
Fallis, Mary A.	30, Oct. 1856	28, Oct.	5- 8m		L5	
Falls, James	5, July 1849	June	12		L3	
Falls, James	12, July 1849	July	12		L3	
Falmer, Valentine	19, July 1849	July	46		L3	
Fanner, (child of Jacob)	7, Feb. 1833	Feb.	5		L1	
Fanning, A. (Col)	20, Aug. 1846	19, Aug.	58		L3	
Fanning, Michael	5, July 1855	July			L3	
Fanshaw, Ann	30, Sept 1852	26, Sept	65	*	L3	
Faran, Charles (Mrs)	21, Apr. 1817	10, Apr.	35		L3	
Faran, Charles P.	8, Jan. 1846	1, Jan.	85	*	L1	
Faris, Mary Paulina	14, June 1849	5, June			L3	
Farland, (man)	29, Jan. 1852	24, Jan.			L1	
Farley, Bridget	9, Mar. 1848	Mar.	48		L3	
Farley, Hudson	8, Nov. 1832	Nov.	3m		L1	
Farley, John	20, Dec. 1825		probate		L4	
Farley, Mary	9, Mar. 1848	Mar.	3m		L3	
Farley, Patrick	18, July 1850	July	35		L3	
Farley, William W.	29, Jan. 1852		estate		L3	
Farley, William W.	1, June 1854		estate		L3	
Farley, William W.	14, Aug. 1856		probate		L6	
Farlow, Eveline Louisa	20, July 1848	17, July	5- 9m- 1d		L3	
Farmer, Isaac	13, June 1810				L3	
Farmer, James	23, Dec. 1847	Dec.	1		L3	
Farmer, James	26, Sept 1850	Sept	63		L3	
Farmer, James	14, June 1838		probate		L4	
Farmer, John	4, July 1810				L3	
Farmsworth, Frank	11, May 1854	30, Apr.	infant		L3	
Farnham, Caroline Elizabeth	20, July 1843	15, July	7w		L3	
Farnham, Charles A.	21, 28, Dec. 1843	16, Dec.			L3	
Farnham, Margaret P.	22, Apr. 1847	18, Apr.	23		L3	Aydelott
Farnsworth, Jerry D.	19, Feb. 1852				L3	
Farquhar, A. Virginia	26, June 1851	23, June			L3	
Farquhar, J. Aug.	27, July 1843	23, July	29		L3	
Farquhar, Jane Ann	20, Nov. 1834	Nov.	8- 7m		L1	
Farquhar, Lydia	11, Jan. 1844	29, Dec.	41		L3	
Farrar, Henry M.	22, July 1841		estate		L3	
Farrar, Samuel	14, Feb. 1839	Feb.	33		L3	
Farrar, Thomas M.	9, Sept 1841	29, Aug.	37		L3	
Farrel, William H.	29, July 1847	July	7m		L3	
Farrell, Anthony	27, Dec. 1849		estate		L3	
Farrell, Anthony	27, Feb. 1851		estate		L3	
Farrell, Daniel	25, Oct. 1832	20, Oct.			L2	
Farrell, James	11, Apr. 1850	Apr.	27		L3	
Farrell, James	9, Apr. 1857		probate		L3	
Farrell, James	4, Sept 1851	1, Sept			L3	
Farrell, Michael	8, Jan. 1852	3, Jan.	48	*	L3	
Farrell, Michael	11, July 1850	July	3m		L3	
Farrell, Thomas	5, Nov. 1846	Oct.	30		L3	
Farren, Ann	26, Oct. 1837	Oct.	43		L4	
Farrer, Andrew	22, Aug. 1844		estate		L3	

Name	Notice Date	Death Date	Age		Page	Maiden Name
Farrer, John	11, May 1848	May	44		L3	
Farrer, Nancy	8, Apr. 1852	25, June			L4	
Farrin, Eliza	11, Aug. 1853	11, Aug.	5		L3	
Farris, James	11, July 1833		probate		L3	
Farrow, A.S.	18, July 1844	16, July	42		L3	
Farrow, Elizabeth Shore	30, June 1842	22, June			L3	
Farrow, William H.	20, Apr. 1843	11, Apr.	2m-22d		L3	
Faulkner, Emma Jacobs	15, May 1845	11, May	6w- 1d		L3	
Faulkner, Neil	20, May 1852	11, May			L3	
Faulkner, Sarah	3, Aug. 1843	27, July	3w- 1d		L3	
Faux, Abraham	10, May 1849	May	37		L3	
Faw, John	9, Oct. 1834	Sept	46		L1	
Fawcet, Thomas	6, Apr. 1843	Mar.	39		L3	
Fawcett, Henrietta Shotwell	8, July 1847	30, June	infant		L3	
Fawcett, Price H.	19, Jan. 1854	4, Jan.	43	*	L3	
Fawcett, Smith	22, May 1834		estate		L3	
Fay, Charles	14, Aug. 1856		probate		L6	
Fay, William	20, Aug. 1840	31, July	60		L3	
Feak, Samuel B.	9, Dec. 1841		estate		L3	
Fear, William	6, Sept 1814		estate		L2	
Featherman, John	12, June 1845	June	24		L3	
Febiger, Annie	15, Feb. 1844	5, Feb.			L3	Fisher
Febiger, Caroline	21, Oct. 1852	15, Oct.	23		L3	
Febiger, Mary Pleasants	20, Aug. 1857	16, Aug.	7m		L3	
Fecheimer, A.	6, Mar. 1856		probate		L3	
Fechheimer, Abraham	21, Dec. 1854		estate		L3	
Fedeerlein, George	10, Dec. 1846	Dec.	57		L3	
Feely, Patrick	1, Feb. 1849	Jan.	25		L3	
Feeney, Patrick	29, Apr. 1847	Apr.	40		L3	
Feeny, Bridget	3, June 1847	May	3		L3	
Feeny, John	19, Feb. 1857	12, Feb.	32	*	L3	
Feeny, John	7, May 1857		probate		L3	
Feeny, Thomas	3, June 1847	May	1- 6m		L3	
Fegan, Daniel	18, Jan. 1849	25, Dec.			L3	
Feilage, Maria Ann	29, June 1848	June	24		L3	
Feldhans, Peter	18, Jan. 1849	Jan.	24		L3	
Feldkamp, Henry	10, Jan. 1856		probate		L3	
Felk, Henry	25, June 1846	June	20		L3	
Fenner, Alexander	9, Aug. 1855		probate		L3	
Fenner, Cornelius George (Rev)	7, Jan. 1847	3, Jan.			L3	
Fenton, Alfred T.	8, Nov. 1838		probate		L3	
Fenton, Debora	3, Sept 1846	22, Aug.	93	*	L3	Freeman
Fenton, Joseph Brush	2, Mar. 1848	25, Feb.			L3	
Fenton, Rowell	11, July 1833		probate		L3	
Fenwick, (Bishop)	4, Oct. 1832	26, Sept			L3	
Ferances, Daniel	19, July 1849	July	40		L3	
Ferber, John	25, Jan. 1849	Jan.	26		L3	
Ferguson, (Mr)	25, Oct. 1832	17, Oct.			L4	
Ferguson, Abijah Franklin	3, Mar. 1836	28, Feb.			L3	
Ferguson, Addison M.	15, Aug. 1833	Aug.			L1	
Ferguson, Alexander	11, Sept 1851	7, Sept	72		L3	
Ferguson, Arthur	14, Nov. 1833		estate		L3	
Ferguson, Daniel Rodney	14, Dec. 1854	21, Nov.	65	*	L3	
Ferguson, Edward	22, Mar. 1838		probate		L3	

Name	Notice Date	Death Date	Age		Page	Maiden Name
Ferguson, Hester	10, Dec. 1857		estate		L3	
Ferguson, Hugh	6, May 1852	2, May	60		L3	
Ferguson, James	4, Sept 1856		probate		L5	
Ferguson, Louisa	6, Feb. 1845	5, Feb.	37	*	L3	King
Ferguson, Lucy	25, Sept 1856		estate		L8	
Ferguson, Matilda Hamilton	8, July 1852	1, July			L3	
Ferguson, Nancy	1, Aug. 1833	July	21		L1	
Ferguson, Perry	28, Mar. 1850	Mar.	27		L3	
Ferguson, Robert	11, July 1844	July	23		L3	
Ferguson, Samuel	21, Mar. 1839	Mar.	23		L3	
Ferguson, William	23, Oct. 1851	22, Oct.	25		L4	
Feriter, Margaret	31, July 1851	July	24		L3	
Fernading, John	19, July 1849	July	22		L3	
Ferrel, William	1, Nov. 1832		estate		L3	
Ferrell, Felix	12, July 1849	July	50		L3	
Ferrell, Thomas	28, June 1849	June	20		L3	
Ferren, Nancy	20, June 1833	June	35		L1	
Ferrill, John	11, May 1837		estate		L4	
Ferrin, Mary A.	26, July 1832	July	3		L1	
Ferris, Abram	23, Mar. 1843	17, Mar.			L3	
Ferris, Abram (Col)	22, Oct. 1857	8, Oct.	70		L3	
Ferris, Andrew	5, July 1849		estate		L3	
Ferris, Andrew (Capt)	21, June 1849	15, June	70		L3	
Ferris, Ann	7, Sept 1848	31, Aug.	63		L3	
Ferris, Catharine	29, Oct. 1857	20, Oct.	76		L3	
Ferris, Elsy	27, Sept 1855	19, Sept	78		L3	
Ferris, Ezra (Dr)	23, Apr. 1857	19, Apr.	74		L3	
Ferris, Harriet	15, Sept 1842	5, Sept	26		L3	Foreman
Ferris, Henrietta	5, June 1851		21		L3	
Ferris, Henry	14, Dec. 1824		probate		L3	
Ferris, Jacob Ewing	28, Sept 1854	19, Sept	2- 9m		L3	
Ferris, James	13, Feb. 1840		probate		L3	
Ferris, James Ewing	30, Oct. 1845	20, Oct.	14m		L3	
Ferris, John	11, Feb. 1841		estate		L3	
Ferris, John	3, Feb. 1848	1, Feb.	infant		L3	
Ferris, John (Col)	4, Feb. 1841	24, Dec.	62	*	L3	
Ferris, John J.	20, Aug. 1857	Aug.	71		L3	
Ferris, Joseph	30, June 1831		estate		L3	
Ferris, Joseph	15, Sept 1831		estate		L3	
Ferris, Rhoda	20, Mar. 1845			*	L3	
Ferry, Riley	18, Oct. 1832	Oct.			L3	
Fertel, John	1, Nov. 1832	27, Oct.			L3	
Fessenden, Benjamin B.	15, May 1851	6, May	43		L3	
Fetherton, John	5, Feb. 1857		probate		L3	
Fetters, Philip	11, Oct. 1849	Oct.	20		L3	
Ficker, John B.	27, Nov. 1845	Nov.	25		L3	
Field, Marium	24, May 1838	May	76		L3	
Field, Sophia	1, Nov. 1832	Oct.	1- -20d		L2	
Field, William H.	26, Aug. 1841	24, Aug.	1- 1m		L3	
Fields, Henry	27, Nov. 1856	20, Nov.	21		L3	
Fields, John	24, Aug. 1837	Aug.	83		L3	
Fierlein, Philip F.	8, Oct. 1857	1, Oct.	51		L3	
Fiestag, Martin	31, May 1849	May	54		L3	
Fifield, Mary Abbey	6, Aug. 1840	30, July	7		L3	

Name	Notice Date	Death Date	Age		Page	Maiden Name
Fifield, Nancy O.	2, Mar. 1848	25, Feb.	45		L3	
Fifield, William Henry	16, Apr. 1840	10, Apr.	4- 1m- 4d		L3	
Figg, Catherine	18, Oct. 1832	16, Oct.	9		L3	
Filkly, Fred.	27, Nov. 1834	Nov.	28		L1	
Fillson, John F.	22, Sept 1836		estate		L4	
Filpman, Bernard	27, Nov. 1834	Nov.	8m		L1	
Filson, John L.	22, Mar. 1838		probate		L3	
Finan, Patrick	28, Oct. 1847	Oct.			L3	
Finch, Francis Melhado	22, June 1848	28, May	8m-18d		L3	
Finch, Jane	2, Aug. 1832	July	25		L1	
Finch, Philip Young	7, Feb. 1850	31, Jan.	10-11m		L3	
Finch, Warren G.	16, Mar. 1843	10, Mar.	34		L3	
Finch, William	3, May 1849	18, Apr.			L3	
Finch, William McLeod	6, Aug. 1846		10m		L3	
Findlay, Elizabeth	22, 29, July 1847	18, July	34		L3	Patterson
Findlay, James (Gen)	31, Dec. 1835	28, Dec.			L3	
Findlay, Mary Jane	2, Nov. 1848	29, Oct.		*	L3	
Findley, Robert	14, June 1849	June	32		L3	
Fine, Thomas B.	8, Feb. 1855	4, Feb.	26		L3	
Finger, Matthias	15, Nov. 1849	Nov.	19		L3	
Finkbine, Letetia	1, Aug. 1839	31, July	67		L3	
Finkbine, Mary M.	11, Nov. 1852	4, Nov.			L3	
Finlay, H.M.	19, Mar. 1857	11, Mar.			L3	
Finlay, James	6, Dec. 1855		probate		L3	
Finlay, Jane	6, Dec. 1855		probate		L3	
Finley, Amelia F.	28, Aug. 1851	20, Aug.		*	L3	
Finley, Garret	6, Mar. 1851	Feb.	35		L3	
Finley, Jane Ellen	30, Oct. 1845	28, Oct.	5m-19d		L3	
Finley, Lizzie M.	8, Sept 1853	6, Sept			L3	
Finley, Thomas	23, Sept 1852	17, Sept	72		L3	
Finns, Nicholas	10, Jan. 1850	Jan.	22		L3	
Fischer, John	8, Feb. 1844	25, Jan.	74		L3	
Fischer, Ulrick	11, Nov. 1841	Oct.	23		L3	
Fish, George W.	16, Oct. 1834	Oct.	10m		L1	
Fish, George W.	12, Nov. 1846	Nov.	28		L3	
Fishback, John	29, Aug. 1850	Aug.	26		L3	
Fisher, (Mrs)	25, Oct. 1832	19, Oct.			L2	
Fisher, Alice	16, May 1850	9, May	73		L3	
Fisher, Alicia	16, July 1846	July	9		L3	
Fisher, Andrew	7, June 1849	May	42		L3	
Fisher, Anna Caroline	23, Jan. 1851	20, Jan.			L3	
Fisher, Anna Carrington	8, May 1845	7, May	4		L3	
Fisher, Brownlow	14, May 1808		estate		L1	
Fisher, Brownlow	4, Oct. 1809		estate		L1	
Fisher, Brownlow	7, Mar. 1808	5, Mar.			L3	
Fisher, Daniel	29, Jan. 1846	Jan.	24		L3	
Fisher, Daniel	29, Apr. 1847	Apr.	32		L3	
Fisher, Elias F.	15, Apr. 1847	5, Apr.	51		L3	
Fisher, Elizabeth	9, May 1844	Apr.	2		L3	
Fisher, Frederick	11, Oct. 1849	Oct.	48		L3	
Fisher, James	18, Oct. 1832	15, Oct.			L3	
Fisher, John	18, June 1846	June	3		L3	
Fisher, John	9, May 1844	Apr.	4		L3	
Fisher, Joseph	14, June 1849	June	26		L3	

Name	Notice Date	Death Date	Age		Page	Maiden Name
Fisher, Julia	18, June 1846	June	16m		L3	
Fisher, Lewis Weld	13, Sept 1855	5, Sept			L3	
Fisher, Miers	1, Nov. 1827		estate		L3	
Fisher, Nancy	19, July 1855	14, July	62		L3	
Fisher, Noah	16, July 1846	July	5		L3	
Fisher, Peter Schuyler	4, May 1854	3, May	3		L3	
Fisher, Richard	27, June 1839	June	22		L3	
Fisher, S.	26, Nov. 1829		estate		L3	
Fisher, Samuel	20, Mar. 1828		estate		L3	
Fisher, Samuel	27, Sept 1827	22, Sept			L3	
Fisher, Sophia	23, Feb. 1827	18, Feb.	24		L3	
Fishfoot, Sophia	19, Sept 1850		estate		L3	
Fisk, Amos	19, Aug. 1825		estate		L3	
Fisk, Amos	19, Dec. 1826		probate		L3	
Fisk, Amos	9, Aug. 1825	8, Aug.		*	L3	
Fisk, Ann	18, Jan. 1844	12, Jan.	72		L3	
Fitch, Daniel	28, June 1849	June	59		L3	
Fitch, Harris	13, Apr. 1854	16, Apr.	60		L3	
Fitch, Pulliel	29, Aug. 1833	Aug.	20		L1	
Fitch, Rachel	15, Aug. 1833	Aug.	57		L1	
Fitch, Simon	8, Apr. 1852	4, Apr.			L3	
Fiter, Bernard	7, Aug. 1834	July			L3	
Fithean, Sarah D.	31, Apr. 1845	23, Apr.	57		L3	
Fitzerman, Henry	21, Oct. 1847	Oct.	17		L3	
Fitzgerald, David	18, July 1850	July	40		L3	
Fitzgerald, Susan Coulter	27, Apr. 1854	23, Apr.	4- 7m- 4d		L3	
Fitzmiller, John	31, Dec. 1857	3, Dec.	78		L3	
Fitzpatric, Michael	14, June 1849	June	58		L3	
Fitzpatrick, Bridget	27, Mar. 1845	Mar.	2m		L3	
Fitzpatrick, M.	22, Aug. 1833	Aug.			L4	
Fitzworth, Jacob	27, Sept 1838	Sept	50		L3	
Flack, John	21, Sept 1848	Sept	63		L3	
Flagg, (Mrs)	25, Oct. 1832	20, Oct.			L2	
Flagg, Luwratha	29, Aug. 1833	Aug.	4m		L1	
Flagg, Mary	15, Aug. 1833	Aug.	23		L1	
Flakis, Teleney	23, May 1833	May	4		L4	
Flamming, Edward	15, Nov. 1832	Nov.			L1	
Flanagan, Mary	17, Oct. 1850	Oct.	7		L3	
Flanders, William H.	23, Dec. 1847	Dec.	19		L3	
Flanigan, Denis	26, June 1851	June	19		L3	
Flanigan, Michael	30, Jan. 1851	Jan.	19		L3	
Flannagan, John	30, Mar. 1849	Mar.	40		L3	
Flannegan, Catharine	20, Feb. 1851	Feb.	36		L3	
Flannegan, Matthew	31, May 1849	May	28		L3	
Flaterness, Barnard	28, Sept 1848	Sept	38		L3	
Fleak, Peter	26, Sept 1826		probate		L3	
Fleetwood, Mary Columbia	19, Aug. 1852		26	*	L3	
Fleishamer, George	18, July 1850	July	42		L3	
Fleming, Isaac	19, July 1832	July	35		L1	
Fleming, James	3, June 1847	May	21		L3	
Fleming, James	28, Mar. 1850	Mar.	25		L3	
Fleming, Mary	26, Feb. 1852	Feb.	20		L4	
Fleming, Mary Jane	5, Feb. 1857	4, Feb.	81		L3	
Fleming, Thomas (Capt)	14, Dec. 1837	5, Dec.	88	*	L3	

Name	Notice Date	Death Date	Age	Page	Maiden Name
Flemming, Bridget	18, July 1850	July	23	L3	
Fletcher, (child of Mary)	7, Feb. 1833	Feb.	1d	L1	
Fletcher, Albert M.	24, Sept 1840	23, Sept	23	L3	
Fletcher, Rosanna F.	7, June 1849	1, June	infant	L3	
Fletcher, Winslow	14, Aug. 1856	26, July	42	L5	
Fliintham, William	8, Mar. 1838	1, Mar.	75	L3	
Flinn, Ann	5, July 1849	June	10w	L3	
Flinn, Archibald	17, Oct. 1839		estate	L3	
Flinn, Bridgett	26, July 1849	July	35	L3	
Flinn, David	27, Oct. 1831		probate	L1	
Flinn, George	21, Feb. 1850	Feb.	30	L3	
Flinn, John	10, June 1847	June	21	L3	
Flinn, John	14, June 1849	June	31	L3	
Flinn, John	11, June 1846	June	63	L3	
Flinn, Julia	25, July 1850	July	55	L3	
Flinn, Martin	1, Nov. 1832	24, Oct.		L1	
Flinn, Rose	1, Nov. 1849	Oct.	40	L3	
Flinn, Stephen	27, Oct. 1831		probate	L1	
Flinn, Stephen	15, Aug. 1850		estate	L3	
Flinn, Stephen	9, June 1836		probate	L3	
Flinn, William	9, June 1836		probate	L3	
Flinn, William	14, Feb. 1839		probate	L3	
Flint, Ann	7, Sept 1848	6, Sept	84	L3	
Flint, Hezekiah	5, Oct. 1843	30, Sept	73	L3	
Flint, Timothy	3, Sept 1840	Aug.	60	L1	
Flomerfelt, Elizabeth	19, Apr. 1825		estate	L3	
Flomerfelt, Peter	27, Oct. 1831		probate	L1	
Flomerfelt, Peter	20, Dec. 1825		probate	L4	
Flood, Betsy	19, July 1849	July	40	L3	
Flood, John	15, Nov. 1849	Nov.	17	L3	
Flood, Thomas	24, Feb. 1842	Feb.	30	L3	
Flood, William (Gen)	29, Aug. 1821	4, Aug.	89	L3	
Florer, John N.	2, Feb. 1854	31, Jan.	44	L3	
Florer, William	24, Aug. 1848	22, Aug.	63	L3	
Flowers, (child of Harriet)	22, Feb. 1849	Feb.	stillborn	L3	
Flowers, Catharine B.	18, Sept 1828		estate	L3	
Flowers, Elizabeth	14, June 1849	June	50	L3	
Flowers, M.	8, Jan. 1829		estate	L3	
Flowers, Michael	9, Aug. 1827		estate	L3	
Floyd, Ellen	23, Aug. 1855	20, Aug.	88	* L3	
Floyd, Lydia	23, Aug. 1855	15, Aug.	67	L3	
Floyd, Lydia	9, Apr. 1857		probate	L3	
Floyd, Thomas	7, Aug. 1851	4, Aug.		L4	
Flummerfelt, Peter	3, Oct. 1823		estate	L3	
Fly, Joseph	26, July 1832	July		L1	
Flynn, Catharine	31, May 1849	May	20	L3	
Foberry, Herman	17, Jan. 1850	Jan.	44	L3	
Foder, David	11, Oct. 1832	5, Oct.		L2	
Fogerty, Patrick	6, Dec. 1849	Nov.	50	L3	
Fogle, Francis	3, Oct. 1844	Sept	42	L3	
Fogt, John	15, Jan. 1846	Jan.	30	L3	
Folbre, Nelson D.	16, Mar. 1854	3, Mar.		L3	
Foley, Isaac	14, Jan. 1836		estate	L3	
Foley, James G.	5, Nov. 1857	30, Oct.	73	L3	

Name	Notice Date	Death Date	Age		Page	Maiden Name
Foley, Timothy	31, Oct. 1850	Oct.	30		L3	
Folger, Charles C.	3, June 1841	2, June	17		L3	
Folger, David	22, Aug. 1833		estate		L3	
Folger, Elenora	28, Apr. 1842	27, Apr.			L3	
Folger, Elihu	18, Jan. 1838		estate		L3	
Folger, Elizabeth	22, June 1837		estate		L3	
Folger, Elizabeth	14, Feb. 1839		probate		L3	
Folger, Eunice	19, Oct. 1813	10, Oct.	16		L3	
Folger, Frederick	16, Jan. 1851	31, Oct.	21		L3	
Folger, Hepsey	21, Feb. 1823	16, Feb.	68	*	L3	
Folger, Hepzabeth	8, May 1834		estate		L4	
Folger, Hepzebah	29, Aug. 1833	Aug.	71		L1	
Folger, M.E.	21, Feb. 1828	Feb.			L1	
Folger, Mary	11, Mar. 1823	3, Mar.		*	L3	
Folger, Nancy W.	20, Jan. 1853	12, Jan.	55		L3	
Folger, Richard	5, Aug. 1841		estate		L3	
Folger, Tristram	29, Apr. 1816		estate		L1	
Folger, Tristram	18, Mar. 1815		estate		L3	
Foller, John G.	4, Mar. 1847	Feb.	28		L3	
Follic, Isaac	22, Mar. 1838		probate		L3	
Follis, Elisha	26, July 1849	July	54		L3	
Fonver, John	11, July 1833		probate		L3	
Foor, Jacob H.	23, Dec. 1852	30, Nov.	48		L3	
Foote, Dan	27, June 1823		estate		L3	
Foote, Dan	9, Jan. 1824		estate		L3	
Foote, Dan	14, Dec. 1824		probate		L3	
Foote, G.A.	13, Nov. 1834	Nov.	5- 8m		L1	
Foote, Isaac E.	26, Oct. 1837		estate		L3	
Foote, John Ellis	26, Sept 1850	24, Sept	6-10m		L3	
Foote, Jordena H.	10, Nov. 1853	1, Nov.	27		L3	
Foote, Thomas G.	6, Mar. 1851	3, Mar.	8- 4m- 3d		L3	
Foote, William G.	9, Dec. 1847	1, Dec.	7m- 9d		L3	
Forbes, James C.	18, Oct. 1832	15, Oct.			L3	
Forbes, William	26, Sept 1826		probate		L3	
Forbus, Edward L.	19, July 1849	11, July	20		L3	
Ford, Catharine	16, Aug. 1849	Aug.	5m		L3	
Ford, Jesse	18, Oct. 1832	15, Oct.			L3	
Ford, Jonathan	30, Dec. 1814		estate		L1	
Ford, Jonathan	8, Apr. 1816		estate		L3	
Ford, Nathan	4, Oct. 1825	2, Oct.	20	*	L3	
Ford, Patrick	13, Sept 1849	Sept	18		L3	
Ford, R.B. (Rev)	23, Oct. 1845	12, Oct.	30	*	L3	
Ford, Sarah	27, July 1843	July	21		L3	
Forden, Christopher	8, Nov. 1838		probate		L3	
Fore, Emeline M.	17, May 1849	13, May	32		L3	
Fore, L.B.	31, Mar. 1853	26, Mar.	86		L3	
Fore, L.B.	5, Feb. 1857		probate		L3	
Fore, Mary	30, Dec. 1847	19, Dec.	81	*	L3	
Foreman, Jonathan	4, June 1857		probate		L3	
Forewell, Augustus	29, Aug. 1850	Aug.	45		L3	
Forgaty, Michael	26, July 1849	July	36		L3	
Forgey, Edgar Sinton	15, July 1852	10, July	4- 4m		L3	
Forhaffer, Frederick	28, Aug. 1834	Aug.	1m		L1	
Forly, John	16, May 1833	May	45		L1	

Name	Notice Date	Death Date	Age		Page	Maiden Name
Forn, John	31, Jan. 1850	Jan.	37		L3	
Forquer, George	20, Sept 1838	12, Sept			L3	
Forrel, Josephine	20, Sept 1832	Sept	10m		L1	
Forrell, John	29, Aug. 1850	Aug.	50		L3	
Forrester, Robert	4, Aug. 1817		estate		L3	
Forrester, Robert	23, Oct. 1828		estate		L4	
Forrin, David	29, Nov. 1849	Nov.	21		L3	
Forringer, George	17, July 1845	July	37		L3	
Forsha, John Henry	27, Mar. 1828	Mar.	4m		L1	
Forster, Annie Lydia	11, June 1846	2, June	2m-14d		L3	
Forster, Julia Seaton	17, Oct. 1850	14, Oct.	22m		L3	
Fortmann, Mary	15, Oct. 1857	13, Oct.	44		L3	
Fortney, Mary	12, Feb. 1852	7, Feb.			L3	
Forwell, Georgiana	24, Oct. 1850	Oct.	1m		L3	
Fosdick, Charles Updike	8, Jan. 1835	6, Jan.	20		L3	
Fosdick, Ella	24, July 1851	16, July	3		L3	
Fosdick, Ella	25, Dec. 1851	20, Dec.	15m		L3	
Fosdick, Ezekiel	4, Aug. 1853	31, July	65		L3	
Fosdick, Henry N.	9, Sept 1841	8, Sept	33		L3	
Fosdick, Henry N.	14, Oct. 1841		estate		L3	
Fosdick, Richard	24, Aug. 1837	20, Aug.	72	*	L2	
Fosdick, Richard L'Hommedieu	13, Oct. 1842	4, Oct.	6		L3	
Fosdick, Samuel	18, Nov. 1847	14, Nov.	2		L3	
Foster, (Judge)	4, 18, Sept 1851	28, Aug.	88		L4	
Foster, Amanda	8, June 1854	1, June			L3	
Foster, Ann	18, July 1833	July	48		L2	
Foster, Ann Maria	25, Nov. 1847	23, Nov.	25		L3	Huntington
Foster, Catharine D. Stanhope	10, Nov. 1826	15, Oct.	9m- 3d		L3	
Foster, Catherine	20, Sept 1832	Sept	10m		L1	
Foster, Eliza	9, May 1850	Apr.	43		L3	
Foster, Elizabeth	1, Aug. 1850	20, July			L3	
Foster, Elizabeth Lytle	6, Dec. 1855	27, Nov.			L3	
Foster, Emily F.	2, Feb. 1854	30, Jan.	31		L3	
Foster, Harriet C.	6, Dec. 1832	Dec.	1- 6m		L1	
Foster, Henry	27, July 1848	July	70		L3	
Foster, Henry Kilgour	3, Mar. 1853	26, Feb.	20		L3	
Foster, James	27, July 1843	15, July			L3	
Foster, Jeremiah	19, Dec. 1810		estate		L3	
Foster, Joseph	25, Oct. 1832	Oct.			L1	
Foster, Joseph C.	19, July 1849	18, July	48	*	L3	
Foster, Kate Wilkins	14, Aug. 1851	6, Aug.			L3	
Foster, Mary Ann	24, June 1852	19, June			L3	
Foster, Sarah	1, Mar. 1849	26, Feb.	88		L3	
Foster, Thomas	23, Oct. 1834	Oct.	1- 3m		L2	
Foster, Thomas F.	25, Nov. 1825	13, Nov.	30	*	L3	
Foster, Thomas F.	9, Dec. 1825		estate		L3	
Foster, William	28, Mar. 1839	Mar.	22		L3	
Foster, William H.	7, Oct. 1852	26, Sept	19		L3	
Foster, William L.	3, May 1855		probate		L3	
Foster, Zebulon	4, Apr. 1833	Mar.	1- 3m		L1	
Fotrell, Jacob	9, Aug. 1838		probate		L3	
Foulds, William H.	20, Sept 1838	2, Sept		*	L3	
Foulk, Thomas	19, Sept 1833	Sept	1- 9m		L4	
Foulke, Cassandra M.	20, Sept 1825	18, Sept			L3	

Name	Notice Date	Death Date	Age	Page	Maiden Name
Foulke, Frank	23, Aug. 1855	16, Aug.	10m	L3	
Foulke, Lydia	19, Jan. 1854	16, Jan.	2	L3	
Foulke, Thomas D.	22, Dec. 1831		estate	L4	
Foundlan, William	9, Aug. 1849	July	1w	L3	
Fountain, Garrett A.	25, Feb. 1847	Feb.	3m	L3	
Fountain, Thomas Corwine	19, July 1849	13, July	-8	L3	
Fowler, Emanuel	29, Aug. 1833		estate	L3	
Fowler, Emily	17, Aug. 1848	Aug.	5m	L3	
Fowler, George	30, Nov. 1819		estate	L3	
Fowler, Henry	25, July 1833	July	55	L1	
Fowler, James H.	13, June 1833	June	2- 2m	L1	
Fowler, Jesse	27, Dec. 1849	Dec.	45	L3	
Fowler, Libby	24, Sept 1840	Sept	37	L3	
Fowler, Thomas	26, Mar. 1840		estate	L3	
Fowles, G.W.	8, July 1847	5, July	16	L3	
Fox, Arthur	23, Aug. 1849	Aug.	28	L3	
Fox, Charles	15, Feb. 1808	Feb.		L3	
Fox, Ely	23, Dec. 1847	Dec.	52	L3	
Fox, James	8, Dec. 1842	Dec.	23	L3	
Fox, John	27, Jan. 1848	Jan.	30	L3	
Fox, Julia	19, Jan. 1843	12, Jan.	2-10m	L3	
Fox, Mary Jane	27, Aug. 1846	20, Aug.	19	L3	
Fox, Ralph	27, Dec. 1849	Dec.	29	L3	
Fox, Sarah	4, Oct. 1833	Sept	11m	L1	
Fox, Sarah	5, Aug. 1852	July	70	L3	
Foy, Patrick	5, Dec. 1850	Nov.	23	L3	
Frab, Ferdinand	8, Oct. 1846	Sept	34	L3	
France, Adele A.	11, July 1850	6, July	21	L3	
Frances, James H.	18, Jan. 1849	Jan.	42	L3	
Franche, (child of Susan)	18, July 1833	July	stillborn	L2	
Francis, David	6, Jan. 1853	3, Jan.		L3	
Francis, Enoch	7, Feb. 1828	Feb.	37	L1	
Francisco, (child of Calvin)	2, Oct. 1834	Sept		L4	
Francisco, Frederick	28, Aug. 1834	Aug.	5m- 4d	L1	
Francisco, Rosetta	15, Aug. 1833	Aug.	4- 7m	L1	
Frandy, Peter	9, July 1846	June	43	L3	
Frank, David	2, May 1839	Apr.	60	L3	
Frank, John	6, Sept 1855	30, Aug.		L3	
Frankenstein, J.A.	2, June 1842	29, May	53	L3	
Frankland, Thomas	29, July 1852	18, July	54	* L3	
Franklin, Benjamin	12, July 1849	July	3	L3	
Franklin, Benjamin	25, Apr. 1850	Apr.	20	L3	
Franklin, Lucinda Jane	23, Aug. 1849	Aug.	11m	L3	
Franklin, Walter	10, Aug. 1843	Aug.	15m	L3	
Frazee, (Mr)	18, Oct. 1832	11, Oct.		L1	
Frazee, Israel	18, Oct. 1832	11, Oct.		L1	
Frazee, Joseph	12, Nov. 1835		estate	L3	
Frazer, Edwin M.	18, Sept 1845	13, Sept	1- 4m	L3	
Frazer, Frances Ella	1, Nov. 1855	17, Oct.	15m	L3	
Frazer, John	11, Sept 1845	Sept	39	L3	
Frazer, Peter	12, Feb. 1857		estate	L3	
Frazer, Peter K.	10, Dec. 1857		probate	L3	
Frazer, Samuel G.	1, Mar. 1855	21, Feb.	43	L3	
Frazier, Charles O.	13, Feb. 1851	4, Feb.		L3	

Name	Notice Date	Death Date	Age	Page	Maiden Name
Frazier, James	23, Jan. 1851	19, Jan.	64	L3	
Frazier, William	10, Jan. 1850	Jan.	30	L3	
Fred, John	15, June 1813	7, June		L3	
Frederick, Henry	25, July 1833	July	2	L1	
Frederick, John	31, Oct. 1850	Oct.	37	L3	
Free, Charles W.	20, Nov. 1856	18, Nov.	4m- 3d	L3	
Free, Kate	26, May 1853	22, May	1-10m	L3	
Free, Polly	18, Oct. 1832	15, Oct.		L3	
Free, Thomas Elwood	28, Apr. 1853	21, Apr.	2- 4m	L3	
Freeland, John	18, July 1850	July	38	L3	
Freeland, Mary	7, Feb. 1833	Feb.	50	L1	
Freely, (child of John)	25, July 1850	July	6d	L3	
Freeman, C. (Dr)	22, June 1843	7, June		L3	
Freeman, John	10, Apr. 1845	Apr.	32	L3	
Freeman, Louisa E.	24, June 1847			L3	
Freeman, Martha	14, June 1849	June	4	L3	
Freeman, Thomas	21, Feb. 1850	Feb.	40	L3	
Freeman, Thomas	5, Oct. 1854	30, Sept	65	L3	
Fregloe, Christian	29, Nov. 1832	Nov.	1	L1	
French, Edward	16, Nov. 1837	Nov.	2m	L3	
French, Jedediah Sanger	27, Apr. 1848	18, Apr.	18	L3	
French, John Maynard	22, Oct. 1840	21, Oct.	5	L3	
French, Laura H.	20, 27, May 1847	18, May	7m-26d	L3	
French, Sarah	26, Nov. 1846	21, Nov.	14- 4m	L3	
French, William Bradford	17, Nov. 1853	11, Nov.	3- 9m	L3	
French, Z.P.	7, Dec. 1837		probate	L3	
Fresh, John A.	15, Feb. 1838	Feb.	22	L3	
Frey, (child of Jacob)	29, Aug. 1833	Aug.	5m	L1	
Frey, John L.	10, Jan. 1856		probate	L3	
Frick, Arithene	25, Apr. 1833	Apr.	59- 8m	L1	
Frick, John	25, Oct. 1832	16, Oct.		L4	
Fricker, (daughter of N.)	1, Nov. 1832	28, Oct.	6	L2	
Friedenblaum, Michael	8, June 1848	May	60	L3	
Friedler, Herman	22, Feb. 1849	Feb.	18	L3	
Friek, Valentine	19, Oct. 1848	Oct.	46	L3	
Friermutte, Joseph	2, Sept 1852	Aug.	31	L3	
Fries, Christopher	26, Nov. 1846	Nov.	18	L3	
Friethoff, Anna M.	11, July 1850	July	74	L3	
Frieze, Frederick	16, May 1850	May		L3	
Frink, Amanda	26, Oct. 1843			L3	
Friteline, (child of Henry)	2, Feb. 1843	Jan.	stillborn	L3	
Fritman, Dorotha	12, July 1849	July	40	L3	
Fritz, George	17, Aug. 1843	Aug.	80	L3	
Fritz, Henry	11, Nov. 1852	Oct.	5	L3	
Froelin, Charles	13, Sept 1855	7, Sept		L3	
Frohmingk, Anthony	12, July 1849	July	20	L3	
Fromeier, Henry	26, Sept 1850	Sept	26	L3	
Froome, Jane	1, May 1851	25, Apr.		L3	
Froome, Mary Elizabeth	5, July 1849	27, June	1- 9m	L3	
Frost, George	19, May 1842	May		L3	
Frost, Isaac	6, Sept 1825		estate	L3	
Frost, Robert	8, Oct. 1846	Sept	33	L3	
Frost, Robert	22, Aug. 1844	11, Aug.	*	L3	
Frost, Solomon	22, Mar. 1838	Mar.	63	L3	

Name	Notice Date	Death Date	Age	Page	Maiden Name
Frown, Augustus	28, Aug. 1834	Aug.		L1	
Frown, Augustus (Mrs)	28, Aug. 1834	Aug.		L1	
Fry, (Mrs)	25, Oct. 1832	17, Oct.		L1	
Fry, George F.	25, Oct. 1832	Oct.	1- 3m	L1	
Fry, John	6, Nov. 1834	Oct.	24	L1	
Fry, Mary	16, Oct. 1834	Oct.	7	L1	
Fry, Mary Ann	4, Feb. 1847	3, Feb.	39	L3	
Fry, Nathan	15, Aug. 1833		estate	L3	
Fry, Zaver	30, July 1840	July	26	L3	
Fuchs, Franz	6, Aug. 1857		probate	L3	
Fucks, Conrad	14, Aug. 1856		probate	L6	
Fugate, Hosea	7, Aug. 1834	July	6	L3	
Fullbright, Marion	5, Aug. 1847	July	10	L3	
Fuller, Amelia Wallace	27, Aug. 1857	25, Aug.	37	L3	
Fuller, Belle	10, Aug. 1854		10	L3	
Fuller, Ezekiel	21, July 1853	18, July		L3	
Fuller, John	13, May 1847	6, May	70	L3	
Fuller, Laury Ann	2, May 1839	Apr.	4	L3	
Fuller, William Henry	21, Aug. 1845	17, Aug.	8m- 5d	L3	
Fullerton, (child of A.)	8, Nov. 1832	Nov.	stillborn	L1	
Fulton, Andrew (Rev)	10, Nov. 1818		estate	L3	
Fulton, Emmor	28, Aug. 1851	12, Aug.	14	L4	
Fulton, Robert	11, Mar. 1815	23, Feb.	42	L3	
Fulton, Robert	24, Sept 1846	19, Sept	68	L3	
Fulton, William	31, July 1851	July	19	L3	
Fulwelder,	7, Aug. 1834	July		L3	
Funk, Eliza Ely Selden	1, Mar. 1838	24, Feb.		L3	
Funk, Elizabeth	26, July 1832	July	71	L1	
Funk, John	17, Aug. 1837	Aug.	30	L3	
Furguson, Lydia	4, Jan. 1844	29, Dec.	41	L3	
Furlong, Patrick	26, July 1849	July		L3	
Furrill, Hannah	5, Feb. 1857		probate	L3	
Furrow, Harriet	27, Oct. 1842	8, Oct.	25	L3	Johnston
Furser, Maria L.	14, Feb. 1833	Feb.	12d	L1	
Fyffe, Martha	29, July 1852	27, July	6m-10d	L3	
Gable, Barbara	11, July 1839	June	32	L3	
Gabriel, Edwin William	17, Dec. 1846	13, Dec.	5- 6m	L3	
Gaddiss, Jane	3, Apr. 1845	Mar.	3	L3	
Gadsden, Christopher (Gen)	15, Oct. 1805	28, Aug.	82	L3	
Gage, James	11, Jan. 1855			L3	
Gage, Julia Webster	21, Aug. 1845	13, Aug.	2- 4m	L3	
Gain, Patrick	25, May 1848	May	1	L3	
Gainbolista, Copello	8, Aug. 1850	July	1- 6m	L3	
Gaines, (Mrs)	1, Nov. 1832	29, Oct.		L3	
Gaines, Eliza	30, Aug. 1849	Aug.	20	L3	
Gaines, Isham	25, Oct. 1832	21, Oct.		L3	
Gaines, Mary H.	26, Apr. 1855	19, Apr.	60	L3	
Gaines, Nancy	12, Sept 1833	Sept	20	L1	
Gaines, Richard (Mrs)	9, June 1812	7, June		* L3	
Gaither, Ann E.	2, Oct. 1834	Sept	7m	L4	
Gaither, George Miller	10, Apr. 1845	4, Apr.	3- 3m	L3	
Galbaugh, Margaret	25, July 1833	July	2	L1	
Galbreath, (child of Hugh)	20, Sept 1827	Sept	11m	L1	

Name	Notice Date	Death Date	Age	Page		Maiden Name
Gale, Cornelia Jane	18, Feb. 1847	9, Feb.	2-11m-10d		L3	
Gale, George	19, July 1832	July	52		L1	
Galieck, Anna	4, Aug. 1853	19, July			L3	
Gallagher, Adam	10, Aug. 1837	July	30		L3	
Gallagher, Effie	18, May 1848	18, May	4		L3	
Gallagher, Fanny Goodman	1, Mar. 1849	25, Feb.	2- 4m		L3	
Gallagher, J.B. (Rev)	8, Feb. 1849	2, Jan.			L3	
Gallagher, John	25, May 1848	21, May	2		L3	
Gallagher, John Adamson	1, June 1848	27, May	5- 2m		L3	
Gallagher, Julia A.	5, Mar. 1846	4, Mar.	21		L3	
Gallagher, Margaret	28, June 1849	24, June			L3	
Gallagher, Mary A.	15, Sept 1853				L3	
Gallagher, Patrick	26, Aug. 1847	Aug.	24		L3	
Gallagher, Rachel S.	9, Aug. 1855	7, Aug.	47		L3	
Galligan, Edward	29, Oct. 1846	Oct.	29		L3	
Galligan, Thomas	8, Aug. 1850	July	33		L3	
Galligher, (child of Philip)	24, July 1851	13, July	7d		L3	
Galligher, Mary Sayre	24, July 1851	13, July	21		L3	
Gallop, John S.	1, Aug. 1833	July	56		L1	
Galloway, James	16, Aug. 1838	7, Aug.	89		L3	
Galloway, Margaret	21, Mar. 1850	10, Mar.	80	*	L3	
Gallup, Elizabeth S.	7, Aug. 1834	July	19		L3	
Gallup, Josiah D.	16, July 1846	4, July		*	L3	
Gally, Thomas	23, Aug. 1849				L2	
Galstin, John	3, Apr. 1851	Mar.	30		L3	
Galston, Catharine	10, Apr. 1851	Apr.	29		L3	
Gamage, Samuel	5, Apr. 1825		estate		L3	
Gamage, Samuel, Jr.	7, May 1824	24, Apr.	42		L2	
Gamble, David	23, Aug. 1849	15, Aug.	22		L3	
Gamble, George	16, Feb. 1843	8, Feb.	76	*	L3	
Gamble, Joseph	15, Sept 1853	8, Sept			L3	
Gamble, Mary	12, Nov. 1857	9, Nov.	84		L3	
Gamble, William	2, Aug. 1849	24, July	75		L3	
Gamble, William	22, June 1837		probate		L3	
Gammel, Fred.	23, Feb. 1854	5, Dec.	64		L3	
Gammel, Thomas	10, Apr. 1828	Apr.	32		L1	
Ganber, John	15, Feb. 1849	Feb.	40		L3	
Ganes, Hubbard P.	27, Sept 1849	Sept	64		L3	
Gano, A.G. (Mrs)	11, May 1837	10, May			L3	
Gano, Aaron G.	7, Dec. 1854		57		L3	
Gano, Charles B.	16, Mar. 1848	11, Mar.	9m-21d		L3	
Gano, Emily S.	28, Apr. 1842		2-10m		L3	
Gano, Harriet K.	13, Mar. 1856		3		L3	
Gano, John A. (Dr)	11, July 1844	10, July	45		L3	
Gano, John S. (Gen)	9, Jan. 1822	1, Jan.	56	*	L3	
Gano, Lizzie	7, Aug. 1851	30, July	19m		L3	
Gano, Mary	2, July 1857	27, June	80		L3	
Gano, Mary D.	14, Dec. 1843	30, Nov.			L3	
Gano, Rebecca L.	2, June 1836	25, May	2		L1	
Gano, Richard	15, Nov. 1832	Nov.	7m		L1	
Gano, Richard M. (Gen)	6, Nov. 1815	22, Oct.	41		L1	
Gano, Stephen	5, Jan. 1813		estate		L3	
Gano, Stephen (Lt)	15, Sept 1812	9, Sept			L3	
Ganter, John D.	10, Jan. 1850	Jan.	35		L3	

Name	Notice Date	Death Date	Age	Page	Maiden Name
Gard, (man)	10, June 1852	9, June		L3	
Gard, Caleb	7, May 1805	1, May	estate	L2	
Gard, Gersham	20, Dec. 1825		probate	L4	
Gard, Gershom	12, Jan. 1827		estate	L3	
Gard, Moses	8, 22, Sept 1853	June		L3	
Gardener, William J.	4, July 1833	June	18	L2	
Gardiner, Alexander	9, Dec. 1852			L3	
Gardiner, Charles	6, Feb. 1851		estate	L3	
Gardiner, James	4, Apr. 1850	Mar.	18	L3	
Gardinier, Benjamin	4, Feb. 1825	24, Jan.		* L3	
Gardner, (Mr)	25, Oct. 1832	10, Oct.		L1	
Gardner, (Mr)	18, Oct. 1832	12, Oct.		L2	
Gardner, Benjamin	14, May 1829		estate	L3	
Gardner, Catherine	13, Sept 1832	Sept	1- 7m	L1	
Gardner, Frances	15, July 1852	12, July	18- 4m-16d	L3	
Gardner, Henry	22, May 1834	May	56	L4	
Gardner, John	6, Feb. 1851	Jan.	25	L3	
Gardner, John	30, Jan. 1851	24, Jan.		L3	
Gardner, John H.	16, Feb. 1854	14, Feb.	32	* L3	
Gardner, John H.	9, Aug. 1855		probate	L3	
Gardner, Josiah	14, Feb. 1833		estate	L3	
Gardner, Peter	31, July 1851	July	32	L3	
Garey, Timothy	11, Mar. 1847	Mar.	51	L3	
Garfforth, John	5, July 1849	June	50	L3	
Gariffin, James	5, Sept 1839		probate	L3	
Garland, James	8, Apr. 1812		estate	L1	
Garmore, Jacob	14, Mar. 1850	Mar.	19	L3	
Garran, Michael	19, Apr. 1849	Apr.	35	L3	
Garrard, J.D.	11, Feb. 1836		estate	L3	
Garrard, Jeptha D.	18, June 1846		estate	L3	
Garrard, Jeptha D.	14, Feb. 1839		probate	L3	
Garrard, Jeptha D.	4, Feb. 1836	27, Jan.		L4	
Garrard, William	7, Dec. 1837		probate	L3	
Garresey, James P.	1, July 1847	June	3w	L3	
Garretson, Caroline W.	4, Apr. 1844	28, Mar.	9m-23d	L3	
Garretson, Jonathan	8, Jan. 1857		probate	L3	
Garrett, John C.	9, Aug. 1838	24, July	infant	L3	
Garrett, Nancy Caroline	13, July 1843	5, July	17	L3	
Garrish, Francis B.	18, Oct. 1832	13, Oct.	63	L2	
Garrison, Elijah	19, May 1842		estate	L3	
Garrison, Harriet	25, Oct. 1832	20, Oct.		L2	
Garrison, Margaret A.	12, July 1849	9, July		L3	Handy
Garrison, Susan M.	23, Dec. 1852	17, Dec.		L3	
Garrist, (child)	25, Oct. 1849	Oct.	stillborn	L3	
Garrs, Caleb	5, June 1845	May	55	L3	
Garvy, John	8, July 1847	June	3	L3	
Gaskill, Patrick	15, Aug. 1850	Aug.	7m	L3	
Gasler, William	5, Sept 1833	Aug.		L1	
Gass, John George	1, Aug. 1844	July	53	L3	
Gassam, Hannah	22, Aug. 1850	Aug.	4	L3	
Gassaway, Agnes Louise	24, Mar. 1853	17, Mar.	7m-14d	L3	
Gassaway, Charles Griffith	13, Dec. 1855	10, Dec.	16m	L3	
Gassaway, Elizabeth	1, Oct. 1846	29, Sept	1- -19d	L3	
Gassaway, Lucy Clay	25, Jan. 1849	19, Jan.	15m	L3	

Name	Notice Date	Death Date	Age		Page	Maiden Name
Gassaway, Olivia Jane	9, June 1853	5, June	24- 6m		L3	
Gassaway, William Ridgeley	18, July 1850	12, July	1- - 5d		L3	
Gassel, Louisa	26, May 1842	May	39		L3	
Gaston, Hugh	7, Feb. 1839		estate		L4	
Gaston, I.R.	8, Jan. 1857		probate		L3	
Gaston, John	29, June 1837		estate		L3	
Gaston, John	18, Apr. 1839		probate		L3	
Gaston, John	7, Apr. 1836		estate		L4	
Gaston, John R.	18, Mar. 1841		estate		L3	
Gaston, John R.	29, May 1834		probate		L3	
Gaston, Thomas	11, Sept 1834	Aug.	23		L1	
Gatch, Elizabeth	17, July 1811	July			L3	
Gatch, Maria	1, Nov. 1849	17, Oct.	58		L3	
Gates, Abner	22, June 1837		probate		L3	
Gates, Andrew	8, Nov. 1838	Oct.	2-10m		L3	
Gates, Dorothy	21, Apr. 1853	18, Apr.	77		L3	
Gates, Horatio (Gen)	5, May 1806	10, Apr.	78		L3	
Gates, Maria	8, Oct. 1846	Sept	35		L3	
Gates, Sarah	14, Aug. 1856		estate		L5	
Gates, Spencer S.	11, Aug. 1842	5, Aug.	34	*	L3	
Gates, Stanton	10, Apr. 1851	Apr.	25		L3	
Gaukle, John W.	31, July 1851	27, July			L3	
Gaurdner, Garner G.	22, Aug. 1833	Aug.	1- 1m-16d		L4	
Gavin, Thomas	17, May 1855	10, May			L3	
Gaxey, Robert	1, Aug. 1833	July	25		L1	
Gaylord, Franklin W.	9, Apr. 1840	2, Apr.		*	L3	
Gaylord, Lucy S.	20, Nov. 1851	13, Nov.			L3	
Gazley, James (Mrs)	29, Dec. 1817	24, Dec.			L2	
Gearing, Godfrey	26, July 1849	July	29		L3	
Gearing, John	17, Jan. 1850	Jan.	43		L3	
Geary, Mahalean	18, May 1843	May	3		L3	
Geddes, Caroline	10, Sept 1846	Sept	10m		L3	
Geddes, John	3, Sept 1846	Aug.	35		L3	
Geddes, Mary Ella	13, May 1841	8, May	9m- 4d		L3	
Geddes, Sarah Ida	1, Aug. 1844	28, July	2- -10d		L3	
Gedge, Frederick G.	16, Nov. 1854	9, Nov.			L3	
Geding, Isaac	8, Aug. 1833	July	39- 6m		L1	
Gedney, Julia Ann	22, Aug. 1833	Aug.	10- 6m		L4	
Gee, Rosel	11, July 1833	July	70		L1	
Geever, Michael	20, Jan. 1848	Jan.	20		L3	
Geffroy, Kate Allen	8, Apr. 1852	30, Mar.	16m-19d		L3	
Geffs, Robert	23, Dec. 1847	Dec.	19		L3	
Gehring, George	30, Apr. 1846	Apr.	24		L3	
Gehrum, Philip J.	19, July 1849	July	83		L3	
Geiger, John G.	10, Dec. 1857		probate		L3	
Geiger, Mary S.	13, Apr. 1854	23, Mar.			L3	Stewart
Geiler, Louisa	9, Aug. 1849	July	1- 3m		L3	
Geinsheimer, Peter	15, Oct. 1857	Oct.			L3	
Geir, Henry B.	28, June 1849	23, June			L3	
Geisendorff, Julia	29, Sept 1853	22, Sept	35-11m		L3	
Geiss, David	6, Dec. 1832	Dec.			L1	
Geizer, Samuel	14, June 1849	June	87		L3	
Gell, Edward S.	28, May 1857	20, May	70		L3	
Gengembre, Cornelia Elizabeth	17, Sept 1857	12, Sept	14m		L3	

Name	Notice Date	Death Date	Age		Page	Maiden Name
Gentle, William T.	28, Feb. 1850		estate		L3	
Gentzer, Edward	18, Apr. 1850	Apr.	37		L3	
Geole, Elizabeth	11, Sept 1834	Aug.	1- 4m		L1	
George, Stephen	21, May 1846	20, May			L3	
Gerardy, George	26, Aug. 1847	Aug.	50		L3	
Gere, Isaac	30, Jan. 1851	21, Jan.	48	*	L3	
Gerleman, John H.	16, Oct. 1856		probate		L6	
German, Caleb	17, Mar. 1826		probate		L3	
German, Caleb	19, Dec. 1826		probate		L3	
Gerrard, Isaac	7, Mar. 1808	Jan.			L3	
Gerry, Elbridge	13, Dec. 1814	12, Dec.			L3	
Gertsenson, Mary	5, Sept 1833	Aug.	6m		L1	
Gest, George	13, Sept 1832	Sept	22		L1	
Gest, Jacob	23, Feb. 1843	12, Feb.	53	*	L3	
Gest, Margaretta	19, July 1849	5, July	38		L3	Biggs
Gest, Melissa S.	4, Feb. 1841	22, Jan.	19		L3	Bryan
Gester, Clayton	24, Dec. 1846	Dec.	11		L3	
Gettier, George	18, Apr. 1839		probate		L3	
Getty, Clarinda	19, Jan. 1843	5, Jan.	36		L3	
Getz, John	11, Apr. 1844	Apr.	32		L3	
Getzer, Herman	2, July 1846	June	39		L3	
Geyer, Josephine	4, July 1833	June	15d		L2	
Ghynkey, Jane	9, June 1842	May	27		L3	
Gibbon, Leonard	26, Sept 1844	10, Sept	33	*	L3	
Gibbons, Isabella W.	15, Aug. 1850	13, Aug.	25		L3	
Gibbons, Laura Ann	16, Aug. 1855	13, Aug.	21		L3	
Gibbons, William Edward	9, Aug. 1855	4, Aug.	13m- 4d		L3	
Gibbs, Eliza Ann	4, Mar. 1847	24, Feb.	29		L3	Eaton
Gibbs, Henry R.	5, Oct. 1848	Sept	38		L3	
Gibbs, Justus	29, Nov. 1838		estate		L3	
Gibbs, Margaret	21, Oct. 1847	Oct.	83		L3	
Gibbs, Nixon	4, Oct. 1833	Sept	30		L1	
Gibhard, Appollonia	6, Dec. 1838	Nov.	26		L4	
Gibins, Thomas	18, July 1850	July	35		L3	
Gibreath, Hugh	29, Nov. 1832	Nov.	40		L1	
Gibson, Ann	14, Sept 1854	10, Sept	62		L3	
Gibson, Florella	27, Nov. 1856	24, Nov.	35		L3	
Gibson, Isaac, Jr.	7, June 1814		estate		L1	
Gibson, James	14, Feb. 1839		probate		L3	
Gibson, James	13, Feb. 1840		probate		L3	
Gibson, Jane	12, Oct. 1848	11, Oct.	37	*	L3	
Gibson, John	2, Aug. 1849	26, July	72		L3	
Gibson, Joseph	23, May 1844	May	45		L3	
Gibson, Martha	10, June 1841	29, May			L3	
Gibson, Mary L.	26, Sept 1833	Sept	6- 1m-14d		L4	
Gibson, Phebe	14, Oct. 1847	10, Oct.	23		L3	
Gibson, Rebecca	26, Oct. 1843	21, Oct.	58		L3	
Gibson, Sarah Ann	19, Apr. 1855	10, Apr.	31		L3	
Gibson, Smith	27, July 1848	July	30		L3	
Gibson, William	7, Dec. 1848	Nov.	48		L3	
Gibson, William	12, Oct. 1837		estate		L3	
Gibson, William	9, Aug. 1838		probate		L3	
Gibson, William Bylie	24, Aug. 1854	21, Aug.	5m-15d		L3	
Gideon, James A.	26, Sept 1833	Sept	9m		L4	

Name	Notice Date	Death Date	Age		Page	Maiden Name
Gidy, Isaac	19, Apr. 1849	Apr.			L3	
Gie, John	1, Aug. 1833	July	32		L1	
Gilbert, Chauncy G. (Dr)	16, Sept 1847	12, Sept	32	*	L3	
Gilbert, Henry	28, Sept 1848	Sept	23		L3	
Gilbert, John	26, Feb. 1846	Feb.	26		L3	
Gilbert, John	4, Sept 1856	estate			L5	
Gilbert, Joseph	19, Sept 1850	14, Sept	76		L3	
Gilbert, Joseph	7, June 1855	probate			L3	
Gilbert, Mary	1, Aug. 1833	July	79		L1	
Gilbert, Samuel	28, Oct. 1847	Oct.	23		L3	
Gilbert, Sarah	16, Dec. 1847	9, Dec.	64		L3	
Gilbreath, (heirs)	9, June 1836	probate			L3	
Gilbreath, Edward	18, Jan. 1849	Jan.	40		L3	
Gilbreath, Hugh	16, Apr. 1835	estate			L3	
Giles, Charles	29, Nov. 1855	estate			L3	
Giles, Charles	6, Dec. 1855	probate			L3	
Gilkeg, Benjamin	30, Aug. 1832	Aug.	4- 9m		L1	
Gilkey, James	4, Jan. 1849	Dec.	62		L3	
Gilkey, Sarah E.	1, Nov. 1832	25, Oct.	10		L1	
Gilkison, George	2, May 1833	Apr.	40		L1	
Gill, Henry	7, May 1846	Apr.	27		L3	
Gill, John	13, Nov. 1850	Nov.	26		L3	
Gill, Mary	28, June 1849	June	3m		L3	
Gill, Mary	25, Oct. 1832	15, Oct.			L4	
Gill, Michael	6, Sept 1849	Aug.	20		L3	
Gill, Reuben	27, Nov. 1834	Nov.	50		L1	
Gilland, Thomas	29, Nov. 1832	Nov.			L1	
Gillens, Patrick	12, Oct. 1848	Oct.	35		L3	
Giller, Patrick	20, Nov. 1850	Nov.	54		L3	
Gillespie, James (Col)	12, Feb. 1805				L3	
Gililnad, David	9, Apr. 1829	estate			L3	
Gillingham, Anne	6, Nov. 1851	4, Nov.	23		L3	
Gillingham, Eliza	5, Aug. 1852	19, July			L3	Gillingham
Gillingham, Sarah	16, Oct. 1851	8, Oct.	21		L3	
Gillmore, Mathew	22, Oct. 1846	Oct.	25		L3	
Gilman, James	29, May 1851	28, May			L3	
Gilman, Mary Phebe	16, July 1846	11, July	infant		L3	
Gilman, Samuel Edward	3, Oct. 1850	1, Oct.	5	*	L3	
Gilmore, Francis	13, Aug. 1846	8, Aug.	62	*	L3	
Gilmore, Gurden R.	23, May 1839	estate			L3	
Gilmore, Gurdon R.	7, Mar. 1850	2, Mar.	38		L3	
Gilmore, Gurdon R.	16, Jan. 1851	estate			L3	
Gilmore, Gurdon R.	5, Nov. 1857	probate			L3	
Gilmore, Gurdon R.	25, Oct. 1832	21, Oct.			L3	
Gilmore, Hiram	15, Feb. 1849	11, Feb.	30		L3	
Gilmore, John	14, June 1838	probate			L4	
Gilmore, Joseph	12, Feb. 1846	Feb.	20		L3	
Gilmore, Julius K.	15, Feb. 1849	6, Feb.	2m		L3	
Gilmore, Martha	14, Aug. 1845	Aug.	45		L3	
Gilmore, Martha	13, Nov. 1850	estate			L3	
Gilmore, Mary	10, Sept 1857	probate			L3	
Gilmore, Phebe	1, Nov. 1849	30, Oct.	65		L3	
Gilmore, Robert McGinnis	18, Oct. 1849	14, Oct.	infant		L3	
Gilpin, Charles T.	16, June 1853	11, June	8		L3	

Name	Notice Date	Death Date	Age	Page	Maiden Name
Gilpin, Leman	20, June 1839	June	45	L3	
Gilpin, Luella	27, Mar. 1851	24, Mar.	1- 9m	L3	
Gimpel, Frederick	26, June 1851	June	29	L3	
Ginsen, Ann	28, Nov. 1833	Nov.	2m-14d	L4	
Giraldin, Carrie	14, May 1857	10, May	infant	L3	
Girard, Charles	11, Feb. 1847	Feb.	32	L3	
Girard, Stephen	4, Jan. 1832	Dec.		L3	
Gist, Thomas	7, Feb. 1839	Jan.	53	L3	
Given, Evan Edward	21, Feb. 1850	Feb.	33	L3	
Given, Sarah	15, Sept 1836		probate	L3	
Glancey, James	28, Sept 1854	26, Sept		L3	
Glancy, William A.	2, Sept 1852	27, Aug.		L3	
Glasco, Joseph D.	26, Sept 1833	Sept	2m-13d	L4	
Glasco, Serepta J.	11, July 1833	July	1- 2m	L1	
Glascoe, James Dill	7, July 1842	4, July	7-10m	L3	
Glascoe, Josephine	7, July 1842	3, July	2- 3m	L3	
Glasgo, John	9, June 1842	May	45	L3	
Glass, (Mrs)	25, July 1833	July	40	L1	
Glass, John	14, Oct. 1830		estate	L3	
Glass, Susan	2, May 1833	Apr.	2	L1	
Glasson, Alexander	6, Dec. 1832	Dec.		L1	
Glassord, William	26, Sept 1844	Sept		L3	
Glatz, Henry A.	7, Feb. 1856		probate	L3	
Glause, Benjamin	27, Mar. 1845	Mar.	27	L3	
Gleason, Norman C.	24, Aug. 1843	Aug.		L3	
Gleason, Thomas	29, Aug. 1850	28, Aug.		L1	
Gleason, Timothy	26, June 1851	June	22	L3	
Glenn, Hugh	13, June 1833	June	41	L1	
Glenn, Hugh	20, Nov. 1834		estate	L3	
Glenn, Hugh	6, June 1833			L4	
Glenn, James	9, Mar. 1813		estate	L3	
Glenn, John	27, July 1843	July	50	L3	
Glenn, Jonathan	28, June 1849	June	2	L3	
Glenn, Lawrence	19, Apr. 1849	17, Apr.		L2	
Glenn, Martin	3, Sept 1857			L3	
Glenn, Robert	25, Oct. 1832	Oct.		L4	
Glenn, William	18, Jan. 1849	14, Jan.	43	L3	
Glenney, Samuel	15, Nov. 1855	9, Nov.	52	L3	
Glidden, Adele	5, Feb. 1852	31, Jan.	2- 3m	L3	
Glidden, George C.	7, Dec. 1854	28, Nov.	17	L3	
Glidden, Mary Ellen	19, Mar. 1857	15, Mar.	*	L3	Robison
Glockler, Jacob F.	9, Apr. 1857		probate	L3	
Glockner, Philip	10, Dec. 1857		probate	L3	
Glord, Xavier	19, Aug. 1852	Aug.	28	L3	
Glossin, (child of Therese)	31, Jan. 1850	Jan.	stillborn	L3	
Glover, Elias	9, Oct. 1811	5, Oct.		L3	
Glover, Isabella H.	9, Aug. 1855		29	L3	Miller
Glover, John	20, Sept 1832	Sept	14d	L1	
Glover, Seding	20, Oct. 1842	Oct.	40	L3	
Gluson, (child)	8, Aug. 1833	July		L1	
Goatee, Betsey	17, Mar. 1842	Mar.	39	L3	
Goble, Abigail Ann	6, June 1839	May	9m	L2	
Goble, Daniel P.	21, Mar. 1839	Mar.	35	L3	
Goble, Jeremiah	24, Dec. 1857	21, Dec.	52	L3	

Name	Notice Date	Death Date	Age	Page	Maiden Name
Godard, A. (Col)	12, June 1851	8, June		* L3	
Goddard, Francis E.	25, Sept 1845	15, Sept	55	L3	
Godfrey, Samuel	20, Nov. 1850	Nov.	67	L3	
Godley, Charles Edwin	16, Jan. 1851	11, Jan.	2- 2m	L3	
Goedke, B.H.	9, Aug. 1855		probate	L3	
Goehring, Hart	1, Oct. 1846	Sept	31	L3	
Goen, Henry	8, Jan. 1846	Dec.	19	L3	
Goephert, Jacob	13, Sept 1849	Sept	67	L3	
Goetchler, (Mrs)	8, Sept 1853	5, Sept		L3	
Goforth, Aaron	25, Dec. 1811		estate	L2	
Goforth, Aaron	13, Nov. 1811	10, Nov.	36	L3	
Goforth, Aaron	5, Dec. 1850		estate	L3	
Goforth, Aaron	14, Dec. 1824		probate	L3	
Goforth, Elizabeth	8, Aug. 1850	4, Aug.	81	L3	
Goforth, Samuel L.	1, Nov. 1832	Oct.	8	L2	
Goforth, William	3, Nov. 1807	2, Nov.	76	* L2	
Goforth, William	17, Nov. 1807	2, Nov.	76	L3	
Goforth, William (Dr)	19, May 1817	12, May		L3	
Gohling, John F.	1, Nov. 1832	25, Oct.		L1	
Gold, John	13, July 1854	6, July	67	L3	
Gold, John	12, Oct. 1824		4d	L3	
Gold, Michael	26, Feb. 1857			L3	
Gold, Nathan	14, Jan. 1818		estate	L2	
Goldenberg, John	11, May 1854	3, May		L3	
Golding, Barnabas	22, Mar. 1838		probate	L3	
Goldsborough, Charles H.	1, May 1851	30, Apr.		L3	
Goldsmith, J.L.	9, Mar. 1854	8, Mar.		L3	
Goldsmith, Lewis	7, May 1857		probate	L3	
Goldsmith, Lewis	14, Aug. 1856		probate	L6	
Goldsmith, Nancy	9, July 1857	28, June	67	L3	
Goldsmith, Rebecca A.	13, Feb. 1851	5, Feb.	32	L3	
Goldsworthy, Margaret	14, Aug. 1856	7, Aug.	43	L5	
Gole, Joseph	3, July 1845	June	53	L3	
Golliher, George	1, Aug. 1850	July	40	L3	
Gooch, Horace	13, Jan. 1848	11, Jan.	56	L3	
Good, (child of Mrs.)	25, July 1833	July	stillborn	L1	
Good, Jane	27, Apr. 1848	26, Apr.		L3	
Good, Joseph H.	30, Aug. 1849	Aug.	20	L3	
Good, Margaret	15, Aug. 1833	Aug.	1-10m	L1	
Goodacre, Philip	26, July 1849	July	18	L3	
Goodall, Charles	9, Dec. 1847	Dec.	33	L3	
Goodall, George O'Neil (Dr)	19, Jan. 1854	5, Jan.	43	L3	
Goode, Mary	9, July 1857	7, July	infant	L3	
Goodenow, John M.	26, July 1838	25, July	56	L3	
Goodheart, Jacob	3, Jan. 1856	31, Dec.	32	L3	
Goodhue, George	23, June 1842	17, June	3	L3	
Goodhue, Julia Ann Maria	19, Jan. 1843	14, Jan.	15m	L3	
Goodin, Daniel R.	30, Dec. 1852	7, Dec.		L3	
Goodin, Harriet A.	2, Mar. 1854	25, Feb.		L3	
Goodloe, Joseph	9, July 1857		probate	L3	
Goodlow, (child of Hannah)	13, Feb. 1845	Feb.	1m	L3	
Goodman, Blanche Foster	9, Aug. 1855	21, July		L3	
Goodman, Edwin Adams	10, Feb. 1848	31, Jan.	5m	L3	
Goodman, Harriet W.	10, Oct. 1850	1, Oct.	51	L3	

Name	Notice Date	Death Date	Age		Page	Maiden Name
Goodman, Horace H.	11, Jan. 1849	3, Jan.	63		L3	
Goodman, Maria M.	23, Nov. 1848	20, Nov.	53		L3	
Goodman, Mary	26, July 1849	20, July	infant		L3	
Goodman, Mary	2, Oct. 1834	Sept	6m		L4	
Goodman, Mary Tarbell	25, Apr. 1844	15, Apr.	7		L3	
Goodman, Thomas	16, Sept 1847	Sept	25		L3	
Goodman, William Austin	25, Apr. 1844	15, Apr.	5		L3	
Goodrich, Jeremiah	9, May 1844		estate		L3	
Goodrich, Jeremiah	20, Feb. 1845		estate		L3	
Goodrich, Jeremiah	20, May 1812		estate		L4	
Goodrich, Sarah Amanda	17, July 1845	7, July	1- 8m		L3	
Goodridge, Luther C.	22, Aug. 1839	13, Aug.	19	*	L3	
Goods, Peter	26, Jan. 1837	Jan.	40		L3	
Goodson, Margaret	12, Mar. 1846	17, Mar.	30		L3	
Goodspede, William	16, Mar. 1849	Mar.	4		L3	
Goodwin, Edward	1, Aug. 1833	July	35		L1	
Goodwin, Edward	19, July 1849	July	35		L3	
Goodwin, Harriet	23, Apr. 1846	20, Apr.	36		L3	
Goodwin, James K.	25, Sept 1845	24, Sept	34		L3	
Goodwin, John	28, Aug. 1834	Aug.	9m		L1	
Goodwin, Marietta Sophia	11, May 1843	25, Apr.	25- 6m		L3	
Goodwin, Mary	13, Nov. 1834	Nov.	1m		L1	
Goodwin, Mary	11, July 1844	July	9d		L3	
Goodwin, Nathan	11, Feb. 1841	Feb.	17		L3	
Goodwin, Oliver (Dr)	15, Mar. 1838	11, Mar.	78		L3	
Goor, Wlater	5, Feb. 1857	29, Jan.	24	*	L3	
Gorden, J.	12, Aug. 1847	Aug.	45		L3	
Gorden, Mary	23, Mar. 1848	Mar.	38		L3 ,	
Gorden, Rosetta	20, July 1848	July	9m		L3	
Gorden, William	3, Jan. 1833	Dec.	3- 6m		L4	
Gordon, (child)	8, Nov. 1832	Nov.	1- 6m		L1	
Gordon, Archibald	12, June 1845		estate		L3	
Gordon, Archibald	4, Feb. 1836	20, Jan.			L4	
Gordon, Edmond Wood	7, July 1842	3, July	4- 8m- 4d		L3	
Gordon, Elizabeth P.	2, May 1833	Apr.	10m		L1	
Gordon, George	29, Dec. 1842	21, Dec.	79		L3	
Gordon, George	14, Feb. 1839		probate		L3	
Gordon, George	3, Sept 1840		probate		L3	
Gordon, H.G.	21, Sept 1837		probate		L4	
Gordon, Henry	13, Nov. 1850	Nov.	30		L3	
Gordon, Horatio G.	7, Aug. 1834	July	28- 3m		L3	
Gordon, Horatio G.	9, Aug. 1838		probate		L3	
Gordon, Horatio G.	4, Sept 1834		estate		L4	
Gordon, Mary	24, May 1849	20, May			L3	
Gordon, Mary F.	2, Aug. 1855		estate		L3	
Gordon, Mary F.	9, Aug. 1855		probate		L3	
Gordon, Mary R.	25, Apr. 1833	Apr.	6m		L1	
Gordon, Peggy	23, Nov. 1843	Nov.	54		L3	
Gordon, Sally W.	9, Mar. 1819	6, Mar.			L3	
Gordon, Susan	29, June 1848	June	8m		L3	
Gordon, Thomas Phillips	29, June 1843	28, June	19m		L3	
Gordon, William L.	6, Aug. 1857		probate		L3	
Gores, S.	15, Aug. 1833	Aug.	21		L1	
Gorham, Parsons	1, June 1837	31, May	60		L3	

Name	Notice Date	Death Date	Age		Page	Maiden Name
Gorman, Catharine	10, Apr. 1851	Apr.	5w		L3	
Gorman, Daniel	6, Jan. 1848	Dec.	58		L3	
Gorman, Edward	18, May 1848	May	35		L3	
Gorman, Henry B.	20, June 1850		estate		L3	
Gorman, Hugh	5, Mar. 1857		probate		L3	
Gorman, James	5, Nov. 1857		probate		L3	
Gorman, James	5, June 1851	27, May			L3	
Gorman, James	1, Sept 1853	20, Aug.			L3	
Gorman, John	8, Aug. 1833	July	37		L1	
Gorman, Patrick	23, Sept 1847	Sept	20		L3	
Gorman, William	5, Sept 1844	27, Aug.	26m		L3	
Gormly, B.	18, Apr. 1839		probate		L3	
Gorrell, Joseph H.	12, Dec. 1839		estate		L1	
Goshorn, Adelia Ann	19, Dec. 1844	16, Nov.	20		L3	
Goshorn, Anthony H.	13, Sept 1832	Sept	10m-12d		L1	
Goshorn, William, Jr.	5, June 1851	29, May			L3	
Goslin, (child of Mr.)	2, Aug. 1832	July			L1	
Gosman, Catharine	18, July 1833	July	25		L2	
Gosman, Samuel	16, Oct. 1834	Oct.	26		L1	
Gossin, Eldora	22, June 1854	16, June	2- 5m		L3	
Gottermutte, Philip	22, Oct. 1840	Oct.	28		L3	
Gottschalk, Augustus	12, July 1849	July	23		L3	
Goudy, Samuel	29, May 1834		probate		L3	
Goudy, William	20, June 1850	June	37		L3	
Gouge, Benjamin	27, Nov. 1834	Nov.	35		L1	
Gough, Edward Purcell	6, July 1854	28, June	3m-27d		L3	
Goulcher, Emanuel	24, June 1841		estate		L3	
Goulcher, Emanuel	7, July 1842		estate		L3	
Goulcher, Rebecca	7, July 1842		estate		L3	
Gould, Albert Stone	18, Sept 1851	10, Sept	1- 2m- 1d		L3	
Gould, Annie Lizzie	15, Oct. 1857	11, Oct.	3- 9m- 6d		L3	
Gould, Jesse	25, Jan. 1838	12, Jan.	82	*	L3	
Gould, John Calvin	27, Nov. 1856	20, Nov.	13m		L3	
Gould, Lauretha Theresa	29, July 1852	20, July	1w- 5d		L3	
Gould, Nathan	13, Oct. 1821		estate		L3	
Gould, Nathan	7, Sept 1824		probate		L3	
Goulden, Joanna	5, Aug. 1852	July	28		L3	
Goulding, James	30, Mar. 1813		estate		L2	
Gourdin, L.J.	5, Dec. 1833		estate		L3	
Gourdin, L.J.	6, Nov. 1834		estate		L3	
Gourdin, Lewis J.	28, May 1840		estate		L3	
Gourdin, Louis J.	1, Nov. 1832	24, Oct.			L1	
Gourgas, J.M.	31, Dec. 1846		81	*	L3	
Gourgas, Jacob	17, Nov. 1821	16, Nov.			L3	
Gove, Amos	19, May 1853	15, May	55		L3	
Gove, Ann Eliza	25, Jan. 1838	20, Jan.	6		L3	
Gove, Lucinda Maria	25, Jan. 1838	16, Jan.	4		L3	
Govels, James	11, July 1850	July	32		L3	
Goves, Amos	9, June 1853		estate		L3	
Gowdy, Catharine	23, Oct. 1834	Oct.	71		L2	
Gowdy, Samuel	11, July 1833		probate		L3	
Gowdy, Theodore	25, July 1850	23, July	45		L3	
Gowern, Jane	1, Aug. 1844	July	42		L3	
Gowers, Sarah Jane	19, July 1832	July	9m- 3d		L1	

Name	Notice Date	Death Date	Age	Page	Maiden Name
Gowey, John	18, July 1850	July	14m	L3	
Grace, (Mrs)	25, Oct. 1832	18, Oct.		L1	
Grace, John W.	8, Nov. 1855	probate		L3	
Grace, John W.	4, Sept 1856	probate		L5	
Grade, James M.	24, May 1849	May	50	L3	
Grady, Matthew	31, May 1849	May	28	L3	
Graff, David McKnight	16, Apr. 1846	10, Apr.	8	L3	
Graff, Mary A.	3, Sept 1857	26, Aug.	6m-27d	L3	
Grafflen, Lizzie R.	16, July 1857	14, July	13	L3	
Grafton, Mary	25, July 1850	July	18	L3	
Graham, Archibald	9, Feb. 1832	7, Feb.	22	L1	
Graham, Elizabeth	28, July 1817	21, July		L3	
Graham, Ellen F.	23, 30, Oct. 1856	21, Oct.		L5	
Graham, George (Major)	27, June 1839	11, June	74	L3	
Graham, James	23, Mar. 1848	Mar.	33	L3	
Graham, John	27, Feb. 1851	Feb.	30	L3	
Graham, John	9, Nov. 1837	18, Oct.	42	L4	
Graham, Maria Espy	27, Apr. 1843	25, Apr.	1- -20d	L3	
Graham, Mary Jane	31, Mar. 1836	29, Mar.		L3	
Graham, Mary L.	3, Aug. 1843	20, July		L3	
Graham, Ruth	18, July 1833	July	30	L2	
Graham, Thomas	10, Oct. 1844	estate		L3	
Graham, William Ridgely	2, Oct. 1851	24, Sept	23	L3	
Graif, Henry	15, July 1852	9, July		L3	
Granden, A.P.	22, Jan. 1852	20, Jan.		L3	
Grandin, Philip Augustus	24, June 1847	20, June	14	L3	
Granes, Frederic	25, July 1833	July	24	L1	
Grange, Ann	15, Aug. 1833	Aug.	1- 1m	L1	
Granger, Ralph	21, Dec. 1843	7, Dec.	53	L3	
Grannahan, John	10, Aug. 1843	Aug.	24	L3	
Grant, Alexander	17, Jan. 1850	estate		L3	
Grant, Alfred	30, Aug. 1849	Aug.	30	L3	
Grant, Benjamin	18, Oct. 1832	12, Oct.		L2	
Grant, Benjamin	27, Dec. 1832	estate		L3	
Grant, John	22, Feb. 1844	Feb.	29	L3	
Grant, William	6, Sept 1827	estate		L2	
Grant, William	25, Oct. 1849	estate		L3	
Grant, William	13, June 1850	estate		L3	
Grany, Mary	17, May 1849	May	3	L3	
Graves, Frances	15, Sept 1853	10, Sept		L3	
Graves, George	11, Dec. 1851	10, Dec.		L4	
Graves, Margaret H.	29, Aug. 1833	Aug.	16- 5m	L1	
Graves, William	21, Sept 1848	Sept	21	L3	
Graveson, Charles Wilson	29, Oct. 1857	23, Oct.	4- -10d	L3	
Gray, Cynthia Raymond	30, Mar. 1854	28, Mar.	28	L3	
Gray, David	5, Mar. 1857	probate		L3	
Gray, Elizabeth Thurston	20, May 1852	18, May	19	L3	
Gray, James	18, July 1833	July	22	L2	
Gray, James	9, Oct. 1845	Sept	32	L3	
Gray, James	14, Mar. 1844	Mar.	37	L3	
Gray, James R.	17, Sept 1846	Sept	11m	L3	
Gray, John D.	19, Jan. 1843	9, Jan.		L3	
Gray, Joseph	28, Nov. 1844	19, Nov.	38	L3	
Gray, Joseph	13, July 1843	July	65	L3	

Name	Notice Date	Death Date	Age	Page	Maiden Name
Gray, Julia Stone	10, Sept 1857	3, Sept	4m	L3	
Gray, Martin	4, Nov. 1841	Oct.	55	L3	
Gray, Michael	27, Feb. 1851	Feb.	13	L3	
Gray, Samuel	9, June 1836		probate	L3	
Grayson, William	26, Nov. 1808	3, Nov.	28	L3	
Grealy, Mary	21, June 1849	June	19	L3	
Greathouse, James	21, Sept 1843	Sept	18m	L3	
Greeley, Arthur Young	26, July 1849	12, July	4- 3m	L3	
Green, (Miss)	15, Mar. 1855	14, Mar.		L3	
Green, Alfred	31, Aug. 1822	3, July	*	L3	
Green, Andrew	12, Aug. 1841	Aug.	29	L3	
Green, Dixon	3, Sept 1808		estate	L2	
Green, George	18, July 1850	July	35	L3	
Green, George	18, Oct. 1832	Oct.	2- 6m	L4	
Green, Gustavus	23, Oct. 1834	Oct.	1- 6m	L2	
Green, Joseph	30, Jan. 1845	Jan.	57	L3	
Green, Lorenzo	10, Aug. 1837	July	24	L3	
Green, Maria J.	8, May 1851	7, May		L3	
Green, Marmaduke	24, Sept 1846	16, Sept	64	L3	
Green, Mary A.	1, Jan. 1852			L3	
Green, Michael	22, Mar. 1838		probate	L3	
Green, Silas	5, May 1831		estate	L3	
Green, William	11, July 1833	July		L1	
Greenbed, Mary	12, Sept 1833	Sept	1- 6m	L1	
Greene, Elizabeth	4, Jan. 1832	1, Jan.		L3	
Greene, Emma	1, June 1848	29, May	3	L3	
Greene, Maria T.	1, July 1841	26, June	31- 9m	L3	
Greene, Philip	28, Apr. 1807	9, Apr.		L3	
Greene, Thomas	19, Nov. 1824	20, Oct.		L3	
Greene, William	11, Oct. 1838		estate	L3	
Greener, John	27, Oct. 1831		probate	L1	
Greener, John	3, Nov. 1831		estate	L4	
Greenham, Daniel	15, Mar. 1814		estate	L3	
Greenham, Joseph	17, Jan. 1850		estate	L3	
Greenham, Joseph	21, Aug. 1856		estate	L5	
Greenleaf, Hannah	15, Jan. 1857	13, Jan.	69	L3	
Greenleaf, James	28, Sept 1843	17, Sept	78	L3	
Greenleaf, Samuel	19, Aug. 1847	Aug.	52	L3	
Greenlee, John	30, June 1842	June	40	L3	
Greenup, George	5, Nov. 1857		probate	L3	
Greenwald, John	8, July 1852	30, June		L3	
Greenwood, Howard Whales	10, Sept 1835	31, Aug.	23	L1	Hill
Greenwood, Margaret Howard	14, Apr. 1842	5, Apr.	7	L3	
Greer, Dixon	11, May 1824		estate	L3	
Greer, James P.	27, Oct. 1831		probate	L1	
Greer, James P.	6, Aug. 1829		estate	L3	
Greer, John	3, Mar. 1817		estate	L4	
Greer, John	11, Mar. 1823		estate	L4	
Greer, Samuel	12, Mar. 1840	Mar.	30	L3	
Greery, Bartley	21, Apr. 1853	15, Apr.	26	L3	
Gregg, Aaron (Capt)	8, Jan. 1805			L3	
Gregg, Amos	21, Sept 1837		probate	L4	
Gregg, Ann Eliza	27, May 1847	24, May	33-11m-17d	L3	
Gregg, Charlotte	18, July 1844	14, July	19	L3	

Name	Notice Date	Death Date	Age	Page	Maiden Name
Gregg, David B.	28, Feb. 1850		estate	L3	
Gregg, George W.	7, May 1846	Apr.	2	L3	
Gregg, Thomas M.	16, Nov. 1843	30, Oct.		L3	
Gregg, Thomas R.	27, Sept 1827		65	L1	
Gregg, William (Rev)	8, Jan. 1857	27, Dec.	92- 7m	L3	
Greggs, Herman	7, Oct. 1847	Sept	34	L3	
Gregory, Caroline H.	28, Oct. 1852	24, Oct.		L3	
Gregory, Elizabeth R.	25, July 1844	14, July	28	L3	
Gregory, Ellen Antoinette	23, July 1840	15, July		L3	
Gregory, Henry Hill	26, Dec. 1850	18, Dec.		L3	
Gregory, Henry M.	2, Aug. 1849	29, July	65	L3	
Gregory, Presley	24, Mar. 1853	17, Mar.	90	L3	
Gregory, Sarah	16, Jan. 1851	11, Jan.		L3	
Gregory, Thomas	25, July 1844	15, July	10	L3	
Gregory, Walter	1, Oct. 1857	21, Sept	45	L3	
Gribbald, John	18, Oct. 1832	Oct.		L3	
Gribble, Benjamin	25, July 1839	July	22	L3	
Gridwold, Stanley	9, Oct. 1815	21, Aug.		L3	
Griffin, Bridget	14, June 1849	June	20	L3	
Griffin, D.	5, Mar. 1857		probate	L3	
Griffin, David	6, Mar. 1856		probate	L3	
Griffin, David	9, Nov. 1854	6, Nov.		L3	
Griffin, James	15, May 1834		estate	L3	
Griffin, John	20, Sept 1849	Sept	22	L3	
Griffin, John	23, Mar. 1854	6, Mar.	27- 5m-27d	L3	
Griffin, Peter	9, July 1857		probate	L3	
Griffin, Rosetta	14, June 1849	June	9	L3	
Griffin, Thomas	28, Nov. 1850	Nov.	35	L3	
Griffin, Wineford	5, Sept 1850	Aug.	2	L3	
Griffith, (child of Jane)	23, Mar. 1849	Mar.	1w	L3	
Griffith, (son of Lewis R.)	17, Oct. 1850		4	L3	
Griffith, Benjamin	28, Jan. 1841	Jan.	25	L3	
Griffith, Benjamin	9, Aug. 1838		probate	L3	
Griffith, John	26, Feb. 1852	15, Feb.		L3	
Griffith, Maria	21, June 1849	June	30	L3	
Griffith, Mary	31, Oct. 1833	Oct.	56	L4	
Griffith, Samuel T.	3, May 1855		probate	L3	
Griffith, William	24, Sept 1846		estate	L3	
Griffith, William	21, Sept 1837		probate	L4	
Griffiths, William	7, Aug. 1834	July	24	L3	
Grigar, Margaret	5, July 1849	June	2w	L3	
Griggs, Jane	5, July 1849	June	24	L3	
Grim, Charles	22, Jan. 1816			L1	
Grima, (child of John)	8, Oct. 1846	Sept	stillborn	L3	
Grimes, Edward	10, Mar. 1853	Feb.	56	L3	
Grimes, James	9, June 1836		probate	L3	
Grimes, John T.	27, Apr. 1848	Apr.	infant	L3	
Grimes, Robert	24, June 1841		estate	L3	
Grimes, Robert F.	8, July 1841		estate	L3	
Grimes, Robert F.	11, Apr. 1844		estate	L3	
Grinck, Conrad	5, May 1853	4, May		L3	
Griner, (Mr. & Mrs.)	5, May 1853			L1	
Grismore, George	23, Feb. 1837		probate	L3	
Grismore, George	8, Nov. 1838		probate	L3	

Name	Notice Date	Death Date	Age	Page	Maiden Name
Grisson, (man)	10, May 1849	May		L3	
Grisson, Henrietta	10, May 1849	May	28	L3	
Gristall, Margaret	12, July 1849	July		L3	
Griswald, James F.	13, Nov. 1811	16, Oct.	22	L3	
Griswold, Elizabeth	11, Sept 1822	18, Aug.	62	L3	
Griswold, Nathaniel	3, Sept 1846	Aug.	74	L3	
Groben, Christopher	21, Feb. 1850		estate	L3	
Groeninger, Louis	5, Mar. 1857		probate	L3	
Groep, (child)	22, Aug. 1833	Aug.	stillborn	L4	
Groesbeck, (child)	23, Oct. 1834	Oct.		L2	
Groesbeck, Jacob Burnet	12, Feb. 1846	4, Feb.	3- 5m	L3	
Groesbeck, John H.	3, Feb. 1848	30, Jan.	4- -24d	L3	
Groesbeck, Mary	14, Sept 1854	6, Sept	60	L3	
Groesbeck, Mary A.	16, Dec. 1852	7, Dec.	14- 2m	L3	
Groesbeck, William J.	16, Oct. 1845	9, Oct.	10m	L3	
Groff, Sarah	18, July 1833	July	6m	L2	
Groff, Sarah	21, Nov. 1833		estate	L3	
Groff, Sarah	13, Feb. 1840		probate	L3	
Grogan, George	7, May 1857		probate	L3	
Grogan, George L.	6, Mar. 1856		probate	L3	
Grogan, Maria	20, Oct. 1853	12, Oct.	30	L3	
Grogan, Mary E.	6, Nov. 1845	Oct.	1- 6m	L3	
Gronan, Edward	27, Sept 1849	Sept	35	L3	
Groshon, Belinda	2, Feb. 1822	31, Jan.		L3	
Gross, (boy)	9, Aug. 1849	4, Aug.		L2	
Gross, Augustus G.	6, May 1847	29, Apr.		L3	
Gross, Jacob	11, Mar. 1841	Feb.		L3	
Gross, John	18, Feb. 1847	9, Feb.	39	* L3	
Gross, John	3, June 1847		estate	L3	
Gross, John Woodward	8, Dec. 1836	3, Dec.	21m	L2	
Gross, Julia Augusta	1, Mar. 1838	24, Feb.	9	L3	
Gross, Veronica	8, May 1851	30, Apr.		L3	
Grotgan, Dederick	24, Sept 1846	Sept	28	L3	
Grougple, Ellen	1, Aug. 1850	July	46	L3	
Grove, Clement	24, Sept 1846	Sept	25	L3	
Grover, Adam	8, Oct. 1857		probate	L3	
Grover, Hepza Dana	3, Oct. 1844	30, Sept	20	L3	Andrews
Grow, George	1, Aug. 1839	July	22	L3	
Growschytz, John	2, Nov. 1843	Oct.	28	L3	
Gruba, Sabina	5, July 1849	June	53	L3	
Grube, John	7, Mar. 1850	Feb.	21	L3	
Grube, Louis	29, Aug. 1850	Aug.	30	L3	
Gruple, Jacob	16, Nov. 1848	Nov.	40	L3	
Gschwind, Maria	7, Aug. 1834	July	25	L3	
Guard, John	8, Nov. 1855		probate	L3	
Guav, (child)	4, July 1833	June		L2	
Guesnard, Marie	7, Apr. 1836		estate	L3	
Guesnard, Marie	21, Sept 1837		probate	L4	
Guest, Henry	2, Aug. 1820	9, July	61	L3	
Guest, James	8, Aug. 1810		estate	L2	
Guest, Lydia	12, Oct. 1822	9, Oct.	50	L3	
Guian, Michael	5, Dec. 1850	Nov.	18	L3	
Guibert, Henry	13, Mar. 1851	4, Mar.	21- 5m	L3	
Guider, Abraham	31, May 1849	May	20	L3	

Name	Notice Date	Death Date	Age		Page	Maiden Name
Guidi, Nelly Allen	27, Aug. 1857	18, Aug.	19m-29d		L3	
Guier, Anthony	7, Sept 1848	Aug.	52		L3	
Guiges, (Mr)	31, May 1820	30, Apr.			L3	
Guild, Hester Louisa	21, Aug. 1856	18, Aug.	13m		L5	
Guild, Malinda	14, Aug. 1856	12, Aug.			L5	
Guilford, Nathan	21, Dec. 1854	18, Dec.	68		L3	
Guilmartin, William X.	25, July 1844	19, July	22		L3	
Guilmartin, William X.	12, Sept 1844				L3	
Guin, Eleanor	18, Sept 1834	Sept	41-10m-18d		L1	
Guion, Benjamin Coombs	28, June 1849	24, June	31		L3	
Guion, David Barton	22, Jan. 1852	15, Jan.	14m		L3	
Guiou, Susan	18, Oct. 1849	14, Oct.	6m-22d		L3	
Gule, Levin	8, Aug. 1833	July	20		L1	
Gulick, John	24, May 1838	14, May	72	*	L3	
Gulick, John	3, Sept 1840		probate		L3	
Gunckel, Elizabeth	7, Jan. 1847	30, Dec.	40		L3	
Gunkel, (man)	20, Apr. 1854	18, Apr.			L3	
Gunn, Sarah	18, Oct. 1832	10, Oct.			L4	
Gunning, Robert	16, Feb. 1827		probate		L3	
Gunsaulis, Elizabeth	3, Jan. 1833	Dec.	52		L4	
Gury, Charles	26, Aug. 1847	17, Aug.	1- 3m		L3	
Gusling, Elizabeth	9, Aug. 1849	July	28		L3	
Guthrie, (son of Pres.)	2, June 1853	31, May	10		L3	
Guthrie, Elizabeth	25, July 1850	19, July		*	L3	
Guthrie, George	14, Aug. 1851	8, Aug.	8		L3	
Guthrie, Hannah	28, July 1817	23, July			L3	
Guthrie, James	10, Aug. 1837	July	25		L3	
Guthrie, Martha	28, May 1846	21, May	60	*	L3	
Guthrie, P.N. (Capt)	31, Dec. 1857	29, Dec.	38		L3	
Guthrie, Robert (Capt)	14, Apr. 1842	13, Apr.	59		L3	
Guthrie, William W.	24, Dec. 1857				L3	
Guy, Fred.	18, Oct. 1832	11, Oct.			L1	
Gwaltney, Josiah	25, July 1823	14, July	51		L3	
Gwin, James	2, Aug. 1832	July	1- 7m		L1	
Gwinn, Mary Flagg	1, Sept 1842	18, Aug.	18m- 8d		L3	
Gwynne, (child of Matilda)	9, Dec. 1847	Dec.	4w		L3	
Gwynne, A.E.	3, Feb. 1855	30, Jan.			L3	
Gwynne, David (Major)	30, Aug. 1849	21, Aug.			L3	
Gwynne, Elizabeth	29, Apr. 1847	16, Apr.	88		L3	
Gwynne, Lewellyn M.	10, Jan. 1856		estate		L3	
Gwynne, Llewellen M.	12, Mar. 1857		estate		L3	
Gwynne, Lwellynn M.	13, Dec. 1855		48		L3	
Gwynne, Martha Ann	6, Apr. 1843	3, Apr.			L3	
Gwynne, Thomas	8, July 1825	5, July			L3	
Haak, John	28, Mar. 1839	Mar.	21		L3	
Habersham, Joseph (Col)	22, Jan. 1816	18, Nov.	65		L1	
Habig, Anthony	7, June 1855		probate		L3	
Habig, Wendel	7, Feb. 1856		probate		L3	
Hack, George	6, June 1850	May	37		L3	
Hackel, Catherine	28, June 1849	June	3		L3	
Hacket, Casper H.	5, Nov. 1857		probate		L3	
Hacket, Humphries	7, Aug. 1834	July	32		L3	
Hacket, Isaac	25, Oct. 1832	Oct.	26		L1	

Name	Notice Date	Death Date	Age		Page	Maiden Name
Hackett, Abigail	21, Sept 1843	19, Sept	58		L3	
Hackett, John	2, Mar. 1848	Feb.	36		L3	
Hacking, William	6, Sept 1849	Aug.	5		L3	
Hackman, Jacob	25, Dec. 1845	Dec.	32		L3	
Haddlesey, Elizabeth	28, June 1849	22, June	22		L3	
Haddlesey, Elizabeth Ann	13, Apr. 1848	5, Apr.	2-11m		L3	
Haddox, S.M.	10, Aug. 1843	25, July			L3	
Hadley, John	23, June 1853				L3	
Hadley, William	27, Sept 1849	Sept	45		L3	
Hadly, M.J.	8, Aug. 1833	July	16		L1	
Haem, (son of Michael)	13, May 1852	8, May	7		L3	
Hafer, Henry	19, Apr. 1825		estate		L3	
Hafer, Henry	9, Feb. 1837		estate		L3	
Hafer, Henry	22, Mar. 1838		estate		L3	
Hafer, Mary	6, Oct. 1807	4, Oct.			L3	
Hafer, Rosana	5, June 1822	22, May	78	*	L3	
Hafien, Andrew	23, Oct. 1834	Oct.	33		L2	
Hafley, William	1, Aug. 1833	July	4		L1	
Hagal, George	19, July 1849	July	43		L3	
Hagal, Margaret	27, Aug. 1846	Aug.	44		L3	
Hagan, Charles	6, Sept 1849	Aug.	50		L3	
Hagan, Eliza	14, Sept 1843	Sept	48		L3	
Hagan, Margaret	11, Apr. 1850	Apr.	1		L3	
Haganson, William	25, Apr. 1850	Apr.	24		L3	
Hagar, Phebe Ann	4, Oct. 1849	Sept	48		L3	
Hageman, A.S.	8, Jan. 1857		probate		L3	
Hageman, Adrian	3, Oct. 1810		estate		L4	
Hageman, Adrian S.	6, Mar. 1856		estate		L3	
Hageman, Christian	27, July 1813	4, July	37		L3	
Hageman, Christian	23, Feb. 1837		probate		L3	
Hagerman, Adrian	26, Sept 1826		probate		L3	
Hagerty, John H.	24, Dec. 1840	17, Dec.	45		L3	
Hagerty, Patrick	14, Dec. 1848	Dec.	22		L2	
Hagerty, Patrick	14, June 1855				L3	
Hagerty, William	4, July 1850	June			L3	
Haggert, John	9, Oct. 1834	Sept	41- 6m		L1	
Haggerty, Michael	26, July 1849	July	61		L3	
Hagget, Isaac	27, Nov. 1834	Nov.	39		L1	
Hahn, Max	14, Aug. 1856		probate		L6	
Hahn, Max.	9, Apr. 1857		probate		L3	
Hahn, Paul F.	7, June 1855		probate		L3	
Hahn, Stephen	9, Apr. 1857		probate		L3	
Haifleigh, Frederick	16, Mar. 1809		estate		L3	
Haifleigh, Frederick	19, Jan. 1809	16, Jan.			L3	
Hailey, James	25, Oct. 1832	19, Oct.			L2	
Hailman, Sarah	18, Apr. 1839		estate		L3	
Hailman, Simon	13, Sept 1838	6, Sept	72		L3	
Haines, Amos	24, Apr. 1822		estate		L3	
Haines, Elias H.	24, Nov. 1853	13, Nov.			L3	
Haines, Jacob	29, June 1854	17, June	77		L3	
Haines, Reuben	16, Nov. 1837	Nov.	39		L3	
Haines, Robert	20, Dec. 1825		probate		L4	
Haines, Sarah	6, June 1833	May	29- 6m		L2	
Haines, William M.	26, Dec. 1833	Dec.	9- 2m		L4	

Name	Notice Date	Death Date	Age		Page	Maiden Name
Haire, Jacob	24, June 1852	1, June	62		L3	
Haire, Jacob	17, June 1852		estate		L3	
Haire, Jacob	10, Nov. 1853		estate		L3	
Haire, Thomas	18, June 1846	1, June	27		L3	
Haire, Thomas	2, July 1846	June			L3	
Hait, Henry	30, Jan. 1851		estate		L3	
Hale, John (Rev)	25, Jan. 1838	Jan.		*	L3	
Hale, Samuel W. Jackson	10, Nov. 1842	3, Nov.	6- -11d		L4	
Hale, Thomas	11, Feb. 1841	1, Feb.	60	*	L3	
Hales, Mary Ann	17, Aug. 1848	10, Aug.	44		L3	
Haley, Anne	30, Aug. 1838	Aug.	5m		L3	
Haley, Ellen	12, Oct. 1848	Oct.	6w		L3	
Haley, Michael	13, Sept 1849	Sept	24		L3	
Halfield, Anna Maria	20, June 1844	19, June	infant		L3	
Halfolder, John	26, Oct. 1848	Oct.	28		L3	
Hall, (Mrs)	18, Oct. 1832	12, Oct.			L1	
Hall, (Mrs)	19, Jan. 1843	3, Jan.			L3	Prince
Hall, Alice E.	20, Mar. 1845	18, Mar.	4- 9m		L3	
Hall, Anna L.	19, Aug. 1852	15, Aug.	53		L3	
Hall, Charles	18, Oct. 1849	Oct.	30		L3	
Hall, Charles	12, Mar. 1846	Mar.	9m		L3	
Hall, Dudley	13, Nov. 1851	3, Nov.	11m		L3	
Hall, Eliza M.	8, Apr. 1847	1, Apr.	32		L3	
Hall, Elizabeth	7, Aug. 1834	July	29		L3	
Hall, Elizabeth	1, Apr. 1847	Mar.	34		L3	
Hall, Elizabeth	14, June 1849	June	1w		L3	
Hall, Elizabeth	1, May 1811	Apr.			L3	
Hall, Elizabeth	9, June 1842	May		.	L3	
Hall, Harvey	4, Dec. 1851		estate		L3	
Hall, Harvey	9, Nov. 1848	8, Nov.			L3	
Hall, Hetty Jane	29, Sept 1853	14, Sept			L3	
Hall, James	19, July 1849	July	33		L3	
Hall, James	13, Jan. 1848	Jan.	82		L3	
Hall, James	11, Sept 1845	9, Sept	7m		L3	
Hall, James C.	8, Sept 1853	1, Sept			L3	
Hall, Jane	27, Jan. 1824				L3	
Hall, Joseph	27, Apr. 1848	Apr.	27		L3	
Hall, Lizzie	29, Jan. 1857	25, Jan.	2- 4m		L3	
Hall, Malinda	14, Feb. 1833	Feb.	5		L1	
Hall, Nancy	11, Oct. 1832	7, Oct.			L2	
Hall, Nancy	18, Oct. 1832	Oct.	34		L4	
Hall, Nancy Jane	31, Aug. 1837	Aug.	5		L4	
Hall, Samuel	14, Nov. 1839		estate		L3	
Hall, Samuel M.	1, Jan. 1829		estate		L3	
Hall, Stephen	27, Oct. 1831		probate		L1	
Hall, Stephen	25, Dec. 1828	25, Dec.			L4	
Hall, Stephen M.	11, Feb. 1847	5, Feb.	46	*	L3	
Hall, William	18, May 1854	12, May			L3	
Hall, William Oliver	30, May 1839	18, May	8m		L2	
Hallam, Mary	26, Nov. 1857	18, Nov.			L3	Rainey
Hallam, Sarah	23, July 1824	15, July	42		L3	
Hallam, Sidney Ann	13, Dec. 1849	7, Dec.	32		L3	Gilpin
Hallam, Thomas	12, Mar. 1857	9, Mar.	9- 7m- 9d		L3	
Haller, Elizabeth	9, July 1857		probate		L3	

Name	Notice Date	Death Date	Age	Page	Maiden Name
Haller, Peter	9, July 1857		probate	L3	
Halley, (child of Washington)	29, Aug. 1833	Aug.		L1	
Halley, Allen	13, Jan. 1807	4, Jan.	18	L3	
Halley, David S.	22, Dec. 1842	19, Dec.	52	L3	
Halley, Eliza J.	14, Mar. 1833	Mar.	5-11m	L1	
Halley, Hillory	17, Feb. 1848	Feb.	58	L3	
Halley, Josiah	21, Mar. 1821		estate	L4	
Halley, Josiah (Major)	11, Nov. 1816	6, Nov.		L3	
Halley, Margueretta	25, Mar. 1847	23, Mar.	77	L3	
Halley, Maria	30, July 1819	28, July		L3	
Halley, Samuel	21, Sept 1813		estate	L1	
Halley, Samuel	20, Jan. 1817		estate	L3	
Halley, Samuel (Capt)	20, May 1812	26, Apr.	47	L3	
Halley, Washington G.	20, Mar. 1856	11, Mar.	51	L3	
Halley, Washington G.	14, May 1857		estate	L3	
Halley, Washington G.	10, Sept 1857		probate	L3	
Hallgath, John	3, May 1855	24, Apr.	74	* L3	
Halliday, Horace C.	12, July 1849	6, July	6w- 5d	L3	
Halliday, James P.	2, Nov. 1843	20, Oct.	20	L3	
Halpin, (child of Eliza)	24, Oct. 1839	Sept	3w	L3	
Halpin, Eliza	31, Oct. 1839	Oct.	21	L3	
Halsey, John B.	24, Oct. 1844	13, Sept	31	L3	
Halsey, Luther	24, Jan. 1833		estate	L4	
Halstead, James	5, Feb. 1816		estate	L3	
Halstein, Joseph	16, Oct. 1851	10, Oct.		L3	
Hambo, Stephen	10, Sept 1857		probate	L3	
Hamer, Caroline M.	28, Dec. 1848	Dec.	3m	L3	
Hamer, Christiana	24, July 1845	July	40	L3	
Hamer, Lydia B.	16, Jan. 1845	3, Jan.		L3	
Hamer, Matthias	24, July 1845	July	36	L3	
Hamer, Thomas M.	28, Aug. 1851			L3	
Hamilton, (child of Alexander)	27, Feb. 1845	Feb.	stillborn	L3	
Hamilton, (child of Ann)	22, May 1845	May	stillborn	L3	
Hamilton, (child of H.)	15, Oct. 1857	11, Oct.		L3	
Hamilton, Andrew	23, Mar. 1843		estate	L3	
Hamilton, Charles	26, July 1849	July	22	L3	
Hamilton, Charles	31, May 1849	May	55	L3	
Hamilton, Charles	4, July 1850	June	75	L3	
Hamilton, Charles	27, June 1850			L3	
Hamilton, Edward	18, Oct. 1849	Oct.	39	L3	
Hamilton, Edward	25, Mar. 1847	17, Mar.	53	L3	
Hamilton, Edwin S.	12, Mar. 1857	8, Mar.		L3	
Hamilton, Israel	20, Oct. 1842	11, Oct.		L3	
Hamilton, Jacob	27, Oct. 1842	Oct.	30	L3	
Hamilton, James	23, Oct. 1834	Oct.	12	L2	
Hamilton, James	8, June 1837	June	28	L2	
Hamilton, James	17, May 1849	May	29	L3	
Hamilton, Joanna	10, Oct. 1844	6, Oct.	69	L3	
Hamilton, John	30, July 1840	11, July	27	L3	
Hamilton, John	23, Mar. 1849	Mar.	40	L3	
Hamilton, John	26, Feb. 1852	Feb.	29	L4	
Hamilton, Lewis L.	13, Sept 1832	Sept	33- 7m	L1	
Hamilton, Margaret	25, Dec. 1811	4, Nov.		L3	
Hamilton, Martha Ludlow	2, Sept 1852	29, Aug.		L3	

Name	Notice Date	Death Date	Age		Page	Maiden Name
Hamilton, Mary T.	13, July 1843	11, July	20		L3	
Hamilton, Matilda	8, July 1852	1, July			L3	
Hamilton, Paul	29, July 1816	30, June			L3	
Hamilton, Ruth	11, Oct. 1832	5, Oct.			L2	
Hamilton, Samuel	22, Aug. 1850	Aug.	40		L3	
Hamilton, Stephen	25, Jan. 1849	Jan.	49		L3	
Hamilton, William	15, Mar. 1838	Mar.	8		L3	
Hamilton, William	1, Nov. 1832	18, Oct.	14		L3	
Hamline, Mary Adelia	27, Mar. 1845	21, Mar.	infant		L3	
Hamm, George	10, May 1849	May			L3	
Hammer, Conrad	1, June 1854	26, May	27		L3	
Hammon, (child of Aaron)	17, Oct. 1844	Oct.	stillborn		L3	
Hammond, (woman)	11, Sept 1851	3, Sept			L4	
Hammond, C.	11, June 1840		estate		L3	
Hammond, Charles	9, Apr. 1840	Apr.	61	*	L3	
Hammond, Ellen	15, Aug. 1833	Aug.	36		L1	
Hammond, Henry	29, Oct. 1829	22, Oct.	20		L3	
Hammond, John	28, June 1849	June	75		L3	
Hammond, Joseph	6, July 1848	3, July	58		L3	
Hammond, Mary	9, Aug. 1849	July	55		L3	
Hammond, Michael	10, May 1849	May	40		L3	
Hammond, Nancy	17, Aug. 1848	15, Aug.	65		L3	
Hammond, Nancy	16, Nov. 1848		estate		L3	
Hammond, Sally C.	1, Aug. 1826	31, July			L3	
Hammond, Theodore W.	26, Feb. 1857	24, Feb.	23	*	L3	
Hammond, Timothy	7, Aug. 1834	July	43		L3	
Hammond, Timothy	4, Sept 1834		estate		L4	
Hammott, Andrew S.	7, Dec. 1843	4, Dec.	41		L3	
Hamon, (child of Aaron)	28, July 1842	July	stillborn		L3	
Hampson, James (Capt)	6, Apr. 1843	26, Mar.			L3	
Hampson, Jefferson	27, Sept 1849	21, Sept			L3	
Hams, Jacob	3, May 1855		probate		L3	
Hamtramck, John Francis (Col)	13, Sept 1827		estate		L3	
Han, (child of Mary)	14, Feb. 1833	Feb.	8d		L1	
Hanagan, Jeffrey	10, May 1849	May	18		L3	
Hanagan, Judith	18, Oct. 1849	Oct.	35		L3	
Hanahan, Cornelius	12, July 1849	July	35		L3	
Hancock, Ann	2, Apr. 1846	Mar.	4		L3	
Hancock, Edith	31, May 1849	May	44		L3	
Hancock, John	6, Oct. 1842	Sept	12		L3	
Hancock, Maria	30, Apr. 1846	Apr.	10		L3	
Hand, David	20, Aug. 1840	18, Aug.			L3	
Hand, Elmore W.	25, July 1839		estate		L3	
Hand, William	6, Aug. 1840		estate		L3	
Handland, Catharine	25, Oct. 1838	Oct.	80		L3	
Handley, Joanna	11, Feb. 1818	5, Feb.			L3	
Handley, Nathaniel P.	22, Dec. 1817	18, Dec.			L2	
Handley, Patrick	25, Oct. 1849	Oct.	32		L3	
Handy, Anna	20, Aug. 1857	17, Aug.	19m		L3	
Handy, Anna Huston	8, Feb. 1855	1, Feb.	15m-18d		L3	
Handy, Betsey	25, Apr. 1850	Apr.	82		L3	
Handy, Charles	10, Aug. 1854	4, Aug.			L3	
Handy, Edward J.	3, Apr. 1856	31, Mar.	34		L3	
Handy, Henry	20, Nov. 1845	12, Nov.			L3	

Name	Notice Date	Death Date	Age		Page	Maiden Name
Handy, Thomas	10, Mar. 1853	Feb.			L3	
Haney, Charlotte	10, Apr. 1828	Apr.	10m		L1	
Hanley, James C.	16, Oct. 1834		estate		L3	
Hanly, Joseph Charles	30, July 1857	29, July	1- 9m-14d		L3	
Hanna, Charles A.	23, Nov. 1848	10, Nov.			L3	
Hanna, Henry	6, May 1847	28, Apr.	22m		L3	
Hanna, James	6, May 1847	29, Apr.	5		L3	
Hanna, John Andre (Gen)	10, Sept 1805	23, Aug.			L4	
Hannaford, Henry Stranger	7, Aug. 1856	31, July	10m- 9d		L5	
Hannefe, James	14, Feb. 1839	Feb.	43		L3	
Hanny, Patrick	11, July 1839	June	23		L3	
Hanselman, Margaret	13, Aug. 1857		90	*	L3	
Hanson, Alexander C.	11, May 1819	23, Apr.			L3	
Hanson, Charles	1, June 1843	May	29		L3	
Hanson, Elizabeth	28, Jan. 1847	Jan.	35		L3	
Hanson, Harriet	24, July 1834	8, July	19- 8m	*	L1	Case
Hany, George	15, July 1852	July	20		L3	
Hany, John Bird	4, July 1850	June	30		L3	
Harbaugh, Virginia Morgan	20, June 1844	18, June	infant		L3	
Harberer, Joseph	24, Feb. 1853	19, Feb.			L3	
Harbeson, Augusta C.	3, Nov. 1853	30, Oct.			L3	
Harbeson, James Gorman	26, Oct. 1843	25, Oct.	infant		L3	
Harbeson, Jane Morris	28, Feb. 1839	21, Feb.	3		L3	
Harbeson, Julia S.	3, Nov. 1853	29, Oct.			L3	
Harbeson, Robert White	19, Apr. 1845	11, Apr.		*	L3	
Harcoat, Richard	28, Nov. 1833	Nov.	1- -15d		L4	
Harden, Mary	16, May 1833	May	25		L1	
Hardie, John Alexis	24, July 1845	15, July	1- 8m		L3	
Hardin, Mary Ann	14, May 1846	May	30		L3	
Harding Jonathan D.	18, Apr. 1844		estate		L3	
Harding, Bernard	1, Nov. 1849	Oct.	48		L3	
Harding, Cassandra	25, Oct. 1832	16, Oct.			L4	
Harding, Charles Edwin	27, July 1854	16, July	2-11m		L3	
Harding, Columbus	21, Sept 1837	Sept	39		L4	
Harding, Frances	27, Feb. 1851	18, Feb.			L3	
Harding, Francis J.	27, July 1854	21, July	1- 4m-17d		L3	
Harding, Jonathan D.	20, Dec. 1838		estate		L3	
Harding, Jonathan D.	9, June 1853		estate		L3	
Harding, Joseph	22, Aug. 1833	Aug.	41		L4	
Harding, Josiah	29, Aug. 1833		estate		L3	
Harding, Josiah	16, Oct. 1834		estate		L3	
Harding, Louise	18, Aug. 1853	16, Aug.	infant		L3	
Harding, Mary Elizabeth	4, Dec. 1845	27, Nov.	infant		L3	
Harding, Mary P.C.	25, July 1850	20, July			L3	
Harding, Reuben	23, Nov. 1848	Nov.	79		L3	
Hardness, John	6, May 1841	Apr.	27		L3	
Hardy, Eliza Jane	30, Oct. 1856	27, Oct.			L5	
Hardy, Elizabeth	25, July 1850	15, July	56		L3	
Hardy, John	7, Dec. 1837	Nov.	37		L3	
Hardy, John Henry	5, July 1855	2, July	15m		L3	
Hare, Horace D.	29, Nov. 1832	Nov.	5		L1	
Hargeiger, Catharine	3, Sept 1857				L3	
Hargill, S. (Miss)	29, Jan. 1852	28, Jan.			L3	
Hargood, George	25, Dec. 1845	Dec.	26		L3	

Name	Notice Date	Death Date	Age		Page	Maiden Name
Hargot, (child of Nich.)	26, July 1849	July	1- 9m		L3	
Hargrave, Adelaide	24, Jan. 1850	Jan.	25		L3	
Hargraves, Ann	13, Sept 1849	10, Sept	73		L3	
Hargraves, Maxwell	16, May 1833		estate		L3	
Hargraves, Maxwell	22, Mar. 1838		probate		L3	
Harighen, James	24, July 1851	15, July			L4	
Harin, James	10, June 1847	June	30		L3	
Harker, Caroline	19, Oct. 1848	Oct.	30		L3	
Harkins, Alfred	9, Aug. 1838		probate		L3	
Harkness, Aurora	20, Mar. 1856		estate		L3	
Harkness, Eliza A.	19, July 1849	15, July	26	*	L3	Harkness
Harkness, Emma	23, Feb. 1854	18, Feb.			L3	
Harkness, Sarah Voorhees	18, Feb. 1836	16, Feb.			L3	
Harkness, William	6, Mar. 1856	3, Mar.	33		L3	
Harkness, William	5, July 1855		probate		L3	
Harkness, William	1, Dec. 1853	30, Nov.			L3	
Harlak, Anna	23, Oct. 1834	Oct.	43		L2	
Harman, Nancy	28, Aug. 1845	Aug.	33		L3	
Harner, (family of Henry)	6, June 1844	31, May			L2	
Harnes, Frederick	23, Dec. 1852				L3	
Harness, Michael	15, Sept 1836		probate		L3	
Harness, Mitchell	21, Nov. 1839		probate		L3	
Harney, Nancy	15, Aug. 1833	Aug.	20		L1	
Harper, Alexander M.	28, Mar. 1850	Mar.	35		L3	
Harper, Charles	19, July 1832	July	30		L1	
Harper, George	24, Oct. 1821	1, Aug.			L3	
Harper, James	11, July 1833		probate		L3	
Harper, James	25, Oct. 1832	21, Oct.			L3	
Harper, James	24, Oct. 1839		estate		L4	
Harper, John	10, Sept 1857		probate		L3	
Harper, Julia Ann	21, Aug. 1845	Aug.	22		L3	
Harper, Mary	19, Dec. 1826		probate		L3	
Harper, Robert	8, Apr. 1816		estate		L3	
Harper, Samuel	2, Dec. 1823		estate		L3	
Harper, William	24, Feb. 1806		estate		L3	
Harper, William	5, Aug. 1841		estate		L3	
Harran, Michael	31, May 1849	May	32		L3	
Harring, Aaron	29, Aug. 1833	Aug.	27		L1	
Harrington, John	24, Oct. 1850	Oct.	25		L3	
Harrington, William	2, Dec. 1825		estate		L3	
Harris, (child of H.)	2, May 1839	Apr.	1w		L3	
Harris, (child of James)	25, Oct. 1832	Oct.	stillborn		L1	
Harris, (child of James)	19, Sept 1833	Sept	1d		L4	
Harris, (Mr)	1, Nov. 1832	23, Oct.			L4	
Harris, Bucklin C.	13, Apr. 1854	31, Mar.	58		L3	
Harris, Cora	15, July 1852	13, July	6m- 4d		L3	
Harris, Edwin	12, Jan. 1837		probate		L3	
Harris, Edwin B.	6, Mar. 1851	23, Feb.	35		L3	
Harris, Eliza W.	17, Apr. 1851	10, Apr.	29		L3	
Harris, Francis Coldstream	5, Apr. 1849	26, Mar.	15- 7m		L3	
Harris, George Worling	20, Sept 1827	Sept	3m		L1	
Harris, Hannah	8, Apr. 1847	Mar.	32		L3	
Harris, Henry	13, Aug. 1846	Aug.	3m		L3	
Harris, Horatio T.	22, Nov. 1855	19, Nov.	57		L3	

Name	Notice Date	Death Date	Age		Page	Maiden Name
Harris, Jefferson	17, May 1855	10, May			L3	
Harris, John	3, Aug. 1837	July	49		L3	
Harris, John	10, May 1849	May			L3	
Harris, Joseph	26, July 1849	July	60		L3	
Harris, Joseph	9, Sept 1847	Aug.	8- 6m		L3	
Harris, Joseph	6, Oct. 1821		estate		L3	
Harris, Joseph	9, Sept 1825		probate		L3	
Harris, Joseph	9, June 1836		probate		L3	
Harris, Joseph	17, July 1845	15, July		*	L3	
Harris, Louisa	27, Jan. 1842	Jan.	5		L3	
Harris, Mary E.J.	27, Mar. 1828	Mar.	3m		L1	
Harris, Noah	31, Mar. 1821	26, Mar.	66	*	L3	
Harris, Peter	14, May 1846	May	55		L3	
Harris, Phoebe	25, Feb. 1836	24, Feb.			L3	
Harris, Robert Q.	1, Aug. 1850	July	40		L3	
Harris, Thomas (Rev)	25, Oct. 1832	19, Oct.			L2	
Harris, William	21, Nov. 1839		probate		L3	
Harris, William	8, Mar. 1855	7, Mar.			L3	
Harris, William C.	18, Sept 1834	Sept	1- -17d		L1	
Harrison, (child of James S.)	12, Aug. 1847	Aug.	1w		L3	
Harrison, (Mrs)	25, Oct. 1832	19, Oct.			L1	
Harrison, Algernon K. (Dr)	7, May 1846	2, Apr.	25		L3	
Harrison, Anna Lizzie	23, Jan. 1851	19, Jan.	infant		L3	
Harrison, Anna Tartt	10, Aug. 1843	8, Aug.			L3	
Harrison, Benjamin	28, Sept 1854	7, Sept	17		L3	
Harrison, Benjamin (Dr)	25, June 1840	17, June	34		L3	
Harrison, Carter B.	22, Aug. 1839	12, Aug.			L1	
Harrison, Carter B.	26, July 1855	24, July	11m		L3	
Harrison, Charles	22, Jan. 1846	21, Jan.	22		L3	
Harrison, Charles L.	15, Aug. 1833	Aug.	2- 3m		L1	
Harrison, Ebenezer, Jr.	15, May 1834	May	1		L4	
Harrison, Edmund	19, July 1855	15, July			L3	
Harrison, Edmund Jones	3, Dec. 1824	27, Nov.	24		L3	
Harrison, Elizabeth S.	23, Jan. 1851	20, Jan.			L3	Stockton
Harrison, Emma	6, Oct. 1842	28, Sept			L3	
Harrison, Frances	4, Oct. 1849	27, Sept			L3	
Harrison, George F.	14, June 1855				L3	
Harrison, Han Annie	17, July 1851	9, July	19		L3	
Harrison, J.	26, Aug. 1852	25, Aug.			L3	
Harrison, Job	8, Nov. 1838		probate		L3	
Harrison, John Cleves Symmes	4, Nov. 1830	30, Oct.			L2	
Harrison, John P.	6, Sept 1849	2, Sept			L3	
Harrison, Laura	15, Oct. 1840	14, Oct.	infant		L3	
Harrison, Margaret	29, Nov. 1832	Nov.	1- 6m		L1	
Harrison, Maria	25, Sept 1845	Sept	26		L3	
Harrison, Martha	11, Sept 1834	Aug.	8		L1	
Harrison, Martha	15, June 1848	June	6		L3	
Harrison, Mary A.	13, Sept 1832	Sept	11		L1	
Harrison, Mary A.	4, Apr. 1833	Mar.	28		L1	
Harrison, Mary Ella	23, July 1857	20, July			L3	
Harrison, Mary J.	20, May 1847	19, May	34		L3	
Harrison, Mary R.	7, Aug. 1851	30, July	50		L3	
Harrison, Oliver	18, July 1833	July	4- 2m		L2	
Harrison, Patrick	18, Oct. 1832	14, Oct.			L2	

Name	Notice Date	Death Date	Age	Page	Maiden Name
Harrison, Richard	1, Oct. 1829		estate	L4	
Harrison, Virginia B.	15, Sept 1853	22, Aug.	23	L3	Quin
Harrison, Wiliam H., Jr.	11, Oct. 1838		estate	L3	
Harrison, William Henry	12, Apr. 1849	18, Mar.	21	L3	
Harrison, William Henry (Gen)	23, Dec. 1841		estate	L3	
Harrold, John	29, Apr. 1847	Apr.	31	L3	
Harron, Robert	20, Apr. 1843	Apr.	40	L3	
Harsh, Fordus	29, Nov. 1832	Nov.	15	L1	
Harsh, Frederica	8, Nov. 1832	30, Oct.	7	L4	
Harst, Henry	1, Nov. 1832	Oct.		L3	
Harst, Jacob	1, Nov. 1832	Oct.		L3	
Hart, (Mr)	31, Aug. 1854	13, July		L3	
Hart, Abram B.	7, Feb. 1856			L3	
Hart, Andrew	26, Mar. 1840	Mar.	55	L3	
Hart, Barbara	4, Oct. 1849	3, Oct.	76	L3	
Hart, Bloomy	16, June 1842	7, June	17m	L3	
Hart, Eliza Ann	3, Aug. 1843	July	1- 6m	L3	
Hart, F.C.	8, Nov. 1855		probate	L3	
Hart, Frederick	10, Aug. 1843	Aug.	3m	L3	
Hart, Frederick	11, Mar. 1852	7, Mar.		L3	
Hart, Frederick C.	25, Mar. 1852		estate	L3	
Hart, George Pugh	18, May 1848	15, May	3- 9m	L3	
Hart, Hannah	29, Apr. 1852	28, Apr.	12	L3	
Hart, Jacob	22, June 1837		probate	L3	
Hart, Jacob	14, Jan. 1836		estate	L4	
Hart, Joseph	19, July 1849	July	33	L3	
Hart, Martha Ann	4, Feb. 1847	Jan.	16m	L3	
Hart, Mary	20, Apr. 1848	Apr.	25	L3	
Hart, Mary H.	18, Sept 1851	6, Sept		L3	Powers
Hart, Samuel	6, July 1843	8, July	73	L3	
Hart, Thomas	10, Sept 1857		probate	L3	
Harthorn, Peter	23, Nov. 1837		estate	L3	
Hartinkat, John	22, Aug. 1833	Aug.	42	L4	
Hartkoff, Margarethe	18, Sept 1834	Sept	21- 6m	L1	
Hartley, Abraham	14, Sept 1854	8, Sept	36	L3	
Hartley, Isabella	18, May 1854	17, May	infant	L3	
Hartley, Joseph	9, Aug. 1849	July	6	L3	
Hartley, Mary	22, Sept 1853	21, Sept	13m	L3	
Hartley, Mary	11, Oct. 1849	Oct.	15m	L3	
Hartly, James	12, July 1849		estate	L3	
Hartly, James	19, July 1849		estate	L3	
Hartman, Catharine M.	15, Sept 1842	Sept	21	L3	
Hartman, Charles	4, Apr. 1833	Mar.	1- 6m	L1	
Hartman, George	9, Aug. 1849	July	29	L3	
Hartmeyer, Francis	25, Jan. 1849	Jan.	61	L3	
Hartney, Mary A.	1, Aug. 1850	July	3m	L3	
Harton, Kate	25, May 1854	19, May		L3	Vanausdol
Hartshorn, Grate	26, Nov. 1846	20, Nov.	58	L3	
Hartshorn, Julia B.	13, June 1833	June	6m	L1	
Hartshorn, Peter	2, Apr. 1840	1, Apr.	58	L3	
Hartshorn, Warren	9, Apr. 1857		probate	L3	
Hartshorne, Martin Baum	27, Aug. 1846	19, Aug.	3- 3m	L3	
Hartshorne, Warren	15, Mar. 1855	11, Mar.	71- 8m- 6d	L3	
Hartshorne, William	17, Nov. 1836	8, Nov.	61	L4	

Name	Notice Date	Death Date	Age		Page	Maiden Name
Hartshorne, William Burrows	26, May 1842	25, May	8m- 8d		L3	
Hartshorne, William Saunders	21, Mar. 1850	20, Mar.	19m		L3	
Hartwell, Abbott Lawrence	8, Apr. 1847	31, Mar.	1		L3	
Hartwell, Alice B.	14, Sept 1843	7, Sept	28		L3	Athearn
Hartwell, Anne	13, Apr. 1848	10, Apr.	infant		L3	
Hartwell, Anne	5, Dec. 1844	4, Dec.			L3	
Hartwell, Caroline S.	20, Aug. 1840	17, Aug.		*	L3	
Hartwell, Eliza W.	6, May 1847	3, May	34		L3	
Hartwell, Frances Baymiller	23, Sept 1847	22, Sept	7m- 5d		L3	
Hartwell, George H.	19, Oct. 1848		estate		L3	
Hartwell, George Henry	12, Dec. 1844	7, Dec.	15m		L3	
Hartwell, Peter P.	29, July 1841	10, July			L3	
Hartzell, (Mrs)	18, Oct. 1832	16, Oct.			L3	
Harvey, (man)	28, July 1853	27, July			L3	
Harvey, Andrew	20, Sept 1849	14, Sept	67	*	L3	
Harvey, Andrew	8, Nov. 1838		probate		L3	
Harvey, Christopher	1, Nov. 1820		estate		L3	
Harvey, Edward	14, Oct. 1847	Oct.	34		L3	
Harvey, John A.	28, Aug. 1834	Aug.	1- 8m		L1	
Harvey, William R.	28, Aug. 1845	22, Aug.	20		L3	
Harvie, Arthur	15, Oct. 1857		estate		L3	
Harwood, William Sherman	28, Feb. 1839	Feb.	2		L3	
Hasch, Andrew	9, Apr. 1857		probate		L3	
Haseltine, Anne Lizzie	20, Jan. 1853	14, Jan.	3-10m-10d		L3	
Haseltine, Charlie Sherman	14, May 1857	10, May	5- 5m		L3	
Haskins, Eliza	26, Sept 1833	Sept	33		L4	
Hasluck, Fidelia VanDyke	7, Sept 1848	15, Aug.	26		L3	
Hasluck, Sidney Vandyke W.	7, Dec. 1843	26, Nov.	8m		L3	
Hassan, Judah	15, Aug. 1833	Aug.	32		L1	
Hassard, Mary Snelling	13, Jan. 1853	5, Jan.	9m-27d		L3	
Hassenau, John	5, Nov. 1857		probate		L3	
Hassey, James	15, June 1848	June	41		L3	
Hassinger, James	5, Mar. 1857		probate		L3	
Hastie, Janet	28, June 1855	20, June	58	*	L3	
Hastings, Abel	13, Mar. 1851	Mar.	53		L3	
Hastings, Daniel	12, Feb. 1846	7, Feb.	71	*	L3	
Hastings, Elizabeth D.	14, Feb. 1833	Feb.	8- -12d		L1	
Hastings, Jane	9, Nov. 1848	1, Nov.	38	*	L3	
Hastings, Nathan	14, Sept 1854	6, Sept	72		L3	
Hatch, Abner	5, Oct. 1819	26, Sept	66	*	L3	
Hatch, George	24, Mar. 1806	18, Mar.	17		L3	
Hatch, Harlan	13, Feb. 1845	21, Dec.	40		L3	
Hatch, Herr	4, July 1850	June	35		L3	
Hatch, Jane	19, Mar. 1819	15, Mar.			L3	
Hatch, Jerusha A.	12, Apr. 1849	9, Apr.			L3	
Hatch, John	22, Apr. 1847	14, Apr.	63		L3	
Hatch, Nancy	14, Aug. 1856		probate		L6	
Hatcher, Archibald	28, Dec. 1854	27, Dec.			L3	
Hatchett, Elizabeth	31, May 1849	May	25		L3	
Hatfield, Hannah	7, Sept 1854	3, Sept			L3	
Hatfield, Jane	18, July 1844	10, July	24		L3	
Hatfield, Mary Jane	18, Dec. 1851	10, Dec.	infant		L3	
Hatfield, William Henry	6, Mar. 1856	27, Feb.	5-11m		L3	
Hathaway, Henry	9, Aug. 1855		probate		L3	

Name	Notice Date	Death Date	Age	Page	Maiden Name
Hathaway, Warren	2, Oct. 1834	Sept	20	L4	
Hathorn, James	3, Jan. 1839		estate	L3	
Hathorn, Peter	5, Sept 1839		probate	L3	
Hation, Susan	11, Oct. 1832	1, Oct.		L2	
Hatman, (Mrs)	5, Aug. 1852	July	30	L3	
Hatman, Caroline	2, Oct. 1834	Sept		L4	
Hatt, Kineth	19, Oct. 1837		estate	L3	
Hatt, Sames	29, Aug. 1850	Aug.	6	L3	
Hatter, Jacob	25, Apr. 1850	Apr.	24	L3	
Hatter, Joseph	10, Sept 1857		probate	L3	
Hatton, Rachel	21, Dec. 1848	13, Dec.	62	L3	
Hauch, John	9, Sept 1847	Aug.	23	L3	
Haudley, Lewis	14, July 1853	13, July		L3	
Haufman, (child of J.)	15, Nov. 1832	Nov.	2	L1	
Haufman, Margaretta	15, Aug. 1833	Aug.	40	L1	
Haughmiere, Christiana	22, July 1847	July	4m	L3	
Haughton, Anne	8, Nov. 1855	5, Nov.	2- 1m	L3	
Haughton, Charles Lewis	28, Mar. 1839	27, Mar.	1-10m	L3	
Haughton, M.A. (Mrs)	14, May 1857	10, May	44	L3	
Hausler, Lewis	16, Aug. 1849	Aug.	37	L3	
Hautic, Ernst	9, Aug. 1849	July	69	L3	
Haven, Mary Colburn	10, Aug. 1854	25, July	infant	L3	
Haver, John (Capt)	19, Jan. 1854	4, Jan.		L3	
Hawes, Elliott Hastings	7, Oct. 1847	4, Oct.		L3	
Hawkens, Carvel	19, Dec. 1826		probate	L3	
Hawkes, Margaret	14, Sept 1837	Sept	35	L4	
Hawkins, Andrew J.	8, Mar. 1849	16, Feb.		L3	
Hawkins, Benjamin (Col)	15, July 1816	6, June		L3	
Hawkins, Carvil	14, Sept 1813		estate	L3	
Hawkins, Carvil	11, July 1833		probate	L3	
Hawkins, Joseph	25, Dec. 1815		estate	L3	
Hawkins, Joseph	19, Dec. 1826		probate	L3	
Hawkins, Josiah	27, Oct. 1831		probate	L1	
Hawkins, Lydia R.	17, July 1845	7, July	30- -7d	L3	
Hawkins, Mary J.	19, Dec. 1850	Dec.	31	L3	
Hawkins, Nancy	2, Aug. 1832	July	25	L1	
Hawkins, Richard	20, Dec. 1825		probate	L4	
Hawkins, Robert	7, Oct. 1847			L2	
Hawkins, William	14, Feb. 1839	7, Feb.	32	L3	
Hawley, Daniel Webster	8, June 1837	29, May	10m	L2	
Hawn, Harriet	12, Mar. 1840	29, Feb.		L3	
Hawthorn, Mary Sallie	27, Aug. 1857	19, Aug.	7	L3	
Hay, (child of Jane)	24, Aug. 1843	Aug.	15m	L3	
Hay, Elizabeth	2, Oct. 1834	Sept		L4	
Hay, George	23, Jan. 1845		estate	L3	
Hay, George	7, Oct. 1830			L3	
Hay, Washington	9, Apr. 1857		probate	L3	
Haycock, Hamilton	30, Aug. 1838		estate	L3	
Hayden, Alfred	31, May 1832		estate	L4	
Hayden, Christopher	10, Nov. 1818		estate	L3	
Hayden, Daniel	24, Nov. 1836		estate	L3	
Hayden, Daniel	12, Jan. 1837		probate	L3	
Hayden, Daniel	14, Feb. 1839		probate	L3	
Hayden, Edith May	27, Nov. 1851	17, Nov.	2- -14d	L3	

Name	Notice Date	Death Date	Age	Page	Maiden Name
Hayden, Georgetta L.	26, Feb. 1852	Feb.	12	L4	
Hayden, Marian	23, May 1833	May	71	L4	
Hayden, S.B.	8, Feb. 1855	31, Jan.	44	L3	
Hayden, William	9, Aug. 1838		probate	L3	
Hayes, Frances G.	8, Aug. 1850	July	1- 6m	L3	
Hayes, Roswell P. (Dr)	27, Apr. 1837		estate	L4	
Hayman, Stephen B.	30, Aug. 1855			L3	
Haynes, Frederick	31, Aug. 1837	Aug.	47	L4	
Haynes, Manley B.	15, Aug. 1839		estate	L3	
Haynes, Manley B.	1, Aug. 1839	31, July		L3	
Hays, Charles	10, Mar. 1853	8, Mar.		L3	
Hays, Ezra	21, Dec. 1813		estate	L1	
Hays, Joseph	9, June 1812		estate	L3	
Hays, Nancy	7, Feb. 1833	Feb.	25	L1	
Hays, Oliver	11, July 1833		probate	L3	
Hays, William	3, May 1849	Apr.	36	L3	
Hayt, Cornelius	5, Nov. 1846	Oct.	5	L3	
Hayt, Samuel	25, Oct. 1832	Oct.	15	L1	
Haythorn, John	30, Sept 1820		estate	L3	
Hazard, Ebenezer	7, July 1817	13, June	73	L2	
Hazard, Maria	19, June 1851	17, June	*	L3	
Hazard, Marion Isabella	20, Sept 1855	10, Sept	6- 4m- 7d	L3	
Hazard, William Snelling	23, Nov. 1854	15, Nov.	10- 1m- 5d	L3	
Hazel, Gerhard H.	18, July 1850	July	47	L3	
Hazelrig, Clarissa	16, Mar. 1854	8, Mar.		L3	
Hazelton, Mary Emma	10, June 1852	2, June	9	L3	
Hazelton, Susan Gordon	10, June 1852	2, June	7	L3	
Hazen, Alfred	16, Aug. 1849	Aug.	14m	L3	
Hazen, Ann Maria	7, Aug. 1834	July	2- 2m	L3	
Hazen, Levi	17, July 1851	9, July	94	L3	
Hazen, Nathan L.	1, Jan. 1852		estate	L3	
Hazen, Nathan L.	24, Feb. 1842	18, Feb.	infant	L3	
Hazen, Nathaniel L.	25, Dec. 1851	17, Dec.	42	L3	
Hazlett, Robert	22, Nov. 1855	15, Nov.	43	L3	
Hazlewood, Fanny	15, Jan. 1857	12, Jan.		L3	
Hazzard, Thomas K.	20, Dec. 1825		probate	L4	
Headley, J.B. (Mrs)	13, Mar. 1851	27, Feb.	*	L3	Piatt
Healy, James	7, June 1849	May	40	L3	
Heamer, Herman H.	8, Aug. 1833	July	7m	L1	
Heaps, John	2, Aug. 1820			L3	
Heath, David	9, Nov. 1819		estate	L3	
Heath, Elizabeth	22, Aug. 1833	Aug.	65	L4	
Heath, James	13, Jan. 1817		estate	L3	
Heath, Levi	8, Dec. 1818		estate	L1	
Heath, Sarah	7, Feb. 1856		estate	L3	
Heath, Sarah	5, Mar. 1857		probate	L3	
Heath, Thomas	11, July 1850		estate	L3	
Heath, William	7, June 1855		probate	L3	
Heaton, Charles Wright	30, June 1853	10, June	5- 7m	L3	
Heaton, George	26, Aug. 1841	25, Aug.		L3	
Heaton, John	1, Aug. 1833	July	39	L1	
Hebenstreit, Philip	2, Aug. 1855		estate	L3	
Heckart, Charles	6, Jan. 1848	Dec.	17	L3	
Heckinger, Joseph	6, Aug. 1846	2, Aug.	80	L3	

Name	Notice Date	Death Date	Age		Page	Maiden Name
Hedden, Frances	2, Feb. 1843	25, Jan.	25		L3	
Hedger, Margaret	8, Aug. 1833	July	20		L1	
Hedger, Sarah Belle	5, Oct. 1854	1, Oct.	2- -19d		L3	
Hedger, Thomas	2, June 1836	29, May		*	L3	
Hedges, Mary	26, Oct. 1854	20, Oct.	72		L3	
Hedly, Agness	1, Feb. 1849	23, Jan.			L3	
Hedwig, Phillip	10, Apr. 1856		probate		L3	
Heeket, Anna C.	9, Oct. 1834	Sept	76		L1	
Heeth, Charlotte	25, July 1850	July	25		L3	
Heetkamp, Hendrikas	22, Jan. 1852	Jan.	24		L3	
Hefer, Christian M.	18, July 1833	July	3-10m		L2	
Heffed, Ellen	10, Mar. 1853	Feb.	38		L3	
Hefferns, Dennis	19, Aug. 1852	Aug.	33		L3	
Heffner, Patrick	8, Dec. 1853	5, Dec.			L3	
Hefler, Everhart	18, Aug. 1842	Aug.	42		L3	
Hefley, Elizabeth	26, Jan. 1843	24, Jan.	infant		L3	
Hefley, John	12, Dec. 1833	Dec.	68		L4	
Hegeman, A.S.	10, Jan. 1856		probate		L3	
Hegeman, Emily	23, May 1833	May			L3	
Hegeman, Jane	23, May 1833	7, May			L3	
Hegeman, Juliet	23, May 1833				L3	
Hegerty, William	27, June 1850	24, June			L3	
Heggie, Thomas	5, Feb. 1857	27, Jan.	42		L3	
Heggins, William	18, Oct. 1832	14, Oct.			L2	
Heghtower, (child of London)	8, Feb. 1849	Jan.	stillborn		L3	
Hegt, Francis	23, May 1850		estate		L3	
Hei, Margaret	15, Aug. 1833	Aug.	30		L1	
Hei, Peter	15, Aug. 1833	Aug.	2- 6m		L1	
Heidelbach, Leonora	1, Nov. 1855	30, Oct.	4- -3d		L3	
Heidelbach, Simon	4, Sept 1856		probate		L5	
Heidelback, Simon	28, June 1849	26, June	31		L3	
Heiffer, (Mrs)	1, Nov. 1832	29, Oct.			L3	
Heigerman, Barney	29, Feb. 1844	Feb.	40		L3	
Heighway, Mary E.	4, Sept 1851	12, Aug.	24	*	L3	
Heighway, Mary E.	14, Aug. 1851	11, Aug.	25- -15d		L3	
Heighway, Samuel	30, Dec. 1816		estate		L3	
Heil, Lewis	8, Aug. 1850	July	12		L3	
Heilman, John	14, Oct. 1841	Oct.	34		L3	
Heininger, Peter	16, Nov. 1837	Nov.	45		L3	
Heinselman, Gizor	24, Jan. 1850	Jan.	22		L3	
Held, Leonard	31, July 1845	July	33		L3	
Helencamp, H.	18, May 1854	14, May	60		L3	
Helfbein, Catharine	26, July 1849	July	73		L3	
Hell, Daniel	15, Aug. 1850	Aug.	1		L3	
Hellman, Elizabeth	14, May 1846	May	39		L3	
Hellman, Joseph	4, Feb. 1847	Jan.	23		L3	
Hellstern, Eliza	19, July 1849	July	23		L3	
Helm, John	11, June 1840	3, Apr.	79	*	L4	
Helman, Jane D.	3, Apr. 1851	Mar.	5		L3	
Helmick, James	22, Apr. 1847	Apr.	2		L3	
Helmkamp, Frederick	23, Nov. 1848	Nov.	51		L3	
Helseh, John	13, Jan. 1848	Jan.	65		L3	
Hemborn, (child)	25, July 1850	July	3w		L3	
Hemmey, Michael	14, Oct. 1841	Oct.	41		L3	

Name	Notice Date	Death Date	Age		Page	Maiden Name
Hemminger, Joseph N.	3, Dec. 1857	5, Nov.	25		L3	
Hemphill, (Mrs)	25, Oct. 1832	20, Oct.			L2	
Hemphill, Joseph	9, June 1842	19, May	73		L3	
Hendershott, Sarah E.	10, Oct. 1844	4, Oct.	17		L3	
Henderson, Alexander	11, Dec. 1815	22, Nov.	79		L3	
Henderson, Ann	15, Nov. 1832	Nov.	14- 7m		L1	
Henderson, Ann	8, Nov. 1832	31, Oct.	14		L4	
Henderson, Charles	25, May 1848	May	2		L3	
Henderson, Edward	11, Jan. 1849	Jan.	20		L3	
Henderson, Edward A.	4, Jan. 1849	26, Dec.	24		L3	
Henderson, James	20, Apr. 1837		estate		L3	
Henderson, James	11, Nov. 1841		estate		L3	
Henderson, James	13, Jan. 1853		estate		L3	
Henderson, James	6, Apr. 1837	3, Apr.			L3	
Henderson, James	28, Mar. 1844	14, Mar.			L3	
Henderson, James	26, July 1838		estate		L4	
Henderson, Louis F.	4, Apr. 1844	29, Mar.	13		L3	
Henderson, Mary	28, Oct. 1847	Oct.	33		L3	
Henderson, Mary A.	28, June 1849	June	19		L3	
Henderson, Mary W.	7, June 1849	24, May	69	*	L3	
Henderson, Mary W.	31, May 1849	23, May			L3	
Henderson, Nancy	28, June 1849	June	1w		L3	
Henderson, Robert	1, Mar. 1849	Feb.	55		L3	
Henderson, Sarah Jane	10, June 1847	June	7		L3	
Henderson, Stephen	28, Dec. 1843	Dec.			L3	
Henderson, Thomas	7, Dec. 1843	6, Dec.	76		L3	
Hendley, Lily	26, Nov. 1857	23, Nov.	3- -19d		L3	
Hendreckson, William	21, June 1849	June	25		L3	
Hendrick, Patrick	23, Feb. 1843	Feb.	26		L3	
Henesy, John	17, Dec. 1840	Dec.	64		L3	
Hengehold, William	18, Apr. 1850		estate		L3	
Henison, Bridget	18, July 1850	July	16		L3	
Henkle, John D.	6, Nov. 1834	Oct.	1		L1	
Hennegrdeff, Margaret	13, Dec. 1832	Dec.	2		L1	
Hennessey, Margaret	5, July 1849	June	37		L3	
Hennessy, Patrick	23, Aug. 1849	Aug.	7		L3	
Henny, John S.	24, June 1847	June	18m		L3	
Henrey, Joseph	20, June 1833	June	3m		L1	
Henrie, William H.	16, Nov. 1854	15, Nov.	54		L3	
Henry, (Mr)	18, Oct. 1832	14, Oct.			L3	
Henry, Catharine	18, July 1833	July	37		L2	
Henry, Elizabeth	9, Feb. 1837	Jan.	36		L3	
Henry, Jane	12, Jan. 1854	5, Jan.	49		L3	
Henry, Joel	25, Oct. 1832	19, Oct.			L2	
Henry, John	20, Dec. 1838	Dec.	58		L3	
Henry, John	1, Nov. 1832	30, Oct.			L3	
Henry, Ruth A.	31, Aug. 1854	25, Aug.			L3	
Henry, Samuel	4, May 1848	2, May	52		L3	
Henry, William	15, Nov. 1832	Nov.	1- 8m		L1	
Henry, William H.	17, Sept 1846	Sept	28		L3	
Henrys, Clinton	14, Mar. 1833	Mar.	4- 9m		L1	
Henshaw, William	11, July 1839		estate		L3	
Henshaw, William	22, July 1841		estate		L3	
Hensley, Sarah	3, Nov. 1853	30, Oct.	39		L3	

Name	Notice Date	Death Date	Age		Page	Maiden Name
Henson, Herman	5, Dec. 1850		estate		L3	
Henton, (child of John)	7, Aug. 1834	July	1- 6m		L3	
Henton, William	12, Apr. 1814		estate		L3	
Hepenauer, Jacob	3, Aug. 1848	July	39		L3	
Herdman, John	25, Oct. 1832	23, Oct.			L3	
Herman, Hiniah	30, Aug. 1832	Aug.	20		L1	
Hermann, Gabriel	6, Sept 1855		probate		L3	
Herndon, Maria Louisa	30, Jan. 1851	23, Jan.	21		L3	Taylor
Herner, Daniel	2, Jan. 1840	Dec.	30		L2	
Heron, William M.	23, Aug. 1838	29, July		*	L3	
Herr, Sarah	24, Aug. 1843	15, Aug.			L3	
Herrick, Alonzo	16, Aug. 1849	Aug.	20		L3	
Herring, Alexander	10, Sept 1835		estate		L3	
Herritage, Benjamin	17, Apr. 1856	15, Apr.	28		L3	
Herrod, John H.	25, Nov. 1847				L2	
Herron, Anna Maria	30, Dec. 1852	22, Dec.	2- 1m		L3	
Herron, Charlie	15, Oct. 1857	8, Oct.	17m		L3	
Herron, Harriet M.	3, July 1851	24, June	7m		L3	
Herron, John	9, July 1857		probate		L3	
Herron, Joseph Trimble	11, Mar. 1852	4, Mar.	4- 6m		L3	
Herron, Otho M.	5, Sept 1839		probate		L3	
Herron, Thomas	28, Mar. 1844	Mar.	50		L3	
Herron, William H.	6, Nov. 1845	Oct.	3m		L3	
Hertzogg, (Mrs)	1, Nov. 1832	26, Oct.			L1	
Hervey, James	18, Oct. 1832	14, Oct.			L2	
Herwan, Daniel	14, Feb. 1850	Feb.	28		L3	
Herzey, Mary	8, Aug. 1833	July			L1	
Hess, Charles	25, July 1850	July	26		L3	
Hess, Herman	1, Aug. 1850	July	6w		L3	
Hesse, Bernard	8, July 1841		estate		L3	
Hesselwood, George	6, Dec. 1832	Dec.	1- 8m		L1	
Heston, (child)	10, Jan. 1828	Jan.	1d		L4	
Hetherington, George (Mrs)	10, Mar. 1853	6, Mar.			L3	
Hetrick, George	7, June 1814		estate		L1	
Heuer, Sarah A.	31, Dec. 1857		estate		L3	
Heuer, William A.	9, Aug. 1838		probate		L3	
Heuss, William	11, July 1850	July	23		L3	
Hewdoe, Lewis	2, Jan. 1840	26, Dec.			L1	
Hewes, Roxanna	20, Dec. 1814	18, Dec.	21		L3	
Hewett, Charlotte	18, July 1833	July	29- 2m		L2	
Hewett, Sarah E.	18, July 1833	July	10m-11d		L2	
Hewit, Catharine	21, Oct. 1847	Oct.	37		L3	
Hewitt, Hiram	3, Jan. 1833	Dec.	35		L4	
Hewlett, Anna Maria	15, June 1854	7, June	3		L3	
Hewlett, Sarah A.	22, June 1854	14, June			L3	
Hewson, Bethnel Washburn	8, June 1848	3, June	2- -12d		L3	
Hewson, Bethuel H.	1, Oct. 1846	29, Sept	42		L3	
Hewson, Emily L.	23, Aug. 1855	17, Aug.		*	L3	Williams
Hey, Bartholomew	19, July 1832	July	1m		L1	
Hey, Bartholomew	9, Feb. 1837	4, Feb.	38		L3	
Hey, Bartholomew	9, Feb. 1837		estate		L3	
Hey, Michael	26, Jan. 1837	23, Jan.	33		L3	
Hey, Michael	9, Feb. 1837		estate		L3	
Heysinger, Michael	25, Mar. 1847	Mar.			L3	

Name	Notice Date	Death Date	Age	Page	Maiden Name
Heyterdreyden, Peter	8, Aug. 1850	July	80	L3	
Heywood, Sarah B.	1, Nov. 1849	25, Oct.	25	L3	
Hiat, Simon	8, Apr. 1847	Mar.	27	L3	
Hiatt, Charles	27, Sept 1849	19, Sept	*	L3	
Hiatt, John	15, Aug. 1850	Aug.	25	L3	
Hibben, Arnold W.	11, Sept 1845		estate	L3	
Hickebreath, Theodore	24, Jan. 1850	Jan.	16m	L3	
Hickey, David	2, May 1850	Apr.	45	L3	
Hickey, John	20, Sept 1849	Sept	24	L3	
Hickey, Thomas	20, Feb. 1851	Feb.	20	L3	
Hickman, Jacob	20, July 1848	July	17	L3	
Hickman, Joseph	11, July 1850		estate	L3	
Hickman, Joseph	14, June 1838		probate	L4	
Hicks, (Mrs)	2, May 1833	Apr.	38	L1	
Hicks, Benjamin	22, Aug. 1850	Aug.	18	L3	
Hicks, James	20, Aug. 1846	13, Aug.	10m-13d	L3	
Hicks, James	13, Feb. 1840		probate	L3	
Hicks, John	24, Aug. 1848	17, Aug.	42	L3	
Hicks, Martha A.	29, Apr. 1852	11, Apr.		L3	Harrison
Hicks, Robert	24, Sept 1840	23, Sept	91	L3	
Hicks, Samuel	18, Jan. 1849	Jan.		L3	
Hicks, Thomas	28, Apr. 1817	13, Apr.		L3	
Hicks, William	8, Aug. 1833	July	10	L1	
Hicks, William	18, Apr. 1850	Apr.	23	L3	
Hicks, William H.	7, Mar. 1850	Feb.	21	L3	
Hiderman, Herman	15, Feb. 1844	Feb.	38	L3	
Hidgeway, (child of T.S.)	30, Aug. 1832	Aug.	3- - 5d	L1	
Hie, John	23, Dec. 1847	Dec.	32	L3	
Hieatt, George Whitfield	16, Dec. 1847	11, Dec.	6	L3	
Hiel, Adam	16, May 1850	May	70	L3	
Hiel, George	18, July 1833	July	10m	L2	
Higbee, Ann	10, July 1845	2, July	39	L3	
Higbee, Charles	4, Mar. 1841	14, Feb.	73	L3	
Higbee, Elizabeth Ann	22, June 1843	20, June	24	L3	Kellum
Higgenbottom, George	13, Apr. 1848	Apr.	39	L3	
Higgins, A. (Dr)	9, Nov. 1822	Nov.	27	L3	
Higgins, John Joliffe (Gen)	9, July 1857	2, July		L3	
Higgins, John M.	23, Apr. 1840	Apr.	58	L3	
Higgins, Margaret E.	17, Feb. 1848	14, Feb.		L3	
Higgins, Mary	20, Nov. 1850	Nov.	49	L3	
Higgins, Nathaniel	20, Aug. 1829		estate	L3	
Higgins, Patrick	7, Dec. 1848	Nov.	28	L3	
Higgins, Patrick	28, Mar. 1850	Mar.	35	L3	
Higgins, William	25, Feb. 1847		estate	L3	
Highfield, Joseph	15, Feb. 1838		estate	L3	
Highfill, Sarah A.	26, Mar. 1846	19, Mar.	61	L3	
Highland,	26, July 1849	July	1- 6m	L3	
Highland, (child of Anthony)	7, Nov. 1810	4, Nov.	child	L3	
Highland, Andrew	8, June 1848	May	1	L3	
Highlands, William	8, July 1841		estate	L3	
Hightower, Reuben	20, Aug. 1846	Aug.	2	L3	
Highway, Caroline	3, Feb. 1848	30, Jan.		L3	
Hilbert, Patrick	15, July 1852	July	19	L3	
Hilditch, Samuel	12, Dec. 1810		estate	L2	

Name	Notice Date	Death Date	Age		Page	Maiden Name
Hilditch, Samuel	19, Sept 1826		estate		L3	
Hilditch, Samuel	10, Oct. 1810	6, Oct.			L3	
Hildreth, George	27, June 1839	24, May	56	*	L3	
Hildreth, George	20, June 1839		estate		L3	
Hill, (child of Ceclia)	18, Mar. 1847	Mar.	stillborn		L3	
Hill, (daughter of Martin)	1, Oct. 1857	30, Sept			L3	
Hill, (son of Benjamin)	29, July 1841	13, July	17d		L3	
Hill, Alice K.	17, Aug. 1837	16, July	24	*	L3	Rhodes
Hill, Ann M.	15, Aug. 1826	23, July			L3	Mason
Hill, Anne	20, Feb. 1851	12, Feb.	18		L3	
Hill, Benjamin	9, Aug. 1838		probate		L3	
Hill, Benjamin	18, Apr. 1839		probate		L3	
Hill, Benjamin Holton	29, Sept 1842	21, Sept	5m		L3	
Hill, Caroline	9, Feb. 1843	30, Jan.	infant		L3	
Hill, Charles Duval	30, June 1853	24, June	7m		L3	
Hill, Daniel	30, Aug. 1832		estate		L4	
Hill, David	26, Aug. 1852	19, Aug.			L3	
Hill, Edwin	18, Jan. 1849	9, Jan.	9d		L3	
Hill, Elizabeth R.	19, Jan. 1843	17, Jan.	20		L3	
Hill, Emeline	30, Nov. 1848	Nov.	30		L3	
Hill, Emily Odger	24, Feb. 1853	21, Feb.	7m- 3d		L3	
Hill, George	19, Mar. 1846	12, Mar.	6m		L3	
Hill, H.W. (Prof)	17, May 1849	13, May			L3	
Hill, Helen Maria	15, June 1843	7, June	13m		L3	
Hill, Herman	29, Nov. 1849	Nov.			L3	
Hill, Jonathan	22, Dec. 1831	8, Dec.		*	L4	
Hill, Mary E.	29, Jan. 1857	22, Jan.	43- -9d		L3	
Hill, Reeve	6, June 1833	May	12		L2	
Hill, Robert S.	2, May 1844	Apr.	45		L3	
Hill, Rowland	5, Dec. 1833		estate		L4	
Hill, W.B.	19, July 1838	16, July	49	*	L3	
Hillet, Frederick	19, Oct. 1837	Oct.	59		L3	
Hilliard, Thomas	25, Oct. 1832	21, Oct.			L3	
Hillmas, Zebulon	20, Dec. 1825		probate		L4	
Hills, Charles	13, Nov. 1834	Nov.	30		L1	
Hills, Mary C.	28, Nov. 1833	30, Oct.	25	*	L4	
Hilt, Lewis	16, Mar. 1837		estate		L3	
Hilton, Daniel	8, Oct. 1846	Sept	43		L3	
Hilton, John, Jr.	23, May 1844	16, May	12		L3	
Hinchman, Mary	29, Sept 1853	26, Sept	27		L3	
Hinds, Jamse	3, Sept 1840		probate		L3	
Hine, Moses	15, Feb. 1849	Feb.	22		L3	
Hine, Sheldon	25, June 1846	31, May	54	*	L3	
Hines, Christian	4, Apr. 1850	Mar.	36		L3	
Hines, John	3, Nov. 1807		estate		L2	
Hines, Samuel	3, Dec. 1840		probate		L3	
Hinkle, Ann Jane	23, Apr. 1846	22, Apr.	3- 1m		L3	
Hinkle, Elizabeth	1, July 1847	23, June	65		L3	
Hinkle, Frances	28, June 1849	June	37		L3	
Hinman, Elizabeth	10, Feb. 1853	3, Feb.	60		L3	
Hinman, Kate E.	28, Aug. 1856	22, Aug.			L5	
Hinsdale, Elizabeth	1, Apr. 1841	21, Mar.	62	*	L3	
Hinsdale, Harriet	20, Nov. 1856	9, Nov.	71		L3	
Hinsdale, Mary J.	8, Dec. 1836	7, Dec.	15	*	L3	

Name	Notice Date	Death Date	Age		Page	Maiden Name
Hinsdill, Adelaide Kellogg	3, Sept 1846	2, Sept	16	*	L3	
Hinton, Eliza	13, Dec. 1832	Dec.	21		L1	
Hinton, I.T. (Rev)	16, Sept 1847	28, Aug.	48		L3	
Hirch, Henry	7, May 1857		probate		L3	
Hirsch, Henry	16, Oct. 1856		probate		L6	
Hirschner, (child of George)	7, Aug. 1834	July	4		L3	
Hisse, William	31, Jan. 1850	Jan.	20		L3	
Hissock, Peter	9, Aug. 1849	July	48		L3	
Hitchcliff, Joseph	28, Mar. 1850	Mar.	24		L3	
Hitchens, George	19, Jan. 1854	31, Dec.	72		L3	
Hite, Abraham (Capt)	26, July 1832	12, July	77		L4	
Hixon, Elizabeth	5, Sept 1850	Aug.	21		L3	
Hixson, William	12, Sept 1850	Sept	5w		L3	
Hoadley, Laura	23, June 1853	19, June	18-10m-14d		L3	
Hobart, Anne Newell	25, Mar. 1847	18, Mar.		*	L3	
Hobart, Edward Everett	10, Aug. 1854	3, Aug.	2-10m		L3	
Hobart, Frances Wells	10, June 1852	9, June	12		L3	
Hobart, James Holbrook	17, Aug. 1854	16, Aug.	17m		L3	
Hobart, Katharine Lawrence	23, Feb. 1854	20, Feb.	10- 6m		L3	
Hobbs, Sarah	25, July 1833	July	9		L1	
Hobbs, William	20, Sept 1827	Sept	24		L1	
Hobson, George	14, June 1838		probate		L4	
Hobson, John	13, Oct. 1831		estate		L2	
Hobson, John	11, July 1833		probate		L3	
Hockmeyer, (Mrs)	18, Nov. 1852				L3	
Hoddard, Joseph	25, July 1833	July	43		L1	
Hodel, (child)	14, Feb. 1833	Feb.	5		L1	
Hodel, Elizabeth	14, Feb. 1833	Feb.	11		L1	
Hodel, Johanna	14, Feb. 1833	Feb.	25		L1	
Hodges, Rufus	16, Jan. 1845	8, Jan.			L3	
Hodgson, (son of W.Q.)	31, Mar. 1842	21, Mar.	11m-14d		L3	
Hodgson, B.H.	12, Dec. 1839	22, Nov.	34		L3	
Hodgson, Benjamin H.	12, Dec. 1839		estate		L1	
Hodgson, Ellen Augusta Margaret	17, Oct. 1844	13, Oct.			L3	
Hodgson, J.T.	18, May 1848		estate		L3	
Hodgson, John	25, Aug. 1842	Aug.	3w		L3	
Hodler, Henry	17, July 1845	16, July			L3	
Hodson, John	14, Apr. 1842	Apr.	12m		L3	
Hodson, William	18, July 1833	July	22		L2	
Hofeggert, Barbara	25, July 1850	July	78		L3	
Hoff, (child of Anthony)	8, Aug. 1839	July	9m		L3	
Hoffer, (child of Fred)	26, Sept 1833	Sept	4d		L4	
Hoffer, (child of Fred)	26, Sept 1833	Sept	stillborn		L4	
Hoffman, (Mr)	20, Apr. 1848	17, Apr.			L2	
Hoffman, Adam	12, July 1849	July	49		L3	
Hoffman, Andrew	5, May 1831		estate		L3	
Hoffman, Armitte	31, Dec. 1846	Dec.	8		L3	
Hoffman, Barney	29, Nov. 1849	Nov.	24		L3	
Hoffman, Cornelius	17, Mar. 1826		probate		L3	
Hoffman, Frederick	25, July 1850	July			L3	
Hoffman, Jacob	26, July 1849	July	60		L3	
Hoffman, John	3, Sept 1846	Aug.	32		L3	
Hoffman, John	11, Nov. 1825		estate		L3	
Hoffman, John	5, Jan. 1854		estate		L3	

Name	Notice Date	Death Date	Age		Page	Maiden Name
Hoffman, John	20, Dec. 1825		probate		L4	
Hoffman, John H.	12, Jan. 1837		probate		L3	
Hoffman, Margaret	20, Aug. 1840	Aug.	1		L3	
Hoffman, Peter	15, Apr. 1847	Apr.	32		L3	
Hoffman, Peter	29, May 1834		probate		L3	
Hoffman, Sarah A.	31, Apr. 1845	Apr.	7m		L3	
Hoffmeister, Henry	24, Sept 1857	23, Sept	40		L3	
Hoffmier, Peter	12, July 1849	July	40		L3	
Hoffner, Caroline	29, May 1834		probate		L3	
Hoffner, Delilah	29, May 1834		probate		L3	
Hoffner, George	13, Mar. 1856		estate		L3	
Hoffner, Jacob	9, July 1846	29, June	81	*	L3	
Hoffner, James M.	26, July 1832	July	1- 4m		L1	
Hoffner, John	1, Aug. 1850	17, July	62		L3	
Hofsis, John	10, Apr. 1851	Apr.	36		L3	
Hog, Michael	31, July 1845	July	5d		L3	
Hogan, Dennis	29, Aug. 1844	Aug.	40		L3	
Hogan, Matthew	10, Apr. 1851	Apr.	65		L3	
Hogan, Patrick	19, Apr. 1849	Apr.	40		L3	
Hogan, William	24, Jan. 1850	Jan.	25		L3	
Hogbroth, Henry	10, Mar. 1853	Feb.	67		L3	
Hogue, Elijah	20, Jan. 1848	Jan.	21		L3	
Holabird, Amos B.	23, Sept 1852	18, Sept	65		L3	
Holabird, Caroline	5, July 1849	1, July	48		L3	
Holcomb, Alice Penthea	14, Oct. 1847	4, Oct.	infant		L3	
Holcomb, Jonathan (Dr)	14, Oct. 1847	1, Oct.	86	*	L3	
Holcomb, Mary Ann	13, Nov. 1834	Nov.	21- 3m		L1	
Holcomb, Ozea	29, Aug. 1833	Aug.	1		L1	
Holcum, Cornelia	30, Mar. 1848	Mar.	25		L3	
Holden, Amos P.	7, Oct. 1852	2, Oct.	46		L3	
Holden, Amos P.	3, May 1855		probate		L3	
Holden, Cornelia Prichard	4, Jan. 1844	31, Dec.	7- 6m		L3	
Holden, Fanny	9, Apr. 1857	8, Apr.	7m		L3	
Holden, George	8, Nov. 1855		probate		L3	
Holden, Hellen Seymore	23, Nov. 1848	16, Nov.	6- 6m		L3	
Holden, Ira	4, Jan. 1849	30, Dec.	15m		L3	
Holden, Ira R.	27, Apr. 1854	25, Apr.	2- 9m		L3	
Holden, Mary Jane	3, Mar. 1853	27, Feb.	43		L3	
Holden, Nehemiah	20, Nov. 1850	10, Nov.	88		L3	
Holden, Richard T.	4, Apr. 1823		estate		L3	
Holderfield, (child of Mr)	7, Aug. 1834	July	2m		L3	
Holderfield, William	7, Aug. 1834	July	5		L3	
Hole, Isabel	5, July 1849		estate		L3	
Hole, John	14, June 1814		estate		L3	
Hole, John	15, Nov. 1809		estate		L4	
Hole, Margaret	26, Apr. 1849	18, Apr.	53- 6m		L3	
Holeman, Barney	8, Aug. 1850	July	29		L3	
Holland, James	19, May 1853	15, May			L3	
Holland, Palmer	18, July 1850	11, July	39		L3	
Holland, Palmer	18, July 1850		estate		L3	
Holland, Rutledge	17, May 1855		14		L3	
Hollenbeck, C.F.	6, Mar. 1856		probate		L3	
Hollenbrant, John	28, June 1849	June	67		L3	
Holley, Edmund	11, Sept 1834	Aug.	16		L1	

Name	Notice Date	Death Date	Age		Page	Maiden Name
Holley, Elizabeth	28, Nov. 1844	21, Nov.			L3	
Holley, Emily	11, Jan. 1844	Jan.	16		L3	
Holley, Mary	17, Dec. 1846	14, Dec.	45		L3	
Holley, Mary	13, Dec. 1849	5, Dec.	58		L3	
Holley, Mary	10, Sept 1846	2, Sept	61		L3	Austin
Holley, Nathaniel, Jr.	19, Oct. 1843	17, Oct.			L3	
Holley, William Augustus	8, Feb. 1838	7, Feb.	19		L3	
Hollgath, Amelia	26, Nov. 1857	23, Nov.	77- 9m	*	L3	
Holliday, Mary Ella	30, Aug. 1855	28, Aug.	3- 3m		L3	
Holliday, William	7, Apr. 1853	5, Apr.	55		L3	
Hollingsworth, Charles Lemuel	20, July 1854	13, July	10m-13d		L3	
Hollingsworth, Valentine M.	25, Oct. 1849	9, Oct.	21		L3	
Hollister, Mary Ann	27, Jan. 1853	26, Jan.			L3	
Hollman, John	6, Mar. 1856		probate		L3	
Hollman, Magdalena	6, Mar. 1856		probate		L3	
Hollmann, Henry	5, July 1849	June	30		L3	
Holloway, Isaiah	19, Mar. 1846	Mar.	33		L3	
Hollowell, Orlando	13, Mar. 1851	5, Mar.	34		L3	
Holly, Mary A.	27, Dec. 1849	17, Dec.	24		L3	
Holm, Andrew Leonard	3, Nov. 1831		estate		L3	
Holman, E.	6, Mar. 1856		probate		L3	
Holman, Sarah	23, Sept 1852	16, Sept			L3	
Holmer, Sarah	7, Aug. 1834	July	31		L3	
Holmes, (Mrs)	18, Oct. 1832	10, Oct.	40		L4	
Holmes, Edward H.	11, Aug. 1842	4, Aug.	23m		L3	
Holmes, Ella	21, May 1857	18, May	2		L3	
Holmes, Hamden A.	27, Aug. 1840	Aug.	27		L3	
Holmes, James M.	24, Mar. 1806	17, Mar.			L3	
Holmes, Julia F.	8, May 1845	3, May	9		L3	
Holmes, Kate	19, Oct. 1854	13, Oct.	1- -28d		L3	
Holmes, Leonard	22, June 1843		47		L3	
Holmes, Lucy	27, Dec. 1832	Dec.	9m		L1	
Holmes, Patrick	28, Mar. 1850	Mar.	37		L3	
Holmes, Peter	2, Oct. 1845	Sept	36		L3	
Holmes, William	25, Aug. 1842		estate		L3	
Holmes, William	14, July 1842	13, July		*	L3	
Holroyd, E.B. (Mrs)	19, July 1849	10, July	30		L3	
Holroyde, Hannah	31, Aug. 1854	29, Aug.			L3	
Holsall, James	8, Aug. 1850	July	30		L3	
Holt, Carrie B.	20, Apr. 1854		8m-12d		L3	
Holt, Elizabeth	10, Dec. 1857		probate		L3	
Holt, William	8, Oct. 1846	30, Sept	55	*	L3	
Holt, William	22, Oct. 1846		estate		L3	
Holtzinger, George W.	9, June 1853		estate		L3	
Homer, James	31, Aug. 1848	Aug.	32		L3	
Homer, Jonathan (Rev)	24, Aug. 1843	10, Aug.	84		L3	
Hoober, (child of Isaac)	20, June 1833	June	12d		L1	
Hoober, Elizabeth	23, May 1833	May	6-10m		L4	
Hood, John	18, Dec. 1834		estate		L2	
Hood, John	14, Dec. 1837		estate		L3	
Hood, John	5, Sept 1839		probate		L3	
Hood, John	11, Jan. 1838		estate		L4	
Hood, Lewis P.	26, Sept 1833	Sept	80		L4	
Hood, Richard W.	24, July 1845	July	25		L3	

Name	Notice Date	Death Date	Age		Page	Maiden Name
Hood, William	8, June 1837	June	1		L2	
Hook, Frederick	25, Oct. 1832	Oct.	19		L1	
Hooke, Mercy	8, Aug. 1833	July	24		L1	
Hooks, Barbara	15, June 1837	June	1d		L4	
Hoole, John Edmund	24, Aug. 1854	17, Aug.	7m		L3	
Hoole, Mary E.	9, Oct. 1834	Sept	25		L1	
Hoole, Samuel	8, Aug. 1839		estate		L3	
Hoole, Samuel	3, Dec. 1840		probate		L3	
Hoole, William R.	2, Oct. 1834	Sept	1- 9m-13d		L4	
Hoon, Mary Isabella	19, May 1853	12, May	7- 6m		L3	
Hooper, John	28, Aug. 1845	Aug.	11m		L3	
Hooper, Sarah	13, Nov. 1845	5, Nov.	68		L3	
Hoople, Eliza Jane	21, May 1857	12, May	32		L3	
Hoover, Edward S.	10, Dec. 1840	Nov.	5m		L3	
Hoover, Felix	4, Nov. 1847				L1	
Hoover, Jacob	1, Sept 1842	Aug.	4w		L3	
Hopgood, James	20, June 1844	June	3		L3	
Hopkins, Ann	1, Aug. 1833	July	37		L1	
Hopkins, Augustus	7, Apr. 1842		estate		L3	
Hopkins, Augustus	3, Mar. 1842	2, Mar.			L3	
Hopkins, B.W.	13, Feb. 1840		probate		L3	
Hopkins, Benjamin	29, Nov. 1832		estate		L2	
Hopkins, Benjamin	18, Oct. 1832	13, Oct.			L2	
Hopkins, Benjamin	5, Sept 1839		probate		L3	
Hopkins, Benjamin W.	3, Sept 1840		probate		L3	
Hopkins, E.D.	17, Jan. 1850		estate		L3	
Hopkins, Edward	18, Oct. 1832	Oct.			L2	
Hopkins, Eliza	4, May 1848	Apr.	23		L3	
Hopkins, Frances Gardner	7, Jan. 1836	16, Dec.	41		L3	Ruffin
Hopkins, John	10, May 1849	May	21		L3	
Hopkins, John	17, Dec. 1840	Dec.	45		L3	
Hopkins, John Estaugh	19, Apr. 1845	14, Apr.			L3	
Hopkins, Mary	18, Oct. 1832	13, Oct.			L2	
Hopkins, Mary	13, Dec. 1838	5, Dec.	61		L4	
Hopkins, Mary Olivia	11, Dec. 1851	8, Dec.	22- 6m-15d	*	L3	Spafford
Hopkins, Samuel H.	11, Apr. 1844	Apr.	44		L3	
Hopkins, Thomas	4, Oct. 1849	Sept	30		L3	
Hopkins, William M.	25, July 1850	17, July	20		L3	
Hopkson, Abbey	12, Oct. 1854	9, Oct.	70		L3	
Hopper, Charles W.	26, Jan. 1854	12, Jan.	49		L3	
Hopper, Henry	24, Nov. 1836		estate		L3	
Hopper, Janet	7, July 1853	2, July	35		L3	
Hopper, John C.	14, Feb. 1828	Feb.	1- 3m		L1	
Hopper, Samuel	17, May 1849	May	28		L3	
Hoppiken, James	15, July 1847	July	35		L3	
Hopping, Luther	5, June 1851	18, May	69	*	L3	
Hopple, Anna M.	1, Nov. 1855	26, Oct.	80		L3	
Hopple, Richard B.	9, May 1844	8, May			L3	
Hopwood, William T.	16, Oct. 1834	Oct.	2		L1	
Hordock, Susan	7, Sept 1837	Aug.	20		L3	
Horman, Frederick	4, June 1857		probate		L3	
Horn, (man)	1, Apr. 1847	28, Mar.			L3	
Horn, Elizabeth	25, July 1833	July	6		L1	
Horn, Mary Ann	10, Jan. 1828	Jan.	1- -18d		L4	

Name	Notice Date	Death Date	Age		Page	Maiden Name
Horn, Patrick	13, Mar. 1845	Mar.	30		L3	
Horn, Zachariah	23, May 1850	May	19		L3	
Horne, Catharine E.	25, Apr. 1833	Apr.	3- 8m		L1	
Horne, Joseph	11, Apr. 1833	Apr.	3- 4m		L1	
Horney, Eleanor	8, Aug. 1833	July	1- 6m		L1	
Hornor, Isaac J.	1, Dec. 1826	9, Nov.	29		L3	
Horr, Julia	1, Aug. 1850	July	2		L3	
Horrocks, E.	15, Nov. 1832	Nov.	18		L1	
Horrocks, Frances A.	2, Aug. 1832	July	1- 3m		L1	
Horrocks, John Freeland	11, Mar. 1847	9, Mar.	25		L3	
Horrocks, Mary Jane	6, Dec. 1832	Dec.	6- 6m		L1	
Horton, Jonathan K.	24, Feb. 1848	23, Feb.	71	*	L3	
Horton, Milton	9, Sept 1852	3, Sept	3- - 3d		L3	
Horton, Nicholas T.	23, July 1857	21, July			L3	
Horton, Sarah	22, May 1845	20, May			L3	
Horts, Frederick W.	2, May 1850	Apr.	8d		L3	
Hosea, Anna Cora	19, Jan. 1854	18, Jan.	3- 2m		L3	
Hosea, Emma Gallagher	12, Jan. 1854	8, Jan.	9m		L3	
Hosea, Robert	16, Mar. 1848	12, Mar.	61		L3	
Hosea, Robert	20, Apr. 1848		estate		L3	
Hosick, (woman)	10, Mar. 1853	9, Mar.			L3	
Hosmer, Victoria	28, July 1842	July	18m		L3	
Hoss, Lene	30, May 1850	May	1m		L3	
Host, Joseph	12, July 1849	July	28		L3	
Hotchkiss, (child of Silas C)	3, Jan. 1833	Dec.	1d		L4	
Hotchkiss, Augusta	14, June 1849	11, June		*	L3	
Hotchkiss, D.C.	21, Feb. 1850	14, Feb.	46		L3	
Hotchkiss, George	20, June 1839	9, June	56	*	L3	
Hotchkiss, Silas C.	13, Nov. 1856	7, Nov.	51		L3	
Hotson, Daniel	2, Mar. 1854	7, Feb.	64		L3	
Hotzer, Henry	6, Sept 1855		probate		L3	
Houke, Adam	29, Mar. 1855	27, Mar.			L3	
Houmeboy, James	10, Mar. 1853	Feb.	30		L3	
House, Caroline	26, Feb. 1852	18, Feb.	2- 4m		L3	
Houseman, Louis	28, Aug. 1851	24, Aug.			L3	
Houslet, Leonard	4, May 1854	29, Apr.			L3	
Houston, Hiram	7, May 1846	3, May	23		L3	
Houston, Mary Ann	4, Oct. 1838	2, Oct.			L3	
Houston, Robert	14, Mar. 1839	Mar.	33		L3	
Houtsberger, Kitty	1, Oct. 1819	13, Sept			L3	
Howard, Andrew	10, Jan. 1828	Jan.	15		L4	
Howard, Anna	13, Jan. 1853	6, Jan.	89		L3	
Howard, Charles	7, Apr. 1853	30, Mar.	5- 3m		L3	
Howard, Eliza	3, Jan. 1850	Dec.	27		L3	
Howard, Freeman	2, Mar. 1843	Feb.	24		L3	
Howard, George	18, Oct. 1838		estate		L3	
Howard, George W.	21, Apr. 1853	13, Apr.	1- 3m		L3	
Howard, John	28, June 1849	June	67		L3	
Howard, Levi H.	23, Feb. 1854	5, Feb.	59	*	L3	
Howard, Lydia	8, May 1828	May	38		L1	
Howard, Mary	7, Aug. 1834	July	33		L3	
Howard, Sally	22, Aug. 1833	12, Aug.	35		L1	Harthorn
Howard, William	7, May 1840	Apr.			L3	
Howarth, Alice	12, Nov. 1846	5, Nov.	7- 6m		L3	

Name	Notice Date	Death Date	Age		Page	Maiden Name
Howarth, Sarah Ann	3, Sept 1846	25, Aug.		*	L3	
Howe, Abigail	27, Sept 1832	27, Sept	39		L1	
Howe, Clara	8, Dec. 1853	13, Nov.		*	L3	Pierson
Howe, Hammond	5, July 1855		probate		L3	
Howe, John	8, Oct. 1829		estate		L3	
Howe, John F.	6, Oct. 1853		estate		L3	
Howe, Maria	29, Dec. 1842	21, Dec.	35		L3	
Howe, S.G.	19, July 1838	9, July	5m		L3	
Howel, Adam	30, Dec. 1814		estate		L3	
Howel, Anne	8, Dec. 1807	2, Dec.			L2	
Howel, Eliza	9, Feb. 1809	7, Feb.			L3	
Howel, Silas (Major)	15, Apr. 1812	10, Apr.			L3	
Howell, Alice Maud	6, Aug. 1846	31, July	15m		L3	
Howell, Clarissa H.	12, Sept 1850	3, Sept			L3	
Howell, Daniel G.	3, Feb. 1826		estate		L3	
Howell, Elias	30, May 1844	16, May			L3	
Howell, Hannah	21, Feb. 1850	18, Feb.	97		L3	
Howell, Jacob H.	2, Dec. 1830		estate		L3	
Howell, Lemuel	16, May 1850	May	35		L3	
Howell, Lewis	13, Nov. 1834	Nov.	46		L1	
Howell, Lewis	4, Dec. 1834		estate		L3	
Howell, Lewis	11, June 1835		estate		L3	
Howell, Mary	21, Mar. 1844	18, Mar.	48		L3	
Howell, Stephen	3, Mar. 1836	1, Mar.	35		L3	
Howes, Hiram	14, Mar. 1833		estate		L3	
Howk, Michael	12, Feb. 1812		estate		L2	
Howk, Michael	2, June 1812		estate		L3	
Howland, Eloise	3, Apr. 1856	4, Mar.	19		L3	Lockwood
Howland, Mary Emma	3, Apr. 1856	4, Mar.	9m		L3	
Howorth, Ruth	26, Feb. 1857	18, Feb.			L3	
Hoy, Charles W.	9, July 1857	1, July	33		L3	
Hoyt, John H.	6, Sept 1855	20, Aug.	21	*	L3	
Hubbard, Christopher S.	11, Sept 1845	3, Sept	39		L3	
Hubbard, Jane	6, Apr. 1848	4, Apr.	77		L3	
Hubbard, Joshua (Dr)	17, May 1849		67		L3	
Hubbard, L.V.	26, Apr. 1849	17, Apr.			L3	
Hubbell, Daniel Gano	8, Sept 1853	6, Sept	28		L3	
Hubbell, Gabriel	8, May 1828	May	37		L1	
Hubbell, Martha P.	10, May 1855	1, May	16m		L3	
Hubbell, N.S.	12, Apr. 1855	11, Apr.	61	*	L3	
Hubbell, Nathaniel S.	12, Apr. 1855	9, Apr.	61		L3	
Hubbell, Stephen H.	6, June 1850	30, May	37		L3	
Hubbell, T. Borden	2, Oct. 1856	29, Sept			L1	
Hubbell, Thomas	20, Jan. 1842		95	*	L3	
Hubbell, Thomas Borden	2, Oct. 1856	29, Sept	38		L5	
Hubbs, Ceanne	6, June 1833	May	1- 6m		L2	
Hubbs, Leopold	28, Mar. 1850	Mar.	34		L3	
Hubel, Anthony	20, Mar. 1851	Mar.			L3	
Huber, Eary	21, June 1849	June	27		L3	
Huber, Martha Louise	25, Dec. 1856	16, Dec.	19		L3	Cary
Hudbleer, George	18, July 1833	July	47		L2	
Huddart, Amelia	1, Apr. 1847	31, Mar.	3m		L3	
Huddart, John	8, Aug. 1833	July	1- 5m		L1	
Huddart, Joseph	22, Aug. 1833		estate		L3	

Name	Notice Date	Death Date	Age	Page	Maiden Name
Huddart, Joseph	24, May 1838		estate	L3	
Huddleston, John	18, Apr. 1850	Apr.	40	L3	
Hudson, Albert	4, Apr. 1850	Mar.	18	L3	
Hudson, Francis	3, Sept 1846	Aug.	3	L3	
Hudson, Guy	1, Jan. 1835		estate	L3	
Hudson, Guy	23, June 1836		estate	L3	
Hudson, Ira	15, Feb. 1849	Feb.	38	L3	
Hudson, James	19, July 1849	July	40	L3	
Hudson, John	29, July 1847	23, July	80	L3	
Hudson, Mary Ann	15, May 1834	May	17	L4	
Hudson, Robert	18, Oct. 1849	Oct.	35	L3	
Hudson, Sarah A.	27, Feb. 1851	Feb.	2m	L3	
Huer, William A.	16, Feb. 1837		estate	L3	
Hueston, Paul	9, Jan. 1845		estate	L3	
Hueston, Samuel L.	22, Mar. 1838		probate	L3	
Huey, Robert	9, June 1807		estate	L2	
Huff, George	24, Aug. 1848	Aug.	23	L3	
Huffman, Andrew	11, July 1833		probate	L3	
Huffman, Elias	19, Oct. 1848		estate	L3	
Huffman, Elias	23, Aug. 1849		estate	L3	
Huffman, Robert	5, Feb. 1835		estate	L3	
Huffman, Robert	7, Dec. 1837		probate	L3	
Hugeanyer, Mary	27, Feb. 1851	Feb.	45	L3	
Huggerford, C.O.	21, Sept 1837		probate	L4	
Hughes, Ada Louisa	17, May 1849	10, May	infant	L3	
Hughes, Barbour	6, Jan. 1848		estate	L3	
Hughes, Catharine	12, Nov. 1857	5, Nov.		L3	
Hughes, Charles John (Lt)	26, Sept 1839	22, Sept		L3	
Hughes, Edward	11, Apr. 1839	Apr.	25	L3	
Hughes, Ellen M.	18, July 1833	July	1- 9m	L2	
Hughes, Harbour	9, Dec. 1847		estate	L3	
Hughes, Henry	11, July 1844	July	30	L3	
Hughes, James	22, Nov. 1855	14, Nov.		L3	
Hughes, James (Rev)	19, May 1821	2, May		L3	
Hughes, John	9, June 1836		probate	L3	
Hughes, Mary	1, Aug. 1833	July	55	L1	
Hughes, Michael	14, Mar. 1850	Mar.	16	L3	
Hughes, Rachael B.	26, Apr. 1855	21, Apr.		L3	
Hughes, Rebecca	3, Sept 1857	28, Aug.	81- 3m-10d	L3	
Hughes, Richard	24, Oct. 1850		estate	L3	
Hughey, John	3, Oct. 1844	Sept	13	L3	
Hughey, Samuel	10, Oct. 1844	Oct.	1	L3	
Hughs, Thomas	27, Dec. 1849	Dec.	26	L3	
Hugo, Jane	9, Feb. 1854	13, Dec.		L3	
Huhn, Henry	5, Mar. 1857		probate	L3	
Hukill, Nancy	19, July 1849	16, July	57	L3	
Hulbert, Amelia	11, July 1850	9, July	34	L3	
Hulbert, Mary Ellen	24, Sept 1846	20, Sept	16m	L3	
Hulbert, Stephen	3, June 1818		estate	L2	
Hulent, Samuel	25, July 1833	July		L1	
Hull, (Mrs)	22, Jan. 1816	4, Dec.		L1	
Hull, Julius	15, July 1852	8, July		L3	
Hull, Lucy Amelia	22, July 1852	11, July	29-11m-22d *	L3	Ives
Hull, M.C.	20, May 1847	25, Apr.	37	L3	

Name	Notice Date	Death Date	Age		Page	Maiden Name
Hull, Morris N.B.	2, Aug. 1820	1, Aug.			L3	
Hull, Stella Amelia	7, Aug. 1856	4, Aug.	13m-15d		L5	
Hull, Stetta Abby	12, Dec. 1850	8, Dec.	4- 7m-12d		L3	
Hulm, Barnard	31, May 1849	May	35		L3	
Hulse, Ebenezer	15, Oct. 1857	8, Oct.	72		L3	
Hulseman, Dorothy	1, Nov. 1832	Oct.	20		L2	
Hultzschar, John	12, July 1849	July	58		L3	
Humble, Mary A.	8, Oct. 1857	4, Oct.	69		L3	
Humekamp, Catharine	20, Sept 1849	Sept	28		L3	
Humes, Elizabeth Marshal	8, Apr. 1852	24, Mar.			L3	Shaw
Humes, John (Mrs)	6, Jan. 1806	29, Dec.			L3	
Humpfelt, (Mr)	25, Oct. 1832	19, Oct.			L2	
Humphreys, David (Gen)	18, Mar. 1818	21, Feb.			L3	
Humphreys, Elizabeth	30, Aug. 1832	Aug.	32- 1m-12d		L1	
Humphreys, Jane	19, July 1849	July	9m		L3	
Humphreys, John	11, Apr. 1810		estate		L2	
Humphreys, John	27, May 1847	May	46		L3	
Humphreys, John	31, Oct. 1810		estate		L3	
Hunkeviller, George	3, July 1851	June	55		L3	
Hunnewell, Martha Ann	5, Mar. 1840	19, Feb.	19	*	L3	
Hunt, (child of John F.)	20, June 1833	June	stillborn		L1	
Hunt, Abijah	24, July 1811	9, June			L3	
Hunt, Anna M.	17, July 1851	23, June	17		L3	
Hunt, Anna M.	7, Aug. 1851	23, June	17		L3	
Hunt, B.P.	24, Dec. 1840	6, Dec.	27		L3	
Hunt, B.V. (Dr)	4, Jan. 1849				L3	
Hunt, Catharine	29, Nov. 1838		estate		L3	
Hunt, Charles H.	1, Aug. 1850	18, July			L3	
Hunt, Charlotte	30, Jan. 1851	21, Jan.	87	*	L3	
Hunt, Cornelia A.	23, Nov. 1854	20, Nov.			L3	
Hunt, Daniel	6, Nov. 1834		estate		L4	
Hunt, Eliza	12, Nov. 1829	29, Oct.	59	*	L2	
Hunt, Eliza Louisa	8, Nov. 1814	31, Oct.	15		L3	
Hunt, Flavel	11, Nov. 1841	4, Nov.	60	*	L3	
Hunt, George N.	21, Oct. 1825		estate		L4	
Hunt, Hannah	7, Aug. 1834	July	32- 1m		L3	
Hunt, Henry	7, Aug. 1834	July	4		L3	
Hunt, Henry L.	11, Oct. 1838	10, Oct.		*	L3	
Hunt, Isaac	11, Dec. 1851		estate		L3	
Hunt, Isaac	5, Mar. 1857		probate		L3	
Hunt, James	19, July 1849	July	32		L3	
Hunt, James	19, Sept 1833	Sept	10m		L4	
Hunt, James A.	28, June 1849	June	33		L3	
Hunt, Jane	7, June 1855	2, June	42		L3	
Hunt, Jeremiah	17, Feb. 1824		estate		L1	
Hunt, John	4, Feb. 1847	Jan.	69		L3	
Hunt, John C.S.	25, Oct. 1832	Oct.	11m		L1	
Hunt, John G.	3, Apr. 1851	27, Feb.	4		L3	
Hunt, Joshua	4, July 1833	June	76		L2	
Hunt, Lewis	13, Nov. 1856	22, Oct.	68		L3	
Hunt, Louisa	3, July 1851	12, June	39	*	L3	
Hunt, Mary H.	25, Sept 1845	23, Sept	52		L3	
Hunt, Priscilla Ann	7, Apr. 1836		estate		L4	
Hunt, Rebecca	1, July 1847	June	55		L3	

Name	Notice Date	Death Date	Age		Page	Maiden Name
Hunt, Reuben	22, Sept 1836		estate		L4	
Hunt, Samuel F.	16, Apr. 1835		estate		L3	
Hunt, Samuel F.	29, Sept 1836		estate		L3	
Hunt, Seth	21, May 1846	9, Apr.	66		L3	
Hunt, Timothy	21, Feb. 1850	Feb.	65		L3	
Hunter, George	6, Dec. 1855		probate		L3	
Hunter, John	26, June 1851	June	35		L3	
Hunter, Lydia	5, July 1849	June	10		L3	
Hunter, Mary	3, Aug. 1843	27, July	infant		L3	
Hunter, Phoebe	1, Feb. 1844		84	*	L3	Bryant
Hunter, Robert	15, Oct. 1846	Oct.	15m		L3	
Hunter, Samuel	25, Oct. 1832	Oct.	55		L1	
Hunter, Serona	19, Sept 1850	17, Sept	4		L3	
Hunter, Thomas	12, Jan. 1819		estate		L4	
Hunter, William	6, Dec. 1849	29, Nov.		*	L3	
Hunter, William L.	24, Oct. 1850		estate		L3	
Hunting, Richard	16, Oct. 1845		1-10m		L3	
Huntington, E.	28, Oct. 1852	1, Oct.	63		L3	
Huntington, Janette Humphreys	28, Jan. 1847	21, Jan.	19- 1m		L3	Canfield
Huntington, Samuel	7, July 1817	7, June	49		L2	
Huntington, Thomas Wolcott	4, Feb. 1847	27, Jan.	10d		L3	
Huntress, Daniel W.	3, July 1845				L3	
Huntsman, Amanda H.	23, June 1853	17, June	17		L3	
Hurd, (child of Chester P.)	30, Aug. 1832	Aug.	1d		L1	
Hurd, Ada	13, July 1854	21, June	1- 7m-26d		L3	
Hurd, Robert S.	29, July 1852	27, July			L3	
Hurd, Sally	16, Apr. 1846	8, Apr.	2- 9m-15d		L3	
Hurde, John	10, Aug. 1843	Aug.	35		L3	
Hurdus, Adam (Rev)	7, Sept 1843	30, Aug.	84		L3	
Hurdus, Hannah	3, Nov. 1836	2, Nov.	74		L3	
Hurdus, James	23, May 1850	14, May	62		L3	
Hurdus, James	8, Nov. 1855		probate		L3	
Hurford, John	3, Nov. 1807	27, Oct.	42		L3	
Hurin, Enos	16, June 1842		estate		L3	
Hurley, Daniel	14, Aug. 1845	Aug.	54		L3	
Hurley, Mary	21, June 1849	June	51		L3	
Hurley, Theodore	19, Dec. 1850		estate		L3	
Hurmiler, John	6, Jan. 1848	Dec.	14		L3	
Hurst, Thomas	28, Sept 1848	22, Sept	3		L3	
Hurst, Valentine	11, Mar. 1852	8, Mar.			L3	
Husch, John	7, Feb. 1856		probate		L3	
Huss, James	14, Aug. 1856		probate		L6	
Hussey, Edith	15, Nov. 1832	Nov.	20		L1	
Hussey, John B.	25, Oct. 1832	Oct.	33		L1	
Huston, Andrew	23, Mar. 1854	13, Mar.	63		L3	
Huston, Martha	29, July 1841	18, July			L3	Carne
Huston, Mary	21, Oct. 1847	18, Oct.	3- 7m		L3	
Huston, Nancy A.	7, Aug. 1834	July	2- 1m		L3	
Hutchenson, James	29, Aug. 1850	Aug.	4- 6m		L3	
Hutchenson, William	9, Oct. 1834	Sept	1- 1m		L1	
Hutcheson, John	4, Apr. 1850	Mar.	16		L3	
Hutchins, (Mrs)	8, Nov. 1832	Nov.	25		L1	
Hutchins, Anthony (Col)	1, Jan. 1805	15, Dec.	80		L3	
Hutchins, Harriet	27, Mar. 1828	Mar.	3m		L1	

Name	Notice Date	Death Date	Age		Page	Maiden Name
Hutchinson, Anna Gertrude	21, Dec. 1848	13, Dec.	3- 3m		L3	
Hutchinson, E.	15, Jan. 1835		estate		L3	
Hutchinson, Edward	14, Feb. 1839	12, Feb.	44		L3	
Hutchinson, George	13, Feb. 1840	1, Feb.			L3	
Hutchinson, John	30, Dec. 1830		estate		L3	
Hutchinson, Jonathan	3, Dec. 1840		estate		L3	
Hutchinson, Robert	22, June 1837		probate		L3	
Hutchinson, Romeyn Stafford	5, Dec. 1850	29, Nov.	2- 3m		L3	
Hutchinson, Ruth	4, Feb. 1836	3, Feb.	22	*	L3	
Hutchinson, Thomas	2, Apr. 1829		estate		L3	
Hutchinson, William(heirs of)	15, Sept 1836		probate		L3	
Hutchison, Harriet	12, Sept 1850	Sept	9		L3	
Hutton, Peregrine	2, Aug. 1820	1, Aug.			L3	
Hutton, Robert	18, Oct. 1832	Oct.	49		L4	
Hutton, Sarah Ann	12, Nov. 1857	7, Nov.	41		L3	
Hyatt, (child of Caleb)	8, Aug. 1833	July			L1	
Hyatt, (Mrs)	25, Oct. 1832	20, Oct.			L2	
Hyatt, Adaline	23, Oct. 1834	Oct.	6- 9m		L2	
Hyatt, Jesse	11, Apr. 1833	Apr.	45		L1	
Hyatt, John T.	12, Jan. 1854	5, Jan.	2- 3m-15d		L3	
Hyatt, Squire	16, Aug. 1838		estate		L3	
Hyatt, Squire	3, Sept 1840		probate		L3	
Hyde, (Mrs)	1, Nov. 1832	25, Oct.			L1	
Hyde, James	11, Dec. 1856	6, Dec.	23	*	L3	
Hyde, William	31, May 1849	May	23		L3	
Hyle, George	23, Aug. 1838	Aug.	30		L3	
Hymore, John	18, July 1833	July	36		L2	
Hynan, Elizabeth	23, Aug. 1849	Aug.	28		L3	
Ibbs, James	15, Nov. 1849	Nov.	30		L3	
Iglehart, Aaron Gano	11, July 1839	5, July	11m-24d		L3	
Iglehart, Frances Jane	28, Jan. 1841	21, Jan.	16m-24d		L3	
Iglehart, Henry Gibbons	19, Oct. 1848	7, Oct.			L3	
Iglehart, Jane	24, Apr. 1851	19, Apr.	70	*	L3	
Iglehart, John S.	31, Mar. 1853		estate		L3	
Iglehart, Mary Esther	13, June 1844	6, June	17m-13d		L3	
Iler, (child of Mrs)	25, Oct. 1832	22, Oct.	5		L3	
Iler, (Mrs)	25, Oct. 1832	21, Oct.			L3	
Iler, George	25, Oct. 1832	22, Oct.			L3	
Ilgner, Theodore Ernest	20, June 1839		estate		L3	
Ilus, Francis	20, Dec. 1838	Dec.	33		L3	
Imlay, Sally	5, Dec. 1810	29, Nov.			L3	
Immel, Jacob	17, July 1845	10, July	50		L3	
Incell, Mary Ann	17, Jan. 1850	12, Jan.			L2	
Indecut, Joseph	20, Sept 1832	Sept	54		L1	
Ingalls, Julia A.	24, May 1855	8, May	33	*	L3	Fink
Ingalls, William	3, Apr. 1856	27, Mar.	40- 6m		L3	
Ingalsbe, Sarah	28, June 1849	22, June			L3	
Ingalsbe, Sarah Augusta	27, Jan. 1848	19, Jan.	2- 3m		L3	
Ingersoll, James	7, Feb. 1856		probate		L3	
Ingle, Almy J.	17, Aug. 1848	Aug.	2		L3	
Ingleking, Henry	28, Sept 1837		estate		L3	
Ingleking, Henry	22, Mar. 1838		probate		L3	
Ingles, Thomas	2, Nov. 1854	20, Oct.	30		L3	

Name	Notice Date	Death Date	Age		Page	Maiden Name
Inglis, Frederick	29, Aug. 1833	Aug.	28		L1	
Ingram, Louisa	28, Aug. 1845	Aug.	3m		L3	
Ingram, Peter	31, Apr. 1845	Apr.	51		L3	
Ingram, Samuel	16, Oct. 1834	Oct.	21		L1	
Innis, Francis	14, May 1829		estate		L3	
Iratabos, Maurice	23, Feb. 1837		probate		L3	
Ireland, (child of Sarah)	12, Feb. 1846	Feb.	5d		L3	
Ireland, (Mr)	18, Oct. 1832	Oct.			L2	
Ireland, Aaron	20, Apr. 1813		estate		L3	
Ireland, Aaron	7, Sept 1813		estate		L3	
Ireland, George	12, Apr. 1855	23, Jan.	20- 9m	*	L3	
Ireton, Alicia	16, Oct. 1851	15, Oct.	19		L3	
Irish, John R.	5, July 1849	June	53		L3	
Ironhart, John	22, Mar. 1838	Mar.	38		L3	
Irons, Laura A.	16, Nov. 1843	9, Nov.	5		L3	
Irons, Sarah	8, Feb. 1844	7, Feb.			L3	
Irvin, William W.	7, Apr. 1842	Mar.	63		L3	
Irvine, Callender (Gen)	21, Oct. 1841	9, Oct.			L3	
Irvine, John	17, June 1841	June	12		L3	
Irwin, (child of Abby)	16, Sept 1847	Sept	4		L3	
Irwin, Amelia	10, Sept 1846	3, Sept			L3	
Irwin, Ann	25, Feb. 1847	23, Feb.		*	L3	
Irwin, Archibald	9, 16, Sept 1852	4, Sept	56		L3	
Irwin, Archibald, Jr.	16, Sept 1852	7, Sept	46		L3	
Irwin, Catharine	4, Dec. 1851		estate		L3	
Irwin, Catharine Allemong	20, Nov. 1851	10, Nov.	85		L3	
Irwin, Catharine Whiteman	22, Aug. 1850	20, Aug.	1- - 8d		L3	
Irwin, Emily A.	19, June 1851	12, June			L3	Jones
Irwin, George	9, July 1846	June	33		L3	
Irwin, Green W.	24, May 1849	May	24		L3	
Irwin, James	1, Aug. 1833	July	35		L1	
Irwin, James	16, Nov. 1843	9, Nov.	86		L3	
Irwin, James	30, June 1812		estate		L3	
Irwin, James M. (Capt)	16, Aug. 1855	12, Aug.	44		L3	
Irwin, John Vanlear	24, Jan. 1839	19, Jan.	32		L3	
Irwin, Laura Eliza	25, May 1843	18, May	2- 1m-17d		L3	
Irwin, Louisa	4, July 1850	2, July	18		L3	
Irwin, Mary	20, Sept 1825	17, Sept			L3	
Irwin, Mary Jane	16, Dec. 1847	13, Dec.			L3	
Irwin, Mathew Vanlear	30, Mar. 1813	28, Mar.			L3	
Irwin, Thomas	21, Feb. 1839		estate		L3	
Irwin, Thomas	5, Sept 1839		probate		L3	
Irwin, William	8, Aug. 1833	July	2		L1	
Irwin, William	8, Aug. 1833	July	1- 6m		L1	
Irwin, William	28, Jan. 1841	27, Jan.	7		L3	
Irwin, William	22, Nov. 1827		estate		L3	
Irwin, William	24, Feb. 1831		estate		L3	
Irwin, William	12, Jan. 1837		probate		L3	
Irwin, William	23, July 1824	15, July			L3	
Irwin, William	17, Apr. 1856	12, Apr.			L3	
Irwin, William (Major)	14, Dec. 1854	12, Dec.	48		L3	
Isham, William A.	8, Aug. 1833	July	2		L1	
Israel, Alexander	23, Oct. 1834	Oct.	12		L2	
Israel, Elizabeth	27, Apr. 1843	Apr.	48		L3	

Name	Notice Date	Death Date	Age		Page	Maiden Name
Iuppenlatz, George	9, Aug. 1849	6, Aug.	69		L3	
Ives, (Mrs)	25, Oct. 1832	23, Oct.			L3	
Jack, Isaac	12, Jan. 1837		probate		L3	
Jack, Isaac	7, Apr. 1836		estate		L4	
Jackson, (child of Mary)	31, Dec. 1846	Dec.			L3	
Jackson, (Mrs. Gen)	1, Jan. 1829	22, Dec.			L2	
Jackson, David	28, Jan. 1841	12, Jan.	49		L3	
Jackson, David, Jr.	9, Aug. 1855		probate		L3	
Jackson, Deborah C.	13, July 1854	4, July	84		L3	
Jackson, DeWitt Clinton	28, Feb. 1826	25, Feb.	infant		L3	
Jackson, Ella E.	28, July 1853	21, July	4- 5m		L3	
Jackson, Fanny B.C.	9, Feb. 1854	8, Feb.			L3	
Jackson, Fanny B.C.	16, Oct. 1856		probate		L6	
Jackson, Fanny R.C.	5, July 1855		probate		L3	
Jackson, George	2, Sept 1852	Aug.	2		L3	
Jackson, George A.	11, Oct. 1838	10, Oct.	31	*	L3	
Jackson, Henrietta	17, Oct. 1839	Oct.	33		L3	
Jackson, Isaac H.	1, Nov. 1849	26, Oct.	79	*	L3	
Jackson, Jacob	2, Aug. 1838	July	24		L3	
Jackson, James	18, May 1854		10-10m		L3	
Jackson, James	27, Jan. 1842		estate		L3	
Jackson, Jerry	25, Aug. 1842				L1	
Jackson, John	1, Aug. 1833	July	32		L1	
Jackson, Jonathan	11, Jan. 1849	Jan.	35		L3	
Jackson, Margaret	1, Apr. 1847	Mar.	11m		L3	
Jackson, Mariana	3, Dec. 1857	25, Nov.	62		L3	
Jackson, Mary	6, Nov. 1834	Oct.	16		L1	
Jackson, Robert	7, June 1855		probate		L3	
Jackson, Rosanna	31, Oct. 1839	Oct.	3m		L3	
Jackson, Salisbury	25, July 1850	July	26		L3	
Jackson, Samuel G.	22, Dec. 1853	14, Dec.	55		L3	
Jackson, Sarah	21, June 1838	17, June	53	*	L3	
Jackson, Sarah A.	2, Aug. 1849	24, July	51		L3	
Jackson, Sarah Clock	21, Dec. 1854	1, Dec.	51	*	L3	
Jackson, Similin	13, Jan. 1848	Jan.	25		L3	
Jackson, Thomas	16, Oct. 1834	Oct.	33		L1	
Jackson, William	4, Oct. 1833	Sept	1- 7m		L1	
Jackson, William	18, Oct. 1832	11, Oct.			L1	
Jackson, William	26, Sept 1833	Sept	1- 7m		L4	
Jackson, William R.	17, June 1852	14, June	66		L3	
Jacobs, Charles	16, Feb. 1827		probate		L3	
Jacobs, Freelove H.	19, Apr. 1849	15, Apr.	32		L3	
Jacobs, Hans	28, Aug. 1851	24, Aug.			L4	
Jacobs, Harriet Lilie	14, Oct. 1847	13, Oct.	13m		L3	
Jacobs, Jacob	12, Sept 1833	Sept	24		L1	
Jacobs, John	17, Mar. 1826		probate		L3	
Jacobs, N.	24, May 1849	May			L3	
Jacox, Sarah Ann	6, Apr. 1843	Mar.	2		L3	
James, Abner Clark	31, Mar. 1853	30, Mar.	37		L3	
James, Ann Eliza	14, June 1849	8, June			L3	
James, David	7, May 1840	Apr.	2		L3	
James, David	9, Sept 1825		probate		L3	
James, Elizabeth	2, Oct. 1851	23, Sept	56	*	L3	

Name	Notice Date	Death Date	Age		Page	Maiden Name
James, Ellzey L.(Lt)	25, Apr. 1810	9, Apr.	25	*	L3	
James, Fanny Hedden	4, July 1850	30, June	2- 1m- 8d		L3	
James, Henry	1, Aug. 1833	July	21		L1	
James, Henry	9, Jan. 1845	31, Dec.	11m		L3	
James, Hugh	6, Sept 1855		probate		L3	
James, Isaac	9, Apr. 1846	Mar.	57		L3	
James, John Keating	17, June 1841	11, June	2-10m		L3	
James, John W.	18, Oct. 1832	Oct.	25		L4	
James, Kate	15, Nov. 1855	12, Nov.			L3	
James, Lemuel	8, Aug. 1833	July	12		L1	
James, Levi	2, Aug. 1849	27, July	73		L3	
James, Lucy Audubon	14, Oct. 1847	5, Oct.	19m-10d		L3	
James, Margaret K.	15, Aug. 1839	12, Aug.			L3	
James, Mary	30, Nov. 1854	24, Nov.	infant		L3	
James, Mary Ann	16, Feb. 1854	10, Feb.	3- 4m		L3	
James, Mary Ellen	4, July 1850	27, June	8m		L3	
James, Michael	2, June 1853	26, May			L3	
James, Patrick	11, Nov. 1841	Oct.	29		L3	
James, Philip	19, July 1849	July	1- 9m		L3	
James, Pierson Wood	19, Feb. 1857	12, Feb.	6- 1m		L3	
James, Rachael	31, July 1851	29, July			L3	
James, Reuben Langdon	30, Dec. 1852	25, Dec.	2- 4m		L3	
James, Richard	16, Oct. 1856		probate		L6	
James, Sarah Augusta	19, June 1845	18, June	infant		L3	
James, Thomas	13, June 1833	June	27		L1	
James, Thomas	23, Feb. 1843	15, Feb.	89		L3	
James, Thomas	6, Sept 1838	1, Sept		*	L3	
James, Thomas E.	1, Aug. 1833	July	13d		L1	
James, William	7, Sept 1843	Aug.	37	*	L3	
James, William S.	27, Mar. 1851	Mar.	35		L3	
Jameson, E.	18, Oct. 1832	13, Oct.			L2	
Jameson, Peter	30, Dec. 1847				L3	
Jamieson, Edward	1, Nov. 1832		estate		L3	
Jamieson, Edward	20, Aug. 1835		estate		L3	
Jamieson, Edward	17, Mar. 1836		estate		L3	
Jamieson, Edward	29, May 1834		probate		L3	
Jamis, Joseph	22, Nov. 1838		estate		L3	
Jamison, Edward	21, Sept 1837		probate		L4	
Jamison, John	10, June 1841				L3	
Jamison, Mahala	9, Feb. 1854	5, Jan.	41		L3	
Janes, Zachariah	12, Feb. 1852	2, Feb.	21- 4m		L3	
Janeway, (Mrs)	18, Oct. 1832	14, Oct.			L2	
Janny, Rudolph	10, Oct. 1844	Oct.	38		L3	
Janson, Anthony	3, May 1849	Apr.	45		L3	
January, William Huston	12, Nov. 1846	4, Nov.	28		L3	
Jaques, Charles D.	20, Apr. 1854	9, Apr.	52		L3	
Jaquess, Martha	28, Oct. 1847	24, Oct.	48		L3	
Jasper, Conrad	19, Oct. 1837	Oct.	32		L3	
Jasper, Conrad	5, Sept 1839		probate		L3	
Jay, Peter A.	2, Mar. 1843	20, Feb.			L3	
Jay, Priscilla	9, Mar. 1854		30		L3	
Jefferies, Constantine	28, Aug. 1851	26, Aug.	58		L3	
Jefferies, Constantine	26, Apr. 1855		estate		L3	
Jefferies, John C.	12, Apr. 1855	5, Apr.	37- 6m		L3	

Name	Notice Date	Death Date	Age		Page	Maiden Name
Jefferies, John C.	29, Apr. 1852	24, Apr.	8m- 6d		L3	
Jeffers, (Mrs)	25, Apr. 1833	Apr.	37		L1	
Jefferson, Garret	11, July 1833		probate		L3	
Jefferson, Hannah	23, Aug. 1838	Aug.	55		L3	
Jefferson, Henry	6, Sept 1855	1, Sept			L3	
Jefferson, Thomas	21, July 1826	4, July			L3	
Jeffres, Constantine	10, Dec. 1857		probate		L3	
Jeffries, Amos	18, July 1833	July	12		L2	
Jeffries, Constantine	4, Sept 1851		estate		L3	
Jeffries, Constantine	7, June 1855		probate		L3	
Jeffries, John C.	26, Apr. 1855		estate		L3	
Jeggi, Magdalena	18, Apr. 1850	Apr.	11w		L3	
Jenkins, Benjamin	17, Mar. 1826		probate		L3	
Jenkins, Benjamin	26, Sept 1826		probate		L3	
Jenkins, Benjamin	20, Dec. 1825		probate		L4	
Jenkins, Henry	28, Apr. 1853	25, Apr.	30		L3	
Jenkins, Henry	5, May 1853				L3	
Jenkins, Justus	5, July 1849		estate		L3	
Jenkins, Justus	28, Mar. 1850		estate		L3	
Jenks, Emma	26, Nov. 1840	21, Nov.	19	*	L3	
Jenks, James P.	23, Oct. 1851				L4	
Jennings, Elmore Y.	29, July 1847	16, July	25		L3	
Jennings, Isaac	31, Oct. 1839		estate		L3	
Jennings, Sarah	10, Dec. 1824	16, Nov.	43		L3	
Jennings, Z.M.	29, Nov. 1838	Nov.	38		L3	
Jenson, Henry	9, Nov. 1848	Oct.	29		L3	
Jenz, Jacob	3, Oct. 1850	Sept	44		L3	
Jessop, Aaron	21, Jan. 1836		estate		L3	
Jessup, (child of Stephen)	18, Aug. 1806	2, Aug.	5		L3	
Jessup, Isaac	2, June 1806		estate		L2	
Jessup, Isaac	6, Jan. 1806	31, Dec.			L3	
Jessup, John	19, Dec. 1826		probate		L3	
Jessup, Samuel	28, July 1817	25, July			L3	
Jewel, James C.B.	3, 10, July 1845	June	4m		L3	
Jewett, Charles Sedgwick	18, Dec. 1845	13, Dec.	3- 6m		L3	
Jewett, Mary	22, Mar. 1838	15, Mar.	23- -13d		L3	Ferris
Jewill, Levi	3, Mar. 1842	Feb.	32		L3	
Jibb, Seth	6, Dec. 1838	Nov.	8m		L4	
Jocelin, Mary E.	26, Apr. 1849	Apr.	16d		L3	
Jocelyn, Aug.	1, Nov. 1832	27, Oct.			L3	
Jogan, Anthony	18, Oct. 1820	11, Oct.		*	L3	
Johannes, Henry	7, June 1855		probate		L3	
John, Abijah	22, June 1837		probate		L3	
John, Levi	19, Dec. 1826		probate		L3	
John, Nancy	14, Sept 1813	28, Aug.	23		L3	Smith
John, Samuel	7, Aug. 1834	July	27		L3	
Johns, Margaretta Jane	14, Dec. 1854	22, Nov.			L3	Shaaff
Johnson, (child of Elizabeth)	17, Feb. 1848	Feb.	3w		L3	
Johnson, (child of Joseph)	9, June 1842	May	3m		L3	
Johnson, Alexander	12, Nov. 1846	Nov.	44		L3	
Johnson, Alfred	19, Apr. 1845	Apr.	3w		L3	
Johnson, Ann	25, July 1850	July			L3	
Johnson, Ann F.	27, Sept 1838	25, Sept	30		L3	
Johnson, Anna Louisa	16, Nov. 1848	7, Nov.	38		L3	Biggs

Name	Notice Date	Death Date	Age	Page	Maiden Name
Johnson, Archibald (Rev)	17, Aug. 1819	16, Aug.		L3	
Johnson, Charles	7, Dec. 1848	Nov.	50	L3	
Johnson, Christopher A.	25, July 1821	22, July	21	L3	
Johnson, Cornelius	1, June 1813	16, May	75	L3	
Johnson, David	30, Aug. 1855	26, Aug.	70	L3	
Johnson, David	22, Mar. 1838		probate	L3	
Johnson, E.	29, May 1834		probate	L3	
Johnson, E.B.	21, Nov. 1839		estate	L3	
Johnson, Elisa A.	26, Jan. 1854	8, Jan.	64	L3	
Johnson, Elizabeth	20, Jan. 1853		50	L3	
Johnson, Elizabeth Peebles	19, Mar. 1857	16, Mar.	3	L3	
Johnson, Francis	2, June 1842	14, May		L3	
Johnson, George	30, Aug. 1849		estate	L3	
Johnson, George Alexander	19, Apr. 1849	15, Apr.		L3	
Johnson, George H.	3, Apr. 1845	Mar.	1- 6m	L3	
Johnson, Harding	10, Dec. 1857	6, Dec.		L3	
Johnson, Harriet Law	9, Feb. 1837	14, Dec.		L3	
Johnson, Henry	5, Sept 1844	Aug.	30	L3	
Johnson, J.B.	13, June 1833	June	3- 5m	L1	
Johnson, James	3, Nov. 1842	Oct.	44	L3	
Johnson, James	28, Apr. 1817	5, Apr.		L3	
Johnson, James M.	30, Mar. 1854	17, Mar.	34	L3	
Johnson, Jo. H.	5, Sept 1833	Aug.	57	L1	
Johnson, John	19, July 1849	July	6	L3	
Johnson, John	24, Jan. 1850	Jan.	32	L3	
Johnson, John	7, Aug. 1834	July	40	L3	
Johnson, John	27, Sept 1814		estate	L4	
Johnson, John M.	14, Dec. 1837	Dec.	46	L3	
Johnson, Joseph	21, Dec. 1837		estate	L3	
Johnson, Joseph J.	30, Sept 1852	25, Sept	47	L3	
Johnson, Lewis M.	10, Sept 1857		probate	L3	
Johnson, Lizzie Frances	5, Aug. 1852	28, July	1-11m	L3	
Johnson, Margaret	17, Oct. 1850	Oct.	4	L3	
Johnson, Margaret	31, Aug. 1843	Aug.	1- 6m	L3	
Johnson, Margaret	2, Oct. 1834	Sept		L4	
Johnson, Maria L.	13, Sept 1838	31, Aug.		L3	Olmsted
Johnson, Mary Ann	23, Mar. 1843	Mar.	20	L3	
Johnson, Michael H.	26, Jan. 1843	18, Jan.	25	L3	
Johnson, Moses	25, Oct. 1832	19, Oct.		L2	
Johnson, Richard	7, June 1855		probate	L3	
Johnson, Robert	25, July 1833	July	36	L1	
Johnson, Robert (Col)	6, Nov. 1815	15, Oct.	71	* L1	
Johnson, Sarah A.	26, Dec. 1850	Dec.	31	L3	
Johnson, Susan	2, May 1839	Apr.	3	L3	
Johnson, Susan	13, Apr. 1848	Apr.	45	L3	
Johnson, Thomas	28, Dec. 1843	Dec.	22	L3	
Johnson, Thomas	20, Nov. 1822		estate	L3	
Johnson, Thomas H.	19, Jan. 1843	11, Jan.	4	L3	
Johnson, Walter	21, Mar. 1823		estate	L3	
Johnson, Walter	26, Sept 1826		probate	L3	
Johnson, Walter	19, Dec. 1826		probate	L3	
Johnson, Wealthy	30, Nov. 1837	Nov.	43	L3	
Johnson, William	4, July 1833	June	7m	L2	
Johnson, William	26, June 1851	June	2	L3	

Name	Notice Date	Death Date	Age		Page	Maiden Name
Johnson, William	12, Aug. 1852	Aug.	35		L3	
Johnson, William	25, Apr. 1850	Apr.	38		L3	
Johnston, (child of Stephen)	29, Aug. 1833	Aug.	2d		L1	
Johnston, Alexander	20, Dec. 1825		probate		L4	
Johnston, Alexander R.	20, July 1848	11, July			L3	
Johnston, Anna	26, Aug. 1852	23, Aug.	5m		L3	
Johnston, Benjamin H.	19, Jan. 1854	8, Jan.	38- 1m-23d		L3	
Johnston, Campbell	26, Oct. 1843	15, Oct.			L3	
Johnston, Catharine E.	26, July 1849	July	47		L3	
Johnston, Charles E.	7, Aug. 1834	July	6		L3	
Johnston, Clarina	7, 14, May 1846	4, May			L3	
Johnston, David	12, Jan. 1837		probate		L3	
Johnston, Elizabeth	22, Mar. 1855	13, Mar.	25	*	L3	
Johnston, Elizabeth W.	12, Sept 1833	Sept	2- 7m-14d		L1	
Johnston, Frank	26, June 1851	22, June	3- 8m		L3	
Johnston, George Wallace	22, Oct. 1846	19, Oct.	5		L3	
Johnston, Henry Mallory	13, Dec. 1855		5		L3	
Johnston, James D.	10, Sept 1835			*	L2	
Johnston, Jerusha (Mrs)	27, July 1854	26, July			L3	
Johnston, John	24, Aug. 1854	20, Aug.	28		L3	
Johnston, Joseph	5, Sept 1839		probate		L3	
Johnston, Malinda D.	28, Aug. 1851	24, Aug.	27		L3	
Johnston, Margaret D.	28, June 1849	22, June	22		L3	
Johnston, Mariana Margaret	28, Nov. 1844	25, Nov.	3- 3m		L3	
Johnston, Nicholas	19, Dec. 1826		probate		L3	
Johnston, Nicholas	16, Feb. 1827		probate		L3	
Johnston, Parmeli	2, Sept 1852	Aug.	38		L3	
Johnston, Phebe	27, Oct. 1831		probate		L1	
Johnston, Rachael	6, Aug. 1840	24, July	57		L3	
Johnston, Rachel	18, July 1833	July	65		L2	
Johnston, Samuel (Rev)	30, May 1833	22, May			L1	
Johnston, Samuel (Rev)	6, June 1833	May	43		L2	
Johnston, Sarah Jane	31, Dec. 1846	22, Dec.	17		L3	
Johnston, Stephen	9, Aug. 1849	2, Aug.			L2	
Johnston, Stephen (Lt)	13, Apr. 1848				L3	
Johnston, Thomas Alexander	14, Sept 1843	6, Sept			L3	
Johnston, Walter	17, Sept 1857	13, Sept	11m-22d		L3	
Johnston, William	11, Oct. 1838		estate		L3	
Joice, Elizabeth	30, Aug. 1814		estate		L3	
Jolley, Edward	4, Aug. 1836	25, July	39		L1	
Jolley, Edward	28, July 1836	25, July			L3	
Jolliffe, John	24, June 1852				L3	
Jolly, John	2, Dec. 1841	29, Nov.	72		L3	
Jonas, Benjamin	21, May 1846	14, May	81	*	L3	
Jonas, Z.S.	22, Aug. 1833	Aug.	2- -3d		L4	
Jones, (a Welshman)	18, July 1850	4, July			L3	
Jones, (child of Castilly)	2, Oct. 1834	Sept	8d		L4	
Jones, (child of Frances)	17, Dec. 1846	Dec.	2w		L3	
Jones, (child of George W.)	13, Nov. 1834	Nov.			L1	
Jones, (child of Jane)	30, July 1840	July	stillborn		L3	
Jones, (child of Margaret)	13, Mar. 1851	Mar.	stillborn		L3	
Jones, (Mrs)	25, Oct. 1832	20, Oct.			L2	
Jones, Alfred	8, May 1851	6, May	27		L3	
Jones, Caroline Aydelott	21, Dec. 1848	17, Dec.	2- 2m		L3	

Name	Notice Date	Death Date	Age		Page	Maiden Name
Jones, Catharine	3, Sept 1840		probate		L3	
Jones, Charles	12, Dec. 1850		infant		L3	
Jones, Dorothea	9, May 1850	Apr.	2		L3	
Jones, Elijah	7, Feb. 1850	2, Feb.			L3	
Jones, Elizabeth	31, Mar. 1853	25, Mar.	21		L3	
Jones, Elizabeth	14, Aug. 1845	Aug.	27		L3	
Jones, Ella McNeal	29, Nov. 1832	Nov.	3m-18d		L1	
Jones, Emeline	15, Nov. 1849	Nov.	35		L3	
Jones, Enoch H.	19, Aug. 1847	13, Aug.		*	L3	
Jones, Euseba	11, July 1839	9, July	70	*	L3	
Jones, Frederick	29, Aug. 1850	Aug.	3w		L3	
Jones, George	25, Apr. 1850	Apr.	24		L3	
Jones, George T.	30, Aug. 1832	Aug.	2- 3m		L1	
Jones, George W.	2, Dec. 1820	1, Dec.	24	*	L3	
Jones, George W.	5, Sept 1839		probate		L3	
Jones, George W., Jr.	18, Aug. 1836	17, Aug.			L1	
Jones, Hannah	27, Nov. 1851	25, Nov.			L3	
Jones, Hannah More	18, Oct. 1849	12, Oct.			L3	Aydelott
Jones, Harriet	12, Sept 1844	Sept	29		L3	
Jones, Harriet E.	15, Aug. 1850	7, Aug.	42		L3	
Jones, Henry	28, Mar. 1850	Mar.	48		L3	
Jones, Henry	1, Nov. 1838		estate		L3	
Jones, Henry	7, May 1840		probate		L3	
Jones, Henry	1, Nov. 1838	27, Oct.			L3	
Jones, Henry H.	16, July 1835		estate		L3	
Jones, Henry H.	12, Jan. 1837		probate		L3	
Jones, Hiram	1, Nov. 1832	24, Oct.			L1	
Jones, Isaac	15, Nov. 1832	Nov.	52		L1	
Jones, James	28, Dec. 1848	Dec.	28		L3	
Jones, James	19, Sept 1844	Sept	2- 6m		L3	
Jones, James	4, Nov. 1825		estate		L4	
Jones, James	20, Dec. 1825		probate		L4	
Jones, James (Rev)	13, Nov. 1856	7, Nov.			L3	
Jones, James L.	10, Sept 1857		probate		L3	
Jones, James T.	29, Aug. 1833	Aug.	11m		L1	
Jones, Jane	12, June 1851	8, June	33-10m		L3	
Jones, John	6, May 1847	Apr.	2		L3	
Jones, John	7, Mar. 1839	Feb.	40		L3	
Jones, John	7, Apr. 1821		estate		L3	
Jones, John	29, Sept 1821		estate		L3	
Jones, John	19, Dec. 1826		estate		L3	
Jones, John	17, Mar. 1826		probate		L3	
Jones, John	19, Dec. 1826		probate		L3	
Jones, John	7, May 1857		probate		L3	
Jones, John	20, Dec. 1825		probate		L4	
Jones, John (Col)	7, Sept 1824		probate		L3	
Jones, John (Col)	31, Mar. 1821	24, Mar.			L3	
Jones, John C.	23, Nov. 1854	21, Nov.			L3	
Jones, John H.	2, Oct. 1845	24, Sept			L3	
Jones, John L.	15, Sept 1836		probate		L3	
Jones, John R.	15, Nov. 1832	Nov.	9- 5m		L1	
Jones, John T.	18, July 1833	July	2-10m		L2	
Jones, John T.	12, Jan. 1837		probate		L3	
Jones, John W.	8, Aug. 1850	July	37		L3	

Name	Notice Date	Death Date	Age		Page	Maiden Name
Jones, Jonathan	19, June 1845	18, June	3		L3	
Jones, Joseph	26, Apr. 1814		estate		L2	
Jones, Katharine Ogden	12, Nov. 1846	11, Nov.	14m		L3	
Jones, Kesiah	1, Aug. 1850	July	44		L3	
Jones, Laura	18, Oct. 1832	13, Oct.			L2	
Jones, Lorenzo	26, Oct. 1837	6, Oct.			L3	
Jones, M.	15, Nov. 1849	Nov.			L3	
Jones, Margaret A.	26, Jan. 1854	11, Jan.	67		L3	
Jones, Maria	30, Apr. 1829		estate		L3	
Jones, Maria Louisa	15, Aug. 1833	Aug.	1- 7m		L1	
Jones, Martha Elizabeth	6, July 1854	29, June			L3	
Jones, Mary	15, Aug. 1833	Aug.	1- 2m		L1	
Jones, Mary	13, Nov. 1850	Nov.	26		L3	
Jones, Mary	3, Apr. 1851	26, Mar.	55		L3	
Jones, Mary	15, Sept 1836		probate		L3	
Jones, Mary (heirs of)	9, June 1836		probate		L3	
Jones, Mary B.	24, Oct. 1850	13, Oct.	23		L3	Grigg
Jones, Mary E.	9, May 1839	Apr.	3m		L3	
Jones, Maurice	27, Mar. 1845	Mar.	24		L3	
Jones, Meriwether	23, Sept 1806	9, Sept			L3	
Jones, Moses	7, Sept 1824		probate		L3	
Jones, Moses	12, Jan. 1837		probate		L3	
Jones, Nancy	15, Aug. 1833	Aug.	5- 4m		L1	
Jones, Nancy	9, Apr. 1857		probate		L3	
Jones, Nancy	9, May 1826	5, May			L3	
Jones, Nathaniel	23, Nov. 1854	21, Nov.			L3	
Jones, Oliver	13, Apr. 1848	8, Apr.			L3	
Jones, Philip	11, July 1833		probate		L3	
Jones, Phillip	28, Sept 1843	21, Sept	48	*	L3	
Jones, R.	15, Jan. 1852				L3	
Jones, Rachael B.	17, Dec. 1846	13, Dec.	63	*	L3	
Jones, Rebecca A.	12, Sept 1833	Sept	2- 6m		L1	
Jones, Richard	5, July 1849	June	37		L3	
Jones, Robert	23, Nov. 1854	21, Nov.			L3	
Jones, Robert T.	15, May 1834	May	4m- 5d		L4	
Jones, Salmon	7, June 1849	4, June			L3	
Jones, Samuel	5, Dec. 1833	Nov.	25		L3	
Jones, Samuel Davis	19, Oct. 1822	14, Oct.			L3	
Jones, Sarah B.	2, Dec. 1816	19, Nov.			L3	
Jones, Stephen	3, May 1855	1, May	42		L3	
Jones, Stephen Johnston	12, Feb. 1846		1- 4m- 7d		L3	
Jones, Thalibone	18, Aug. 1831	10, Aug.	24		L4	
Jones, Thomas	14, Feb. 1839	Feb.	24		L3	
Jones, Thomas	29, May 1834		probate		L3	
Jones, Thomas C.	11, Aug. 1836		estate		L3	
Jones, Thomas C.	9, Aug. 1838		probate		L3	
Jones, Thomas G. (Rev)	7, Aug. 1845	10, July	67		L3	
Jones, Thomas W.	11, Feb. 1847	7, Feb.		*	L3	
Jones, William	4, July 1833	June	26		L2	
Jones, William	12, June 1845	June	8m		L3	
Jones, William A.	6, Dec. 1832	Dec.	24- 4m		L1	
Jones, William D.	23, Nov. 1854	18, Nov.	62	*	L3	
Jones, William D.	24, Dec. 1840	14, July	66- 1m- 8d	*	L3	
Jones, William Henry	28, May 1824	19, May			L2	

Name	Notice Date	Death Date	Age	Page	Maiden Name
Jones, William Henry	16, Aug. 1849	11, Aug.	3m	L3	
Jones, Willie Donald	17, Apr. 1856	14, Apr.	2-10m-18d	L3	
Jonnor, (child)	8, Aug. 1833	July		L1	
Jonte, Jannette C.	5, Dec. 1833	Nov.	1d	L3	
Joos, Walburga	16, Oct. 1856		probate	L6	
Jordan, Caleb D.	13, Oct. 1831		estate	L3	
Jordan, Harriet D.	20, Feb. 1845	15, Feb.	58	L3	
Jordan, James	15, Feb. 1838		estate	L3	
Jordan, James	9, May 1839		estate	L3	
Jordan, William	21, June 1849	June	50	L3	
Joseph, Charles	12, July 1849	July	32	L3	
Joseph, Samuel	10, Mar. 1826		estate	L3	
Joseph, Samuel	28, Feb. 1826	23, Feb.		*	L3
Josephs, Susan	25, Oct. 1832	22, Oct.		L3	
Joslin, (child of Jacob)	1, Aug. 1833	July	28d	L1	
Joso, (child of Rosana)	24, June 1847	June	stillborn	L3	
Joyce, Robert	5, Nov. 1829		estate	L3	
Joyce, Thomas	15, Sept 1836		probate	L3	
Judkins, Edith	29, Oct. 1857	22, Oct.		L3	
Judkins, Rachel	26, Mar. 1835	20, Mar.	44	L1	
Judkins, Silas F.	5, Feb. 1852	1, Feb.		L3	
Judkins, Susan	18, Jan. 1838	16, Jan.		L3	
Julian, Mary	9, Feb. 1854	8, Jan.	69	L3	
Julian, Mary Ann	1, Aug. 1833	July	22	L1	
Jund, Lewis	3, Jan. 1828	Jan.	48	L1	
Jungman, J.E.	11, July 1850	8, July	54	L3	
Junker, George	17, May 1849	May	26	L3	
Jury, Mary	28, Feb. 1839	Feb.	56	L3	
Justice, Amanda	5, Sept 1850	7, Aug.	22	L3	
Justice, Anna Rebecca	22, July 1852	21, July	11m-10d	L3	
Justice, Enoch P.	25, Sept 1851		34	L3	
Justice, Enoch P.	11, Dec. 1851		estate	L3	
Justice, Jesse	17, July 1851		estate	L3	
Justice, Phebe F.	11, July 1833	July	4- 8m-22d	L1	
Justiniani, L. (Rev)	26, July 1855	18, July		L3	
Justis, Thomas	30, Sept 1847	26, Sept		L2	
Kaeltering, Ann	21, June 1849	June	25	L3	
Kaeppner, Peter	23, Oct. 1834	Oct.	54- 6m	L2	
Kaerber, George	14, June 1849	June	77	L3	
Kagall, Catharine	8, Aug. 1833	July	1	L1	
Kahman, H.	12, Aug. 1852	Aug.	36	L3	
Kahn, Peter	5, Aug. 1852	July	40	L3	
Kail, (child of Michael)	6, Feb. 1851	Jan.	1d	L3	
Kain, Daniel (Major)	23, Mar. 1843	11, Mar.	70	*	L3
Kairman, Anthony	14, June 1849	June	70	L3	
Kallers, George	28, Apr. 1853			L3	
Kalley, William	6, Sept 1827	Sept	6	L1	
Kaltenbacher, Matilda	27, Aug. 1857	24, Aug.		L3	
Kane, Conrad	18, Jan. 1844	Jan.	40	L3	
Kane, Thomas	1, Mar. 1849	Feb.	27	L3	
Kannon, Martha	13, Nov. 1834	Nov.	36	L1	
Karns, Samuel	22, June 1837		probate	L3	
Karr, John	14, Aug. 1856		probate	L6	

Name	Notice Date	Death Date	Age		Page	Maiden Name
Kattenhorn, Martin	20, Feb. 1845		estate		L3	
Kattenhorn, Martin	13, Jan. 1848		estate		L3	
Kaufman, A.M.	10, Dec. 1857		probate		L3	
Kaufman, Loretta	11, July 1850	4, July	25		L3	
Kautz, David	4, Oct. 1849	1, Oct.	68		L3	
Kautz, Jacob	9, Dec. 1820		estate		L3	
Kauzer, Conrad	8, Oct. 1857		probate		L3	
Kavanaugh, Daniel	9, Apr. 1857		probate		L3	
Kavanaugh, Morris	17, Jan. 1850	Jan.	50		L3	
Keagan, Thomas	25, Jan. 1849	Jan.	33		L3	
Kean, James	31, Oct. 1823	29, Oct.	74		L3	
Kean, Lucinda	16, July 1846	July	8		L3	
Keaohl, Barbara	11, July 1833	July	22		L1	
Kear, Phillip	25, July 1850	July	23		L3	
Kearnan, Barney	15, Aug. 1844	Aug.	30		L3	
Kearns, George	29, Apr. 1847	Apr.	1		L3	
Kearns, George	6, May 1847	Apr.	36		L3	
Keating, John	29, May 1845	28, May	76		L3	
Keating, Luke	12, Aug. 1847	Aug.	22		L3	
Kebler, John Elliott	22, May 1851	13, May	17m		L3	
Keck, J.P.	4, July 1833	26, June	26	*	L1	
Keckeler, Theophilus	27, July 1854	23, July	55		L3	
Keckler, Harry Clifford	18, 25, Sept 1856	15, Sept	2- 5m		L5	
Keefe, Edward	31, July 1845	July	28		L3	
Keel, Benjamin	3, Nov. 1842		estate		L3	
Keeler, Silas W.	5, Oct. 1848	Sept	33		L3	
Keenan, James	8, Oct. 1846	Sept	24		L3	
Keenan, John	16, May 1850	May	45		L3	
Keene, William H.	8, July 1847	June	11m		L3	
Keeney, John	23, Aug. 1849	Aug.	40		L3	
Kegan, Patrick	14, Oct. 1841	Oct.	43		L3	
Kehoe, Samuel	13, July 1822		estate		L3	
Keiffe, Sarah	13, Aug. 1846	12, Aug.	30		L3	
Keil, J.	20, July 1837	July	30		L4	
Keim, Julia	27, Feb. 1851	21, Feb.	36		L3	
Keim, Peter	17, May 1849	9, May	44		L3	
Keiser, John	19, May 1842	May	28		L3	
Keiser, Peter	20, Mar. 1851	13, Mar.			L3	
Keizer, John	21, Feb. 1856	13, Feb.	84		L3	
Kelee, Henry	9, May 1850	Apr.	40		L3	
Kell, Benjamin	9, Aug. 1849	3, Aug.	76		L3	
Kellam, Phebe C.	16, Nov. 1854	29, Oct.	42		L3	
Keller, (child of Nicholas)	6, Apr. 1837	Apr.	1d		L4	
Keller, George L.	12, Sept 1833	Sept	5m		L1	
Keller, Jacob	16, June 1853	11, June	53		L3	
Kelley, (Mrs)	29, Aug. 1833	Aug.			L1	
Kelley, Barney	15, Feb. 1838	Feb.	37		L3	
Kelley, Caroline	23, Feb. 1854	17, Feb.			L3	
Kelley, James	18, Sept 1834		estate		L3	
Kelley, John	12, Mar. 1840	2, Mar.			L3	
Kelley, Michael	3, July 1851	June	40		L3	
Kelley, Oliver	19, Oct. 1824		estate		L1	
Kelley, Oliver	28, Feb. 1828		estate		L3	
Kelley, Patrick	27, July 1837	July	48		L3	

Name	Notice Date	Death Date	Age	Page	Maiden Name
Kelley, Thomas	16, Nov. 1837	Nov.	36	L3	
Kellogg, (child)	1, Aug. 1833	July		L1	
Kellogg, Albert	30, Dec. 1847	23, Dec.	6- 8m- 9d	L3	
Kellogg, Eliza Simons	29, Aug. 1850	20, Aug.	13m-15d	L3	
Kellogg, Lizzie	8, July 1852	2, July		L3	
Kellogg, Louisa	12, July 1838	July	1- 2m	L3	
Kellogg, Mary	23, Oct. 1834	Oct.	2m	L2	
Kellogg, Miner	24, June 1852	21, June	3- 6m	L3	
Kellogg, Miner Edmund	8, Dec. 1842	5, Dec.	3- 5m	L3	
Kellogg, Virginia	25, July 1850	23, July	8	L3	
Kelly, (child of Rachel)	21, Nov. 1839	Nov.	stillborn	L3	
Kelly, (Miss)	27, Dec. 1832	Dec.	18	L1	
Kelly, (Mrs)	25, Oct. 1832	16, Oct.		L4	
Kelly, Abram	30, Nov. 1854		estate	L3	
Kelly, Abram	6, Aug. 1857		probate	L3	
Kelly, Adelphia	15, Nov. 1849	Nov.	5m	L3	
Kelly, Ann Eliza	17, Apr. 1851	14, Apr.	21	L3	
Kelly, Betsey	13, Nov. 1834	Nov.	70	L1	
Kelly, Bridget	1, Aug. 1850	July	40	L3	
Kelly, Bridget	18, July 1850	July	45	L3	
Kelly, Bridget	29, Aug. 1850	Aug.		L3	
Kelly, Catharine	19, Aug. 1852	Aug.	2	L3	
Kelly, Catharine	23, Aug. 1849	Aug.	27	L3	
Kelly, Cecilia	3, June 1847	May	25	L3	
Kelly, Christopher	12, July 1849	July	9	L3	
Kelly, Edward	6, Mar. 1851	Feb.	33	L3	
Kelly, Ellen S.	1, Oct. 1846	Sept	4m	L3	
Kelly, Francis	22, June 1848	June	27	L3	
Kelly, Hannah A.	26, Apr. 1849	Apr.	4	L3	
Kelly, James	25, Apr. 1839		estate	L2	
Kelly, James	31, Apr. 1845	Apr.	1- 6m	L3	
Kelly, James	9, June 1836		probate	L3	
Kelly, James	3, Dec. 1840		probate	L3	
Kelly, James	25, Jan. 1855	19, Jan.		L3	
Kelly, John	17, Mar. 1853	12, Mar.	30	L3	
Kelly, Joseph	10, Jan. 1856		probate	L3	
Kelly, M.L.	8, Aug. 1833	July	5m	L1	
Kelly, Margaret	15, July 1852	July	2	L3	
Kelly, Mary	8, Aug. 1850	July	26	L3	
Kelly, Mary	21, Nov. 1833	Nov.	74	L3	
Kelly, Mary Ann	12, Dec. 1850	4, Dec.	43	L3	
Kelly, Mary Jane	5, Sept 1844	4, Sept		L3	
Kelly, Michael	1, Nov. 1849	Oct.	22	L3	
Kelly, Michael	2, Sept 1852	Aug.	3m	L3	
Kelly, Nathaniel	5, Apr. 1849	Mar.	25	L3	
Kelly, Owen	29, May 1845	May	40	L3	
Kelly, Patrick	1, Feb. 1849	Jan.	28	L3	
Kelly, Peter	7, June 1849	May		L3	
Kelly, Philip	26, Oct. 1843	Oct.	21	L3	
Kelly, Samuel P.	31, Aug. 1854		21	L3	
Kelly, Sarah	8, Feb. 1849	Jan.	38	L3	
Kelly, Serena	22, June 1848	June	27	L3	
Kelly, Thomas	18, Jan. 1849	Jan.	33	L3	
Kelly, Thomas	27, Sept 1849	Sept	36	L3	

Name	Notice Date	Death Date	Age	Page	Maiden Name
Kelly, Thomas	5, Dec. 1826	2, Dec.		L3	
Kelly, William	3, Jan. 1850	Dec.	26	L3	
Kelly, William	13, Oct. 1853	2, Oct.		L3	
Kelsey, (child of Jessey)	1, Aug. 1833	July	1- 6m	L1	
Kelsey, (child)	13, Feb. 1851	Feb.	20m	L3	
Kelsey, Thomas C.	28, Sept 1824	12, Sept		L3	
Kelso, John	11, Nov. 1852	Oct.	9m	L3	
Kelso, Margaret	16, Mar. 1854	4, Mar.		L3	
Kelton, Elizabeth	3, Feb. 1848	Jan.	85	L3	
Kelvey, Eliza	6, Jan. 1848	Dec.	8	L3	
Kemper, (son)	1, Nov. 1832	22, Oct.	3	L4	
Kemper, Caleb	6, Dec. 1832		estate	L3	
Kemper, Caleb	15, Jan. 1835		estate	L3	
Kemper, Caleb	25, Oct. 1832	16, Oct.		L4	
Kemper, David Rice	13, Sept 1849	8, Sept	57	L3	
Kemper, Elnathan	16, Oct. 1834		estate	L3	
Kemper, James (Rev)	6, Nov. 1834		estate	L3	
Kemper, Judith Hathaway	5, Mar. 1846	1, Mar.	*	L3	
Kemper, Nancy	4, Jan. 1849	31, Dec.	75	L3	
Kemper, Peggy	7, May 1805	3, May		L2	
Kemper, Peter	30, July 1829	23, July	87	L2	
Kemper, Peter H.	10, Jan. 1856		probate	L3	
Kemper, Peter H.	8, Jan. 1857		probate	L3	
Kemper, Rebecca L.	10, Apr. 1851	3, Apr.		L3	
Kemper, Stephen	23, Jan. 1845	20, Jan.	73	L3	
Kenady, Ann	15, Aug. 1850	Aug.	50	L3	
Kenady, John	16, Feb. 1837	Feb.	21	L4	
Kenady, Patrick	25, May 1848	May	41	L3	
Kenard, Mary	8, Apr. 1847	Mar.	23	L3	
Kendall, Richard G.	14, Aug. 1856		probate	L6	
Kendall, Robert H.	29, May 1851		estate	L3	
Kendall, Sarah Ayres	13, Feb. 1845	8, Feb.	9	L3	
Kendrick, Sarah M.	24, Apr. 1851	20, Apr.		L3	
Kendrick, William L.	26, Jan. 1854	3, Jan.	35	L3	
Kenedy, Charles	11, Oct. 1838		estate	L3	
Kenedy, Patrick	21, June 1849	June	25	L3	
Kenedy, Philip	19, July 1838	July	21	L3	
Kenedy, Timothy	23, Mar. 1849	Mar.	40	L3	
Kenessman, Catharine P.	6, June 1833	May	27- 5m	L2	
Kenis, Sophia	7, Aug. 1834	July	20	L3	
Keniston, Lowell	18, Feb. 1841	Feb.	35	L3	
Kenley, Catharine	7, Mar. 1850	Feb.	61	L3	
Kennard, (child of James)	26, Nov. 1846	Nov.	1w	L3	
Kennard, John	22, Apr. 1847	Apr.	14	L3	
Kennedy, David	8, Nov. 1855		probate	L3	
Kennedy, Ellen	27, Apr. 1854	19, Apr.	19- 1m	L3	
Kennedy, P.	8, Jan. 1857		probate	L3	
Kennedy, Robert West	24, Oct. 1850	16, Oct.	17	L3	
Kennedy, Stephen	18, Oct. 1832	12, Oct.		L2	
Kennedy, Thomas	24, Mar. 1853	20, Mar.		L3	
Kenner, George R.	28, Oct. 1852	25, Sept		L3	
Kenner, Sarah Bella	29, Apr. 1852	26, Mar.	16- 4m	L3	
Kenner, William Butler	6, Oct. 1853	26, Sept		L3	
Kennett, Elizabeth G.	13, June 1844	10, June		L3	

Name	Notice Date	Death Date	Age		Page	Maiden Name
Kenney, James	26, July 1849	July	40		L3	
Kenney, Jefferson	24, Apr. 1827	19, Apr.			L3	
Kenney, Joseph	19, Sept 1833	Sept	15d		L4	
Kenniston, James	8, Nov. 1838		probate		L3	
Kenny, Michael	19, July 1849	July	23		L3	
Kenny, Robert (Capt)	2, June 1807	30, May			L3	
Kent, Amelia Elizabeth	31, Apr. 1845	30, Apr.	7- 9m		L3	
Kent, Amelia Mary	10, Aug. 1837	9, Aug.	20		L3	Ernst
Kent, Annie Benjamin	2, Aug. 1849	29, July	26		L3	
Kent, Charles Woodward	25, Nov. 1847	10, Nov.	18m-10d		L3	
Kent, Charlotte	18, May 1848	10, May	78	*	L3	
Kent, Elizabeth	25, July 1850	17, July			L3	
Kent, Elizabeth D.	24, June 1841	20, June	58		L3	
Kent, Ellen	22, Feb. 1849	16, Feb.	30		L3	
Kent, John	3, Dec. 1835	2, Dec.			L4	
Kent, Louisa Elgel	12, July 1849	July	7m		L3	
Kent, Louisa F.	16, Mar. 1854	8, Mar.	32		L3	
Kent, Luke	7, July 1842		estate		L3	
Kent, William Henry	6, Aug. 1857	2, Aug.	21		L3	
Kently, (Mr)	28, Aug. 1834	Aug.	67		L1	
Kenyon, William	19, Mar. 1824		estate		L3	
Kenyon, William	26, Sept 1826		probate		L3	
Keordall, Amanda M.	4, July 1833	June	5d		L2	
Kepner, George	27, Apr. 1854	22, Apr.			L3	
Kerdoff, Amanda	26, July 1855	18, July	34		L3	
Kereding, Anna	21, June 1849	June	1		L3	
Kereit, John	13, Dec. 1849	Dec.	24		L3	
Kerford, Bernard	7, Aug. 1834	July			L3	
Kerns, Samuel	12, Feb. 1835		estate		L4	
Kerr, Emily	22, Apr. 1847		estate		L3	
Kerr, Frances	28, Nov. 1833	Nov.	22		L4	
Kerr, George	28, Aug. 1834	Aug.	2m- 7d		L1	
Kerr, George	20, June 1844	19, June	47		L3	
Kerr, George	22, Apr. 1847		estate		L3	
Kerr, George	2, July 1857				L3	
Kerr, John D.	8, Oct. 1857		probate		L3	
Kerr, Mary	6, July 1843	5, July		*	L3	
Kerr, Mary	13, July 1843	30, June		*	L3	
Kerr, Rebecca	21, Sept 1843	15, Sept			L3	
Kerr, William	13, Feb. 1840		probate		L3	
Kerwin, Morris	18, Apr. 1850	Apr.	28		L3	
Kesley, (Mrs)	15, Aug. 1833	Aug.	84		L1	
Kesley, William (Rev)	7, Oct. 1841	24, Sept	57		L3	
Kesse, Ann	12, July 1849	July	40		L3	
Kesse, Henry G.	18, July 1850	July	40		L3	
Kessler, Herman (Capt)	13, Apr. 1848				L3	
Kestler, James	16, Aug. 1849	Aug.	3- 3m		L3	
Ketchum, (man)	20, June 1844	June	21		L3	
Key, Harriet	26, July 1832	July	34		L1	
Key, Ryley	6, Sept 1838	Aug.	26		L3	
Keys, (Miss)	25, Oct. 1832	18, Oct.			L1	
Keys, George	29, Nov. 1838	Nov.	22		L3	
Keys, James	27, Feb. 1827		estate		L3	
Keys, Jane	31, Dec. 1857	28, Dec.	70		L3	

Name	Notice Date	Death Date	Age		Page	Maiden Name
Keys, John Finley	18, Sept 1851	16, Sept	3- 8m		L3	
Keys, Richard	6, May 1830	28, Apr.	74	*	L4	
Keys, Sarah Ann	14, June 1838	June	1		L3	
Keysor, John	27, Sept 1849	Sept	30		L3	
Keysor, John	21, June 1849	June	66		L3	
Kibby, Emma Louisa	6, Sept 1827	Sept	15m		L1	
Kibby, Jarvis	28, July 1831		estate		L1	
Kidd, John	9, Feb. 1819	7, Feb.	72		L3	
Kidd, John	19, Oct. 1819		estate		L3	
Kidd, John	7, Sept 1824		probate		L3	
Kidd, Pamela Augusta	21, Apr. 1817	16, Apr.			L3	
Kidd, Pinkham	23, Aug. 1855	15, Aug.	22		L3	
Kidder, Salla	14, Feb. 1850	31, Jan.		*	L3	Atherton
Kief, Alice	30, May 1850	May	22		L3	
Kiefer, Louisa	27, Feb. 1851	Feb.	34		L3	
Kiersted, Jeremiah	20, Feb. 1834		estate		L4	
Kiersted, Jeremiah	5, Mar. 1835		estate		L4	
Kieser, Francis	7, June 1849	May	69		L3	
Kiger, Francis	12, July 1849	July	42		L3	
Kilbourne, James	2, May 1850	24, Apr.	80		L3	
Kilday, Edward	4, May 1848	Apr.	55		L3	
Kiles, Delia	13, Sept 1832	Sept	24		L1	
Kiles, Jane	25, Feb. 1841	Feb.	14		L3	
Kiles, Julia	15, Aug. 1850	Aug.	2		L3	
Kiles, Mary	4, Apr. 1844	Mar.	55		L3	
Kiley, Julia	22, Apr. 1852	20, Apr.	22		L3	
Kilgore, Charles	6, Oct. 1807	2, Oct.			L3	
Kilgour, Catharine	28, Dec. 1848	24, Dec.	78		L3	
Kilgour, Charlotte Townsend	31, Oct. 1839	25, Oct.	2- 7m		L3	
Kilgour, David	22, May 1834	May			L4	
Kilgour, Henry	17, Aug. 1837	11, Aug.	75		L3	
Kilgour, Joseph	8, Aug. 1833	July	63		L1	
Kilgour, Sarah	1, Sept 1821	14, Aug.	52		L3	
Killers, Nancy	18, July 1850	July	4		L3	
Killers, Peter F.	18, July 1850	July	26		L3	
Killers, Sybelia	18, July 1850	July	14		L3	
Killin, Edwin Gower	9, July 1846	8, July	infant		L3	
Kiloh, Mary Ann	21, Oct. 1847	18, Oct.		*	L3	
Kilroy, James	31, May 1849	May	20		L3	
Kimbal, Susanna	15, Nov. 1832	Nov.	28		L1	
Kimball,	20, Aug. 1857				L3	
Kimball, Abel	24, Nov. 1853	27, Sept	35		L3	
Kimball, Charles	27, Jan. 1842	20, Jan.	29		L3	
Kimball, Clarissa Ellen	8, June 1843	31, May	13		L3	
Kimball, Elizabeth	20, July 1837	July	45		L4	
Kimball, Fanny	30, Jan. 1851	17, Jan.	67		L3	
Kimball, Lula	24, Nov. 1853	1, Sept	4		L3	
Kimball, Mary A.	24, Nov. 1853	9, Sept	28		L3	
Kimball, Mary Elizabeth	7, Jan. 1836	30, Dec.			L1	
Kimball, Richard	7, Sept 1837	Aug.	50		L3	
Kimball, William	19, Oct. 1822		estate		L3	
Kimball, William	28, Aug. 1822	24, Aug.		*	L3	
Kimbell, John	20, June 1850	June	35		L3	
Kincade, (man)	4, Nov. 1852				L3	

Name	Notice Date	Death Date	Age		Page	Maiden Name
Kindal, James	13, Feb. 1840		probate		L3	
Kiner, (child of Nathaniel)	7, Aug. 1834	July	19d		L3	
King, (child of Judeth)	9, Jan. 1845	Dec.	4		L3	
King, (Mrs)	1, Nov. 1832	29, Oct.			L3	
King, Alexander	15, Feb. 1808	Feb.			L3	
King, Andrew	19, Sept 1850	12, Sept			L3	
King, Ann R.	3, Apr. 1856	24, Mar.			L3	
King, Charles	2, June 1842	May	30		L3	
King, Cynthia Ann	12, Dec. 1850	10, Dec.	39		L3	Dodson
King, Cyrus (Gen)	19, May 1817		44		L3	
King, Deliliah	19, Feb. 1846	Feb.	15m		L3	
King, Edward (Gen)	18, Feb. 1836	13, Feb.	40		L3	
King, Emily A.	14, Mar. 1833	Mar.	5		L1	
King, Frances Elizabeth	3, Nov. 1853	17, Oct.			L3	
King, George	5, Dec. 1844	4, Dec.	40		L3	
King, James	20, Oct. 1831	17, Oct.	4		L3	
King, John Dodson	6, Mar. 1851	1, Mar.	7m		L3	
King, John W.	27, Sept 1838	16, Sept			L3	
King, John W. (Dr)	28, Sept 1854	24, Sept	65		L3	
King, Joseph	1, Nov. 1832	28, Oct.			L3	
King, Julia	29, Aug. 1850	Aug.	36		L3	
King, Margaret W.	28, Nov. 1850	20, Nov.	27		L3	
King, Mary	28, Aug. 1834	Aug.	31		L1	
King, Mary	22, Aug. 1833	Aug.	49		L4	
King, Mary A.	17, Oct. 1844	Oct.	1		L3	
King, Mary B.	21, Aug. 1815	19, Aug.			L3	Richardson
King, Polly Jane	31, Aug. 1843	Aug.	18		L3	
King, Rufus	18, May 1827	29, Apr.	73		L4	
King, Samuel	24, Dec. 1857	22, Dec.			L1	
King, Samuel	16, July 1857	9, July	51		L3	
King, Sarah Ann	12, June 1845	June	4m		L3	
King, Susan	23, Aug. 1849		estate		L3	
King, William	8, July 1852	17, June	84	*	L3	
King, William	18, Oct. 1832	Oct.	2- -12d		L4	
Kingson, (child of Thomas)	29, Aug. 1833	Aug.	stillborn		L1	
Kinkaid, Jane	14, Mar. 1844	9, Mar.	35		L3	
Kinkead, Mary D.	4, May 1854	28, Mar.	36- 1m-13d		L3	Gay
Kinkerd, (Mrs)	9, Dec. 1852	2, Dec.			L3	
Kinley, Mary Ann	12, Nov. 1857	11, Nov.	25- 8m		L3	
Kinmont, Alexander	27, Sept 1838	16, Sept			L1	
Kinmont, Alexander	18, Apr. 1839		estate		L3	
Kinmont, Alexander	3, Dec. 1840		probate		L3	
Kinmont, Alexander	20, Sept 1838	16, Sept			L3	
Kinney, Henry (Rev)	16, Nov. 1854	24, Oct.			L3	
Kinney, Joseph Newcomb	13, Nov. 1850	5, Nov.	2		L3	
Kinsey, Edward Dodson	18, July 1850	12, July	infant		L3	
Kinsey, Sarah Ann	5, Mar. 1840		26	*	L3	McFarland
Kirby, (daughter of James)	15, Nov. 1809	7, Nov.	4		L3	
Kirby, Elizabeth	13, July 1843	July	87		.L3	
Kirby, Ephraim	15, Jan. 1805	20, Oct.			L3	
Kirby, Hannah	4, Jan. 1844	30, Dec.	32		L3	
Kirby, John H.	21, Oct. 1852	2, Sept			L3	
Kirby, Julia	4, Feb. 1836	31, Jan.	infant		L3	
Kirby, Mary Jane	16, Dec. 1852	13, Dec.	8- 1m-23d		L3	

Name	Notice Date	Death Date	Age	Page	Maiden Name
Kirby, Richard	15, Aug. 1833	Aug.	30	L1	
Kirby, Robert	16, May 1833	May	62	L1	
Kirchmer, Francis	7, Aug. 1851	2, Aug.		L3	
Kirchmer, Joseph	7, Aug. 1851	2, Aug.		L3	
Kirchner, Louis	14, Aug. 1856		probate	L6	
Kirk, Fred.	15, Aug. 1833	Aug.	2- 6m	L1	
Kirk, John	8, Jan. 1857		probate	L3	
Kirk, John	6, Aug. 1857		probate	L3	
Kirk, Thomas	27, Sept 1838	Sept	72	L3	
Kiroy, Hannah	7, Aug. 1834	July	5- 6m	L3	
Kirsch, George	21, Sept 1848	Sept	30	L3	
Kirtland, Turhand	12, Sept 1844	17, Aug.	89	* L3	
Kisner, William	13, Sept 1832	Sept	37	L1	
Kistner, John	11, Nov. 1852	Oct.	36	L3	
Kitchel, Benajah	25, Jan. 1814	22, Jan.	37	L3	
Kitchel, Calvin	6, Oct. 1807		estate	L4	
Kitchel, Luther	15, Jan. 1805	12, Jan.		L3	
Kitchell, Asa	10, Nov. 1807	7, Nov.		L3	
Kitchell, Benajah	19, Dec. 1826		probate	L3	
Kitchell, Benejah	7, June 1814		estate	L1	
Kitchell, John	18, June 1805		estate	L3	
Kitchell, John	19, Feb. 1805	8, Feb.		L3	
Kitchell, Luther	12, Feb. 1805		estate	L3	
Kitchell, Moses	2, Jan. 1840		estate	L3	
Kitchen, W.P. (Dr)	16, Oct. 1856	8, Oct.		L1	
Kitcher, Thomas	11, July 1833		probate	L3	
Kittering, Mary	18, July 1850	July	43	L3	
Kittridge, Sarah T.	2, Aug. 1849	26, July		L3	
Kitts, Joseph	16, Mar. 1848	Mar.	24	L3	
Kius, (Mrs)	7, Aug. 1834	July	44	L3	
Klamroth, Anthony	28, June 1849	June	65	L3	
Kleckner, Henry	26, July 1849	July	28	L3	
Kleger, Christian	9, Apr. 1857		probate	L3	
Klein, Frederick	7, May 1857		probate	L3	
Kleineberg, Joseph	7, Feb. 1856		probate	L3	
Klenck, George	17, Feb. 1848	Feb.	50	L3	
Klien, George	21, June 1849	June	18	L3	
Klimmas, Moritz	26, Feb. 1852	Feb.	69	L4	
Klimpetre, (boy)	24, July 1851	17, July	15	L3	
Kline, (child of Jacob)	27, Mar. 1828	Mar.	1d	L1	
Kline, Carl	4, July 1844	June	26	L3	
Kline, Henry C.	18, Mar. 1852	5, Mar.	6m- 8d	L3	
Kline, Lawrence	26, July 1849	July	55	L3	
Kline, Nancy G.	1, Apr. 1852	28, Mar.	29	L3	
Klineman, Frederick	12, July 1855	6, July		L3	
Kling, George	8, Oct. 1857		probate	L3	
Kling, Lawrence	23, Apr. 1846	Apr.	40	L3	
Klingler, Jacob	16, Aug. 1849	Aug.	30	L3	
Klink, William	13, May 1852	7, May		L3	
Kloppel, Charles (Mrs)	21, Dec. 1848			L1	
Kloppenburg, Henry	31, July 1851	July	41	L3	
Klosman, Aug.	31, July 1845	July	26	L3	
Klump, Anthony	19, Sept 1833	Sept		L4	
Klumpp, Gottlieb	6, Dec. 1849	Nov.	34	L3	

Name	Notice Date	Death Date	Age		Page	Maiden Name
Knaft, Margaret	8, July 1847	June	4		L3	
Knapp, (child of Sarah J.)	6, Mar. 1851	Feb.	9d		L3	
Knapp, Ann E.	11, July 1850	July	25		L3	
Knapp, Ansel	30, Aug. 1849	Aug.	8m		L3	
Knapp, John	7, July 1853	5, July			L3	
Knapp, Philipina	3, Apr. 1856		estate		L3	
Knapp, Philippina	9, Apr. 1857		probate		L3	
Knau, John	7, Feb. 1856		probate		L3	
Knealing, (child of Eleanor)	18, July 1833	July	stillborn		L2	
Knell, Valentine	2, May 1850	Apr.	40		L3	
Kneves, Sarah	1, Aug. 1833	July	11		L1	
Knight, (Mr)	18, Oct. 1832	15, Oct.			L2	
Knight, (Mrs)	25, Oct. 1832	19, Oct.			L3	
Knight, (Mrs)	5, May 1853	4, May			L3	
Knight, Aaron	25, Aug. 1807	10, Aug.			L3	
Knight, Abby H.	31, Oct. 1850	25, Oct.			L3	Jones
Knight, Cordelia Frances	10, July 1845	3, July	8m		L3	
Knight, Frances Gates Adamson	6, May 1847	3, May	33		L3	
Knight, George W.	18, July 1833	July	7		L2	
Knight, Henrietta	9, Sept 1847	Aug.	5w		L3	
Knight, Henry	15, Apr. 1841	6, Apr.	32	*	L3	
Knight, Henry	6, May 1841		estate		L3	
Knight, John	11, Mar. 1852	Mar.	50		L4	
Knight, Jonathan	19, Dec. 1826		probate		L3	
Knight, Lydia	18, Sept 1834	Sept	25		L1	
Knight, Thomas	17, May 1849	May	35		L3	
Knight, William	1, June 1848	May	25		L3	
Knight, William Henry	25, Mar. 1841	18, Mar.	22m		L3	
Knobber, John H.	9, Aug. 1855		probate		L3	
Knobber, John H.	6, Dec. 1855		probate		L3	
Knoblaugh, John	16, June 1842	June	43		L3	
Knocks, John	15, Nov. 1832	Nov.	37		L1	
Knodel, Catharine	11, July 1850	July	11w		L3	
Knolton, T.C.	20, Sept 1849	Sept	35		L3	
Knopp, Jacob	2, Mar. 1848	Feb.	40		L3	
Knouer, Henry	11, Nov. 1847	Nov.	38		L3	
Knowles, Benjamin	20, Sept 1832		estate		L3	
Knowles, Jemima	1, Nov. 1832	25, Oct.			L1	
Knowles, Jonas	13, Nov. 1850	12, Nov.			L3	
Knowles, Mary	22, Aug. 1833	Aug.	1- 1m		L4	
Knowles, William	1, Nov. 1832	Oct.			L2	
Knowles, William	31, Aug. 1848	24, Aug.	44	*	L3	
Knowles, William	17, Jan. 1833		estate		L3	
Knowlton, Elizabeth	26, Oct. 1843	22, Oct.	44	*	L3	
Knowlton, Emma A.	14, Aug. 1851	8, Aug.	17m		L3	
Knowlton, Samuel	8, Jan. 1857	4, Jan.	74	*	L3	
Knowlton, Sarah	15, Aug. 1833	Aug.	10m		L1	
Knowlton, Sherman	25, July 1850	19, July	29-11m		L3	
Knox, James	2, Oct. 1815		estate		L4	
Knox, John	21, Feb. 1850	Feb.	33		L3	
Knox, John	16, May 1844		59		L3	
Knox, W.P.	12, Oct. 1843	11, Oct.	40	*	L3	
Knox, William	14, Feb. 1850	Feb.	83		L3	
Knoxes, James M.	5, July 1849		estate		L3	

Name	Notice Date	Death Date	Age	Page	Maiden Name
Knudson, George	22, Aug. 1839	Aug.	23	L3	
Knueman, Mary	5, Dec. 1833	Nov.	40	L3	
Kochner, Jacob	2, Nov. 1837	Oct.	34	L4	
Koeffer, John	12, Apr. 1849	Apr.	27	L3	
Koehler, Gottlib	5, July 1849	June	44	L3	
Koehler, John	14, Feb. 1850	Feb.	29	L3	
Koellein, Josephine	5, Nov. 1857		probate	L3	
Koellein, Josephine	10, Dec. 1857		probate	L3	
Kofer, Louisa M.	28, Aug. 1834	Aug.	1	L1	
Koffer, Romanus	6, Aug. 1846	July	42	L3	
Kogan, Thomas	16, May 1850	May	21	L3	
Kollock, Henry (Rev)	21, Jan. 1820	29, Dec.		L2	
Kolp, Adam	3, Dec. 1857	2, Dec.	35	L3	
Kolp, J.C.	5, May 1853			L1	
Koonsweiler, Conrad	14, Mar. 1844	Mar.	24	L3	
Kopp, Peter	31, Mar. 1842	Mar.	28	L3	
Korle, Ann	9, Oct. 1834	Sept	2m	L1	
Korte, John G.	10, Sept 1857		probate	L3	
Kountz, Catharine	2, Feb. 1843	Jan.	35	L3	
Koush, Thomas	9, May 1850	Apr.	2	L3	
Kracht, Frederick	16, May 1850	May		L3	
Kramer, David	8, Nov. 1832	Nov.	5- 5m	L1	
Kramer, Sarah	16, Oct. 1851	1, Oct.	28	L3	
Krapp, Frederick	2, Apr. 1857	1, Apr.	23	L3	
Kraus, Jacob	9, July 1857		probate	L3	
Kraus, Leonard	21, Apr. 1842	Apr.	2- 6m	L3	
Krausbeig, (man)	25, Aug. 1853	20, Aug.		L3	
Krause, George C.	6, Dec. 1855		probate	L3	
Krause, Louis	1, Nov. 1849	Oct.	26	L3	
Kreitz, Amelia	8, Mar. 1849	Feb.	6m	L3	
Kress, John	26, July 1849		estate	L3	
Kritzner, Conrad	8, Feb. 1844	Jan.	43	L3	
Kroeger, Adolphus	10, June 1847	June	35	L3	
Kroeger, James J.	15, Feb. 1849	Feb.	1- 6m	L3	
Krouse, Henry	17, June 1835		estate	L4	
Krozier, Herman	24, Sept 1846	Sept	21	L3	
Krueger, Emil	6, Dec. 1855		probate	L3	
Kruep, Bernard	24, Oct. 1850		estate	L3	
Kruse, Henry	16, Mar. 1848	Mar.	36	L3	
Kruser, Frederick	3, Jan. 1833	Dec.	2	L4	
Kuchlein, Catharine	23, Mar. 1849	Mar.	39	L3	
Kueller, Christian	10, May 1849	May	46	L3	
Kugleman, D.	15, Aug. 1833	Aug.	2	L1	
Kugler, Elizabeth	7, May 1846	26, Apr.	66	L3	
Kugler, Matilda Caroline	5, Nov. 1840	24, Oct.	32- 9m	L2	Brower
Kugler, Matthias	9, Mar. 1854	7, Mar.	76	L3	
Kuhlman, Theodore	28, June 1849	June	38	L3	
Kuhn, Andrew	20, Feb. 1851	Feb.	23	L3	
Kuhn, Gotleb	28, Sept 1848	Sept	66	L3	
Kuhn, Joseph	14, May 1846	May	20	L3	
Kuhn, Joseph	5, July 1849	June	23	L3	
Kuhn, William	19, Sept 1833	Sept	30	L4	
Kull, John	23, Sept 1847	Sept	25	L3	
Kumler, Henry (Rev)	19, Jan. 1854	8, Jan.	80	L3	

Name	Notice Date	Death Date	Age	Page	Maiden Name
Kuntz, Joseph	6, Nov. 1845	Oct.	58		L3
Kunz, John	6, Apr. 1843	Mar.	27		L3
Kunzman, Anthony	24, Dec. 1840	Dec.	51		L3
Kurop, William	28, Aug. 1834	Aug.	1- 7m		L1
Kutz, Jacob	28, June 1849	June			L3
Kyes, Sarah	9, July 1857	2, July	66		L3
Kyle, Jane	10, Sept 1840	17, Aug.	47		L3
Kyle, William	9, Dec. 1847	Dec.	52		L3
Kyler, George	10, May 1820		estate		L3
Kyler, George	11, July 1833		probate		L3
Kyles, Thomas	11, Apr. 1839	Apr.	23		L3
Labadino, Angelo	11, Oct. 1849	Oct.	29		L3
Labaw, Derick	7, Mar. 1839		estate		L4
LaBoiteaux, John V.	28, Feb. 1856	26, Feb.	19m-14d		L3
LaBoyteaux, A.A. (Mrs)	11, July 1850	8, July			L3
Laboyteaux, Peter	10, May 1814		estate		L2
Labrot, Marie Estelle F.	9, Sept 1847	4, Sept	13m-15d		L3
Lachlan, Sarah Anne	15, Mar. 1855	11, Mar.	23	*	L3
Lackey, Alexis H.	23, Aug. 1814		estate		L3
Lacock, Abner	4, May 1837		67		L2
Laferty, James	14, June 1849	June	6		L3
Lafferty, Charles	9, Aug. 1849	July	1- 9m		L3
Lafferty, James M.	28, Dec. 1848	Dec.	22		L3
Lafferty, Lydia	28, June 1849	June	36		L3
Lagere, Peter	15, Nov. 1832	Nov.			L1
LaGrate, Moses	30, Jan. 1845	Jan.	26		L3
Laharaun, Henry	5, July 1855		probate		L3
Lahey, John	28, Mar. 1850	Mar.	24		L3
Lahmas, John	31, Dec. 1857		estate		L3
Lahmering, J.H.	17, Jan. 1856		estate		L3
Lahmering, J.H.	10, Apr. 1856		probate		L3
Lahy, John	16, Sept 1852	12, Sept			L3
Laird, Elmira	4, July 1833	June	1- 5m		L2
Laird, Joshua	16, Aug. 1849		estate		L3
Laird, William J.	26, Feb. 1852	Feb.	26		L4
Lakeman, Daniel	1, Mar. 1855	22, Feb.	75	*	L3
Lakeman, Susannah	19, July 1855	13, July	35	*	L3
Lakeman, Willard	27, Dec. 1855	23, Dec.	6m- 5d		L3
Lakenbock, Francis	18, Sept 1834	Sept	25		L1
Lamaire, George	6, Dec. 1832	Dec.	5m- 4d		L1
Laman, Matthew	25, May 1843	May	35		L3
Laman, Michael	4, Oct. 1849	Sept	32		L3
Lamb, Charles Weatley	28, Aug. 1856	23, Aug.	4- 5m		L5
Lamb, James	19, July 1849	July	55		L3
Lamb, Mary	28, Aug. 1834	Aug.	15		L1
Lambert, Daniel	7, Sept 1824		probate		L3
Lambert, Susan	17, Jan. 1850	Jan.	25		L3
Lammert, William	9, Apr. 1846	Mar.	25		L3
Lamon, Charles	12, July 1849	July	50		L3
Lamont, Mary Wall	27, Jan. 1848	25, Jan.	17m		L3
Lampas, William	8, June 1822		estate		L3
Lamper, Eliza	18, Apr. 1850	Apr.	18		L3
Lancaster, Hugh	5, Nov. 1840		estate		L2

Name	Notice Date	Death Date	Age	Page	Maiden Name
Lancaster, John F.	6, Nov. 1839		estate	L3	
Lancaster, William	21, Nov. 1844		estate	L3	
Lancaster, William P.	12, Feb. 1846		estate	L3	
Lance, John	25, Aug. 1842	Aug.	10w	L3	
Land, Elenor	21, Mar. 1844	18, Mar.		L3	
Land, John	21, Dec. 1848	17, Dec.	66	L3	
Land, Mary Ann	28, Apr. 1842	25, Apr.		L3	
Landerberger, Christian	9, Aug. 1838	July	40	L3	
Landis, James	12, Sept 1833	Sept	4	L1	
Landon, Moses	3, Dec. 1857			L3	
Landrigan, John	12, Dec. 1833	Dec.		L4	
Landrum, Mahala	3, May 1849	1, May		L3	
Lane, Ann	17, Jan. 1850		estate	L3	
Lane, Ann	6, June 1850	29, May		L3	
Lane, David	31, July 1851	July	28	L3	
Lane, Eleanor	13, June 1833	June	35	L1	
Lane, George	18, Feb. 1818		estate	L3	
Lane, Henry	1, Aug. 1844		26	L3	
Lane, John	19, Apr. 1845	Apr.	35	L3	
Lane, Richard	7, Aug. 1834	July	6	L3	
Lane, Rufus	24, Dec. 1846	Dec.	22	L3	
Lane, William	18, Sept 1845	Sept	7	L3	
Lang, James	15, July 1841	July	69	L3	
Lang, James	16, Oct. 1856		probate	L6	
Langarl, Anne	23, May 1833	May	25	L4	
Langarl, William	20, Dec. 1825		probate	L4	
Langdon, Catharine W.	19, Oct. 1848	13, Oct.	54	L3	
Langdon, Emma	15, Mar. 1855	10, Mar.	10- -12d	L3	
Langdon, Jesse Lee	10, June 1823	4, June		L3	
Langdon, John	12, Jan. 1837		probate	L3	
Langdon, John	3, Nov. 1831		estate	L4	
Langdon, Mary E.	14, Sept 1843	Sept	1	L3	
Langdon, Nancy (Mrs)	16, Mar. 1824	7, Mar.	30	L3	
Langdon, Solomon	15, Sept 1817		estate	L3	
Langdon, Solomon	16, Mar. 1822		estate	L4	
Langdon, Solomon (Rev)	14, Oct. 1816	8, Oct.	40	* L3	
Langdon, Solomon (Rev)	25, Nov. 1816		estate	L3	
Langdon, William L.	18, Oct. 1832	Oct.		L4	
Langewisch, Conrad	26, July 1849	July	47	L3	
Langfritz, John	1, Nov. 1849	Oct.	27	L3	
Langley, Edward	6, Nov. 1845	1, Nov.	63	* L3	
Langley, John	9, Dec. 1847	26, Nov.		L1	
Langman, Philip	18, July 1844	July	63	L3	
Langsing, Oliver	1, Aug. 1833	July	2-11m	L1	
Langstaff, Elizabeth Euphemia	2, Dec. 1852	27, Nov.	5- -10d	L3	
Langstaff, Henry Clay	2, Apr. 1846	1, Apr.	3- 7m	L3	
Langstaff, William Harrison	29, Apr. 1852	28, Apr.	1-11m-24d	L3	
Langton, John	20, Mar. 1851	Mar.	26	L3	
Langtry, Julia Ann	2, Aug. 1832	July	1- 2m	L1	
Langtry, Samuel	25, May 1843	17, May	20	L3	
Lanier, Elizabeth G.	23, Apr. 1846	15, Apr.		L3	
Lanphear, Lucinda	25, Mar. 1841	20, Mar.	57	L3	
Lanphear, Susan A.	18, Oct. 1838	17, Oct.		L3	
Lansing, Catharine	10, Oct. 1850	23, Sept	81	L3	

Name	Notice Date	Death Date	Age		Page	Maiden Name
Lansing, D.C. (Rev)	26, Mar. 1857	19, Mar.	72		L3	
Lansing, Maria Hubbard	10, Oct. 1850	24, Sept	10		L3	
Lansing, Sanders	10, Oct. 1850	19, Sept	85	*	L3	
Lansing, William Alexander	10, Oct. 1850	20, Sept	18		L3	
Lantz, Frederick J.	3, July 1845	June	56		L3	
Lanz, Theodore	4, Sept 1856		probate		L5	
Lape, Benjamin	5, July 1821		estate		L3	
Lape, Benjamin	9, June 1821	7, June			L3	
Lape, Jacob	8, Aug. 1833	July	36		L1	
Lapham, Darius	25, July 1850	20, July	42		L3	
Lapham, Nancy L.	20, Nov. 1845	14, Nov.	31		L3	
Lapham, Phebe F.	16, Dec. 1847	30, Nov.	13- 5m		L3	
Lapham, Rachel Allen	12, Jan. 1837		4m- 4d		L3	
Lapham, Seneca	5, 19, Jan. 1854	30, Dec.	70		L3	
Lapham, William	15, Mar. 1855	9, Mar.	37- 4m- 9d		L3	
Lapp, Simon	7, June 1855		probate		L3	
Lappenty, (child)	22, Aug. 1833	Aug.	infant		L4	
Laquey, Elexis H.	4, Jan. 1814		estate		L2	
Large, Ann	13, Nov. 1850	Nov.	65		L3	
Large, Barbary	19, Sept 1833	Sept	64		L4	
Large, Lucinda	10, May 1849	May	20m		L3	
Larimore, James S. (Dr)	27, May 1841	12, May	27		L3	
Lark, Sebastian	19, July 1849	July	30		L3	
Larkin, James	13, Mar. 1851	8, Mar.			L3	
Larkin, John	22, Aug. 1850	Aug.	1- 3m		L3	
Larkin, William	14, June 1849	June			L3	
Larkins, Emeline	1, July 1847	23, June			L3	
Larkins, Hannah	24, July 1845	July	35		L3	
Larkins, Patrick	24, July 1845	July	38		L3	
Larnard, J.H.	7, Sept 1848	3, Sept			L3	
Larow, John	3, Sept 1840		estate		L3	
Lartis, Barrell	22, July 1847	July	2m		L3	
Lartis, Mary	29, July 1847	July	44		L3	
Lasselle, Julia Riddey D.	10, Nov. 1842	26, Oct.	54		L4	DeBosseron
Latham,	23, Feb. 1854				L3	
Latham, Robert	17, July 1845	July	51		L3	
Lathrop, Jane	11, Dec. 1851	2, Dec.			L3	
Lathrop, Joshua	28, Aug. 1856	20, Aug.	69		L5	
Latshaw, Andrew	5, Apr. 1849	Mar.	40		L3	
Latta, John	10, Jan. 1828	Jan.	47		L4	
Latta, S.A. (Dr)	1, July 1852	26, June			L3	
Lauenstein, Henry J.	7, May 1857		probate		L3	
Laughlin, Michael	9, July 1857		probate		L3	
Laurison, Andrew	12, July 1849	July	7		L3	
Laurison, Ann	12, July 1849	July	35		L3	
Laurison, Charles	12, July 1849	July	11		L3	
Lavery, John	20, Sept 1849	Sept	25		L3	
Lavin, Lawrence	27, Feb. 1851	Feb.	58		L3	
Law, Benjamin	4, June 1857		probate		L3	
Law, William	28, Dec. 1848	Dec.	24		L3	
Law, William	5, July 1849	June	38		L3	
Lawler, Ann	22, June 1837		probate		L3	
Lawler, Mary	20, Feb. 1851	Feb.	22		L3	
Lawless, Sarah	21, Aug. 1845	Aug.	30		L3	

Name	Notice Date	Death Date	Age	Page	Maiden Name
Lawless, Thomas	25, Jan. 1849	Jan.	25		L3
Lawner, Bartlett	5, July 1849	June	25		L3
Lawrence, Alanson I.M.	26, Nov. 1840	14, Oct.	21		L3
Lawrence, Ann E.	17, Feb. 1848	Feb.	1		L3
Lawrence, Ann S.	15, Aug. 1833	Aug.	2m-10d		L1
Lawrence, Anna M.	21, Dec. 1843	12, Dec.	16		L3
Lawrence, Anna O.	18, Sept 1845	13, Sept	50		L3
Lawrence, Charles	3, Aug. 1843	July	30		L3
Lawrence, Edmond	22, Aug. 1850	Aug.	3		L3
Lawrence, Edward	20, July 1848	18, July	31		L3
Lawrence, Jonathan	29, May 1834		probate		L3
Lawrence, Lorenzo (Dr)	29, Dec. 1836	21, Dec.	44		L3
Lawrence, Lydia	18, July 1833	July	52		L2
Lawrence, P.K.	10, June 1841	19, May			L3
Lawrence, Richard	13, Apr. 1848	Apr.	67		L3
Lawrence, Robert	23, Feb. 1837		probate		L3
Lawrence, Sophia W.	26, Dec. 1833	Dec.	5- 7m- 2d		L4
Lawrence, William DeWitt	16, Apr. 1846	13, Apr.	11m- 4d		L3
Laws, Panter	15, Jan. 1857	3, Jan.	72	*	L3
Lawson, Fenton	4, Aug. 1853	30, July	46		L3
Lawson, Louisa C.	17, Dec. 1846	20, Nov.	34		L3
Lawson, Peter P.	23, Mar. 1854	13, Mar.	81- 9m		L3
Lawson, Thomas	26, Jan. 1843	Jan.	22		L3
Lawson, Thomas	10, June 1841	9, June	53		L3
Lawson, Thomas	17, June 1841		estate		L3
Lawson, Thomas, Jr.	23, Dec. 1852	21, Dec.	35		L3
Lawson, William	20, June 1833	June	10m		L1
Lawson, William	15, Aug. 1850	Aug.	32		L3
Lay, John	17, Aug. 1848	Aug.	40		L3
Layer, Frederick	25, Feb. 1841	Feb.	25		L3
Layman, (man)	11, Aug. 1853	9, Aug.			L3
Layman, Sirah B.	3, May 1849		estate		L3
Lazarus, Frank	18, Mar. 1847	13, Mar.	5m		L3
Lea, James	4, Oct. 1825	30, Sept	66		L3
Lea, James M.	11, July 1833		probate		L3
Lea, Thomas G.	24, Oct. 1844		estate		L3
Lea, Thomas G.	3, Oct. 1844	30, Sept			L3
Leach,	16, Aug. 1849	Aug.	6m		L3
Leach, Charles E.	27, Jan. 1848	18, Jan.	3- 6m		L3
Leach, Charlotte	25, July 1839	July	20		L3
Leach, Harriet	25, July 1839	July	18		L3
Leach, Joseph	24, Feb. 1848	20, Feb.	39		L3
Leach, L.D.	28, June 1849	20, June	32		L3
Leake, Louis	20, Feb. 1851		estate		L3
Leaman, Calvin	8, Aug. 1844	4, Aug.	1		L3
Leaman, Peter	13, Feb. 1822		estate		L3
Leanord, Benjamin C.	23, Jan. 1845	14, Jan.	52	*	L3
Lear, St.	16, Nov. 1854	26, Oct.			L3
Lear, Tobias	4, Nov. 1816	22, Sept			L3
Leard, Enoch	20, Sept 1832	Sept	1- 6m		L1
Leasure, John	25, July 1839	July	52		L3
Leatenberger, Simon	14, Apr. 1853	11, Apr.			L3
Leavitt, Rufus	11, Mar. 1847	8, Mar.	7		L3
Leckey, Alexander	20, Dec. 1825		probate		L4

Name	Notice Date	Death Date	Age		Page	Maiden Name
Leckey, Andrew	20, Dec. 1825		probate		L4	
Lecount, David	28, May 1857	26, May	73	*	L3	
Lecount, Henry	14, July 1853				L3	
Leddy, Margaret	20, Mar. 1851	Mar.	9		L3	
Ledman, Samuel F.	30, Nov. 1848		estate		L3	
Ledyard, H.L.	3, Sept 1840		probate		L3	
Lee, Adam	23, Feb. 1837		probate		L3	
Lee, Augustus	26, June 1851	June			L3	
Lee, Betsy C.	9, Nov. 1837	2, Nov.	35		L3	
Lee, Caroline R.	22, Aug. 1833	Aug.	1- 2m		L4	
Lee, Charles	11, Sept 1834	Aug.	1m		L1	
Lee, Clinton W.	23, Oct. 1851	15, Oct.	26		L3	
Lee, David	10, Jan. 1856		probate		L3	
Lee, David	8, Oct. 1857		probate		L3	
Lee, Edmund J.	8, June 1843				L3	
Lee, Edward	13, Aug. 1846	Aug.	40		L3	
Lee, Eliza Ann	7, Mar. 1850	Feb.	25		L3	
Lee, Eliza Ann	13, Jan. 1853	6, Jan.	82		L3	
Lee, George M.	23, July 1846	July	8m		L3	
Lee, Harriet Brown	13, June 1833	June	8m		L1	
Lee, James	7, Mar. 1850	Feb.	25		L3	
Lee, James	21, Aug. 1851	14, Aug.			L4	
Lee, Jane	25, Oct. 1827	Oct.	7m		L2	
Lee, Jane	15, Nov. 1849	12, Nov.	48		L3	
Lee, Jane	1, Feb. 1849	21, Jan.			L3	
Lee, Jesse (Rev)	28, Oct. 1816	12, Sept	59		L2	
Lee, John	14, June 1849	June	38		L3	
Lee, John	8, June 1854	3, June	74	*	L3	
Lee, John G.	20, Sept 1827	12, Sept	24	*	L1	
Lee, Lewis H.	22, Nov. 1832		estate		L3	
Lee, Lewis H.	25, Oct. 1832	21, Oct.			L3	
Lee, Manirva	3, Aug. 1843	July	36		L3	
Lee, Minerva Jane	10, Aug. 1843	Aug.	2		L3	
Lee, Preston	8, Oct. 1846	Sept	21		L3	
Lee, Reuben	15, May 1834	May	3- 6m		L4	
Lee, Richard	2, June 1806				L3	
Lee, Rickard,	30, May 1844	May	10m		L3	
Lee, Robert	27, Sept 1838	22, Sept	21	*	L3	
Lee, Samuel	19, Dec. 1826		probate		L3	
Lee, Thomas	22, Nov. 1849	Nov.	70		L3	
Lee, William	27, Mar. 1828	Mar.	31		L1	
Lee, William H.	19, Aug. 1847	12, Aug.	21- 6m		L3	
Leebody, (Mrs)	23, May 1833	May	60		L4	
Leech, Sophronia	10, Oct. 1850	2, Oct.			L3	
Leeper, Clements	29, Aug. 1844		estate		L3	
Leeper, Clements	26, Mar. 1846		estate		L3	
Leet, John	16, May 1850	May	20		L3	
Lefavour, Clementine	15, Jan. 1852	4, Jan.	24		L3	
Leffel, Maria	28, Aug. 1834	Aug.	30		L1	
Leffinguell, Orville E.	9, May 1839	Apr.	34		L3	
Leffler, Joseph	19, July 1849	July	41		L3	
Leffler, William	10, Jan. 1850	25, Dec.			L2	
Lefler, Catharine	2, Aug. 1832	July	1- 2m		L1	
Left, Elizabeth	15, Aug. 1839	Aug.	18m		L3	

Name	Notice Date	Death Date	Age		Page	Maiden Name
Leger, William F.	12, Sept 1850	Sept	27		L3	
Legg, (son of Thomas)	1, July 1852	30, June	6		L3	
Legg, William	6, Mar. 1856		estate		L3	
Legg, William	6, Aug. 1857		probate		L3	
Legg, William	14, Aug. 1856		probate		L6	
Legg, William	11, Sept 1856		estate		L8	
Legget, James	15, Aug. 1833	Aug.	35		L1	
Lehman, Bernard H.	15, Oct. 1846	Oct.	52		L3	
Lehman, Jane	21, Feb. 1828	Feb.	2m		L1	
Lehmus, Daniel	12, Feb. 1846	Feb.	61		L3	
Leib, Michael	21, Jan. 1823	18, Jan.	63		L2	
Leibee, John	11, July 1844		estate		L3	
Leiber, Joseph	21, Dec. 1848	Dec.	25		L3	
Leiber, Lewis	27, Sept 1849	Sept	35		L3	
Leibert, Joseph B.	28, July 1806	25, July			L3	
Leiby, George	14, Dec. 1837		estate		L4	
Leidy, Tobias W.	4, July 1850	29, June	47		L3	
Leien, Frank	21, June 1849	June	33		L3	
Leinning, John B.	21, Nov. 1833	Nov.	18		L3	
Lemaire, Amanda M.	11, July 1850	7, July	32		L3	
Lemaire, Louis	12, Oct. 1854	5, Oct.	51		L3	
Leman, Andrew	26, Sept 1826		probate		L3	
Lemmon, Alexis	16, Oct. 1856		probate		L6	
Lemmon, Charles	27, Feb. 1845	Feb.	50		L3	
Lemon, Sarah Jane	11, Sept 1834	Aug.	1- 6m		L1	
Lendly, Mary	2, Sept 1852	Aug.	1		L3	
Lennig, Henry	15, Aug. 1850	Aug.	55		L3	
Lennox, Margaret	3, Feb. 1853		15		L3	
Lennox, Tom	25, Oct. 1849	19, Oct.			L3	
Lentz, Catharine	15, July 1841	July	3m		L3	
Leny, Thomas M.	5, July 1849	June	42		L3	
Leonard, Alexander	9, Apr. 1857		probate		L3	
Leonard, Catharine	12, Feb. 1852	7, Feb.			L3	
Leonard, Charles	20, June 1850	14, June	5		L3	
Leonard, Eliphalet (Capt)	14, Dec. 1837		70	*	L3	
Leonard, John	30, May 1850	May	45		L3	
Leonard, Margaret	5, Sept 1833	Aug.	30		L1	
Leonard, Owen	22, July 1847	July	22		L3	
LePage, Edwin	22, Aug. 1826	21, Aug.	28		L3	
Lernbar, Joseph	22, Aug. 1850	Aug.	43		L3	
Leser, A.	5, Mar. 1857		probate		L3	
Leser, Andrew	20, Nov. 1851		estate		L3	
Leser, Andrew	22, Feb. 1855		estate		L3	
Leslie, Andrew	17, Mar. 1842	13, Mar.	7w		L3	
Leslie, Emma	27, July 1843	19, July			L3	
Leslie, Jeremiah	12, Feb. 1857	5, Feb.			L3	
Leslie, Margaret Spence	4, Sept 1851	28, Aug.	39		L3	
Leslie, Norman	26, June 1851	21, June	5m		L3	
Leslie, Rachel A.	8, Sept 1853	27, Aug.			L3	
Leslie, William	4, Feb. 1847	21, Jan.	30	*	L3	
Lestor, Joanna	23, Mar. 1849	Mar.	30		L3	
Leter, George	7, Aug. 1834	July	2		L3	
Levalara, John	8, Nov. 1855		probate		L3	
Levin, Lewis	24, Dec. 1829	2, Dec.	30	*	L3	

Name	Notice Date	Death Date	Age	Page	Maiden Name
Levings, Noah (Rev)	18, Jan. 1849	9, Jan.	53	L3	
Levy, (child of Rachel)	1, July 1841	June	2m	L3	
Lewell, Margaret	28, Apr. 1853	26, Apr.		L3	
Lewis, (child of Samuel)	30, Aug. 1832	Aug.	3d	L1	
Lewis, Abigail	2, Mar. 1843	21, Feb.	73	L3	
Lewis, Alexander	9, May 1850	Apr.	41	L3	
Lewis, Alexander P.	10, May 1855	6, May	36	L3	
Lewis, Andrew P.	6, Sept 1855	27, Aug.	20	L3	
Lewis, Ann	28, Feb. 1856	20, Feb.	74	L3	
Lewis, Anstay	11, Apr. 1821	7, Apr.	26	L3	
Lewis, Eleanor Parke	29, July 1852	17, July	74	L3	Custis
Lewis, Eliza	7, Dec. 1848	Nov.	29	L3	
Lewis, Elizabeth G.	16, Sept 1847	12, Sept	19	L3	
Lewis, F.W.	1, Aug. 1833	July	30	L1	
Lewis, Frances S.	13, Jan. 1853	6, Jan.	21	L3	
Lewis, James	4, June 1857	probate		L3	
Lewis, Jane	22, Oct. 1857	17, Oct.	26	L3	
Lewis, Jane	23, Feb. 1854	19, Jan.	34	L3	
Lewis, John	12, Sept 1833	Sept	7d	L1	
Lewis, John	2, Nov. 1843	Oct.	30	L3	
Lewis, John	10, July 1851	2, July	71	L3	
Lewis, Jonathan	18, Sept 1845	3, Sept	79	* L3	
Lewis, Joseph T. (Rev)	13, Nov. 1850	4, Nov.		L3	
Lewis, Leah	19, Oct. 1848	Oct.	1	L3	
Lewis, Lydia	13, Sept 1849	Sept	43	L3	
Lewis, Margaret (Mrs)	1, Nov. 1832	26, Oct.		L1	
Lewis, Margaret T.	22, Apr. 1847	Apr.	14m	L3	
Lewis, Mark	16, Nov. 1837	11, Nov.	23	* L3	
Lewis, Martha J.	29, Oct. 1846	27, Oct.	22	L3	
Lewis, Mary Aurelia	9, May 1844	4, Apr.	39	L3	Mayo
Lewis, Mira Albina	30, May 1850	22, May	16- 6m	L3	
Lewis, Nancy Marcella	9, Mar. 1848	1, Mar.	18- 3m	L3	
Lewis, Oliver	1, Nov. 1832	25, Oct.		L1	
Lewis, Peter	22, Jan. 1852	7, Jan.	17	L3	
Lewis, Philip	14, Nov. 1826	10, Nov.		L3	
Lewis, Samuel	1, Nov. 1832	Oct.	85	L2	
Lewis, Samuel	3, Aug. 1854	28, July	56	L3	
Lewis, Samuel	21, Feb. 1856	probate		L3	
Lewis, Samuel	5, Mar. 1857	probate		L3	
Lewis, Samuel Henry	4, Dec. 1845	27, Nov.	4-11m	L3	
Lewis, Samuel Henry	16, July 1857	11, July	8-10m	L3	
Lewis, Serina	2, Jan. 1840	1, Jan.		L2	
Lewis, Theodore K.	18, 25, Apr. 1844	11, Apr.	16	* L3	
Lewis, Watson	27, June 1839	estate		L3	
Lewis, Watson	30, July 1840	estate		L3	
Lewis, Watson	20, June 1839	14, June		L3	
Lewis, William H.S.	16, Dec. 1852	13, Dec.	22m	L3	
Lewis, William Y.	14, May 1846			L1	
Lewton, Abraham	3, Sept 1840	probate		L3	
L'Hommedieu, Charles	15, Dec. 1817	estate		L3	
L'Hommedieu, Charles	13, Apr. 1813	10, Apr.		* L3	
L'Hommedieu, Charles Hammond	10, Sept 1840	9, Sept	10m-13d	L3	
L'Hommedieu, Louis Francis	7, June 1855	29, May	21m	L3	
L'Hommedieu, Mary	5, Mar. 1840	21, Feb.	2- 4m	L3	

Name	Notice Date	Death Date	Age		Page	Maiden Name
L'Hommedieu, Mary C.	17, Aug. 1843	25, July	77		L3	
L'Hommedieu, Richard F.	11, Feb. 1847		estate		L3	
L'Hommedieu, Richard F.	1, Mar. 1849		estate		L3	
L'Hommedieu, Samuel	11, Oct. 1838		estate		L3	
L'Hommedieu, Samuel	7, May 1840		probate		L3	
L'Hommedieu, Sarah S.	17, Oct. 1839	16, Oct.	14m		L3	
L'Hommedieu, Sylvester	7, Feb. 1828	16, Jan.			L1	
L'Hommedieu, Sylvester	5, Mar. 1840	28, Feb.	8		L3	
Lhorton, Peter	5, Aug. 1852	6, July	66		L3	
Lias, Benjamin	1, Feb. 1849	Jan.	24		L3	
Liban, Jacob	30, Dec. 1847	Dec.	42		L3	
Libeau, Charles	2, Oct. 1856		estate		L6	
Libeau, V.G.W.	5, Mar. 1857		probate		L3	
Libo, John H.	2, May 1839	Apr.	33		L3	
Lidwell, Israel	1, Nov. 1832	23, Oct.			L4	
Lieman, Gotleeb	8, Oct. 1840	Sept	71		L3	
Liggett, Elizabeth	28, Oct. 1852	22, Oct.	27		L3	
Liggett, J.S. (Dr)	23, Oct. 1845	26, Sept			L3	
Liggett, James	17, May 1849	16, May	30		L3	
Liggins, Beverly, Jr.	21, June 1838	June	12		L3	
Light, Almira	19, Jan. 1854	23, Dec.	42		L3	Manning
Light, Martin	19, Apr. 1845		estate		L3	
Light, Mary	19, July 1849	July	14d		L3	
Light, Mary	18, Apr. 1844	14, Apr.			L3	Montague
Lightfoot, Eliza	1, Nov. 1838	Oct.	43		L3	
Lightfoot, Montraville	25, Oct. 1832	Oct.	2		L1	
Lilie, P.H.	16, Oct. 1856		probate		L6	
Lilley, Julia Ann	2, May 1833	Apr.	2		L1	
Lilley, Rachel	11, Jan. 1838	7, Jan.			L3	
Lilley, William P.	25, Apr. 1833	Apr.	4- 8m		L1	
Limming, Benjamin	25, Dec. 1815		estate		L3	
Limpus, Elizabeth M.	2, Mar. 1854	14, Feb.	33		L3	
Lims, Charles H.	1, Nov. 1832	27, Oct.			L3	
Linch, Fanny	1, Nov. 1832	26, Oct.			L1	
Linck, John	25, Oct. 1832	19, Oct.			L2	
Lincoln, Francis Seymour	11, Oct. 1849	6, Oct.	16m-13d		L3	
Lincoln, William (Dr)	26, Apr. 1814		estate		L2	
Lind, Andrew	31, Oct. 1839		estate		L3	
Lindenburg, Francis	25, July 1844	July	32		L3	
Lindenger, John	12, July 1849	July	26		L3	
Lindinger, Magdalena	12, July 1849	July	28		L3	
Lindlay, Abraham	12, Nov. 1846	23, Oct.	84	*	L3	
Lindley, Dodd	22, June 1843		estate		L3	
Lindley, Eliza	19, Aug. 1852	Aug.	6		L3	
Lindley, Sarah	4, Jan. 1838	16, Dec.	58	*	L3	
Lindley, William	12, Aug. 1852	Aug.	19m		L3	
Lindman, Larbie	18, July 1833	July	16		L2	
Lindo,	11, Dec. 1856				L3	
Lindo, A.A.	12, July 1849	8, July	73	*	L3	
Lindsay, (child of Jane)	8, May 1828	May	1d		L1	
Lindsay, Elizabeth T.	20, May 1847	12, May	44		L3	
Lindsay, Letitia Catharine	20, Sept 1849	14, Sept	13		L3	
Lindsay, Mortimer	3, June 1847	May	7m		L3	
Lindsay, Thomas	16, July 1857		estate		L3	

Name	Notice Date	Death Date	Age		Page	Maiden Name
Lindsay, William R.	28, Oct. 1847	Oct.	29		L3	
Lindsey, Eliza	24, Sept 1840	12, Sept			L3	
Lindsey, Thomas	18, June 1857	12, June	50		L3	
Line, Margarette	20, July 1854	2, May	88	*	L3	
Linehin, Brien	20, Mar. 1851	Mar.	25		L3	
Lines, Orrin P.	16, May 1839	May	29	*	L3	
Linett, John	4, Nov. 1847	Oct.	45		L3	
Link, Harper	25, May 1837	May	27		L2	
Linn, (child of Abraham)	6, Sept 1849	Aug.	9m		L3	
Linn, John	25, May 1848	May			L3	
Linton, William	16, Mar. 1848	12, Mar.	67		L3	
Lippincott, David A.	8, Nov. 1838		probate		L3	
Lisdade, Richard	13, June 1833	June	1- 1m		L1	
Lisdom, John	23, Jan. 1845		estate		L3	
List, Ludwig	5, Oct. 1837	Sept	33		L4	
Lister, Richard	28, June 1849	June			L3	
Liston, Mary	11, July 1850	July	22		L3	
Litchfield, Jacob	5, Oct. 1837	Sept	21		L4	
Litman, Rudolph	21, Dec. 1837	Dec.	60		L3	
Littell, William T.	29, Apr. 1830		estate		L4	
Litter, John	22, June 1848	10, June	77		L3	
Little, Benjamin	18, Oct. 1832	Oct.			L1	
Little, Christopher	26, July 1849	July	45		L3	
Little, Isaac	6, July 1843	June	9m		L3	
Little, James M.	3, Sept 1840		probate		L3	
Little, Jane	1, Oct. 1840	22, Sept		*	L3	
Little, Joseph	5, Mar. 1846				L3	
Little, William	28, Nov. 1833	19, Nov.	43	*	L4	
Liverpool, (Mr)	1, Nov. 1832	27, Oct.			L2	
Liverpool, John	8, Nov. 1832	Nov.	65		L1	
Liverpool, William Henry	24, Apr. 1856	13, Apr.	31		L3	
Livezey, Elizabeth B.	9, Sept 1852	5, Sept			L3	
Livingston, (child of R.H.)	13, Sept 1832	Sept			L1	
Livingston, Ann	24, Oct. 1807	4, Sept	32		L3	
Livingston, John F.	20, Sept 1832	Sept	2m-14d		L1	
Livingston, Robert B.	21, Mar. 1850		estate		L3	
Livingston, Robert B.	30, Jan. 1851		estate		L3	
Lize, Indian	3, Jan. 1850	Dec.			L3	
L'Jean, Bernard	18, July 1833	July	32		L2	
Lloyd, Amelia Mansell	27, Sept 1855		34		L3	
Lloyd, Dasha	17, Sept 1846	Sept	45		L3	
Lloyd, John	4, May 1848	Apr.	32		L3	
Loar, G.	14, June 1838		probate		L4	
Loar, George	15, Sept 1836		estate		L3	
Loar, George	7, Dec. 1837		probate		L3	
Loar, George	13, Feb. 1840		probate		L3	
Loathain, John	4, Jan. 1814		estate		L2	
Loather, William	14, Feb. 1850	Feb.	20		L3	
Lobson, Matthew	9, Oct. 1834	Sept	45		L1	
Locke, Anna Elizabeth	24, Sept 1857	16, Sept	2- 3m		L3	
Locke, James	18, Feb. 1841	Feb.	22		L3	
Locke, John (Dr)	21, Aug. 1856				L1	
Locke, John M.	12, Oct. 1837	Oct.	26		L4	
Lockhart, John	25, Apr. 1833	Apr.	28		L1	

Name	Notice Date	Death Date	Age	Page	Maiden Name
Lockwood, Edwin	25, Oct. 1832	18, Oct.		L1	
Lockwood, James	9, Apr. 1857	probate		L3	
Lockwood, Mary Amanda	27, Mar. 1856	22, Mar.	5- 6m-17d	L3	
Lockwood, Susan Ellen	8, May 1851	2, May		L3	
Lockwood, Thomas Ambrose	11, May 1848	3, May	5m-23d	L3	
Lodge, Catharine B.	26, Oct. 1843	19, Oct.	26	L3	
Lodge, Gordon	11, Sept 1834	Aug.	2-11m- 9d	L1	
Lodge, James	21, Jan. 1836	estate		L3	
Lodge, Seline	13, Oct. 1818	6, Oct.		L3	
Lodge, Susan	26, July 1827	13, July		L3	
Lodwick, Eliza B.	9, Oct. 1851	2, Oct.	60	L3	
Lodwick, William	16, June 1831	11, June		L2	
Lodwick, William	28, July 1831	estate		L3	
Lodwick, William	16, June 1842	estate		L3	
Loechter, Herman	27, Nov. 1851	estate		L3	
Loefner, Francisca	23, July 1857	21, July	25	L3	Koehler
Loffland, Brantson	6, Feb. 1811	estate		L1	
Lofland, Brantson	5, Jan. 1809	estate		L2	
Lofsinger, Albert	24, May 1849	May	20	L3	
Lofthouse, Larry	19, July 1849	July	35	L3	
Lofthouse, William	25, Mar. 1852	estate		L3	
Lofthouse, William	23, Apr. 1857	estate		L3	
Logan, David B.	13, Sept 1838	Sept	27	L3	
Logan, John W.	30, Oct. 1845	26, Oct.	42	L3	
Logan, Margaret	25, Jan. 1855	25, Nov.	69	L3	
Logan, Maria D.	10, May 1855	2, May		L3	
Logeree, Peter	8, Nov. 1832	31, Oct.		L4	
Lohmyer, William	8, Oct. 1846	Sept	31	L3	
Lohryan, (child)	8, Aug. 1833	July		L1	
Loke, N.	9, Mar. 1854	26, Feb.		L3	
Lonaman, Leo	16, Oct. 1851	12, Oct.		L3	
Londerloch, John	20, Sept 1827	Sept	66	L1	
Long, (child of Nancy)	18, Mar. 1847	Mar.	2m	L3	
Long, Agness	18, Dec. 1828	estate		L1	
Long, Agness	9, Aug. 1838	probate		L3	
Long, Andrew	8, Oct. 1857	probate		L3	
Long, Charles	15, Aug. 1833	Aug.	43	L1	
Long, Ellen Madaline	1, Aug. 1850	28, July	infant	L3	
Long, Henry	18, Oct. 1832	16, Oct.		L3	
Long, Herman	1, Feb. 1825	estate		L3	
Long, Jacob	15, May 1834	estate		L3	
Long, John D.	27, Sept 1827	2- 8m		L1	
Long, Michael	28, Sept 1822	estate		L3	
Long, Stephen L'Hommedieu	12, Sept 1833	1, Sept	5	L4	
Longe, Frederick G.	9, Nov. 1848	Oct.	38	L3	
Longhurst, Henry	9, Oct. 1851	30, Sept		L4	
Longmeyer, John H.	14, Oct. 1847	Oct.	30	L3	
Longshore, John	9, Aug. 1838	probate		L3	
Longwell, William	1, Aug. 1833	July	2-10m	L1	
Longworth, Elizabeth	27, Nov. 1834	Nov.	1	L1	
Lonokes, (child of Arton)	3, Jan. 1833	Dec.	9m	L4	
Looker, Allison C.	15, July 1852	9, July	30	L3	
Looker, Frances Jane	2, Apr. 1846	28, Mar.	8m- 9d	L3	
Looker, James Harvey	6, Mar. 1827	3, Mar.		L3	

Name	Notice Date	Death Date	Age		Page	Maiden Name
Looker, John M.	22, Dec. 1812	17, Dec.		*	L3	
Looker, Otheniel	8, Nov. 1849	12, Oct.	36		L3	
Looker, R.A.	9, June 1836		probate		L3	
Looker, R.A.	12, Jan. 1837		probate		L3	
Looker, Robert A.	11, June 1835		estate		L3	
Looker, Sally	20, July 1813	14, July		*	L3	
Looker, Silas C.	15, Oct. 1840		estate		L3	
Loomis, William Dorwin	30, Nov. 1837	21, Nov.	6m- 2d		L3	
Loos, Ferdinand	20, Sept 1849	Sept	40		L3	
Lopez, Matthew	16, May 1833	May	45		L1	
Lord, Charles	10, Jan. 1828	Jan.	40		L4	
Lord, Frederic French	17, Feb. 1848	13, Feb.	4-10m		L3	
Lord, J.K. (Rev)	19, July 1849	13, July	30		L2	
Lord, Mary C.	30, Nov. 1854	23, Nov.	17		L3	
Lord, Thomas W.	27, Dec. 1855	21, Dec.	56		L3	
Lord, Thomas W.	10, Jan. 1856		estate		L3	
Lord, Thomas W.	6, Aug. 1857		probate		L3	
Lorentz, Magdalena	25, Jan. 1855	12, Jan.	79		L3	
Lorenzo, Balshaser	11, Mar. 1852	Mar.	61		L4	
Loring, David	25, Jan. 1849	22, Jan.	64		L3	
Loring, David	8, Feb. 1849	22, Jan.	64	*	L3	
Loring, David	23, Mar. 1849		estate		L3	
Loring, George	5, Oct. 1843	14, Aug.		*	L3	
Loring, James L.	21, Apr. 1853				L3	
Lorton, Mary E.	8, Aug. 1833	July	1- -12d		L1	
Losh, Lot	6, Nov. 1851		estate		L3	
Loucers, Andrew	29, Aug. 1833	Aug.	56		L1	
Lough, Joseph	27, Sept 1820	3, Aug.	40	*	L3	
Loughead, Theodore	5, Feb. 1857	28, Jan.	1m-18d		L3	
Louis, William B.	11, Jan. 1849	Jan.	40		L3	
Lounsberg, Cornelius H.	3, Jan. 1856		estate		L3	
Lounsbery, Louisa Brooke	11, Mar. 1847	7, Mar.	2- - 1d		L3	
Love, Henry	9, Apr. 1846		estate		L3	
Love, Peter	4, Jan. 1814		estate		L4	
Love, Richard (Capt)	19, Jan. 1843				L3	
Love, Rufus K.	3, Aug. 1854	2, Aug.			L3	
Lovejoy, Abigail W.	11, Mar. 1852	30, Jan.	33		L3	
Lovejoy, Henry B.	19, May 1842	7, May	23		L3	
Lovejoy, James	1, Aug. 1844	July	9m		L3	
Lovejoy, Samuel	7, May 1840		probate		L3	
Lovejoy, Samuel (heirs of)	14, June 1838		probate		L4	
Lovejoy, William George	11, Nov. 1847	6, Nov.	26		L3	
Lovelace, Sarah Maria	13, Feb. 1840	7, Feb.	18		L3	
Lovelace, Seneca	8, May 1828	May	37		L1	
Lovelace, Seneca	18, Dec. 1845	14, Dec.	28		L3	
Lovelace, William	2, Mar. 1843	26, Feb.	3m		L3	
Lovell, Clara Smith	26, Apr. 1855	23, Apr.	43		L3	
Lovell, Downes	16, Apr. 1840	9, Apr.	4-10m		L3	
Lovell, Phebe	13, Dec. 1849	Dec.	46		L3	
Lovell, William	29, Aug. 1850	Aug.	26		L3	
Lover, Francis	24, Sept 1846	Sept	60		L3	
Lovet, Moses	31, Aug. 1848	Aug.	40		L3	
Lovet, Washington	23, Aug. 1849	Aug.	20		L3	
Lovett, William	2, May 1850	Apr.	62		L3	

Name	Notice Date	Death Date	Age		Page	Maiden Name
Loving, Richard	1, June 1848	May	19		L3	
Low, Ebenezer	3, Dec. 1840		probate		L3	
Lowcks, George W.	17, Dec. 1846	Dec.	33		L3	
Lowe, Augustine	24, Dec. 1857	20, Dec.	20		L3	
Lowe, Ebenezer	18, July 1839		estate		L4	
Lowe, George	9, July 1857		probate		L3	
Lowe, Mary	7, Feb. 1839		estate		L3	
Lowery, Rebecca	11, Nov. 1841	21, Sept	43		L3	
Lowrie, Amanda C.	14, Mar. 1839	6, Mar.	23m-22d		L3	
Lowry, Charles F.	25, May 1837	May	24		L2	
Lowry, David	18, Oct. 1832	14, Oct.			L2	
Lowry, Francis	14, Aug. 1845	Aug.	36		L3	
Lowry, Isabella Ann	26, July 1825	23, July	2		L3	
Lowry, John C.	31, Mar. 1853	25, Mar.			L3	
Lowry, John Kyle	30, Mar. 1848	29, Mar.	29		L3	
Lowry, Samuel	8, Oct. 1857	5, Oct.	70		L3	
Lowry, Thomas	27, Dec. 1849	Dec.	24		L3	
Lowry, Thomas	5, Sept 1839	Aug.	27		L3	
Loyd, David	27, Dec. 1838	Dec.	23		L3	
Loyes, Chester	21, June 1849	June	42		L3	
Lucas, Dinah	4, Aug. 1842	Aug.	14m		L3	
Lucas, James	20, June 1844	June	34		L3	
Lucassic, Morris	26, Feb. 1857				L3	
Luce, Elijah W.	10, Aug. 1837		estate		L3	
Luckey, Eliza Ann	25, Oct. 1832	17, Oct.	7		L4	
Luckey, Obediah Jennings	15, Feb. 1844	14, Feb.	22		L3	
Lucky, William H.	8, Aug. 1833	July	2		L1	
Luders, Martin	30, Aug. 1838	Aug.	39		L3	
Ludlam, Providence	8, Dec. 1818		estate		L3	
Ludlow, Henry	20, Aug. 1835		estate		L3	
Ludlow, Israel	5, Sept 1810		estate		L2	
Ludlow, Israel	19, May 1853	(d.1804)	39		L3	
Ludlow, Israel	25, Aug. 1817		estate		L4	
Ludlow, Israel (Col)	1, Nov. 1809		estate		L2	
Ludlow, Israel L.	30, Apr. 1846	21, Apr.	40	*	L3	
Ludlow, J.C.	26, Aug. 1841	15, Aug.			L3	
Ludlow, James C.	26, Aug. 1841	15, Aug.	42	*	L3	
Ludlow, James C.	11, Mar. 1847		estate		L3	
Ludlow, John	5, Nov. 1857		probate		L3	
Ludlow, John	18, Sept 1851	14, Sept			L3	
Ludlow, Josephine C.	11, Dec. 1845	7, Dec.			L3	
Ludlow, Worcester	15, Oct. 1846	9, Oct.	8m-10d		L3	
Ludlum, Augusta Victoria	13, Feb. 1851	29, Jan.			L3	
Ludlum, Henry	7, Sept 1824		probate		L3	
Ludlum, Joseph	22, Aug. 1833	Aug.	21		L4	
Ludo, Susan	14, Mar. 1850	Mar.	48		L3	
Lugenbuhl, William	4, Sept 1834		estate		L4	
Luke, Clementine	10, Feb. 1848	2, Feb.	25		L3	
Luken, H.	10, Mar. 1853				L3	
Luken, H.H.	5, May 1853	Apr.			L3	
Lukes, John	25, June 1846	June	70		L3	
Lumber, B.	26, July 1849	July			L3	
Lummas, Catharine	9, Aug. 1849	July	30		L3	
Lumsden, Alexander	21, Dec. 1843	10, Dec.	16- 6m-21d		L3	

Name	Notice Date	Death Date	Age	Page	Maiden Name
Lumsden, Mary Jane	24, Sept 1840	8, Sept	6m-21d	L3	
Lumson, (child of Ann)	27, May 1847	May	2w	L3	
Lupton, Anna Buck	3, May 1849	27, Apr.	11m	L3	
Lupton, Harriet Lawrence	20, July 1837	16, July	7m-16d	L3	
Lupton, Harriet O.	8, Dec. 1836	2, Dec.	20	L3	Lawrence
Lupton, Mary F.	24, May 1849	3, May	32	L3	Leslie
Lurty, William M.	11, Feb. 1847	1, Feb.	15	L3	
Lusk, Lorin	4, Sept 1851	31, Aug.	22	L3	
Luterbaker, Barbara	5, June 1845	May	3w	L3	
Lutes, Mary	25, May 1848	May	27	L3	
Luth, Mary Emma	5, July 1849	June	4- 6m	L3	
Luthrop, Aburier	1, Aug. 1833	July	2- -20d	L1	
Lutmeir, John	3, Aug. 1837	July	40	L3	
Lutz, Casper	20, Jan. 1848	Jan.	33	L3	
Luzenburg, Mary L.	21, June 1849	19, June	20	L3	
Luzier, Joseph	31, Aug. 1837	Aug.	35	L4	
Lyberger, Josiah	16, July 1846	July	1- 6m	L3	
Lyberger, Sally	3, Sept 1846	Aug.	70	L3	
Lybrand, Edwin W.P.	18, Mar. 1847	9, Mar.	6	L3	
Lyburger, William	6, Aug. 1846	July	6	L3	
Lycum, (child of John)	31, Jan. 1850	Jan.		L3	
Lyens, Isaac	5, Feb. 1852		estate	L3	
Lyens, Isaac	31, Mar. 1853		estate	L3	
Lyens, Isaac	26, July 1855		estate	L3	
Lyle, Agnes	25, July 1850	22, July		* L3	
Lyle, Mary Jane	23, Aug. 1849	Aug.	25	L3	
Lynch, Bazabel	1, Feb. 1838	Jan.	37	L3	
Lynch, Dennis	6, June 1850	May	33	L3	
Lynch, Honora	20, Feb. 1851	Feb.	30	L3	
Lynch, Hugh	26, July 1849	July	18	L3	
Lynch, John	19, Mar. 1857	14, Mar.	16	L3	
Lynch, Mary	22, July 1847	July	2	L3	
Lynch, Nicholas	8, July 1847	June	7	L3	
Lynch, Patrick	23, Aug. 1849	Aug.	24	L3	
Lynch, Peter	10, Feb. 1848	25, Jan.	31	L3	
Lynch, Thomas	19, Oct. 1848	Oct.		L3	
Lyne, Catharine	6, Dec. 1838	Nov.	26	L4	
Lynes, Debrah	5, Apr. 1855		80	L3	
Lynes, William	27, Jan. 1842		estate	L3	
Lynk, Andrew	9, June 1836		probate	L3	
Lynk, Elmira	20, Sept 1838	Sept	9	L3	
Lynn, Eliza Catharine	10, July 1845	10, June	3- 8m-13d	L3	
Lynn, Mary Ann	31, July 1845	23, July	1- 5m-15d	L3	
Lynn, Matthew	1, Nov. 1832	28, Oct.		L2	
Lyon, (child of Mr)	7, Aug. 1834	July		L3	
Lyon, Benjamin	18, Sept 1834	Sept	60	L1	
Lyon, Charles	1, July 1847	June	56	L3	
Lyon, Eliza	10, Sept 1840	7, Sept		L3	
Lyon, James	28, Oct. 1841		esate	L3	
Lyon, James M.	24, Jan. 1856	9, Jan.		L3	
Lyon, John	12, July 1849	July	2	L3	
Lyon, Moses	28, Oct. 1841	27, Oct.		L3	
Lyon, Myraett	8, Jan. 1835	4, Jan.	34- 5m- 1d	L2	Hitchcock
Lyons, Henry	13, Sept 1832	Sept	38	L1	

Name	Notice Date	Death Date	Age		Page	Maiden Name
Lyons, J.	6, Sept 1855		probate		L3	
Lyons, James	23, Sept 1841	22, Sept	87		L3	
Lyons, Joseph	15, Mar. 1838		estate		L3	
Lyons, Mary	30, Dec. 1825		67		L3	
Lyons, Michael	13, Apr. 1848	Apr.	33		L3	
Lyons, Spencer Clark	6, Mar. 1845	19, Feb.	21- 8m		L3	
Lyst, John	2, Nov. 1819		estate		L3	
Lyst, John	20, Dec. 1825		probate		L4	
Lytle, Andrew J.	23, June 1842	2, June	26		L3	
Lytle, Eliza N.	19, May 1821	15, May			L3	
Lytle, Elizabeth R.	24, Nov. 1842	21, Nov.	22		L6	
Lytle, John S.	13, May 1841		estate		L3	
Lytle, Joseph C.	17, Nov. 1842	28, Oct.	24		L6	
Lytle, Margaret	19, June 1851	14, June	79		L3	
Lytle, Margaret Haines	17, July 1851	14, June		*	L3	
Lytle, Margaretta	12, Apr. 1832	7, Apr.			L3	
Lytle, Rowan	6, Apr. 1813	27, Mar.	infant		L3	
Lytle, S.S. (Mrs)	20, June 1833	June	24		L1	
Lytle, William	18, Sept 1828	13, Sept	18		L3	
Lytle, William H.	6, 27, June 1826	3, June	24	*	L3	
Macady, (Mrs)	8, Aug. 1833	July			L1	
MacAlester, Eliza Ann	17, Sept 1835	31, Aug.			L1	Lytle
MacCracken, Eliza B.	12, Sept 1850	7, Sept	26		L3	Brooks
MacDonald, Thomas Rogerson	20, Aug. 1857	16, Aug.	4m- 6d		L3	
MacEwen, Duncan	17, Sept 1857	22, Aug.			L3	
Macey, Charles	26, Oct. 1848	Oct.	30		L3	
Macey, George	1, Jan. 1816		estate		L3	
Machel, Windel	8, Nov. 1832	Nov.	26		L1	
Machesney, John (Major)	9, Dec. 1816	18, Sept			L3	
Macim, Emme	15, May 1834	May	27		L4	
Mack, Cornelia	1, Sept 1853	14, Aug.	infant		L3	
Mack, James	11, Apr. 1850	Apr.	40		L3	
Mack, Margaret	8, Oct. 1846	30, Sept	101		L3	
Macke, Henry	31, Dec. 1846	Dec.	23		L3	
Macke, Henry	3, May 1855		probate		L3	
Macken, Jane	15, Nov. 1849	Nov.	25		L3	
Macken, John	13, Apr. 1848	Apr.	44		L3	
Mackey, Alexander	13, Mar. 1811	Mar.		*	L3	
Mackie, Mary	30, June 1842	20, June		*	L3	Conyers
Mackie, William	27, Dec. 1849		estate		L3	
Macklin, Henry	10, Sept 1857		probate		L3	
Macklin, Henry	10, Dec. 1857		probate		L3	
Maclarland, William	18, Sept 1834	Sept	20		L1	
Maclay, James Johnson	27, Aug. 1846	18, Aug.	30	*	L3	
MacMaster, Gilbert (Rev)	30, Mar. 1854	17, Mar.	77		L3	
Macosman, (child of Chaplen M)	13, Dec. 1832	Dec.	stillborn		L1	
Macozy, (child of Ann)	18, Oct. 1832	Oct.	stillborn		L4	
Macracken, James C.	28, Oct. 1852	5, Oct.	32		L3	
Macswell, William	14, Oct. 1852		50		L3	
Mactunkids, Anne	20, Sept 1832	Sept	33		L1	
Macy, Eliza S.	25, June 1846	21, June			L3	
Macy, Elizabeth	12, June 1851	1, June	79- 6m	*	L3	
Madarie, William	9, Aug. 1838		probate		L3	

Name	Notice Date	Death Date	Age		Page	Maiden Name
Madden, Daniel	26, June 1851	June	27		L3	
Madden, William	15, Mar. 1814		estate		L3	
Maddigan, Edward	24, Dec. 1840	Dec.	20		L3	
Madding, Thomas	20, Sept 1849	Sept	40		L3	
Maddox, Delia	9, Jan. 1851	12, Dec.			L3	Miller
Maddox, John	26, July 1832	July	50		L1	
Maddy, Michael	31, Dec. 1846	Dec.			L3	
Madeira, George D.	18, Oct. 1827	Oct.	11m		L3	
Madeira, Jacob	23, Jan. 1830	30, Dec.	35		L2	
Madigars, John	1, June 1848	May	38		L3	
Madira, Mary	14, Feb. 1856	13, Feb.	59		L3	
Madison, George	28, Oct. 1816	14, Oct.			L2	
Madison, John	13, Feb. 1822		estate		L3	
Madison, Margaret	13, Dec. 1838	5, Dec.			L4	
Madison, Margaret Fenecia	4, Sept 1856	31, Aug.	22		L5	
Madison, Reuben	19, July 1838		estate		L4	
Madon, Mary	18, Jan. 1849	Jan.	11m		L3	
Magentanz, Christian	6, Dec. 1849	Nov.	22		L3	
Magfield, Elizabeth	26, Nov. 1846	Nov.	50		L3	
Magill, Catherine	12, July 1849	8, July	60	*	L3	
Magill, Francis	21, Oct. 1841	Oct.	27		L3	
Magill, James	5, Nov. 1840	15, Oct.	23		L2	
Maginnis, Peter	26, Aug. 1847	Aug.	43		L3	
Magle, William	7, Aug. 1834	July	47		L3	
Mahady, (Mrs)	1, Aug. 1833	July			L1	
Mahaley, Michael	30, Nov. 1848	Nov.	26		L3	
Mahan, Francis	29, June 1848	June	35		L3	
Mahan, John	30, Aug. 1849				L2	
Mahan, Michael	11, Dec. 1856				L3	
Mahan, William	6, Aug. 1857		probate		L3	
Mahana, Timothy	3, May 1849	Apr.	23		L3	
Mahaney, Haley	18, Sept 1834	Sept	1		L1	
Mahaney, William	18, Sept 1834	Sept	47		L1	
Mahar, Margaret	26, June 1851	June	25		L3	
Mahar, Michael	11, Apr. 1850	Apr.	3		L3	
Mahar, Patrick	11, Apr. 1850	Apr.	10		L3	
Mahar, Patrick	11, Apr. 1850	Apr.	13		L3	
Mahard, (Mrs)	15, Aug. 1833	Aug.			L1	
Mahard, Ann	8, Aug. 1833	5, Aug.			L2	
Mahard, John	31, Dec. 1846	July	76	*	L3	
Mahard, John	24, Sept 1846		estate		L3	
Mahary, Patrick	21, Feb. 1850	Feb.	2- 6m		L3	
Maher, John	5, Sept 1844	Aug.	27		L3	
Maher, Martin	9, Nov. 1837		estate		L3	
Mahon, Rozetta	27, Apr. 1854	23, Apr.	9m		L3	
Mahon, Stephen	30, Oct. 1856	27, Oct.			L5	
Mahon, Symuel Cobb	27, Apr. 1854	25, Apr.	4		L3	
Mahoney, John	30, Aug. 1849	Aug.	28		L3	
Mahoney, John	3, May 1849	Apr.	36		L3	
Mahoney, Michael	13, Apr. 1848	Apr.	36		L3	
Mahorney, Sarah	11, Feb. 1847	Feb.	34		L3	
Main, John	18, July 1833	July	42		L2	
Main, John	22, Aug. 1833		estate		L4	
Mair, John	18, Sept 1834	Sept	14- 7m		L1	

Name	Notice Date	Death Date	Age		Page	Maiden Name
Maitland, John	25, Apr. 1850	Apr.	33		L3	
Maize, Sarah	23, Oct. 1845	Oct.	35		L3	
Majer, William	31, Jan. 1850	Jan.	18		L3	
Majors, Charles L.	2, Aug. 1832	July	2- 5m		L1	
Makin, Thomas	15, Aug. 1833	Aug.	40		L1	
Makintosh, Steven D.	4, Nov. 1841	17, Oct.			L3	
Malally, John	20, Dec. 1849	16, Dec.			L2	
Malana, Ann	3, July 1851	June	20		L3	
Malbring, Sarah	23, Oct. 1834	Oct.	32		L2	
Malcolm, Joseph	7, Oct. 1847	Sept	33		L3	
Malcom, Chandler Holbrook	19, Jan. 1843	3, Jan.	2- 3m		L3	
Malcomb, William	11, Dec. 1851	9, Dec.			L4	
Maley, John	1, Dec. 1853		85		L1	
Maley, Michael O.	8, Mar. 1838	Feb.	55		L3	
Maley, Sarah	3, Apr. 1851	30, Mar.	52		L3	Enyart
Maley, Thomas	10, Apr. 1851	Apr.	45		L3	
Mallang, James	3, Jan. 1833	Dec.	35		L4	
Mallory, Ann H.	26, Nov. 1857	18, Nov.	42		L3	
Malone, Julia H.	21, June 1855	15, June	23		L3	See
Malone, Michael	13, Aug. 1846	Aug.	22		L3	
Malone, William	30, May 1850	May	23		L3	
Maloney, Johnson	10, Mar. 1853	Feb.	22		L3	
Malony, Daniel	16, Sept 1852	9, Sept	38		L3	
Malony, Michael	27, Dec. 1849	Dec.	48		L3	
Maloy, Mary	20, Nov. 1850	Nov.	25		L3	
Man, Abel	15, Nov. 1832	Nov.			L1	
Manahan, William	26, July 1849	July	5		L3	
Manchester, Elias	9, Apr. 1846	14, Mar.	90	*	L3	
Mandell, Joseph	25, Oct. 1832	17, Oct.			L4	
Mandler, Philip	9, Aug. 1855		probate		L3	
Maney, John	18, Jan. 1849	Jan.	28		L3	
Mangeals, John	16, Jan. 1845		48		L3	
Manion, Margaret	14, May 1846	May	73		L3	
Mann, Charles Edward	8, Feb. 1844	4, Feb.	3m-26d		L3	
Mann, Elizabeth	8, Aug. 1833	July	5		L1	
Mann, H.C. (Dr)	2, May 1850	21, Dec.		*	L3	
Mann, Hartley	5, June 1845	1, June	32		L3	
Mann, John	15, Dec. 1808		estate		L3	
Mann, Leah P.	27, Jan. 1842	24, Jan.	27		L3	
Mann, Sarah Ada	31, May 1855	23, May	4- 2m-19d		L3	
Manning, Anna	19, Jan. 1854	21, Dec.	92		L3	
Manning, Clarinda	15, Sept 1853	10, Sept	21		L3	
Manning, Elizabeth	5, Oct. 1837	Sept	9		L4	
Manning, Nathan	6, Oct. 1812		estate		L3	
Manning, Patrick	5, July 1849	June	36		L3	
Manning, Thomas	19, Jan. 1854	23, Dec.	91		L3	
Manning, William	25, Apr. 1850	Apr.	35		L3	
Mansell, William H.	19, 26, July 1832	July	11d		L1	
Mansfield, Elizabeth	2, May 1850	12, Apr.	74	*	L3	Phipps
Mansfield, Elizabeth	3, Oct. 1850		estate		L3	
Mansfield, John Fenno (Capt)	15, 21, Sept 1812	14, Sept	25		L3	
Mansfield, Lawrence	25, Jan. 1849	Jan.	49		L3	
Mansfield, Mary	16, Mar. 1837	10, Mar.			L3	
Mansfield, Roswell	9, Oct. 1845		estate		L3	

Name	Notice Date	Death Date	Age	Page	Maiden Name
Manuel, Thomas	7, Dec. 1848		estate	L3	
Manuel, Thomas	3, Aug. 1848	28, July		L3	
March, Joseph	2, Oct. 1834	Sept	44	L4	
March, Joseph H.	9, Oct. 1834		estate	L3	
Marchant, Nathan	2, Aug. 1832	July	7m- 1d	L1	
Marchant, Nathan	3, July 1834		estate	L3	
Marchant, Nathan	1, Nov. 1832	27, Oct.		L3	
Marchant, Samuel L.	25, Aug. 1853	18, Aug.	40	L3	
Marilard, Christian	8, Aug. 1833	July	17	L1	
Mariman, Elizabeth	6, Nov. 1834	Oct.		L1	
Mark, Nathaniel	25, Oct. 1832	Oct.	80	L1	
Markland, Charles	18, Apr. 1839		probate	L3	
Markland, Garah	24, Jan. 1839		estate	L3	
Markland, Garah	5, Sept 1839		probate	L3	
Markland, Thomas	11, July 1833		probate	L3	
Markland, Thomas	22, Mar. 1838		probate	L3	
Marks, (Mr)	1, Nov. 1832	24, Oct.		L1	
Marks, Joseph	17, Apr. 1856	14, Apr.		L3	
Marks, William	15, July 1852		35	L3	
Markward, Charles	3, Aug. 1843	26, July	45	L3	
Marlay, Francis	22, Nov. 1855	14, Nov.	3-11m	L3	
Marony, Mary	11, May 1837	10, May	12	L3	
Maroony, Margaret	12, July 1849	July	6	L3	
Marringer, Henry	23, Aug. 1838	Aug.	26	L3	
Marrion, Louisa	19, July 1849	July	25	L3	
Marrion, Mary	19, July 1849	July	1	L3	
Marsh, Alwilda H.	29, Oct. 1857	23, Oct.	8	L3	
Marsh, Calvin	16, Oct. 1856		probate	L6	
Marsh, Charles	22, Aug. 1850	Aug.	35	L3	
Marsh, Charles	19, Mar. 1857	16, Mar.	1- 8m	L3	
Marsh, Charles	8, Feb. 1820		estate	L3	
Marsh, Enos	5, July 1855		probate	L3	
Marsh, Harriet S.	5, July 1849	1, July	38	L3	
Marsh, Harry Blatchford	5, Sept 1850	28, Aug.	6- 7m	L3	
Marsh, Jeremiah	22, Dec. 1808		estate	L1	
Marsh, Joseph Jones	21, July 1853	19, July	1- -12d	L3	
Marsh, Martha	6, June 1833	May	5m	L2	
Marsh, Polly	12, Dec. 1810	27, Nov.		L2	
Marsh, Samuel	6, Jan. 1817	31, Dec.	15	L3	
Marsh, Sidney	6, Dec. 1849	Nov.	42	L3	
Marsh, Thomas	1, Nov. 1832	27, Oct.		L3	
Marsh, Thomas W.	20, Jan. 1848	18, Jan.	47	* L3	
Marsh, William Crossman	17, Feb. 1853	2, Feb.	1-11m	L3	
Marshal, Charles	8, Aug. 1833	July	55	L1	
Marshall, Abner	21, Oct. 1847	Oct.	26	L3	
Marshall, Alfred King	3, Apr. 1856	26, Mar.	infant	L3	
Marshall, George S.	11, July 1833	July	3m-15d	L1	
Marshall, Herman	10, June 1847	June	34	L3	
Marshall, Leah P.	20, Apr. 1824	16, Apr.		L3	
Marshall, Libeus	22, Oct. 1819		estate	L3	
Marshall, Margaret	31, July 1845	July	18	L3	
Marshall, Martin	29, Sept 1853	19, Sept	77	* L3	
Marshall, Martin Key	4, Jan. 1855	31, Dec.	7m- 5d	L3	
Marshall, Matilda B.	9, Mar. 1843	1, Mar.	59	L3	

Name	Notice Date	Death Date	Age		Page	Maiden Name
Marshall, Thomas	29, Dec. 1842	Dec.	38		L3	
Marshall, Vincent C.	15, Feb. 1844		estate		L3	
Marshall, Vincent C. (Dr)	11, Jan. 1844	8, Jan.	50		L3	
Marshall, William P.	10, May 1849	6, May	30- 5m	*	L3	
Marston, Francis	27, Mar. 1851	25, Mar.	35	*	L3	
Marston, Mary Ann	22, Nov. 1855	14, Nov.	53	*	L3	Vail
Martin, (child of Arthur)	20, June 1833	June	stillborn		L1	
Martin, (child of Thomas)	11, Sept 1834	Aug.	stillborn		L1	
Martin, (Mr)	1, Nov. 1832	25, Oct.			L1	
Martin, Abigail Mary	5, Feb. 1816	30, Jan.			L3	
Martin, Andrew	1, Nov. 1849	Oct.	50		L3	
Martin, Annie	30, Oct. 1851	27, Oct.	22		L3	
Martin, Arthur	16, Mar. 1848	11, Mar.	57		L3	
Martin, Caroline	20, Apr. 1848	Apr.	1d		L3	
Martin, Clara V.	30, Mar. 1854	28, Mar.	20		L3	
Martin, E. (Mrs)	19, June 1851	13, June	56		L3	
Martin, E.H.	2, Oct. 1851	27, July			L4	
Martin, Elizabeth	26, Jan. 1837	22, Jan.	30		L3	
Martin, Francis	29, May 1834		probate		L3	
Martin, Francis D.	29, May 1834		probate		L3	
Martin, Franky P.	15, Jan. 1857	9, Jan.	5		L3	
Martin, G.W.	29, May 1834		probate		L3	
Martin, George	25, Oct. 1849	Oct.	54		L3	
Martin, George	30, Mar. 1843	17, Mar.		*	L3	
Martin, George W.	14, Feb. 1839		probate		L3	
Martin, Hannah Jane	25, Dec. 1845	19, Dec.	21		L3	
Martin, Henry	10, Apr. 1851	Apr.	32		L3	
Martin, Jacob O.	29, May 1834		probate		L3	
Martin, Jacob O.	9, Aug. 1838		probate		L3	
Martin, James	31, July 1851	July	35		L3	
Martin, Jefferson	9, July 1846	June	32		L3	
Martin, Jeremiah	15, Dec. 1808		estate		L3	
Martin, John	12, Aug. 1847	7, Aug.	23	*	L3	
Martin, John	21, June 1849	June	30		L3	
Martin, John	14, June 1838		probate		L4	
Martin, John M.	7, Oct. 1841	15, Sept		*	L3	
Martin, Joseph	17, June 1847	8, June	70		L3	
Martin, Joseph	22, Sept 1853	1, Sept			L3	
Martin, Julia Elma	18, Jan. 1838	17, Jan.			L3	
Martin, Letitia	31, Oct. 1828	24, Oct.			L3	
Martin, Maria	9, Feb. 1813	8, Feb.	6m-14d		L3	
Martin, Mary	21, Sept 1848	Sept	19m		L3	
Martin, Mary Ann	4, Oct. 1838	Sept	3		L3	
Martin, Merric	3, June 1816		estate		L1	
Martin, Nancy Blair	23, Sept 1852	15, Sept	93		L3	
Martin, Oliver	20, Apr. 1854	10, Apr.	56		L3	
Martin, Oliver	1, Oct. 1829		estate		L4	
Martin, Oliver, Sen.	14, May 1829	13, May			L1	
Martin, Phebe E.	11, Sept 1845	Sept	1		L3	
Martin, Samuel	15, June 1848	June	35		L3	
Martin, Samuel M.	27, Dec. 1825		estate		L3	
Martin, Samuel M.	16, Feb. 1827		probate		L3	
Martin, Samuel M.	25, Nov. 1825	24, Nov.			L3	
Martin, Samuel S.	18, Sept 1834	Sept	9m-21d		L1	

Name	Notice Date	Death Date	Age	Page	Maiden Name
Martin, Simon	9, Oct. 1834	Sept	31	L1	
Martin, Thomas (Major)	26, Jan. 1819	18, Jan.	68	L3	
Martin, Thomas Henry	21, Mar. 1839	14, Mar.		L3	
Martin, William	9, Jan. 1845	Dec.		L3	
Martin, Zerelda	1, Nov. 1855	24, Oct.	36	L3	
Martinson, Frederick	7, Oct. 1847	Sept	22	L3	
Martyn, Richard	1, June 1837	25, May	34	L3	
Masher, (chilf of Elijah)	2, May 1833	Apr.	2d	L1	
Mason, Anna S.	23, Mar. 1824	22, Mar.	21	L3	Fosdick
Mason, Benjamin	28, Oct. 1847	18, Oct.	76	L3	
Mason, Eunice	18, July 1850	12, July		L3	
Mason, George	22, Aug. 1833	Aug.	2- 5m	L4	
Mason, James	8, Aug. 1833	July		L1	
Mason, James	19, May 1842	May	30	L3	
Mason, James M.	3, Aug. 1837		estate	L3	
Mason, James M.	13, Feb. 1840		probate	L3	
Mason, James M.	10, Sept 1840		estate	L4	
Mason, James M. (Dr)	29, June 1837	28, June		L2	
Mason, Jane	22, Aug. 1833	Aug.	6	L4	
Mason, Joel	17, Dec. 1846	12, Dec.	38	L3	
Mason, Joseph	18, Apr. 1821	16, Apr.	58	L3	
Mason, Mary Ann	23, Feb. 1854	3, Feb.	49- - 4d	L3	
Mason, Sarah	20, Apr. 1843	19, Apr.	74	L3	
Mason, Stevens T.	19, Jan. 1843	4, Jan.		L3	
Mason, Trueman E. (Dr)	24, Sept 1846	20, Sept	38	L3	
Massey, Thomas	8, Nov. 1832	Nov.	64	L1	
Massie, Joseph	5, Jan. 1837		55	L3	
Masson, James	27, Oct. 1853	26, Oct.		L3	
Masters, Joseph	18, July 1850	July	35	L3	
Matchett, C.F.	26, Sept 1839	18, Sept	33	* L3	
Matchett, Catharine M.	11, Nov. 1841	10, Nov.	43	* L3	
Matchett, Charles F.	6, Nov. 1839		estate	L3	
Mather, Joseph	5, Mar. 1857		probate	L3	
Mathers, John	16, Oct. 1834	Oct.	35	L1	
Mathers, Mary Ann	17, Sept 1857	15, Sept	61	L3	
Mathews, (Mr)	1, Nov. 1832	25, Oct.		L1	
Mathews, Agnes	6, Dec. 1832	Dec.	69	L1	
Mathews, Clara Curtis	14, June 1849	3, June	1	L3	
Mathews, George	7, July 1817		estate	L3	
Mathews, Thomas J.	18, Nov. 1852	10, Nov.	65	L3	
Mathews, Vincent (Gen)	1, Oct. 1846	23, Sept	80	* L3	
Matix, Fites	2, May 1833	Apr.	29	L1	
Matson, Eliza R.	19, July 1849	14, July	34	L3	
Matson, Enoch	13, Aug. 1808		estate	L2	
Matson, James	29, May 1834		probate	L3	
Matson, James	12, Apr. 1832		estate	L4	
Matson, John	14, Jan. 1847	10, Jan.	78	L3	
Matson, Mary	9, Oct. 1851	4, Oct.	75	L3	
Matt, John	9, Aug. 1838	July	35	L3	
Mattharal, Jane	22, Aug. 1833	Aug.	67	L4	
Matthee, Charles A.	24, July 1851	22, July		L3	
Matthes, John F.	9, Apr. 1857		probate	L3	
Matthews, Albert	5, June 1851	3, June	19m- 8d	L3	
Matthews, Charles	1, Nov. 1832	27, Oct.		L3	

Name	Notice Date	Death Date	Age		Page	Maiden Name
Matthews, Dorrance	3, Apr. 1845	25, Mar.	31		L3	
Matthews, Edward L.	28, Oct. 1830		estate		L3	
Matthews, Edwin Stanley	6, Jan. 1853	28, Dec.			L3	
Matthews, Harriet J.	20, Nov. 1822	12, Nov.			L3	
Matthews, Ida I.	3, Apr. 1845	22, Mar.	24- 3m	*	L3	Irwin
Matthews, James	22, Feb. 1838	Feb.	36		L3	
Matthews, Jane	18, Aug. 1853	13, Aug.			L3	
Matthews, John	31, Oct. 1844		estate		L3	
Matthews, John	9, Sept 1825		probate		L3	
Matthews, Nehemiah	6, Sept 1827	Sept	26		L1	
Matthews, Samuel	25, Apr. 1850	Apr.	21		L3	
Matthews, Sarah	13, May 1847	8, May	49		L3	
Matthews, Sarah Ann	21, June 1849	12, June	28		L3	
Matthews, Thomas	23, Nov. 1837	Nov.	59		L3	
Matthews, Thomas	11, July 1833		probate		L3	
Matthews, William	15, July 1852	5, July			L3	
Matthewson, Ann	11, July 1850	July	99		L3	
Mattilon, Jacob	5, Feb. 1805	7, Jan.	95		L2	
Mattox, Joseph H.	4, Apr. 1833	Mar.	5		L1	
Matux, William	6, Nov. 1834	Oct.	24		L1	
Maugh, John	18, Oct. 1832	14, Oct.			L2	
Maulsbury, Samuel	14, June 1838		probate		L4	
Maver, James R.	27, Apr. 1843	25, Apr.	17m		L3	
Maw, Jacob	14, June 1838		probate		L4	
Maxey, William	8, May 1834		estate		L3	
Maxey, William	10, Sept 1835		estate		L3	
Maxwell, Elizabeth	15, Dec. 1842	14, Dec.	75		L5	
Maxwell, Sophia Barbauld	1, Nov. 1832	16, Oct.			L3	Henderson
Maxwell, William	21, Mar. 1844	7, Mar.	48		L3	
Maxwell, William (Col)	13, Sept 1809	10, Sept	42		L3	
May, Andrew	18, Apr. 1839		probate		L3	
May, David	30, Aug. 1849	Aug.	21		L3	
Mayer, Catharine	17, Mar. 1853	12, Mar.	69		L3	
Mayer, Frederick	28, Aug. 1834	Aug.	6m		L1	
Mayer, Frederick	7, Aug. 1834	July	2		L3	
Mayer, Henry	7, Aug. 1834	July	21		L3	
Mayer, Jacob	27, June 1839	June	22		L3	
Mayer, John D.	22, Aug. 1833	Aug.	2		L4	
Mayer, Thomas	7, Aug. 1834	July			L3	
Mayes, John	8, Aug. 1850		estate		L3	
Mayes, John	30, Oct. 1851		estate		L3	
Mayes, Margaret H.	13, Dec. 1855		estate		L3	
Mayhew, Benjamin	8, Aug. 1833	July	45		L1	
Mayhew, Eber	10, June 1841	6, June			L3	
Mayhew, Joseph	7, May 1857		probate		L3	
Mayhew, Nathaniel	4, July 1833		estate		L4	
Mayhew, Nathaniel	21, Sept 1837		probate		L4	
Mayhew, William	18, Mar. 1852	17, Mar.		*	L4	
Mayhood, John	25, Oct. 1832	Oct.			L1	
Mayhood, Rebecca	16, May 1833	May	51		L1	
Maylan, Martin	13, Mar. 1851	Mar.	23		L3	
Maynahan, Michael	29, Nov. 1855	20, Oct.			L3	
Mayo, Daniel Dudley	9, Sept 1841	26, Aug.	33		L3	
Mayo, Elizabeth	19, Oct. 1854	11, Oct.	36		L3	

Name	Notice Date	Death Date	Age	Page	Maiden Name
Mayo, Frances M.	13, Dec. 1838	27, Nov.		L4	St.Clair
Mayo, Joseph	23, Mar. 1848		estate	L3	
Mayo, Sarah	25, Oct. 1849	Oct.	19	L3	
Mayo, Seth	3, Jan. 1823		estate	L2	
Mayville, Francis	3, Sept 1846	Aug.	1	L3	
Maze, James	18, Sept 1845	Sept	4	L3	
Mazeen, Ezekiel	26, May 1826	2, May	27	L3	
McAffel, Cochram	1, Nov. 1832	29, Oct.		L3	
McAfferty, James	27, Mar. 1845	Mar.	25	L3	
McAfferty, Thomas	6, Aug. 1846	July	25	L3	
McAlpin, Edward	3, Oct. 1826	2, Oct.		L3	
McAlpin, James	13, Oct. 1853	30, Sept		L3	
McAlpin, James Andrew	23, July 1857	15, July	3- 7m	L3	
McAlpin, Pierson Spining	13, Aug. 1857	6, Aug.	11m	L3	
McArthurs, William D.	2, Aug. 1832	July	8m- 9d	L1	
McAuley, George	29, Aug. 1833	Aug.	35	L1	
McAvoy, Richard	9, May 1850	Apr.	35	L3	
McAwee, (Mr)	1, Aug. 1833	July		L1	
McBane, George	16, Feb. 1843	Feb.	80	L3	
McBride, (child of Lyman)	27, Dec. 1832	Dec.	2	L1	
McBride, (Mr)	1, Nov. 1832	25, Oct.		L1	
McBride, Charles	23, Aug. 1849	Aug.	21	L3	
McBride, James Faran	12, Mar. 1857	4, Mar.	14m- 2d	L3	
McBride, Mary Jane	2, Aug. 1832	July	1- 3m	L1	
McBride, Simpson	1, June 1837		77	L3	
McByrnes, Alexander	3, Jan. 1833	Dec.	40	L4	
McCabe, Catharine	21, Feb. 1850	Feb.	69	L3	
McCabe, John	20, Mar. 1856		estate	L3	
McCabe, Leander	31, Aug. 1848	Aug.	22	L3	
McCague, James	3, Aug. 1854	8, June	25	L3	
McCail, Judith	11, Oct. 1849	Oct.	60	L3	
McCaine, Alexander (Mrs)	22, May 1815	17, May		L3	
McCall, Alexander	3, Aug. 1854	30, July	86	L3	
McCall, Archibald	21, Sept 1843	12, Sept	51	L3	
McCall, Hugh	24, Jan. 1850	Jan.	38	L3	
McCall, Rachael	29, Jan. 1852	28, Jan.	83- 3m	L3	
McCall, Thomas	7, Feb. 1850	Jan.	1- 6m	L3	
McCalla, Elizabeth	21, Apr. 1806	2, Apr.		L3	
McCalley, William	11, Jan. 1844	Jan.	56	L3	
McCammon, Edmond	1, Nov. 1832	Oct.	1-11m	L2	
McCammon, James	14, Aug. 1856		probate	L6	
McCan, James (Dr)	18, Jan. 1844	5, Jan.	57	* L3	
McCan, John	9, Oct. 1834	Sept	2m	L1	
McCandless, James	2, Feb. 1843	30, Jan.	40	L3	
McCandless, James	23, Mar. 1843		estate	L3	
McCandless, Uriah	4, May 1843		50	L3	
McCann, (Miss)	12, Jan. 1854	5, Jan.	16	L3	
McCann, John	9, Aug. 1849	July	29	L3	
McCann, John	27, Apr. 1854	21, Apr.		L3	
McCann, Margaret	16, Nov. 1848	Nov.	18m	L3	
McCann, William H.	14, Sept 1837	Sept	10m	L4	
McCarden, Michael	8, Dec. 1842	Dec.	26	L3	
McCarthy, Florence	5, Mar. 1857		probate	L3	
McCarthy, John	24, Apr. l845	Apr.	29	L3	

Name	Notice Date	Death Date	Age		Page	Maiden Name
McCartney, Elizabeth	1, Aug. 1833	July			L1	
McCartney, Mary	1, Nov. 1832	Oct.	82		L2	
McCarty,	26, July 1855	21, July	child		L3	
McCarty, Barney	25, July 1850	July	29		L3	
McCarty, John	11, Apr. 1833	Apr.	38		L1	
McCarty, John	8, Nov. 1849	Oct.	25		L3	
McCarty, John	19, July 1849	July	40		L3	
McCarty, John	12, Oct. 1848	11, Oct.	2- 2m		L3	
McCarty, John	3, Feb. 1853	25, Jan.			L3	
McCarty, Mary	11, Oct. 1849	Oct.	4		L3	
McCarty, Mary	6, Feb. 1851	Jan.	47		L3	
McCarty, Peter	15, Jan. 1852				L3	
McCarty, Sarah H.	9, Feb. 1854	7, Dec.	25		L3	Taylor
McCarty, Thomas	19, Sept 1850	Sept	29		L3	
McCarty, Thomas	10, Mar. 1853	12, Mar.			L3	
McCasher, Andrew	11, Dec. 1845	Dec.	40		L3	
McCauhey, Samuel	25, Feb. 1847	20, Feb.			L3	
McCauley, Sarah	18, Jan. 1814	13, Jan.			L3	
McCelpin, James	18, Oct. 1832	Oct.	66		L4	
McChesney, John	26, Nov. 1808		estate		L3	
McChesney, Mary	8, Aug. 1850	4, Aug.	84		L3	
McCibben, Jane M.	18, July 1833	July	1- 9m		L2	
McClain, Hugh	3, Sept 1840		probate		L3	
McClardy, Neil	1, Oct. 1857	29, Sept			L3	
McClaskey, Henry	16, July 1808	6, July			L3	
McClave, David (Dr)	25, Sept 1851		33- 5m-15d	*	L3	
McClave, John	18, July 1844	30, June	72- 8m		L3	
McClave, Mary M.	25, Sept 1851	10, Aug.	11m-24d		L3	
McClave, Thomas	25, Sept 1851	1, Sept	16d		L3	
McClay, James	2, Feb. 1843	Jan.	29		L3	
McClean, John	17, Mar. 1826		probate		L3	
McClean, Margaret	8, May 1834		estate		L3	
McClelan, William	7, June 1855		probate		L3	
McCleland, Betsey	7, Aug. 1834	July	35		L3	
McClelland, Elizabeth	18, Sept 1834				L4	
McClelland, Samuel	21, Aug. 1851	17, Aug.		*	L3	
McClellon, Laura	25, July 1850	July	4m		L3	
McClenon, John	25, Oct. 1838	Oct.	28		L3	
McCloon, John	1, Apr. 1847	Mar.	40		L3	
McCloskey, Henry	10, Sept 1808		estate		L3	
McCloud, (sons of Lawson)	5, Mar. 1857	9, Feb.			L1	
McCluer, Samuel	29, Dec. 1818		estate		L4	
McClune, Mahala	17, Oct. 1844	Oct.	6		L3	
McClure, Elizabeth Hardy	10, Feb. 1853		23		L3	
McClure, Frank	17, Dec. 1857		estate		L3	
McClure, Frank S.	10, Dec. 1857	6, Dec.	30		L3	
McClure, James	15, Oct. 1846	Oct.			L3	
McClure, Margaret Catharine	23, Dec. 1847	19, Dec.	15		L3	
McClure, Margaret D.	2, Mar. 1854	20, Feb.	26		L3	
McClure, Michael	16, May 1850	May	21		L3	
McClusky, Patrick	2, May 1844	Apr.	48		L3	
McCollum, Thomas	15, Sept 1836		probate		L3	
McComas, J. Parker (Capt)	25, Aug. 1853	15, Aug.	24		L3	
McComas, Mary Ellen	22, Feb. 1844	21, Feb.	1-11m		L3	

Name	Notice Date	Death Date	Age	Page	Maiden Name
McComas, William Henry	13, Mar. 1851	2, Mar.		L3	
McCombs, Robert	3, May 1855		probate	L3	
McConkey, B.M.	10, Apr. 1856		probate	L3	
McConkey, Benjamin M.	20, Dec. 1855		estate	L3	
McConn, Joseph	7, Mar. 1844	Feb.	32	L3	
McConnell, John	30, Nov. 1848	Nov.	26	L3	
McConnell, John	13, July 1843	July	14m	L3	
McConnell, Lucinda Caroline	19, Aug. 1852	17, Aug.	infant	L3	
McConnell, Patrick	17, Nov. 1853	15, Nov.		L3	
McConnell, Paul Jones	22, Mar. 1855	15, Mar.	9m-26d	L3	
McConney, Triens	27, Sept 1849	Sept	39	L3	
McCoombes, Elias C.	2, Dec. 1805	29, Nov.	9	L3	
McCoombs, Robert	13, Sept 1855		estate	L3	
McCord, Asenath Brown	22, Apr. 1847	17, Apr.	30	L3	
McCord, Emily Elizabeth	28, Dec. 1848	19, Dec.	2- 6m	L3	
McCord, Hepsa Louisa	29, Aug. 1850	26, Aug.	12	L3	
McCord, Mary	31, May 1849	May	20	L3	
McCorkle, Thomas	8, Oct. 1840		estate	L3	
McCormae, John	26, Feb. 1852	Feb.	26	L4	
McCormic, John	21, Aug. 1815		estate	L2	
McCormick, Adelaide Augusta	8, Apr. 1847	2, Apr.		L3	
McCormick, Charles H.	18, Oct. 1849	11, Oct.	43	L3	
McCormick, Dennis	17, Aug. 1854	1, Aug.	40	* L3	
McCormick, Elizabeth	15, Aug. 1844	25, July	41- 8m	L3	Moore
McCormick, Evans	29, Sept 1836	28, Sept	31	L3	
McCormick, Francis	9, Feb. 1837		estate	L3	
McCormick, George	8, Feb. 1825		estate	L4	
McCormick, James	21, Mar. 1850	Mar.	22	L3	
McCormick, James	9, Apr. 1846	Mar.	30	L3	
McCormick, John	22, Oct. 1857	Oct.		L3	
McCormick, John (Mrs)	26, Aug. 1852			L3	
McCormick, Joseph	1, Aug. 1833	July	28	L1	
McCormick, Leah E.	30, Jan. 1845	Jan.	4	L3	
McCormick, Margaret	22, Nov. 1849	Nov.	7	L3	
McCormick, Margaret	27, Mar. 1845	6, Mar.	55	* L3	Ellison
McCormick, Mary	26, Aug. 1852	19, Aug.	62	L3	
McCormick, Samuel (Col)	1, May 1851	30, Apr.	74	* L3	
McCormick, Sarah Ann	25, July 1839		estate	L3	
McCormick, William	5, July 1849	28, June		L3	
McCorny, Hugh	14, Mar. 1850	Mar.	18	L3	
McCowan, John	18, Jan. 1849	Jan.	25	L3	
McCowan, Mary	31, Mar. 1842		estate	L4	
McCowen, Mary	26, Nov. 1840		estate	L3	
McCown, James	7, Sept 1843	Aug.	33	L3	
McCown, John	6, Feb. 1845	Jan.	27	L3	
McCoy, John	18, Oct. 1832	14, Oct.		L2	
McCoy, William	12, July 1849	July	44	L3	
McCracken, Charlotte	20, Mar. 1845	5, Mar.	45	L3	
McCracken, F.	15, Nov. 1832	Nov.	1- 8m	L1	
McCracken, Fannie Belle	3, Sept 1857	30, Aug.	13m-15d	L3	
McCracken, Henry	23, Jan. 1845	18, Jan.	10m	L3	
McCracken, Rebecca	4, Mar. 1847	Feb.	31	* L3	Turner
McCreary, Cornelia Lucinda	2, May 1850	25, Apr.	34	L3	
McCrew, William	1, Nov. 1832	Oct.		L2	

Name	Notice Date	Death Date	Age	Page	Maiden Name
McCristal, William H.	24, May 1855		estate	L3	
McCrum, Thomas	17, Dec. 1846	Dec.	32	L3	
McCudden, William	14, Oct. 1847	Oct.		L3	
McCue, (3 sisters)	16, July 1846			L3	
McCullom, Thomas G.	21, Sept 1848	17, Sept	63	L3	
McCullough, John	26, Dec. 1826		estate	L3	
McCullough, Julia	3, Aug. 1854	23, July	8	L3	
McCullough, Mary	12, Apr. 1849	8, Apr.	87	L3	
McCullough, Parthena	5, Sept 1839		probate	L3	
McCullough, Patrick	3, Feb. 1848	2, Feb.		L3	
McCullough, Robert	1, Jan. 1829		estate	L3	
McCullough, Sampson	26, Sept 1826		probate	L3	
McCullough, Sampson	19, Dec. 1826		probate	L3	
McCullough, Thomas	8, Apr. 1812		estate	L3	
McCullum,	13, Nov. 1834	Nov.	45	L1	
McCune, Cornelius	19, Apr. 1849	Apr.	18	L3	
McCune, William	15, Nov. 1809		estate	L3	
McDermit, Thomas	18, Oct. 1849	Oct.	17	L3	
McDermod, William	7, Oct. 1841	Sept	39	L3	
McDermont, John	18, June 1846	June	14m	L3	
McDermont, Mary	25, Oct. 1832	20, Oct.		L2	
McDermot, Isaac Henry	22, Sept 1842	16, Sept	11m- 1d	L3	
McDermot, Patrick M.	15, June 1848	June	30	L3	
McDevit, Mary Ann	8, Nov. 1849	Oct.	30	L3	
McDonald, (child of Eliza)	21, Feb. 1839	Feb.	1d	L3	
McDonald, (man)	25, May 1854			L3	
McDonald, Andrew J.	14, Feb. 1839	Feb.	22	L3	
McDonald, Anthony	24, Oct. 1850	Oct.	60	L3	
McDonald, Archibald	30, Apr. 1808	29, Apr.		L3	
McDonald, Barnard	22, June 1837		probate	L3	
McDonald, Barney	11, July 1850	July	20	L3	
McDonald, Barney	5, Dec. 1850	Nov.	50	L3	
McDonald, Bridget	3, May 1849	Apr.	35	L3	
McDonald, Bridget	8, July 1852	30, June		L3	
McDonald, Catharine	23, May 1850	22, Mar.		L3	
McDonald, Collin	21, Mar. 1844	8, Feb.		L3	
McDonald, D.K. (Rev)	27, Dec. 1849	19, Dec.	39	L3	
McDonald, Henderson (Capt)	18, Mar. 1852	3, Mar.		* L3	
McDonald, James	18, July 1850	July	30	L3	
McDonald, Joanna	18, July 1850	July	1- 6m	L3	
McDonald, John	3, May 1849	Apr.	40	L3	
McDonald, John	22, Aug. 1850	Aug.	1- 6m	L3	
McDonald, John	18, May 1854	12, May		L3	
McDonald, Joseph	20, June 1850	June	5	L3	
McDonald, Joseph	3, Apr. 1845	Mar.	45	L3	
McDonald, Margery	19, July 1849	13, July	49	* L3	
McDonald, Mary	16, May 1850	May	6	L3	
McDonald, Walter	1, Aug. 1833	July		L1	
McDonald, Walter	16, Aug. 1838	Aug.	45	L3	
McDonald, William	4, Dec. 1851	31, Oct.	50	* L3	
McDonald, William Alexander	10, June 1847	1, June	21	L3	
McDonley, Sarah A.	6, June 1833	May	22	L2	
McDonough, (child of Pat)	19, July 1849	July	2w	L3	
McDonough, Bridget	17, Aug. 1848	Aug.	40	L3	

Name	Notice Date	Death Date	Age	Page	Maiden Name
McDonough, Patrick	29, July 1841	July	35	L3	
McDonough, Rose Lee	18, Oct. 1849	Oct.	39	L3	
McDougal, Aucberzew	9, Oct. 1834	Sept	18- 9m	L1	
McDowel, Henrietta	8, Nov. 1832	Nov.	45	L1	
McDowell, Amanda V.	19, July 1855	3, July		L3	
McDowell, Joshua	30, Aug. 1832	Aug.	55	L1	
McDuffie, T.	22, Oct. 1857	18, Oct.		L3	
McDusky, (Mr)	18, Oct. 1832	16, Oct.		L3	
McElheny, Daniel	20, Sept 1838	Sept	38	L3	
McElroy, Rose	11, July 1850	July	37	L3	
McElroy, Thomas	22, Sept 1853	Aug.		L3	
McElroy, William	28, June 1849	June	14m	L3	
McFall, Margaret	8, Feb. 1849	2, Feb.	49	L3	
McFarlan, Anne Frances	9, Feb. 1854	31, Jan.		L3	
McFarland,	21, Sept 1848	Sept	35	L3	
McFarland, Catharine	3, Oct. 1850	29, Sept	74	L3	
McFarland, James	20, June 1839		estate	L1	
McFarland, James	30, Apr. 1846		estate	L3	
McFarland, James	3, Sept 1840		probate	L3	
McFarland, James	26, Mar. 1846	24, Mar.		L3	
McFarland, R.T.	12, Oct. 1854	27, Sept		L3	
McFarland, Robert	13, Aug. 1846	Aug.	32	L3	
McFarland, Stephen (Col)	15, Nov. 1832	7, Nov.	61	* L1	
McFarland, Susan	8, Aug. 1839	28, July		L3	
McFarland, Thomas	9, June 1817		estate	L3	
McFarland, Thomas	15, Apr. 1818		estate	L3	
McFarland,(daughter of Judge)	29, Sept 1807	21, Sept	3	L3	
McFeeley, Richard	3, Sept 1840		probate	L3	
McGahern, Rose	15, July 1847	July	2	L3	
McGahill, Richard	22, Apr. 1847	16, Apr.	32	L3	
McGarvey, William	1, Nov. 1832		estate	L3	
McGary, Catharine	31, Oct. 1839		estate	L3	
McGary, Martin	10, Feb. 1848	Feb.	23	L3	
McGaughey, Samuel	15, Apr. 1847		estate	L3	
mcGeagh, Eliza Jane	7, July 1853	1, July	64	L3	
McGechin, William	12, July 1849	8, July	19m- 9d	L3	
McGedrick, James	24, Aug. 1843	Aug.	1	L3	
McGee, Bridget	23, Dec. 1847	Dec.	18	L3	
McGee, John	2, Sept 1852	Aug.	36	L3	
McGhee, Eliza	6, Mar. 1845	Feb.	30	L3	
McGhee, William	26, July 1832	July	1- 3m	L1	
McGill, John	23, Dec. 1847	Dec.	40	L3	
McGill, Milo	5, Apr. 1855	2, Apr.	28	L3	
McGill, Neille	10, Jan. 1856		probate	L3	
McGill, Patrick	17, Aug. 1854	16, Aug.	45	L3	
McGill, Robert	28, Mar. 1839		estate	L3	
McGill, William	23, Oct. 1834	Oct.	14	L2	
McGill, William Y.	30, Mar. 1848	Mar.	44	L3	
McGilliard, John	5, Sept 1839		probate	L3	
McGinley, Patrick	9, Aug. 1849	3, Aug.	73	L3	
McGinn, John	13, Jan. 1853	7, Jan.		L3	
McGinn, Michael	28, Dec. 1848	Dec.	25	L3	
McGinnis, Elizabeth	22, Aug. 1833	Aug.	35	L4	
McGinty, John	14, Sept 1848	Sept	30	L3	

Name	Notice Date	Death Date	Age		Page	Maiden Name
McGlade, Thomas	5, Aug. 1847	July	3m		L3	
McGlaughlin, William	25, Oct. 1832	20, Oct.			L2	
McGlothlin, William	19, Mar. 1846		estate		L3	
McGonagle, George	15, July 1847	July	3		L3	
McGoughy, John	29, July 1847	July	24		L3	
McGow, Thomas	8, June 1848	May	26		L3	
McGowan, Wilson (Col)	20, June 1844	26, May			L3	
McGowen, James	9, May 1850	Apr.	35		L3	
McGowen, Michael	14, Feb. 1839	Feb.	47		L3	
McGran, Michael	15, Aug. 1833	Aug.	30		L1	
McGraw, Michael	24, Oct. 1833		estate		L3	
McGregor, (child of Nancy J.)	20, Jan. 1848	Jan.	2m		L3	
McGregor, (dau. of Farquhan)	4, Sept 1856	31, Aug.	1- 1m-24d		L5	
McGregor, Helen	18, Nov. 1847	14, Nov.	35		L3	
McGrew, Alexander	16, Nov. 1843		estate		L3	
McGrew, Alvira L.	20, Apr. 1824	9, Apr.			L3	
McGrew, James	17, Dec. 1846	Dec.	35		L3	
McGrew, John B.	12, Mar. 1857	11, Mar.			L3	
McGrew, Margaret Amelia	11, 18, Sept 1834	4, Sept	41		L1	
McGrew, Margaret R.	19, June 1845	15, June	32	*	L3	Gallagher
McGrew, Ross	22, Oct. 1846	17, Oct.	16m- 7d		L3	
McGrew, Sarah	15, Dec. 1836	10, Dec.	29		L3	
McGrew, Thomas B.	19, Mar. 1857	10, Mar.	65		L3	
McGrew, William	31, Oct. 1833	Oct.	2- 3m-13d		L4	
McGuff, Bridget	17, May 1849	May	18		L3	
McGuff, Bridget	10, May 1849	May	60		L3	
McGuffey, Alexander	15, Mar. 1855	1, Mar.	88		L3	
McGuffey, Charles S.	25, Sept 1851	15, Sept	15		L3	
McGuffey, Harriet S.	11, July 1850	3, July			L3	
McGuire, Isaac	31, Dec. 1835	27, Dec.			L3	
McGuire, James	3, May 1849	Apr.	32		L3	
McGury, Martin	8, Mar. 1849	Feb.	'25		L3	
McHamon, (Mr)	8, Aug. 1833	July			L1	
McHaran, Michael	29, June 1848	June	46		L3	
McHendry, Mary	28, Oct. 1816	17, Oct.			L2	
McHenry, Amos N.	7, June 1855		probate		L3	
McHenry, Sarah	28, June 1849	26, June			L3	
McHugh, Bridget	7, June 1855		probate		L3	
McHugh, Catharine	9, Mar. 1848	Mar.	40		L3	
McHugh, Michael	20, Nov. 1851	15, Nov.			L3	
McHugh, Sarah	12, July 1849	July	20		L3	
McHugh, William	7, June 1855		probate		L3	
McIcin, William	13, Apr. 1848	Apr.	21		L3	
McIlroy, Enos	2, Oct. 1828		estate		L4	
McIlvaine, Emerson	20, Oct. 1853	9, Oct.	51		L3	
McIntire, David	19, July 1849	July			L3	
McIntire, Duncan	7, May 1840		probate		L3	
McIntire, James	2, Aug. 1832	July	32		L1	
McIntire, James	10, Nov. 1842	Nov.	28		L4	
McIntire, Joseph	17, Oct. 1850	Oct.	38		L3	
McIntire, Joseph	18, Oct. 1832	Oct.			L4	
McIntire, William T.	20, Dec. 1825		probate		L4	
McIntosh, Lachlan (Gen)	14, Apr. 1806	20, Feb.	80		L3	
McIntyre, Catharine	18, Nov. 1841	Nov.	41		L3	

Name	Notice Date	Death Date	Age		Page	Maiden Name
McIntyre, Duncan	14, June 1838	7, June	38	*	L3	
McIntyre, Joseph	11, Oct. 1832	7, Oct.			L2	
McKean, Neil	14, Oct. 1841	Oct.	28		L3	
McKean, Thomas	14, July 1817	24, June			L3	
McKee, (Mr)	28, Oct. 1816	10, Oct.	82		L2	
McKee, Andrew	1, Nov. 1832	25, Oct.			L1	
McKee, Francis	13, Feb. 1851	9, Feb.			L3	
McKee, James	24, May 1814		estate		L4	
McKee, James	14, Aug. 1856		probate		L6	
McKee, Jane	2, Feb. 1854	23, Jan.	53		L3	
McKee, Mary C.	25, May 1837	14, May			L2	
McKee, Rebecca	3, Sept 1840		probate		L3	
McKee, Samuel	26, Feb. 1852		estate		L3	
McKeever, John	15, July 1847	July	25		L3	
McKennell, James (Capt)	2, Feb. 1843	28, Jan.	80	*	L3	
McKenzie, John	15, July 1852	July	22		L3	
McKenzie, John	22, Oct. 1824	3, Oct.	80	*	L3	
McKenzie, Marian Bowers	24, Feb. 1842	23, Feb.	4- 7m-23d		L3	
McKenzie, Mary R.	13, June 1850	7, June	40	*	L3	Boyle
McKim, Elizabeth	27, Aug. 1824	20, Aug.	65	*	L2	
McKim, Nathaniel	17, Mar. 1836	8, Mar.	38	*	L4	
McKinley, James	28, May 1840	May	42		L3	
McKinley, Jane	16, May 1833	May	46		L1	
McKinley, John	28, Dec. 1848	Dec.	55		L3	
McKinnell, Caroline Bailey	11, Oct. 1849	30, Sept	11m		L3	
McKinnell, Charles	13, May 1852	3, May	33		L3	
McKinnell, Mary	13, May 1852	9, May	77		L3	
McKinnell, William	26, July 1855		estate		L3	
McKinnell, William	16, Aug. 1855		estate		L3	
McKinnell, William	17, Jan. 1850	3, Jan.			L3	
McKinney, Archibald (Dr)	5, Dec. 1833	Nov.	53		L3	
McKinnon, Simeon	5, Jan. 1818	2, Jan.	22	*	L3	
McKinsey, A.	14, Mar. 1833	Mar.	14d		L1	
McKnight, Ann Holland	22, Apr. 1852	10, Apr.	infant		L3	
McKnight, David	19, 23, May 1821	13, May	61		L3	
McKnight, William	22, Feb. 1849	Feb.	23		L3	
McKog, Eliza	15, Aug. 1833	Aug.	2- 9m		L1	
McKoy, Alex.	18, Oct. 1832	13, Oct.			L2	
McKoy, Matilda	7, Aug. 1834	July	1-10m		L3	
McKoy, Samuel	16, Oct. 1834	Oct.	13		L1	
McLain, Allen	19, Jan. 1854	16, Oct.	73		L3	
McLain, Martha	9, Aug. 1838	July	29		L3	
McLane, John	16, July 1824	10, July			L2	
McLasty, John	19, July 1849	July	13m		L3	
McLaughlin, Addison	5, Dec. 1833	Nov.	11		L3	
McLaughlin, Catharine	1, Nov. 1832	28, Oct.			L2	
McLaughlin, Catharine	25, July 1850	July	20		L3	
McLaughlin, Charles	4, Jan. 1844	26, Dec.			L3	
McLaughlin, Dolly	31, May 1849	May	2		L3	
McLaughlin, Ellen	31, May 1849	May	8		L3	
McLaughlin, John	24, May 1809		estate		L2	
McLaughlin, Margaret	22, Jan. 1852	Jan.	40		L3	
McLaughlin, Mary	18, Dec. 1845	9, Dec.	97		L3	
McLaughlin, Michael	8, Dec. 1842	Dec.	43		L3	

Name	Notice Date	Death Date	Age	Page	Maiden Name
McLaughlin, Neil	18, Oct. 1838	Oct.	33	L3	
McLaughlin, Rachel	6, Feb. 1845	Jan.	45	L3	
McLaughlin, Thomas	14, Dec. 1848	Dec.	12	L2	
McLean, Ann	10, July 1851			L3	
McLean, Anna	30, Dec. 1852	24, Dec.	5- 6m-11d	L3	
McLean, Caroline T.	17, 24, Apr. 1856	15, Apr.		L3	Burnet
McLean, James	15, Aug. 1833	Aug.	47	L1	
McLean, James Alexander	28, Dec. 1843	27, Dec.	19	L3	
McLean, Ludlow	15, Oct. 1846	13, Oct.	9m- 3d	L3	
McLean, Margaret	15, Sept 1836		probate	L3	
McLean, Nathaniel Collins	24, Sept 1846	18, Sept	11m	L3	
McLean, Nicholas	9, Aug. 1855		probate	L3	
McLean, Nicholson	27, July 1854	20, July	45	L3	
McLean, Nicholson	17, Aug. 1854		estate	L3	
McLean, Rebecca Burnet	14, Aug. 1851	11, Aug.		L3	
McLean, Robert	3, Aug. 1854		estate	L3	
McLean, Robert	10, Apr. 1856		probate	L3	
McLean, William	28, Feb. 1839	14, Feb.	7m	L3	
McLear, Mary	23, Oct. 1845	Oct.	30	L3	
McLeigh, Joseph	29, Aug. 1844	Aug.	27	L3	
McLenan, Bernard	6, Mar. 1856		probate	L3	
McLenan, Bernard	15, July 1847	13, July		L3	
McLeon, Robert	4, June 1857		estate	L3	
McLilley, J.	26, Dec. 1833	Dec.	80	L4	
McLone, Mary	27, Sept 1849	Sept	38	L3	
McLure, Felix G.	18, Nov. 1847	18, Nov.	24	L3	
McMackin, James	14, Aug. 1856		probate	L6	
McMahan, James	5, Oct. 1843	Sept	25	L3	
McMahon, Edward	7, Aug. 1834	July		L3	
McMahon, Elizabeth	7, Aug. 1834	July		L3	
McMahon, Frederick S.	7, May 1846	Apr.	27	L3	
McMahon, Hugh	1, Nov. 1832	27, Oct.		L2	
McMakin, James	18, Aug. 1853	10, Aug.	77	L3	
McMan, Anthony	24, July 1851	17, July	17	L3	
McMannis, (Mrs)	8, Aug. 1833	July		L1	
McMannis, Dennis	22, June 1848	June	2	L3	
McMannis, John	8, Aug. 1833	July	4	L1	
McMannus, James	23, May 1850	May	25	L3	
McManus, Margaret	23, May 1850	May	51	L3	
McMaster, Gilbert	5, July 1855		probate	L3	
McMasters, (Mr)	25, Oct. 1832	21, Oct.	4	L2	
McMasters, Elizabeth	25, July 1833	July	4	L1	
McMasters, William	18, July 1833	July	45	L2	
McMechan, Sarah	24, July 1851	13, July	35	L3	
McMicken, Charles	12, June 1851	8, June	8m-26d	L3	
McMickle, John	3, Sept 1840	Aug.	25	L3	
McMickle, William	4, Oct. 1833	Sept	30	L1	
McMillan, James Renwick	26, Apr. 1849			L3	
McMillen, John	16, May 1844		estate	L3	
McMillen, William Arthur	18, Nov. 1847	16, Nov.	19m	L3	
McMillen, Willie	13, Aug. 1857	11, Aug.	5m	L3	
McMinchey, William	29, Dec. 1836		estate	L3	
McMinn, Francis	27, Oct. 1831		probate	L1	
McMullen, (child of John)	18, Nov. 1852	15, Nov.		L3	

Name	Notice Date	Death Date	Age	Page	Maiden Name
McMullen, Samuel (Mrs)	12, Sept 1810	5, Sept	38	L3	
McMullin, Patrick	1, Feb. 1849	Jan.	25	L3	
McMurchey, William	8, Nov. 1838		probate	L3	
McMurchy, (Mr)	1, Aug. 1833	July		L1	
McMurchy, William	1, Aug. 1833		estate	L3	
McMurchy, William	22, Mar. 1838		probate	L3	
McMurphy, Mary Catharine	27, May 1847	20, May	6- 8m	L3	
McMurphy, Samuel S.	21, Jan. 1847	13, Jan.	28	L3	
McMurphy, Theodore W.	12, Oct. 1848	5, Oct.	34	L3	
McMurray, Joseph	13, May 1823		estate	L3	
McMurry, Eli	4, July 1850	June	34	L3	
McNair, James	18, Aug. 1853	11, Aug.	64	* L3	
McNairy, John	16, Nov. 1837	10, Oct.	75	L3	
McNalley, Charles	9, Mar. 1854	3, Mar.		L3	
McNally, Catharine	10, May 1849	May	25	L3	
McNally, Francis	29, Aug. 1844	Aug.	29	L3	
McNally, John	10, Feb. 1848	Feb.	40	L3	
McNally, Thomas	27, Apr. 1854			L3	
McNamarrow, Hetty	14, Feb. 1839	Feb.	66	L3	
McNaughton, Isaac	5, Sept 1839	1, Sept	33	* L3	
McNeal, James	9, Oct. 1834	Sept	38	L1	
McNealy,	11, Mar. 1852	Mar.	30	L4	
McNealy, (man)	11, Mar. 1852	2, Mar.	30	L4	
McNealy, William	9, Jan. 1851	Dec.	22	L3	
McNeely, Lorenzo	24, Dec. 1840	18, Dec.	3	L3	
McNeely, Mary	1, Nov. 1832	24, Oct.		L4	
McNeil, John (Gen)	7, Mar. 1850	2, Mar.	66	* L3	
McNeil, Mary L.	18, July 1850	14, July		L3	
McNichol, Peter	9, July 1857		probate	L3	
McNickle, John K.	4, July 1850	30, June		L3	
McNickle, Letitia	18, July 1850	11, July		L3	
McNicol, Catharine	21, Dec. 1848	15, Dec.	61	L3	
McNicoll, Elizabeth C.	6, Apr. 1854	1, Apr.	23	L3	
McNicoll, Peter	12, Feb. 1852	6, Feb.	81	L3	
McNutt, Margaret	20, July 1822	18, July	19	L3	
McNutt, Mary	26, Dec. 1833	Dec.	56	L4	
McPeck, Daniel	9, Aug. 1814		estate	L3	
McPherson, Ann	1, Aug. 1833	July	77	L1	
McQuaid, John	27, Nov. 1845	Nov.	34	L3	
McQuaid, Michael	13, Aug. 1846	Aug.	45	L3	
McQuarters, (man)	26, Aug. 1847			L1	
McQueed, George	30, May 1850	May	24	L3	
McQuellan, James	25, Oct. 1849	Oct.	41	L3	
McQuigg, Charles	19, July 1832	July	23	L1	
McQuillen, James	26, Dec. 1844	Dec.	42	L3	
McQuillon, Jane	22, Nov. 1849	Nov.		L3	
McQuilty, Nancy	9, Feb. 1854	3, Jan.	47	L3	
McQuinly, Elizabeth	15, Feb. 1838	Feb.	7	L3	
McQuithy, Ansel	9, Sept 1847	Aug.	44	L3	
McRae, James	27, July 1837	July	33	L3	
McRoberts, David	8, May 1834		estate	L4	
McRoberts, Samuel	30, Mar. 1843	28, Mar.	40	L3	
McRoberts, William James	20, Sept 1855	18, Sept	2- 5m	L3	
McRubill, Jeremiah	9, Jan. 1851	Dec.	27	L3	

Name	Notice Date	Death Date	Age		Page	Maiden Name
McShane, Philip	31, Aug. 1848	Aug.	34		L3	
McShay, Hugh	5, Aug. 1852	July	1		L3	
McSorley, John	26, Mar. 1846	20, Mar.	20		L3	
McStrevack, John	20, Apr. 1843	Apr.	25		L3	
McTaggert, John H.	8, Feb. 1855	2, Feb.	1- 2m- 1d		L3	
McTavish, Donald	22, Jan. 1816	22, May			L1	
McVay, James	1, Jan. 1846	Dec.	34		L3	
McVeigh, Margaret	21, Feb. 1850	Feb.	66		L3	
McWilliam, Patrick	19, Apr. 1849	17, Apr.			L2	
McWilliams, Elizabeth	8, Mar. 1855	2, Mar.	39		L3	Hammond
McWilliams, Patrick	26, Apr. 1849	Apr.	22		L3	
Mead, (Mrs)	25, Oct. 1832	16, Oct.			L4	
Mead, B.C. (Mrs)	28, Mar. 1839	22, Mar.	64	*	L3	
Mead, Henry	19, Apr. 1849	Apr.	45		L3	
Meade, Anastasia	23, Aug. 1849	9, Aug.		*	L3	Stewart
Meader, Margum	13, Sept 1832	Sept	27		L1	
Meads, John D.	7, May 1857	3, May	31		L3	
Meakings, Mary Elizabeth	15, July 1852	4, July	10		L3	
Meal, Charles Wesley	3, Jan. 1856	27, Dec.	3- 5w		L3	
Meara, Thomas	27, Sept 1838		estate		L3	
Mearl, Magdebanon	6, Dec. 1832	Dec.	2m-15d		L1	
Mears, Andrew	27, Sept 1849	Sept	37		L3	
Mears, John	10, Dec. 1857		probate		L3	
Mears, John	14, Aug. 1856		estate		L5	
Mears, John	16, Oct. 1856		probate		L6	
Mears, Thomas C.	28, Aug. 1845	Aug.	26		L3	
Meason, Isaac	20, Mar. 1845	26, Feb.	72		L3	
Meason, Isaac	24, Feb. 1842	21, Feb.			L3	
Meason, Mary	28, Dec. 1843	15, Dec.	4		L3	
Medaris, Martha	23, Apr. 1857	16, Apr.	30- 3m		L3	
Medary, Jacob (Gen)	1, Apr. 1847				L3	
Medary, Joseph	8, Jan. 1857		probate		L3	
Medary, Mary	7, Dec. 1854	4, Dec.	57		L3	
Medary, Mary	10, Sept 1857		probate		L3	
Medary, William	12, Apr. 1849	6, Apr.	54		L3	
Medary, William	6, Dec. 1855		probate		L3	
Meddock, Abijah	18, May 1837		estate		L3	
Meddock, Abijah	9, Aug. 1838		estate		L3	
Meddock, Abijah	3, Dec. 1840		probate		L3	
Meddock, Patsey	3, Apr. 1811	28, Mar.			L3	
Medearis, Prior	23, May 1850		estate		L3	
Medearis, Prior	26, Jan. 1854		estate		L3	
Medery, Nathaniel	19, Feb. 1846	11, Feb.	42		L3	
Medistredor, Bernard	29, Aug. 1833	Aug.	16		L1	
Meeds, Samuel	25, Sept 1856	16, Sept	68		L5	
Meek, E.M.	9, Oct. 1834	Sept	8m		L1	
Meek, Hugh	19, Apr. 1814		estate		L2	
Meek, Mary Ann	11, Sept 1834	Aug.	21		L1	
Meeker, Amanda R.	13, Jan. 1842	6, Jan.			L3	
Meeker, Caroline	27, May 1841	26, May	11	*	L3	
Meeker, Elizabeth	5, Oct. 1837		estate		L3	
Meeker, Elizabeth	21, Nov. 1839		probate		L3	
Meeker, Harvey	13, June 1833	June	29		L1	
Meeker, Hervey	6, June 1833				L4	

Name	Notice Date	Death Date	Age		Page	Maiden Name
Meeker, John	22, June 1837		probate		L3	
Meeker, John C.	1, June 1848		estate		L3	
Meeker, John, Jr.	9, June 1836		probate		L3	
Meeker, Margaret	13, Sept 1855	11, Sept	64	*	L3	
Meeker, Randolph	9, Feb. 1809	25, Jan.	25		L3	
Meeker, Vannelia James	21, Nov. 1844	19, Nov.	12		L3	
Meekings, B.H.	14, Aug. 1856		probate		L6	
Meeks, Dorothea	11, Nov. 1841	4, Nov.	62	*	L3	Spencer
Meevan, Patrick	8, Aug. 1850	July	50		L3	
Megill, Robert	15, Aug. 1833	Aug.	40		L1	
Megle, Joseph	7, May 1857		probate		L3	
Meguier, Mary Frances	19, Apr. 1845	11, Apr.	11m-24d		L3	
Mehen, Wilson	12, Feb. 1852	10, Feb.			L3	
Mehl, Anne	20, Sept 1832	Sept	8		L1	
Meier, F.M. (Mrs)	8, Nov. 1838	4, Nov.	27		L3	
Melanephy, Constantine	25, Oct. 1832	19, Oct.			L1	
Melchars, John	11, Apr. 1850	Apr.			L3	
Melchor, William	29, Jan. 1846	Jan.	31		L3	
Melendy, James	9, Nov. 1848	6, Nov.	57		L3	
Melendy, James	4, June 1857		probate		L3	
Melford, William (Dr)	19, July 1849	16, July	48- 9m		L3	
Melish, Anna Belle	27, Jan. 1853	21, Dec.			L3	
Mellen, Edward Clark	9, Dec. 1847	1, Dec.			L3	
Mellen, Isabel	7, 14, June 1849	19, May	6m		L3	
Mellen, Isabel	28, Dec. 1854	24, Dec.			L3	
Mellen, John	26, July 1849	July	5		L3	
Mellen, William	13, May 1852	7, May	69		L3	
Mellon, Joshur	21, Mar. 1850	Mar.	35		L3	
Melose, Amelia M.	31, Oct. 1833	Oct.	5m		L4	
Meloy, Asa	9, Mar. 1854	23, Feb.	54		L3	
Meloy, Asa W.	2, Mar. 1854	21, Feb.	50		L3	
Melville, Eugene	14, Apr. 1853	Apr.	28		L3	
Mencer, Charles	12, Sept 1850	Sept	44		L3	
Mencer, George	18, May 1848	May	4m		L3	
Menden, Dorothy	22, Mar. 1838		probate		L3	
Mendenall, George	11, July 1850	6, July	17m		L3	
Mendenhall, Elizabeth	24, Feb. 1853	21, Feb.	4m		L3	
Mendenhall, Laura Jane	8, May 1845	4, May	2		L3	
Menken, Alexander	9, Oct. 1834	7, Oct.	75	*	L3	
Menken, Eliza	29, Nov. 1832	Nov.	32		L1	
Menken, Solomon	11, Dec. 1856		estate		L3	
Menken, Solomon	5, Feb. 1857		probate		L3	
Menkin, Solomon	22, Dec. 1853	19, Dec.	66		L3	
Mennessier, Francis	12, Apr. 1814		estate		L3	
Mennessier, Francis	13, Dec. 1814		estate		L3	
Mennie, James	15, July 1852	8, July		*	L3	
Menninger, John H.	16, Oct. 1856		probate		L6	
Mentle, Mary A.	22, Aug. 1850	Aug.	1		L3	
Menzler, (child of Jacob)	25, Dec. 1856	22, Dec.	3		L3	
Mercer, John	4, June 1808		estate		L3	
Mercer, John	23, Jan. 1827		estate		L3	
Mercer, John	17, Mar. 1826		probate		L3	
Mercer, Jon.	28, May 1824		estate		L3	
Mercer, William	2, Feb. 1843	Jan.	39		L3	

Name	Notice Date	Death Date	Age		Page	Maiden Name
Meriweather, James H.	6, Mar. 1856		probate		L3	
Meriweather, Nicholas	14, Aug. 1851		estate		L3	
Meroney, John (Mrs)	1, Mar. 1855	17, Feb.	76		L3	
Merrefield, Joseph	30, Sept 1825	22, Sept	55	*	L3	
Merrel, Daniel	4, Sept 1815		estate		L3	
Merrell, Benjamin A.	13, Sept 1838		estate		L3	
Merrell, Horace	22, Nov. 1838	31, Oct.			L3	
Merrell, John	22, Feb. 1814		estate		L1	
Merrell, Levisa	22, Nov. 1838	14, Nov.	20		L3	Stockbridge
Merrell, Mary Frances	8, Aug. 1850	2, Aug.	10m-23d		L3	
Merrell, Sophia E.H.	8, Aug. 1850	31, July	32		L3	
Merrell, Warren Kellogg	21, Oct. 1852	14, Oct.	2m-26d		L3	
Merrick, J.F.	15, Dec. 1836	24, Nov.	22		L3	
Merrie, Ellen A.	25, Apr. 1850	23, Apr.			L3	
Merrie, James B.	13, May 1830	12, May	21		L4	
Merrie, Robert	23, Nov. 1837		estate		L3	
Merrifield, Alden Spooner	26, June 1845	22, June	33	*	L3	
Merrill, Alexander	20, June 1833	June	1- 9m		L1	
Merrill, Benjamin A.	22, July 1841		estate		L3	
Merrill, Dan	31, Mar. 1817		estate		L3	
Merrill, Dan.	18, Oct. 1832	11, Oct.			L1	
Merrill, Ellen	20, Nov. 1834	Nov.	1- 2m		L1	
Merrill, Joseph S.	13, Mar. 1851		estate		L3	
Merrill, Moody	29, May 1828	May	55		L2	
Merringer, George	6, Dec. 1855		probate		L3	
Merrit, (child of Isaac)	25, June 1808	4, June	2- 6m		L3	
Merrit, Jesse	6, Aug. 1808		estate		L3	
Merritt, E. (heirs of)	22, Mar. 1838		probate		L3	
Merritt, Elizabeth	15, Sept 1836		probate		L3	
Merritt, Elizabeth	22, Mar. 1838		probate		L3	
Merritt, Elizabeth	2, Oct. 1834	Sept	36		L4	
Merritt, Elizabeth	4, Dec. 1834		estate		L4	
Merritt, Louisa Jane	18, Oct. 1832	Oct.	5m		L4	
Merriweather, (son of Nicholas)	26, Jan. 1843	22, Jan.	infant		L3	
Merriweather, James Hood	24, Dec. 1846	21, Dec.	36		L3	
Merriweather, Rowan	13, Apr. 1848	9, Apr.			L3	
Merriwether, John	26, Jan. 1854	12, Jan.	79		L3	
Merry, Ann	7, Aug. 1834	July	26		L3	
Merry, John	21, Sept 1837		probate		L4	
Merryman, John	11, Jan. 1844	4, Jan.	50		L3	
Mess, Christopher	14, June 1849	June	38		L3	
Messinger, Jason	19, Mar. 1857		estate		L3	
Mestoffsky, Simon	14, Aug. 1856		probate		L6	
Metcalf, Agnes	24, Dec. 1840	22, Dec.	infant		L3	
Metcalf, Amos	12, Mar. 1857	7, Mar.	54		L3	
Metcalf, Joseph	5, Sept 1839		probate		L3	
Metcalfe, Ann	4, Mar. 1841	3, Mar.			L3	
Metcalfe, Ellen May	3, May 1855	1, May	7m-19d		L3	
Metcalfe, William	3, Dec. 1857	30, Nov.	69		L3	
Meter, Aaron	4, Nov. 1847	Oct.	41		L3	
Meter, Christian	13, Sept 1849	Sept	37		L3	
Methver, John (Mrs)	15, Mar. 1855	14, Mar.			L3	
Metzel, Frank	2, June 1853	1, June			L3	
Mevery, David	15, Nov. 1832	Nov.	37		L1	

Name	Notice Date	Death Date	Age		Page	Maiden Name
Meyer, Francis	23, Nov. 1848	Nov.	27		L3	
Meyer, Frederick	14, Oct. 1841	Oct.	21		L3	
Meyer, Jacob	15, Nov. 1832	Nov.	32		L1	
Meyer, John	23, May 1850	May	27		L3	
Meyer, Joseph	14, Dec. 1848	Dec.	24		L2	
Meyers, Mary	14, Oct. 1852	10, Oct.			L3	Clark
Meyers, Weseel	28, Aug. 1851	25, Aug.	62		L3	
Meyn, Anthony	4, Sept 1856		probate		L5	
Meysonbug, Richard	19, Sept 1850	Sept	37		L3	
Miall, Nathaniel	5, July 1849	June	47		L3	
Michael, (child of Amanda)	20, Feb. 1851	Feb.	3d		L3	
Michael, Jacob	4, Jan. 1849	Dec.	49		L3	
Michael, John	20, Sept 1832	Sept	1-10m-25d		L1	
Michael, Michael	9, May 1850	Apr.			L3	
Michael, Paul	28, June 1814		estate		L3	
Michaels, Amanda	13, Mar. 1851	Mar.	36		L3	
Michaels, Henry	20, Feb. 1851	Feb.	23		L3	
Mickmickle, Margaret	26, July 1849	July	52		L3	
Middaugh, Henry	18, Jan. 1844	Jan.	18		L3	
Middleton, (Dr)	28, Aug. 1834	Aug.			L1	
Middleton, John	25, Oct. 1832	19, Oct.			L2	
Middleton, John	22, Nov. 1832		estate		L3	
Middleton, Thomas	4, Feb. 1847	28, Jan.	57	*	L3	
Middleton, William	23, July 1835		estate		L4	
Middleton, William T.	6, Nov. 1834		estate		L3	
Middleton, William T.	31, Mar. 1836		estate		L4	
Middleton, William T.	14, June 1838		probate		L4	
Middlewood, Caroline	14, Aug. 1851	13, Aug.	1- 9m		L3	
Middlewood, Henry	21, Nov. 1833	Nov.	53		L3	
Mier, (child of John)	1, Aug. 1833	July	stillborn		L1	
Miers, (child of S.)	26, Dec. 1833	Dec.	stillborn		L4	
Milbis, Napoleon B.	12, Nov. 1840		estate		L3	
Milder, (boy)	28, Apr. 1853				L3	
Miler, C.C.	18, Oct. 1832	14, Oct.			L3	
Miles, Ann	30, Oct. 1851	23, Oct.			L3	
Miles, Benjamin	12, Feb. 1835		estate		L3	
Miles, Benjamin	9, June 1836		probate		L3	
Miles, Burnet	12, Oct. 1848	2, Oct.	26	*	L3	
Miles, Edward	7, Mar. 1850	Feb.	45		L3	
Miles, John	21, Aug. 1828		estate		L1	
Miles, Judah	3, Dec. 1840		probate		L3	
Miles, Mary Yorke	1, June 1843	26, May	23m		L3	
Miles, Robert	11, Apr. 1844	Apr.	36		L3	
Miles, Sarah	9, Aug. 1838		estate		L3	
Milholland, (Mr)	11, Oct. 1832	1, Oct.			L2	
Miliken, Henrietta	4, May 1848	Apr.	34		L3	
Millar, Clara Bell	14, Dec. 1854	11, Dec.	4		L3	
Millar, John	2, June 1853	28, May			L3	
Millard, Dennis	18, Nov. 1841	Nov.	30		L3	
Millason, Isabella	12, Sept 1833	Sept	6m		L1	
Miller, (child of Daniel)	12, June 1845	June	stillborn		L3	
Miller, (child of William)	26, Apr. 1849	Apr.	1w		L3	
Miller, (child)	11, Sept 1834	Aug.			L1	
Miller, (Mr)	6, Apr. 1819	3, Apr.			L2	

Name	Notice Date	Death Date	Age		Page	Maiden Name
Miller, Adam	13, Dec. 1838	Dec.	68		L4	
Miller, Alexander	23, Aug. 1849	Aug.	33		L3	
Miller, Alexander	16, Sept 1841	22, Aug.	55		L3	
Miller, Andrew Jackson	10, Nov. 1842	6, Nov.	25		L4	
Miller, Arabella	31, Apr. 1845	Apr.	10m		L3	
Miller, Augustus	30, Nov. 1848	Nov.	33		L3	
Miller, Catharine	30, Oct. 1845	28, Oct.	42		L3	
Miller, Catharine	3, Nov. 1853	30, Oct.			L3	
Miller, Charles B.	26, July 1855	21, July	infant		L3	
Miller, Charles W.	1, Apr. 1847	18, Mar.	37		L3	
Miller, Christian	30, Oct. 1845	Oct.	26		L3	
Miller, Christian	9, Dec. 1847	Dec.	47		L3	
Miller, Christopher	16, Aug. 1849	Aug.	40		L3	
Miller, Christopher	20, Sept 1838	Sept	48		L3	
Miller, Daniel	19, Jan. 1854	11, Oct.	85		L3	
Miller, Edward	25, Oct. 1838	Oct.	68		L3	
Miller, Edward (Capt)	11, July 1823	7, July			L3	
Miller, Eliza Ann	20, Sept 1849	13, Sept			L3	
Miller, Elizabeth	2, Jan. 1824	31, Dec.			L2	
Miller, George	10, Apr. 1856		probate		L3	
Miller, George H.	1, Mar. 1849	24, Feb.	22		L3	
Miller, George Washington	24, Feb. 1848	21, Feb.	7m		L3	
Miller, Halsey B.	10, Sept 1857		probate		L3	
Miller, Halsey Benton	9, Nov. 1854	2, Nov.			L3	
Miller, Henry	13, Jan. 1842	Jan.	19		L3	
Miller, Henry	29, Feb. 1844	Feb.	52		L3	
Miller, Henry	17, May 1849	May	52		L3	
Miller, Henry	23, Mar. 1837		estate		L3	
Miller, Henry	21, Sept 1837	Sept	24		L4	
Miller, Ichabod B.	26, Dec. 1839	4, Dec.	75	*	L1	
Miller, Isaac C.	6, Mar. 1845	3, Mar.	infant		L3	
Miller, J.R.	10, Nov. 1836		estate		L3	
Miller, Jacob	29, June 1848	June	23		L3	
Miller, James	4, Oct. 1849	Sept	35		L3	
Miller, James	9, Dec. 1852				L3	
Miller, James Lawrence (Dr)	13, Jan. 1848	30, Dec.	26		L3	
Miller, Jane	16, Mar. 1849	Mar.	49		L3	
Miller, John	29, Jan. 1846	Jan.	28		L3	
Miller, John	23, Feb. 1837		probate		L3	
Miller, John L.	6, Apr. 1848	Mar.	21		L3	
Miller, John M.	29, July 1852		estate		L3	
Miller, John R.	8, Nov. 1838		probate		L3	
Miller, Joseph	14, Aug. 1856		probate		L6	
Miller, Joseph B.	27, May 1847	23, May		*	L2	
Miller, Joseph B.	10, June 1847	June	26		L3	
Miller, Joshua	7, Dec. 1848	Nov.	18		L3	
Miller, Levi	2, May 1850	Apr.	25		L3	
Miller, Levi	3, Aug. 1843	July			L3	
Miller, Lewis	27, Nov. 1845	Nov.	24		L3	
Miller, Magdalen	6, May 1847	Apr.	76		L3	
Miller, Margaret	11, July 1850	July	60		L3	
Miller, Mary	27, July 1843	July	25		L3	
Miller, Mary A.E.	20, Nov. 1856	16, Nov.			L3	
Miller, Nancy	8, May 1845	Apr.	43		L3	

Name	Notice Date	Death Date	Age		Page	Maiden Name
Miller, Nancy	27, Mar. 1845	Mar.	53		L3	
Miller, Ruth	20, May 1847	May	46		L3	
Miller, Samuel R.	28, Sept 1843	23, Sept	55		L3	
Miller, Sarah Ridgely	1, Feb. 1838	31, Jan.			L3	
Miller, Simon	9, July 1857		probate		L3	
Miller, Sophia B.	10, Nov. 1853	7, Nov.	24		L3	
Miller, Susan	9, Aug. 1855	4, Aug.	52		L3	
Miller, Theobald	10, Aug. 1843				L3	
Miller, Timothy	18, June 1846	June	35		L3	
Miller, Ursula	18, July 1850	14, July	67	*	L3	
Miller, Ursula	12, Sept 1850		estate		L3	
Miller, W.R.	1, Apr. 1852	18, Mar.			L3	
Miller, William	17, May 1849	May	20		L3	
Miller, William (Judge)	15, May 1845	12, May	83	*	L3	
Millin, (child)	2, Oct. 1834	Sept			L4	
Mills, Abizen	29, May 1834		probate		L3	
Mills, Abner	7, Dec. 1837		probate		L3	
Mills, Abraham	19, July 1832	July	23		L1	
Mills, Huldah Gazley	3, July 1845	30, June	30		L3	
Mills, Isaac	16, Feb. 1843	20, Jan.	77		L3	
Mills, Isaac	9, Apr. 1835		estate		L3	
Mills, Isaac	23, Feb. 1837		probate		L3	
Mills, Isaac	12, July 1849	1, July			L3	
Mills, James	27, Sept 1849	21, Sept		*	L3	
Mills, Jane	23, May 1833	May	2		L4	
Mills, John	8, Dec. 1842	Dec.			L3	
Mills, John R. (Major)	27, June 1810	23, June			L3	
Mills, Joshua (Dr)	11, May 1843	29, Apr.	46		L3	
Mills, Kate	13, Apr. 1854	11, Apr.	10m-16d		L3	
Mills, Mary	5, Oct. 1837	29, Sept	62		L3	
Mills, P.E.	12, Jan. 1837		probate		L3	
Mills, Peter	11, Nov. 1847	2, Nov.			L3	
Mills, Rebekah	2, Feb. 1809	27, Jan.			L3	
Mills, Robert	26, Sept 1833	Sept	37		L4	
Mills, Sallie A.	21, June 1849	12, June	32		L3	
Mills, Sarah Delia	9, Aug. 1838	24, July	3- 9m		L3	
Mills, Sarah Delia	10, Jan. 1856	29, Dec.			L3	
Mills, William P.	18, July 1850		estate		L3	
Mills, William P.	3, May 1855		probate		L3	
Mills, William R.P.	16, Jan. 1827		estate		L3	
Millspaugh, William	9, June 1836		probate		L3	
Millspaugh, William	12, Jan. 1837		probate		L3	
Milot, Patrick	22, June 1837		probate		L3	
Milward, Mary	26, Dec. 1839	Dec.	5		L3	
Milwood, Mary	3, July 1851	26, June			L3	
Minague, Michael	25, Jan. 1849	Jan.	18		L3	
Mineer, George	18, Nov. 1841	Nov.	19		L3	
Miner, Caroline A.	23, Dec. 1852	31, May			L3	
Miner, Emma	12, July 1849	8, July	12m		L3	
Minet, Julius C.	11, Aug. 1842	31, July	6m-11d		L3	
Minor, John D.	25, June 1857	17, June	13m- 7d		L3	
Minor, John D.	29, Aug. 1850	26, Aug.	infant		L3	
Minor, Martha Clark	24, Apr. 1845	20, Apr.	2- 1m		L3	
Minor, Martha J.	3, Aug. 1843	26, July	21		L3	

Name	Notice Date	Death Date	Age		Page	Maiden Name
Minor, Sallie McLean	28, Apr. 1853	24, Apr.			L3	
Minor, Thomas H.	14, Dec. 1848	10, Dec.	38		L2	
Minor, Thomas H.	25, Jan. 1849		estate		L3	
Minor, William	8, Nov. 1849	Oct.	27		L3	
Minshal, John	14, Apr. 1853	11, Apr.	31		L3	
Minshall, Griffith	3, Feb. 1817		estate		L3	
Minster, William S.	30, Mar. 1848		estate		L3	
Mirler, E.	8, Aug. 1833	July	40		L1	
Mirrielies, Eliza Margaretta	13, July 1848	25, June	infant		L3	
Misener, Jacob	5, Feb. 1816		estate		L3	
Misner, Jacob	17, Mar. 1826		probate		L3	
Mitchel, Jacob	6, June 1833	May	31		L2	
Mitchel, Mary	5, Sept 1833	Aug.	1- 4m		L1	
Mitchel, Robert	9, Nov. 1837		estate		L3	
Mitchel, Simeon	12, Nov. 1835		estate		L3	
Mitchel, Stella	10, Apr. 1851	1, Apr.	7m-11d		L3	
Mitchell, Andrew	16, May 1844	5, May	60		L3	
Mitchell, Anthony	4, May 1848	Apr.	50		L3	
Mitchell, Emma Louisa	30, Sept 1852	26, Sept			L3	
Mitchell, Evodine	12, July 1855	5, July			L3	
Mitchell, Franklin	3, 10, Nov. 1853	1, Nov.	14		L3	
Mitchell, George	23, May 1833	May	6		L4	
Mitchell, Hannah	27, Sept 1855	10, Aug.	79	*	L3	
Mitchell, Hannah	16, Aug. 1855	15, Aug.	81	*	L3	
Mitchell, J.C.	7, Sept 1843	17, Aug.		*	L3	
Mitchell, James	21, Aug. 1856	14, Aug.	28		L5	
Mitchell, Jethro	7, Feb. 1833	Feb.			L1	
Mitchell, John	1, Mar. 1849		estate		L3	
Mitchell, John B.	21, June 1838	June			L3	
Mitchell, Kate W.	6, Mar. 1856	3, Mar.			L3	
Mitchell, Mary	21, Sept 1854	20, Sept	2- 6m		L3	
Mitchell, Minturn Post	14, Mar. 1844	10, Mar.	13m		L3	
Mitchell, Newton W.	20, Jan. 1853	18, Jan.	2-10m		L3	
Mitchell, Phebe	1, Aug. 1833	July	41		L1	
Mitchell, Robert	19, Apr. 1832		estate		L3	
Mitchell, Sarah S.	19, Feb. 1846	11, Feb.	28		L3	
Mitchell, Simeon	22, Mar. 1838		probate		L3	
Mitchell, Simeon	21, Sept 1837		probate		L4	
Mitchell, Thomas	1, Aug. 1833	July	42		L1	
Mitchell, Thomas	29, Aug. 1833		estate		L3	
Mitchell, Thomas	15, May 1834		estate		L3	
Mitchell, Thomas	17, Mar. 1826		probate		L3	
Mitchell, Thomas	22, June 1837		probate		L3	
Mitchell, Thomas G.	21, July 1853	20, July			L3	
Mitchell, William	27, Oct. 1831		probate		L1	
Mitchell, William	18, May 1843		estate		L3	
Mitchell, William Henry	3, Feb. 1853	1, Feb.	12- 1m-13d		L3	
Mitchild, John	1, Aug. 1833	July	3		L1	
Mittio, Joseph	6, Apr. 1837	Apr.	42		L4	
Mix, John	18, July 1850	July			L3	
Mixer, Ebenezer	25, Apr. 1850	12, Apr.	61		L3	
Mixer, Ebenezer	2, May 1850		estate		L3	
Mizner, Lansing Gaine	2, Mar. 1848	16, Feb.	19		L3	
Mizner, Mary G.	2, Apr. 1857	20, Mar.	57		L3	

Name	Notice Date	Death Date	Age		Page	Maiden Name
Modler, Holde	1, Aug. 1850	July	3		L3	
Moerlin, Conrad	9, July 1857		probate		L3	
Moffett, Nathaniel	1, Nov. 1832	26, Oct.			L1	
Moffit, Anna M.	24, June 1847	June	56		L3	
Mogenheimer, Margaret	22, Oct. 1846	Oct.	38		L3	
Moghen, Patrick	30, Mar. 1849	Mar.	33		L3	
Mohler, Alonzo	19, Feb. 1829	12, Feb.		*	L1	
Mohn, Frederick	19, Aug. 1847	Aug.	29		L3	
Mohn, Peter	10, Apr. 1856		probate		L3	
Moiles, William	26, July 1849	July	40		L3	
Moline, Andrew	24, Feb. 1848	Feb.	30		L3	
Mollering, Frederick	31, July 1845	July	25		L3	
Molleston, Henry	3, Dec. 1819	1, Dec.			L2	
Molony, Lucy	9, Mar. 1848	4, Mar.	3- 5m		L3	
Molyneaux, Samuel	5, Sept 1823	7, Aug.	63		L3	
Molyneaux, Sarah	5, Sept 1823	5, Aug.	53		L3	
Monagon, John	11, Apr. 1850	Apr.	1d		L3	
Monahan, Anthony	15, July 1847	July	36		L3	
Mondhank, Henry	6, Feb. 1840	Jan.	64		L3	
Monegan, Jane	12, July 1849	July	40		L3	
Moneypeny, James	11, July 1850	July	19		L3	
Moning, John H.	8, Jan. 1857		probate		L3	
Monkhouse, John S.	4, Apr. 1839	Mar.	35		L3	
Monroe, Augustus	26, Oct. 1843	Oct.	34		L3	
Monroe, Ebenezer	19, July 1825	25, June	73		L3	
Monroe, Joseph B.	12, Apr. 1855	3, Apr.			L3	
Monsarray, Ann	1, Mar. 1838	18, Feb.			L3	
Montage, James	19, Jan. 1843	12, Jan.	21- 2m-27d		L3	
Montague, Frederick	18, Sept 1834	Sept	1		L1	
Montfort, (Mr)	20, Apr. 1848	16, Apr.			L2	
Montgomery, David	10, Nov. 1812		estate		L4	
Montgomery, Eunice	26, Aug. 1847	Aug.	4- 6m		L3	
Montgomery, Henry	8, July 1847	June	2- 6m		L3	
Montgomery, Joseph G.	8, Apr. 1847	Mar.	40		L3	
Montgomery, Margaret Y.	8, Oct. 1857	1, Oct.	17	*	L3	
Montgomery, Maria Francis Ann	28, Dec. 1854	26, Dec.	3- 6m		L3	
Montgomery, Mary A.	22, Jan. 1846	15, Jan.			L3	
Montgomery, Perry	30, May 1839	May	27		L2	
Montgomery, Philip M.	11, Sept 1845	Sept	35		L3	
Montooth, (child of Sarah)	5, Sept 1833	Aug.	7m		L1	
Montooth, Mary Ann	29, Aug. 1833	Aug.	6		L1	
Mooney, James	17, Mar. 1842	Mar.	44		L3	
Mooney, Mary A.	15, Jan. 1857	8, Jan.		*	L3	Dakin
Moor, (child of Richard M.)	14, Mar. 1833	Mar.	1d		L1	
Moor, Charles	6, Dec. 1849	30, Nov.	35		L2	
Moor, Charles	13, Dec. 1849	Dec.	35		L3	
Moor, John L.	29, Nov. 1832	Nov.	2- 6m		L1	
Moore, (child of James)	31, July 1851	July	3		L3	
Moore, (child of Jane)	17, Jan. 1850	Jan.	3w		L3	
Moore, (daughter of Hugh)	31, Mar. 1807	22, Mar.	infant		L3	
Moore, Adam	3, Jan. 1850	28, Dec.	71		L3	
Moore, Adam	22, June 1822		estate		L3	
Moore, Adam	17, Jan. 1850		estate		L3	
Moore, Adam	6, July 1854		estate		L3	

Name	Notice Date	Death Date	Age		Page	Maiden Name
Moore, Adam	6, Mar. 1856		probate		L3	
Moore, Ann	16, Nov. 1843	14, Nov.			L3	
Moore, Augustus	13, Dec. 1855	3, Dec.	76		L3	
Moore, Barbara	4, Feb. 1841	28, Jan.	61	*	L3	Schroeder
Moore, Benjamin F.	19, Oct. 1854	22, Sept	20		L3	
Moore, Bentard	11, July 1833		probate		L3	
Moore, Chloe	24, Nov. 1853	13, Nov.	73		L3	
Moore, David	15, Aug. 1844		estate		L3	
Moore, David	20, Mar. 1845		estate		L3	
Moore, David	7, May 1846		estate		L3	
Moore, E.	8, Jan. 1857		probate		L3	
Moore, Eli	27, July 1848		estate		L3	
Moore, Eliza Ann	3, Apr. 1845		estate		L3	
Moore, Eliza Ann	5, June 1845	4, June			L3	
Moore, Elizabeth	18, July 1833	July	45		L2	
Moore, Emily C.	28, Apr. 1853	22, Apr.	infant		L3	
Moore, George	29, Aug. 1833	Aug.	2- 3m		L1	
Moore, George	7, Mar. 1844		estate		L3	
Moore, George W.	13, Sept 1849		estate		L3	
Moore, Harriet	20, Mar. 1851	14, Mar.	infant		L3	
Moore, Heman A.	11, Apr. 1844	3, Apr.			L3	
Moore, Hester Ann	1, Nov. 1832	23, Oct.			L4	
Moore, Hugh	31, Dec. 1857		estate		L3	
Moore, Hugh	7, Feb. 1856		probate		L3	
Moore, Hugh (Capt)	29, June 1854	26, June	81-10m		L3	
Moore, Hugh Montgomery	20, Sept 1855		estate		L3	
Moore, I.	8, Aug. 1833	July	48		L1	
Moore, Isaac	17, May 1849	May	38		L3	
Moore, Isaac	7, Jan. 1836		estate		L3	
Moore, Isaac	22, June 1837		probate		L3	
Moore, Isaac	3, Sept 1840		probate		L3	
Moore, Isaac	21, Sept 1837		probate		L4	
Moore, Isaac	14, June 1838		probate		L4	
Moore, Isabella	19, Nov. 1857	14, Nov.	57		L3	
Moore, Isabella	24, Dec. 1857		estate		L3	
Moore, J.T.	2, Nov. 1854	17, Oct.		*	L3	
Moore, James	14, June 1838		probate		L4	
Moore, James Edgar	13, June 1844	7, June	21	*	L3	
Moore, Jane	8, Mar. 1849	Feb.	6m		L3	
Moore, John	12, Mar. 1846	Mar.	20		L3	
Moore, John	18, Oct. 1832	15, Oct.			L3	
Moore, John	22, July 1852	17, July			L3	
Moore, John D.	12, Aug. 1841	2, Aug.	56		L3	
Moore, Jonathan	21, June 1849	16, June	64	*	L3	
Moore, Joseph	21, Feb. 1856	5, Feb.			L3	
Moore, Linus	8, Apr. 1841	6, Apr.			L3	
Moore, Lydia	19, Jan. 1854	20, Dec.	68		L3	
Moore, Margaret	21, June 1849	June	5		L3	
Moore, Maria Ann	29, Aug. 1833	Aug.	6		L1	
Moore, Mary Ann	19, Jan. 1854	5, Jan.	2- 3m		L3	
Moore, Mary H.	11, Apr. 1850	4, Apr.	28		L3	Hulburd
Moore, Mary J.	6, Aug. 1840	July	2w		L3	
Moore, Mary S.	28, Aug. 1834	Aug.	49		L1	
Moore, Mary Symmes	14, Aug. 1834	Aug.	49		L3	

Name	Notice Date	Death Date	Age	Page	Maiden Name
Moore, Mary Symmes	14, Sept 1843	10, Sept	infant	L3	
Moore, Michael A.	16, June 1842	June	24	L3	
Moore, Nancy	1, Aug. 1833	July	27	L1	
Moore, Nancy A.	6, June 1833	May	2	L2	
Moore, Patrick	21, Apr. 1806		estate	L3	
Moore, Patrick	29, Sept 1807		estate	L3	
Moore, Patrick	14, Apr. 1806	9, Apr.		L3	
Moore, Raphael M.	13, July 1854		estate	L3	
Moore, Raphel Mengs	29, June 1854	25, June	24	L3	
Moore, Richard C. (Bishop)	25, Nov. 1841	12, Nov.		L3	
Moore, Robert	21, Sept 1854	13, Sept	30	L3	
Moore, Robert	27, Mar. 1845		estate	L3	
Moore, Robert	10, May 1825		estate	L4	
Moore, Sallie F.	18, Dec. 1856	12, Dec.	26	L3	
Moore, Samuel	26, Sept 1850		estate	L3	
Moore, Samuel V.	11, July 1833		probate	L3	
Moore, Susan Emily Wright	3, May 1855	29, Apr.	26- 3m	L3	
Moore, Susan North	11, Apr. 1850	24, Mar.		L3	
Moore, Vincent R.	13, Feb. 1851	10, Feb.	30	L3	
Moore, William	11, July 1850	July	21	L3	
Moore, William	6, Mar. 1851	Feb.	21	L3	
Moore, William	7, May 1840	Apr.	23	L3	
Moore, William	1, Aug. 1839	28, July	infant	L3	
Moorehead, Samuel	22, June 1837		probate	L3	
Moores, John	4, Aug. 1836		estate	L3	
Moores, John	7, Dec. 1837		probate	L3	
Moores, Linus F.	8, July 1841		estate	L3	
Moorhead, Boanerges	30, Jan. 1845	23, Jan.		L3	
Moorhead, Maria M.	17, May 1849	2, May	6- 2m	L3	
Moorhead, Robert (Dr)	13, Feb. 1845	9, Feb.	51	L3	
Moorhead, Samuel	22, Mar. 1838		probate	L3	
Moorhead, William	25, Oct. 1832	18, Oct.		L1	
Moorman, Maria Doretta	24, May 1849	22, May	24	L3	
Moosbey, Mary	17, Oct. 1844	Oct.		L3	
Moran, Eliza	24, Oct. 1850	Oct.	18	L3	
Moran, John	16, Mar. 1854	15, Mar.		L3	
Moran, Peter	13, June 1850	June	26	L3	
Morcellas, Theodore	25, July 1850	July	23	L3	
Mordica, David Moses	23, July 1846	July	4	L3	
Morehead, (Gov)	4, Jan. 1855			L3	
Morehead, Anne	9, Feb. 1843	27, Jan.	63	L3	
Morehead, Robert	8, Aug. 1844	July	25	L3	
Morehouse, Charlotte R.	25, Sept 1856	20, Sept	14m	L5	
Morehouse, Lucy A.	15, Mar. 1855	7, Mar.	2- 6m	L3	
Morehouse, Oscar	22, July 1847	18, July	22	L3	
Moreland, John T.	12, Sept 1833	Sept	3m-12d	L1	
Moren, Edward	17, May 1849	May	26	L3	
Morfit, William	1, Feb. 1849	Jan.	37	L3	
Morgan, Ann B.	1, Nov. 1855	28, Oct.		L3	
Morgan, Charlotte	1, Dec. 1842	30, Nov.	infant	L3	
Morgan, Collins	26, Apr. 1849	Apr.	22	L3	
Morgan, Edward	15, July 1847	July	31	L3	
Morgan, Edward Jordan	12, Jan. 1837	4, Jan.	6	L3	
Morgan, Edward Smith	13, Sept 1849	30, Aug.	1- -20d	L3	

Name	Notice Date	Death Date	Age		Page	Maiden Name
Morgan, George	14, Sept 1854	7, Sept	37		L3	
Morgan, Harriet	12, July 1849	10, July		*	L3	Stone
Morgan, John	1, Dec. 1831		estate		L3	
Morgan, John	9, Apr. 1835		estate		L3	
Morgan, John	19, May 1836		estate		L3	
Morgan, John	3, Dec. 1840		probate		L3	
Morgan, John	23, May 1850				L3	
Morgan, John	7, Feb. 1839		estate		L4	
Morgan, John	14, June 1838		probate		L4	
Morgan, John (Gen)	5, May 1817	13, Apr.			L3	
Morgan, John S. (Col)	24, June 1852	17, June	54		L3	
Morgan, Luther D. (Rev)	19, Jan. 1854	19, Dec.			L3	
Morgan, Margaretta C.	31, Aug. 1854	18, July	30	*	L3	
Morgan, Mary Stuart	18, Feb. 1847	23, Jan.	36- 1m	*	L3	Jennings
Morgan, Morgan	21, Dec. 1848	Dec.	40		L3	
Morgan, Richard (Capt)	15, June 1819		estate		L3	
Morgan, Sarah	7, Dec. 1848	Nov.	16		L3	
Morgan, Sarah Ann	23, Oct. 1834	Oct.	15		L2	
Morgan, Thomas	10, Apr. 1856		probate		L3	
Moritz, Joseph	7, July 1842		estate		L3	
Morley, Elizabeth	22, May 1834	May	39		L4	
Morow, Mary Ann	11, Feb. 1847	2, Feb.	22- -4d		L3	
Morrell, Abraham	2, Mar. 1854		estate		L3	
Morrell, Abram	2, Feb. 1854	26, Jan.			L3	
Morrell, O.H.	12, Aug. 1847	3, Aug.	33		L3	
Morrell, O.H.	7, Dec. 1848		estate		L3	
Morrell, Thaddeus C.	3, Aug. 1848	21, July			L3	
Morrey, Laney	8, Apr. 1841	Mar.	44		L3	
Morris, (Mr)	7, Oct. 1847	6, Oct.			L2	
Morris, Abigail	26, May 1842	25, May			L3	
Morris, Alexander	22, Feb. 1849		estate		L3	
Morris, Caroline S.	31, Dec. 1857	9, Dec.			L3	Drummond
Morris, David	10, Apr. 1851		18		L3	
Morris, David	16, Mar. 1843	4, Mar.	54		L3	
Morris, Ellen	21, July 1836	10, July	3		L3	
Morris, Frank	19, July 1849	July	37		L3	
Morris, Frederick	27, Aug. 1857	24, Aug.		*	L3	
Morris, Gourverneur	2, Dec. 1816	7, Nov.	65		L3	
Morris, Henry E.	6, Mar. 1856	28, Feb.	32		L3	
Morris, James C.	23, Oct. 1828		estate		L2	
Morris, James C.	23, Apr. 1829		estate		L3	
Morris, James C.	17, Nov. 1831		estate		L3	
Morris, James C.	8, Nov. 1838		probate		L3	
Morris, James C.	14, June 1838		probate		L4	
Morris, Jane	14, June 1838		probate		L4	
Morris, Jane B.	22, June 1843	15, June	39		L3	Dunlevy
Morris, John	8, Aug. 1833	July	14- 6m		L1	
Morris, Jonathan	7, Feb. 1833	Feb.	51		L1	
Morris, Jonathan	14, Jan. 1833		estate		L3	
Morris, Lucien B.	10, Nov. 1842				L4	
Morris, Martha B.	27, Sept 1855	20, Aug.			L3	
Morris, Mary	29, Aug. 1839	Aug.	29		L3	
Morris, Mary	12, Oct. 1824		32		L3	
Morris, Mary	27, Jan. 1848	26, Jan.			L3	

Name	Notice Date	Death Date	Age	Page	Maiden Name
Morris, Mary Ann	1, May 1828		6- 7m	L1	
Morris, Mary C.	16, Oct. 1851	26, Sept	40	L3	
Morris, Robert	4, Aug. 1853	19, July	38	L3	
Morris, Robert	2, June 1806	28, May		L3	
Morris, Sarah	5, Feb. 1857			L3	
Morrison, (child of David)	8, Aug. 1833	July	stillborn	L1	
Morrison, Alexander	18, Sept 1834		estate	L3	
Morrison, Caroline	3, Jan. 1850	Dec.	20m	L3	
Morrison, Christiana	11, Sept 1834	Aug.	55	L1	
Morrison, Edward	16, Aug. 1849	Aug.	5w	L3	
Morrison, Ellen Em.	31, Aug. 1848	Aug.	21	L3	
Morrison, George (Capt)	4, May 1848	25, Apr.		L3	
Morrison, Harriet	7, Sept 1848	Aug.	3w	L3	
Morrison, Harriett	13, Jan. 1848	5, Jan.	35	L3	
Morrison, Isaac	20, Dec. 1825		probate	L4	
Morrison, Jacob	15, Nov. 1855	9, Nov.	74	L3	
Morrison, James	7, May 1857		probate	L3	
Morrison, James	9, July 1857		probate	L3	
Morrison, John	9, May 1850	2, May		L3	
Morrison, Josephine	15, Feb. 1855	10, Feb.	21	L3	
Morrison, M. (Mrs)	1, Aug. 1833	July	55	L1	
Morrison, M.S. (Mrs)	25, Oct. 1832	19, Oct.		L2	
Morrison, Margaret	6, May 1847	Apr.	60	L3	
Morrison, Mary	7, Feb. 1850	Jan.	2	L3	
Morrison, Mary Ann	15, Aug. 1833	Aug.	23	L1	
Morrison, Moses	29, May 1834		probate	L3	
Morrison, Moses	9, June 1836		probate	L3	
Morrison, William	2, Nov. 1854	31, Oct.	51	L3	
Morrison, William C.	7, July 1836		estate	L3	
Morrison, William C.	7, Dec. 1837		probate	L3	
Morrison, William C.	21, Sept 1837		probate	L4	
Morrison, William McCormick	5, June 1845	31, May	8m-19d	L3	
Morrit, Rebecca F.	19, Sept 1833	Sept	2- 5m	L4	
Morrow, Jeremiah, Jr.	3, Aug. 1843	26, July	33	L3	
Morrow, Mary Elizabeth	25, July 1844	24, July	18m	L3	
Morrow, T.V. (Dr)	15, Aug. 1850		estate	L3	
Morrow, Thomas V.	18, July 1850	16, July	48	L3	
Morse,	3, May 1849	2, May	20	L2	
Morse, (Mrs)	25, Oct. 1832	19, Oct.		L1	
Morse, Eleazer	2, Dec. 1823	1, Dec.	22	L3	
Morse, Lewis	13, Nov. 1851		estate	L3	
Morse, Lewis	5, July 1855		probate	L3	
Morse, Lewis	9, July 1857		probate	L3	
Morse, Mary	25, Oct. 1832	18, Oct.		L1	
Morse, Phebe	18, Jan. 1844	14, Jan.	40	L3	
Morse, Sarah R.	20, Apr. 1843	12, Apr.	24	L3	
Morse, Stephen	5, June 1845	May	60	L3	
Morsell, Elizabeth	7, July 1831	4, July	2- 2m	L3	
Morsell, James C.	5, Mar. 1835		estate	L3	
Morserrat, George	19, Apr. 1849	12, Apr.		L3	
Morten, Henry, Sen.	27, Apr. 1837		estate	L4	
Mortimer, Emma	25, Oct. 1832	23, Oct.		L3	
Mortimer, Mary Ann	8, Aug. 1833	July	10	L1	
Mortimer, William	1, Nov. 1838		estate	L3	

Name	Notice Date	Death Date	Age		Page	Maiden Name
Mortiz, Catharine	11, July 1850	July	27		L3	
Morton, Abraham	15, Feb. 1844	11, Feb.	25		L3	
Morton, Charles William	19, Jan. 1854	16, Jan.	11w		L3	
Morton, Daniel	26, May 1853	20, May		*	L3	
Morton, David	28, May 1846	May	45		L3	
Morton, Henry, Sen.	13, Feb. 1840		probate		L3	
Morton, James	12, Aug. 1847	7, Aug.			L3	
Morton, Rebecca	25, Oct. 1849	Oct.	18		L3	
Mosby, Benjamin	17, July 1815	10, July	38		L3	
Mosby, Littleberry	21, July 1842	14, July	33		L3	
Mosby, Littlebury	11, Aug. 1842		estate		L3	
Mosby, Napoleon B.	3, July 1845	30, June			L3	
Moseman, Joseph	30, Aug. 1832	Aug.	22		L1	
Moses, Hetty	10, Nov. 1836	6, Nov.		*	L3	Block
Moses, Julia Frances	22, Feb. 1844	21, Feb.	15m		L3	
Moses, Margaretta	7, Mar. 1850	2, Mar.	34		L3	
Mosher, Charles Linnaeus	11, June 1857	12, Apr.	24		L3	
Moss, Henry	26, Mar. 1840		estate		L3	
Moss, Henry	19, Mar. 1840	19, Mar.			L3	
Moss, James	2, July 1840	June	37		L3	
Moss, Mary Alice	7, July 1853	1, July	6m-28d		L3	
Moss, R. Louisa	4, Jan. 1849	26, Dec.	24	*	L3	
Moss, Richard	25, Jan. 1813	16, Oct.			L3	
Moss, William	31, Oct. 1850		estate		L3	
Moss, William	25, Jan. 1855		estate		L3	
Moss, William	4, June 1857		probate		L3	
Mossman, William	8, Nov. 1855		probate		L3	
Mott, Emeline	13, Dec. 1849	Dec.	24		L3	
Mott, Mary	25, Oct. 1849	Oct.	1d		L3	
Mott, Samuel	11, Nov. 1841	23, Oct.	60		L3	
Motz, George W. (Major)	27, Sept 1849	6, July			L3	
Mound, John Adair	25, Oct. 1832	22, Oct.			L3	
Mount, Eliza	15, Oct. 1857	6, Oct.			L3	
Mount, William	26, Sept 1850	Sept	34		L3	
Mount, William	30, Nov. 1843	22, Nov.	48		L3	
Mounts, Joseph	1, Apr. 1847	19, Mar.	66	*	L3	
Mounts, Providence	19, Jan. 1854	1, Dec.	58	*	L3	
Mouton, John	1, Aug. 1850	28, July	4m-14d		L3	
Mow, (child of Samuel)	2, Aug. 1832	July	1- 4m		L1	
Mowry, Olive W.	15, Apr. 1841	12, Apr.	25		L3	
Mowry, Olive W.	20, May 1841				L3	
Mowton, James	18, July 1850	9, July	3m-25d		L3	
Moyer, Charles A.	21, Oct. 1841	Oct.	5m		L3	
Muchmore, Samuel	7, Dec. 1837		probate		L3	
Muchmore, Samuel	13, May 1812		estate		L4	
Muchmore, Stephen	14, Jan. 1847		estate		L3	
Mudge, Enoch	5, Nov. 1857	31, Oct.	60		L3	
Mudge, Landon R.	13, Dec. 1832	Dec.	9m- 9d		L1	
Muggeridge, (Mrs)	25, Oct. 1832	21, Oct.			L3	
Mulaley, (child of Joseph)	22, Aug. 1833	Aug.	1- 6m		L4	
Muldoon, John	23, Aug. 1849	Aug.	20		L3	
Mulford, Edmund B.	21, Nov. 1833	Nov.	1- -13d		L3	
Mulford, Elizabeth M.	8, Aug. 1850	9, July	26		L3	
Mulford, Emma C.	8, July 1841	29, June	14m- 4d		L3	

Name	Notice Date	Death Date	Age		Page	Maiden Name
Mulford, Lewis	19, Aug. 1820	18, Aug.	69	*	L3	
Mulholland, Daniel	19, Apr. 1849	Apr.	32		L3	
Mulkins, Elizabeth	11, July 1850	July	55		L3	
Mull, Martha	11, July 1833		probate		L3	
Mullalley, John	21, Feb. 1850		estate		L3	
Mullay, Hugh (Lt)	17, July 1845	11, July	94		L3	
Mulleck, Charles	18, Oct. 1832	Oct.	49		L4	
Mullen, Catharine	20, May 1852	13, May		*	L3	
Mullen, Emma	4, Oct. 1849	30, Sept	4- 5m		L3	
Mullen, Mary	1, Nov. 1832	24, Oct.			L1	
Mullen, Thomas	6, Mar. 1851	Feb.	35		L3	
Mulligan, (child of P.)	22, Aug. 1833	Aug.			L4	
Mulligan, Patrick	29, Nov. 1849	26, Nov.	30		L2	
Mulligan, Patrick	6, Dec. 1849	Nov.	35		L3	
Mulliner, Samuel L.	11, Aug. 1842		estate		L3	
Mumford, Paul	24, Sept 1805	20, Aug.	72		L3	
Munday, Benjamin	5, July 1849	June	50		L3	
Mundhenck, (Mrs)	18, Oct. 1832	15, Oct.			L2	
Mundia, Patrick	25, Oct. 1832	19, Oct.			L2	
Mundorf, Davis	23, Jan. 1851	Jan.	43		L3	
Munford, Mary	1, Nov. 1832	28, Oct.	4		L3	
Munford, Robert	25, Oct. 1832	22, Oct.			L3	
Munhall, Lucy A.	20, July 1848	July	5m		L3	
Munnigan, Barney	20, Mar. 1851	Mar.	67		L3	
Munro, Jane	10, Feb. 1848	6, Feb.	18	*	L3	
Munsell, Levi	19, Apr. 1849	1, Mar.	87		L2	
Munson, George Augustus	28, July 1842	22, July	15m		L3	
Muntooth, Mary Ann	15, June 1848	June	9m		L3	
Murch, Valentine	9, July 1857		probate		L3	
Murdock, George L. (Dr)	9, May 1850	6, May	60		L3	
Murdock, Lizzie H.	9, Sept 1852	8, Sept			L3	
Murphey, Edward	5, July 1849	June	33		L3	
Murphey, Ellen	13, Dec. 1849	Dec.	20		L3	
Murphey, Greenbury	16, May 1844	May	5		L3	
Murphey, William H.	22, Apr. 1847	Apr.	2		L3	
Murphy, (child of Mary)	12, Dec. 1850	Dec.	stillborn		L3	
Murphy, (Mr)	18, Oct. 1832	15, Oct.			L3	
Murphy, Andrew	15, May 1834	May	6		L4	
Murphy, Ann	3, Apr. 1851	Mar.	30		L3	
Murphy, Anthony	18, July 1850	July	24		L3	
Murphy, Catharine	21, June 1849	June	29		L3	
Murphy, Cornelius	8, Mar. 1849	28, Feb.	63		L3	
Murphy, David	24, July 1851	18, July			L4	
Murphy, Edmund	11, Apr. 1850	Apr.	48		L3	
Murphy, Edward	20, Mar. 1851	Mar.			L3	
Murphy, Henry	1, Nov. 1832	Oct.			L3	
Murphy, Hugh	14, Aug. 1851		estate		L3	
Murphy, J.W.	4, July 1850	27, June	34		L3	
Murphy, John	4, Apr. 1850	Mar.	18		L3	
Murphy, John	4, Apr. 1850	Mar.	27		L3	
Murphy, John	7, June 1849	May	28		L3	
Murphy, John	16, Mar. 1849	Mar.	36		L3	
Murphy, John	21, June 1849	June	1- 6m		L3	
Murphy, John	25, Aug. 1842		estate		L3	

Name	Notice Date	Death Date	Age		Page	Maiden Name
Murphy, John W.	29, Aug. 1850		estate		L3	
Murphy, Joseph W.	18, Sept 1834		estate		L3	
Murphy, Joseph W.	4, Feb. 1836		estate		L4	
Murphy, Lewis, Jr.	22, Aug. 1844	16, Aug.	infant		L3	
Murphy, Mary	20, Feb. 1851	Feb.	26		L3	
Murphy, Mary	19, Dec. 1850	Dec.			L3	
Murphy, Michael	26, Apr. 1849	Apr.	21		L3	
Murphy, Neal	13, Feb. 1840		probate		L3	
Murphy, Patrick	8, June 1848	May	27		L3	
Murphy, Patrick	12, Dec. 1850	Dec.	45		L3	
Murphy, Patrick	23, Jan. 1851	Jan.	50		L3	
Murphy, Patrick	15, Apr. 1847	Apr.	63		L3	
Murphy, Robert Yeatman	25, May 1843	19, May	10m		L3	
Murphy, Sarah T.	4, Apr. 1844	30, Mar.			L3	
Murphy, Thomas	2, May 1839	Apr.	35		L3	
Murphy, William	15, Aug. 1850	Aug.	25		L3	
Murphy, William	21, June 1849	June	39		L3	
Murphy, William (Dr)	15, Dec. 1808	12, Dec.			L3	
Murray, Andrew	23, Oct. 1834	Oct.	29		L2	
Murray, Bernard	3, Apr. 1845	16, Mar.	76		L3	
Murray, Harriet	26, Mar. 1840	17, Mar.			L3	
Murray, James L.	11, Jan. 1838			*	L3	
Murray, John	8, June 1848	May	17		L3	
Murray, John Ellis	6, Oct. 1853	1, Oct.			L3	
Murray, Joseph D.	5, July 1849	3, July	84		L3	
Murray, Reuben J.	22, Apr. 1847	20, Apr.	37		L3	
Murray, Susan	19, Sept 1844	31, Aug.			L3	
Murrell, David	25, Oct. 1849		estate		L3	
Murrell, Robert	20, Apr. 1848		estate		L3	
Murrey, John	15, Nov. 1849	Nov.	38		L3	
Murry, Edmund	18, Apr. 1850	Apr.	25		L3	
Murry, Elizabeth	23, May 1839		3m		L3	
Murry, John	19, June 1845	June	6m		L3	
Murry, Phebe Ann	19, June 1845	June	17		L3	
Murry, Thomas	21, Mar. 1850	Mar.	58		L3	
Muscroft, Eleanor	25, July 1833	July	22		L1	
Muscroft, George	21, Apr. 1842	17, Apr.	58	*	L3	
Muscroft, George	9, Mar. 1843		estate		L3	
Muscroft, H.F.	18, Oct. 1832	12, Oct.			L2	
Musgrave, Hiram	3, Jan. 1850	Dec.	6w		L3	
Musgrove, Mary Jane	23, Mar. 1849	Mar.	1		L3	
Musler, Mary Magdalene	11, July 1850	7, July	4		L3	
Musselman, Mary	5, Dec. 1833	Nov.	53		L3	
Mussey, Joseph	10, Jan. 1856	3, Jan.	39		L3	
Muzzy, John	19, Sept 1833	Sept			L4	
Myer (child)	5, Sept 1833	Aug.	2		L1	
Myer, Henry	13, May 1847	May	3w		L3	
Myer, Peter	5, Nov. 1846	Oct.	34		L3	
Myers, (child)	18, July 1833	July			L2	
Myers, Adam	8, Nov. 1838		probate		L3	
Myers, Caroline	4, May 1843	1, May	7		L3	
Myers, Diana	26, July 1832	July	28		L1	
Myers, Elizabeth	24, Oct. 1839		estate		L4	
Myers, Frederick	7, Mar. 1844	Feb.	23		L3	

Name	Notice Date	Death Date	Age		Page	Maiden Name
Myers, Frederick	24, Aug. 1843	Aug.	25		L3	
Myers, George	5, Aug. 1852				L3	
Myers, Henry	13, Nov. 1834	Nov.	4		L1	
Myers, Henry	16, Sept 1847	Sept	23		L3	
Myers, Henry	29, May 1845	May	30		L3	
Myers, Henry	29, June 1837	June	20		L4	
Myers, Jacob	29, Aug. 1833	Aug.			L1	
Myers, John	27, Oct. 1831		probate		L1	
Myers, John	8, Jan. 1857		probate		L3	
Myers, John R.	2, Oct. 1856	27, Sept	37		L5	
Myers, Joseph	21, Sept 1837		probate		L4	
Myers, Louise	2, Oct. 1851	30, Sept			L3	
Myers, Marcus	22, Oct. 1840	Oct.	6		L3	
Myers, Maria S.	13, Sept 1832	Sept	1- 5m-12d		L1	
Myers, Mary	25, Aug. 1842	17, Aug.	45		L3	
Myers, Richard	21, Feb. 1839	Feb.	60		L3	
Myers, Ruth	9, June 1836		probate		L3	
Myers, Sarah E.	7, Aug. 1834	July	6- 2m		L3	
Myers, William (Mrs)	23, Feb. 1854	4, Feb.			L3	
Myres, Andrew	4, Apr. 1844		estate		L3	
Myres, Charles	26, July 1849	July	6- 3m		L3	
Myrick, Eunice	7, Aug. 1845	3, Aug.	65		L3	
Naber, Haman	5, June 1851	31, May			L3	
Nagel, Knedes	23, Oct. 1834	Oct.	1- 3m- 9d		L2	
Nailor, (Mr)	25, Oct. 1832	18, Oct.			L1	
Nancarrow, John	19, Feb. 1805	14, Feb.	63		L3	
Napier, E.W.	30, Mar. 1849		estate		L3	
Napoleon, Sarah	19, Apr. 1849	Apr.			L3	
Narry, Patrick	5, Apr. 1849	Mar.	34		L3	
Nash, Eliza Delia	20, Nov. 1850	16, Nov.	38	*	L3	Hannahs
Nash, John	28, Feb. 1839	20, Feb.	70		L3	
Nash, John	8, Apr. 1852	3, Apr.			L3	
Nash, Lewis	11, Jan. 1838	Dec.	33		L3	
Nash, William	15, Aug. 1833	Aug.	29		L1	
Nason, Mary C.	10, Mar. 1853	3, Mar.			L3	
Nathaw, James	1, Aug. 1850	July	3		L3	
Naughton, James M.	14, Mar. 1833	Mar.	39		L1	
Nauman, Henry	9, May 1850	Apr.	36		L3	
Nave, M.S.	12, Feb. 1829		estate		L4	
Navis, Patrick	7, Sept 1848	Aug.	21		L3	
Nead, Patrick	15, Feb. 1838		estate		L3	
Nead, Patrick	1, Feb. 1838	24, Jan.			L3	
Neal, (Mr)	25, Oct. 1832	20, Oct.			L2	
Neal, Eleazar	5, Sept 1833	Aug.	14d		L1	
Neal, John	21, Dec. 1854	28, Nov.	81		L3	
Nealand, Thomas	12, July 1849	July	50		L3	
Neale, George	25, Apr. 1833	Apr.	1-10m		L1	
Neave, Alexander	18, Jan. 1820	15, Jan.	22- 5m-24d		L3	
Neave, Charles	17, Dec. 1857	12, Dec.	33		L3	
Neave, Charles, Jr.	26, Dec. 1833	Dec.	3		L4	
Neave, Lizzie	16, Feb. 1854	14, Feb.	8m- 2d		L3	
Neave, Louisa	8, Aug. 1833	July	3- 8m		L1	
Neave, Martha W.	10, May 1855	3, May	26		L3	Whipple

Name	Notice Date	Death Date	Age		Page	Maiden Name
Neave, Mary S.	25, Mar. 1841	9, Mar.	8- 6m		L3	
Neave, Oliver M.	18, Feb. 1841	9, Feb.	8m		L3	
Neave, Sarah	20, Apr. 1843	12, Apr.	13m		L3	
Neave, T.M.	3, Sept 1857	27, Aug.	23		L3	
Neave, Thomas Jefferson	4, Dec. 1828	3, Dec.	2m		L1	
Neavelle, Emma Clay	1, June 1848	29, May	19	*	L3	Clay
Nebel, Daniel	13, Sept 1838	Sept	35		L3	
Neely, Benjamin	28, June 1849	June	22		L3	
Neff, Elizabeth Clifford W.	28, Jan. 1841	27, Jan.	infant		L3	
Neff, George W.	20, Nov. 1850		estate		L3	
Neff, George W.	23, Jan. 1851		estate		L3	
Neff, Isabella	14, Mar. 1844	6, Mar.			L3	
Neff, Juliana Wayne	16, Feb. 1837	15, Feb.	4- 4m- 7d		L4	
Neff, Nicholas W.J.	28, June 1855	23, June	infant		L3	
Neff, William	27, Nov. 1856	25, Nov.	66		L3	
Neff, William	13, Nov. 1856	9, Nov.			L3	
Nehemiah, David	15, Nov. 1832	Nov.	67		L1	
Neil, Mary	19, Oct. 1854	16, Oct.	44	*	L3	
Neill, Sarah Elizabeth	12, Oct. 1843	Oct.	3m-11d		L3	
Neillord, Patrick	12, July 1849	July	53		L3	
Neilson, Elenor	15, Apr. 1847	13, Apr.			L3	
Neiman, William	27, Sept 1849	Sept	2- 6m		L3	
Neise, A. (Dr)	12, July 1849	July			L3	
Neisse, A.	5, July 1849	4, July	35		L2	
Neitzel, John	27, Sept 1849	Sept	34		L3	
Nelleneer, Henry	11, Nov. 1852	Oct.	30		L3	
Nelson, (Mr)	11, Oct. 1832	6, Oct.			L2	
Nelson, Ann	11, Feb. 1847	Feb.	18m		L3	
Nelson, Caroline	23, Nov. 1848	Nov.	11		L3	
Nelson, Elizabeth	3, May 1849	25, Apr.	66		L3	
Nelson, Jane	24, May 1849	May	50		L3	
Nelson, John	25, July 1833	July	33		L1	
Nelson, John	3, Dec. 1840		probate		L3	
Nelson, John	27, Sept 1832		estate		L4	
Nelson, John	15, May 1834		estate		L4	
Nelson, John	1, Jan. 1835		estate		L4	
Nelson, John	14, June 1838		probate		L4	
Nelson, Nancy	10, June 1847	June	13		L3	
Nelson, Sarah	18, May 1848	May	21		L3	
Nelson, Virginia	18, Mar. 1847	Mar.	19		L3	
Nelson, William	20, Apr. 1822		estate		L4	
Neptune, Sarah	23, May 1844	May	28		L3	
Nesbit, (Mr)	25, Oct. 1832	19, Oct.			L2	
Nettson, Henry	25, Oct. 1832	21, Oct.			L2	
Neumire, Edward	1, June 1848	May	6		L3	
Nevill, Agnes	28, Aug. 1845	20, Aug.	17	*	L3	
Nevill, Alfred	23, Jan. 1851	19, Jan.	15		L3	
Nevill, Eliza	17, Oct. 1850	11, Oct.	12		L3	
Nevill, Joseph	25, Dec. 1851	15, Dec.	57		L3	
Neville, Charles Dickens	17, Mar. 1842	5, Mar.	7m		L3	
Neville, Elbridge Lawrence	2, Dec. 1847	26, Nov.	18m		L3	
Neville, John	5, Nov. 1840	Oct.	29		L2	
Neville, Morgan	18, Apr. 1839		estate		L3	
Neville, Presley (Gen)	8, Dec. 1818	1, Dec.	63		L3	

Name	Notice Date	Death Date	Age	Page	Maiden Name
Newberry, Horace P.	13, Nov. 1834	Nov.	11m	L1	
Newbold,	19, Mar. 1846	Mar.	9m	L3	
Newcomb, Jesse	15, Apr. 1812	11, Apr.	35	L3	
Newcomb, Jesse	22, Apr. 1812		estate	L3	
Newcomb, William	7, Dec. 1843	Dec.	26	L3	
Newell, Abigail	21, Mar. 1839	14, Mar.	50	L3	
Newell, Benjamin	7, Feb. 1828		estate	L3	
Newell, James	17, July 1851	13, July		L3	
Newell, Samuel	20, May 1847	11, Apr.	67	* L3	
Newell, Samuel	18, Apr. 1839		probate	L3	
Newell, Samuel	14, June 1838		probate	L4	
Newell, Thomas	25, Mar. 1847	24, Mar.	58	L3	
Newell, William H.	8, July 1852	5, July	33	L3	
Newhall, Edward	8, Mar. 1855	1, Mar.	60	L3	
Newhall, Edward	5, Apr. 1855	1, Apr.	60	* L3	
Newhall, Edward	24, May 1855		estate	L3	
Newhall, John	8, July 1841	June	62	L3	
Newhall, Margaret Adeline	28, Dec. 1848	24, Dec.	19	L3	
Newhold, Sophia	27, Mar. 1828	Mar.	41	L1	
Newman, Arthur	27, July 1848	July	22	L3	
Newman, Mary	22, Dec. 1836		22	L3	
Newsteckel, Eliza	28, June 1849	June	30	L3	
Newton, (child of James)	8, Aug. 1833	July	stillborn	L1	
Newton, (child of James)	6, Dec. 1832	Dec.		L1	
Newton, Abby B.	13, May 1830	7, May	32	L3	Wood
Newton, Martin	23, Jan. 1851	Jan.	24	L3	
Newton, Thomas	6, Aug. 1857		probate	L3	
Newton, Thomas C.	26, July 1849		estate	L3	
Neyes, Charles C.	7, Feb. 1856		probate	L3	
Nichol, Arthur	31, May 1849	May	7m	L3	
Nichol, Francis	13, May 1812		estate	L4	
Nichol, Margaret	31, May 1849	May	20	L3	
Nicholas, Charles M.	24, Oct. 1850		estate	L3	
Nicholas, Josiah	14, Nov. 1844	13, Nov.		* L3	
Nichols, Arthur Huon	24, Sept 1840	18, Sept	7m	L3	
Nichols, Benoni	30, Sept 1847	Sept	34	L3	
Nichols, Charles	24, Oct. 1850	Oct.	30	L3	
Nichols, Charles M.	7, Mar. 1850	26, Feb.	29	L3	
Nichols, Clarence B.	12, Sept 1844	1, Sept	3	L3	
Nichols, Ellen Amanda	2, Oct. 1845	29, Sept	22m	L3	
Nichols, George W.	8, July 1841	June	32	L3	
Nichols, Nathan	22, June 1822		estate	L3	
Nichols, Samuel	29, Sept 1812	22, Sept		L3	
Nicholson, John G.	12, July 1849	July	43	L3	
Nicholson, Robert	24, Dec. 1835		estate	L4	
Nicholson, Thomas	23, Oct. 1834	Oct.	36	L2	
Nicholson, William Rozelle	19, July 1849	12, July	11m	L3	
Nickan, (child of John)	14, Feb. 1828	Feb.	1d	L1	
Nickels, Mary W.	29, Nov. 1849	21, Nov.	1- 8m	L3	
Nicoll, Edward	6, Sept 1820	2, Sept		* L3	
Nicolson, John	16, Sept 1841	9, Sept		L3	
Nieblinger, Charles	9, Aug. 1849	July	36	L3	
Nieburn, Elizabeth	31, Oct. 1833	Oct.		L4	
Niehaus, Joseph	8, Jan. 1857		probate	L3	

Name	Notice Date	Death Date	Age		Page	Maiden Name
Niemann, Frederick Wilhelm	9, June 1853		estate		L3	
Niemeyer, Conrad	8, Dec. 1842	Dec.	22		L3	
Nihar, Philip	23, July 1846	July	1- 6m		L3	
Niles, Charles M.	22, June 1848	21, June	17		L3	
Niles, Daniel H.	10, May 1855	3, May	43		L3	
Niles, Daniel H.	7, May 1857		probate		L3	
Niles, Judson	2, Dec. 1847	24, Nov.	21		L3	
Niles, Sarah H.	31, Aug. 1843	19, Aug.	28		L3	
Nilferan, George J.	6, Nov. 1834	Oct.	28		L1	
Nimmo, Matthew	13, Feb. 1845		estate		L3	
Nixon, Catherine Matilda	26, July 1849	16, July			L3	
Nixon, Ellen B.	7, Oct. 1841	5, Oct.			L3	
Nixon, Wilson (Mrs)	13, May 1841	8, May	85	*	L3	
Noble, A.	15, Aug. 1833	Aug.	1- 7m		L1	
Noble, Asiel	9, May 1839		estate		L3	
Noble, Horace	2, Mar. 1854	25, Feb.	83		L3	
Noble, Horace	16, Oct. 1856		probate		L6	
Noble, James	17, Mar. 1831	19, Feb.	48		L4	
Noble, Susan	7, Nov. 1844	Oct.	46		L3	
Noble, Trusuman	15, May 1815		estate		L3	
Noble, William	24, Dec. 1829		estate		L1	
Noble, William	17, Dec. 1846	Dec.	42		L3	
Noble, William	7, May 1840		probate		L3	
Noe, (Mrs)	25, Oct. 1832	19, Oct.			L2	
Noe, Constant	25, July 1833	July	62		L1	
Noe, Peter	18, Aug. 1853	15, Aug.			L3	
Noe, Rachel	12, Dec. 1850	Dec.	36		L3	
Noel, William T.	26, Oct. 1843	16, Oct.			L3	
Noikabuer, Charles	1, Aug. 1850	July	26		L3	
Nolan, Betsy	26, July 1849	July	35		L3	
Nolan, Patrick	10, Mar. 1853	Feb.	24		L3	
Noland, Bridget	31, May 1849	May	21		L3	
Nold, Henry	27, Aug. 1846	19, Aug.	59		L3	
Nolen, Timothy	22, Aug. 1833	Aug.	40		L4	
Nolin, Patrick	13, June 1850	June	25		L3	
Nolker, John G.	3, Apr. 1851	Mar.	23		L3	
Noonan, Mary	28, Aug. 1834	Aug.	38		L1	
Noonan, Timothy	4, Mar. 1841	Feb.	34		L3	
Nordike, (child of J.)	19, July 1832	July	5		L1	
Nordman, Barnard	19, Sept 1850	Sept	23		L3	
Norfolk, Benjamin	9, Feb. 1854	25, Jan.	60		L3	
Norford, Richard	7, Mar. 1850	2, Mar.			L2	
Norman, Elizabeth	12, Sept 1850	Sept	3		L3	
Norris, Alexander	7, Dec. 1848	5, Dec.	77		L3	
Norris, Aquilla	29, Apr. 1812		estate		L3	
Norris, Catharine	15, Nov. 1849	8, Nov.			L3	
Norris, Elizabeth	11, Apr. 1850	7, Apr.	49	*	L3	
Norris, Elizabeth Ratcliff	5, Nov. 1846	30, Oct.	5- 2m-16d		L3	
Norris, George	25, Feb. 1841	Feb.	21	*	L3	
Norris, George Henry	9, July 1846	4, July	11- 3m		L3	
Norris, Gursham	12, Jan. 1837		probate		L3	
Norris, John	18, Oct. 1827	Oct.	2		L3	
Norris, John Summerfield	6, Oct. 1853	29, Sept	29		L3	
Norris, Uriah	7, June 1849	May	37		L3	

Name	Notice Date	Death Date	Age		Page	Maiden Name
Norris, William B.	5, Apr. 1849	30, Mar.	25- 3m		L3	
Northay, Richard	16, Nov. 1837	Nov.	45		L3	
Northrup, William Henry	22, Oct. 1846	15, Oct.	19m		L3	
Norton, Harriet	27, Oct. 1817	22, Oct.		*	L3	
Norton, James	19, Mar. 1846	Mar.	34		L3	
Norton, Lewis	26, June 1845	June	2m		L3	
Norton, Martha	11, Sept 1845	Sept	29		L3	
Norton, Rebecca	7, June 1849	30, May			L3	
Norvell, Catharine Mary	13, Oct. 1842	2, Oct.	27		L3	
Norvell, Lipscomb	16, Mar. 1843	2, Mar.	87	*	L3	
Nott, Henry	11, July 1850	July	31		L3	
Nott, John	1, Aug. 1850	July	1- 6m		L3	
Nourse, Elizabeth M.	8, Apr. 1847	4, Apr.	4		L3	
Nourse, George	27, May 1852		estate		L3	
Nourse, George	5, Jan. 1854		estate		L3	
Nourse, Samuel Purcell	31, Jan. 1856	28, Jan.	17		L3	
Nowland, Mary	25, Oct. 1827	Oct.	42		L2	
Noyes, Joseph	19, Aug. 1820	19, Aug.	25	*	L3	
Nuckols, John	6, Dec. 1855		probate		L3	
Nuessein, Charles	28, Nov. 1850	Nov.	29		L3	
Nugent, William	19, July 1849	July	42		L3	
Nukins, Lucy	14, Mar. 1833	Mar.	80		L1	
Nutall, Mary H.	7, Feb. 1850	Jan.	10m		L3	
Nutt, Adam	7, Dec. 1837		probate		L3	
Nutt, Edward J.	19, July 1849	July	35		L3	
Nutt, Nancy	7, Dec. 1837		probate		L3	
Nutt, Nancy	5, Sept 1839		probate		L3	
Nutting, Eliza	18, Oct. 1827	Oct.	13m		L3	
Nutting, Stephen	9, Aug. 1832		estate		L3	
Nye, (child of Henry)	4, Jan. 1849	30, Dec.	2m		L3	
Nye, (Mrs)	18, Oct. 1832	16, Oct.			L3	
Nye, Maria	15, Apr. 1852	12, Apr.	34	*	L3	Lawrence
Nye, Simon H.	2, Dec. 1847	24, Nov.	7		L3	
Nye, Thomas	11, Mar. 1852	26, Feb.			L3	
Oakley, Charles	8, June 1837	June	21		L2	
O'Banon, John	26, Nov. 1819		estate		L4	
Oberdorf, Francis	13, May 1847	10, May	5m-18d		L3	
Oberdorf, Sarah	19, Sept 1844	11, Sept	56		L3	
Oberhen, Wilhelmina	15, Jan. 1857	7, Jan.	63		L3	
Obold, (Mrs)	1, Nov. 1832	23, Oct.			L4	
O'Briant, Andrew J.	19, Dec. 1850	Dec.	31		L3	
O'Brien, Dennis	14, May 1846	May	24		L3	
O'Brien, Michael	4, July 1850	June	33		L3	
O'Brien, Thomas	3, May 1849	2, May			L2	
O'Bryon, E.D.	30, Aug. 1849	24, Aug.	47		L3	
Ocheltree, Hannah Hunt	3, June 1847	27, May	32		L3	
Ochletree, Alonzo T.	29, July 1841	20, July	16m		L3	
O'Connel, Dinnes (Mrs)	31, May 1849	27, May			L3	
O'Connel, Mary Ann	6, Sept 1849	Aug.	29		L3	
O'Connel, Patrick	8, Aug. 1833	July	32		L1	
O'Connell,	18, Jan. 1849	Jan.			L3	
O'Connell, Charles	14, Feb. 1850	Feb.	30		L3	
O'Connell, Dennis	5, July 1855		probate		L3	

Name	Notice Date	Death Date	Age	Page	Maiden Name
O'Connell, Honora	16, Jan. 1851	13, Jan.	64	L3	
O'Connell, John	9, May 1850	Apr.	22	L3	
O'Connell, William	30, May 1850	May	24	L3	
O'Conner, Daniel	27, Jan. 1848	Jan.	25	L3	
O'Conner, Jeremiah	22, June 1837		probate	L3	
O'Conner, Patrick	29, Aug. 1850	Aug.	2	L3	
O'Conner, Timothy	31, Oct. 1839	Oct.	46	L3	
O'Connor, Mary Ann	2, Oct. 1834	Sept	3	L4	
Odell, Caroline Louisa	7, May 1840	1, May	21m-24d	L3	
Oder, William	19, Apr. 1849	Apr.	31	L3	
O'Donald, Daniel	17, Aug. 1848	Aug.	25	L3	
O'Driscoll, Louisa	28, Feb. 1856	22, Feb.	10- 3m	L3	
Oehler, Simon	14, Aug. 1856		probate	L6	
Oerkues, Anton	25, Dec. 1845	Dec.	24	L3	
Oertels, Jacob	10, Apr. 1856		probate	L3	
O'Ferrall, John	20, Feb. 1811		estate	L3	
O'Ferrall, John	7, Sept 1824		probate	L3	
O'Ferrall, John	24, Oct. 1810	17, Oct.		L3	
O'Ferralls, John	14, Dec. 1824		probate	L3	
O'Ferrel, John	16, Feb. 1827		probate	L3	
Offeorbider, Dorophas	5, Sept 1833	Aug.	30	L1	
Ogan, Jonathan	25, Nov. 1852	12, Nov.	21	L3	
Ogden, Albert	27, Nov. 1845	Nov.	23	L3	
Ogden, Ann Eliza	7, Nov. 1844	4, Nov.	17	L3	
Ogden, Caroline	29, Aug. 1833	Aug.	3	L1	
Ogden, Charles Edward	25, Apr. 1850	19, Apr.	6m	L3	
Ogden, David	20, Oct. 1836		estate	L3	
Ogden, David	29, May 1834		probate	L3	
Ogden, David	9, Aug. 1838		probate	L3	
Ogden, Henry A.	8, Sept 1853	30, Aug.		L3	
Ogden, Isaac A. (Rev)	2, Nov. 1854	15, Oct.	75	L3	
Ogden, James S.	2, Aug. 1849		estate	L3	
Ogg, Loyd	8, Sept 1806		estate	L3	
O'Hagan, Patrick	5, July 1849	June		L3	
O'Hara, Dominic	19, Mar. 1857	14, Mar.	60	L3	
O'Hara, Ezra	15, May 1851	11, May		L3	
O'Hara, Joseph H.	28, May 1846	21, May	13	L3	
O'Hara, Thomas	11, July 1850	July	34	L3	
O'Hara, W.A.	6, Aug. 1857		probate	L3	
O'Hara, William	5, Apr. 1855	1, Apr.	51	L3	
Ohe, Caroline	15, Aug. 1833	Aug.	8m	L1	
O'Herron, Michael	20, Apr. 1848	Apr.	15	L3	
O'Keefe, Dennis	6, Dec. 1855		probate	L3	
O'Lary, Daniel	21, June 1849	June	42	L3	
Oldendoff, Frederick W.	19, July 1849	July	29	L3	
Oldendorff, Fred. W.	19, July 1849	July	3	L3	
Older, George	19, July 1849	July	35	L3	
Oldham, James	17, Aug. 1837	Aug.	10	L3	
Oldham, Mordica	15, June 1848	June	45	L3	
Oldham, T.J.	3, Oct. 1850	Sept	20	L3	
Oldman, George	7, June 1849	30, May		L3	
Olds, Joseph	6, May 1847	27, Apr.	52	L3	
O'Leary, Caroline G.	15, Apr. 1852	12, Apr.	23	L3	
Olinger, Peter	6, Mar. 1856		probate	L3	

Name	Notice Date	Death Date	Age		Page	Maiden Name
Oliphant, William	3, Feb. 1853				L3	
Oliver, Catharine	18, July 1850	July	2		L3	
Oliver, Daniel	23, June 1842	1, June	54		L3	
Oliver, Eliza	28, Apr. 1853	22, Apr.	56		L3	
Oliver, Elizabeth	18, July 1850	July	2		L3	
Oliver, Joseph F.	1, Oct. 1840	23, Sept	29		L3	
Oliver, Lycurgis H.	23, Nov. 1837	14, Nov.	19	*	L3	
Oliver, Mary J.	5, Sept 1833	Aug.	13d		L1	
Oliver, Nicholas	20, July 1837	July	40		L4	
Oliver, Sarah B.	23, Apr. 1840	Apr.	10m		L3	
Oliver, Sarah Maria	14, Feb. 1828	Feb.	20		L1	
Oliver, Washington	2, Apr. 1846	28, Mar.	27		L3	
Oliver, William (Major)	1, Jan. 1852	28, Dec.	64		L3	
Oliver, William (Mrs)	5, May 1853				L3	Ruffin
Ollison, (Capt)	30, Dec. 1852	29, Dec.			L3	
Olmstead, Henry	10, Sept 1846	5, Sept	36	*	L3	
Olmsted, Henry	22, Oct. 1846		estate		L3	
Olmsted, Henry	18, Jan. 1849		estate		L3	
Olmsted, Hetty	13, Sept 1838	3, Sept			L3	
Olney, E.W. (Dr)	27, Feb. 1845	19, Feb.	38		L3	
Olver, Samuel L.	2, Oct. 1856	2, Sept	26		L5	
O'Neal,	23, Mar. 1849	Mar.	11d		L3	
O'Neal, Garret	3, July 1851	June	30		L3	
O'Neal, James	6, June 1833	May	3- 2m		L2	
O'Neal, James	21, Sept 1837		probate		L4	
O'Neal, John	21, Nov. 1844	Nov.	40		L3	
O'Neal, Margaret	8, Mar. 1849	Feb.	25		L3	
O'Neal, Mary	24, May 1849	May	22		L3	
O'Neal, William	12, 19, Oct. 1843			*	L3	
O'Neil, Eliza	16, Oct. 1851	12, Oct.			L3	
O'Neil, John	19, July 1849	July	38		L3	
O'Niel, John	31, July 1845	July	22		L3	
Oniel, Margaret	21, Nov. 1833	Nov.	35		L3	
Onis, Federica Merklein	9, June 1817	22, May			L2	
Oppenheimer, Catharine	12, July 1849	5, July	64		L3	
Oppenheimer, Emanuel	28, Feb. 1856	26, Feb.	77		L3	
Oppliger, Christian	3, Apr. 1845	Mar.	30		L3	
Orange, Elizabeth	16, Oct. 1845	15, Oct.			L3	
Orange, Jane	29, May 1828	May	9m		L2	
Orange, Jane Augusta	2, June 1836	31, May	infant		L3	
Orcutt, Alvin H.	11, Sept 1845		estate		L3	
O'Reilly, P.	7, Jan. 1836	31, Dec.	43	*	L1	
O'Reilly, Patrick	19, Apr. 1845		estate		L3	
Organ, John	24, Oct. 1844	Oct.	21		L3	
Orhman, Daniel	24, Dec. 1846	Dec.	76		L3	
O'Rielly, Patrick	7, May 1840		probate		L3	
Orlick, (child of George)	4, Apr. 1850	Mar.	3d		L3	
Orlopp, Paulina Henrietta	13, Mar. 1856	8, Mar.	2m-11d		L3	
Ormsby, Betsy	29, Dec. 1853	22, Dec.	75		L3	
Orr, Amelia	15, July 1847	16, June	33		L3	Pierson
Orr, James	18, Oct. 1832	15, Oct.			L3	
Orr, John	24, Feb. 1853	19, Feb.	19		L3	
Orr, Rachel	9, Aug. 1838	July	33		L3	
Orr, Robert	21, May 1857		estate		L3	

Name	Notice Date	Death Date	Age		Page	Maiden Name
Orr, Robert	14, 21, Aug. 1856	7, Aug.	86	*	L5	
Orr, Winthrop G.	5, Mar. 1840		estate		L3	
Orr, Winthrop G.	5, Mar. 1840	19, Feb.			L3	
Orth, Adam	5, Feb. 1857		probate		L3	
Orthe, Theodore	29, Aug. 1844	Aug.			L3	
Osborn, E.F. (Mrs)	26, June 1851				L3	
Osborne, (child of John)	14, Nov. 1839	2, Nov.	6		L3	
Osborne, Anna Richards	8, Mar. 1849	1, Mar.	78	*	L3	
Osborne, William H.	23, Oct. 1851	15, Oct.	22		L3	
O'Shaughnessy, Thomas	3, June 1847	May	22		L3	
O'Shea, Emanuel	6, Nov. 1845	Oct.	40		L3	
O'Shortnessey, John	30, Jan. 1851	Jan.	35		L3	
Oskamp, Theodore	6, Dec. 1855		probate		L3	
Oskamp, Theodore	6, Mar. 1856		probate		L3	
Oslen, Joseph	12, Sept 1833	Sept	1- 2m		L1	
Osta, John	8, Aug. 1850	28, July			L3	
Ostrander, Catharine M.	26, Mar. 1857	Mar.	50		L3	
O'Strandler, Charles	22, Jan. 1846	21, Jan.			L1	
Ott, Otho	16, Apr. 1857	7, Apr.	47		L3	
Ottenheimer, Morris	6, Aug. 1846		32		L3	
Otter, Jacob	19, Dec. 1826		probate		L3	
Otto, Harriette A.	23, Oct. 1834	Oct.	22		L2	
Oustoby, William E.	10, Dec. 1840	9, Dec.	46	*	L3	
Outcalt, Mary Ellen	2, July 1846	23, June	4		L3	
Overaker, Catharine	6, Dec. 1849	4, Dec.	18m		L3	
Overend, (Mrs)	15, Aug. 1833	Aug.	59		L1	
Overend, John	14, June 1838		estate		L3	
Overman, Amos	21, Sept 1848	Sept	40		L3	
Owen, Allison	26, Feb. 1857	21, Feb.	53		L3	
Owen, Charles Allison	28, Nov. 1844	26, Nov.	2		L3	
Owen, Edward	13, Nov. 1850	Nov.	35		L3	
Owen, Kesiah A.	17, June 1852	15, June	32		L3	
Owen, Susan Pendleton	11, Aug. 1842	4, Aug.	1		L3	
Owen, Wash	24, May 1849	May	30		L3	
Owens, Anna Belle	15, Mar. 1855	7, Mar.			L3	
Owens, Chauncy B.	10, Dec. 1857		probate		L3	
Owens, David E.	11, July 1833		probate		L3	
Owens, Elizabeth	25, July 1844	20, July	7m-21d		L3	
Owens, Ellen	3, May 1849	Apr.	25		L3	
Owens, Jane	3, July 1845	27, June	22		L3	
Owens, Jane	30, Nov. 1848	26, Nov.	36		L3	
Owens, John	1, Aug. 1839	July	57		L3	
Owens, John Q.	1, Aug. 1833	July	3m		L1	
Owens, Martha J.	12, Feb. 1857	4, Feb.	38		L3	
Owens, Mary A.	24, Aug. 1848	20, Aug.			L3	
Owens, Mary H.	22, Mar. 1855	20, Mar.	2- 8m		L3	
Owens, Michael	3, May 1849	Apr.	36		L3	
Owens, Richard	26, July 1849		estate		L3	
Ownes, Lucy	4, Mar. 1841	25, Feb.	38		L3	
Pace, Catharine	24, Nov. 1842	16, Nov.	58		L6	
Pace, James	22, June 1843	16, June			L3	
Packer, Reuben	1, Aug. 1839	July	37		L3	
Paddack, Lucretia	25, July 1850	17, July			L3	

Name	Notice Date	Death Date	Age		Page	Maiden Name
Paddack, Samuel	9, Aug. 1849		61		L3	
Paddack, Sarah	20, Aug. 1846	15, Aug.	21- 6m-11d		L3	
Paddock, Benjamin	31, May 1832		estate		L3	
Paddock, William C.	10, May 1855	2, May	21		L3	
Padgett, Daniel W.	2, Dec. 1841	26, Nov.			L3	
Page, Francis A.	12, Apr. 1849	9, Apr.	18		L3	
Page, Joseph R., Jr.	12, Sept 1833	Sept	46		L1	
Page, Lewis	5, Apr. 1849	Mar.	24		L3	
Page, Samuel	5, Sept 1839		probate		L3	
Page, Sarah	29, May 1845	May	50		L3	
Page, Thomas	9, Apr. 1857		probate		L3	
Paine, Charles Faris	13, Apr. 1854	10, Apr.			L3	
Paine, Ed. (Gen)	23, Sept 1841	28, Aug.	89		L3	
Paine, Thomas	21, June 1809	8, June			L3	
Painter, (son of Jacob)	16, Nov. 1854	15, Nov.	14		L3	
Palerson, (child of Ludlow)	11, July 1833	July	7m		L1	
Palfrey, George W.	25, Sept 1851				L4	
Palmer, (child of Eliza)	29, Aug. 1850	Aug.	3w		L3	
Palmer, Barnabas	9, Dec. 1816		96		L3	
Palmer, Benjamin	7, Aug. 1845	July	68		L3	
Palmer, C.B.	15, Aug. 1850		estate		L3	
Palmer, Elizabeth	25, Feb. 1847	Feb.	3m		L3	
Palmer, James	29, Aug. 1850	Aug.	17		L3	
Palmer, James	27, Dec. 1838	Dec.	34		L3	
Palmer, M.	25, Oct. 1832	Oct.			L1	
Palmer, Maria	14, Apr. 1842	11, Apr.	32		L3	
Palmer, Mary	26, Jan. 1854	11, Jan.	77		L3	
Palmer, Reuben	28, Sept 1843	Sept	14		L3	
Palmer, Seneca	15, Nov. 1832	Nov.	12		L1	
Palmer, Seneca	7, Feb. 1856		estate		L3	
Palmer, Thomas	27, Aug. 1846	26, Aug.	70	*	L3	
Palmer, Thomas B. (Capt)	17, Aug. 1837	25, July			L1	
Pancoast, Edward	28, Mar. 1839	Mar.	30		L3	
Pancoast, Sidonias	1, Apr. 1847	23, Mar.	85	*	L3	
Pangburn, Nancy	7, Feb. 1856		estate		L3	
Panning, Edward A.	27, May 1841		estate		L3	
Pape, Edward	27, Nov. 1845	Nov.	34		L3	
Parcel, (Mrs)	1, Nov. 1832	30, Oct.			L3	
Parcell, Mary	8, Aug. 1850	July	50		L3	
Paree, (child of Joseph)	26, Sept 1833	Sept	1-11m		L4	
Parent, John	7, Sept 1848	Aug.	35		L3	
Park, Culbertson	21, Sept 1837		probate		L4	
Park, Elizabeth	19, Dec. 1826		probate		L3	
Park, Margaret	18, Dec. 1856	11, Dec.	37		L3	
Park, Mary	20, Mar. 1856	17, Mar.			L3	
Park, Thomas	1, Nov. 1832	27, Oct.			L2	
Parker, (boy)	9, Aug. 1849	8, Aug.	16		L2	
Parker, Angeline	8, Oct. 1857		probate		L3	
Parker, Angeline	4, May 1854	25, Apr.			L3	
Parker, Ann	20, May 1847	May	72		L3	
Parker, C. (Mrs)	27, June 1839	22, June			L3	
Parker, Cecilia	29, Apr. 1847	Apr.	76		L3	
Parker, Charles W.	6, Sept 1849	Aug.	50		L3	
Parker, Edward	26, Nov. 1846	23, Nov.		*	L3	

Name	Notice Date	Death Date	Age		Page	Maiden Name
Parker, Emma	19, Jan. 1854	16, Jan.	1- 9m-11d		L3	
Parker, George	22, Jan. 1816	31, Oct.	23		L1	
Parker, George W.	12, June 1845		estate		L3	
Parker, Henry B.	25, July 1833	July	33		L1	
Parker, Jane	24, May 1849	23, May	17- 5m		L3	
Parker, John M.	3, Aug. 1848	July	17		L3	
Parker, John M.	30, July 1835		estate		L3	
Parker, John M.	12, Feb. 1835		estate		L4	
Parker, Joseph	13, Apr. 1843	Apr.	25		L3	
Parker, Joseph	22, Aug. 1833		estate		L4	
Parker, Major	24, May 1838	May	30		L3	
Parker, Nancy	1, Nov. 1832	23, Oct.			L4	
Parker, Rebecca	25, Apr. 1850	Apr.	60		L3	
Parker, Robert C.	2, Aug. 1824	1, Aug.			L3	
Parker, Stephen	25, Oct. 1832	20, Oct.			L2	
Parker, William	18, Jan. 1844	15, Jan.	38		L3	
Parker, William	2, Oct. 1834	Sept			L4	
Parkeson, (child of John)	4, July 1833	June	3d		L2	
Parkhurst, Charles Lewis	13, Dec. 1838	4, Dec.	21m		L4	
Parks, Jane	5, July 1849	25, June		*	L3	
Parks, Magbury	8, Oct. 1846	Sept	44		L3	
Parks, Martin P. (Lt)	8, July 1852	5, July			L3	
Parks, Matilda M.	21, Nov. 1833	Nov.	6		L3	
Parmelee, Helen F.	12, May 1842	30, Apr.	20m		L3	
Parmelle, Rosewell	5, Sept 1850	Aug.	38		L3	
Parr, Adam	16, July 1857	13, July	20		L3	
Parr, John Adam	2, Aug. 1855		estate		L3	
Parrett, Bridget	12, Dec. 1850	Dec.	2		L3	
Parrish,	31, May 1849	30, May			L3	
Parrish, (Rev)	21, Oct. 1847	17, Oct.			L3	
Parrish, Catharine	29, Apr. 1847	Apr.	31		L3	
Parrish, Elizabeth Ann F.	26, Aug. 1852	24, Aug.	26		L3	
Parrish, Patsy	7, May 1846	Apr.	52		L3	
Parrish, Petsy	22, Jan. 1846	Jan.	95		L3	
Parrish, William V.	21, Feb. 1850	19, Feb.	2		L3	
Parriss, John	31, Aug. 1854	1, July	85	*	L3	
Parry, Ewd.	26, Aug. 1841	10, Aug.	30		L3	
Parson, Sarah	22, May 1827		17		L3	
Parsons, Julia E.	18, June 1857	9, June	27	*	L3	Edwards
Parsons, Sarah	16, Oct. 1834		estate		L3	
Parsons, William	13, July 1824	9, July	56		L3	
Parvain, W.S.	8, Aug. 1833	July	11		L1	
Parvin, (child of Dr.)	1, Aug. 1833	July			L1	
Parvin, Holmes	13, Oct. 1842		estate		L3	
Parvin, Holmes (Dr)	10, Feb. 1842	4, Feb.			L3	
Parvin, Samuel T.	15, Nov. 1855	12, Nov.	37		L3	
Patch, Zulima Lawrence	27, July 1848	19, July	16m		L3	
Paterson, William	1, Jan. 1846	Dec.	21		L3	
Patrick, Clara Ada	27, June 1850	21, June	18m-24d		L3	
Patrick, James DeBrette	4, July 1850	2, July	2-10m		L3	
Patrick, John	11, Feb. 1847	Feb.	33		L3	
Patrorih, (child of Peter)	26, June 1845	June	stillborn		L3	
Pattent, (Mrs)	18, Oct. 1832	14, Oct.			L2	
Patterson, (child of Isaac)	23, Aug. 1838	Aug.	2d		L3	

Name	Notice Date	Death Date	Age	Page	Maiden Name
Patterson, (child)	8, Aug. 1833	July	5	L1	
Patterson, (Miss)	25, Oct. 1832	20, Oct.		L2	
Patterson, Andrew	3, Dec. 1857	24, Nov.	55	L3	
Patterson, Andrew	11, Oct. 1820		estate	L3	
Patterson, Andrew	13, Sept 1827		estate	L3	
Patterson, Anna Sophia	5, Feb. 1852	28, Jan.		L3	
Patterson, Charles N.	13, June 1850	6, June		L3	
Patterson, Cornelia A.	25, Apr. 1833	Apr.	2- 5m	L1	
Patterson, James	24, May 1855		estate	L3	
Patterson, Jane Ann	10, June 1852	3, June	19	L3	
Patterson, John	12, July 1849	July	6	L3	
Patterson, Joseph	10, Feb. 1848	Feb.	28	L3	
Patterson, Josephine	22, Apr. 1847	20, Apr.	18	L3	
Patterson, Margaret	21, June 1849	June	3m	L3	
Patterson, Martha	28, Aug. 1834	Aug.	11m	L1	
Patterson, Martha	29, Aug. 1850	Aug.	23	L3	
Patterson, Mary	13, Jan. 1842	7, Jan.	57	* L3	
Patterson, R.	18, Oct. 1832	13, Oct.		L2	
Patterson, Samuel	15, June 1827		estate	L3	
Patterson, Samuel	28, Dec. 1837		estate	L3	
Patterson, Samuel	15, July 1841	2, June		L3	
Patterson, William	25, July 1833	July	11m	L1	
Pattin, (Mr)	15, Aug. 1833	Aug.		L1	
Patton, Ann	4, July 1827	3, July		L2	
Patton, John	18, July 1850	11, July	38	L3	
Patton, Robert	23, Feb. 1837		probate	L3	
Patton, Thomas	3, May 1855		probate	L3	
Patton, William	12, Nov. 1805	25, Oct.		L3	
Patton, William Humphreys	13, Jan. 1848	5, Jan.	5	L3	
Paul, Jacob	17, May 1849	May	48	L3	
Paul, James (Col)	29, July 1841	23, July	81	L3	
Paul, Jane	18, Oct. 1832	11, Oct.		L4	
Paul, Susan	1, Jan. 1846	24, Dec.		* L3	Carothers
Paulding, John	18, Mar. 1818	20, Feb.		L3	
Paull, Henry	9, Oct. 1834	Sept		L1	
Paull, Henry	15, Sept 1836		probate	L3	
Paver, George W.	12, July 1855	25, June	45	L3	
Pawner, Abigail	28, Feb. 1828		estate	L2	
Paxson, Robert	30, Mar. 1813	Mar.	25	L3	
Payne, Richard	24, Nov. 1842	Nov.	2	L6	
Payne, Robert	11, May 1848	May	74	L3	
Payne, Robert	26, Feb. 1812		estate	L3	
Payne, Thomas	16, Aug. 1838	Aug.	24	L3	
Peabody, Emily Lea	10, Oct. 1844	6, Oct.	25	L3	Lea
Peabody, Hiram	14, 21, July 1842	9, July	26	* L3	
Peabody, Samuel	8, Nov. 1849	Oct.	40	L3	
Peach, Mary	26, Mar. 1846	Mar.	31	L3	
Peach, William	18, July 1844	July	1- 6m	L3	
Peacock, Gemima	15, Apr. 1847	9, Apr.		L3	
Peale, Edmund	2, Oct. 1851	25, Sept		* L3	
Peale, Mary Ann	13, Nov. 1850	8, Nov.		L3	
Pearce, Alice	6, Mar. 1851	27, Feb.	35	L3	
Pearce, Catharine	11, Dec. 1845	10, Dec.		L3	
Pearce, Elizabeth	7, June 1855	5, June		L3	Owens

Name	Notice Date	Death Date	Age		Page	Maiden Name
Pearce, Henry Gardner	10, May 1849	5, May	2- 6m		L3	
Pearce, James	25, Mar. 1852	20, Mar.	1- 9m		L3	
Pearce, Lura	8, Aug. 1850	1, Aug.	25		L3	
Pearce, Nancy Cary	26, Nov. 1846	23, Nov.	5- 7m		L3	
Pearce, Rosana	1, July 1847	June	1		L3	
Pearce, Thomas	14, Nov. 1839	6, Nov.	30		L3	
Pearce, Wilfred Lee	12, Aug. 1847	8, Aug.	8m		L3	
Pearcy, William	12, June 1845	24, Jan.		*	L3	
Pearson, Hester Ann	16, Aug. 1855	12, Aug.	44		L3	
Pearson, Jane J.	10, Jan. 1828	Jan.	3m		L4	
Pease, Aseneath	1, Nov. 1855	10, Oct.	74		L3	
Pease, Charles	1, Dec. 1817		estate		L2	
Peaseiki, Weadimer	27, Apr. 1843	Apr.	42		L3	
Pebbles, Thomas	3, Jan. 1810	30, Dec.		*	L3	
Peck, Henry	7, May 1846	Apr.	70		L3	
Peck, John	18, Jan. 1849	Jan.	60		L3	
Peck, Perry	4, July 1844	June	22		L3	
Peck, William	11, June 1857	2, June	59		L3	
Peck, William K.	25, June 1846	17, June	38	*	L3	
Peckham, Henry William	6, June 1844	25, May	6m		L3	
Pedrick, James	11, Sept 1845		estate		L3	
Peebles, Howard Stephenson	14, Jan. 1847	8, Jan.	3		L3	
Peebles, Isaac	27, Oct. 1831	19, Oct.	38	*	L1	
Peebles, John	5, Nov. 1846	22, Oct.	77	*	L3	
Peebles, Lucy	28, Sept 1848	23, Sept	27		L3	
Peel, Samuel Foster	20, Jan. 1853	9, Jan.	6- 5m- 7d		L3	
Peinter, Peter	12, July 1849	July	27		L3	
Peirce, Elvina	11, July 1850	July	14		L3	
Peirce, Martha	23, July 1840	July	7m		L3	
Peirce, Thomas	28, Mar. 1850	21, Mar.	64		L3	
Peirce, Thomas	11, Apr. 1850		estate		L3	
Peiser, John	23, June 1842	June	28		L3	
Pekles, Sarah J.	15, Nov. 1832	Nov.	5m		L1	
Pelham, Mary Jane	22, Nov. 1855	28, Oct.	39	*	L3	Fisher
Pelsor, Mary	2, Oct. 1834	Sept	9m		L4	
Pencell, Dennis	17, Mar. 1826		probate		L3	
Pendelton, Robert	4, July 1850	June	33		L3	
Pendleton, Frances Jones	15, Mar. 1838	21, Jan.	15m		L3	
Pendleton, Jane F.	11, July 1839	7, July		*	L3	
Pendleton, Jesse Hunt	10, Jan. 1839	7, Jan.	infant		L3	
Pendrick, Charles	4, 18, Sept 1845	1, Sept	30		L3	
Penel, Catharine Elizabeth	6, Jan. 1853	31, Dec.	32		L3	
Penington, John	9, Sept 1841	4, Sept	65	*	L3	
Penn, Clarissa	26, Dec. 1844	Dec.	24		L3	
Penn, H.L.	9, July 1857	29, June			L3	
Penn, Thomas Granville	10, Apr. 1851	7, Apr.	26- 6m		L3	
Penn, William	1, Feb. 1844	4, Jan.	51		L3	
Pennell, James M. (Dr)	30, Apr. 1857	4, Apr.	53		L3	
Pennell, William	5, Mar. 1846	Feb.	3w		L3	
Penniman, Dorinda W.	8, Sept 1842	16, Aug.	51	*	L3	
Penniman, Obediah	9, Aug. 1838		probate		L3	
Penniman, Obediah	5, Sept 1839		probate		L3	
Pennington, John	2, Oct. 1845	25, Sept	28		L3	
Penrose, Samuel	24, Feb. 1853				L3	

Name	Notice Date	Death Date	Age	Page	Maiden Name
Pentecost, A.E.	30, Mar. 1854	17, Mar.	23	L3	
Peplow, Edward P.	5, Apr. 1849	Mar.	48	L3	
Pepper, Henry	15, Nov. 1832	Nov.	36	L1	
Percell, John	18, Jan. 1849	Jan.	22	L3	
Percival, William W.	3, Dec. 1846	Nov.	26	L3	
Perda, Daniel	20, Mar. 1845	Mar.	4	L3	
Perin, O.G.	22, Feb. 1855	19, Feb.	infant	L3	
Perkins, Emily Elizabeth	11, Jan. 1838	10, Jan.		L3	
Perkins, Jacob	6, Sept 1849	30, July	83	L3	
Perkins, James H.	24, Jan. 1850		estate	L3	
Perkins, Samuel G.	3, June 1847	24, May	80	L3	
Perkins, Simon (Gen)	12, Dec. 1844	22, Nov.	60	L3	
Perlee, Peter	8, Nov. 1849		estate	L3	
Perlee, Peter	7, May 1857		probate	L3	
Pernell, Thomas	3, Sept 1840		probate	L3	
Perpin, Aaron F.	18, Sept 1851	16, Sept	24	L3	
Perren, James	4, July 1833	June	7- 9m	L2	
Perret, Phillip H.	11, Apr. 1826	6, Apr.		* L3	
Perrin, Amos	22, June 1837		probate	L3	
Perritt, Amie	12, Dec. 1850	Dec.	30	L3	
Perry, (Commodore)	8, Oct. 1819	23, Aug.		L3	
Perry, Elizabeth	27, Sept 1855	26, Sept	77	L3	
Perry, Ella	15, June 1854	9, June	10- 7m	L3	
Perry, Freeman (Dr)	16, Aug. 1825	27, July	63	* L3	
Perry, Jackson	8, Aug. 1833	July	2	L1	
Perry, John	29, May 1834		probate	L3	
Perry, Joshua H.	13, June 1844		55	L3	
Perry, Lyman	13, Jan. 1853	6, Jan.	46	L3	
Perry, Mary	8, Feb. 1849	Jan.	38	L3	
Perry, Mary Ann	22, July 1847	July	3- 6m	L3	
Perry, Oliver H.	6, June 1833	May	3m	L2	
Perry, Priscila M.	25, July 1850	July	60	L3	
Perry, Samuel	19, Apr. 1855	12, Apr.	72	L3	
Perry, Samuel	7, May 1857		probate	L3	
Perry, Sarah	11, Apr. 1850	Apr.	20	L3	
Perry, Selina S.	7, Aug. 1834	July	12-11m	L3	
Perry, William	28, Jan. 1841	Jan.	27	L3	
Perry, William	3, Mar. 1806		estate	L3	
Perry, William	26, Jan. 1809		estate	L3	
Perry, William	13, Jan. 1806	6, Jan.		* L3	
Person, Helen Claudine	23, Dec. 1847	16, Dec.	7- 5m- 3d	L3	
Person, VanBuren	7, Oct. 1847	6, Oct.	1- - 6d	L3	
Person, William Klein	10, Feb. 1848	7, Feb.	5- 8m	L3	
Pesicoll, Frank	19, July 1849	July	24	L3	
Peter, Martha Custis	20, July 1854	13, July	77	L3	
Peter, William	17, Feb. 1853	7, Feb.		L3	
Petereim, John	26, Aug. 1847	Aug.	38	L3	
Peters, (son of David)	12, July 1809	9, July		L3	
Peters, Augustus Benoit	15, Apr. 1847	6, Apr.	12- 3m	L3	
Peters, Christopher	10, June 1852		estate	L3	
Peters, George	26, June 1851	June	17	L3	
Peters, Hugh	16, June 1831	June		L2	
Peters, Mathias	19, July 1849	July		L3	
Peters, William	10, June 1847	27, May	38	L3	

Name	Notice Date	Death Date	Age	Page	Maiden Name
Petershan, Israel	25, Oct. 1849	Oct.	7m	L3	
Petershans, David C.	26, July 1849	July	3	L3	
Peterson, John	17, Oct. 1844	Oct.		L3	
Peterson, Peter	12, Mar. 1840	Mar.	35	L3	
Petess, Samuel	15, Aug. 1833	Aug.	35	L1	
Pettis, David	25, Apr. 1844	Apr.	57	L3	
Pettit, Agnes	8, Aug. 1850	July	49	L3	
Pettit, Albert	2, Jan. 1845	22, Dec.	37	L3	
Pettit, Jerome Seymore	12, July 1849	4, July	2- 6m	L3	
Pettit, M.S. (Dr)	18, Aug. 1817	28, July		L3	
Pettit, Mary Ann	24, July 1851	17, July	36	L3	
Pettit, Sarah Bella	5, July 1849	30, June	5- 2m-13d	L3	
Pettit, Tharesa Ann	20, June 1833	June	1- 1m	L1	
Petz, William	2, June 1842	May	26	L3	
Peyton, Ran (Col)	30, July 1846	27, July		L3	
Pfaus, Constantine	16, Aug. 1849	Aug.	35	L3	
Pfeffner, Catharine	25, July 1850	July	25	L3	
Pfeifer, Barbara	13, Dec. 1849	Dec.	32	L3	
Pfeifer, John	12, Dec. 1850	Dec.	26	L3	
Pfeiff, Charles	26, July 1849	July	2	L3	
Pfitzer, Charles	11, July 1850	July	30	L3	
Phalen, Daniel	14, Aug. 1856	probate		L6	
Phares, S.S.	13, Sept 1855			L3	
Phares, Washington	25, June 1857	estate		L3	
Pharis, (child of Joseph)	7, Aug. 1834	July	stillborn	L3	
Phelan, Patrick	16, Mar. 1849	Mar.	26	L3	
Phelps, Ann	19, July 1838	estate		L4	
Phelps, Charles	23, Nov. 1854	19, Nov.	74	* L3	
Phelps, Charles	25, Jan. 1855	estate		L3	
Phelps, Charles	10, Jan. 1856	probate		L3	
Phelps, Charles	5, Feb. 1857	probate		L3	
Phelps, Harriet E.	21, Oct. 1847	10, Oct.		L3	
Phelps, Joseph Henry	16, Mar. 1837	8, Mar.		L3	
Phelps, Martha G.	8, Aug. 1833	July	50	L1	
Phelps, Phebe	15, Nov. 1832	Nov.	67	L1	
Phelps, Samuel Cowdrey	29, July 1841	14, July	14m	L3	
Phelps, Samuel W.	20, Apr. 1837	12, Apr.	54	L3	
Pherson, Margaret	2, Aug. 1832	July		L1	
Philips, E.H.	27, Sept 1849	21, Sept		L3	Gregg
Philips, Joseph	25, Jan. 1844	Jan.	13	L3	
Philips, Joseph	1, Feb. 1844	Jan.	13	L3	
Philips, Richard	8, Aug. 1833	July	34	L1	
Phillips, (child of Miles)	22, May 1834	May	1- 1m	L4	
Phillips, (child of Phelina)	3, Mar. 1842	Feb.		L3	
Phillips, (man)	15, Apr. 1852			L3	
Phillips, (Mrs)	16, May 1810	May		L3	
Phillips, Benjamin	16, May 1844	9, May		* L3	
Phillips, Benjamin C.	1, Aug. 1850	estate		L3	
Phillips, Charlotte M.	24, Jan. 1850	19, Jan.		L3	
Phillips, Helen	24, Oct. 1844	18, Oct.	5	L3	
Phillips, James	15, Feb. 1849	Feb.	20	L3	
Phillips, James M.	25, Mar. 1847	Mar.		L3	
Phillips, Jessee B.	22, Apr. 1847	Apr.	4m	L3	
Phillips, John	18, Nov. 1841	Nov.	36	L3	

Name	Notice Date	Death Date	Age	Page	Maiden Name
Phillips, John	31, May 1849	May	40	L3	
Phillips, Joseph	31, Aug. 1854	26, Aug.		L3	
Phillips, Mariah	22, Sept 1842	20, Sept	26	L3	
Phillips, Rufus J.	14, Feb. 1850	9, Feb.	27	L3	
Phillips, S.C. (Mrs)	7, Oct. 1852	26, Sept	49	L3	
Phillips, Sarah E.	23, Oct. 1834	Oct.	4	L2	
Phillips, Thomas	21, Feb. 1828	Feb.	51	L1	
Phillips, Thomas	20, July 1822	18, July		L3	
Phillips, William	24, Aug. 1843	Aug.	43	L3	
Phillips, William	7, May 1840		probate	L3	
Phillips, William	12, July 1855	5, July		L3	
Piat, Daniel	15, Oct. 1808	8, Oct.		L3	
Piatt, Daniel	19, Jan. 1809		estate	L2	
Piatt, Elizabeth	30, Nov. 1854	23, Nov.	78	L3	
Piatt, Frances	6, Feb. 1851		estate	L3	
Piatt, Jacob	4, Sept 1834	16, Aug.	88	* L1	
Piatt, Jacob Wykoff	4, June 1857	28, May	57	L3	
Piatt, John	12, Jan. 1809	10, Jan.	3	L3	
Piatt, John H.	22, Mar. 1822		estate	L3	
Piatt, John H.	26, Dec. 1826		estate	L3	
Piatt, John H.	30, Apr. 1829		estate	L3	
Piatt, Margaret	3, Mar. 1842	2, Mar.	76	L3	
Piatt, Martha	31, Mar. 1842		estate	L3	
Piatt, William M.	29, Dec. 1842	17, Dec.	17	L3	
Pickard, John	6, Mar. 1856		probate	L3	
Pickens, Elizabeth	20, Aug. 1846	Aug.	25	L3	
Picker, Maria G.	14, Feb. 1833	Feb.	1- 1m-16d	L1	
Picket, Maria Garniss	7, Feb. 1833	2, Feb.	13m-15d	L2	
Pickett, (Mrs)	18, Oct. 1832	Oct.		L3	
Pickins, John	26, July 1838	July	45	L3	
Pickle, George	20, Dec. 1825		probate	L4	
Pickleburger, Magdalen	1, Apr. 1847	Mar.	65	L3	
Pidgeon, John H.	1, Oct. 1857	30, Sept		L3	
Pierce, (Mrs)	8, Aug. 1833	July		L1	
Pierce, Alica	15, Nov. 1832	Nov.	26	L1	
Pierce, Arthur F.	11, July 1850	3, July	10m	L3	
Pierce, Charles	15, July 1841	July	9m	L3	
Pierce, Charles J.	13, Nov. 1834	Nov.	11- 6m	L1	
Pierce, Eliza	27, Sept 1809		19	L3	
Pierce, Elizabeth M.	8, Feb. 1844	7, Feb.		L3	
Pierce, James	14, June 1855			L3	
Pierce, John (Rev)	6, Sept 1849	24, Aug.	77	L3	
Pierce, John O.	18, Jan. 1855	9, Jan.	69	L3	
Pierce, Joseph (Capt)	4, July 1850	23, June	41- 1m	L3	
Pierce, Joseph (Mrs)	7, Oct. 1841	23, Sept		* L3	
Pierce, Julia	2, Dec. 1841	24, Nov.	2- 7m	L3	
Pierce, Maria A.	1, Aug. 1833	July	1- -15d	L1	
Pierce, Mary	18, Jan. 1855	25, Dec.	59	L3	
Pierce, Mary S.	16, Aug. 1849	12, July		L3	
Pierce, Mary Shreve	19, July 1849	12, July		L3	
Pierce, Sally	7, Oct. 1841	23, Sept	55	L3	
Pierce, Samuel R.	29, May 1834		probate	L3	
Pierce, William	18, Oct. 1832	12, Oct.		L1	
Pierce, William H.	19, Feb. 1846	13, Feb.	19-10m	L3	

Name	Notice Date	Death Date	Age	Page	Maiden Name
Pierpont, Charles H.	8, Nov. 1849	13, Oct.		L3	
Pierson, Amanda	13, Dec. 1832	Dec.	3	L1	
Pierson, Clara Elizabeth	14, Apr. 1853	7, Apr.	9m- 3d	L3	
Pierson, David	18, Dec. 1834		estate	L2	
Pierson, David	14, July 1836		estate	L3	
Pierson, David	23, Feb. 1837		probate	L3	
Pierson, E.H.	4, Nov. 1830		estate	L4	
Pierson, Ebenezer	8, Jan. 1829		estate	L3	
Pierson, Ebenezer H.	28, July 1831		estate	L3	
Pierson, Elizabeth	30, Aug. 1832	Aug.	1- 6m	L1	
Pierson, Jesse	10, Apr. 1856		probate	L3	
Pierson, John	10, Apr. 1856		probate	L3	
Pierson, Nancy	9, Mar. 1854	29, Feb.		L3	
Pierson, Sarah C.	26, Aug. 1847	18, Aug.		L3	
Pierson, Sineas	28, July 1807	16, July	27	L3	
Pierson, Sineus	27, Mar. 1856		estate	L3	
Pike, Clara H.	29, Apr. 1847	18, Apr.	65	L3	
Pike, Isabella	3, Jan. 1810	25, Dec.	55	L3	
Pike, Joseph	21, Nov. 1844	Nov.	40	L3	
Pike, Sallie	9, Dec. 1852	5, Dec.	4- 1m- 4d	L3	
Piles, William H.	14, Mar. 1850	Mar.	32	L3	
Pind, (child of R.)	14, Mar. 1833	Mar.	stillborn	L1	
Pindell, Catharine	5, Sept 1839		estate	L3	
Pindell, George	6, Dec. 1849	Nov.		L3	
Pine, Lazarus	17, Dec. 1840		estate	L3	
Pine, Lazarus	7, Jan. 1841		estate	L3	
Pingree, Mary Ann	17, Dec. 1840	12, Dec.	17	L3	Halley
Pinkerton, James	9, Oct. 1845	Sept	40	L3	
Pinkney, Charles C. (Gen)	6, Sept 1825	16, Aug.		L3	
Pinkston, (Mr)	25, Oct. 1832	17, Oct.		L1	
Pinkston, Willes	1, Nov. 1832	Oct.	28	L2	
Pinney, George	30, Sept 1852	26, Sept	18	L3	
Pioncon, John N.	25, July 1850	July	35	L3	
Piper, William M.	4, July 1850	June	1	L3	
Pister, Henry	3, July 1845	June	86	L3	
Pitcher, Nancy	20, Apr. 1824	14, Apr.		L3	
Pitman, Jonathan	22, Mar. 1838		probate	L3	
Pitner, Elizabeth	21, June 1849	June	53	L3	
Pitner, George	21, June 1849	June	48	L3	
Pitt, (child of C.)	2, Aug. 1832	July	10m	L1	
Place, Eliza	8, Aug. 1833	July	1- -5d	L1	
Place, Elizabeth	13, Nov. 1856	22, Oct.		L3	Landis
Plater, William	14, June 1849	June	25	L3	
Plato, Hanibal	20, Feb. 1845	Feb.	57	L3	
Pleasants, John Hampden	12, Mar. 1846			L3	
Pleasants, Mary	19, May 1842	18, May	38	L3	
Ploeger, John C.	24, June 1847	June	37	L3	
Plume, Lutitia	15, May 1834	May	39	L4	
Plummer, Elizabeth G.	15, Oct. 1840	22, Sept		L3	
Poindexter, Theodore	21, Sept 1854	4, Sept	*	L3	
Poinier, Henry	22, Aug. 1833	Aug.	1-11m	L4	
Poinier, Isaac	12, Feb. 1857	4, Feb.	77	L3	
Poinier, Jane R.	15, Mar. 1855	25, Feb.	69	L3	
Poinier, John	24, Sept 1840	9, Sept	infant	L3	

Name	Notice Date	Death Date	Age		Page	Maiden Name
Poinsett, Joel R.	1, Jan. 1852	12, Dec.	73		L1	
Poland, Agnes Ann	19, Mar. 1857	15, Mar.	11m		L3	
Poland, Andrew S.	15, Nov. 1832	Nov.	12		L1	
Poland, Joseph Patrick	28, May 1857	22, May	3- 3m		L3	
Poland, William H.	25, Oct. 1832	22, Oct.			L3	
Polfry, (Mrs)	8, Aug. 1833	July			L1	
Polke, William	11, May 1843	26, Apr.	68		L3	
Pollard, Alfred N.	19, June 1851	13, June	43		L3	
Pollard, John	22, Aug. 1833	Aug.	2m		L4	
Pollock, James S.	17, Jan. 1856	13, Jan.	6- 5m		L3	
Pollock, John	20, Apr. 1843		estate		L3	
Pollock, Martha S.	17, July 1851	10, July			L3	
Pollock, Stephen	28, Nov. 1850	Nov.	20		L3	
Pomeroy, Catharine Coolidge	20, Jan. 1842	16, Jan.	1- 3m		L3	
Pomeroy, Clarissa	29, Jan. 1852	20, Jan.	81	*	L3	
Pomeroy, Elizabeth	26, June 1851	23, June	11m		L3	
Pomeroy, Elizabeth R.	18, Nov. 1852	7, Nov.			L3	Worthington
Pomeroy, Samuel Wyllis	17, June 1841		78	*	L3	
Pompey, Eliza	1, July 1852	25, June	54		L3	
Pond, Albert W.	11, Mar. 1852	8, Mar.	16		L3	
Pond, Elizabeth	22, Mar. 1855	15, Mar.	54		L3	
Pool, Charles	18, July 1833	July	15		L2	
Pool, Sophia	20, Nov. 1834	Nov.	40		L1	
Pool, William	9, Mar. 1854	28, Feb.	89		L3	
Poor, (Mr)	23, Oct. 1834	Oct.			L2	
Poor, Erastus	7, 14, Feb. 1850	23, Jan.	53		L3	
Poor, Noah	5, June 1851	4, June			L3	
Pope, Thomas	10, Apr. 1856		estate		L3	
Poplar, Malinda	3, Oct. 1850	Sept	85		L3	
Poppe, John D.	6, Dec. 1855		probate		L3	
Poppingburg, William	20, Apr. 1848	Apr.	34		L3	
Port, (Mrs)	25, Oct. 1832	16, Oct.			L4	
Port, Cheshire	25, Oct. 1832	15, Oct.	98		L4	
Port, Christian	25, July 1833	July	100		L1	
Portal, Jacob Sebastian	22, July 1847	July	24		L3	
Porter, Edward Philbrick	27, June 1850	24, June	3m-15d		L3	
Porter, Hannah	15, Sept 1842	Sept			L3	
Porter, Jonathan L.	30, Sept 1847	26, Sept			L2	
Porter, Martha Ann	29, July 1841	July	2		L3	
Porter, Nancy K.	11, Mar. 1852	8, Mar.		*	L3	
Porter, William	29, May 1834		probate		L3	
Portlow, Alonza	6, Jan. 1848	Dec.	12		L3	
Portselle, Anton	19, Aug. 1852	Aug.	33		L3	
Posey, Charles	12, July 1849	July	2		L3	
Potee, Elizabeth	26, June 1845	June	36		L3	
Potter, Elderkin	30, Oct. 1845	15, Oct.			L3	
Potter, Elizabeth	26, July 1832	July	21		L1	
Potter, Joseph	7, Sept 1824		probate		L3	
Potter, Mary Virginia	29, May 1851	20, May	5		L3	
Potter, Milton	18, Oct. 1832	13, Oct.			L2	
Potter, William	1, Apr. 1847	18, Mar.	75		L3	
Potts, James	22, Feb. 1838	Feb.	60		L3	
Potts, John	3, May 1855		probate		L3	
Potts, John	4, June 1857		probate		L3	

Name	Notice Date	Death Date	Age	Page	Maiden Name
Potts, John	9, July 1857		probate	L3	
Pouder, John	9, Aug. 1838		probate	L3	
Pough, David William	1, Aug. 1833	July	5	L1	
Poundsford, William	21, June 1838	June	48	L3	
Pounsford, Sarah	29, Nov. 1832	Nov.	34	L1	
Pourtal, Rordy	17, Aug. 1848	Aug.	14	L3	
Powel, James	4, July 1833	June	2- 3m-14d	L2	
Powell, Elizabeth	30, Mar. 1849	Mar.	50	L3	
Powell, Hiram	8, May 1845	Apr.	31	L3	
Powell, Jonathan	28, Oct. 1816		estate	L3	
Powell, Mary Elizabeth	26, Feb. 1857	18, Feb.	10m-22d	L3	
Powell, Norman	14, Sept 1848	Sept	18	L3	
Powell, Selina W.	7, Aug. 1856	29, July	46	L5	
Powell, Thomas	28, Mar. 1850	20, Mar.		L3	
Powell, William	3, Jan. 1833	Dec.	34	L4	
Power, James	21, Nov. 1823		estate	L4	
Powers, Catharine M.	18, Feb. 1836	25, Jan.	8- 3m- 9d	L3	
Powers, Charles E.	11, Mar. 1847	Mar.	18	L3	
Powers, Edward	1, May 1828		41	L1	
Powers, Hiram	9, Oct. 1834	Sept	38	L1	
Powers, John	1, Nov. 1832	25, Oct.	72	L1	
Powers, Maria Louisa	14, Aug. 1845	10, Aug.	3-10m	L3	
Powers, Mary Ann	14, Sept 1848	Sept	26	L3	
Powers, Patrick	27, June 1850	June	24	L3	
Powers, Patrick	25, July 1850	July	38	L3	
Powers, Sarah	29, Mar. 1825	20, Mar.	57	* L3	
Powers, Stephen	3, Sept 1819	30, Aug.	51	L3	
Powers, Thankful	25, Apr. 1850	Apr.	60	L3	
Powers, William S.	7, Aug. 1851	30, July		L3	
Powlesson, Peter	5, Mar. 1857		probate	L3	
Powner, John	5, May 1821		estate	L3	
Powner, John	7, Sept 1824		probate	L3	
Praetorius, Edward	7, Aug. 1851	3, Aug.		L3	
Prater, Henry	5, July 1849	June	22	L3	
Prather, John G.	18, Mar. 1847	31, Jan.	23	L3	
Pratt, Jeremiah T. (Rev)	19, Jan. 1854	17, July		L3	
Pratt, Nathan	21, Feb. 1850	Feb.	3w	L3	
Presner, Joseph	12, July 1849	July	30	L3	
Prestley, Jane M.	28, July 1853	25, July		L3	
Prestley, William H.	25, Mar. 1852	19, Mar.	5m	L3	
Preston, Harry	25, Oct. 1832	22, Oct.		L3	
Preston, James	6, Feb. 1845	Jan.	25	L3	
Preston, John P.	23, Feb. 1837		probate	L3	
Price, (Mr)	15, Nov. 1832	Nov.	60	L1	
Price, Anna Maria	29, Oct. 1846	Oct.	16	L3	
Price, Carrie F.	24, Aug. 1854	21, Aug.		L3	
Price, Daniel	25, June 1840		estate	L3	
Price, David	4, May 1822		estate	L3	
Price, David	25, June 1840		estate	L3	
Price, Elizabeth	25, Jan. 1844	16, Jan.	34	L3	
Price, Erastus W.	8, Nov. 1855		probate	L3	
Price, Eunice	8, Aug. 1850	July	54	L3	
Price, Evan	29, Dec. 1821		estate	L3	
Price, Frances D.	17, May 1849	11, May	29- 6m	L3	

Name	Notice Date	Death Date	Age		Page	Maiden Name
Price, Hannah Fisher	1, Aug. 1850	25, July	57		L3	
Price, Hezekiah	22, June 1837		probate		L3	
Price, Jacob F. (Rev)	10, June 1847	27, May			L3	
Price, James	28, Aug. 1834	Aug.	3		L1	
Price, James	11, Oct. 1832	5, Oct.			L2	
Price, James A.	3, Apr. 1828		estate		L3	
Price, John	19, July 1832	July	54		L1	
Price, John	4, June 1857		68	*	L3	
Price, John	16, Oct. 1834		estate		L3	
Price, John W.	27, Oct. 1831		probate		L1	
Price, Margaret	5, Oct. 1848	Sept	40		L3	
Price, Maria	3, Apr. 1811	29, Mar.			L3	
Price, Nancy	24, Mar. 1806	22, Mar.	30		L3	
Price, Sarah	12, June 1828		24		L3	
Price, Sarah	9, May 1839	8, May	74	*	L3	
Price, Watkin	1, Jan. 1852	27, Dec.	46		L3	
Price, William	12, Sept 1833	Sept	4m		L1	
Price, William	5, Sept 1839		probate		L3	
Priest, Joseph	20, June 1844	June	18		L3	
Priestly, Timothy (Rev)	22, Apr. 1816				L1	
Prince, Joseph	19, Sept 1833	Sept	45		L4	
Prince, Sally	30, Apr. 1808	21, Apr.			L3	Conn
Pringe, (Mrs)	17, Aug. 1854	26, July			L3	Harrod
Prisch, Daniel	5, Sept 1839		probate		L3	
Pritchard, Elizabeth	25, July 1850	July	9m		L3	
Pritchet, Nicholas	1, July 1841	June	35		L3	
Probes, Perry	2, Aug. 1832	July	4- 6m		L1	
Procter, Martha	1, Nov. 1832	Oct.	32		L2	
Procter, Thomas Harley	23, Apr. 1857	18, Apr.	42		L3	
Proctor, Alfred	23, Oct. 1834	Oct.	22		L2	
Proebster, Caroline	10, Sept 1857		probate		L3	
Proffitt, George H.	16, Sept 1847	7, Sept			L3	
Prosky, Henry	10, June 1852	4, June			L3	
Prout, George Brown	7, Sept 1848	Aug.	26		L3	
Prouty, Phineas	18, Oct. 1832	12, Oct.			L1	
Pruck, John	9, Mar. 1837	Mar.	62		L3	
Pruden, David	11, July 1833		probate		L3	
Pruden, William	7, June 1855		probate		L3	
Pruzier, Magdalena	12, July 1849	July	44		L3	
Pryer, Moses	9, Aug. 1838		probate		L3	
Pugh, (child of L.)	1, Nov. 1832	26, Oct.			L3	
Pugh, (Mrs)	1, Nov. 1832	24, Oct.			L4	
Pugh, David	9, Nov. 1819	5, Nov.			L3	
Pugh, J.W.	5, Mar. 1857	25, Feb.			L3	
Pugh, John	27, Sept 1855	24, Sept	76-11m-17d	*	L3	
Pugh, Lot	10, Apr. 1851	3, Apr.	60		L3	
Pugh, Michael	14, Nov. 1844	12, Nov.			L3	
Pugh, Nancy	1, Apr. 1816	27, Mar.			L3	
Pugh, Penelope A.	15, Aug. 1833	Aug.	1		L1	
Pugh, Samuel	19, Sept 1833	Sept	3- 6m		L4	
Pugh, Samuel Miller	2, Apr. 1846	1, Apr.	14m-18d		L3	
Pugsby, David	29, Jan. 1852	24, Jan.			L3	
Pullan, John	24, Feb. 1842	23, Jan.	24		L3	
Pullan, John	30, June 1842		estate		L3	

Name	Notice Date	Death Date	Age		Page	Maiden Name
Pullan, Thomas	1, Mar. 1838		estate		L3	
Pullan, Thomas	25, Jan. 1838	27, Dec.			L3	
Pully, (Mrs)	7, Aug. 1834	July			L3	
Pumphrey, Nicholas F.	15, Apr. 1847	10, Apr.	25		L3	
Punshon, Elizabeth	31, Dec. 1846	22, Dec.	68		L3	
Punshon, Robert (Rev)	3, Aug. 1848	2, Aug.	72		L3	
Purcel, John	23, Feb. 1837		probate		L3	
Purcell, John	9, Aug. 1838		probate		L3	
Pursel, John	7, June 1855		probate		L3	
Pursell, Joseph	20, Jan. 1831		estate		L2	
Putnam, David	10, Apr. 1856	31, Mar.	87	*	L3	
Pye, Sarah	26, July 1832	July	2-10m		L1	
Pyle, Rebecca	17, Sept 1846	Sept	42		L3	
Pyle, Susan	7, Feb. 1856		probate		L3	
Pyne, Mary Jane	12, Sept 1833	Sept	3m		L1	
Quail, Robert	31, Oct. 1850	Oct.	67		L3	
Quamby, Salina	29, Aug. 1833	Aug.	11m-12d		L1	
Quaris, Sarah	23, Sept 1847	Sept	9		L3	
Quarls, Susan	25, Oct. 1832	23, Oct.			L3	
Quarter, William (Bishop)	20, Apr. 1848				L3	
Questa, Catharine	31, July 1845	July	33		L3	
Questa, J.B.	4, June 1857		probate		L3	
Questa, John	9, Apr. 1857		probate		L3	
Questa, John B.	10, Dec. 1857		probate		L3	
Quigley, (child of Hannah)	21, Nov. 1833	Nov.	1d		L3	
Quinlan, John	2, Mar. 1848	Feb.	33		L3	
Quinn, Alice	26, June 1851	June	10m		L3	
Quinn, Charles Henry	15, Feb. 1855	11, Feb.	5- 6m-30d		L3	
Quinn, Elizabeth	15, Aug. 1850	13, Aug.	66		L3	
Quinn, Ellen	21, June 1849	June	3		L3	
Quinn, George W.	27, Dec. 1855	13, Dec.			L3	
Quinn, James	21, June 1849	June	30		L3	
Quinn, John	28, June 1849	June	1		L3	
Quinn, Mary	18, July 1850	July	3		L3	
Quinn, Michael	27, June 1850	June	10		L3	
Quinn, Patrick	6, Dec. 1855		probate		L3	
Quinn, Patrick	10, Sept 1857		probate		L3	
Quinslow, Jonathan	24, Apr. 1851	23, Apr.			L3	
Quinton, James	25, Oct. 1832	22, Oct.			L3	
Quinton, Littleton	30, Apr. 1857	26, Apr.	77	*	L3	
Quirk, William	13, Mar. 1851	Mar.	22		L3	
Rachael, Herman H.	29, June 1848	June	35		L3	
Racken, Barbara	8, Jan. 1846	Dec.	57		L3	
Rackett, Joshua Y.	19, July 1849	15, July	72		L3	
Racop, Terescok	1, Aug. 1850	July	1		L3	
Radcliff, Harriett	2, Jan. 1851	29, Dec.		*	L3	
Radcliff, William	26, Aug. 1852	19, Aug.			L3	
Raeb, Anna Maria	6, Nov. 1834	Oct.	7- 7m-18d		L1	
Rag, Robert	3, Jan. 1833	Dec.	30		L4	
Ragin, John M.	24, Nov. 1853	17, Nov.			L3	
Ragley, Talever	23, May 1833	May	47		L4	
Rainforth, William	22, June 1837		probate		L3	

Name	Notice Date	Death Date	Age		Page	Maiden Name
Rainforth, William	3, Dec. 1840		probate		L3	
Rains, Nancy	11, May 1848	2, May	86		L3	
Rakit, John	12, Aug. 1852	Aug.	40		L3	
Rambo, Lucinda	3, Nov. 1836		15		L3	
Rampy (child of Mr)	7, Aug. 1834	July			L3	
Ramsay, David (Dr)	29, May 1815	8, May	66		L3	
Ramsay, John	11, July 1833		probate		L3	
Ramsay, John	15, Sept 1836		probate		L3	
Ramsay, Margaret Jane	12, Aug. 1841	Aug.	5		L3	
Ramsay, Nathan	12, Jan. 1813		estate		L2	
Ramsay, Samuel	20, Oct. 1831		estate		L3	
Ramsay, Samuel (Dr)	24, Feb. 1831		estate		L3	
Ramsay, Susan Emma	8, Jan. 1846	4, Jan.	24		L3	
Ramsay, Thomas (Capt)	8, Sept 1818	6, Aug.			L2	
Ramsay, William	22, Apr. 1825	21, Apr.			L3	
Ramsay, William	20, Jan. 1831		estate		L4	
Ramsdale, John	18, Apr. 1850		estate		L3	
Ramsdell, Clarissa	24, Feb. 1848	Feb.	25		L3	
Ramsey, Elizabeth	20, Mar. 1845	17, Mar.	6		L3	
Ramsey, Elizabeth	7, June 1849	29, May	77		L3	
Ramsey, Elizabeth Juliana	16, Dec. 1816	6, Dec.			L2	
Ramsey, Francis H.	13, June 1844	7, June			L3	
Ramsey, John (Col)	8, Sept 1831	29, Aug.	53		L1	
Ramsey, Tirzah Alvord	20, July 1843	13, July	14m		L3	
Ranabon, Jane	28, Aug. 1834	Aug.			L1	
Rand, Maria	18, Sept 1834	Sept			L1	
Randall, Lydia	29, Aug. 1833	Aug.	41- 4m		L1	
Randle, William, Jr.	16, Dec. 1852	9, Dec.	4		L3	
Rands, Mary Delafield	19, Sept 1850	12, Sept	62		L3	
Raney, Margaret	1, Dec. 1842	16, Nov.	30	*	L3	Morrow
Rankens, Robert	15, Aug. 1850	Aug.	22		L3	
Rankin, William	2, Aug. 1849	23, July	51	*	L3	
Rankin, William	9, Aug. 1849		estate		L3	
Rannells, Sarah Jane	25, Feb. 1836	24, Feb.	18		L1	
Ranney, Catharine M.	8, Dec. 1842	6, Dec.	20m-13d		L3	
Ranney, Clara	31, Apr. 1845	30, Apr.	21m-11d		L3	
Ranney, Mary Eliza	20, Mar. 1851	14, Mar.	11- 9m		L3	
Ranshin, John	20, Apr. 1848	Apr.	30		L3	
Ranster, Robert	10, Apr. 1856		probate		L3	
Rapee, Esther	15, July 1847	July	16		L3	
Raper, Holley	5, Dec. 1850	29, Nov.	32		L3	
Raper, Holly	17, Apr. 1856		estate		L3	
Raper, Millisent	25, Aug. 1853	17, Aug.			L3	
Raper, William H. (Rev)	19, Feb. 1852	11, Feb.	58		L3	
Rapp, John	17, Sept 1846	Sept	39		L3	
Rappelyea, Mary C.	1, Aug. 1833	July	36		L1	
Rariden, James	30, Oct. 1856	26, Oct.	53		L5	
Rassender, Louisa	24, May 1849	May	17		L3	
Rathmann, Henry	23, Aug. 1849	Aug.	26		L3	
Ratsterken, Oliver	14, May 1846	May	11		L3	
Rattigan, John	8, June 1848	May	1m		L3	
Raulman, Barnard	27, Sept 1849	Sept	3- 6m		L3	
Rausch, Phillip	2, Dec. 1852		estate		L3	
Rawlings, A.W. (Dr)	3, July 1845	21, June	38		L3	

Name	Notice Date	Death Date	Age		Page	Maiden Name
Rawlings, Hezekiah	25, Jan. 1849	Jan.	14		L3	
Rawlins, (child of Hugh)	25, July 1833	July	16d		L1	
Rawlins, John Rogers	25, Mar. 1818	4, Mar.		*	L3	
Rawson, Charles Grindal	24, Mar. 1853	20, Mar.	4m-16d		L3	
Rawson, Hannah Child	25, Dec. 1856	21, Dec.	11		L3	
Ray, Catharine	5, July 1855	29, June			L3	
Ray, Charles	14, Aug. 1845	Aug.	1d		L3	
Ray, Henry	4, Apr. 1839	Mar.	13		L3	
Ray, James B.	10, Aug. 1848	4, Aug.	54		L3	
Ray, Joseph (Dr)	19, Apr. 1855	19, Apr.	48		L3	
Ray, Lemuel B.	5, Aug. 1852		26		L3	
Ray, Margaret Jane	8, Sept 1853	3, Sept			L3	Baker
Ray, Susan	2, May 1839	Apr.	18m		L3	
Ray, Valentine	19, Feb. 1852	13, Feb.			L3	
Ray, William	10, Apr. 1851	3, Apr.			L3	
Raymond, Cornelia Maria	23, May 1850	17, May	1		L3	
Raymond, Frank Macy	11, July 1850	4, July	8		L3	
Raymond, Franklin W.	27, Sept 1849	20, Sept	16m		L3	
Raymond, Helen	24, July 1845	17, July	17m		L3	
Raymond, Henry Hamline	8, June 1848	5, June	7-11m-26d		L3	
Raymond, Martha H.	24, May 1849	16, May	32		L3	Macy
Raymond, Mary Constantia	25, July 1850	18, July	7- 7m		L3	
Raymond, Reginold Heber	8, May 1851	1, May	12		L3	
Raymond, S.M.	2, Aug. 1849	27, July	40		L3	
Raynes, Joseph	17, May 1849	8, May	45	*	L3	
Read, (child of Sarah)	17, Jan. 1850	Jan.	stillborn		L3	
Read, Aaron	21, Oct. 1847	Oct.	43		L3	
Read, David	9, Aug. 1849	July	35		L3	
Read, Francis	25, Feb. 1836	20, Feb.	37		L2	
Read, Francis	5, Sept 1839		probate		L3	
Read, James	19, Sept 1850	10, Sept	48		L3	
Read, James	21, Feb. 1839	Feb.	50		L3	
Read, James (Col)	1, Jan. 1805				L3	
Read, John	10, Jan. 1856	3, Dec.		*	L3	
Read, John M.	16, Mar. 1848	Mar.	16m		L3	
Read, Ruth	14, Aug. 1845	Aug.	28		L3	
Read, Sarah	23, Dec. 1847	Dec.	45		L3	
Read, William George	16, Apr. 1846	7, Apr.	46		L3	
Reader, Melvin	11, Sept 1834	Aug.	10m		L1	
Ready, Ellen	23, Mar. 1849	Mar.	8m-15d		L3	
Reagin, Nathaniel	12, Aug. 1847	Aug.	35		L3	
Reaitner, (woman)	9, Aug. 1849	July	50		L3	
Reaker, Utman	11, July 1850	July	21		L3	
Ream, Samuel	25, Sept 1845	18, Sept			L3	
Rebekah, Mary Ann	4, Apr. 1833	Mar.	8m-20d		L1	
Rechstein, Daniel	3, Jan. 1850	Dec.	29		L3	
Reckett, Louisa	12, July 1849	10, July	72		L3	
Reclor, Frederick	1, Nov. 1832	26, Oct.			L1	
Rector, Nelson (Major)	5, Feb. 1816	17, Nov.			L3	
Reddick, Richard P.	25, July 1833	July	5		L1	
Redding, Catharine M.	21, Nov. 1833	Nov.	3		L3	
Redding, Harriet	21, May 1846	May	19		L3	
Reddish, Sarah	8, Nov. 1838		probate		L3	
Reddish, Stephen	8, Nov. 1838		probate		L3	

Name	Notice Date	Death Date	Age	Page	Maiden Name
Reddish, Thomas	10, Nov. 1831	17, Aug.		L2	
Reddish, Thomas	20, Apr. 1837		estate	L3	
Reddish, Thomas	29, Nov. 1838		estate	L3	
Reddish, Thomas	7, May 1840		probate	L3	
Reddish, Thomas (heirs of)	23, Feb. 1837		probate	L3	
Redfield, Ann	28, Oct. 1841	23, Oct.		* L3	
Redhead, James Clarke	1, Nov. 1855	24, Oct.	38	L3	
Redhead, John	22, Apr. 1852	19, Apr.	75	L3	
Redhead, John Wesley	2, Aug. 1849	25, July	28	L3	
Redinbo, Adam	17, Mar. 1836		estate	L3	
Redinbo, Adam	23, Feb. 1837		probate	L3	
Redington, Isaac F.	2, May 1850	Dec.		L3	
Redman, Patrick	28, Sept 1848	Sept	52	L3	
Redman, William Boone	9, Mar. 1854	7, Mar.	7- 6m-21d	L3	
Redmand, John	8, Aug. 1833	July	28	L1	
Ree, Marion	4, Nov. 1847	1, Nov.	16m	L3	
Reed, (child of Isaac)	5, Nov. 1846	Oct.	stillborn	L3	
Reed, (child of John)	20, Sept 1832	Sept	3	L1	
Reed, (child of Sarah A.)	13, July 1843	July	7w	L3	
Reed, Agnes	5, Oct. 1854	2, Oct.	74	L3	
Reed, Ann M.	15, May 1834	May	26	L4	
Reed, Charles J.	30, Apr. 1846	Apr.	5d	L3	
Reed, Daniel	4, Apr. 1844	Mar.	1	L3	
Reed, Elizabeth	7, Sept 1854	30, Aug.	39	* L3	Beebee
Reed, Elizabeth	27, Dec. 1832		estate	L3	
Reed, Hamilton	25, Mar. 1816		estate	L1	
Reed, Henry	2, July 1846		estate	L3	
Reed, Hensey	12, July 1849	July	14	L3	
Reed, Hugh	25, Oct. 1849	Oct.	31	L3	
Reed, Jane	19, July 1855	11, July		L3	
Reed, John (Lt)	23, Mar. 1854	4, Mar.	90	L3	
Reed, Joseph	2, Feb. 1843	7, Jan.	95	* L3	
Reed, Louis Henry	25, Feb. 1841	18, Feb.	12	L3	
Reed, Luther	10, May 1814		estate	L1	
Reed, Luther	18, Dec. 1815		estate	L3	
Reed, Martin	25, July 1850	July	20	L3	
Reed, Mary	31, Dec. 1846	Dec.	22	L3	
Reed, Mary Ann	30, Aug. 1832	Aug.	18	L1	
Reed, N.C.	2, Feb. 1854	28, Jan.		L3	
Reed, Nelson	22, May 1851		estate	L3	
Reed, Oglen Livingston	26, Sept 1833	Sept	1- 6m	L4	
Reed, Rachel	6, Oct. 1807	25, Sept		L3	
Reed, Rosanda P.	19, Apr. 1849	Apr.	24	L3	
Reed, Susan C.	16, Aug. 1849	14, Aug.	30	L3	
Reeder, (man)	19, Nov. 1857	18, Nov.		L3	
Reeder, (Mrs)	8, Nov. 1832	30, Oct.		L4	
Reeder, Alfred	8, Apr. 1841		estate	L3	
Reeder, Alfred S.	21, Apr. 1842		estate	L3	
Reeder, Anne	21, July 1821	6, July	76	L3	
Reeder, Eratus S.	26, July 1832	July	11m-11d	L1	
Reeder, George McAlpin	5, Apr. 1849	28, Mar.	21m	L3	
Reeder, Henson	27, Oct. 1812		estate	L2	
Reeder, Henson	19, June 1811		estate	L3	
Reeder, John	15, Nov. 1832	Nov.	32	L1	

Name	Notice Date	Death Date	Age		Page	Maiden Name
Reeder, Julia Symmes	14, Mar. 1844	9, Mar.	55		L3	
Reeder, Mary	18, Jan. 1808	17, Jan.			L3	
Reeder, Micajah	12, Oct. 1843		65		L3	
Reeder, Nathaniel	15, Sept 1836		probate		L3	
Reeder, Nathaniel	12, Jan. 1837		probate		L3	
Reemelin, Matilda	17, Sept 1857	15, Sept	13		L3	
Rees, Elias	11, July 1833		probate		L3	
Rees, George	25, Feb. 1847	Feb.	31		L3	
Rees, Samuel	1, Oct. 1846		estate		L3	
Reese, (son of G.W.)	10, June 1852	8, June			L3	
Reese, David T.	20, Sept 1827	Sept	14m		L1	
Reese, Edward J.	4, Mar. 1841	Feb.	27		L3	
Reese, Granville	16, June 1842	June	34		L3	
Reese, Henry	4, May 1854	27, Apr.			L3	
Reese, John	8, Aug. 1833	July	4		L1	
Reese, John	26, Sept 1833	Sept	26		L4	
Reese, Margaret Morgan	29, July 1847	26, July	3- 8m		L3	
Reeves, Electra	26, July 1849	21, July			L2	
Reeves, Florence May	23, June 1853	21, June	1- 7m-22d		L3	
Reeves, George	20, Oct. 1853	14, Oct.	60		L3	
Reeves, Jane	22, Nov. 1838	Nov.	24		L3	
Reeves, Josias	14, Oct. 1841	22, Sept	81	*	L3	
Reeves, Thomas B.	6, Nov. 1834	Oct.	11m		L1	
Reggs, Mary Ann	25, July 1844	July	25		L3	
Reginier, Julius	16, Mar. 1854	17, Feb.	50		L3	
Regisinger, Joseph	10, Jan. 1850	3, Jan.			L2	
Rehfuss, L.	5, Mar. 1857		probate		L3	
Rehfuss, L. (Dr)	2, Aug. 1855	31, July	49		L3	
Rehfuss, Louis	2, Oct. 1856		estate		L8	
Reich, John	8, Jan. 1857		probate		L3	
Reichard, Martin	12, Oct. 1848	Oct.	48		L3	
Reichs, John	7, June 1855		probate		L3	
Reid, John (Major)	12, Feb. 1816	18, Jan.			L3	
Reid, Robert Raymond	29, July 1841	1, July	48		L3	
Reiley, Joseph H.	30, Mar. 1849	21, Mar.			L3	
Reilly, Elizabeth	6, May 1830	29, Apr.			L3	
Reilly, Thomas	20, Aug. 1835		estate		L3	
Reilly, Thomas	27, Sept 1838		estate		L3	
Reilly, Thomas	22, Mar. 1838		probate		L3	
Reilly, Thomas	7, Jan. 1836		estate		L4	
Reily, Catharine	27, Jan. 1848	22, Jan.	28		L3	Campbell
Reily, Jenny	2, Feb. 1854	20, Jan.	7		L3	
Reily, John	24, May 1849	May	24		L3	
Reinland, Mathias	21, Sept 1848	Sept	60		L3	
Reinlin, Anthony	5, Feb. 1857		probate		L3	
Reister, Isaac S.	13, Mar. 1845	5, Mar.	3-10m-21d		L3	
Remington, Betsy	18, Mar. 1847	17, Mar.		*	L3	
Remington, John R.	3, Nov. 1853	18, Oct.			L3	
Rempper, (boy)	1, Jan. 1852	28, Dec.	12		L3	
Remring, Catharine	5, Feb. 1852	28, Jan.			L4	
Remspark, Mary	29, Aug. 1844	Aug.	16		L3	
Rench, Harriet	26, July 1849	July	40		L3	
Rendell, Charles	5, Nov. 1846	Oct.	21		L3	
Rendinger, Barbara	9, Aug. 1855		probate		L3	

Name	Notice Date	Death Date	Age		Page	Maiden Name
Renick, George James	1, Feb. 1844	25, Jan.	61		L3	
Reno, Samuel W.	3, May 1855		probate		L3	
Reno, Samuel W.	6, Sept 1855		probate		L3	
Reno, Samuel W.	4, June 1857		probate		L3	
Renshaw, Augusta A.	15, Sept 1853	31, Aug.	19- 6m		L3	
Renshaw, James	19, Sept 1833	Sept	9m		L4	
Renshaw, Mary Ann	10, Feb. 1848	Feb.	28		L3	
Renton, James	19, Mar. 1857		estate		L3	
Rentz, Adam K.	6, June 1844	May	50		L3	
Rentz, Elizabeth	29, Apr. 1847	Apr.	10m		L3	
Repperdine, John	13, Dec. 1849	Dec.	34		L3	
Resor, Edward	5, July 1849	27, June	infant		L3	
Resor, Jacob	18, Feb. 1836	5, Feb.	2		L3	
Resor, Jacob	16, Jan. 1845	1, Jan.	61		L3	
Resor, James	29, Jan. 1846	Jan.	23		L3	
Resor, Lydia	18, July 1844	12, July	23		L3	
Resor, Reuben P.	24, Feb. 1853	12, Feb.	40		L3	
Resor, Reuben P.	3, Mar. 1853	21, Feb.	40		L3	
Resor, Reuben P.	9, Aug. 1855		probate		L3	
Resor, Walter Gordon	29, June 1848	29, June			L3	
Rex, George	26, Sept 1844		estate		L3	
Reynolds, Amanda	2, Aug. 1838	1, Aug.	10		L3	
Reynolds, David	9, May 1850	28, Apr.	35		L3	
Reynolds, Edward	7, Feb. 1833	Feb.	3- 6m		L1	
Reynolds, Elizabeth	27, Nov. 1834	Nov.	7		L1	
Reynolds, Elizabeth	18, July 1826	7, July	19	*	L3	Guest
Reynolds, G.K.	9, Aug. 1855		probate		L3	
Reynolds, John	27, Dec. 1855	21, Dec.	80- 8m		L3	
Reynolds, John D.W.	19, Jan. 1822	16, Jan.			L3	
Reynolds, John P.	10, May 1849	9, May	54		L3	
Reynolds, Joseph R.	1, Feb. 1849	25, Jan.			L1	
Reynolds, Mary B.	30, May 1839	25, May	19		L2	
Rhees, Morgan I. (Rev)	15, Jan. 1805				L3	
Rhinehart, (Mrs)	7, Sept 1854	3, Sept			L3	
Rhoades, Edward	22, Sept 1836	21, Sept	24	*	L4	
Rhoarback, Philip	26, Aug. 1847	Aug.	29		L3	
Rhodes, Frances A.	19, Feb. 1852	18, Feb.	34- 5m		L3	
Rhodes, Jennie G.	13, Mar. 1856	27, Jan.			L3	Webb
Rhodes, John	14, Mar. 1826		estate		L3	
Rhodes, John W.	5, Nov. 1840	16, Oct.	infant		L2	
Rhodes, Stephen S.	8, June 1848	May	75		L3	
Rhodes, William H.	25, Dec. 1851	27, Nov.	33	*	L3	
Rhomers, John	19, July 1849	July	37		L3	
Rice, (child of Jacob)	12, Oct. 1824		infant		L3	
Rice, Aaron B.	6, June 1833	May	33		L2	
Rice, Abigail	23, Oct. 1856	3, Oct.	56		L5	Hunt
Rice, Decries	11, Jan. 1844	Jan.	36		L3	
Rice, George	18, Oct. 1832	Oct.	30		L4	
Rice, James	13, Jan. 1842	24, Dec.	116-7m		L3	
Rice, John	5, July 1849	June	47		L3	
Rice, John	15, Feb. 1838		estate		L3	
Rice, Josiah	4, Nov. 1847	Oct.	30		L3	
Rice, Mary Catharine	13, Apr. 1843	Apr.	20		L3	
Rice, Mary K.	26, Dec. 1839	20, Dec.			L3	

Name	Notice Date	Death Date	Age		Page	Maiden Name
Rice, Mary Una	7, Oct. 1852	3, Oct.	1-11m		L3	
Rice, Michael	1, Nov. 1855	28, Oct.			L3	
Rice, William P.	1, June 1843	31, May		*	L3	
Richards, (child of Mary)	11, Jan. 1844	Jan.	stillborn		L3	
Richards, Andrew	24, July 1845	July	24		L3	
Richards, Charles Frederick	6, Sept 1855	5, Sept	16m		L3	
Richards, Chester	14, Dec. 1848	Dec.	52		L2	
Richards, Elizabeth	10, Oct. 1850	8, Oct.			L3	
Richards, Emma W.	21, Sept 1854	12, Sept			L3	
Richards, J.P.	18, Oct. 1832	13, Oct.			L2	
Richards, Janet	23, Mar. 1819	21, Mar.			L3	
Richards, John W.	16, Feb. 1854	24, Jan.	51		L3	
Richards, Joseph	16, Feb. 1827		probate		L3	
Richards, Lydia H.	2, May 1850	25, Apr.		*	L3	Williamson
Richards, Susan Huntington	11, Dec. 1845	3, Dec.	infant		L3	
Richardson, Adah Frances	16, Dec. 1852	8, Dec.	2- -8d		L3	
Richardson, Alfred	19, July 1849	16, July	15m		L3	
Richardson, Andrew	25, Oct. 1832	19, Oct.			L2	
Richardson, Charles	5, Sept 1833	Aug.	2- 6m-13d		L1	
Richardson, Charles	3, Feb. 1848	Jan.	9m		L3	
Richardson, Edmund Lawrence	6, June 1850	2, June	infant		L3	
Richardson, Eliza	15, Nov. 1832	Nov.	39		L1	
Richardson, Lawrence	24, Aug. 1848	15, Aug.	infant		L3	
Richardson, Malachiah	10, May 1814		estate		L2	
Richardson, Mary	18, Mar. 1847	Mar.	83		L3	
Richardson, Mary	20, Aug. 1857	13, Aug.	21- 8m		L3	
Richardson, Mary A.	15, Aug. 1833	Aug.	28		L1	
Richardson, Mary Ann	10, May 1849	May	40		L3	
Richardson, Reuben	26, May 1842	May	67		L3	
Richardson, Robert (Rev)	21, June 1855	17, June	83		L3	
Richardson, Silas	2, May 1833	Apr.	55		L1	
Richardson, Smith	15, Nov. 1832	Nov.	20- 2m		L1	
Richardson, Susannah	25, July 1833	July	22		L1	
Richardson, Thomas P.	30, Mar. 1854	25, Feb.	28		L3	
Richardson, W.G.	9, July 1857	8, July			L1	
Richardson, W.R.	28, Mar. 1839	Mar.	26		L3	
Richardson, William	7, Feb. 1850	Jan.	40		L3	
Richardson, William H. (Dr)	25, Sept 1845	21, Sept			L3	
Riche, Elizabeth	10, Apr. 1851	Apr.	62		L3	
Richeson, John	22, Aug. 1833	Aug.	stillborn		L4	
Richey, Elizabeth S.	1, Aug. 1850	25, July			L3	
Richey, Mary	12, Jan. 1837		probate		L3	
Richey, Randal	9, Aug. 1855	4, Aug.	57		L3	
Richman, Elizabeth	9, Apr. 1857	5, Apr.			L3	
Richter, Cassimer	15, Feb. 1849	Feb.	36		L3	
Rick, Philip	13, Sept 1832	Sept	80		L1	
Rickey, Elizabeth	10, Aug. 1843	1, Aug.	12m	*	L3	
Rickey, Randol	11, Oct. 1838	6, Oct.	3		L3	
Rickey, Samuel	11, Oct. 1838	14, Sept	9m		L3	
Rickoff, Elizabeth	9, Sept 1852	5, Sept	26		L3	
Riddle, (Col)	5, May 1853		estate		L3	
Riddle, David W.	15, Oct. 1846	8, Oct.	24		L3	
Riddle, Edward R.	3, Feb. 1855	28, Jan.	3- 4m		L3	
Riddle, Elisha	28, Sept 1837	Sept	47		L4	

Name	Notice Date	Death Date	Age	Page	Maiden Name
Riddle, John	28, Oct. 1847		estate	L3	
Riddle, John	3, May 1855		probate	L3	
Riddle, John	10, Sept 1857		probate	L3	
Riddle, John (Col)	24, June 1847	17, June	86	* L2,3	
Riddle, John C.	20, Sept 1838	14, Sept	9m	L3	
Riddle, John, Sen.	7, Feb. 1856		probate	L3	
Riddle, Lewis	25, Oct. 1832	Oct.		L4	
Riddle, Nancy	12, Sept 1810	7, Sept	28	L3	
Riddle, Richard J.	18, July 1833	July	20	L2	
Riddle, Robert	20, Aug. 1846	14, Aug.		* L3	
Riddle, Sarah	3, 10, July 1845	30, June		L3	
Riddle, Tallmadge A.	19, Apr. 1849	14, Apr.	2- 3m	L3	
Riddle, Thomas J.	8, Oct. 1857		probate	L3	
Ridenbaugh, Samuel	4, Aug. 1842	Aug.		L3	
Ridenour, Clara Isadore	16, Apr. 1857	13, Apr.	10m-16d	L3	
Ridenour, Samuel (Major)	15, Aug. 1850	30, July	57	* L3	
Rider, (man)	29, Jan. 1852	24, Jan.		L1	
Ridgely, A.	23, Nov. 1843	22, Nov.		L3	
Ridgely, Charlotte S.	24, May 1849	22, May	26	L3	
Ridgeway, Mary A.	30, Aug. 1832	Aug.	19- 7m-14d	L1	
Ridgway, Jacob	11, May 1843	30, Apr.	75	L3	
Ridington, Edward	15, July 1847	July	3	L3	
Riechter, Charles G.	25, July 1850	July	29	L3	
Riely, William	16, June 1807		estate	L1	
Rienke, William	10, Dec. 1857		probate	L3	
Riffinbark, Peter	28, Jan. 1841		37	L3	
Rigdon, Charles	24, Sept 1846	Sept	70	L3	
Rigg, William	6, Mar. 1851	Feb.	21	L3	
Riggle, George	1, Jan. 1812		estate	L2	
Riggle, George	17, Mar. 1826		probate	L3	
Riggle, Jacob	12, Sept 1839		estate	L3	
Riggles, George	20, Dec. 1825		probate	L4	
Rigney, Catharine	24, Jan. 1850	Jan.	28	L3	
Rigney, Thomas	27, May 1847	May	28	L3	
Riker, Samuel	7, May 1857		probate	L3	
Riley, Archibald	23, Feb. 1843	Feb.		L3	
Riley, Barnard	7, Jan. 1847	Dec.	50	L3	
Riley, Clara Jane	24, Mar. 1853	18, Mar.	7	L3	
Riley, Elizabeth	11, Jan. 1855	24, Dec.		L3	
Riley, Erastus	7, Nov. 1826	5, Nov.	30	L3	
Riley, Hugh	27, Mar. 1851	Mar.	55	L3	
Riley, J.	1, Nov. 1838		estate	L3	
Riley, James	5, Apr. 1849	Mar.	32	L3	
Riley, John	20, Aug. 1846	Aug.	2	L3	
Riley, John	30, May 1850	May	25	L3	
Riley, John	18, July 1850	July	48	L3	
Riley, John	17, Jan. 1850	Jan.	67	L3	
Riley, John Edward	8, Nov. 1849	2, Nov.	2m- 3d	L3	
Riley, Patrick	18, July 1850	July	24	L3	
Riley, Patrick	16, Aug. 1849	Aug.	27	L3	
Riley, S.A.	29, Nov. 1855	22, Nov.	16m-16d	L3	
Riley, Thomas	22, Dec. 1842	Dec.	47	L3	
Riley, Timothy	23, Mar. 1849	Mar.	35	L3	
Rimenock, Henry	28, Mar. 1839	Mar.	1	L3	

Name	Notice Date	Death Date	Age		Page	Maiden Name
Rinas, Elisha	13, Sept 1832	Sept	13m-13d		L1	
Rindge, Sarah A.M.	14, Aug. 1856		probate		L6	
Rindge, Sarah Ann	17, Jan. 1850	9, Jan.		*	L3	
Rinear, John	30, Aug. 1832	Aug.	11m		L1	
Rineer, James	26, Sept 1833	Sept	43		L4	
Ringen, Conrad	7, June 1855		probate		L3	
Ringgold, Alexander	25, Oct. 1832	19, Oct.			L1	
Ringgold, Frederick G.	22, Aug. 1850	20, Aug.			L3	
Ringgold, Mary A.H.	20, Mar. 1845	17, Mar.	5- 2m-15d		L3	
Ringgold, Samuel F.	15, July 1847	6, July	21		L3	
Ringold, P.G.	7, Feb. 1856		probate		L3	
Rinney, Thomas	1, Apr. 1852	29, Mar.	4		L3	
Rinning, Hearnam H.	7, Feb. 1833	Feb.	33		L1	
Ripking, Gerhard	6, Dec. 1855		probate		L3	
Ripley, Ezra (Rev)	7, Oct. 1841	21, Sept	90		L3	
Ripley, Nathaniel	18, Aug. 1826	15, Aug.	59		L3	
Rippee, Ann	5, Aug. 1847	July	46		L3	
Risk, Charlotte C.	30, Jan. 1822		estate		L3	
Risk, Charlotte C.L.	17, Mar. 1826		probate		L3	
Risk, David	17, Mar. 1826		probate		L3	
Risk, David (Rev)	5, Jan. 1819		estate		L3	
Risk, Henderson	8, Aug. 1833	July	35		L1	
Rittenhouse, F.H.	7, Dec. 1843	4, Dec.	25		L3	
Rittenhouse, Jefferson	25, June 1846	15, June	40		L3	
Ritter, John	6, Apr. 1854	23, Mar.	22		L3	
Rivers, (child of Joshua)	20, June 1839	June	2w		L3	
Rivers, Joshua	30, Apr. 1846	Apr.	47		L3	
Rivers, Pamelia	1, Aug. 1839	July	27		L3	
Rizer, Amaka	7, Dec. 1837		probate		L3	
Roach, (child of Catharine)	12, Sept 1839	Sept	1d		L3	
Roach, Garret	11, July 1850	July	32		L3	
Roach, Ira	18, Jan. 1844	Jan.	2m		L3	
Roach, Thomas	6, Dec. 1849	Nov.	29		L3	
Roarke, Louisa	1, July 1847	30, June			L3	
Roat, Henry	30, Sept 1847	Sept	21		L3	
Robb, Isaaac	2, Mar. 1809	18, Feb.			L3	
Robb, Jesse	10, Jan. 1828	Jan.	28		L4	
Robb, William	30, Aug. 1838	Aug.	40		L3	
Robbins, (Mrs)	16, July 1808	12, July		*	L3	
Robbins, Charlotte	25, June 1846	20, June		*	L3	Whiting
Robbins, Elizabeth P.	2, Feb. 1854	13, Jan.	28		L3	
Robbins, Francis	10, Nov. 1853	8, Nov.	39		L3	
Robbins, J.	15, Sept 1818	20, Aug.			L3	
Robbins, William Lynd	17, Feb. 1853	10, Feb.	5-11m		L3	
Rober, (man)	23, Mar. 1854	18, Mar.			L3	
Robert, Simon	3, Nov. 1842	Oct.			L3	
Roberts, A.F.	17, Sept 1846	11, Sept			L3	
Roberts, David E.	22, Dec. 1853	15, Dec.		*	L3	
Roberts, Elizabeth	13, Nov. 1834	Nov.	49		L1	
Roberts, Hannah	13, Nov. 1834	Nov.	35		L1	
Roberts, Hannah	8, Aug. 1833	July	1- 6m		L1	
Roberts, Hives John	10, Mar. 1853	Feb.	58		L3	
Roberts, Jane	1, Nov. 1832	29, Oct.			L3	
Roberts, John	20, Nov. 1850	Nov.	35		L3	

Name	Notice Date	Death Date	Age		Page	Maiden Name
Roberts, John	3, May 1855		probate		L3	
Roberts, John	8, Oct. 1857		probate		L3	
Roberts, Joseph	31, Aug. 1848	24, Aug.	50		L3	
Roberts, Joseph	28, Dec. 1843	Dec.	10m		L3	
Roberts, Lewis	16, Oct. 1845	Oct.	25		L3	
Roberts, Perry	7, Aug. 1845	July	18		L3	
Roberts, Richard	27, July 1843	July	11m		L3	
Roberts, Stephen	9, Mar. 1843	5, Mar.	34		L3	
Robertson, D.	11, Nov. 1852	Oct.	20		L3	
Robertson, Isabella	9, Feb. 1837	7, Feb.			L3	
Robertson, Jeoffrey (Capt)	9, Dec. 1816	31, Aug.			L3	
Robertson, John	20, Feb. 1845	19, Feb.	49		L3	
Robertson, Robert A.	22, Sept 1853	3, Sept	36	*	L3	
Robertson, Robert Alexander	8, Sept 1853	3, Sept			L3	
Robertson, Thomas	5, Nov. 1846	31, Oct.	64		L3	
Robertson, William	7, Sept 1837		estate		L3	
Robertson, William	5, Sept 1839		probate		L3	
Robey, Malinda	17, July 1845	July	3d		L3	
Robins, Cornelia	1, Nov. 1832	25, Oct.			L1	
Robins, Ephraim	20, Feb. 1845	19, Feb.			L3	
Robins, John	19, July 1832	July	21		L1	
Robins, John Newton	11, Feb. 1823	9, Feb.	26		L3	
Robinson, (child of William)	19, Jan. 1809	16, Jan.	infant		L3	
Robinson, A.F.	4, May 1843	1, May	38		L3	
Robinson, Archibald	18, Dec. 1811		estate		L3	
Robinson, Archibald	2, Mar. 1813		estate		L3	
Robinson, Archibald	7, Dec. 1843	6, Dec.			L3	
Robinson, Asa	25, July 1826		estate		L3	
Robinson, Asa H.	26, Sept 1826		probate		L3	
Robinson, Asa H.	16, Feb. 1827		probate		L3	
Robinson, Asa H.	25, Sept 1822		estate		L4	
Robinson, Caroline	5, Sept 1850	Aug.	29		L3	
Robinson, Catharine	1, Apr. 1847		estate		L3	
Robinson, Christina	2, Mar. 1848	Feb.	5		L3	
Robinson, Elizabeth	16, Oct. 1828	14, Oct.			L3	
Robinson, Elizabeth A.	29, May 1845	May	3		L3	
Robinson, Ellen	24, Jan. 1856	13, Jan.	34		L3	Bond
Robinson, Enos	24, Aug. 1848	Aug.	35		L3	
Robinson, Frances J.	31, Jan. 1856	27, Jan.			L3	Dunn
Robinson, James	15, Nov. 1849	Nov.	29		L3	
Robinson, James	28, Oct. 1847	Oct.	34		L3	
Robinson, James	3, July 1851	June			L3	
Robinson, James C.	4, June 1857		probate		L3	
Robinson, James H.	6, June 1833	May	3- 8m		L2	
Robinson, John	17, May 1849	May	11		L3	
Robinson, John	18, Apr. 1850	Apr.	30		L3	
Robinson, John	10, Dec. 1846	Dec.	38		L3	
Robinson, John	5, Mar. 1846	Feb.	42	*	L3	
Robinson, John	22, Jan. 1857	21, Jan.	94		L3	
Robinson, John D.	19, July 1849	14, July			L3	
Robinson, Joshua	2, Nov. 1843	Oct.	68		L3	
Robinson, Julia A.M.	2, Aug. 1849	30, July	22		L3	
Robinson, Julius Henry	23, Oct. 1845	16, Oct.	8- 5m		L3	
Robinson, Lucy B.	9, Mar. 1854	5, Mar.	infant		L3	

Name	Notice Date	Death Date	Age	Page	Maiden Name
Robinson, Lydia	25, Oct. 1838	Oct.	37	L3	
Robinson, Malvina	22, May 1851	17, May	4m-21d	L3	
Robinson, Marshal A.	6, Sept 1832	31, Aug.	1- 2m	L2	
Robinson, Martha	20, Apr. 1843	Apr.		L3	
Robinson, Mary	11, July 1850	July	24	L3	
Robinson, Randolph	12, Apr. 1849	Apr.	30	L3	
Robinson, Samuel (heirs of)	8, Nov. 1838		probate	L3	
Robinson, Samuel (Rev)	11, Sept 1845	1, Sept	60	L3	
Robinson, Thomas	1, June 1837		23	L3	
Robinson, Thomas	22, Oct. 1840	Oct.	33	L3	
Robinson, William	19, Dec. 1826		probate	L3	
Robinson, William S.	10, Aug. 1843	3, Aug.	2- 5m	L3	
Robison, Hester Anne	14, Feb. 1828	Feb.	5w	L1	
Robison, Margaret	23, Oct. 1834	Oct.	54	L2	
Robison, Samuel	16, Oct. 1828		estate	L4	
Robison, Sophia	19, Sept 1844	Sept	6m	L3	
Robson, William	1, Nov. 1832	Oct.	10m	L2	
Roby, (child of Malindy)	16, Aug. 1849	Aug.	5d	L3	
Roche, Susan	12, Sept 1833	Sept		L1	
Rockenfield, John	11, Jan. 1849		estate	L3	
Rockey, Charles R.	19, Feb. 1846	31, Jan.	6- 3m-25d	L3	
Rockey, Mary	4, Mar. 1847	28, Feb.	48	L3	
Rockey, Sarah Hall	1, June 1837	25, May	infant	L3	
Rodecker, Catharine	19, July 1832	July	2m	L1	
Rodes, Catharine	16, Nov. 1854	5, Nov.	93	L3	
Rodgers, A.W.	23, Feb. 1854	Dec.	47	L3	
Rodgers, Hiram	9, Aug. 1855		probate	L3	
Rodgers, John	5, Mar. 1857		probate	L3	
Rodgers, Milton	5, Apr. 1855	30, Mar.		L3	
Rodgers, Samuel	9, Sept 1825		probate	L3	
Rodman, Joseph	23, Oct. 1834	Oct.	24	L2	
Rodman, Samuel B.	6, Sept 1849	Aug.	35	L3	
Roe, Edward	16, May 1839	May	30	L3	
Roedter, Henry	23, July 1857	18, July		L3	
Roetker, Frederick	20, Sept 1849	Sept	25	L3	
Roetker, Joseph	1, Feb. 1849	Jan.	29	L3	
Roff, Mary H.	7, Aug. 1834	July	3- 2m-23d	L3	
Rogate, Jacob	25, May 1837	May	33	L2	
Rogers,	8, May 1828	May	infant	L1	
Rogers, (Mrs)	25, Oct. 1832	20, Oct.		L2	
Rogers, Alfred (Capt)	5, July 1849	10, June	30	L3	
Rogers, Ann	17, May 1849	16, May		L3	
Rogers, C.M.	18, Oct. 1827	Oct.	8m	L3	
Rogers, Caroline L.	29, Apr. 1852	22, Apr.		L3	
Rogers, Charles Henry	4, July 1850	1, July	27	L3	
Rogers, Charles Leonard	28, June 1855	22, June	1	L3	
Rogers, David	11, May 1824		estate	L3	
Rogers, David	22, Aug. 1823	19, Aug.		* L3	
Rogers, Ebenezer	9, July 1857	7, July	86	L3	
Rogers, Ebenezer L.	13, Oct. 1842	Oct.	22	L3	
Rogers, Eunice S.	20, Sept 1825	16, Sept		L3	
Rogers, George	24, May 1849	May	44	L3	
Rogers, George (Rev)	9, July 1846	6, July	42	L3	
Rogers, Henry	25, Oct. 1832	20, Oct.		L2	

Name	Notice Date	Death Date	Age	Page	Maiden Name
Rogers, Hiram	24, Feb. 1848	21, Feb.	40	L3	
Rogers, James	25, Apr. 1850	Apr.	40	L3	
Rogers, James (Capt)	4, Oct. 1820	8, Sept		L3	
Rogers, John C.	17, Sept 1857	11, Sept	48	L3	
Rogers, Josiah	2, Oct. 1834	Sept		L4	
Rogers, Laura D.	19, Sept 1833	Sept	1- 2m- 4d	L4	
Rogers, Margaret C.	5, July 1855	28, June		L3	
Rogers, Ralph	13, Feb. 1840	Feb.	76	L3	
Rogers, Robert	9, Feb. 1854	31, Jan.	68	L3	
Rogers, Samuel	18, Oct. 1832	12, Oct.		L1	
Rogers, Samuel	2, May 1826		estate	L3	
Rogers, Samuel	19, Jan. 1827		estate	L3	
Rogers, Samuel	9, June 1836		probate	L3	
Rogers, Thomas	18, Jan. 1849	Jan.	2	L3	
Rohan, Mary Ann	2, Mar. 1854	25, Feb.	40	L3	
Rohlfering, Mary	4, Sept 1856		probate	L5	
Rohn, Francis	8, Aug. 1850	July	1- 6m	L3	
Rohn, Philip	8, Aug. 1850	July	41	L3	
Rohs, John	14, Dec. 1837	Dec.	22	L3	
Roism, William	29, Nov. 1832	Nov.	28	L1	
Rolison, William	1, Aug. 1833	July	35	L1	
Rolker, Emeline Anna	18, June 1846	13, June	18	* L3	Hastings
Roll, Edmund	17, Mar. 1826		probate	L3	
Roll, Edward	20, Jan. 1831		estate	L2	
Roll, Edward	14, Dec. 1824		probate	L3	
Roll, Edward	8, Nov. 1838		probate	L3	
Roll, Edward	20, Dec. 1825		probate	L4	
Roll, Edward C.	10, Apr. 1856		probate	L3	
Roll, Edward C.	3, Aug. 1854	29, July		L3	
Roll, Edward M.	24, Sept 1840	10, Sept	3- 1m	L3	
Roll, Isaac M.	22, May 1845	17, May	17m-14d	L3	
Roll, John	6, Dec. 1832	Dec.	22	L1	
Roll, Julia Ann	5, Dec. 1844	30, Nov.	25	L3	
Roll, Wick (idiot)	23, Feb. 1837		probate	L3	
Rollen, Uriah	26, July 1849	July	45	L3	
Roller, John	2, Feb. 1854	11, Jan.	48	L3	
Rolling, Harman	5, June 1851	31, May		L3	
Rollins, Elizabeth	29, Nov. 1849	24, Nov.		L2	
Rollins, Laura	23, May 1844	May	30	L3	
Rollins, Mary A.	18, Jan. 1849	Jan.	6	L3	
Rolton, (child)	8, Aug. 1833	July	5	L1	
Romain, James	28, Feb. 1839	Feb.	33	L3	
Romine, Jackson	13, July 1848	July	21	L3	
Rond, Ann	23, Oct. 1834	Oct.	58	L2	
Roney, Dominick	8, Nov. 1849	Oct.		L3	
Roney, John B.	6, Nov. 1851	28, Oct.	18	L3	
Roney, Michael	24, 31, July 1845	July	18	L3	
Roney, Michael	11, Apr. 1850	Apr.	60	L3	
Roney, Patrick	4, Apr. 1850	Mar.	26	L3	
Roning, Joanna	26, July 1849	July	40	L3	
Ronnebaum, John B.	11, Mar. 1847		estate	L3	
Ronnebaum, John H.	13, Aug. 1857	6, Aug.	50	L3	
Ronnebaum, John H.	20, Aug. 1857		estate	L3	
Roob, Lawrence	21, Feb. 1850	Feb.	22	L3	

Name	Notice Date	Death Date	Age		Page	Maiden Name
Roosa, Jacob R.	10, Apr. 1856		probate		L3	
Root, Daniel	21, June 1838		estate		L3	
Root, Daniel	3, Jan. 1839		estate		L3	
Root, Daniel	13, Feb. 1840		probate		L3	
Roots, Edward North	24, July 1851	10, July	18m		L3	
Roots, Gertrude Jane	4, July 1844	16, June			L3	
Ropes, Abigail Pickman	10, Feb. 1842	1, Feb.	25d		L3	
Ropes, John	27, Jan. 1842	16, Jan.	2- 4m-19d		L3	
Rosa, Franklin	24, June 1841	20, June	1- 5m-23d		L3	
Rosberry,	8, July 1847	June			L3	
Rose, Embrey Clay	16, Mar. 1849	11, Mar.	4m-19d		L3	
Rose, H.A. Maria	1, Nov. 1832	Oct.	2- 1m-17d		L2	
Rose, Harriet	6, Aug. 1846	5, Aug.			L3	
Rose, Luther	1, Oct. 1857	27, Sept	69		L3	
Rose, Oloisius	5, Nov. 1846	Oct.	64		L3	
Rosegrant, John	7, June 1814		estate		L3	
Rosenbush, Mary	10, Apr. 1856		probate		L3	
Roskin, Amelia	5, July 1849	June	7		L3	
Ross, (Miss)	23, May 1833	May	10		L4	
Ross, Ann P.	16, Mar. 1854	7, Mar.	40		L3	
Ross, Anne	22, Oct. 1805	13, Sept	34	*	L3	
Ross, Annie Martin	10, June 1852	5, June	1- 6m		L3	
Ross, Britton	23, Nov. 1837		estate		L3	
Ross, Britton	14, Feb. 1839		probate		L3	
Ross, Clara M.	5, Nov. 1857	27, Oct.	23		L3	Murray
Ross, Daniel	9, Aug. 1855		probate		L3	
Ross, David	5, May 1853	28, Apr.			L3	
Ross, David	8, Nov. 1832	30, Oct.			L4	
Ross, Elizabeth	14, Feb. 1833	Feb.	33		L1	
Ross, Ella	15, June 1854	14, June	5- 1m- 5d		L3	
Ross, G.	8, Jan. 1857		probate		L3	
Ross, Georgiana	24, Apr. 1851	16, Apr.	36		L3	
Ross, Georgiana	10, Sept 1857		probate		L3	
Ross, Hepsibah	12, Mar. 1846	5, Mar.	42		L3	
Ross, Jacob	8, Nov. 1855		estate		L3	
Ross, Jacob	6, Sept 1855		probate		L3	
Ross, Jane	22, Aug. 1833	Aug.	43		L4	
Ross, Jesse W.	29, Nov. 1855	13, Nov.	43		L3	
Ross, John	25, Oct. 1832	19, Oct.	7		L2	
Ross, John (Dr)	14, June 1814		estate		L1	
Ross, Kate Adan	25, Mar. 1852	15, Mar.			L3	
Ross, Martha Jane	19, May 1853	17, May	5- 8m		L3	
Ross, Mary Daly	24, Feb. 1848	22, Feb.	7m-22d		L3	
Ross, Mary Jane	22, Aug. 1833	Aug.			L4	
Ross, Patton	6, Aug. 1840		estate		L3	
Ross, Tracy	25, May 1848	18, May	2-10m-27d		L3	
Ross, William	6, Dec. 1832	Dec.	64		L1	
Ross, William	9, Aug. 1838		estate		L3	
Ross, William	22, Mar. 1838		probate		L3	
Ross, William	5, Sept 1839		probate		L3	
Ross, William H.	5, Apr. 1849	31, Mar.	41		L3	
Ross, William H.	8, Jan. 1857		probate		L3	
Ross, William H.	10, Sept 1857		probate		L3	
Rossell, William	9, July 1840	20, June	80		L3	

Name	Notice Date	Death Date	Age	Page	Maiden Name
Rotchford, Patrick	23, Nov. 1848	Nov.	20	L3	
Roth, Joseph Augustus	11, Mar. 1847	4, Mar.	3- 1m- 9d	L3	
Rottman, Peter	1, Feb. 1849	Jan.	23	L3	
Rouch, John	13, June 1850	June	24	L3	
Roudabush, Catharine	22, Feb. 1844	21, Feb.		*	L3	
Rourk, (child of Mary)	4, July 1844	June	9d	L3	
Rouse, Magdalena	12, July 1849	July	62	L3	
Routingrass, Henry	13, Nov. 1834	Nov.	2	L1	
Rovsa, Jacob R.	5, July 1855		probate	L3	
Rowan, Anne	19, July 1849	14, July	77	L3	Lytle
Rowan, Hill	8, Aug. 1833	2, Aug.		L4	
Rowan, Robert	19, Dec. 1826		probate	L3	
Rowan, Robert, Jr.	30, Dec. 1823		estate	L3	
Rowan, William	16, June 1836	12, June	31	L3	
Rowan, William	8, Aug. 1833	2, Aug.		L4	
Rowcroft, Victoria Sophia	23, Aug. 1855	15, Aug.	3m	L3	
Rowe, Charles Joseph	19, July 1849	16, July	44	L3	
Rowe, Elizabeth M.	1, Aug. 1850	July	27	L3	
Rowe, James S.	15, Oct. 1835	3, Oct.		L1	
Rowe, Margaret	12, June 1845	6, June	7m	L3	
Rowe, Margaret	2, Oct. 1834	Sept		L4	
Rowen, Eliza	30, Aug. 1832	Aug.	39	L1	
Rowlsen, John	11, July 1833		probate	L3	
Roy, Eufrosina	10, Feb. 1848	Feb.	34	L3	
Roy, John	1, Aug. 1833	July	37	L1	
Roy, Mary M.	10, Sept 1846	Sept	4w	L3	
Ruben, Joseph	12, Aug. 1841	Aug.	35	L3	
Rubrus, Jeremiah	26, July 1849	July	20	L3	
Ruby, Adam	7, Aug. 1834	July		L3	
Rucker, Amos	18, Oct. 1832	13, Oct.		L2	
Rucker, Mary Jane	19, Apr. 1849	4, Apr.	34	L3	Heckewelder
Rucker, Sarah	18, May 1843	May	35	L3	
Rude, Samuel W.	12, Mar. 1835		estate	L3	
Rude, Samuel W.	15, Sept 1836		probate	L3	
Rue, Amelia	4, Jan. 1844	Dec.	30	L3	
Ruf, Isidore	10, Sept 1857		probate	L3	
Ruff, Eliza	18, July 1833	July	1- 6m	L2	
Ruffin, Mary Rockey	26, July 1849	20, July		L3	
Ruffin, Oliver Perry	27, Feb. 1845	21, Feb.		L3	
Ruffin, Samuel N.	4, Oct. 1849	27, Sept	41	L3	
Ruffin, Sarah	13, Sept 1838	Sept	20	L3	
Ruffin, Sarah A.	17, Nov. 1853	8, Nov.	43	L3	
Ruffin, William (Major)	7, Aug. 1834	25, July	66	L3	
Ruffner, Abraham	26, Jan. 1854	23, Jan.	73	L3	
Ruffner, David (Col)	16, Feb. 1843	8, Feb.		L3	
Ruffner, Marine	24, Apr. 1856	18, Apr.		L3	
Ruffner, Martha J.	21, June 1855	20, June		L3	
Rugg, L.H.	13, Sept 1855	7, Sept		L3	
Rugg, Samuel	29, Sept 1812	22, Sept		L3	
Ruhl, George	7, Dec. 1843	Dec.	44	L3	
Rule, Anna Clayton	14, Feb. 1850	7, Feb.	20m	L3	
Ruley,	18, Dec. 1856		14	L3	
Rumpler, George C.	8, Oct. 1857		probate	L3	
Rumpler, John F.	8, Oct. 1857		probate	L3	

Name	Notice Date	Death Date	Age		Page	Maiden Name
Rumpler, John K.	4, June 1857		probate		L3	
Rung, Jacob	6, Dec. 1832	Dec.			L1	
Runyan, (Dr)	6, Dec. 1855				L3	
Runyan, John	14, July 1853	9, July			L3	
Runyan, William	30, Sept 1852		estate		L3	
Runyan, William	9, Apr. 1857		probate		L3	
Rupel, Samuel	2, May 1833	Apr.	21		L1	
Ruse, Frances	1, Aug. 1833	July	3m		L1	
Rush, Benjamin (Dr)	4, May 1813	19, Apr.			L3	
Rush, Rachel	2, July 1846	June	45		L3	
Rusk, Martha E.	13, Dec. 1832	Dec.	4		L1	
Rusk, Rebecca	30, Aug. 1832	Aug.	4m		L1	
Rusner, Joseph	4, Nov. 1841	Oct.	53		L3	
Russel, James	19, Dec. 1826		probate		L3	
Russel, James	21, Sept 1837		probate		L4	
Russel, James	1, Nov. 1832	24, Oct.			L4	
Russel, Robert	4, July 1850	June	34		L3	
Russel, Thomas	26, Sept 1826		probate		L3	
Russell, (child of James)	6, June 1810	3, June	infant		L2	
Russell, Caroline	23, Apr. 1840	Apr.	24		L3	
Russell, Charles	7, Oct. 1841	Sept	32		L3	
Russell, Charles	24, Oct. 1850	Oct.	44		L3	
Russell, Elizabeth	9, Feb. 1819	7, Feb.			L3	
Russell, George W. (Capt)	11, Dec. 1815				L3	
Russell, Howard	29, Aug. 1850	24, Aug.	13m		L3	
Russell, James	16, Feb. 1837		estate		L3	
Russell, James	18, Apr. 1839		probate		L3	
Russell, Jane W.	16, Nov. 1843	8, Nov.			L3	
Russell, John	23, Oct. 1845	Oct.	19		L3	
Russell, John	12, July 1849	July	35		L3	
Russell, John W.	28, Dec. 1848	Dec.	54		L3	
Russell, Margaret	26, Sept 1850	Sept	6w		L3	
Russell, Mary	1, Aug. 1833	July	19		L1	
Russell, Mary Elizabeth	18, Dec. 1845	14, Dec.	17	*	L3	Copping
Russell, Mary Elizabeth	8, Jan. 1852	3, Jan.			L3	Hillyer
Rust, Benjamin	23, Oct. 1851	19, Oct.			L4	
Rust, Jane B.	8, Dec. 1842	7, Dec.			L3	Morris
Rust, Joseph G.	23, Jan. 1851	18, Jan.	41		L3	
Rust, Joseph G.	4, Sept 1851		estate		L3	
Rust, Paul	21, Aug. 1856	18, Aug.	73		L5	
Rust, William	18, Sept 1834	Sept	1		L1	
Rutherford, Elizabeth P.	19, Apr. 1845	Apr.	3m		L3	
Rutherford, Isaac Stricker	13, May 1841	10, May	13m		L3	
Rutherford, Margaret Elizabeth	24, Feb. 1842	11, Feb.	13		L3	
Rutherford, Peter	16, Oct. 1845	Oct.	45		L3	
Rutherford, Thomas M.	1, Mar. 1855	26, Feb.	50		L3	
Rutherford, Thomas Miers Bush	24, Feb. 1842	18, Feb.	5		L3	
Rutschman, Joseph	18, Jan. 1849	Jan.	25		L3	
Ryall, Charles	18, June 1846	10, June	29		L3	
Ryall, William	24, 31, Oct. 1844	21, Oct.	35	*	L3	
Ryan, Catharine	4, Apr. 1850	Mar.	2- 6m		L3	
Ryan, Charles	31, May 1849	May	24		L3	
Ryan, Daniel	29, Aug. 1850	Aug.	2		L3	
Ryan, James	13, Dec. 1849	Dec.	22		L3	

Name	Notice Date	Death Date	Age	Page	Maiden Name
Ryan, James	11, July 1850	July	28	L3	
Ryan, James	28, Jan. 1847	Jan.	38	L3	
Ryan, Jane	16, July 1846	July	5	L3	
Ryan, John	8, Mar. 1849	Feb.	55	L3	
Ryan, John	27, Mar. 1851	Mar.	5- 6m	L3	
Ryan, Judith	28, Mar. 1850	Mar.	16	L3	
Ryan, Mary	28, Mar. 1850	Mar.	40	L3	
Ryan, Robert	26, Sept 1844	Sept		L3	
Ryan, Sarah	24, Apr. l845	Apr.	2	L3	
Ryan, Thomas	3, July 1851	June	52	L3	
Ryan, William	23, May 1850	May	22	L3	
Ryan, William	10, July 1845	8, July	80	L3	
Ryan, William, Jr.	15, Sept 1836		probate	L3	
Rybolt, Jacob	11, July 1833		probate	L3	
Ryerdon, Thomas	15, Nov. 1849	Nov.	20	L3	
Ryland, James	7, June 1855	1, June	78	L3	
Ryland, Joseph P.	19, Sept 1833	Sept	50	L4	
Rynearson, John	18, June 1829		estate	L4	
Rynearson, Mary A.	10, June 1847	June	35	L3	
Ryon, William	23, Feb. 1837		probate	L3	
Sackett, Lectus	23, Feb. 1854	3, Feb.	63	L3	
Sackett, Letus	9, Mar. 1854	3, Feb.	60	L3	
Sackett, Margaret	1, July 1852	24, June	60	L3	
Sacks, Emma J.	17, May 1849	May	22	L3	
Sadd, Elijah	17, Feb. 1848	Feb.	20	L3	
Safford, Mary H.	1, May 1851	20, Apr.		L3	Beecher
Sahan, John	13, Apr. 1848	Apr.	26	L3	
Saintjohn, John S.	4, May 1848	Apr.	2- 3m	L3	
Salisbury, (Mrs)	1, Aug. 1833	July	45	L1	
Salisbury, Alex.	28, July 1836		estate	L3	
Salisbury, Alexander	10, Dec. 1835		estate	L3	
Salley, Harvey	18, Dec. 1845	Dec.	24	L3	
Salley, William	27, July 1837	July	22	L3	
Salmon, Ann E.	31, May 1849	May	2- 6m	L3	
Salmon, Barbara	28, June 1849	June	50	L3	
Salmon, Francis M.	11, June 1846	June	2	L3	
Salmon, John	22, Oct. 1835		estate	L4	
Salmon, Sarah Jane	23, July 1846	July	10	L3	
Salsbury, Morea	13, June 1844	June	80	L3	
Salter, Thomas	29, June 1854	26, June	44	L3	
Salters, (Mr)	18, Oct. 1832	Oct.		L2	
Sammons, James	5, Feb. 1857		probate	L3	
Sampson, Ann Maria	23, July 1840	15, July		L3	
Sampson, Anna Maria	8, Feb. 1844	7, Feb.	39	L3	
Sampson, Aquila W.	10, Apr. 1856	3, Apr.		L3	
Sampson, Ellen Perry	28, May 1846	23, May	20m	L3	
Sampson, Henry	27, June 1839	June	8m	L3	
Sampson, James	12, Dec. 1839	Dec.	26	L3	
Sampson, Joseph S.	22, Nov. 1849	16, Nov.	50	L3	
Sampson, Mary Ann Hastings	24, Aug. 1837	20, Aug.	8m	L3	
Sampson, Merrit	25, Apr. 1850	Apr.	31	L3	
Sampson, Nathan	12, Nov. 1857	8, Nov.	51	L3	
Sampson, Nathan A.	1, Aug. 1833	July	11m- 4d	L1	

Name	Notice Date	Death Date	Age		Page	Maiden Name
Sampson, Siloma	25, Apr. 1850	Apr.	54		L3	
Sanborn, Bessie	7, May 1857	1, May	2		L3	
Sanborn, Edward J.	12, Mar. 1840			*	L3	
Sandback, Richard	20, June 1850	June			L3	
Sanders, (child of Oscar)	30, Dec. 1847	Dec.	4		L3	
Sanders, Caroline A.	5, July 1838	26, June	14m-20d		L3	
Sanders, Caroline W.	6, July 1837	30, June	29		L3	
Sanders, Charles	22, Aug. 1850	Aug.	3		L3	
Sanders, George	8, July 1841	June	19		L3	
Sanders, George A.	5, July 1849	June	5m		L3	
Sanders, Hezekiah	4, May 1837		estate		L3	
Sanders, Hezekiah	15, Sept 1836		probate		L3	
Sanders, Hezekiah	9, Aug. 1838		probate		L3	
Sanders, John	7, June 1849	May	21		L3	
Sanders, John	16, May 1850	May	24		L3	
Sanders, Margaret M.	9, Sept 1847	Aug.	22		L3	
Sanders, Nathan	19, May 1806	16, May	23		L3	
Sanders, Paul R.	22, Aug. 1850	13, Aug.			L3	
Sanders, Tanner	30, Mar. 1849	Mar.	24		L3	
Sanderson, Mary Ann	7, Sept 1843	3, Sept			L3	
Sandford, David	5, Nov. 1805	11, Oct.	22		L3	
Sanford, Eliza	1, Oct. 1846	Sept	32		L3	
Sanford, Sarah Ann	14, Mar. 1844	2, Mar.		*	L3	
Sanford, Thomas (Gen)	15, Dec. 1808	11, Dec.			L3	
Sargent, (child of the widow)	11, Apr. 1833	Apr.	1- 2m		L1	
Sargent, David	22, Mar. 1838		probate		L3	
Sargent, Emaline	5, Sept 1833	Aug.	7		L1	
Sargent, John B.	22, May 1851		estate		L3	
Sargent, Lizzie Chapman	29, Jan. 1857	22, Jan.	6-10m		L3	
Sargent, Sallie	22, July 1852	19, July	9m		L3	
Sargent, Sarah B.	18, Nov. 1841	17, Nov.			L3	
Sargent, Thomas F.	26, Dec. 1850	22, Dec.	2- 2m		L3	
Sargent, William	23, Mar. 1843		estate		L3	
Sarle, Albert Henry	7, Oct. 1847	6, Oct.	3- 9m		L3	
Sarver, (child of Elisha)	18, Oct. 1827	Oct.	4d		L3	
Sasser, John	1, Feb. 1849	Jan.	29		L3	
Sater, (child of Joseph)	18, Sept 1834	Sept	2m		L1	
Sater, Hannah	6, Dec. 1855		probate		L3	
Satterly, Margaret Baron	2, Aug. 1838	29, July	16m		L3	
Satterly, Stephen	12, Apr. 1832	8, Apr.	7		L3	
Saul, Guy	22, June 1848	June	34		L3	
Saully, Patrick	8, Aug. 1833	July	50		L1	
Saunders, Elihu	17, Feb. 1807		estate		L2	
Saunders, Francis	1, Mar. 1849	Feb.	32		L3	
Saunders, George	20, Feb. 1845	16, Feb.	74		L3	
Saunders, J.D.	2, Apr. 1846	30, Mar.			L3	
Saunders, John D.	13, Dec. 1855		estate		L3	
Saunders, Mary	17, Aug. 1854	9, Aug.			L3	
Saunders, Mary King	6, Jan. 1817	3, Jan.	infant		L3	
Saunders, Sue W.	19, July 1855	1, July			L3	
Sauton, Edward	22, Aug. 1833	Aug.	1- 3m		L4	
Savage, John Ceborn	16, Aug. 1849	9, Aug.	10- 3m-17d		L3	
Savage, Joseph	25, Oct. 1832	20, Oct.			L2	
Savage, Joseph	1, Nov. 1832	23, Oct.	4		L4	

Name	Notice Date	Death Date	Age		Page	Maiden Name
Savage, Robert	29, May 1828	May	2		L2	
Sawtell, Theophilus	31, Aug. 1843	Aug.	2- 8m		L3	
Sawyer, Levi G.	22, May 1845	May	7		L3	
Sawyer, Willie	6, Aug. 1857	3, Aug.	18m		L3	
Sawyler, Nathaniel	6, Oct. 1853	3, Oct.	69- 5m-23d	*	L3	
Saxe, Paul	11, Dec. 1856	6, Dec.			L3	
Saxon, Catharine	26, July 1849	July	25		L3	
Sayre, Ananias	20, May 1816	14, May	26		L3	
Sayre, Julia A.V.	25, July 1850	18, July			L3	
Sayre, Leonard	26, Jan. 1822	10, Jan.	59		L3	
Sayre, Leonard	6, Mar. 1827		estate		L3	
Sayre, Levi	1, Nov. 1827		estate		L3	
Sayre, Thomas (heirs of)	15, Sept 1836		probate		L3	
Sayre, William	24, Sept 1829		estate		L4	
Sayre, William D.	21, May 1857	7, May	17m		L3	
Sayres, Ananias	9, Sept 1816		estate		L3	
Scanlan, Michael	14, Sept 1848	Sept	33		L3	
Scanlin, Edward	23, June 1853				L3	
Scanlin, Michael	12, Oct. 1848	Oct.	31		L3	
Scanlin, Thomas	10, Apr. 1851	1, Apr.			L1	
Scarborough, Anne Hoadley	13, Aug. 1846	6, Aug.	11m-10d		L3	
Scarborough, Charles Springer	27, Mar. 1856	21, Mar.	infant		L3	
Schadt, George Henry	7, June 1855		probate		L3	
Schaffer, (child of Adam)	19, July 1832	July	9		L1	
Schaffer, Gustav H.	15, June 1854				L3	
Schaler, Henry	23, Jan. 1851	Jan.	42		L3	
Schaller, Ferdinand	24, Nov. 1842	Nov.	43		L6	
Schanbek, Philip	8, Aug. 1850	July	50		L3	
Schardellmann, William	22, Mar. 1838		probate		L3	
Scheeneck, Ludwig	14, Oct. 1847	Oct.	36		L3	
Scheid, Philip J.	6, Dec. 1855		probate		L3	
Scheidler, G.V.	15, Feb. 1849	12, Feb.	39		L3	
Schenck, Daniel	12, July 1838		estate		L3	
Schenck, Daniel	13, Feb. 1840		probate		L3	
Schenck, Elizabeth R.	9, Mar. 1854	6, Mar.	78		L3	
Schenck, William C. (Gen)	17, Jan. 1821	12, Jan.			L3	
Schenck, Woodhull S. (Lt)	17, May 1849	11, May		*	L3	
Schenks, John	26, June 1851	June	40		L3	
Schenter, William	20, July 1848	July	18		L3	
Scheur, Casper	20, July 1848	July	25		L3	
Schewlenberg, (child of Henry)	7, Feb. 1833	Feb.	4d		L1	
Schielck, Gertrude	12, July 1849	July	48		L3	
Schierberg, Fred.	7, Feb. 1856		probate		L3	
Schiller, Anthony	14, Mar. 1850	Mar.	35		L3	
Schillinger, Alexana	19, Aug. 1852		estate		L3	
Schlanstedt, Christopher	24, May 1849	May	22		L3	
Schlee, George	7, June 1855		probate		L3	
Schleicher, Ann C.	24, July 1845	July	45		L3	
Schlenker, Paul	8, Apr. 1847	Mar.	37		L3	
Schmeede, Maria	10, Nov. 1842	Nov.	51		L4	
Schmidt, Bernard	17, July 1851		estate		L3	
Schmidt, David Griffin	30, May 1850	27, May	5		L3	
Schmidt, Henry W.	10, Mar. 1853	Feb.	32		L3	
Schmidt, Peter	28, Jan. 1841	Jan.	49		L3	

Name	Notice Date	Death Date	Age		Page	Maiden Name
Schmidt, Valentine	16, Mar. 1849	Mar.	19		L3	
Schmude, Henrietta	17, Nov. 1842	Nov.	21		L6	
Schnapp, Leonard	10, Aug. 1843	Aug.	26		L3	
Schneck, Jacob	4, Aug. 1842	Aug.	27		L3	
Schneckener, William	31, July 1845	July	25		L3	
Schneider, Catharine	21, June 1849	June	25		L3	
Schneider, Gottlieb	30, Mar. 1854	Mar.	50		L3	
Schneider, William	5, July 1849	June	23		L3	
Schnippel, Barnard	9, Aug. 1855		probate		L3	
Schnoors, Frederick	3, Dec. 1846	Nov.	23		L3	
Schoff, William	24, July 1845	July	26		L3	
Schofield, Hugh	17, Mar. 1836		estate		L4	
Schofield, Samuel	25, July 1833	July	22		L1	
Schooley, Edward Rockwell	16, Aug. 1855	12, Aug.	1-10m		L3	
Schooley, John	22, Mar. 1838		probate		L3	
Schooley, Nathaniel S.	9, Apr. 1857		probate		L3	
Schooley, Samuel	12, Jan. 1837		probate		L3	
Schoots, Jacob	14, June 1849	June	32		L3	
Schoover, Frederick	8, Aug. 1833	July	23		L1	
Schraffenberg, John	9, Sept 1847	Aug.	30		L3	
Schreiber, John	19, Apr. 1849	Apr.	16		L3	
Schreiber, Lemuel William	4, July 1850	3, July	19	*	L3	
Schreiber, Mary	21, June 1849	June	32		L3	
Schreiner, Charles	3, May 1849	Apr.	49		L3	
Schrek, George	8, Aug. 1850	July	2m		L3	
Schrenck, Robert C.	10, Sept 1846	3, Sept	21m		L3	
Schriver, Adam	15, Oct. 1840	Oct.	18		L3	
Schriver, Milchoir	15, Oct. 1840	Oct.	22		L3	
Schroeder, John B.	16, Oct. 1856		probate		L6	
Schrol, John	18, Oct. 1832	15, Oct.			L3	
Schrott, Catharine	12, Aug. 1852	Aug.	62		L3	
Schrout, Catherine	15, Aug. 1833	Aug.	60		L1	
Schrumm, Michael	30, Jan. 1851	Jan.	35		L3	
Schuff, Conrad	23, Nov. 1848	Nov.	48		L3	
Schug, Jacob	9, Aug. 1849		estate		L3	
Schug, Jacob	1, Jan. 1852		estate		L3	
Schule, Elizabeth	22, Jan. 1852	Jan.	45		L3	
Schuler, Jacob	30, Nov. 1848	Nov.	24		L3	
Schuler, John	20, Nov. 1850	Nov.	23		L3	
Schultz, Ann	8, Aug. 1833	27, July		*	L1	Bowers
Schultz, Ann E.	8, Aug. 1833	July	26		L1	
Schultz, Barnard	19, Sept 1850	Sept	28		L3	
Schultz, Caroline Matilda	12, Feb. 1846	7, Feb.	28		L3	
Schultz, Charles	26, Jan. 1837	Jan.	35		L3	
Schultz, Conrad	4, Apr. 1850	3, Apr.	80		L3	
Schultz, Daniel	27, Apr. 1848	Apr.	38		L3	
Schultz, Elizabeth	28, Aug. 1856	16, Aug.	87- -6d	*	L5	
Schultz, John	30, Oct. 1851	16, Oct.	9		L4	
Schultz, William	30, May 1839	May	37		L2	
Schultze,	12, Dec. 1850	11, Dec.			L3	
Schulze, Frederic Maximillian	17, Jan. 1850	4, Jan.	17		L3	
Schuman, Philip	8, Oct. 1846	Sept	23		L3	
Schunk, Jacob	23, Aug. 1849	Aug.	34		L3	
Schutte, Anthony	18, Apr. 1850		estate		L3	

Name	Notice Date	Death Date	Age		Page	Maiden Name
Schuyler, Clara	28, Aug. 1851	21, Aug.	10m		L3	
Schwalm, A.	6, Mar. 1856		probate		L3	
Schwarty, Nicholas	28, Aug. 1834	Aug.	1- 5m		L1	
Schwartz, Jacob	27, Apr. 1837		25		L3	
Schwartz, Maria Ann	27, Oct. 1821	21, Oct.			L3	
Schwartze, Mary G.	27, Apr. 1848	26, Apr.	23		L3	Weatherby
Schwegman, Joseph	6, Aug. 1857		probate		L3	
Schwegman, Joseph	16, Oct. 1856		probate		L6	
Schwenker, A.D.	22, Aug. 1850		estate		L3	
Schwinker, Henry	14, Mar. 1850	Mar.	22		L3	
Sciles, Edith	11, July 1850	July	25		L3	
Scofield, James	28, Sept 1822		estate		L3	
Scofield, Martin	8, July 1847	June	3- 6m		L3	
Scofield, Richard	18, Jan. 1849	Jan.	28		L3	
Scofield, Richard	3, Sept 1840		probate		L3	
Scoggin, Elisha	20, Dec. 1825		probate		L4	
Scoley, Bridget	21, June 1849	June	21		L3	
Scolland, Bridget	21, Mar. 1850	Mar.	37		L3	
Scora, Mary Ann	16, Aug. 1849	Aug.	35		L3	
Scott, (child of Mary)	16, May 1850	May	stillborn		L3	
Scott, Abigail F.	2, Dec. 1830	20, Nov.	30		L4	
Scott, Alexander	11, Mar. 1852	Mar.	40		L4	
Scott, Ann	27, Sept 1855	18, Sept	70		L3	
Scott, Dinah	4, Dec. 1845	1, Dec.	24		L3	
Scott, Elizabeth	1, Jan. 1852	20, Dec.	67	*	L3	
Scott, Elizabeth	30, Mar. 1848	26, Mar.	94		L3	
Scott, Elizabeth	13, Apr. 1848	26, Mar.	94		L3	
Scott, Enoc B.	27, Apr. 1848		estate		L3	
Scott, Fanny	25, Oct. 1832	19, Oct.			L2	
Scott, George	29, Nov. 1832	Nov.			L1	
Scott, George	1, Apr. 1841	Mar.	2		L3	
Scott, George Holmes	18, Oct. 1838	13, Oct.	19		L3	
Scott, George, Jr.	11, Jan. 1849	4, Jan.		*	L3	
Scott, Granville	20, Mar. 1845	Mar.	22		L3	
Scott, James	7, Oct. 1841	7, Oct.	41	*	L3	
Scott, James	15, Aug. 1850		estate		L3	
Scott, James	4, Sept 1834		estate		L4	
Scott, James	14, June 1838		probate		L4	
Scott, James Chambers	15, Sept 1817	6, Sept	22		L3	
Scott, John	27, Oct. 1831		probate		L1	
Scott, John	6, Dec. 1849	Nov.	40		L3	
Scott, John	9, June 1836		probate		L3	
Scott, John	15, May 1834	May	37		L4	
Scott, John M. (Col)	12, Jan. 1813	20, Dec.			L3	
Scott, Josiah	13, Sept 1855		estate		L3	
Scott, L.M.	4, June 1857		probate		L3	
Scott, Margaret	25, Jan. 1844	20, Jan.			L3	
Scott, Mary	22, Aug. 1850	14, Aug.			L3	
Scott, Michael	1, Aug. 1833	July	83		L1	
Scott, Nancy	8, Aug. 1833	July	19		L1	
Scott, Naomi	25, June 1846	17, June	61	*	L3	
Scott, Nelson	21, June 1849	June			L3	
Scott, Robert	3, Jan. 1828	Jan.	19		L1	
Scott, Robert	12, Aug. 1847	4, Aug.	31		L3	

Name	Notice Date	Death Date	Age		Page	Maiden Name
Scott, Samuel (Col)	8, Mar. 1855		62		L3	
Scott, Samuel H.	23, Nov. 1848	Nov.	23		L3	
Scott, Solomon	22, Apr. 1841	Apr.	120		L3	
Scott, Thomas	4, Nov. 1852	25, Oct.	86		L3	
Scott, Thomas	28, Oct. 1852	25, Oct.			L3	
Scott, Thomas	12, Feb. 1852	5, Feb.			L4	
Scott, William	30, Oct. 1845	Oct.	33		L3	
Scott, Winfield	24, Aug. 1848	Aug.	2m		L3	
Scroggs, Albert	21, Dec. 1854	12, Dec.	26		L3	
Scruggs, Edward A.	28, Dec. 1837	17, Dec.	22	*	L3	
Scudder, Henry	14, Dec. 1824		probate		L3	
Scudder, Henry	19, Dec. 1826		probate		L3	
Scuelly, Humphreys	5, Sept 1833	Aug.	56		L1	
Scull, Edward (Dr)	22, Jan. 1816	28, Nov.	28		L1	
Scully, Patrick	8, Aug. 1833	July			L1	
Scully, Patrick	3, Apr. 1851	Mar.	20		L3	
Scully, Thomas	3, July 1845	28, June	25		L3	
Scurlock, Jared	29, Jan. 1846	Jan.	24		L3	
Seagraves, Charles	13, May 1847	May	23		L3	
Seaman, (child)	16, Oct. 1834	Oct.	3d		L1	
Seaman, Hester A.	19, Sept 1850	Sept	20		L3	
Seaman, John	25, Apr. 1823		estate		L3	
Seaman, John	20, Dec. 1825		probate		L4	
Seaman, William	22, Feb. 1849	Feb.	30		L3	
Seamans, Nathan	26, Oct. 1837		estate		L3	
Seamonds, Joshua	22, Aug. 1839	Aug.	35		L3	
Searle, Charles E.	20, Jan. 1848	18, Jan.	3- 6m		L3	
Sears, Angeline B.	21, Dec. 1848	17, Dec.			L3	
Sears, Benjamin	19, Dec. 1826		probate		L3	
Sears, Helen G.	5, Nov. 1857	30, Oct.			L3	Graff
Seavey, Amos W.	24, Jan. 1850			*	L3	
Secrist, Theresa A.	15, July 1852	12, July	33		L3	
Sedam, Cornelius R.	29, July 1823		estate		L3	
Sedam, Cornelius R. (Col)	23, May 1823	10, May	64	*	L3	
Sedam, Elizabeth	30, May 1810	29, May			L3	
Sedam, Isaac	20, Dec. 1827		estate		L3	
Sedbrook, Chaney	10, Mar. 1853	Feb.	60		L3	
Sedgwick, Stephen	27, Mar. 1822	22, Mar.	38		L3	
Sedsberry, Andrew F.	6, June 1833	May	22		L2	
Seebers, Herman	9, Apr. 1857		probate		L3	
Seebers, Herman	6, Aug. 1857		probate		L3	
Seegar, Benjamin D.	26, July 1832	July	1m		L1	
Seekner, (son of Josiah)	19, Feb. 1852	12, Feb.	15		L4	
Seeley, Elizabeth	18, Apr. 1821				L3	
Seeley, Mason G.	18, Apr. 1821	22, Mar.			L3	
Seely, Edson	26, July 1832	July	23		L1	
Seely, Morris	29, July 1847	July	47		L3	
Seemer, Jacob	12, Aug. 1841	Aug.	21		L3	
Seever, Henry	14, Mar. 1833	Mar.	8- 9m		L1	
Sefton, Elizabeth	13, Jan. 1842		estate		L3	
Sefton, Henry	9, June 1836		probate		L3	
Sefton, Henry	12, Jan. 1837		probate		L3	
Sefton, Henry	22, June 1837		probate		L3	
Sehon, John L. (Major)	10, June 1847	17, May	77	*	L3	

Name	Notice Date	Death Date	Age	Page	Maiden Name
Seib, W. (Rev)	30, Nov. 1843	29, Nov.		L3	
Seibert, Henry	12, July 1849	July	47	L3	
Seifert, Otto	3, Aug. 1854	29, July	11m	L3	
Seig, George Burke	15, Jan. 1852	12, Jan.	10w	L3	
Seig, Mary	21, June 1849	17, June	67	L3	
Seig, Mary Ann	4, July 1850	27, June	38	L3	
Seig, Peter	21, Dec. 1848	15, Dec.	68	L3	
Seivenspenner, John	9, May 1850	Apr.	29	L3	
Selden, Alanson Douglass	22, Apr. 1852	16, Apr.	53	L3	
Selden, Cary	8, June 1843	26, May	61	L3	
Selden, Joseph	24, June 1847	June	37	L3	
Selden, Sophia Hunt	13, May 1852	4, May	4- - 4d	L3	
Selius, Barnard	4, Sept 1845	Aug.	35	L3	
Seller, John	15, Oct. 1840	Oct.	45	L3	
Sellers, Eleanor Parrish	23, Aug. 1855	21, Aug.	19	L3	
Sellers, Sarah	1, Mar. 1855	31, Jan.	72	L3	
Sellers, Thomas	9, Oct. 1834	Sept	26	L1	
Sellers, William	11, July 1844	1, July		L3	
Sellew, John Y.	25, Dec. 1851	24, Dec.		L4	
Sellew, Lucy Virginia	14, Oct. 1847		4-10m	L3	
Sellew, Washington L. Fayette	29, Apr. 1847	14, Apr.	23	L3	
Sellin, Frederick H.	7, June 1855	4, June	39	L3	
Sellinger, Andrew (Mrs)	20, Mar. 1856		26	L3	
Sellman, Elizabeth	17, Oct. 1844	9, Oct.	64	L3	
Sellman, John (Dr)	7, 14, Feb. 1828	6, Feb.	64	L1	
Selman, Mary G.	14, Mar. 1833	Mar.	14-10m	L1	
Selomker, John	7, Aug. 1834	July	1- 4m	L3	
Seloy (child of Charles)	22, Aug. 1833	Aug.	stillborn	L4	
Selter, (son of J.A.)	26, Feb. 1852	14, Feb.	3	L3	
Seltz, Jacob	13, July 1843	July	38	L3	
Selver, John N.	21, Sept 1843	Sept	65	L3	
Selves, Charles Michael	1, June 1843	31, May	2	L3	
Selves, George	11, Dec. 1856	4, Dec.	21	L3	
Selves, Sarah Ellen	18, Dec. 1845	14, Dec.	1- 9m	L3	
Selves, Sophia	3, Apr. 1845	27, Mar.	18	L3	
Semple, Helen M.	7, June 1849	3, June		L3	Wallace
Semple, Mariann B.	14, Dec. 1854	7, Dec.		L3	
Senion, John E.	19, Apr. 1845	11, Apr.	28	L3	
Senteny, William	12, Nov. 1840		estate	L3	
Sepley, John	21, July 1842	July	48	L3	
Serafini, Mary	23, Dec. 1830	12, Dec.	39	L2	
Seraton, Dominic	25, Oct. 1832	19, Oct.		L2	
Sergant, (child of Mr)	4, Oct. 1833	Sept	8d	L1	
Serimgour, David	16, May 1833	May	3- 6m	L1	
Sermerman, (child of Jacob)	20, Nov. 1834	Nov.	1d	L1	
Serron, Robert	18, July 1833	July	30	L2	
Serterni, Martin	29, July 1852			L3	
Sesinger, Benedict	28, Aug. 1845	Aug.	31	L3	
Sester, Thomas	8, Mar. 1849	Feb.	25	L3	
Setterling, Frederick	8, June 1848	May	15m	L3	
Severn, Joseph	29, Jan. 1846	21, Jan.	62	L3	
Severns, Edward	12, Sept 1850	Sept	34	L3	
Seward, B.J.	1, Apr. 1841	24, Feb.		L3	
Seward, James	2, Feb. 1809		estate	L3	

Name	Notice Date	Death Date	Age	Page	Maiden Name
Sexton, (child of John)	4, Sept 1845	Aug.	6w	L3	
Seybold, Emanuel F.	16, Oct. 1851	13, Oct.	39	L3	
Seybold, Frederick	14, July 1853	9, July		L3	
Seymour, Daniel	25, Oct. 1832	16, Oct.	4	L4	
Shackelford, Henrettes	20, June 1833	June	34	L1	
Shackleford, George T. (Lt)	5, Oct. 1848	28, Sept	18	* L3	
Shadd, Edwin Ashton	30, June 1853	23, June	4- 2m	L3	
Shaddinger, George	26, Mar. 1857	25, Mar.	68	L3	
Shaddinger, Sarah	9, Feb. 1854	17, Dec.	65- 5m	L3	
Shadduck, Charles	10, Aug. 1843	27, July		L3	
Shaeffer, Daniel	26, Sept 1826		probate	L3	
Shafer, Elizabeth	28, June 1849	June	28	L3	
Shafer, Jonas	7, Oct. 1847	Sept	26	L3	
Shafer, Melchior	18, Apr. 1850	Apr.	5m	L3	
Shaffer, Anderson	8, Dec. 1842	Dec.	40	L3	
Shaffer, Anna	25, July 1850	July	7	L3	
Shaffer, Catharine Ellen	11, Aug. 1842	1, Aug.	9m	L3	
Shaffer, Daniel	24, Oct. 1821		estate	L4	
Shaffer, George Nicholas	1, Jan. 1852	29, Dec.		L3	
Shaffer, Henry	30, Mar. 1848	Mar.	40	L3	
Shaffer, John	25, July 1850	July	6	L3	
Shaffer, Louis	31, Mar. 1831		estate	L3	
Shaffer, Michael	25, July 1850	July	36	L3	
Shaffer, William	4, Oct. 1833	Sept	4m-15d	L1	
Shaffler, Arnold	24, Dec. 1840	Dec.	51	L3	
Shalley, Samuel	15, June 1848	June	30	L3	
Shally, Elizabeth	24, June 1841	19, June		L3	
Shally, Louis H. (Capt)	4, Mar. 1847	25, Feb.		L3	
Shally, Susan F. Sharpless	26, Dec. 1839	25, Dec.		L3	
Shampeela, Louis	4, Oct. 1849	Sept	43	L3	
Shane, (child of Henry)	22, Aug. 1833	Aug.		L4	
Shane, (Mrs)	1, Aug. 1833	July		L1	
Shane, Mary	18, July 1844	15, July	62	L3	
Shanehart, John	11, Jan. 1838	Dec.	28	L3	
Shankland, Rhoad	2, May 1826		estate	L2	
Shanklin, John	9, Sept 1847		81	L3	
Shanklin, John, Jr.	27, Dec. 1832		estate	L3	
Shanks, Louisa	12, Mar. 1840	Mar.	1- 8m	L3	
Shannon, John	12, Aug. 1852	Aug.	1	L3	
Share, James	11, Oct. 1832	7, Oct.		L2	
Sharp, Delia Frances	24, July 1834	23, July	1- 3m-19d	L4	
Sharp, Elizabeth	20, Sept 1832	Sept	11m	L1	
Sharp, James	9, June 1836		probate	L3	
Sharp, Mary Jane	23, Jan. 1851	Jan.	18m	L3	
Sharp, Nathan	9, Aug. 1849	3, Aug.	63	L3	
Sharp, William	13, Apr. 1848	Apr.	36	L3	
Sharpe, James	19, Sept 1833	Sept	26	L4	
Sharpe, Sarah Ann	19, Feb. 1857	15, Feb.		L3	
Sharpless, Margaret	25, Jan. 1844		estate	L3	
Sharpless, Thomas	8, Nov. 1832	Nov.	35	L1	
Sharpless, Thomas	29, Nov. 1832		estate	L2	
Shartridge, George W.	25, Oct. 1832	Oct.	12	L1	
Shatolis, William J.	9, Aug. 1849	July	3	L3	
Shattuck, Charles Perry	10, Aug. 1843		estate	L3	

Name	Notice Date	Death Date	Age	Page	Maiden Name
Shaw, Anna	16, Oct. 1834	Oct.	11m-15d	L1	
Shaw, Annie G.	12, Apr. 1855	3, Apr.		L3	
Shaw, Daniel	28, Aug. 1856	20, Aug.	60	L5	
Shaw, Elizabeth	28, Nov. 1833	Nov.	34	L4	
Shaw, Henry	12, Apr. 1849	Apr.	27	L3	
Shaw, Henry	14, Nov. 1839	6, Nov.	28 *	L3	
Shaw, Henry	13, May 1841		estate	L3	
Shaw, James	4, Jan. 1844	Dec.	26	L3	
Shaw, John	7, Sept 1848	Aug.	25	L3	
Shaw, Mary C.	5, Nov. 1857	2, Nov.	13	L3	
Shaw, Robert	15, Jan. 1857	8, Jan.	19	L3	
Shaw, Thomas	14, June 1849	8, June		L3	
Shaw, William	1, Sept 1842	Aug.	20	L3	
Shaw, William	5, Sept 1839		probate	L3	
Shawk, (child of Abel)	23, Oct. 1834	Oct.	stillborn	L2	
Shawk, (child of Abigail)	12, Sept 1833	Sept	1d	L1	
Shawk, Anna M.	10, Oct. 1844	9, Oct.		L3	
Shawk, Mary	15, Nov. 1832	Nov.	9	L1	
Shays, Frances B.	23, Mar. 1849	15, Mar.	54	L3	
Shays, Frederick Augustus	3, Nov. 1842	13, Oct.	16- 9m	L3	
Shays, John	13, Feb. 1851	6, Feb.	65	L3	
Shays, John	6, Mar. 1851		estate	L3	
Shays, John Mount	11, May 1854	7, May	8	L3	
Shea, Thomas	16, Sept 1847	Sept	24	L3	
Shea, William	28, Oct. 1847	Oct.	25	L3	
Sheardin, Thomas	19, Apr. 1849	Apr.	49	L3	
Shearer, James	18, Oct. 1832	Oct.	43	L4	
Shearer, John	6, July 1854	26, Mar.		L3	
Shearman, Charles	4, Apr. 1833	Mar.	10m	L1	
Shearwin, Cynthia J.	16, Aug. 1849	Aug.	14	L3	
Sheas, Richard	13, Nov. 1850	Nov.	23	L3	
Sheckels, John	11, July 1833	July	28	L1	
Shedley, Fred.	26, July 1849	July	30	L3	
Sheehen, Thomas	7, June 1849	May	55	L3	
Sheeney, Thadeus	12, Apr. 1849	Apr.	40	L3	
Sheets, Levi	26, Apr. 1849	Apr.	21	L3	
Sheets, Philip	29, Sept 1842	Sept	52	L3	
Sheffey, Guttlevey	19, Aug. 1852	Aug.	26	L3	
Shehane, (child of Mary)	17, May 1849	May	stillborn	L3	
Shehane, Mary	17, May 1849	May	25	L3	
Shelden, Chrispin	31, Aug. 1848	Aug.	16	L3	
Sheldon, James M.	26, Nov. 1846	Nov.	18m	L3	
Shell, Mary Juliet	24, Aug. 1843	4, Aug.	20m	L3	
Shell, Sarah Sailor	24, Aug. 1843	20, Aug.		L3	
Shelton, Fleming	31, Oct. 1850	Oct.		L3	
Shelton, John O.	19, July 1855	11, July	48	L3	
Shemin, Sylvester	31, May 1849	May	17	L3	
Shepard, Edwin	25, July 1850	23, July	38 *	L3	
Shepard, Edwin	12, Sept 1850		estate	L3	
Shepardson, Mary Harriet	23, Aug. 1849	16, Aug.	1- -24d	L3	
Shepherd, David	13, Mar. 1845	6, Mar.	62	L3	
Shepherd, Frances A.	1, July 1841	29, June		L3	
Shepherd, George	13, June 1839		estate	L3	
Shepherd, John	26, June 1851	June	1m	L3	

Name	Notice Date	Death Date	Age		Page	Maiden Name
Shepherd, Morris L.	12, Aug. 1841	11, Aug.			L3	
Shepherd, Uriel C.	15, Mar. 1838	13, Mar.	9- 3m		L3	
Shepherd, Zerelda	26, Aug. 1841	30, July			L3	
Sheppard, Augustus L. (Capt)	1, Feb. 1849	21, Jan.			L3	
Sheppard, James	8, Jan. 1857		probate		L3	
Shepperd, John G.	18, Dec. 1845	12, Dec.	20		L3	
Sherer, Thomas	7, July 1853	June			L3	
Sheridan, James S.	22, Sept 1853	Aug.			L3	
Sheridan, Mary	21, June 1849	June	40		L3	
Sheridan, Orren	10, June 1847	June	24		L3	
Sheriff, James	1, July 1841	June	33		L3	
Sherlock, Martha Ann	15, Oct. 1857	14, Oct.	9		L3	
Sherlock, Martha Ann	5, July 1849	28, June	10m		L3	
Sherlock, Martha Ann	31, Aug. 1848	21, Aug.			L3	
Sherman, Eliza	28, May 1846	May	15m		L3	
Sherman, John	18, July 1850	July	6m		L3	
Sherman, Joseph Edwin	7, Sept 1848	6, Sept	5m-16d		L3	
Sherman, Mary Ann	4, May 1848	1, May	27	*	L3	Gitchell
Sherrer, Caroline	7, Feb. 1850	Jan.	29		L3	
Sherridan, James B.	5, Apr. 1849	Mar.	30		L3	
Sherry, Edward	26, Oct. 1848	Oct.	40		L3	
Sherwin, Willington W.	19, July 1849	July	19		L3	
Sherwood, Aris B.	23, Mar. 1849	18, Mar.	18m-15d		L3	
Sherwood, Christian Alice	1, Mar. 1849	24, Feb.	4		L3	
Sherwood, James R.	27, July 1848	20, July	44		L3	
Sherwood, Mathew H.	29, Jan. 1846	25, Jan.	25		L3	
Sherwood, Robert Revell	25, July 1850	23, July	1		L3	
Shewell, Edward	9, Nov. 1854	30, Oct.			L3	
Shewell, Lowell A.	23, June 1853	21, June	13		L3	
Shieftods, Catharine M.	8, Aug. 1833	July	2		L1	
Shield, Eliza	9, May 1844	8, May			L3	
Shield, Ida	24, June 1847	23, June	11m		L3	
Shields, Laura	14, July 1853	4, July			L3	
Shields, Virginia J.	17, June 1852	10, June			L3	
Shingledecker, Abigail	16, Aug. 1838	8, Aug.	103-1m-16d	*	L3	
Shingledecker, Isaac	28, Aug. 1834	Aug.	50		L1	
Shingledecker, Isaac	2, Oct. 1834		estate		L4	
Shinn, Charles	13, Nov. 1834		estate		L3	
Shinn, Hannah	22, Aug. 1833	Aug.	2- 6m		L4	
Shinn, William H.	13, July 1848	July	5		L3	
Shipler, John F.	20, July 1854	13, July	21- 1m- 2d		L3	
Shipley, Ann	3, Aug. 1854	29, July	93- 9m-19d		L3	
Shipley, Caroline	1, June 1843	24, May	4m		L3	
Shipley, Emeline V.	16, June 1853	12, June	21- 4m		L3	
Shipley, Henry Bonsall	11, July 1850	7, July	13m-20d		L3	
Shipley, Mary A.	26, June 1851	June	2m		L3	
Shipley, Mary Emily	8, June 1843	4, June	30- -16d		L3	
Shipley, Sarah	4, Jan. 1855	30, Dec.	67		L3	
Shipley, William	23, Mar. 1854	3, Mar.		*	L3	
Shipman, William	21, May 1835		estate		L3	
Shipman, William	23, Feb. 1837		probate		L3	
Shipp, Samuel A.M.	23, Mar. 1843	9, Mar.			L3	
Shippin, William	25, Aug. 1812		estate		L2	
Shoat, (child of James)	18, Oct. 1827	Oct.	4m		L3	

Name	Notice Date	Death Date	Age	Page	Maiden Name
Shodel, Henry	29, Aug. 1844	Aug.	58	L3	
Shoemaker, Adam	22, July 1852	20, July		L3	
Shoemaker, Charles	29, July 1847	22, July	20	L3	
Shoemaker, Jos.	8, Oct. 1846	Sept	34	L3	
Shoemaker, Samuel	16, Nov. 1848	Nov.	22	L3	
Shoenberger, (girl)	11, Nov. 1847	4, Nov.		L1	
Shoenberger, Jane	30, Jan. 1851	27, Jan.	5- 4m	L3	
Shoester, John	15, July 1847	July	22	L3	
Sholl, David	5, Nov. 1857		probate	L3	
Sholl, David	27, Mar. 1856	20, Mar.		L3	
Shook, Hiram	21, Sept 1848	Sept	21	L3	
Shoolfield, Honora A.	14, July 1853	13, July		L3	
Shores, David	7, June 1849	May	27	L3	
Short, Ann M.	9, Aug. 1849	July	1- 6m	L3	
Short, Betsy B.	1, Oct. 1846	27, Sept		L3	
Short, Mathew	19, Feb. 1846	Feb.	35	L3	
Short, Peyton	13, Jan. 1831		estate	L3	
Short, Robert	9, May 1839	Apr.	50	L3	
Short, Thornton	31, Aug. 1854	20, Aug.	9m-22d	L3	
Short, William	25, Oct. 1832	16, Oct.		L4	
Shortridge, Eliza Ann	16, Oct. 1828	14, Oct.		L3	
Shotten, Edward	10, June 1847	June	51	L3	
Shotwell, John T.	3, Oct. 1850		estate	L3	
Shotwell, John T. (Dr)	1, Aug. 1850	23, July		L3	
Shoultz, Frederick	9, Aug. 1849	July	1	L3	
Shoup, George	14, July 1853	7, July	43	L3	
Shreeve, Caleb Howard	26, Nov. 1857	16, Nov.		L3	
Shreve, Thomas	21, Jan. 1847	20, Jan.	77	* L3	
Shriver, Elizabeth	8, Oct. 1840	Sept	38	* L3	
Shriver, Margaret	8, Oct. 1840	Sept	17	* L3	
Shropshire, Sarah E.	4, Dec. 1845	27, Nov.		L3	
Shroyer, George	11, Oct. 1838	28, Sept		L3	
Shuey, Adam C. (Dr)	16, Oct. 1856	23, Sept	28	* L5	
Shuey, Catharine	16, Feb. 1854	3, Feb.	26	L3	
Shull, Reuben	10, June 1852		estate	L3	
Shull, Reuben	28, June 1849		estate	L4	
Shulte, John Beman	5, Oct. 1848	Sept	47	L3	
Shultz, Conrad	26, Sept 1839	9, Sept	85	L3	
Shupe, Samuel	16, Sept 1847	Sept	46	L3	
Shurrager, George W.	20, Dec. 1855	15, Dec.	44	L3	
Shurtleff, Benjamin (Dr)	29, Apr. 1847	12, Apr.	73	L3	
Shute, Milton	5, Nov. 1857	4, Nov.	5	L3	
Shute, Milton	30, Aug. 1855		estate	L3	
Shute, Milton	9, Apr. 1857		probate	L3	
Shuts, Milton	9, Aug. 1855	8, Aug.	35	L3	
Sickly, James	3, Jan. 1850	Dec.	24	L3	
Sidebothom, (child of Joseph)	2, June 1842	May	3m	L3	
Sidel, Henry	21, June 1849	June	25	L3	
Sidell, Elizabeth Ann	9, Mar. 1854	1, Mar.	30- 2m-14d	L3	Cline
Sides, Eliza	4, Oct. 1849	1, Oct.	37	L3	
Sidle, Thornton	11, June 1846	June	30	L3	
Siebern, C.M. Lucy	26, July 1849	18, July	22	L3	
Siewers, Frank	19, Jan. 1854	16, Jan.	4- 6m	L3	
Sigerson, Theodore M.	2, Dec. 1852	26, Nov.	10	L3	

Name	Notice Date	Death Date	Age		Page	Maiden Name
Siglow, John	6, June 1850	May	20		L3	
Silben, Conrad	18, Oct. 1838	Oct.	35		L3	
Siler, Henry	11, Sept 1834	Aug.	23		L1	
Sill, Mary	7, Dec. 1843	6, Dec.	33		L3	
Silliman, George	13, Aug. 1846	Aug.	53		L3	
Silliman, George W.	24, Nov. 1842	26, Oct.	34		L6	
Silliman, Isabella E.	18, Nov. 1841	9, Nov.	18		L3	
Silliman, Wyllis	24, Nov. 1842	13, Nov.	65		L6	
Sillirs, John Bernhardt	8, June 1854	1, June			L3	
Sills, Richard	1, Nov. 1832	23, Oct.			L1	
Silman, Abel	28, Apr. 1853	27, Apr.			L3	
Silman, Lewis	1, Oct. 1846	Sept	29		L3	
Silock, Jacob	2, July 1846	June	27		L3	
Silsbee, Bell	4, July 1850	26, June	1		L3	
Silsbee, Charles Houston	23, Apr. 1846	21, Apr.	1- 1m		L3	
Silsbee, Harriet Anna	3, Nov. 1842	27, Oct.	8m		L3	
Silsbee, John W.	11, Oct. 1838		estate		L3	
Silsbee, John W.	13, Feb. 1840		probate		L3	
Silsbee, John W.	27, Sept 1838	26, Sept			L3	
Silver, Elias	22, June 1837		probate		L3	
Silver, Elizabeth	27, Dec. 1849		estate		L3	
Silver, John	8, June 1827		estate		L3	
Silvers, Elias	12, May 1836		estate		L4	
Silvers, James	1, Jan. 1852		estate		L3	
Silvester, Sally	30, Apr. 1808	21, Apr.		*	L3	
Silvey, A.D.	15, Apr. 1847	10, Apr.	24	*	L3	
Silvey, George	2, Nov. 1843	Oct.	27		L3	
Simes, Charles W.	15, Oct. 1840	Oct.	24		L3	
Simeson, Barney	24, Feb. 1848		estate		L3	
Simmons, A.H.	29, July 1841	23, July		*	L3	
Simmons, Abigail E.	2, Aug. 1855	31, July	40		L3	
Simmons, George	22, Mar. 1838		probate		L3	
Simmons, John	12, July 1849	July	23		L3	
Simmons, Martha G.	2, Mar. 1848	23, Feb.			L2	
Simmons, Robert	5, Dec. 1826	2, Dec.			L3	
Simms, Michael	8, Jan. 1846	Dec.	23		L3	
Simms, William	3, May 1855	27, Apr.	57		L3	
Simon, Henry J.	30, Mar. 1854				L3	
Simon, Isaac	5, Nov. 1857		probate		L3	
Simons,	8, Aug. 1833	July	36		L1	
Simons, Jane	25, May 1837	May	23		L2	
Simons, Lucy C.	3, 10, July 1845	June	32		L3	
Simonson, Aaron	8, Jan. 1852		estate		L3	
Simonton, Theophilus	6, Dec. 1855	6, Dec.	87	*	L3	
Simpkinson, Elizabeth	23, Jan. 1845	20, Jan.		*	L3	
Simpson, Alexander	22, Aug. 1833	Aug.	9		L4	
Simpson, Catharine	8, June 1848	5, June	20		L3	
Simpson, Elizabeth	18, Sept 1834	Sept	57		L1	
Simpson, James	18, Oct. 1832	13, Oct.			L2	
Simpson, James	10, May 1849	May	21		L3	
Simpson, James	8, July 1847	June	25		L3	
Simpson, John	11, Apr. 1839	Apr.	35		L3	
Simpson, Sarah J.	6, June 1833	May	2		L2	
Sims, James	3, Mar. 1831		estate		L3	

Name	Notice Date	Death Date	Age	Page	Maiden Name
Sims, James	3, May 1832		estate	L3	
Sims, James	14, Feb. 1839		probate	L3	
Sims, John	26, May 1817		estate	L1	
Simson, Margaret	27, Jan. 1848	Jan.	53	L3	
Sincox, James	12, Mar. 1840		estate	L4	
Singer, Catharine E.	18, July 1833	July	14	L2	
Singleton, Benjamin	28, Nov. 1850	Nov.	2m	L3	
Singleton, Sarah	26, Sept 1850	Sept	17d	L3	
Sink, Christopher	3, June 1847	May	58	L3	
Sintenburg, Ann Maria	1, Aug. 1833	July	19	L1	
Sinton, Jane	2, 9, June 1853	28, May	27	L3	
Sipe, Charles	12, Oct. 1813		estate	L2	
Sirokum, Barny	13, Dec. 1849	Dec.	30	L3	
Sirp, Francis	19, July 1849	July	36	L3	
Sisson, James	22, Aug. 1823	19, Aug.	35	L3	
Sisson, James	26, Sept 1826		probate	L3	
Sisson, Orrin	9, Aug. 1838		probate	L3	
Sisson, Reuben	29, June 1848	June	26	L3	
Sivessy, John	23, Mar. 1848	Mar.	42	L3	
Sizer, Searian	1, Aug. 1833	July	3- 2m	L1	
Skaates, Abigail	12, Sept 1833	Sept	24	L1	
Skaats, John	3, Aug. 1854	1, Aug.	8- 5m	L3	
Skaats, Margret Emma	17, Aug. 1854	14, Aug.	4	L3	
Skillman, Benjamin	4, June 1829		estate	L3	
Skillman, Jacob	9, Feb. 1822		estate	L3	
Skillman, Jacob	29, May 1834		probate	L3	
Skillman, Samuel	13, Feb. 1824		estate	L4	
Skillman, Thomas	11, July 1833		probate	L3	
Skilsman, Isaac N.	7, Jan. 1841		estate	L3	
Skinn, (child of Samuel)	16, June 1842	June	stillborn	L3	
Skinner, Ambrose	16, Oct. 1845	Oct.	15	L3	
Skinner, George	5, Aug. 1816		estate	L3	
Skivington, William	31, Jan. 1810	29, Jan.	56	L3	
Skull, John	25, May 1843	17, May	7- 6m-24d	L3	
Slack, James	20, Mar. 1851	Mar.	1- 6m	L3	
Slack, Margaretta D.	21, Mar. 1839	4, Mar.	*	L3	Heard
Slade, Henry A.	12, Oct. 1837	20, Sept		L3	
Slaigh, Isabella	4, Oct. 1833	Sept	2	L1	
Slanger, Frederick	21, Feb. 1850	Feb.	60	L3	
Slater, William	8, May 1828	May	17	L1	
Slaughter, Abraham	30, Dec. 1830		estate	L3	
Slaughter, Abraham	17, Mar. 1826		probate	L3	
Slaughter, William	8, Apr. 1841		estate	L3	
Slayback, A. (Dr)	29, Aug. 1839	28, Aug.	50	L3	
Slayback, A. (Dr)	26, Dec. 1839		estate	L3	
Slayback, Solomon	7, Sept 1824		probate	L3	
Sleag, Robert M.	18, Oct. 1832	11, Oct.		L1	
Sleaper, Oscar	5, Apr. 1849	1, Apr.	10m- 1d	L3	
Sleicker, George	7, May 1846	Apr.	46	L3	
Sleven, Elizabeth J.	30, Nov. 1848	Nov.	7m	L3	
Slevin, Ann	3, Apr. 1845	26, Mar.	7m	L3	
Slevin, Louisa	16, Oct. 1851	15, Oct.	infant	L3	
Slevin, Patrick H.	15, Feb. 1855	11, Feb.	24	L3	
Slevin, Tully Daniel	17, Mar. 1853	10, Mar.	79	L3	

Name	Notice Date	Death Date	Age		Page	Maiden Name
Slick, John	23, July 1846	July	36		L3	
Slicter, (Mr)	19, May 1853	16, May			L3	
Slinebrow, Frederick	26, Dec. 1850	Dec.	14d		L3	
Sloan, James	2, Mar. 1854	1, Mar.	35		L3	
Sloat, (child of George)	8, Aug. 1833	July	1d		L1	
Sloate, Mary A.	8, Aug. 1833	July	22- 6m		L1	
Slocum, Martha	9, July 1846	June	16		L3	
Sloo, Harriett	22, May 1815	20, May			L3	
Sloop, Catharine	25, May 1843	20, May	78		L3	
Sloop, Samuel	16, Apr. 1840	10, Apr.	39		L3	
Sloop, Samuel	23, Apr. 1840		estate		L3	
Sluvin, William	12, Sept 1833	Sept			L1	
Sly, Jane	2, Aug. 1838	July	25		L3	
Sly, Jane	14, Feb. 1839		probate		L3	
Small, Hannah	2, Oct. 1834	Sept			L4	
Smart, James R.	12, Jan. 1837		probate		L3	
Smart, Louisa	19, Mar. 1857	16, Mar.	36		L3	
Smidt, John	10, Dec. 1857		probate		L3	
Smith, (child of Acturn)	21, Nov. 1833	Nov.	14d		L3	
Smith, (child of Eliza)	8, July 1841	June	stillborn		L3	
Smith, (child of Elizabeth)	22, Sept 1842	Sept	stillborn		L3	
Smith, (child of Elizabeth)	22, Feb. 1844	Feb.	stillborn		L3	
Smith, (child of Mary)	20, Apr. 1848	Apr.	6w		L3	
Smith, (child of Phebe)	11, Oct. 1838	Oct.	1d		L3	
Smith, (child of Samuel)	9, Oct. 1834	Sept	15d		L1	
Smith, (child)	16, Oct. 1834	Oct.	9d		L1	
Smith, (daughter of Mrs)	25, Oct. 1832	19, Oct.	5		L1	
Smith, (Mrs)	25, Oct. 1832	19, Oct.			L2	
Smith, Abner	18, July 1850	July	41		L3	
Smith, Ada Eliza	9, Apr. 1857	7, Apr.	3-10m-21d		L3	
Smith, Ada Louisa	3, Feb. 1855	25, Jan.	3- 6m		L3	
Smith, Adam	31, Dec. 1846	Dec.	64		L3	
Smith, Albert	29, Jan. 1846	Jan.	23		L3	
Smith, Albert	24, June 1847	June	20m		L3	
Smith, Albert T.	27, Sept 1855		10- -14d		L3	
Smith, Alex	4, Apr. 1833	Mar.	1- 6m		L1	
Smith, Amy P.	3, Mar. 1853	24, Feb.	37		L3	
Smith, Angelina	5, Aug. 1852	10, July	21m		L3	
Smith, Ann	23, Mar. 1848	Mar.	23		L3	
Smith, Ann	1, Oct. 1840	Sept	35		L3	
Smith, Ann	4, Jan. 1844	15, Dec.		*	L3	
Smith, Anna	15, Nov. 1855	4, Oct.	49-10m	*	L3	
Smith, Arnold Charles	13, June 1844	12, June	6		L3	
Smith, Benjamin Y.	12, July 1838	2, July			L3	
Smith, Bridget	3, July 1851	June	39		L3	
Smith, Broadfoot	18, Aug. 1831		estate		L3	
Smith, Burrows	10, Oct. 1823	9, Oct.			L3	
Smith, Caroline	7, Aug. 1845	July	3		L3	
Smith, Caroline Walker	20, Mar. 1845	18, Mar.	4- 6m		L3	
Smith, Catharine	15, Nov. 1849	10, Nov.	76		L3	
Smith, Catharine Eliza	7, Apr. 1826				L3	
Smith, Charles	18, July 1850	July	24		L3	
Smith, Charles	25, July 1839	July	30		L3	
Smith, Charles Edward	23, Aug. 1855	18, Aug.	2m		L3	

Name	Notice Date	Death Date	Age		Page	Maiden Name
Smith, Charles Osmond	23, Dec. 1847	19, Dec.	15m- 9d		L3	
Smith, Charles S.	24, Apr. 1851	17, Apr.	26		L3	
Smith, Charles T.	15, July 1841	21, June	22		L3	
Smith, Charlotte	9, May 1821	5, May			L3	
Smith, Chester	30, Mar. 1854	4, Feb.	27		L3	
Smith, Christian	20, Dec. 1825		probate		L4	
Smith, Christopher	11, July 1850	July	1m		L3	
Smith, Christopher	31, Mar. 1853		estate		L3	
Smith, Conrad	27, Apr. 1854	21, Apr.			L3	
Smith, Constantine	29, Jan. 1816		estate		L3	
Smith, Cyrus N.	11, May 1819	4, May			L3	
Smith, Daniel	18, Oct. 1849	15, Oct.			L2	
Smith, Daniel	25, Oct. 1849				L3	
Smith, David	16, Oct. 1815				L1	
Smith, Deborah	1, Nov. 1832	23, Oct.			L4	
Smith, Edmund C.	25, July 1833	July			L1	
Smith, Edmund C.	29, Apr. 1847	23, Apr.	23- 4m		L3	
Smith, Edmund C.	12, Sept 1833		estate		L3	
Smith, Edward	17, Sept 1857	9, Sept			L3	
Smith, Elenor	23, Mar. 1837	Mar.	4		L3	
Smith, Eli (Dr)	5, Mar. 1857	11, Jan.			L1	
Smith, Elizabeth	19, July 1855	10, July	39		L3	
Smith, Elizabeth	21, Aug. 1845	13, Aug.	42		L3	
Smith, Elizabeth	21, Dec. 1824	19, Dec.	78		L3	
Smith, Ellen	13, Sept 1855	6, Sept	26		L3	
Smith, Emily	13, Sept 1832	Sept	1- 2m- 4d		L1	
Smith, Fannie H.	13, Feb. 1851	10, Feb.	14m		L3	
Smith, Fanny	9, May 1839	30, Apr.			L3	
Smith, Frances E.	3, Feb. 1848	29, Jan.	18		L3	Coleman
Smith, Francis	13, Feb. 1845		20		L3	
Smith, Garnett	31, July 1851	26, July	80		L3	
Smith, George	21, Dec. 1837	Dec.	35		L3	
Smith, George	2, May 1850	28, Apr.	68	*	L3	
Smith, George (Capt)	10, Apr. 1828	1, Apr.	70	*	L2	
Smith, George H.	7, Aug. 1856	30, July	22m		L5	
Smith, George Lucky	5, Oct. 1854	3, Oct.	infant		L3	
Smith, Green H.	30, Aug. 1832	Aug.	58		L1	
Smith, H.W.	27, Nov. 1856	1, Nov.	36		L3	
Smith, Hannah	14, Feb. 1828	Feb.	2		L1	
Smith, Hanson	26, Oct. 1848	Oct.	22		L3	
Smith, Helen Sargent	11, Oct. 1838	10, Oct.	17m		L3	
Smith, Helen Virginia	9, July 1857	8, July	22- 8m		L3	
Smith, Henry	13, June 1833	June	23		L1	
Smith, Henry	12, Mar. 1840	Mar.	8m		L3	
Smith, Henry	18, Oct. 1832	15, Oct.			L3	
Smith, Henry	7, July 1853				L3	
Smith, Henry H.	23, Jan. 1845	15, Jan.	3- 6m		L3	
Smith, Hulda	16, June 1806	1, May	43		L3	
Smith, Isaac	24, Aug. 1854		estate		L3	
Smith, Isabella	16, June 1853	15, June	20- 5m		L3	
Smith, Jacob	25, July 1833	July	9m		L1	
Smith, Jacob	11, July 1844	July	42		L3	
Smith, Jacob	16, Oct. 1856		probate		L6	
Smith, James	25, July 1833	July	46		L1	

Name	Notice Date	Death Date	Age		Page	Maiden Name
Smith, James	1, Aug. 1833	July			L1	
Smith, James	3, Mar. 1842	Feb.	17		L3	
Smith, James	29, July 1847	July	20		L3	
Smith, James	29, Jan. 1846	Jan.	23		L3	
Smith, James	22, Aug. 1833		estate		L3	
Smith, James	28, Apr. 1807	25, Apr.			L3	
Smith, James	21, July 1807		estate		L4	
Smith, James Bailey	13, May 1830	11, May	7- 3m- 9d		L3	
Smith, James P.	14, Feb. 1839		probate		L3	
Smith, Jane	18, July 1833	July	52		L2	
Smith, Jane	24, July 1845	July	24		L3	
Smith, Jane	10, Jan. 1856	2, Dec.		*	L3	
Smith, Jane P.	25, May 1843	18, May			L3	
Smith, Jesse	2, Apr. 1835		estate		L3	
Smith, Jesse	7, May 1840		probate		L3	
Smith, Jesse	7, Jan. 1841	22, Dec.			L3	
Smith, Jesse (Dr)	1, 8, Aug. 1833	31, July	40		L1	
Smith, Jesse H.	22, Mar. 1838		probate		L3	
Smith, Jessee M.	12, Sept 1833		estate		L3	
Smith, Joanna	25, Mar. 1841	14, Mar.	53	*	L3	Morrill
Smith, John	6, Nov. 1834	Oct.	40		L1	
Smith, John	2, July 1829	26, June	30	*	L2	
Smith, John	6, Aug. 1846	July	20		L3	
Smith, John	8, Aug. 1850	July	22		L3	
Smith, John	11, Oct. 1838	Oct.	31		L3	
Smith, John	6, Aug. 1846	July	35		L3	
Smith, John	20, Nov. 1845	Nov.	38		L3	
Smith, John	20, Apr. 1848	Apr.	45		L3	
Smith, John	6, Aug. 1829		estate		L3	
Smith, John	12, Aug. 1841		estate		L3	
Smith, John	29, July 1841	28, July			L3	
Smith, John	3, Feb. 1848	25, Jan.			L3	
Smith, John	23, Feb. 1854				L3	
Smith, John Armor	25, Mar. 1841	12, Mar.	3		L3	
Smith, John J.	6, Feb. 1851	Jan.	30		L3	
Smith, John L.	9, Aug. 1855		probate		L3	
Smith, John L.	8, Aug. 1850	28, July			L3	
Smith, John R.	5, Feb. 1835		estate		L4	
Smith, Joseph H. (Dr)	19, Feb. 1846	18, Feb.	54		L3	
Smith, Josiah D.	15, Apr. 1847	12, Apr.	16		L3	
Smith, Julia	3, July 1845	25, June	6m		L3	
Smith, Justin	4, Jan. 1855	29, Dec.	75		L3	
Smith, Justus	7, Oct. 1823			*	L3	
Smith, Lavina Carll	28, Jan. 1841	27, Jan.	infant		L3	
Smith, Lemuel	3, Jan. 1833	13, Dec.			L2	
Smith, Lewis	9, July 1846	June	23		L3	
Smith, Lilla	5, Dec. 1850	30, Nov.	2-10m		L3	
Smith, Lockwood W.	20, Nov. 1828		estate		L3	
Smith, Louise	12, Aug. 1847	31, July	17m		L3	
Smith, Lovicy	18, Aug. 1821	16, Aug.			L3	
Smith, Lyman J.	9, Oct. 1845	Sept	15m		L3	
Smith, Marcus	6, Dec. 1855	27, Nov.			L3	
Smith, Margaret	1, Nov. 1832	Oct.	14		L2	
Smith, Margaret	3, Oct. 1850	Sept	15		L3	

Name	Notice Date	Death Date	Age	Page	Maiden Name
Smith, Margaret A.	22, Aug. 1850	Aug.	8m	L3	
Smith, Margaret J.	5, Sept 1833	Aug.	1- 2m	L1	
Smith, Martha	9, Sept 1841		estate	L3	
Smith, Martha J.	8, Aug. 1833	July	3-11m	L1	
Smith, Mary	16, May 1833	May	43	L1	
Smith, Mary	16, Aug. 1849	11, Aug.	58	L3	
Smith, Mary	14, May 1857	11, May	72	L3	
Smith, Mary A.	1, Nov. 1832	Oct.	25	L2	
Smith, Mary Ann	20, Sept 1838	Sept	4d	L3	
Smith, Mary Ella	3, June 1852	30, May		L3	
Smith, Mary J.	8, June 1848	May	23	L3	
Smith, Michael	3, Oct. 1850	Sept	56	L3	
Smith, Nancy M.	11, July 1833	July	14d	L1	
Smith, Nathan E.	14, Feb. 1833	Feb.	3m	L1	
Smith, Oliver C.	25, Apr. 1823		estate	L3	
Smith, Oliver C.	8, Apr. 1823	3, Apr.		L3	
Smith, Oscar	29, May 1845	May	17	L3	
Smith, Patrick	8, Sept 1831	30, Aug.		L1	
Smith, Patrick	10, Sept 1857	5, Sept	14	L3	
Smith, Peter	15, Aug. 1850	Aug.	4w	L3	
Smith, Priscilla	24, June 1847	June	17	L3	
Smith, Reuben	19, July 1832	July	30	L1	
Smith, Reuben	11, July 1850	July	35	L3	
Smith, Rhoda	20, Sept 1827	Sept	38	L1	
Smith, Robert	8, Aug. 1833	July	63	L1	
Smith, Robert	19, Dec. 1850	Dec.	20	L3	
Smith, Robert	14, June 1814		estate	L3	
Smith, Robert	18, Feb. 1836		estate	L3	
Smith, Robert	21, Sept 1837		probate	L4	
Smith, Robert H. (Dr)	12, Jan. 1813		estate	L3	
Smith, Robert S.	26, Nov. 1846	Nov.	46	L3	
Smith, Safronia B.	20, July 1848	15, July		* L3	
Smith, Samuel	20, Nov. 1850	Nov.	50	L3	
Smith, Samuel Wilshire	24, Feb. 1853	18, Feb.	5w	L3	
Smith, Sarah	22, Nov. 1849	9, Nov.	72	* L3	
Smith, Sarah Jane	12, Sept 1833	Sept	7- 8m-11d	L1	
Smith, Simon	3, Aug. 1848	July		L3	
Smith, T.B.	7, Dec. 1837		probate	L3	
Smith, T.J.	11, Oct. 1838		estate	L3	
Smith, Thomas	26, Feb. 1846	21, Feb.		L3	
Smith, Thomas	25, Oct. 1832	Oct.		L4	
Smith, Thomas B.	8, Nov. 1838		probate	L3	
Smith, Thomas B.	18, Apr. 1839		probate	L3	
Smith, Thomas Sargent	18, Dec. 1845	15, Dec.	10- 3m	L3	
Smith, Vannelia James	24, Oct. 1844	23, Oct.	infant	L3	
Smith, William	21, Feb. 1828	Feb.	29	L1	
Smith, William	1, Jan. 1846	23, Dec.	23	L3	
Smith, William	5, Jan. 1837		25	L3	
Smith, William	2, May 1850	Apr.	4m	L3	
Smith, William	30, May 1850	May	9m	L3	
Smith, William	26, Sept 1826		probate	L3	
Smith, William	16, Feb. 1827		probate	L3	
Smith, William	14, Dec. 1837	1, Dec.		L3	
Smith, William	21, Jan. 1847	Jan.		L3	

Name	Notice Date	Death Date	Age		Page	Maiden Name
Smith, William (Dr)	14, Mar. 1850	5, Mar.	66	*	L3	
Smith, William (Dr)	11, Apr. 1850		estate		L3	
Smith, William B.	20, June 1844	10, June			L3	
Smith, William C.	2, Oct. 1811	28, Sept			L3	
Smith, William F.	29, Aug. 1850	24, Aug.	28		L3	
Smith, William H.	6, July 1822		estate		L3	
Smith, William Henry H.	25, Mar. 1841	7, Mar.	11m		L3	
Smith, William O.	15, Aug. 1839	Aug.	35		L3	
Smith, William R.	30, July 1840	24, July	7m		L3	
Smith, William R.	10, Apr. 1856		probate		L3	
Smith, William R.	7, June 1849	3, June			L3	
Smith, William Richard	26, Aug. 1852	22, Aug.			L3	
Smith, William T.	17, Jan. 1850	1, Dec.	19		L3	
Smith, Wright	20, Nov. 1845	16, Nov.	62		L3	
Smith, Wright	12, Nov. 1846		estate		L3	
Smith, Wright	4, Sept 1856		probate		L5	
Smitherman, John	14, Feb. 1839		probate		L3	
Smoltz, Mary	17, Jan. 1850	10, Jan.			L2	
Smoot, David B.	14, Dec. 1824	13, Dec.			L3	
Snee, Mary	1, Aug. 1850	July	60		L3	
Sneed, (child of Cynthia)	7, Mar. 1844	Feb.			L3	
Snelling, James G. (Capt)	30, Aug. 1855	25, Aug.			L3	
Snethen, Nicholas (Rev)	19, June 1845	30, May	76		L3	
Snethen, Susannah Hood	19, Oct. 1843	26, Sept			L3	
Snider, (daughter)	1, Nov. 1832	24, Oct.	5		L1	
Snider, Daniel	29, May 1828	May	40		L2	
Snider, Elizabeth	24, May 1849	May	68		L3	
Snider, John M.	5, July 1855		probate		L3	
Sniveley, John H.	19, Sept 1844	Sept	1- 6m		L3	
Snoke, Arlan	15, Nov. 1832	Nov.	5		L1	
Snook, Anthony	11, Sept 1834	Aug.			L1	
Snow, James	6, Oct. 1821		estate		L3	
Snow, Lemuel	7, Sept 1824	3, Sept	65	*	L3	
Snowden, Roland G. Mitchell	31, Mar. 1853	23, Mar.	infant		L3	
Snowden, Sidney	2, Mar. 1854	27, Feb.			L3	
Snyder, (child of Susan)	23, Feb. 1843	Feb.	1m		L3	
Snyder, (man)	13, Jan. 1848	Jan.			L3	
Snyder, (Mrs)	1, Nov. 1832	24, Oct.			L1	
Snyder, Elizabeth	1, May 1828		20		L1	
Snyder, G.F.	30, July 1857	29, July	74		L3	
Snyder, George	27, Apr. 1854	22, Apr.	3		L3	
Snyder, George	7, Dec. 1848	Nov.	47		L3	
Snyder, Jacob	2, Jan. 1845	Dec.	48		L3	
Snyder, John	23, Jan. 1851	Jan.	86		L3	
Snyder, Samuel	17, Nov. 1842	Nov.	40		L6	
Soerg, Catharine	26, July 1849	July	25		L3	
Sogler, John	18, July 1833	July	2m		L2	
Sohn, E. (Mrs)	27, Dec. 1849	23, Dec.	73	*	L3	
Solar, Margaret	5, Aug. 1852	July	2		L3	
Soller, Catharine	29, Aug. 1833	Aug.	12d		L1	
Solomons, Jacob	15, Sept 1853				L3	
Solsman, Christian	2, Aug. 1832	July	4d		L1	
Solson, Henry	11, May 1848	May	20		L3	
Somerville, Archibald	15, Sept 1836		probate		L3	

Name	Notice Date	Death Date	Age	Page	Maiden Name
Sommer, Archibald	26, Dec. 1833		estate	L3	
Soreek (child)	1, Nov. 1832	24, Oct.	9	L1	
Sorosley, Lucy	11, July 1833	July	2- 5m	L1	
Sorter, Thomas	29, May 1834		probate	L3	
Souders, Daniel	11, Oct. 1838		estate	L3	
Souders, Daniel	3, Sept 1840		probate	L3	
Souders, Dennis K.	18, Oct. 1832	Oct.	1- 2m	L4	
South, William	6, Nov. 1811		estate	L3	
Southard, Emala	1, Nov. 1832	Oct.	1- 4m	L2	
Southell, Charles	28, July 1842	July	1- 8m	L3	
Southgate, Edward S.	20, May 1852	14, May	42- 4m	L3	
Southgate, H.H.	12, Apr. 1855	8, Apr.		L3	
Southgate, Julia	11, Sept 1851	6, Sept		L3	Watson
Southgate, Orville	8, Aug. 1850	2, Aug.	18	L3	
Southgate, Richard	9, Aug. 1855	5, Aug.	50	L3	
Southgate, Richard	6, Aug. 1857		estate	L3	
Southgate, William Wright	2, Jan. 1845	26, Dec.		L3	
Southwick, Amos	3, Sept 1846	22, Aug.	72	L1	
Sowders, Catharine	18, July 1850	July	26	L3	
Sowders, Jacob	18, July 1850	July	3	L3	
Sowers, Joseph Andrew	24, Nov. 1853	17, Nov.	16m	L3	
Sowers, Philip	15, Mar. 1832		estate	L3	
Spader, Peter	2, Mar. 1848		estate	L3	
Spader, Peter	21, June 1849		estate	L3	
Spahr, Amanda	20, June 1833	June	2- 4m	L1	
Spalding, Emma Celia	2, June 1853	25, May	1	L3	
Spalding, Henry P.	21, May 1846		28	* L3	
Spalding, Laura L.	24, June 1847	18, June	18m-27d	L3	
Spalman, David	18, Oct. 1832	11, Oct.		L1	
Sparks, Isaac	7, Dec. 1837		probate	L3	
Sparks, John H.	29, May 1834		probate	L3	
Sparks, Louisa	15, Nov. 1832	Nov.	8m-17d	L1	
Speakman, Mary W.	20, May 1841	26, Apr.	37	L3	
Spear, Emma	18, June 1846	11, June	3- -19d	L3	
Spears, Gamaliel Bailey	21, Aug. 1856	13, Aug.		L5	
Specht, Noyes	18, Oct. 1832	12, Oct.		L2	
Speck, Anthony	8, Nov. 1849	Oct.	26	L3	
Speckler, (son of Martin)	18, Mar. 1852		3- 6m	L4	
Speer, Harriet	24, Sept 1846	Sept	15m	L3	
Speer, John G.	4, June 1835		estate	L4	
Speer, Sarah Ann	18, June 1857	14, June	22	L3	
Spegler, George	18, June 1846	June	25	L3	
Spence, George	29, Apr. 1847	Apr.	35	L3	
Spence, John	24, Oct. 1839	Sept	43	L3	
Spence, Stephen	8, Nov. 1838		estate	L3	
Spence, Stephen	13, Feb. 1840		probate	L3	
Spence, Thomas	27, June 1850	June	2	L3	
Spencer, (child of Mr)	25, Oct. 1832	16, Oct.	3	L4	
Spencer, Alexander O.	21, Oct. 1841	12, Oct.	28	L3	
Spencer, Ann Eliza	23, May 1833	May	18	L4	
Spencer, Electra	1, Feb. 1849	28, Jan.	63	L3	
Spencer, Emily	23, Aug. 1849	Aug.	4	L3	
Spencer, John	5, July 1849	June	22	L3	
Spencer, John C.	28, Aug. 1856	24, Aug.	47	L5	

Name	Notice Date	Death Date	Age		Page	Maiden Name
Spencer, Maria Antoinette	13, May 1847	7, May	15m		L3	
Spencer, Ogden	28, June 1849	25, June	8		L3	
Spencer, Oliver	14, June 1814		estate		L3	
Spencer, Oliver	30, Oct. 1811		estate		L4	
Spencer, Oliver (Col)	30, Jan. 1811	22, Jan.	74		L3	
Spencer, Oliver (Col)	6, Feb. 1811	22, Jan.	74	*	L3	
Spencer, Robert G.	25, Oct. 1832	Oct.	1- 2m		L1	
Spencer, Robert Halsted	15, June 1837	11, June	2		L3	
Spencer, Samuel	20, Aug. 1829		estate		L3	
Spencer, William	8, Feb. 1838	Feb.	67		L3	
Spencer, William Halsted	24, Sept 1840	13, Sept	1- 3m		L3	
Spener, James	8, Aug. 1833	July	18		L1	
Spenser, Polly	16, May 1833	May	51		L1	
Spicet, Charles H.	23, Feb. 1854	15, Jan.	28	*	L3	
Spicet, Charles H. (Mrs)	23, Feb. 1854	18, Oct.			L3	
Spidel, Jacob	18, Oct. 1832	13, Oct.			L2	
Spiles, Barney	26, July 1849	July	56		L3	
Spiller, Benjamin	20, Sept 1827	Sept	8m		L1	
Spining, Pierson	29, Jan. 1857	21, Jan.	71		L3	
Spinning, Ichabod	22, Oct. 1819		estate		L3	
Spinning, Ichabod	11, May 1822		estate		L3	
Spinning, Ichabod	12, Jan. 1819	9, Jan.			L3	
Spinning, James D.	24, Feb. 1826	19, Feb.			L3	
Spinning, John J.	15, Sept 1836		probate		L3	
Spinning, John P.	10, Sept 1829		estate		L3	
Spinning, Jonathan	27, Apr. 1837		estate		L4	
Spinning, Newton	31, Oct. 1810	27, Sept			L3	
Spinning, Sarah Gano	2, Dec. 1847	23, Nov.	84		L3	
Spoffard, Moody	21, Nov. 1839		estate		L3	
Sponcher, Mary	5, Sept 1833	Aug.	3- 2m		L1	
Spooner, Francis L.	3, Jan. 1856	26, Dec.			L3	
Spooner, Francis M.	6, Dec. 1855	1, Dec.	30	*	L3	Leonard
Spooner, Lemuel Reed	23, June 1853	18, June	12		L3	
Spooner, Reed	29, Oct. 1835		estate		L3	
Spooner, Reed	22, June 1837		probate		L3	
Spooner, Reed	22, Mar. 1838		probate		L3	
Spooner, Sarah L.	8, Aug. 1850	31, July		*	L3	Leonard
Spooner, Sarah P.	9, July 1846	24, June	50	*	L3	Hinman
Spooner, Susannah	1, Aug. 1833	July	1-11m		L1	
Spragg, John	29, May 1834		probate		L3	
Sprags, John	15, Aug. 1833	Aug.	43		L1	
Sprague, Elizabeth	12, July 1849	5, July	17		L3	
Sprahn, Mary	17, Oct. 1844	Oct.	30		L3	
Sprick, Henry	9, Aug. 1849	July	28		L3	
Sprigg, Samuel	10, Aug. 1843	2, Aug.	59		L3	
Sprigman, Abigail	18, Dec. 1815	11, Dec.	23		L3	
Sprigman, Sarah	28, Apr. 1826	25, Apr.			L3	
Springer, C.G.	10, Apr. 1856		probate		L3	
Springer, Catharine	3, Feb. 1853	30, Jan.			L3	
Springer, Charles G.	15, Feb. 1855		estate		L3	
Springer, Charles Gordon	26, July 1849	21, July			L3	
Springer, Edward	22, July 1847		estate		L3	
Springer, Jacob	7, Sept 1824		probate		L3	
Springer, John	4, July 1850	June	52		L3	

Name	Notice Date	Death Date	Age	Page	Maiden Name
Springer, Mary Elizabeth	7, July 1842	2, July	16m	L3	
Sprong, David	26, May 1842		estate	L3	
Sprout, Elizabeth	18, Oct. 1832	16, Oct.		L3	
Spugg, James D.M.	14, Mar. 1833	Mar.	2	L1	
Spurrier, Thomas	4, Jan. 1820		estate	L3	
Squier, Ezekiel	10, Aug. 1819	10, July		L3	
Squire, Elizabeth B.	3, Dec. 1857	20, Nov.		L3	
Squire, William B.	28, June 1855	24, June	49	L3	
Sraggeny, Richard	25, May 1848	May	37	L3	
Srofel, Peter	18, July 1833	July	47	L2	
St.Clair, Ann	15, May 1834	May	1m- 5d	L4	
St.Clair, Arthur	9, Sept 1841	24, Aug.	38	L3	
St.Clair, Arthur	30, Sept 1820	26, Sept		L3	
St.Clair, Arthur	10, Mar. 1821		estate	L4	
St.Clair, Eliza L.	7, Mar. 1839	28, Feb.		L3	
St.Clair, George	19, Aug. 1825		estate	L3	
St.Clair, George	11, July 1833		probate	L3	
St.Clair, George (heirs of)	14, June 1838		probate	L4	
St.John, Deyo	3, May 1855		probate	L3	
Staal, Sebastian	9, Sept 1847	Aug.	25	L3	
Stabler, David	9, Aug. 1855		probate	L3	
Stabler, James	30, Nov. 1848	Nov.	37	L3	
Stabler, John	8, Aug. 1833	July	30	L1	
Stabler, Vincent	17, Nov. 1842	Nov.	35	L6	
Stacey, Betsey	24, Nov. 1842	23, Nov.	28	L6	
Stackhouse, Sarah E.	22, Dec. 1853	18, Dec.	27	L3	
Staebler, John F.	15, Aug. 1833	Aug.	3- 5m	L1	
Stafford, Catharine	27, June 1839	June	5m	L3	
Stafford, Peter	10, Aug. 1837	July	50	L3	
Stafford, William	18, Jan. 1849	Jan.	21	L3	
Stagemiller, James	19, July 1849	July		L3	
Stagg, Daniel	3, May 1855	27, Apr.	81	L3	
Stagg, Daniel	9, Aug. 1855		estate	L3	
Stagg, Daniel	5, Nov. 1857		estate	L3	
Stagg, Daniel	16, Oct. 1856		probate	L6	
Stagg, Susan	24, Oct. 1850	18, Oct.		L3	
Stagg, Susan R.	25, Sept 1856	17, Sept		L5	
Stagg, Warren Percy	20, July 1854	15, July	1- 8m- 4d	L3	
Stahl, Frederick W.G.	21, Aug. 1856		estate	L6	
Stainbreak, Arma M.	27, July 1848	July	19	L3	
Stait, John S.	14, June 1849	June	74	L3	
Stalee, John L.	5, July 1855		probate	L3	
Staley, John L.	1, June 1854	26, May		L3	
Stall, George W. (Lt)	9, Feb. 1819	6, Feb.		L3	
Stammer,	25, Apr. 1850	Apr.	32	L3	
Stanbery, Henry	11, Nov. 1852	8, Nov.	17	L3	
Standifer, James (Col)	31, Aug. 1837	20, Aug.		L3	
Stanfield, John	18, Oct. 1832	13, Oct.		L2	
Stanford, (child of Nancy)	8, Feb. 1838	Feb.	6w	L3	
Stanford, Richard	29, Apr. 1816	9, Apr.	47	L3	
Stanislaus, Anna Maria	30, Sept 1852	30, Sept	46	L3	
Stanley, Charlotte	15, Jan. 1846	9, Jan.	43	L3	
Stanley, Elisha	23, Nov. 1843	18, Nov.	19	L3	
Stanley, Frederick Judson	19, Feb. 1846	14, Feb.	infant	L3	

Name	Notice Date	Death Date	Age	Page	Maiden Name
Stanley, Mary	9, Sept 1847	2, Sept	52		L3	
Stanley, Thomas M.	19, July 1849		estate		L3	
Stanley, William (Major)	10, May 1814	8, May			L3	
Stannus, Ephraim D.	12, July 1855	6, July	25- 7m		L3	
Stannus, Mary Jessop	15, June 1843	8, June	9		L3	
Stansbury, Caroline E.	5, July 1849	24, June	24		L3	Burch
Stansbury, Thomas J.	30, Mar. 1849	24, Mar.	38		L3	
Stanton, Edward	28, Mar. 1844	13, Mar.			L3	
Stanton, Mary	29, Aug. 1850	Aug.	7d		L3	
Stanton, Patrick	7, Oct. 1847	Sept	52		L3	
Stanton, Peter	30, May 1850	May	40		L3	
Stanus, Ephraim	6, Aug. 1857		probate		L3	
Stanwood, Mehitable	14, Oct. 1847	3, Oct.		*	L3	
Staplesburg, Henry	23, July 1846	July	21		L3	
Stapleton, (child of James)	28, June 1849	June	stillborn		L3	
Star, John	14, Sept 1848	Sept	33		L3	
Starbuck, Sarah Ann	25, Nov. 1852	18, Nov.	20- 4m-16d		L3	
Starbuck, Sophia	28, June 1855	27, June	9m		L3	
Stark, Abraham (Capt)	11, Feb. 1847	3, Feb.	67	*	L3	
Stark, Peter	23, Mar. 1843	19, Mar.			L3	
Starling, Lyne	30, Nov. 1848	29, Oct.			L1	
Starly, Amanda M.	25, Apr. 1833	Apr.	3- 8m		L1	
Starr, Elizabeth	29, Aug. 1850	13, Aug.	11m		L3	
Starr, Henry	2, Oct. 1851		estate		L3	
Starr, Henry	22, Nov. 1855		estate		L3	
Starr, Henry	4, Sept 1851	30, Aug.			L3	
Starr, John	7, Dec. 1837	26, Oct.	64	*	L3	
Starr, John W.	31, Dec. 1846				L3	
Starr, Lydia S.	25, July 1850	5, July	25		L3	
Starr, Marion Elizabeth	9, Jan. 1845	21, Dec.	2m		L3	
Starr, William Penn	21, Aug. 1856	19, Aug.	22		L5	
Stars, W.H. (Rev)	30, Mar. 1854	6, Mar.			L3	
Staughen, Samuel	15, Oct. 1846	Oct.	1m		L3	
Staughton, J.M.	5, Sept 1833		estate		L3	
Staughton, James	9, June 1836		probate		L3	
Staughton, James M. (Dr)	22, Aug. 1833	Aug.	33- 4m		L4	
Staughton, Louisa	7, June 1855		probate		L3	
Staughton, Louisa	15, Sept 1853	8, Sept			L3	
Stead, John Kirk	4, Nov. 1841	Oct.	21		L3	
Stearns, Anna Russell	20, May 1852	13, May	13m		L3	
Stearns, James	10, Aug. 1848	13, July	20		L3	
Steban, Henry	12, Oct. 1837	Oct.	31		L4	
Stebbins, Norman B.	8, Jan. 1852	5, Jan.		*	L3	
Stede, Nancy	5, Sept 1833	Aug.	14		L1	
Stedele, Johann Nep.	26, Jan. 1854	22, Jan.	45	*	L3	
Stedman, (child)	18, Aug. 1853				L3	
Stedman, Abby Huntington	13, Nov. 1856	30, Oct.			L3	Porter
Stedman, Frank Porter	7, Dec. 1848	1, Dec.	13m-17d		L3	
Steele, (boy)	9, Aug. 1849	8, Aug.	16		L2	
Steele, Mary Chase	8, May 1845	2, May	infant		L3	
Steele, Mary Jane	4, May 1822	25, Apr.	23		L3	Rowan
Steele, Mary Jane	8, Aug. 1833	2, Aug.			L4	
Steele, Peter	5, July 1849	June	22		L3	
Steelman, Andrew	4, Jan. 1844	1, Jan.	20- 4m-16d		L3	

Name	Notice Date	Death Date	Age		Page	Maiden Name
Steelman, Ann Eliza	29, Dec. 1842	20, Dec.	17		L3	
Steer, Elizabeth L.	2, Feb. 1843	30, Jan.	22		L3	
Steer, Samuel	5, Sept 1839		probate		L3	
Stegner, Henry	7, Aug. 1834	July	37		L3	
Stehle, John	16, May 1850	May	25		L3	
Steinbaugh, Ernst	21, June 1849	June	28		L3	
Steinbeck, Wilhelmina	24, June 1847	June	42		L3	
Steiner, Rachael	4, July 1850	27, June	66		L3	
Steinhoff, Louis	12, July 1849	July	28		L3	
Steinman, Henry	12, July 1849	July	3- 6m		L3	
Steinman, John	12, July 1849	July	7		L3	
Steinmetz, Phillip	15, Aug. 1839	Aug.	27		L3	
Stephan, Peter	5, Aug. 1852	July	63		L3	
Stephens, (child of Henry)	28, Nov. 1833	Nov.	1d		L4	
Stephens, Catharine	6, Apr. 1848	Mar.	11m		L3	
Stephens, Charles	6, Mar. 1856	21, Feb.	53	*	L3	
Stephens, Eliza	2, Apr. 1840	1, Apr.			L3	
Stephens, Ephraim M.	13, Nov. 1834		estate		L3	
Stephens, George W.	11, Jan. 1844	Jan.	9w		L3	
Stephens, Isaac	8, Jan. 1852	31, Dec.	72		L3	
Stephens, Mary	21, June 1849	June	48		L3	
Stephens, Susan F.	25, Oct. 1832	Oct.	4		L4	
Stephenson, Alonzo	29, Apr. 1847	Apr.	31		L3	
Stephenson, Caroline	5, July 1849	28, June	20		L3	
Stephenson, Ebenezer	18, Oct. 1832	12, Oct.			L1	
Stephenson, Edward	7, Oct. 1841	Sept	21		L3	
Stephenson, Eliza	12, Mar. 1857	8, Mar.	69		L3	
Stephenson, Nimrod	23, Aug. 1849		estate		L3	
Stephenson, Stephen	18, Apr. 1839		probate		L3	
Stephenson, Thomas	24, May 1814		estate		L3	
Sterling, Eliza	14, Oct. 1852	3, Oct.	55		L3	
Stern, (child of Richard)	8, Aug. 1833	July	5		L1	
Sterret, Abigail	8, Aug. 1850	31, July			L3	
Sterret, John	30, May 1850	May	32		L3	
Sterrett, Eugenia J.	11, Feb. 1847	4, Feb.	2- 6m		L3	
Sterrett, Jane B.	1, Oct. 1840	30, Sept	29		L3	Keys
Sterrett, John	28, June 1849	23, June	55		L3	
Sterrett, Robert	17, July 1851	10, July	11m-17d		L3	
Sterrette, Jane	22, Feb. 1849	20, Feb.	25		L3	
Stevens, Ann	9, June 1836		probate		L3	
Stevens, Caleb	8, Nov. 1838		estate		L3	
Stevens, Caleb	27, June 1839		estate		L3	
Stevens, Charles W.	7, Sept 1848	31, Aug.	7- 6m		L3	
Stevens, Edwin	31, Aug. 1848	23, Aug.	3- 9m		L3	
Stevens, H.E. (Capt)	20, Mar. 1856		31		L3	
Stevens, Hannah	15, Feb. 1838	4, Jan.			L3	
Stevens, John	9, June 1836		probate		L3	
Stevens, Louisa	8, Oct. 1840	28, Sept	25		L3	
Stevens, Martha Jane	25, Dec. 1856	23, Dec.	11- -19d		L3	
Stevens, Martha Sampson	9, Nov. 1848	1, Nov.			L3	
Stevens, Mary A.	10, May 1855	1, May	51		L3	
Stevens, Phebe	30, Apr. 1857	3, Apr.	18-10m		L3	Hand
Stevens, Sarah B.	27, Sept 1849	20, Sept	26		L3	
Stevens, Seth B.	2, Mar. 1854	25, Feb.			L3	

Name	Notice Date	Death Date	Age	Page	Maiden Name
Stevens, Thomas	4, Oct. 1827		estate	L2	
Stevens, Thomas (heirs of)	15, Sept 1836		probate	L3	
Stevens, William L.	3, Dec. 1840		estate	L3	
Stevenson, Louisiana Symmes S.	31, Aug. 1848	26, Aug.	5- 5m	L3	
Stevenson, Nimrod	20, Nov. 1851		estate	L3	
Stevenson, Robert John	20, Dec. 1849	17, Dec.	20	L3	
Stevenson, Samuel Winston	2, Feb. 1854	30, Jan.	4- -10d	L3	
Stevenson, Sarah	13, Jan. 1848	6, Jan.	23	L3	Phillips
Steward, Edward K.	22, Feb. 1855	12, Feb.		L3	
Steward, James	26, Aug. 1831		estate	L2	
Steward, Lewis	3, Mar. 1842	Feb.	36	L3	
Steward, William Taylor	4, Feb. 1841	28, Jan.	infant	L3	
Stewart, (child of Elizabeth)	23, Apr. 1840	Apr.	8d	L3	
Stewart, Alexander	20, June 1850	June	35	L3	
Stewart, Alice	26, May 1842	May	33	L3	
Stewart, Amanda	24, Aug. 1848	Aug.	3m	L3	
Stewart, Barbary	25, Apr. 1844	Apr.	30	L3	
Stewart, Charles	24, May 1849	May	35	L3	
Stewart, Charles D.	30, Dec. 1852	26, Dec.	32	L3	
Stewart, Daniel S.	20, July 1848	July		L3	
Stewart, David	11, July 1850	July	28	L3	
Stewart, David R.	6, 13, Apr. 1854	30, Mar.	76	L3	
Stewart, David T.	25, Mar. 1847	17, Mar.	20	L3	
Stewart, Debora	2, Aug. 1832	July	27-11m	L1	
Stewart, Edward	17, June 1847	June	42	L3	
Stewart, Elizabeth	31, Oct. 1833	Oct.	60	L4	
Stewart, Hannah	1, Nov. 1855	25, Oct.	59	L3	
Stewart, James	15, July 1847	July	83	L3	
Stewart, James	7, May 1835	4, May		L3	
Stewart, Jane	23, June 1842	June	4m	L3	
Stewart, John	11, July 1850	July	28	L3	
Stewart, John	15, Oct. 1840	Oct.	29	L3	
Stewart, John	9, May 1850	Apr.	67	L3	
Stewart, John	9, Aug. 1855	31, July	1- 5m-21d	L3	
Stewart, John	26, Sept 1826		probate	L3	
Stewart, John	29, Aug. 1810		estate	L5	
Stewart, Joseph	6, Oct. 1831	1, Oct.	33	* L3	
Stewart, Joseph	11, Nov. 1841	Oct.	1- 5m	L3	
Stewart, Joseph	4, Oct. 1832		estate	L3	
Stewart, K.F. (Dr)	13, May 1852	18, Mar.		L3	
Stewart, Mary A.	14, June 1849	June	18	L3	
Stewart, Nathan	21, Mar. 1850		estate	L3	
Stewart, W.S.	19, Mar. 1857	11, Mar.		L3	
Stewart, William	14, July 1853	11, July		L3	
Stewart, William C.	6, June 1850	29, May	50	L3	
Stewart, William C.	4, July 1850		estate	L3	
Stewart, William L.	18, Sept 1834	Sept	40	L1	
Stibbins, Ziba	6, July 1819		estate	L3	
Stibbs, Ann	10, Feb. 1842	29, Jan.	60	L3	
Stibbs, Samuel	1, Nov. 1855	29, Oct.	79	L3	
Stickney, Moses P.	19, July 1849	July	40	L3	
Stickney, Rosanna	30, May 1850	May	35	L3	
Stienbraker, Henry	22, Aug. 1850	17, Aug.		L3	
Stienbush, John	16, Nov. 1848	Nov.	42	L3	

Name	Notice Date	Death Date	Age	Page	Maiden Name
Stier, Magdalen	9, Aug. 1849	July	44	L3	
Stille, Conrad	10, Apr. 1856		probate	L3	
Stille, John	2, Sept 1852	25, Aug.	48	L3	
Stillman, Adam	19, July 1849	July	40	L3	
Stillman, Charles A.	7, Aug. 1834	July	1- 8m	L3	
Stills, (child of Jane)	1, Apr. 1847	Mar.	2w	L3	
Stimpson, William Hooper	13, Dec. 1814	10, Dec.	10	L3	
Stinson, Martha	4, Mar. 1841	Feb.		L3	
Stinson, Robert	25, Sept 1845	Sept	32	L3	
Stites, anna	17, July 1811	6, July	39	L3	
Stites, Benjamin	5, Mar. 1846	18, Feb.	74	L3	
Stites, Benjamin	30, Apr. 1805		estate	L3	
Stites, Benjamin	7, Sept 1824		probate	L3	
Stites, Benjamin	19, Dec. 1826		probate	L3	
Stites, John G.	11, July 1833	July	15- 2m	L1	
Stites, Mary M.	26, Nov. 1857	21, Nov.	52	L3	
Stith, Mordica	16, Sept 1841	Sept	11	L3	
Stitt, Samuel	26, Aug. 1847	21, Aug.	78	L3	
Stitt, Samuel	14, Oct. 1847		estate	L3	
Stitt, Samuel	10, Apr. 1856		probate	L3	
Stockell, Lovena H.	2, May 1844	Apr.	11m	L3	
Stocklin, Charles	27, Aug. 1857			L3	
Stocklin, Charles	10, Sept 1857	5, Sept		L3	
Stockton, Horatio	8, Jan. 1816	1, Dec.	18	L3	
Stoddard, David	17, June 1847	10, June		L3	
Stoddard, Lemuel	16, June 1806	June	20	L3	
Stoddart, John, Jr.	25, July 1833	July		L1	
Stokes, John	27, May 1830	24, May	56	L3	
Stokes, Montfort	8, Dec. 1842	4, Dec.	81	L3	
Stokes, Robert	14, Sept 1837	Sept	26	L4	
Stoll, Sasis	12, July 1849	July	37	L3	
Stoltzer, (boy)	1, Aug. 1850	27, July		L3	
Stoms, Alfred A.	28, Jan. 1847	24, Jan.	29	L3	
Stone, A.G.	29, Aug. 1839	Aug.	30	L3	
Stone, Aaron	13, Feb. 1851	18, Jan.	88	L3	
Stone, Abigail Maria	2, Aug. 1849	26, July	76	* L3	Storrs
Stone, Charles	9, Oct. 1834	Sept	17	L1	
Stone, Charles	9, Nov. 1848	31, Oct.	92	* L3	
Stone, David	14, Nov. 1839	3, Nov.	63	L3	
Stone, Eli	14, Oct. 1841	22, Sept	38	* L3	
Stone, Ethan	22, Apr. 1852	20, Apr.	85	L2	
Stone, Ethan	29, Apr. 1852	20, Apr.	85	L3	
Stone, Ethan	8, Oct. 1857		probate	L3	
Stone, Hannah	22, Aug. 1850	8, Aug.	64	L3	
Stone, Harriet B.	30, Sept 1825	28, Sept		L3	
Stone, Henry	20, Dec. 1855	12, Dec.	31	L3	
Stone, Henry B.	6, Mar. 1851		estate	L3	
Stone, John C.	8, Apr. 1852	25, Mar.	11	L3	
Stone, Louis	7, Aug. 1834	July	68	L3	
Stone, Mary	8, Nov. 1838	7, Nov.	75	L3	
Stone, Patience	23, Oct. 1834	Oct.	41	L2	
Stone, Wilmot	1, Aug. 1833	July	38	L1	
Stone, Wilmot	3, Sept 1840		probate	L3	
Stone, Wilmot, Jr.	5, Sept 1844	29, Aug.	11- 9m	L3	

Name	Notice Date	Death Date	Age		Page	Maiden Name
Stonebraker, Nancy	3, Jan. 1856	27, Dec.	62		L3	
Stonebreaker, (Mr)	18, Oct. 1832	15, Oct.			L3	
Storer, J.P.B. (Rev)	4, Apr. 1844	17, Mar.			L3	
Storer, Margaret	8, Oct. 1840	21, Sept	75	*	L3	
Storer, Sarah C.	12, Oct. 1843	11, Oct.			L3	
Storms, Daniel	2, July 1805		estate		L3	
Storrs, Seth (Col)	15, Mar. 1838	9, Oct.	82	*	L3	
Story, Daniel (Rev)	5, Feb. 1805	30, Dec.	40		L2	
Story, James	3, July 1851	27, June	35		L3	
Story, Jane	27, Sept 1849	Sept	24		L3	
Storz, Jacob	11, July 1850	July	35		L3	
Stothart, John D.	19, May 1842	15, May		*	L3	
Stotkamp, Henry	27, Mar. 1851	Mar.	30		L3	
Stout, Aaron	16, Aug. 1814		estate		L3	
Stout, Caroline Augusta	14, Sept 1843	3, Sept	25		L3	
Stout, Eliza C.	14, May 1846	5, May	24	*	L3	
Stout, Elizabeth	25, May 1837	17, May			L2	
Stout, John	11, July 1833		probate		L3	
Stout, Jonathan	11, Aug. 1817	26, July			L3	
Stout, Kate	11, Dec. 1851	9, Dec.	6m		L3	
Stout, Mary	4, Apr. 1833	Mar.	9m- 7d		L1	
Stout, Reuben	22, Mar. 1838		probate		L3	
Stout, Samuel	18, Oct. 1832	12, Oct.			L2	
Stout, Samuel	17, Jan. 1833		estate		L3	
Stout, Sarah	5, Dec. 1833	Nov.	24		L3	
Stout, Thomas H.	22, Aug. 1833	Aug.	4- 7m		L4	
Stout, William	27, Oct. 1831		probate		L1	
Stout, William	20, Dec. 1827		estate		L3	
Stoutenburgh, John H.	9, July 1824		estate		L3	
Stoutenburgh, John H.	18, July 1823	16, July	29	*	L3	
Stoutenburgh, John H.	20, Dec. 1825		probate		L4	
Stowe, William	27, July 1837	July	30		L3	
Strabe, Philip	11, May 1848	May	50		L3	
Strader, Abby	10, June 1841	9, June			L3	
Strader, Charles	29, Nov. 1832	Nov.	5		L1	
Strader, David P. (Dr)	2, Sept 1852				L3	
Strader, John Jacob	2, Nov. 1854	27, Oct.	21		L3	
Strader, Mary Jane	12, Jan. 1854	5, Jan.			L3	
Strader, William	11, Mar. 1847	Mar.	29		L3	
Strait, Eliza	1, Nov. 1832	Oct.	1- 6m		L2	
Strait, George W.	20, Nov. 1834	Nov.	3- 3m		L1	
Strathers, Presly	29, Jan. 1846	Jan.	27		L3	
Stratsford, Joseph	26, July 1849	July	49		L3	
Stratton, Elias	1, Dec. 1807	23, Nov.			L3	
Stratton, Hannah	1, Aug. 1833	July	56		L1	
Stratton, Job	7, Sept 1824		probate		L3	
Stratton, Josiah J.	13, Nov. 1850	9, Nov.	45	*	L3	
Stratton, Mary	20, Sept 1832	Sept	1		L1	
Stratton, Mary	28, Dec. 1807	22, Dec.			L3	
Stratton, Robert B.	2, Aug. 1832	July	7d		L1	
Strause, John H.	27, Aug. 1857	20, Aug.	36		L3	
Straw, Abraham	17, Dec. 1846	Dec.	87		L3	
Strawbeck, John	29, Aug. 1833	Aug.	20		L1	
Strawder, Joseph	16, Feb. 1854	1852			L3	

Name	Notice Date	Death Date	Age		Page	Maiden Name
Streaker, William	6, Nov. 1834	Oct.			L1	
Street, George	4, Mar. 1841	Feb.	35		L3	
Streicher, Mary	16, May 1850	May	26		L3	
Strenber, Jacob	21, Dec. 1848	Dec.	48		L3	
Stricker, Henry	12, July 1849	July	26		L3	
Strickland, Maria W.	11, Jan. 1849	8, Jan.			L3	Cooke
Strickland, Sarah	22, Aug. 1839	Aug.	50		L3	
Strickle, Jacob	28, Dec. 1854	15, Dec.	73		L3	
Strobridge, George	13, Nov. 1845	11, Nov.	31		L3	
Strobridge, George	11, Dec. 1845		estate		L3	
Strobridge, James Gordon	24, May 1849	16, May	23		L3	
Strobridge, Nelson	9, May 1844	30, Apr.	25		L3	
Strong, Barnabas	7, July 1821		estate		L3	
Strong, David F.	21, June 1855	12, June	14		L3	
Strong, Edward	20, Nov. 1851	14, Nov.			L4	
Strong, Elizabeth	8, Oct. 1840	Sept	20		L3	
Strong, George D.	14, Feb. 1850	9, Feb.	51		L3	
Strong, George D.	21, Mar. 1850	9, Feb.	51	*	L3	
Strong, Mary Huntington	16, Jan. 1851	13, Jan.			L3	Richards
Strong, William	28, Dec. 1848	Dec.	18		L3	
Strong, William	13, Oct. 1818		estate		L3	
Strong, William C.	28, July 1853	25, July	30		L3	
Stroughton, (Mr)	7, Jan. 1820	6, Jan.			L3	
Stroup, Clemens	31, Apr. 1845	Apr.	62		L3	
Stroup, John	24, Apr. 1845	Apr.	45		L3	
Strowder, Joseph	16, Sept 1852	15, Sept			L3	
Strowhouver, (Mrs)	25, Oct. 1832	19, Oct.			L2	
Strub, John	3, Sept 1840	Aug.	4- 8m		L3	
Strul, (Mrs)	7, Feb. 1828	Feb.	40		L1	
Stuard, Jane	8, Aug. 1833	July	2- -24d		L1	
Stuart, Jane	23, Feb. 1843	17, Feb.			L3	
Stuart, Joseph	17, Nov. 1831		estate		L3	
Stuart, Nathaniel	6, July 1837	1, July	68	*	L3	
Stubblefield, W.W.	13, Apr. 1843	8, Apr.			L3	
Stubbs, James R.	8, June 1848	4, May	53	*	L3	
Stubert, Clarissa	24, Aug. 1854	19, Aug.	43		L3	
Stubewehr, Mary	28, Jan. 1847	Jan.	36		L3	
Stull, Angeline	18, Apr. 1844	Apr.	5		L3	
Stump, William	15, Sept 1836		probate		L3	
Sturdivant, Elias E.	15, Aug. 1850	Aug.	37		L3	
Sturgess, Simeon B.	20, Mar. 1845	16, Mar.	43	*	L3	
Sturgis, Lewis B.	11, Apr. 1844	30, Mar.	81		L3	
Stuyvesant, Moses S.	5, Oct. 1848		estate		L3	
Sudmier, John B.	5, July 1855		probate		L3	
Sugenbaugh, William	7, Aug. 1834	July	31		L3	
Sullivan, (child of H.W.)	26, Sept 1833	Sept	stillborn		L4	
Sullivan, Andrew	18, Apr. 1850	Apr.	32		L3	
Sullivan, Ann	5, July 1849	June	35		L3	
Sullivan, Ann	12, June 1845	June	39		L3	
Sullivan, Daniel	28, Nov. 1850	Nov.	42		L3	
Sullivan, Daniel	3, Sept 1819	1, Sept	96	*	L3	
Sullivan, Dennis	21, June 1849	June	28		L3	
Sullivan, George W.	31, Apr. 1845	Apr.	26		L3	
Sullivan, Giles	29, Aug. 1850	Aug.	47		L3	

Name	Notice Date	Death Date	Age		Page	Maiden Name
Sullivan, James	12, Feb. 1835	10, Dec.			L1	
Sullivan, James	28, Mar. 1850	Mar.	25		L3	
Sullivan, James	12, Mar. 1846	Mar.	32		L3	
Sullivan, Jane	26, Nov. 1846	19, Nov.	76		L3	
Sullivan, John	8, Aug. 1833	July			L1	
Sullivan, John	19, Feb. 1835		estate		L3	
Sullivan, John (Deacon)	12, Feb. 1835	22, Dec.			L1	
Sullivan, Mary S.	25, Sept 1851	16, Sept			L3	Groesbeck
Sullivan, Michael	20, Jan. 1848	Jan.	33		L3	
Sullivan, Thomas W.	12, Nov. 1846	Nov.	22		L3	
Sullivan, William C.	20, July 1837	July	9		L4	
Summerfield, Joseph	13, June 1844	June	1		L3	
Summerfield, Mary	27, Aug. 1846	Aug.	1		L3	
Summers, Lewis	14, Sept 1843	Sept	65		L3	
Sumner, Alexander B.	30, July 1840	22, July	52	*	L3	
Sumner, Waterman	2, June 1842	May	38		L3	
Sunders, Sally Ann	23, Oct. 1834	Oct.	2- 9m		L2	
Suplee, Rebecca	9, Aug. 1809	29, July		*	L3	
Susanra, Arina P.	6, June 1833	May	48		L2	
Suter, (child of J.Z.)	18, Dec. 1851	13, Dec.	13m		L3	
Suttles, (Mr)	18, Oct. 1832	16, Oct.			L3	
Suydam, Cornelius R.	27, Nov. 1845	12, Nov.	53		L3	
Swabb, Adam	4, Apr. 1839		estate		L3	
Swads, William	6, June 1833	May	29		L2	
Swaigly, John	8, Aug. 1833	July	50		L1	
Swain, Charles Barnard	9, July 1846	6, July	15m- 6d		L3	
Swain, Charles C.	4, Apr. 1833	Mar.	2		L1	
Swain, Joseph	5, Sept 1839		probate		L3	
Swain, Joseph	14, July 1836		estate		L4	
Swain, Louisa Martha	4, Oct. 1833	Sept	21d		L1	
Swain, Sarah	23, Oct. 1834	Oct.	20		L2	
Swain, Solomon (Capt)	19, Aug. 1825	8, Aug.	55	*	L3	
Swale, (Miss)	25, Oct. 1832	21, Oct.			L2	
Swallow, Christian	5, Oct. 1848	Sept	22		L3	
Swallow, Mary	26, July 1849	July	52		L3	
Swan, Caleb (Major)	21, Dec. 1809	29, Nov.			L3	
Swan, Ebenezer G.	8, Aug. 1850	4, Aug.			L3	
Swan, George	13, Feb. 1840		19		L1	
Swaney, George	15, July 1852	July	2		L3	
Swartz, E.	28, June 1849	June	1		L3	
Swartz, Henry	28, June 1849	June	4		L3	
Swartz, Henry	7, Sept 1848	Aug.	44		L3	
Swartz, James	28, June 1849	June	5		L3	
Swartz, Nicholas	28, June 1849	June	2- 6m		L3	
Swartz, Rebecca	16, Aug. 1838	Aug.	1- 6m		L3	
Swartz, Valentine	28, June 1849	June	50		L3	
Swasey, Alice Drake	26, May 1853	22, May	4- 6m		L3	
Swasey, Ella Maria	16, Sept 1852	13, Sept	5- 9m-13d		L3	
Swasey, John	1, Feb. 1849	21, Jan.	68		L3	
Swasey, Samuel	3, Aug. 1843	28, July	3		L3	
Swasey, William B.	17, Feb. 1848	12, Feb.	3		L3	
Swathzalder, George	2, Mar. 1837				L4	
Sweeney, Ann	1, June 1843	May	38		L3	
Sweeney, Charles	10, Feb. 1848				L2	

Name	Notice Date	Death Date	Age		Page	Maiden Name
Sweeney, Constantine	9, June 1853	4, June			L3	
Sweeney, Frederick O.	30, Jan. 1845	Jan.	40		L3	
Sweeney, James	6, Apr. 1848	Mar.	30		L3	
Sweeney, Mary	20, Nov. 1850	Nov.	20		L3	
Sweet, Stephen W.	30, Nov. 1843	23, Nov.	64		L3	
Sweetland, William	28, Aug. 1834	Aug.	27		L1	
Sweets, (child of Absulom)	4, July 1833	June	3m		L2	
Swift, Calvin	20, May 1830		estate		L3	
Swift, Calvin	31, Dec. 1824	24, Dec.			L3	
Swift, Jedediah B.	16, Mar. 1843	7, Mar.	66	*	L3	
Swift, Martha P.	27, July 1854	25, July	38		L3	
Swift, Reuben	8, Oct. 1829		estate		L3	
Swift, Reuben	23, Dec. 1830		estate		L3	
Swift, Susan	12, Feb. 1852	10, Feb.	36		L3	Cary
Swift, Thomas Truxton	29, Oct. 1857	28, Oct.	40		L3	
Swift, Thomas Truxton	5, Nov. 1857	27, Oct.	40		L3	
Swing, David	25, Oct. 1832	23, Oct.			L3	
Swing, James	12, June 1828	8, June			L4	
Swing, Samuel	24, Aug. 1819		estate		L3	
Swing, Samuel	2, July 1824		estate		L3	
Swing, Samuel	20, Jan. 1826		estate		L3	
Swink, John	26, July 1855	22, July			L3	
Swishard, Elizabeth	26, July 1849	July	80		L3	
Switzer, Clarinda O.	10, Feb. 1848	Feb.	2		L3	
Switzer, George	10, Jan. 1850	Jan.	6		L3	
Switzer, George W.	9, Mar. 1848	Mar.	4		L3	
Switzer, Victoria	29, Nov. 1849	Nov.	19		L3	
Syer, Rachel	18, Oct. 1832	Oct.	55		L4	
Sykes, William	2, Oct. 1845	25, Sept	44		L3	
Sylvester, Charles	26, July 1832	July	38		L1	
Sylyaster, Rachel	21, Mar. 1850	Mar.	45		L3	
Symmes, (man)	21, Aug. 1851				L4	
Symmes, Celadon	24, Aug. 1837	Aug.	65		L3	
Symmes, Daniel	19, May 1817	11, May	51	*	L3	
Symmes, Daniel	15, Feb. 1838	10, Feb.	5m		L3	
Symmes, Daniel	9, June 1817		estate		L3	
Symmes, Daniel	11, Feb. 1820		estate		L3	
Symmes, Daniel	23, Apr. 1829		estate		L3	
Symmes, Daniel	16, Feb. 1827		probate		L3	
Symmes, Ethan Allen	2, Mar. 1837	25, Feb.	7- 6m		L3	
Symmes, Harriet Louisa	5, Aug. 1852	28, July	25		L3	
Symmes, John Cleves	8, May 1815		estate		L1	
Symmes, John Cleves	1, Mar. 1814	26, Mar.			L3	
Symmes, Timothy	26, Sept 1823	18, Sept	27		L3	
Symmes, William	7, Nov. 1810		estate		L2	
Symmes, William	23, Mar. 1809	15, Mar.	35		L3	
Symmes, William	29, Dec. 1812		estate		L4	
Symonds, Isaac	12, Jan. 1837		probate		L3	
Symonds, Lewis	23, Nov. 1837		estate		L3	
Symonds, Morris	13, Nov. 1856	9, Nov.			L3	
Taber, Jethro W.	9, Aug. 1855		estate		L3	
Taber, Jethro W.	5, Feb. 1857		probate		L3	
Tabler, John	3, Aug. 1848	July	21		L3	

Name	Notice Date	Death Date	Age	Page	Maiden Name
Tabor, George	5, Feb. 1852			L3	
Tabor, George	6, Jan. 1853	5, Jan.		L3	
Tabous, Caroline	13, Sept 1832	Sept	1- 6m	L1	
Tachrenhas, Louisa C.	16, Nov. 1848	Nov.	18	L3	
Taft, Alphonzo	6, Mar. 1851	2, Mar.	9m-20d	L3	
Taft, Daniel	26, Jan. 1854	19, Jan.	55	* L1	
Taft, Daniel	26, Jan. 1854	19, Jan.	55	L3	
Taft, John	22, Aug. 1844	Aug.	46	L3	
Taft, Mary	7, Dec. 1848	29, Nov.	infant	L3	
Taft, Nancy M.	3, June 1847	31, May	63	L3	
Taft, Samuel Davenport	10, Apr. 1856	7, Apr.	14m	L3	
Taggart, Martha	5, Jan. 1854	20, Dec.	60	L3	Lowery
Tague, Andrew	10, Apr. 1856		probate	L3	
Tailer, Leonard	18, Oct. 1832	13, Oct.		L2	
Tait, (Mrs)	1, Aug. 1833	July		L1	
Tait, Caroline M.	14, Mar. 1833	Mar.	1- -7d	L1	
Tait, James, Sen.	20, Dec. 1827		estate	L3	
Talbot, Isham	5, Oct. 1837	2, Oct.		L3	
Talbott, Samuel	25, Oct. 1849	24, Oct.	77	L3	
Talbott, Sarah Jane	4, Feb. 1847	3, Feb.	10m- 3d	L3	
Tallon, Michael T.	14, Sept 1843	10, Sept		* L3	
Talor, Martha A.	1, Aug. 1833	July	50	L1	
Tanenberger, (child of Sophia)	24, Dec. 1857	Dec.	infant	L3	
Taney, Jonas	28, Feb. 1850		estate	L3	
Taney, Lewis	27, Sept 1838	23, Sept		L3	
Tanier, Richard	11, Mar. 1852	Mar.	21	L4	
Tannabill, Adamson	25, Oct. 1832	22, Oct.		L3	
Tanner, Almon	15, Aug. 1833	Aug.	7	L1	
Tanner, Anthony	13, July 1848	July	2	L3	
Tanner, Orwill	15, Aug. 1833	Aug.	3	L1	
Tanner, Susan	27, July 1848	July	4w	L3	
Tappan, Betsey	25, June 1840			L3	
Tapscoff, James	12, Feb. 1816		estate	L3	
Tarbell, Joseph	11, Dec. 1815	25, Nov.		L3	
Tarehollen, (Mrs)	2, Oct. 1834	Sept		L4	
Tarrant, L.M.	13, May 1830	20, Apr.	34	L3	
Tarrant, L.M.	12, July 1838		estate	L3	
Tarrant, Larkin M.	7, Oct. 1830		estate	L3	
Tarring, Deborah	13, Dec. 1849	Dec.	45	L3	
Tasemine, John P.	14, Feb. 1828	Feb.		L1	
Taskey, William	7, Aug. 1834	July		L3	
Tasnach, Jacob	21, Feb. 1828	Feb.	25	L1	
Tate, (child of George)	2, May 1833	Apr.	stillborn	L1	
Tate, Jane	29, Aug. 1833		estate	L3	
Tatem, Charles	8, May 1845	29, Apr.	73	L3	
Tatem, Charles	4, May 1837	30, Apr.	8m	L3	
Tatem, Charles, Jr.	7, Apr. 1836		estate	L4	
Tatem, Henry I.	18, Aug. 1853	11, Aug.	52	L3	
Tatem, Henry L.	6, Sept 1855		probate	L3	
Tatem, John	26, Oct. 1837	7, Oct.	39	L4	
Tatem, Rachel	26, July 1838	25, July		L3	
Tatspaw, Peter	12, Sept 1833	Sept	25	L1	
Tauflec, Peter	27, Dec. 1832	Dec.	45	L1	
Taulman, Harmanus	20, Dec. 1825		probate	L4	

Name	Notice Date	Death Date	Age		Page	Maiden Name
Taulman, Joseph	17, Mar. 1826		probate		L3	
Taulman, Joseph	19, Dec. 1826		probate		L3	
Taulman, Joseph	9, June 1836		probate		L3	
Taulman, Joseph	13, Oct. 1818	28, Sept			L3	
Taulman, Joseph	20, Dec. 1825		probate		L4	
Taulman, Peter	9, June 1836		probate		L3	
Taylor, Abby	9, Jan. 1851	Dec.	7		L3	
Taylor, Alanson	23, May 1833	May	33		L4	
Taylor, Amos B.	24, Oct. 1821	20, Oct.			L3	
Taylor, Anne Harrison	25, Feb. 1847	20, Feb.		*	L3	Tyler
Taylor, Archibald R.	6, Nov. 1834		estate		L3	
Taylor, Archibald R.	30, June 1836		estate		L3	
Taylor, Bartholomew	14, Oct. 1847	5, Oct.	94	*	L3	
Taylor, Caleb	8, Mar. 1849		estate		L3	
Taylor, Catharine	19, Jan. 1843	12, Jan.		*	L3	
Taylor, Charles	31, July 1851	July	25		L3	
Taylor, Charles Telford	20, Feb. 1845	16, Feb.	9m-16d		L3	
Taylor, Edmund (Major)	9, Oct. 1811	1, Oct.			L3	
Taylor, Elizabeth C.	9, Aug. 1855	1, Aug.	40		L3	
Taylor, Elizabeth Jane	27, May 1847	18, May	5		L3	
Taylor, Elizabeth L.	23, Mar. 1848	18, Mar.	13m		L3	
Taylor, Ellen	8, Mar. 1855	4, Mar.	9		L3	
Taylor, Emily R.	22, Jan. 1852	9, Jan.			L3	Rogers
Taylor, Ernestine	19, Oct. 1854	28, Sept	12		L3	
Taylor, Fletcher S.	11, Apr. 1833	Apr.	1m-21d		L1	
Taylor, Frances Eliza	5, June 1845	30, May	1		L3	
Taylor, George K.	11, Dec. 1815				L3	
Taylor, Griffin	9, Apr. 1808		estate		L3	
Taylor, Harriet A.	21, May 1846	May	1- 6m		L3	
Taylor, Henry	17, Oct. 1844	Oct.	30		L3	
Taylor, Isaac N.	14, Sept 1854	27, Aug.			L3	
Taylor, James	23, Aug. 1838	Aug.	27		L3	
Taylor, James	16, Nov. 1854	11, Nov.	69	*	L3	
Taylor, James	19, July 1849	July	3- 6m		L3	
Taylor, James (Capt)	6, Apr. 1843	23, Mar.	74	*	L3	
Taylor, James (Gen)	9, Nov. 1848	8, Nov.	80	*	L3	
Taylor, Jane	19, July 1849	July	10		L3	
Taylor, Jane	25, July 1850	July	33		L3	
Taylor, John	12, Oct. 1848	11, Oct.	50	*	L3	
Taylor, John	21, Dec. 1848		estate		L3	
Taylor, John	22, Oct. 1857	20, Oct.			L3	
Taylor, Joseph	30, June 1842	25, June	91	*	L3	
Taylor, Lilie Anne	26, July 1849	July	7		L3	
Taylor, Lucinda	9, Apr. 1846	Mar.	18		L3	
Taylor, Lucy Harrison	19, July 1855	23, June	66		L3	Singleton
Taylor, Margaret W.	27, Aug. 1857	18, Aug.	8		L3	
Taylor, Mark P.	4, Aug. 1853	2, Aug.			L3	
Taylor, Mark Pringle	4, Dec. 1845	29, Nov.			L3	
Taylor, Mary	13, Sept 1832	Sept	38		L1	
Taylor, Mary	8, Nov. 1832	Nov.	4- 1m		L1	
Taylor, Mary Ann	16, Aug. 1849	Aug.	30		L3	
Taylor, Mellicent	4, May 1848	1, May			L3	
Taylor, Nicholas	3, Feb. 1848	Jan.	31		L3	
Taylor, Orson	29, Jan. 1846	20, Jan.	36		L3	

Name	Notice Date	Death Date	Age		Page	Maiden Name
Taylor, Philip R.	6, Nov. 1834		estate		L3	
Taylor, Ralph	11, Mar. 1847	9, Mar.	54	*	L3	
Taylor, Richard A.	5, Nov. 1840	29, Oct.	23		L2	
Taylor, Robert	18, Apr. 1850	Apr.	27		L3	
Taylor, Roldan Gard	29, May 1845	22, May	7- 5m		L3	
Taylor, Samuel	18, Apr. 1839		probate		L3	
Taylor, Sarah Jane	6, Aug. 1857	30, July	29		L3	
Taylor, Sarah M.	19, Sept 1850	11, Sept	13m- 4d		L3	
Taylor, Thomas	28, Apr. 1817		77		L3	
Taylor, Thomas	2, Sept 1830		estate		L3	
Taylor, Thomas	1, June 1854		estate		L3	
Taylor, Townsend	23, May 1833	May	45		L4	
Taylor, William	30, Apr. 1846	Apr.			L3	
Taylor, William W.	3, Oct. 1850	Sept	30		L3	
Teaniman, John	23, Aug. 1849	Aug.	25		L3	
Teany, Charlotte	26, Feb. 1857	17, Feb.			L3	
Teater, Christiana	30, July 1829	10, July	40		L1	
Teater, William	16, Sept 1825	8, Sept	23		L3	
Teats, Charles	5, May 1853				L1	
Teboe, Philip	16, Apr. 1840	Apr.	30		L3	
Tebon, Uriah	11, June 1835		estate		L4	
Tedlie, Jane	27, Aug. 1846	15, Aug.	90	*	L3	
Tedrow, Allen	9, Oct. 1834	Sept	20		L1	
Tedrow, Isaac	1, Aug. 1833	July	48		L1	
Teetre, Archibald	19, July 1832	July	2		L1	
Teifel, Joseph	13, Aug. 1857				L3	
Telford, Catlyna Totten	18, Mar. 1847	10, Mar.	infant		L3	
Telford, Charles L.	16, Aug. 1849	5, Aug.		*	L3	
Teller, John	6, Aug. 1857	4, Aug.			L3	
Temple, Frances H.	6, Apr. 1848	3, Apr.			L3	
Temple, Lucinda S.	24, Dec. 1857	19, Dec.			L3	
Temple, W.H. Clay	1, Apr. 1847	24, Mar.	2- 9m		L3	
Temple, Warren	11, Sept 1834	Aug.	1- -19d		L1	
Templeton, George	18, Oct. 1832	13, Oct.			L2	
Templin, Agness	24, Feb. 1826	6, Feb.	88	*	L3	
Terrell, Elizabeth	11, Oct. 1849	Oct.	28		L3	
Terrell, Mary	9, Nov. 1848	Oct.	27		L3	
Terry, Hugh J.	18, May 1854	12, May	61		L3	
Terry, May	10, Nov. 1842	Nov.	27		L4	
Terry, William	27, Nov. 1851		estate		L3	
Terry, William	5, July 1855		probate		L3	
Terry, William, Jr.	6, Mar. 1856		probate		L3	
Terry, William, Sen.	29, Jan. 1852		estate		L3	
Terry, William, Sen.	6, Dec. 1855		probate		L3	
Terwillegar, Nathaniel	13, Apr. 1809		estate		L3	
Terwillegar, Nathaniel	5, Sept 1839		probate		L3	
Teton, Shadrach	15, Nov. 1832	Nov.			L1	
Teurrence, (Mrs)	8, Aug. 1833	July			L1	
Thacher, Peter O.	9, Mar. 1843	23, Feb.	66		L3	
Thacker, Alven	12, Nov. 1846	Nov.	28		L3	
Thacker, John	4, Oct. 1838		estate		L3	
Thallman, Frederick	12, Sept 1850	Sept	45		L3	
Thamer, Catharine E.	22, Aug. 1850	Aug.	1		L3	
Tharp, Jane	3, Feb. 1848	30, Jan.	50		L3	

Name	Notice Date	Death Date	Age		Page	Maiden Name
Tharp, Mary VanMatre	15, Mar. 1855	10, Mar.	58	*	L3	
Tharpe, Sarah	5, Dec. 1833	Nov.	11m-14d		L3	
Thatcher, Ann P.	22, Aug. 1833	Aug.	2m		L4	
Thatcher, David	29, Apr. 1823		estate		L3	
Thatcher, David	17, Mar. 1826		probate		L3	
Thatcher, Justin M.	13, Nov. 1850	8, Nov.	45		L3	
Thatcher, Phebe K.	20, Feb. 1834	16, Feb.	19		L3	
Thathey, Elizabeth	1, Nov. 1832	Oct.	3		L2	
Thayer, Charles	17, Feb. 1848	14, Feb.	7- 1m		L3	
Thayer, Isaac	4, June 1857	3, June	65		L3	
Thayer, Oliver	27, Aug. 1846	Aug.	38		L3	
Thayer, Zebdial	27, Mar. 1845	22, Mar.	60		L3	
Thennedy, Michael Ignatius	26, Sept 1850	23, Sept	6m		L3	
Thering, Theodore	15, Aug. 1850	Aug.	61		L3	
Thers, Jacob	14, June 1849	June	38		L3	
Theurer, Jacob	5, July 1849	June	30		L3	
Thiebe, Christopher	9, Aug. 1855			*	L3	
Thielmann, Christian	7, June 1855		probate		L3	
Thirkield, James E.	29, June 1854	21, June	70		L3	
Thockey, James	3, Jan. 1850	Dec.	35		L3	
Thole, Ann M.	30, Aug. 1849	Aug.	15		L3	
Thomas,	12, July 1809				L3	
Thomas, (Mrs)	5, Jan. 1854	30, Dec.			L2	
Thomas, Abel J.	11, June 1857	5, June	62		L3	
Thomas, Ann	31, Oct. 1850	Oct.			L3	
Thomas, Ashbel	1, Aug. 1850	29, July			L3	
Thomas, Augusta Fanshaw	26, Nov. 1846	23, Nov.	6		L3	
Thomas, Boyd	4, June 1857		probate		L3	
Thomas, Charles A.	30, Oct. 1845	29, Oct.	3- 1m-16d		L3	
Thomas, Charles Edward	23, Jan. 1851	15, Jan.	infant		L3	
Thomas, E. Sidney	23, Mar. 1848	10, Mar.			L3	
Thomas, E.S.	30, Oct. 1845	22, Oct.	71		L3	
Thomas, Elizabeth	18, Oct. 1838	Oct.	42		L3	
Thomas, Henry	27, Sept 1849	Sept	24		L3	
Thomas, Isabella	8, Aug. 1833	July	2- 5m		L1	
Thomas, J.R.	9, Oct. 1834	Sept	39		L1	
Thomas, James	12, Apr. 1814		estate		L2	
Thomas, James	11, July 1850	July	30		L3	
Thomas, James	2, Dec. 1816		estate		L3	
Thomas, James	31, Mar. 1842		estate		L3	
Thomas, John	31, Jan. 1850	Jan.	9		L3	
Thomas, John	6, Apr. 1848	Mar.	33		L3	
Thomas, John	30, Dec. 1847	Dec.	40		L3	
Thomas, John	8, Aug. 1850	July	41		L3	
Thomas, John F.	14, Nov. 1839		estate		L3	
Thomas, John Finlay	31, Oct. 1839	21, Oct.	25		L3	
Thomas, Laura Anna	3, Mar. 1853	28, Feb.	4m-11d		L3	
Thomas, Margaret	30, Jan. 1851	28, Jan.	57	*	L3	
Thomas, Margaret	26, July 1849	24, July	69		L3	
Thomas, Mary	3, July 1851	June	40		L3	
Thomas, Mary Ann	3, Apr. 1851	19, Mar.			L3	Reeder
Thomas, Mary Elizabeth	17, Aug. 1843	12, Aug.	15m		L3	
Thomas, Perry	11, Jan. 1849	Jan.	22		L3	
Thomas, Rebecca M.	22, June 1848	18, June	36		L3	

Name	Notice Date	Death Date	Age	Page	Maiden Name
Thomas, Richard	30, Jan. 1840	Jan.	28	L3	
Thomas, Richard	5, July 1855		probate	L3	
Thomas, Richard	8, Nov. 1855		probate	L3	
Thomas, Richard	9, June 1853	5, June		L3	
Thomas, Sarah M.	15, Feb. 1855	11, Feb.		L3	
Thomas, Sophronia Belles	8, Apr. 1852	4, Apr.	11m-15d	L3	
Thomas, William	25, July 1850	July	6	L3	
Thomas, William C.	9, June 1836		probate	L3	
Thomas, William F.	18, Sept 1834	Sept	40	L1	
Thomas, William H.	25, Jan. 1849	19, Jan.	16m	L3	
Thomason, Charles W.	13, July 1848	July	13m	L3	
Thompson, (child of Ann)	20, Aug. 1846	Aug.	stillborn	L3	
Thompson, (child of Jane)	3, Jan. 1833	Dec.	1	L4	
Thompson, Alfred	26, July 1832	July	25	L1	
Thompson, Ann	7, Aug. 1834	July	54	L3	
Thompson, Arthur	26, Dec. 1839	Dec.	18	L3	
Thompson, Benjamin	17, May 1849	14, May	33	L3	
Thompson, Benjamin	20, Jan. 1821		estate	L3	
Thompson, Benjamin	16, Nov. 1822		estate	L4	
Thompson, Caleb	19, Feb. 1805		estate	L1	
Thompson, Charles	31, Apr. 1845	Apr.	68	L3	
Thompson, Charles	31, Aug. 1824	16, Aug.		L3	
Thompson, Charles	15, June 1837	June	24	L4	
Thompson, Charles H.	4, Jan. 1849	1, Jan.	4m	L3	
Thompson, Cornelia	21, June 1849	15, June	10w	L3	
Thompson, David M.	13, Aug. 1857	29, June		L3	
Thompson, Elijah (Col)	13, Feb. 1840	28, Jan.		L3	
Thompson, George	11, July 1833	July	14d	L1	
Thompson, George W.	11, June 1846	June	28	L3	
Thompson, H.	21, Feb. 1828	Feb.	30	L1	
Thompson, Hannah	1, Aug. 1833	July	60	L1	
Thompson, Harvey	17, Feb. 1853			L3	
Thompson, Henry Robert	9, Mar. 1854	7, Mar.	9m	L3	
Thompson, James	4, May 1848	Apr.	45	L3	
Thompson, James J.	15, June 1843	June	3- 6m	L3	
Thompson, Jessie	29, May 1851	27, May	8m-14d	L3	
Thompson, John	25, July 1850	July	31	L3	
Thompson, John	25, Jan. 1838		estate	L3	
Thompson, John	3, Sept 1840		estate	L3	
Thompson, John	3, Sept 1840	25, Aug.		L3	
Thompson, John (Rev)	19, Jan. 1843	3, Jan.		L3	
Thompson, John L.	9, Nov. 1854	7, Nov.	*	L3	
Thompson, Josiah	7, Aug. 1834	July	30	L3	
Thompson, Mary	1, July 1852	26, June	infant	L3	
Thompson, Matilda B.	22, Sept 1842	Sept	27	L3	
Thompson, Robert	12, July 1855	4, July		L3	
Thompson, Sarah Ann	3, June 1841	2, June	15- 5m	L3	
Thompson, Sarah Ann	11, July 1844	July	2w	L3	
Thompson, Sarah Janny	21, Aug. 1851	15, Aug.	4- 6m	L3	
Thompson, Seth	9, Aug. 1838	July	40	L3	
Thompson, Susannah	18, Oct. 1832	Oct.	18	L4	
Thompson, Thomas	19, Apr. 1814		estate	L1	
Thompson, Thomas	6, Apr. 1837		estate	L3	
Thompson, Thomas	22, Mar. 1838		probate	L3	

Name	Notice Date	Death Date	Age	Page	Maiden Name
Thompson, William	18, Nov. 1841	Nov.	10	L3	
Thompson, William	25, July 1810	22, July	27	L3	
Thompson, William A.	1, Aug. 1839	July	39	L3	
Thompson, William B.	27, Sept 1827		35	L1	
Thompson, William L.F.	9, July 1857		probate	L3	
Thoms, Isabella	15, 22, Aug. 1833	14, Aug.	3- 1m	L4	
Thoms, James	16, May 1839		estate	L3	
Thoms, James	9, May 1839	8, May		L3	
Thoms, William	15, Aug. 1833	Aug.	10m	L1	
Thoms, William	12, Oct. 1848		estate	L3	
Thoms, William	20, May 1852		estate	L3	
Thoms, William	31, Aug. 1848	30, Aug.		L3	
Thomson, Elizabeth	11, May 1854	8, May		L3	
Thomson, Ella	11, May 1854	9, May		L3	
Thomson, George	19, July 1849	13, July	7	L3	
Thomson, James	3, July 1851		estate	L3	
Thomson, James	7, May 1857		probate	L3	
Thomson, Patrick	2, Aug. 1838		estate	L3	
Thore, Martha Jane	17, Aug. 1843	Aug.	22	L3	
Thorn, Alexander	5, Apr. 1849	Mar.	25	L3	
Thorn, Mary F.	27, July 1843	July	5m	L3	
Thorndike, William	7, Sept 1824		probate	L3	
Thorndike, William (Dr)	20, Oct. 1818		estate	L3	
Thornley, Alice	12, July 1849	July	8m	L3	
Thornley, Philip L.	4, Apr. 1850	Mar.	26	L3	
Thornton, Beryam	7, Dec. 1843		estate	L3	
Thornton, Hannah Kirby	25, Sept 1856	21, Sept	7- 1m- 9d	L5	
Thornton, Jane	1, Dec. 1842		estate	L3	
Thornton, Joseph	1, Aug. 1821	26, July		L3	
Thornton, Lewis	29, Nov. 1849	Nov.		L3	
Thornton, Martha Elizabeth	5, Apr. 1849	28, Mar.	6	L3	
Thornton, Mary	8, Dec. 1842	16, Nov.	34	L3	Harrison
Thornton, Mary S.H.	24, Nov. 1842	16, Nov.		L6	Harrison
Thorp, (Mrs)	22, Aug. 1833	Aug.		L4	
Thorp, Andrew	15, Sept 1836		estate	L3	
Thorp, Andrew	30, Jan. 1845		estate	L3	
Thorp, Andrew	30, Aug. 1835		estate	L4	
Thorp, David (heirs of)	15, Sept 1836		probate	L3	
Thorp, Elias	28, Aug. 1834		estate	L4	
Thorp, Elizabeth	20, June 1850	15, June	18	L3	
Thorp, Elvira	20, July 1848	16, July	22	L3	
Thorp, Ezekiel	13, June 1833	June	53	L1	
Thorp, Ezekiel	20, June 1833		estate	L3	
Thorp, Ezekiel	12, Jan. 1837		probate	L3	
Thorp, Ezekiel	6, June 1833	29, May		L4	
Thorp, Herbert A.	6, May 1852	2, May	8- -25d	L3	
Thorp, J.D. (heirs of)	14, June 1838		probate	L4	
Thorp, Jane	7, Mar. 1850	2, Mar.	26	L3	
Thorp, John D.	27, Nov. 1828		estate	L3	
Thorp, Mary E.	27, Dec. 1832	Dec.	1- 2m	L1	
Thorpe, Martha Ellen	27, Oct. 1853	19, Oct.		L3	
Thorpe, Mary E.	25, Mar. 1847	19, Mar.	5- 6m	L3	
Thrall, Norman	13, July 1848	July	35	L3	
Threlkeld, Caroline	13, Jan. 1842	12, Jan.	3- 3m	L3	

Name	Notice Date	Death Date	Age		Page	Maiden Name
Throckmorton, Adalin Laura	2, Aug. 1849	28, July	14m		L3	
Throop, George B.	2, Mar. 1854	23, Feb.	62		L3	
Thurber, Samuel N.	14, Sept 1854	10, Sept	49		L3	
Thurman, Pleasant (Rev)	21, Feb. 1856	18, Feb.	73		L3	
Tibb, (child of Ebenezer)	27, Mar. 1828	Mar.	infant		L1	
Tibbat, (child of John)	8, Aug. 1833	July	1m- 5d		L1	
Tibbatts, Eliza Longworth	27, Mar. 1845	22, Mar.	infant		L3	
Tibbatts, Mary	16, Nov. 1854	10, Nov.			L3	
Tibbatts, Thomas	4, Mar. 1841	25, Feb.	83		L3	
Tibbens, Elizabeth	7, Sept 1824		probate		L3	
Tibbetts, Samuel	1, June 1824	23, May	86	*	L2	
Tibbitts, Nathaniel	27, Aug. 1824	23, Aug.	34		L3	
Tibbs, (Mrs)	16, July 1808	10, July	90		L3	
Tibbs, Emily	14, Mar. 1839	Mar.	7w		L3	
Tibbs, Samuel	11, Dec. 1834		estate		L3	
Tibbs, Samuel	16, Apr. 1835		estate		L3	
Ticer, Lucy	26, Feb. 1852	Feb.	78		L4	
Tichenor, Gabriel	15, Feb. 1855		estate		L3	
Tichenor, Gabriel	10, Sept 1857		probate		L3	
Tiebout, James W.	18, Oct. 1832	13, Oct.			L2	
Tiernan, Michael	19, Apr. 1845	14, Apr.	62		L3	
Tierney, Barney	19, Apr. 1849	Apr.	28		L3	
Tierney, Patrick	26, June 1851	June	30		L3	
Tiffin, Mary	23, July 1808	15, July			L3	
Tift, William	17, Dec. 1846	21, Nov.	30		L3	
Tiley, F.	12, Apr. 1855	9, Apr.	79		L3	
Tiley, Francis	12, Apr. 1855	9, Apr.	79		L3	
Tillotson, Augusta	21, Aug. 1851	16, Aug.	3- 2m		L3	
Tillotson, C.R.	6, Sept 1855		probate		L3	
Tillotson, Edward R.	29, July 1852	22, July	32		L3	
Tillottson, James	1, Jan. 1852	28, Dec.			L3	
Tillson, Mary	15, Oct. 1857	Oct.			L3	
Tilney, Charles H.	7, Feb. 1856	1, Feb.	20m- 3d		L3	
Tilten, Francis	6, Apr. 1854	4, Apr.	63		L3	
Tilton, William	6, July 1819		estate		L3	
Tilton, William	18, June 1819	7, June		*	L3	
Timberlick, Philip	3, Sept 1846	Aug.	85		L3	
Timmerman, (child of David)	19, July 1832	July	1		L1	
Timmis, Henry	21, Mar. 1839	Mar.	39		L3	
Timmons, Elisha	20, July 1837	July	36		L4	
Tindall, Mary	15, Nov. 1832	Nov.	60		L1	
Tindle, Catherine	8, Aug. 1833	July	29		L1	
Tingley, Henry	7, Apr. 1853	6, Apr.			L3	
Tinker, Lucy	30, Nov. 1848	27, Nov.	16		L3	
Tipton, Elizabeth	27, May 1847	18, May	68		L3	
Tipton, Joshua	18, Oct. 1832	13, Oct.	52		L2	
Tisdale, L. (Dr)	19, Sept 1833	28, Aug.		*	L1	
Titcomb, Miriam	8, Jan. 1857	2, Jan.	56		L3	
Titus, Elizabeth	29, Nov. 1849	24, Nov.			L2	
Titus, Timothy S.	6, Dec. 1855		probate		L3	
Tizzard, Elizabeth	20, Feb. 1851	10, Feb.	61- 1m-18d		L3	
Tizzard, Samuel	6, June 1844	10, May	57	*	L3	
Tobes, George	17, Aug. 1848	Aug.	26		L3	
Tobey, Charles	30, Nov. 1843	4, Nov.			L3	

Name	Notice Date	Death Date	Age	Page	Maiden Name
Tobey, George H.	10, Sept 1857	6, Sept	35	L3	
Tobosing, John	9, Apr. 1846	Mar.	30	L3	
Toby, (son of Mr)	25, Oct. 1832	22, Oct.	6	L3	
Toby, Ardina T.	27, Apr. 1848	18, Apr.	42	L3	
Todd, Catharine V.	13, Apr. 1854			L3	
Todd, John	6, Aug. 1857		probate	L3	
Todd, Joseph	17, July 1845	12, July		L3	
Todd, Presly	1, Aug. 1839	July	30	L3	
Toddhunter, Thomas	12, July 1838	7, July		L3	
Todhunter, Margaret A.	21, Nov. 1833	Nov.	4	L3	
Toliver, Ann	25, July 1850	July	24	L3	
Toliver, Martha	14, July 1842	July	10	L3	
Toliver, William	22, Feb. 1844	Feb.	2	L3	
Tollen, (child of Michael)	16, Oct. 1834	Oct.	14d	L1	
Toller, Michael	31, Mar. 1842	Mar.	39	L3	
Tomlesour, J.	1, Aug. 1833	July	16	L1	
Tomlinson, (child of T.)	28, Aug. 1834	Aug.	11m	L1	
Tomlinson, J.C.	20, Sept 1838	9, Aug.	*	L3	
Tomlinson, John F.	6, Aug. 1857		probate	L3	
Tompkins, Daniel D.	28, June 1825	11, June	51	L3	
Tompkins, Ella	5, Aug. 1852	31, July	18m	L3	
Tompkins, George F.	22, June 1837		probate	L3	
Tompkins, James Bingham	7, Apr. 1853	4, Apr.	18	L3	
Tompkinson, George	27, June 1850	June	45	L3	
Tompson, John	20, Aug. 1840	Aug.	24	L3	
Toney, Jonas	5, July 1849	3, July		L3	
Tool, Edward	17, Feb. 1853	11, Feb.		L3	
Tool, James	8, Nov. 1849	Oct.	23	L3	
Toppin, (child of William)	9, Sept 1841	Aug.	1- 4m	L3	
Topping, Jane A.	9, Aug. 1855	3, Aug.	46	L3	
Torance,	23, May 1833	May	33	L4	
Torbert, Simpson (Col)	1, Mar. 1838	23, Feb.	*	L3	
Torbit, John S.	16, Mar. 1854	26, Feb.	88	L3	
Tornto, Constantine	13, Nov. 1851	8, Nov.		L4	
Torrence, Eaton	26, June 1851	June	2w	L3	
Torrence, George P.	30, Aug. 1855	27, Aug.	74	L3	
Torrence, John	17, July 1811		estate	L3	
Torrence, Mary	27, Oct. 1842	30, Sept	80	L3	
Torrence, Mary Findlay	16, Aug. 1849	8, Au.g	1-10m	L3	
Torrence, Thomas Finley	25, Apr. 1844	22, Apr.	21m	L3	
Torrince, John	30, Jan. 1811		estate	L3	
Totin, John T.	25, July 1833	July	1	L1	
Totten, Joseph	3, July 1811		estate	L3	
Totten, Joseph	8, Nov. 1855		probate	L3	
Totten, Joseph	10, Sept 1857		probate	L3	
Toutelot, Jesse	8, Jan. 1835		estate	L3	
Tower, Gideon	1, July 1847	11, June	94	L3	
Towler, Nancy	16, Feb. 1843	8, Feb.	69	L3	
Towles, Agatha	15, June 1843	9, June	*	L3	
Town, William	25, July 1839	9, July		L3	
Towne, Thomas	10, Sept 1846	29, Aug.	*	L3	
Towns, Joseph	23, May 1844	May	31	L3	
Townsend, George	29, Jan. 1846	29, Dec.	19	L3	
Townsend, Lydia	30, Mar. 1849	24, Mar.	52	L3	

Name	Notice Date	Death Date	Age	Page	Maiden Name
Townsend, Marshall	29, June 1843	June	32	L3	
Townsend, Mary Henrietta	31, May 1849	25, May	5- 2m	L3	
Townsend, Rachel	13, Aug. 1846	Aug.	3	L3	
Townsend, Thomas	19, Sept 1833		estate	L3	
Townsend, Thomas	6, Nov. 1834		estate	L3	
Townshend, (Mrs)	14, July 1853			L3	
Townsley, William	2, June 1807		estate	L2	
Toy, Benjamin R.	23, Dec. 1852	14, Dec.	30	L3	
Toy, Benjamin R.	9, Apr. 1857		probate	L3	
Toy, John	1, Feb. 1838		estate	L3	
Toy, John	18, Apr. 1839		probate	L3	
Tracey, William L.	10, Dec. 1835		estate	L3	
Tracy, Mary	20, Nov. 1845	5, Nov.	43	L3	
Tracy, Samuel M.	8, Jan. 1857	25, Dec.	63	L3	
Tracy, William D.	12, July 1849	8, July	16	L3	
Tracy, William L.	25, Jan. 1838		estate	L3	
Tracy, William L.	7, Dec. 1837		probate	L3	
Trainer, C.	1, Nov. 1832	27, Oct.	12	L3	
Tranbat, Charles	27, July 1848	July	17	L3	
Tranor, Thomas	2, Mar. 1848	23, Feb.	35	L3	
Trash, Thomas Sterne	13, Mar. 1851		22	L3	
Tratsbas, Maurice	22, Mar. 1838		probate	L3	
Travis, Ann	16, Aug. 1849	Aug.	30	L3	
Travis, Perry	28, Oct. 1847	Oct.	34	L3	
Treat, Harriet Pool	2, July 1840	1, July	16d	L3	
Treat, Samuel Pool	16, May 1839	12, May	2	L3	
Trendle, Adaline	6, May 1847	Apr.	2	L3	
Trener, Nancy	1, Aug. 1850	July	30	L3	
Treusdell, Arnold	30, Apr. 1835		estate	L4	
Trevor, Catharine	12, Oct. 1843	7, Oct.		L3	
Trib, Henry	18, July 1833	July	27	L2	
Trimble, Cyrus	7, Aug. 1834	July	21	L3	
Trimble, John B.	18, Oct. 1827	Oct.	23	L3	
Trimble, Mary	15, Dec. 1842	10, Dec.		L5	McArthur
Trimmer, Rufus A.	26, June 1845	June	20	L3	
Tripp, Elizabeth	1, Aug. 1833	July	57	L1	
Trischler, Nicholas	21, June 1849	June	59	L3	
Trolter, Christopher	13, Mar. 1828		estate	L3	
Tron, Henry	3, Jan. 1828	Jan.	infant	L1	
Trotter, Aness	13, Mar. 1851		estate	L3	
Trotter, Joseph	23, Oct. 1845	Oct.	32	L3	
Trounstine, Elizabeth	20, Dec. 1855	19, Dec.	32	L3	
Trousdale, Joseph	26, Feb. 1857	8, Feb.	36	L3	
Trousdale, Joseph	9, Apr. 1857		probate	L3	
Trousdale, Mary Jane	26, Feb. 1857	6, Jan.	3- 5m	L3	
Trousdale, Sarah	23, Mar. 1843	15, Mar.	43	L3	
Trousdale, Thomas	30, Sept 1847		estate	L3	
Trousdale, Thomas	3, June 1852		estate	L3	
Trow, George	12, Aug. 1841	Aug.	45	L3	
Trowbridge, Archibald	9, July 1857		probate	L3	
Troy, Judy	27, July 1848	July	22	L3	
Truax, David Anton	22, Nov. 1855	17, Nov.	infant	L3	
Truax, Edmund Addison	30, Oct. 1851	25, Oct.	infant	L3	
Truax, Edward Willard	21, May 1857	16, May	4m- 6d	L3	

Name	Notice Date	Death Date	Age		Page	Maiden Name
True, Martha Jane	22, Mar. 1838	Mar.	6		L3	
Truett, David	5, Apr. 1849	1, Apr.	20		L3	
Truman, Elizabeth Hotchkiss	11, July 1839	3, July	4		L3	
Truman, Elizabeth Hotchkiss	12, Aug. 1841	9, Aug.	10m		L3	
Truman, William T.	20, Mar. 1845	16, Mar.	36		L3	
Trump, John	26, July 1849		estate		L3	
Tryon, William R.	23, Nov. 1843	Nov.	30		L3	
Tucker, Benjamin S.	21, Oct. 1847	18, Oct.			L3	
Tucker, E.H.	28, Nov. 1850	24, Nov.	23		L3	
Tucker, Elizabeth	25, Oct. 1832	Oct.	19		L1	
Tucker, Henry	17, Oct. 1844		estate		L3	
Tucker, Henry	28, Nov. 1844		estate		L3	
Tucker, John	5, Sept 1844		estate		L3	
Tucker, John	9, Nov. 1837	Oct.			L4	
Tucker, Marion	8, Mar. 1855	3, Mar.			L3	
Tucker, Martin	14, June 1849	6, June	26	*	L3	
Tucker, Mary	8, Mar. 1849		estate		L3	
Tucker, Willas	13, Nov. 1834	Nov.	30		L1	
Tucker, William	13, Sept 1838	Sept	37		L3	
Tucker, William	27, May 1830	22, May	50	*	L3	
Tudor, Rachel Ann	29, July 1841	16, July	13m		L3	
Tudor, Thomas	25, Feb. 1841	24, Feb.			L3	
Tuff, Sarah	27, July 1837	July	8m		L3	
Tuley, Jane F.	31, Oct. 1844	18, Oct.	21		L3	
Tullinghues, Gertrude	7, Aug. 1834	July			L3	
Tullis, Oliver C.	23, Oct. 1845	16, Oct.	20		L3	
Tumblin, Amanda	9, Aug. 1855	8, Aug.			L3	
Tumy, Charles Marion	8, June 1854	6, June	13- 6m		L3	
Tumy, Julia Caroline	3, July 1851	26, June	infant		L3	
Tumy, Robert G.	12, Nov. 1857	30, Oct.			L3	
Tunis, Nehemiah	11, July 1833		probate		L3	
Tunis, Nehemiah	23, Feb. 1832		estate		L4	
Tunison, Henry	3, May 1855		probate		L3	
Tunnison, Henry	9, Apr. 1857		probate		L3	
Tuohy, Patrick	6, June 1850	May	24		L3	
Tuomy, (boy)	8, Apr. 1852	3, Apr.			L4	
Turbofield, (Mr)	18, Oct. 1832	14, Oct.			L2	
Turdin, Rosey	2, Aug. 1832	July	5- 6m		L1	
Turland, John	21, June 1849	June	29		L3	
Turnbull, Robert J. (Dr)	8, June 1854	4, June			L3	
Turner, (man)	9, Oct. 1851	3, Oct.			L3	
Turner, (Mr)	1, Nov. 1832	27, Oct.			L2	
Turner, (Mrs)	1, Dec. 1842	28, Nov.	67		L3	
Turner, Anna C.	5, July 1849	3, July	17		L3	
Turner, Daniel H.	25, Oct. 1849	Oct.			L3	
Turner, George	18, May 1843		94	*	L3	
Turner, Henry	25, July 1844	July	74		L3	
Turner, Henry C.	11, Jan. 1855	30, Dec.			L3	
Turner, James	11, Oct. 1832	6, Oct.			L2	
Turner, James	18, Oct. 1832	Oct.	55		L4	
Turner, Jesse	18, Jan. 1849	Jan.			L3	
Turner, John	20, Nov. 1850	Nov.	26		L3	
Turner, John D.	14, Feb. 1828	Feb.	infant		L1	
Turner, Jonathan A.	29, Apr. 1847	5, Mar.	32		L3	

Name	Notice Date	Death Date	Age	Page	Maiden Name
Turner, Mary	20, Sept 1849	Sept	23	L3	
Turner, Mary Frances	26, Mar. 1857	11, Mar.	22	L3	
Turner, Michael	24, Jan. 1850	Jan.	34	L3	
Turner, Nancy	8, Dec. 1842	Dec.	45	L3	
Turner, Priscilla A.	4, Apr. 1844	Mar.	2w	L3	
Turner, Sarah	13, Nov. 1850	Nov.	32	L3	
Turner, Susan	21, July 1853	16, July		L3	
Turner, William	8, Apr. 1841	Mar.	35	L3	
Turney, William	31, Oct. 1833	Oct.	3- -7d	L4	
Turpin, P.P. (Gen)	5, Oct. 1848	29, Sept		L3	
Turpin, Philip	14, Feb. 1839		probate	L3	
Turpin, Philip	21, Sept 1837		probate	L4	
Turpin, Phillip	3, Dec. 1840		probate	L3	
Turrill, Ida Celeste	23, Aug. 1855	18, Aug.	9m	L3	
Turry, Mary	18, Oct. 1832	Oct.	49	L4	
Tush, Sarah	26, July 1832	July	31	L1	
Tuttle, E.J.	7, Aug. 1834	July	22	L3	
Tuttle, Ebenezer	23, Aug. 1838		estate	L3	
Tuttle, Ebenezer B.	3, Dec. 1840		probate	L3	
Tuttle, Eliza L.	6, July 1848	1, July	infant	L3	
Tuxford, William	24, Mar. 1842	16, Mar.	44	L3	
Tu-y, John J.	7, Aug. 1834	July	51	L3	
Tweed, Emeline	13, Oct. 1853			L3	
Tweed, Harry C.	4, Dec. 1845	28, Nov.	2- 2m	L3	
Twichell, Rebecca B.	22, Oct. 1840	8, Oct.	27	L3	
Twigh, Mary	22, July 1847	July	14	L3	
Twitchell, Edeliza Hunt	26, July 1838	19, July	infant	L3	
Tyler, Henry	25, Oct. 1832	19, Oct.		L2	
Tyler, John	8, May 1845	Apr.	4	L3	
Tyler, John	8, May 1845	Apr.	32	L3	
Tylor, John J.	26, Sept 1850	Sept	5m	L3	
Tyre, Whitfield	22, Oct. 1840	Oct.	35	L3	
Tyre, Whitfield	26, Aug. 1841		estate	L3	
Tyre, Whitfield	5, Jan. 1843		estate	L3	
Ucutter, Nicholas	30, Nov. 1837	Nov.	21	L3	
Uhl, (boy)	15, July 1852	10, July		L3	
Ulm, Dieterick	8, Nov. 1838		probate	L3	
Ulrey, John	21, Nov. 1844	Nov.	9	L3	
Unberger, (child of Elizabeth)	9, Sept 1852	2, Sept	infant	L3	
Underwood, Daniel	11, Oct. 1832	5, Oct.		L2	
Underwood, Daniel	18, Oct. 1832	Oct.	65	L4	
Underwood, Erastus	15, June 1854	9, June	42	L3	
Underwood, Michael	29, May 1834		probate	L3	
Underwood, Sophia S.	28, Aug. 1834	Aug.	33	L1	
Underwood, William	20, June 1850	June	39	L3	
Underwood, William	9, Sept 1841	Aug.	45	L3	
Unvergayt, Catharine	12, July 1849	July	29	L3	
Unverzagt, Andrew	9, Sept 1847	Aug.	29	L3	
Unverzant, John G.	24, June 1847	June	3m	L3	
Upjohn, James	25, July 1839	24, July	85	L3	
Upjohn, Sarah	6, June 1826	3, June		L3	
Ure, John	31, Aug. 1843	Aug.	58	L3	
Urner, Benjamin	9, July 1857	3, July	62	L3	

Name	Notice Date	Death Date	Age		Page	Maiden Name
Urner, Edward Hall	4, Aug. 1836	25, July	23m-12d		L1	
Urton, Hannah	15, Aug. 1833	Aug.	17- 6m		L1	
Urwiller, Rebecca	13, Nov. 1834	Nov.	30		L1	
Ustick, Stephen C.	16, Nov. 1837	11, Nov.	66	*	L3	
Utes, John	12, Aug. 1852	Aug.	10		L3	
Uthoff, Henry	12, July 1855		29		L3	
Utley, Joseph Addison	14, Sept 1854	5, Sept	19- 4m		L3	
Uxwiller, George	7, Feb. 1833	Feb.	7d		L1	
Vaelker, Henry	23, May 1839		51		L3	
Vail, (child of Mary)	6, Feb. 1851	Jan.	1d		L3	
Vairin, Sarah	18, Apr. 1839	2, Apr.			L3	
Valentine, Aaron	20, Sept 1827	Sept	22m		L1	
Valentine, Aaron	1, Aug. 1850	28, July	52- 9m		L3	
Valentine, Aaron	5, Sept 1850		estate		L3	
Valentine, Aaron	10, Apr. 1856		probate		L3	
Valentine, Baker	28, Aug. 1834	Aug.	2		L1	
Valentine, Charles	11, Dec. 1856	6, Dec.	66		L3	
Valentine, Francis	10, May 1814		estate		L2	
Valentine, John	8, Jan. 1852	21, Oct.			L3	
Valentine, Mary Ann	18, Mar. 1847	17, Mar.	3		L3	
Valiant, Hugh	23, Sept 1847	13, Sept	63	*	L3	
Valiant, Novicey	21, Apr. 1853	15, Apr.	33		L3	
Vallandigham, John D.	14, Apr. 1853	6, Apr.		*	L3	
Vallandingham, (Mr)	22, Mar. 1855	20, Mar.			L3	
Vallandingham, William	27, Apr. 1848	Apr.	19		L3	
Vallere, Henry M.	7, Aug. 1834	July	6m- 5d		L3	
Vallet, Peter	22, Nov. 1825		estate		L3	
Vallett, Peter	4, Oct. 1825	3, Oct.			L3	
Vallette, Henrietta	21, July 1842	15, July	27		L3	
Vallette, Henry Thane	31, Aug. 1837	30, Aug.			L3	
Vallette, Julia	6, Aug. 1846	5, Aug.	35		L3	
Vallette, Sarah Julia	20, Aug. 1846	30, July	34		L3	
Vampels, Amelia A.	18, July 1833	July	4m-17d		L2	
VanAmringe, Mary Euretta	10, Dec. 1857	6, Dec.	8- 9m- 3d		L3	
VanAntwerp, Mary Griffith	14, Dec. 1854	10, Dec.	2- - 17d		L3	
Vanauker, Joseph	11, Aug. 1842		estate		L3	
Vanausdol, Jinnit	5, May 1806		estate		L2	
Vanausdol, Orpha	11, Mar. 1847	6, Mar.	52		L3	
VanBergen, Charles Miles	5, May 1853	28, Apr.	8m		L3	
VanBergen, Henry	20, Apr. 1854	16, Apr.	4- 4m		L3	
VanBergin, Edgar G.	24, Jan. 1856	18, Jan.	19		L3	
VanBoskerck, S. Stuart	27, Feb. 1851		20		L3	
Vance, Harriet D.	30, Aug. 1832	Aug.	32		L1	
Vance, Harrison	23, Sept 1841				L3	
Vance, James	28, Mar. 1839		estate		L3	
Vance, James	11, June 1840		estate		L3	
Vance, James	14, June 1838		probate		L4	
Vance, Joseph C. (Lt)	10, Sept 1840	31, Aug.			L1	
Vance, Mary	28, Mar. 1823	21, Mar.	41		L3	
VanCleave, John	19, Dec. 1850		estate		L3	
VanCleve, John	19, Sept 1850	6, Sept	70		L3	
VanClieve, Anne	2, June 1806		estate		L4	
Vanderlippi, R.C.H.	12, July 1849	July	59		L3	

Name	Notice Date	Death Date	Age		Page	Maiden Name
Vanderpool, (Mr)	17, July 1851	12, July		*	L3	
VanderPool, Mary Ann	16, May 1826	13, May	17		L3	
Vandersol, Andrew	20, Jan. 1848	Jan.	23		L3	
Vandervort, Alice	5, Apr. 1855	11, Mar.	73		L3	
Vandoren, D.B.	15, Nov. 1849		estate		L3	
VanHamm, Clara	24, Feb. 1848	18, Feb.	31	*	L3	Smallwood
VanHorn, John	30, Aug. 1832	Aug.	32		L1	
VanHorn, Mary E.	9, Oct. 1834	Sept	5- 3m		L1	
VanHorne, Mary Elizabeth	9, Oct. 1834	27, Sept	5- 3m		L3	
VanHorne, Thomas B. (Col)	7, Oct. 1841	21, Sept	59	*	L3	
Vanhorner, (boy)	24, July 1851	17, July			L3	
VanHouten, Isaac (Capt)	11, Mar. 1847	9, Mar.			L1	
VanHouten, John P.	1, Aug. 1833		estate		L3	
VanHouten, John P.	20, Aug. 1835		estate		L3	
VanHouten, John P.	18, Aug. 1836		estate		L4	
VanHouton, Augustus	28, Dec. 1843	27, Dec.	12		L3	
VanKirk, Angeline	5, Oct. 1854	28, Sept	16		L3	
Vanlew, Con	14, Apr. 1853				L3	
Vanliew, Ira C.	14, Apr. 1853				L3	
VanLoon, Mary	3, May 1855		probate		L3	
VanMatre, John Henderson	3, June 1847	27, May	13m-15d		L3	
VanMatre, Ruth	8, Aug. 1844	4, Aug.	76		L3	
VanMiddlesworth, John	30, July 1835		estate		L3	
VanNauendooff, Frederick	9, Apr. 1857		probate		L3	
VanNest, Garret	13, Jan. 1817		estate		L3	
Vannier, Hester	11, July 1833		probate		L3	
Vannier, John	19, Dec. 1826		probate		L3	
VanPelt, Alexander	13, Sept 1832	Sept	1- 8m-13d		L1	
Vanpelt, James	8, Aug. 1844	July	50		L3	
VanRenssalear, Philip	25, Jan. 1838	Jan.	60		L3	
Vansant, R.R.	14, Aug. 1856		probate		L6	
Vansant, Sarah	5, Sept 1833	Aug.	1- 4m		L1	
VanSickle, Ralph	13, Aug. 1835		estate		L3	
Vansickle, Ralph	15, Sept 1836		probate		L3	
Vansickle, Ralph	7, Dec. 1837		probate		L3	
Vanslike, Daniel	14, Oct. 1841	21, Sept			L3	
Vantuyl, Charity	12, Feb. 1846		estate		L3	
VanValkenburgh, John	31, Aug. 1854	24, Aug.	64	*	L3	
VanValkenburgh, Mary	28, Feb. 1850	25, Feb.	20		L3	
Vanvickel, Robert	26, Apr. 1814		estate		L2	
VanVickel, Robert	4, Mar. 1815		estate		L3	
VanVolkenburg, J.	17, Oct. 1839	Oct.	50		L3	
VanWart, William	26, May 1842		83		L3	
VanWaters, Isaac	20, Sept 1827	Sept	30		L1	
VanWinkle, Nicholas	6, Aug. 1857		probate		L3	
VanZandt, Benjamin N.	31, Oct. 1839		estate		L3	
VanZandt, Isaac	22, Aug. 1827		estate		L2	
VanZant, John	1, Nov. 1838	Oct.	6		L3	
Varian, Miles B.	9, Aug. 1849	29, July	32		L3	
Varing, Susan	1, Aug. 1833	July	31		L1	
Varner, William	23, Oct. 1834	Oct.	35		L2	
Vasso, Francis	25, Oct. 1832	22, Oct.			L3	
Vattier, Charles	11, Mar. 1841	7, Mar.			L3	
Vattier, Mary F.	18, July 1844	10, July	28		L3	

Name	Notice Date	Death Date	Age	Page	Maiden Name
Vaughan, (child of David G.)	20, Apr. 1843	Apr.	1d	L3	
Vaughan, Claiborne	29, July 1852	6, July	38	L3	
Vaughan, Fanny	17, Aug. 1843	10, Aug.	16m	L3	
Vaughen, John	24, Jan. 1850	Jan.	7w	L3	
Vaughn, George	5, Nov. 1857		probate	L3	
Vawter, Sarah N.	11, Oct. 1838	19, Sept		L3	Neave
Veach, (child of Charles)	8, May 1828	May	3m	L1	
Veard, Peter	18, Nov. 1820		estate	L3	
Veard, Peter	14, Mar. 1821		estate	L3	
Vears, Dianna	28, June 1809	28, May	23	L3	
Veatch, Charles	13, Aug. 1857	12, Aug.	56	L3	
Veets, (man)	16, Mar. 1854			L3	
Veit, John	26, July 1849	July	68	L3	
Velman, Enoch	18, Oct. 1832	15, Oct.		L3	
Verhorff, Augustus (Rev)	4, Dec. 1851	26, Nov.		L3	
Vermeyer, Maria C.	6, Jan. 1848	Dec.	34	L3	
Verplank, John	26, July 1838	July	19	L3	
Vesh, Josephine	6, Feb. 1851	Jan.	40	L3	
Vester, John	4, Sept 1856		probate	L5	
Vewmon, Ruth	2, Oct. 1834	Sept		L4	
Vickers, Mary	16, June 1842		estate	L3	
Vickwire, (Mrs)	25, Oct. 1832	21, Oct.		L3	
Viers, Brice	2, Mar. 1854	22, Feb.	89	L3	
Viers, Elvira	9, Jan. 1851	30, Dec.	55	L3	Hammond
Vina, Santa	17, Jan. 1850	Jan.	50	L3	
Vincent, Bartlett C.	20, Nov. 1828		estate	L3	
Vincent, James	26, Jan. 1837	Jan.	23	L3	
Vining, Cyrene	22, July 1847	11, July	51	L3	
Vinton, Earl D.	15, Nov. 1832	Nov.	41- 1m- 5d	L1	
Virtue, Alexander	26, Apr. 1855	17, Apr.		L3	
Voelkel, John	16, May 1844	May	35	L3	
Vogel, William	21, Oct. 1841	Oct.	26	L3	
Voges, Jacob Herman	18, Sept 1851	10, Sept		L4	
Vogle, Catharine	15, Aug. 1850	Aug.	27	L3	
Vogt, Joseph	30, Aug. 1849	Aug.	45	L3	
Volkel, John	30, May 1844	May	3m	L3	
Volle, Jacob	25, July 1810	22, July		L3	
Volmer, Henry	6, Mar. 1851		estate	L3	
Vonderheide, B.H.	16, Oct. 1856		probate	L6	
VonNauendorff, F.L.	4, Sept 1856		probate	L5	
VonPhul, Lauretta Bodman	13, Aug. 1857	Aug.	7m	L3	
Voorhees, Abraham	23, Feb. 1837		probate	L3	
Voorhees, Amanda	23, Nov. 1837	19, Nov.	2- 4m	L3	
Voorhees, Cornelius	2, Dec. 1805	24, Nov.		L3	
Voorhees, Isabella	11, July 1833	July	23- 6m	L1	
Voorhees, Miny	28, July 1806	19, July	23	L3	
Voorhees, Sarah P.	1, July 1841	27, June	35	L3	
Voorhees, William Henry H.	25, Feb. 1841	18, Feb.	4m	L3	
Voorheese, Eliza A.	8, Nov. 1832	Nov.	7- 2m	L1	
Voorheese, Ralph M.	13, Mar. 1828	5, Mar.		L1	
Voras, John	28, Nov. 1833	Nov.	57	L4	
Vorhee, (child)	1, Nov. 1832	27, Oct.		L2	
Vorhes, Harriet	16, Jan. 1851	8, Jan.	27	L3	Gregg
Voss, Peter M.	19, Mar. 1846	15, Mar.	31	L3	

Name	Notice Date	Death Date	Age		Page	Maiden Name
Vrafeldt, Herman	9, Apr. 1857		probate		L3	
Waalley, Joseph	1, Nov. 1832	25, Oct.			L1	
Waas, Henry	19, July 1849	July	54		L3	
Wade, D.E.	8, Jan. 1857		probate		L3	
Wade, David	19, Dec. 1844		estate		L3	
Wade, David	17, Oct. 1844	13, Oct.			L3	
Wade, David (Mrs)	1, May 1811	Apr.			L3	
Wade, David E.	6, Dec. 1832	Dec.	34		L1	
Wade, David E.	28, July 1842		80		L3	
Wade, David E.	28, July 1842		estate		L3	
Wade, Frances	25, Apr. 1833	Apr.	9m-14d		L1	
Wade, Frances	28, Mar. 1826	5, Mar.	26		L3	Betts
Wade, Harriet Ramsay	2, June 1842	18, May			L3	
Wade, James	19, Oct. 1848	11, Oct.	5m		L3	
Wade, Mary C.	22, Apr. 1825	20, Apr.			L3	
Wade, Mary Elizabeth	21, Dec. 1848	18, Dec.	10- -24d		L3	
Wade, Samuel McCormick	12, Aug. 1841	3, Aug.	infant		L3	
Wade, Stephen Jones	29, June 1848	20, June	13m		L3	
Wade, Stephen Jones	14, Mar. 1850	7, Mar.	3m-16d		L3	
Wade, William	27, July 1843	19, July	infant		L3	
Wade, William W.	28, Sept 1843	26, Sept			L3	
Wadsworth, James	20, June 1844	7, June			L3	
Waggaman, G.B. (Judge)	6, Apr. 1843	23, Mar.			L3	
Waggoner, Aaron	25, Feb. 1847		estate		L3	
Waggoner, Chris.	24, Aug. 1848	Aug.	31		L3	
Waggoner, Christina	21, June 1849	June	32		L3	
Waggoner, James	19, Jan. 1843	20, Jan.	32		L3	
Waggoner, Peter C.	4, June 1857		probate		L3	
Wagner, Christian	19, July 1849		estate		L3	
Wagner, John D.	16, Oct. 1856		probate		L6	
Wagner, Peter C.	10, Dec. 1857		probate		L3	
Wagner, William Jacob	7, Aug. 1851	2, Aug.	16		L3	
Wagoner, Daniel	31, Dec. 1846	Dec.	36		L3	
Wahlors, Rebecca	28, June 1849	June	34		L3	
Waiglos, Ann	4, July 1833	June	77		L2	
Wain, (child of Anthony)	8, Aug. 1833	July	stillborn		L1	
Wait, (child of Richard)	13, Nov. 1834	Nov.	14d		L1	
Waite, William	22, Aug. 1839	Aug.	24		L3	
Wakefield, Alice D.	7, 14, Dec. 1854	30, Nov.		*	L3	Rowan
Wakefield, William	16, Oct. 1856		probate		L6	
Wakefield, William (Col)	12, Apr. 1855	6, Apr.	60		L3	
Walbridge, William G.	31, Aug. 1854	21, Aug.	21		L3	
Wald, Henry	14, Aug. 1856	6, Aug.	48		L5	
Wald, Henry	28, Aug. 1856		estate		L8	
Wald, Theresa	18, Oct. 1832	12, Oct.			L2	
Walden, Baltzer	9, July 1857		probate		L3	
Walder, Thomas	10, Apr. 1851		23		L3	
Waldie, George	6, Nov. 1845	Oct.	30		L3	
Waldo, Anna	26, June 1851	22, June	2m		L3	
Waldo, Arabella	18, Jan. 1844	12, Jan.	28		L3	Lawrence
Waldo, Emma Clark	25, Sept 1845	18, Sept	6- 6m		L3	
Waldron, (man)	21, July 1853	20, July			L3	
Waldsmith, Christian	19, Apr. 1814		estate		L3	

Name	Notice Date	Death Date	Age	Page	Maiden Name
Waldsmith, Christian	12, Apr. 1814	31, Mar.		L3	
Waldsmith, John	19, Apr. 1814		estate	L2	
Waldsmith, John	14, Feb. 1839		probate	L3	
Waldsmith, William	6, Jan. 1817		estate	L4	
Wales, (child of Lucinda)	14, Feb. 1833	Feb.	1m- 4d	L1	
Wales, Arvine	26, Jan. 1854	22, Jan.	69	* L3	
Wales, William	15, Aug. 1833	Aug.	22	L1	
Waley, John	8, Mar. 1849	Feb.	44	L3	
Walingham, Arthur	25, Sept 1851	18, Sept		L4	
Walker, (boy)	25, Oct. 1827	Oct.	9m	L2	
Walker, (child)	6, Nov. 1834	Oct.		L1	
Walker, (Mrs)	25, July 1833	July	35	L1	
Walker, Addie Haughton	8, Jan. 1857	2, Jan.	1	L3	
Walker, Alfred	5, Jan. 1837		estate	L3	
Walker, Alfred	22, June 1837		probate	L3	
Walker, Alfred	24, July 1834		estate	L4	
Walker, Ann	9, Aug. 1849	3, Aug.	15m-10d	L3	
Walker, Ann	21, May 1857		estate	L3	
Walker, Ann Eliza	3, Nov. 1836	31, Oct.		L2	
Walker, Christopher	13, May 1841	9, May	84	* L3	
Walker, David	9, Sept 1825		probate	L3	
Walker, Davis	30, Oct. 1834	27, Oct.	infant	L3	
Walker, Diana	8, Apr. 1847		estate	L3	
Walker, Edwin H.	1, Oct. 1857	29, Sept	8	L3	
Walker, Frederick Brewster	19, Oct. 1848	11, Oct.	14m	L3	
Walker, George	9, June 1836		probate	L3	
Walker, George	25, Apr. 1833		estate	L4	
Walker, James	13, Dec. 1849	Dec.	40	L3	
Walker, James	7, Aug. 1851		60	L3	
Walker, Jane Clark	20, Aug. 1857	17, Aug.	10m	L3	
Walker, Jemima	1, May 1827		estate	L3	
Walker, John	23, June 1853	20, June	54	* L3	
Walker, John	29, May 1834		probate	L3	
Walker, John	9, Aug. 1855		probate	L3	
Walker, John	6, Dec. 1855		probate	L3	
Walker, John	7, Feb. 1856		probate	L3	
Walker, John	9, July 1857		probate	L3	
Walker, John Harvey	27, July 1843	15, July		L3	
Walker, Joseph	14, Mar. 1844	7, Mar.	35	L3	
Walker, Joseph	21, June 1838		estate	L3	
Walker, Joseph	31, Oct. 1844		estate	L3	
Walker, Joseph Brewster	7, Jan. 1847	31, Dec.	38	L3	
Walker, Margaret	14, Oct. 1847	Oct.	4m	L3	
Walker, Margaret	5, Mar. 1857	1, Mar.		L3	
Walker, Martha C.	3, Apr. 1856	28, Mar.		L3	
Walker, Martha E.	28, Jan. 1841	27, Jan.		L3	
Walker, Mary	5, July 1849	June	25	L3	
Walker, Milton Ludlow	22, Dec. 1842	16, Dec.	18m	L3	
Walker, Peter	21, June 1838		estate	L3	
Walker, Peter	3, Dec. 1840		probate	L3	
Walker, Robert J.	18, Dec. 1845	3, Dec.		L3	
Walker, Rockey (Mrs)	13, Jan. 1842	6, Jan.	57	L3	
Walker, Samuel S. (Dr)	18, May 1848	15, May		L3	
Walker, Sears C.	3, Feb. 1853	30, Jan.	48	L3	

Name	Notice Date	Death Date	Age		Page	Maiden Name
Walker, Timothy	17, Jan. 1856	15, Jan.	53		L3	
Walker, Timothy	7, Feb. 1856		estate		L3	
Walker, Timothy	5, Feb. 1857		probate		L3	
Walker, Timothy	8, Oct. 1857		probate		L3	
Walker, Washington	14, Oct. 1841	Oct.	26		L3	
Wall, Cassandra	14, July 1807	11, July			L3	
Wall, Michael	8, Nov. 1849	5, Nov.	27		L2	
Wall, Robert	25, Oct. 1832	19, Oct.			L2	
Wallace, Deborah	31, July 1815	19, July	33		L3	
Wallace, Eliza J.	9, Oct. 1834	Sept	8m		L1	
Wallace, Gavin	9, Aug. 1849	7, Aug.		*	L3	
Wallace, Harriet Scott	3, Aug. 1813	24, July	16		L3	
Wallace, Huldah	21, Mar. 1850	13, Mar.			L3	
Wallace, Jane	23, Sept 1852	16, Sept	76		L3	
Wallace, John S. (Col)	4, Aug. 1836	3, Aug.	71		L1	
Wallace, Mary	28, Aug. 1834	Aug.	10m-14d		L1	
Wallace, Selah	13, Feb. 1840	Feb.	32		L3	
Wallace, William	29, Dec. 1836		estate		L3	
Wallen, Ruth	8, Aug. 1833	July	44		L1	
Wallis, Cassandra	1, Dec. 1821	14, Nov.		*	L3	
Wallis, John J.	28, Oct. 1830	5, Oct.	34	*	L2	
Wallis, Moses	18, Sept 1834		estate		L3	
Wallon, Elizabeth	7, May 1846	29, Apr.	28- 6m		L3	
Wallon, William B.	15, Aug. 1833	Aug.	7m-27d		L1	
Walls, Ann	1, Nov. 1855	30, Oct.	83		L3	
Walls, John (Rev)	26, Jan. 1854	10, Jan.	30		L3	
Walpers, John C.	15, May 1834	May	26		L4	
Walsemairns, Burchard	12, Sept 1833	Sept	6		L1	
Walter, (son of Joseph)	1, Apr. 1847	31, Mar.	infant		L3	
Walter, Brinton	31, Aug. 1843	22, Aug.	8- 8m		L3	
Walter, Celine	18, Sept 1851	11, Sept		*	L3	
Walter, Henry	16, Aug. 1849		estate		L3	
Walter, Henry Gerhard	10, Jan. 1850	9, Jan.	3- 6m		L3	
Walter, Joseph	1, Aug. 1833	July			L1	
Walter, Joseph	23, June 1853	22, June	8		L3	
Walter, Lydia	26, Dec. 1850	2, Dec.	43		L3	Ogden
Walter, Thomas Oliver	24, Apr. 1851	16, Apr.	20m-26d		L3	
Walters, (Mr)	19, July 1849				L2	
Walters, Francis	27, July 1848	July	20		L3	
Walters, Henry	9, Aug. 1849		estate		L3	
Walton, Charles Holley	24, Aug. 1843	23, Aug.	10m-24d		L3	
Walton, Frank Leonard	2, Aug. 1849	27, July	17m-20d		L3	
Walton, George H.	19, June 1845	June	2		L3	
Walton, John C.	17, Oct. 1844	Oct.	57		L3	
Walton, Nathan	13, Dec. 1849	8, Dec.	60		L3	
Walton, Nathaniel	8, July 1841	June	28		L3	
Walton, Sarah M.	13, Apr. 1843	7, Apr.	18		L3	
Walton, Thomas	13, Dec. 1849				L2	
Walton, Thomas	5, July 1849	27, June	37		L3	
Waltz, Charles	1, Apr. 1847	Mar.			L3	
Waltz, John	25, July 1850	July	33		L3	
Waples, William D.	4, Nov. 1841	19, Oct.			L3	
Wappenburgh, Henry	14, June 1849	June	35		L3	
Ward, Aaron	1, Aug. 1833	July	30		L1	

Name	Notice Date	Death Date	Age		Page	Maiden Name
Ward, Asa	28, June 1849	26, June	65	*	L3	
Ward, Bridget	25, July 1850	July	60		L3	
Ward, Clarissa	25, May 1837	May	6		L2	
Ward, Francis	12, Sept 1844	Sept	19		L3	
Ward, George	28, Oct. 1847	21, Oct.		*	L3	
Ward, George	12, Feb. 1852	5, Feb.			L4	
Ward, Israel	8, Jan. 1857	27, Dec.	33		L3	
Ward, Israel	2, July 1846	21, June	84	*	L3	
Ward, James	25, Apr. 1850	Apr.	22		L3	
Ward, John	18, Dec. 1845	Dec.	37		L3	
Ward, Joshua	6, Feb. 1840	Jan.	1		L3	
Ward, Mary	16, Jan. 1811	Jan.			L3	
Ward, Patrick (Mrs)	14, May 1846				L1	
Ward, Prudence	31, Jan. 1850	16, Jan.	72		L3	
Ward, Roxana W.	3, Oct. 1844	19, Sept		*	L3	Blake
Ward, Thomas	15, July 1847	July	84		L3	
Ward, William	11, Nov. 1841	10, Nov.	57	*	L3	
Ward, William M.	15, June 1837	June	45		L4	
Warden, Joseph A.	4, Aug. 1853	30, July			L3	
Warden, Sarah Ann	13, Jan. 1853	6, Jan.	28		L3	
Warder, Jeremiah	20, Sept 1849	11, Sept	70		L3	
Ware, Eliza M.	3, Mar. 1842				L3	
Ware, Henry (Rev)	5, Oct. 1843	29, Sept	49		L3	
Ware, Josiah	29, May 1828	May	infant		L2	
Ware, Priscilla	18, Oct. 1832	14, Oct.			L2	
Ware, Robert	20, Oct. 1842				L3	
Wareham, Joseph	25, Oct. 1832	18, Oct.			L1	
Warfield, David W.	19, Sept 1844	10, Sept	25	*	L3	
Warfield, Joshua	9, Oct. 1845				L3	
Warfield, Seth	23, July 1835		estate		L4	
Warner, Baldwin	16, Oct. 1828		estate		L3	
Warner, Margaret	4, July 1850	23, June	33	*	L3	
Warner, Samuel	7, June 1855		probate		L3	
Warner, Sarah	27, Nov. 1845	24, Nov.	76		L3	
Warner, Sarah C.	9, Oct. 1815	4, Oct.			L3	
Warner, Thomas	7, Aug. 1834	July	25		L3	
Warnke, Fredina	8, Aug. 1833	July	22		L1	
Warnock, James	22, June 1837		probate		L3	
Warnsford, Henry	12, Sept 1833	Sept	18d		L1	
Warren, Elijah	29, Dec. 1836	Dec.	20	*	L3	
Warren, Mary G.	23, May 1850	4, May	43	*	L3	Adamson
Wartman, Dorothy	24, Apr. 1845	14, Apr.	82	*	L3	
Warwick, Robert (Rev)	22, Dec. 1831		estate		L3	
Warwick, Samuel	30, Sept 1847	26, Sept			L2	
Warwick, Samuel W.	14, Oct. 1847		estate		L3	
Warwick, Thomas	26, Dec. 1833	Dec.	50		L4	
Washburn, (child of Elizabeth)	27, Dec. 1832	Dec.	9d		L1	
Washburn, F.W. (Rev)	4, Nov. 1852	22, Oct.	31		L3	
Washburn, Fanny	3, Feb. 1855	29, Jan.	73		L3	
Washington, Ann	12, July 1849	July	50		L3	
Washington, Charles	13, Oct. 1842	Oct.			L3	
Washington, Eliza	8, Aug. 1833	July	25		L1	
Washington, Lucinda	16, June 1842	June	31		L3	
Washington, William (Gen)	2, May 1810	16, Mar.			L3	

Name	Notice Date	Death Date	Age	Page	Maiden Name
Wasserman, Charles	28, Oct. 1847	Oct.	25		L3	
Waterbury, J.G.	9, May 1833		estate		L3	
Waterbury, Joseph G.	13, Sept 1832	Sept	22- 7m		L1	
Waterer, John	7, Aug. 1834	July	20		L3	
Waterfield, Nancy	31, July 1851	July	33		L3	
Waterfield, William H.	3, July 1851	June	6		L3	
Waterman, Jacob	28, Oct. 1841		estate		L3	
Waterman, Sarah	17, Feb. 1853	4, Feb.	92		L3	
Waters, Eliza C.	20, Nov. 1856	16, Nov.			L3	Campbell
Waters, Eliza Jane	23, Feb. 1854	28, Jan.	17		L3	
Waters, John	24, June 1847	June	20		L3	
Watkins, Anna	19, Apr. 1845	Apr.	80		L3	
Watkins, H.C.	26, Apr. 1849	21, Apr.	50		L2	
Watkins, Humphrey C.	19, July 1832	July	1- 6m		L1	
Watkins, J.L. (Dr)	17, Jan. 1856	12, Dec.	65	*	L3	
Watkins, J.L. (Dr)	20, Dec. 1855	12, Dec.		*	L3	
Watkins, John R.	13, July 1854	4, July			L3	
Watkins, Jonathan	23, Aug. 1849	Aug.	22		L3	
Watkins, Thomas H.	1, Nov. 1832	Oct.	5-10m- 4d		L2	
Watson, Ann	20, Dec. 1855	12, Dec.	56		L3	
Watson, Ann	6, Mar. 1856		probate		L3	
Watson, Elizabeth	26, July 1832	July	23		L1	
Watson, Francis	18, June 1846	13, June	22		L3	
Watson, James	13, Sept 1832	Sept	1- 2m		L1	
Watson, James	13, July 1813		estate		L1	
Watson, James	20, July 1854	4, July		*	L3	
Watson, Luman	4, Dec. 1834	Dec.	44		L2	
Watson, Luman	11, Dec. 1834		estate		L3	
Watson, Luman	25, Oct. 1838		estate		L3	
Watson, Luman	19, Mar. 1840		estate		L3	
Watson, Luman	9, June 1836		probate		L3	
Watson, Luman	9, Aug. 1838		probate		L3	
Watson, Luman	13, Feb. 1840		probate		L3	
Watson, Lumen	1, Jan. 1835		estate		L4	
Watson, Margaret	28, Sept 1837	Sept	46		L4	
Watson, Rebecca	11, July 1833	July	27		L1	
Watson, Ruel A.	23, May 1833				L3	
Watson, Sarah	25, Mar. 1841	20, Mar.	44		L3	
Watson, Thomas	21, Feb. 1850	Feb.	42		L3	
Watson, Tommy (Dr)	14, Feb. 1850	13, Feb.			L3	
Watson, William	8, Apr. 1816		estate		L3	
Watson, William H.	15, May 1834	May	4- 8m		L4	
Watson, William W.	7, Feb. 1833	Feb.	2-10m		L1	
Watt, James	28, Dec. 1848	July			L3	
Watterson, Lewis	7, Sept 1837	Aug.	23		L3	
Watts, (child of Mr)	26, Dec. 1833	Dec.	stillborn		L4	
Watts, Maria E.	20, May 1847		1		L3	
Wauhop, Andrew	5, Oct. 1843	2, Oct.	32		L3	
Wave, Eliza J.	3, July 1851	June	27		L3	
Wayburn, Joseph H.	24, June 1847	June			L3	
Wayman, Henry	10, Aug. 1837	July	35		L3	
Wayne, Ann Eliza	1, June 1848	30, May	5m- 3d		L3	
Wayne, Catharine Amelia	22, Aug. 1850	18, Aug.	6		L3	
Weakly, Luella M.	1, Apr. 1847	27, Mar.	8- 4m-16d		L3	

Name	Notice Date	Death Date	Age	Page	Maiden Name
Weargel, Peter	26, July 1849	July	33		L3
Weatherby, Caroline S.	9, Mar. 1837	3, Mar.			L3
Weatherby, Jane	30, Dec. 1852	22, Dec.	84		L3
Weatherby, Phillip G.	19, Nov. 1857	17, Nov.	2- -12d		L3
Weaver, Adam	4, Oct. 1849	Sept	2		L3
Weaver, Catharine	19, Oct. 1848	Oct.	40		L3
Weaver, George	9, Feb. 1854	29, Jan.	84	*	L3
Weaver, Margaret	4, Sept 1845	28, Aug.			L3
Weaver, Philip	8, Nov. 1849	Oct.	6		L3
Weaver, William	20, Sept 1809		estate		L4
Webb, (child of George)	14, Feb. 1828	Feb.	1d		L1
Webb, Elsey	18, Oct. 1832	11, Oct.			L1
Webb, Ferdinand	31, Dec. 1857		estate		L3
Webb, George M.	20, Feb. 1851	Feb.	23		L3
Webb, Jacob	10, Sept 1857		probate		L3
Webb, John	2, June 1806		estate		L4
Webb, John T.	11, Apr. 1850	Apr.	52		L3
Webb, Joseph	20, Mar. 1845		86		L3
Webb, Joseph	26, Mar. 1829		estate		L3
Webb, Joseph	13, June 1839		estate		L3
Webb, Nelson	18, Oct. 1832	15, Oct.			L2
Webb, Stephen	15, Jan. 1835		estate		L3
Webb, Stephen	15, Sept 1836		probate		L3
Webb, William	19, July 1849	July	24		L3
Webb, William	9, Oct. 1811		estate		L3
Webb, William	26, Sept 1826		probate		L3
Webber, David	30, June 1836		estate		L3
Webber, David	9, June 1836		probate		L3
Webber, David	14, Feb. 1839		probate		L3
Webber, Martin	23, June 1853				L3
Webber, W.	10, Sept 1829	9, Sept			L3
Weber, Elizabeth	27, Nov. 1834	Nov.	3		L1
Weber, Henry	3, July 1851	June	35		L3
Weber, John Wendel	29, July 1847	July	35		L3
Weber, William	28, Dec. 1848	Dec.	21		L3
Webster, Daniel	18, Oct. 1838	Oct.	45		L3
Webster, William	21, June 1838		estate		L3
Webster, William	18, Apr. 1839		probate		L3
Weddle, Peter M.	20, May 1847	7, May	59	*	L3
Wedekind, Ernst	26, Sept 1839	Sept	32		L3
Wedilien, Charlotte	22, Apr. 1841	Apr.	10w		L3
Weeks, Job	1, Nov. 1832	24, Oct.			L4
Weeks, Loretta	5, Sept 1833	Aug.	2- -25d		L1
Weeks, Nancy	19, Oct. 1854	12, Oct.	88		L3
Weeks, Wellington	3, Jan. 1856		estate		L3
Weiber, John	7, Aug. 1834	July	2		L3
Weigman, G.W.	30, Nov. 1848	19, Nov.	36		L3
Weilel, Adam	19, July 1849	9, July	46		L3
Weiler, Samuel C.	19, July 1849	July	24		L3
Weily, Mary Annie	16, Nov. 1854	9, Nov.			L3
Weiner, John	30, July 1840	July	65		L3
Weingartner, F.I.	8, Jan. 1857		probate		L3
Weis, Mary	6, Aug. 1857		probate		L3
Weisang, Gerhard H.	28, Aug. 1834	Aug.	21		L1

Name	Notice Date	Death Date	Age		Page	Maiden Name
Weiss, Earnest	27, Nov. 1834	Nov.	25		L1	
Weissinger, George W.	7, Mar. 1850	4, Mar.	43	*	L3	
Weist, Valentine	24, Feb. 1853				L3	
Weitman, Nicholas	30, Mar. 1848	Mar.	61		L3	
Wejer, Herman	31, Dec. 1846	Dec.	27		L3	
Welch, (Capt)	28, Aug. 1811	Aug.			L3	
Welch, Hellen W.	6, Dec. 1838	Nov.	6		L4	
Welch, James	31, July 1845	July	35		L3	
Welch, John	11, Oct. 1838	Oct.	33		L3	
Wellington, James	14, Sept 1843	Sept	25		L3	
Wellington, William H.	27, Oct. 1842	11, Oct.	25	*	L3	
Wellman, F.H.	6, Sept 1855		probate		L3	
Wellman, Pord	15, Nov. 1832	Nov.	55		L1	
Wells, Benjamin	21, Nov. 1833	Nov.	22		L3	
Wells, Benjamin P.	23, Feb. 1832	19, Feb.	26	*	L3	
Wells, Frederika	19, June 1851	13, June	21		L3	
Wells, Horace	13, Jan. 1853	9, Jan.	18m		L3	
Wells, Horace	5, June 1851		estate		L3	
Wells, Horace	7, June 1855		probate		L3	
Wells, Horace	22, May 1851	16, May		*	L3	
Wells, Isaiah	9, Feb. 1854	12, Jan.			L3	
Wells, John	7, Feb. 1850	Jan.	22		L3	
Wells, Lizzie Hoodley	22, Mar. 1855	15, Mar.	27- 7m		L3	
Wells, Oliver	14, July 1836	9, July			L2	
Wells, Sarah	8, Nov. 1832	Nov.	30		L1	
Wells, Thomas	1, Nov. 1838	Oct.	2		L3	
Wells, Zerobabel	22, Dec. 1831		estate		L3	
Welmeyer, Martin	16, Apr. 1840	Apr.	39		L3	
Welsh, (child of Mary)	6, Mar. 1851	Feb.	stillborn		L3	
Welsh, Edmond	19, Sept 1850	Sept	43		L3	
Welsh, Hugh	5, Oct. 1848	Sept	33		L3	
Welsh, J.	29, Aug. 1850	Aug.	23		L3	
Welsh, John	26, Oct. 1843	Oct.	30		L3	
Welsh, John	1, Aug. 1850	July	32		L3	
Welsh, John	17, Sept 1846	Sept	39		L3	
Welsh, Lawrence	20, Sept 1849	Sept	35		L3	
Welsh, Michael	21, June 1849	June	2w		L3	
Welsh, Patrick	26, Apr. 1849	Apr.	25		L3	
Welsh, Patrick	19, July 1849	July	27		L3	
Welsh, William	25, Jan. 1849	Jan.	21		L3	
Welsh, William	1, Mar. 1849	Feb.	1- 6m		L3	
Wembers, Christiana	27, Jan. 1848	Jan.	3		L3	
Wensell, John	17, July 1845	July	20		L3	
Wentworth, John	27, Oct. 1831		probate		L1	
Wentworth, Luther	27, Oct. 1831		probate		L1	
Wentworth, Susan Osgood	13, July 1848	4, July	26	*	L3	Jones
Wenzel, Catharine	11, July 1850	July	40		L3	
Weomikth, William J.	1, Aug. 1850	July	28		L3	
Werber, Julia Ann	30, Sept 1847	Sept	42		L3	
Werk, Athenais Pauline Jos.	22, Nov. 1855	15, Nov.	2- 5m- 2d		L3	
Werk, Peter Michael	12, Apr. 1855	6, Apr.	6w- 6d		L3	
Wertz, Motts	21, Nov. 1833	Nov.			L3	
Wescott, William	14, Dec. 1824		probate		L3	
Wesinger, Elizabeth	1, Nov. 1849	Oct.	1		L3	

Name	Notice Date	Death Date	Age	Page	Maiden Name
West, (child of Polly)	17, Jan. 1850	Jan.	4w	L3	
West, Charles	13, Sept 1832	Sept	7	L1	
West, Edward	4, Nov. 1841	Oct.	40	L3	
West, Elnatham	22, June 1837		probate	L3	
West, Francis B.	13, Apr. 1843		estate	L3	
West, James	23, Apr. 1835		estate	L4	
West, James	30, July 1835		estate	L4	
West, James L.	14, Feb. 1828	Feb.	6m	L1	
West, Lucinda	19, Oct. 1843	17, Oct.		L3	
West, Martha Ann	23, Oct. 1845	Oct.	20	L3	
West, Martha G.	6, May 1847	3, May		L3	Morgan
West, Rebecca	12, June 1828	9, June		L4	
Westco, Theodore	30, Sept 1847	28, Sept	9	L1	
Westcott, Daniel	13, Sept 1832	Sept	21- 6m	L1	
Westcott, James	2, Feb. 1827		estate	L3	
Westemkemp, Lewis	21, July 1853	16, July		L3	
Westerfield, David J.	29, Aug. 1844	27, Aug.	38	L3	
Western, George	7, May 1840		probate	L3	
Westfall, Mary	25, Oct. 1832	19, Oct.		L2	
Westfall, Nicholas	25, Oct. 1832	20, Oct.		L2	
Westlake, Robert	4, Dec. 1828		estate	L3	
Weston, Lewis	9, July 1846	June	70	L3	
Westpeel, (child of Eli)	26, July 1832	July	4m	L1	
Wetherbee, Anna Maria	14, Dec. 1854	4, Dec.	25	L3	Foster
Wetherbee, M.M. (Mrs)	25, July 1850	22, July	32	L3	
Wettekind, Nicholas	29, July 1847	July	28	L3	
Wetzug, Adam	25, July 1850	July	27	L3	
Whaland, Daniel	10, Apr. 1845	Apr.	37	L3	
Whaland, Joseph	21, Mar. 1850	Mar.	22	L3	
Whaler, Kunigunda	12, Nov. 1846	Nov.	31	L3	
Whaley, John	28, Sept 1848	Sept	31	L3	
Whalin, Job	17, May 1849	May	39	L3	
Whalin, Michael	18, July 1850	July	40	L3	
Whaling, Spencer	24, Aug. 1848	Aug.	17	L3	
Whallen, James J.	2, Dec. 1841		estate	L3	
Whallon, Barnabas H.	2, Apr. 1835		estate	L3	
Whallon, Charles W.	18, May 1854		estate	L3	
Whallon, James	5, July 1855		probate	L3	
Whallon, James J.	29, Oct. 1840		estate	L3	
Whallon, James J.	25, Aug. 1842		estate	L3	
Whallon, James J.	3, Mar. 1842		estate	L4	
Whallon, R.H.	9, June 1836		probate	L3	
Whamer, John D.	8, Nov. 1832	Nov.	72	L1	
Whanshaw, James	7, Aug. 1834	July	42	L3	
Wharton, (daughter of Charles)	4, Aug. 1821	1, Aug.		L3	
Wharton, Henry	31, July 1851	12, July	35	L3	
Wharton, Penemiah	1, Nov. 1849	25, Oct.	27	L3	
Wharton, Robert J.	13, July 1854	3, July		L3	
Wheaton, Joseph	17, Feb. 1848	Feb.		L3	
Whedon, Thomas Edwin	1, Aug. 1844	30, July	11m-21d	L3	
Wheeler, Charles Webster	24, Feb. 1853	22, Feb.	3m- 4d	L3	
Wheeler, Elizur (Dr)	5, June 1815	6, May	57	L3	
Wheeler, Harriet	2, Oct. 1845	21, Sept		L3	
Wheeler, Maranda	18, July 1850	July	2	L3	

Name	Notice Date	Death Date	Age		Page	Maiden Name
Wheeler, Stephen	3, Feb. 1807		estate		L3	
Wheeler, Werham	28, Aug. 1834	Aug.	42		L1	
Wheelock, John	19, May 1817	11, Apr.	68		L3	
Wheelwright, Anna	27, July 1843	19, July			L3	
Wheelwright, Rachel	15, July 1841	8, July	infant		L3	
Whelaker, Hariet	5, Sept 1833	Aug.	1- -25d		L1	
Whelan, Bedelia	23, Nov. 1848	18, Nov.	54		L3	
Whelan, Robert	16, Mar. 1822		estate		L4	
Whelpley, David	10, Mar. 1853	23, Feb.			L3	
Whetstone, Clifton Key	13, Sept 1855	9, Sept	infant		L3	
Whetstone, John	16, Dec. 1841	13, Dec.	43	*	L2	
Whetstone, John	21, Apr. 1826		estate		L3	
Whetstone, John	27, Jan. 1842		estate		L3	
Whetstone, John	15, Nov. 1809	9, Nov.			L3	
Whetstone, John (Mrs)	24, Nov. 1807	19, Nov.			L3	
Whetstone, Susan Prince	14, Jan. 1836	13, Jan.	17		L1	
Whetstone, Zelah	6, Dec. 1838		estate		L3	
Whetstone, Zelah	8, Jan. 1857		probate		L3	
Whetten, Jane A.	8, Nov. 1855		probate		L3	
Whetton, Jane Amelia	6, Sept 1855	4, Sept	44		L3	
Whipple, Anson C.	25, May 1819		estate		L3	
Whipple, Barnard	23, Mar. 1848	Mar.	39		L3	
Whipple, Emanuel	18, Dec. 1851	15, Dec.			L3	
Whipple, Enion	20, Apr. 1843	14, Apr.	38		L3	
Whipple, Frances M.	4, May 1843	18, Apr.			L3	Smith
Whipple, Francis	4, Feb. 1847	12, Jan.	40		L3	
Whipple, Hannah Ralster	7, Feb. 1850	27, Jan.			L3	Chase
Whipple, John	18, Oct. 1832	12, Oct.			L2	
Whipple, John	2, Sept 1816		estate		L3	
Whipple, John N.	24, Feb. 1848	Feb.	17		L3	
Whipple, John Newton	17, Feb. 1848	12, Feb.	16		L3	
Whipple, Mollie M.	14, Feb. 1856	7, Feb.	17- 8m		L3	
Whipple, Pamelia	11, Mar. 1852	4, Mar.	46		L3	
Whipple, Sylvina	2, Feb. 1837	20, Jan.	61	*	L3	
Whippy, John	9, May 1833		estate		L3	
Whippy, John	29, Oct. 1835		estate		L3	
Whippy, John	4, Feb. 1836		estate		L3	
Whitaker, John	14, June 1849	10, June	29		L3	
Whitaker, John	19, Apr. 1845	12, Apr.	52	*	L3	
Whitaker, Preston	9, Apr. 1846	Mar.	10d		L3	
Whitaker, William H.	19, Apr. 1855		estate		L3	
Whitcomb, (child of Elenor)	22, Feb. 1844	Feb.	18m		L3	
Whitcomb, John	13, Aug. 1840	Aug.	10		L3	
White, (man)	5, Feb. 1852	25, Jan.			L4	
White, Abigail	28, Aug. 1851	23, Aug.	77		L3	
White, Alfred	17, Sept 1846	Sept	5		L3	
White, Amelia Peabody	9, Apr. 1857	2, Apr.	3		L3	
White, Carrie Hall	6, Dec. 1855	1, Dec.	1- 9m-18d		L3	
White, Catharine	28, Sept 1843	25, Sept	60		L3	
White, Clement	4, Oct. 1838	26, Sept	22m		L3	
White, Cornelia A.	3, July 1845	26, June	17		L3	
White, Edward Peace	27, July 1854	2, July	3		L3	
White, Elizabeth Poole	29, Jan. 1857	20, Jan.	75		L3	
White, Emily Maria	15, Jan. 1857	8, Jan.	2- 7m		L3	

Name	Notice Date	Death Date	Age	Page	Maiden Name
White, Fanny	16, Jan. 1845	12, Jan.		L3	
White, Francis	21, Feb. 1828	Feb.	34	L1	
White, George	31, Dec. 1846	Dec.	30	L3	
White, Harriette Wilson	28, Sept 1848	Sept	2- 3m	L3	
White, Henry	18, Sept 1834	Sept	27	L1	
White, Ira	17, June 1835		estate	L3	
White, Jacob	20, Dec. 1825		probate	L4	
White, Jacob, Jr.	19, Dec. 1826		probate	L3	
White, Jacob, Jr.	16, Feb. 1827		probate	L3	
White, James	25, Jan. 1849	Jan.	27	L3	
White, James	24, Oct. 1844	Oct.	83	L3	
White, James Coolidge	14, Dec. 1848	10, Dec.	2- 3m	L2	
White, John R.	15, July 1841		estate	L3	
White, Jordan	1, Jan. 1852			L3	
White, Joseph	10, Jan. 1833		estate	L3	
White, Joseph	4, June 1808	31, May		L3	
White, Katie	4, Nov. 1852	1, Nov.	4- 8m-14d	L3	
White, Laura A.	19, Jan. 1854	3, Dec.	17	L3	
White, Lizzie	23, Dec. 1852	21, Dec.		L3	
White, Louisa	21, Feb. 1850	Feb.	35	L3	
White, Martha Jane	29, Nov. 1832	Nov.	27- 2m	L1	
White, Peter	6, June 1850	May	24	L3	
White, R.H.	21, June 1849	15, June		L3	
White, Samuel	18, Nov. 1841	30, Oct.	84	* L3	
White, Samuel	25, July 1844	20, July		L3	
White, Sarah J.	31, Jan. 1850	Jan.	2- 6m	L3	
White, Walter R.	17, Jan. 1856	9, Jan.	31	L3	
White, William McClure	25, Mar. 1841	13, Mar.	7m-10d	L3	
Whitehead, Abby	17, Mar. 1853	5, Mar.	78	L3	
Whitehead, Christopher	9, Aug. 1849		estate	L3	
Whitehead, Thomas T.	11, Aug. 1853	9, Aug.	50	L3	
Whitehead, William	18, Nov. 1841		estate	L3	
Whitehead, William	8, Nov. 1855		probate	L3	
Whiteinger, Francis	7, Mar. 1810		estate	L3	
Whiteley, James	15, July 1852	8, July		L3	
Whitelock, Harvey	25, Mar. 1847	Mar.	39	L3	
Whiteman, Benjamin (Gen)	8, 15, July 1852	1, July	84	* L3	
Whiteman, Catharine	30, Sept 1852	21, Sept	81	L3	
Whiteman, Jane Findlay	20, May 1847	11, May	43	L3	
Whiteman, Louisa	15, Nov. 1832	Nov.	29	L1	
Whiteman, Louisa T.	8, Nov. 1832	30, Oct.		L4	
Whiteman, Rebecca	20, May 1841	26, Apr.		L3	Johnston
Whitendale, Mary	13, July 1848	July	35	L3	
Whiteside, John J.	16, May 1844	May	5m	L3	
Whiteside, Robert	22, Nov. 1849	Nov.	32	L3	
Whitewell, J.S.	6, Aug. 1857		probate	L3	
Whitewell, John Sprague	3, Feb. 1853	30, Jan.	57	L3	
Whitfield, James (Bishop)	30, Oct. 1834	19, Oct.	64	L2	
Whitford, Benjamin	19, Sept 1833	Sept	62	L4	
Whiting, Indiana Bel	7, 14, June 1849	25, May		* L3	Sanford
Whiting, Ira M.	7, May 1846	Apr.	2- 6m	L3	
Whiting, John	17, Feb. 1807		estate	L2	
Whiting, Lucinda	9, Apr. 1846	Mar.	10w	L3	
Whitman, Josiah (Dr)	6, Dec. 1838		estate	L3	

Name	Notice Date	Death Date	Age		Page	Maiden Name
Whitman, Josiah (Dr)	25, Oct. 1838	22, Oct.		*	L3	
Whitmer, Casper	4, May 1848	Apr.	21		L3	
Whitney,	23, Feb. 1854				L3	
Whitney, A.T.	6, Dec. 1849	Nov.	18		L3	
Whitney, Lucia M.	5, July 1849	June	42		L3	
Whitney, Mary Clewell	3, Sept 1857	28, Aug.	1-10m		L3	
Whitridge, John C. (Dr)	13, May 1847	29, Apr.	52		L3	
Whitridge, L.W.	13, May 1847	2, May	39		L3	
Whitridge, Peleg (Dr)	13, May 1847	24, Apr.	51		L3	
Whittaker, James	8, Feb. 1849	3, Feb.	72		L3	
Whittemore, Henry R.	17, Apr. 1827	15, Apr.			L3	
Whittemore, L.	25, Oct. 1832	Oct.	66		L1	
Whittemore, Nathan M.	15, May 1834		estate		L3	
Whitten, Rosannah	11, Dec. 1845		38- 5m	*	L3	
Whittermore, Nathan M.	20, June 1833	June	40		L1	
Whittington, Anna C.	19, July 1855	7, July		*	L3	Wright
Whitton, John Burnes (Dr)	28, June 1855	14, June		*	L3	
Wicker, Lawrence S.	1, July 1847	28, June	42		L3	
Wickliffe, Robert, Jr.	12, Sept 1850	29, Aug.	35		L3	
Wickoff, Henry	1, Aug. 1850	July	32		L3	
Wicks, Sarah J.	30, Mar. 1854	17, Mar.	27- 2m- 8d		L3	
Wickuns, Ebenezer	6, June 1850	May	35		L3	
Wickwere, Elizabeth	8, Nov. 1832	Nov.	6m		L1	
Wiebrecht, Godfrea	24, Sept 1846	Sept	23		L3	
Wiedeiner, Amelia	6, Apr. 1854	30, Mar.	1- -21d		L3	
Wiegart, Frederick	20, Jan. 1848	Jan.	40		L3	
Wienhold, Henry	21, June 1849	June	51		L3	
Wier, James	1, Aug. 1850	30, July	86		L3	
Wiessang, John	31, July 1851	July	36		L3	
Wiest, Peter	4, Oct. 1849	Sept	35		L3	
Wigand, Francis	7, June 1855		probate		L3	
Wiggins, Cornelia	6, Mar. 1845	26, Feb.			L3	
Wiggins, John Shackford	8, Dec. 1842	3, Dec.	18		L3	
Wilber, (Mr)	18, Oct. 1832	12, Oct.			L2	
Wilber, John Early	25, July 1850	23, July	6- 9m		L3	
Wilber, Marion Cole	24, Mar. 1853	17, Mar.	infant		L3	
Wilber, Thomas	23, Mar. 1849	Mar.	39		L3	
Wilcox, Diana	20, Jan. 1842	Jan.	28		L3	
Wilcox, Elmira	24, Feb. 1842	Feb.	3m		L3	
Wilcox, Ephraim	25, Oct. 1832	22, Oct.			L3	
Wilcox, Peter	25, Oct. 1832	18, Oct.			L1	
Wilcox, Trueman W.	15, Feb. 1838	12, Feb.	22	*	L3	
Wild, (child of James)	7, Aug. 1851	6, Aug.	2		L4	
Wilde, Jane	17, July 1845	July	21		L3	
Wilder, Ann	28, Aug. 1834	Aug.	34		L1	
Wilder, Susan	22, Aug. 1839	11, Aug.			L3	
Wildey, James	6, Mar. 1845	3, Mar.	38		L3	
Wildie, (child of Lawrence)	1, Aug. 1833	July	stillborn		L1	
Wildman, Edger E.	16, Aug. 1849	8, Aug.		*	L3	
Wildon, James	28, June 1849	June	45		L3	
Wiles, William M.	4, May 1837	30, Apr.	50		L3	
Wiley, Henry	5, June 1845	May	6m		L3	
Wilgus, Mary	12, Oct. 1843	2, Oct.	59		L3	
Wilhelm, Peter	12, Oct. 1843	Oct.	19		L3	

Name	Notice Date	Death Date	Age		Page	Maiden Name
Wilkenson, Hugh E.	5, Mar. 1857		estate		L3	
Wilkerson, Margaret	23, Apr. 1840	Apr.	6		L3	
Wilkey, Celistie	30, Oct. 1845	Oct.	3		L3	
Wilkins, (child of Eliza)	18, July 1833	July	5m		L2	
Wilkins, A.A.	4, Aug. 1842	1, Aug.	49	*	L3	
Wilkins, Andrew A.	11, Aug. 1842		estate		L3	
Wilkins, Mary	23, June 1853	19, June			L3	
Wilkinson, Elizabeth	9, Mar. 1848	Mar.	8m		L3	
Wilkinson, H.E. (Dr)	20, Jan. 1853	14, Jan.			L3	
Wilkinson, Hugh E.	4, Sept 1856		probate		L5	
Wilkinson, James (Gen)	21, Feb. 1826	Dec.			L3	
Wilkinson, Joel T.	7, Feb. 1856		probate		L3	
Wilkinson, John	9, Mar. 1848	Mar.	27		L3	
Wilkinson, Pres	28, Nov. 1850	Nov.	35		L3	
Wilkinson, Samuel	6, Jan. 1853	29, Dec.	24	*	L3	
Will, William	4, July 1850	June	25		L3	
Willard, Samuel (Dr)	18, Feb. 1820	16, Feb.			L3	
Willard, Susan	9, Dec. 1847	5, Dec.			L3	
Willer, Samuel	11, July 1833		probate		L3	
Willet, (child of David)	4, Apr. 1833	Mar.	2		L1	
Willets, Josephine Louisa	8, May 1845	30, Apr.	4m-23d		L3	
Willett, John (Major)	8, June 1854	23, May	85		L3	
Willey, (child of Elijah)	1, Aug. 1833	July	11d		L1	
Willey, (Judge)	29, July 1841	23, July		*	L3	
Willey, Anthony	29, Sept 1842		estate		L3	
Willey, Nathaniel	6, Dec. 1832	Dec.	4- 6m		L1	
Williams,	11, Apr. 1850	Apr.	21		L3	
Williams,	2, July 1808	28, June			L3	
Williams, (child of Abram)	8, May 1828	May	infant		L1	
Williams, (Mr)	5, Dec. 1826	2, Dec.			L3	
Williams, (Mr)	1, Dec. 1853	29, Nov.			L3	
Williams, (soldier)	20, Mar. 1856				L3	
Williams, (son of Jonathan)	28, July 1807	19, July			L3	
Williams, (son of Zadock)	1, Aug. 1850	27, July	15		L3	
Williams, Adelaide	12, Sept 1833	Sept			L1	
Williams, Agnes	4, Sept 1845	Aug.	3		L3	
Williams, C.	8, Jan. 1857		probate		L3	
Williams, C.S.	23, Oct. 1856	17, Oct.			L5	
Williams, Caleb	5, Nov. 1857		probate		L3	
Williams, Cassandra	28, Jan. 1841	27, Jan.			L3	
Williams, Catharine	11, Nov. 1816	7, Nov.			L3	
Williams, Charles	25, Oct. 1838	Oct.	16		L3	
Williams, Daniel	5, Sept 1839		probate		L3	
Williams, E.S. (Dr)	23, July 1846	17, July			L3	
Williams, Edwin S.	22, Nov. 1849	16, Nov.	16		L3	
Williams, Eleanor	16, Feb. 1843	9, Feb.	70		L3	
Williams, Eliza	18, July 1833	July	24		L2	
Williams, Elizabeth	25, May 1848	17, May		*	L3	Ringgold
Williams, Ella	2, Aug. 1832	July	7- -6d		L1	
Williams, Ellis W.	11, Apr. 1833	Apr.	19		L1	
Williams, Emma	18, Nov. 1841		9m		L3	
Williams, Eunice E.	11, Oct. 1849	8, Oct.			L3	
Williams, Fanny	18, Mar. 1847	13, Mar.	18		L3	
Williams, Frances	20, July 1843	14, July	10m		L3	

Name	Notice Date	Death Date	Age		Page	Maiden Name
Williams, Francis B.	7, Apr. 1853	4, Apr.	9m-21d		L3	
Williams, Frank Carroll	21, Mar. 1839	13, Mar.			L3	
Williams, Frederick	7, Sept 1837	Aug.	32		L3	
Williams, Frederick	30, Jan. 1851	Jan.	34		L3	
Williams, G.W.F.M.	20, Sept 1832	Sept	2		L1	
Williams, George	30, May 1839	May	27		L2	
Williams, George	25, Apr. 1850	Apr.	27		L3	
Williams, George	27, Mar. 1845	Mar.	50		L3	
Williams, George	13, Dec. 1849	Dec.	6w		L3	
Williams, George Clement	27, Nov. 1845	19, Nov.	12		L3	
Williams, George Henry	29, Jan. 1852	20, Jan.	5m-15d		L3	
Williams, George L.	18, Jan. 1855	10, Jan.	3		L3	
Williams, Harriet	12, Mar. 1857	6, Mar.	15		L3	
Williams, Henry M.	23, Dec. 1852	21, Dec.	2- -23d		L3	
Williams, Hugh	27, Sept 1849	Sept	21		L3	
Williams, Isaac	19, June 1845	June	31		L3	
Williams, Jacob	9, Mar. 1854	4, Mar.	45		L3	
Williams, Jacob	9, July 1840	6, July	66		L3	
Williams, Jacob	17, Sept 1840		estate		L3	
Williams, James	13, Aug. 1840	Aug.	56		L3	
Williams, James	24, Oct. 1844		estate		L3	
Williams, Jane B.	4, Apr. 1850	28, Mar.		*	L3	Neff
Williams, Joel	4, Jan. 1825		estate		L3	
Williams, John	1, May 1828		18		L1	
Williams, John	12, Mar. 1840	Mar.	34		L3	
Williams, John	5, Aug. 1852	July	35		L3	
Williams, John	23, Mar. 1849	Mar.	52		L3	
Williams, John	12, Aug. 1847		estate		L3	
Williams, John	22, July 1847	15, July			L3	
Williams, John S.	6, Oct. 1853	27, Sept	24		L3	
Williams, Jonathan	11, Oct. 1814		estate		L3	
Williams, Jonathan	8, Apr. 1816		estate		L3	
Williams, Joseph	5, July 1855		probate		L3	
Williams, Joshua	22, Mar. 1838		probate		L3	
Williams, Joshua	14, Feb. 1839		probate		L3	
Williams, Julian	5, Feb. 1852	27, Jan.			L3	
Williams, Levi W.	13, July 1848	July	51		L3	
Williams, Lewis	7, Sept 1824	3, Sept	19		L3	
Williams, Lillie	26, Feb. 1857	17, Feb.	3w- 3d		L3	
Williams, Louisa	8, Mar. 1855	28, Feb.	39		L3	
Williams, Louisa	20, Aug. 1846	Aug.	1- 6m		L3	
Williams, Lydia	4, Nov. 1847	Oct.	23		L3	
Williams, M.C. (Dr)	17, Feb. 1853	11, Feb.	50		L3	
Williams, M.T.	5, July 1855		probate		L3	
Williams, M.T.	5, Feb. 1857		probate		L3	
Williams, Margaret	11, May 1843		36		L3	
Williams, Margaret Ann	16, Jan. 1845	1, Jan.			L3	Jones
Williams, Martha A.	15, Aug. 1833	Aug.	16		L1	
Williams, Martha E.	25, Mar. 1847	Mar.	3w		L3	
Williams, Mary	9, Aug. 1855	7, Aug.	42		L3	
Williams, Mary Ann	17, July 1828	13, July	52		L3	
Williams, Mary Blanche	7, Dec. 1848	29, Nov.	14m-23d		L3	
Williams, Mary Breed	13, Mar. 1856	7, Mar.	5		L3	
Williams, Mary Jane	28, Oct. 1852	20, Oct.	2- 7m-22d		L3	

Name	Notice Date	Death Date	Age		Page	Maiden Name
Williams, Matilda	24, May 1849	May	35		L3	
Williams, Micajah T.	4, July 1844	25, June			L3	
Williams, Michael	12, Sept 1850	Sept	32		L3	
Williams, Moses M.	22, Jan. 1857		estate		L3	
Williams, Nancy	4, Apr. 1833	Mar.	14- 9m		L1	
Williams, Nancy	25, Oct. 1832	21, Oct.			L3	
Williams, Nelson	10, Aug. 1854				L3	
Williams, Peter	9, Mar. 1837	23, Feb.	67		L3	
Williams, Peter	9, Mar. 1837		estate		L3	
Williams, Peter	20, Apr. 1837		estate		L3	
Williams, Peter	9, Aug. 1838		probate		L3	
Williams, Peter	5, Sept 1839		probate		L3	
Williams, Peter	3, Dec. 1840		probate		L3	
Williams, Peter F.	16, July 1846	July	35		L3	
Williams, Rachel	25, July 1833	July	33		L1	
Williams, Rebecca	22, Apr. 1852	20, Apr.	21- 9m		L3	
Williams, Rebecca A.	18, July 1833	July	2m-14d		L2	
Williams, Robert	26, Feb. 1852	Feb.	21		L4	
Williams, Samuel	9, Dec. 1825	3, Dec.	73	*	L3	
Williams, Sarah	5, Sept 1850	Aug.	29		L3	
Williams, Sarah	26, Dec. 1844	16, Dec.	10m		L3	
Williams, Thomas	18, Oct. 1832	13, Oct.			L2	
Williams, Thomas	9, May 1833		estate		L3	
Williams, Thomas	12, Jan. 1837		probate		L3	
Williams, Thomas	8, Nov. 1838		probate		L3	
Williams, Thomas	3, Sept 1840		probate		L3	
Williams, William	27, Dec. 1832	Dec.	21		L1	
Williams, William	9, July 1840	6, July	40		L3	
Williams, William	6, Dec. 1849	Nov.	63		L3	
Williams, William	10, Sept 1840		estate		L3	
Williams, William H.	29, June 1843	June	2w		L3	
Williams, William R.	20, Nov. 1834	Nov.	28	*	L1	
Williamson, Cicelia Wrenn	13, Nov. 1851	9, Nov.		*	L3	
Williamson, Edward	23, Feb. 1854	18, Feb.	infant		L3	
Williamson, Emily R.	4, July 1850	29, June	10m- 7d		L3	
Williamson, Florence Seymour	20, Nov. 1851	13, Nov.			L3	
Williamson, George	29, July 1825	28, July	47		L3	
Williamson, George	31, Oct. 1839	Oct.	8m		L3	
Williamson, George	19, Dec. 1826		probate		L3	
Williamson, James	22, Sept 1853	17, Sept	63		L3	
Williamson, James	2, Nov. 1854	28, Oct.			L3	
Williamson, John	19, Mar. 1846	Mar.	39		L3	
Williamson, John	14, Feb. 1839		probate		L3	
Williamson, Joseph	9, Apr. 1840		estate		L3	
Williamson, Joseph (Lt)	2, Apr. 1840	4, Mar.	85	*	L3	
Williamson, Juliana	20, Jan. 1853	11, Jan.	82	*	L3	
Williamson, Margaret Cook	20, Nov. 1851	13, Nov.			L3	
Williamson, Mary	26, July 1849	19, July		*	L3	Dayton
Williamson, Moses	20, Apr. 1843	Apr.	40		L3	
Williamson, Peter	19, Apr. 1832	7, Apr.			L2	
Williamson, Richard	6, Aug. 1857		probate		L3	
Williamson, Susan A.	24, July 1845	21, July	24		L3	
Williamson, Westley	26, July 1832	July	29		L1	
Williamson, William	27, Sept 1855	24, Sept			L3	

Name	Notice Date	Death Date	Age		Page	Maiden Name
Willink, Wilhelm	13, May 1841	13, Feb.	91		L3	
Willis, Edward	31, Oct. 1850	Oct.	30		L3	
Willis, Elijah	24, May 1855				L3	
Willis, Elijah	5, Feb. 1857	May 1855			L3	
Willis, George	30, Jan. 1851	Jan.	40		L3	
Willis, Mary	22, Aug. 1850	18, Aug.			L3	
Willis, Rachael	25, Oct. 1832	23, Oct.			L3	
Willis, William	19, Jan. 1854	9, Nov.	23		L3	
Willock, Jacob	5, Aug. 1852	July	22		L3	
Wills, John	27, Sept 1832		estate		L3	
Willsey, Henry	8, Nov. 1838		probate		L3	
Wilmares, Cord	8, Nov. 1832	Nov.	6		L1	
Wilmers, John	28, June 1849	June	32		L3	
Wilmes, John Gerard	8, Jan. 1857		probate		L3	
Wilshire, Mary Lizzie	30, Jan. 1851	27, Jan.			L3	
Wilson, (child of McCurdy)	8, Aug. 1833	July	1- 4m		L1	
Wilson, (child of Rachel)	24, Aug. 1843	Aug.	10d		L3	
Wilson, (child of Rachel)	15, Sept 1842	Sept	12d		L3	
Wilson, (child of Sarah)	1, Apr. 1847	Mar.	1d		L3	
Wilson, Abraham	26, Sept 1826		probate		L3	
Wilson, Abram	26, Aug. 1823		estate		L4	
Wilson, Agnes Lacy	19, Dec. 1850	16, Dec.	2- 2m		L3	
Wilson, Amos	2, Aug. 1832	July	11m		L1	
Wilson, Andrew	8, June 1848	May	26		L3	
Wilson, Andrew	25, Feb. 1818		estate		L3	
Wilson, Ann	4, July 1833	June	1- - 3d		L2	
Wilson, Ann	1, Aug. 1850	July	3		L3	
Wilson, Anna	26, June 1845	19, June	8m		L3	
Wilson, Catharine	1, Aug. 1833	July	2		L1	
Wilson, Charles	22, Aug. 1850	Aug.	3		L3	
Wilson, D.	16, Oct. 1856		probate		L6	
Wilson, David	1, Aug. 1850	July	15		L3	
Wilson, David	24, Mar. 1853	20, Mar.	74		L3	
Wilson, David	5, Nov. 1857		probate		L3	
Wilson, E.	5, Dec. 1833	Nov.	1- 5m		L3	
Wilson, Elias J.	16, Dec. 1847	14, Dec.	25		L3	
Wilson, Elias J.	5, Feb. 1857		probate		L3	
Wilson, Eliza	22, July 1847	20, July			L3	
Wilson, Elizabeth	1, Aug. 1833	July	3- 8m		L1	
Wilson, Elizabeth	17, June 1841	June	4m		L3	
Wilson, Frances	16, June 1836	7, June	4		L3	
Wilson, George	16, Aug. 1849	13, Aug.			L2	
Wilson, George M.	26, Aug. 1825	18, July	23	*	L3	
Wilson, Geraldine Frances	25, Sept 1856	13, Sept	24- 6m		L5	Renshaw
Wilson, Harrie Clifford	19, Feb. 1857	14, Feb.			L3	
Wilson, Henry Morten	4, Nov. 1852	3, Nov.			L3	
Wilson, Hugh	6, June 1850	18, May	66		L3	
Wilson, Isaac	4, Apr. 1850	Mar.	68		L3	
Wilson, Isaac	28, Oct. 1852				L3	
Wilson, J.O.	24, 31, July 1851	23, July	30		L3	
Wilson, James	18, July 1833	July	5		L2	
Wilson, James	13, Feb. 1824	12, Feb.	24		L3	
Wilson, James	23, Aug. 1838	Aug.	28		L3	
Wilson, James	19, July 1849	July	43		L3	

Name	Notice Date	Death Date	Age		Page	Maiden Name
Wilson, James	11, Feb. 1841	5, Feb.	78	*	L3	
Wilson, James	8, Aug. 1850	July	6m		L3	
Wilson, James (Capt)	16, Sept 1847	11, Sept			L2	
Wilson, John	13, June 1833	June	40		L1	
Wilson, John	6, June 1850	May	38		L3	
Wilson, John	6, Mar. 1856		probate		L3	
Wilson, John	15, Oct. 1846	14, Oct.			L3	
Wilson, John Henry	5, Feb. 1857	29, Jan.			L3	
Wilson, John M.	1, Aug. 1833	July	1		L1	
Wilson, John N.	7, Mar. 1844	23, Feb.			L3	
Wilson, John R.	25, Sept 1828	17, Sept	26	*	L1	
Wilson, John Thomas	22, Sept 1853	19, Sept	5m-20d		L3	
Wilson, Joseph	25, July 1833	July	35		L1	
Wilson, Joseph	20, Nov. 1850	Nov.	35		L3	
Wilson, Joseph (Dr)	20, Dec. 1849	21, Nov.	38		L3	
Wilson, Joseph S.	7, Aug. 1834		estate		L3	
Wilson, Joshua Lacy (Rev)	20, Aug. 1846	14, Aug.	72		L3	
Wilson, Margaret	29, Nov. 1832	Nov.	2m- 2d		L1	
Wilson, Martha Washington	24, Apr. 1851	12, Apr.	8		L3	
Wilson, Mary	26, Dec. 1839	25, Dec.	44		L3	
Wilson, Mary	31, Dec. 1857	29, Dec.			L3	
Wilson, Mary Jane	6, Aug. 1846	July	23		L3	
Wilson, Mary Jane	22, Oct. 1857	19, Oct.	10-10m		L3	
Wilson, McCraddock	27, May 1847	May	47		L3	
Wilson, Minerva J.	25, Dec. 1856		34		L3	Ruffner
Wilson, Nancy Johnston	28, June 1849	23, June	29		L3	
Wilson, Oliver	3, May 1855	26, Apr.	43		L3	
Wilson, Peter	8, May 1811		estate		L1	
Wilson, Peter	13, Aug. 1835		estate		L3	
Wilson, Philander L.	12, Oct. 1848	4, Oct.	31		L3	
Wilson, Rebecca	14, Sept 1843	Sept	56		L3	
Wilson, Sally M.	27, Nov. 1856	22, Nov.	78		L3	
Wilson, Samuel	22, Jan. 1857	19, Jan.	71		L3	
Wilson, Samuel Henry	10, May 1855	2, May	4m		L3	
Wilson, Sarah	25, July 1850	July	37		L3	
Wilson, Sarah	9, June 1836		probate		L3	
Wilson, Sarah	14, Aug. 1851	11, Aug.			L3	
Wilson, Sarah Ann	9, Aug. 1838		probate		L3	
Wilson, Sarah White	25, Mar. 1841	24, Mar.	79	*	L3	
Wilson, Solomon	26, June 1845	June	29		L3	
Wilson, Thad's	14, Dec. 1819	6, Nov.	57		L3	
Wilson, Thomas	15, Aug. 1833	Aug.	19		L1	
Wilson, Thomas	6, Apr. 1819	3, Apr.			L2	
Wilson, Thomas	27, July 1848	July	22		L3	
Wilson, Thomas	14, July 1853	10, July	53	*	L3	
Wilson, Thomas	3, May 1855		probate		L3	
Wilson, Thomas	9, Aug. 1855		probate		L3	
Wilson, Timothy	9, Apr. 1835		estate		L3	
Wilson, Timothy	22, June 1837		probate		L3	
Wilson, Virginia Belle	18, July 1850	15, July	1- 2m-27d		L3	
Wilson, Walton C.	19, Jan. 1854	23, Dec.	1- 2m- 8d		L3	
Wilson, William	26, Sept 1826		probate		L3	
Wilson, William	9, June 1836		probate		L3	
Wilson, William	13, Feb. 1840		probate		L3	

Name	Notice Date	Death Date	Age		Page	Maiden Name
Wilson, William B.	17, Sept 1857	10, Sept	56		L3	
Wilson, William L.	4, Nov. 1841		estate		L3	
Wilstach, Mary H.	13, Dec. 1832	Dec.	1- 4m		L1	
Wiltsee, (man)	1, June 1854	26, May			L3	
Wiltsee, Thomas	15, Apr. 1847	8, Apr.	49		L3	
Wimer, (child of Richard)	10, Jan. 1828	Jan.	1d		L4	
Wimon, John	19, July 1849	July	22		L3	
Wims, Isaac	30, Jan. 1840	Jan.	60		L3	
Winall, John	16, Aug. 1855	12, Aug.	50		L3	
Winch, John	1, Nov. 1832	26, Oct.			L1	
Winchester, Stephen	23, Sept 1847	10, Sept	42		L3	
Wing, Cornelius	10, Oct. 1823		estate		L3	
Wing, Cornelius	3, Oct. 1823	26, Sept			L3	
Wing, Edward	21, Jan. 1833		estate		L3	
Wing, Isaiah	12, July 1849	3, July	67		L3	
Wing, Joseph	30, Mar. 1822	9, Mar.			L3	
Wingler, Joseph	20, Apr. 1848	Apr.	23		L3	
Winkle, (Professor)	24, Mar. 1853	Mar.			L3	
Winn, Mary Ann	29, Nov. 1832		estate		L3	
Winn, Mary Ann	25, Oct. 1832	23, Oct.			L3	
Winram, Winefield Black	18, July 1844	10, July			L3	
Winright, (Mrs)	25, Oct. 1832	17, Oct.			L1	
Winright, Charles	25, Oct. 1832	20, Oct.	4		L2	
Winship, Henry	8, Aug. 1833	July	26		L1	
Winslow, Alice	4, Aug. 1853	29, July			L3	
Winslow, Henry	23, Dec. 1852	18, Dec.			L3	
Winslow, John	27, Oct. 1831		probate		L1	
Winslow, R.W.	18, Oct. 1832	12, Oct.			L2	
Winslow, Thomas J.	31, Dec. 1835		estate		L3	
Winston, Ann	9, Nov. 1854	6, Nov.			L3	
Winston, D.S.	20, July 1854	June	77		L3	Henry
Winston, Marcia S.	26, Oct. 1837	11, Oct.	19		L3	
Winston, Timothy	10, Dec. 1857		probate		L3	
Winter, (child of Elisha)	8, Aug. 1833	July	2		L1	
Winter, Frederick	2, Dec. 1841	19, Nov.	23	*	L3	
Winter, Mm.	15, Aug. 1833	Aug.	2		L1	
Winterbottom, John	13, Dec. 1855	5, Dec.	37		L3	
Winterhalter, Cassimer	15, Apr. 1847	Apr.	26		L3	
Winters, Eliza	23, Nov. 1843	17, Nov.		*	L3	Mitchell
Winters, James F.	28, Feb. 1835		estate		L3	
Winters, Mary R.	19, July 1849	July	20		L3	
Winters, Robert	15, Jan. 1852	11, Jan.			L3	
Winton, John	11, Dec. 1856	5, Dec.	64-11m-14d		L3	
Winton, Polly	6, Jan. 1806	3, Jan.	17		L3	
Wipper, Henry	20, Sept 1849	Sept	36		L3	
Wisby, Margaret	22, June 1854	14, June			L3	
Wise, Joanna	18, Nov. 1847	15, Nov.	24- 8m-22d		L3	Townsend
Wiseman,	29, Sept 1853	23, Sept			L3	
Wiseman, Margaret	8, Sept 1842	Aug.	2		L3	
Wishart, James	8, Aug. 1850	31, July		*	L3	
Wiskott, William	23, Jan. 1822		estate		L3	
Wisner, George W.	20, Sept 1849	10, Sept	37	*	L3	
Wite, Agnes	2, Oct. 1834	Sept			L4	
Witham, Morris	24, Nov. 1807		estate		L3	

Name	Notice Date	Death Date	Age		Page	Maiden Name
Witham, Morris	7, Mar. 1810		estate		L3	
Withnal, William	11, Sept 1845	Sept	63		L3	
Witman, John	7, Aug. 1834	July	42		L3	
Witschger, Raymond	16, Sept 1847	Sept	42		L3	
Woelfell, John	15, Oct. 1846	Oct.	26		L3	
Wolf, (child of Eliza)	9, Dec. 1847	Dec.	7w		L3	
Wolf, (child)	1, Aug. 1833	July			L1	
Wolf, Adam	10, Dec. 1846	Dec.	30		L3	
Wolf, Catharine	24, Jan. 1850	Jan.	5w		L3	
Wolf, Henry	26, July 1849	July	2- 6m		L3	
Wolf, Henry	26, July 1849	July	4- 6m		L3	
Wolf, Herman	28, June 1849	June	35		L3	
Wolf, J.	27, Aug. 1846	22, Aug.	23	*	L3	Elfelt
Wolf, Jane Emily	6, Sept 1827	Sept	18m		L1	
Wolf, Jane Seymour	24, Feb. 1826	21, Feb.	28		L3	
Wolf, John	7, Dec. 1848	Nov.	39		L3	
Wolf, Joseph	15, Aug. 1844	Aug.	40		L3	
Wolf, Mary	11, Sept 1845	Sept	42		L3	
Wolf, Mary	21, Oct. 1847	Oct.	5w		L3	
Wolf, Nicholas	14, Aug. 1856		probate		L6	
Wolf, Philip	15, Nov. 1849	Nov.	22		L3	
Wolf, W.C.	12, Apr. 1855	3, Apr.	16		L3	
Wolf, William	19, July 1849	July	28		L3	
Wolfe, Johannes	19, July 1849	July	28		L3	
Wolfhart, Barbara	11, July 1850	July	26		L3	
Wolfhart, John	18, July 1850	July	5		L3	
Wolfhart, William	18, July 1850	July	1		L3	
Wolley, (child of Sarah A.)	20, Sept 1827	Sept	22m		L1	
Wolly, Alice	1, Aug. 1833	July	52		L1	
Wolsey, (Mrs)	25, Oct. 1832	22, Oct.			L3	
Wonder, Priscilla	12, Nov. 1857	8, Nov.			L3	
Wonderly, Agatha	3, Feb. 1848	Jan.	32		L3	
Wonns, Catharine	22, June 1848	June	40		L3	
Wood, (child of Josiah)	7, Jan. 1847	Dec.	1w		L3	
Wood, B. Franklin	6, Mar. 1845	26, Feb.	23		L3	
Wood, Charlotte E.	6, Mar. 1845	3, Mar.	37		L3	
Wood, Clarissa	31, Dec. 1840	22, Dec.	21		L3	
Wood, Clarkson F.	25, Aug. 1853	15, Aug.	37		L3	
Wood, Cornelius	27, Sept 1838	24, Sept			L3	
Wood, Ebby Foster	22, Oct. 1857	17, Oct.	4- 7m		L3	
Wood, Emma Louella	4, Jan. 1849	24, Dec.	9		L3	
Wood, Emma Louisa	20, July 1848	19, July	5- - 5d		L3	
Wood, Fanny	30, Aug. 1849	22, Aug.	69	*	L3	
Wood, Franklin W.	15, Sept 1853	12, Sept	5		L3	
Wood, George M.	25, Jan. 1855	20, Jan.	32		L3	
Wood, George M.	14, Feb. 1856		probate		L3	
Wood, George M.	9, Apr. 1857		probate		L3	
Wood, Govneur	3, July 1851	1, July	4m-13d		L3	
Wood, Harriet	29, Aug. 1850	23, Aug.			L3	
Wood, Irene N.	12, Apr. 1849	8, Apr.	10		L3	
Wood, James	18, Oct. 1832	13, Oct.			L2	
Wood, James	6, Sept 1849	Aug.	50		L3	
Wood, John	3, Sept 1808	26, Aug.			L3	
Wood, John Wrenshand	19, July 1849	15, July	15		L3	

Name	Notice Date	Death Date	Age		Page	Maiden Name
Wood, Josiah	20, June 1850	June	28		L3	
Wood, Lewis M.	29, May 1834		probate		L3	
Wood, Lewis M.	15, Sept 1831		estate		L4	
Wood, Louisa Elizabeth	27, June 1850	26, June	4		L3	
Wood, Mary Ann	20, Dec. 1838	14, Dec.	31	*	L3	Withington
Wood, Mary Ann	13, Apr. 1843	6, Apr.	47		L3	
Wood, Mary Jane	5, July 1849	June	22		L3	
Wood, Palemon	23, Aug. 1855		estate		L3	
Wood, Robert C.	20, May 1852	17, May	31		L3	
Wood, S.C.	22, 29, July 1847	20, July	19		L2	
Wood, Sarah	14, Aug. 1851	6, Aug.	71		L3	
Wood, Spencer Asbury	4, May 1837	2, May			L3	
Wood, Stephen (Dr)	16, 23, May 1844	11, May	82	*	L3	
Wood, T.B.	22, 29, July 1847	20, July	30		L2	
Wood, Thomas	3, June 1847	May	45		L3	
Wood, Velma	5, May 1853	2, May	1- 3m		L3	
Wood, Victory	25, Oct. 1849	Oct.	5		L3	
Wood, William	3, May 1849	Apr.	37		L3	
Wood, William	5, Apr. 1849	Mar.	50		L3	
Wood, William	18, June 1857	9, June	50		L3	
Wood, William (Dr)	2, July 1857		estate		L3	
Wood, William A.H.	12, July 1849	11, July	infant		L3	
Woodard, Elizabeth	13, June 1833	June	24		L1	
Woodbridge, Sarah	17, July 1822	12, July	64	*	L3	
Woodburn, Robert	27, Aug. 1846	Aug.	2		L3	
Woodbury, Charles S.	3, Sept 1840		probate		L3	
Woodbury, Esther A.	11, July 1833	July	1- 9m		L1	
Woodfall, Henry Hampton	19, May 1806	12, Dec.	67		L3	
Woodhurst, Ellen	6, Nov. 1845	Oct.	7m		L3	
Woodin, John G. (Capt)	2, Dec. 1847	22, Oct.			L3	
Woodman, James	21, June 1849	June	31		L3	
Woodman, Mary B.	1, Mar. 1855	19, Feb.	39	*	L3	Bangs
Woodrough, Joseph	12, Sept 1833	Sept	20- 6m		L1	
Woodrow, Walter	4, Jan. 1855	28, Dec.	3- 8m		L3	
Woodruff, Archibald	6, Feb. 1845	29, Jan.	72		L3	
Woodruff, Archibald	19, June 1845		estate		L3	
Woodruff, Archibald (Capt)	20, Feb. 1845	29, Jan.	72	*	L3	
Woodruff, Caroline M.	26, July 1855	23, July	29		L3	
Woodruff, Cornelia	18, Feb. 1836	16, Feb.	52		L3	
Woodruff, Daniel J.	19, June 1851	9, June	26		L3	
Woodruff, David	6, Dec. 1855		estate		L3	
Woodruff, Enos	27, July 1843	July	64		L3	
Woodruff, Harriet	19, July 1832	July	1- 3m		L1	
Woodruff, Harry Percy	6, Aug. 1840	30, July	1- 3m		L3	
Woodruff, James LeRoy	19, Feb. 1852	2, Feb.			L3	
Woodruff, John	9, Aug. 1855		estate		L3	
Woodruff, John	7, June 1855		probate		L3	
Woodruff, John G.	13, June 1850	12, June	19m		L3	
Woodruff, John S.	26, May 1853	20, May	53	*	L3	
Woodruff, Jonathan	31, Aug. 1843		74	*	L3	
Woodruff, Jonathan G.	7, June 1855		probate		L3	
Woodruff, Josephine	12, Sept 1833	Sept	9m-21d		L1	
Woodruff, Matilda C.	23, July 1846	July	1- 6m		L3	
Woodruff, Percis	20, June 1844	17, June	32		L3	

Name	Notice Date	Death Date	Age		Page	Maiden Name
Woodruff, Samuel	12, Jan. 1837		probate		L3	
Woodruff, Susan	7, July 1836	5, July	30	*	L3	
Woodruff, Walter Ferguson	25, Mar. 1841	20, Mar.	6- 4m		L3	
Woods, Amanda R.	3, Aug. 1848	July	28		L3	
Woods, Andrew	8, Nov. 1849	Oct.	23		L3	
Woods, Ann Eliza	20, Sept 1838	Sept	3w		L3	
Woods, David	6, May 1841	Apr.	5m		L3	
Woods, George W.	20, June 1844	14, June	23		L3	
Woods, John	31, Aug. 1843	Aug.	1- 8m		L3	
Woods, Lafayette	14, Feb. 1850	Feb.	3		L3	
Woods, Strong F.	19, Oct. 1843	Oct.	35		L3	
Woodson, John	13, Jan. 1848		estate		L3	
Woodson, John	27, Jan. 1848		estate		L3	
Woodward, Abagail	26, Feb. 1852	19, Feb.	67	*	L3	Cutler
Woodward, Ezekiel R.	16, Feb. 1827		probate		L3	
Woodward, Henry H.	26, July 1849	July	16		L3	
Woodward, Lansing	15, Mar. 1855	Mar.			L3	
Woodward, Lemuel, Jr.	15, Oct. 1840	10, Oct.	21	*	L3	
Woodward, Mary S.	6, Mar. 1856	28, Feb.	11m-10d		L3	
Woodward, Samuel M.	10, Nov. 1842	8, Nov.	19	*	L4	
Woodward, William	7, Feb. 1833	Feb.	65		L1	
Woodward, William	18, July 1850	July	27		L3	
Woodward, William Hill	29, Aug. 1839	19, Aug.			L3	
Woodward, William W.	2, Feb. 1837	18, Jan.	68		L4	
Woodworth, Erastus	20, Nov. 1845	Nov.	53		L3	
Woolekind, Dorothy	4, Apr. 1833	Mar.	1m-20d		L1	
Woolen, William	23, Feb. 1854	29, Dec.			L3	
Woolescroft, A.	4, June 1857		probate		L3	
Woolescroft, Absalom	5, Mar. 1857		estate		L3	
Wooley, Joseph	14, May 1835		estate		L3	
Woolley, (child of A.)	21, Feb. 1828	Feb.	1d		L1	
Woolley, John	20, Nov. 1834		estate		L3	
Woolley, John	15, Sept 1836		probate		L3	
Woolley, John (Dr)	29, Aug. 1833	Aug.	46-11m		L1	
Woolley, Martha	12, Oct. 1837		estate		L3	
Woolley, William	9, July 1857		probate		L3	
Woolsey, Frances Virginia	22, Aug. 1844	16, Aug.	5-11m-18d		L3	
Woolsey, Thompson Neave	9, May 1844	28, Apr.	16- 9m		L3	
Woolsey, William Slayback	15, Apr. 1841	14, Apr.	infant		L3	
Woovel, John	7, Aug. 1834	July	24		L3	
Worcester, (child of Jane)	1, Apr. 1841	Mar.	9d		L3	
Worcester, Noah (Dr)	8, Apr. 1847	4, Apr.	36	*	L3	
Worchester, Jane E.	29, Sept 1842	28, Sept	26		L3	
Worhurst, Samuel	18, Sept 1845	Sept	36		L3	
Works, (child of Amey)	1, Jan. 1846	Dec.	2w		L3	
Worland, John	25, Aug. 1842	Aug.	50		L3	
Worley, (daughter of Henry)	20, Oct. 1853	16, Oct.			L3	
Wormsley, Alexander	26, Dec. 1844	Dec.	62		L3	
Worrall, Charles A.	1, Apr. 1847	7, Mar.			L3	
Worst, Martin	24, May 1849	May			L3	
Worthington, Amos	5, Feb. 1852	31, Jan.		*	L3	
Worthington, Benjamin J.	25, Nov. 1847	20, Nov.	33		L3	
Worthington, Catharine D.	16, Oct. 1851	9, Oct.	17		L3	
Worthington, Charles	16, Nov. 1848	10, Nov.	77		L3	

Name	Notice Date	Death Date	Age		Page	Maiden Name
Worthington, David	18, July 1833	July	6		L2	
Worthington, Eleanor	4, Jan. 1849	24, Dec.	72	*	L3	
Worthington, F.A.	16, Oct. 1856		probate		L6	
Worthington, Francis A.	18, Dec. 1851		estate		L3	
Worthington, Julia	10, Apr. 1856	2, Apr.	47		L3	Galloway
Worthington, Mary Ann	6, Nov. 1834	Oct.	32		L1	
Worthington, Mary Ann	30, Oct. 1834	25, Oct.	32		L2	Burnet
Worthington, Mary Ann	9, July 1840	June	1		L3	
Worthington, Samuel	7, Dec. 1848	6, Dec.			L3	
Worthington, William M.	3, Mar. 1842	22, Feb.		*	L3	
Wray, Clara	23, Nov. 1854	17, Nov.	4m		L3	
Wray, James	10, May 1814		estate		L3	
Wrench, William	11, Apr. 1833	Apr.	50		L1	
Wright, (Mrs)	25, Oct. 1832	21, Oct.			L3	
Wright, (son of Crafts)	28, Nov. 1844	27, Nov.	infant		L3	
Wright, Benjamin	20, Sept 1832	Sept	3m		L1	
Wright, Benjamin T.	2, July 1840	12, May	30		L3	
Wright, Catharine	6, Feb. 1845	Jan.	45		L3	
Wright, Charlotte	12, July 1855	8, July	4- 9m		L3	
Wright, Christopher Wilson	2, Nov. 1833		estate		L3	
Wright, Comfort	28, Apr. 1807		estate		L1	
Wright, Daniel W.	3, July 1851	June	30		L3	
Wright, David	21, Sept 1837		probate		L4	
Wright, Eliza	13, Aug. 1846	Aug.	20		L3	
Wright, Emily	15, Nov. 1832	Nov.	9- 5m		L1	
Wright, Fannie Eliza	9, Aug. 1855	28, July	4m-11d		L3	
Wright, Frances	16, Dec. 1852	13, Dec.	57		L3	
Wright, George	8, Aug. 1850	July	3		L3	
Wright, George	16, Sept 1841	Sept	3d		L3	
Wright, Hannah	26, July 1849	20, July			L3	
Wright, Henry W.	7, May 1857		probate		L3	
Wright, James	20, Mar. 1851	Mar.	36		L3	
Wright, James	29, Aug. 1844	16, Aug.	63		L3	
Wright, James Jenkinson	19, June 1845	30, May	64	*	L3	
Wright, Joanna	5, Sept 1850	25, Aug.	38	*	L3	Keane
Wright, John	10, Jan. 1856		probate		L3	
Wright, John	7, Oct. 1852	28, Sept			L3	
Wright, John C.	23, Mar. 1848	21, Feb.	14- 9m		L3	
Wright, John J.	11, Sept 1851	7, Sept	59		L3	
Wright, Joseph	19, Sept 1844	23, Aug.	87	*	L3	
Wright, Lydia Ann	15, Apr. 1847	Apr.	2w		L3	
Wright, Mara Louisa	1, Aug. 1850	28, July			L3	
Wright, Mary	22, July 1847	July	35		L3	
Wright, Mary	8, Aug. 1844	4, Aug.	39		L3	
Wright, Mary Ann	4, July 1850	June	18		L3	
Wright, Mary M.	11, Dec. 1851	5, Dec.	76		L3	
Wright, Samuel	7, June 1849	May	76		L3	
Wright, Stephen	31, Apr. 1845	Apr.	2- 6m		L3	
Wright, Thomas B.	18, Apr. 1844	10, Apr.			L3	
Wright, Thomas C.	24, Oct. 1839	23, Oct.	15m		L3	
Wright, Westley	25, Apr. 1833	Apr.	4		L1	
Wroom, Peter	17, Dec. 1846	Dec.	53		L3	
Wurlitzer, B.W.	24, July 1851	18, July	24		L3	
Wurlitzer, B.W.M.	31, July 1851	July			L3	

Name	Notice Date	Death Date	Age		Page	Maiden Name
Wyatt, Dorothy	11, July 1833	July	63		L1	
Wyatt, Edward	23, Aug. 1849	Aug.	20		L3	
Wyatt, Henry	4, July 1833	June	69		L2	
Wyatt, Mary	5, Sept 1839		probate		L3	
Wyatt, T.G.A.	25, Jan. 1838	Jan.	22		L3	
Wyatt, York	4, June 1857		probate		L3	
Wyeth, Dora P.C.	27, Feb. 1851	20, Feb.			L3	Cooke
Wyeth, Eliza	2, Nov. 1848	18, Oct.	58	*	L3	
Wyeth, Joshua	5, Jan. 1837		estate		L4	
Wyeth, Prentis	29, Aug. 1810	26, Aug.	19	*	L5	
Wyles, Arvine	26, Jan. 1854	22, Jan.	69	*	L3	
Wylie, J.C. (Capt)	6, Mar. 1845	13, Sept			L3	
Wylie, J.C. (Mrs)	6, Mar. 1845	4, Jan.			L3	
Wylie, Samuel (Rev)	28, Oct. 1852	13, Oct.	80		L3	
Wylie, Samuel T.	23, Jan. 1851		estate		L3	
Wylie, Samuel T.	2, Jan. 1851	25, Dec.			L3	
Wylker, John	6, Oct. 1853	29, Sept	48		L3	
Wynne, David	2, Oct. 1851	24, Sept	43		L3	
Wynne, David	8, Nov. 1855		probate		L3	
Wynne, Richard	19, Apr. 1855	6, Apr.	43	*	L3	
Yager, George	18, May 1854	16, May			L3	
Yancey, William H.	14, May 1846	8, May			L3	
Yangor, William	1, Nov. 1849	Oct.	80		L3	
Yardley, Mary A.	19, July 1849	11, July			L3	
Yardley, William	9, Dec. 1852	2, Dec.	22- 4m		L3	
Yardly, Thomas	9, June 1842	8, June	5- 6m- 4d		L3	
Yarnall, Ephraim	22, June 1837		probate		L3	
Yarot, William W.	19, July 1832	July	7m		L1	
Yarwood, Joel	19, Apr. 1849	Apr.	31		L3	
Yates, James	23, Aug. 1849	Aug.	19		L3	
Yeager, Mary	13, Feb. 1851	Feb.	50		L3	
Yearsly, Joseph	20, July 1837	July	28		L4	
Yeatman, Anna Henrietta	27, Aug. 1857	19, Aug.	5m		L3	
Yeatman, Caroline W.B.	26, May 1821	22, May	20		L3	
Yeatman, Griffin	8, Mar. 1849	4, Mar.	79		L3	
Yeatman, Griffin (Mrs)	24, Sept 1808	23, Sept			L3	
Yeatman, Harriet T.	13, Feb. 1851	10, Feb.	16		L3	
Yeatman, Louisa	21, July 1842	9, July	14		L3	
Yeatman, Margaret	18, Nov. 1852	10, Nov.	71-10m		L3	
Yeatman, Thomas	20, June 1833	12, June		*	L2	
Yeatman, Thomas R.	2, Mar. 1843	28, Feb.	20		L3	
Yeatman, Walker	5, Apr. 1849	22, Mar.	21		L3	
Yeatman, Walker	4, Mar. 1841	12, Feb.			L3	
Yetsor, John	8, Nov. 1849	Oct.	35		L3	
Yewell, Elizabeth A.	8, Aug. 1833	July	6		L1	
Yocom, Emily Jane	12, July 1849	5, July	45		L3	
Yokum, Charles	12, July 1849	July	33		L3	
Yorington, E.W.	15, Feb. 1838	Feb.	31		L3	
Yorke, Mary A.	13, July 1837	5, July	21		L3	
Yost, Abraham	20, Aug. 1829		estate		L3	
Yost, James W.	1, Feb. 1849	29, Dec.	40		L3	
Yost, Otto	16, Apr. 1857	13, Apr.			L3	
Young, Anna D.	9, Apr. 1846	1, Apr.			L3	Dean

Name	Notice Date	Death Date	Age	Page	Maiden Name
Young, Charlotte Jane	23, Apr. 1846	17, Apr.	11m	L3	
Young, Clayton	6, Aug. 1846	29, July	2- - 5d	L3	
Young, Ellen Flack	31, Apr. 1845	22, Apr.	13m	L3	
Young, George H.	21, June 1838		estate	L3	
Young, George H.	14, Mar. 1839		estate	L3	
Young, George W.	9, Oct. 1834	Sept	2-10m	L1	
Young, Horace	6, Sept 1849		estate	L3	
Young, Horace	4, June 1857		probate	L3	
Young, Jacob	26, July 1849	July	22	L3	
Young, Jacob	24, Jan. 1850	Jan.	22	L3	
Young, James B.	13, Sept 1832	Sept	7m	L1	
Young, James P.	16, Oct. 1834	Oct.	7	L1	
Young, John	6, Dec. 1832	Dec.		L1	
Young, John	7, Oct. 1847	4, Oct.	44	L3	
Young, John P.	19, July 1832	July	45	L1	
Young, Joseph B.	26, Apr. 1849	Apr.	28	L3	
Young, Julia	8, Aug. 1850	July	49	L3	
Young, Margaret	23, Oct. 1845	16, Oct.	47	L3	
Young, Mary	11, Jan. 1844	Jan.	40	L3	
Young, Matthew	30, Sept 1830		estate	L3	
Young, Peter	3, Dec. 1829		estate	L3	
Young, Peter	8, Nov. 1838		probate	L3	
Young, Philip	28, Sept 1848	Sept	58	L3	
Young, Philip (Dr)	20, Jan. 1848	15, Jan.	27	L3	
Young, Robert	16, July 1846	July	51	L3	
Young, Robert	20, Nov. 1845		estate	L3	
Young, Robert	15, Jan. 1846		estate	L3	
Young, Wheeler P.	27, June 1850	20, June	2- 2m-11d	L3	
Young, William	27, Apr. 1848		estate	L3	
Young, William	25, Jan. 1849		estate	L3	
Young, William A.	9, Oct. 1834	Sept	4- 8m	L1	
Young, William C.	12, Feb. 1835		estate	L3	
Young, William M. (Capt)	16, Nov. 1843	31, Oct.		L3	
Youngs, Rebecca	20, Feb. 1851	16, Feb.	41	L3	
Zane, Lois	3, Dec. 1840		probate	L3	
Zann, Lewis	18, July 1850	July	4	L3	
Zanone, Mary Josephine	24, June 1847	13, June	20m-16d	L3	
Zeager, Louis	28, Dec. 1848	Dec.	23	L3	
Zebold, Louisa	8, Oct. 1840	8, Oct.		L3	
Zeigler, David	2, Oct. 1811	24, Sept	*	L3	
Zeigler, David (Major)	18, Dec. 1811		estate	L3	
Zeigler, Jacob	3, July 1851	June	30	L3	
Zeigler, John	19, July 1849	July	23	L3	
Zeigler, Luceanna	6, Jan. 1821		estate	L3	
Zeigler, Lucyanna	6, Dec. 1820	18, Nov.	53	L3	
Zern, Christian	10, Dec. 1840		estate	L3	
Zesline, J. (Rev)	4, Feb. 1818	31, Jan.		L2	
Zeumer, (child of Christian)	12, Aug. 1852	10, Aug.	3	L3	
Zeumer, (child of Christian)	12, Aug. 1852	10, Aug.	5	L3	
Zeumer, Henry L.	22, Jan. 1846	19, Jan.	38	L3	
Zever, Jacob	29, Aug. 1850	Aug.	43	L3	
Ziegel, Adam	27, June 1850	June	21	L3	
Zierman, Augustus	24, May 1849	May	23	L3	

Name	Notice Date	Death Date	Age		Page	Maiden Name
Zierman, Frederick	26, July 1849	July	25		L3	
Zimmerman, (child of Jane)	14, Dec. 1837	Dec.	1d		L3	
Zimmerman, Richard	7, Mar. 1839	Feb.	40		L3	
Zimmermann, Samuel	2, Apr. 1857		42	*	L3	
Zoefgen, Joseph	20, Dec. 1855		estate		L3	
Zoefgen, Joseph	14, Aug. 1856		probate		L6	
Zumalt, Henry (Col)	5, Apr. 1814	23, Mar.			L3	

Maiden Name	Name	Notice Date	Death Date	Age		Page
Adamson	Warren, Mary G.	23, May 1850	4, May	43	*	L3
Andrews	Grover, Hepza Dana	3, Oct. 1844	30, Sept	20		L3
Athearn	Hartwell, Alice B.	14, Sept 1843	7, Sept	28		L3
Atherton	Kidder, Salla	14, Feb. 1850	31, Jan.		*	L3
Austin	Holley, Mary	10, Sept 1846	2, Sept	61		L3
Aydelott	Farnham, Margaret P.	22, Apr. 1847	18, Apr.	23		L3
Aydelott	Jones, Hannah More	18, Oct. 1849	12, Oct.			L3
Baker	Coray, Cordelia E.	16, Nov. 1854		30		L3
Baker	Ray, Margaret Jane	8, Sept 1853	3, Sept			L3
Baltzell	Dean, Mary J.	29, Sept 1853	17, Sept	23	*	L3
Bangs	Woodman, Mary B.	1, Mar. 1855	19, Feb.	39	*	L3
Bayard	Butler, Cornelia Rutgers	26, July 1849	17, July	31	*	L3
Beebee	Reed, Elizabeth	7, Sept 1854	30, Aug.	39	*	L3
Beecher	Cheever, Margaret L.	1, June 1848	23, May	26		L3
Beecher	Safford, Mary H.	1, May 1851	20, Apr.			L3
Best	Barkley, Elizabeth C.	6, Jan. 1853	24, Dec.			L3
Betts	Wade, Frances	28, Mar. 1826	5, Mar.	26		L3
Biggs	Gest, Margaretta	19, July 1849	5, July	38		L3
Biggs	Johnson, Anna Louisa	16, Nov. 1848	7, Nov.	38		L3
Blake	Ward, Roxana W.	3, Oct. 1844	19, Sept		*	L3
Block	Moses, Hetty	10, Nov. 1836	6, Nov.		*	L3
Bond	Robinson, Ellen	24, Jan. 1856	13, Jan.	34		L3
Bowers	Schultz, Ann	8, Aug. 1833	27, July		*	L1
Boyle	McKenzie, Mary R.	13, June 1850	7, June	40	*	L3
Broadwell	Everett, Amanda M.	22, Oct. 1840	15, Oct.	23		L3
Brooks	MacCracken, Eliza B.	12, Sept 1850	7, Sept	26		L3
Brower	Kugler, Matilda Caroline	5, Nov. 1840	24, Oct.	32- 9m		L2
Bryan	Gest, Melissa S.	4, Feb. 1841	22, Jan.	19		L3
Bryant	Hunter, Phoebe	1, Feb. 1844		84	*	L3
Burch	Stansbury, Caroline E.	5, July 1849	24, June	24		L3
Burnet	Worthington, Mary Ann	30, Oct. 1834	25, Oct.	32		L2
Burnet	McLean, Caroline T.	17, 24, Apr. 1856	15, Apr.			L3
Burrows	Dayton, Julia T.	13, July 1837	5, July			L3
Campbell	Reily, Catharine	27, Jan. 1848	22, Jan.	28		L3
Campbell	Waters, Eliza C.	20, Nov. 1856	16, Nov.			L3
Canfield	Huntington, Janette Humphreys	28, Jan. 1847	21, Jan.	19- 1m		L3
Carne	Huston, Martha	29, July 1841	18, July			L3
Carneal	Burke, Sallie	15, Aug. 1850	11, Aug.			L3
Carothers	Paul, Susan	1, Jan. 1846	24, Dec.		*	L3
Cary	Huber, Martha Louise	25, Dec. 1856	16, Dec.	19		L3
Cary	Swift, Susan	12, Feb. 1852	10, Feb.	36		L3
Case	Hanson, Harriet	24, July 1834	8, July	19- 8m	*	L1
Chase	Whipple, Hannah Ralster	7, Feb. 1850	27, Jan.			L3
Chenoweth	Apperson, Lizzie C.	25, Dec. 1856	15, Dec.			L3
Clark	Burnet, Susan M.	15, Dec. 1853	2, Dec.	33		L3
Clark	Meyers, Mary	14, Oct. 1852	10, Oct.			L3
Clay	Duralde, Martin (Mrs)	18, Oct. 1825	18, Sept			L3
Clay	Neavelle, Emma Clay	1, June 1848	29, May	19	*	L3
Cline	Sidell, Elizabeth Ann	9, Mar. 1854	1, Mar.	30- 2m-14d		L3
Coleman	Smith, Frances E.	3, Feb. 1848	29, Jan.	18		L3
Conn	Prince, Sally	30, Apr. 1808	21, Apr.			L3
Conyers	Mackie, Mary	30, June 1842	20, June		*	L3
Cooke	Strickland, Maria W.	11, Jan. 1849	8, Jan.			L3
Cooke	Wyeth, Dora P.C.	27, Feb. 1851	20, Feb.			L3

Maiden Name	Name	Notice Date	Death Date	Age		Page
Copping	Russell, Mary Elizabeth	18, Dec. 1845	14, Dec.	17	*	L3
Corry	Anderson, Elizabeth	27, Oct. 1842	14, Oct.			L3
Crane	Barney, Electa C.	30, May 1844	21, May		*	L3
Curry	Burnet, Margaret	28, Jan. 1836	26, Dec.		*	L4
Custis	Lewis, Eleanor Parke	29, July 1852	17, July	74		L3
Cutler	Woodward, Abagail	26, Feb. 1852	19, Feb.	67	*	L3
Cutter	Broadwell, Ella Maria	21, May 1857	13, May	34-10m		L3
Dakin	Mooney, Mary A.	15, Jan. 1857	8, Jan.		*	L3
Dayton	Williamson, Mary	26, July 1849	19, July		*	L3
Dean	Young, Anna D.	9, Apr. 1846	1, Apr.			L3
DeBosseron	Lasselle, Julia Riddey D.	10, Nov. 1842	26, Oct.	54		L4
DeGolyer	Barret, Ann	15, July 1847	12, July	42		L3
Doan	Davenport, Ruth	26, June 1845	16, June	40	*	L3
Doddridge	Brannan, Mary E.	9, Apr. 1857	3, Apr.			L3
Dodson	King, Cynthia Ann	12, Dec. 1850	10, Dec.	39		L3
Dorman	Brandon, Maria E.B.	20, Dec. 1838	17, Dec.			L3
Drake	Bedinger, Lavinia	5, June 1822	25, May	25	*	L3
Drummond	Morris, Caroline S.	31, Dec. 1857	9, Dec.			L3
Dunlevy	Morris, Jane B.	22, June 1843	15, June	39		L3
Dunn	Robinson, Frances J.	31, Jan. 1856	27, Jan.			L3
Eaton	Gibbs, Eliza Ann	4, Mar. 1847	24, Feb.	29		L3
Edwards	Atlee, Ann Mackintosh	21, June 1838	30, May	23	*	L3
Edwards	Parsons, Julia E.	18, June 1857	9, June	27	*	L3
Elfelt	Wolf, J.	27, Aug. 1846	22, Aug.	23	*	L3
Ellison	McCormick, Margaret	27, Mar. 1845	6, Mar.	55	*	L3
Enyart	Maley, Sarah	3, Apr. 1851	30, Mar.	52		L3
Ernst	Kent, Amelia Mary	10, Aug. 1837	9, Aug.	20		L3
Ferris	Jewett, Mary	22, Mar. 1838	15, Mar.	23- -13d		L3
Fink	Ingalls, Julia A.	24, May 1855	8, May	33	*	L3
Fisher	Febiger, Annie	15, Feb. 1844	5, Feb.			L3
Fisher	Pelham, Mary Jane	22, Nov. 1855	28, Oct.	39	*	L3
Fithian	Dull, Sarah D.	10, July 1845	6, July	19		L3
Foreman	Ferris, Harriet	15, Sept 1842	5, Sept	26		L3
Fosdick	Mason, Anna S.	23, Mar. 1824	22, Mar.	21		L3
Foster	Wetherbee, Anna Maria	14, Dec. 1854	4, Dec.	25		L3
Fowler	Dalie, Abigail	11, July 1844			*	L3
Freeman	Fenton, Debora	3, Sept 1846	22, Aug.	93	*	L3
Gallagher	McGrew, Margaret R.	19, June 1845	15, June	32	*	L3
Galloway	Worthington, Julia	10, Apr. 1856	2, Apr.	47		L3
Gano	Anderson, Maria J.	14, Oct. 1852	29, Sept			L3
Gay	Kinkead, Mary D.	4, May 1854	28, Mar.	36- 1m-13d		L3
George	Boyd, Agnes	26, Feb. 1852		20	*	L4
Gest	Buckingham, Margaret G.	11, Apr. 1850	8, Apr.	26		L3
Gillingham	Gillingham, Eliza	5, Aug. 1852	19, July			L3
Gilpin	Hallam, Sidney Ann	13, Dec. 1849	7, Dec.	32		L3
Gitchell	Sherman, Mary Ann	4, May 1848	1, May	27	*	L3
Graff	Sears, Helen G.	5, Nov. 1857	30, Oct.			L3
Greenleaf	Cranch, Nancy	28, Sept 1843	16, Sept	71		L3
Gregg	Philips, E.H.	27, Sept 1849	21, Sept			L3
Gregg	Vorhes, Harriet	16, Jan. 1851	8, Jan.	27		L3
Gregory	Catlin, Clara B.	28, Aug. 1845	25, July		*	L3
Grigg	Jones, Mary B.	24, Oct. 1850	13, Oct.	23		L3
Groesbeck	Sullivan, Mary S.	25, Sept 1851	16, Sept			L3
Guest	Reynolds, Elizabeth	18, July 1826	7, July	19	*	L3

Maiden Name	Name	Notice Date	Death Date	Age		Page
Halley	Pingree, Mary Ann	17, Dec. 1840	12, Dec.	17		L3
Hamilton	Carter, Anna E.	9, Feb. 1843	30, Jan.	21- 6m		L3
Hammond	McWilliams, Elizabeth	8, Mar. 1855	2, Mar.	39		L3
Hammond	Viers, Elvira	9, Jan. 1851	30, Dec.	55		L3
Hand	Stevens, Phebe	30, Apr. 1857	3, Apr.	18-10m		L3
Handy	Garrison, Margaret A.	12, July 1849	9, July			L3
Hannahs	Nash, Eliza Delia	20, Nov. 1850	16, Nov.	38	*	L3
Harkness	Harkness, Eliza A.	19, July 1849	15, July	26	*	L3
Harrison	Hicks, Martha A.	29, Apr. 1852	11, Apr.			L3
Harrison	Thornton, Mary	8, Dec. 1842	16, Nov.	34		L3
Harrison	Thornton, Mary S.H.	24, Nov. 1842	16, Nov.			L6
Harrod	Pringe, (Mrs)	17, Aug. 1854	26, July			L3
Harthorn	Howard, Sally	22, Aug. 1833	12, Aug.	35		L1
Hastings	Rolker, Emeline Anna	18, June 1846	13, June	18	*	L3
Heard	Slack, Margaretta D.	21, Mar. 1839	4, Mar.		*	L3
Heath	Bailhache, Elizabeth Harwood	19, July 1849	1, July	52	*	L3
Heckewelder	Rucker, Mary Jane	19, Apr. 1849	4, Apr.	34		L3
Henderson	Maxwell, Sophia Barbauld	1, Nov. 1832	16, Oct.			L3
Henry	Winston, D.S.	20, July 1854	June	77		L3
Hill	Greenwood, Howard Whales	10, Sept 1835	31, Aug.	23		L1
Hillyer	Russell, Mary Elizabeth	8, Jan. 1852	3, Jan.			L3
Hinman	Spooner, Sarah P.	9, July 1846	24, June	50	*	L3
Hitchcock	Lyon, Myraett	8, Jan. 1835	4, Jan.	34- 5m- 1d		L2
Holmes	Browning, Martha Ann	14, Oct. 1847	11, Oct.	23		L3
Hulburd	Moore, Mary H.	11, Apr. 1850	4, Apr.	28		L3
Hunt	Rice, Abigail	23, Oct. 1856	3, Oct.	56		L5
Huntington	Foster, Ann Maria	25, Nov. 1847	23, Nov.	25		L3
Irwin	Matthews, Ida I.	3, Apr. 1845	22, Mar.	24- 3m	*	L3
Ives	Hull, Lucy Amelia	22, July 1852	11, July	29-11m-22d	*	L3
Jennings	Childress, Rebecca	20, Jan. 1848	16, Jan.	30	*	L3
Jennings	Morgan, Mary Stuart	18, Feb. 1847	23, Jan.	36- 1m	*	L3
Johnston	Furrow, Harriet	27, Oct. 1842	8, Oct.	25		L3
Johnston	Whiteman, Rebecca	20, May 1841	26, Apr.			L3
Jones	Black, Harriet	21, Oct. 1841	17, Oct.			L3
Jones	Irwin, Emily A.	19, June 1851	12, June			L3
Jones	Knight, Abby H.	31, Oct. 1850	25, Oct.			L3
Jones	Wentworth, Susan Osgood	13, July 1848	4, July	26	*	L3
Jones	Williams, Margaret Ann	16, Jan. 1845	1, Jan.			L3
Judkins	Comly, Sarah R.	11, Jan. 1849	9, Jan.			L3
Keane	Wright, Joanna	5, Sept 1850	25, Aug.	38	*	L3
Kellum	Higbee, Elizabeth Ann	22, June 1843	20, June	24		L3
Ketchum	Bliss, Elvira	4, Sept 1856	27, Aug.	25		L5
Keys	Sterrett, Jane B.	1, Oct. 1840	30, Sept	29	*	L3
King	Ferguson, Louisa	6, Feb. 1845	5, Feb.	37	*	L3
Knowlton	Eastman, Lydia B.	16, June 1853		54		L3
Koehler	Loefner, Francisca	23, July 1857	21, July	25		L3
Landis	Place, Elizabeth	13, Nov. 1856	22, Oct.			L3
Lawrence	Lupton, Harriet O.	8, Dec. 1836	2, Dec.	20		L3
Lawrence	Nye, Maria	15, Apr. 1852	12, Apr.	34	*	L3
Lawrence	Waldo, Arabella	18, Jan. 1844	12, Jan.	28		L3
Lea	Peabody, Emily Lea	10, Oct. 1844	6, Oct.	25		L3
Leonard	Spooner, Francis M.	6, Dec. 1855	1, Dec.	30	*	L3
Leonard	Spooner, Sarah L.	8, Aug. 1850	31, July		*	L3
Leslie	Lupton, Mary F.	24, May 1849	3, May	32		L3

Maiden Name	Name	Notice Date	Death Date	Age		Page
Levassor	DeBarr, Clara Julia	3, May 1849	23, Apr.	19- 9m-17d		L3
Lewis	Bacon, Maria	18, Apr. 1844	16, Apr.		*	L3
Lockett	Currie, Sarah S.	29, Apr. 1847	22, Apr.	22	*	L3
Lockwood	Howland, Eloise	3, Apr. 1856	4, Mar.	19		L3
Lowery	Taggart, Martha	5, Jan. 1854	20, Dec.	60		L3
Ludlow	Chase, Sarah Bella D.L.	22, Jan. 1852	13, Jan.	32		L3
Lytle	MacAlester, Eliza Ann	17, Sept 1835	31, Aug.			L1
Lytle	Rowan, Anne	19, July 1849	14, July	77		L3
Macy	Raymond, Martha H.	24, May 1849	16, May	32		L3
Manning	Light, Almira	19, Jan. 1854	23, Dec.	42		L3
Mason	Hill, Ann M.	15, Aug. 1826	23, July			L3
Mayo	Carson, Alexina	20, Sept 1855	16, Sept	21		L3
Mayo	Lewis, Mary Aurelia	9, May 1844	4, Apr.	39		L3
McArthur	Trimble, Mary	15, Dec. 1842	10, Dec.			L5
McCormick	Andrews, Mary	27, Aug. 1857	20, Aug.	32		L3
McFarland	Kinsey, Sarah Ann	5, Mar. 1840		26	*	L3
Metcalf	Disney, Anna	5, May 1836	3, May			L3
Miller	Biggs, Catherine	19, July 1849	15, July	25		L3
Miller	Glover, Isabella H.	9, Aug. 1855		29		L3
Miller	Maddox, Delia	9, Jan. 1851	12, Dec.			L3
Mitchell	Winters, Eliza	23, Nov. 1843	17, Nov.		*	L3
Montague	Light, Mary	18, Apr. 1844	14, Apr.			L3
Moore	McCormick, Elizabeth	15, Aug. 1844	25, July	41- 8m		L3
Morgan	Chiles, Elizabeth	16, Nov. 1848	10, Nov.			L3
Morgan	West, Martha G.	6, May 1847	3, May			L3
Morrill	Smith, Joanna	25, Mar. 1841	14, Mar.	53	*	L3
Morris	Rust, Jane B.	8, Dec. 1842	7, Dec.			L3
Morrow	Raney, Margaret	1, Dec. 1842	16, Nov.	30	*	L3
Murray	Ross, Clara M.	5, Nov. 1857	27, Oct.	23		L3
Neave	Vawter, Sarah N.	11, Oct. 1838	19, Sept			L3
Neff	Williams, Jane B.	4, Apr. 1850	28, Mar.		*	L3
Ogden	Walter, Lydia	26, Dec. 1850	2, Dec.	43		L3
Olmsted	Johnson, Maria L.	13, Sept 1838	31, Aug.			L3
Orr	DuBois, Mary C.	16, Apr. 1857	10, Apr.			L3
Owens	Pearce, Elizabeth	7, June 1855	5, June			L3
Pace	Adams, Ellen	16, July 1857	9, July	31	*	L3
Palmer	Bradford, Louisa S.	31, Mar. 1836	29, Mar.	21		L3
Patterson	Findlay, Elizabeth	22, 29, July 1847	18, July	34		L3
Pelham	Bonner, Ann	20, Apr. 1809	2, Apr.			L3
Pemberton	Batchelor, Elizabeth	8, Feb. 1844	4, Feb.	20	*	L3
Phelps	Cheseldine, Martha G.	1, Nov. 1855	30, Oct.		*	L3
Phillips	Stevenson, Sarah	13, Jan. 1848	6, Jan.	23		L3
Phipps	Mansfield, Elizabeth	2, May 1850	12, Apr.	74	*	L3
Piatt	Headley, J.B. (Mrs)	13, Mar. 1851	27, Feb.		*	L3
Pierson	Howe, Clara	8, Dec. 1853	13, Nov.		*	L3
Pierson	Orr, Amelia	15, July 1847	16, June	33		L3
Porter	Stedman, Abby Huntington	13, Nov. 1856	30, Oct.			L3
Powers	Hart, Mary H.	18, Sept 1851	6, Sept			L3
Prince	Hall, (Mrs)	19, Jan. 1843	3, Jan.			L3
Quin	Harrison, Virginia B.	15, Sept 1853	22, Aug.	23		L3
Rainey	Hallam, Mary	26, Nov. 1857	18, Nov.			L3
Reeder	Thomas, Mary Ann	3, Apr. 1851	19, Mar.			L3
Renshaw	Wilson, Geraldine Frances	25, Sept 1856	13, Sept	24- 6m		L5
Rhodes	Anthony, Sarah Aborn	27, July 1854	11, July		*	L3

Maiden Name	Name	Notice Date	Death Date	Age		Page
Rhodes	Hill, Alice K.	17, Aug. 1837	16, July	24	*	L3
Richards	Strong, Mary Huntington	16, Jan. 1851	13, Jan.			L3
Richardson	King, Mary B.	21, Aug. 1815	19, Aug.			L3
Ringgold	Williams, Elizabeth	25, May 1848	17, May		*	L3
Robison	Glidden, Mary Ellen	19, Mar. 1857	15, Mar.		*	L3
Rogers	Chenoweth, Julia	30, Jan. 1851	28, Jan.		*	L3
Rogers	Ebersole, Lydia Ann	18, Mar. 1847	4, Mar.	23	*	L3
Rogers	Taylor, Emily R.	22, Jan. 1852	9, Jan.			L3
Rowan	Steele, Mary Jane	4, May 1822	25, Apr.	23		L3
Rowan	Wakefield, Alice D.	7, 14, Dec. 1854	30, Nov.		*	L3
Ruffin	Hopkins, Frances Gardner	7, Jan. 1836	16, Dec.	41		L3
Ruffin	Oliver, William (Mrs)	5, May 1853				L3
Ruffner	Wilson, Minerva J.	25, Dec. 1856		34		L3
Sanford	Whiting, Indiana Bel	7, 14, June 1849	25, May		*	L3
Schroeder	Moore, Barbara	4, Feb. 1841	28, Jan.	61	*	L3
See	Malone, Julia H.	21, June 1855	15, June	23		L3
Sellman	Conover, Julia Ann E.	31, Mar. 1836	24, Mar.	24- 3m		L1
Sellman	Evans, Elizabeth	27, July 1854	19, July	49		L3
Shaaff	Johns, Margaretta Jane	14, Dec. 1854	22, Nov.			L3
Shaw	Humes, Elizabeth Marshal	8, Apr. 1852	24, Mar.			L3
Sibley	Alling, Sarah Ann	19, July 1849	8, July	30- 7m		L3
Sinard	Corwin, Sarah L.	27, July 1843	14, June	19		L3
Singleton	Taylor, Lucy Harrison	19, July 1855	23, June	66		L3
Smallwood	VanHamm, Clara	24, Feb. 1848	18, Feb.	31	*	L3
Smith	Coombs, Sarah	8, Dec. 1842	27, Nov.			L3
Smith	John, Nancy	14, Sept 1813	28, Aug.	23		L3
Smith	Whipple, Frances M.	4, May 1843	18, Apr.			L3
Spafford	Hopkins, Mary Olivia	11, Dec. 1851	8, Dec.	22- 6m-15d	*	L3
Spencer	Cass, Elizabeth	14, Apr. 1853	31, Mar.	64	*	L3
Spencer	Meeks, Dorothea	11, Nov. 1841	4, Nov.	62	*	L3
St.Clair	Mayo, Frances M.	13, Dec. 1838	27, Nov.			L4
Stephenson	DeForest, Mary	23, Oct. 1856	16, Oct.	42		L5
Stevens	Britt, Frances	26, Mar. 1857	20, Mar.	74	*	L3
Stewart	Geiger, Mary S.	13, Apr. 1854	23, Mar.			L3
Stewart	Meade, Anastasia	23, Aug. 1849	9, Aug.		*	L3
Stockbridge	Merrell, Levisa	22, Nov. 1838	14, Nov.	20		L3
Stockton	Harrison, Elizabeth S.	23, Jan. 1851	20, Jan.			L3
Stoddert	Campbell, Harriet	26, July 1849	17, July	61	*	L3
Stone	Morgan, Harriet	12, July 1849	10, July		*	L3
Storrs	Stone, Abigail Maria	2, Aug. 1849	26, July	76	*	L3
Sullivan	Ewing, (Mrs)	12, Feb. 1835	11, Oct.			L1
Taylor	Clark, Grace A.C.	14, Mar. 1850	8, Mar.	23- 8m		L3
Taylor	Herndon, Maria Louisa	30, Jan. 1851	23, Jan.	21		L3
Taylor	McCarty, Sarah H.	9, Feb. 1854	7, Dec.	25		L3
Temple	Davis, Amelia L.	26, Mar. 1857	22, Mar.			L3
Townsend	Wise, Joanna	18, Nov. 1847	15, Nov.	24- 8m-22d		L3
Tunis	Bowmar, Emeline	18, May 1848	12, May	38		L3
Turner	McCracken, Rebecca	4, Mar. 1847	Feb.	31	*	L3
Tyler	Taylor, Anne Harrison	25, Feb. 1847	20, Feb.		*	L3
Vail	Marston, Mary Ann	22, Nov. 1855	14, Nov.	53	*	L3
Vanausdol	Harton, Kate	25, May 1854	19, May			L3
VanBuren	Convers, Rebecca	17, Oct. 1850	15, Oct.			L3
VanValkenburgh	Burnet, Anna	12, May 1853	3, May	30	*	L3
Wallace	Semple, Helen M.	7, June 1849	3, June			L3

Maiden Name	Name	Notice Date	Death Date	Age		Page
Warden	Becking, Rebecca J.	12, Sept 1850	10, Sept	20		L3
Watson	Southgate, Julia	11, Sept 1851	6, Sept			L3
Weatherby	Schwartze, Mary G.	27, Apr. 1848	26, Apr.	23		L3
Webb	Rhodes, Jennie G.	13, Mar. 1856	27, Jan.			L3
Whipple	Neave, Martha W.	10, May 1855	3, May	26		L3
Whiting	Robbins, Charlotte	25, June 1846	20, June		*	L3
Williams	Hewson, Emily L.	23, Aug. 1855	17, Aug.		*	L3
Williamson	Richards, Lydia H.	2, May 1850	25, Apr.		*	L3
Withington	Wood, Mary Ann	20, Dec. 1838	14, Dec.	31	*	L3
Wood	Coleman, Mary Emma	5, Feb. 1852	31, Jan.		*	L3
Wood	Newton, Abby B.	13, May 1830	7, May	32		L3
Worcester	Every, Anna S.	22, Jan. 1852	14, Jan.	18		L3
Worthington	Pomeroy, Elizabeth R.	18, Nov. 1852	7, Nov.			L3
Wright	Whittington, Anna C.	19, July 1855	7, July		*	L3
Young	Brown, Frances Mary	26, Feb. 1852	20, Feb.			L3

Grooms	Brides	Date of Notice	Page
Aarons, David C.	Craig, Mary Ann	18, Mar. 1847	L3
Abbott, C.S.	Ward, Anna E.	17, May 1855	L3
Abbott, John C.	Thomas, Jane	11, Apr. 1844	L3
Abbott, Wilson	Brown, Sarah	9, Feb. 1854	L3
Abercrombie, Robert	Goble, Dinah	16, Dec. 1829	L3
Abraham, J.	DeYoung, Sarah	9, Sept 1841	L3
Abrams, William H.	Brown, Sarah A.	14, Nov. 1844	L3
Ackerman, Richard	Mann, Catharine W.	10, June 1841	L3
Ackley, William E.	Choate, Carrie	26, July 1855	L3
Acton, Clement J.	Noble, Mary	22, Jan. 1846	L3
Adae, Charles F.	Woods, Ellen	17, Mar. 1842	L3
Adam, Andrew	Brown, Elizabeth	15, Mar. 1838	L3
Adam, George N.	Mendenhall, Mary Ann	16, Feb. 1854	L3
Adams, A.H.	Tiebout, Esther Y.	15, Oct. 1846	L3
Adams, Albert	Bonney, Elizabeth F.	16, Mar. 1854	L3
Adams, Alex H.	Ballard, Mary I.	16, Nov. 1837	L3
Adams, Alfred	Coolidge, Rebecca	5, May 1836	L3
Adams, Charles	Tennent, Sallie	15, Nov. 1855	L3
Adams, Charles F.	Barrett, Eliza (Mrs)	8, June 1843	L3
Adams, Christopher T	Rutherford, Mary J.	10, Mar. 1853	L3
Adams, David T.	Johnson, Josephine	5, May 1853	L3
Adams, Henry J.	Gibson, Abby	23, Sept 1841	L3
Adams, John	Johnston, Mary Ann	11, Nov. 1847	L3
Adams, John Q.	Sefton, Elizabeth N.	13, Apr. 1854	L3
Adams, John Quincy	Dorsy, Mary Ann	25, Feb. 1847	L3
Adams, Thomas Jen.	Bogie, Isabella	23, May 1821	L3
Adams, William	Richardson, Abigail	8, May 1811	L3
Adams, William A.	Cassilly, Mary	20, Oct. 1842	L3
Addams, A. (Dr)	Moffett, Catharine	24, Apr. 1845	L3
Aehle, Charles F.	Macks, Eliza Jane	2, July 1846	L3
Ager, John	Morgan, Mary Ann	22, Oct. 1857	L3
Agin, Burroughs	Smith, Sarah Jane	10, Aug. 1848	L3
Aiken, Charles	Merrill, Martha S.	29, Nov. 1855	L3
Akers, James	Fagin, Mary Ann	2, May 1844	L3
Akin, Macaully	Mix, Chloe P.	8, May 1845	L3
Alcoke, James B.	Creager, Emily	17, Nov. 1842	L6
Alden, George W.(Dr)	Shelton, Amanda C.	27, May 1847	L3
Aldrich, Edwin R.	Rayner, Helen M.	26, Aug. 1852	L3
Allan, John	Bell, Elizabeth	6, Nov. 1851	L3
Allen, Alfred F.	Meers, Sallie Dogget	18, Sept 1845	L3
Allen, Charles Henry	Silsbee, Mary	3, Apr. 1851	L3
Allen, Fernian	Plate, Louisa M.	16, Feb. 1854	L3
Allen, George	Brown, Charlotte	12, Aug. 1847	L3
Allen, George	Egleston, Mary Jane	2, Apr. 1857	L3
Allen, Israel	Marsh, Hannah (Mrs)	29, May 1815	L3
Allen, James G.	Robertson, Louisa	15, June 1854	L3
Allen, John (Dr)	Rudor, C.L.	12, Nov. 1846	L3
Allen, Joseph	Jenkins, (Mrs)	12, Feb. 1805	L3
Allen, Joseph H.	Reynolds, Cornelia	9, July 1857	L3
Allen, L.S. (Dr)	Green, Alvernon H.	23, Sept 1841	L3
Allen, Louis A.	Wise, Margaret Jane	24, Mar. 1853	L3
Allen, Robert E.	Ward, Gerogia E.	8, Nov. 1855	L3
Allen, S.M.	Alvord, Harriet	18, May 1848	L3
Allen, T.C.	Woodruff, Jinne D.	10, June 1852	L3

Grooms	Brides	Date of Notice	Page
Allen, William	Coons, Effie (Mrs)	22, May 1845	L3
Allen, William	Wilcox, Mary Louisa	17, July 1845	L3
Allen, William H.	Mann, Mary Davis	25, Mar. 1841	L3
Alley, Enoch L.	Kruse, Phebe	28, Aug. 1845	L3
Ames, Fisher W.(Dr)	Deshields, Mary Z.	30, Oct. 1851	L3
Anderson, Alexander	Bakewell, Sarah	31, Mar. 1826	L3
Anderson, Andrew	Tewers, Leah (Mrs)	9, Oct. 1834	L2
Anderson, Charles R.	Loring, Eliza	2, June 1842	L3
Anderson, Charles W.	Coleman, Margaret A.	30, Nov. 1848	L3
Anderson, Evan	Lumley, Mary	7, Oct. 1841	L3
Anderson, James	Stillwell, Sarah (Mrs)	13, Apr. 1854	L3
Anderson, Richard C.	Thompson, Agnes	28, June 1855	L3
Anderson, Robert	Bonnel, Rachel V.	19, June 1811	L3
Anderson, Samuel	Phillips, Sarah Ann	10, Nov. 1821	L3
Anderson, Samuel K.	Cilley, Cecilia	19, Nov. 1857	L3
Anderson, W.C.	Yeatman, Anna Maria	25, May 1837	L2
Anderson, Walter	Gengembre, S.	19, June 1851	L3
Anderson, William	Clark, Jane Douglas	12, Oct. 1837	L3
Anderson, Yeatman	Mitchell, Helen M.	4, June 1857	L3
Anderson, Younger	Burrett, M. Louisa	21, Jan. 1847	L3
Andress, Charles	Dodsworth, Mary	17, June 1841	L3
Andress, Charles O.	Weatherby, Amelia F.	12, Feb. 1852	L3
Andress, Charles O.	Wright, Hannah	29, June 1848	L3
Andress, Frederick	Hopkins, Jennie T.	5, Mar. 1857	L3
Andress, Henry W.	Corwine, Anne E.	23, Oct. 1851	L3
Andrew, Peter	Oberdorf, Mary E.	27, Mar. 1845	L3
Andrews, A.H.	Vandyke, L.C.	5, Sept 1850	L3
Andrews, John	Boyd, Elizabeth	7, May 1846	L3
Andrews, R.D.	Thompson, Annie H.	21, Dec. 1854	L3
Andrews, R.H.	White, Eliza M.	6, Jan. 1853	L3
Andrews, Richard	Holmes, Elizabeth P.	6, Aug. 1846	L3
Andrews, Samuel	McCormick, Mary	15, June 1848	L3
Andrews, Seth L. (Dr)	Dike, Amelia	22, Apr. 1852	L3
Angevine, Charles	Skaats, Catharine E.	20, Nov. 1845	L3
Angevine, William	Bonte, Eliza Louisa	21, Feb. 1850	L3
Angle, Solomon	McClure, Julia Ann	18, Dec. 1845	L3
Antram, Alpheus	Bentley, Kate	12, Jan. 1854	L3
Antram, M.T.	Davis, Martha R.	11, Dec. 1856	L3
Antsim, Cyrus	Seely, Eliza	6, Feb. 1851	L3
Apperson, William W.	Chenoweth, Lizzie	14, Aug. 1851	L3
Applegate, Benjamin	White, Frances	12, Aug. 1847	L3
Applegate, John A.	Funk, Elizabeth	6, June 1844	L3
Applegate, John W.	Williams, Mary	20, July 1848	L3
Argo, Ebenezer	Spinning, Hannah	1, Nov. 1849	L3
Arion, C.P.J.	Givens, Lucretia	24, Dec. 1824	L3
Armstrong, Arthur E.	Schillinger, Priscilla	2, Nov. 1837	L4
Armstrong, E.R.T.	Dyer, M. Louisa	20, Oct. 1853	L3
Armstrong, H.G.	Munford, Ella C.	13, July 1854	L3
Armstrong, James	Smith, Sarah	14, Apr. 1820	L3
Armstrong, James S.	Rosyell, Louisa E.	1, July 1847	L3
Armstrong, John	Willis, Susan	28, Dec. 1807	L3
Armstrong, John H.	Russell, Theodosia G	30, Mar. 1849	L3
Armstrong, John W.	Smith, Agnes A.	27, Sept 1838	L3
Armstrong, Lafayette	Dudley, Charlotte	23, Oct. 1845	L3

Grooms	Brides	Date of Notice	Page
Armstrong, Leonard L	Murdock, Adelia	3, Aug. 1848	L3
Armstrong, Robert	Burley, Jane	8, Oct. 1835	L1
Armstrong, Robert G.	Summons, Mary	2, Dec. 1847	L3
Armstrong, Walter	Kautz, Hannah	21, May 1808	L3
Armstrong, William	Halley, Deborah	28, Apr. 1817	L3
Arnet, Mahlon	Talbert, Elizabeth	9, Mar. 1854	L3
Arons, Garret	Damont, Harriet L.	14, Sept 1843	L3
Arons, W.C.	Baldridge, Martha C.	6, Sept 1855	L3
Arthers, Samuel	Debaugee, Mary	11, Mar. 1818	L3
Arthur, B.H.	Morris, Cornelia M.	18, Jan. 1855	L3
Arthur, W.E.	Southgate, Ada	15, Nov. 1855	L3
Arthur, William, Jr.	Parson, Eliza	14, Apr. 1820	L3
Arthurs, Henry	Collins, Emiline	31, Aug. 1843	L3
Ashcroft, Robert	Bruner, Mary A.	4, Nov. 1847	L3
Ashton, Charles	Doggitt, Elizabeth N	23, Mar. 1854	L3
Askey, David	Kitchel, Mary (Mrs)	11, Mar. 1815	L3
Atherton, Abner	Foster, Eliza	18, Sept 1845	L3
Atherton, George	Cooper, Sarah	5, Apr. 1855	L3
Atkins, Richard L.	Warner, Anna S.	3, Sept 1857	L3
Atlee, S. Yorke	Williams, Mary Ann	6, May 1841	L3
Attwell, Roger G.	Fones, Amanda	21, Oct. 1847	L3
Aubery, William A.	Place, Lucy A.	5, Mar. 1840	L3
Augur, James S.	Wainwright, Jerusha	29, Oct. 1846	L3
Auisten, John	Martin, Sarah	3, July 1845	L3
Auld, Thomas	Harper, Ann (Mrs)	6, June 1844	L3
Austen, David	Picket, Cordelia	14, Nov. 1844	L3
Austin, James S.	Murch, Hannah	2, July 1840	L3
Austin, Seneca	Mixer, Julia A. (Mrs)	10, Sept 1840	L3
Averel, Edward	Peers, Sarah	8, Oct. 1840	L3
Avery, Charles L.	Page, Martha	10, June 1847	L3
Avery, Dudley (Dr)	Browne, Mary Ann	31, Mar. 1807	L3
Avery, Leonard S.	Hutchinson, Elizabeth O.	23, Feb. 1843	L3
Avey, Andrew J.	Hildreth, Frances M.	19, May 1853	L3
Aydelote, John H.	Western, Charlotte E	18, Sept 1851	L3
Ayers, Albert B.	Billerbeck, Mary	20, Sept 1855	L3
Aylsworth, Caleb A.	Jocelyn, Augusta	9, Mar. 1854	L3
Ayres, Mark	Mason, Marie	1, Oct. 1846	L3
Ayres, Samuel	Myers, Elizabeth	4, Aug. 1806	L3
Ayres, Stephen S.	Ayres, Elizabeth	24, Apr. 1845	L3
Bachelor, Jonathan R	Larue, Martha	13, May 1816	L3
Bacon, Isaac W.	Wilmuth, Mary Jane	25, Feb. 1847	L3
Bacon, John Henry	Eberle, Catharine	19, Dec. 1833	L2
Bacon, Joseph D.	Brown, Elizabeth	28, Mar. 1850	L3
Badger, William	Rappalee, Mary Ann	15, Oct. 1846	L3
Badgley, William	Wright, Amelia	22, Mar. 1814	L3
Baer, Frederick	Cryer, Mary	8, Nov. 1855	L3
Bagley, Thomas	Murray, Elizabeth	18, Feb. 1847	L3
Bagley, William A.	Weatherby, Rosalinda	27, Sept 1855	L3
Bailey, H.A.	Bacon, Helen B.	6, Sept 1855	L3
Bailey, Hezekiah B.	Griffith, Elizabeth	20, Nov. 1856	L3
Bailey, Isaac S.	Long, Mary E.	8, Oct. 1857	L3
Bailey, M.	Miller, Lizzie (Mrs)	18, June 1857	L3
Bailey, William	Whitehouse, Sarah	16, Jan. 1851	L3

Grooms	Brides	Date of Notice	Page
Bailey, William	Wilson, Margaret Ann	18, July 1844	L3
Bailoche, John	Heath, Eliza	6, Jan. 1817	L3
Baily, Andrew	McCarty, Martha	3, May 1814	L3
Baily, John	Tiebout, Mary (Mrs)	28, July 1836	L3
Bainsell, John	Watkins, Jane	28, Mar. 1839	L3
Baker, Adam	Green, Nancy	23, Dec. 1825	L3
Baker, Charles	Alvord, J.	7, May 1846	L3
Baker, Franklin	Hart, Mary Catharine	9, Jan. 1851	L3
Baker, J.W.	Hutchinson, M.W.	24, Sept 1857	L3
Baker, John	Flint, Esther	7, July 1817	L2
Baker, John W.	Adams, Henrietta P.	17, Oct. 1839	L3
Baker, M.A.	Young, Mollie T.	4, Jan. 1855	L3
Baker, Nathan	Horner, Amelia	13, Aug. 1840	L3
Baker, Reuben	Allen, Elcy H.	1, Sept 1853	L3
Baker, William W.	King, Mary	26, May 1842	L3
Bakewell, William W.	Jaudon, Elizabeth	14, Oct. 1847	L3
Baldock, Milton	Boss, Virginia	10, Feb. 1842	L3
Baldwin, E.C.	Bell, Durinda	26, May 1853	L3
Baldwin, Edward Hy.	Clark, Mary Elizabeth	30, Sept 1852	L3
Baldwin, Edwin J.	Sanderson, Frances	9, Mar. 1854	L3
Baldwin, Henry W.	Holland, Esther (Mrs)	20, Oct. 1853	L3
Baldwin, James H.	Spencer, Rhoda	20, May 1847	L3
Baldwin, John W.	Raxter, Eliza	22, Oct. 1846	L3
Baldwin, O.W.	Pope, Margaret	18, Jan. 1855	L3
Ball, George W.	McNickle, Mary Jane	24, June 1841	L3
Ballance, Charles	England, Elizabeth	4, Feb. 1836	L4
Ballauf, William	Storch, Josephine	17, June 1847	L3
Baner, Jonathan J.	Thomas, Rebecca Ann	21, Sept 1837	L3
Banks, Francis R.	Morley, Lucy Jane	24, Nov. 1853	L3
Banks, Frederick (Dr)	Wiggins, Virinda	29, May 1845	L3
Banks, Tomlin M. (Dr)	Harrison, Clarissa L	18, Apr. 1844	L3
Barber, James H.	Houser, Emaline	4, Nov. 1852	L3
Barbour, Oliver P.	Foulke, Ann Eliza	16, Jan. 1845	L3
Barch, William	Lowe, Elizabeth	23, July 1846	L3
Bard, Sylvester	Mayhew, Louisa P.	13, Nov. 1845	L3
Barfield, William	Bacon, Margaret C.	27, Nov. 1845	L3
Baris, Levi	Bain, Hannah	20, Sept 1855	L3
Barkalow, Gilbert L.	DuBois, Jennie M.	19, Feb. 1857	L3
Barker, Emery B.	Robinson, Martha A.	19, Dec. 1844	L3
Barker, Hiram	Hubbard, Rebecca J.	16, Mar. 1854	L3
Barker, Ozias	Adams, Catharine	30, Mar. 1848	L3
Barker, Thomas C.	Yeatman, Julia	3, May 1814	L3
Barnard, George	Kendall, Sarah W.	18, Jan. 1844	L3
Barnard, J.	Farnsworth, Josephin	30, Nov. 1854	L3
Barnard, William C.	Moody, Mary Louisa	29, May 1851	L3
Barnes, John C.	Starr, Mary	16, Mar. 1849	L3
Barnett, Robert	Jacobs, Elizabeth A.	23, May 1850	L3
Barney, Burchel J.	Boone, Elizabeth	16, Dec. 1829	L3
Barnhart, Daniel	Williams, Anna	15, Sept 1842	L3
Barns, John	Goudy, Ary	21, July 1817	L2
Barns, Samuel	Johnson, Mary	14, Nov. 1839	L1
Barr, Baldwin	Wilson, Catharine	7, Jan. 1847	L3
Barr, Sterret	Moller, Clara P.	16, Sept 1847	L3
Barr, William M.	Dole, Sarah	23, Feb. 1854	L3

Grooms	Brides	Date of Notice	Page
Barr, William V.	Burch, Janetta E.	12, Nov. 1846	L3
Barret, Thomas	Fisher, Elizabeth (Mrs)	26, Nov. 1808	L3
Barrett, Austin C.	Kingsley, Jane E.	15, Feb. 1849	L3
Barrett, William D.	Martin, Sarah C.	15, Aug. 1844	L3
Barrow, Edwin	Knotts, Mary E.	25, Jan. 1849	L3
Bart, Edwin R.	Forbes, Georgiana	25, Jan. 1855	L3
Barton, John O. (Rev)	Boynton, Sarah A.	9, Mar. 1854	L3
Barton, Julius V.	Hand, Mary	18, Apr. 1844	L3
Barwise, Edward K.	Wilson, Matilda E.	8, Apr. 1847	L3
Barwise, Luther T.	Morris, Mary Jane	25, Sept 1851	L3
Bassford, Thomas	Singer, Mary Jane	28, Jan. 1841	L3
Batchelor, William H	Bigelow, Eliza S.	9, Aug. 1855	L3
Bateman, James W.	Turner, O.	2, Dec. 1847	L3
Bateman, Warren M.	Buel, Emma	27, July 1854	L3
Bateman, William D.	Langdon, Mary Jane	18, Aug. 1842	L3
Bates, E.S.	Berresford, Elizabeth	16, Apr. 1840	L3
Bates, Harrison	Cole, Pauline	18, May 1848	L3
Bates, Henry M.	Fawcett, Mary Ann	18, Jan. 1838	L3
Bates, Joshua H.	Hoadly, Elizabeth D.	23, May 1844	L3
Bates, Niles	Greer, Polly	27, Apr. 1809	L3
Bates, William M.	Winn, Sophia	3, Mar. 1842	L3
Bauer, Augustus	Bruce, Elizabeth	16, Nov. 1848	L3
Baumann, John	Riester, Mary	22, June 1854	L3
Baun, J.C.	Achey, Matilda	5, Oct. 1843	L3
Baxter, J. Watson (Dr)	Vorhis, H.L.	18, Dec. 1845	L3
Bayless, Andrew H.	Godman, Ellen	16, Nov. 1854	L3
Bayley, James K.	McKnight, Elizabeth	11, Mar. 1816	L3
Baymiller, Jacob	Thomas, Ann	27, Dec. 1809	L3
Beach, Edward P.	Blachly, Elizabeth A	10, Oct. 1850	L3
Beach, William	Carey, Abby	21, Nov. 1844	L3
Beale, John	Bradford, Sarah	16, Sept 1847	L3
Bealek, Francis M.	Hoffman, Ruth Ann	25, Oct. 1849	L3
Beall, A.W.	Preble, Henrietta	16, Feb. 1854	L3
Beall, Oliver E.	Boog, Mary C.	21, Mar. 1850	L3
Beall, William B.	Low, Mary G.	23, Oct. 1822	L3
Beall, William K.	Harris, Melinda	25, Mar. 1812	L3
Beans, William L.	Clark, Frances	7, June 1849	L3
Beatty, James S.	Devou, Sarah Alice	2, Aug. 1838	L3
Beatty, John	Ward, Mary (Mrs)	15, Oct. 1846	L3
Beaty, James M.	Moffatt, Alletha	23, Mar. 1854	L3
Bechtel, William	Thompson, Emma F.	9, June 1853	L3
Bechtle, Henry C.	Perry, Betsey	19, Feb. 1816	L3
Beck, James	Conaway, Emeline	2, Mar. 1854	L3
Becker, C.F.	Thesing, Marie E.	30, Dec. 1847	L3
Bedinger, B.F. (Dr)	Wade, Sarah	1, July 1820	L3
Bedinger, Henry C.	Drake, Lavinia	9, Sept 1820	L3
Beggs, Joseph P.	Curtis, Mary	26, Aug. 1847	L3
Begraun, T.A.	Thompson, Ann Louise	13, Apr. 1848	L3
Behne, Theodore D.	Poor, Anne	17, Aug. 1854	L3
Beitch, Marcus	Vogelbach, Gertrude	18, May 1854	L3
Bell, James B.	Allen, Adeline	27, Oct. 1853	L3
Bell, Joseph	Foley, Mary	9, Sept 1847	L3
Bell, Thomas	Hornblower, Joanna M.	19, July 1827	L3
Belman, J.C.	Hamlin, Laura	29, Dec. 1853	L3

Grooms	Brides	Date of Notice	Page
Belvel, James	Folger, Harriet	18, Oct. 1838	L3
Beman, I.C.	Williams, Anne S.	20, Sept 1838	L3
Benedict, Alexander	Cleaveland, Sarah	11, Aug. 1842	L3
Benjamin, O.A.	Hartwell, Abia A.	5, Mar. 1857	L3
Bennett, Charles	Noblock, Mary	10, Oct. 1844	L3
Bennett, D.V.	Silsbee, Mary	25, May 1843	L3
Bennett, Daniel R.	Taylor, Jane	3, Feb. 1855	L3
Bennett, George	Kore, Charlotte R.	13, Nov. 1845	L3
Bennett, Thomas S.	Fennimore, Eliza J.	5, Dec. 1850	L3
Bennett, William	Montgomery, Polly	21, Apr. 1821	L3
Bennington, Samuel	Savill, Ellen	13, Sept 1849	L3
Benson, Abraham	Tolbert, Ruth	16, Feb. 1854	L3
Benson, Gabriel	Mills, Abigail	14, Apr. 1820	L3
Benson, James	Nelson, Mary Ann	13, Sept 1849	L3
Benson, Martin	Banks, Elizabeth J.	11, Nov. 1852	L3
Bently, Edward	Horsfall, Elizabeth	7, July 1853	L3
Benton, Oliver	Evans, Nancy	28, Apr. 1817	L3
Beresford, Benjamin	Johnston, Mary Ann	15, Sept 1836	L1
Beresford, Samuel	Wunder, Eliza J.	8, Nov. 1855	L3
Berry, Archibald	Looker, Amelia	12, Mar. 1846	L3
Berry, Hubbard	McKenney, Agnes	21, Apr. 1817	L3
Berry, John H.	Adams, Rachel	18, Dec. 1845	L3
Bettmann, M.	Moehring, Flora	23, Oct. 1845	L3
Betts, John	Kelly, Phebe	18, Nov. 1823	L3
Betts, Joseph W.	Young, Margaret	8, Nov. 1855	L3
Betts, Morgan L.	Wilson, Mary E.	20, July 1854	L3
Betts, Smith	Young, Cynthia Ann	3, Feb. 1848	L3
Bewley, George	Carroll, Mary Ann	3, July 1851	L3
Beyring, F.W. Theo.	Dippel, Mary C.	4, July 1844	L3
Bickham, William D.	Strickle, Maria E.	10, Jan. 1856	L3
Bicknell, Benjamin	Brickett, Loretta J.	27, Nov. 1856	L3
Biddecomer, D.R. (Rev)	Edmondson, Mary Ann	9, June 1842	L3
Bidwell, Gilbert A.	Collins, Emeline	23, Sept 1847	L3
Bigger, John	Cathcart, Louisa	9, Mar. 1854	L3
Biggers, David A.	Lowry, Rebecca Jane	18, June 1857	L3
Biggs, H.W. (Rev)	Poinier, Cornelia S.	25, Aug. 1853	L3
Biggs, Thomas R.	Langdon, Elizabeth	23, Oct. 1851	L3
Biggs, Thomas R.	Miller, Catharine A.	2, Apr. 1846	L3
Billings, Charles F.	Ross, Susannah	25, Feb. 1841	L3
Bingham, John	McDonald, Mary Ann	8, July 1852	L3
Bircham, Daniel	Cropper, Nancy	3, Apr. 1811	L3
Birney, Dion.	Crawford, Sarah	21, Aug. 1845	L3
Birney, William	Hoffman, Kate	19, Nov. 1846	L3
Bishop, John M.(Rev)	North, Lucy D.	19, Nov. 1846	L3
Bishop, William T.	Worrick, Lizzie	24, May 1855	L3
Bissell, William C.	Hamlen, Martha A.	22, Mar. 1855	L3
Blachly, O.B.	Alden, Elizabeth P.	14, June 1825	L3
Black, Adam M. (Dr)	Martin, Isabella H.	7, July 1842	L3
Black, Reuben	Rands, Katharine	25, June 1846	L3
Black, William W.	English, Letitia T.	26, Sept 1844	L3
Blackburn, Edward C.	Norris, Virginia	25, Jan. 1844	L3
Blackburn, J.C. (Dr)	Davey, Eleanor	31, May 1855	L3
Blackburn, Jona	Lyon, Missouri	22, Jan. 1852	L3
Blackly, Joseph W.	Tuttle, Caroline W.	19, Oct. 1822	L3

Grooms	Brides	Date of Notice	Page
Blackston, B.D. (Dr)	Morris, Mary J.	27, Apr. 1848	L3
Blackwell, Henry B.	Stone, Lucy	10, May 1855	L3
Blackwell, Samuel C.	Brown, Antoinette	31, Jan. 1856	L3
Blaghly, J. Warren	Wilmot, Jennie T.	18, Dec. 1856	L3
Blair, A.P.	Winston, Mary E.	8, Jan. 1835	L1
Blair, McLean J.	Walker, Caroline S.	19, Apr. 1845	L3
Blair, Robert	Ewing, Rebecca	18, Dec. 1811	L3
Blake, A. (Rev)	Leonard, Anne J.	16, Sept 1841	L3
Blakely, John	Mount, Nancy	3, July 1845	L3
Blakely, Zerah	Stafford, Mary E.	24, July 1851	L3
Blakemore, John	Denman, Abby	6, Nov. 1845	L3
Blanchard, William A.	Baily, Elmira S.	25, May 1854	L3
Blaney, William	Cobb, Phebe Jane	10, Dec. 1846	L3
Blatchford, Henry S.	Crossman, Martha	20, June 1844	L3
Bleck, R.F.	Caldwell, Ellen J.	21, June 1849	L3
Bliss, Henry	Hazen, Janette (Mrs)	19, Oct. 1854	L3
Bliss, Oliver H.	Douglass, Caroline E	1, Dec. 1842	L3
Bliss, William W.	Taylor, Mary Elizabeth	21, Dec. 1848	L3
Bloss, G.M.D.	McCormick, Lizzie	11, May 1854	L3
Boal, Isaac A.	Potter, Harriet A.	11, May 1854	L3
Boal, Robert, Jr.	Mills, Phoebe H.	6, Jan. 1817	L3
Boal, William M.	Fifield, Francis M.	11, May 1854	L3
Bocking, Adolph H.	Merrell, Nettie	14, July 1853	L3
Bodley, Anthony P.	Talbert, Rebecca W.	26, Jan. 1827	L3
Bogart, Isaac	Holenshade, Jennie C.	20, Nov. 1856	L3
Bogart, Thomas O.	Ayres, Emeline	16, Nov. 1843	L3
Bogert, Isaac	Stewart, Cornelia A.	13, Jan. 1853	L3
Boggs, Joseph R.	Ford, Rachel H.	8, June 1848	L3
Bohrer, Benjamin S.	Luffborough, Eliza	18, Oct. 1820	L3
Bokum, Herman (Rev)	Drummond, Ann R.	20, Feb. 1851	L3
Bolles, William T.	Avey, Eliza J.	10, June 1847	L3
Bond, J.R.H.	Bowlin, Maggie V.	7, May 1857	L3
Bond, John R.S.	Hinton, Annie F.	29, Apr. 1852	L3
Bond, William S.	Cary, Mary Ann (Mrs)	9, Mar. 1854	L3
Bonham, Hervey	Cullum, Chloe	18, Sept 1815	L3
Bonnel, John	Benedict, Sarah E.	20, May 1847	L3
Bonner, David	Reynolds, Elizabeth	24, Mar. 1806	L3
Bonner, Stephen	Hanley, Lucy M.	29, Oct. 1835	L3
Bonte, Peter C.	Blanchard, Frances J	11, May 1843	L3
Boots, Adam	Grieve, Martha	6, Apr. 1854	L3
Borden, Samuel	Zesline, Sarah (Mrs)	16, July 1819	L3
Borgman, Charles H.	Purlier, Pauline	29, Nov. 1855	L3
Boroff, Samuel B.	Crane, Mary E.	22, June 1854	L3
Borrowman, Thomas	Wilson, Isabella	14, Jan. 1847	L3
Bosson, Joseph	Reid, Anna Maria	18, Nov. 1823	L3
Bostick, Edgar M.	Carter, Polly	8, Jan. 1835	L1
Boswell, George W.	McGinnis, Ann Eliza	9, Dec. 1847	L3
Bottom, John	Goosman, Althea	13, Apr. 1848	L3
Boughard, Joseph	Hartman, Margaret	25, Mar. 1816	L3
Bouhane, John C. (Rev)	Harrington, O.E.	20, Nov. 1856	L3
Bourgoin, Alexis J.	Mosier, Elizabeth Y.	21, June 1849	L3
Bowers, Augustus	Cole, Caroline	4, Oct. 1838	L3
Bowers, William	Butt, Lydia	28, July 1817	L3
Bowler, Robert B.	Pendleton, Susan L.	27, Oct. 1842	L3

Grooms	Brides	Date of Notice	Page
Bowlin, William T.	Finch, Jane	18, Jan. 1838	L3
Bowman, Henry Andrew	Eastland, Ann Eliza	30, Mar. 1848	L3
Bowman, William	Grayson, M.E.	2, Dec. 1847	L3
Boyd, Charles	Reeder, Charlotte M.	15, Apr. 1852	L3
Boyd, D.B.	Elliott, Caroline	6, Jan. 1853	L3
Boyden, James C.	Aldrich, Susan	11, June 1857	L3
Boyden, John S.	Gordon, Mary	10, Apr. 1856	L3
Boyer, Jacob	Hunt, Susannah	23, Nov. 1822	L3
Boyer, John	Morris, Esther	7, Jan. 1820	L3
Boylan, James	Halsted, Mary Kerr	18, Jan. 1844	L3
Boylan, Julius A.	Bradley, Mary	9, Dec. 1852	L3
Bozarth, William M.	Newbury, Mary Ann	19, Oct. 1843	L3
Brachman, William	Murphy, Jane	9, Mar. 1854	L3
Brachmann, Henry	Toufly, Rosalie (Mrs)	1, Aug. 1833	L3
Brackenridge, Wm.	Simpson, Mary	23, Nov. 1843	L3
Bradbury, Cornelius	Spinning, Sarah Ann	24, Nov. 1821	L2
Bradbury, George W.	Wright, Anna Rebecca	26, Oct. 1843	L3
Bradbury, V.C.	Winterbottom, Jane A	10, Nov. 1853	L3
Bradford, Daniel	Russell, Eliza	17, Mar. 1807	L3
Bradford, David	Charters, Mary Ann	6, July 1822	L3
Bradley, Lewis A.	Sharpe, Fannie H.	6, July 1854	L3
Bradley, Orlando	Winnie, Lizzie	9, Nov. 1854	L3
Bradwell, Martin	Hamilton, Martha A.	18, May 1848	L3
Brady, Lorenzo D.	Kennon, Caroline	27, Feb. 1845	L3
Branch, Cushman A.	Bacon, Martha	17, Jan. 1850	L3
Brandon, James P.	Dorman, Maria E.	29, Nov. 1838	L3
Brashears, Gassaway	Laws, Amelia	5, Jan. 1837	L3
Brasher, Robert C.	Alter, Mary Ann	8, May 1828	L3
Breedley, Edwin R.	Tillinghast, Anna	27, Sept 1849	L3
Breese, William G.	Wiggins, Adeline	9, July 1840	L3
Brent, C.P. (Dr)	Dale, Annie E.	3, Sept 1857	L3
Brenton, William H.	Bills, Elizabeth T.	20, Sept 1849	L3
Brett, William	White, Adaline	28, Aug. 1845	L3
Brettell, Joseph	Deilkes, Jerusha(Mrs	22, Feb. 1844	L3
Brew, Thomas	Rhoades, Mary Jane	30, Oct. 1851	L3
Brewster, O.S.	Parker, Priscilla	13, Sept 1838	L3
Briant, Lewis	Hatch, Susan F.	4, Nov. 1825	L3
Bridges, Harrison	Gordon, Ellen	17, Aug. 1848	L3
Bridges, Joel H.	Carl, Lavinia	15, Jan. 1846	L3
Briggs, Abraham	Bailey, Jane Shaw	20, Oct. 1842	L3
Briggs, William H.	Suiter, Ellen	24, Feb. 1842	L3
Brigham, Lucius A.	Taylor, Cornelia	3, Oct. 1850	L3
Brigham, Mathias	Crossman, Caroline	6, Oct. 1821	L3
Bright, Ethelbert B.	Reed, Eliza M.	28, Mar. 1839	L3
Brindle, James L.	Brown, Marion	5, Dec. 1844	L3
Brisbane, Benjamin L	Dickson, Sarah Emily	2, Feb. 1854	L3
Broadwell, Charles G	Williamson, Mary J.	9, May 1844	L3
Broadwell, John	Pratt, Betsey	14, Apr. 1817	L3
Broadwell, Jonathan	Capp, Kate	12, June 1851	L3
Broadwell, Samuel J.	Lytle, Elizabeth H.	20, Nov. 1856	L3
Brochamp, Henry	Stewart, Elizabeth	13, Mar. 1856	L3
Brockenbrough, John	Rush, Harriet E.	24, Feb. 1853	L3
Brockman, Jesse S.	Death, Susan A.	16, Mar. 1849	L3
Broks, Theodore M.	McGowan, Maria	2, Dec. 1847	L3

Grooms	Brides	Date of Notice	Page
Bromwell, Henry B.	Aviral, Sarah	26, Dec. 1844	L3
Bronson, George H.	Almy, Catharine B.	7, Jan. 1847	L3
Brookbank, B.F.	Long, Lizzie D.	10, Jan. 1850	L3
Brooke, Reston S.	Parsons, Harriet	5, Apr. 1825	L3
Brookenshire, James	Wallace, Margaret	1, Aug. 1844	L3
Brooks, Daniel	Barwise, Mary Ann	1, Apr. 1823	L3
Brooks, Erastus	Cranch, Margaret D.	1, Feb. 1844	L3
Brooks, Theodore M.	McGowan, Maria (Mrs)	11, Nov. 1847	L3
Brooks, Thomas B.	Shak, Mary S.	13, Aug. 1857	L3
Brooks, Valentine	Hoak, Margaret Ann	18, Jan. 1838	L3
Brooks, W.W.	Hardinge, Rachael	5, Mar. 1846	L3
Brotherton, James H.	Snyder, Anne L.	16, Mar. 1849	L3
Brough, John	Nelson, Caroline A.	21, Sept 1843	L3
Broughard, James	Miller, Betsey	16, Sept 1816	L3
Brown, Anson R. (Dr)	Lundy, Adaline Elizabeth	22, Feb. 1849	L3
Brown, Elnathan W.	Sturgis, Martha E.	30, Nov. 1843	L3
Brown, George H.	Greene, Caroline	3, Sept 1846	L3
Brown, James	Smith, Peggy	29, May 1811	L3
Brown, James	Page, Maria C.	16, Dec. 1830	L4
Brown, James D.	Wilson, Margaret A.	28, Oct. 1852	L3
Brown, John L.	Bliss, Catharine	14, Oct. 1841	L3
Brown, P.Y.	Smith, Frances	26, June 1851	L3
Brown, Randal	Brooks, Cath. A. (Mrs)	7, Sept 1854	L3
Brown, Richard F.	Smith, Elizabeth	30, July 1840	L3
Brown, Robert P.	Galloway, Sarah A.	9, Nov. 1837	L3
Brown, Samuel	Beanham, Mary A.	9, Feb. 1854	L3
Brown, Samuel C.	Davis, Martha E.	12, Dec. 1850	L3
Brown, Sidney B.	West, Elizabeth C.	30, Mar. 1848	L3
Brown, Thomas	Josselyn, Melcena	30, Nov. 1854	L3
Brown, Thomas E.	Gano, Maria	25, May 1854	L3
Brown, William	Holmes, Maria	25, Apr. 1850	L3
Brown, William (Dr)	Thomas, Cecilia A.	21, July 1853	L3
Brown, William H.	Finch, Frances M.	10, Oct. 1850	L3
Brown, William H.	Reeves, Ellen T.	10, Nov. 1842	L4
Brown, William P.	Hoogland, Minerva	9, Dec. 1847	L3
Browne, Samuel J.	Barker, Esther (Mrs)	9, May 1839	L3
Browning, George T.	Holmes, Martha A.	9, Apr. 1846	L3
Brownson, James (Rev)	Maclay, Sarah Ellen	6, Apr. 1843	L3
Bruce, Benjamin	Tumy, Caroline M.	29, Jan. 1846	L3
Bruce, Isaac	Ray, Catharine W.	7, Nov. 1844	L3
Bruen, Luther R.	Forrer, Augusta	15, Dec. 1853	L3
Bruner, Moses	Rex, Maria C.	22, July 1816	L2
Brunner, Alpheus A.	Carr, Sophia W.	2, July 1857	L3
Bryan, Thomas B.	Page, Jennie Byrd	5, Dec. 1850	L3
Bryant, Alfred	Hughes, Mary H.	20, June 1850	L3
Bryant, Isaac F.	Howard, Catharine	28, Feb. 1856	L3
Bryant, William	Wilson, Jane (Mrs)	3, Feb. 1848	L3
Bryarby, Charles W.	Reck, Emma L.	10, Apr. 1845	L3
Bryson, Ambrose M.	Walker, Ann Mary	28, Jan. 1841	L3
Bryson, Isaac	Armstrong, Isabella	1, Oct. 1857	L3
Buchanan, Alfred	Kinneon, Mary P.	22, Nov. 1855	L3
Buchanan, Charles M.	Wheeler, Emily	18, June 1857	L3
Buchanan, John	Lee, Margaret B.	11, May 1843	L3
Buchanan, Robert	Riggle, Sarah Jane	13, May 1847	L3

Grooms	Brides	Date of Notice	Page
Buchanan, W.A.	Bryon, Sallie C.O.	28, Oct. 1852	L3
Buckingham, E.J.	Doyle, Emaline Ad.	20, Mar. 1851	L3
Buckingham, John I.	Guest, Margaret	11, Apr. 1844	L3
Buckles, Dean	Bennett, Nancy	16, Feb. 1854	L3
Buckner, Thomas	Perry, Caroline	8, July 1820	L3
Budd, W.G.	Stevenson, Mollie	2, Feb. 1854	L3
Budden, Edward	Oiriel, Charlotte	27, Aug. 1857	L3
Buel, Lucius C.	Whitman, Jane S.	20, Mar. 1851	L3
Buell, George P.	Lane, Ann	25, June 1824	L3
Buffington, Francis	Merril, Caroline	2, Feb. 1854	L3
Buist, Thomas	Downard, Eliza	21, Nov. 1844	L3
Bullock, Benjamin	Hansell, Susan B.	23, Oct. 1856	L5
Bunnel, Benjamin	Robeson, Margaret	10, Nov. 1821	L3
Burch, James K. (Dr)	Drummond, Maria	25, July 1839	L3
Burch, William	McNutt, Sarah	15, Aug. 1810	L3
Burchard, Asa	Burchard, Emily	24, Nov. 1842	L6
Burckhardt, Frederic	Kittridge, Kate	29, June 1854	L3
Burdsal, Caleb S.	Beach, Mary K.	24, Sept 1846	L3
Burdsal, Elijah	Leathers, Lucy	16, Oct. 1845	L3
Burdsal, Henry W.	Morales, Ana	13, Apr. 1848	L3
Burdsal, James S.	Wood, Mary E.	16, May 1850	L3
Burdsal, Solomon B.	Denny, Elizabeth	6, May 1847	L3
Burdsal, Stephen W.	Turner, Ann Maria	25, Feb. 1836	L3
Burgess, George H.	Scott, Annie	25, Sept 1856	L5
Burgoyne, E.M.	Cummins, Sarah	22, Jan. 1857	L3
Burgoyne, John	Greene, Jennie C.	24, Feb. 1853	L3
Burke, Glendy	Carneal, Sallie	20, June 1844	L3
Burke, William (Rev)	Lane, Mary (Mrs)	25, Aug. 1842	L3
Burnet, David S.	Gano, Mary	31, Mar. 1830	L3
Burnet, Isaac G.	Gordon, Catharine	24, Oct. 1807	L3
Burnet, Jacob	Duncan, Mary S.	13, Nov. 1856	L3
Burnet, Robert W.	Groesbeck, Margaret	27, Oct. 1836	L2
Burnet, William	Clark, Susan Maria	11, Feb. 1841	L3
Burnet, William	Schooley, Mary	22, Oct. 1857	L3
Burnett, Jacob	Lynd, Mary S.	31, Apr. 1845	L3
Burnham, Nathan C.	Pancoast, Mary A.	3, Nov. 1842	L3
Burns, James A.	Oldham, Irene	29, Nov. 1855	L3
Burns, John H.	Gibson, Louisa H.	5, Feb. 1857	L3
Burogyne, Horatio	Stewart, Nancy	28, Apr. 1821	L2
Burr, C. Chauncey	Kellum, Celia	9, Jan. 1851	L3
Burr, Edward M.	Richey, Frances B.	26, Aug. 1852	L3
Burr, Joseph S.	Berrell, Ellen T.	27, Apr. 1843	L3
Burrett, R.T.	Bates, Lizzie	23, Dec. 1852	L3
Burroughs, Thomas N.	Perry, Ann D. (Mrs)	27, Aug. 1846	L3
Burrows, John A.D.	Dudley, Louisa	15, June 1843	L3
Burrows, Joseph H.	Schenck, Lucy H.	29, Aug. 1844	L3
Burt, Andrew	Gano, Sarah Anne	10, Feb. 1807	L3
Burton, Edwin M.	Ford, Lucy L.	6, Feb. 1851	L3
Bush, E.T.	Dosey, Susan	19, Aug. 1847	L3
Bush, James Foster	Chandler, M. Melissa	20, Mar. 1851	L3
Bush, O.N.	Tucker, Hattie D.	13, July 1854	L3
Bushnell, A.L.	Rhoades, Mary E.	4, Sept 1851	L3
Bushnell, Joseph	McFadden, Kate E.	20, Apr. 1854	L3
Bushnell, Simeon M.	Collier, Elizabeth	26, Feb. 1857	L3

Grooms	Brides	Date of Notice	Page
Bussall, A.T.	Harding, Mina	7, Aug. 1856	L5
Butler, Charles	Schenck, Mary B.	13, Feb. 1845	L3
Butler, E.S.	Smith, Margaret J.	25, Feb. 1847	L3
Butler, James D.	Bevis, Mary	31, Mar. 1853	L3
Butler, James J.	Russell, Mary	25, July 1850	L3
Butler, James J.	Rutgers, Cornelia	2, Jan. 1845	L3
Butler, James Jones	Bayard, Cornelia R.	16, Jan. 1845	L3
Butler, James Oliver	Ryder, Margaret	26, Jan. 1843	L3
Butler, Joseph C.	Laverty, Alice B.	9, Sept 1847	L3
Butler, Selar	Peabody, Sarah	30, Jan. 1851	L3
Butler, Thomas S.	Patterson, Jane	2, Dec. 1841	L3
Butterfield, Algeron	Veatch, Ann Maria	28, Dec. 1843	L3
Buttles, Lucien	Disney, Mary E.	20, June 1844	L3
Byers, Israel	Abbot, Mary	25, Sept 1811	L3
Cady, C.W.	Kiersted, A.A.	17, Nov. 1842	L6
Cady, D. Knight	Farrell, M. Ellen	29, Oct. 1857	L3
Cady, John N.	Clingman, Ann Eliza	5, June 1845	L3
Cady, John N.	Craner, Louisa S.	6, Sept 1849	L3
Cahill, James	Carroll, Dorcas	30, Sept 1847	L3
Cake, Charles T.	Hull, Louisa Jane	14, Mar. 1839	L3
Caldow, Robert	McGregor, Margaret	24, Sept 1840	L3
Caldwell, James C.	Bunker, Rebecca R.	1, Nov. 1849	L3
Caldwell, John D.	Templeton, Margaret	23, Oct. 1845	L3
Caldwell, Robert	Avery, Ann	31, Mar. 1807	L3
Caldwell, Sandford	Broadus, Sarah B.	2, Mar. 1854	L3
Caldwell, Thomas L.	Clifford, Mary Jane	15, June 1822	L3
Calhoun, James	Sanxay, Charlotte	5, Sept 1844	L3
Callihan, Henry (Dr)	Metcalfe, Sarah H.	11, Jan. 1844	L3
Camac, P.S.	Parker, Julia A.	10, Nov. 1842	L4
Camp, Samuel J.	Baker, Hannah M.	29, Aug. 1850	L3
Campbell, (Capt)	Suiter, Mary	24, Feb. 1842	L3
Campbell, Carey A.	Armstrong, Mary Ann	13, Sept 1827	L3
Campbell, E.B.	Haydon, N.B.	24, Nov. 1842	L6
Campbell, Edwin R.	Wright, Sarah Jane	24, May 1849	L3
Campbell, Hiram	Woodrow, Sarah Elizabeth	9, May 1844	L3
Campbell, James	Cordry, Mary (Mrs)	10, Jan. 1839	L3
Campbell, John L.	Parmely, Sylvia	16, Jan. 1845	L3
Campbell, John S.	Morris, Mary Ann	9, Feb. 1854	L3
Campbell, Lewis D.	Reily, Jane	14, Jan. 1836	L2
Campbell, Thomas	Pool, Amanda (Mrs)	9, Feb. 1854	L3
Capen, Charles	Collins, Catharine	12, Feb. 1829	L3
Capp, Henry B.	Butler, Lucy	18, Feb. 1823	L3
Carbert, Thomas (Rev)	Scott, Catharine	2, Oct. 1845	L3
Carel, John	Johnson, Nancy	1, Apr. 1823	L3
Carey, George	Tapley, Caroline M.	27, July 1848	L3
Carey, M.T. (Dr)	Burnet, Cornelia	13, Nov. 1856	L3
Carey, Wilson	Brown, Maria Elizabeth	13, Feb. 1851	L3
Carleton, Enoch	Brown, Jemima	16, Oct. 1845	L3
Carlisle, John	Wilson, Isabel	15, Nov. 1855	L3
Carman, Benjamin	Adamson, Catharine	18, Feb. 1820	L3
Carmichael, Neil	Linfoot, Rosetta	29, Dec. 1842	L3
Carnahan, James A.P.	Cummings, Sarah S.	24, Sept 1846	L3
Carneal, Lewis	Lawrence, Maria	4, Dec. 1845	L3

Grooms	Brides	Date of Notice	Page
Carnes, Cyrus	Hemminger, Eliza	26, Jan. 1854	L3
Carnes, Peter	Whitney, Harriet	31, Mar. 1842	L3
Carpenter, C.	McPeak, Anna	14, Sept 1848	L3
Carpenter, Isaac B.	Ellmaker, Susan	29, June 1837	L2
Carr, Francis	Upjohn, Mary Ann	3, Aug. 1822	L3
Carrick, David S.	Baker, Jane E.	11, July 1850	L3
Carroll, Foster (Dr)	Lynch, Anna M.	31, Oct. 1850	L3
Carroll, Robert W.	Conaway, Lydia B.	28, Sept 1854	L3
Carroll, Thomas	Manning, Mary	13, Nov. 1851	L3
Carson, Charles	Dicks, Sarah	19, Jan. 1854	L3
Carson, E.T.	Mayo, Alexina	19, May 1853	L3
Carson, Oliver H.	McManama, Sallie	21, May 1857	L3
Carson, William (Dr)	Whiteman, Louisa	19, Oct. 1854	L3
Carter, E. Henry	Stokes, Emma	19, Dec. 1844	L3
Carter, G.W.	Wishart, Margaretta	31, Mar. 1842	L3
Carter, J. Hamilton	White, Louisa C.	13, Sept 1849	L3
Carter, James H.	Roberts, Margaret	6, Jan. 1848	L3
Carter, James S.	Brickell, M. Louisa	7, Apr. 1853	L3
Carter, Lewis R.	Fleming, Ellis M.	12, June 1827	L3
Carter, Samuel	McClure, Frances S.	15, Sept 1821	L3
Carter, Samuel R.	Taylor, Mary L.	4, Jan. 1855	L3
Carter, T. Jarvis	Woolsen, Emm C.	29, May 1851	L3
Cartrite, William	Raper, Margaret	16, Feb. 1854	L3
Carver, Henry E.	Glascoe, Kitty Ann	31, Oct. 1839	L3
Cary, John	Urno, Mary	19, Jan. 1854	L3
Cary, S.F. (Gen)	Stillwell, Eliza	7, June 1849	L3
Cary, Samuel F.	Allen, Maria Louisa	27, Oct. 1836	L3
Case, John	McGuigan, Mary Ann	8, Oct. 1840	L3
Casey, Charles E.	Minere, Sarah	9, Dec. 1847	L3
Casey, Louis E.	Gratehouse, Ellen	6, Dec. 1855	L3
Cassatt, John W.	Wunder, Susan D.	24, Dec. 1857	L3
Cassel, John F.	Moore, Eliza F.	1, July 1847	L3
Casto, Jonathan	Dodge, Frances Ann	9, Dec. 1847	L3
Caswell, Benjamin	Hodges, Lydia T.	24, Apr. 1851	L3
Cathcart, David	Sherwin, Charlotte	4, Feb. 1818	L2
Center, Hartzill H.	Slaughter, Sarah	22, Feb. 1849	L3
Chadbourne, Benjamin	Boutelle, Laurette L	7, Sept 1854	L3
Chalmers, Horatio S.	Turner, Elizabeth A.	30, Sept 1825	L3
Chamberlain, William	Bigler, Sallie L.	16, Sept 1852	L3
Chamberlaine, James	Moore, Caroline	3, Oct. 1823	L3
Chambers, Charles C.	Jonte, Louisa E.	30, Nov. 1854	L3
Chambers, Pius	Chamberlain, Hannah	21, Nov. 1844	L3
Champian, Thomas	Moore, Martha	28, Nov. 1826	L3
Champlin, C.C.	Jones, Nettie A.	8, Feb. 1855	L3
Chandler, John (Rev)	Hopkins, Charlotte	17, Sept 1846	L3
Chapin, Humeston	Hunt, Sarah	20, Jan. 1842	L3
Chapman, John Q.A.	Cofflin, Elizabeth	18, Sept 1845	L3
Chapman, William	Niles, Helen M.	23, Oct. 1856	L5
Chapman, William B.	Crossman, Margaret	18, Apr. 1839	L3
Chapman, William J.	Evens, Louisa Anna	29, Nov. 1838	L3
Chase, S.P.	Ludlow, Sarah Bella	19, Nov. 1846	L3
Chatfield, William H	Disney, Mary A.	30, Nov. 1854	L3
Cheetham, John	Briggs, Mary Ann	20, Oct. 1842	L3
Cheever, Daniel	Appleton, Ann J.	26, Mar. 1846	L3

Grooms	Brides	Date of Notice	Page
Cheever, John H.	Noble, Lizzie	10, Nov. 1853	L3
Chenoweth, J.S.	Leach, Julia	22, Dec. 1853	L3
Chenoweth, Richard	Hough, Jane H.	21, Nov. 1844	L3
Chester, J.H.	Wilshire, M.A.	28, Feb. 1856	L3
Childs, C.J. (Dr)	Baldridge, Elizabeth	18, Mar. 1847	L3
Childs, John R.	Wood, Frances P.	11, Sept 1845	L3
Childs, William E.	Tait, Eliza	8, June 1837	L1
Chiles, Hamlet W.	Payne, Eddie A.	25, Feb. 1847	L3
Chipman, Horace G.	Bennett, Maria J.	6, Dec. 1849	L3
Chisman, Edward T.	Stone, Amelia C.	29, Oct. 1846	L3
Chittenden, Edward F	Rogers, Julia M.	18, Feb. 1836	L3
Chittenden, Henry A.	Gano, Henrietta	3, Oct. 1844	L3
Christian, George H.	Clark, Rebecca	9, Mar. 1854	L3
Christie, John	O'Reiley, Cecelia	7, Jan. 1847	L3
Christopher, Alex.	Brown, Sarah A.	16, Aug. 1855	L3
Churchill, A.W.	Land, Ellen	19, Mar. 1840	L3
Churchill, David	McKim, Frances A.C.	25, Feb. 1825	L3
Chute, James	Clapp, Martha	27, Oct. 1817	L3
Cist, Francis J.	Wilson, Mary	20, Nov. 1856	L3
Cist, L.J.	Renshaw, Mary S.	27, May 1847	L3
Claflin, George D.	Weed, Sophia B.	7, Sept 1854	L3
Clark, Andrew	McCullough, Mary	16, Feb. 1854	L3
Clark, Augustus	Sargent, Selina B.	14, Mar. 1839	L3
Clark, Benjamin F.	Bevens, Julian	16, Feb. 1837	L3
Clark, Caleb B.	Mayhew, Angeline	2, Apr. 1829	L2
Clark, Enos B.	Dickson, Mary	18, Sept 1845	L3
Clark, George	Bagott, Nancy C.	21, Aug. 1845	L3
Clark, George	Clark, Lydia	27, May 1847	L3
Clark, George W.	King, Sarah C.	13, Feb. 1840	L3
Clark, Henry	Folger, Eliza	22, June 1824	L3
Clark, Henry S.	Bigler, Anne L.	8, June 1854	L3
Clark, J.C.	Lamb, Jane D.	4, Dec. 1845	L3
Clark, James	Harrison, Mary	24, Feb. 1848	L3
Clark, James	Niles, Christina	16, Jan. 1845	L3
Clark, James A.	Willett, Sarah A.	27, Feb. 1845	L3
Clark, John	Mattox, Cordelia	17, Mar. 1853	L3
Clark, John	Walsh, Martha	28, Aug. 1845	L3
Clark, John E.	Valentine, Phebe P.	24, Jan. 1856	L3
Clark, Orgia	Muchmore, Sarah (Mrs)	3, Aug. 1813	L3
Clark, Perry	Holland, Melissa J.	8, Aug. 1850	L3
Clark, Thomas	Baldwin, Margaret R.	19, Mar. 1840	L3
Clark, Thomas	Honeywell, Eliza	25, Oct. 1825	L3
Clark, Walter	McConnell, Eliza	3, Mar. 1836	L2
Clark, William H.	Barr, Eliza A.	18, Sept 1856	L5
Clark, William Penn	Crummey, Caroline V.	9, June 1842	L3
Clark, William Y.	Arthur, Sallie J.	17, Apr. 1851	L3
Clark, William Y.	Conter, Grace Ann	11, Feb. 1847	L3
Clarke, John	Haymon, Susan	29, May 1845	L3
Clarke, Orlando (Rev)	Lyman, Henrietta	21, Aug. 1856	L5
Clarke, R.W.	Pollard, Sarah T.D.	26, Jan. 1843	L3
Clarkson, C.F.	Colescott, Elizabeth	24, May 1849	L3
Clarkson, John D.	Cox, Rebecca Ann	20, June 1850	L3
Clarkson, William O.	Gregory, Mary A.	21, May 1834	L4
Clason, Lewis W.	Rutledge, Lucy Jane	28, Oct. 1847	L3

Grooms	Brides	Date of Notice	Page
Clay, Ralph A.	Gassaway, Lucy Ann	21, Oct. 1841	L3
Clayton, Richard	Jenkins, Jane	2, Feb. 1843	L3
Clayton, Richard	Jenkins, Mary Ann	4, Apr. 1844	L3
Clayton, William	Cropper, Louisa C.	20, Nov. 1850	L3
Clement, William B.	Meads, Eliza Jane	7, Sept 1843	L3
Clement, William H.	Smith, Caroline	11, Sept 1851	L3
Clements, Nelson	Jones, Emily	8, June 1854	L3
Clemmer, J.H.	Clement, Jane	23, Oct. 1845	L3
Cleveland, George P.	Scott, Henrietta E.	27, Nov. 1834	L2
Cleveland, John (Dr)	Chamberlain, Juliana	28, Nov. 1844	L3
Cline, John	Shannon, Isabella	17, Aug. 1813	L3
Cloon, Samuel	Clemons, Martha Ann	12, Aug. 1847	L3
Clossin, David L.	Kain, Almira	4, Dec. 1845	L3
Clough, John P.	Stout, Louisa	27, Apr. 1854	L3
Clutch, John V.	Housel, Eliza	7, Nov. 1844	L3
Clyde, Andrew	Lovelace, Louisa C.	28, Dec. 1843	L3
Cobb, Jedediah	Morrill, Ann Maria	13, June 1826	L3
Cochnower, John	Barton, Amanda M.	23, Sept 1852	L3
Cochran, William	Foster, Elizabeth M.	8, May 1851	L3
Coddington, G.W.	Hulbert, Mary	21, June 1849	L3
Coe, Stephen W.	Miller, Lydia L.	17, Aug. 1848	L3
Coffeen, John Q.A.	Crane, Mary F.	20, Nov. 1856	L3
Coffeen, Zeloma	Swallow, Elizabeth	8, Jan. 1857	L3
Coffin, Dennis H.B.	McKee, Noami	8, Jan. 1846	L3
Coffin, Joseph H.	Maltry, Sophia	17, Feb. 1848	L3
Coffin, W.G.	Israel, Hannah	7, May 1840	L3
Cogy, Joseph (Dr)	Wood, Abbey C.	1, July 1820	L3
Cohoon, Robert	Dalton, Eliza	15, June 1837	L3
Colburn, Charles L.	Symmes, Mary S.	5, Aug. 1847	L3
Colburn, Perry	Hilts, Lydia	28, Mar. 1850	L3
Colburn, W.T.	Thomas, S.E.	20, Feb. 1845	L3
Colby, George W.	Kendall, Samantha E.	27, Nov. 1851	L3
Colby, Joseph	Booth, Pamela	24, Feb. 1807	L3
Colby, Zerebabel	Campbell, Sarah (Mrs)	3, Aug. 1813	L3
Cole, Jacob F.	Swan, Helen A.	11, July 1850	L3
Cole, John F.	Shaw, Ellen	23, Feb. 1854	L3
Coleman, Andrew (Rev)	Walton, Lydia H.	3, Oct. 1844	L3
Coleman, John	Reynolds, Mary L.	12, Feb. 1857	L3
Coleman, John W.	Woodward, Lucia Anna	30, Oct. 1834	L1
Coleman, Robert J.	Carlisle, Ann M.	11, Apr. 1844	L3
Coleman, Thomas	Hay, Mary A.	9, June 1853	L3
Coles, Abraham	Thomas, Emily	20, June 1839	L3
Colles, James	Blachly, Mary J.	1, Nov. 1855	L3
Collett, William R.	Suydam, Ann Eliza	22, Aug. 1833	L1
Collier, Allen	How, Susan C.	30, Sept 1852	L3
Collier, Charles B.	Chapin, Sarah E.	1, Oct. 1857	L3
Collier, D.	Tylor, Lizzie H.	24, Jan. 1856	L3
Collier, William E.	Pouder, Elizabeth	22, May 1851	L3
Collingwood, John	Lester, Emma	11, Feb. 1841	L3
Collins, Amos	Swing, Priscilla	26, Mar. 1819	L3
Collins, Charles	Driskill, Caroline	26, Jan. 1843	L3
Collins, Edmund	Taylor, Elizabeth (Mrs)	11, Aug. 1842	L3
Collins, Hiram B.	McCord, Jane D.	26, Jan. 1854	L3
Collins, Isaac C.	Ruth, Emily H.	5, Feb. 1852	L3

Grooms	Brides	Date of Notice	Page
Collins, John A.	Case, Laura G.	18, Mar. 1847	L3
Collins, John C.	Wakelam, Anna M.	1, Dec. 1853	L3
Collins, Joseph H.	Judkins, Martha A.	18, Jan. 1849	L3
Collins, Philip	Gardner, Martha Jane	11, May 1848	L3
Collins, William	Kelley, Jane	2, Dec. 1847	L3
Collins, William O.	Wever, Catharine W.	30, Nov. 1843	L3
Collord, James	Thorn, Mary	10, Aug. 1819	L3
Collord, W.A.	Severns, Rebecca	15, Oct. 1846	L3
Colter, Aaron A.	Burdsal, Margaret	14, Oct. 1852	L3
Colvin, Thomas	Conn, Hannah (Mrs)	11, July 1826	L3
Combs, John S. (Dr)	Frazee, Cynthia	9, Sept 1852	L3
Comly, James D.	Pennington, Francis	27, Sept 1849	L3
Comly, Richard N.	Sanders, Julia E.	16, May 1833	L4
Comly, William F.	Judkins, Sarah R.	27, Oct. 1836	L3
Compton, William A.	Vanausdoll, Caroline	28, Dec. 1837	L3
Comstock, William H.	Foote, Catharine A.	27, May 1847	L3
Conant, E.L.	Hurdus, Maria	31, Oct. 1826	L3
Conclin, Caleb	Williams, Margaret	9, Mar. 1824	L3
Conclin, William	Leslie, Maria E.	12, Dec. 1850	L3
Cones, Joseph	Woodruff, Phoebe	13, May 1852	L3
Cones, W.M.	Orange, Rebecca H.	3, Mar. 1853	L3
Cones, William M.	Thompson, Margaret	11, Dec. 1845	L3
Cones, William W.	Branch, Elizabeth L.	3, Oct. 1844	L3
Conklin, Henry M.	Martin, Harriet N.	7, Mar. 1850	L3
Conklin, I.C.	Patton, Matilda L.	17, Mar. 1853	L3
Conklin, John T.	Cregar, Rebecca Ann	23, Dec. 1852	L3
Conklin, S.F. (Dr)	King, Margaret M.	2, Oct. 1851	L3
Conkling, Isaac V.	Carman, Mary	11, Mar. 1847	L3
Conkling, R.	Armstrong, Elizabeth (Mrs)	13, Nov. 1850	L3
Conkling, R.	Kenton, Lucie A.	20, Nov. 1845	L3
Conkling, Stephen	Forgy, Mary	30, Mar. 1848	L3
Conner, Thomas H.(Dr	Robinson, Ellen	8, May 1845	L3
Conover, James F.	Evans, Hannah	3, Nov. 1853	L3
Conway, Wilton A.	Burns, Laura	22, Oct. 1846	L3
Conwell, Ira (Dr)	Soule, Martha S.	6, Apr. 1843	L3
Conwell, LaFayette	Disney, Annie	7, Feb. 1850	L3
Cook, Anthony	Cornish, Martha	2, Oct. 1845	L3
Cook, Austin	Davis, Lucinda	20, Sept 1827	L1
Cook, Edward	Hill, Mary W.	7, Aug. 1856	L5
Cook, G.T.	McKeag, Ann	8, June 1843	L3
Cook, Samuel	Dollin, Frances	11, Nov. 1820	L3
Cook, Theodore	Semple, Anna G.	2, Oct. 1856	L5
Cook, W.H.	Ewing, Emma A.	30, Oct. 1856	L5
Cook, William J.	Chandler, Sarah Jane	20, Mar. 1851	L3
Cooke, David B.	Hageman, Mary B.	16, Nov. 1848	L3
Coolidge, William	Philpot, Elizabeth	11, May 1843	L3
Coolidge, William H.	Wilson, Mary J.	17, Apr. 1851	L3
Coombs, Alfred D.	Frankenstein, Maria	24, May 1849	L3
Coombs, Ollman	Davis, Mahula	14, Dec. 1848	L2
Cooper, Daniel	Burnet, Sophia	24, Sept 1805	L3
Cooper, E. Samuel	Martin, Mary E.	29, July 1841	L3
Cooper, James	Oliver, Frances E.	30, Apr. 1840	L3
Cooper, James	Palmer, Mary E.	8, Nov. 1855	L3
Cooper, Jonas	Price, Elizabeth	29, Dec. 1821	L3

Grooms	Brides	Date of Notice	Page
Copelan, Harvey	Pickering, Lucinda	16, Feb. 1854	L3
Copelen, George W.	Young, Elizabeth R.	4, July 1850	L3
Copelen, Isaac C.	Young, Nancy (Mrs)	5, Sept 1850	L3
Corben, William	Hayes, Ann	26, Mar. 1819	L3
Corbin, James B.	Smith, Mary A.	15, Sept 1853	L3
Cordell, C.M.	Burr, Orvelia K.	10, Aug. 1843	L3
Cornell, John P.	Chapin, Sylvia	2, June 1842	L3
Correl, J.	Lewis, B.	28, Oct. 1825	L2
Corry, Thomas F.	Collins, Harriet	13, Aug. 1846	L3
Corwin, Daniel	Johnson, Elizabeth (Mrs)	6, Feb. 1840	L3
Corwine, David M.	Stout, Margaret Elizabeth	24, Aug. 1848	L3
Corwine, Samuel L.	Thomas, Belle	3, Aug. 1854	L3
Cory, Jonathan L.	Ross, Esther	21, Apr. 1820	L3
Cosgrove, John N.	Gardner, Susan	9, Jan. 1845	L3
Cottam, Richard	Ladley, Lydia Ann	7, Oct. 1841	L3
Cottam, Richard	Rolef, Mary E.	9, May 1844	L3
Cotton, Charles B.	Gallagher, Jennie M.	27, Dec. 1855	L3
Cotty, William	Leeds, Elizabeth	8, Mar. 1849	L3
Coulson, Edward	Smith, Maria	31, Dec. 1846	L3
Councellor, John	Fosdick, Sarah (Mrs)	30, Dec. 1806	L3
Courteney, Samuel G.	Dickinson, Lydia L.	30, Sept 1852	L3
Covert, D'Estaing	Conklin, Eunice	14, June 1855	L3
Cowling, Richard	Brush, Mary	24, May 1849	L3
Cox, Edward	Sweetland, Eliza	30, July 1857	L3
Cox, Jerome	Powell, Lizzie	17, Apr. 1851	L3
Cox, R.S.	Schell, Hannah F.	3, Feb. 1855	L3
Cox, Rudolph	Roberts, Lucy B.	11, Oct. 1838	L3
Crabee, Alexander	Hardy, Elizabeth	9, Feb. 1854	L3
Craft, J.W.	Applegate, Ellen	3, June 1847	L3
Craig, J.W.	Vickers, Emeline J.	30, Mar. 1854	L3
Craig, James H.	Burnside, Elvira J.	18, May 1848	L3
Craig, Robert S.	Hansfall, Anna	13, Nov. 1856	L3
Craig, William S.	Thompson, Jane M.	2, Apr. 1829	L2
Craighead, Samuel	Schenck, Jeannette A	10, Feb. 1853	L3
Cramer, George R.	Hollenshade, Catharine E.	20, Sept 1849	L3
Cranch, John	Appleton, Charlotte	24, Apr. 1845	L3
Crane, Henry	Hanks, Zeniah	20, Dec. 1838	L3
Crane, James C.	Holden, Emma A.	2, July 1857	L3
Crane, Joseph H.	Elliot, Julia Ann E.	19, July 1809	L3
Crane, Oliver	Crane, Abigail	15, Apr. 1812	L3
Crary, Georgy	Taylor, Eliza Jane	5, Sept 1844	L3
Craut, Henry	Hubbert, Jannet C.	30, Apr. 1840	L3
Craven, Gershom S.	Mulford, Harriet P.	16, Sept 1820	L3
Crawford, Andrew	Walker, Georgina	7, Sept 1848	L3
Crawford, Henry B.	Rich, Eliza L.	23, Feb. 1854	L3
Crawford, John	Smith, Susan E.	9, Oct. 1851	L3
Crawford, Leonard	Kidder, Mary W.	13, Nov. 1851	L3
Crawford, Levi S.	Hamilton, Anna M.	18, Dec. 1845	L3
Crawford, William	McPherson, Mary Jane	28, Sept 1848	L3
Crawson, James	Mackey, Maria (Mrs)	21, Aug. 1811	L3
Creagh, Job	Williamson, Emily	29, Nov. 1849	L3
Creighton, W.H.	Woodbridge, Ellen	8, June 1843	L3
Crew, James	Bowen, Mary J.	13, Sept 1849	L3
Crew, Peter J.	Bowen, Virginia	30, Mar. 1854	L3

Grooms	Brides	Date of Notice	Page
Crockett, Alden	Conner, Nelle V.	18, Dec. 1851	L3
Crosby, Joshua E.	Stibbs, Sarah Ann	9, June 1836	L3
Crosley, Henry	Russell, Adeline	7, Feb. 1850	L3
Crossen, Peter B.	Holland, Laura E.	10, Aug. 1854	L3
Crowell, Martin	Rayl, Polly	25, Apr. 1810	L3
Cruzan, Benjamin W.	Dumm, Catharine A.	7, Feb. 1839	L3
Culberston, William	Ebersol, Mary Jane	12, Jan. 1854	L3
Cummings, Caleb P.	Campton, Cynthia Ann	10, Feb. 1842	L3
Cummings, George W.	Campbell, Rebecca J.	13, May 1847	L3
Cummins, J.W.	Colby, Caroline	20, Mar. 1845	L3
Cunningham, Andrew	Hutchens, Lucretia	23, June 1853	L3
Cunningham, E.W.	Swift, Lucy	27, Sept 1838	L3
Cunningham, Francis	Bryant, Caroline	8, Mar. 1855	L3
Cunningham, J.H.	Fosdick, Harriet (Mrs)	10, Sept 1846	L3
Cunningham, John P.	Letter, Eleanor D.	2, Feb. 1843	L3
Cunningham, T.E.	Hyatt, Elizabeth S.	23, Feb. 1854	L3
Curd, Thomas H.	Payne, Amanda G.	19, May 1853	L3
Curd, William O.	Johnson, Eliza E.	16, Apr. 1846	L3
Curme, Arthur A.	Nicholas, Libby J.	30, Oct. 1856	L5
Curtis, Herschel C.	Schatzman, Julia A.	29, Jan. 1846	L3
Curtis, Joseph A.	Jackson, Maria N.	15, Oct. 1846	L3
Curtiss, L.G.	Browne, Frances M.	9, Sept 1847	L3
Curwen, Maskell E.	Wright, Mary T.	24, May 1855	L3
Cushard, William	Kennedy, Mary Ellen	26, Jan. 1854	L3
Custenbarder, Daniel	Miller, Catharine	26, Jan. 1854	L3
Daily, Nathaniel	Daily, Emeline	30, Oct. 1851	L3
Dakes, H.J.	Conkling, Eliza Jane	15, Feb. 1838	L3
Dale, Henry S.	Holabird, Emeline	22, Jan. 1852	L3
Dalton, James	Halley, Lauretta E.	25, May 1848	L3
Dana, Charles A.	MacDaniel, Eunice	2, Apr. 1846	L3
Danby, Charles	Griffiths, Caroline	5, May 1853	L3
Dandridge, Alexander	Pendleton, Martha E.	11, May 1843	L3
Daniels, Archer D.	Ramsdale, Mary	7, Dec. 1843	L3
Daniels, Hector L.	O'Neill, Julia F.	26, Nov. 1846	L3
Dare, Clement	Penton, Rebecca Jane	20, Feb. 1845	L3
Darling, John	Gillett, Cynthia A.	6, Oct. 1842	L3
Darling, Thomas	Anderson, Margaret	14, July 1836	L3
Darr, Francis	Gross, Josephine	6, Dec. 1855	L3
Darr, Joseph	Armstrong, Kate	14, Feb. 1850	L3
Darst, Jacob	Darst, Anna B. (Mrs)	17, Dec. 1857	L3
Darst, Jacob B.	Black, Rebecca	27, Sept 1849	L3
Dart, George L.	Edday, Hannah (Mrs)	22, July 1852	L3
Dart, George L.	Weirick, Sallie H.	20, Apr. 1848	L3
Daughlade, John L.A.	Siebenthal, Anna (Mrs)	20, Feb. 1824	L3
Davenport, Cyrus	Stephens, Mary Ann	15, July 1847	L3
Davenport, Darius	Burr, Emma C.	21, Apr. 1820	L3
Davenport, Darius G.	Mulford, Mary R.	2, June 1853	L3
Davies, Joseph	Glasgow, Mary	1, Apr. 1823	L3
Daviess, William	Thompson, M.W.R.	31, Oct. 1839	L3
Davis, Charles	Goodin, Elizabeth	13, May 1852	L3
Davis, George H.	Child, Elizabeth F.	28, May 1846	L3
Davis, George W.	Brooks, Mary W.	16, Mar. 1848	L3
Davis, H.M.F.	Gano, Nancy	7, Nov. 1844	L3

Grooms	Brides	Date of Notice	Page
Davis, Henry F.	Kellogg, Almira S.	19, Mar. 1840	L3
Davis, James Ward	Perry, Virginia	4, Oct. 1849	L3
Davis, John M.	Cooper, Clara A.	23, Nov. 1848	L3
Davis, Joseph	Brown, Eliza	30, June 1821	L3
Davis, Joshua	Tilton, Mary	5, Sept 1850	L3
Davis, Joshua	Tilton, Mary	12, Sept 1850	L3
Davis, Judson	Merrill, Adaline	25, Sept 1856	L5
Davis, Samuel	Boorall, Elizabeth	5, Feb. 1852	L3
Davis, Thomas	Cameron, Kate J.	24, July 1851	L3
Davis, Timothy	O'Ferrall, Jane B.	26, Nov. 1857	L3
Davis, Werter R.(Rev	Russell, Minerva	18, May 1843	L3
Davisson, A.W. (Dr)	Charters, Anna L.	30, Nov. 1837	L3
Davisson, Thomas	White, Elvira	12, Nov. 1846	L3
Dawson, W.W. (Dr)	Hand, Margaret	15, May 1851	L3
Day, George W.	Brown, Elizabeth L.	10, Jan. 1850	L3
Day, George W.	Kerns, Henrietta	19, Oct. 1843	L3
Day, Travis B.	Guss, Sarah	23, Feb. 1854	L3
Day, Willard G.	Catchcart, Caroline	10, May 1855	L3
Dayton, Eli (Dr)	Wood, Catharine	21, Feb. 1839	L3
Deaven, Thomas	Young, Honor (Mrs)	12, Nov. 1829	L3
Debarr, J.H. Diss	Levassor, Clara J.	25, May 1848	L3
DeCamp, Job	Jacobs, Margaret E.	9, May 1844	L3
DeCamp, John	Hildreth, Serena A.	6, June 1844	L3
DeCamp, Lambert	Garwood, Lydia	11, Sept 1856	L5
Decker, Josiah	Wiltberger, Susan (Mrs)	18, May 1822	L3
DeCourcy, Oliver M.	Belt, Isabella W.	2, Dec. 1847	L3
Dedrick, David	Campbell, Mary	15, May 1845	L3
Dedrick, William(Dr)	Ashworth, Lois	9, Feb. 1837	L3
Deebugin, Henry	Kelsy, Sarosa	22, July 1816	L2
Deeds, Isaac W.	Rogers, Ann Eliza	9, May 1818	L3
DeForest, William	Higdon, Eliza J.	29, Oct. 1857	L3
DeGolzee, Watts	Boyle, Sophia	27, Dec. 1855	L3
DeGraw, Abraham	Cornelius, Mary	13, Jan. 1842	L3
Degraw, P.G.	Miller, Lizzie A.	18, Nov. 1847	L3
DeGrummond, G.W.	Justus, Angeline	5, Aug. 1852	L3
Delap,	Moyer,	30, Dec. 1847	L3
Delaplaine, Joseph	Livingston, Jane Ann	14, Oct. 1806	L3
Dellinger, A.F.	McMurray, Catharine	4, Aug. 1836	L3
Demoss, Peter	Scogin, Polly	25, Apr. 1810	L3
Denen, James M.	Muckelvar, Nancy	17, Mar. 1842	L3
Denise, Denise	Schenck, Mary Eliza	5, Oct. 1843	L3
Dennhard, John	Blair, Minerva	21, Nov. 1844	L3
Dennis, Benjamin (Dr)	Bessom, Charlotte	8, Feb. 1838	L3
Dennis, Jacob J.	Wakefield, Margaret	17, Oct. 1850	L3
Dennis, John	Mallally, Elizabeth	13, Nov. 1845	L3
Denny, McHenry Hall	Conroy, Elizabeth Anna	29, June 1843	L3
DeSerisy, Louis	Reed, Margaret A.	4, Sept 1845	L3
Deshler, Charles G.	King, Flora	5, June 1845	L3
Desilver, J. Ford	Geiger, Lavinia M.	12, Dec. 1844	L3
Develin, James	Pike, Lucy A.	27, Nov. 1856	L3
Dewey, James W.	Stinton, Mary E.	26, Jan. 1854	L3
DeWitt, G.V.H.	Pierson, Mary Ann	21, May 1819	L3
Dexter, Charles	Harbeson, Anna	7, June 1855	L3
Dial, William C.(Dr)	Simmons, Sallie A.	22, Nov. 1855	L3

Grooms	Brides	Date of Notice	Page
Dick, William A.	Atkins, Rebecca A.	23, Oct. 1851	L3
Dickerson, Charles D	Cox, Amelia S.	19, Apr. 1855	L3
Dickey, George	Hartnan, Solona	16, Feb. 1854	L3
Dickinson, William S	Bishop, Ella T.	24, May 1855	L3
Dickson, Charles	Baily, Salley	13, Dec. 1849	L3
Dickson, James M.	Taylor, Caroline	12, Nov. 1846	L3
Dickson, Thomas	Graham, Hannah	6, July 1843	L3
Dill, Joseph	Putnam, Levina	1, Oct. 1824	L3
Dill, Samuel	Knowles, Sarah Ann	29, Dec. 1842	L3
Dill, William J.	Smith, Ann F.	10, Jan. 1850	L3
Dillen, John	Mitchell, Margaret	16, Feb. 1854	L3
Dills, W.R.	Forbus, Maggie F.	18, Dec. 1856	L3
Dilworth, Joseph	Richardson, Louisa M.	17, Jan. 1850	L3
Dimmick, Charles W.	Kilbreath, Caroline	6, June 1839	L2
Dimond, Cornelius R.	Carter, Adelia	30, Apr. 1846	L3
Disney, T. Bishop	Tift, Laura Rebecca	8, Nov. 1855	L3
Distin, William L.	Lehmanowsky, Anna S.	21, Sept 1837	L4
Doan, Isaac	Cooke, Isabella	6, Dec. 1838	L3
Dobson, Benjamin	Leech, Sarah	22, Apr. 1847	L3
Dodd, George S.	Bourne, Annie	1, Sept 1853	L3
Dodd, James	Gibbs, C.H.	31, Dec. 1840	L3
Dodd, William	Hart, Jane P.	14, Feb. 1856	L3
Dodd, William	Hinman, Eliza P.	27, Dec. 1838	L3
Dodds, Preston C.	Prickett, Matilda A.	16, Feb. 1854	L3
Dodge, Ossian	Lyon, Ettie	13, July 1854	L3
Dodge, William	McFarland, Sarah	8, Aug. 1850	L3
Dodson, Edward	Rose, Pamela	30, Dec. 1806	L3
Dodson, William B.	Starbuck, Deborah	9, Dec. 1825	L3
Doering, Charles H.	McLaughlin, Nancy J.	19, Oct. 1843	L3
Doggett, James F.	Cathell, Laura	18, Sept 1845	L3
Dohrman, Arnold H.	Collier, Elizabeth M	27, May 1841	L3
Dolson, Jacob	Marshall, Hetty Ann	18, May 1827	L3
Dominick, George	Enyart, M.C.	17, June 1852	L3
Donahou, John W.	Reeder, Caroline B.	1, Mar. 1849	L3
Donaldson, Francis T	Beck, Ann G.	29, Nov. 1849	L3
Donaldson, Frank	Guilford, Anna	15, Oct. 1846	L3
Donaldson, George	Guilford, Appeline	3, June 1847	L3
Donaldson, Thomas	Parker, Susanna E.	7, Sept 1837	L3
Donaldson, William	Reakirt, Arabella C.	26, Mar. 1857	L3
Doniphan, David A.	McGroarty, Mary Ann	16, Jan. 1845	L3
Donnavau, Corydon	Doughty, Rachel	1, Aug. 1839	L3
Donnel, W.S.H.	Smith, Rosa M.	12, Jan. 1854	L3
Donogh, James B.	Hannaford, Eliza	6, Mar. 1845	L3
Donogh, John P.	Mahard, Esther	12, Nov. 1835	L1
Donogh, Robert P.	Coleman, Elizabeth	2, Mar. 1843	L3
Doolittle, Charles A	Fitzpatrick, Mary A.	28, Dec. 1848	L3
Doolittle, Henry	Powell, Amelia	27, May 1852	L3
Dopp, Solomon	VanDuston, Isabella	3, Feb. 1848	L3
Dorfeuille, J.	Davis, Janette	14, May 1824	L3
Dosch, Daniel	Emerson, Charlotte	18, Apr. 1850	L3
Doty, John	Lawson, Hannah	28, Jan. 1847	L3
Doty, Thomas	Cornick, Peggy	14, Apr. 1807	L4
Doughty, George E.	Fingland, Louisa	11, Sept 1851	L3
Doughty, William M.	Guthrie, Martha	23, Nov. 1843	L3

Grooms	Brides	Date of Notice	Page
Douglas, James M.	Brown, Eliza	28, Dec. 1843	L3
Douglass, James M.	Corry, Eleanor	21, Feb. 1850	L3
Douglass, Samuel M.	Corry, Eleanor	14, Feb. 1850	L3
Downer, William	Wattson, Ann Delia	20, May 1841	L3
Downing, Hollis	Ross, Frances Ellen	9, Mar. 1854	L3
Downs, Arthur D.	Mitchell, Cora	8, Jan. 1857	L3
Doyle, Michael	Lightfoot, Susan (Mrs)	20, June 1844	L3
Dozier, E. (Dr)	Eubank, Maria (Mrs)	10, June 1816	L3
Drake, Aaron	Harrison, Ann	31, Mar. 1821	L3
Drake, Charles D.	Cross, Margaret (Mrs)	23, Mar. 1843	L3
Drake, Daniel (Dr)	Cisson, Harriet	28, Dec. 1807	L3
Drake, Josiah	Kugler, Catharine	2, May 1833	L1
Drake, William	Spooner, Lucy J.	27, Sept 1855	L3
Dransfield, Henry F.	Ruffner, Eliza Ann	11, May 1848	L3
Drew, William C.	Armstrong, Mary G.	15, Dec. 1817	L3
Driesbach,	Walters, Sallie A.	11, May 1854	L3
Driver, James S.	Shingledecker, Jem.	17, Aug. 1848	L3
Driver, Lucien	Shingledecker, Mary	11, Apr. 1844	L3
Duberly, John	Garritson, Sarah L.	26, May 1842	L3
Duble, John A.	Reynolds, Clara J.	12, Aug. 1847	L3
Dubois, George (Rev)	McIlvaine, Mary Coxe	24, Aug. 1848	L3
Dubois, John	McKinney, Frances (Mrs)	17, Jan. 1850	L3
Dudley, Ambrose (Col)	Cuny, Clarissa (Mrs)	13, July 1837	L3
Dudley, James M.	Lewis, Mary Ann	2, Feb. 1843	L3
Duffield, Charles	Cloon, Sarah E.	31, Mar. 1842	L3
Duffield, J.J.	Pienier, Eliza	26, May 1836	L3
Dufour, Oliver	Ruter, Amanda S.	12, May 1842	L3
Dugan, John A.	Gilliams, Susan L.	14, Oct. 1852	L3
Duhme, Herman	McNicoll, Mary A.	18, Feb. 1847	L3
Dumass, Benjamin	Pettit, Maria	15, Oct. 1819	L3
Dunbar, John	Clarke, Elizabeth	27, Apr. 1848	L3
Dunbar, Seth	Mahew, Hannah	3, June 1820	L3
Duncan, John E.	Connell, Susan E.	15, Sept 1853	L3
Duncan, Lucius C.	Smith, Mary Rebecca	28, Sept 1854	L3
Duncan, Richard A.	Bradbury, Mary P.	11, Nov. 1852	L3
Duncan, W.C. (Dr)	Langley, Eliza A.	8, May 1845	L3
Dunham, Joseph C.	Stevens, E.A.	6, Apr. 1848	L3
Dunham, William	McLean, Eliza L.	18, Feb. 1841	L3
Dunhapst, John H.	Belmer, Rebecca	22, Sept 1853	L3
Dunlap, Charles C.	Meadowcroft, Mary A.	30, Oct. 1851	L3
Dunlap, Joseph L.	Clingman, Anna Maria	12, Sept 1850	L3
Dunn, Lewis	Bailey, Mary (Mrs)	1, June 1848	L3
Dunn, Samuel	Rich, Caroline (Mrs)	22, Jan. 1852	L3
Dunnington, Alex.	Ratliffe, Nancy (Mrs)	2, Mar. 1854	L3
Dunseth, John	Hat, Mary	5, Dec. 1844	L3
Dunseth, Lewis	Hawkins, Louisa	23, Apr. 1840	L3
Dunsmore, Joseph	Ward, Margaret A.	9, Feb. 1854	L3
Durbin, John P. (Rev)	Cook, Frances	20, Sept 1827	L3
Dusenbury, Cornelius	Loevieson, Maria	27, Nov. 1845	L3
Duval, John	Pottinger, Mary Ann	7, Feb. 1856	L3
Duvall, L.W.	Doyal, Emma D.	15, Dec. 1853	L3
Dye, Andrew	Martin, Elizabeth	19, July 1814	L3
Dyer, A.F.	Morse, Mary Jane	24, Feb. 1848	L3
Dyer, Elisha Isaac	Gregory, Frances	11, Mar. 1841	L3

Grooms	Brides	Date of Notice	Page
Dymond, R.	Glenn, Lizzie	12, July 1855	L3
Earenfight, John	Huntington, Jane	7, Mar. 1839	L3
Earhart, J.S.	Patterson, Anna R.	24, Mar. 1853	L3
Easton, George	Palmer, Florinda C.	6, June 1839	L2
Eaton, George C.	Harrison, Bessie S.	10, June 1847	L3
Eaton, John	Scott, Jane	6, Jan. 1848	L3
Eaton, Joseph O.	Goodman, Emma	14, June 1855	L3
Eberle, Richard	Higbee, Theodosia W.	10, Dec. 1840	L3
Ebrert, Isaac (Rev)	Easton, Eliza	3, June 1841	L3
Eccles, Henry	Johnston, Jane	8, July 1847	L3
Eckert, Daniel	Stites, Pheby	31, Aug. 1822	L3
Eckert, John	Berry, Charlotte	16, Nov. 1848	L3
Eckstein, Frederick	Holabird, Harriet	3, Dec. 1857	L3
Edington, George	Calendar, Theresa	24, Dec. 1857	L3
Edmeston, William	Bromwell, Loui	7, July 1853	L3
Edminster, James C.	Robinson, Louisa J.	6, Apr. 1854	L3
Edwards, Clement R.	Booth, Sarah C.	11, Aug. 1853	L3
Edwards, Edwin	Risinger, Sarah W.	27, May 1847	L3
Edwards, James	Adams, Lucy	16, Jan. 1845	L3
Edwards, John M.	Philpot, Anna	4, July 1844	L3
Edwards, Joseph R.	Chamberlin, Mary	28, Mar. 1839	L3
Edwards, Samuel	Parmetar, Aurelia M.	26, May 1842	L3
Edwards, William	Browne, Charlotte	25, Mar. 1812	L3
Edwards, William C.	Hoagland, Catharine	7, Nov. 1844	L3
Eichelberger, Martin	Burk, Mary Jane	18, June 1857	L3
Elder, Edward D.	Beman, Louise F.	15, Aug. 1844	L3
Elder, James	Powlon, Rosanna	2, May 1844	L3
Eldickin, John C.	Morrison, Mary	17, Feb. 1848	L3
Eliott, William J.	White, Charlotte (Mrs)	19, Sept 1850	L3
Elliott, Conrad B.	Chappell, M. Louisa	24, Jan. 1856	L3
Elliott, F.R.	Hopkins, Sophia	26, Feb. 1846	L3
Elliott, W.L.	Jones, Harriet E.	29, Oct. 1846	L3
Elliott, William	Perkey, Harriet	19, Oct. 1843	L3
Ellis, George L.	Collins, Hester	9, Feb. 1854	L3
Ellis, Henry	Hicks, Charlotte A.	20, July 1854	L3
Ellis, James S.	Kain, Susan	28, Apr. 1842	L3
Ellis, John	Breckenridge, S.M.	6, Oct. 1853	L3
Ellis, John W.	Lindlay, Caroline	20, Nov. 1845	L3
Ellis, Rowland	Hartshorne, Sallie J	16, Feb. 1854	L3
Ellis, Simon	Millin, Sarah	6, Apr. 1854	L3
Ellis, Thomas	Sommerville, Mary	31, July 1851	L3
Ells, John	Patterson, Eleanor K.	21, July 1842	L3
Ellsbery, Andrew (Dr)	Clark, Jane	8, May 1851	L3
Elmaker, Horace	Armstrong, Eliza M.	19, Oct. 1843	L3
Elstner, John	Rarns, Mary	14, Mar. 1823	L3
Elstner, Joseph	Sterritt, Sallie J.	23, Dec. 1852	L3
Elston, William	McKee, Emma	26, May 1842	L3
Elyea, John	Stumps, Jane	1, Mar. 1838	L3
Embich, Michael D.	Stanislaus, Catharine	22, Feb. 1855	L3
Embick, Michael D.	Pine, Matilda M.	27, Jan. 1842	L3
Embree, Jesse	Dickinson, Mary	29, Sept 1818	L2
Emerson, Allison	Walker, Hannah E.	15, June 1848	L3
Emerson, Edwin S.	Ryan, Julia	17, Apr. 1851	L3

Grooms	Brides	Date of Notice	Page
Emerson, Henry	Benbridge, Eveline	3, Jan. 1828	L1
Emerson, Natham	Barber, Catharine W.	31, Aug. 1837	L3
Emrie, J.R.	Longwell, Emma	9, Dec. 1847	L3
English, Benajah	Ross, Nancy	1, June 1819	L3
English, Mizeal	Arnold, Melinda	30, Mar. 1854	L3
English, Samuel	Trout, Susan	15, Apr. 1812	L3
Enneking, John B.	Heuer, Lizzie	15, Feb. 1855	L3
Enness, John B.	Barr, Susan	21, Aug. 1811	L3
Enness, John B.	Clingman, Susan	13, Oct. 1826	L3
Eppley, James B.	Wilson, Sophronia Z.	24, Nov. 1853	L3
Epply, Jacob	Crane, Sarah (Mrs)	2, Mar. 1848	L3
Epply, John P.	Mansur, Harriet L.	12, Sept 1844	L3
Ernest, Jacob	Swager, Elizabeth	14, June 1849	L3
Ernst, A.H.	Otis, Sarah H.	7, Oct. 1841	L3
Ernst, Andrew H.	Heffley, Elizabeth	9, June 1817	L2
Ernst, Franklin	Hopper, Jemima	27, May 1841	L3
Ernst, Jacob	McMaster, Sarah	27, Mar. 1851	L3
Erwin, J. Warner	Borden, Caroline A.	29, Aug. 1850	L3
Este, David K.	Harrison, Lucy S.	5, Oct. 1819	L3
Este, David K.	Houston, Eliza P.	9, Apr. 1840	L3
Estep, Richard	Noble, Mary F.	7, July 1842	L3
Estep, Thomas	Smith, Sarah Y.	10, Feb. 1842	L3
Eustis, William	Langdon, Caroline	17, Oct. 1810	L3
Evans, Daniel D.	Lewis, Ann Eliza	25, July 1844	L3
Evans, David	Brown, Sarah	21, Oct. 1820	L3
Evans, John	Dillon, Elizabeth	11, Oct. 1838	L3
Evans, Owen	Roe, Sallie A.	24, Dec. 1846	L3
Evans, Robert	Armstrong, Anna E.	8, May 1851	L3
Evans, William	Backus, Martha	24, Nov. 1812	L3
Evans, William L.	Sibley, Caroline	10, Apr. 1851	L3
Evens, P.	Bishop, Sophronia S.	16, June 1853	L3
Everest, B.B.	Harley, Fannie B.	15, June 1854	L3
Everett, John	Chenoweth, Laura R.	9, July 1857	L3
Everett, William H.	Broadwell, Amanda M.	23, Mar. 1837	L4
Ewing, A.H.	Baum, Mary P.	13, June 1833	L3
Ewing, James	Conn, Patty (Mrs)	5, Nov. 1808	L3
Ewing, James H	Russell, Sarah V.	25, Apr. 1844	L3
Ewing, John H.	Kimball, Augusta	11, June 1846	L3
Fabian, Robert L.	Johnston, Emily	9, Oct. 1851	L3
Fagaly, Lewis C.	Shields, Sarah A.M.	17, May 1855	L3
Fairbanks,	Miles, Polly	28, Mar. 1810	L3
Fairman, L. (Dr)	Todd, Mary L.	12, Mar. 1824	L2
Falconer, Cyrus (Dr)	Woods, Mary	17, Oct. 1839	L3
Fallon, James J	Harris, Nanny	21, June 1855	L3
Fanshaw, William D.	Higgins, M. Louise	22, July 1847	L3
Faran, James J.	Russell, Angeline	2, Apr. 1840	L3
Faries, J.C.	Garret, Martha	30, Mar. 1854	L3
Faris, Thomas	Doerrer, Rachel	7, Aug. 1845	L3
Farnham, Charles A.	Aydelotte, Margaret	30, June 1842	L3
Farnsworth, Thomas R	Thomson, Nannie H.	17, June 1852	L3
Farquhar, William P.	Sampson, Mary	10, Sept 1835	L3
Farris, Robert P.	Bowen, Eliza S.	10, Aug. 1848	L3
Faulkner, Jeremiah	Jacobs, Ann E.	26, Nov. 1840	L3

Grooms	Brides	Date of Notice	Page
Fay, Edwin D.	Chew, Elizabeth Ann	25, Sept 1851	L3
Febiger, George	Fisher, Eliza Ann	16, June 1842	L3
Febiger, George L.	Pleasants, Frances	8, Nov. 1855	L3
Febriger, George L.	Smith, Caroline A.	12, Apr. 1849	L3
Fee, William M.	Pinney, Emeliza E.	9, Oct. 1851	L3
Fenwick, David	Gregg, Eliza M.	2, Mar. 1854	L3
Ferguson, A.F.	Jolly, Ellen	26, Jan. 1854	L3
Ferguson, Abijah	Kemper, Susan M.	25, Mar. 1816	L3
Ferguson, Addison M.	Perry, Catharine	6, Feb. 1824	L3
Ferguson, Charles	Arbeguson, Mary E.	15, Oct. 1857	L3
Ferguson, E.A.	Moore, Agnes A.	25, Sept 1851	L3
Ferguson, John	Moore, Sarah J.	11, Jan. 1849	L3
Ferguson, Robert G.	Farley, Angerone	16, July 1857	L3
Ferguson, William G.	Hildreth, Eliza Jane	25, May 1848	L3
Ferris, Abraham	Wheeler, Rhoda	29, Sept 1807	L3
Ferris, E.H. (Dr)	Colbow, Frances H.	15, Nov. 1849	L3
Ferris, E.H. (Dr)	McCullough, Matilda	29, Dec. 1853	L3
Ferris, J.S.	Ewing, Martha Ann	11, Apr. 1839	L3
Ferris, John	Minshall, Mary F.	22, Apr. 1847	L3
Ferris, William J.	Bartlett, Emily	18, Apr. 1833	L3
Ferris, William J.	Brown, Eliza Ann	26, Dec. 1839	L3
Ferson, John L.	Mather, Caroline M.	26, Jan. 1854	L3
Fessenden, Benjamin	Leverett, Charlotte	3, Dec. 1829	L3
Field, Henry S.	Williams, Mary (Mrs)	11, Dec. 1851	L3
Field, Richard	Blaique, M.D.	27, Oct. 1842	L3
Field, Thomas M.(Dr)	Adair, Maria Jane	27, June 1850	L3
Field, William R.	Howard, Mary Ann	13, Sept 1827	L3
Filley, Lucius L.	Jones, Christiana	30, Mar. 1849	L3
Finch, Charles C.	Farmer, Miranda	25, Feb. 1847	L3
Finch, Joel	Saxton, Harriet S.	4, July 1844	L3
Finch, Marcus A.	Howell, Amelia F.	27, Sept 1849	L3
Finch, Pardin M.	Allen, Rebecca	13, Nov. 1845	L3
Findlay, Samuel B.	Duncan, Elizabeth	14, Dec. 1837	L3
Fine, John	Shoyer, Mary Jane	14, Oct. 1847	L3
Finley, William	Graves, Martha (Mrs)	16, Feb. 1854	L3
Fishback, O.T.	Evans, Louisa	24, May 1855	L3
Fishback, William P.	McMaine, Mary L.	22, Feb. 1855	L3
Fisher, Charles	Brigham, Julia R.	2, Nov. 1833	L2
Fisher, Daniel M.	Johnson, Sarah P.	30, Apr. 1846	L3
Fisher, David	Guion, Wealthy (Mrs)	25, Dec. 1856	L3
Fisher, George	Myers, Anna S.	16, Nov. 1854	L3
Fisher, Henry C.	Haven, Caroline S.	6, July 1848	L3
Fisher, Homer	Williamson, Orphia E	15, Jan. 1857	L3
Fisher, John W.	Day, Mary E.	28, Feb. 1850	L3
Fisher, Mirza	Bolls, Emeline	1, Feb. 1828	L1
Fisher, Robert I.	Jameson, Catharine	4, Feb. 1836	L2
Fisher, Samuel S.	Crossett, Aurelia	16, Oct. 1856	L5
Fisher, William L.	Reynolds, Sarah	27, Dec. 1814	L3
Fisher, William M.	Elstner, Louise	9, Sept 1852	L3
Fisk, John F.	Johnson, Elizabeth S	20, Oct. 1842	L3
Fitz, Rudolph H.	Howard, Elmina F.	28, May 1857	L3
Flagg, Jared B.	Montague, Sarah R.	20, Jan. 1842	L3
Flagg, William J.	Longworth, Eliza	29, Aug. 1850	L3
Flake, Aaron	Tharp, Polly	24, Oct. 1810	L3

Grooms	Brides	Date of Notice	Page
Flemming, William J.	Allen, Mary	26, Dec. 1823	L3
Fletcher, Addison C.	Fuller, Lizzie F.	13, Apr. 1854	L3
Fletcher, Calvin	Munroe, Bernice	12, Aug. 1816	L2
Flinn, Jesse	Wilson, Sarah Ann	22, Apr. 1847	L3
Florer, Robert C.	Rand, Emeline	21, Feb. 1839	L3
Flynt, H.S.	Hulburd, Helen M.	13, Oct. 1853	L3
Folger, Charles R.	Brown, Jane D.	1, Oct. 1840	L3
Follin, Augustus	Reeder, Caroline A.	16, Sept 1847	L3
Folsom, Samuel	Davis, Sophia	2, Dec. 1847	L3
Foot, Joseph	Hardesty, Rebeckah	28, Dec. 1813	L3
Foote, Andrew R.	Ware, Abigail	21, Sept 1837	L3
Foote, Charles B.	Hall, Sarah E.	10, Apr. 1851	L3
Foote, H.E. (Dr)	Agniel, Louise	22, May 1851	L3
Foote, T.M. (Dr)	Wilkeson, Julia (Mrs)	19, June 1851	L3
Forbes, James	Hall, Mary	20, Mar. 1856	L3
Forbes, Joseph	Crooks, Margaret	30, Nov. 1813	L3
Ford, Samuel	Brown, Ellen	10, May 1855	L3
Ford, Smith	Fox, Frances L.	24, June 1847	L3
Fording, Christopher	Hutchinson, Casandra	28, June 1814	L3
Fordney, Beates	Seaman, Mary Ann (Mrs)	16, Oct. 1845	L3
Fore, P.G. (Dr)	Moore, Emeline	12, Dec. 1839	L3
Foree, Thomas P.	Ball, Ann P.	17, Feb. 1848	L3
Forker, James	Link, Jane	5, Aug. 1847	L3
Forl, James	McCray, Emeline	26, Jan. 1854	L3
Forrer, Samuel	Howard, Sarah H.	10, Feb. 1826	L3
Forshey, C.C.	Williams, Martha	7, Sept 1843	L3
Forster, Thomas G.	Clingman, Laura M.	3, Oct. 1844	L3
Fortman, Harman	Duncan, Margaret	9, May 1844	L3
Fosdick, Charles R.	Bingham, Fannie S.	13, Oct. 1853	L3
Fosdick, Henry H.	Goldson, Margaret K.	30, Jan. 1845	L3
Fosdick, Henry N.	Harkness, Harriet	4, Feb. 1836	L2
Fosdick, Sylvester L	Raymond, Harriet R.	19, May 1821	L3
Fosdick, William	Tiley, Amelia Ann	16, Sept 1841	L3
Foster, A.M.	Sawain, M. Louise	27, Nov. 1851	L3
Foster, David	Allen, Martha Ann	16, Sept 1852	L3
Foster, Francis F.	Follett, Eliza W.	30, Mar. 1854	L3
Foster, Horton J.	Hawes, Mercy Ann	24, June 1852	L3
Foster, J.G.	Sanders, Emily F.	20, Mar. 1851	L3
Foster, J.G.	Shepperd, Mary E.	20, Sept 1855	L3
Foster, James	Bargelt, Susannah	28, May 1846	L3
Foster, N. (Dr)	Lytle, Josephine R.	28, Apr. 1853	L3
Foster, Thomas W.	Burford, M.J.	31, Dec. 1857	L3
Foster, William S.	Stratton, Catharine	15, Sept 1853	L3
Foulds, Thomas H.	Hubbell, Mary E.	15, Sept 1853	L3
Foulger, Seth	Clasby, Lydia	14, Apr. 1820	L3
Foulks, George W.	Manning, Jemima	28, Oct. 1847	L3
Fowler, John	Sharp, S. Caroline	26, Aug. 1847	L3
Fox, Charles	Miller, Mary	10, Dec. 1824	L2
Fox, James	White, Margaret Ann	2, Oct. 1856	L5
Francis, Thomas	Preston, Mary Ann	31, Aug. 1843	L3
Francisco, Albert N.	Covert, Minverva T.	19, Dec. 1844	L3
Franklin, John	DeForrest, Julia	4, Apr. 1826	L3
Franklin, William	Smith, Mary Eliza	16, Sept 1841	L3
Fraser, Alexander J.	Miles, Pamela E.	9, June 1853	L3

Grooms	Brides	Date of Notice	Page
Fraser, Volney J.	Brickell, Lydia Ann	31, Apr. 1845	L3
Frazer, D.M. (Dr)	Clarke, Minerva J.	21, Aug. 1845	L3
Frazer, James A.	McCormick, Elizabeth	15, June 1848	L3
Frazer, John	Fletcher, Rosanna B.	22, May 1845	L3
Frazier, A.S.	Stewart, Hannah	26, Dec. 1844	L3
Frazier, Alexander	Ludlow, Eliza	4, Sept 1845	L3
Free, A.C.	Kirby, Emily R.	19, Mar. 1857	L3
Freeman, W.D.	Shaw, Margaret S.	9, Aug. 1855	L3
French, Cornelius R.	Browne, Esther	23, Aug. 1809	L2
French, J.H.	Smith, Kate C.	22, Sept 1853	L3
French, William H.	Stacy, Mary Elizabeth	1, Nov. 1849	L3
Fries, Silvester	Leibee, Selone (Mrs)	20, Nov. 1845	L3
Frintz, Michael	Munroe, Cornelia A.	19, Aug. 1847	L3
Fristoe, J.W.	Mason, Mary E.	9, Aug. 1855	L3
Frizzell, Hugh W.	Slayback, Hannah W.	20, July 1854	L3
Froome, Samuel	Redhead, Jane	10, Dec. 1840	L3
Frost, George W.	Stevens, Angelina A.	13, Jan. 1853	L3
Fry, Benjamin St.	Baldwin, Eliza N.	23, Sept 1852	L3
Fry, J. Reese	Nevens, Cornelia	17, June 1841	L3
Fuller, George S.	Truesdale, Mary L.	23, Oct. 1856	L5
Fuller, John W.	Peck, Delia	30, Sept 1847	L3
Fuller, Robert C.	Martin, Laura Attila	22, Apr. 1847	L3
Fuller, William F.	Gorden, Amelia W.	18, Aug. 1842	L3
Fullerton, William R	Lyon, Fanny Cornelia	7, Aug. 1851	L3
Fulton, Alexander	Bullitt, Sally	4, Oct. 1809	L3
Fulweiler, John	Moore, Frances Ann	20, Dec. 1838	L3
Funk, Henry B.	Johnston, Eliza (Mrs)	4, Apr. 1839	L3
Furnas, Robert W.	McComas, Mary E.	6, Nov. 1845	L3
Gabriel, Edwin T.	Patton, Philinda	10, Jan. 1839	L3
Gaddis, Maxwell P.	Parrott, Josephine	17, May 1849	L3
Gaff, John	Kelly, Anna S.	5, Nov. 1857	L3
Gaines, E.P. (Gen)	Whitney, Myra C. (Mrs)	16, May 1839	L3
Gaines, Henry	Carson, Achsah Jane	22, Apr. 1847	L3
Gaines, Richard	Cheney, Clarinda	2, May 1844	L3
Galbreath, James	Howells, Lucy S.	11, Jan. 1855	L3
Gallagher, F.R. (Dr)	Fingland, Maggie	5, July 1855	L3
Gallagher, George W.	Baker, Clara P.	15, Feb. 1849	L3
Gallagher, George W.	Hall, Julia A.	27, Nov. 1845	L3
Gallagher, John M.	Cushing, Hannah L.	16, Oct. 1834	L2
Gallagher, Phillip	Burnham, Mary Sayre	21, Jan. 1847	L3
Gallagher, Thomas J.	Collins, Mary E.	30, Dec. 1847	L3
Gallagher, William	Doughty, Matilda	26, Nov. 1857	L3
Gallespie, Philander	Parker, Lizzie	23, Nov. 1854	L3
Galway, William	Borden, Mary E.	27, Aug. 1857	L3
Galy, Andrew	Fountain, Charlotte	17, July 1845	L3
Gano, Aaron	Burley, Frances	20, May 1818	L2
Gano, Aaron G.	Storer, Sophia	25, July 1844	L3
Gano, Charles L.	Harkness, Jane	30, Nov. 1843	L3
Gano, Daniel	Lawrence, Rebecca	30, Sept 1816	L3
Gano, Daniel, Jr.	Price, Margaret S.	13, Apr. 1848	L3
Gano, Gazzam	Stewart, Hannah	28, July 1853	L3
Gano, Howell	Wilshire, Elizabeth	20, Apr. 1848	L3
Gano, John S.	Bastable, Mary Jane	11, Mar. 1841	L3

Grooms	Brides	Date of Notice	Page
Gano, Stephen	French, Sarah L.F.	10, May 1855	L3
Gant, John	Hewes, Tabitha	8, Dec. 1812	L3
Gard, Benjamin M.	Ward, Julia M.	10, Dec. 1857	L3
Gardener, Lafayette	Robinson, Isabella	30, Oct. 1851	L3
Gardiner, J.B. (Dr)	Fontaine, Susan (Mrs)	28, Apr. 1842	L3
Gardner, Colin	Hemphill, Jane (Mrs)	12, July 1849	L3
Gardner, James	Walker, Rebecca	8, Jan. 1857	L3
Gardner, Richard	Sisson, Mary	4, Aug. 1817	L3
Gardner, William J.	Craig, Elizabeth J.	24, May 1849	L3
Garesche, Alexander	VanZandt, Laura C.	10, May 1849	L3
Garrard, Jeptha D.	Ludlow, Sarabella	20, Aug. 1824	L3
Garrard, William	Howe, Bella	5, Mar. 1857	L3
Garrett, Charles R.	Conn, Virginia V.	12, May 1853	L3
Garrett, E.J.	Smith, Mary	26, May 1842	L3
Garrison, D.L.	Richards, Mary E.	10, May 1855	L3
Garrison, John W.	Handy, Margaret A.	6, Nov. 1845	L3
Gartrell, Charles H.	Finch, Ella F.	31, Jan. 1856	L3
Gartzell, Henry C.	Pogue, Lida J.	3, Nov. 1853	L3
Garwood, Nicholas	Rollin, Mary A.	17, June 1847	L3
Gaskill, John C.	Singer, Catharine	2, Jan. 1845	L3
Gassaway, David	Crane, Anna	13, Nov. 1851	L3
Gassaway, George	McEwen, Olivia J.	24, July 1851	L3
Gassaway, Henry C.	Allen, Elizabeth	19, Sept 1844	L3
Gaston, Isaac N.	Henry, S. Cornelia	12, June 1851	L3
Gatch, Francis M.	Barber, Salina	9, Jan. 1851	L3
Gatch, Thomas (Capt)	Barber, Sarah	26, Apr. 1814	L3
Gatchell, Horatio (Dr)	Crane, Anna Maria	1, Dec. 1842	L3
Gatton, Zachariah	Miller, Sarah K.	15, Apr. 1847	L3
Gaylord, Thomas G.	Groesbeck, Lucy S.	8, May 1851	L3
Gebhart, Isaac	Price, Martha W.	12, Jan. 1854	L3
Geisendorff, Conrad	Smith, Sarah H.	18, Jan. 1855	L3
Gemeny, R.D.	Kesley, Margaret	10, Sept 1846	L3
Gengembre, H.P.	Doisy, Charlotte E.	19, June 1851	L3
Gest, Andrew M.	Fish, Sarah B. (Mrs)	16, Mar. 1848	L3
Gest, Jonas C.	Hollis, Harriet B.	26, Sept 1844	L3
Gest, Joseph J.	Bailey, Sue A.	8, Feb. 1855	L3
Gettier, George	Coffman, Mary	21, Oct. 1820	L3
Getz, John	Cochrane, Mary Ann	22, Feb. 1838	L3
Gibbons, Joseph G.	Carpenter, Anna M.	29, Jan. 1852	L3
Gibbs, Edward G.	Kelpan, Mary Jane	14, Oct. 1841	L3
Gibbs, Ira B.	Clark, Margaret M.	15, June 1848	L3
Gibbs, William F.	Eaton, Eliza Ann	17, Mar. 1836	L3
Gibson, Alexander	Greene, Eliza S.	14, Nov. 1844	L3
Gibson, Henry H.	Miller, Mary A.	13, Oct. 1853	L3
Gibson, James E.	Carlisle, Antoinette	15, Oct. 1857	L3
Gibson, Stephen	VanZant, Martha (Mrs)	22, Mar. 1855	L3
Gibson, Thomas	Graham, Florilla	26, June 1845	L3
Gibson, William	McCormick, Anne	29, Apr. 1852	L3
Gilbert, A.W.	Richards, Elizabeth A.	25, May 1848	L3
Gilbert, Samuel E.	Manson, Cordelia F.	19, Aug. 1847	L3
Gilbert, Thomas	Kelley, Elizabeth	19, June 1845	L3
Giles, Benjamin	Longshore, Rachel C.	4, Nov. 1847	L3
Gill, William	Cushing, Lucie W.	6, Apr. 1854	L3
Gillespie, George D.	Lathrop, Rebecca P.	5, June 1845	L3

Grooms	Brides	Date of Notice	Page
Gillet, P.G.	Phipps, E.M.	11, May 1854	L3
Gillett, G.W. (Rev)	Wharton, Marianne	8, June 1848	L3
Gilman, William	Stearnes, Bulah Ann	6, Mar. 1845	L3
Gilmore, George W.	Martin, Clara	28, Mar. 1850	L3
Gilmore, Gurdon R.	Butler, Melvina	13, Sept 1838	L3
Gilmore, James	Stibb, Mary Jane	21, July 1842	L3
Giraldin, Charles	Higgins, Ellen	6, Mar. 1851	L3
Girton, John	Butterworth, Edith	24, Feb. 1848	L3
Gist, Robert C.	Dosey, Mary	18, Jan. 1832	L4
Gitchell, Joseph R.	Collins, Caroline	8, Feb. 1849	L3
Givens, D.A.	Keler, Margaret	28, June 1855	L3
Glancy, Harvey M.	Death, Hannah Jane	7, Sept 1854	L3
Glass, William	Lape, Elizabeth	14, Apr. 1821	L3
Glenn, Isaac Drake	Hays, Jane	21, Feb. 1850	L3
Glenn, James	Sayre, Ann	20, May 1820	L3
Glezen, Eben K.	Gilbert, Abby T.	22, June 1843	L3
Glidden, D.A.	Robinson, Mary Ellen	24, Aug. 1848	L3
Goddard, John F.	Daniel, Mary L.V.	7, Sept 1837	L3
Godden, Edward	Smart, Mary W.	23, May 1844	L3
Godley, George H.	Smith, Carrie B.	24, Dec. 1857	L3
Godley, John	McHenry, Mary	28, June 1820	L3
Goepper, Leopold	Pendry, Susan B.	23, Dec. 1852	L3
Goforth, Poole	Gordon, Dolly E.	16, Sept 1825	L3
Goheen, Charles	Certain, Mary	11, July 1850	L3
Golding, Aaron	Garrish, Sophia	6, Mar. 1822	L3
Golding, Robert J.	Steele, Lydia Ann	5, Nov. 1846	L3
Goldson, George	Markland, Matilda	6, Nov. 1845	L3
Gomez, Eusebio J.	Flash, Sarah J.	4, Jan. 1849	L3
Gooch, Henry	Stoddart, Clarissa	3, June 1841	L3
Gooch, John S.	Oldrieve, Prothesia	16, June 1853	L3
Good, John	Cooke, Helen M.	17, May 1849	L3
Good, Robert	Kelly, Susan A.	14, Nov. 1839	L1
Goode, John F.	Walton, Elizabeth	9, Feb. 1854	L3
Goodhue, G.W.	Graves, Elizabeth S.	6, May 1847	L3
Goodhue, William	Knoblaugh, Margaret	20, Sept 1849	L3
Goodin, Samuel H.	Green, Ellen	24, Sept 1840	L3
Goodlett, Nicholas	Mitchell, Melinda	16, Feb. 1854	L3
Goodman, Frank	Foster, Alice H.	20, Mar. 1851	L3
Goodman, John S.	Price, Mary	9, Oct. 1851	L3
Goodman, Moses	Foster, Sallie C.	1, Apr. 1852	L3
Goodman, Timothy S.	Shipman, Julia E.	19, Oct. 1848	L3
Goodman, W. Augustus	Grandin, Lucy A.	15, July 1847	L3
Gordon, Goerge (Col)	Werner, Ellen Agnes	16, June 1836	L3
Gordon, James	Gray, Catharine	9, Feb. 1854	L3
Gore, John H.	Morehead, Lucy A.	24, Sept 1846	L3
Gorham, William F.	Daggett, Eliza Jane	22, Apr. 1847	L3
Gorman, Jonathan H.	Harris, Rosetta	22, Oct. 1857	L3
Goshing, Samuel M.	Smith, Susan M.	9, Nov. 1848	L3
Goshorn, James M.	Carnahan, Margaret K.	13, Aug. 1846	L3
Gosling, George	Weibling, Clarissa C	6, Mar. 1845	L3
Gossin, Benjamin F.	Hillhouse, Susan	10, July 1845	L3
Gossin, Henry	Bowman, Catharine	3, Nov. 1821	L3
Gotchell, Alfred	Richardson, Rosetta	19, Mar. 1857	L3
Gould, John	Stone, Eunice Ann	7, Oct. 1847	L3

Grooms	Brides	Date of Notice	Page
Gould, John P.	Brooks, Caroline	5, June 1845	L3
Gould, Levi G.	Vanausdol, Emily	25, Jan. 1855	L3
Gould, Thomas	Johnson, Peggy	16, May 1810	L3
Grace, John William	Heaslett, Ruth A.	9, Sept 1841	L3
Graham, James	Neville, Cornelia	17, Oct. 1844	L3
Graham, Thomas	Symmes, Elizabeth (Mrs)	5, Oct. 1819	L3
Graham, William A.	VanHamm, Sarah	3, June 1847	L3
Grames, C.W.	Bureau, Emelia R.	28, Aug. 1851	L3
Granger, John L.	Iddings, Eliza (Mrs)	7, July 1842	L3
Grant, Charles	Collier, Emma C.	15, June 1848	L3
Grant, Edward B.	Duval, Cornelia	26, Apr. 1855	L3
Grant, John H.	Swearingen, Ellen	21, Nov. 1844	L3
Graves, James M.	Graves, Sarah Jane	27, May 1841	L3
Graves, Joseph A.	Harrison, Anne C.	8, Dec. 1842	L3
Gray, Alfred W.	Bradbury, Elmira	28, Mar. 1850	L3
Gray, J. Presley	Hoyt, Louise	11, Dec. 1856	L3
Gray, Robert	Huie, Mary	12, Apr. 1855	L3
Gray, Robert P.	Clark, Lucinda W.	2, Feb. 1854	L3
Gray, Robert P.	Denman, Elizabeth	10, Apr. 1851	L3
Greatwood, G.	Oakes, (Miss)	25, Sept 1811	L3
Green, George	Dilse, Jane	13, Mar. 1845	L3
Green, George	Hoover, Lucy	24, Dec. 1840	L3
Green, Jared B.	Corson, Henrietta	21, June 1855	L3
Green, John K.	Stewart, Jane T.	11, Nov. 1841	L3
Green, John W.	Smith, Martha M.	24, Feb. 1848	L3
Green, Samuel F.	Volander, Frances	17, Jan. 1850	L3
Green, Stephen A.	Lovejoy, Mary	10, June 1847	L3
Green, William N.	Stockwell, Elizabeth B.	26, Nov. 1840	L3
Greene, Caleb	Tunis, Caroline	15, Oct. 1840	L3
Greene, Williard L.	Stone, Annes	18, Sept 1845	L3
Greer, William P.	Armstrong, Theodosia	11, Mar. 1847	L3
Gregg, Stephen	Williamson, Harriet	15, Apr. 1812	L3
Greggory, David (Rev)	Bury, Elizabeth	5, Feb. 1852	L3
Gregory, Francis H.	Holibird, Caroline S.	5, July 1849	L3
Gregory, Uriah	Sprague, Maria B.	29, Nov. 1849	L3
Gridley, Ethan S.	Anderson, Mary	3, Oct. 1850	L3
Grieves, John G.	Longley, Amanda	11, Mar. 1847	L3
Griffin, David	Griffing, Mary	23, Apr. 1846	L3
Griffin, John	Ottenheimer, Louisa	3, Sept 1846	L3
Griffith, A.R.	White, Elemina	2, Aug. 1855	L3
Griffith, James	McDaniel, Mary Ann	26, Dec. 1810	L3
Griffith, Romulus R.	Meriweather, L. (Mrs)	1, June 1848	L3
Griffith, Romulus R.	Merriwether, Rachel	29, June 1827	L3
Griffiths, Romulus R	Meriweather, Louisa	25, May 1848	L3
Grimes, Alexander	Gordon, Bell Frances	7, July 1817	L2
Groat, Francis	Anderson, M.	18, Apr. 1844	L3
Groesbeck, Abraham	Burnham, Ann Eliza	10, Sept 1846	L3
Groesbeck, Herman J.	Benoist, Rosina E.	19, Oct. 1837	L3
Groesbeck, William S	Burnet, Elizabeth	9, Nov. 1837	L4
Grover, George W.	Andrews, Hepza Dana	30, May 1844	L3
Groves, William J.	Beall, Margaret	17, Sept 1846	L3
Grow, William S.	Thomas, Martha M.	2, Dec. 1847	L3
Grubbs, William B.	Coleman, Lizzie	27, Dec. 1855	L3
Grundy, R.C. (Rev)	Kemper, E. Suzette	1, June 1848	L3

Grooms	Brides	Date of Notice	Page
Guelich, Lewis	Phillips, Mary A.	21, Oct. 1852	L3
Guibert, Ben. J.	Norris, Fannie	20, Oct. 1853	L3
Guiou, Benjamin	Wright, Eliza S.	11, May 1843	L3
Guiteau, John Wilson	Tyner, Missouri	22, Jan. 1857	L3
Gunn, John C.	Jarnagin, Clarissa H	30, Apr. 1835	L2
Guthrie, Benjamin F.	Pearce, Amelia J.	26, Oct. 1848	L3
Guthrie, Charles W.	Ewing, Mary L.	30, Mar. 1854	L3
Guthrie, M.W.	VandeWater, Maria	2, June 1853	L3
Guthrie, Robert	McKee, Kate	2, May 1850	L3
Guy, Alexander	Wade, Susan A.L.	31, Mar. 1830	L3
Guzsi, John R.	McKim, Emma	12, Mar. 1846	L3
Gwathmey, Alfred	Keats, Georgiana	28, Oct. 1847	L3
Gwin, Evan	Field, Nancy	27, May 1847	L3
Gwynne, David (Major)	Talbert, Sophia	13, Feb. 1845	L3
Hackleman, John	Adams, Sally	24, Oct. 1810	L3
Hackley, James M.	Wells, Rebecca	5, May 1817	L3
Hadley, Milton E.	Phillips, Jane	6, Apr. 1854	L3
Hafer, Henry	Schwartz, Charlotte	30, Jan. 1824	L2
Hagan, Marcelus B.	Lewis, Almira	18, Sept 1851	L3
Haggott, John P.(Dr)	McAroy, Mary B.	9, Nov. 1837	L3
Hahn, Paul F.	Mansell, Alice M.	6, Mar. 1845	L3
Haile, Andrew J.	Smith, Lucy A.	19, May 1842	L3
Haines, Amos	Carr, Angeline	16, Mar. 1854	L3
Haines, Amos	Whetstone, Mary	10, Aug. 1813	L3
Haines, Josiah	Marsh, Lydia	10, Feb. 1821	L3
Haire, E.	Wright, Mary M.	10, June 1852	L3
Halderman, W.N.	Metcalf, Elizabeth	7, Nov. 1844	L3
Hale, William B.	Parker, Jennie	13, Sept 1855	L3
Hales, Charles	Lewis, Margaretha H.	7, June 1849	L3
Hall, Dudley	Vincent, Hannah M.	22, Nov. 1855	L3
Hall, Henry E.	White, Elizabeth E.	12, Jan. 1854	L3
Hall, James	Alexander, Mary (Mrs)	12, Sept 1839	L3
Hall, John	Dunseth, Ann	26, Mar. 1846	L3
Hall, John C.	Dicks, Cornelia	7, Dec. 1843	L3
Hall, John C.	Faulkner, Sarah Ann	7, Oct. 1841	L3
Hall, Joseph	Caswell, Margaretta	15, Dec. 1842	L5
Hall, Mitchell	Seymour, C. Jane	6, June 1850	L3
Hall, Richard M.	Brooks, Clara B.	4, June 1857	L3
Hall, Samuel W.	Haines, Sarah M.	5, July 1849	L3
Hall, William	Kinkaid, Mary	19, May 1853	L3
Halley, David J.	Betts, Mary	8, Apr. 1812	L3
Halley, Samuel B.	Hathaway, Harriet	11, Nov. 1841	L3
Halsey, D.W.	Budd, Sally J.	13, July 1854	L3
Halstead, John	Marsh, Ann (Mrs)	10, Jan. 1823	L3
Halsted, M.	Banks, Mary V.	5, Mar. 1857	L3
Halverstaty, William	Wolf, Christiana	30, Mar. 1854	L3
Hamilton, James	Hunt, Margaret	8, Aug. 1810	L3
Hamilton, John	Gatch, Jenny	1, Nov. 1855	L3
Hamilton, John	Harrison, Cordelia	13, Oct. 1853	L3
Hamilton, Milton	Piatt, Nancy	21, Feb. 1850	L3
Hamilton, Turner	Jackson, Kate	11, Aug. 1853	L3
Hamlen, Shephard (Dr)	Valentine, Elizabeth	20, Nov. 1850	L3
Hamlin, Henry H.	Flagg, Mary E.	12, Jan. 1854	L3

Grooms	Brides	Date of Notice	Page
Hamm, John	Mount, Louisa	14, July 1853	L3
Hammill, J.R.	Bratton, Mary E.	16, Feb. 1854	L3
Hammond, Andrew	Henderson, Eliza	24, Aug. 1837	L3
Hammond, Robert H.	Woods, Martha J.	23, Feb. 1854	L3
Hammond, Smallwood C	Moorhead, Elizabeth B.	14, Jan. 1836	L4
Hancint, David	Bellows, Mary	8, Dec. 1836	L3
Hancock, John	Jones, Elizabeth	9, Aug. 1855	L3
Hand, Amos	Gour, Lumy	11, Aug. 1817	L3
Hand, Ellis	Evans, Ellen S.	27, May 1847	L3
Hand, George R.	Scudder, Sarah L.	28, Jan. 1841	L3
Handy, F.H.	Davenport, Serena B.	1, Mar. 1849	L3
Handy, R.J.H.	Cummings, Eliza	15, Feb. 1844	L3
Handy, Robert D.	Torrence, Eliza Jane	24, Apr. 1851	L3
Handy, Truman	Blakeslee, Marietta	24, Oct. 1850	L3
Hankins, William J.	Morris, Belle	18, Nov. 1852	L3
Hanks, Albert S.	Jungman, Anna S.	6, May 1847	L3
Hanks, George L.	Bunce, Julia A.	19, May 1836	L2
Hann, George W.	Robinson, Margaret B	16, Sept 1847	L3
Hannaford, John W.	Peck, Harriet J.	27, Aug. 1857	L3
Hannaford, Roger	Wardle, Susan F.	3, Jan. 1856	L3
Hannaford, W.M.	Ballard, Anne R.	21, Feb. 1850	L3
Hansalman, Christian	Hansalman, Christena	28, Mar. 1823	L3
Hansell, Wm. F.(Rev)	Niles, Cornelia	8, Feb. 1855	L3
Harbaugh, H.M.	Hales, Mary A.	9, May 1839	L3
Harberson, Robert W.	Stapley, Elizabeth	2, May 1844	L3
Harbeson, Matthew L.	Morris, Jane	20, Oct. 1831	L1
Harce, Robert	McCorkle, Polly	17, Aug. 1813	L3
Hard, Edward	Duncan, Hattie M.	26, July 1855	L3
Hardesty, Samuel	Emily, Nancy Ann	22, Dec. 1842	L3
Harding, Joseph C.	Baldwin, Cornelia A.	10, Oct. 1850	L3
Harding, Lyman	Shepherd, Mary P.C.	12, Jan. 1837	L3
Harding, William H.	Immel, Harriet	18, Dec. 1845	L3
Hardy, John C. (Dr)	Swan, Lucie G.	15, Jan. 1852	L3
Hare, John P.	Brown, Elizabeth	6, Apr. 1854	L3
Hargan, James	Simns, Esther Ann	31, Oct. 1850	L3
Harkness, Charles	Harkness, Eliza A.	6, July 1843	L3
Harkness, H.	Baker, Louise	17, Aug. 1854	L3
Harkness, William	Odell, Aurora S.	21, Sept 1848	L3
Harmar, Josiah	Lanman, Sarah Coit	21, Oct. 1830	L3
Harning, Hilesy	Grice, Susan	16, Feb. 1854	L3
Harp, David	Smith, Harriet	28, Oct. 1847	L3
Harper, James S.	McMillan, Mollie E.	7, Aug. 1856	L5
Harran, John	McCauley, Mary Jane	11, Feb. 1847	L3
Harrington, James S.	Spalding, Caroline C	18, Feb. 1847	L3
Harris, Caleb K.	Davis, Mary Jane	19, Nov. 1846	L3
Harris, Daniel	Salvin, Elizabeth T.	2, Sept 1852	L3
Harris, Edward	James, Sarah	27, Oct. 1842	L3
Harris, John W.	Jackson, Alice Ann	28, Jan. 1841	L3
Harris, Thomas M. (Dr)	Miller, Elizabeth	3, Mar. 1836	L2
Harris, Timothy (Rev)	Linnel, Sarah	13, Sept 1809	L3
Harris, William	Stuart, Mary	3, Mar. 1842	L3
Harrison, George	Reynolds, Rebecca	14, Jan. 1820	L3
Harrison, George W.	Davis, Maria Louisa	18, Dec. 1845	L3
Harrison, George W.	Morrison, Ann E. (Mrs)	18, Apr. 1839	L3

Grooms	Brides	Date of Notice	Page
Harrison, Gustavus	Moss, Minerva	20, Mar. 1851	L3
Harrison, Henry	St.Clair, Margaret	30, Sept 1841	L3
Harrison, Henry B.	Gibson, Sarah Elizabeth	11, Feb. 1847	L3
Harrison, Hiram	Baker, Margaret Anne	17, Sept 1846	L3
Harrison, J. Findlay	Alston, Caroline W.	28, Sept 1848	L3
Harrison, J.C.S.	Pike, Clarissa B.	5, Oct. 1819	L3
Harrison, John Pitts	Merrie, Mary Ann	24, May 1838	L3
Harrison, John Scott	Irwin, Elizabeth R.	18, Aug. 1831	L3
Harrison, John Scott	Johnson, Lucretia K.	31, Dec. 1824	L3
Harrison, Lerner B.	Goodman, Fanny M.	9, June 1853	L3
Harrison, Livingston	Pierson, Mary R.	26, Oct. 1822	L3
Harrison, W.H.	Torrence, Mary P.	3, July 1845	L3
Harrison, William H.	Irwin, Jane Findlay	9, Mar. 1824	L3
Harrold, William	Jones, Margaret	8, June 1843	L3
Harsha, Thomas F.	Lumley, Sarah	25, July 1844	L3
Harshberger, Jacob	Short, M.E.	26, Jan. 1854	L3
Hart, Henry N.	Church, Jane Elizabeth	4, Oct. 1838	L3
Hart, Henry R.	Dodd, Mary E.	15, June 1848	L3
Hart, Matthew	Moreland, Mary Ann	12, Feb. 1846	L3
Hart, Samuel	Pugh, Mary A.	10, June 1841	L3
Hart, William	Saffin, Susan L.	24, Oct. 1850	L3
Harter, L.F.	Williams, Catharine	12, July 1849	L3
Hartgrove, Nelson	McMillen, Catharine	26, May 1842	L3
Hartpense, Isaac	Meginnis, Margaret	23, Feb. 1837	L4
Hartshorn, James	Davis, Sarah	4, May 1822	L3
Hartwell, A.C.L.	Chaloner, Ann E.	19, Dec. 1844	L3
Hartwell, J. William	Baymiller, Mary T.	27, Nov. 1845	L3
Hartwell, J.W.	Athearn, Abia B.	2, Nov. 1837	L3
Hartwell, John W.	Oliver, Elizabeth T.	4, Mar. 1847	L3
Hartwell, Shattuck	Mussey, Catharine S.	2, Aug. 1849	L3
Harvey, George	Morten, Tabitha A.	23, Mar. 1843	L3
Harvey, James M.	South, Amanda	27, Feb. 1851	L3
Harvey, Thomas	Abernathy, Betsey	24, Oct. 1810	L3
Harvie, Charles S.	Kramer, Clarion W.	8, June 1843	L3
Harwood, William S.	Horsley, Martha A.	8, Sept 1853	L3
Haskins, Charles	Raphael, Adelaide	1, July 1847	L3
Hasluck, D.S.	VanDyke, Fidelia R.	9, June 1842	L3
Hastings, John L.	Tendell, Charlotte	30, Jan. 1845	L3
Hastings, Lanford W.	Tolar, Charlotte C.	22, Feb. 1849	L3
Hatch, George	Avery, Rachel (Mrs)	9, May 1839	L3
Hatch, William S.	Cooper, Rebecca J.	27, July 1848	L3
Hatfield, David T.	Ayres, Sarah	13, July 1848	L3
Hatfield, George	Trousdale, Hannah	13, Sept 1849	L3
Hatfield, George	Backheuser, Mary	30, Oct. 1856	L5
Hathaway, Curtis B.J	Colby, Lydia D.	26, June 1845	L3
Hathaway, Eleazer	Abbott, Rachel	27, July 1822	L3
Hathaway, Henry	Corn, Lydia	21, Mar. 1821	L3
Hathaway, Henry, Jr.	Hubbell, Jane	6, Mar. 1827	L3
Hauk, Columbus B.	Norton, Joanna	8, Feb. 1844	L3
Haven, Augustus	Longmoor, Ellen	1, Nov. 1849	L3
Haven, Charles H.	Thatcher, Julia Ann	9, Apr. 1846	L3
Haven, James L.	Paddack, Rebecca	4, July 1850	L3
Haven, Langdon H.	Symmes, Elizabeth	4, Dec. 1845	L3
Hawekotte, Henry	Wallace, Sarah E.	13, Nov. 1856	L3

Grooms	Brides	Date of Notice	Page
Hawes, Dan	Pile, Josephine S.	22, Oct. 1846	L3
Hawie, Charles S.	Cramer, Clarion M.	8, June 1843	L3
Hawkins, David	Conklin, Annie M.	9, July 1857	L3
Hawkins, Theobald E.	Munday, Mary A.	7, Dec. 1854	L3
Hawkins, William	Magee, Catharine	8, Oct. 1857	L3
Hawn, Emanuel	Colvin, Hannah (Mrs)	29, Sept 1842	L3
Hawpe, George(Major)	Wilson, Rebecca	21, Nov. 1844	L3
Haws, J.M. (Capt)	Southgate, Maria J.	5, Feb. 1857	L3
Hawthorne, Lee Roy	Smith, J. Loue	3, Jan. 1856	L3
Hay, Joseph	Machett, Sophia A.	15, Dec. 1842	L5
Hayden, Alfred	Burley, Esther B.	8, June 1827	L3
Hayes, Samuel	Blockson, Mary Ann	7, Feb. 1839	L3
Hayford, William H.	Bushnell, Hannah V.	4, July 1850	L3
Hayman, H.C.	Castner, Jane	24, Sept 1846	L3
Hayne, B.J. (Dr)	Hawes, Olivia (Mrs)	1, Apr. 1852	L3
Hays, Nelson B.	Blackiston, Rachel A	20, May 1847	L3
Hays, R.B.	Webb, Lucy W.	6, Jan. 1853	L3
Haywood, Samuel M.	Bennett, Eliza M.	18, Mar. 1847	L3
Hazen, Alfred W.	Camp, Elizabeth	16, Sept 1847	L3
Hazen, Theodore S.	McAlee, Mary A.	12, Jan. 1854	L3
Hazen, William L.	Mills, Julia L.	4, Nov. 1847	L3
Hazlett, John	Noble, Sarah Jane	9, Nov. 1848	L3
Hazzard, John F.	Tyner, Louisiana	3, Mar. 1853	L3
Head, James Edward	Smith, Mary Jane N.	29, July 1847	L3
Healy, Jesse	Ray, Ann W.	17, Oct. 1844	L3
Heard, J. Wilson	McCracken, Sarah	12, Aug. 1841	L3
Hearn, Beverly	Joiner, Pennie	27, June 1810	L3
Heaver, William	Ross, Margaret (Mrs)	25, Feb. 1847	L3
Heckewelder, Thomas	Sayre, Polly	27, Feb. 1811	L3
Hedges, Clayborn	Drennan, Sarah J. (Mrs)	11, Feb. 1847	L3
Heferman, Thomas N.	Zebold, Mary E.	14, Oct. 1852	L3
Hefley, Isaac	Butler, Ann Augusta	19, Jan. 1837	L3
Heighway, A.E. (Dr)	Culbertson, Josephine	7, Dec. 1854	L3
Heighway, S. Mercer	Hawkins, Caroline	29, Dec. 1842	L3
Helm, C.J. (Major)	Whistler, Louisa A.	22, June 1854	L3
Hempstead, Samuel B.	Hamilton, Mary Ann	2, Apr. 1846	L3
Henderson, Joseph	Treece, Mary A.	2, Feb. 1854	L3
Henning, John	Pollock, Rebecca S.	20, Nov. 1856	L3
Henrie, Arthur	Sisson, Grace	25, Sept 1811	L3
Henry, David	Andrews, Martha Jane	2, Aug. 1849	L3
Henry, John	McLenan, Jane	18, Feb. 1847	L3
Herman, Samuel	Morgan, Abbie C.	27, Apr. 1854	L3
Heron, John	Robertson, Jane	14, June 1849	L3
Herrick, Hiram N.	Wakefield, Mary E.	16, Feb. 1854	L3
Herron, James H.	Fuller, Josephine S.	21, Sept 1854	L3
Herron, John W.	Collins, Harnietta A	16, Mar. 1854	L3
Hervey, Thomas	Prouty, Ann Janette	4, Jan. 1844	L3
Herzog, William	Schaffer, Catharine	5, Nov. 1846	L3
Hewlett, Jeremiah S.	Huntington, Sarah A.	20, Oct. 1842	L3
Hewson, John H.	McIlvaine, Emily R.	17, Jan. 1856	L3
Heytep, Solomon	Mose, Catharine Ann	6, Apr. 1854	L3
Hibben, J. Harry	Conkling, Mary L.	30, Aug. 1855	L3
Hickman, E.R.	Schnetz, Anna A.	20, Aug. 1857	L3
Hickox, Hiram S.	Slack, Rebecca (Mrs)	1, Apr. 1852	L3

Grooms	Brides	Date of Notice	Page
Hicks, James	Harrison, Martha A.	23, June 1842	L3
Hicks, James	Whetstone, Ruth	5, Jan. 1809	L3
Hiester, J.P. (Dr)	Rauch, P.B. (Mrs)	1, Aug. 1844	L3
Higby, James B.	Stonemats, Sarah	17, Feb. 1848	L3
Higden, Henry H.	Lee, Jane Ann	28, Mar. 1844	L3
Higgins, William H.	Wright, Mary Jane	24, Dec. 1857	L3
Hight, George W.	Vance, Mary	26, Aug. 1816	L3
Hill, Benjamin	Death, Arachne	23, Nov. 1854	L3
Hill, David	Gilmore, Elizabeth	26, Feb. 1846	L3
Hill, Edward D.	Foote, Alice E.	12, Feb. 1857	L3
Hill, Edward H.	Lehmanowsky, Paulina	16, Nov. 1843	L3
Hill, Edward H.	VanDuzen, Elizabeth	25, Mar. 1841	L3
Hill, F.D. (Dr)	Woodruff, Rozella	22, June 1854	L3
Hill, Francis M.	Parms, Winnie Ann	9, Mar. 1854	L3
Hill, Francis S.	Babcock, Electa W.	4, Feb. 1847	L3
Hill, James	Taylor, Mary Ann	8, May 1845	L3
Hill, Joseph S.	McKinnell, Anna	10, July 1845	L3
Hill, Robert	Goshorn, Elizabeth	16, Mar. 1854	L3
Hill, W.F.	Lytle, Rebecca A.	3, Sept 1846	L3
Hillerman, William J	Robinson, Elizabeth (Mrs)	8, Mar. 1849	L3
Hillhouse, James	Swinson, Margaret C.	16, Jan. 1845	L3
Hills, Townsend	Cochran, Eliza	25, July 1844	L3
Hilton, George	Laverty, Honora W.	23, June 1842	L3
Hilton, George	Luce, Mary E.	27, Jan. 1853	L3
Hilton, Thomas	Morton, Anne (Mrs)	12, Dec. 1844	L3
Hilts, Charles	Calvin, Anna	6, Oct. 1853	L3
Hinckle, Phillip	Gaither, Martha	2, Jan. 1851	L3
Hinde, Thomas S.	Bradford, Belinda	25, Oct. 1809	L3
Hine, L.A.	Chapin, Helen	18, Nov. 1847	L3
Hinman, E.B.	Duble, Kate S.	1, Apr. 1852	L3
Hinsch, Augustus F.	Denman, Louisa Eve.	5, May 1836	L3
Hinsdale, John T.	Loring, Susan M.	8, Dec. 1836	L3
Hipple, Benjamin	King, Amanda	21, Sept 1843	L3
Hitchler, John	McCann, Rosella Ann	26, Aug. 1847	L3
Hite, Charles P.	Heaton, Virginia	23, Mar. 1854	L3
Hixson, James	Randle, Mary	14, Mar. 1844	L3
Hoadly, George	Perry, Mary B.	21, Aug. 1851	L3
Hoffman, Allen	Gilman, Barbara A.	14, Oct. 1847	L3
Hoffman, Jacob	Whitney, Abby	23, Sept 1841	L3
Hoffner, Jacob	Marsden, Elizabeth	3, June 1820	L3
Hoffner, John	King, Nancy	27, Feb. 1811	L3
Hogan, David	Watts, Virginia	21, Nov. 1833	L3
Hoke, Abraham	Arnot, Mary B.	20, Apr. 1848	L3
Holcomb, Asa	Sullivan, Mary	1, Apr. 1816	L3
Holden, R.A.	Wells, Aurelia	29, Sept 1836	L4
Holdzkorn, William	Laird, Amanda	26, Feb. 1846	L3
Hole, James	Compton, Rachel	12, Sept 1810	L3
Holenshade, John H.	Oulton, Emily	12, Feb. 1857	L3
Holliday, Joseph	Smith, S.M.	27, May 1847	L3
Holliday, Nathan	Stanbery, Charlotte	22, Oct. 1840	L3
Hollister, Edward	Perry, Martha H.	22, Feb. 1849	L3
Hollister, G.B.	Strait, Laura Burton	14, Aug. 1851	L3
Holloday, Uriah B.	Fryer, Mary	2, Feb. 1854	L3
Holmes, Benjamin	Nolan, Susan C.	6, Aug. 1857	L3

Grooms	Brides	Date of Notice	Page
Holmes, Charles S.	Russell, Helen M.	20, Oct. 1853	L3
Holmes, Ezekiel B.	Symsor, Christiana	20, Nov. 1845	L3
Holmes, Francis M.	Ogden, Fannie L.	18, Oct. 1849	L3
Holmes, James H.	Stroman, Sarah A.	10, Nov. 1853	L3
Holmes, R.S. (Dr)	Walker, Annie M.	24, Oct. 1850	L3
Holmes, William	Buffington, Elizabeth	11, Nov. 1847	L3
Holmes, William N.	Graham, Ella	22, Aug. 1850	L3
Holt, George H.	Ray, Anna	15, Apr. 1852	L3
Homans, Benjamin	Williams, Fanny E.	24, Aug. 1854	L3
Homans, S. Southard	Gillette, Martha B.	30, Jan. 1851	L3
Honore, Francis (Capt)	Lockwood, Matilda D.	8, Dec. 1818	L3
Hood, D. Burr	Waggoner, Mattie A.	3, Feb. 1855	L3
Hooker, Edward	Loring, Georgiana	30, Dec. 1852	L3
Hoole, Joseph	Graham, Lucy Ann	1, Mar. 1838	L3
Hooper, Samuel S.	Irwin, Elizabeth S.	30, Nov. 1848	L3
Hooper, William	Lee, Anne S.	13, July 1854	L3
Hoopes, Edward L.	Downard, Malinda B.	17, Nov. 1831	L2
Hoping, E.N.	Andrews, Harriet	26, Jan. 1854	L3
Hopkins, Ben E.	Grover, Mary E.	7, Feb. 1856	L3
Hopkins, James	Vannoy, Sarah	9, Feb. 1854	L3
Hopkins, John (Rev)	Perry, Mary C.	26, Nov. 1840	L3
Hopkins, Lewis C.	Whetstone, Julia M.	6, Feb. 1851	L3
Hopkins, Richard R.	Baldridge, Mary L.	18, Mar. 1847	L3
Hopkins, William H.	Ruffin, Frances	26, Apr. 1814	L3
Hopkins, William R.	Hobbs, Laura W.	21, July 1842	L3
Hopper, Joseph L.	Dicks, Mary Jane	11, Jan. 1838	L3
Hopper, Morris	Westlake, Susan	22, Mar. 1838	L3
Hopple, Jacob	Tudor, Ann C.	4, Jan. 1844	L3
Hopple, Matthew	Payne, Penelope V.	2, Aug. 1855	L3
Horass, Fintin	Swenny, Eliza Jane	2, July 1846	L3
Horne, Daniel H.	Coffin, Anna B.	21, Feb. 1839	L3
Horne, John R.	McConnell, Amanda M.	26, May 1842	L3
Horney, Daniel	Calhoun, Elizabeth	25, Oct. 1849	L3
Horniman, Henry	Fletcher, Margaret	20, Sept 1849	L3
Horrocks, John F.	Fagely, Harriet	24, Aug. 1843	L3
Horton, Benjamin M.	Hart, Carrie	9, Sept 1852	L3
Horton, David C.	Dumont, Matilda	25, Mar. 1852	L3
Horton, Henry Hall	McRobert, Lucitty J.	27, Nov. 1845	L3
Hoskeir, Isaac A.	Winton, Jane M.	19, Oct. 1843	L3
Hoster, Joseph C.	Voorhis, Maggie	13, Sept 1855	L3
Hotchkiss, Henry O.	Sawyier, Mary A.	3, June 1841	L3
Hovey, James	Morrow, Ursula	4, July 1844	L3
Howard, James N.	Irwin, Mary W.	12, May 1842	L3
Howard, James P.	Pagget, Elizabeth (Mrs)	18, Apr. 1844	L3
Howard, Nicholas	Hart, Henrietta	21, Oct. 1841	L3
Howarth, James	Leadbetter, Sarah A.	9, Oct. 1834	L2
Howden, Robert	Pest, Ann	9, Nov. 1854	L3
Howe, F.S. (Rev)	Pierson, Clara	28, Mar. 1844	L3
Howe, Hammond	Price, S.J.	13, Sept 1838	L3
Howe, John F.	Hunt, Mary Ann	6, Feb. 1840	L3
Howe, Robert	Peabody, Mary	27, May 1852	L3
Howell, Daniel G.	Lyall, Jane Eliza	25, Aug. 1818	L2
Howell, Edward	Owens, Mary Ann	16, Feb. 1837	L3
Howell, G.W.	Fenton, Josephine R.	8, Sept 1842	L3

Grooms	Brides	Date of Notice	Page
Howell, H. Scott	Redman, Anna Lizzie	26, Oct. 1854	L3
Howell, Rozel P.	Hall, Hulda A. (Mrs)	11, Nov. 1847	L3
Howell, William F.	Applegate, Sallie C.	16, July 1857	L3
Howes, Josiah	Parks, Grizella	17, June 1852	L3
Howland, Charles H.	Conclin, Mary A.	11, Mar. 1852	L3
Hoy, John F.	Clarke, Ladonia C.	11, Mar. 1847	L3
Hoyt, J.W.	Sampson, E.O.	7, Dec. 1854	L3
Hubbard, L.V.	Lee, Annie E.	26, Oct. 1848	L3
Hubbel, Harry H.	Bauman, Kate	26, July 1855	L3
Hubbell, Thomas B.	Benson, Elizabeth A.	2, Jan. 1845	L3
Hubbell, William T.	Willson, Mary Jane	16, Oct. 1851	L3
Huber, Charles B.	Cary, Martha Louisa	20, Sept 1855	L3
Hudson, Ed	Miller, Risyiah	2, Dec. 1841	L3
Hudson, John	Jones, Ann C. (Mrs)	21, Apr. 1820	L3
Hudson, William	Harton, Margaret Ann	20, Mar. 1845	L3
Hueston, William M.	Gorman, Anna Maria	18, Feb. 1836	L3
Huey, George J.	Whetstone, Hannah E.	22, Oct. 1840	L3
Hughart, John	Russell, Mary E.	10, Nov. 1853	L3
Hughes, Charles T.	Hughey, Emily H.	19, Aug. 1847	L3
Hughes, Edward J.	Lewis, Elizabeth	18, Sept 1845	L3
Hughes, Ezekiel	Ewing, Mary	16, July 1805	L3
Hughes, J.W.	Martin, Almira L.	28, June 1855	L3
Hughes, John	Burt, Sarah A. (Mrs)	22, Sept 1817	L3
Hughes, L.F.	Lewis, Mary	18, Sept 1845	L3
Hugle, James	Murry, Frances	23, Oct. 1856	L5
Hulbert, William P.	Bowne, Carrie M.	11, Mar. 1852	L3
Hulburd, H.H.	Corwin, R.S.	13, Oct. 1853	L3
Hulings, Perry	Cook, Elizabeth	18, May 1848	L3
Hull, D.P.	Riley, Sarah A.	27, May 1847	L3
Hull, George M.	Bell, Rebecca Jane	12, Apr. 1855	L3
Hull, James M.	Turner, Ann	19, Mar. 1846	L3
Hulse, James	Oldaker, Roxolina	9, Feb. 1854	L3
Hune, Henry	Lutz, Susan	9, Nov. 1854	L3
Hungarford, Richard	Shaw, Sarah	6, Mar. 1811	L3
Hunt, Charles H.	Clark, Sarah A.	30, Mar. 1849	L3
Hunt, Freeman	Parmenter, Elizabeth T.	27, Oct. 1853	L3
Hunt, John	Harrison, Zebuline A	17, Dec. 1840	L3
Hunt, Ralph P.	VanderPool, Adareen	24, Mar. 1826	L3
Hunt, Randal	Ludlow, Ruhannah	20, July 1854	L3
Hunt, Thomas E.	Lewis, Elizabeth R.	12, June 1851	L3
Hunter, Moses	Hammond, Catharine	23, Feb. 1843	L3
Hunter, N.D.	Herbst, Caroline	19, Mar. 1840	L3
Hunter, William	Taylor, A.E.	16, Mar. 1854	L3
Hunter, William	Wright, Sophia	23, Apr. 1846	L3
Hunter, William G.	Brown, Mary Ann	28, Dec. 1843	L3
Hunter, William M.	Ashton, Caroline A.	29, Feb. 1844	L3
Huntington, Henry D.	Johnston, Sarah H.	14, May 1846	L3
Huntington, John C.	Mitchell, Mary	7, Sept 1848	L3
Huntington, John M.	Canfield, Janette	9, Oct. 1845	L3
Huntington, John M.	Canfield, Janette H.	2, Oct. 1845	L3
Huntington, Spencer	Williamson, Frances	7, Dec. 1848	L3
Huntington, Thomas S	Byington, Malvina	21, June 1855	L3
Huntington, William	Johnston, Mary E.	4, Sept 1851	L3
Hurd, L.	Nicholas, Mary E.	28, Aug. 1845	L3

Grooms	Brides	Date of Notice	Page
Hurdus, George	Hershew, Elizabeth	10, Aug. 1813	L3
Hurley, John H.	Downs, Mary E.	10, May 1855	L3
Hurtt, F.W.	Ives, Sarah B.	15, Feb. 1855	L3
Huser, John	Thacker, Patty	16, Sept 1816	L3
Huston, H.	Hilton, S.E.	13, Apr. 1854	L3
Huston, James H.	Smith, Clarissa	5, Jan. 1809	L3
Hutchins, A.S.	Avery, Henrietta B.	2, Jan. 1845	L3
Hutton, John	Stapley, Ann	6, July 1843	L3
Hyeth, Peyton	Cooke, Deborah	8, Oct. 1840	L4
Hyter, Abraham	Phares, Nancy	5, June 1816	L3
Iglehart, N.P.	Gano, Frances Mary	27, July 1837	L3
Impey, Robert	Stanbery, Frances	22, Oct. 1840	L3
Ingalsbe, L.	Mullen, Sarah B.	21, Nov. 1844	L3
Ingersoll, Henry	Harrod, Elizabeth	23, Mar. 1848	L3
Ingols, Chester	Bishop, Ada	2, Feb. 1819	L3
Ingram, James	Fee, Melvina R.	20, Oct. 1853	L3
Innes, D.K.	Hand, Harriet A.	6, May 1847	L3
Innis, Robert B.	Williams, Laura Jane	17, Jan. 1850	L3
Irwin, A.R. (Capt)	Reilly, Mary Ann	17, Dec. 1846	L3
Irwin, Archibald	Jones, Emily Albina	26, June 1828	L3
Irwin, Archibald	Sumwalt, Martha (Mrs)	13, Nov. 1850	L3
Irwin, James M.	Adams, Sarah Ann	14, Jan. 1836	L1
Irwin, John V.	Eaton, Anna Jane	4, Oct. 1838	L3
Irwin, Thomas	Pomeroy, Mary Russel	14, Jan. 1836	L1
Irwin, William	Ramsey, Sarah L.	23, Aug. 1838	L3
Irwin, William	Smith, Mary Jane	18, Jan. 1832	L4
Is--g, Daniel	McMahon, Elizabeth	16, June 1817	L3
Jackson, Charles	Joycelin, Mary H.	18, May 1822	L3
Jackson, Charles J.	Paris, Mary E.	17, Dec. 1857	L3
Jackson, James	Craig, Charlotte E.	30, Dec. 1852	L3
Jackson, James	Miller, Sarah A.	23, Dec. 1847	L3
Jackson, John G.	Meigs, Mary	22, Aug. 1810	L3
Jackson, Joseph	Stewart, Susan V.	18, Apr. 1850	L3
Jacobs, John	Ireland, Rebecca	3, July 1811	L3
Jacobs, S.C.	Davis, Mary M.	26, Feb. 1857	L3
James, A.C.	Ernst, Mary A.	15, Oct. 1840	L3
James, David A.	Bakewell, Elizabeth	3, June 1841	L3
James, John H.	Bailey, Abbey	12, Aug. 1825	L3
James, Joseph	Picket, Sarah Jane	11, Sept 1845	L3
James, Joseph J.	Keating, Margaret	4, July 1826	L3
James, L.A. (Dr)	Gibson, Elmira J.	17, Feb. 1848	L3
James, U.P.	Wood, Olive H.	13, May 1847	L3
Jamison, Robert	Johnson, Mary J.	6, Apr. 1854	L3
Jaquess, John	Handy, Mary E.	20, Apr. 1848	L3
Jeffries, John C.	Vanausdol, Mary R.	21, Apr. 1842	L3
Jenifer, Benjamin	Coddington, Sarah A.	24, Dec. 1840	L3
Jenkins, James	Littlefield, Mary L.	3, July 1845	L3
Jenkins, Richard	Millin, Lucinda	6, Apr. 1854	L3
Jenkins, Riley	Davis, Nancy	13, June 1850	L3
Jenkins, Thomas	Mitchell, Mary Ann	1, Nov. 1855	L3
Jenkins, Thomas C.	Piatt, Carrie C.	20, Nov. 1856	L3
Jennings, Charles P.	Burnet, Gertrude G.	15, Sept 1842	L3

Grooms	Brides	Date of Notice	Page
Jennings, T.M.	Cleary, Mary A.	31, May 1855	L3
Jessup, D.B. (Dr)	James, Martha J.	24, Dec. 1846	L3
Jessup, Thomas C.	Hart, Isabella	1, Nov. 1855	L3
Jocelyn, Augustus	Richardson, Laura M.	22, Dec. 1831	L2
John, E.D.	Parry, Sarah R.	11, Mar. 1841	L3
Johns, James C.	Thompson, Ann	14, Apr. 1842	L3
Johnson, Alexander B	Purcell, Harriet	25, Dec. 1845	L3
Johnson, Archibald	Ferguson, Amelia R.	9, July 1819	L3
Johnson, Campbell	Sandford, J.	3, Feb. 1824	L3
Johnson, Cary	Jessup, Rebecca	15, Sept 1806	L3
Johnson, Charles	Henry, Rebecca	22, Oct. 1846	L3
Johnson, David	Biggs, Anna Louisa	2, Dec. 1847	L3
Johnson, Edward B.	Kelly, Emily E.	12, Nov. 1857	L3
Johnson, G. Brainerd	Townsend, Caroline	15, June 1843	L3
Johnson, Henry W.	Oldrieve, Emilia	24, June 1852	L3
Johnson, James A.	White, Catharine L.	17, Feb. 1848	L3
Johnson, John	Frost, Harriet S.	14, Mar. 1850	L3
Johnson, Joseph J.	James, Anna D.	10, Apr. 1845	L3
Johnson, Rufus S.	Cromwell, Laura	6, Apr. 1854	L3
Johnson, Samuel	Jessup, Phebe	7, Nov. 1810	L3
Johnson, Samuel	Moulton, Elizabeth	11, Jan. 1844	L3
Johnson, William A.	Gano, Lucretia	11, Feb. 1847	L3
Johnston, Alexander	Betts, Abigail R.	6, Mar. 1851	L3
Johnston, Archibald	McMeen, Mary A.	29, Mar. 1855	L3
Johnston, George	Hoy, Frances	31, Dec. 1857	L3
Johnston, J.W.	Patterson, Mary	4, Nov. 1841	L3
Johnston, John	Gregg, Lamira J.	2, Mar. 1854	L3
Johnston, John R.	Addleman, Mahala	23, Feb. 1854	L3
Johnston, Joseph M.	Pettit, Mary A.	8, Jan. 1846	L3
Johnston, Samuel	Wilson, Margaretta E	6, Dec. 1820	L3
Johnston, William S.	Butterfield, Jane	5, Dec. 1850	L3
Jonas, Joseph	Oppenheim, Martha	29, Nov. 1838	L3
Jonas, Joseph	Scixas, Rachael A.	23, Dec. 1823	L3
Jonas, W.H.	Louderback, C. (Mrs)	13, Aug. 1857	L3
Jones, Alanson	Dryden, Selina	11, May 1854	L3
Jones, Cadwalader	Rees, Ann	29, Oct. 1846	L3
Jones, Charles	Stewart, Laura	29, Sept 1842	L3
Jones, Charles A.	Ludlow, Charlotte C.	20, July 1843	L3
Jones, E.A. (Dr)	Metcalfe, Jane R.	8, May 1845	L3
Jones, George	Erickson, Sarah	28, Oct. 1852	L3
Jones, George G.	Aydelotte, Hannah	30, Oct. 1845	L3
Jones, George H.	Hughes, Mollie B.	17, Dec. 1857	L3
Jones, George W.	Kittridge, M. Louise	25, Apr. 1844	L3
Jones, George W.	Wilkinson, Amanda	20, Dec. 1838	L3
Jones, Gilbert R.	Decker, Caroline	11, Dec. 1845	L3
Jones, J. Dan.	Bell, Margaretta	22, Sept 1853	L3
Jones, J.J.	Norman, Sarah E.	12, Sept 1850	L3
Jones, J.N.	Edwards, Mary	11, May 1848	L3
Jones, James W.	Morehouse, Mary E.	15, Jan. 1857	L3
Jones, John	Bryant, Milly	11, Feb. 1820	L3
Jones, John D.	Johnson, Elizabeth	30, Sept 1823	L3
Jones, John G.	Brewster, Elizabeth	23, Apr. 1846	L3
Jones, John T.	Lawrence, Ann B.	30, June 1821	L3
Jones, Michael	McGuire, Louisa W.	23, Mar. 1854	L3

Grooms	Brides	Date of Notice	Page
Jones, Morris	Teirnan, Margaret	12, Aug. 1841	L3
Jones, R.	Hibben, L.	2, Jan. 1851	L3
Jones, Richard	Stephenson, Nancy	23, Mar. 1854	L3
Jones, Robert	Myers, Frances Jane	29, June 1843	L3
Jones, Rufus A.	Thompson, Sarah E.	26, Oct. 1848	L3
Jones, Samuel A.	Osborn, Mary Ann	25, Sept 1851	L3
Jones, Thomas C.	Tait, Mary	26, May 1836	L3
Jones, William	Coleman, Sarah B.	19, June 1815	L3
Jones, William C.	Whitehead, Eliza F.	9, Apr. 1840	L3
Jones, William D.	Longworth, Charlotte	17, Mar. 1821	L3
Jones, William M.	Cheesman, Rachael W.	11, Feb. 1841	L3
Jonte, Robert	Stout, Harriet	22, Sept 1853	L3
Jordan, Daniel B.	Ramsdale, Juliann	10, May 1832	L3
Joyce, James	Jones, Lucretia	14, June 1855	L3
Judah, Judah	Mortz, Caroline	7, Sept 1843	L3
Judkins, William	Palmer, Mary M.	9, Sept 1841	L3
Judy, George H.	Richardson, Rebecca	2, Feb. 1854	L3
Juppenlatz, George	Alther, Anna Catharine	20, Jan. 1817	L3
Justice, Enoch P.	DeCamp, Charlotte	14, Sept 1848	L3
Justice, Leonidas	Corley, Caroline E.	5, Jan. 1854	L3
Karrmann, William	Winter, Eliza	27, Nov. 1845	L3
Kauffman, J.L.	Barrett, Hannah E.	10, Aug. 1848	L3
Kaugger, Christian	Eha, Mary	3, Nov. 1853	L3
Kautz, Jacob	Miller, Hannah	27, Jan. 1806	L3
Kavney, Lewis	Johnson, Maria E.	20, Sept 1849	L3
Keating, John	Wheelright, Mary (Mrs)	28, Apr. 1826	L3
Keats, Clarence G.	James, Mary A.	20, Jan. 1853	L3
Kebler, John	Abbott, Lucy E.	3, Sept 1846	L3
Keckeler, Theophilus	Manser, Mary A.	15, July 1852	L3
Keckler, Adolphus T.	Ryland, Louisa	28, July 1853	L3
Keckley, William Hy.	Simpson, Elizabeth	13, Feb. 1845	L3
Keelor, Alexis	Steedman, Alvena P.	15, Oct. 1857	L3
Keely, George W.	Wells, Sue	21, Mar. 1850	L3
Keenan, John W.	Baer, E.F.	13, Mar. 1851	L3
Keeshan, John	Carrigan, Hannah	3, Feb. 1853	L3
Keith, Isaac	Williams, Charlotte	28, Jan. 1847	L3
Kelley, John H.	Hill, Elizabeth A.	16, Mar. 1854	L3
Kellogg, Charles H.	Todd, Margaret	11, Nov. 1847	L3
Kellogg, Henry S.	Cochran, Margaret E.	6, Jan. 1831	L2
Kelly, William F.	Harding, Emilie D.	18, June 1857	L3
Kelsall, Thomas	Gooch, Emma	20, Nov. 1845	L3
Kelsey, Chauncey	McElvain, Mary	24, Apr. 1845	L3
Kelsey, Naaman	Barber, Sarah Jane	19, May 1842	L3
Kelso, Charles A.	Thurston, Mary	16, Feb. 1854	L3
Kemper, Augustus S.	Bradbury, Mary	7, June 1855	L3
Kemper, Charles H.	Terry, Margaret	9, Sept 1847	L3
Kemper, Henry L.	Martin, Lizzie	20, Dec. 1855	L3
Kemper, J.L.	Metcalfe, Mary J.	19, Aug. 1847	L3
Kemper, Peter, Jr.	Davis, (Mrs)	2, Feb. 1809	L3
Kendrick, Charles S.	Ludlow, Amanda	19, Dec. 1844	L3
Kendrick, Oscar (Dr)	Clark, Mary A.	12, July 1849	L3
Keneday, Lester	McQuilty, Martha Ann	13, Feb. 1845	L3
Kenedy, Joseph	Kenny, Mary (Mrs)	24, Oct. 1807	L3

Grooms	Brides	Date of Notice	Page
Kenna, Edward	Lewis, Margery J.	24, June 1847	L3
Kenneday, Charles	Delaplane, Margaret	23, Mar. 1854	L3
Kennedy, James	Hudson, Sarah	16, Sept 1820	L3
Kennedy, John	Marshall, Louisa	19, Oct. 1837	L3
Kennedy, Samuel	Wall, Lizzie R.	27, Apr. 1854	L3
Kennet, William (Dr)	McKee, Martha J.	11, May 1854	L3
Kennett, John	Gassaway, Elizabeth G.	20, Nov. 1834	L1
Kenny, Joseph (Capt)	Collins, Mary Jane	27, June 1839	L3
Kent, Luke	Ernst, Adeline E.	9, July 1840	L3
Kernes, Thomas	Scowdon, Sarah Ann	31, Dec. 1835	L3
Kerr, Robert	Heffernan, Anna M.	24, Aug. 1854	L3
Kerr, Thomas	Armstrong, Rebecca	26, Sept 1839	L3
Ketchum, William P.	King, Elizabeth J.	13, Apr. 1848	L3
Kettler, William	Love, Mary Ann	28, Feb. 1856	L3
Key, William J.	Reid, Agness	28, Dec. 1843	L3
Keys, R.W.	Sterrett, M. Eunice	21, May 1846	L3
Keys, Samuel B.	Baker, Julia A.	15, Jan. 1852	L3
Kibly, Timothy	Brown, Susan J.	31, July 1845	L3
Kidd, Edwin T.	Ebersole, Mary	3, May 1855	L3
Kiderlen, William L.	Longworth, Lucia C.	22, June 1848	L3
Killough, J. (Dr)	Brownrigg, C.	10, Aug. 1837	L3
Killough, James (Dr)	Davis, Mary Christin	16, Sept 1841	L3
Kiloh, John	Wright, Anna	4, Sept 1851	L3
Kimball, John F.	Hankins, Maria M.	25, Apr. 1844	L3
Kinder, William R.	Long, Agnes	21, Oct. 1852	L3
King, D. Cleaves	Dodson, Cynthia Ann	14, June 1849	L3
King, Edward	Worthington, Sarah A	20, May 1816	L3
King, Edward A.	McNaughton, Sarah M.	3, June 1841	L3
King, J. Willard	Welton, Margaret	27, Jan. 1848	L3
King, James	Park, Elizabeth	5, Jan. 1827	L3
King, James W.	Bennefield, Elizabet	20, June 1844	L3
King, Rufus	Rives, Margaret	25, May 1843	L3
King, Thomas W.	Neil, Elizabeth J.	10, Apr. 1845	L3
Kinkaid, Thomas J.	Bowers, Nancy	19, Mar. 1846	L3
Kinsey, Abram G.	Rogers, Isabella	23, Oct. 1856	L5
Kinsey, David	Pocock, Julia Ann	9, Feb. 1843	L3
Kinsey, Edward	Pocock, Temperance	28, Jan. 1841	L3
Kinsey, Joseph	Ammidown, A. Frances	8, Jan. 1852	L3
Kinsey, William G.	Evans, Ann	31, Apr. 1845	L3
Kirby, Clinton	Crawford, Anna M.	21, June 1855	L3
Kirby, Thomas	Pearce, Mary	17, Nov. 1842	L6
Kirk, John W.	Hubbard, Annie (Mrs)	27, July 1854	L3
Kirker, Thomas, Jr.	Stevenson, Jane	27, Dec. 1832	L3
Kirkhart, John	Oldaker, Mary E.	9, Feb. 1854	L3
Kirkland, John A.	Smith, Anna R.	26, Apr. 1855	L3
Kirkup, Joseph	Stanley, Emma	2, Jan. 1851	L3
Kirman, John	Bradley, Maria (Mrs)	27, Dec. 1855	L3
Kitchell, Wickliff	Ross, Elizabeth	26, Feb. 1812	L3
Kite, Thomas	Bragg, Margaret	31, Aug. 1848	L3
Kizer, Andy J.	Annis, Imogen	25, June 1857	L3
Kline, Benneville	Fagin, Nannie G.	26, Dec. 1850	L3
Kline, Benneville	Winans, Mary	31, Dec. 1857	L3
Knapp, Alvin C.	Martin, Eliza	7, Nov. 1844	L3
Kneeland, Philo N.	Barringer, Caroline	23, Apr. 1846	L3

Grooms	Brides	Date of Notice	Page
Knies, John K.	Pointer, Mary Ann	1, July 1820	L3
Knight, Benjamin	Marsh, Margaret	11, May 1848	L3
Knight, George H.	Kiloh, Ann	13, Nov. 1850	L3
Knight, James D.	Wilson, Louisa A.	5, Nov. 1840	L2
Knisely, Abram J.	Hastings, Rebecca	5, Feb. 1857	L3
Knowlton, C.C.	Hastings, Sarah P.	6, Sept 1855	L3
Knowlton, Cyrus	Dodge, Adaline	28, Sept 1848	L3
Knowlton, Sherman	Monahon, Dorcas	20, May 1847	L3
Knox, James H.	Thomas, Adaline E.	10, Dec. 1840	L3
Kovatz, Augusta (Lt)	Wallace, Martha N.	25, Nov. 1852	L3
Kreider, David L.	Graham, Rebecca	26, Sept 1839	L3
Kugler, David	Marlay, Malinda	24, Sept 1846	L3
Kyle, John	Carson, Margaret	21, May 1857	L3
Kyler, George	Stonemitz, Debby	14, Dec. 1807	L3
LaBoiteaux, Andrew	Wood, Matilda B.	13, Dec. 1855	L3
LaBoyteaux, Isaac N.	McLenan, Margaret	27, Nov. 1856	L3
Labrot, Auguste	Cromwell, Elizabeth	28, Nov. 1844	L3
Lackey, Ira	Merrit, Catharine	22, June 1822	L3
Ladd, William H.	White, Jean M.	5, Aug. 1847	L3
Lakin, John S.	Ricker, Leontine C.	8, Apr. 1852	L3
Lamont, Roger	Wall, Elizabeth	30, Mar. 1843	L3
Lamothe, Bernard (Dr)	Stockdale, Elizabeth	15, Apr. 1847	L3
Landis, Henry	Tunis, Susan	24, Mar. 1817	L3
Landon, Daniel	McCollom, Nancy	9, Feb. 1809	L3
Lane, Andrew	Rogers, Semor A.	24, Sept 1840	L3
Langdon, Elam P.	Cromwell, Ann	17, Oct. 1821	L3
Langdon, Oliver	Bassett, Catharine W.	3, Sept 1824	L2
Langdon, Oliver(Rev)	Brown, Nancy	7, May 1808	L3
Langtry, William	Beresford, (Miss)	19, Oct. 1822	L3
Lanham, W.W.	Fee, Mary	3, Nov. 1853	L3
Lanphear, Edward P.	Lewis, Rebecca S.	7, Nov. 1844	L3
Lape, Jacob S.	Rockwood, Amanda J.	1, Jan. 1852	L3
Lape, William H.	Taylor, Martha A.	24, June 1847	L3
Lapham, William	Bevan, M.J.	19, Aug. 1852	L3
Lardner, Henry (Dr)	Keys, Mary Ann	6, Sept 1838	L3
Larimore, Robert	Stoddard, Amelia N.	18, Sept 1851	L3
Larkin, S.F.	Jtark, Julia	22, May 1851	L3
Latham, Lorenzo	Latham, Mary A.	1, Aug. 1826	L3
Lathrop, Gardner	Hudson, Margaret (Mrs)	14, Mar. 1839	L3
Lathrop, Martin D.	Wright, Rebecca	18, Feb. 1815	L3
Latta, Alexander B.	Parson, Elizabeth A.	28, Oct. 1847	L3
Latta, Finley	Smith, Eliza Ann	25, Mar. 1841	L3
Lattimore, S.A.	Larrabee, Ellen	19, Aug. 1852	L3
Laue, C.M.	Snyder, Lizzie	7, May 1857	L3
Lawder, John B.	Sheldon, Rebecca A.	26, May 1842	L3
Lawrence, Albert G.	Sterling, Charlotte	29, June 1848	L3
Lawrence, H.K.	Vinton, Pamela W.	1, Feb. 1849	L3
Lawrence, Henry	Barclay, Mary D.	8, June 1843	L3
Lawrence, Henry	Hill, Elizabeth	13, Apr. 1854	L3
Lawrence, John H.	Moore, Amelia C.	12, Sept 1850	L3
Lawrence, Robert	Suydant, Lydia (Mrs)	29, Jan. 1829	L1
Lawrence, William	Ramsey, Margaret E.	5, Aug. 1847	L3
Lawrence, William C.	Fertig, Catharine A. (Mrs)	6, May 1841	L3

Grooms	Brides	Date of Notice	Page
Laws, Edward (Dr)	Nelson, Mary	31, May 1855	L3
Laws, James H.	Langdon, Sarah A.	23, Oct. 1851	L3
Lawson, F.H.	McDougal, Annie R.	5, Feb. 1857	L3
Lawson, George	Sterrett, Mary Jane	6, July 1854	L3
Lawson, Joseph	Birdsall, Sarah Ann	28, Dec. 1843	L3
Lawson, L.M. (Dr)	Robinson, Ann Eliza	17, Aug. 1848	L3
Layton, James M.	Raymond, Cora O.	9, Jan. 1851	L3
Lea, Henry	Trumbull, Louisa J.	11, Sept 1845	L3
Lea, Henry C.	Jaudon, Anna C.	30, May 1850	L3
Lea, James H.	Campbell, Ellen	12, May 1836	L2
Lea, James M.	Ellis, Mary Caroline	6, May 1852	L3
Leaf, William	Linscott, Marybe	9, Feb. 1854	L3
Leake, J. Bloomfield	Hawkins, Cordelia	12, Oct. 1854	L3
Leary, John J.O.	Collison, Caroline G	17, Oct. 1850	L3
Leavitt, John M.	Brooks, Bithia	5, Oct. 1848	L3
LeCain, Fred G.	Thomas, Eliza	12, Mar. 1857	L3
Ledman, Samuel F.	Sayre, Ann	18, Oct. 1838	L3
Lee, R.W.	Omstead, Martha B.	28, Sept 1848	L3
Lee, Samuel C.	Baker, Anna Maria	20, Apr. 1854	L3
Lee, Samuel M.	Arcambal, Paulina	3, Dec. 1829	L3
Leeds, Jesse J.	Eshelman, Sarah A.	23, Mar. 1854	L3
Leeka, Philip	Thomas, Ruth	12, Jan. 1854	L3
Lefferson, James B.	Shafor, Catharine	4, Oct. 1849	L3
Lehmer, James D.	Isham, Jane B.	9, Aug. 1849	L3
Leitch, William	Porter, Mary Elizabeth	12, Mar. 1846	L3
Lemaire, Isaac K.	Kirby, Jane	14, Oct. 1847	L3
Leman, Washington H.	Diters, Mary	26, Sept 1844	L3
Leming, James	Harrison, Kiziah	11, Aug. 1817	L3
Lemon, Randall	Porter, Mary Jane	11, Feb. 1847	L3
Lennan, D.B.	Sampson, Belle	8, Mar. 1855	L3
Leonard, John D.	Avy, Margaret	17, July 1845	L3
Leonard, William	Meritt, Eliza R.	24, Dec. 1857	L3
Leslie, James	Marsh, Rachael A.	22, July 1852	L3
Letford, John S.	Jones, Jane	23, July 1846	L3
Leuthstrom, William	Carey, Letitia E.	19, Sept 1844	L3
Levassor, Armond P.	Taylor, Louisa	16, Jan. 1845	L3
Levy, Alexander	Jacobs, Isabella	4, Aug. 1836	L3
Levy, J.L.	Marks, Sarah Edwitha	18, Apr. 1839	L3
Lewis, A. (Capt)	Mayo, Mary A.	15, Oct. 1829	L4
Lewis, B.F.	Sheppard, Ella V.	13, Nov. 1856	L3
Lewis, Charles F.	Kiloh, Maria E.	15, Nov. 1849	L3
Lewis, Frank	Godley, Kate T.	24, Sept 1857	L3
Lewis, G.W.	Baldwin, Virginia L.	28, Oct. 1847	L3
Lewis, George N.	Forward, Martha	13, Nov. 1856	L3
Lewis, John Loyd	Wheeler, Cornelia D.	11, Jan. 1844	L3
Lewis, Marcus	Burr, Mary H.	16, Apr. 1857	L3
Lewis, Richard	Hatch, Jenny P.	29, Sept 1853	L3
Lewis, Robert L.	Hubbard, Anna Sarah	9, July 1846	L3
Lewis, Samuel	Goforth, Charlotte K	8, Aug. 1823	L3
Lewis, Thatcher	Bennett, Elizabeth A	5, Nov. 1846	L3
Lewis, William	Mix, Eliza (Mrs)	14, Feb. 1839	L3
L'Hommedieu, Charles	Howell, Elmira	23, Oct. 1828	L3
L'Hommedieu, S.S.	Hammond, Alma	29, Apr. 1830	L2
L'Hommedieu, Samuel	Swift, Eliza	27, June 1826	L3

Grooms	Brides	Date of Notice	Page
Liebern, John N.	Steinkamp, Elizabeth	30, Jan. 1845	L3
Lilley, John	Taylor, Mary Ann	12, Apr. 1849	L3
Lillie, John	Ormiston, Elizabeth	16, Feb. 1854	L3
Lincoln, T.D.	Clark, Mary S.	28, Aug. 1845	L3
Lindley, Jacob	Ellicott, Catharine	28, Oct. 1847	L3
Lindly, Abraham	L'Hommedieu, S. (Mrs)	6, Mar. 1822	L3
Lindman, Lewis T.	Donaldson, Mary	22, Apr. 1847	L3
Lindsay, H.R.	Lewis, Augusta M.	18, Sept 1851	L3
Lindsay, John	Parker, Elizabeth	18, Apr. 1844	L3
Lindsay, Robert	Dunnelly, Betsy (Mrs)	13, Nov. 1850	L3
Lindsay, Samuel	Turner, Edith	29, July 1847	L3
Linton, Benjamin	Brockman, Susan (Mrs)	23, Nov. 1854	L3
Liter, Adam	Foster, Sarah C.	23, July 1846	L3
Little, Benjamin	Perkins, Elizabeth	29, Dec. 1812	L3
Little, George	Miles, Caroline	28, Jan. 1841	L3
Little, James S.	Griffith, Jane C.	15, Jan. 1857	L3
Little, Joseph B.	Stockum, Harriet J.	31, Apr. 1845	L3
Livezy, I.W.	Lee, E.	6, Jan. 1853	L3
Livingston, James	Templeton, Nancy	27, Oct. 1812	L3
Lloyd, James Tilford	Lloyd, Heloise	21, May 1857	L3
Locke, John (Dr)	Dallas, Mary E. (Mrs)	28, Sept 1854	L3
Lockwood, Daniel	Shays, Frances C.	8, June 1837	L2
Lockwood, Daniel H.	Mulford, Gabriella	28, Dec. 1848	L3
Lockwood, F.T.	Baldwin, Emily	27, Nov. 1856	L3
Lodge, Caleb T.	Irwin, Sarah W.	14, Aug. 1828	L3
Lodge, John	Arion, Susanna	18, Aug. 1817	L3
Lodge, Laban	Piatt, Catharine S.	13, May 1823	L3
Logan, C.A. (Dr)	Shaw, Zoe	13, Apr. 1854	L3
Logan, David O.	Price, Harriet	26, Jan. 1854	L3
Logan, L.	Hubbard, Catharine S	26, Jan. 1843	L3
Logan, Thomas A.	Thornton, Jinny	19, May 1853	L3
Long, George W.	Shuff, Margaret	2, Mar. 1854	L3
Long, Jacob	L'Hommedieu, Maria M.	13, June 1826	L3
Long, William	Baker, Elizabeth	13, July 1843	L3
Longfellow, Henry W.	Appleton, Fanny E.	27, July 1843	L3
Longley, Elias	Vater, Elizabeth M.	20, May 1847	L3
Longshore, Abner	O'Neal, Mary Anne	4, May 1848	L3
Longworth, Joseph	Rives, Anna	27, May 1841	L3
Longworth, Nicholas	Connor, Susan	28, Dec. 1807	L3
Looker, Allison C.	Hough, Rachel	11, Mar. 1816	L3
Looker, Benjamin F.	Phares, Naomi	5, June 1816	L3
Looker, Thomas H.	Brigham, Lucilia S.	21, May 1857	L3
Loomis, D.W.	Dilworth, Eliza W.	1, Apr. 1847	L3
Lord, Henry C.	Wright, Eliza B.	1, July 1852	L3
Lord, Russell E.	Scott, Lizzie	8, Feb. 1849	L3
Loring, Allen	Oliver, Eliza Ann	27, May 1841	L3
Louderback, Jacob P.	Pittick, Mariamar C.	23, Feb. 1843	L3
Louis, A.	Mayer, Juliet	20, Oct. 1842	L3
Lounsbury, James	Leonard, Hannah A.	3, Oct. 1850	L3
Love, Robert A.	Laby, Scilla	3, Apr. 1851	L3
Lovejoy, Henry B.	Neblett, Sarah S.	8, July 1841	L3
Lovejoy, Thatcher	Tindall, Eliza Ann	7, May 1819	L3
Lovell, John D.	Hamet, Ellen B.	11, Sept 1834	L1
Lovell, Oliver S.	Russell, Sarah Jane	19, Jan. 1843	L3

Grooms	Brides	Date of Notice	Page
Lovie, Henri	Rechie, Mary	15, Sept 1853	L3
Lowe, George W.	Wright, Mary W.	6, Nov. 1845	L3
Lowe, John G.	Thruston, M.L. (Mrs)	18, May 1843	L3
Lowe, P.T.	Butler, Julia A.	27, Apr. 1843	L3
Lowell, James R.	White, Maria	9, Jan. 1845	L3
Lowndes, John	Howell, Catharine	6, Jan. 1817	L3
Lowry, George W.	Whitehead, Maria	23, Mar. 1848	L3
Lowry, John A.	Morecraft, Emily	6, Mar. 1845	L3
Loyd, John F. (Rev)	Miller, Mary E.	27, Apr. 1854	L3
Lubenstein, Isaac	Wolf, Adeline	31, Oct. 1844	L3
Lucas, Edward	Meline, Catharine A.	22, Feb. 1838	L3
Luckett, William G.	Goode, Martha Jane	22, Feb. 1844	L3
Luckey, John S.	Walker, Amelia Ann	9, May 1839	L3
Ludlow, George C.	Ludlum, Alzina A.	18, July 1844	L3
Ludlow, James C.	Dunlop, Josephine	9, Apr. 1819	L3
Lumsden, F. Af.	Spedden, Blanche	19, Jan. 1843	L3
Lupton, D.B.	Neave, Anna E.	11, Apr. 1839	L3
Lupton, Nathan	Boylew, Ann (Mrs)	30, Dec. 1847	L3
Lupton, Thomas	Nedy, Elizabeth	29, Nov. 1838	L3
Lusk, Thomas	Wartman, Elizabeth (Mrs)	22, Nov. 1838	L3
Lusk, Uzal B.	Meady, Eliza (Mrs)	1, Apr. 1847	L3
Lyan, Andrew Madison	Ross, Mary Ann C.	16, Nov. 1848	L3
Lynch, Augustine	Wampole, Isabella	9, Apr. 1840	L3
Lynes, William	Mears, Mary	21, Aug. 1811	L3
Lynn, John B.	Stone, Mary Elizabeth	3, Feb. 1848	L3
Lynn, John F.	Hall, M.G.	1, Nov. 1849	L3
Lytle, Edward H.	Shoenberger, Elizabeth	4, Oct. 1838	L3
Lytle, Robert T.	Haines, Elizabeth S.	2, Dec. 1825	L3
MacAlester, Charles	Lytle, Eliza Ann	19, Oct. 1824	L3
MacCracken, John	Brooks, Eliza	29, Apr. 1847	L3
MacDonald, Alexander	Richardson, Anna J.	30, Dec. 1852	L3
Mackay, John	Rowland, Mildred (Mrs)	31, May 1855	L3
Macomb, David B.	Worthington, Mary T.	1, Apr. 1816	L3
Macready, Robert	Stone, Dollie M.	20, Sept 1855	L3
Maddux, Lewis	Wilders, Loretta	2, Mar. 1854	L3
Madeira, J.	Dashiell, Mary Y.	26, Nov. 1824	L3
Magee, Jacob	Nicholas, Margaret	25, Aug. 1817	L2
Maggini, John C.(Dr)	McCloskey, Mary Ann	5, Dec. 1844	L3
Maghee, J.H.	Parker, Ellen	8, Jan. 1835	L1
Magill, Wesley W.	Cooke, Mary S.	25, Mar. 1847	L3
Magurk, Michael J.	McOliff, M. Cecilia	6, May 1841	L3
Mahaffey, Robert	Kellogg, Frances A.	9, Sept 1852	L3
Mahon, Stephen	Cobb, Kate	4, May 1848	L3
Majop, Francis (Dr)	Bennett, Ellen (Mrs)	23, Mar. 1854	L3
Major, John	Moss, Lucinda	13, Apr. 1848	L3
Mallard, Henry	Cross, Esther E.	17, June 1841	L3
Mallory, W.L.	Dudley, Bettie F.	22, Jan. 1857	L3
Malone, H.B.	See, Julia H.	1, Dec. 1853	L3
Malone, James F.	Magers, Jane	11, May 1854	L3
Malone, William H.	Kinsey, Jane G.	28, Nov. 1844	L3
Maloney, Daniel	Stevens, Sarah	31, Dec. 1840	L3
Mann, Isaac	Ludlow, Mary Ann	6, June 1810	L3
Mann, John	Mitchell, Ann	5, June 1851	L3

Grooms	Brides	Date of Notice	Page
Mann, Lowell A.	Folger, Eunice	1, Apr. 1841	L3
Mann, Marshall	Bartlett, Elizabeth	15, Feb. 1814	L3
Mansfield, Edward D.	Worthington, Margaret	9, May 1839	L3
Manypenny, William	Brunson, Maria	16, Feb. 1854	L3
Manzies, Samuel G.	Winston, Sarah Ann	8, Jan. 1835	L1
Mapes, Joel M.	Spinks, Elizabeth J.	25, Nov. 1847	L3
Mar, George W.	Hubbell, Elizabeth A	26, Oct. 1854	L3
March, George P.	Stanford, Sarah Jane	5, Oct. 1848	L3
Markland, Benjamin	Rogers, Fanny	22, Mar. 1814	L3
Markland, Simeon	Stevens, Alvira Jane	18, Mar. 1847	L3
Markward, James	Churchill, Abigail W	22, Oct. 1846	L3
Marlay, John F.(Rev)	Crendiff, Lizzie	15, Sept 1853	L3
Marlay, Joseph K.	McReynolds, Mary E.	18, Sept 1856	L5
Marpe, C.A.C.	Lovejoy, Harriet N.	8, Dec. 1842	L3
Marple, Jerome H.	Atchison, Sarah G.	15, Apr. 1847	L3
Marpless, Charles	Lyon, Melinda	6, Apr. 1854	L3
Marsh, Alanson	Woodruff, M. Louisa	23, May 1839	L3
Marsh, Alfred A.	Jones, Harriet	11, Sept 1851	L3
Marsh, C.P.	Baldridge, Laura S.	15, Jan. 1852	L3
Marsh, Charles	Langdon, Lucy	21, Sept 1812	L3
Marsh, David	Little, Mary	27, Aug. 1840	L3
Marsh, Isaac	Folger, Margaret M.	11, Jan. 1844	L3
Marsh, Luther H.	Haskell, Elizabeth J	8, Jan. 1857	L3
Marsh, Moses	Bonnel, Phebe	13, Apr. 1813	L3
Marsh, Nathan B.	Crossman, Elizabeth	10, Nov. 1842	L4
Marsh, Richard	Robinson, Mary Ann	9, Mar. 1854	L3
Marsh, Theodore	Cunningham, Rachel	27, Nov. 1845	L3
Marshall, Alfred	Morrison, Kate	11, June 1857	L3
Marshall, Edward C.	Chalfant, Josephine	9, Dec. 1852	L3
Marshall, James B.	Moore, Mary Ann	15, Oct. 1829	L4
Marshall, N.T. (Dr)	Soward, Elizabeth	7, May 1846	L3
Marshall, Peter	Boyd, Ellen	12, May 1842	L3
Marshall, Robert	Spalding, Jane (Mrs)	16, Mar. 1848	L3
Marshall, Robert M.	Davey, Mary A.	25, Nov. 1852	L3
Marshall, Samuel (Dr)	Stevenson, Mary C.	25, May 1854	L3
Marshall, Vincent C.	Cassilly, Ann S.	23, Dec. 1825	L3
Marshall, Vincent C.	Pugh, Leah	22, July 1820	L3
Martin, Alfred	Daniels, Elizabeth	26, Nov. 1840	L3
Martin, Charles T.	Ball, Jeanette V.	4, Oct. 1838	L3
Martin, Fernando K.	Dunn, Zion M.	17, Oct. 1844	L3
Martin, Francis	Irwin, Elizabeth	13, May 1816	L3
Martin, George	Bonsall, Mary P.	4, Oct. 1849	L3
Martin, Henry (Capt)	Cole, Maria	21, Sept 1843	L3
Martin, John B.	Brown, Adeline	19, Sept 1850	L3
Martin, John R.	Newman, Adaline	5, Mar. 1846	L3
Martin, Oliver	Coffin, Sarah	27, Oct. 1817	L3
Martin, Thomas F.	Leonard, Jane (Mrs)	6, Apr. 1848	L3
Martin, Thomas J.	Hazlett, Harriet M.	29, Oct. 1846	L3
Martin, William	Greer, Peggy	27, Apr. 1809	L3
Marvell, Henry W.	Belsh, Sarah Ann	2, July 1846	L3
Marvin, John P.	Tappan, Eliza R.	13, Feb. 1845	L3
Mason, A.J.	Hogue, Matilda	10, Apr. 1856	L3
Mason, Cuthbert H.	Bowman, Mary	12, Apr. 1855	L3
Mason, Edwin	Smith, Henrietta S.	16, Sept 1852	L3

Grooms	Brides	Date of Notice	Page
Mason, Lyman	Mussy, Mary L.	2, June 1853	L3
Mason, Zelotes H.	Newman, Christina	28, Dec. 1837	L3
Massalski, Joseph	Powers, Frances	7, July 1836	L4
Massey, Thomas Edwin	Medary, Sarah A.	28, Jan. 1847	L3
Matlock, Bowen	Cook, Elizabeth P.	20, Apr. 1843	L3
Matson, John	Anderson, Mary	22, Oct. 1808	L3
Matson, William D.	Rice, Eliza A.	23, Nov. 1837	L3
Matthews, Charles H.	Briggs, Alice H.	27, Aug. 1857	L3
Matthews, Fitch J.	Parrott, Frances A.	4, June 1857	L3
Matthews, George	Clifton, Rebecca	6, Sept 1855	L3
Matthews, James	Ellis, Jane	28, Oct. 1847	L3
Matthews, Jesse	Sones, Rebecca	16, Feb. 1854	L3
Matthews, Joseph M.	Saunders, Martha (Mrs)	16, Feb. 1854	L3
Matthews, T.J.	Brown, Isabella	3, Oct. 1823	L3
Matthews, W.	Orr, Eliza (Mrs)	16, July 1840	L3
Maurer, F.	Tilley, Josephine	17, Oct. 1850	L3
Maurer, George	Gerhart, Christiana	23, Jan. 1845	L3
Maxwell, George	Adams, Submit	21, Sept 1837	L3
Maxwell, Hugh B.	Henderson, Sophia	11, Oct. 1832	L4
Mayer, Adolph A.	Philipson, Rosa A.	9, Nov. 1848	L3
Mayhew, E.C.	Witmer, Sarah A.	22, Jan. 1857	L3
Mayhew, Thomas R.	Bassett, Margaret M.	3, Dec. 1846	L3
Maynard, John F.	Whitcomb, Esther A.	9, Feb. 1854	L3
Maynard, Rufus	Jones, Elizabeth (Mrs)	21, Sept 1854	L3
Mayronne, O.F.	Eberle, Margaret	5, Nov. 1840	L2
McAlister, William R	Reeder, Mary S.	6, Mar. 1845	L3
McAllaster, Henry	Peaslee, Rebecca Ann	16, Feb. 1854	L3
McAlpin, George W.	Spinning, E.L.	11, July 1850	L3
McBirney, Hugh	Johnston, Isabella M.	15, Nov. 1849	L3
McBratney, Robert	Palmer, Mary	6, Apr. 1848	L3
McBride, Henry R.	Ewing, Sarah V.	22, July 1852	L3
McBride, William D.	Comly, Fannie B. (Mrs)	25, May 1854	L3
McCalla, William H.	English, Mary Jane	21, Feb. 1856	L3
McCammon, William	Fowler, Jane	12, Feb. 1852	L3
McCane, John	Strawbridge, Jane	8, Apr. 1812	L3
McCarty, John	Soward, Maria C.	29, May 1845	L3
McCarty, Wm. (Rev)	Philips, Sarah	28, July 1806	L3
McCasland, John F.	Cochran, Charlotte	23, Feb. 1854	L3
McCauly, James	Bonnel, Sarah	13, Apr. 1813	L3
McClain, Edward A.	Robinson, Elizabeth	8, Jan. 1846	L3
McClain, James	Morehead, Eliza	13, Jan. 1824	L3
McClaskey, John	Hyland, Marianne (Mrs)	22, June 1843	L3
McClean, John	Edwards, Rebecca	7, Apr. 1807	L3
McClean, Nathaniel	Nut, Hetty	17, Jan. 1810	L3
McClintock, Andrew T.	Cist, Augusta B.	27, May 1841	L3
McClure, Alexander	Sweet, Martha	26, July 1838	L3
McClure, M.L.	Colledge, T.J.	9, Mar. 1854	L3
McConkey, Benjamin M	Morsell, Hester C.	6, July 1843	L3
McCorkle, John	Walker, Margaret	27, Dec. 1814	L3
McCormick, Benjamin	Schulze, Adelaid	10, Sept 1857	L3
McCormick, Edward	Parsons, Olivia Jane	9, May 1850	L3
McCormick, J.B.	Martin, Mary A.	6, Apr. 1854	L3
McCormick, Thomas J.	Hunter, Eunice	20, Jan. 1842	L3
McCracken, Robert B.	Turner, Rebecca	8, June 1843	L3

Grooms	Brides	Date of Notice	Page
McCreary, James K.	Howell, Elizabeth C.	18, Jan. 1838	L3
McCreight, Thomas	McMurry, Catharine	9, Feb. 1809	L3
McCulloch, Robert	Merrie, Jane	30, July 1819	L3
McCullough, T.	Girton, Lizzie L.	21, Aug. 1851	L3
McCullough, William	Piatt, Arabella S.	19, May 1826	L3
McCullum, John	Andrew, Ellen G.	2, Jan. 1851	L3
McDaniel, William	Alexander, Charlotte	9, Feb. 1854	L3
McDermot, William L.	Gill, Sarah Dell	15, July 1847	L3
McDonald, Harrison	Davis, Julia Maria	25, Apr. 1844	L3
McDonald, Hugh	Carroll, Kate	18, June 1857	L3
McDonald, Isaac	Owens, Jane	31, Dec. 1840	L3
McDougal, Addison B.	Turner, Emily J.	25, Jan. 1844	L3
McDowell, J.H.	Rodes, Belle	6, Jan. 1853	L3
McDowell, John	Achey, M.E.	23, Sept 1852	L3
McDowell, Joseph N.	Drake, Amanda	3, Apr. 1827	L3
McDowell, Malcolm	Gordon, Jennie	6, May 1852	L3
McDowell, Robert V.	Pinkstun, Mary Ann	10, Dec. 1857	L3
McDuffie, J.T.	Price, Mary A.	14, July 1853	L3
McElvain, John	Kelsey, Ellen (Mrs)	12, Oct. 1854	L3
McFarland, Demas L.	Heaton, Nancy (Mrs)	9, Mar. 1854	L3
McFarlane, James	Liddell, Margaret	10, Aug. 1854	L3
McFeely, James (Dr)	Miniear, Mary	13, Sept 1849	L3
McFerran, J.C. (Lt)	Green, Rose H.	10, Oct. 1844	L3
McGechin, Thomas	Bishop, Thalia	28, Dec. 1843	L3
McGibbens, David	Sharp, Mary A.	21, Oct. 1847	L3
McGowan, John H.	Green, Mary E.	5, July 1855	L3
McGrew, Alex	Hall, Carolina C.	10, Dec. 1840	L3
McGrew, Alexander	Fisher, Alvira L.	12, Jan. 1822	L3
McGrew, Alexander	Osborn, Margaret A.	19, Apr. 1825	L3
McGrew, Henry C.	Dick, Jane	11, June 1846	L3
McGrew, J.S.	Cord, Mary (Mrs)	17, Apr. 1851	L3
McGrew, James	Lundy, Nancy	23, Mar. 1849	L3
McGrew, Joseph	Gilkey, Mary Elizabeth	25, Apr. 1850	L3
McGrew, William C.	Osburn, Mary Ann	11, Feb. 1841	L3
McHenry, Enoch	Goulding, Rhoda (Mrs)	21, July 1817	L2
McHenry, John	Harrison, Ellen S.	30, Nov. 1854	L3
McIntyre, George	Moore, Sarah C.	6, Mar. 1845	L3
McIntyre, Peter	Mackie, Mary D.	6, Mar. 1845	L3
McKay, Jacob F.	Spangler, Lucy V.	9, Feb. 1854	L3
McKay, Ralph	Sterling, Mary Ann	28, Jan. 1841	L3
McKean, Alexander	Loring, Catharine	22, Apr. 1818	L3
McKean, James	Lodwick, Jane E.	18, June 1846	L3
McKee, Robert	Bonte, Hannah R.	30, Jan. 1845	L3
McKee, William	Conway, Elizabeth	31, July 1845	L3
McKeely, James H.	Park, Margaret	5, Jan. 1854	L3
McKenna, J. Theodore	Duval, Mary Isabella	2, Feb. 1854	L3
McKenzie, A.	Davis, Rachael	13, May 1852	L3
McKenzie, J.M. (Dr)	Washington, Marion W	18, May 1854	L3
McKinlay, James	Lang, Margaret	3, Nov. 1836	L3
McKinle, John (Rev)	Lanphear, Frances	9, May 1839	L3
McKinnell, Charles	Bailey, Mary B.T.	4, Nov. 1847	L3
McKinney, John (Col)	Taylor, Polly T.	24, Mar. 1817	L3
McKinney, John T.	Mayo, Sarah A.	13, June 1821	L3
McKoy, Theodore	Collins, Amelia Ann	15, Jan. 1846	L3

Grooms	Brides	Date of Notice	Page
McLain, Josiah	Whiterow, Mary P.	24, Feb. 1848	L3
McLane, Henry	Scott, Eliza	19, June 1851	L3
McLaughlin, C.A.	Ball, Ann H.	3, Nov. 1842	L3
McLaughlin, Zenas K.	Parker, Elizabeth Ann	30, Jan. 1845	L3
McLean, John	Garrard, Sarah B. (Mrs)	18, May 1843	L3
McLean, N.H.	Kilbreth, Sallie G.	18, June 1857	L3
McLean, Nathaniel	Burnet, Caroline	13, Sept 1838	L3
McLean, Robert L.	Guise, Maria Louisa	25, Apr. 1850	L3
McLean, Sylvester	Cox, Sarah Elizabeth	22, Oct. 1857	L3
McLenan, William	Doherty, Catharine	24, Jan. 1850	L3
McMahan, James	Jones, Ann Maria	15, June 1813	L3
McMahan, John	Griswold, Alice Ann	1, Oct. 1846	L3
McMaken, M.C.	Clark, Elizabeth	22, July 1852	L3
McMaster, Gilbert	Lewis, Pauline	26, Apr. 1855	L3
McMean, William	Fairchild, Polly	7, Mar. 1810	L3
McMellen, Isaac	Parker, Mary	1, Aug. 1844	L3
McMichael, Isaac	Hazen, Amelia	30, Mar. 1848	L3
McMullen, Samuel	McMullen, Martha	18, Apr. 1850	L3
McMurchy, William	Harvey, Janet	22, Dec. 1831	L4
McMurphey, A.T. (Rev)	Bennett, Eleanor	18, Apr. 1844	L3
McMurphey, J.W.	Bennet, Mary	22, May 1845	L3
McMurphy, Samuel S.	Hubbell, Mary C.F.	26, Sept 1839	L3
McNair, Alexander	Johnston, Agnes	19, Jan. 1854	L3
McNight, John	Greenwell, Anne	25, Feb. 1815	L1
McNutt, Charles	Burch, Elizabeth	15, Aug. 1810	L3
McNutt, James	Torrence, Rebecca	12, Dec. 1810	L2
McNutt, James	Johnson, Laura	6, Feb. 1845	L3
McQueen, James	Lawrence, Elizabeth	5, Sept 1850	L3
McTiernan, James	Shears, Jane	2, Oct. 1851	L3
McWilliams, Matthew	Hammond, Elizabeth	2, Nov. 1848	L3
Mead, John	Smith, Mary Rebecca	5, Oct. 1843	L3
Meade, Nathaniel B.	Stewart, Anastasia L	12, Oct. 1848	L3
Meadows, James	Edmonds, Emily	2, Mar. 1854	L3
Means, Thomas	Stewart, Ann J.	17, Feb. 1848	L3
Medaris, John (Dr)	Perry, Martha	8, Mar. 1849	L3
Medary, George W.	Moody, Margaret C.	15, Feb. 1849	L3
Medary, John M.	Dubois, Lorinda H.	28, May 1846	L3
Medary, William	Walker, Mary	26, Nov. 1819	L3
Meddock, Abijah	Duvall, Rachel	5, Feb. 1812	L2
Meek, Alexander A.	McCullough, Patty	1, Dec. 1807	L3
Meek, John P.	Lanter, Georgiana	6, July 1843	L3
Meeker, John C.	Miller, Amelia	1, Oct. 1840	L3
Meeker, Moses	Shackelton, Eliza P.	6, Apr. 1837	L3
Meley, Jonathan	Carson, Jane	25, Mar. 1841	L3
Melindy, P.	Coddington, Martha F	29, Oct. 1846	L3
Meline, James F.	Rogers, Mary Elizabeth	3, Sept 1846	L3
Melish, Thomas J.	Bromwewll, Maria V.	24, May 1849	L3
Mellen, William C.	Brewster, Angeline C	30, Apr. 1857	L3
Mellen, William P.	Clarke, Isabel	17, Sept 1846	L3
Mercer, Lucius	Smith, Sarah B.	26, Jan. 1854	L3
Meredith, J.R.	Collier, Annie	13, Jan. 1853	L3
Merrell, Ashbel S.	Hill, Sophia E.	14, Oct. 1841	L3
Merrill, A.S.	Kellogg, Rhoda W.	30, Oct. 1851	L3
Merrill, Daniel	Bright, Nancy	12, Mar. 1829	L2

Grooms	Brides	Date of Notice	Page
Merrill, Robert, Jr.	Poineer, Adeline	18, July 1826	L3
Merrit, James P.J	Crossley, Rachel	31, Aug. 1822	L3
Merriweather, N.	Yeatman, Sarah Jane	26, Dec. 1839	L3
Merser, Robert	Dobson, Ann	10, June 1847	L3
Merwin, Anson W.	Charters, Anna L.	10, June 1841	L3
Merwin, George B.	Wood, Loretta	9, Aug. 1838	L3
Metcalf, Eli P.	Kemper, Fanny C.	20, Mar. 1851	L3
Metcalf, James	Edwards, Ann	23, Mar. 1843	L3
Meyers, J.H.	Ellis, E.J.	19, Jan. 1854	L3
Meyrick, William	Collins, Mary	16, June 1853	L3
Michael, D.C. (Capt)	Bacon, A.E.	19, Dec. 1850	L3
Middleton, Elijah C.	Lovejoy, Mary Jane	27, Apr. 1848	L3
Middleton, William	Mason, Ann	20, Feb. 1822	L2
Midlen, William	McBride, Eliza	15, Sept 1842	L3
Miles, Reason S.	Tatem, Catharine	4, Mar. 1847	L3
Miller, Alfred	Gaskill, Susannah	24, Apr. 1845	L3
Miller, Charles W.	Conover, Lavina (Mrs)	10, Sept 1846	L3
Miller, Emanuel J.	Taylor, Sarah K.	20, June 1839	L3
Miller, Halsey B.	Williams, Mary Ann E.	24, Dec. 1846	L3
Miller, Henry	Moore, Jane	3, July 1811	L3
Miller, Henry B.	Reeves, Mary	10, June 1841	L3
Miller, Henry F.	Statenfield, Elizabeth	9, Sept 1852	L3
Miller, Jacob	Kyler, Susannah	13, Jan. 1806	L3
Miller, James R.	Bonte, Sarah A.	13, May 1847	L3
Miller, John	Cutting, Mary Ann	30, Oct. 1856	L5
Miller, John F.	Chess, Mary W.	27, Aug. 1857	L3
Miller, John V.	Grannis, Sarah M.	11, Jan. 1849	L3
Miller, Joseph	Derrough, Mary (Mrs)	16, May 1850	L3
Miller, Martin	Long, Nancy	31, Oct. 1810	L3
Miller, Richard	O'Ferrall, Catharine	22, Nov. 1825	L3
Miller, Samuel	Pickering, Emeline M	23, May 1839	L3
Miller, T.H.	Crumbaugh, Sarah	30, Mar. 1854	L3
Miller, Thane	Jungman, Fanny E.	10, Aug. 1848	L3
Miller, William	Thurman, N.E.	18, Jan. 1855	L3
Miller, Z.B.	Nicholas, Huldah	18, Apr. 1844	L3
Milliken, Minor	Mollyneaux, Mary B.	11, Sept 1856	L5
Mills, James R.	Thornton, Elvira	22, July 1852	L3
Mills, Thornton (Rev)	Whittelsey, Ann (Mrs)	2, Nov. 1854	L3
Milne, George	Grinnell, Helen Elizabeth	16, Sept 1847	L3
Miner, John L.	Wright, Mary	2, Nov. 1837	L3
Miner, Thomas H.	Baldridge, Rebecca	5, Dec. 1844	L3
Minett, Julius C.	Thompson, Sarah	20, July 1837	L3
Minnear, John W.	Bowman, Margaret P.	25, Mar. 1847	L3
Minor, John D.	McLean, Mary B.	4, Jan. 1844	L3
Mirrielees, George	Lumsden, Sara	11, Oct. 1849	L3
Mitchel, Samuel	Gram, Mary	16, Feb. 1854	L3
Mitchell, J. McD.	Crawford, Margaret J	18, May 1843	L3
Mitchell, J.W.	Whitehead, Mary Jane	13, Jan. 1848	L3
Mitchell, James	Howell, Virginia J.	1, Apr. 1852	L3
Mitchell, John S.	Black, Nancy	2, Nov. 1837	L3
Mitchell, Micajah B.	Ward, Frances M.	7, May 1846	L3
Mitchell, Samuel	Gram, Mary A.	26, Jan. 1854	L3
Mitchell, Thomas G.	Coffin, Martha Elizabeth	22, Oct. 1846	L3
Mitchell, Walter(Rev	Evans, Mary Eliza	2, Nov. 1848	L3

Grooms	Brides	Date of Notice	Page
Mitchell, William	Scott, Jane A.	6, Apr. 1848	L3
Mitchell, William F.	Coleman, Elizabeth A	26, Feb. 1852	L3
Mitchell, William H.	Goodloe, Louisa	12, Oct. 1854	L3
Mix, James	Covey, Helen M.	11, May 1854	L3
Mix, W.H.	Craimer, Elizabeth	23, Oct. 1856	L5
Mixer, S.F. (Dr)	Knowlton, Mary E.	3, Mar. 1853	L3
Mixter, Ebenezer	Janes, Deborah	2, Sept 1816	L3
Mode, William	Peirce, Priscilla	9, Mar. 1854	L3
Moffat, James C.	Matthews, Mary Blair	2, Jan. 1851	L3
Moffett, James S.	Hoffner, Elizabeth M.	9, Mar. 1843	L3
Mollen, Joseph	Thomas, Mary	3, Apr. 1811	L3
Molster, Cornelius	Finch, Sarah Ann	21, Nov. 1844	L3
Monk, Samuel	Case, Harriet R.	7, Jan. 1847	L3
Montague, Thomas	Bacon, Sarah	16, Dec. 1847	L3
Montgomery, Henry J.	Smith, Thomasina C.	16, Sept 1852	L3
Moody, James E.	Parker, Margaret L.	24, July 1851	L3
Moody, William M.	Balee, Omanthis	13, Sept 1855	L3
Moonert, Augustus	Seymour, Sarah	14, Sept 1848	L3
Mooney, D.H.	Dakin, Mary A.	12, Oct. 1854	L3
Moore, Adam	Dodsworth, Eliza	25, Mar. 1852	L3
Moore, Adrian	Evans, Susannah	10, Apr. 1845	L3
Moore, Arthur	Utz, Isabella	13, Aug. 1857	L3
Moore, Augustus O.	Green, Harriet C.	16, Oct. 1851	L3
Moore, Augustus O.	Hulburd, Mary Eliza	9, Sept 1841	L3
Moore, Charles L.	Harrison, Lydia C.	22, Sept 1853	L3
Moore, Francis M.	Hilton, Maria (Mrs)	25, June 1857	L3
Moore, George W.	Terry, Sarah	10, Feb. 1826	L3
Moore, Hugh	Symmes, (Miss)	2, Dec. 1805	L3
Moore, Isaac	Meranda, Amanda	9, Nov. 1854	L3
Moore, J.C.S. (Dr)	Wright, Susan Emily	19, June 1851	L3
Moore, James C.	DeCamp, Phoebe A.	10, May 1855	L3
Moore, John M.	Smith, Fanny O.	20, Apr. 1848	L3
Moore, John M.	Wilshire, Sallie	15, June 1854	L3
Moore, John, Jr.	Langley, Mary	8, Mar. 1838	L3
Moore, Joseph A.	Williamson, Margaret	30, Dec. 1847	L3
Moore, Nathan	Kelley, Clarissa	13, Oct. 1818	L3
Moore, Robert	Moffett, Anna	31, Jan. 1856	L3
Moore, Robert M.	Price, Anna Eliza	4, May 1843	L3
Moore, T.S.	Regor, Prudence A.	10, Dec. 1840	L3
Moore, Thomas H.	Gordon, Lydia Ann	7, Jan. 1847	L3
Moore, Thomas L.	Adams, Jennie K.	30, June 1853	L3
Moore, W.H.	Ward, Mary	11, Mar. 1815	L3
Moore, William (Rev)	Forbes, Elizabeth W.	21, Oct. 1847	L3
Moore, William H.	Butterworth, Virgina	26, Feb. 1852	L3
Moore, William H.	Eaton, Anna J. Irwin	15, Aug. 1844	L3
Moorhead, John	Humphreys, Susan (Mrs)	23, Dec. 1830	L4
More, William	Anderson, Margaret	4, Aug. 1817	L3
Morgan, Andrew J.	Moore, Lucinda	12, June 1845	L3
Morgan, Daniel H.	Gordon, Mary	16, Oct. 1856	L5
Morgan, Edward S.	Smith, Lizzy G.	3, June 1847	L3
Morgan, George W.	Smith, Kate	21, Sept 1854	L3
Morgan, Henry	Yeatman, Elizabeth	11, May 1843	L3
Morgan, Hugh	Smith, Ann B.	26, May 1842	L3
Morgan, Isaac	Wood, Eliza	17, Nov. 1817	L3

Grooms	Brides	Date of Notice	Page
Morgan, Samuel J.	Quinton, Ella A.	25, Sept 1856	L5
Morrell, A.	Ware, Anna Maria	10, Dec. 1840	L3
Morrell, Daniel J.	Stackhouse, Susanna	20, Feb. 1845	L3
Morrill, H.E. (Dr)	Langdon, Cynthia	18, Nov. 1841	L3
Morrill, Nahum	Barnard, Mary	24, Sept 1840	L3
Morris, Charles N.	Brachman, Rosalie	27, Sept 1855	L3
Morris, Daniel	McLaughlin, Elizabeth	26, May 1807	L3
Morris, Edward C.	Ely, Anna L.	9, July 1857	L3
Morris, Henry C.	Hunter, Charlotte	30, Oct. 1845	L3
Morris, J.F.	Skillman, Sarah E.	21, June 1855	L3
Morris, Jacob	Graham, Susan M.	25, June 1846	L3
Morris, John C.	Beauman, Mary	27, May 1847	L3
Morris, Joseph S.	Burton, Mattie S.	5, Feb. 1857	L3
Morris, Lorenzo D.	Smith, Hannah	22, June 1843	L3
Morris, Robert H.	Wright, Martha E.	7, Apr. 1853	L3
Morris, William R.	Powers, Lydia S.	13, May 1823	L3
Morrison, D. Wallis	Whitney, M.J.	19, Nov. 1857	L3
Morrison, James	Richey, Belle	20, Apr. 1854	L3
Morrison, James C.	McCormick, Lydia S.	5, Oct. 1843	L3
Morrison, Joseph	Moore, Jane	22, June 1854	L3
Morrison, William	Debolt, Elizabeth	27, Jan. 1807	L3
Morrow, R.A.	Jones, Marie A.	18, Nov. 1852	L3
Morse, Bennett W.	Dickinson, M. Ellen	30, Sept 1852	L3
Morse, Charles E.	Hardie, Sarah	17, Sept 1846	L3
Morse, George W.	Hemphill, Mary	28, Aug. 1845	I3
Morse, Increase	Whittaker, Caroline	6, June 1850	L3
Morse, Stephen	Cook, Sarah J.	19, Dec. 1850	L3
Morsell, James C.	Johnson, Amelia	26, Dec. 1823	L3
Morten, Thomas	Booth, Eliza	25, Nov. 1847	L3
Morton, Aaron Gano	Spencer, Mary Elizabeth	21, Dec. 1843	L3
Morton, Wellington	Calling, Jane Ann	4, Mar. 1841	L3
Morton, William R.	Henderson, Mary A.	7, Jan. 1847	L3
Morton, William R.	Lee, Mary M.	6, June 1850	L3
Mosby, Napoleon B.	Mosby, Ann (Mrs)	18, Apr. 1844	L3
Moses, Benjamin	Block, Esther	21, Jan. 1836	L1
Moses, Simpson P.	Tucker, Lizzie C.	19, July 1849	L3
Moss, Horace H.	McCreary, R. Louisa	5, Aug. 1847	L3
Moss, Lewis	Smith, Martha	8, Feb. 1849	L3
Motz, George W.	Dennison, Mary Ang.	25, Apr. 1844	L3
Mount, Robert M.	Shephert, Nancy	19, Jan. 1843	L3
Moyer, Lewis H.	Helvering, Christina	9, Mar. 1854	L3
Moylich, Frank	Snyder, Margaret	16, Feb. 1854	L3
Mufford, Howell	Riddle, Lucinda	6, June 1844	L3
Mulford, John P.	Parvin, Ruth H.	4, Jan. 1838	L3
Mullen, James	Rees, Mollie M.	5, Nov. 1857	L3
Mungall, John	Goddin, Ann	5, Feb. 1846	L3
Muntz, Jeremiah	Cain, Ellen A.	28, Jan. 1841	L3
Murdoch, J.	Bartlett, Mary E.	5, Dec. 1850	L3
Murdock, Joseph	King, Louise	24, Nov. 1853	L3
Murphey, A.J.	Snowden, Nancy	12, Jan. 1854	L3
Murphy, Andrew	Nixon, Rachel E.	16, Feb. 1854	L3
Murphy, Archibald	McCane, Sarah	1, Feb. 1825	L3
Murphy, Lewis	Cole, Adela	17, Mar. 1853	L3
Murray, William H.	Brown, Jane	1, Nov. 1849	L3

Grooms	Brides	Date of Notice	Page
Murray, William P.	Conwell, Carrie S.	9, June 1853	L3
Murrell, Thomas	Beatty, Eliza	23, Aug. 1849	L3
Musat, Charles	Lord, Susan	19, July 1855	L3
Muselman, Edward M.	McIntire, Mary E.	6, July 1854	L3
Musgrave, William B.	Fosdick, Anna M.	14, Aug. 1856	L5
Mussey, William H.	Lindsly, Carrie W.	28, May 1857	L3
Mustard, Alexander	Gaiter, Sophia	28, Dec. 1843	L3
Mustin, C.C.L.	Pickering, Maria	9, Aug. 1855	L3
Myer, Lewis Henry (Rev)	Tressel, Sarah Mary	12, Aug. 1823	L3
Myers, Abraham	Moses, Sarah Ann	5, July 1838	L3
Myers, Elkunah	Owens, Mary Ann Jane	12, July 1849	L3
Myers, Henry W.	Fehleisen, Matilda	14, Oct. 1852	L3
Myers, Isaac	Graham, Jane	15, Jan. 1846	L3
Myers, John	Brooks, Mary	21, Oct. 1820	L3
Myers, Joseph	Goodwin, Susan	8, July 1823	L3
Myers, Simon	Bill, Betsey	30, Dec. 1806	L3
Myers, William W.	Nash, Anna E.	4, Nov. 1852	L3
Nason, Cyrus	Conklin, Mary A.	8, Jan. 1852	L3
Nason, Cyrus	Jones, Harriet E.	2, Aug. 1855	L3
Nathorst, John	Ross, Charlotte	18, Apr. 1844	L3
Naudain, W.M.(Dr)	Esselstine, Cornelia	5, July 1855	L3
Neave, Charles	Caldwell, Jane R.	8, June 1827	L3
Neave, Charley	Whipple, Martha L.	18, Dec. 1851	L3
Neave, Martin	Force, Mary N.	16, Oct. 1845	L3
Neave, Thomson	Medaris Lizzie J.	5, Nov. 1857	L3
Neff, Ambrose W.	Smith, Rebecca	29, Aug. 1850	L3
Neff, George W.	Stanbery, Clara	10, Jan. 1856	L3
Neff, Peter	Biggs, Sarah	7, Mar. 1850	L3
Neff, Peter Rudolph	Burnet, Caroline	14, July 1853	L3
Neff, William	Keller, Sarah	9, Mar. 1854	L3
Neff, William C.	Thomas, Ellen B.	23, Feb. 1854	L3
Neff, William Howard	Wallace, Lucy	28, Nov. 1850	L3
Neighbours, James	Hopkins, Caroline	30, Aug. 1825	L3
Neil, Robert E.	Sullivant, Jane M.	8, June 1843	L3
Neil, William A.	Nevins, Mary L.	30, June 1853	L3
Nelson, Herron (Dr)	Sellman, Harriet Key	31, Dec. 1857	L3
Nesbit, William P.	Farris, Elizabeth	30, Oct. 1845	L3
Nesmith, Thomas A.	Lamotte, Eliza	5, July 1855	L3
Neville, John S.	Hayes, Charlotte A.	27, Jan. 1842	L3
Newcomb, John M.	Shields, Julia M.	29, Jan. 1846	L3
Newhall, Charles H.	Russell, Mary Jane	25, Mar. 1852	L3
Newkirk, Matthew	St.Clair, Nancy M.	9, Mar. 1837	L3
Nias, Raymond	Gilman, Lizzie S.	17, Aug. 1854	L3
Nicholas, Charles M.	Bruen, Joanna	1, Aug. 1844	L3
Nichols, John D.	Rice, Frances P.	2, Sept 1831	L2
Nichols, Luther	Whittaker, Anna	9, July 1846	L3
Nichols, S.S.	Atlee, Elizabeth J.	4, Mar. 1841	L3
Nicholson, Henry (Dr)	Askien, Mary	19, June 1845	L3
Nicholson, Thomas	Goble, Elizabeth	7, Oct. 1847	L3
Niles, William B.	Scull, Letitia	1, Dec. 1853	L3
Nimmo, Edward L.	Henderson, Ellen G.	26, May 1842	L3
Nippert, August	Knapp, Virginia	30, July 1857	L3
Nixon, Alexander B.	Bigham, Margaret G.	25, Sept 1845	L3

Grooms	Brides	Date of Notice	Page
Nixon, John S.	Clemens, Mary A.	18, Sept 1851	L3
Nixon, Martin	Brown, Matilda	25, Feb. 1847	L3
Nixon, Wilson K.	Greenwood, Martha	20, July 1854	L3
Noble, David	Kerr, Rebecca	28, Apr. 1817	L3
Noel, Henry A.	Waterman, Susan B.	4, July 1844	L3
Nordhoff, Charles	Letford, Eliza J.	27, Aug. 1857	L3
Norris, Charles C.	Yeatman, Sarah Lucy	18, Apr. 1839	L3
Norris, Charles P.	Johnston, Essa E.	5, Nov. 1857	L3
North, Peter	Stall, Emma	18, Mar. 1847	L3
Northrop, William W.	Stone, Melissa B.	16, Nov. 1843	L3
Norton, O.D. (Dr)	Burt, Juliet	26, Oct. 1854	L3
Nutts, Jacob	Blair, Sarah E.	27, Nov. 1845	L3
Nye, George W. (Dr)	Conklin, Emily C.	10, July 1851	L3
Nye, Henry	Ball, Harriet	30, June 1853	L3
Oakley, Lester	Rose, Parmelia D.	15, Feb. 1844	L3
Oalley, John	Macgerry, Margaret	19, Aug. 1820	L3
Oates, John	Stauffer, Josephine	3, Jan. 1856	L3
Oberdorf, Elias	Lewis, Fanny	20, July 1843	L3
O'Connell, Daniel A.	Shultz, Mary B.	11, Aug. 1853	L3
O'Connor, John H.	Higgins, Margaret	6, Dec. 1855	L3
O'Connor, John X.	Higgins, Margaret	29, Nov. 1855	L3
Odlin, Woodbridge	Thompson, Lizzie	30, Mar. 1854	L3
O'Donnell, Hugh	Pitcher, Laura	12, Oct. 1837	L4
Ogborn, W. Elwood	Slocum, Elizabeth F.	11, June 1846	L3
Ogden, E.H.	Wood, Harriet S.	13, July 1848	L3
Ogden, Henry S.	Wood, Julia E.	23, Jan. 1851	L3
Ogden, Henry T.	Holby, Nancy	19, Sept 1850	L3
Ogden, James	Hall, Margaret	5, Jan. 1818	L3
Ogden, Lewis B.	Hardy, Isabella	17, June 1847	L3
Ogden, Robert B.	Harr, Julia W.	23, Sept 1847	L3
Olcott, Edward R.	Gosman, Elizabeth (Mrs)	22, July 1852	L3
Olds, C.N.	Williams, Mary B.	16, Sept 1852	L3
Oliver, David (Dr)	Wade, Mary	26, Feb. 1816	L3
Oliver, David W.	Harrison, Mary A.	8, Dec. 1853	L3
Oliver, M.W.	Gere, Anna E.	4, July 1850	L3
Oliver, William (Capt)	Ruffin, Eliza	26, Apr. 1814	L3
Oliver, William D.	Davis, Mary Jane	13, May 1847	L3
Olmstead, H.B.	Lawson, Ellen	4, Sept 1856	L5
Openlander, Chris.	Horman, Mary M.	3, June 1847	L3
Oppenlander, Chris.	Holman, Mary M.	17, June 1847	L3
Orange, Benjamin	Beresford, Elizabeth	26, June 1828	L3
Orr, Arthur	Clingman, Eliza	3, Oct. 1844	L3
Orr, John	Kiloh, Henrietta	17, July 1851	L3
Orr, Robert M.	Weer, Esther Ann	18, July 1844	L3
Orr, Thomas	Munford, Eliza Jane	1, Aug. 1844	L3
Orr, Thomas J. (Dr)	Grandin, Mary E.	28, Dec. 1837	L3
Orr, William M.	Dixon, Elizabeth	29, Dec. 1817	L2
Orvis, Clark	Holley, M.H.	3, Dec. 1857	L3
Osborn, Archibald K.	Marshall, Missouri A	12, Nov. 1846	L3
Osborne, John H.	Belcher, Elizabeth	29, Sept 1853	L3
Osborne, Thos. (Rev)	Allibone, Mary	23, Oct. 1822	L3
Osburn, Stephen	Scribner, Sarah B.	21, Oct. 1847	L3
Oswald, Matthew H.	Bennett, Lucy	19, Dec. 1844	L3

Grooms	Brides	Date of Notice	Page
Ottenheimer, Morris	Oppenheimer, Lydia	21, Dec. 1837	L3
Otter, Abraham(Capt)	Miller, Julia Ann	6, July 1837	L3
Owen, Charles	Mariani, Louisa	1, July 1852	L3
Owen, Chauncey B.	Gedge, Mary A.	22, Sept 1853	L3
Owen, John	Murray, Isabella	8, Feb. 1838	L3
Owen, John	Punshon, Jane	9, May 1839	L3
Owen, John H.	Bower, Virginia S.	28, Oct. 1847	L3
Owens, John P.	Black, Jane	2, Feb. 1843	L3
Owens, John P.	McAllister, Helen J.	23, Nov. 1848	L3
Owens, Richard	Cummins, Mary A.	29, Oct. 1846	L3
Packard, Henry	Cowan, Sarah	9, July 1846	L3
Packard, S.S.	Crocker, Marion	14, Mar. 1850	L3
Paddack, Alexander	Crumsey, Mary A.	14, July 1853	L3
Paddock, W.R.	Hodgson, Mary Abby	12, Sept 1850	L3
Page, Andrew Jackson	Yocum, Elizabeth	3, Oct. 1844	L3
Paine, Daniel	Tess, Rebecca	8, Nov. 1814	L3
Palmer, Abraham	Nehemiah, Sarah	2, May 1844	L3
Palmer, Charles L.	Tincher, Caroline	20, June 1850	L3
Palmer, George F.	Robinson, Sarah F.	30, Oct. 1856	L5
Palmer, John	Kamper, Sophia	27, Apr. 1813	L3
Palmer, John J.	Harvey, E.G.	27, Jan. 1848	L3
Palmer, Solon	Becket, Mary A.	17, July 1851	L3
Palmer, William E.	Shaw, Martha E.	22, Oct. 1857	L3
Palmerton, Homer	Stewart, Clarinda V.	15, May 1828	L3
Pancoast, George	Archer, Lizzie P.	13, Jan. 1853	L3
Pane, George W.	King, Amanda J.	1, Aug. 1844	L3
Paris, Peter	Reese, Mary Jane	1, July 1847	L3
Parke, Samuel S.	Lee, Clara	30, Aug. 1849	L3
Parker, Alexander C.	Noble, Melissia O.	9, Nov. 1848	L3
Parker, Daniel	Gillespie, Kate	11, Nov. 1847	L3
Parker, David M.	Dungan, Harriet	29, Feb. 1844	L3
Parker, Frederick	Langland, Margaret	5, Mar. 1846	L3
Parker, J.A. (Dr)	Lindley, Joanna	17, Oct. 1823	L3
Parker, Luther	Bevan, Louisa A.	10, Apr. 1851	L3
Parker, T.H.	Cheever, Mary J.	1, Nov. 1849	L3
Parker, William	Luse, Angeline (Mrs)	13, Feb. 1840	L3
Parker, William	Woodruff, Catharine	8, Nov. 1838	L3
Parker, William G.	Leeds, Ann	18, Apr. 1844	L3
Parmele, Hervey	Fernival, Martha	20, May 1816	L3
Parr, John C.	Butler, Emily	10, Nov. 1853	L3
Parrot, Horace	Matthews, Rebecca	19, Jan. 1854	L3
Parrott, George	Sinks, Belle	12, Nov. 1857	L3
Parry, Owen L.	Goodhue, Miranda	4, Dec. 1845	L3
Parsell, George	Gibbs, Mary P.	6, Sept 1838	L3
Parsens, George M.	Swan, Jane	2, Nov. 1843	L3
Parsons, Enoch	Horner, Sarah A.E.	28, Oct. 1852	L3
Partridge, Charles A	Peck, Mary G.	27, May 1852	L3
Partridge, Sanford S	Moore, Mary	29, Jan. 1852	L3
Parvin, Samuel T.	Brown, Lucinda H.	14, Sept 1848	L3
Patmore, John	Satcher, Marian	9, Sept 1847	L3
Patrick, Holmes C.	Taylor, Mary Jane	30, Oct. 1851	L3
Patrick, J.W.	Grace, Ruth A.	28, May 1857	L3
Patten, Alpheus	Davis, Amanda	1, Oct. 1846	L3

Grooms	Brides	Date of Notice	Page
Patten, Matthew	Ludlow, Betsey	22, Oct. 1808	L3
Patterson, John K.	Bliss, Sarah T.	29, Jan. 1829	L1
Patterson, R.J.	Clark, Lucy	27, July 1848	L3
Patton, Andrew H.	Griffis, Sarah Ann	14, Aug. 1851	L3
Pawson, Thomas	Weeks, Rebecca	11, Nov. 1847	L3
Payge, John	Cooke, Nancy	8, Jan. 1846	L3
Payne, Edmond	Martin, Margaret	23, Mar. 1854	L3
Peabody, Herbert C.	Lea, Emily L.	28, Jan. 1841	L3
Peach, Henry G.	Coffin, Esther E.	9, July 1840	L3
Peachey, Henry	Cummins, Jennett	18, July 1850	L3
Peacock, David C.	Follin, Mirian F.	13, Apr. 1854	L3
Peacock, Simeon	Langdon, Mollie G.	19, Mar. 1857	L3
Peacock, William H.	Browner, Sophia J.	17, June 1847	L3
Pearce, Christopher	Sackett, Jane Ann	22, Oct. 1840	L3
Pearce, Henry	Owens, Elizabeth	19, Aug. 1847	L3
Pearce, Henry	Owens, Sallie J.	8, Jan. 1857	L3
Pearce, James	Goss, Mary	20, May 1847	L3
Pearce, John	Bagott, Alice	12, Aug. 1841	L3
Pearson, John	Brokenshire, Mary A.	1, Oct. 1846	L3
Pease, John B.	Dibrell, Elizabeth W	2, Mar. 1837	L3
Peck, A.F.	Todd, Caroline	6, Oct. 1842	L3
Peck, Charles A.	Potter, Adeline E.	17, Mar. 1842	L3
Peebles, Joseph R.	Straub, Mary C.	29, Feb. 1844	L3
Peebles, William S.	Stephenson, Lucy	4, Nov. 1841	L3
Peebles, William S.	Tift, Delia Annie	17, June 1852	L3
Pelton, John	Hann, Catharine	13, May 1816	L3
Pendleton, Edmund	Morgan, Cornelia M.	20, Feb. 1845	L3
Pendleton, Elliott	Gaylord, Mary E.	13, Nov. 1850	L3
Pendleton, George H.	Key, Alice	11, June 1846	L3
Pendleton, N.G.	James, Anne	20, May 1841	L3
Pendleton, Nathaniel	Hunt, Jane F.	13, May 1820	L3
Pendry, John L.	Rockey, Catharine O.	17, June 1847	L3
Penny, George	Taylor, Jane	8, Jan. 1857	L3
Pepper, James H.	Schooley, Rebecca R.	7, Nov. 1844	L3
Peregrine, J.S.(Rev)	DeGraw, Rebecca	20, Aug. 1857	L3
Perigo,	McCready, S.V.	9, Nov. 1854	L3
Perin, Franklin	McMicken, Mary	4, July 1844	L3
Perin, Lyman	Wilson, Maria Louisa	19, Apr. 1849	L3
Perrine, Robert	Miller, Lucinda(Mrs)	13, July 1843	L3
Perry, A.F.	Williams, Elizabeth	23, Mar. 1843	L3
Perry, Benjamin P.	Reynolds, Elizabeth	4, July 1850	L3
Perry, Samuel	Cunningham, Eliza A.	16, Mar. 1848	L3
Perry, Samuel	Thew, Mary B.	19, Aug. 1816	L3
Perry, Samuel	Wallace, Mary	11, Oct. 1809	L3
Peter, William	King, Sarah (Mrs)	31, Oct. 1844	L3
Peters, Henry J.	Huyler, Marianne	13, Feb. 1845	L3
Peters, William C.	Barrett, Lucy D.	20, Aug. 1857	L3
Pettiner, Matthew	DeCamp, Sarah B.	5, Mar. 1857	L3
Pettit, John W.	Kenneallie, Mary J.	30, Aug. 1855	L3
Pettit, Theodore	Bailey, Martha F.	17, Mar. 1853	L3
Peyton, Buford	Cochenour, Elizabeth	9, Mar. 1843	L3
Peyton, Francis H.	Luke, Harriet A.	31, Oct. 1839	L3
Pharis, Washington	Looker, Pamela C.	8, Apr. 1812	L3
Phelps, S.W.	Drake, Harriet E.	5, May 1836	L3

Grooms	Brides	Date of Notice	Page
Phelps, Winslow S.	Foster, Susan W.	16, Mar. 1837	L3
Philip, Bernhard	Purlier, Elizabeth	11, Sept 1845	L3
Phillips, Benjamin C	Etherington, Susan C.	4, Apr. 1850	L3
Phillips, David (Rev)	Matthews, Elizabeth (Mrs)	14, Sept 1848	L3
Phillips, Isaac	Martin Mary Ann (Mrs)	2, Dec. 1852	L3
Phillips, W.H.	Hill, Martha P.	12, Nov. 1846	L3
Phillips, William	Kautz, Margaret D.	18, Aug. 1853	L3
Phillips, William	Symmonds, Esther E.	22, Sept 1842	L3
Phillipson, Simon	Stoy, Susan	12, Mar. 1808	L3
Philpot, William	Hammatt, Ann M.	10, Apr. 1845	L3
Phipps, Gardner	Enyart, Rebecca A.	14, Mar. 1839	L3
Phipps, William R.	Reynolds, Lydia B.	5, June 1851	L3
Piatt, Abraham S.	Piatt, Hannah A.	26, Nov. 1840	L3
Piatt, J.W.	DeValcourt, Martha E	7, Sept 1837	L3
Piatt, Jacob	Hubbell, Mary A.	3, Mar. 1853	L3
Piatt, John H.	Willis, Martha Ann	27, July 1813	L3
Piatt, William	Allen, Mary L.	18, Dec. 1851	L3
Pickens, James S.	Smith, Catharine	27, Aug. 1857	L3
Pickens, John	Carlisle, Nancy	23, Apr. 1805	L3
Pierce, Elijah	Bartle, Eliza	9, Feb. 1809	L3
Pierce, Harvey	Dickinson, Sarah	26, Sept 1844	L3
Pierce, James	Smith, Louisa	20, Apr. 1848	L3
Pierce, James	Wood, Mary Eliza	2, Mar. 1843	L3
Pierce, Joseph(Capt)	Shreve, Mary	7, July 1831	L3
Pierce, Thomas B.	Wheeler, Mary Jane	9, Oct. 1845	L3
Pierce, William	Jackson, Evelina	15, Sept 1836	L3
Pierson, Charles E.	Moore, Nancy M.	20, Nov. 1845	L3
Pierson, Daniel B.	Lathrop, Lydia H.	24, Jan. 1850	L3
Pigman, William P.	Sprigman, M. Theresa	12, Jan. 1854	L3
Pike Samuel N.	Miller, Ellen P.	5, Nov. 1846	L3
Pike, John W.	Raines, Vashti N.	30, Mar. 1854	L3
Pike, Samuel T.	Simpson, Genett	22, Feb. 1855	L3
Pindell, Daniel	Sterling, Elizabeth	21, Oct. 1841	L3
Pingree, E.M. (Rev)	Halley, Mary Ann	22, Oct. 1840	L3
Pitman, Edward G.	Barrett, Alvira J.	18, Dec. 1856	L3
Place, Lucius H.	Landis, Elizabeth	13, Feb. 1845	L3
Platt, William H.	Smith, Amelia	10, May 1855	L3
Pleasants, Samuel E.	Biggs, Mary	19, May 1821	L3
Plummer, Aaron	Ousley, Martha	9, Feb. 1854	L3
Polley, Charles C.	Orr, Mary Jane	8, Oct. 1846	L3
Pollock, John	Butler, Martha Sarah	21, Aug. 1845	L3
Pollock, John D.	McLean, Mattie	10, Jan. 1856	L3
Pomeroy, Robert	Jenkins, Mary C.	6, Feb. 1840	L3
Pomroy, Caleb M.	Simpson, Nancy	16, Oct. 1834	L1
Pond, Augustus	Blaique, Sophia	19, May 1842	L3
Pond, H. Aug.	Hubbard, Julie E.	24, Oct. 1850	L3
Pool, James	Cilley, Emily	11, June 1857	L3
Pope, J.P.	Mooklar, Anna	20, Oct. 1853	L3
Porter, J.H.	Bonsall, L.T.	30, Mar. 1849	L3
Porter, William H.	Halsted, Mary Louisa	21, July 1853	L3
Portner, Henry A.	Caswell, Mary H.	17, May 1855	L3
Posey, Oliver	Patterson, Sallie E.	5, Nov. 1857	L3
Pottenger, Harden	Milholland, Mary	16, Feb. 1854	L3
Potter, Courtland W.	Umpheries, Annie E.	9, Feb. 1854	L3

Grooms	Brides	Date of Notice	Page
Potter, Henry E.	Finn, Anna E.	22, Oct. 1857	L3
Potter, James H.	Gulick, Mary (Mrs)	19, Oct. 1843	L3
Potter, Joseph T(Dr)	Longworth, Elizabeth M.	28, Sept 1848	L3
Potter, Thaddeus	Smith, Nancy Jane	9, Feb. 1854	L3
Potter, William H.	Clark, Elizabeth	26, June 1845	L3
Potts, William Henry	Stephens, Hannah	2, Feb. 1837	L4
Poucher, Isaiah	Gresh, Catharine	6, Apr. 1854	L3
Powars, John	Lehman, Sybilla	27, Nov. 1834	L2
Powell, Ellick	Merrick, Elizabeth (Mrs)	15, Sept 1821	L3
Powell, Henry	Berrall, Susan	19, Aug. 1852	L3
Powell, James	Foley, Anna M.	26, Apr. 1855	L3
Powell, Joseph	Hallowell, Louisa R.	29, June 1843	L3
Powell, W.S.	Ross, Ellen Luella	26, Jan. 1843	L3
Powell, William	Barrall, Mary	26, Apr. 1855	L3
Powell, William F.	Dulhagen, Elizabeth	21, Dec. 1848	L3
Power, John T.	Clarke, Fannie	5, Nov. 1857	L3
Powers, Aaron	Colby, Martha	24, Feb. 1807	L3
Powers, B.F.	Bosson, Catharine M.	1, Dec. 1818	L3
Pragoff, William	Plasket, Mary Jemima	12, Sept 1833	L1
Pratt, Albert C.	Bidwell, Pennie	31, May 1855	L3
Prentiss, Charles S.	Smith, Mary F.	26, Jan. 1854	L3
Prescott, T.O. (Rev)	Mackie, Jessie	19, July 1849	L3
Prestley, James (Rev)	Tagart, Jane Mary	7, May 1846	L3
Prestley, William H.	Burgoyne, Ann Jane	5, Mar. 1857	L3
Preston, A.J.	Raguet, Lillie	19, Jan. 1854	L3
Preston, Edmund J.	Bryant, Lydia	16, Dec. 1847	L3
Price, James P.	Dana, Frances	16, Nov. 1843	L3
Price, John E.	Baker, Mattie L.	7, Apr. 1853	L3
Price, Patrick	Byrne, Catharine	29, Aug. 1850	L3
Price, Philip	Malsbery, Maria (Mrs)	30, June 1806	L3
Price, Rees B.	Seiter, Mary Louisa	22, Jan. 1857	L3
Price, Thomas	Hindman, Susan	29, Feb. 1844	L3
Price, William T.	McHenry, Eliza A.G.	17, Oct. 1826	L3
Prichard, George A.	Colby, Hannah S.	27, May 1841	L3
Priley, William	Stevens, Elizabeth	25, May 1848	L3
Prill, John	Best, Sarah	3, Jan. 1810	L3
Prince, Joseph W.	Washburn, Harriet J.	31, May 1849	L3
Pritchard, Rees	Hamilton, Margaret	18, Sept 1845	L3
Pritchett, Jeremiah	Wooley, Julia Ann	15, Apr. 1852	L3
Probasco, Henry	Carrington, Julia A.	3, Sept 1840	L3
Pruden, Andrew	Powell, Mary Ann	26, Aug. 1841	L3
Pugh, George E.	Chalfant, Therese	29, Nov. 1855	L3
Pugh, James B.	Moore, Sophia D.	21, July 1853	L3
Pugh, Jordan A.	Miller, Sarah Belle	9, June 1842	L3
Pugh, William H.	Stewart, Ella F.	10, Apr. 1856	L3
Pull, Charles	Fithian, Sarah P.	31, Mar. 1842	L3
Pullan, Joseph	Philbeck, Eliza	5, Aug. 1847	L3
Pullan, Richard B.	Donaldson, Jessie	3, May 1849	L3
Pullman, John	Maloney, Fellitia	9, May 1844	L3
Punshon, John W.	Langdon, Ruth	28, Nov. 1844	L3
Purdy, John E.	Pigman, Caroline F.	20, Apr. 1854	L3
Purser, John	Dunlap, E.	28, Aug. 1845	L3
Purvis, John	Douglass, Eliza Ann	30, Nov. 1843	L3
Pygall, George V.	Clements, Balinda	18, Dec. 1845	L3

Grooms	Brides	Date of Notice	Page
Pyle, Alexander	Baldwin, Ellenora	13, May 1852	L3
Quaill, John	Hey, Ann (Mrs)	25, July 1839	L3
Querry, Charles D.	Burton, Frances E.	2, Feb. 1854	L3
Quinn, J.J. (Dr)	Slevin, Maria L.	8, July 1852	L3
Rader, Levi	Foreman, Sarah E.	12, Jan. 1854	L3
Rall, George S.	Cary, Estelle M.	22, Nov. 1855	L3
Ralston, James H.	Hill, Sarah J.	31, Dec. 1857	L3
Rammelsberg, Frederick	Lape, Sarah M.	21, Apr. 1842	L3
Ramsay, William E.	Punshon, Mary E.	9, Sept 1847	L3
Ramsey, C. Sample	Peters, Anna Maria	16, Sept 1841	L3
Ramsey, James B.	Gondor, Eveline A.	31, Oct. 1850	L3
Rance, Elijah (Rev)	Spencer, Dorothy	19, Jan. 1854	L3
Randolph, Thomas	Lawrence, Catharine	27, June 1810	L3
Ranger, Richard	Goodman, Elizabeth	26, Sept 1850	L3
Rankin, William	Laing, Matilda Ann	4, Nov. 1847	L3
Rankin, William	Stevens, Ellen	10, June 1841	L3
Rannells, Charles S.	Wardour, Mary A.	26, May 1842	L3
Rannells, D.W. (Dr)	Clarkson, Mary E.	24, Jan. 1839	L3
Ranney, Moses	Luckey, Catharine M.	16, Mar. 1837	L3
Ransey, Cunningham S	Bagley, Ann H.	17, May 1825	L3
Raper, Holley	Ramsey, Mary	14, Mar. 1844	L3
Rapp, Joseph M.	Hill, Elizabeth S.	23, Aug. 1855	L3
Rasland, Benjamin F.	Ellis, Jane Maria	27, Nov. 1845	L3
Rathburn, Charles B.	Howard, Delila (Mrs)	20, Sept 1855	L3
Rawson, Joseph	Richards, Mary W.	6, Dec. 1838	L3
Ray, Daniel G.	Weaver, Josephine A.	17, May 1855	L3
Ray, James M.	Johnson, Sophia (Mrs)	20, Dec. 1855	L3
Raymond, David S.	Facemire, Matilda	18, May 1822	L3
Read, Francis	Morton, Mary Ann	8, Aug. 1823	L3
Reddish, Stevenson	Bofinger, Kate E.	23, June 1853	L3
Reddish, Thomas	Waters, Phebe (Mrs)	1, Feb. 1825	L3
Reed, Cyrus	Lowe, Lavinia Ann	13, Aug. 1857	L3
Reed, Daniel	Scott, Ann	12, Feb. 1805	L3
Reed, Edwin O.	Taylor, Mary C.	23, Dec. 1847	L3
Reed, Enos B.	Ireland, Mary W.	5, June 1845	L3
Reed, Erastus R.	Moore, Jennie C.	5, May 1853	L3
Reed, George M.	Lodge, Indiana	13, July 1854	L3
Reed, James H.T.	Collins, Jane	20, Jan. 1848	L3
Reed, Joseph	Sedam, Eliza	28, Jan. 1847	L3
Reed, Robert C.	Haleman, Julia	20, May 1818	L2
Reeder, Charles A.	McCullough, Ellen	4, Feb. 1841	L3
Reeder, Jacob	Crane, Frances	19, Feb. 1816	L3
Reeder, Jesse	Kennedy, Mary	19, May 1807	L3
Reeder, Jesse	McKnight, Mary	15, Apr. 1816	L3
Reese, George L.	Oldson, Mary Ann	2, Jan. 1845	L3
Reeves, Mark E.	Middleton, Caroline	13, Sept 1849	L3
Reid, G.M.	Case, Henrietta	6, Apr. 1854	L3
Reid, Henry	Replogle, Sarah Ann	9, Mar. 1854	L3
Reilly, Thomas	Haines, Joanna	18, Jan. 1832	L4
Reily, John	Hunter, Nancy	16, Mar. 1809	L3
Reily, Kobert	Campbell, Katharine	2, May 1844	L3
Reinlein, A.	Hullfish, Kate M.	5, Nov. 1857	L3

Grooms	Brides	Date of Notice	Page
Renck, J.M.	Werstelle, Corinne D	1, Oct. 1857	L3
Renout, Charles E.	Renard, Elizabeth	17, July 1851	L3
Renshaw, William	Morrison, Emily M.	8, June 1848	L3
Requa, George	Clapp, Sarah T.	11, Nov. 1823	L3
Resin, Samuel	Smith, Catharine	10, May 1855	L3
Resor, Jacob	Sissbee, Anna	23, Oct. 1845	L3
Restieaux, William	Kennedy, Jennetta	21, Aug. 1856	L5
Reynolds, Benjamin B	Guest, Elizabeth	10, Mar. 1826	L3
Reynolds, John P.	Bebb, Eliza A.	24, Nov. 1842	L6
Reynolds, Joseph	Este, Lucy Ann	16, Feb. 1843	L3
Reynolds, Lemuel	Fisher, Emeline S.	23, Apr. 1824	L2
Reynolds, R.S.	Lansdale, Martha	12, Sept 1823	L3
Reynolds, Reuben	Griffith, Elizabeth	5, Apr. 1825	L3
Reynolds, Sacket	Guest, Mary Ann	22, Oct. 1819	L3
Reynolds, William A.	Johnston, Rachael	9, June 1836	L3
Rhakirt, Charles C.	Whetstone, Caroline	10, June 1852	L3
Rhodes, James F.	Kingman, Sarah A.	5, Feb. 1852	L3
Rhodes, Thomas F.	Smith, Eliza B.	11, July 1839	L3
Rhodes, William	Merrill, Lydia S.	7, July 1853	L3
Rianhard, Louis A.	Benbridge, Kate E.	13, Aug. 1857	L3
Rianhard, W.E.	Bassett, Jane	24, Feb. 1848	L3
Rice, Eliphaet L.	Harrison, Sallie P.	6, Jan. 1848	L3
Rice, William P.	Vose, Mary R.	10, Jan. 1839	L3
Richards, Channing	Williamson, Lydia H.	16, Mar. 1837	L3
Richards, Charles A.	Weston, Emma	8, Sept 1853	L3
Richards, Edward	Bashour, Serena A.	15, Oct. 1857	L3
Richards, Giles	Lloyd, Eleanor H.	11, Nov. 1820	L3
Richards, John (Capt)	Northrop, Adaline	6, Aug. 1846	L3
Richards, Joseph(Dr)	Wise, Anna Maria	20, July 1854	L3
Richards, Randolph	Green, Laura L.	25, June 1857	L3
Richards, William	Gibson, Jenette	4, Feb. 1818	L2
Richardson, Charles	Graham, Hannah B.	10, Apr. 1851	L3
Richardson, Francis	Conclin, Louisa	22, Apr. 1847	L3
Richardson, Richard	Knox, Mary Ann	27, Mar. 1828	L3
Richardson, Samuel	Lawrence, Mary Elizabeth	23, Sept 1847	L3
Ricker, Gustavus	Hughes, Elizabeth M.	19, June 1851	L3
Rickoff, Andrew J.	Davis, R. Flora	16, Oct. 1856	L5
Ricks, Nathaniel W.	Winston, Mary L.	5, Mar. 1846	L3
Riddle, Adam N.	Cook, Elizabeth	7, May 1835	L4
Riddle, Andrew	Miller, Martha	2, Dec. 1847	L3
Riddle, Cyrus	Foster, Laura B.	3, May 1855	L3
Riddle, George W.	Orr, Lydia S.	2, Jan. 1851	L3
Riddle, John R.	Marshall, Jane	5, Dec. 1810	L3
Ridenour, William	Bevis, Ann Elizabeth	11, Sept 1851	L3
Ridgeley, William	Graham, Sarah M.	28, Oct. 1825	L2
Ridgely, A.	Hayes, Frances A.	7, Sept 1843	L3
Ridgely, Fred. W.	Isett, Harriet L.	9, Nov. 1854	L3
Ridgely, T. Graham	Baer, Debbie L.	23, Oct. 1851	L3
Riegel, John P.	Hawley, Mary C.	1, Nov. 1855	L3
Rifner, James M.	Cilley, Martha A.	15, Sept 1853	L3
Riggs, Simpson	Cullum, Sarah Ann	13, Sept 1849	L3
Riley, Patrick	Hughes, Caroline	23, Mar. 1854	L3
Riley, Shepherd G.	Ward, Harriet	12, Aug. 1847	L3
Rinehart, John	Cottam, Margaret	9, Mar. 1843	L3

Grooms	Brides	Date of Notice	Page
Ringer, Joab	Ellis, Emeline	16, Nov. 1854	L3
Ringgold, T.G.	Gilmore, Clara	8, Jan. 1857	L3
Rinsford, Thomas C.	Williams, Margaret R	2, Jan. 1845	L3
Risk, D. (Rev)	Ludlow, Charlotte (Mrs)	15, Dec. 1808	L3
Risk, E.F.	Murdock, Jane H.	7, May 1846	L3
Risser, Daniel (Rev)	Gregory, Harriet	23, Nov. 1854	L3
Ritchie, Casper	Moore, Elizabeth	11, Aug. 1853	L3
Rives, Landon (Dr)	Watts, Letitia G.	7, Feb. 1850	L3
Robbins, Charles E.	Sullivan, Sallie Y.	6, Apr. 1854	L3
Robbins, Ephraim	Burnet, Eliza	17, June 1820	L3
Robbins, John V.	Ford, Annastatia	26, Dec. 1850	L3
Robbins, Samuel(Rev)	Burlingame, Patty	17, Oct. 1810	L3
Roberts, Charles J.	LeBoutillier, Anne	13, July 1848	L3
Robertson, Alexander	Stephenson, Matilda	7, June 1855	L3
Robertson, William	Russell, Eliza	4, Oct. 1849	L3
Robinson, Charles D.	Tuttle, Elizabeth A.	3, Sept 1846	L3
Robinson, Henry H.	Glancy, Josephine	13, Jan. 1848	L3
Robinson, J.S.	Carlin, Hester	22, Nov. 1855	L3
Robinson, John (Dr)	McGee, Mary Jane	14, May 1846	L3
Robinson, John A.	Bond, Ellen J.	28, Oct. 1852	L3
Robinson, John C.	Martin, Almira	23, Mar. 1849	L3
Robinson, Samuel	Delacroix, Victorine	24, Apr. 1845	L3
Robinson, Solon	Evans, M. (Mrs)	22, May 1828	L1
Robinson, Webster	Seever, Anna	8, Oct. 1857	L3
Robinson, William H.	Marshall, Mary J.	12, May 1853	L3
Robison, John	Hull, Mary	21, Dec. 1837	L3
Robson, William H.	Parsons, Mary E.	23, Apr. 1857	L3
Rockey, Henry	Perry, Margaret J.	30, Jan. 1851	L3
Rockey, Henry	Ruffin, Mary	11, Nov. 1820	L3
Rodes, Philip A.	Moore, Eliza	9, Feb. 1854	L3
Rodgers, Charles G.	Fallis, Hattie E.	3, Dec. 1857	L3
Rodgers, Thomas	Kenvyn, Rachel	2, Mar. 1854	L3
Rodiffer, Joseph	Ruff, Ann Maria	28, Jan. 1841	L3
Rodriquez, Francis P	Magine, Mary Jos.	14, Nov. 1844	L3
Roe, Daniel	Mason, Mary	2, Aug. 1824	L3
Roe, Daniel	Smith, Emily	7, Nov. 1821	L3
Roe, John J. (Capt)	Wright, Martha Ann	31, Aug. 1837	L3
Roelker, Frederick	Hastings, Emily	5, Mar. 1846	L3
Rofelty, William J.	Markland, Catharine	23, Nov. 1848	L3
Rogers, Harry V.	Holliday, Emma	23, July 1857	L3
Rogers, John W.	Shane, Mary Jane	22, Apr. 1847	L3
Rogers, Joseph H.	McIlvain, Mary R.	22, Jan. 1846	L3
Rogers, L.M. (Dr)	Ebersole, Annie	23, Oct. 1851	L3
Rogers, R.	Miller, Catharine J.	25, July 1850	L3
Rogers, Solomon	Hubbell, Sarah	1, Aug. 1826	L3
Roll, Edward C.	Riddle, Eliza Jane	15, Jan. 1846	L3
Romeril, Charles E.	Looker, Emmeline	14, Apr. 1826	L3
Roof, Joseph A.(Rev)	Sweitzer, Caroline	16, Nov. 1854	L3
Rooker, J.J. (Dr)	Lyle, M. Jennie	22, Oct. 1857	L3
Ropes, Nathaniel	Brown, Sarah Evans	14, July 1826	L3
Rose, Erasmus (Dr)	Kuhn, Sarah	12, Apr. 1849	L3
Rose, Thomas	Drake, Rebecca A.	18, May 1848	L3
Rose, Timothy	Price, Harriet	25, Mar. 1818	L3
Rosenstiel, Lewis S.	Menkin, Rosina	12, Feb. 1846	L3

Grooms	Brides	Date of Notice	Page
Ross, A.N. (Dr)	Dodd, Louisa Jane	6, Nov. 1845	L3
Ross, Andrew	Dailey, Martha Ann	28, Jan. 1841	L3
Ross, John L.	Waldo, Fannie W.	7, Sept 1848	L3
Ross, Robert D.	Todd, Caroline F.	21, Sept 1848	L3
Ross, S.R.	Kinney, Elizabeth	16, Sept 1847	L3
Ross, Thomas	Wing, Sarah H.	6, Apr. 1848	L3
Rotherbusch, Philip	Darr, M. Amelia	30, Dec. 1847	L3
Rowan, Matthew B.	Osborn, Ann	28, Oct. 1847	L3
Rowe, Ebenezer	Angevine, Eliza	10, Oct. 1850	L3
Rowe, Stanhope S.	Thomas, Frances Mary	12, Aug. 1841	L3
Rowland, George E.	Sheeler, Kate	7, June 1849	L3
Rowland, T.	Miller, Sarah J.	16, Nov. 1854	L3
Rowland, W.F.	Bailey, Catharine W.	22, June 1843	L3
Rowse, John B.	Silver, Margaret M.	25, Dec. 1845	L3
Ruffner, Henry	Perry, Jemima C.	15, May 1851	L3
Ruffner, Morgan	Letter, Mary Eliza	2, Nov. 1843	L3
Ruggles, Henry B.	Heilig, Jane	27, Dec. 1855	L3
Rumsey, Joseph A.	Blue, Sarah S.	26, Jan. 1854	L3
Runge, William	Scheidler, (Mrs)	1, Aug. 1850	L3
Runkle, Ralph	Piatt, H.J.	23, Jan. 1830	L2
Russel, Jonathan	Smith, Lydia	28, Apr. 1817	L3
Russel, Samuel	Crane, Mary	14, Oct. 1825	L3
Russell, H.W.	French, Eliza (Mrs)	29, July 1847	L3
Russell, Henry W.	Tait, Jane	9, Sept 1841	L3
Russell, John	Winter, Maria	13, Nov. 1845	L3
Russell, John H.W.	Ryland, Mary S.	7, Dec. 1848	L3
Russell, William	L'Hommedieu, E. (Mrs)	24, June 1847	L3
Rust, Joseph G.	Morris, Jane	9, June 1836	L3
Rust, William B.	Winston, Mary	23, Sept 1852	L3
Rutter, William	Woodruff, Eliza	10, Feb. 1842	L3
Ryan, John B.	Blakely, Mary Louisa	20, Sept 1855	L3
Ryan, Matthew	Beresford, Mary	6, June 1844	L3
Rybolt, William	Agin, Frances Ann	15, Oct. 1857	L3
Saeon, Ambrose	Cary, Jane	19, Jan. 1854	L3
Sage, George R.	Corwin, Eva A.	31, May 1855	L3
Sage, Henry W.	Hinkle, Lizzie	30, Oct. 1856	L5
Samuels, Solomon	Gratz, Rachel (Mrs)	7, Sept 1843	L3
Sanborn, John S.	Cooke, Eliza W.	31, Dec. 1846	L3
Sanders, Alford	Sandford, Antoinette	14, Apr. 1842	L3
Sanders, David A.	Wright, Lucy	16, Aug. 1838	L3
Sanderson, George	Hardinge, Henriette	19, Oct. 1854	L3
Sandford, Alfred	Martin, Susan L.	26, Dec. 1810	L3
Sanford, Alonson J.	D'Orfeuille, Jenny	14, June 1855	L3
Sanford, Charles S.	Judson, Susan A.	19, Apr. 1855	L3
Sanford, D.W.C.	Slayback, Elizabeth	1, Feb. 1849	L3
Sanford, Edwin	Miller, Janet	24, Feb. 1848	L3
Santmyer, Joseph P.	Haynes, Mary E.	14, June 1855	L3
Sanxay, Frederick	Whipple, Mary	18, Mar. 1818	L3
Sanxy, Theodore	Perry, Hetty A.	2, June 1842	L3
Sargeant, Charles H.	Lawson, Hannah	23, June 1842	L3
Sargent, Edward	Smith, Mary J.	9, Oct. 1845	L3
Saunders, R.C.	Lewis, Ellen M.	30, Sept 1841	L3
Saunders, William	Richardson, Elizabeth F.	24, Nov. 1812	L3

Grooms	Brides	Date of Notice	Page
Sawyer, Joseph A.	Hallowell, Mary R.	30, Jan. 1840	L3
Saxton, Joseph C.	Harding, Sarah B. (Mrs)	10, Jan. 1826	L3
Sayers, John	Brooks, Jane (Mrs)	11, May 1843	L3
Sayre, George E.	Nicholas, Ruth W.	15, June 1854	L3
Sayre, William H.	Gallagher, Emma B.	7, Dec. 1854	L3
Scammerhorn, Joseph	Harn, Anna Belle	19, Dec. 1850	L3
Schaefer, Charles B.	Cobb, Annie M.	12, Dec. 1850	L3
Scharbach, Jaque	Drone, Mary Magdalena	19, Dec. 1821	L3
Schenck, Aaron L.	Wood, Maria P.	3, Aug. 1822	L3
Schenck, B.G.	Dubois, Phebe Jane	19, Jan. 1843	L3
Schenck, John C.	Barkalon, Elizabeth	29, Aug. 1844	L3
Schenck, John N.C.	Schenck, Phebe W.	12, Oct. 1843	L3
Schenck, Noah Hunt	Pendleton, Anna H.	20, Nov. 1850	L3
Schenck, William R.	Reeder, Phebe W.	7, Sept 1822	L3
Schenck, Woodhull	Miller, Jeannette A.	21, Oct. 1841	L3
Schillinger, William	Cones, Frances Mary	3, June 1841	L3
Schillinger, William	Lovejoy, Mary (Mrs)	3, Nov. 1836	L3
Schofield, W.S. (Dr)	Brown, Lucy	9, Apr. 1846	L3
Schooley, John C.	Isham, E.T.	30, May 1844	L3
Schoolfield, John Q.	Simms, Honora A.	1, Jan. 1846	L3
Schoolfield, Joseph	Clark, Sarah A.	16, Sept 1852	L3
Schrock, Silas	Colston, Sarah A.	6, Sept 1855	L3
Schultz, Charles	Bowers, Ann Elizabeth	13, Feb. 1827	L3
Schultz, Henry (Dr)	Bixler, Caroline	17, Mar. 1836	L3
Schultz, William J.	Spencer, Maria F.	16, June 1842	L3
Schuster, Paul	Shwebel, Eliza	18, Sept 1851	L3
Schwartze, F.W.	Weatherby, Mary G.	15, Apr. 1847	L3
Scott, Chasteen	Fowler, Abigail	24, June 1816	L3
Scott, David B.	Vanausdol, Naomi R.	27, Oct. 1853	L3
Scott, John H.	Haslam, Anna	23, Mar. 1854	L3
Scott, John L.	Stevens, Jane M.	21, Oct. 1841	L3
Scott, Josiah	Austin, Susan E.	7, May 1846	L3
Scott, Winfield	Mayo, Maria D.	21, Apr. 1817	L3
Scovill, Amon L.	Whipple, Harriet E.	29, Dec. 1842	L3
Scudder, Sidney	Potter, Ann Jane	18, Feb. 1847	L3
Searles, Daniel	McFarland, Jane	14, Dec. 1807	L3
Sears, Clinton (Rev)	Brooks, Angeline	9, June 1842	L3
Sears, Clinton W.	Graff, Helen C.	19, Sept 1850	L3
Seccomb, E.	Bessom, Hannah P.	26, June 1845	L3
Seccomb, E.	Bessom, Hannah P.	3, July 1845	L3
Secrist, John M.	Schruke, Sophia	20, Nov. 1850	L3
Secrist, Peter	Mankey, Lydia A.	3, Aug. 1843	L3
See, William H.	Belangee, Hannah M.	1, Oct. 1846	L3
Sehon, Edmund W.	McLean, Caroline A.	12, Sept 1833	L4
Seibert, Christian	McKim, Sarah T.	2, Jan. 1845	L3
Seig, George B.	Conklin, Jerusha H.	6, June 1850	L3
Selby, Charles	Gephart, Elizabeth	16, Feb. 1854	L3
Selby, Samuel	Gephart, Amanda	16, Feb. 1854	L3
Sellars, Eliphalet D	Moberly, Asenath S.	9, Mar. 1854	L3
Sellers, Norris	Patterson, Amanda	9, Feb. 1854	L3
Sellers, William W.	Lacey, Caroline M.	5, Nov. 1857	L3
Sellman, Carberry J.	Smith, Mary Ann	27, Oct. 1831	L4
Semple, James A.	Laudeman, Maggie H.	24, Jan. 1856	L3
Servis, James	Bradford, Margaret	23, Apr. 1840	L3

Grooms	Brides	Date of Notice	Page
Servis, John P.	Strange, Rhoda Ellen	23, Feb. 1854	L3
Sewell, John W.	Perkins, Harriet M.	9, Sept 1852	L3
Sexton, Charles	Woodward, Elizabeth	19, July 1855	L3
Seybold, Emanuel F.	Zimmerman, Catharine	10, June 1847	L3
Seymour, Henry F.	Skiff, Ruby S.	5, Oct. 1843	L3
Shaddinger, Anderson	Rose, Isabel	20, Aug. 1846	L3
Shaffer, William	Lewis, Susan	7, Aug. 1845	L3
Shane, William	Lawson, Maria	1, June 1827	L2
Sharpless, Thomas	Sayre, Margaret	27, Nov. 1822	L3
Shattuck, William B.	Richardson, Elizabeth C.	30, May 1850	L3
Shaw, Hezekiah (Rev)	Halstead, Rebecca	9, Oct. 1811	L3
Shaw, John	Wright, Elizabeth	12, Apr. 1814	L3
Shaw, John A.	Rutherford, Virginia	28, May 1846	L3
Shaw, W.M.	Elmaker, Eliza (Mrs)	12, Feb. 1852	L3
Shawley, Lewis	Sharpless, Susan	21, May 1829	L3
Shays, Charles M.	Resor, Gertrude C.	29, Oct. 1857	L3
Shays, J.W.	Crane, Susan T.	14, Mar. 1844	L3
Shays, John	Iglehart, Mary Ann	20, Nov. 1850	L3
Shearer, Michael K.	Grinson, Anna	9, May 1839	L3
Shelden, Edward A.	Gregory, Sarah A.	27, Nov. 1851	L3
Sheldon, J.A.	Price, Mary	5, Oct. 1848	L3
Shepard, Oscar F.	Bicknell, Hattie	26, Feb. 1857	L3
Shepherd, Chauncey B	Armstrong, Eliza (Mrs)	15, Apr. 1841	L3
Shepherd, J.W.	Offley, Rachel	14, Oct. 1852	L3
Shepherd, M.L.	O'Reilly, Catharine	18, Jna. 1838	L3
Shepherd, Stephen	Smith, Sarah	7, Oct. 1841	L3
Shepherd, William	Long, Catharine	23, Feb. 1854	L3
Sheppard, Edwin F.	Ewing, Mary Jane	28, Dec. 1848	L3
Sherlock, James L.	Cleburne, Anna	17, Mar. 1853	L3
Sherlock, Thomas	Redhead, Martha Ann	1, Apr. 1847	L3
Sherlock, Thomas	Turpin, Nancy C. (Mrs)	30, Sept 1852	L3
Sherman, Charles T.	Williams, Eliza Jane	11, Feb. 1841	L3
Sherman, L.P.	Gitchell, Mary A.	19, Apr. 1845	L3
Sherriff, Anthony C.	Lovejoy, Sarah (Mrs)	7, Jan. 1847	L3
Shever, John	Cordingly, Marcian A	28, July 1842	L3
Shillito, John	Wallace, Mary	26, May 1836	L3
Shipley, John P.	Russell, Emeline V.	12, Oct. 1848	L3
Shipley, John W.	Deane, Agnes	20, Oct. 1836	L1
Shipley, Joseph	Kiles, Sarah Anne	26, Aug. 1825	L3
Shipley, Murray	Taylor, Hannah D.	29, May 1851	L3
Shoemaker, J.W.	Middleton, Elizabeth J.	9, Feb. 1854	L3
Short, J. Cleves	Mitchell, Mary Ann	2, Aug. 1849	L3
Shotwell, George H.	Tudor, Mary Elizabeth A.	17, Nov. 1836	L3
Shreve, Charles U.	McCandless, Sallie B	5, Feb. 1852	L3
Shultz, Henry (Dr)	Litherbury, Matilda	17, Sept 1846	L3
Shumaker, Michael	Piatt, Juliet E.	25, July 1850	L3
Shumard, B.F. (Dr)	Allen, Lizzie M.	2, Dec. 1852	L3
Shumard, John	Miller, Caroline	9, Sept 1852	L3
Shumway, Horatio G.	Johnston, Augusta	18, Dec. 1856	L3
Siebern, St. W.	Bauman, Mary Ann	12, Oct. 1854	L3
Sigerson, John	Schillinger, Philomena	3, Nov. 1836	L3
Sigerson, Wallace	Magaw, Anna Maria	26, Nov. 1840	L3
Sigerson, William	Elliott, Mary B.	30, Nov. 1837	L3
Silsbee, Samuel (Dr)	Whipple, Hannah	8, July 1841	L3

Grooms	Brides	Date of Notice	Page
Silvers, Aaron	Buchanan, Eliza	30, Oct. 1815	L3
Simmons, L.C.	Wylier, Anna C.	23, Oct. 1856	L5
Simms, Robert E.	Smith, Mary Ann	17, Feb. 1848	L3
Simons, Frank	Dullhagen, Annie	27, Sept 1855	L3
Simonton, Richard	Smith, Edith C. (Mrs)	12, Dec. 1844	L3
Simonton, William	Wilson, Maria	9, Sept 1816	L3
Simpkinson, Charles	Roseboom, Martha R.	31, Dec. 1857	L3
Simpson, George B.F.	Todd, Abbie	20, Dec. 1855	L3
Simpson, J.A.	Jackson, Caroline M.	20, June 1850	L3
Simpson, John A.	Martin, Sidney M.	2, June 1826	L3
Single, William S.	Dodge, Fannie E.	14, Feb. 1856	L3
Singleton, Henry	Fitzgerald, Elizabet	13, Dec. 1849	L3
Sinks, Randolph M.	Frazier, Mary	9, Sept 1852	L3
Skaggs, Henry H.	Bacon, Calista	25, Jan. 1855	L3
Skelton, Josiah W.	Ormon, Eliza	11, Aug. 1812	L3
Skiles, Thomas H.	Strickland, Mary Ada	14, May 1857	L3
Skillman, Henry M.	Foster, Augusta V.	20, Mar. 1856	L3
Skinner, Ralston	Wiggins, Emma Louisa	9, July 1857	L3
Slane, Alexander	Bradford, Mary Ann	29, July 1847	L3
Slater, William F.	Hitt, Mary A.	1, Apr. 1841	L3
Slevin, R.D.	Orange, Martha	31, July 1851	L3
Slocum, Alfred (Dr)	Bacon, Harriet M.	7, Sept 1854	L3
Slocum, J. Jeremiah	L'Hommedieu, Sallie	15, June 1854	L3
Slough, John P.	McLean, Arabella S.	3, Feb. 1853	L3
Smallwood, Samuel N.	Curtis, Eliza M.	1, Jan. 1846	L3
Smallwood, William A	Douglas, Mary L. (Mrs)	5, Mar. 1846	L3
Smiley, Robeson	Lfiff, Clarasy	9, Oct. 1845	L3
Smith, C.W.	Brown, Lottie W.	6, Dec. 1855	L3
Smith, Charles J.	Marshall, Evaline P.	11, Mar. 1852	L3
Smith, Charles S.	Ackerman, Catharine	12, Jan. 1854	L3
Smith, Chester	Preston, Mary Ann E.	12, Apr. 1849	L3
Smith, Daniel J.	Brickley, Sarah E.	12, Apr. 1849	L3
Smith, DeWitt C.	Getz, Elizabeth	28, Oct. 1847	L3
Smith, F.	Rice, Lucy	11, May 1822	L3
Smith, George R.	Kemp, Salome	30, May 1839	L2
Smith, Henry	Lester, Martha	14, Dec. 1837	L3
Smith, Hezekiah	Cox, Amy	23, Jan. 1845	L3
Smith, Hiram W.	Howell, Delia W.	13, July 1848	L3
Smith, J. Freeman	Wood, Phebe M.	28, Aug. 1845	L3
Smith, J.B. Clark	Crowell, Elenor B.	17, July 1845	L3
Smith, J.H.	Arnold, Mary Jane	23, Mar. 1849	L3
Smith, James Douglas	Hooper, Lizzie	13, July 1854	L3
Smith, James F.	Jeremiah, Martha W.	15, Apr. 1847	L3
Smith, James M.	Poinier, Jane	22, May 1845	L3
Smith, James R.	James, Angelina	18, May 1843	L3
Smith, James R.	Nixon, Elizabeth A.	15, Apr. 1847	L3
Smith, James R.	Nixon, Elizabeth Adelia	8, Apr. 1847	L3
Smith, John L.	Dana, Mary	31, Oct. 1823	L3
Smith, Joseph	Harris, Mary	15, Feb. 1844	L3
Smith, Joseph	Patterson, Lizzie S.	10, May 1855	L3
Smith, Joseph	Vantrees, Catharine	19, May 1807	L3
Smith, Joseph K.	Bell, Melinda	8, June 1824	L3
Smith, Justus	Chapman, Fanny	28, Oct. 1820	L3
Smith, Lorenzo D.	DeBeck, Mary E.L.	13, Dec. 1855	L3

Grooms	Brides	Date of Notice	Page
Smith, Lucian	Hadley, Mary M.	24, Sept 1857	L3
Smith, N.T.	Lovett, Elizabeth	18, Feb. 1847	L3
Smith, Oliver	Hulse, Ruth Ann	21, Aug. 1822	L3
Smith, Oliver	Carroll, Sallie J.	25, Sept 1856	L5
Smith, R.G.	Marshall, Laura C.	15, Sept 1853	L3
Smith, S.	Harris, Sue W.	4, Dec. 1851	L3
Smith, S.W.	Rice, Susan C.	8, Sept 1842	L3
Smith, Samuel W.	Woolley, Caroline	10, Apr. 1845	L3
Smith, Spencer	Wainwright, Ruth	3, June 1841	L3
Smith, T. Gardner	James, Vannelia	5, Sept 1850	L3
Smith, Thomas	Dollin, Jane	11, Nov. 1820	L3
Smith, Thomas	Otsen, Margaret	9, Mar. 1848	L3
Smith, Thomas K.	McCullough, Elizabeth B.	11, May 1848	L3
Smith, W. Henry	Glascock, Mary Jane	27, Oct. 1842	L3
Smith, Walter	Irwin, Eliza	7, Jan. 1847	L3
Smith, William	Allen, Nancy	18, Feb. 1841	L3
Smith, William	Beebe, Lydia	4, Jan. 1855	L3
Smith, William	Broadwell, Mary Eliz	11, July 1844	L3
Smith, William	Folger, Eliza Ann	3, Jan. 1821	L3
Smith, William	McDonogh, Maria	8, May 1845	L3
Smith, William B.	Sedam, Mary Jane	2, Oct. 1851	L3
Smith, William F.	Hervey, Frances A.	15, Oct. 1846	L3
Smith, William H(Dr)	Crawford, Martha Ann	4, July 1844	L3
Smith, William H.	Lamb, Elizabeth	30, Mar. 1849	L3
Smith, William P.	Hill, Sereptia	1, June 1848	L3
Smith, William R.	Watson, Caroline	27, Dec. 1838	L3
Smith, Winthrop B.	Sargent, Mary	13, Nov. 1834	L2
Snedaker, Samuel B.	Turner, Ann	14, Aug. 1845	L3
Snedicher, Isaac	Smith, Susanna	30, Aug. 1855	L3
Snow, Henry	Lynd, Catharine L.	21, Nov. 1844	L3
Snow, Lemuel	Langdon, Lorendo	16, Sept 1816	L3
Snowdon, Sidney	Mitchell, Eliza	31, Aug. 1837	L3
Snowdon, T.M.	Cutler, Mary E.	6, Sept 1855	L3
Snyder, Charles W.	Norris, Mary E.	22, Dec. 1842	L3
Snyder, George	Garoutee, Sarah M.	5, Apr. 1855	L3
Snyder, Thomas	Carver, Mary Ann	15, May 1827	L3
Southard, Isaac	Mitchell, Sarah	12, Nov. 1846	L3
Southgate, Richard H	Watson, Julia	4, Jan. 1844	L3
Spahr, Benjamin	Plummer, Mary B.	9, Jan. 1845	L3
Spalding, Henry P.	Cole, Jane	12, Aug. 1841	L3
Sparks, J.C. (Dr)	Latta, Mary E.	12, May 1853	L3
Sparks, Jesse	Forbs, Ann Eliza	2, Apr. 1857	L3
Sparks, Joseph K(Dr)	Goodwin, Elizabeth (Mrs)	8, May 1827	L3
Spear, Samuel B.	Barrett, Lucy D.	19, May 1836	L2
Spear, Samuel B.	Carey, Rachel	21, July 1842	L3
Speck, Adolphus C.	Taylor, Naomi	16, Feb. 1854	L3
Speer, John	McMahan, Elizabeth D.	28, July 1842	L3
Spencer, O.M.	Coombs, Emily	5, Oct. 1837	L3
Spencer, Oliver	Oliver, (Miss)	15, Jan. 1805	L3
Spencer, Peter L.	Butterworth, Mary A.	25, Apr. 1844	L3
Spining, Charles E.	Baker, Mary A.	21, May 1846	L3
Spining, F.A.	Tosso, Adele	16, Jan. 1851	L3
Spinning, William	Worley, Margarety E.	31, May 1849	L3
Spoffard, A.R.	Partridge, Sarah P.	23, Sept 1852	L3

Grooms	Brides	Date of Notice	Page
Spofford, Jacob F.	Springer, Elizabeth (Mrs)	5, Nov. 1846	L3
Spooner, Thomas	Leonard, Frances M.	30, Oct. 1851	L3
Spooner, Thomas	Leonard, Sarah	15, Sept 1842	L3
Spooner, William L.	Smith, Catharine	5, Nov. 1840	L2
Sprague, Andrew W.	Watkins, Lydia	24, Feb. 1842	L3
Sprague, J.R.	Hardinge, Sarah	16, May 1850	L3
Sprigman, J.A.	Singer, Sallie A.	24, May 1855	L3
Sprigman, Peter A.	Harris, Abigail	6, Feb. 1811	L3
Sprong, David	Harris, Elizabeth A.	6, Apr. 1837	L3
Sproul, Hasht	Traber, Mary Ann	27, June 1839	L3
Squire, William B.	Barnard, Elizabeth M	8, Apr. 1841	L3
St.Clair, George	Flint, Esther	27, Dec. 1809	L3
St.Clair, John	Crooker, Ann	20, Sept 1827	L3
St.Johns, Job	Newbury, Lydia A.	24, Dec. 1840	L3
Stagg, Henry	Davis, Isabella	24, Nov. 1842	L6
Stagg, Lewis	Mattox, Maggie C.	10, Feb. 1853	L3
Stall, George W.	Haifligh, Barbara	12, May 1806	L3
Stanberry, Henry	Bond, Cecilia K.	29, July 1841	L3
Stanbury, John S.	Burch, Caroline E.	5, Dec. 1844	L3
Stanley, Frederick	Lanphear, Mary A.	5, Oct. 1843	L3
Stanley, George S.	Maywood, Mary	28, June 1849	L3
Stanley, Thomas	Yeo, Jane	10, May 1855	L3
Stanley, William	Waterman, Julia	24, Mar. 1807	L3
Stannus, Richard G.	Walker, Margaret	30, Dec. 1847	L3
Stannus, Thomas J.	McGregor, Helen	7, Nov. 1844	L3
Stansberry, John	Cooper, Mary Jane	23, Feb. 1854	L3
Stapp, Edwin	Akers, Elvira	13, Mar. 1845	L3
Starbuck, Calvin W.	Webster, Nancy	9, Jan. 1845	L3
Starlin, Israel	Wilson, Margaretta	11, Dec. 1811	L3
Starling, Samuel	Stewart, Sarah	9, Mar. 1854	L3
Starr, David L. (Dr)	Harper, Sarah J.	31, May 1849	L3
Stebbens, Uriah	Pence, Sarah Jane	9, Mar. 1854	L3
Stedman, George T.	Porter, Abby H.	20, Feb. 1845	L3
Steelman, Hosea	Bowring, Elizabeth J	13, Aug. 1857	L3
Steer, R.A.	King, Alice J.	20, Dec. 1855	L3
Steman, Jacob	Stake, Mary	20, Apr. 1819	L3
Stephens, Benjamin R	Smith, Jerusha	23, Jan. 1851	L3
Stephens, Charles	Martin, Rhoda	12, Sept 1810	L3
Stephens, Elihu	Sampson, Martha	3, Oct. 1844	L3
Stephens, Ephraim M.	Mayhew, Aceneth	8, June 1827	L3
Stephens, Estep	Williams, Charlotte	28, Aug. 1851	L3
Stephens, Isaac	Middleton, Lydia	28, Oct. 1847	L3
Stephens, Isaac	Pullan, Eliza	16, May 1839	L3
Stephens, Jacob	Speer, Caroline M.	17, Nov. 1836	L3
Stephens, John M.	Strahan, Catharine A	7, Aug. 1845	L3
Stephens, Marcus	Butler, Charlotte	18, Feb. 1823	L3
Stephenson, Andrew C	Davis, Harriet Ann	21, Oct. 1847	L3
Stephenson, H.W.	Dorman, Sarah Ann	21, Feb. 1839	L3
Sterling, Samuel G.	Smith, Eliza	22, Dec. 1842	L3
Sterrett, A. McD.	McCreary, Elizabeth	5, Aug. 1847	L3
Sterrett, Benjamin	Maclay, Catharine	6, Apr. 1843	L3
Sterrett, Robert	Duke, Eugenia J.	20, Sept 1827	L1
Stettinius, John L.	Olmsted, Eloise B.	22, June 1854	L3
Stevens, E.	Perrine, Sarah	7, Oct. 1841	L3

Grooms	Brides	Date of Notice	Page
Stevens, Elijah	Ramsay, Hannah	12, Mar. 1829	L2
Stevens, Hiram E.	White, Wealthy Ann	18, July 1844	L3
Stevens, J.P.	Bosley, Emily	27, Apr. 1854	L3
Stevens, Thomas A.	DeCamp, Mary Anna	12, Feb. 1852	L3
Stevens, William L.	Gallaugher, Sarah B.	7, Jan. 1823	L2
Stevenson, B.D.	Ogden, Maggie M.	23, Apr. 1857	L3
Stevenson, Henry D.	Hand, Elizabeth	18, May 1848	L3
Stevenson, John W.	Winston, Sibella	29, June 1843	L3
Stevenson, Joseph D.	Watkins, Mary	13, Nov. 1850	L3
Stewart, Benjamin M.	Parker, Mary L.	30, Sept 1852	L3
Stewart, Charles	Dawson, Martha Ann	12, Apr. 1849	L3
Stewart, Charles S.	Lister, Elizabeth	2, Mar. 1854	L3
Stewart, Ephiram	Phillips, Belle	5, July 1855	L3
Stewart, G.H. (Dr)	Newton, Sophia F.	24, July 1845	L3
Stewart, K.F.	VanDyke, Ellen	8, June 1848	L3
Stewart, M.A.	Meara, Catharine M.	5, June 1845	L3
Stewart, Martin	Babbs, Eliza	27, Sept 1809	L3
Stewart, Samuel M.	Riley, Amanda	9, May 1844	L3
Stewart, William A.	Homer, Elizabeth	21, Oct. 1841	L3
Stewart, William C.	Conkling, Mary F.	13, Dec. 1855	L3
Stewart, William S.	Guilford, Belle E.	25, Nov. 1852	L3
Stickney, J. Charles	Clifford, Abby Anna	16, June 1836	L3
Stiles, Francis	Arnet, Elizabeth	7, Apr. 1853	L3
Stille, D.P.	McMicken, Lizzie	18, Dec. 1856	L3
Stillie, J.	Hamilton, Caroline F	19, May 1842	L3
Stillman, George K.	Nottingham, Mary	12, Feb. 1846	L3
Stillman, O.D.	Talbott, Hester Ann	19, July 1838	L3
Stillwell, T. Neal	Conwell, Winnie K.	28, Oct. 1852	L3
Stinson, Charles	Graham, Rachel	19, Oct. 1837	L3
Stipley, Henry H.	Bonsall, Anna H.	29, June 1848	L3
Stites, Hezekiah	Ferris, Mary	10, Sept 1846	L3
Stites, Robert	Parker, Eunice	24, Aug. 1843	L3
Stockton, J.B.	Miner, M.J.	7, Sept 1848	L3
Stockton, Phillip	Cunningham, Kate	21, Feb. 1856	L3
Stoddart, David	VanAmringe, Eliza J.	23, Feb. 1854	L3
Stoms, William	Mears, Eliza Lucinda	19, Oct. 1837	L3
Stone, B.T.	Williams, Hannah M.	20, Sept 1838	L3
Stone, Dan	Farnsworth, Augusta	10, Dec. 1824	L2
Stone, F.H.	Fairchild, Catharine	20, Aug. 1840	L3
Stone, Hubbard	Meader, Miriam	21, Sept 1854	L3
Stone, James S.	Phinney, Mary L.	21, June 1838	L3
Stone, Leaverett G.	Eckert, Josephine	21, Aug. 1856	L5
Stone, R.H.	Landrum, Sarah W.	3, Dec. 1846	L3
Stonemitz, David H.	Ogden, Ruth N.	22, July 1816	L2
Stoops, Pleasant	Furry, Hannah	9, Feb. 1854	L3
Stoops, Stephen M.	Stewart, Phebe (Mrs)	23, Mar. 1854	L3
Storer, Belamy	Barton, Euretta Lou.	30, Sept 1820	L3
Storer, Bellamy	Drinker, Elizabeth	21, May 1846	L3
Stoton, Eli	Scofield, Emeline	13, Nov. 1845	L3
Stoughton, Joseph	Hanbee, Nancy	11, Aug. 1817	L3
Stout, Elisha	Brown, Phebe	14, Mar. 1810	L3
Stout, Ephraim B.	Dounn, Mattie	3, Apr. 1856	L3
Stout, Henry D.	Pennington, Elizabet	13, Feb. 1845	L3
Stout, Horace	Agnew, Emely	11, Sept 1834	L1

Grooms	Brides	Date of Notice	Page
Stout, Jesse D.	Thomas, Mary Ann	30, Nov. 1848	L3
Stout, Nathaniel R.	Peck, Emily P.	6, May 1847	L3
Stow, E.	Moore, Peggy	24, Mar. 1807	L3
Stowe, Daniel C.	Moore, Mary	18, Oct. 1849	L3
Strader, P. Wilson	Hubbard, Cornelia F.	26, Jan. 1843	L3
Straeffer, Jacob M.	Caley, Rebecca	1, Dec. 1836	L4
Straeffer, Michael	Dressel, Elizabeth	2, June 1831	L1
Strange, John (Rev)	Waller, Ruth	8, Sept 1812	L2
Stratton, Jeriel R.	Babb, Emeline	3, Sept 1846	L3
Stratton, Josiah J.	Lee, Susan M.	5, Jan. 1827	L3
Stratton, Samuel S.	Reed, Sarah A.	11, May 1854	L3
Strickle, Abraham E.	Goodwin, Caroline	6, Jan. 1831	L3
Strickler, George W.	Dicks, Mary Ellen	24, Feb. 1842	L3
Strickler, George W.	Johnson, Mary B.	18, Nov. 1847	L3
Strickler, John	Ruckle, Catharine C.	18, Aug. 1842	L3
Strobridge, H.	Wright, Jane Isabell	9, Oct. 1845	L3
Strong, Charles L.	Ingram, A.C. (Mrs)	19, Nov. 1857	L3
Strong, Ebenezer B.	Glover, Catharine B.	5, Mar. 1846	L3
Strong, Edward K.	Fine, Elizabeth	22, July 1852	L3
Strong, Jonathan M.	Graham, Adelia	6, Jan. 1848	L3
Strowder, Z.B.	Harrison, Elizabeth S.	26, Jan. 1843	L3
Strowhuver, George	Allison, Patsey	6, Apr. 1813	L3
Stryker, Joseph M.	Gardner, E.A.	18, May 1848	L3
Stuart, Ewing T.	Adams, Roberta Charlotte	14, June 1849	L3
Stuart, John	Bradbury, Eliza C.	26, Feb. 1852	L3
Sturgus, John J.	McNulty, M. Louisa	24, Dec. 1857	L3
Suhr, H.W. (Rev)	Ordeman, Methe	12, June 1845	L3
Suit, Nathaniel	Collier, Nancy	12, Dec. 1810	L2
Sullivan, Algernon	Hammond, Mary M.	27, Dec. 1855	L3
Sullivan, Algernon S	Groesbeck, Mary S.	9, Jan. 1851	L3
Sullivan, Hiram	Haven, Georgetta	28, May 1846	L3
Summerwell, Robert K	Easton, Rebecca	28, Dec. 1854	L3
Susan, Thomas	Harnbrook, Mary Anne	24, Aug. 1843	L3
Sutherland, Robert	Pennell, Emma	28, June 1855	L3
Sutton, Demetrius A.	Grant, Caroline A.	3, Jan. 1821	L3
Sutton, Edward	Lawrence, Amanda (Mrs)	20, Apr. 1848	L3
Sutton, Joseph M.	Nicholas, Lydia Ann	24, May 1849	L3
Swafford, James	Wheeler, Harriet Ann	10, Jan. 1823	L3
Swain, Alonzo	Buchanan, Elvira	31, Dec. 1840	L3
Swain, William P.	Morgan, Sarah	2, Aug. 1849	L3
Swan, John M.	Roads, Elizabeth H.	5, Nov. 1846	L3
Swartz, John T.	Evans, M. Anna	31, Dec. 1857	L3
Swasey, Moses	Martin, Maria R. (Mrs)	5, Nov. 1840	L2
Swazey, Hazen	Allen, Sophia	11, Sept 1822	L3
Sweat, John	Moore, Matilda	5, Dec. 1844	L3
Sweeny, John	Wheeland, Elvira	9, Jan. 1845	L3
Swift, Briggs	Hubbell, Martha P.	24, Sept 1846	L3
Swift, Briggs	McCullough, Jane	18, June 1857	L3
Swift, Charles	Witherup, Anna C.	10, Sept 1857	L3
Swift, Henry A.	Livingston, Ruth	18, Sept 1851	L3
Swift, John	Williams, Euretta F.	16, Apr. 1857	L3
Swift, Thomas T.	Holabird, Jenette	13, Sept 1849	L3
Swing, Jeremiah	Erwin, Olivia	26, July 1827	L3
Swormsted, Leroy (Rev)	Cummins, Ann (Mrs)	14, Jan. 1825	L3

Grooms	Brides	Date of Notice	Page
Sykes, Charles	Jones, Martha Ann	5, Apr. 1849	L3
Symmes, Henry	Sedam, Melinda	17, Sept 1846	L3
Symmes, Peyton S.	Close, Hannah B.	25, May 1819	L3
Taft, Alphonso	Torrey, Louise M.	5, Jan. 1854	L3
Tait, George	Morrison, Eliza D.	20, May 1830	L3
Talasfero, Charles W	Slack, M. Josephine	12, Dec. 1839	L3
Talbert, Aaron S.	Wolfe, Eveline H.	5, Nov. 1846	L3
Talbot, Isham	Thomason, Adelaide	28, Apr. 1817	L3
Talbott, Isaiah L.	Rutherford, Sarah J.	7, Jan. 1847	L3
Talbott, W.H.	Tinker, Elizabeth	30, Mar. 1848	L3
Taliaferro, W.T.(Dr)	Ramsey, Eliza (Mrs)	27, Apr. 1843	L3
Tappin, Benjamin	George, Maggie	2, Oct. 1856	L5
Tapscott, George W.	St.Clair, Margaret B	21, July 1836	L2
Tarrant, Larkin M.	Tunis, Emeline	24, Jan. 1826	L3
Tate, J.H.	Chenoweth, Maggie	19, May 1853	L3
Tatem, Henry L.	Hall, Sarah Ann	2, Nov. 1833	L4
Tatem, John	Leibey, Mary	26, Aug. 1823	L3
Tathem, G.W.	Bryns, Margaret W.	17, Nov. 1836	L3
Tatin, Simon C.	Francis, Sarah (Mrs)	11, Sept 1845	L3
Taylor, A.M.	Shoemaker, Elizabeth R.	14, Sept 1848	L3
Taylor, Charles A.	Smith, Rebecca F.	15, Oct. 1857	L3
Taylor, Eli	Marsh, Hannah M.	7, Jan. 1836	L2
Taylor, Gabriel A.	Miller, Sarah Jane	23, Sept 1847	L3
Taylor, George	Nesmith, Margaret	6, June 1844	L3
Taylor, George R.	Nesmith, Margaret M.	6, June 1844	L3
Taylor, Henry W.	Kemper, Mary V.	23, Oct. 1851	L3
Taylor, Isaac N.	Fauber, Elizabeth	9, Feb. 1854	L3
Taylor, J.B.	Farrar, Martha	23, Mar. 1854	L3
Taylor, James	Shipley, Elizabeth C	31, Oct. 1844	L3
Taylor, James W.	Langford, Chloe	23, Oct. 1845	L3
Taylor, James W.	Symmes, Louisiana	2, Aug. 1832	L3
Taylor, John	Day, Dianthy	5, Sept 1844	L3
Taylor, John C.	Harvie, Caroline	28, Aug. 1851	L3
Taylor, John C.	Sterns, Fanny L.	3, Apr. 1851	L3
Taylor, Joseph	Chamberlain, Elizabeth	27, Mar. 1828	L3
Taylor, Joseph B.	Ligget, Sophia Susan	30, Jan. 1845	L3
Taylor, Mahlon R.	Lyon, Elizabeth W.	8, Dec. 1836	L3
Taylor, R.M.W.	Menefee, Frances A.	7, Sept 1843	L3
Teach, David	Moorman, Emily	12, Jan. 1854	L3
Teal, Samuel R.	Revill, Amelia	12, July 1827	L1
Tealen, Robert	Parker, Ann	10, Jan. 1839	L3
Teasdale, William	Cook, Eliza	1, Mar. 1838	L3
Teater, Henry	Buchanan, Christiana	12, Aug. 1816	L2
Telford, Charles L.	Totten, Susan M.	24, Nov. 1842	L6
Temple, Charles W.	Protsman, Annie	1, Nov. 1855	L3
Templeton, William C	Hawkins, Eliza	19, Dec. 1833	L3
Terrell, William G.	Thornton, Mary (Mrs)	20, Nov. 1850	L3
Terry, Reuben	Enness, Mary	18, Sept 1815	L3
Terwilliger, Nathaniel	Whitesides, Mary	28, July 1807	L3
Tharp, Jacob	VanMetre, Mary	4, July 1844	L3
Thatcher, David	Flint, Julia	15, Mar. 1814	L3
Thayer, Henry	Wood, Susan M.	23, Apr. 1840	L3
Thayer, William H.	Sharp, Jennie	8, Nov. 1855	L3

Grooms	Brides	Date of Notice	Page
Themin, C.F.	Follenius, Catharine	23, May 1844	L3
Thielman, John	Fehleisen, Amelia	14, May 1857	L3
Thirkield, Thornton	Mooney, Mary	26, Dec. 1844	L3
Thistlewaite, James	Punshon, Rachel	16, Feb. 1837	L3
Thomas, Cal. W.	Keck, Sallie C.	30, Aug. 1855	L3
Thomas, D.	Pearce, Jane	9, Mar. 1854	L3
Thomas, Daniel G.	Taylor, Anna	27, Dec. 1849	L3
Thomas, E. Sydney	Morris, Rebecca	3, Feb. 1848	L3
Thomas, George	Jackson, Elizabeth	15, Feb. 1814	L3
Thomas, James	Merrit, Margaret	27, Oct. 1812	L3
Thomas, Jesse B.	Hamtrammack, Rebecca	24, Feb. 1807	L3
Thomas, John	Callaghan, Ellen	28, Dec. 1854	L3
Thomas, John R.	Hager, Abigail	29, Dec. 1821	L3
Thomas, John S.	Burley, Margaret	27, Oct. 1817	L3
Thomas, Joseph	McCollum, Elizabeth	9, June 1853	L3
Thomas, Joseph H.	Hudson, Mary E.	30, Dec. 1847	L3
Thomas, Reuben	Foor, Amanda P.	30, Aug. 1855	L3
Thomas, Robert	Whitney, Elizabeth (Mrs)	20, May 1847	L3
Thomas, Samuel P.	Brown, Mary A.	7, Sept 1854	L3
Thomas, Terrill	Williams, Sarah	4, June 1857	L3
Thompson, David W.	Mayhew, Agnes (Mrs)	26, May 1842	L3
Thompson, Francis	Norris, Martha	9, Sept 1847	L3
Thompson, James	Todd, Ann D.	22, Nov. 1849	L3
Thompson, James R.	Hartley, Rachael M.	16, Sept 1841	L3
Thompson, Marcus	Gorman, Matilda	3, Mar. 1842	L3
Thompson, Moses F.	Reakirt, Anna Maria	24, Feb. 1853	L3
Thompson, R.E.	Ryland, Caroline	6, Sept 1849	L3
Thompson, S.J.	Keys, Eveline A.	7, Feb. 1850	L3
Thompson, Samuel	Newport, Sarah E.	12, Jan. 1854	L3
Thompson, Samuel G.	Smith, Mary Ann	25, Mar. 1847	L3
Thompson, Thomas	Nancarrow, Polly	24, Feb. 1806	L3
Thompson, William H.	Dart, Harriet N.	24, Apr. 1845	L3
Thompson, William H.	Graham, Laura	22, May 1845	L3
Thomson, John C.	Storms, Rody	30, Nov. 1854	L3
Thomson, Robert	Gardner, Margaret B.	1, Aug. 1850	L3
Thomson, William	Sterling, Julia C.	27, Apr. 1843	L3
Thorne, Ellwood E.	Bennett, Sallie	21, Feb. 1856	L3
Thornton, J.H.F.(Dr)	Carpenter, Eliza	16, Jan. 1845	L3
Thornton, John H(Dr)	Harrison, Mary S.	12, Mar. 1829	L2
Thornton, Joseph	West, Mary	23, Dec. 1825	L3
Thornton, Joseph L.	Corbin, Mary M.	5, Oct. 1854	L3
Thornton, Tyrrel	Carey, Rosetta Jane	24, Dec. 1835	L1
Thorp, David W.	Reed, Angeline F.	6, Nov. 1845	L3
Thorp, George S.	Miller, Fanny B.	23, Sept 1852	L3
Thorp, John F. (Dr)	Wood, Eliza Jane	19, Oct. 1843	L3
Thorp, John T.	Tiley, Emma	14, July 1836	L3
Thorp, William A.	Israel, Mary M.	31, Oct. 1839	L3
Thorpe, Coleman	Miner, Cynthia H.	2, Oct. 1845	L3
Thorpe, Oliver	Adkins, Julia A. (Mrs)	28, Sept 1848	L3
Thorpe, Truman B.	Kingston, Margaret	12, Aug. 1841	L3
Thrasher, Daniel W.	Fisher, Carrie	31, Jan. 1856	L3
Thurber, Samuel	Lawrence, Mary A. (Mrs)	29, Dec. 1842	L3
Tibbatts, John W.	Taylor, Ann	7, Jan. 1825	L3
Tibbets, Robert	Pangburn, Martha	14, Mar. 1823	L3

Grooms	Brides	Date of Notice	Page
Tibbits, Samuel	Richardson, Isabella	23, Oct. 1845	L3
Tichenor, Edward J.	Craven, Rebecca Jane	12, Jan. 1854	L3
Tiley, Francis	Hughes, Sarah (Mrs)	21, Oct. 1841	L3
Tilley, D.B.	Moore, Rebecca Ann	4, June 1857	L3
Tillinghast, William	Laughton, Anne	19, Dec. 1850	L3
Tillotson, Edward R.	Schooley, Augusta	5, Dec. 1844	L3
Tilton, James	Adams, Isabella	12, Oct. 1848	L3
Tingey, Thomas	Craven, Ann Evelina	21, Apr. 1817	L3
Tobey, George H.	Lewis, Jane	30, Dec. 1847	L3
Tobin, Edward M.	Brown, Merium J.	4, May 1854	L3
Tobin, William J.	Doherty, Mary Ann	24, Apr. 1856	L3
Tod, Samuel	Wallace, Henrietta H	15, Sept 1818	L3
Todd, (Dr)	Church, Lydia	29, May 1828	L3
Todd, Alexander	Washington, Virginia	29, Sept 1853	L3
Todd, Charles S.	Shelby, Letitia	1, July 1816	L3
Todd, James M.	Rennick, Allisonia	3, June 1847	L3
Todd, John	Kemper, Nancy	30, June 1806	L3
Todd, John P.	Smith, Frances M.	23, Nov. 1837	L3
Todd, William	Gorman, Cordelia A.	21, Sept 1854	L3
Todhunter, Thomas	Hanley, Margaret	19, Feb. 1816	L3
Todhunter, William	Herzog, Elizabeth	5, Nov. 1846	L3
Tolbert, Martin	Morrow, Amanda	9, Mar. 1848	L3
Tolle, W.B.	Seymour, S. Emily	13, Nov. 1850	L3
Tompkins, A.F.	Ball, Flora	24, Dec. 1846	L3
Tompkins, Garretson	Phillips, Frances	13, Aug. 1857	L3
Toplis, William	Clough, Harriet	27, Sept 1855	L3
Tounly, Major J.	Allen, Harriet	22, Nov. 1838	L3
Townes, Robert J.	Eggleston, Pattie C.	15, Jan. 1846	L3
Townsend, Albert J.	Black, Honour A.	21, May 1846	L3
Townsend, John	Casett, Catharine S.	19, Apr. 1845	L3
Townsend, Louis	Warren, Elizabeth A.	9, Dec. 1852	L3
Townsend, Oliver	Symonds, Charlotte	22, Nov. 1849	L3
Traber, Henry	Beard, Ann	2, Mar. 1837	L3
Traber, Joseph	David, Louise	5, Feb. 1857	L3
Traber, Joseph	Ogle, Harriet	27, Nov. 1845	L3
Traber, R.	Cullen, M.A.	7, May 1857	L3
Tranor, Thomas	Boyd, Maria J.	21, Oct. 1841	L3
Tranter, James	Worchester, Lucy	3, May 1849	L3
Trask, Keah B.	McDonough, Lizzie	17, Aug. 1854	L3
Treatt, Isaac	North, Jane W. (Mrs)	26, Aug. 1841	L3
Tredway, William M.	Jobe, Mary Jane	20, Oct. 1842	L3
Trevor, Samuel	Bidwell, Margaret (Mrs)	1, June 1848	L3
Trice, Solomon	Herring, Margaret A.	12, Feb. 1829	L3
Trim, Nathaniel N.	Clark, Sarah Louisa	18, July 1844	L3
Trimble, Cary A.	McArthur, Mary	11, Jan. 1838	L3
Trimble, William H.	Buckingham, Martha H	25, June 1846	L3
Troup, P. (Dr)	Coovert, Abigail	21, Jan. 1836	L4
Truax, Edmund A.	Mason, Lucretia	30, May 1850	L3
True, Moses	Clark, Nancy	7, May 1846	L3
Trusdale, Charles	Sennett, Helen M.	26, July 1849	L3
Tschudy, James H.	Walker, Martha A.	22, Apr. 1852	L3
Tucker, Amos	Glascoe, Sarah F.	21, Oct. 1847	L3
Tucker, Elbridge (Rev)	Hallam, Rosannah	28, Nov. 1850	L3
Tucler, Daniel E.	Monroe, Maria	24, Nov. 1821	L2

Grooms	Brides	Date of Notice	Page
Tuite, Aaron G.	Howard, Mary Elizabeth	2, Mar. 1848	L3
Tuite, Thomas J.	Costigan, Alicia M.	15, Aug. 1844	L3
Tull, Beverly W.	Michell, Catharine R	27, Aug. 1857	L3
Tumy, J.C.	Conkling, Rosalinda	4, Jan. 1849	L3
Turner, Charles	Johnson, Ursula N.	28, Dec. 1854	L3
Turner, R.F.	Beebe, Sarah	29, Dec. 1853	L3
Turner, Samuel	Wiltsee, Rachel S.	14, Mar. 1844	L3
Turner, Samuel C.	Williamson, Mary Ann	20, Feb. 1845	L3
Turner, William	Morris, Jane C.	25, Nov. 1825	L3
Turpin, John W.	Swain, Elizabeth B.	9, Mar. 1854	L3
Turrill, Horatio B.	Buck, Marilla	6, Mar. 1856	L3
Tuston, Charles	Boyer, Elenor	27, Jan. 1807	L3
Tuttle, G.P.	Clark, Sarah Jane	9, Sept 1847	L3
Tuttle, Samuel (Rev)	Camp, Amelia	17, June 1841	L3
Tweed, J.P.	VanDyke, Jane Carol.	20, Oct. 1836	L2
Tyler, George	Reed, Mary Ann	13, Apr. 1854	L3
Tyrrel, John	Blackford, Sarah	7, Apr. 1806	L3
Tyson, James L.	Drinker, Caroline	2, Apr. 1840	L3
Tytus, Francis J.	Butler, Sarah	1, Dec. 1842	L3
Underwood, Franklin	Cobb, Julia C.	19, Apr. 1855	L3
Underwood, John	Smith, Eve	26, May 1842	L3
Urner, Benjamin	Arnold, Abby	19, Aug. 1852	L3
Usher, Peter	Dury, Martha Jane	20, Dec. 1827	L2
Valleau, C.M.	Sprigman, Augusta C.	27, May 1841	L3
Vallentine, Lewis	Dunn, Elizabeth	21, Apr. 1842	L3
Vallet, Henry	Carley, Sarah Julia	2, Oct. 1828	L3
VanAntwerp, L.	Cleneay, Maria F.	12, Sept 1850	L3
Vanausdol, Angus W.	King, Mary	17, Aug. 1848	L3
Vanausdol, Garret	Gazley, Julia	12, Aug. 1847	L3
Vanausdol, Garret	Vanhorn, Jane (Mrs)	9, Feb. 1854	L3
VanBergen, Henry	Benjamin, Julia Mary	23, Oct. 1845	L3
VanBergen, Joseph B.	Boal, Mary F.	30, Oct. 1851	L3
VanCamp, Cornelius	Hahn, Mary	9, Jan. 1845	L3
VanCamp, John	Reed, Elizabeth	30, Oct. 1856	L5
Vance, William A.	Burr, Matilda	27, May 1852	L3
VanDeventer, P.L.	Walls, Emily	5, Dec. 1844	L3
VanDusen, J.	Smith, Sophia	15, May 1845	L3
VanDuzen, Sylvenus	Bryan, Mary	21, Dec. 1843	L3
VanHamm, Washington	Minor, Rebecca	16, Jan. 1851	L3
VanHorn, William K.	Ewing, Rebecca	5, May 1807	L3
VanKuren, Edward	Duncan, Susan M.	14, June 1849	L3
Vanloon, Samuel T.	McDowell, Rachel L.	19, Oct. 1843	L3
VanMatre, Daniel	Henderson, Maria	2, May 1833	L1
VanMiddlesworth, Hy.	Cook, Eliza	12, Aug. 1816	L2
Vansant, Joseph T.	Davis, Phebe	17, July 1845	L3
Vantuile, Isaac	Carnahan, Ellen	12, Aug. 1847	L3
VanTuyl, Abram	Shoup, Emma	9, Mar. 1854	L3
VanValkenburgh, Hy.	Thompson, Eliza	15, June 1854	L3
Varian, Charles M.	Goodwin, Eliza	29, Oct. 1829	L3
Vassar, William	Brickett, Mary	20, Nov. 1850	L3
Vattier, John L. (Dr)	Moore, Anna Maria	18, Dec. 1845	L3
Veatch, Charles W.	Wood, Mary E.	15, Sept 1853	L3

Grooms	Brides	Date of Notice	Page
Venable, John W.	Farnsworth, Sarah E.	12, Nov. 1846	L3
Venable, Samuel (Dr)	Patterson, Margaret	19, May 1807	L3
Verner, James	Hopper, Caroline	28, Feb. 1850	L3
Vinnedge, Isaac H.	Snively, Cordelia	23, Feb. 1854	L3
Vogelbach, F.H.	Hergenrother, Catharine	18, May 1854	L3
VonPhul, Henry	Stout, Esther A.	6, Apr. 1843	L3
Voorhees, Isaac	Gregg, Harriet	8, Apr. 1841	L3
Voorhees, John	Canine, Margaret	6, Apr. 1854	L3
Voorheese, Ralph M.	Kirker, Mary	23, Apr. 1824	L2
Voorhis, Daniel B.	Barnwell, Mary M.	18, Nov. 1852	L3
Vowell, Ebenezer	Heighway, Eliza	31, Jan. 1810	L3
Wade, David S.	Barton, Ann (Mrs)	31, Mar. 1826	L3
Wade, John M.	Peyton, Harriet Jane	22, Aug. 1844	L3
Wadsworth, Joshua (Dr)	Magaw, Sarah Jane	24, Nov. 1842	L6
Wagaman, Eli	Leasure, Mary Ann	26, Jan. 1854	L3
Wagener, James	Miller, Elizabeth A.	16, Feb. 1854	L3
Walden, Baltzer, C.	Streeter, Julia Ann	1, Nov. 1838	L3
Waldo, Fred. A.(Dr)	Leonard, Frances	10, Sept 1846	L3
Waldo, Fred. Aug.	Lawrence, Arabella H	24, Jan. 1833	L4
Waldo, Frederick J.	Egleston, Martha	23, Dec. 1852	L3
Waldsmith, Hannes	Elliot, Margaret	28, May 1808	L3
Wales, John W.	Noble, Matilda (Mrs)	27, Apr. 1837	L3
Walker, Charles	Boffendeck, Rebecca	10, Aug. 1848	L3
Walker, Daniel J.	Chumley, Catharine	6, July 1848	L3
Walker, George W.	Ward, Mary L.	25, Mar. 1841	L3
Walker, James	Smith, Mary Ann	18, July 1850	L3
Walker, James	Fraser, Susan W.	23, Oct. 1856	L5
Walker, John	Finch, Adeline A.	2, Jan. 1845	L3
Walker, John	Wiswell, Isabella	31, July 1845	L3
Walker, John S.	Upham, Harriet H.	8, June 1848	L3
Walker, Lewis S.	Taylor, Mary	18, Nov. 1841	L3
Walker, Samuel J.	Southgate, Martha C.	6, Sept 1849	L3
Walker, Timothy	Wood, Ellen P.	19, Mar. 1840	L3
Walker, William	Mason, Matilda (Mrs)	20, Apr. 1854	L3
Walker, William H.	Spinning, Frances M.	2, June 1836	L1
Walker, William S.	Lingle, Susan E.	2, Feb. 1854	L3
Walkly, Nelson (Dr)	Gardner, Anna M.	21, Jan. 1847	L3
Wallace, Robert	Sterret, Jane E.	10, June 1816	L3
Walsh, Simon W.	Avery, Eliza Browne	16, Feb. 1837	L3
Walter, William	McCall, Mary A.	30, June 1842	L3
Walters, Marquis D.	Brittingham, Eleanor	6, May 1847	L3
Walters, Mitchell	Hilton, Caroline	8, Dec. 1842	L3
Walton, Charles	Blake, Sarah N.H.	14, Mar. 1839	L3
Walton, Elias J.	Carter, Susan B.	9, Nov. 1837	L4
Walton, George	Woodruff, Mary Ann	25, Feb. 1847	L3
Wandell, William	Hailman, Leah	30, Aug. 1825	L3
Wann, Samuel	Gamble, Jane	10, Jan. 1850	L3
Ward, George W.	Harris, Josephine	24, June 1847	L3
Ward, James W.	Lea, Catharine M.	6, July 1848	L3
Ward, Josiah	Mead, Rebecca	29, Oct. 1846	L3
Ward, L.B.	Starr, Elizabeth	26, July 1849	L3
Ward, Morris	Bramble, Mary	15, Feb. 1814	L3
Ward, Squire	Moore, Maria	11, Mar. 1815	L3

Grooms	Brides	Date of Notice	Page
Ward, Thomas	Fuller, Mariette	15, Aug. 1839	L3
Ward, William M.	Yeatman, Caroline	7, June 1849	L3
Warden, Americus	Kerdolff, Eleanor A.	12, Sept 1844	L3
Warden, Lewis	Camron, Louisa Ann	8, Apr. 1841	L3
Warden, Robert B.	Kerdolff, Catharine	19, Oct. 1843	L3
Warden, William W.	Medary, Catharine E.	10, Oct. 1844	L3
Ware, Henry	Johnson, Isabella	14, Oct. 1847	L3
Ware, Thomas	Patterson, Isabella	2, Feb. 1854	L3
Ware, Thomas C.	Motz, Angie (Mrs)	26, Feb. 1852	L3
Warfield, Thomas B.	Carneal, Alice	26, July 1838	L3
Waring, George	McCracken, Eliza	14, Jan. 1836	L2
Warner, James H.	Sutherland, Elizabeth	11, Nov. 1847	L3
Warren, Cyrus M.	Ross, Lydia	20, Sept 1849	L3
Warren, George	Ware, Abigail	24, Aug. 1819	L3
Warrington, Lewis	King, Carey	21, Apr. 1817	L3
Wartmann, J.W.	Graham, Mary	5, Feb. 1857	L3
Warwick, Samuel H.	Niles, Mary L.	6, Feb. 1827	L2
Washington, George	Wharton, Mary E.	19, Oct. 1837	L3
Washington, John F.	MacKenzie, Ellen B.	6, July 1854	L3
Wasson, William A.	Dunlap, Parthenia	11, Dec. 1856	L3
Waterhouse, John(Dr)	Hardin, Hester	8, Oct. 1857	L3
Waterhouse, Josiah	Sloop, Elizabeth	9, Feb. 1822	L3
Waters, James	Brown, Elizabeth	18, Oct. 1849	L3
Watkin, Henry	Fry, Laura A.	2, June 1853	L3
Watson, E.J.	Bumpass, Sarah G.	17, Mar. 1842	L3
Watson, John	Fredly, Elizabeth	7, July 1817	L2
Watson, Jonathan S.	Fate, Harriet F.	5, July 1855	L3
Watt, Anthony	Murphy, Melinda	14, Oct. 1852	L3
Watt, Hugh	Murry, Margaret	30, Mar. 1854	L3
Watt, James	Thomas, Frances Ann	16, June 1836	L3
Watts, John R.	Carnelly, Catharine	14, Nov. 1844	L3
Watts, William	Thompson, Amelia L.	26, Dec. 1844	L3
Way, James C.	Ellis, Mary Ann	14, Feb. 1839	L3
Wayman, Henry W.	Rogers, Elizabeth	31, Apr. 1845	L3
Wayne, Anthony	Hitchcock, Sarah E.	12, June 1851	L3
Wayne, Charles	Quinton, Sarah Ann	29, May 1828	L1
Wayne, Edward S.	Wayne, Elizabeth	26, Feb. 1846	L3
Wayne, Henry	Perry, Elizabeth C.	2, Nov. 1854	L3
Wayne, Joseph W.	Gove, Mary F.	12, Aug. 1852	L3
Weaks, Henry	Cox, Rebecca M.	28, Feb. 1823	L3
Weatherby, Charles S	Wood, Mary A.	29, Nov. 1855	L3
Weatherby, Philip G.	Jackson, Mary Jane	9, Sept 1847	L3
Weaver, Israel	Smith, Phebe Jane	25, Sept 1845	L3
Weaver, Phillip	Snider, Calista	10, May 1855	L3
Webb, C.C.	Hord, Harriet L.	6, Jan. 1848	L3
Webb, Henry	Stratton, Mary P.	11, Nov. 1847	L3
Webb, John G.	Payne, Permelia	31, Oct. 1844	L3
Webb, Joseph	Moland, Louisa	18, Aug. 1817	L3
Webb, William H.	Wallace, Phebe F.	6, July 1837	L1
Webber, George H.	Stuart, Jane M.	30, Mar. 1849	L3
Weber, Daniel	Davis, Hannah D.	13, Mar. 1856	L3
Webster, Edmund W.	Corey, Jane H.	9, Mar. 1848	L3
Wedley, George B.	Champion, Mary	23, Oct. 1856	L5
Weed, P.L.	Mudge, Caroline W.	27, June 1850	L3

Grooms	Brides	Date of Notice	Page
Weeks, Eben	Conkling, A. Rebecca	23, Oct. 1845	L3
Weeks, Edward A.	Carnes, Lucy P.	9, June 1853	L3
Weeks, Thomas J.	Dunseth, Mary	22, Nov. 1849	L3
Weibling, Herman G.	McFall, Anna	8, Jan. 1852	L3
Weissinger, George W	Poignand, Eliza	30, Sept 1847	L3
Weissmann, Frederick	Kattenhorn, Sophia	5, Nov. 1857	L3
Welch, William H.	Adams, Elizabeth E.	9, Feb. 1854	L3
Well, William F.	Priest, Sarah Maria	16, Mar. 1854	L3
Weller, John B.	Taylor, Susan P.	10, Apr. 1845	L3
Wells, A.H.	Hutton, Jane	28, Sept 1848	L3
Wells, Erastus H.	Hyatt, Maria Anna	26, Oct. 1843	L3
Wells, Horace	Whipple, Sarah H.	22, Mar. 1822	L3
Wells, Oliver, Sen.	Tudor, Elizabeth	27, June 1826	L3
Wells, William	Dutton, Amanda L.	11, Jan. 1838	L3
Wells, William	Henderson, Charlotte	21, Dec. 1843	L3
Wentworth, Mark H.	Jones, Susan Osgood	8, Aug. 1844	L3
Wentworth, Samuel S.	Hunt, Margaret P.	17, Feb. 1848	L3
Wesco, Franklin	Mills, Mary	9, Mar. 1854	L3
Wescott, Leonard W.	Miller, Ann	16, Mar. 1849	L3
West, Albert	Webb, Kate H.	26, Dec. 1850	L3
West, D.S.	Morgan, Martha G.	8, Apr. 1841	L3
West, Isaac E.	Howell, Sallie C.	25, May 1854	L3
West, Samuel	Allison, Rebecca (Mrs)	1, Sept 1817	L3
West, Samuel	Williams, Elizabeth (Mrs)	9, June 1853	L3
West, W. (Rev)	Carr, Mary Ann (Mrs)	9, Apr. 1840	L3
Westcott, Ebenezer	Collier, Sarah	23, Sept 1816	L3
Weston, John A.	Lewis, Amelia	16, Nov. 1848	L3
Wetherbee, Francis W	Foster, Anna Maria	8, Sept 1853	L3
Wetherow, John	Murphy, Margaret J.	26, Feb. 1852	L3
Weyer, Josiah S.	King, Margaret	14, Mar. 1844	L3
Weymouth, J.H.	Shellman, Rachael	30, Mar. 1854	L3
Wharton, Clifton	Ormsby, Oliveretta	30, Aug. 1838	L3
Wharton, Henry	Miner, Mary	1, Aug. 1839	L3
Wharton, Robert J.	Brooks, Jane Frances	13, June 1850	L3
Wharton, Robert J.	Honeywell, Nina M.	28, May 1846	L3
Whateley, Henry	Littlebury, Sarah	23, June 1853	L3
Whedon, E.H.	Arnold, Mary O.	17, Nov. 1842	L6
Wheeler, B.D. (Dr)	Allen, Eliza	23, Mar. 1843	L3
Wheeler, Wilber B.	Gordon, Julia M.	6, Jan. 1848	L3
Wheeler, William O.	Higgins, Marie A.	19, Feb. 1857	L3
Wheelock, Daniel W.	Pierce, Eunice	3, Nov. 1817	L3
Wheelwright, James R	James, Sarah F.	21, Nov. 1839	L3
Whetstone, F.D.S.	Cook, Mary J.	8, Jan. 1852	L3
Whetstone, John	Hopkins, Julia M.	22, Nov. 1809	L3
Whetstone, Richard A	Smith, Marion G.	6, May 1847	L3
Whetstone, Thomas H.	Mears, Esther R.	24, Sept 1840	L3
Whicher, William C.	Patterson, Sarah N.	21, Nov. 1844	L3
Whipple, Elijah	Comstock, Elizabeth	31, Mar. 1807	L3
Whipple, George	Drew, Isabella	7, Aug. 1856	L5
Whipple, Samuel D.	Conkling, Eliza	15, Oct. 1819	L3
Whipple, Sumner	Webber, Harriet	23, Dec. 1820	L3
Whitcomb, George B.	Barclay, Anne E.	24, Sept 1846	L3
White, Albert S.	Randolph, Harriet W.	9, Feb. 1843	L3
White, Amos	Harding, Susan	21, Dec. 1807	L3

Grooms	Brides	Date of Notice	Page
White, Carleton	Dunn, Lizzie H.	26, Nov. 1857	L3
White, Frank M.	Lewis, Serena A.	14, June 1855	L3
White, Henry	Duckworth, Keziah C.	16, Dec. 1847	L3
White, Isaac H.	Ryder, Caroline	17, Aug. 1848	L3
White, James B.	McCanless, Mary	6, Apr. 1854	L3
White, John F. (Dr)	Wade, Harriet	10, Apr. 1845	L3
White, Joseph (Rev)	Patterson, Eliza	10, Nov. 1842	L4
White, Julian	Shays, Sallie C.	5, July 1855	L3
White, Peter A.	Woolley, M.	27, Nov. 1856	L3
White, William	Hargy, Mary Jane	25, Feb. 1847	L3
White, William E.	Seymour, Emila	3, Mar. 1821	L3
Whitecross, William	Stuart, Lilly	8, Jan. 1857	L3
Whitehouse, Joseph	Foy, Bridget C.	1, Jan. 1852	L3
Whiteman, Benjamin	Cassilly, Henrietta	20, Sept 1838	L3
Whiteman, Lewis	Harrison, Jane F. (Mrs)	7, July 1842	L3
Whiteman, William J.	Hall, Fanny	3, July 1851	L3
Whitford, Foster	Story, Sally (Mrs)	22, Apr. 1847	L3
Whiting, Augustus	Swan, Sarah	2, Nov. 1843	L3
Whitney, Rodney	Storrs, Sarah W.	30, Apr. 1857	L3
Whitney, William B.	Clerrell, Laura M.	30, Nov. 1854	L3
Whitridge, William	Hook, Mary	9, Oct. 1834	L2
Whittaret, Joseph	Beresford, Sarah	19, Aug. 1847	L3
Whittemore, N.M.	Thornton, Elvira	19, Nov. 1824	L3
Whitten, Robert	Kenny, Eliza	18, Jan. 1855	L3
Whittier, Thomas	Barber, Charlotte R.	13, Sept 1849	L3
Whitton, John Burns	Robertsn, Mary H.	23, May 1839	L3
Wicker, Lawrence S.	Thompson, Eliza M.	2, Oct. 1828	L3
Widney, Steven	Williams, Eliza Jane	9, Jan. 1845	L3
Wiedemer, F.X.	Fortman, Mary Louisa	10, June 1852	L3
Wightman, A.F.	Burgundy, Phoebe	8, Feb. 1844	L3
Wigley, Henry	Kimball, Susan (Mrs)	22, Jan. 1846	L3
Wilby, Joseph H.	Hinman, Mary H.	9, Sept 1847	L3
Wilcox, John	Lynes, Elizabeth	24, Apr. 1811	L3
Wilkins, S.C.	Price, Clementine A.	10, Feb. 1848	L3
Wilkinson, Nathaniel	Brown, Letitia A.	15, Oct. 1846	L3
Willard, A.F.	Filson, Martha Ellen	19, Jan. 1854	L3
Willets, Lindley M.	Spillard, Elizabeth	19, Nov. 1857	L3
Willey, Harrison	Willey, Mary	9, May 1810	L3
Willi, Samuel	Musick, Lucinda	15, May 1827	L3
Williams, C. Butler	Darst, Mary E.	12, Apr. 1849	L3
Williams, Cornelius	Shipman, Tryphene	8, Sept 1806	L3
Williams, Courtland	Gatch, Elizabeth	11, July 1839	L3
Williams, Cyrus M.	Neff, Jane B.	1, July 1847	L3
Williams, Cyrus M.	Pollard, Mary Eliza	19, Aug. 1852	L3
Williams, D.C.	Bishop, Jane	16, Oct. 1845	L3
Williams, E. (Dr)	McGrew, Sallie B.	9, Apr. 1857	L3
Williams, Elmore	Harrison, Isabella	23, Sept 1816	L3
Williams, Francis B.	Ellis, Mary	19, Oct. 1848	L3
Williams, George F.	Harris, Tillie E.	23, Oct. 1856	L5
Williams, John	Barker, Esther B.A.	2, Jan. 1851	L3
Williams, John	Bliss, Harriet L.	24, Oct. 1844	L3
Williams, John A.	Jones, Margaret F.	11, May 1837	L3
Williams, Micajah T.	Jones, Hannah	11, Mar. 1818	L3
Williams, Miles	Whann, Mary V.D.	14, Feb. 1850	L3

Grooms	Brides	Date of Notice	Page
Williams, Miles	Hudson, Eunice Elizabeth	13, Dec. 1838	L4
Williams, Milo G.	Loring, Mary F.	27, Oct. 1842	L3
Williams, Milton L.	Cleaver, Caroline C.	25, Apr. 1850	L3
Williams, Minot	Ballard, Hannah E.	14, Jan. 1820	L3
Williams, S.B.	Johnson, Caroline E.	23, May 1844	L3
Williams, Samuel R.	Harding, Sarah T.	24, July 1851	L3
Williams, Simeon B.	Johnston, Cornelia	6, July 1848	L3
Williams, Victor	Allen, Sarah	31, July 1851	L3
Williams, William	Evans, Anna D.	27, Jan. 1848	L3
Williams, William	Kirkpatrick, Cynthia	9, Mar. 1854	L3
Williams, William	Thompson, Hannah	19, June 1845	L3
Williams, William B.	Reid, Isabella M.	14, May 1857	L3
Williams, William E.	Graven, Eliza	4, Jan. 1855	L3
Williams, William G.	Davis, Mary Ann	19, Aug. 1847	L3
Williams, William G.	Heaslitt, Sarah	11, Dec. 1845	L3
Williamson, Alex. W.	Shane, Araminta E.	21, Oct. 1847	L3
Williamson, E.H.	Clingman, Lydia	9, Jan. 1851	L3
Williamson, James T.	Spencer, E.M.	11, Jan. 1855	L3
Williamson, Joseph M	Boyle, Mary	26, Dec. 1833	L1
Williamson, Obid C.	Frazer, Martha Ann	16, Oct. 1845	L3
Williamson, Ovid C.	Frazer, Etna M.	27, Apr. 1848	L3
Williamson, Sheridan	Aucbez, Cinderella	14, Aug. 1851	L3
Williamson, William	Hobart, Caroline	30, Nov. 1848	L3
Wills, William	Venable, Hannah	6, Apr. 1854	L3
Wilmans, Henry	Stickney, Charlotte	31, Dec. 1840	L3
Wilsey, Rufus	Dunseth, Elizabeth A	18, Mar. 1847	L3
Wilshire, George	Clemons, Clarinda	14, Aug. 1845	L3
Wilshire, Samuel	Turpin, Mary F.	9, Jan. 1851	L3
Wilshire, William	Wilkins, Frances M.	31, Aug. 1843	L3
Wilson, Alexander	Bradley, Kate L.	8, June 1854	L3
Wilson, Alexander	Cotty, Elizabeth	25, Mar. 1841	L3
Wilson, Allan	Christie, Janet	16, June 1836	L3
Wilson, Benjamin R.	Peck, Adeline A.	1, Nov. 1849	L3
Wilson, Charles	Renshaw, Geraldine F	15, Apr. 1852	L3
Wilson, David	Coleman, Lucy Rice	28, Feb. 1823	L3
Wilson, Edward J.	Peck, Amanda	23, Sept 1847	L3
Wilson, Henry	Medary, E. Virginia	14, Dec. 1843	L3
Wilson, Hiram	Hobbs, Elizabeth H.	29, Oct. 1846	L3
Wilson, Imla D.	Danvers, Minerva	16, Feb. 1854	L3
Wilson, J. Plume	James, Amanda M.	10, Feb. 1848	L3
Wilson, J.W.	Smith, H.C.	27, May 1847	L3
Wilson, James K.	Keys, Virginia	24, June 1852	L3
Wilson, Jesse P.	Ruffner, Minerva J.	2, Mar. 1848	L3
Wilson, John James	Nicholson, Susannah	8, July 1847	L3
Wilson, John S.	Seybold, Isabella	2, Mar. 1854	L3
Wilson, Joseph	Resor, Elizabeth	30, Mar. 1824	L2
Wilson, Joseph L.	Horner, Caroline	18, Dec. 1845	L3
Wilson, Lemuel	Bywaters, Amanda G.	14, Oct. 1841	L3
Wilson, Nathan	Slack, Hannah (Mrs)	16, Mar. 1854	L3
Wilson, Oliver	Barlow, Eliza F.	14, July 1842	L3
Wilson, S. Ramsey	Bell, Mary Kate	5, Feb. 1852	L3
Wilson, Samuel	Laird, Rebecca	28, Aug. 1845	L3
Wilson, Steward	Calhoun, Sarah Ann	16, Oct. 1845	L3
Wilson, William B.	Keys, Mary B.	13, Apr. 1827	L3

Grooms	Brides	Date of Notice	Page
Wilson, William W.	Fitzgerald, N. (Mrs)	9, Dec. 1847	L3
Wiltse, John F.	Lyon, Susan Emily	30, Oct. 1845	L3
Wiltsee, William P.	Spinning, Sarah E.	26, Jan. 1854	L3
Winall, George W.	Medarra, Susanna	16, July 1840	L3
Winall, Jesse B.	Brown, Kate	30, Mar. 1848	L3
Winans, Henry C.	Dakin, Lucy E.	16, Feb. 1854	L3
Winchell, George D.	Weeks, Susan Ann	6, May 1847	L3
Winchester, C.C.	Kelly, Susan H.	25, Nov. 1852	L3
Winder, W.W.	Harrison, Vallie	25, June 1857	L3
Wing, Benjamin G.	Gregg, Margaret	6, Mar. 1845	L3
Wing, Edward	Bradford, Margaret	2, Apr. 1824	L3
Winkler, John	Buck, Elizabeth	15, Dec. 1853	L3
Winram, Robert H.	Black, Winefield	18, Apr. 1839	L3
Winslow, James	Laurie, Margaret D.	25, Mar. 1847	L3
Winston, A.V.	Smith, Alice	18, Jan. 1855	L3
Winston, John P.	Smith, Julia S.	7, Sept 1837	L3
Winston, Leonidas W.	Holt, Ada Eliza	18, Jan. 1855	L3
Winston, Samuel	Martin, Mary F.	4, May 1822	L3
Winter, George	Corbin, Emeline	11, Dec. 1856	L3
Winters, James	Baily, Martha	13, Nov. 1815	L3
Winters, John	Rex, Anna S.	22, July 1816	L2
Winters, John H.	Bates, S. Louella	18, June 1857	L3
Wintrade, John B.	Kinney, Lucy S.	27, Aug. 1846	L3
Wise, John T. (Dr)	Perry, Mary Ann	25, Nov. 1852	L3
Wiseman, Thomas	Remlinger, Mary	17, Feb. 1848	L3
Wisener, James G.	Dolph, Mary Ann	11, July 1850	L3
Wisner, Harry C.	Keznor, Lizzie	26, Nov. 1857	L3
Witherby, Luther	Brown, Julia Ann	6, Dec. 1820	L3
Withers, Rolla M.	Scott, Susan C.	4, May 1848	L3
Wolf, Jacob	Lyndscey, Cynthia	27, Mar. 1851	L3
Wolf, Michael	Seymour, Jane	4, June 1824	L3
Wolfe, John Henry	Carter, Mary E.	18, Sept 1851	L3
Wolff, Charles H.	Swarmstedt, Sarah A.	23, Oct. 1845	L3
Wolff, George H.	Fyffe, Elizabeth R.	15, Sept 1853	L3
Wood, Alfred	Clark, Anna	27, Oct. 1836	L3
Wood, Augustus	Cathell, Elizabeth	11, July 1850	L3
Wood, George	Bates, Mary Matilda	4, May 1843	L3
Wood, John C.	Collins, Mary G.	18, Jan. 1855	L3
Wood, John C.	Comteyon, Sarah	23, Mar. 1843	L3
Wood, John M.	Copelen, Isabel C.	25, Jan. 1844	L3
Wood, L.	Waterman, Louisa C.	14, Dec. 1854	L3
Wood, William	Craven, Abigail	1, June 1843	L3
Woodbury, George W.	Leech, Ann E.	5, May 1853	L3
Woodrow, David T.	Cromwell, Louisa	8, Oct. 1840	L3
Woodrow, N.A.	Kissick, M.J.	18, Dec. 1856	L3
Woodruff, Charles S.	Jenks, Charlotte R.	12, Aug. 1841	L3
Woodruff, Edward	White, Harriet S.	25, Dec. 1845	L3
Woodruff, James L.	Hughes, Elizabeth	17, Dec. 1846	L3
Woodruff, John S.	Young, Caroline	8, Nov. 1849	L3
Woods, Andrew	Evans, Margaret	24, Feb. 1848	L3
Woods, William H.	Wayne, Mary	1, Mar. 1855	L3
Woods, William W.	Tait, Lizzie A.	26, Apr. 1855	L3
Woodward, E.W.	Miller, Harriet	1, Mar. 1855	L3
Woodward, Josiah L.	Granden, Susan A.	13, Nov. 1856	L3

Grooms	Brides	Date of Notice	Page
Woodworth, Emmet C.	Bell, Amelia	17, Nov. 1853	L3
Woodworth, George	Read, Mattie L.	30, Oct. 1856	L5
Woodworth, W.L.	Thorp, Margaret	30, Jan. 1840	L3
Woodyard, Milton J.	Gilderslieve, Sarah	22, May 1845	L3
Woolley, Charles	Forman, Eliza	3, Oct. 1823	L3
Woolley, Charles W.	Strader, Mollie F.	27, Nov. 1856	L3
Woolley, Joseph N.	Church, Elizabeth	18, May 1848	L3
Woolley, Lell H.	Sawtell, Lydia Jane	14, Apr. 1853	L3
Worden, William	Wherritt, Sallie	23, Mar. 1854	L3
Work, Frank	Wood, Ellen	5, Mar. 1857	L3
Worthington, James T	Galloway, M. Julia	11, Dec. 1828	L2
Worthington, James T	Postlethwait, Anne M	26, Sept 1850	L3
Worthington, James T	Read, Martha A. (Mrs)	11, Dec. 1856	L3
Worthington, Lewis	Pierce, Sally Ann	12, Oct. 1837	L4
Worthington, Vachel	Burnet, Mary Ann	27, May 1825	L3
Wrenn, Allen S.	Taylor, Parthena	22, May 1845	L3
Wright, Abram L.	O'Neil, Clara M.	12, Jan. 1854	L3
Wright, Arthur W.	Dunn, Harriet L.	15, Jan. 1846	L3
Wright, Augustus S.	Lake, Ellen R.	1, Dec. 1853	L3
Wright, Benjamin F.	Lakeman, Alice H.	26, Feb. 1857	L3
Wright, Charles A.	Doerer, Paulina	20, May 1847	L3
Wright, David W.	Stephens, Mary M.	10, Apr. 1851	L3
Wright, Frederick A.	Bailey, Isabella R.	21, Aug. 1856	L5
Wright, John F.(Rev)	Smith, Eliza (Mrs)	12, Feb. 1846	L3
Wright, John R.	Smith, Mary E.	12, June 1851	L3
Wright, Joseph F.	Gano, Mary	15, May 1851	L3
Wright, N.	Thew, Caroline A.	21, Apr. 1820	L3
Wright, Noah	Ferris, Maria L.	11, Sept 1845	L3
Wright, Samuel	Miller, Emilia	10, Nov. 1853	L3
Wright, Sylvanus	Goodman, Frances P.	28, Jan. 1825	L3
Wright, Tilman	Agnew, Anna F.	27, Dec. 1855	L3
Wright, William H.	Conwell, Elizabeth E	20, Nov. 1856	L3
Wright, William H.	Kemper, Charlotte L.	23, May 1850	L3
Wright, William S.	Taylor, Lydia S.	19, Sept 1844	L3
Wright, Williamson	Moore, Lucy	7, June 1855	L3
Wykoff, Garret P.	Coxe, Phebe	26, Dec. 1810	L3
Wyman, N.R.	Hale, Mary	26, Feb. 1852	L3
Wynne, Jabez E.	McClary, Sarah E.	26, Nov. 1857	L3
Wynne, John	Barnard, Sarah	31, May 1849	L3
Wysong, Henry M.	Woodring, Sarah M.	19, Jan. 1854	L3
Yardley, Kirkbridge	Harris, Sarah Jane	11, Dec. 1851	L3
Yates, Charles J.	Sare, Mary Ann	14, Mar. 1844	L3
Yeatman, Thomas Hy.	Hartzell, Elizabeth	13, Feb. 1827	L3
Yeatman, Walker	Burrows, Frances M.	6, Mar. 1822	L3
Yocum, Horatio N.	Neal, Georgiana	29, Oct. 1857	L3
Yocum, W.D.	Barney, Louisa M.	25, Dec. 1856	L3
Youart, Samuel	McKnight, Eliza	28, Mar. 1810	L3
Youmans, M.G.	Platt, Mary K.	19, Mar. 1857	L3
Young, A.P. (Col)	Hutchinson, Julia H.	9, July 1857	L3
Young, Charles	Cleveland, Nancy	12, Oct. 1848	L3
Young, George H.	Smith, Lucy Ann	23, Oct. 1834	L2
Young, Isaac	McLean, Eliza	25, Jan. 1844	L3
Young, J. Wesley	Nelson, Delila W.	7, Dec. 1843	L3

Grooms	Brides	Date of Notice	Page
Young, John	Doig, Elizabeth	9, Aug. 1849	L3
Young, John B.	Anan, Elizabeth	7, Mar. 1850	L3
Young, Joseph G.	Langdon, Mary Jane	11, Feb. 1841	L3
Young, Nicholas	Kerby, Elizabeth (Mrs)	24, Aug. 1854	L3
Young, Robert A.	McCormick, Mary	12, Feb. 1857	L3
Young, William P.	Davis, Charlotte E.	25, July 1844	L3
Zachos, John C.	Canfield, Harriet T.	9, Aug. 1849	L3
Zimmerman, John	Ritter, Lina	12, July 1855	L3

Brides	Grooms	Date of Notice	Page
Abbot, Mary	Byers, Israel	25, Sept 1811	L3
Abbott, Lucy E.	Kebler, John	3, Sept 1846	L3
Abbott, Rachel	Hathaway, Eleazer	27, July 1822	L3
Abernathy, Betsey	Harvey, Thomas	24, Oct. 1810	L3
Achey, M.E.	McDowell, John	23, Sept 1852	L3
Achey, Matilda	Baun, J.C.	5, Oct. 1843	L3
Ackerman, Catharine	Smith, Charles S.	12, Jan. 1854	L3
Adair, Maria Jane	Field, Thomas M.(Dr)	27, June 1850	L3
Adams, Catharine	Barker, Ozias	30, Mar. 1848	L3
Adams, Elizabeth E.	Welch, William H.	9, Feb. 1854	L3
Adams, Henrietta P.	Baker, John W.	17, Oct. 1839	L3
Adams, Isabella	Tilton, James	12, Oct. 1848	L3
Adams, Jennie K.	Moore, Thomas L.	30, June 1853	L3
Adams, Lucy	Edwards, James	16, Jan. 1845	L3
Adams, Rachel	Berry, John H.	18, Dec. 1845	L3
Adams, Roberta Charlotte	Stuart, Ewing T.	14, June 1849	L3
Adams, Sally	Hackleman, John	24, Oct. 1810	L3
Adams, Sarah Ann	Irwin, James M.	14, Jan. 1836	L1
Adams, Submit	Maxwell, George	21, Sept 1837	L3
Adamson, Catharine	Carman, Benjamin	18, Feb. 1820	L3
Addleman, Mahala	Johnston, John R.	23, Feb. 1854	L3
Adkins, Julia A. (Mrs)	Thorpe, Oliver	28, Sept 1848	L3
Agin, Frances Ann	Rybolt, William	15, Oct. 1857	L3
Agnew, Anna F.	Wright, Tilman	27, Dec. 1855	L3
Agnew, Emely	Stout, Horace	11, Sept 1834	L1
Agniel, Louise	Foote, H.E. (Dr)	22, May 1851	L3
Akers, Elvira	Stapp, Edwin	13, Mar. 1845	L3
Alden, Elizabeth P.	Blachly, O.B.	14, June 1825	L3
Aldrich, Susan	Boyden, James C.	11, June 1857	L3
Alexander, Charlotte	McDaniel, William	9, Feb. 1854	L3
Alexander, Mary (Mrs)	Hall, James	12, Sept 1839	L3
Allen, Adeline	Bell, James B.	27, Oct. 1853	L3
Allen, Elcy H.	Baker, Reuben	1, Sept 1853	L3
Allen, Eliza	Wheeler, B.D. (Dr)	23, Mar. 1843	L3
Allen, Elizabeth	Gassaway, Henry C.	19, Sept 1844	L3
Allen, Harriet	Tounly, Major J.	22, Nov. 1838	L3
Allen, Lizzie M.	Shumard, B.F. (Dr)	2, Dec. 1852	L3
Allen, Maria Louisa	Cary, Samuel F.	27, Oct. 1836	L3
Allen, Martha Ann	Foster, David	16, Sept 1852	L3
Allen, Mary	Flemming, William J.	26, Dec. 1823	L3
Allen, Mary L.	Piatt, William	18, Dec. 1851	L3
Allen, Nancy	Smith, William	18, Feb. 1841	L3
Allen, Rebecca	Finch, Pardin M.	13, Nov. 1845	L3
Allen, Sarah	Williams, Victor	31, July 1851	L3
Allen, Sophia	Swazey, Hazen	11, Sept 1822	L3
Allibone, Mary	Osborne, Thos. (Rev)	23, Oct. 1822	L3
Allison, Patsey	Strowhuver, George	6, Apr. 1813	L3
Allison, Rebecca (Mrs)	West, Samuel	1, Sept 1817	L3
Almy, Catharine B.	Bronson, George H.	7, Jan. 1847	L3
Alston, Caroline W.	Harrison, J. Findlay	28, Sept 1848	L3
Alter, Mary Ann	Brasher, Robert C.	8, May 1828	L3
Alther, Anna Catharine	Juppenlatz, George	20, Jan. 1817	L3
Alvord, Harriet	Allen, S.M.	18, May 1848	L3
Alvord, J.	Baker, Charles	7, May 1846	L3

Brides	Grooms	Date of Notice	Page
Ammidown, A. Frances	Kinsey, Joseph	8, Jan. 1852	L3
Anan, Elizabeth	Young, John B.	7, Mar. 1850	L3
Anderson, M.	Groat, Francis	18, Apr. 1844	L3
Anderson, Margaret	Darling, Thomas	14, July 1836	L3
Anderson, Margaret	More, William	4, Aug. 1817	L3
Anderson, Mary	Gridley, Ethan S.	3, Oct. 1850	L3
Anderson, Mary	Matson, John	22, Oct. 1808	L3
Andrew, Ellen G.	McCullum, John	2, Jan. 1851	L3
Andrews, Harriet	Hoping, E.N.	26, Jan. 1854	L3
Andrews, Hepza Dana	Grover, George W.	30, May 1844	L3
Andrews, Martha Jane	Henry, David	2, Aug. 1849	L3
Angevine, Eliza	Rowe, Ebenezer	10, Oct. 1850	L3
Annis, Imogen	Kizer, Andy J.	25, June 1857	L3
Applegate, Ellen	Craft, J.W.	3, June 1847	L3
Applegate, Sallie C.	Howell, William F.	16, July 1857	L3
Appleton, Ann J.	Cheever, Daniel	26, Mar. 1846	L3
Appleton, Charlotte	Cranch, John	24, Apr. 1845	L3
Appleton, Fanny E.	Longfellow, Henry W.	27, July 1843	L3
Arbeguson, Mary E.	Ferguson, Charles	15, Oct. 1857	L3
Arcambal, Paulina	Lee, Samuel M.	3, Dec. 1829	L3
Archer, Lizzie P.	Pancoast, George	13, Jan. 1853	L3
Arion, Susanna	Lodge, John	18, Aug. 1817	L3
Armstrong, Anna E.	Evans, Robert	8, May 1851	L3
Armstrong, Eliza (Mrs)	Shepherd, Chauncey B	15, Apr. 1841	L3
Armstrong, Eliza M.	Elmaker, Horace	19, Oct. 1843	L3
Armstrong, Elizabeth (Mrs)	Conkling, R.	13, Nov. 1850	L3
Armstrong, Isabella	Bryson, Isaac	1, Oct. 1857	L3
Armstrong, Kate	Darr, Joseph	14, Feb. 1850	L3
Armstrong, Mary Ann	Campbell, Carey A.	13, Sept 1827	L3
Armstrong, Mary G.	Drew, William C.	15, Dec. 1817	L3
Armstrong, Rebecca	Kerr, Thomas	26, Sept 1839	L3
Armstrong, Theodosia	Greer, William P.	11, Mar. 1847	L3
Arnet, Elizabeth	Stiles, Francis	7, Apr. 1853	L3
Arnold, Abby	Urner, Benjamin	19, Aug. 1852	L3
Arnold, Mary Jane	Smith, J.H.	23, Mar. 1849	L3
Arnold, Mary O.	Whedon, E.H.	17, Nov. 1842	L6
Arnold, Melinda	English, Mizeal	30, Mar. 1854	L3
Arnot, Mary B.	Hoke, Abraham	20, Apr. 1848	L3
Arthur, Sallie J.	Clark, William Y.	17, Apr. 1851	L3
Ashton, Caroline A.	Hunter, William M.	29, Feb. 1844	L3
Ashworth, Lois	Dedrick, William(Dr)	9, Feb. 1837	L3
Askien, Mary	Nicholson, Henry (Dr)	19, June 1845	L3
Atchison, Sarah G.	Marple, Jerome H.	15, Apr. 1847	L3
Athearn, Abia B.	Hartwell, J.W.	2, Nov. 1837	L3
Atkins, Rebecca A.	Dick, William A.	23, Oct. 1851	L3
Atlee, Elizabeth J.	Nichols, S.S.	4, Mar. 1841	L3
Aucbez, Cinderella	Williamson, Sheridan	14, Aug. 1851	L3
Austin, Susan E.	Scott, Josiah	7, May 1846	L3
Avery, Ann	Caldwell, Robert	31, Mar. 1807	L3
Avery, Eliza Browne	Walsh, Simon W.	16, Feb. 1837	L3
Avery, Henrietta B.	Hutchins, A.S.	2, Jan. 1845	L3
Avery, Rachel (Mrs)	Hatch, George	9, May 1839	L3
Avey, Eliza J.	Bolles, William T.	10, June 1847	L3
Aviral, Sarah	Bromwell, Henry B.	26, Dec. 1844	L3

Brides	Grooms	Date of Notice	Page
Avy, Margaret	Leonard, John D.	17, July 1845	L3
Aydelotte, Hannah	Jones, George G.	30, Oct. 1845	L3
Aydelotte, Margaret	Farnham, Charles A.	30, June 1842	L3
Ayres, Elizabeth	Ayres, Stephen S.	24, Apr. 1845	L3
Ayres, Emeline	Bogart, Thomas O.	16, Nov. 1843	L3
Ayres, Sarah	Hatfield, David T.	13, July 1848	L3
Babb, Emeline	Stratton, Jeriel R.	3, Sept 1846	L3
Babbs, Eliza	Stewart, Martin	27, Sept 1809	L3
Babcock, Electa W.	Hill, Francis S.	4, Feb. 1847	L3
Backheuser, Mary	Hatfield, George	30, Oct. 1856	L5
Backus, Martha	Evans, William	24, Nov. 1812	L3
Bacon, A.E.	Michael, D.C. (Capt)	19, Dec. 1850	L3
Bacon, Calista	Skaggs, Henry H.	25, Jan. 1855	L3
Bacon, Harriet M.	Slocum, Alfred (Dr)	7, Sept 1854	L3
Bacon, Helen B.	Bailey, H.A.	6, Sept 1855	L3
Bacon, Margaret C.	Barfield, William	27, Nov. 1845	L3
Bacon, Martha	Branch, Cushman A.	17, Jan. 1850	L3
Bacon, Sarah	Montague, Thomas	16, Dec. 1847	L3
Baer, Debbie L.	Ridgely, T. Graham	23, Oct. 1851	L3
Baer, E.F.	Keenan, John W.	13, Mar. 1851	L3
Bagley, Ann H.	Ransey, Cunningham S	17, May 1825	L3
Bagott, Alice	Pearce, John	12, Aug. 1841	L3
Bagott, Nancy C.	Clark, George	21, Aug. 1845	L3
Bailey, Abbey	James, John H.	12, Aug. 1825	L3
Bailey, Catharine W.	Rowland, W.F.	22, June 1843	L3
Bailey, Isabella R.	Wright, Frederick A.	21, Aug. 1856	L5
Bailey, Jane Shaw	Briggs, Abraham	20, Oct. 1842	L3
Bailey, Martha F.	Pettit, Theodore	17, Mar. 1853	L3
Bailey, Mary (Mrs)	Dunn, Lewis	1, June 1848	L3
Bailey, Mary B.T.	McKinnell, Charles	4, Nov. 1847	L3
Bailey, Sue A.	Gest, Joseph J.	8, Feb. 1855	L3
Baily, Elmira S.	Blanchard, William A.	25, May 1854	L3
Baily, Martha	Winters, James	13, Nov. 1815	L3
Baily, Salley	Dickson, Charles	13, Dec. 1849	L3
Bain, Hannah	Baris, Levi	20, Sept 1855	L3
Baker, Anna Maria	Lee, Samuel C.	20, Apr. 1854	L3
Baker, Clara P.	Gallagher, George W.	15, Feb. 1849	L3
Baker, Elizabeth	Long, William	13, July 1843	L3
Baker, Hannah M.	Camp, Samuel J.	29, Aug. 1850	L3
Baker, Jane E.	Carrick, David S.	11, July 1850	L3
Baker, Julia A.	Keys, Samuel B.	15, Jan. 1852	L3
Baker, Louise	Harkness, H.	17, Aug. 1854	L3
Baker, Margaret Anne	Harrison, Hiram	17, Sept 1846	L3
Baker, Mary A.	Spining, Charles E.	21, May 1846	L3
Baker, Mattie L.	Price, John E.	7, Apr. 1853	L3
Bakewell, Elizabeth	James, David A.	3, June 1841	L3
Bakewell, Sarah	Anderson, Alexander	31, Mar. 1826	L3
Baldridge, Elizabeth	Childs, C.J. (Dr)	18, Mar. 1847	L3
Baldridge, Laura S.	Marsh, C.P.	15, Jan. 1852	L3
Baldridge, Martha C.	Arons, W.C.	6, Sept 1855	L3
Baldridge, Mary L.	Hopkins, Richard R.	18, Mar. 1847	L3
Baldridge, Rebecca	Miner, Thomas H.	5, Dec. 1844	L3
Baldwin, Cornelia A.	Harding, Joseph C.	10, Oct. 1850	L3

Brides	Grooms	Date of Notice	Page
Baldwin, Eliza N.	Fry, Benjamin St.	23, Sept 1852	L3
Baldwin, Ellenora	Pyle, Alexander	13, May 1852	L3
Baldwin, Emily	Lockwood, F.T.	27, Nov. 1856	L3
Baldwin, Margaret R.	Clark, Thomas	19, Mar. 1840	L3
Baldwin, Virginia L.	Lewis, G.W.	28, Oct. 1847	L3
Balee, Omanthis	Moody, William M.	13, Sept 1855	L3
Ball, Ann H.	McLaughlin, C.A.	3, Nov. 1842	L3
Ball, Ann P.	Foree, Thomas P.	17, Feb. 1848	L3
Ball, Flora	Tompkins, A.F.	24, Dec. 1846	L3
Ball, Harriet	Nye, Henry	30, June 1853	L3
Ball, Jeanette V.	Martin, Charles T.	4, Oct. 1838	L3
Ballard, Anne R.	Hannaford, W.M.	21, Feb. 1850	L3
Ballard, Hannah E.	Williams, Minot	14, Jan. 1820	L3
Ballard, Mary I.	Adams, Alex H.	16, Nov. 1837	L3
Banks, Elizabeth J.	Benson, Martin	11, Nov. 1852	L3
Banks, Mary V.	Halsted, M.	5, Mar. 1857	L3
Barber, Catharine W.	Emerson, Natham	31, Aug. 1837	L3
Barber, Charlotte R.	Whittier, Thomas	13, Sept 1849	L3
Barber, Salina	Gatch, Francis M.	9, Jan. 1851	L3
Barber, Sarah	Gatch, Thomas (Capt)	26, Apr. 1814	L3
Barber, Sarah Jane	Kelsey, Naaman	19, May 1842	L3
Barclay, Anne E.	Whitcomb, George B.	24, Sept 1846	L3
Barclay, Mary D.	Lawrence, Henry	8, June 1843	L3
Bargelt, Susannah	Foster, James	28, May 1846	L3
Barkalon, Elizabeth	Schenck, John C.	29, Aug. 1844	L3
Barker, Esther (Mrs)	Browne, Samuel J.	9, May 1839	L3
Barker, Esther B.A.	Williams, John	2, Jan. 1851	L3
Barlow, Eliza F.	Wilson, Oliver	14, July 1842	L3
Barnard, Elizabeth M	Squire, William B.	8, Apr. 1841	L3
Barnard, Mary	Morrill, Nahum	24, Sept 1840	L3
Barnard, Sarah	Wynne, John	31, May 1849	L3
Barney, Louisa M.	Yocum, W.D.	25, Dec. 1856	L3
Barnwell, Mary M.	Voorhis, Daniel B.	18, Nov. 1852	L3
Barr, Eliza A.	Clark, William H.	18, Sept 1856	L5
Barr, Susan	Enness, John B.	21, Aug. 1811	L3
Barrall, Mary	Powell, William	26, Apr. 1855	L3
Barrett, Alvira J.	Pitman, Edward G.	18, Dec. 1856	L3
Barrett, Eliza (Mrs)	Adams, Charles F.	8, June 1843	L3
Barrett, Hannah E.	Kauffman, J.L.	10, Aug. 1848	L3
Barrett, Lucy D.	Spear, Samuel B.	19, May 1836	L2
Barrett, Lucy D.	Peters, William C.	20, Aug. 1857	L3
Barringer, Caroline	Kneeland, Philo N.	23, Apr. 1846	L3
Bartle, Eliza	Pierce, Elijah	9, Feb. 1809	L3
Bartlett, Elizabeth	Mann, Marshall	15, Feb. 1814	L3
Bartlett, Emily	Ferris, William J.	18, Apr. 1833	L3
Bartlett, Mary E.	Murdoch, J.	5, Dec. 1850	L3
Barton, Amanda M.	Cochnower, John	23, Sept 1852	L3
Barton, Ann (Mrs)	Wade, David S.	31, Mar. 1826	L3
Barton, Euretta Lou.	Storer, Belamy	30, Sept 1820	L3
Barwise, Mary Ann	Brooks, Daniel	1, Apr. 1823	L3
Bashour, Serena A.	Richards, Edward	15, Oct. 1857	L3
Bassett, Catharine W.	Langdon, Oliver	3, Sept 1824	L2
Bassett, Jane	Rianhard, W.E.	24, Feb. 1848	L3
Bassett, Margaret M.	Mayhew, Thomas R.	3, Dec. 1846	L3

Brides	Grooms	Date of Notice	Page
Bastable, Mary Jane	Gano, John S.	11, Mar. 1841	L3
Bates, Lizzie	Burrett, R.T.	23, Dec. 1852	L3
Bates, Mary Matilda	Wood, George	4, May 1843	L3
Bates, S. Louella	Winters, John H.	18, June 1857	L3
Baum, Mary P.	Ewing, A.H.	13, June 1833	L3
Bauman, Kate	Hubbel, Harry H.	26, July 1855	L3
Bauman, Mary Ann	Siebern, St. W.	12, Oct. 1854	L3
Bayard, Cornelia R.	Butler, James Jones	16, Jan. 1845	L3
Baymiller, Mary T.	Hartwell, J. William	27, Nov. 1845	L3
Beach, Mary K.	Burdsal, Caleb S.	24, Sept 1846	L3
Beall, Margaret	Groves, William J.	17, Sept 1846	L3
Beanham, Mary A.	Brown, Samuel	9, Feb. 1854	L3
Beard, Ann	Traber, Henry	2, Mar. 1837	L3
Beatty, Eliza	Murrell, Thomas	23, Aug. 1849	L3
Beauman, Mary	Morris, John C.	27, May 1847	L3
Bebb, Eliza A.	Reynolds, John P.	24, Nov. 1842	L6
Beck, Ann G.	Donaldson, Francis T	29, Nov. 1849	L3
Becket, Mary A.	Palmer, Solon	17, July 1851	L3
Beebe, Lydia	Smith, William	4, Jan. 1855	L3
Beebe, Sarah	Turner, R.F.	29, Dec. 1853	L3
Belangee, Hannah M.	See, William H.	1, Oct. 1846	L3
Belcher, Elizabeth	Osborne, John H.	29, Sept 1853	L3
Bell, Amelia	Woodworth, Emmet C.	17, Nov. 1853	L3
Bell, Durinda	Baldwin, E.C.	26, May 1853	L3
Bell, Elizabeth	Allan, John	6, Nov. 1851	L3
Bell, Margaretta	Jones, J. Dan.	22, Sept 1853	L3
Bell, Mary Kate	Wilson, S. Ramsey	5, Feb. 1852	L3
Bell, Melinda	Smith, Joseph K.	8, June 1824	L3
Bell, Rebecca Jane	Hull, George M.	12, Apr. 1855	L3
Bellows, Mary	Hancint, David	8, Dec. 1836	L3
Belmer, Rebecca	Dunhapst, John H.	22, Sept 1853	L3
Belsh, Sarah Ann	Marvell, Henry W.	2, July 1846	L3
Belt, Isabella W.	DeCourcy, Oliver M.	2, Dec. 1847	L3
Beman, Louise F.	Elder, Edward D.	15, Aug. 1844	L3
Benbridge, Eveline	Emerson, Henry	3, Jan. 1828	L1
Benbridge, Kate E.	Rianhard, Louis A.	13, Aug. 1857	L3
Benedict, Sarah E.	Bonnel, John	20, May 1847	L3
Benjamin, Julia Mary	VanBergen, Henry	23, Oct. 1845	L3
Bennefield, Elizabet	King, James W.	20, June 1844	L3
Bennet, Mary	McMurphey, J.W.	22, May 1845	L3
Bennett, Eleanor	McMurphey, A.T. (Rev)	18, Apr. 1844	L3
Bennett, Eliza M.	Haywood, Samuel M.	18, Mar. 1847	L3
Bennett, Elizabeth A	Lewis, Thatcher	5, Nov. 1846	L3
Bennett, Ellen (Mrs)	Majop, Francis (Dr)	23, Mar. 1854	L3
Bennett, Lucy	Oswald, Matthew H.	19, Dec. 1844	L3
Bennett, Maria J.	Chipman, Horace G.	6, Dec. 1849	L3
Bennett, Nancy	Buckles, Dean	16, Feb. 1854	L3
Bennett, Sallie	Thorne, Ellwood E.	21, Feb. 1856	L3
Benoist, Rosina E.	Groesbeck, Herman J.	19, Oct. 1837	L3
Benson, Elizabeth A.	Hubbell, Thomas B.	2, Jan. 1845	L3
Bentley, Kate	Antram, Alpheus	12, Jan. 1854	L3
Beresford, (Miss)	Langtry, William	19, Oct. 1822	L3
Beresford, Elizabeth	Orange, Benjamin	26, June 1828	L3
Beresford, Mary	Ryan, Matthew	6, June 1844	L3

Brides	Grooms	Date of Notice	Page
Beresford, Sarah	Whittaret, Joseph	19, Aug. 1847	L3
Berrall, Susan	Powell, Henry	19, Aug. 1852	L3
Berrell, Ellen T.	Burr, Joseph S.	27, Apr. 1843	L3
Berresford, Elizabeth	Bates, E.S.	16, Apr. 1840	L3
Berry, Charlotte	Eckert, John	16, Nov. 1848	L3
Bessom, Charlotte	Dennis, Benjamin (Dr)	8, Feb. 1838	L3
Bessom, Hannah P.	Seccomb, E.	26, June 1845	L3
Bessom, Hannah P.	Seccomb, E.	3, July 1845	L3
Best, Sarah	Prill, John	3, Jan. 1810	L3
Betts, Abigail R.	Johnston, Alexander	6, Mar. 1851	L3
Betts, Mary	Halley, David J.	8, Apr. 1812	L3
Bevan, Louisa A.	Parker, Luther	10, Apr. 1851	L3
Bevan, M.J.	Lapham, William	19, Aug. 1852	L3
Bevens, Julian	Clark, Benjamin F.	16, Feb. 1837	L3
Bevis, Ann Elizabeth	Ridenour, William	11, Sept 1851	L3
Bevis, Mary	Butler, James D.	31, Mar. 1853	L3
Bicknell, Hattie	Shepard, Oscar F.	26, Feb. 1857	L3
Bidwell, Margaret (Mrs)	Trevor, Samuel	1, June 1848	L3
Bidwell, Pennie	Pratt, Albert C.	31, May 1855	L3
Bigelow, Eliza S.	Batchelor, William H	9, Aug. 1855	L3
Biggs, Anna Louisa	Johnson, David	2, Dec. 1847	L3
Biggs, Mary	Pleasants, Samuel E.	19, May 1821	L3
Biggs, Sarah	Neff, Peter	7, Mar. 1850	L3
Bigham, Margaret G.	Nixon, Alexander B.	25, Sept 1845	L3
Bigler, Anne L.	Clark, Henry S.	8, June 1854	L3
Bigler, Sallie L.	Chamberlain, William	16, Sept 1852	L3
Bill, Betsey	Myers, Simon	30, Dec. 1806	L3
Billerbeck, Mary	Ayers, Albert B.	20, Sept 1855	L3
Bills, Elizabeth T.	Brenton, William H.	20, Sept 1849	L3
Bingham, Fannie S.	Fosdick, Charles R.	13, Oct. 1853	L3
Birdsall, Sarah Ann	Lawson, Joseph	28, Dec. 1843	L3
Bishop, Ada	Ingols, Chester	2, Feb. 1819	L3
Bishop, Ella T.	Dickinson, William S	24, May 1855	L3
Bishop, Jane	Williams, D.C.	16, Oct. 1845	L3
Bishop, Sophronia S.	Evens, P.	16, June 1853	L3
Bishop, Thalia	McGechin, Thomas	28, Dec. 1843	L3
Bixler, Caroline	Schultz, Henry (Dr)	17, Mar. 1836	L3
Blachly, Elizabeth A	Beach, Edward P.	10, Oct. 1850	L3
Blachly, Mary J.	Colles, James	1, Nov. 1855	L3
Black, Honour A.	Townsend, Albert J.	21, May 1846	L3
Black, Jane	Owens, John P.	2, Feb. 1843	L3
Black, Nancy	Mitchell, John S.	2, Nov. 1837	L3
Black, Rebecca	Darst, Jacob B.	27, Sept 1849	L3
Black, Winefield	Winram, Robert H.	18, Apr. 1839	L3
Blackford, Sarah	Tyrrel, John	7, Apr. 1806	L3
Blackiston, Rachel A	Hays, Nelson B.	20, May 1847	L3
Blaique, M.D.	Field, Richard	27, Oct. 1842	L3
Blaique, Sophia	Pond, Augustus	19, May 1842	L3
Blair, Minerva	Dennhard, John	21, Nov. 1844	L3
Blair, Sarah E.	Nutts, Jacob	27, Nov. 1845	L3
Blake, Sarah N.H.	Walton, Charles	14, Mar. 1839	L3
Blakely, Mary Louisa	Ryan, John B.	20, Sept 1855	L3
Blakeslee, Marietta	Handy, Truman	24, Oct. 1850	L3
Blanchard, Frances J	Bonte, Peter C.	11, May 1843	L3

Brides	Grooms	Date of Notice	Page
Bliss, Catharine	Brown, John L.	14, Oct. 1841	L3
Bliss, Harriet L.	Williams, John	24, Oct. 1844	L3
Bliss, Sarah T.	Patterson, John K.	29, Jan. 1829	L1
Block, Esther	Moses, Benjamin	21, Jan. 1836	L1
Blockson, Mary Ann	Hayes, Samuel	7, Feb. 1839	L3
Blue, Sarah S.	Rumsey, Joseph A.	26, Jan. 1854	L3
Boal, Mary F.	VanBergen, Joseph B.	30, Oct. 1851	L3
Boffendeck, Rebecca	Walker, Charles	10, Aug. 1848	L3
Bofinger, Kate E.	Reddish, Stevenson	23, June 1853	L3
Bogie, Isabella	Adams, Thomas Jen.	23, May 1821	L3
Bolls, Emeline	Fisher, Mirza	1, Feb. 1828	L1
Bond, Cecilia K.	Stanberry, Henry	29, July 1841	L3
Bond, Ellen J.	Robinson, John A.	28, Oct. 1852	L3
Bonnel, Phebe	Marsh, Moses	13, Apr. 1813	L3
Bonnel, Rachel V.	Anderson, Robert	19, June 1811	L3
Bonnel, Sarah	McCauly, James	13, Apr. 1813	L3
Bonney, Elizabeth F.	Adams, Albert	16, Mar. 1854	L3
Bonsall, Anna H.	Stipley, Henry H.	29, June 1848	L3
Bonsall, L.T.	Porter, J.H.	30, Mar. 1849	L3
Bonsall, Mary P.	Martin, George	4, Oct. 1849	L3
Bonte, Eliza Louisa	Angevine, William	21, Feb. 1850	L3
Bonte, Hannah R.	McKee, Robert	30, Jan. 1845	L3
Bonte, Sarah A.	Miller, James R.	13, May 1847	L3
Boog, Mary C.	Beall, Oliver E.	21, Mar. 1850	L3
Boone, Elizabeth	Barney, Burchel J.	16, Dec. 1829	L3
Boorall, Elizabeth	Davis, Samuel	5, Feb. 1852	L3
Booth, Eliza	Morten, Thomas	25, Nov. 1847	L3
Booth, Pamela	Colby, Joseph	24, Feb. 1807	L3
Booth, Sarah C.	Edwards, Clement R.	11, Aug. 1853	L3
Borden, Caroline A.	Erwin, J. Warner	29, Aug. 1850	L3
Borden, Mary E.	Galway, William	27, Aug. 1857	L3
Bosley, Emily	Stevens, J.P.	27, Apr. 1854	L3
Boss, Virginia	Baldock, Milton	10, Feb. 1842	L3
Bosson, Catharine M.	Powers, B.F.	1, Dec. 1818	L3
Bourne, Annie	Dodd, George S.	1, Sept 1853	L3
Boutelle, Laurette L	Chadbourne, Benjamin	7, Sept 1854	L3
Bowen, Eliza S.	Farris, Robert P.	10, Aug. 1848	L3
Bowen, Mary J.	Crew, James	13, Sept 1849	L3
Bowen, Virginia	Crew, Peter J.	30, Mar. 1854	L3
Bower, Virginia S.	Owen, John H.	28, Oct. 1847	L3
Bowers, Ann Elizabeth	Schultz, Charles	13, Feb. 1827	L3
Bowers, Nancy	Kinkaid, Thomas J.	19, Mar. 1846	L3
Bowlin, Maggie V.	Bond, J.R.H.	7, May 1857	L3
Bowman, Catharine	Gossin, Henry	3, Nov. 1821	L3
Bowman, Margaret P.	Minnear, John W.	25, Mar. 1847	L3
Bowman, Mary	Mason, Cuthbert H.	12, Apr. 1855	L3
Bowne, Carrie M.	Hulbert, William P.	11, Mar. 1852	L3
Bowring, Elizabeth J	Steelman, Hosea	13, Aug. 1857	L3
Boyd, Elizabeth	Andrews, John	7, May 1846	L3
Boyd, Ellen	Marshall, Peter	12, May 1842	L3
Boyd, Maria J.	Tranor, Thomas	21, Oct. 1841	L3
Boyer, Elenor	Tuston, Charles	27, Jan. 1807	L3
Boyle, Mary	Williamson, Joseph M	26, Dec. 1833	L1
Boyle, Sophia	DeGolzee, Watts	27, Dec. 1855	L3

Brides	Grooms	Date of Notice	Page
Boylew, Ann (Mrs)	Lupton, Nathan	30, Dec. 1847	L3
Boynton, Sarah A.	Barton, John O. (Rev)	9, Mar. 1854	L3
Brachman, Rosalie	Morris, Charles N.	27, Sept 1855	L3
Bradbury, Eliza C.	Stuart, John	26, Feb. 1852	L3
Bradbury, Elmira	Gray, Alfred W.	28, Mar. 1850	L3
Bradbury, Mary	Kemper, Augustus S.	7, June 1855	L3
Bradbury, Mary P.	Duncan, Richard A.	11, Nov. 1852	L3
Bradford, Belinda	Hinde, Thomas S.	25, Oct. 1809	L3
Bradford, Margaret	Servis, James	23, Apr. 1840	L3
Bradford, Margaret	Wing, Edward	2, Apr. 1824	L3
Bradford, Mary Ann	Slane, Alexander	29, July 1847	L3
Bradford, Sarah	Beale, John	16, Sept 1847	L3
Bradley, Kate L.	Wilson, Alexander	8, June 1854	L3
Bradley, Maria (Mrs)	Kirman, John	27, Dec. 1855	L3
Bradley, Mary	Boylan, Julius A.	9, Dec. 1852	L3
Bragg, Margaret	Kite, Thomas	31, Aug. 1848	L3
Bramble, Mary	Ward, Morris	15, Feb. 1814	L3
Branch, Elizabeth L.	Cones, William W.	3, Oct. 1844	L3
Bratton, Mary E.	Hammill, J.R.	16, Feb. 1854	L3
Breckenridge, S.M.	Ellis, John	6, Oct. 1853	L3
Brewster, Angeline C	Mellen, William C.	30, Apr. 1857	L3
Brewster, Elizabeth	Jones, John G.	23, Apr. 1846	L3
Brickell, Lydia Ann	Fraser, Volney J.	31, Apr. 1845	L3
Brickell, M. Louisa	Carter, James S.	7, Apr. 1853	L3
Brickett, Loretta J.	Bicknell, Benjamin	27, Nov. 1856	L3
Brickett, Mary	Vassar, William	20, Nov. 1850	L3
Brickley, Sarah E.	Smith, Daniel J.	12, Apr. 1849	L3
Briggs, Alice H.	Matthews, Charles H.	27, Aug. 1857	L3
Briggs, Mary Ann	Cheetham, John	20, Oct. 1842	L3
Brigham, Julia R.	Fisher, Charles	2, Nov. 1833	L2
Brigham, Lucilia S.	Looker, Thomas H.	21, May 1857	L3
Bright, Nancy	Merrill, Daniel	12, Mar. 1829	L2
Brittingham, Eleanor	Walters, Marquis D.	6, May 1847	L3
Broadus, Sarah B.	Caldwell, Sandford	2, Mar. 1854	L3
Broadwell, Amanda M.	Everett, William H.	23, Mar. 1837	L4
Broadwell, Mary Eliz	Smith, William	11, July 1844	L3
Brockman, Susan (Mrs)	Linton, Benjamin	23, Nov. 1854	L3
Brokenshire, Mary A.	Pearson, John	1, Oct. 1846	L3
Bromwell, Loui	Edmeston, William	7, July 1853	L3
Bromwewll, Maria V.	Melish, Thomas J.	24, May 1849	L3
Brooks, Angeline	Sears, Clinton (Rev)	9, June 1842	L3
Brooks, Bithia	Leavitt, John M.	5, Oct. 1848	L3
Brooks, Caroline	Gould, John P.	5, June 1845	L3
Brooks, Cath. A. (Mrs)	Brown, Randal	7, Sept 1854	L3
Brooks, Clara B.	Hall, Richard M.	4, June 1857	L3
Brooks, Eliza	MacCracken, John	29, Apr. 1847	L3
Brooks, Jane (Mrs)	Sayers, John	11, May 1843	L3
Brooks, Jane Frances	Wharton, Robert J.	13, June 1850	L3
Brooks, Mary	Myers, John	21, Oct. 1820	L3
Brooks, Mary W.	Davis, George W.	16, Mar. 1848	L3
Brown, Adeline	Martin, John B.	19, Sept 1850	L3
Brown, Antoinette	Blackwell, Samuel C.	31, Jan. 1856	L3
Brown, Charlotte	Allen, George	12, Aug. 1847	L3
Brown, Eliza	Davis, Joseph	30, June 1821	L3

Brides	Grooms	Date of Notice	Page
Brown, Eliza	Douglas, James M.	28, Dec. 1843	L3
Brown, Eliza Ann	Ferris, William J.	26, Dec. 1839	L3
Brown, Elizabeth	Adam, Andrew	15, Mar. 1838	L3
Brown, Elizabeth	Bacon, Joseph D.	28, Mar. 1850	L3
Brown, Elizabeth	Hare, John P.	6, Apr. 1854	L3
Brown, Elizabeth	Waters, James	18, Oct. 1849	L3
Brown, Elizabeth L.	Day, George W.	10, Jan. 1850	L3
Brown, Ellen	Ford, Samuel	10, May 1855	L3
Brown, Isabella	Matthews, T.J.	3, Oct. 1823	L3
Brown, Jane	Murray, William H.	1, Nov. 1849	L3
Brown, Jane D.	Folger, Charles R.	1, Oct. 1840	L3
Brown, Jemima	Carleton, Enoch	16, Oct. 1845	L3
Brown, Julia Ann	Witherby, Luther	6, Dec. 1820	L3
Brown, Kate	Winall, Jesse B.	30, Mar. 1848	L3
Brown, Letitia A.	Wilkinson, Nathaniel	15, Oct. 1846	L3
Brown, Lottie W.	Smith, C.W.	6, Dec. 1855	L3
Brown, Lucinda H.	Parvin, Samuel T.	14, Sept 1848	L3
Brown, Lucy	Schofield, W.S. (Dr)	9, Apr. 1846	L3
Brown, Maria Elizabeth	Carey, Wilson	13, Feb. 1851	L3
Brown, Marion	Brindle, James L.	5, Dec. 1844	L3
Brown, Mary A.	Thomas, Samuel P.	7, Sept 1854	L3
Brown, Mary Ann	Hunter, William G.	28, Dec. 1843	L3
Brown, Matilda	Nixon, Martin	25, Feb. 1847	L3
Brown, Merium J.	Tobin, Edward M.	4, May 1854	L3
Brown, Nancy	Langdon, Oliver(Rev)	7, May 1808	L3
Brown, Phebe	Stout, Elisha	14, Mar. 1810	L3
Brown, Sarah	Abbott, Wilson	9, Feb. 1854	L3
Brown, Sarah	Evans, David	21, Oct. 1820	L3
Brown, Sarah A.	Abrams, William H.	14, Nov. 1844	L3
Brown, Sarah A.	Christopher, Alex.	16, Aug. 1855	L3
Brown, Sarah Evans	Ropes, Nathaniel	14, July 1826	L3
Brown, Susan J.	Kibly, Timothy	31, July 1845	L3
Browne, Charlotte	Edwards, William	25, Mar. 1812	L3
Browne, Esther	French, Cornelius R.	23, Aug. 1809	L2
Browne, Frances M.	Curtiss, L.G.	9, Sept 1847	L3
Browne, Mary Ann	Avery, Dudley (Dr)	31, Mar. 1807	L3
Browner, Sophia J.	Peacock, William H.	17, June 1847	L3
Brownrigg, C.	Killough, J. (Dr)	10, Aug. 1837	L3
Bruce, Elizabeth	Bauer, Augustus	16, Nov. 1848	L3
Bruen, Joanna	Nicholas, Charles M.	1, Aug. 1844	L3
Bruner, Mary A.	Ashcroft, Robert	4, Nov. 1847	L3
Brunson, Maria	Manypenny, William	16, Feb. 1854	L3
Brush, Mary	Cowling, Richard	24, May 1849	L3
Bryan, Mary	VanDuzen, Sylvenus	21, Dec. 1843	L3
Bryant, Caroline	Cunningham, Francis	8, Mar. 1855	L3
Bryant, Lydia	Preston, Edmund J.	16, Dec. 1847	L3
Bryant, Milly	Jones, John	11, Feb. 1820	L3
Bryns, Margaret W.	Tathem, G.W.	17, Nov. 1836	L3
Bryon, Sallie C.O.	Buchanan, W.A.	28, Oct. 1852	L3
Buchanan, Christiana	Teater, Henry	12, Aug. 1816	L2
Buchanan, Eliza	Silvers, Aaron	30, Oct. 1815	L3
Buchanan, Elvira	Swain, Alonzo	31, Dec. 1840	L3
Buck, Elizabeth	Winkler, John	15, Dec. 1853	L3
Buck, Marilla	Turrill, Horatio B.	6, Mar. 1856	L3

Brides	Grooms	Date of Notice	Page
Buckingham, Martha H	Trimble, William H.	25, June 1846	L3
Budd, Sally J.	Halsey, D.W.	13, July 1854	L3
Buel, Emma	Bateman, Warren M.	27, July 1854	L3
Buffington, Elizabeth	Holmes, William	11, Nov. 1847	L3
Bullitt, Sally	Fulton, Alexander	4, Oct. 1809	L3
Bumpass, Sarah G.	Watson, E.J.	17, Mar. 1842	L3
Bunce, Julia A.	Hanks, George L.	19, May 1836	L2
Bunker, Rebecca R.	Caldwell, James C.	1, Nov. 1849	L3
Burch, Caroline E.	Stanbury, John S.	5, Dec. 1844	L3
Burch, Elizabeth	McNutt, Charles	15, Aug. 1810	L3
Burch, Janetta E.	Barr, William V.	12, Nov. 1846	L3
Burchard, Emily	Burchard, Asa	24, Nov. 1842	L6
Burdsal, Margaret	Colter, Aaron A.	14, Oct. 1852	L3
Bureau, Emelia R.	Grames, C.W.	28, Aug. 1851	L3
Burford, M.J.	Foster, Thomas W.	31, Dec. 1857	L3
Burgoyne, Ann Jane	Prestley, William H.	5, Mar. 1857	L3
Burgundy, Phoebe	Wightman, A.F.	8, Feb. 1844	L3
Burk, Mary Jane	Eichelberger, Martin	18, June 1857	L3
Burley, Esther B.	Hayden, Alfred	8, June 1827	L3
Burley, Frances	Gano, Aaron	20, May 1818	L2
Burley, Jane	Armstrong, Robert	8, Oct. 1835	L1
Burley, Margaret	Thomas, John S.	27, Oct. 1817	L3
Burlingame, Patty	Robbins, Samuel(Rev)	17, Oct. 1810	L3
Burnet, Caroline	McLean, Nathaniel	13, Sept 1838	L3
Burnet, Caroline	Neff, Peter Rudolph	14, July 1853	L3
Burnet, Cornelia	Carey, M.T. (Dr)	13, Nov. 1856	L3
Burnet, Eliza	Robbins, Ephraim	17, June 1820	L3
Burnet, Elizabeth	Groesbeck, William S	9, Nov. 1837	L4
Burnet, Gertrude G.	Jennings, Charles P.	15, Sept 1842	L3
Burnet, Mary Ann	Worthington, Vachel	27, May 1825	L3
Burnet, Sophia	Cooper, Daniel	24, Sept 1805	L3
Burnham, Ann Eliza	Groesbeck, Abraham	10, Sept 1846	L3
Burnham, Mary Sayre	Gallagher, Phillip	21, Jan. 1847	L3
Burns, Laura	Conway, Wilton A.	22, Oct. 1846	L3
Burnside, Elvira J.	Craig, James H.	18, May 1848	L3
Burr, Emma C.	Davenport, Darius	21, Apr. 1820	L3
Burr, Mary H.	Lewis, Marcus	16, Apr. 1857	L3
Burr, Matilda	Vance, William A.	27, May 1852	L3
Burr, Orvelia K.	Cordell, C.M.	10, Aug. 1843	L3
Burrett, M. Louisa	Anderson, Younger	21, Jan. 1847	L3
Burrows, Frances M.	Yeatman, Walker	6, Mar. 1822	L3
Burt, Juliet	Norton, O.D. (Dr)	26, Oct. 1854	L3
Burt, Sarah A. (Mrs)	Hughes, John	22, Sept 1817	L3
Burton, Frances E.	Querry, Charles D.	2, Feb. 1854	L3
Burton, Mattie S.	Morris, Joseph S.	5, Feb. 1857	L3
Bury, Elizabeth	Greggory, David (Rev)	5, Feb. 1852	L3
Bushnell, Hannah V.	Hayford, William H.	4, July 1850	L3
Butler, Ann Augusta	Hefley, Isaac	19, Jan. 1837	L3
Butler, Charlotte	Stephens, Marcus	18, Feb. 1823	L3
Butler, Emily	Parr, John C.	10, Nov. 1853	L3
Butler, Julia A.	Lowe, P.T.	27, Apr. 1843	L3
Butler, Lucy	Capp, Henry B.	18, Feb. 1823	L3
Butler, Martha Sarah	Pollock, John	21, Aug. 1845	L3
Butler, Melvina	Gilmore, Gurdon R.	13, Sept 1838	L3

Brides	Grooms	Date of Notice	Page
Butler, Sarah	Tytus, Francis J.	1, Dec. 1842	L3
Butt, Lydia	Bowers, William	28, July 1817	L3
Butterfield, Jane	Johnston, William S.	5, Dec. 1850	L3
Butterworth, Edith	Girton, John	24, Feb. 1848	L3
Butterworth, Mary A.	Spencer, Peter L.	25, Apr. 1844	L3
Butterworth, Virgina	Moore, William H.	26, Feb. 1852	L3
Byington, Malvina	Huntington, Thomas S	21, June 1855	L3
Byrne, Catharine	Price, Patrick	29, Aug. 1850	L3
Bywaters, Amanda G.	Wilson, Lemuel	14, Oct. 1841	L3
Cain, Ellen A.	Muntz, Jeremiah	28, Jan. 1841	L3
Caldwell, Ellen J.	Bleck, R.F.	21, June 1849	L3
Caldwell, Jane R.	Neave, Charles	8, June 1827	L3
Calendar, Theresa	Edington, George	24, Dec. 1857	L3
Caley, Rebecca	Straeffer, Jacob M.	1, Dec. 1836	L4
Calhoun, Elizabeth	Horney, Daniel	25, Oct. 1849	L3
Calhoun, Sarah Ann	Wilson, Steward	16, Oct. 1845	L3
Callaghan, Ellen	Thomas, John	28, Dec. 1854	L3
Calling, Jane Ann	Morton, Wellington	4, Mar. 1841	L3
Calvin, Anna	Hilts, Charles	6, Oct. 1853	L3
Cameron, Kate J.	Davis, Thomas	24, July 1851	L3
Camp, Amelia	Tuttle, Samuel (Rev)	17, June 1841	L3
Camp, Elizabeth	Hazen, Alfred W.	16, Sept 1847	L3
Campbell, Ellen	Lea, James H.	12, May 1836	L2
Campbell, Katharine	Reily, Kobert	2, May 1844	L3
Campbell, Mary	Dedrick, David	15, May 1845	L3
Campbell, Rebecca J.	Cummings, George W.	13, May 1847	L3
Campbell, Sarah (Mrs)	Colby, Zerebabel	3, Aug. 1813	L3
Campton, Cynthia Ann	Cummings, Caleb P.	10, Feb. 1842	L3
Camron, Louisa Ann	Warden, Lewis	8, Apr. 1841	L3
Canfield, Harriet T.	Zachos, John C.	9, Aug. 1849	L3
Canfield, Janette	Huntington, John M.	9, Oct. 1845	L3
Canfield, Janette H.	Huntington, John M.	2, Oct. 1845	L3
Canine, Margaret	Voorhees, John	6, Apr. 1854	L3
Capp, Kate	Broadwell, Jonathan	12, June 1851	L3
Carey, Abby	Beach, William	21, Nov. 1844	L3
Carey, Letitia E.	Leuthstrom, William	19, Sept 1844	L3
Carey, Rachel	Spear, Samuel B.	21, July 1842	L3
Carey, Rosetta Jane	Thornton, Tyrrel	24, Dec. 1835	L1
Carl, Lavinia	Bridges, Joel H.	15, Jan. 1846	L3
Carley, Sarah Julia	Vallet, Henry	2, Oct. 1828	L3
Carlin, Hester	Robinson, J.S.	22, Nov. 1855	L3
Carlisle, Ann M.	Coleman, Robert J.	11, Apr. 1844	L3
Carlisle, Antoinette	Gibson, James E.	15, Oct. 1857	L3
Carlisle, Nancy	Pickens, John	23, Apr. 1805	L3
Carman, Mary	Conkling, Isaac V.	11, Mar. 1847	L3
Carnahan, Ellen	Vantuile, Isaac	12, Aug. 1847	L3
Carnahan, Margaret K.	Goshorn, James M.	13, Aug. 1846	L3
Carneal, Alice	Warfield, Thomas B.	26, July 1838	L3
Carneal, Sallie	Burke, Glendy	20, June 1844	L3
Carnelly, Catharine	Watts, John R.	14, Nov. 1844	L3
Carnes, Lucy P.	Weeks, Edward A.	9, June 1853	L3
Carpenter, Anna M.	Gibbons, Joseph G.	29, Jan. 1852	L3
Carpenter, Eliza	Thornton, J.H.F.(Dr)	16, Jan. 1845	L3

Brides	Grooms	Date of Notice	Page
Carr, Angeline	Haines, Amos	16, Mar. 1854	L3
Carr, Mary Ann (Mrs)	West, W. (Rev)	9, Apr. 1840	L3
Carr, Sophia W.	Brunner, Alpheus A.	2, July 1857	L3
Carrigan, Hannah	Keeshan, John	3, Feb. 1853	L3
Carrington, Julia A.	Probasco, Henry	3, Sept 1840	L3
Carroll, Dorcas	Cahill, James	30, Sept 1847	L3
Carroll, Kate	McDonald, Hugh	18, June 1857	L3
Carroll, Mary Ann	Bewley, George	3, July 1851	L3
Carroll, Sallie J.	Smith, Oliver	25, Sept 1856	L5
Carson, Achsah Jane	Gaines, Henry	22, Apr. 1847	L3
Carson, Jane	Meley, Jonathan	25, Mar. 1841	L3
Carson, Margaret	Kyle, John	21, May 1857	L3
Carter, Adelia	Dimond, Cornelius R.	30, Apr. 1846	L3
Carter, Mary E.	Wolfe, John Henry	18, Sept 1851	L3
Carter, Polly	Bostick, Edgar M.	8, Jan. 1835	L1
Carter, Susan B.	Walton, Elias J.	9, Nov. 1837	L4
Carver, Mary Ann	Snyder, Thomas	15, May 1827	L3
Cary, Estelle M.	Rall, George S.	22, Nov. 1855	L3
Cary, Jane	Saeon, Ambrose	19, Jan. 1854	L3
Cary, Martha Louisa	Huber, Charles B.	20, Sept 1855	L3
Cary, Mary Ann (Mrs)	Bond, William S.	9, Mar. 1854	L3
Case, Harriet R.	Monk, Samuel	7, Jan. 1847	L3
Case, Henrietta	Reid, G.M.	6, Apr. 1854	L3
Case, Laura G.	Collins, John A.	18, Mar. 1847	L3
Casett, Catharine S.	Townsend, John	19, Apr. 1845	L3
Cassilly, Ann S.	Marshall, Vincent C.	23, Dec. 1825	L3
Cassilly, Henrietta	Whiteman, Benjamin	20, Sept 1838	L3
Cassilly, Mary	Adams, William A.	20, Oct. 1842	L3
Castner, Jane	Hayman, H.C.	24, Sept 1846	L3
Caswell, Margaretta	Hall, Joseph	15, Dec. 1842	L5
Caswell, Mary H.	Portner, Henry A.	17, May 1855	L3
Catchcart, Caroline	Day, Willard G.	10, May 1855	L3
Cathcart, Louisa	Bigger, John	9, Mar. 1854	L3
Cathell, Elizabeth	Wood, Augustus	11, July 1850	L3
Cathell, Laura	Doggett, James F.	18, Sept 1845	L3
Certain, Mary	Goheen, Charles	11, July 1850	L3
Chalfant, Josephine	Marshall, Edward C.	9, Dec. 1852	L3
Chalfant, Therese	Pugh, George E.	29, Nov. 1855	L3
Chaloner, Ann E.	Hartwell, A.C.L.	19, Dec. 1844	L3
Chamberlain, Elizabeth	Taylor, Joseph	27, Mar. 1828	L3
Chamberlain, Hannah	Chambers, Pius	21, Nov. 1844	L3
Chamberlain, Juliana	Cleveland, John (Dr)	28, Nov. 1844	L3
Chamberlin, Mary	Edwards, Joseph R.	28, Mar. 1839	L3
Champion, Mary	Wedley, George B.	23, Oct. 1856	L5
Chandler, M. Melissa	Bush, James Foster	20, Mar. 1851	L3
Chandler, Sarah Jane	Cook, William J.	20, Mar. 1851	L3
Chapin, Helen	Hine, L.A.	18, Nov. 1847	L3
Chapin, Sarah E.	Collier, Charles B.	1, Oct. 1857	L3
Chapin, Sylvia	Cornell, John P.	2, June 1842	L3
Chapman, Fanny	Smith, Justus	28, Oct. 1820	L3
Chappell, M. Louisa	Elliott, Conrad B.	24, Jan. 1856	L3
Charters, Anna L.	Davisson, A.W. (Dr)	30, Nov. 1837	L3
Charters, Anna L.	Merwin, Anson W.	10, June 1841	L3
Charters, Mary Ann	Bradford, David	6, July 1822	L3

Brides	Grooms	Date of Notice	Page
Cheesman, Rachael W.	Jones, William M.	11, Feb. 1841	L3
Cheever, Mary J.	Parker, T.H.	1, Nov. 1849	L3
Cheney, Clarinda	Gaines, Richard	2, May 1844	L3
Chenoweth, Laura R.	Everett, John	9, July 1857	L3
Chenoweth, Lizzie	Apperson, William W.	14, Aug. 1851	L3
Chenoweth, Maggie	Tate, J.H.	19, May 1853	L3
Chess, Mary W.	Miller, John F.	27, Aug. 1857	L3
Chew, Elizabeth Ann	Fay, Edwin D.	25, Sept 1851	L3
Child, Elizabeth F.	Davis, George H.	28, May 1846	L3
Choate, Carrie	Ackley, William E.	26, July 1855	L3
Christie, Janet	Wilson, Allan	16, June 1836	L3
Chumley, Catharine	Walker, Daniel J.	6, July 1848	L3
Church, Elizabeth	Woolley, Joseph N.	18, May 1848	L3
Church, Jane Elizabeth	Hart, Henry N.	4, Oct. 1838	L3
Church, Lydia	Todd, (Dr)	29, May 1828	L3
Churchill, Abigail W	Markward, James	22, Oct. 1846	L3
Cilley, Cecilia	Anderson, Samuel K.	19, Nov. 1857	L3
Cilley, Emily	Pool, James	11, June 1857	L3
Cilley, Martha A.	Rifner, James M.	15, Sept 1853	L3
Cisson, Harriet	Drake, Daniel (Dr)	28, Dec. 1807	L3
Cist, Augusta B.	McClintock, Andrew T.	27, May 1841	L3
Clapp, Martha	Chute, James	27, Oct. 1817	L3
Clapp, Sarah T.	Requa, George	11, Nov. 1823	L3
Clark, Anna	Wood, Alfred	27, Oct. 1836	L3
Clark, Elizabeth	McMaken, M.C.	22, July 1852	L3
Clark, Elizabeth	Potter, William H.	26, June 1845	L3
Clark, Frances	Beans, William L.	7, June 1849	L3
Clark, Jane	Ellsbery, Andrew (Dr)	8, May 1851	L3
Clark, Jane Douglas	Anderson, William	12, Oct. 1837	L3
Clark, Lucinda W.	Gray, Robert P.	2, Feb. 1854	L3
Clark, Lucy	Patterson, R.J.	27, July 1848	L3
Clark, Lydia	Clark, George	27, May 1847	L3
Clark, Margaret M.	Gibbs, Ira B.	15, June 1848	L3
Clark, Mary A.	Kendrick, Oscar (Dr)	12, July 1849	L3
Clark, Mary Elizabeth	Baldwin, Edward Hy.	30, Sept 1852	L3
Clark, Mary S.	Lincoln, T.D.	28, Aug. 1845	L3
Clark, Nancy	True, Moses	7, May 1846	L3
Clark, Rebecca	Christian, George H.	9, Mar. 1854	L3
Clark, Sarah A.	Hunt, Charles H.	30, Mar. 1849	L3
Clark, Sarah A.	Schoolfield, Joseph	16, Sept 1852	L3
Clark, Sarah Jane	Tuttle, G.P.	9, Sept 1847	L3
Clark, Sarah Louisa	Trim, Nathaniel N.	18, July 1844	L3
Clark, Susan Maria	Burnet, William	11, Feb. 1841	L3
Clarke, Elizabeth	Dunbar, John	27, Apr. 1848	L3
Clarke, Fannie	Power, John T.	5, Nov. 1857	L3
Clarke, Isabel	Mellen, William P.	17, Sept 1846	L3
Clarke, Ladonia C.	Hoy, John F.	11, Mar. 1847	L3
Clarke, Minerva J.	Frazer, D.M. (Dr)	21, Aug. 1845	L3
Clarkson, Mary E.	Rannells, D.W. (Dr)	24, Jan. 1839	L3
Clasby, Lydia	Foulger, Seth	14, Apr. 1820	L3
Cleary, Mary A.	Jennings, T.M.	31, May 1855	L3
Cleaveland, Sarah	Benedict, Alexander	11, Aug. 1842	L3
Cleaver, Caroline C.	Williams, Milton L.	25, Apr. 1850	L3
Cleburne, Anna	Sherlock, James L.	17, Mar. 1853	L3

Brides	Grooms	Date of Notice	Page
Clemens, Mary A.	Nixon, John S.	18, Sept 1851	L3
Clement, Jane	Clemmer, J.H.	23, Oct. 1845	L3
Clements, Balinda	Pygall, George V.	18, Dec. 1845	L3
Clemons, Clarinda	Wilshire, George	14, Aug. 1845	L3
Clemons, Martha Ann	Cloon, Samuel	12, Aug. 1847	L3
Cleneay, Maria F.	VanAntwerp, L.	12, Sept 1850	L3
Clerrell, Laura M.	Whitney, William B.	30, Nov. 1854	L3
Cleveland, Nancy	Young, Charles	12, Oct. 1848	L3
Clifford, Abby Anna	Stickney, J. Charles	16, June 1836	L3
Clifford, Mary Jane	Caldwell, Thomas L.	15, June 1822	L3
Clifton, Rebecca	Matthews, George	6, Sept 1855	L3
Clingman, Ann Eliza	Cady, John N.	5, June 1845	L3
Clingman, Anna Maria	Dunlap, Joseph L.	12, Sept 1850	L3
Clingman, Eliza	Orr, Arthur	3, Oct. 1844	L3
Clingman, Laura M.	Forster, Thomas G.	3, Oct. 1844	L3
Clingman, Lydia	Williamson, E.H.	9, Jan. 1851	L3
Clingman, Susan	Enness, John B.	13, Oct. 1826	L3
Cloon, Sarah E.	Duffield, Charles	31, Mar. 1842	L3
Close, Hannah B.	Symmes, Peyton S.	25, May 1819	L3
Clough, Harriet	Toplis, William	27, Sept 1855	L3
Cobb, Annie M.	Schaefer, Charles B.	12, Dec. 1850	L3
Cobb, Julia C.	Underwood, Franklin	19, Apr. 1855	L3
Cobb, Kate	Mahon, Stephen	4, May 1848	L3
Cobb, Phebe Jane	Blaney, William	10, Dec. 1846	L3
Cochenour, Elizabeth	Peyton, Buford	9, Mar. 1843	L3
Cochran, Charlotte	McCasland, John F.	23, Feb. 1854	L3
Cochran, Eliza	Hills, Townsend	25, July 1844	L3
Cochran, Margaret E.	Kellogg, Henry S.	6, Jan. 1831	L2
Cochrane, Mary Ann	Getz, John	22, Feb. 1838	L3
Coddington, Martha F	Melindy, P.	29, Oct. 1846	L3
Coddington, Sarah A.	Jenifer, Benjamin	24, Dec. 1840	L3
Coffin, Anna B.	Horne, Daniel H.	21, Feb. 1839	L3
Coffin, Esther E.	Peach, Henry G.	9, July 1840	L3
Coffin, Martha Elizabeth	Mitchell, Thomas G.	22, Oct. 1846	L3
Coffin, Sarah	Martin, Oliver	27, Oct. 1817	L3
Cofflin, Elizabeth	Chapman, John Q.A.	18, Sept 1845	L3
Coffman, Mary	Gettier, George	21, Oct. 1820	L3
Colbow, Frances H.	Ferris, E.H. (Dr)	15, Nov. 1849	L3
Colby, Caroline	Cummins, J.W.	20, Mar. 1845	L3
Colby, Hannah S.	Prichard, George A.	27, May 1841	L3
Colby, Lydia D.	Hathaway, Curtis B.J	26, June 1845	L3
Colby, Martha	Powers, Aaron	24, Feb. 1807	L3
Cole, Adela	Murphy, Lewis	17, Mar. 1853	L3
Cole, Caroline	Bowers, Augustus	4, Oct. 1838	L3
Cole, Jane	Spalding, Henry P.	12, Aug. 1841	L3
Cole, Maria	Martin, Henry (Capt)	21, Sept 1843	L3
Cole, Pauline	Bates, Harrison	18, May 1848	L3
Coleman, Elizabeth	Donogh, Robert P.	2, Mar. 1843	L3
Coleman, Elizabeth A	Mitchell, William F.	26, Feb. 1852	L3
Coleman, Lizzie	Grubbs, William B.	27, Dec. 1855	L3
Coleman, Lucy Rice	Wilson, David	28, Feb. 1823	L3
Coleman, Margaret A.	Anderson, Charles W.	30, Nov. 1848	L3
Coleman, Sarah B.	Jones, William	19, June 1815	L3
Colescott, Elizabeth	Clarkson, C.F.	24, May 1849	L3

Brides	Grooms	Date of Notice	Page
Colledge, T.J.	McClure, M.L.	9, Mar. 1854	L3
Collier, Annie	Meredith, J.R.	13, Jan. 1853	L3
Collier, Elizabeth	Bushnell, Simeon M.	26, Feb. 1857	L3
Collier, Elizabeth M	Dohrman, Arnold H.	27, May 1841	L3
Collier, Emma C.	Grant, Charles	15, June 1848	L3
Collier, Nancy	Suit, Nathaniel	12, Dec. 1810	L2
Collier, Sarah	Westcott, Ebenezer	23, Sept 1816	L3
Collins, Amelia Ann	McKoy, Theodore	15, Jan. 1846	L3
Collins, Caroline	Gitchell, Joseph R.	8, Feb. 1849	L3
Collins, Catharine	Capen, Charles	12, Feb. 1829	L3
Collins, Emeline	Bidwell, Gilbert A.	23, Sept 1847	L3
Collins, Emiline	Arthurs, Henry	31, Aug. 1843	L3
Collins, Harnietta A	Herron, John W.	16, Mar. 1854	L3
Collins, Harriet	Corry, Thomas F.	13, Aug. 1846	L3
Collins, Hester	Ellis, George L.	9, Feb. 1854	L3
Collins, Jane	Reed, James H.T.	20, Jan. 1848	L3
Collins, Mary	Meyrick, William	16, June 1853	L3
Collins, Mary E.	Gallagher, Thomas J.	30, Dec. 1847	L3
Collins, Mary G.	Wood, John C.	18, Jan. 1855	L3
Collins, Mary Jane	Kenny, Joseph (Capt)	27, June 1839	L3
Collison, Caroline G	Leary, John J.O.	17, Oct. 1850	L3
Colston, Sarah A.	Schrock, Silas	6, Sept 1855	L3
Colvin, Hannah (Mrs)	Hawn, Emanuel	29, Sept 1842	L3
Comly, Fannie B. (Mrs)	McBride, William D.	25, May 1854	L3
Compton, Rachel	Hole, James	12, Sept 1810	L3
Comstock, Elizabeth	Whipple, Elijah	31, Mar. 1807	L3
Comteyon, Sarah	Wood, John C.	23, Mar. 1843	L3
Conaway, Emeline	Beck, James	2, Mar. 1854	L3
Conaway, Lydia B.	Carroll, Robert W.	28, Sept 1854	L3
Conclin, Louisa	Richardson, Francis	22, Apr. 1847	L3
Conclin, Mary A.	Howland, Charles H.	11, Mar. 1852	L3
Cones, Frances Mary	Schillinger, William	3, June 1841	L3
Conklin, Annie M.	Hawkins, David	9, July 1857	L3
Conklin, Emily C.	Nye, George W. (Dr)	10, July 1851	L3
Conklin, Eunice	Covert, D'Estaing	14, June 1855	L3
Conklin, Jerusha H.	Seig, George B.	6, June 1850	L3
Conklin, Mary A.	Nason, Cyrus	8, Jan. 1852	L3
Conkling, A. Rebecca	Weeks, Eben	23, Oct. 1845	L3
Conkling, Eliza	Whipple, Samuel D.	15, Oct. 1819	L3
Conkling, Eliza Jane	Dakes, H.J.	15, Feb. 1838	L3
Conkling, Mary F.	Stewart, William C.	13, Dec. 1855	L3
Conkling, Mary L.	Hibben, J. Harry	30, Aug. 1855	L3
Conkling, Rosalinda	Tumy, J.C.	4, Jan. 1849	L3
Conn, Hannah (Mrs)	Colvin, Thomas	11, July 1826	L3
Conn, Patty (Mrs)	Ewing, James	5, Nov. 1808	L3
Conn, Virginia V.	Garrett, Charles R.	12, May 1853	L3
Connell, Susan E.	Duncan, John E.	15, Sept 1853	L3
Conner, Nelle V.	Crockett, Alden	18, Dec. 1851	L3
Connor, Susan	Longworth, Nicholas	28, Dec. 1807	L3
Conover, Lavina (Mrs)	Miller, Charles W.	10, Sept 1846	L3
Conroy, Elizabeth Anna	Denny, McHenry Hall	29, June 1843	L3
Conter, Grace Ann	Clark, William Y.	11, Feb. 1847	L3
Conway, Elizabeth	McKee, William	31, July 1845	L3
Conwell, Carrie S.	Murray, William P.	9, June 1853	L3

Brides	Grooms	Date of Notice	Page
Conwell, Elizabeth E	Wright, William H.	20, Nov. 1856	L3
Conwell, Winnie K.	Stillwell, T. Neal	28, Oct. 1852	L3
Cook, Eliza	VanMiddlesworth, Hy.	12, Aug. 1816	L2
Cook, Eliza	Teasdale, William	1, Mar. 1838	L3
Cook, Elizabeth	Hulings, Perry	18, May 1848	L3
Cook, Elizabeth	Riddle, Adam N.	7, May 1835	L4
Cook, Elizabeth P.	Matlock, Bowen	20, Apr. 1843	L3
Cook, Frances	Durbin, John P. (Rev)	20, Sept 1827	L3
Cook, Mary J.	Whetstone, F.D.S.	8, Jan. 1852	L3
Cook, Sarah J.	Morse, Stephen	19, Dec. 1850	L3
Cooke, Deborah	Hyeth, Peyton	8, Oct. 1840	L4
Cooke, Eliza W.	Sanborn, John S.	31, Dec. 1846	L3
Cooke, Helen M.	Good, John	17, May 1849	L3
Cooke, Isabella	Doan, Isaac	6, Dec. 1838	L3
Cooke, Mary S.	Magill, Wesley W.	25, Mar. 1847	L3
Cooke, Nancy	Payge, John	8, Jan. 1846	L3
Coolidge, Rebecca	Adams, Alfred	5, May 1836	L3
Coombs, Emily	Spencer, O.M.	5, Oct. 1837	L3
Coons, Effie (Mrs)	Allen, William	22, May 1845	L3
Cooper, Clara A.	Davis, John M.	23, Nov. 1848	L3
Cooper, Mary Jane	Stansberry, John	23, Feb. 1854	L3
Cooper, Rebecca J.	Hatch, William S.	27, July 1848	L3
Cooper, Sarah	Atherton, George	5, Apr. 1855	L3
Coovert, Abigail	Troup, P. (Dr)	21, Jan. 1836	L4
Copelen, Isabel C.	Wood, John M.	25, Jan. 1844	L3
Corbin, Emeline	Winter, George	11, Dec. 1856	L3
Corbin, Mary M.	Thornton, Joseph L.	5, Oct. 1854	L3
Cord, Mary (Mrs)	McGrew, J.S.	17, Apr. 1851	L3
Cordingly, Marcian A	Shever, John	28, July 1842	L3
Cordry, Mary (Mrs)	Campbell, James	10, Jan. 1839	L3
Corey, Jane H.	Webster, Edmund W.	9, Mar. 1848	L3
Corley, Caroline E.	Justice, Leonidas	5, Jan. 1854	L3
Corn, Lydia	Hathaway, Henry	21, Mar. 1821	L3
Cornelius, Mary	DeGraw, Abraham	13, Jan. 1842	L3
Cornick, Peggy	Doty, Thomas	14, Apr. 1807	L4
Cornish, Martha	Cook, Anthony	2, Oct. 1845	L3
Corry, Eleanor	Douglass, James M.	21, Feb. 1850	L3
Corry, Eleanor	Douglass, Samuel M.	14, Feb. 1850	L3
Corson, Henrietta	Green, Jared B.	21, June 1855	L3
Corwin, Eva A.	Sage, George R.	31, May 1855	L3
Corwin, R.S.	Hulburd, H.H.	13, Oct. 1853	L3
Corwine, Anne E.	Andress, Henry W.	23, Oct. 1851	L3
Costigan, Alicia M.	Tuite, Thomas J.	15, Aug. 1844	L3
Cottam, Margaret	Rinehart, John	9, Mar. 1843	L3
Cotty, Elizabeth	Wilson, Alexander	25, Mar. 1841	L3
Covert, Minverva T.	Francisco, Albert N.	19, Dec. 1844	L3
Covey, Helen M.	Mix, James	11, May 1854	L3
Cowan, Sarah	Packard, Henry	9, July 1846	L3
Cox, Amelia S.	Dickerson, Charles D	19, Apr. 1855	L3
Cox, Amy	Smith, Hezekiah	23, Jan. 1845	L3
Cox, Rebecca Ann	Clarkson, John D.	20, June 1850	L3
Cox, Rebecca M.	Weaks, Henry	28, Feb. 1823	L3
Cox, Sarah Elizabeth	McLean, Sylvester	22, Oct. 1857	L3
Coxe, Phebe	Wykoff, Garret P.	26, Dec. 1810	L3

Brides	Grooms	Date of Notice	Page
Craig, Charlotte E.	Jackson, James	30, Dec. 1852	L3
Craig, Elizabeth J.	Gardner, William J.	24, May 1849	L3
Craig, Mary Ann	Aarons, David C.	18, Mar. 1847	L3
Craimer, Elizabeth	Mix, W.H.	23, Oct. 1856	L5
Cramer, Clarion M.	Hawie, Charles S.	8, June 1843	L3
Cranch, Margaret D.	Brooks, Erastus	1, Feb. 1844	L3
Crane, Abigail	Crane, Oliver	15, Apr. 1812	L3
Crane, Anna	Gassaway, David	13, Nov. 1851	L3
Crane, Anna Maria	Gatchell, Horatio (Dr)	1, Dec. 1842	L3
Crane, Frances	Reeder, Jacob	19, Feb. 1816	L3
Crane, Mary	Russel, Samuel	14, Oct. 1825	L3
Crane, Mary E.	Boroff, Samuel B.	22, June 1854	L3
Crane, Mary F.	Coffeen, John Q.A.	20, Nov. 1856	L3
Crane, Sarah (Mrs)	Epply, Jacob	2, Mar. 1848	L3
Crane, Susan T.	Shays, J.W.	14, Mar. 1844	L3
Craner, Louisa S.	Cady, John N.	6, Sept 1849	L3
Craven, Abigail	Wood, William	1, June 1843	L3
Craven, Ann Evelina	Tingey, Thomas	21, Apr. 1817	L3
Craven, Rebecca Jane	Tichenor, Edward J.	12, Jan. 1854	L3
Crawford, Anna M.	Kirby, Clinton	21, June 1855	L3
Crawford, Margaret J	Mitchell, J. McD.	18, May 1843	L3
Crawford, Martha Ann	Smith, William H(Dr)	4, July 1844	L3
Crawford, Sarah	Birney, Dion.	21, Aug. 1845	L3
Creager, Emily	Alcoke, James B.	17, Nov. 1842	L6
Cregar, Rebecca Ann	Conklin, John T.	23, Dec. 1852	L3
Crendiff, Lizzie	Marlay, John F.(Rev)	15, Sept 1853	L3
Crocker, Marion	Packard, S.S.	14, Mar. 1850	L3
Cromwell, Ann	Langdon, Elam P.	17, Oct. 1821	L3
Cromwell, Elizabeth	Labrot, Auguste	28, Nov. 1844	L3
Cromwell, Laura	Johnson, Rufus S.	6, Apr. 1854	L3
Cromwell, Louisa	Woodrow, David T.	8, Oct. 1840	L3
Crooker, Ann	St.Clair, John	20, Sept 1827	L3
Crooks, Margaret	Forbes, Joseph	30, Nov. 1813	L3
Cropper, Louisa C.	Clayton, William	20, Nov. 1850	L3
Cropper, Nancy	Bircham, Daniel	3, Apr. 1811	L3
Cross, Esther E.	Mallard, Henry	17, June 1841	L3
Cross, Margaret (Mrs)	Drake, Charles D.	23, Mar. 1843	L3
Crossett, Aurelia	Fisher, Samuel S.	16, Oct. 1856	L5
Crossley, Rachel	Merrit, James P.J	31, Aug. 1822	L3
Crossman, Caroline	Brigham, Mathias	6, Oct. 1821	L3
Crossman, Elizabeth	Marsh, Nathan B.	10, Nov. 1842	L4
Crossman, Margaret	Chapman, William B.	18, Apr. 1839	L3
Crossman, Martha	Blatchford, Henry S.	20, June 1844	L3
Crowell, Elenor B.	Smith, J.B. Clark	17, July 1845	L3
Crumbaugh, Sarah	Miller, T.H.	30, Mar. 1854	L3
Crummey, Caroline V.	Clark, William Penn	9, June 1842	L3
Crumsey, Mary A.	Paddack, Alexander	14, July 1853	L3
Cryer, Mary	Baer, Frederick	8, Nov. 1855	L3
Culbertson, Josephine	Heighway, A.E. (Dr)	7, Dec. 1854	L3
Cullen, M.A.	Traber, R.	7, May 1857	L3
Cullum, Chloe	Bonham, Hervey	18, Sept 1815	L3
Cullum, Sarah Ann	Riggs, Simpson	13, Sept 1849	L3
Cummings, Eliza	Handy, R.J.H.	15, Feb. 1844	L3
Cummings, Sarah S.	Carnahan, James A.P.	24, Sept 1846	L3

Brides	Grooms	Date of Notice	Page
Cummins, Ann (Mrs)	Swormsted, Leroy (Rev)	14, Jan. 1825	L3
Cummins, Jennett	Peachey, Henry	18, July 1850	L3
Cummins, Mary A.	Owens, Richard	29, Oct. 1846	L3
Cummins, Sarah	Burgoyne, E.M.	22, Jan. 1857	L3
Cunningham, Eliza A.	Perry, Samuel	16, Mar. 1848	L3
Cunningham, Kate	Stockton, Phillip	21, Feb. 1856	L3
Cunningham, Rachel	Marsh, Theodore	27, Nov. 1845	L3
Cuny, Clarissa (Mrs)	Dudley, Ambrose (Col)	13, July 1837	L3
Curtis, Eliza M.	Smallwood, Samuel N.	1, Jan. 1846	L3
Curtis, Mary	Beggs, Joseph P.	26, Aug. 1847	L3
Cushing, Hannah L.	Gallagher, John M.	16, Oct. 1834	L2
Cushing, Lucie W.	Gill, William	6, Apr. 1854	L3
Cutler, Mary E.	Snowdon, T.M.	6, Sept 1855	L3
Cutting, Mary Ann	Miller, John	30, Oct. 1856	L5
Daggett, Eliza Jane	Gorham, William F.	22, Apr. 1847	L3
Dailey, Martha Ann	Ross, Andrew	28, Jan. 1841	L3
Daily, Emeline	Daily, Nathaniel	30, Oct. 1851	L3
Dakin, Lucy E.	Winans, Henry C.	16, Feb. 1854	L3
Dakin, Mary A.	Mooney, D.H.	12, Oct. 1854	L3
Dale, Annie E.	Brent, C.P. (Dr)	3, Sept 1857	L3
Dallas, Mary E. (Mrs)	Locke, John (Dr)	28, Sept 1854	L3
Dalton, Eliza	Cohoon, Robert	15, June 1837	L3
Damont, Harriet L.	Arons, Garret	14, Sept 1843	L3
Dana, Frances	Price, James P.	16, Nov. 1843	L3
Dana, Mary	Smith, John L.	31, Oct. 1823	L3
Daniel, Mary L.V.	Goddard, John F.	7, Sept 1837	L3
Daniels, Elizabeth	Martin, Alfred	26, Nov. 1840	L3
Danvers, Minerva	Wilson, Imla D.	16, Feb. 1854	L3
Darr, M. Amelia	Rotherbusch, Philip	30, Dec. 1847	L3
Darst, Anna B. (Mrs)	Darst, Jacob	17, Dec. 1857	L3
Darst, Mary E.	Williams, C. Butler	12, Apr. 1849	L3
Dart, Harriet N.	Thompson, William H.	24, Apr. 1845	L3
Dashiell, Mary Y.	Madeira, J.	26, Nov. 1824	L3
Davenport, Serena B.	Handy, F.H.	1, Mar. 1849	L3
Davey, Eleanor	Blackburn, J.C. (Dr)	31, May 1855	L3
Davey, Mary A.	Marshall, Robert M.	25, Nov. 1852	L3
David, Louise	Traber, Joseph	5, Feb. 1857	L3
Davis, (Mrs)	Kemper, Peter, Jr.	2, Feb. 1809	L3
Davis, Amanda	Patten, Alpheus	1, Oct. 1846	L3
Davis, Charlotte E.	Young, William P.	25, July 1844	L3
Davis, Hannah D.	Weber, Daniel	13, Mar. 1856	L3
Davis, Harriet Ann	Stephenson, Andrew C	21, Oct. 1847	L3
Davis, Isabella	Stagg, Henry	24, Nov. 1842	L6
Davis, Janette	Dorfeuille, J.	14, May 1824	L3
Davis, Julia Maria	McDonald, Harrison	25, Apr. 1844	L3
Davis, Lucinda	Cook, Austin	20, Sept 1827	L1
Davis, Mahula	Coombs, Ollman	14, Dec. 1848	L2
Davis, Maria Louisa	Harrison, George W.	18, Dec. 1845	L3
Davis, Martha E.	Brown, Samuel C.	12, Dec. 1850	L3
Davis, Martha R.	Antram, M.T.	11, Dec. 1856	L3
Davis, Mary Ann	Williams, William G.	19, Aug. 1847	L3
Davis, Mary Christin	Killough, James (Dr)	16, Sept 1841	L3
Davis, Mary Jane	Harris, Caleb K.	19, Nov. 1846	L3

Brides	Grooms	Date of Notice	Page
Davis, Mary Jane	Oliver, William D.	13, May 1847	L3
Davis, Mary M.	Jacobs, S.C.	26, Feb. 1857	L3
Davis, Nancy	Jenkins, Riley	13, June 1850	L3
Davis, Phebe	Vansant, Joseph T.	17, July 1845	L3
Davis, R. Flora	Rickoff, Andrew J.	16, Oct. 1856	L5
Davis, Rachael	McKenzie, A.	13, May 1852	L3
Davis, Sarah	Hartshorn, James	4, May 1822	L3
Davis, Sophia	Folsom, Samuel	2, Dec. 1847	L3
Dawson, Martha Ann	Stewart, Charles	12, Apr. 1849	L3
Day, Dianthy	Taylor, John	5, Sept 1844	L3
Day, Mary E.	Fisher, John W.	28, Feb. 1850	L3
Deane, Agnes	Shipley, John W.	20, Oct. 1836	L1
Death, Arachne	Hill, Benjamin	23, Nov. 1854	L3
Death, Hannah Jane	Glancy, Harvey M.	7, Sept 1854	L3
Death, Susan A.	Brockman, Jesse S.	16, Mar. 1849	L3
Debaugee, Mary	Arthers, Samuel	11, Mar. 1818	L3
DeBeck, Mary E.L.	Smith, Lorenzo D.	13, Dec. 1855	L3
Debolt, Elizabeth	Morrison, William	27, Jan. 1807	L3
DeCamp, Charlotte	Justice, Enoch P.	14, Sept 1848	L3
DeCamp, Mary Anna	Stevens, Thomas A.	12, Feb. 1852	L3
DeCamp, Phoebe A.	Moore, James C.	10, May 1855	L3
DeCamp, Sarah B.	Pettiner, Matthew	5, Mar. 1857	L3
Decker, Caroline	Jones, Gilbert R.	11, Dec. 1845	L3
DeForrest, Julia	Franklin, John	4, Apr. 1826	L3
DeGraw, Rebecca	Peregrine, J.S.(Rev)	20, Aug. 1857	L3
Deilkes, Jerusha(Mrs	Brettell, Joseph	22, Feb. 1844	L3
Delacroix, Victorine	Robinson, Samuel	24, Apr. 1845	L3
Delaplane, Margaret	Kenneday, Charles	23, Mar. 1854	L3
Denman, Abby	Blakemore, John	6, Nov. 1845	L3
Denman, Elizabeth	Gray, Robert P.	10, Apr. 1851	L3
Denman, Louisa Eve.	Hinsch, Augustus F.	5, May 1836	L3
Dennison, Mary Ang.	Motz, George W.	25, Apr. 1844	L3
Denny, Elizabeth	Burdsal, Solomon B.	6, May 1847	L3
Derrough, Mary (Mrs)	Miller, Joseph	16, May 1850	L3
Deshields, Mary Z.	Ames, Fisher W.(Dr)	30, Oct. 1851	L3
DeValcourt, Martha E	Piatt, J.W.	7, Sept 1837	L3
Devou, Sarah Alice	Beatty, James S.	2, Aug. 1838	L3
DeYoung, Sarah	Abraham, J.	9, Sept 1841	L3
Dibrell, Elizabeth W	Pease, John B.	2, Mar. 1837	L3
Dick, Jane	McGrew, Henry C.	11, June 1846	L3
Dickinson, Lydia L.	Courteney, Samuel G.	30, Sept 1852	L3
Dickinson, M. Ellen	Morse, Bennett W.	30, Sept 1852	L3
Dickinson, Mary	Embree, Jesse	29, Sept 1818	L2
Dickinson, Sarah	Pierce, Harvey	26, Sept 1844	L3
Dicks, Cornelia	Hall, John C.	7, Dec. 1843	L3
Dicks, Mary Ellen	Strickler, George W.	24, Feb. 1842	L3
Dicks, Mary Jane	Hopper, Joseph L.	11, Jan. 1838	L3
Dicks, Sarah	Carson, Charles	19, Jan. 1854	L3
Dickson, Mary	Clark, Enos B.	18, Sept 1845	L3
Dickson, Sarah Emily	Brisbane, Benjamin L	2, Feb. 1854	L3
Dike, Amelia	Andrews, Seth L. (Dr)	22, Apr. 1852	L3
Dillon, Elizabeth	Evans, John	11, Oct. 1838	L3
Dilse, Jane	Green, George	13, Mar. 1845	L3
Dilworth, Eliza W.	Loomis, D.W.	1, Apr. 1847	L3

Brides	Grooms	Date of Notice	Page
Dippel, Mary C.	Beyring, F.W. Theo.	4, July 1844	L3
Disney, Annie	Conwell, LaFayette	7, Feb. 1850	L3
Disney, Mary A.	Chatfield, William H	30, Nov. 1854	L3
Disney, Mary E.	Buttles, Lucien	20, June 1844	L3
Diters, Mary	Leman, Washington H.	26, Sept 1844	L3
Dixon, Elizabeth	Orr, William M.	29, Dec. 1817	L2
Dobson, Ann	Merser, Robert	10, June 1847	L3
Dodd, Louisa Jane	Ross, A.N. (Dr)	6, Nov. 1845	L3
Dodd, Mary E.	Hart, Henry R.	15, June 1848	L3
Dodge, Adaline	Knowlton, Cyrus	28, Sept 1848	L3
Dodge, Fannie E.	Single, William S.	14, Feb. 1856	L3
Dodge, Frances Ann	Casto, Jonathan	9, Dec. 1847	L3
Dodson, Cynthia Ann	King, D. Cleaves	14, June 1849	L3
Dodsworth, Eliza	Moore, Adam	25, Mar. 1852	L3
Dodsworth, Mary	Andress, Charles	17, June 1841	L3
Doerer, Paulina	Wright, Charles A.	20, May 1847	L3
Doerrer, Rachel	Faris, Thomas	7, Aug. 1845	L3
Doggitt, Elizabeth N	Ashton, Charles	23, Mar. 1854	L3
Doherty, Catharine	McLenan, William	24, Jan. 1850	L3
Doherty, Mary Ann	Tobin, William J.	24, Apr. 1856	L3
Doig, Elizabeth	Young, John	9, Aug. 1849	L3
Doisy, Charlotte E.	Gengembre, H.P.	19, June 1851	L3
Dole, Sarah	Barr, William M.	23, Feb. 1854	L3
Dollin, Frances	Cook, Samuel	11, Nov. 1820	L3
Dollin, Jane	Smith, Thomas	11, Nov. 1820	L3
Dolph, Mary Ann	Wisener, James G.	11, July 1850	L3
Donaldson, Jessie	Pullan, Richard B.	3, May 1849	L3
Donaldson, Mary	Lindman, Lewis T.	22, Apr. 1847	L3
D'Orfeuille, Jenny	Sanford, Alonson J.	14, June 1855	L3
Dorman, Maria E.	Brandon, James P.	29, Nov. 1838	L3
Dorman, Sarah Ann	Stephenson, H.W.	21, Feb. 1839	L3
Dorsy, Mary Ann	Adams, John Quincy	25, Feb. 1847	L3
Dosey, Mary	Gist, Robert C.	18, Jan. 1832	L4
Dosey, Susan	Bush, E.T.	19, Aug. 1847	L3
Doughty, Matilda	Gallagher, William	26, Nov. 1857	L3
Doughty, Rachel	Donnavau, Corydon	1, Aug. 1839	L3
Douglas, Mary L. (Mrs)	Smallwood, William A	5, Mar. 1846	L3
Douglass, Caroline E	Bliss, Oliver H.	1, Dec. 1842	L3
Douglass, Eliza Ann	Purvis, John	30, Nov. 1843	L3
Dounn, Mattie	Stout, Ephraim B.	3, Apr. 1856	L3
Downard, Eliza	Buist, Thomas	21, Nov. 1844	L3
Downard, Malinda B.	Hoopes, Edward L.	17, Nov. 1831	L2
Downs, Mary E.	Hurley, John H.	10, May 1855	L3
Doyal, Emma D.	Duvall, L.W.	15, Dec. 1853	L3
Doyle, Emaline Ad.	Buckingham, E.J.	20, Mar. 1851	L3
Drake, Amanda	McDowell, Joseph N.	3, Apr. 1827	L3
Drake, Harriet E.	Phelps, S.W.	5, May 1836	L3
Drake, Lavinia	Bedinger, Henry C.	9, Sept 1820	L3
Drake, Rebecca A.	Rose, Thomas	18, May 1848	L3
Drennan, Sarah J. (Mrs)	Hedges, Clayborn	11, Feb. 1847	L3
Dressel, Elizabeth	Straeffer, Michael	2, June 1831	L1
Drew, Isabella	Whipple, George	7, Aug. 1856	L5
Drinker, Caroline	Tyson, James L.	2, Apr. 1840	L3
Drinker, Elizabeth	Storer, Bellamy	21, May 1846	L3

Brides	Grooms	Date of Notice	Page
Driskill, Caroline	Collins, Charles	26, Jan. 1843	L3
Drone, Mary Magdalena	Scharbach, Jaque	19, Dec. 1821	L3
Drummond, Ann R.	Bokum, Herman (Rev)	20, Feb. 1851	L3
Drummond, Maria	Burch, James K. (Dr)	25, July 1839	L3
Dryden, Selina	Jones, Alanson	11, May 1854	L3
Duble, Kate S.	Hinman, E.B.	1, Apr. 1852	L3
DuBois, Jennie M.	Barkalow, Gilbert L.	19, Feb. 1857	L3
Dubois, Lorinda H.	Medary, John M.	28, May 1846	L3
Dubois, Phebe Jane	Schenck, B.G.	19, Jan. 1843	L3
Duckworth, Keziah C.	White, Henry	16, Dec. 1847	L3
Dudley, Bettie F.	Mallory, W.L.	22, Jan. 1857	L3
Dudley, Charlotte	Armstrong, Lafayette	23, Oct. 1845	L3
Dudley, Louisa	Burrows, John A.D.	15, June 1843	L3
Duke, Eugenia J.	Sterrett, Robert	20, Sept 1827	L1
Dulhagen, Elizabeth	Powell, William F.	21, Dec. 1848	L3
Dullhagen, Annie	Simons, Frank	27, Sept 1855	L3
Dumm, Catharine A.	Cruzan, Benjamin W.	7, Feb. 1839	L3
Dumont, Matilda	Horton, David C.	25, Mar. 1852	L3
Duncan, Elizabeth	Findlay, Samuel B.	14, Dec. 1837	L3
Duncan, Hattie M.	Hard, Edward	26, July 1855	L3
Duncan, Margaret	Fortman, Harman	9, May 1844	L3
Duncan, Mary S.	Burnet, Jacob	13, Nov. 1856	L3
Duncan, Susan M.	VanKuren, Edward	14, June 1849	L3
Dungan, Harriet	Parker, David M.	29, Feb. 1844	L3
Dunlap, E.	Purser, John	28, Aug. 1845	L3
Dunlap, Parthenia	Wasson, William A.	11, Dec. 1856	L3
Dunlop, Josephine	Ludlow, James C.	9, Apr. 1819	L3
Dunn, Elizabeth	Vallentine, Lewis	21, Apr. 1842	L3
Dunn, Harriet L.	Wright, Arthur W.	15, Jan. 1846	L3
Dunn, Lizzie H.	White, Carleton	26, Nov. 1857	L3
Dunn, Zion M.	Martin, Fernando K.	17, Oct. 1844	L3
Dunnelly, Betsy (Mrs)	Lindsay, Robert	13, Nov. 1850	L3
Dunseth, Ann	Hall, John	26, Mar. 1846	L3
Dunseth, Elizabeth A	Wilsey, Rufus	18, Mar. 1847	L3
Dunseth, Mary	Weeks, Thomas J.	22, Nov. 1849	L3
Dury, Martha Jane	Usher, Peter	20, Dec. 1827	L2
Dutton, Amanda L.	Wells, William	11, Jan. 1838	L3
Duval, Cornelia	Grant, Edward B.	26, Apr. 1855	L3
Duval, Mary Isabella	McKenna, J. Theodore	2, Feb. 1854	L3
Duvall, Rachel	Meddock, Abijah	5, Feb. 1812	L2
Dyer, M. Louisa	Armstrong, E.R.T.	20, Oct. 1853	L3
Eastland, Ann Eliza	Bowman, Henry Andrew	30, Mar. 1848	L3
Easton, Eliza	Ebrert, Isaac (Rev)	3, June 1841	L3
Easton, Rebecca	Summerwell, Robert K	28, Dec. 1854	L3
Eaton, Anna J. Irwin	Moore, William H.	15, Aug. 1844	L3
Eaton, Anna Jane	Irwin, John V.	4, Oct. 1838	L3
Eaton, Eliza Ann	Gibbs, William F.	17, Mar. 1836	L3
Eberle, Catharine	Bacon, John Henry	19, Dec. 1833	L2
Eberle, Margaret	Mayronne, O.F.	5, Nov. 1840	L2
Ebersol, Mary Jane	Culberston, William	12, Jan. 1854	L3
Ebersole, Annie	Rogers, L.M. (Dr)	23, Oct. 1851	L3
Ebersole, Mary	Kidd, Edwin T.	3, May 1855	L3
Eckert, Josephine	Stone, Leaverett G.	21, Aug. 1856	L5

Brides	Grooms	Date of Notice	Page
Edday, Hannah (Mrs)	Dart, George L.	22, July 1852	L3
Edmonds, Emily	Meadows, James	2, Mar. 1854	L3
Edmondson, Mary Ann	Biddecomer, D.R. (Rev)	9, June 1842	L3
Edwards, Ann	Metcalf, James	23, Mar. 1843	L3
Edwards, Mary	Jones, J.N.	11, May 1848	L3
Edwards, Rebecca	McClean, John	7, Apr. 1807	L3
Eggleston, Pattie C.	Townes, Robert J.	15, Jan. 1846	L3
Egleston, Martha	Waldo, Frederick J.	23, Dec. 1852	L3
Egleston, Mary Jane	Allen, George	2, Apr. 1857	L3
Eha, Mary	Kaugger, Christian	3, Nov. 1853	L3
Ellicott, Catharine	Lindley, Jacob	28, Oct. 1847	L3
Elliot, Julia Ann E.	Crane, Joseph H.	19, July 1809	L3
Elliot, Margaret	Waldsmith, Hannes	28, May 1808	L3
Elliott, Caroline	Boyd, D.B.	6, Jan. 1853	L3
Elliott, Mary B.	Sigerson, William	30, Nov. 1837	L3
Ellis, E.J.	Meyers, J.H.	19, Jan. 1854	L3
Ellis, Emeline	Ringer, Joab	16, Nov. 1854	L3
Ellis, Jane	Matthews, James	28, Oct. 1847	L3
Ellis, Jane Maria	Rasland, Benjamin F.	27, Nov. 1845	L3
Ellis, Mary	Williams, Francis B.	19, Oct. 1848	L3
Ellis, Mary Ann	Way, James C.	14, Feb. 1839	L3
Ellis, Mary Caroline	Lea, James M.	6, May 1852	L3
Ellmaker, Susan	Carpenter, Isaac B.	29, June 1837	L2
Elmaker, Eliza (Mrs)	Shaw, W.M.	12, Feb. 1852	L3
Elstner, Louise	Fisher, William M.	9, Sept 1852	L3
Ely, Anna L.	Morris, Edward C.	9, July 1857	L3
Emerson, Charlotte	Dosch, Daniel	18, Apr. 1850	L3
Emily, Nancy Ann	Hardesty, Samuel	22, Dec. 1842	L3
England, Elizabeth	Ballance, Charles	4, Feb. 1836	L4
English, Letitia T.	Black, William W.	26, Sept 1844	L3
English, Mary Jane	McCalla, William H.	21, Feb. 1856	L3
Enness, Mary	Terry, Reuben	18, Sept 1815	L3
Enyart, M.C.	Dominick, George	17, June 1852	L3
Enyart, Rebecca A.	Phipps, Gardner	14, Mar. 1839	L3
Erickson, Sarah	Jones, George	28, Oct. 1852	L3
Ernst, Adeline E.	Kent, Luke	9, July 1840	L3
Ernst, Mary A.	James, A.C.	15, Oct. 1840	L3
Erwin, Olivia	Swing, Jeremiah	26, July 1827	L3
Eshelman, Sarah A.	Leeds, Jesse J.	23, Mar. 1854	L3
Esselstine, Cornelia	Naudain, W.M.(Dr)	5, July 1855	L3
Este, Lucy Ann	Reynolds, Joseph	16, Feb. 1843	L3
Etherington, Susan C.	Phillips, Benjamin C	4, Apr. 1850	L3
Eubank, Maria (Mrs)	Dozier, E. (Dr)	10, June 1816	L3
Evans, Ann	Kinsey, William G.	31, Apr. 1845	L3
Evans, Anna D.	Williams, William	27, Jan. 1848	L3
Evans, Ellen S.	Hand, Ellis	27, May 1847	L3
Evans, Hannah	Conover, James F.	3, Nov. 1853	L3
Evans, Louisa	Fishback, O.T.	24, May 1855	L3
Evans, M. (Mrs)	Robinson, Solon	22, May 1828	L1
Evans, M. Anna	Swartz, John T.	31, Dec. 1857	L3
Evans, Margaret	Woods, Andrew	24, Feb. 1848	L3
Evans, Mary Eliza	Mitchell, Walter(Rev	2, Nov. 1848	L3
Evans, Nancy	Benton, Oliver	28, Apr. 1817	L3
Evans, Susannah	Moore, Adrian	10, Apr. 1845	L3

Brides	Grooms	Date of Notice	Page
Evens, Louisa Anna	Chapman, William J.	29, Nov. 1838	L3
Ewing, Emma A.	Cook, W.H.	30, Oct. 1856	L5
Ewing, Martha Ann	Ferris, J.S.	11, Apr. 1839	L3
Ewing, Mary	Hughes, Ezekiel	16, July 1805	L3
Ewing, Mary Jane	Sheppard, Edwin F.	28, Dec. 1848	L3
Ewing, Mary L.	Guthrie, Charles W.	30, Mar. 1854	L3
Ewing, Rebecca	Blair, Robert	18, Dec. 1811	L3
Ewing, Rebecca	VanHorn, William K.	5, May 1807	L3
Ewing, Sarah V.	McBride, Henry R.	22, July 1852	L3
Facemire, Matilda	Raymond, David S.	18, May 1822	L3
Fagely, Harriet	Horrocks, John F.	24, Aug. 1843	L3
Fagin, Mary Ann	Akers, James	2, May 1844	L3
Fagin, Nannie G.	Kline, Benneville	26, Dec. 1850	L3
Fairchild, Catharine	Stone, F.H.	20, Aug. 1840	L3
Fairchild, Polly	McMean, William	7, Mar. 1810	L3
Fallis, Hattie E.	Rodgers, Charles G.	3, Dec. 1857	L3
Farley, Angerone	Ferguson, Robert G.	16, July 1857	L3
Farmer, Miranda	Finch, Charles C.	25, Feb. 1847	L3
Farnsworth, Augusta	Stone, Dan	10, Dec. 1824	L2
Farnsworth, Josephin	Barnard, J.	30, Nov. 1854	L3
Farnsworth, Sarah E.	Venable, John W.	12, Nov. 1846	L3
Farrar, Martha	Taylor, J.B.	23, Mar. 1854	L3
Farrell, M. Ellen	Cady, D. Knight	29, Oct. 1857	L3
Farris, Elizabeth	Nesbit, William P.	30, Oct. 1845	L3
Fate, Harriet F.	Watson, Jonathan S.	5, July 1855	L3
Fauber, Elizabeth	Taylor, Isaac N.	9, Feb. 1854	L3
Faulkner, Sarah Ann	Hall, John C.	7, Oct. 1841	L3
Fawcett, Mary Ann	Bates, Henry M.	18, Jan. 1838	L3
Fee, Mary	Lanham, W.W.	3, Nov. 1853	L3
Fee, Melvina R.	Ingram, James	20, Oct. 1853	L3
Fehleisen, Amelia	Thielman, John	14, May 1857	L3
Fehleisen, Matilda	Myers, Henry W.	14, Oct. 1852	L3
Fennimore, Eliza J.	Bennett, Thomas S.	5, Dec. 1850	L3
Fenton, Josephine R.	Howell, G.W.	8, Sept 1842	L3
Ferguson, Amelia R.	Johnson, Archibald	9, July 1819	L3
Fernival, Martha	Parmele, Hervey	20, May 1816	L3
Ferris, Maria L.	Wright, Noah	11, Sept 1845	L3
Ferris, Mary	Stites, Hezekiah	10, Sept 1846	L3
Fertig, Catharine A. (Mrs)	Lawrence, William C.	6, May 1841	L3
Field, Nancy	Gwin, Evan	27, May 1847	L3
Fifield, Francis M.	Boal, William M.	11, May 1854	L3
Filson, Martha Ellen	Willard, A.F.	19, Jan. 1854	L3
Finch, Adeline A.	Walker, John	2, Jan. 1845	L3
Finch, Ella F.	Gartrell, Charles H.	31, Jan. 1856	L3
Finch, Frances M.	Brown, William H.	10, Oct. 1850	L3
Finch, Jane	Bowlin, William T.	18, Jan. 1838	L3
Finch, Sarah Ann	Molster, Cornelius	21, Nov. 1844	L3
Fine, Elizabeth	Strong, Edward K.	22, July 1852	L3
Fingland, Louisa	Doughty, George E.	11, Sept 1851	L3
Fingland, Maggie	Gallagher, F.R. (Dr)	5, July 1855	L3
Finn, Anna E.	Potter, Henry E.	22, Oct. 1857	L3
Fish, Sarah B. (Mrs)	Gest, Andrew M.	16, Mar. 1848	L3
Fisher, Alvira L.	McGrew, Alexander	12, Jan. 1822	L3

Brides	Grooms	Date of Notice	Page
Fisher, Carrie	Thrasher, Daniel W.	31, Jan. 1856	L3
Fisher, Eliza Ann	Febiger, George	16, June 1842	L3
Fisher, Elizabeth (Mrs)	Barret, Thomas	26, Nov. 1808	L3
Fisher, Emeline S.	Reynolds, Lemuel	23, Apr. 1824	L2
Fithian, Sarah P.	Pull, Charles	31, Mar. 1842	L3
Fitzgerald, Elizabet	Singleton, Henry	13, Dec. 1849	L3
Fitzgerald, N. (Mrs)	Wilson, William W.	9, Dec. 1847	L3
Fitzpatrick, Mary A.	Doolittle, Charles A	28, Dec. 1848	L3
Flagg, Mary E.	Hamlin, Henry H.	12, Jan. 1854	L3
Flash, Sarah J.	Gomez, Eusebio J.	4, Jan. 1849	L3
Fleming, Ellis M.	Carter, Lewis R.	12, June 1827	L3
Fletcher, Margaret	Horniman, Henry	20, Sept 1849	L3
Fletcher, Rosanna B.	Frazer, John	22, May 1845	L3
Flint, Esther	Baker, John	7, July 1817	L2
Flint, Esther	St.Clair, George	27, Dec. 1809	L3
Flint, Julia	Thatcher, David	15, Mar. 1814	L3
Foley, Anna M.	Powell, James	26, Apr. 1855	L3
Foley, Mary	Bell, Joseph	9, Sept 1847	L3
Folger, Eliza	Clark, Henry	22, June 1824	L3
Folger, Eliza Ann	Smith, William	3, Jan. 1821	L3
Folger, Eunice	Mann, Lowell A.	1, Apr. 1841	L3
Folger, Harriet	Belvel, James	18, Oct. 1838	L3
Folger, Margaret M.	Marsh, Isaac	11, Jan. 1844	L3
Follenius, Catharine	Themin, C.F.	23, May 1844	L3
Follett, Eliza W.	Foster, Francis F.	30, Mar. 1854	L3
Follin, Mirian F.	Peacock, David C.	13, Apr. 1854	L3
Fones, Amanda	Attwell, Roger G.	21, Oct. 1847	L3
Fontaine, Susan (Mrs)	Gardiner, J.B. (Dr)	28, Apr. 1842	L3
Foor, Amanda P.	Thomas, Reuben	30, Aug. 1855	L3
Foote, Alice E.	Hill, Edward D.	12, Feb. 1857	L3
Foote, Catharine A.	Comstock, William H.	27, May 1847	L3
Forbes, Elizabeth W.	Moore, William (Rev)	21, Oct. 1847	L3
Forbes, Georgiana	Bart, Edwin R.	25, Jan. 1855	L3
Forbs, Ann Eliza	Sparks, Jesse	2, Apr. 1857	L3
Forbus, Maggie F.	Dills, W.R.	18, Dec. 1856	L3
Force, Mary N.	Neave, Martin	16, Oct. 1845	L3
Ford, Annastatia	Robbins, John V.	26, Dec. 1850	L3
Ford, Lucy L.	Burton, Edwin M.	6, Feb. 1851	L3
Ford, Rachel H.	Boggs, Joseph R.	8, June 1848	L3
Foreman, Sarah E.	Rader, Levi	12, Jan. 1854	L3
Forgy, Mary	Conkling, Stephen	30, Mar. 1848	L3
Forman, Eliza	Woolley, Charles	3, Oct. 1823	L3
Forrer, Augusta	Bruen, Luther R.	15, Dec. 1853	L3
Fortman, Mary Louisa	Wiedemer, F.X.	10, June 1852	L3
Forward, Martha	Lewis, George N.	13, Nov. 1856	L3
Fosdick, Anna M.	Musgrave, William B.	14, Aug. 1856	L5
Fosdick, Harriet (Mrs)	Cunningham, J.H.	10, Sept 1846	L3
Fosdick, Sarah (Mrs)	Councellor, John	30, Dec. 1806	L3
Foster, Alice H.	Goodman, Frank	20, Mar. 1851	L3
Foster, Anna Maria	Wetherbee, Francis W	8, Sept 1853	L3
Foster, Augusta V.	Skillman, Henry M.	20, Mar. 1856	L3
Foster, Eliza	Atherton, Abner	18, Sept 1845	L3
Foster, Elizabeth M.	Cochran, William	8, May 1851	L3
Foster, Laura B.	Riddle, Cyrus	3, May 1855	L3

Brides	Grooms	Date of Notice	Page
Foster, Sallie C.	Goodman, Moses	1, Apr. 1852	L3
Foster, Sarah C.	Liter, Adam	23, July 1846	L3
Foster, Susan W.	Phelps, Winslow S.	16, Mar. 1837	L3
Foulke, Ann Eliza	Barbour, Oliver P.	16, Jan. 1845	L3
Fountain, Charlotte	Galy, Andrew	17, July 1845	L3
Fowler, Abigail	Scott, Chasteen	24, June 1816	L3
Fowler, Jane	McCammon, William	12, Feb. 1852	L3
Fox, Frances L.	Ford, Smith	24, June 1847	L3
Foy, Bridget C.	Whitehouse, Joseph	1, Jan. 1852	L3
Francis, Sarah (Mrs)	Tatin, Simon C.	11, Sept 1845	L3
Frankenstein, Maria	Coombs, Alfred D.	24, May 1849	L3
Fraser, Susan W.	Walker, James	23, Oct. 1856	L5
Frazee, Cynthia	Combs, John S. (Dr)	9, Sept 1852	L3
Frazer, Etna M.	Williamson, Ovid C.	27, Apr. 1848	L3
Frazer, Martha Ann	Williamson, Obid C.	16, Oct. 1845	L3
Frazier, Mary	Sinks, Randolph M.	9, Sept 1852	L3
Fredly, Elizabeth	Watson, John	7, July 1817	L2
French, Eliza (Mrs)	Russell, H.W.	29, July 1847	L3
French, Sarah L.F.	Gano, Stephen	10, May 1855	L3
Frost, Harriet S.	Johnson, John	14, Mar. 1850	L3
Fry, Laura A.	Watkin, Henry	2, June 1853	L3
Fryer, Mary	Holloday, Uriah B.	2, Feb. 1854	L3
Fuller, Josephine S.	Herron, James H.	21, Sept 1854	L3
Fuller, Lizzie F.	Fletcher, Addison C.	13, Apr. 1854	L3
Fuller, Mariette	Ward, Thomas	15, Aug. 1839	L3
Funk, Elizabeth	Applegate, John A.	6, June 1844	L3
Furry, Hannah	Stoops, Pleasant	9, Feb. 1854	L3
Fyffe, Elizabeth R.	Wolff, George H.	15, Sept 1853	L3
Gaiter, Sophia	Mustard, Alexander	28, Dec. 1843	L3
Gaither, Martha	Hinckle, Phillip	2, Jan. 1851	L3
Gallagher, Emma B.	Sayre, William H.	7, Dec. 1854	L3
Gallagher, Jennie M.	Cotton, Charles B.	27, Dec. 1855	L3
Gallaugher, Sarah B.	Stevens, William L.	7, Jan. 1823	L2
Galloway, M. Julia	Worthington, James T	11, Dec. 1828	L2
Galloway, Sarah A.	Brown, Robert P.	9, Nov. 1837	L3
Gamble, Jane	Wann, Samuel	10, Jan. 1850	L3
Gano, Frances Mary	Iglehart, N.P.	27, July 1837	L3
Gano, Henrietta	Chittenden, Henry A.	3, Oct. 1844	L3
Gano, Lucretia	Johnson, William A.	11, Feb. 1847	L3
Gano, Maria	Brown, Thomas E.	25, May 1854	L3
Gano, Mary	Burnet, David S.	31, Mar. 1830	L3
Gano, Mary	Wright, Joseph F.	15, May 1851	L3
Gano, Nancy	Davis, H.M.F.	7, Nov. 1844	L3
Gano, Sarah Anne	Burt, Andrew	10, Feb. 1807	L3
Gardner, Anna M.	Walkly, Nelson (Dr)	21, Jan. 1847	L3
Gardner, E.A.	Stryker, Joseph M.	18, May 1848	L3
Gardner, Margaret B.	Thomson, Robert	1, Aug. 1850	L3
Gardner, Martha Jane	Collins, Philip	11, May 1848	L3
Gardner, Susan	Cosgrove, John N.	9, Jan. 1845	L3
Garoutee, Sarah M.	Snyder, George	5, Apr. 1855	L3
Garrard, Sarah B. (Mrs)	McLean, John	18, May 1843	L3
Garret, Martha	Faries, J.C.	30, Mar. 1854	L3
Garrish, Sophia	Golding, Aaron	6, Mar. 1822	L3

Brides	Grooms	Date of Notice	Page
Garritson, Sarah L.	Duberly, John	26, May 1842	L3
Garwood, Lydia	DeCamp, Lambert	11, Sept 1856	L5
Gaskill, Susannah	Miller, Alfred	24, Apr. 1845	L3
Gassaway, Elizabeth G.	Kennett, John	20, Nov. 1834	L1
Gassaway, Lucy Ann	Clay, Ralph A.	21, Oct. 1841	L3
Gatch, Elizabeth	Williams, Courtland	11, July 1839	L3
Gatch, Jenny	Hamilton, John	1, Nov. 1855	L3
Gaylord, Mary E.	Pendleton, Elliott	13, Nov. 1850	L3
Gazley, Julia	Vanausdol, Garret	12, Aug. 1847	L3
Gedge, Mary A.	Owen, Chauncey B.	22, Sept 1853	L3
Geiger, Lavinia M.	Desilver, J. Ford	12, Dec. 1844	L3
Gengembre, S.	Anderson, Walter	19, June 1851	L3
George, Maggie	Tappin, Benjamin	2, Oct. 1856	L5
Gephart, Amanda	Selby, Samuel	16, Feb. 1854	L3
Gephart, Elizabeth	Selby, Charles	16, Feb. 1854	L3
Gere, Anna E.	Oliver, M.W.	4, July 1850	L3
Gerhart, Christiana	Maurer, George	23, Jan. 1845	L3
Getz, Elizabeth	Smith, DeWitt C.	28, Oct. 1847	L3
Gibbs, C.H.	Dodd, James	31, Dec. 1840	L3
Gibbs, Mary P.	Parsell, George	6, Sept 1838	L3
Gibson, Abby	Adams, Henry J.	23, Sept 1841	L3
Gibson, Elmira J.	James, L.A. (Dr)	17, Feb. 1848	L3
Gibson, Jenette	Richards, William	4, Feb. 1818	L2
Gibson, Louisa H.	Burns, John H.	5, Feb. 1857	L3
Gibson, Sarah Elizabeth	Harrison, Henry B.	11, Feb. 1847	L3
Gilbert, Abby T.	Glezen, Eben K.	22, June 1843	L3
Gildersllieve, Sarah	Woodyard, Milton J.	22, May 1845	L3
Gilkey, Mary Elizabeth	McGrew, Joseph	25, Apr. 1850	L3
Gill, Sarah Dell	McDermot, William L.	15, July 1847	L3
Gillespie, Kate	Parker, Daniel	11, Nov. 1847	L3
Gillett, Cynthia A.	Darling, John	6, Oct. 1842	L3
Gillette, Martha B.	Homans, S. Southard	30, Jan. 1851	L3
Gilliams, Susan L.	Dugan, John A.	14, Oct. 1852	L3
Gilman, Barbara A.	Hoffman, Allen	14, Oct. 1847	L3
Gilman, Lizzie S.	Nias, Raymond	17, Aug. 1854	L3
Gilmore, Clara	Ringgold, T.G.	8, Jan. 1857	L3
Gilmore, Elizabeth	Hill, David	26, Feb. 1846	L3
Girton, Lizzie L.	McCullough, T.	21, Aug. 1851	L3
Gitchell, Mary A.	Sherman, L.P.	19, Apr. 1845	L3
Givens, Lucretia	Arion, C.P.J.	24, Dec. 1824	L3
Glancy, Josephine	Robinson, Henry H.	13, Jan. 1848	L3
Glascock, Mary Jane	Smith, W. Henry	27, Oct. 1842	L3
Glascoe, Kitty Ann	Carver, Henry E.	31, Oct. 1839	L3
Glascoe, Sarah F.	Tucker, Amos	21, Oct. 1847	L3
Glasgow, Mary	Davies, Joseph	1, Apr. 1823	L3
Glenn, Lizzie	Dymond, R.	12, July 1855	L3
Glover, Catharine B.	Strong, Ebenezer B.	5, Mar. 1846	L3
Goble, Dinah	Abercrombie, Robert	16, Dec. 1829	L3
Goble, Elizabeth	Nicholson, Thomas	7, Oct. 1847	L3
Goddin, Ann	Mungall, John	5, Feb. 1846	L3
Godley, Kate T.	Lewis, Frank	24, Sept 1857	L3
Godman, Ellen	Bayless, Andrew H.	16, Nov. 1854	L3
Goforth, Charlotte K	Lewis, Samuel	8, Aug. 1823	L3
Goldson, Margaret K.	Fosdick, Henry H.	30, Jan. 1845	L3

Brides	Grooms	Date of Notice	Page
Gondor, Eveline A.	Ramsey, James B.	31, Oct. 1850	L3
Gooch, Emma	Kelsall, Thomas	20, Nov. 1845	L3
Goode, Martha Jane	Luckett, William G.	22, Feb. 1844	L3
Goodhue, Miranda	Parry, Owen L.	4, Dec. 1845	L3
Goodin, Elizabeth	Davis, Charles	13, May 1852	L3
Goodloe, Louisa	Mitchell, William H.	12, Oct. 1854	L3
Goodman, Elizabeth	Ranger, Richard	26, Sept 1850	L3
Goodman, Emma	Eaton, Joseph O.	14, June 1855	L3
Goodman, Fanny M.	Harrison, Lerner B.	9, June 1853	L3
Goodman, Frances P.	Wright, Sylvanus	28, Jan. 1825	L3
Goodwin, Caroline	Strickle, Abraham E.	6, Jan. 1831	L3
Goodwin, Eliza	Varian, Charles M.	29, Oct. 1829	L3
Goodwin, Elizabeth (Mrs)	Sparks, Joseph K(Dr)	8, May 1827	L3
Goodwin, Susan	Myers, Joseph	8, July 1823	L3
Goosman, Althea	Bottom, John	13, Apr. 1848	L3
Gorden, Amelia W.	Fuller, William F.	18, Aug. 1842	L3
Gordon, Bell Frances	Grimes, Alexander	7, July 1817	L2
Gordon, Catharine	Burnet, Isaac G.	24, Oct. 1807	L3
Gordon, Dolly E.	Goforth, Poole	16, Sept 1825	L3
Gordon, Ellen	Bridges, Harrison	17, Aug. 1848	L3
Gordon, Jennie	McDowell, Malcolm	6, May 1852	L3
Gordon, Julia M.	Wheeler, Wilber B.	6, Jan. 1848	L3
Gordon, Lydia Ann	Moore, Thomas H.	7, Jan. 1847	L3
Gordon, Mary	Boyden, John S.	10, Apr. 1856	L3
Gordon, Mary	Morgan, Daniel H.	16, Oct. 1856	L5
Gorman, Anna Maria	Hueston, William M.	18, Feb. 1836	L3
Gorman, Cordelia A.	Todd, William	21, Sept 1854	L3
Gorman, Matilda	Thompson, Marcus	3, Mar. 1842	L3
Goshorn, Elizabeth	Hill, Robert	16, Mar. 1854	L3
Gosman, Elizabeth (Mrs)	Olcott, Edward R.	22, July 1852	L3
Goss, Mary	Pearce, James	20, May 1847	L3
Goudy, Ary	Barns, John	21, July 1817	L2
Goulding, Rhoda (Mrs)	McHenry, Enoch	21, July 1817	L2
Gour, Lumy	Hand, Amos	11, Aug. 1817	L3
Gove, Mary F.	Wayne, Joseph W.	12, Aug. 1852	L3
Grace, Ruth A.	Patrick, J.W.	28, May 1857	L3
Graff, Helen C.	Sears, Clinton W.	19, Sept 1850	L3
Graham, Adelia	Strong, Jonathan M.	6, Jan. 1848	L3
Graham, Ella	Holmes, William N.	22, Aug. 1850	L3
Graham, Florilla	Gibson, Thomas	26, June 1845	L3
Graham, Hannah	Dickson, Thomas	6, July 1843	L3
Graham, Hannah B.	Richardson, Charles	10, Apr. 1851	L3
Graham, Jane	Myers, Isaac	15, Jan. 1846	L3
Graham, Laura	Thompson, William H.	22, May 1845	L3
Graham, Lucy Ann	Hoole, Joseph	1, Mar. 1838	L3
Graham, Mary	Wartmann, J.W.	5, Feb. 1857	L3
Graham, Rachel	Stinson, Charles	19, Oct. 1837	L3
Graham, Rebecca	Kreider, David L.	26, Sept 1839	L3
Graham, Sarah M.	Ridgeley, William	28, Oct. 1825	L2
Graham, Susan M.	Morris, Jacob	25, June 1846	L3
Gram, Mary	Mitchel, Samuel	16, Feb. 1854	L3
Gram, Mary A.	Mitchell, Samuel	26, Jan. 1854	L3
Granden, Susan A.	Woodward, Josiah L.	13, Nov. 1856	L3
Grandin, Lucy A.	Goodman, W. Augustus	15, July 1847	L3

Brides	Grooms	Date of Notice	Page
Grandin, Mary E.	Orr, Thomas J. (Dr)	28, Dec. 1837	L3
Grannis, Sarah M.	Miller, John V.	11, Jan. 1849	L3
Grant, Caroline A.	Sutton, Demetrius A.	3, Jan. 1821	L3
Gratehouse, Ellen	Casey, Louis E.	6, Dec. 1855	L3
Gratz, Rachel (Mrs)	Samuels, Solomon	7, Sept 1843	L3
Graven, Eliza	Williams, William E.	4, Jan. 1855	L3
Graves, Elizabeth S.	Goodhue, G.W.	6, May 1847	L3
Graves, Martha (Mrs)	Finley, William	16, Feb. 1854	L3
Graves, Sarah Jane	Graves, James M.	27, May 1841	L3
Gray, Catharine	Gordon, James	9, Feb. 1854	L3
Grayson, M.E.	Bowman, William	2, Dec. 1847	L3
Green, Alvernon H.	Allen, L.S. (Dr)	23, Sept 1841	L3
Green, Ellen	Goodin, Samuel H.	24, Sept 1840	L3
Green, Harriet C.	Moore, Augustus O.	16, Oct. 1851	L3
Green, Laura L.	Richards, Randolph	25, June 1857	L3
Green, Mary E.	McGowan, John H.	5, July 1855	L3
Green, Nancy	Baker, Adam	23, Dec. 1825	L3
Green, Rose H.	McFerran, J.C. (Lt)	10, Oct. 1844	L3
Greene, Caroline	Brown, George H.	3, Sept 1846	L3
Greene, Eliza S.	Gibson, Alexander	14, Nov. 1844	L3
Greene, Jennie C.	Burgoyne, John	24, Feb. 1853	L3
Greenwell, Anne	McNight, John	25, Feb. 1815	L1
Greenwood, Martha	Nixon, Wilson K.	20, July 1854	L3
Greer, Peggy	Martin, William	27, Apr. 1809	L3
Greer, Polly	Bates, Niles	27, Apr. 1809	L3
Gregg, Eliza M.	Fenwick, David	2, Mar. 1854	L3
Gregg, Harriet	Voorhees, Isaac	8, Apr. 1841	L3
Gregg, Lamira J.	Johnston, John	2, Mar. 1854	L3
Gregg, Margaret	Wing, Benjamin G.	6, Mar. 1845	L3
Gregory, Frances	Dyer, Elisha Isaac	11, Mar. 1841	L3
Gregory, Harriet	Risser, Daniel (Rev)	23, Nov. 1854	L3
Gregory, Mary A.	Clarkson, William O.	21, May 1834	L4
Gregory, Sarah A.	Shelden, Edward A.	27, Nov. 1851	L3
Gresh, Catharine	Poucher, Isaiah	6, Apr. 1854	L3
Grice, Susan	Harning, Hilesy	16, Feb. 1854	L3
Grieve, Martha	Boots, Adam	6, Apr. 1854	L3
Griffing, Mary	Griffin, David	23, Apr. 1846	L3
Griffis, Sarah Ann	Patton, Andrew H.	14, Aug. 1851	L3
Griffith, Elizabeth	Bailey, Hezekiah B.	20, Nov. 1856	L3
Griffith, Elizabeth	Reynolds, Reuben	5, Apr. 1825	L3
Griffith, Jane C.	Little, James S.	15, Jan. 1857	L3
Griffiths, Caroline	Danby, Charles	5, May 1853	L3
Grinnell, Helen Elizabeth	Milne, George	16, Sept 1847	L3
Grinson, Anna	Shearer, Michael K.	9, May 1839	L3
Griswold, Alice Ann	McMahan, John	1, Oct. 1846	L3
Groesbeck, Lucy S.	Gaylord, Thomas G.	8, May 1851	L3
Groesbeck, Margaret	Burnet, Robert W.	27, Oct. 1836	L2
Groesbeck, Mary S.	Sullivan, Algernon S	9, Jan. 1851	L3
Gross, Josephine	Darr, Francis	6, Dec. 1855	L3
Grover, Mary E.	Hopkins, Ben E.	7, Feb. 1856	L3
Guest, Elizabeth	Reynolds, Benjamin B	10, Mar. 1826	L3
Guest, Margaret	Buckingham, John I.	11, Apr. 1844	L3
Guest, Mary Ann	Reynolds, Sacket	22, Oct. 1819	L3
Guilford, Anna	Donaldson, Frank	15, Oct. 1846	L3

Brides	Grooms	Date of Notice	Page
Guilford, Appeline	Donaldson, George	3, June 1847	L3
Guilford, Belle E.	Stewart, William S.	25, Nov. 1852	L3
Guion, Wealthy (Mrs)	Fisher, David	25, Dec. 1856	L3
Guise, Maria Louisa	McLean, Robert L.	25, Apr. 1850	L3
Gulick, Mary (Mrs)	Potter, James H.	19, Oct. 1843	L3
Guss, Sarah	Day, Travis B.	23, Feb. 1854	L3
Guthrie, Martha	Doughty, William M.	23, Nov. 1843	L3
Hadley, Mary M.	Smith, Lucian	24, Sept 1857	L3
Hageman, Mary B.	Cooke, David B.	16, Nov. 1848	L3
Hager, Abigail	Thomas, John R.	29, Dec. 1821	L3
Hahn, Mary	VanCamp, Cornelius	9, Jan. 1845	L3
Haifligh, Barbara	Stall, George W.	12, May 1806	L3
Hailman, Leah	Wandell, William	30, Aug. 1825	L3
Haines, Elizabeth S.	Lytle, Robert T.	2, Dec. 1825	L3
Haines, Joanna	Reilly, Thomas	18, Jan. 1832	L4
Haines, Sarah M.	Hall, Samuel W.	5, July 1849	L3
Hale, Mary	Wyman, N.R.	26, Feb. 1852	L3
Haleman, Julia	Reed, Robert C.	20, May 1818	L2
Hales, Mary A.	Harbaugh, H.M.	9, May 1839	L3
Hall, Carolina C.	McGrew, Alex	10, Dec. 1840	L3
Hall, Fanny	Whiteman, William J.	3, July 1851	L3
Hall, Hulda A. (Mrs)	Howell, Rozel P.	11, Nov. 1847	L3
Hall, Julia A.	Gallagher, George W.	27, Nov. 1845	L3
Hall, M.G.	Lynn, John F.	1, Nov. 1849	L3
Hall, Margaret	Ogden, James	5, Jan. 1818	L3
Hall, Mary	Forbes, James	20, Mar. 1856	L3
Hall, Sarah Ann	Tatem, Henry L.	2, Nov. 1833	L4
Hall, Sarah E.	Foote, Charles B.	10, Apr. 1851	L3
Hallam, Rosannah	Tucker, Elbridge (Rev)	28, Nov. 1850	L3
Halley, Deborah	Armstrong, William	28, Apr. 1817	L3
Halley, Lauretta E.	Dalton, James	25, May 1848	L3
Halley, Mary Ann	Pingree, E.M. (Rev)	22, Oct. 1840	L3
Hallowell, Louisa R.	Powell, Joseph	29, June 1843	L3
Hallowell, Mary R.	Sawyer, Joseph A.	30, Jan. 1840	L3
Halstead, Rebecca	Shaw, Hezekiah (Rev)	9, Oct. 1811	L3
Halsted, Mary Kerr	Boylan, James	18, Jan. 1844	L3
Halsted, Mary Louisa	Porter, William H.	21, July 1853	L3
Hamet, Ellen B.	Lovell, John D.	11, Sept 1834	L1
Hamilton, Anna M.	Crawford, Levi S.	18, Dec. 1845	L3
Hamilton, Caroline F	Stillie, J.	19, May 1842	L3
Hamilton, Margaret	Pritchard, Rees	18, Sept 1845	L3
Hamilton, Martha A.	Bradwell, Martin	18, May 1848	L3
Hamilton, Mary Ann	Hempstead, Samuel B.	2, Apr. 1846	L3
Hamlen, Martha A.	Bissell, William C.	22, Mar. 1855	L3
Hamlin, Laura	Belman, J.C.	29, Dec. 1853	L3
Hammatt, Ann M.	Philpot, William	10, Apr. 1845	L3
Hammond, Alma	L'Hommedieu, S.S.	29, Apr. 1830	L2
Hammond, Catharine	Hunter, Moses	23, Feb. 1843	L3
Hammond, Elizabeth	McWilliams, Matthew	2, Nov. 1848	L3
Hammond, Mary M.	Sullivan, Algernon	27, Dec. 1855	L3
Hamtrammack, Rebecca	Thomas, Jesse B.	24, Feb. 1807	L3
Hanbee, Nancy	Stoughton, Joseph	11, Aug. 1817	L3
Hand, Elizabeth	Stevenson, Henry D.	18, May 1848	L3

Brides	Grooms	Date of Notice	Page
Hand, Harriet A.	Innes, D.K.	6, May 1847	L3
Hand, Margaret	Dawson, W.W. (Dr)	15, May 1851	L3
Hand, Mary	Barton, Julius V.	18, Apr. 1844	L3
Handy, Margaret A.	Garrison, John W.	6, Nov. 1845	L3
Handy, Mary E.	Jaquess, John	20, Apr. 1848	L3
Hankins, Maria M.	Kimball, John F.	25, Apr. 1844	L3
Hanks, Zeniah	Crane, Henry	20, Dec. 1838	L3
Hanley, Lucy M.	Bonner, Stephen	29, Oct. 1835	L3
Hanley, Margaret	Todhunter, Thomas	19, Feb. 1816	L3
Hann, Catharine	Pelton, John	13, May 1816	L3
Hannaford, Eliza	Donogh, James B.	6, Mar. 1845	L3
Hansalman, Christena	Hansalman, Christian	28, Mar. 1823	L3
Hansell, Susan B.	Bullock, Benjamin	23, Oct. 1856	L5
Hansfall, Anna	Craig, Robert S.	13, Nov. 1856	L3
Harbeson, Anna	Dexter, Charles	7, June 1855	L3
Hardesty, Rebeckah	Foot, Joseph	28, Dec. 1813	L3
Hardie, Sarah	Morse, Charles E.	17, Sept 1846	L3
Hardin, Hester	Waterhouse, John(Dr)	8, Oct. 1857	L3
Harding, Emilie D.	Kelly, William F.	18, June 1857	L3
Harding, Mina	Bussall, A.T.	7, Aug. 1856	L5
Harding, Sarah B. (Mrs)	Saxton, Joseph C.	10, Jan. 1826	L3
Harding, Sarah T.	Williams, Samuel R.	24, July 1851	L3
Harding, Susan	White, Amos	21, Dec. 1807	L3
Hardinge, Henriette	Sanderson, George	19, Oct. 1854	L3
Hardinge, Rachael	Brooks, W.W.	5, Mar. 1846	L3
Hardinge, Sarah	Sprague, J.R.	16, May 1850	L3
Hardy, Elizabeth	Crabee, Alexander	9, Feb. 1854	L3
Hardy, Isabella	Ogden, Lewis B.	17, June 1847	L3
Hargy, Mary Jane	White, William	25, Feb. 1847	L3
Harkness, Eliza A.	Harkness, Charles	6, July 1843	L3
Harkness, Harriet	Fosdick, Henry N.	4, Feb. 1836	L2
Harkness, Jane	Gano, Charles L.	30, Nov. 1843	L3
Harley, Fannie B.	Everest, B.B.	15, June 1854	L3
Harn, Anna Belle	Scammerhorn, Joseph	19, Dec. 1850	L3
Harnbrook, Mary Anne	Susan, Thomas	24, Aug. 1843	L3
Harper, Ann (Mrs)	Auld, Thomas	6, June 1844	L3
Harper, Sarah J.	Starr, David L. (Dr)	31, May 1849	L3
Harr, Julia W.	Ogden, Robert B.	23, Sept 1847	L3
Harrington, O.E.	Bouhane, John C. (Rev)	20, Nov. 1856	L3
Harris, Abigail	Sprigman, Peter A.	6, Feb. 1811	L3
Harris, Elizabeth A.	Sprong, David	6, Apr. 1837	L3
Harris, Josephine	Ward, George W.	24, June 1847	L3
Harris, Mary	Smith, Joseph	15, Feb. 1844	L3
Harris, Melinda	Beall, William K.	25, Mar. 1812	L3
Harris, Nanny	Fallon, James J	21, June 1855	L3
Harris, Rosetta	Gorman, Jonathan H.	22, Oct. 1857	L3
Harris, Sarah Jane	Yardley, Kirkbridge	11, Dec. 1851	L3
Harris, Sue W.	Smith, S.	4, Dec. 1851	L3
Harris, Tillie E.	Williams, George F.	23, Oct. 1856	L5
Harrison, Ann	Drake, Aaron	31, Mar. 1821	L3
Harrison, Anne C.	Graves, Joseph A.	8, Dec. 1842	L3
Harrison, Bessie S.	Eaton, George C.	10, June 1847	L3
Harrison, Clarissa L	Banks, Tomlin M. (Dr)	18, Apr. 1844	L3
Harrison, Cordelia	Hamilton, John	13, Oct. 1853	L3

Brides	Grooms	Date of Notice	Page
Harrison, Elizabeth S.	Strowder, Z.B.	26, Jan. 1843	L3
Harrison, Ellen S.	McHenry, John	30, Nov. 1854	L3
Harrison, Isabella	Williams, Elmore	23, Sept 1816	L3
Harrison, Jane F. (Mrs)	Whiteman, Lewis	7, July 1842	L3
Harrison, Kiziah	Leming, James	11, Aug. 1817	L3
Harrison, Lucy S.	Este, David K.	5, Oct. 1819	L3
Harrison, Lydia C.	Moore, Charles L.	22, Sept 1853	L3
Harrison, Martha A.	Hicks, James	23, June 1842	L3
Harrison, Mary	Clark, James	24, Feb. 1848	L3
Harrison, Mary A.	Oliver, David W.	8, Dec. 1853	L3
Harrison, Mary S.	Thornton, John H(Dr)	12, Mar. 1829	L2
Harrison, Sallie P.	Rice, Eliphaet L.	6, Jan. 1848	L3
Harrison, Vallie	Winder, W.W.	25, June 1857	L3
Harrison, Zebuline A	Hunt, John	17, Dec. 1840	L3
Harrod, Elizabeth	Ingersoll, Henry	23, Mar. 1848	L3
Hart, Carrie	Horton, Benjamin M.	9, Sept 1852	L3
Hart, Henrietta	Howard, Nicholas	21, Oct. 1841	L3
Hart, Isabella	Jessup, Thomas C.	1, Nov. 1855	L3
Hart, Jane P.	Dodd, William	14, Feb. 1856	L3
Hart, Mary Catharine	Baker, Franklin	9, Jan. 1851	L3
Hartley, Rachael M.	Thompson, James R.	16, Sept 1841	L3
Hartman, Margaret	Boughard, Joseph	25, Mar. 1816	L3
Hartnan, Solona	Dickey, George	16, Feb. 1854	L3
Harton, Margaret Ann	Hudson, William	20, Mar. 1845	L3
Hartshorne, Sallie J	Ellis, Rowland	16, Feb. 1854	L3
Hartwell, Abia A.	Benjamin, O.A.	5, Mar. 1857	L3
Hartzell, Elizabeth	Yeatman, Thomas Hy.	13, Feb. 1827	L3
Harvey, E.G.	Palmer, John J.	27, Jan. 1848	L3
Harvey, Janet	McMurchy, William	22, Dec. 1831	L4
Harvie, Caroline	Taylor, John C.	28, Aug. 1851	L3
Haskell, Elizabeth J	Marsh, Luther H.	8, Jan. 1857	L3
Haslam, Anna	Scott, John H.	23, Mar. 1854	L3
Hastings, Emily	Roelker, Frederick	5, Mar. 1846	L3
Hastings, Rebecca	Knisely, Abram J.	5, Feb. 1857	L3
Hastings, Sarah P.	Knowlton, C.C.	6, Sept 1855	L3
Hat, Mary	Dunseth, John	5, Dec. 1844	L3
Hatch, Jenny P.	Lewis, Richard	29, Sept 1853	L3
Hatch, Susan F.	Briant, Lewis	4, Nov. 1825	L3
Hathaway, Harriet	Halley, Samuel B.	11, Nov. 1841	L3
Haven, Caroline S.	Fisher, Henry C.	6, July 1848	L3
Haven, Georgetta	Sullivan, Hiram	28, May 1846	L3
Hawes, Mercy Ann	Foster, Horton J.	24, June 1852	L3
Hawes, Olivia (Mrs)	Hayne, B.J. (Dr)	1, Apr. 1852	L3
Hawkins, Caroline	Heighway, S. Mercer	29, Dec. 1842	L3
Hawkins, Cordelia	Leake, J. Bloomfield	12, Oct. 1854	L3
Hawkins, Eliza	Templeton, William C	19, Dec. 1833	L3
Hawkins, Louisa	Dunseth, Lewis	23, Apr. 1840	L3
Hawley, Mary C.	Riegel, John P.	1, Nov. 1855	L3
Hay, Mary A.	Coleman, Thomas	9, June 1853	L3
Haydon, N.B.	Campbell, E.B.	24, Nov. 1842	L6
Hayes, Ann	Corben, William	26, Mar. 1819	L3
Hayes, Charlotte A.	Neville, John S.	27, Jan. 1842	L3
Hayes, Frances A.	Ridgely, A.	7, Sept 1843	L3
Haymon, Susan	Clarke, John	29, May 1845	L3

Brides	Grooms	Date of Notice	Page
Haynes, Mary E.	Santmyer, Joseph P.	14, June 1855	L3
Hays, Jane	Glenn, Isaac Drake	21, Feb. 1850	L3
Hazen, Amelia	McMichael, Isaac	30, Mar. 1848	L3
Hazen, Janette (Mrs)	Bliss, Henry	19, Oct. 1854	L3
Hazlett, Harriet M.	Martin, Thomas J.	29, Oct. 1846	L3
Heaslett, Ruth A.	Grace, John William	9, Sept 1841	L3
Heaslitt, Sarah	Williams, William G.	11, Dec. 1845	L3
Heath, Eliza	Bailoche, John	6, Jan. 1817	L3
Heaton, Nancy (Mrs)	McFarland, Demas L.	9, Mar. 1854	L3
Heaton, Virginia	Hite, Charles P.	23, Mar. 1854	L3
Heffernan, Anna M.	Kerr, Robert	24, Aug. 1854	L3
Heffley, Elizabeth	Ernst, Andrew H.	9, June 1817	L2
Heighway, Eliza	Vowell, Ebenezer	31, Jan. 1810	L3
Heilig, Jane	Ruggles, Henry B.	27, Dec. 1855	L3
Helvering, Christina	Moyer, Lewis H.	9, Mar. 1854	L3
Hemminger, Eliza	Carnes, Cyrus	26, Jan. 1854	L3
Hemphill, Jane (Mrs)	Gardner, Colin	12, July 1849	L3
Hemphill, Mary	Morse, George W.	28, Aug. 1845	l3
Henderson, Charlotte	Wells, William	21, Dec. 1843	L3
Henderson, Eliza	Hammond, Andrew	24, Aug. 1837	L3
Henderson, Ellen G.	Nimmo, Edward L.	26, May 1842	L3
Henderson, Maria	VanMatre, Daniel	2, May 1833	L1
Henderson, Mary A.	Morton, William R.	7, Jan. 1847	L3
Henderson, Sophia	Maxwell, Hugh B.	11, Oct. 1832	L4
Henry, Rebecca	Johnson, Charles	22, Oct. 1846	L3
Henry, S. Cornelia	Gaston, Isaac N.	12, June 1851	L3
Herbst, Caroline	Hunter, N.D.	19, Mar. 1840	L3
Hergenrother, Catharine	Vogelbach, F.H.	18, May 1854	L3
Herring, Margaret A.	Trice, Solomon	12, Feb. 1829	L3
Hershew, Elizabeth	Hurdus, George	10, Aug. 1813	L3
Hervey, Frances A.	Smith, William F.	15, Oct. 1846	L3
Herzog, Elizabeth	Todhunter, William	5, Nov. 1846	L3
Heuer, Lizzie	Enneking, John B.	15, Feb. 1855	L3
Hewes, Tabitha	Gant, John	8, Dec. 1812	L3
Hey, Ann (Mrs)	Quaill, John	25, July 1839	L3
Hibben, L.	Jones, R.	2, Jan. 1851	L3
Hicks, Charlotte A.	Ellis, Henry	20, July 1854	L3
Higbee, Theodosia W.	Eberle, Richard	10, Dec. 1840	L3
Higdon, Eliza J.	DeForest, William	29, Oct. 1857	L3
Higgins, Ellen	Giraldin, Charles	6, Mar. 1851	L3
Higgins, M. Louise	Fanshaw, William D.	22, July 1847	L3
Higgins, Margaret	O'Connor, John H.	6, Dec. 1855	L3
Higgins, Margaret	O'Connor, John X.	29, Nov. 1855	L3
Higgins, Marie A.	Wheeler, William O.	19, Feb. 1857	L3
Hildreth, Eliza Jane	Ferguson, William G.	25, May 1848	L3
Hildreth, Frances M.	Avey, Andrew J.	19, May 1853	L3
Hildreth, Serena A.	DeCamp, John	6, June 1844	L3
Hill, Elizabeth	Lawrence, Henry	13, Apr. 1854	L3
Hill, Elizabeth A.	Kelley, John H.	16, Mar. 1854	L3
Hill, Elizabeth S.	Rapp, Joseph M.	23, Aug. 1855	L3
Hill, Martha P.	Phillips, W.H.	12, Nov. 1846	L3
Hill, Mary W.	Cook, Edward	7, Aug. 1856	L5
Hill, Sarah J.	Ralston, James H.	31, Dec. 1857	L3
Hill, Sereptia	Smith, William P.	1, June 1848	L3

Brides	Grooms	Date of Notice	Page
Hill, Sophia E.	Merrell, Ashbel S.	14, Oct. 1841	L3
Hillhouse, Susan	Gossin, Benjamin F.	10, July 1845	L3
Hilton, Caroline	Walters, Mitchell	8, Dec. 1842	L3
Hilton, Maria (Mrs)	Moore, Francis M.	25, June 1857	L3
Hilton, S.E.	Huston, H.	13, Apr. 1854	L3
Hilts, Lydia	Colburn, Perry	28, Mar. 1850	L3
Hindman, Susan	Price, Thomas	29, Feb. 1844	L3
Hinkle, Lizzie	Sage, Henry W.	30, Oct. 1856	L5
Hinman, Eliza P.	Dodd, William	27, Dec. 1838	L3
Hinman, Mary H.	Wilby, Joseph H.	9, Sept 1847	L3
Hinton, Annie F.	Bond, John R.S.	29, Apr. 1852	L3
Hitchcock, Sarah E.	Wayne, Anthony	12, June 1851	L3
Hitt, Mary A.	Slater, William F.	1, Apr. 1841	L3
Hoadly, Elizabeth D.	Bates, Joshua H.	23, May 1844	L3
Hoagland, Catharine	Edwards, William C.	7, Nov. 1844	L3
Hoak, Margaret Ann	Brooks, Valentine	18, Jan. 1838	L3
Hobart, Caroline	Williamson, William	30, Nov. 1848	L3
Hobbs, Elizabeth H.	Wilson, Hiram	29, Oct. 1846	L3
Hobbs, Laura W.	Hopkins, William R.	21, July 1842	L3
Hodges, Lydia T.	Caswell, Benjamin	24, Apr. 1851	L3
Hodgson, Mary Abby	Paddock, W.R.	12, Sept 1850	L3
Hoffman, Kate	Birney, William	19, Nov. 1846	L3
Hoffman, Ruth Ann	Bealek, Francis M.	25, Oct. 1849	L3
Hoffner, Elizabeth M.	Moffett, James S.	9, Mar. 1843	L3
Hogue, Matilda	Mason, A.J.	10, Apr. 1856	L3
Holabird, Emeline	Dale, Henry S.	22, Jan. 1852	L3
Holabird, Harriet	Eckstein, Frederick	3, Dec. 1857	L3
Holabird, Jenette	Swift, Thomas T.	13, Sept 1849	L3
Holby, Nancy	Ogden, Henry T.	19, Sept 1850	L3
Holden, Emma A.	Crane, James C.	2, July 1857	L3
Holenshade, Jennie C.	Bogart, Isaac	20, Nov. 1856	L3
Holibird, Caroline S.	Gregory, Francis H.	5, July 1849	L3
Holland, Esther (Mrs)	Baldwin, Henry W.	20, Oct. 1853	L3
Holland, Laura E.	Crossen, Peter B.	10, Aug. 1854	L3
Holland, Melissa J.	Clark, Perry	8, Aug. 1850	L3
Hollenshade, Catharine E.	Cramer, George R.	20, Sept 1849	L3
Holley, M.H.	Orvis, Clark	3, Dec. 1857	L3
Holliday, Emma	Rogers, Harry V.	23, July 1857	L3
Hollis, Harriet B.	Gest, Jonas C.	26, Sept 1844	L3
Holman, Mary M.	Oppenlander, Chris.	17, June 1847	L3
Holmes, Elizabeth P.	Andrews, Richard	6, Aug. 1846	L3
Holmes, Maria	Brown, William	25, Apr. 1850	L3
Holmes, Martha A.	Browning, George T.	9, Apr. 1846	L3
Holt, Ada Eliza	Winston, Leonidas W.	18, Jan. 1855	L3
Homer, Elizabeth	Stewart, William A.	21, Oct. 1841	L3
Honeywell, Eliza	Clark, Thomas	25, Oct. 1825	L3
Honeywell, Nina M.	Wharton, Robert J.	28, May 1846	L3
Hoogland, Minerva	Brown, William P.	9, Dec. 1847	L3
Hook, Mary	Whitridge, William	9, Oct. 1834	L2
Hooper, Lizzie	Smith, James Douglas	13, July 1854	L3
Hoover, Lucy	Green, George	24, Dec. 1840	L3
Hopkins, Caroline	Neighbours, James	30, Aug. 1825	L3
Hopkins, Charlotte	Chandler, John (Rev)	17, Sept 1846	L3
Hopkins, Jennie T.	Andress, Frederick	5, Mar. 1857	L3

Brides	Grooms	Date of Notice	Page
Hopkins, Julia M.	Whetstone, John	22, Nov. 1809	L3
Hopkins, Sophia	Elliott, F.R.	26, Feb. 1846	L3
Hopper, Caroline	Verner, James	28, Feb. 1850	L3
Hopper, Jemima	Ernst, Franklin	27, May 1841	L3
Hord, Harriet L.	Webb, C.C.	6, Jan. 1848	L3
Horman, Mary M.	Openlander, Chris.	3, June 1847	L3
Hornblower, Joanna M.	Bell, Thomas	19, July 1827	L3
Horner, Amelia	Baker, Nathan	13, Aug. 1840	L3
Horner, Caroline	Wilson, Joseph L.	18, Dec. 1845	L3
Horner, Sarah A.E.	Parsons, Enoch	28, Oct. 1852	L3
Horsfall, Elizabeth	Bently, Edward	7, July 1853	L3
Horsley, Martha A.	Harwood, William S.	8, Sept 1853	L3
Hough, Jane H.	Chenoweth, Richard	21, Nov. 1844	L3
Hough, Rachel	Looker, Allison C.	11, Mar. 1816	L3
Housel, Eliza	Clutch, John V.	7, Nov. 1844	L3
Houser, Emaline	Barber, James H.	4, Nov. 1852	L3
Houston, Eliza P.	Este, David K.	9, Apr. 1840	L3
How, Susan C.	Collier, Allen	30, Sept 1852	L3
Howard, Catharine	Bryant, Isaac F.	28, Feb. 1856	L3
Howard, Delila (Mrs)	Rathburn, Charles B.	20, Sept 1855	L3
Howard, Elmina F.	Fitz, Rudolph H.	28, May 1857	L3
Howard, Mary Ann	Field, William R.	13, Sept 1827	L3
Howard, Mary Elizabeth	Tuite, Aaron G.	2, Mar. 1848	L3
Howard, Sarah H.	Forrer, Samuel	10, Feb. 1826	L3
Howe, Bella	Garrard, William	5, Mar. 1857	L3
Howell, Amelia F.	Finch, Marcus A.	27, Sept 1849	L3
Howell, Catharine	Lowndes, John	6, Jan. 1817	L3
Howell, Delia W.	Smith, Hiram W.	13, July 1848	L3
Howell, Elizabeth C.	McCreary, James K.	18, Jan. 1838	L3
Howell, Elmira	L'Hommedieu, Charles	23, Oct. 1828	L3
Howell, Sallie C.	West, Isaac E.	25, May 1854	L3
Howell, Virginia J.	Mitchell, James	1, Apr. 1852	L3
Howells, Lucy S.	Galbreath, James	11, Jan. 1855	L3
Hoy, Frances	Johnston, George	31, Dec. 1857	L3
Hoyt, Louise	Gray, J. Presley	11, Dec. 1856	L3
Hubbard, Anna Sarah	Lewis, Robert L.	9, July 1846	L3
Hubbard, Annie (Mrs)	Kirk, John W.	27, July 1854	L3
Hubbard, Catharine S	Logan, L.	26, Jan. 1843	L3
Hubbard, Cornelia F.	Strader, P. Wilson	26, Jan. 1843	L3
Hubbard, Julie E.	Pond, H. Aug.	24, Oct. 1850	L3
Hubbard, Rebecca J.	Barker, Hiram	16, Mar. 1854	L3
Hubbell, Elizabeth A	Mar, George W.	26, Oct. 1854	L3
Hubbell, Jane	Hathaway, Henry, Jr.	6, Mar. 1827	L3
Hubbell, Martha P.	Swift, Briggs	24, Sept 1846	L3
Hubbell, Mary A.	Piatt, Jacob	3, Mar. 1853	L3
Hubbell, Mary C.F.	McMurphy, Samuel S.	26, Sept 1839	L3
Hubbell, Mary E.	Foulds, Thomas H.	15, Sept 1853	L3
Hubbell, Sarah	Rogers, Solomon	1, Aug. 1826	L3
Hubbert, Jannet C.	Craut, Henry	30, Apr. 1840	L3
Hudson, Eunice Elizabeth	Williams, Miles	13, Dec. 1838	L4
Hudson, Margaret (Mrs)	Lathrop, Gardner	14, Mar. 1839	L3
Hudson, Mary E.	Thomas, Joseph H.	30, Dec. 1847	L3
Hudson, Sarah	Kennedy, James	16, Sept 1820	L3
Hughes, Caroline	Riley, Patrick	23, Mar. 1854	L3

Brides	Grooms	Date of Notice	Page
Hughes, Elizabeth	Woodruff, James L.	17, Dec. 1846	L3
Hughes, Elizabeth M.	Ricker, Gustavus	19, June 1851	L3
Hughes, Mary H.	Bryant, Alfred	20, June 1850	L3
Hughes, Mollie B.	Jones, George H.	17, Dec. 1857	L3
Hughes, Sarah (Mrs)	Tiley, Francis	21, Oct. 1841	L3
Hughey, Emily H.	Hughes, Charles T.	19, Aug. 1847	L3
Huie, Mary	Gray, Robert	12, Apr. 1855	L3
Hulbert, Mary	Coddington, G.W.	21, June 1849	L3
Hulburd, Helen M.	Flynt, H.S.	13, Oct. 1853	L3
Hulburd, Mary Eliza	Moore, Augustus O.	9, Sept 1841	L3
Hull, Louisa Jane	Cake, Charles T.	14, Mar. 1839	L3
Hull, Mary	Robison, John	21, Dec. 1837	L3
Hullfish, Kate M.	Reinlein, A.	5, Nov. 1857	L3
Hulse, Ruth Ann	Smith, Oliver	21, Aug. 1822	L3
Humphreys, Susan (Mrs)	Moorhead, John	23, Dec. 1830	L4
Hunt, Jane F.	Pendleton, Nathaniel	13, May 1820	L3
Hunt, Margaret	Hamilton, James	8, Aug. 1810	L3
Hunt, Margaret P.	Wentworth, Samuel S.	17, Feb. 1848	L3
Hunt, Mary Ann	Howe, John F.	6, Feb. 1840	L3
Hunt, Sarah	Chapin, Humeston	20, Jan. 1842	L3
Hunt, Susannah	Boyer, Jacob	23, Nov. 1822	L3
Hunter, Charlotte	Morris, Henry C.	30, Oct. 1845	L3
Hunter, Eunice	McCormick, Thomas J.	20, Jan. 1842	L3
Hunter, Nancy	Reily, John	16, Mar. 1809	L3
Huntington, Jane	Earenfight, John	7, Mar. 1839	L3
Huntington, Sarah A.	Hewlett, Jeremiah S.	20, Oct. 1842	L3
Hurdus, Maria	Conant, E.L.	31, Oct. 1826	L3
Hutchens, Lucretia	Cunningham, Andrew	23, June 1853	L3
Hutchinson, Casandra	Fording, Christopher	28, June 1814	L3
Hutchinson, Elizabeth O.	Avery, Leonard S.	23, Feb. 1843	L3
Hutchinson, Julia H.	Young, A.P. (Col)	9, July 1857	L3
Hutchinson, M.W.	Baker, J.W.	24, Sept 1857	L3
Hutton, Jane	Wells, A.H.	28, Sept 1848	L3
Huyler, Marianne	Peters, Henry J.	13, Feb. 1845	L3
Hyatt, Elizabeth S.	Cunningham, T.E.	23, Feb. 1854	L3
Hyatt, Maria Anna	Wells, Erastus H.	26, Oct. 1843	L3
Hyland, Marianne (Mrs)	McClaskey, John	22, June 1843	L3
Iddings, Eliza (Mrs)	Granger, John L.	7, July 1842	L3
Iglehart, Mary Ann	Shays, John	20, Nov. 1850	L3
Immel, Harriet	Harding, William H.	18, Dec. 1845	L3
Ingram, A.C. (Mrs)	Strong, Charles L.	19, Nov. 1857	L3
Ireland, Mary W.	Reed, Enos B.	5, June 1845	L3
Ireland, Rebecca	Jacobs, John	3, July 1811	L3
Irwin, Eliza	Smith, Walter	7, Jan. 1847	L3
Irwin, Elizabeth	Martin, Francis	13, May 1816	L3
Irwin, Elizabeth R.	Harrison, John Scott	18, Aug. 1831	L3
Irwin, Elizabeth S.	Hooper, Samuel S.	30, Nov. 1848	L3
Irwin, Jane Findlay	Harrison, William H.	9, Mar. 1824	L3
Irwin, Mary W.	Howard, James N.	12, May 1842	L3
Irwin, Sarah W.	Lodge, Caleb T.	14, Aug. 1828	L3
Isett, Harriet L.	Ridgely, Fred. W.	9, Nov. 1854	L3
Isham, E.T.	Schooley, John C.	30, May 1844	L3
Isham, Jane B.	Lehmer, James D.	9, Aug. 1849	L3

Brides	Grooms	Date of Notice	Page
Israel, Hannah	Coffin, W.G.	7, May 1840	L3
Israel, Mary M.	Thorp, William A.	31, Oct. 1839	L3
Ives, Sarah B.	Hurtt, F.W.	15, Feb. 1855	L3
Jackson, Alice Ann	Harris, John W.	28, Jan. 1841	L3
Jackson, Caroline M.	Simpson, J.A.	20, June 1850	L3
Jackson, Elizabeth	Thomas, George	15, Feb. 1814	L3
Jackson, Evelina	Pierce, William	15, Sept 1836	L3
Jackson, Kate	Hamilton, Turner	11, Aug. 1853	L3
Jackson, Maria N.	Curtis, Joseph A.	15, Oct. 1846	L3
Jackson, Mary Jane	Weatherby, Philip G.	9, Sept 1847	L3
Jacobs, Ann E.	Faulkner, Jeremiah	26, Nov. 1840	L3
Jacobs, Elizabeth A.	Barnett, Robert	23, May 1850	L3
Jacobs, Isabella	Levy, Alexander	4, Aug. 1836	L3
Jacobs, Margaret E.	DeCamp, Job	9, May 1844	L3
James, Amanda M.	Wilson, J. Plume	10, Feb. 1848	L3
James, Angelina	Smith, James R.	18, May 1843	L3
James, Anna D.	Johnson, Joseph J.	10, Apr. 1845	L3
James, Anne	Pendleton, N.G.	20, May 1841	L3
James, Martha J.	Jessup, D.B. (Dr)	24, Dec. 1846	L3
James, Mary A.	Keats, Clarence G.	20, Jan. 1853	L3
James, Sarah	Harris, Edward	27, Oct. 1842	L3
James, Sarah F.	Wheelwright, James R	21, Nov. 1839	L3
James, Vannelia	Smith, T. Gardner	5, Sept 1850	L3
Jameson, Catharine	Fisher, Robert I.	4, Feb. 1836	L2
Janes, Deborah	Mixter, Ebenezer	2, Sept 1816	L3
Jarnagin, Clarissa H	Gunn, John C.	30, Apr. 1835	L2
Jaudon, Anna C.	Lea, Henry C.	30, May 1850	L3
Jaudon, Elizabeth	Bakewell, William W.	14, Oct. 1847	L3
Jenkins, (Mrs)	Allen, Joseph	12, Feb. 1805	L3
Jenkins, Jane	Clayton, Richard	2, Feb. 1843	L3
Jenkins, Mary Ann	Clayton, Richard	4, Apr. 1844	L3
Jenkins, Mary C.	Pomeroy, Robert	6, Feb. 1840	L3
Jenks, Charlotte R.	Woodruff, Charles S.	12, Aug. 1841	L3
Jeremiah, Martha W.	Smith, James F.	15, Apr. 1847	L3
Jessup, Phebe	Johnson, Samuel	7, Nov. 1810	L3
Jessup, Rebecca	Johnson, Cary	15, Sept 1806	L3
Jobe, Mary Jane	Tredway, William M.	20, Oct. 1842	L3
Jocelyn, Augusta	Aylsworth, Caleb A.	9, Mar. 1854	L3
Johnson, Amelia	Morsell, James C.	26, Dec. 1823	L3
Johnson, Caroline E.	Williams, S.B.	23, May 1844	L3
Johnson, Eliza E.	Curd, William O.	16, Apr. 1846	L3
Johnson, Elizabeth	Jones, John D.	30, Sept 1823	L3
Johnson, Elizabeth (Mrs)	Corwin, Daniel	6, Feb. 1840	L3
Johnson, Elizabeth S	Fisk, John F.	20, Oct. 1842	L3
Johnson, Isabella	Ware, Henry	14, Oct. 1847	L3
Johnson, Josephine	Adams, David T.	5, May 1853	L3
Johnson, Laura	McNutt, James	6, Feb. 1845	L3
Johnson, Lucretia K.	Harrison, John Scott	31, Dec. 1824	L3
Johnson, Maria E.	Kavney, Lewis	20, Sept 1849	L3
Johnson, Mary	Barns, Samuel	14, Nov. 1839	L1
Johnson, Mary B.	Strickler, George W.	18, Nov. 1847	L3
Johnson, Mary J.	Jamison, Robert	6, Apr. 1854	L3
Johnson, Nancy	Carel, John	1, Apr. 1823	L3

Brides	Grooms	Date of Notice	Page
Johnson, Peggy	Gould, Thomas	16, May 1810	L3
Johnson, Sarah P.	Fisher, Daniel M.	30, Apr. 1846	L3
Johnson, Sophia (Mrs)	Ray, James M.	20, Dec. 1855	L3
Johnson, Ursula N.	Turner, Charles	28, Dec. 1854	L3
Johnston, Agnes	McNair, Alexander	19, Jan. 1854	L3
Johnston, Augusta	Shumway, Horatio G.	18, Dec. 1856	L3
Johnston, Cornelia	Williams, Simeon B.	6, July 1848	L3
Johnston, Eliza (Mrs)	Funk, Henry B.	4, Apr. 1839	L3
Johnston, Emily	Fabian, Robert L.	9, Oct. 1851	L3
Johnston, Essa E.	Norris, Charles P.	5, Nov. 1857	L3
Johnston, Isabella M.	McBirney, Hugh	15, Nov. 1849	L3
Johnston, Jane	Eccles, Henry	8, July 1847	L3
Johnston, Mary Ann	Beresford, Benjamin	15, Sept 1836	L1
Johnston, Mary Ann	Adams, John	11, Nov. 1847	L3
Johnston, Mary E.	Huntington, William	4, Sept 1851	L3
Johnston, Rachael	Reynolds, William A.	9, June 1836	L3
Johnston, Sarah H.	Huntington, Henry D.	14, May 1846	L3
Joiner, Pennie	Hearn, Beverly	27, June 1810	L3
Jolly, Ellen	Ferguson, A.F.	26, Jan. 1854	L3
Jones, Ann C. (Mrs)	Hudson, John	21, Apr. 1820	L3
Jones, Ann Maria	McMahan, James	15, June 1813	L3
Jones, Christiana	Filley, Lucius L.	30, Mar. 1849	L3
Jones, Elizabeth	Hancock, John	9, Aug. 1855	L3
Jones, Elizabeth (Mrs)	Maynard, Rufus	21, Sept 1854	L3
Jones, Emily	Clements, Nelson	8, June 1854	L3
Jones, Emily Albina	Irwin, Archibald	26, June 1828	L3
Jones, Hannah	Williams, Micajah T.	11, Mar. 1818	L3
Jones, Harriet	Marsh, Alfred A.	11, Sept 1851	L3
Jones, Harriet E.	Elliott, W.L.	29, Oct. 1846	L3
Jones, Harriet E.	Nason, Cyrus	2, Aug. 1855	L3
Jones, Jane	Letford, John S.	23, July 1846	L3
Jones, Lucretia	Joyce, James	14, June 1855	L3
Jones, Margaret	Harrold, William	8, June 1843	L3
Jones, Margaret F.	Williams, John A.	11, May 1837	L3
Jones, Marie A.	Morrow, R.A.	18, Nov. 1852	L3
Jones, Martha Ann	Sykes, Charles	5, Apr. 1849	L3
Jones, Nettie A.	Champlin, C.C.	8, Feb. 1855	L3
Jones, Susan Osgood	Wentworth, Mark H.	8, Aug. 1844	L3
Jonte, Louisa E.	Chambers, Charles C.	30, Nov. 1854	L3
Josselyn, Melcena	Brown, Thomas	30, Nov. 1854	L3
Joycelin, Mary H.	Jackson, Charles	18, May 1822	L3
Jtark, Julia	Larkin, S.F.	22, May 1851	L3
Judkins, Martha A.	Collins, Joseph H.	18, Jan. 1849	L3
Judkins, Sarah R.	Comly, William F.	27, Oct. 1836	L3
Judson, Susan A.	Sanford, Charles S.	19, Apr. 1855	L3
Jungman, Anna S.	Hanks, Albert S.	6, May 1847	L3
Jungman, Fanny E.	Miller, Thane	10, Aug. 1848	L3
Justus, Angeline	DeGrummond, G.W.	5, Aug. 1852	L3
Kain, Almira	Clossin, David L.	4, Dec. 1845	L3
Kain, Susan	Ellis, James S.	28, Apr. 1842	L3
Kamper, Sophia	Palmer, John	27, Apr. 1813	L3
Kattenhorn, Sophia	Weissmann, Frederick	5, Nov. 1857	L3
Kautz, Hannah	Armstrong, Walter	21, May 1808	L3

Brides	Grooms	Date of Notice	Page
Kautz, Margaret D.	Phillips, William	18, Aug. 1853	L3
Keating, Margaret	James, Joseph J.	4, July 1826	L3
Keats, Georgiana	Gwathmey, Alfred	28, Oct. 1847	L3
Keck, Sallie C.	Thomas, Cal. W.	30, Aug. 1855	L3
Keler, Margaret	Givens, D.A.	28, June 1855	L3
Keller, Sarah	Neff, William	9, Mar. 1854	L3
Kelley, Clarissa	Moore, Nathan	13, Oct. 1818	L3
Kelley, Elizabeth	Gilbert, Thomas	19, June 1845	L3
Kelley, Jane	Collins, William	2, Dec. 1847	L3
Kellogg, Almira S.	Davis, Henry F.	19, Mar. 1840	L3
Kellogg, Frances A.	Mahaffey, Robert	9, Sept 1852	L3
Kellogg, Rhoda W.	Merrill, A.S.	30, Oct. 1851	L3
Kellum, Celia	Burr, C. Chauncey	9, Jan. 1851	L3
Kelly, Anna S.	Gaff, John	5, Nov. 1857	L3
Kelly, Emily E.	Johnson, Edward B.	12, Nov. 1857	L3
Kelly, Phebe	Betts, John	18, Nov. 1823	L3
Kelly, Susan A.	Good, Robert	14, Nov. 1839	L1
Kelly, Susan H.	Winchester, C.C.	25, Nov. 1852	L3
Kelpan, Mary Jane	Gibbs, Edward G.	14, Oct. 1841	L3
Kelsey, Ellen (Mrs)	McElvain, John	12, Oct. 1854	L3
Kelsy, Sarosa	Deebugin, Henry	22, July 1816	L2
Kemp, Salome	Smith, George R.	30, May 1839	L2
Kemper, Charlotte L.	Wright, William H.	23, May 1850	L3
Kemper, E. Suzette	Grundy, R.C. (Rev)	1, June 1848	L3
Kemper, Fanny C.	Metcalf, Eli P.	20, Mar. 1851	L3
Kemper, Mary V.	Taylor, Henry W.	23, Oct. 1851	L3
Kemper, Nancy	Todd, John	30, June 1806	L3
Kemper, Susan M.	Ferguson, Abijah	25, Mar. 1816	L3
Kendall, Samantha E.	Colby, George W.	27, Nov. 1851	L3
Kendall, Sarah W.	Barnard, George	18, Jan. 1844	L3
Kenneallie, Mary J.	Pettit, John W.	30, Aug. 1855	L3
Kennedy, Jennetta	Restieaux, William	21, Aug. 1856	L5
Kennedy, Mary	Reeder, Jesse	19, May 1807	L3
Kennedy, Mary Ellen	Cushard, William	26, Jan. 1854	L3
Kennon, Caroline	Brady, Lorenzo D.	27, Feb. 1845	L3
Kenny, Eliza	Whitten, Robert	18, Jan. 1855	L3
Kenny, Mary (Mrs)	Kenedy, Joseph	24, Oct. 1807	L3
Kenton, Lucie A.	Conkling, R.	20, Nov. 1845	L3
Kenvyn, Rachel	Rodgers, Thomas	2, Mar. 1854	L3
Kerby, Elizabeth (Mrs)	Young, Nicholas	24, Aug. 1854	L3
Kerdolff, Catharine	Warden, Robert B.	19, Oct. 1843	L3
Kerdolff, Eleanor A.	Warden, Americus	12, Sept 1844	L3
Kerns, Henrietta	Day, George W.	19, Oct. 1843	L3
Kerr, Rebecca	Noble, David	28, Apr. 1817	L3
Kesley, Margaret	Gemeny, R.D.	10, Sept 1846	L3
Key, Alice	Pendleton, George H.	11, June 1846	L3
Keys, Eveline A.	Thompson, S.J.	7, Feb. 1850	L3
Keys, Mary Ann	Lardner, Henry (Dr)	6, Sept 1838	L3
Keys, Mary B.	Wilson, William B.	13, Apr. 1827	L3
Keys, Virginia	Wilson, James K.	24, June 1852	L3
Keznor, Lizzie	Wisner, Harry C.	26, Nov. 1857	L3
Kidder, Mary W.	Crawford, Leonard	13, Nov. 1851	L3
Kiersted, A.A.	Cady, C.W.	17, Nov. 1842	L6
Kilbreath, Caroline	Dimmick, Charles W.	6, June 1839	L2

Brides	Grooms	Date of Notice	Page
Kilbreth, Sallie G.	McLean, N.H.	18, June 1857	L3
Kiles, Sarah Anne	Shipley, Joseph	26, Aug. 1825	L3
Kiloh, Ann	Knight, George H.	13, Nov. 1850	L3
Kiloh, Henrietta	Orr, John	17, July 1851	L3
Kiloh, Maria E.	Lewis, Charles F.	15, Nov. 1849	L3
Kimball, Augusta	Ewing, John H.	11, June 1846	L3
Kimball, Susan (Mrs)	Wigley, Henry	22, Jan. 1846	L3
King, Alice J.	Steer, R.A.	20, Dec. 1855	L3
King, Amanda	Hipple, Benjamin	21, Sept 1843	L3
King, Amanda J.	Pane, George W.	1, Aug. 1844	L3
King, Carey	Warrington, Lewis	21, Apr. 1817	L3
King, Elizabeth J.	Ketchum, William P.	13, Apr. 1848	L3
King, Flora	Deshler, Charles G.	5, June 1845	L3
King, Louise	Murdock, Joseph	24, Nov. 1853	L3
King, Margaret	Weyer, Josiah S.	14, Mar. 1844	L3
King, Margaret M.	Conklin, S.F. (Dr)	2, Oct. 1851	L3
King, Mary	Baker, William W.	26, May 1842	L3
King, Mary	Vanausdol, Angus W.	17, Aug. 1848	L3
King, Nancy	Hoffner, John	27, Feb. 1811	L3
King, Sarah (Mrs)	Peter, William	31, Oct. 1844	L3
King, Sarah C.	Clark, George W.	13, Feb. 1840	L3
Kingman, Sarah A.	Rhodes, James F.	5, Feb. 1852	L3
Kingsley, Jane E.	Barrett, Austin C.	15, Feb. 1849	L3
Kingston, Margaret	Thorpe, Truman B.	12, Aug. 1841	L3
Kinkaid, Mary	Hall, William	19, May 1853	L3
Kinneon, Mary P.	Buchanan, Alfred	22, Nov. 1855	L3
Kinney, Elizabeth	Ross, S.R.	16, Sept 1847	L3
Kinney, Lucy S.	Wintrade, John B.	27, Aug. 1846	L3
Kinsey, Jane G.	Malone, William H.	28, Nov. 1844	L3
Kirby, Emily R.	Free, A.C.	19, Mar. 1857	L3
Kirby, Jane	Lemaire, Isaac K.	14, Oct. 1847	L3
Kirker, Mary	Voorheese, Ralph M.	23, Apr. 1824	L2
Kirkpatrick, Cynthia	Williams, William	9, Mar. 1854	L3
Kissick, M.J.	Woodrow, N.A.	18, Dec. 1856	L3
Kitchel, Mary (Mrs)	Askey, David	11, Mar. 1815	L3
Kittridge, Kate	Burckhardt, Frederic	29, June 1854	L3
Kittridge, M. Louise	Jones, George W.	25, Apr. 1844	L3
Knapp, Virginia	Nippert, August	30, July 1857	L3
Knoblaugh, Margaret	Goodhue, William	20, Sept 1849	L3
Knotts, Mary E.	Barrow, Edwin	25, Jan. 1849	L3
Knowles, Sarah Ann	Dill, Samuel	29, Dec. 1842	L3
Knowlton, Mary E.	Mixer, S.F. (Dr)	3, Mar. 1853	L3
Knox, Mary Ann	Richardson, Richard	27, Mar. 1828	L3
Kore, Charlotte R.	Bennett, George	13, Nov. 1845	L3
Kramer, Clarion W.	Harvie, Charles S.	8, June 1843	L3
Kruse, Phebe	Alley, Enoch L.	28, Aug. 1845	L3
Kugler, Catharine	Drake, Josiah	2, May 1833	L1
Kuhn, Sarah	Rose, Erasmus (Dr)	12, Apr. 1849	L3
Kyler, Susannah	Miller, Jacob	13, Jan. 1806	L3
Laby, Scilla	Love, Robert A.	3, Apr. 1851	L3
Lacey, Caroline M.	Sellers, William W.	5, Nov. 1857	L3
Ladley, Lydia Ann	Cottam, Richard	7, Oct. 1841	L3
Laing, Matilda Ann	Rankin, William	4, Nov. 1847	L3

Brides	Grooms	Date of Notice	Page
Laird, Amanda	Holdzkorn, William	26, Feb. 1846	L3
Laird, Rebecca	Wilson, Samuel	28, Aug. 1845	L3
Lake, Ellen R.	Wright, Augustus S.	1, Dec. 1853	L3
Lakeman, Alice H.	Wright, Benjamin F.	26, Feb. 1857	L3
Lamb, Elizabeth	Smith, William H.	30, Mar. 1849	L3
Lamb, Jane D.	Clark, J.C.	4, Dec. 1845	L3
Lamotte, Eliza	Nesmith, Thomas A.	5, July 1855	L3
Land, Ellen	Churchill, A.W.	19, Mar. 1840	L3
Landis, Elizabeth	Place, Lucius H.	13, Feb. 1845	L3
Landrum, Sarah W.	Stone, R.H.	3, Dec. 1846	L3
Lane, Ann	Buell, George P.	25, June 1824	L3
Lane, Mary (Mrs)	Burke, William (Rev)	25, Aug. 1842	L3
Lang, Margaret	McKinlay, James	3, Nov. 1836	L3
Langdon, Caroline	Eustis, William	17, Oct. 1810	L3
Langdon, Cynthia	Morrill, H.E. (Dr)	18, Nov. 1841	L3
Langdon, Elizabeth	Biggs, Thomas R.	23, Oct. 1851	L3
Langdon, Lorendo	Snow, Lemuel	16, Sept 1816	L3
Langdon, Lucy	Marsh, Charles	21, Sept 1812	L3
Langdon, Mary Jane	Bateman, William D.	18, Aug. 1842	L3
Langdon, Mary Jane	Young, Joseph G.	11, Feb. 1841	L3
Langdon, Mollie G.	Peacock, Simeon	19, Mar. 1857	L3
Langdon, Ruth	Punshon, John W.	28, Nov. 1844	L3
Langdon, Sarah A.	Laws, James H.	23, Oct. 1851	L3
Langford, Chloe	Taylor, James W.	23, Oct. 1845	L3
Langland, Margaret	Parker, Frederick	5, Mar. 1846	L3
Langley, Eliza A.	Duncan, W.C. (Dr)	8, May 1845	L3
Langley, Mary	Moore, John, Jr.	8, Mar. 1838	L3
Lanman, Sarah Coit	Harmar, Josiah	21, Oct. 1830	L3
Lanphear, Frances	McKinle, John (Rev)	9, May 1839	L3
Lanphear, Mary A.	Stanley, Frederick	5, Oct. 1843	L3
Lansdale, Martha	Reynolds, R.S.	12, Sept 1823	L3
Lanter, Georgiana	Meek, John P.	6, July 1843	L3
Lape, Elizabeth	Glass, William	14, Apr. 1821	L3
Lape, Sarah M.	Rammelsberg, Frederick	21, Apr. 1842	L3
Larrabee, Ellen	Lattimore, S.A.	19, Aug. 1852	L3
Larue, Martha	Bachelor, Jonathan R	13, May 1816	L3
Latham, Mary A.	Latham, Lorenzo	1, Aug. 1826	L3
Lathrop, Lydia H.	Pierson, Daniel B.	24, Jan. 1850	L3
Lathrop, Rebecca P.	Gillespie, George D.	5, June 1845	L3
Latta, Mary E.	Sparks, J.C. (Dr)	12, May 1853	L3
Laudeman, Maggie H.	Semple, James A.	24, Jan. 1856	L3
Laughton, Anne	Tillinghast, William	19, Dec. 1850	L3
Laurie, Margaret D.	Winslow, James	25, Mar. 1847	L3
Laverty, Alice B.	Butler, Joseph C.	9, Sept 1847	L3
Laverty, Honora W.	Hilton, George	23, June 1842	L3
Lawrence, Amanda (Mrs)	Sutton, Edward	20, Apr. 1848	L3
Lawrence, Ann B.	Jones, John T.	30, June 1821	L3
Lawrence, Arabella H	Waldo, Fred. Aug.	24, Jan. 1833	L4
Lawrence, Catharine	Randolph, Thomas	27, June 1810	L3
Lawrence, Elizabeth	McQueen, James	5, Sept 1850	L3
Lawrence, Maria	Carneal, Lewis	4, Dec. 1845	L3
Lawrence, Mary A. (Mrs)	Thurber, Samuel	29, Dec. 1842	L3
Lawrence, Mary Elizabeth	Richardson, Samuel	23, Sept 1847	L3
Lawrence, Rebecca	Gano, Daniel	30, Sept 1816	L3

Brides	Grooms	Date of Notice	Page
Laws, Amelia	Brashears, Gassaway	5, Jan. 1837	L3
Lawson, Ellen	Olmstead, H.B.	4, Sept 1856	L5
Lawson, Hannah	Doty, John	28, Jan. 1847	L3
Lawson, Hannah	Sargeant, Charles H.	23, June 1842	L3
Lawson, Maria	Shane, William	1, June 1827	L2
Lea, Catharine M.	Ward, James W.	6, July 1848	L3
Lea, Emily L.	Peabody, Herbert C.	28, Jan. 1841	L3
Leach, Julia	Chenoweth, J.S.	22, Dec. 1853	L3
Leadbetter, Sarah A.	Howarth, James	9, Oct. 1834	L2
Leasure, Mary Ann	Wagaman, Eli	26, Jan. 1854	L3
Leathers, Lucy	Burdsal, Elijah	16, Oct. 1845	L3
LeBoutillier, Anne	Roberts, Charles J.	13, July 1848	L3
Lee, Anne S.	Hooper, William	13, July 1854	L3
Lee, Annie E.	Hubbard, L.V.	26, Oct. 1848	L3
Lee, Clara	Parke, Samuel S.	30, Aug. 1849	L3
Lee, E.	Livezy, I.W.	6, Jan. 1853	L3
Lee, Jane Ann	Higden, Henry H.	28, Mar. 1844	L3
Lee, Margaret B.	Buchanan, John	11, May 1843	L3
Lee, Mary M.	Morton, William R.	6, June 1850	L3
Lee, Susan M.	Stratton, Josiah J.	5, Jan. 1827	L3
Leech, Ann E.	Woodbury, George W.	5, May 1853	L3
Leech, Sarah	Dobson, Benjamin	22, Apr. 1847	L3
Leeds, Ann	Parker, William G.	18, Apr. 1844	L3
Leeds, Elizabeth	Cotty, William	8, Mar. 1849	L3
Lehman, Sybilla	Powars, John	27, Nov. 1834	L2
Lehmanowsky, Anna S.	Distin, William L.	21, Sept 1837	L4
Lehmanowsky, Paulina	Hill, Edward H.	16, Nov. 1843	L3
Leibee, Selone (Mrs)	Fries, Silvester	20, Nov. 1845	L3
Leibey, Mary	Tatem, John	26, Aug. 1823	L3
Leonard, Anne J.	Blake, A. (Rev)	16, Sept 1841	L3
Leonard, Frances	Waldo, Fred. A.(Dr)	10, Sept 1846	L3
Leonard, Frances M.	Spooner, Thomas	30, Oct. 1851	L3
Leonard, Hannah A.	Lounsbury, James	3, Oct. 1850	L3
Leonard, Jane (Mrs)	Martin, Thomas F.	6, Apr. 1848	L3
Leonard, Sarah	Spooner, Thomas	15, Sept 1842	L3
Leslie, Maria E.	Conclin, William	12, Dec. 1850	L3
Lester, Emma	Collingwood, John	11, Feb. 1841	L3
Lester, Martha	Smith, Henry	14, Dec. 1837	L3
Letford, Eliza J.	Nordhoff, Charles	27, Aug. 1857	L3
Letter, Eleanor D.	Cunningham, John P.	2, Feb. 1843	L3
Letter, Mary Eliza	Ruffner, Morgan	2, Nov. 1843	L3
Levassor, Clara J.	Debarr, J.H. Diss	25, May 1848	L3
Leverett, Charlotte	Fessenden, Benjamin	3, Dec. 1829	L3
Lewis, Almira	Hagan, Marcelus B.	18, Sept 1851	L3
Lewis, Amelia	Weston, John A.	16, Nov. 1848	L3
Lewis, Ann Eliza	Evans, Daniel D.	25, July 1844	L3
Lewis, Augusta M.	Lindsay, H.R.	18, Sept 1851	L3
Lewis, B.	Correl, J.	28, Oct. 1825	L2
Lewis, Elizabeth	Hughes, Edward J.	18, Sept 1845	L3
Lewis, Elizabeth R.	Hunt, Thomas E.	12, June 1851	L3
Lewis, Ellen M.	Saunders, R.C.	30, Sept 1841	L3
Lewis, Fanny	Oberdorf, Elias	20, July 1843	L3
Lewis, Jane	Tobey, George H.	30, Dec. 1847	L3
Lewis, Margaretha H.	Hales, Charles	7, June 1849	L3

Brides	Grooms	Date of Notice	Page
Lewis, Margery J.	Kenna, Edward	24, June 1847	L3
Lewis, Mary	Hughes, L.F.	18, Sept 1845	L3
Lewis, Mary Ann	Dudley, James M.	2, Feb. 1843	L3
Lewis, Pauline	McMaster, Gilbert	26, Apr. 1855	L3
Lewis, Rebecca S.	Lanphear, Edward P.	7, Nov. 1844	L3
Lewis, Serena A.	White, Frank M.	14, June 1855	L3
Lewis, Susan	Shaffer, William	7, Aug. 1845	L3
Lfiff, Clarasy	Smiley, Robeson	9, Oct. 1845	L3
L'Hommedieu, E. (Mrs)	Russell, William	24, June 1847	L3
L'Hommedieu, Maria M.	Long, Jacob	13, June 1826	L3
L'Hommedieu, S. (Mrs)	Lindly, Abraham	6, Mar. 1822	L3
L'Hommedieu, Sallie	Slocum, J. Jeremiah	15, June 1854	L3
Liddell, Margaret	McFarlane, James	10, Aug. 1854	L3
Ligget, Sophia Susan	Taylor, Joseph B.	30, Jan. 1845	L3
Lightfoot, Susan (Mrs)	Doyle, Michael	20, June 1844	L3
Lindlay, Caroline	Ellis, John W.	20, Nov. 1845	L3
Lindley, Joanna	Parker, J.A. (Dr)	17, Oct. 1823	L3
Lindsly, Carrie W.	Mussey, William H.	28, May 1857	L3
Linfoot, Rosetta	Carmichael, Neil	29, Dec. 1842	L3
Lingle, Susan E.	Walker, William S.	2, Feb. 1854	L3
Link, Jane	Forker, James	5, Aug. 1847	L3
Linnel, Sarah	Harris, Timothy (Rev)	13, Sept 1809	L3
Linscott, Marybe	Leaf, William	9, Feb. 1854	L3
Lister, Elizabeth	Stewart, Charles S.	2, Mar. 1854	L3
Litherbury, Matilda	Shultz, Henry (Dr)	17, Sept 1846	L3
Little, Mary	Marsh, David	27, Aug. 1840	L3
Littlebury, Sarah	Whateley, Henry	23, June 1853	L3
Littlefield, Mary L.	Jenkins, James	3, July 1845	L3
Livingston, Jane Ann	Delaplaine, Joseph	14, Oct. 1806	L3
Livingston, Ruth	Swift, Henry A.	18, Sept 1851	L3
Lloyd, Eleanor H.	Richards, Giles	11, Nov. 1820	L3
Lloyd, Heloise	Lloyd, James Tilford	21, May 1857	L3
Lockwood, Matilda D.	Honore, Francis (Capt)	8, Dec. 1818	L3
Lodge, Indiana	Reed, George M.	13, July 1854	L3
Lodwick, Jane E.	McKean, James	18, June 1846	L3
Loevieson, Maria	Dusenbury, Cornelius	27, Nov. 1845	L3
Long, Agnes	Kinder, William R.	21, Oct. 1852	L3
Long, Catharine	Shepherd, William	23, Feb. 1854	L3
Long, Lizzie D.	Brookbank, B.F.	10, Jan. 1850	L3
Long, Mary E.	Bailey, Isaac S.	8, Oct. 1857	L3
Long, Nancy	Miller, Martin	31, Oct. 1810	L3
Longley, Amanda	Grieves, John G.	11, Mar. 1847	L3
Longmoor, Ellen	Haven, Augustus	1, Nov. 1849	L3
Longshore, Rachel C.	Giles, Benjamin	4, Nov. 1847	L3
Longwell, Emma	Emrie, J.R.	9, Dec. 1847	L3
Longworth, Charlotte	Jones, William D.	17, Mar. 1821	L3
Longworth, Eliza	Flagg, William J.	29, Aug. 1850	L3
Longworth, Elizabeth M.	Potter, Joseph T(Dr)	28, Sept 1848	L3
Longworth, Lucia C.	Kiderlen, William L.	22, June 1848	L3
Looker, Amelia	Berry, Archibald	12, Mar. 1846	L3
Looker, Emmeline	Romeril, Charles E.	14, Apr. 1826	L3
Looker, Pamela C.	Pharis, Washington	8, Apr. 1812	L3
Lord, Susan	Musat, Charles	19, July 1855	L3
Loring, Catharine	McKean, Alexander	22, Apr. 1818	L3

Brides	Grooms	Date of Notice	Page
Loring, Eliza	Anderson, Charles R.	2, June 1842	L3
Loring, Georgiana	Hooker, Edward	30, Dec. 1852	L3
Loring, Mary F.	Williams, Milo G.	27, Oct. 1842	L3
Loring, Susan M.	Hinsdale, John T.	8, Dec. 1836	L3
Louderback, C. (Mrs)	Jonas, W.H.	13, Aug. 1857	L3
Love, Mary Ann	Kettler, William	28, Feb. 1856	L3
Lovejoy, Harriet N.	Marpe, C.A.C.	8, Dec. 1842	L3
Lovejoy, Mary	Green, Stephen A.	10, June 1847	L3
Lovejoy, Mary (Mrs)	Schillinger, William	3, Nov. 1836	L3
Lovejoy, Mary Jane	Middleton, Elijah C.	27, Apr. 1848	L3
Lovejoy, Sarah (Mrs)	Sherriff, Anthony C.	7, Jan. 1847	L3
Lovelace, Louisa C.	Clyde, Andrew	28, Dec. 1843	L3
Lovett, Elizabeth	Smith, N.T.	18, Feb. 1847	L3
Low, Mary G.	Beall, William B.	23, Oct. 1822	L3
Lowe, Elizabeth	Barch, William	23, July 1846	L3
Lowe, Lavinia Ann	Reed, Cyrus	13, Aug. 1857	L3
Lowry, Rebecca Jane	Biggers, David A.	18, June 1857	L3
Luce, Mary E.	Hilton, George	27, Jan. 1853	L3
Luckey, Catharine M.	Ranney, Moses	16, Mar. 1837	L3
Ludlow, Amanda	Kendrick, Charles S.	19, Dec. 1844	L3
Ludlow, Betsey	Patten, Matthew	22, Oct. 1808	L3
Ludlow, Charlotte (Mrs)	Risk, D. (Rev)	15, Dec. 1808	L3
Ludlow, Charlotte C.	Jones, Charles A.	20, July 1843	L3
Ludlow, Eliza	Frazier, Alexander	4, Sept 1845	L3
Ludlow, Mary Ann	Mann, Isaac	6, June 1810	L3
Ludlow, Ruhannah	Hunt, Randal	20, July 1854	L3
Ludlow, Sarabella	Garrard, Jeptha D.	20, Aug. 1824	L3
Ludlow, Sarah Bella	Chase, S.P.	19, Nov. 1846	L3
Ludlum, Alzina A.	Ludlow, George C.	18, July 1844	L3
Luffborough, Eliza	Bohrer, Benjamin S.	18, Oct. 1820	L3
Luke, Harriet A.	Peyton, Francis H.	31, Oct. 1839	L3
Lumley, Mary	Anderson, Evan	7, Oct. 1841	L3
Lumley, Sarah	Harsha, Thomas F.	25, July 1844	L3
Lumsden, Sara	Mirrielees, George	11, Oct. 1849	L3
Lundy, Adaline Elizabeth	Brown, Anson R. (Dr)	22, Feb. 1849	L3
Lundy, Nancy	McGrew, James	23, Mar. 1849	L3
Luse, Angeline (Mrs)	Parker, William	13, Feb. 1840	L3
Lutz, Susan	Hune, Henry	9, Nov. 1854	L3
Lyall, Jane Eliza	Howell, Daniel G.	25, Aug. 1818	L2
Lyle, M. Jennie	Rooker, J.J. (Dr)	22, Oct. 1857	L3
Lyman, Henrietta	Clarke, Orlando (Rev)	21, Aug. 1856	L5
Lynch, Anna M.	Carroll, Foster (Dr)	31, Oct. 1850	L3
Lynd, Catharine L.	Snow, Henry	21, Nov. 1844	L3
Lynd, Mary S.	Burnett, Jacob	31, Apr. 1845	L3
Lyndscey, Cynthia	Wolf, Jacob	27, Mar. 1851	L3
Lynes, Elizabeth	Wilcox, John	24, Apr. 1811	L3
Lyon, Elizabeth W.	Taylor, Mahlon R.	8, Dec. 1836	L3
Lyon, Ettie	Dodge, Ossian	13, July 1854	L3
Lyon, Fanny Cornelia	Fullerton, William R	7, Aug. 1851	L3
Lyon, Melinda	Marpless, Charles	6, Apr. 1854	L3
Lyon, Missouri	Blackburn, Jona	22, Jan. 1852	L3
Lyon, Susan Emily	Wiltse, John F.	30, Oct. 1845	L3
Lytle, Eliza Ann	MacAlester, Charles	19, Oct. 1824	L3
Lytle, Elizabeth H.	Broadwell, Samuel J.	20, Nov. 1856	L3

Brides	Grooms	Date of Notice	Page
Lytle, Josephine R.	Foster, N. (Dr)	28, Apr. 1853	L3
Lytle, Rebecca A.	Hill, W.F.	3, Sept 1846	L3
MacDaniel, Eunice	Dana, Charles A.	2, Apr. 1846	L3
Macgerry, Margaret	Oalley, John	19, Aug. 1820	L3
Machett, Sophia A.	Hay, Joseph	15, Dec. 1842	L5
MacKenzie, Ellen B.	Washington, John F.	6, July 1854	L3
Mackey, Maria (Mrs)	Crawson, James	21, Aug. 1811	L3
Mackie, Jessie	Prescott, T.O. (Rev)	19, July 1849	L3
Mackie, Mary D.	McIntyre, Peter	6, Mar. 1845	L3
Macks, Eliza Jane	Aehle, Charles F.	2, July 1846	L3
Maclay, Catharine	Sterrett, Benjamin	6, Apr. 1843	L3
Maclay, Sarah Ellen	Brownson, James (Rev)	6, Apr. 1843	L3
Magaw, Anna Maria	Sigerson, Wallace	26, Nov. 1840	L3
Magaw, Sarah Jane	Wadsworth, Joshua (Dr)	24, Nov. 1842	L6
Magee, Catharine	Hawkins, William	8, Oct. 1857	L3
Magers, Jane	Malone, James F.	11, May 1854	L3
Magine, Mary Jos.	Rodriquez, Francis P	14, Nov. 1844	L3
Mahard, Esther	Donogh, John P.	12, Nov. 1835	L1
Mahew, Hannah	Dunbar, Seth	3, June 1820	L3
Mallally, Elizabeth	Dennis, John	13, Nov. 1845	L3
Maloney, Fellitia	Pullman, John	9, May 1844	L3
Malsbery, Maria (Mrs)	Price, Philip	30, June 1806	L3
Maltry, Sophia	Coffin, Joseph H.	17, Feb. 1848	L3
Mankey, Lydia A.	Secrist, Peter	3, Aug. 1843	L3
Mann, Catharine W.	Ackerman, Richard	10, June 1841	L3
Mann, Mary Davis	Allen, William H.	25, Mar. 1841	L3
Manning, Jemima	Foulks, George W.	28, Oct. 1847	L3
Manning, Mary	Carroll, Thomas	13, Nov. 1851	L3
Mansell, Alice M.	Hahn, Paul F.	6, Mar. 1845	L3
Manser, Mary A.	Keckeler, Theophilus	15, July 1852	L3
Manson, Cordelia F.	Gilbert, Samuel E.	19, Aug. 1847	L3
Mansur, Harriet L.	Epply, John P.	12, Sept 1844	L3
Mariani, Louisa	Owen, Charles	1, July 1852	L3
Markland, Catharine	Rofelty, William J.	23, Nov. 1848	L3
Markland, Matilda	Goldson, George	6, Nov. 1845	L3
Marks, Sarah Edwitha	Levy, J.L.	18, Apr. 1839	L3
Marlay, Malinda	Kugler, David	24, Sept 1846	L3
Marsden, Elizabeth	Hoffner, Jacob	3, June 1820	L3
Marsh, Ann (Mrs)	Halstead, John	10, Jan. 1823	L3
Marsh, Hannah (Mrs)	Allen, Israel	29, May 1815	L3
Marsh, Hannah M.	Taylor, Eli	7, Jan. 1836	L2
Marsh, Lydia	Haines, Josiah	10, Feb. 1821	L3
Marsh, Margaret	Knight, Benjamin	11, May 1848	L3
Marsh, Rachael A.	Leslie, James	22, July 1852	L3
Marshall, Evaline P.	Smith, Charles J.	11, Mar. 1852	L3
Marshall, Hetty Ann	Dolson, Jacob	18, May 1827	L3
Marshall, Jane	Riddle, John R.	5, Dec. 1810	L3
Marshall, Laura C.	Smith, R.G.	15, Sept 1853	L3
Marshall, Louisa	Kennedy, John	19, Oct. 1837	L3
Marshall, Mary J.	Robinson, William H.	12, May 1853	L3
Marshall, Missouri A	Osborn, Archibald K.	12, Nov. 1846	L3
Martin Mary Ann (Mrs)	Phillips, Isaac	2, Dec. 1852	L3
Martin, Almira	Robinson, John C.	23, Mar. 1849	L3

Brides	Grooms	Date of Notice	Page
Martin, Almira L.	Hughes, J.W.	28, June 1855	L3
Martin, Clara	Gilmore, George W.	28, Mar. 1850	L3
Martin, Eliza	Knapp, Alvin C.	7, Nov. 1844	L3
Martin, Elizabeth	Dye, Andrew	19, July 1814	L3
Martin, Harriet N.	Conklin, Henry M.	7, Mar. 1850	L3
Martin, Isabella H.	Black, Adam M. (Dr)	7, July 1842	L3
Martin, Laura Attila	Fuller, Robert C.	22, Apr. 1847	L3
Martin, Lizzie	Kemper, Henry L.	20, Dec. 1855	L3
Martin, Margaret	Payne, Edmond	23, Mar. 1854	L3
Martin, Maria R. (Mrs)	Swasey, Moses	5, Nov. 1840	L2
Martin, Mary A.	McCormick, J.B.	6, Apr. 1854	L3
Martin, Mary E.	Cooper, E. Samuel	29, July 1841	L3
Martin, Mary F.	Winston, Samuel	4, May 1822	L3
Martin, Rhoda	Stephens, Charles	12, Sept 1810	L3
Martin, Sarah	Auisten, John	3, July 1845	L3
Martin, Sarah C.	Barrett, William D.	15, Aug. 1844	L3
Martin, Sidney M.	Simpson, John A.	2, June 1826	L3
Martin, Susan L.	Sandford, Alfred	26, Dec. 1810	L3
Mason, Ann	Middleton, William	20, Feb. 1822	L2
Mason, Lucretia	Truax, Edmund A.	30, May 1850	L3
Mason, Marie	Ayres, Mark	1, Oct. 1846	L3
Mason, Mary	Roe, Daniel	2, Aug. 1824	L3
Mason, Mary E.	Fristoe, J.W.	9, Aug. 1855	L3
Mason, Matilda (Mrs)	Walker, William	20, Apr. 1854	L3
Mather, Caroline M.	Ferson, John L.	26, Jan. 1854	L3
Matthews, Elizabeth (Mrs)	Phillips, David (Rev)	14, Sept 1848	L3
Matthews, Mary Blair	Moffat, James C.	2, Jan. 1851	L3
Matthews, Rebecca	Parrot, Horace	19, Jan. 1854	L3
Mattox, Cordelia	Clark, John	17, Mar. 1853	L3
Mattox, Maggie C.	Stagg, Lewis	10, Feb. 1853	L3
Mayer, Juliet	Louis, A.	20, Oct. 1842	L3
Mayhew, Aceneth	Stephens, Ephraim M.	8, June 1827	L3
Mayhew, Agnes (Mrs)	Thompson, David W.	26, May 1842	L3
Mayhew, Angeline	Clark, Caleb B.	2, Apr. 1829	L2
Mayhew, Louisa P.	Bard, Sylvester	13, Nov. 1845	L3
Mayo, Alexina	Carson, E.T.	19, May 1853	L3
Mayo, Maria D.	Scott, Winfield	21, Apr. 1817	L3
Mayo, Mary A.	Lewis, A. (Capt)	15, Oct. 1829	L4
Mayo, Sarah A.	McKinney, John T.	13, June 1821	L3
Maywood, Mary	Stanley, George S.	28, June 1849	L3
McAlee, Mary A.	Hazen, Theodore S.	12, Jan. 1854	L3
McAllister, Helen J.	Owens, John P.	23, Nov. 1848	L3
McAroy, Mary B.	Haggott, John P.(Dr)	9, Nov. 1837	L3
McArthur, Mary	Trimble, Cary A.	11, Jan. 1838	L3
McBride, Eliza	Midlen, William	15, Sept 1842	L3
McCall, Mary A.	Walter, William	30, June 1842	L3
McCandless, Sallie B	Shreve, Charles U.	5, Feb. 1852	L3
McCane, Sarah	Murphy, Archibald	1, Feb. 1825	L3
McCanless, Mary	White, James B.	6, Apr. 1854	L3
McCann, Rosella Ann	Hitchler, John	26, Aug. 1847	L3
McCarty, Martha	Baily, Andrew	3, May 1814	L3
McCauley, Mary Jane	Harran, John	11, Feb. 1847	L3
McClary, Sarah E.	Wynne, Jabez E.	26, Nov. 1857	L3
McCloskey, Mary Ann	Maggini, John C.(Dr)	5, Dec. 1844	L3

Brides	Grooms	Date of Notice	Page
McClure, Frances S.	Carter, Samuel	15, Sept 1821	L3
McClure, Julia Ann	Angle, Solomon	18, Dec. 1845	L3
McCollom, Nancy	Landon, Daniel	9, Feb. 1809	L3
McCollum, Elizabeth	Thomas, Joseph	9, June 1853	L3
McComas, Mary E.	Furnas, Robert W.	6, Nov. 1845	L3
McConnell, Amanda M.	Horne, John R.	26, May 1842	L3
McConnell, Eliza	Clark, Walter	3, Mar. 1836	L2
McCord, Jane D.	Collins, Hiram B.	26, Jan. 1854	L3
McCorkle, Polly	Harce, Robert	17, Aug. 1813	L3
McCormick, Anne	Gibson, William	29, Apr. 1852	L3
McCormick, Elizabeth	Frazer, James A.	15, June 1848	L3
McCormick, Lizzie	Bloss, G.M.D.	11, May 1854	L3
McCormick, Lydia S.	Morrison, James C.	5, Oct. 1843	L3
McCormick, Mary	Andrews, Samuel	15, June 1848	L3
McCormick, Mary	Young, Robert A.	12, Feb. 1857	L3
McCracken, Eliza	Waring, George	14, Jan. 1836	L2
McCracken, Sarah	Heard, J. Wilson	12, Aug. 1841	L3
McCray, Emeline	Forl, James	26, Jan. 1854	L3
McCready, S.V.	Perigo,	9, Nov. 1854	L3
McCreary, Elizabeth	Sterrett, A. McD.	5, Aug. 1847	L3
McCreary, R. Louisa	Moss, Horace H.	5, Aug. 1847	L3
McCullough, Elizabeth B.	Smith, Thomas K.	11, May 1848	L3
McCullough, Ellen	Reeder, Charles A.	4, Feb. 1841	L3
McCullough, Jane	Swift, Briggs	18, June 1857	L3
McCullough, Mary	Clark, Andrew	16, Feb. 1854	L3
McCullough, Matilda	Ferris, E.H. (Dr)	29, Dec. 1853	L3
McCullough, Patty	Meek, Alexander A.	1, Dec. 1807	L3
McDaniel, Mary Ann	Griffith, James	26, Dec. 1810	L3
McDonald, Mary Ann	Bingham, John	8, July 1852	L3
McDonogh, Maria	Smith, William	8, May 1845	L3
McDonough, Lizzie	Trask, Keah B.	17, Aug. 1854	L3
McDougal, Annie R.	Lawson, F.H.	5, Feb. 1857	L3
McDowell, Rachel L.	Vanloon, Samuel T.	19, Oct. 1843	L3
McElvain, Mary	Kelsey, Chauncey	24, Apr. 1845	L3
McEwen, Olivia J.	Gassaway, George	24, July 1851	L3
McFadden, Kate E.	Bushnell, Joseph	20, Apr. 1854	L3
McFall, Anna	Weibling, Herman G.	8, Jan. 1852	L3
McFarland, Jane	Searles, Daniel	14, Dec. 1807	L3
McFarland, Sarah	Dodge, William	8, Aug. 1850	L3
McGee, Mary Jane	Robinson, John (Dr)	14, May 1846	L3
McGinnis, Ann Eliza	Boswell, George W.	9, Dec. 1847	L3
McGowan, Maria	Broks, Theodore M.	2, Dec. 1847	L3
McGowan, Maria (Mrs)	Brooks, Theodore M.	11, Nov. 1847	L3
McGregor, Helen	Stannus, Thomas J.	7, Nov. 1844	L3
McGregor, Margaret	Caldow, Robert	24, Sept 1840	L3
McGrew, Sallie B.	Williams, E. (Dr)	9, Apr. 1857	L3
McGroarty, Mary Ann	Doniphan, David A.	16, Jan. 1845	L3
McGuigan, Mary Ann	Case, John	8, Oct. 1840	L3
McGuire, Louisa W.	Jones, Michael	23, Mar. 1854	L3
McHenry, Eliza A.G.	Price, William T.	17, Oct. 1826	L3
McHenry, Mary	Godley, John	28, June 1820	L3
McIlvain, Mary R.	Rogers, Joseph H.	22, Jan. 1846	L3
McIlvaine, Emily R.	Hewson, John H.	17, Jan. 1856	L3
McIlvaine, Mary Coxe	Dubois, George (Rev)	24, Aug. 1848	L3

Brides	Grooms	Date of Notice	Page
McIntire, Mary E.	Muselman, Edward M.	6, July 1854	L3
McKeag, Ann	Cook, G.T.	8, June 1843	L3
McKee, Emma	Elston, William	26, May 1842	L3
McKee, Kate	Guthrie, Robert	2, May 1850	L3
McKee, Martha J.	Kennet, William (Dr)	11, May 1854	L3
McKee, Noami	Coffin, Dennis H.B.	8, Jan. 1846	L3
McKenney, Agnes	Berry, Hubbard	21, Apr. 1817	L3
McKim, Emma	Guzsi, John R.	12, Mar. 1846	L3
McKim, Frances A.C.	Churchill, David	25, Feb. 1825	L3
McKim, Sarah T.	Seibert, Christian	2, Jan. 1845	L3
McKinnell, Anna	Hill, Joseph S.	10, July 1845	L3
McKinney, Frances (Mrs)	Dubois, John	17, Jan. 1850	L3
McKnight, Eliza	Youart, Samuel	28, Mar. 1810	L3
McKnight, Elizabeth	Bayley, James K.	11, Mar. 1816	L3
McKnight, Mary	Reeder, Jesse	15, Apr. 1816	L3
McLaughlin, Elizabeth	Morris, Daniel	26, May 1807	L3
McLaughlin, Nancy J.	Doering, Charles H.	19, Oct. 1843	L3
McLean, Arabella S.	Slough, John P.	3, Feb. 1853	L3
McLean, Caroline A.	Sehon, Edmund W.	12, Sept 1833	L4
McLean, Eliza	Young, Isaac	25, Jan. 1844	L3
McLean, Eliza L.	Dunham, William	18, Feb. 1841	L3
McLean, Mary B.	Minor, John D.	4, Jan. 1844	L3
McLean, Mattie	Pollock, John D.	10, Jan. 1856	L3
McLenan, Jane	Henry, John	18, Feb. 1847	L3
McLenan, Margaret	LaBoyteaux, Isaac N.	27, Nov. 1856	L3
McMahan, Elizabeth D.	Speer, John	28, July 1842	L3
McMahon, Elizabeth	Is--g, Daniel	16, June 1817	L3
McMaine, Mary L.	Fishback, William P.	22, Feb. 1855	L3
McManama, Sallie	Carson, Oliver H.	21, May 1857	L3
McMaster, Sarah	Ernst, Jacob	27, Mar. 1851	L3
McMeen, Mary A.	Johnston, Archibald	29, Mar. 1855	L3
McMicken, Lizzie	Stille, D.P.	18, Dec. 1856	L3
McMicken, Mary	Perin, Franklin	4, July 1844	L3
McMillan, Mollie E.	Harper, James S.	7, Aug. 1856	L5
McMillen, Catharine	Hartgrove, Nelson	26, May 1842	L3
McMullen, Martha	McMullen, Samuel	18, Apr. 1850	L3
McMurray, Catharine	Dellinger, A.F.	4, Aug. 1836	L3
McMurry, Catharine	McCreight, Thomas	9, Feb. 1809	L3
McNaughton, Sarah M.	King, Edward A.	3, June 1841	L3
McNickle, Mary Jane	Ball, George W.	24, June 1841	L3
McNicoll, Mary A.	Duhme, Herman	18, Feb. 1847	L3
McNulty, M. Louisa	Sturgus, John J.	24, Dec. 1857	L3
McNutt, Sarah	Burch, William	15, Aug. 1810	L3
McOliff, M. Cecilia	Magurk, Michael J.	6, May 1841	L3
McPeak, Anna	Carpenter, C.	14, Sept 1848	L3
McPherson, Mary Jane	Crawford, William	28, Sept 1848	L3
McQuilty, Martha Ann	Keneday, Lester	13, Feb. 1845	L3
McReynolds, Mary E.	Marlay, Joseph K.	18, Sept 1856	L5
McRobert, Lucitty J.	Horton, Henry Hall	27, Nov. 1845	L3
Mead, Rebecca	Ward, Josiah	29, Oct. 1846	L3
Meader, Miriam	Stone, Hubbard	21, Sept 1854	L3
Meadowcroft, Mary A.	Dunlap, Charles C.	30, Oct. 1851	L3
Meads, Eliza Jane	Clement, William B.	7, Sept 1843	L3
Meady, Eliza (Mrs)	Lusk, Uzal B.	1, Apr. 1847	L3

Brides	Grooms	Date of Notice	Page
Meara, Catharine M.	Stewart, M.A.	5, June 1845	L3
Mears, Eliza Lucinda	Stoms, William	19, Oct. 1837	L3
Mears, Esther R.	Whetstone, Thomas H.	24, Sept 1840	L3
Mears, Mary	Lynes, William	21, Aug. 1811	L3
Medaris Lizzie J.	Neave, Thomson	5, Nov. 1857	L3
Medarra, Susanna	Winall, George W.	16, July 1840	L3
Medary, Catharine E.	Warden, William W.	10, Oct. 1844	L3
Medary, E. Virginia	Wilson, Henry	14, Dec. 1843	L3
Medary, Sarah A.	Massey, Thomas Edwin	28, Jan. 1847	L3
Meers, Sallie Dogget	Allen, Alfred F.	18, Sept 1845	L3
Meginnis, Margaret	Hartpense, Isaac	23, Feb. 1837	L4
Meigs, Mary	Jackson, John G.	22, Aug. 1810	L3
Meline, Catharine A.	Lucas, Edward	22, Feb. 1838	L3
Mendenhall, Mary Ann	Adam, George N.	16, Feb. 1854	L3
Menefee, Frances A.	Taylor, R.M.W.	7, Sept 1843	L3
Menkin, Rosina	Rosenstiel, Lewis S.	12, Feb. 1846	L3
Meranda, Amanda	Moore, Isaac	9, Nov. 1854	L3
Meritt, Eliza R.	Leonard, William	24, Dec. 1857	L3
Meriweather, L. (Mrs)	Griffith, Romulus R.	1, June 1848	L3
Meriweather, Louisa	Griffiths, Romulus R	25, May 1848	L3
Merrell, Nettie	Bocking, Adolph H.	14, July 1853	L3
Merrick, Elizabeth (Mrs)	Powell, Ellick	15, Sept 1821	L3
Merrie, Jane	McCulloch, Robert	30, July 1819	L3
Merrie, Mary Ann	Harrison, John Pitts	24, May 1838	L3
Merril, Caroline	Buffington, Francis	2, Feb. 1854	L3
Merrill, Adaline	Davis, Judson	25, Sept 1856	L5
Merrill, Lydia S.	Rhodes, William	7, July 1853	L3
Merrill, Martha S.	Aiken, Charles	29, Nov. 1855	L3
Merrit, Catharine	Lackey, Ira	22, June 1822	L3
Merrit, Margaret	Thomas, James	27, Oct. 1812	L3
Merriwether, Rachel	Griffith, Romulus R.	29, June 1827	L3
Metcalf, Elizabeth	Halderman, W.N.	7, Nov. 1844	L3
Metcalfe, Jane R.	Jones, E.A. (Dr)	8, May 1845	L3
Metcalfe, Mary J.	Kemper, J.L.	19, Aug. 1847	L3
Metcalfe, Sarah H.	Callihan, Henry (Dr)	11, Jan. 1844	L3
Michell, Catharine R	Tull, Beverly W.	27, Aug. 1857	L3
Middleton, Caroline	Reeves, Mark E.	13, Sept 1849	L3
Middleton, Elizabeth J.	Shoemaker, J.W.	9, Feb. 1854	L3
Middleton, Lydia	Stephens, Isaac	28, Oct. 1847	L3
Miles, Caroline	Little, George	28, Jan. 1841	L3
Miles, Pamela E.	Fraser, Alexander J.	9, June 1853	L3
Miles, Polly	Fairbanks,	28, Mar. 1810	L3
Milholland, Mary	Pottenger, Harden	16, Feb. 1854	L3
Miller, Amelia	Meeker, John C.	1, Oct. 1840	L3
Miller, Ann	Wescott, Leonard W.	16, Mar. 1849	L3
Miller, Betsey	Broughard, James	16, Sept 1816	L3
Miller, Caroline	Shumard, John	9, Sept 1852	L3
Miller, Catharine	Custenbarder, Daniel	26, Jan. 1854	L3
Miller, Catharine A.	Biggs, Thomas R.	2, Apr. 1846	L3
Miller, Catharine J.	Rogers, R.	25, July 1850	L3
Miller, Elizabeth	Harris, Thomas M. (Dr)	3, Mar. 1836	L2
Miller, Elizabeth A.	Wagener, James	16, Feb. 1854	L3
Miller, Ellen P.	Pike Samuel N.	5, Nov. 1846	L3
Miller, Emilia	Wright, Samuel	10, Nov. 1853	L3

Brides	Grooms	Date of Notice	Page
Miller, Fanny B.	Thorp, George S.	23, Sept 1852	L3
Miller, Hannah	Kautz, Jacob	27, Jan. 1806	L3
Miller, Harriet	Woodward, E.W.	1, Mar. 1855	L3
Miller, Janet	Sanford, Edwin	24, Feb. 1848	L3
Miller, Jeannette A.	Schenck, Woodhull	21, Oct. 1841	L3
Miller, Julia Ann	Otter, Abraham(Capt)	6, July 1837	L3
Miller, Lizzie (Mrs)	Bailey, M.	18, June 1857	L3
Miller, Lizzie A.	Degraw, P.G.	18, Nov. 1847	L3
Miller, Lucinda(Mrs)	Perrine, Robert	13, July 1843	L3
Miller, Lydia L.	Coe, Stephen W.	17, Aug. 1848	L3
Miller, Martha	Riddle, Andrew	2, Dec. 1847	L3
Miller, Mary	Fox, Charles	10, Dec. 1824	L2
Miller, Mary A.	Gibson, Henry H.	13, Oct. 1853	L3
Miller, Mary E.	Loyd, John F. (Rev)	27, Apr. 1854	L3
Miller, Risyiah	Hudson, Ed	2, Dec. 1841	L3
Miller, Sarah A.	Jackson, James	23, Dec. 1847	L3
Miller, Sarah Belle	Pugh, Jordan A.	9, June 1842	L3
Miller, Sarah J.	Rowland, T.	16, Nov. 1854	L3
Miller, Sarah Jane	Taylor, Gabriel A.	23, Sept 1847	L3
Miller, Sarah K.	Gatton, Zachariah	15, Apr. 1847	L3
Millin, Lucinda	Jenkins, Richard	6, Apr. 1854	L3
Millin, Sarah	Ellis, Simon	6, Apr. 1854	L3
Mills, Abigail	Benson, Gabriel	14, Apr. 1820	L3
Mills, Julia L.	Hazen, William L.	4, Nov. 1847	L3
Mills, Mary	Wesco, Franklin	9, Mar. 1854	L3
Mills, Phoebe H.	Boal, Robert, Jr.	6, Jan. 1817	L3
Miner, Cynthia H.	Thorpe, Coleman	2, Oct. 1845	L3
Miner, M.J.	Stockton, J.B.	7, Sept 1848	L3
Miner, Mary	Wharton, Henry	1, Aug. 1839	L3
Minere, Sarah	Casey, Charles E.	9, Dec. 1847	L3
Miniear, Mary	McFeely, James (Dr)	13, Sept 1849	L3
Minor, Rebecca	VanHamm, Washington	16, Jan. 1851	L3
Minshall, Mary F.	Ferris, John	22, Apr. 1847	L3
Mitchell, Ann	Mann, John	5, June 1851	L3
Mitchell, Cora	Downs, Arthur D.	8, Jan. 1857	L3
Mitchell, Eliza	Snowdon, Sidney	31, Aug. 1837	L3
Mitchell, Helen M.	Anderson, Yeatman	4, June 1857	L3
Mitchell, Margaret	Dillen, John	16, Feb. 1854	L3
Mitchell, Mary	Huntington, John C.	7, Sept 1848	L3
Mitchell, Mary Ann	Jenkins, Thomas	1, Nov. 1855	L3
Mitchell, Mary Ann	Short, J. Cleves	2, Aug. 1849	L3
Mitchell, Melinda	Goodlett, Nicholas	16, Feb. 1854	L3
Mitchell, Sarah	Southard, Isaac	12, Nov. 1846	L3
Mix, Chloe P.	Akin, Macaully	8, May 1845	L3
Mix, Eliza (Mrs)	Lewis, William	14, Feb. 1839	L3
Mixer, Julia A. (Mrs)	Austin, Seneca	10, Sept 1840	L3
Moberly, Asenath S.	Sellars, Eliphalet D	9, Mar. 1854	L3
Moehring, Flora	Bettmann, M.	23, Oct. 1845	L3
Moffatt, Alletha	Beaty, James M.	23, Mar. 1854	L3
Moffett, Anna	Moore, Robert	31, Jan. 1856	L3
Moffett, Catharine	Addams, A. (Dr)	24, Apr. 1845	L3
Moland, Louisa	Webb, Joseph	18, Aug. 1817	L3
Moller, Clara P.	Barr, Sterret	16, Sept 1847	L3
Mollyneaux, Mary B.	Milliken, Minor	11, Sept 1856	L5

Brides	Grooms	Date of Notice	Page
Monahon, Dorcas	Knowlton, Sherman	20, May 1847	L3
Monroe, Maria	Tucler, Daniel E.	24, Nov. 1821	L2
Montague, Sarah R.	Flagg, Jared B.	20, Jan. 1842	L3
Montgomery, Polly	Bennett, William	21, Apr. 1821	L3
Moody, Margaret C.	Medary, George W.	15, Feb. 1849	L3
Moody, Mary Louisa	Barnard, William C.	29, May 1851	L3
Mooklar, Anna	Pope, J.P.	20, Oct. 1853	L3
Mooney, Mary	Thirkield, Thornton	26, Dec. 1844	L3
Moore, Agnes A.	Ferguson, E.A.	25, Sept 1851	L3
Moore, Amelia C.	Lawrence, John H.	12, Sept 1850	L3
Moore, Anna Maria	Vattier, John L. (Dr)	18, Dec. 1845	L3
Moore, Caroline	Chamberlaine, James	3, Oct. 1823	L3
Moore, Eliza	Rodes, Philip A.	9, Feb. 1854	L3
Moore, Eliza F.	Cassel, John F.	1, July 1847	L3
Moore, Elizabeth	Ritchie, Casper	11, Aug. 1853	L3
Moore, Emeline	Fore, P.G. (Dr)	12, Dec. 1839	L3
Moore, Frances Ann	Fulweiler, John	20, Dec. 1838	L3
Moore, Jane	Miller, Henry	3, July 1811	L3
Moore, Jane	Morrison, Joseph	22, June 1854	L3
Moore, Jennie C.	Reed, Erastus R.	5, May 1853	L3
Moore, Lucinda	Morgan, Andrew J.	12, June 1845	L3
Moore, Lucy	Wright, Williamson	7, June 1855	L3
Moore, Maria	Ward, Squire	11, Mar. 1815	L3
Moore, Martha	Champian, Thomas	28, Nov. 1826	L3
Moore, Mary	Partridge, Sanford S	29, Jan. 1852	L3
Moore, Mary	Stowe, Daniel C.	18, Oct. 1849	L3
Moore, Mary Ann	Marshall, James B.	15, Oct. 1829	L4
Moore, Matilda	Sweat, John	5, Dec. 1844	L3
Moore, Nancy M.	Pierson, Charles E.	20, Nov. 1845	L3
Moore, Peggy	Stow, E.	24, Mar. 1807	L3
Moore, Rebecca Ann	Tilley, D.B.	4, June 1857	L3
Moore, Sarah C.	McIntyre, George	6, Mar. 1845	L3
Moore, Sarah J.	Ferguson, John	11, Jan. 1849	L3
Moore, Sophia D.	Pugh, James B.	21, July 1853	L3
Moorhead, Elizabeth B.	Hammond, Smallwood C	14, Jan. 1836	L4
Moorman, Emily	Teach, David	12, Jan. 1854	L3
Morales, Ana	Burdsal, Henry W.	13, Apr. 1848	L3
Morecraft, Emily	Lowry, John A.	6, Mar. 1845	L3
Morehead, Eliza	McClain, James	13, Jan. 1824	L3
Morehead, Lucy A.	Gore, John H.	24, Sept 1846	L3
Morehouse, Mary E.	Jones, James W.	15, Jan. 1857	L3
Moreland, Mary Ann	Hart, Matthew	12, Feb. 1846	L3
Morgan, Abbie C.	Herman, Samuel	27, Apr. 1854	L3
Morgan, Cornelia M.	Pendleton, Edmund	20, Feb. 1845	L3
Morgan, Martha G.	West, D.S.	8, Apr. 1841	L3
Morgan, Mary Ann	Ager, John	22, Oct. 1857	L3
Morgan, Sarah	Swain, William P.	2, Aug. 1849	L3
Morley, Lucy Jane	Banks, Francis R.	24, Nov. 1853	L3
Morrill, Ann Maria	Cobb, Jedediah	13, June 1826	L3
Morris, Belle	Hankins, William J.	18, Nov. 1852	L3
Morris, Cornelia M.	Arthur, B.H.	18, Jan. 1855	L3
Morris, Esther	Boyer, John	7, Jan. 1820	L3
Morris, Jane	Harbeson, Matthew L.	20, Oct. 1831	L1
Morris, Jane	Rust, Joseph G.	9, June 1836	L3

Brides	Grooms	Date of Notice	Page
Morris, Jane C.	Turner, William	25, Nov. 1825	L3
Morris, Mary Ann	Campbell, John S.	9, Feb. 1854	L3
Morris, Mary J.	Blackston, B.D. (Dr)	27, Apr. 1848	L3
Morris, Mary Jane	Barwise, Luther T.	25, Sept 1851	L3
Morris, Rebecca	Thomas, E. Sydney	3, Feb. 1848	L3
Morrison, Ann E. (Mrs)	Harrison, George W.	18, Apr. 1839	L3
Morrison, Eliza D.	Tait, George	20, May 1830	L3
Morrison, Emily M.	Renshaw, William	8, June 1848	L3
Morrison, Kate	Marshall, Alfred	11, June 1857	L3
Morrison, Mary	Eldickin, John C.	17, Feb. 1848	L3
Morrow, Amanda	Tolbert, Martin	9, Mar. 1848	L3
Morrow, Ursula	Hovey, James	4, July 1844	L3
Morse, Mary Jane	Dyer, A.F.	24, Feb. 1848	L3
Morsell, Hester C.	McConkey, Benjamin M	6, July 1843	L3
Morten, Tabitha A.	Harvey, George	23, Mar. 1843	L3
Morton, Anne (Mrs)	Hilton, Thomas	12, Dec. 1844	L3
Morton, Mary Ann	Read, Francis	8, Aug. 1823	L3
Mortz, Caroline	Judah, Judah	7, Sept 1843	L3
Mosby, Ann (Mrs)	Mosby, Napoleon B.	18, Apr. 1844	L3
Mose, Catharine Ann	Heytep, Solomon	6, Apr. 1854	L3
Moses, Sarah Ann	Myers, Abraham	5, July 1838	L3
Mosier, Elizabeth Y.	Bourgoin, Alexis J.	21, June 1849	L3
Moss, Lucinda	Major, John	13, Apr. 1848	L3
Moss, Minerva	Harrison, Gustavus	20, Mar. 1851	L3
Motz, Angie (Mrs)	Ware, Thomas C.	26, Feb. 1852	L3
Moulton, Elizabeth	Johnson, Samuel	11, Jan. 1844	L3
Mount, Louisa	Hamm, John	14, July 1853	L3
Mount, Nancy	Blakely, John	3, July 1845	L3
Moyer,	Delap,	30, Dec. 1847	L3
Muchmore, Sarah (Mrs)	Clark, Orgia	3, Aug. 1813	L3
Muckelvar, Nancy	Denen, James M.	17, Mar. 1842	L3
Mudge, Caroline W.	Weed, P.L.	27, June 1850	L3
Mulford, Gabriella	Lockwood, Daniel H.	28, Dec. 1848	L3
Mulford, Harriet P.	Craven, Gershom S.	16, Sept 1820	L3
Mulford, Mary R.	Davenport, Darius G.	2, June 1853	L3
Mullen, Sarah B.	Ingalsbe, L.	21, Nov. 1844	L3
Munday, Mary A.	Hawkins, Theobald E.	7, Dec. 1854	L3
Munford, Eliza Jane	Orr, Thomas	1, Aug. 1844	L3
Munford, Ella C.	Armstrong, H.G.	13, July 1854	L3
Munroe, Bernice	Fletcher, Calvin	12, Aug. 1816	L2
Munroe, Cornelia A.	Frintz, Michael	19, Aug. 1847	L3
Murch, Hannah	Austin, James S.	2, July 1840	L3
Murdock, Adelia	Armstrong, Leonard L	3, Aug. 1848	L3
Murdock, Jane H.	Risk, E.F.	7, May 1846	L3
Murphy, Jane	Brachman, William	9, Mar. 1854	L3
Murphy, Margaret J.	Wetherow, John	26, Feb. 1852	L3
Murphy, Melinda	Watt, Anthony	14, Oct. 1852	L3
Murray, Elizabeth	Bagley, Thomas	18, Feb. 1847	L3
Murray, Isabella	Owen, John	8, Feb. 1838	L3
Murry, Frances	Hugle, James	23, Oct. 1856	L5
Murry, Margaret	Watt, Hugh	30, Mar. 1854	L3
Musick, Lucinda	Willi, Samuel	15, May 1827	L3
Mussey, Catharine S.	Hartwell, Shattuck	2, Aug. 1849	L3
Mussy, Mary L.	Mason, Lyman	2, June 1853	L3

Brides	Grooms	Date of Notice	Page
Myers, Anna S.	Fisher, George	16, Nov. 1854	L3
Myers, Elizabeth	Ayres, Samuel	4, Aug. 1806	L3
Myers, Frances Jane	Jones, Robert	29, June 1843	L3
Nancarrow, Polly	Thompson, Thomas	24, Feb. 1806	L3
Nash, Anna E.	Myers, William W.	4, Nov. 1852	L3
Neal, Georgiana	Yocum, Horatio N.	29, Oct. 1857	L3
Neave, Anna E.	Lupton, D.B.	11, Apr. 1839	L3
Neblett, Sarah S.	Lovejoy, Henry B.	8, July 1841	L3
Nedy, Elizabeth	Lupton, Thomas	29, Nov. 1838	L3
Neff, Jane B.	Williams, Cyrus M.	1, July 1847	L3
Nehemiah, Sarah	Palmer, Abraham	2, May 1844	L3
Neil, Elizabeth J.	King, Thomas W.	10, Apr. 1845	L3
Nelson, Caroline A.	Brough, John	21, Sept 1843	L3
Nelson, Delila W.	Young, J. Wesley	7, Dec. 1843	L3
Nelson, Mary	Laws, Edward (Dr)	31, May 1855	L3
Nelson, Mary Ann	Benson, James	13, Sept 1849	L3
Nesmith, Margaret	Taylor, George	6, June 1844	L3
Nesmith, Margaret M.	Taylor, George R.	6, June 1844	L3
Nevens, Cornelia	Fry, J. Reese	17, June 1841	L3
Neville, Cornelia	Graham, James	17, Oct. 1844	L3
Nevins, Mary L.	Neil, William A.	30, June 1853	L3
Newbury, Lydia A.	St.Johns, Job	24, Dec. 1840	L3
Newbury, Mary Ann	Bozarth, William M.	19, Oct. 1843	L3
Newman, Adaline	Martin, John R.	5, Mar. 1846	L3
Newman, Christina	Mason, Zelotes H.	28, Dec. 1837	L3
Newport, Sarah E.	Thompson, Samuel	12, Jan. 1854	L3
Newton, Sophia F.	Stewart, G.H. (Dr)	24, July 1845	L3
Nicholas, Huldah	Miller, Z.B.	18, Apr. 1844	L3
Nicholas, Libby J.	Curme, Arthur A.	30, Oct. 1856	L5
Nicholas, Lydia Ann	Sutton, Joseph M.	24, May 1849	L3
Nicholas, Margaret	Magee, Jacob	25, Aug. 1817	L2
Nicholas, Mary E.	Hurd, L.	28, Aug. 1845	L3
Nicholas, Ruth W.	Sayre, George E.	15, June 1854	L3
Nicholson, Susannah	Wilson, John James	8, July 1847	L3
Niles, Christina	Clark, James	16, Jan. 1845	L3
Niles, Cornelia	Hansell, Wm. F.(Rev)	8, Feb. 1855	L3
Niles, Helen M.	Chapman, William	23, Oct. 1856	L5
Niles, Mary L.	Warwick, Samuel H.	6, Feb. 1827	L2
Nixon, Elizabeth A.	Smith, James R.	15, Apr. 1847	L3
Nixon, Elizabeth Adelia	Smith, James R.	8, Apr. 1847	L3
Nixon, Rachel E.	Murphy, Andrew	16, Feb. 1854	L3
Noble, Lizzie	Cheever, John H.	10, Nov. 1853	L3
Noble, Mary	Acton, Clement J.	22, Jan. 1846	L3
Noble, Mary F.	Estep, Richard	7, July 1842	L3
Noble, Matilda (Mrs)	Wales, John W.	27, Apr. 1837	L3
Noble, Melissia O.	Parker, Alexander C.	9, Nov. 1848	L3
Noble, Sarah Jane	Hazlett, John	9, Nov. 1848	L3
Noblock, Mary	Bennett, Charles	10, Oct. 1844	L3
Nolan, Susan C.	Holmes, Benjamin	6, Aug. 1857	L3
Norman, Sarah E.	Jones, J.J.	12, Sept 1850	L3
Norris, Fannie	Guibert, Ben. J.	20, Oct. 1853	L3
Norris, Martha	Thompson, Francis	9, Sept 1847	L3
Norris, Mary E.	Snyder, Charles W.	22, Dec. 1842	L3

Brides	Grooms	Date of Notice	Page
Norris, Virginia	Blackburn, Edward C.	25, Jan. 1844	L3
North, Jane W. (Mrs)	Treatt, Isaac	26, Aug. 1841	L3
North, Lucy D.	Bishop, John M.(Rev)	19, Nov. 1846	L3
Northrop, Adaline	Richards, John (Capt)	6, Aug. 1846	L3
Norton, Joanna	Hauk, Columbus B.	8, Feb. 1844	L3
Nottingham, Mary	Stillman, George K.	12, Feb. 1846	L3
Nut, Hetty	McClean, Nathaniel	17, Jan. 1810	L3
Oakes, (Miss)	Greatwood, G.	25, Sept 1811	L3
Oberdorf, Mary E.	Andrew, Peter	27, Mar. 1845	L3
Odell, Aurora S.	Harkness, William	21, Sept 1848	L3
O'Ferrall, Catharine	Miller, Richard	22, Nov. 1825	L3
O'Ferrall, Jane B.	Davis, Timothy	26, Nov. 1857	L3
Offley, Rachel	Shepherd, J.W.	14, Oct. 1852	L3
Ogden, Fannie L.	Holmes, Francis M.	18, Oct. 1849	L3
Ogden, Maggie M.	Stevenson, B.D.	23, Apr. 1857	L3
Ogden, Ruth N.	Stonemitz, David H.	22, July 1816	L2
Ogle, Harriet	Traber, Joseph	27, Nov. 1845	L3
Oiriel, Charlotte	Budden, Edward	27, Aug. 1857	L3
Oldaker, Mary E.	Kirkhart, John	9, Feb. 1854	L3
Oldaker, Roxolina	Hulse, James	9, Feb. 1854	L3
Oldham, Irene	Burns, James A.	29, Nov. 1855	L3
Oldrieve, Emilia	Johnson, Henry W.	24, June 1852	L3
Oldrieve, Prothesia	Gooch, John S.	16, June 1853	L3
Oldson, Mary Ann	Reese, George L.	2, Jan. 1845	L3
Oliver, (Miss)	Spencer, Oliver	15, Jan. 1805	L3
Oliver, Eliza Ann	Loring, Allen	27, May 1841	L3
Oliver, Elizabeth T.	Hartwell, John W.	4, Mar. 1847	L3
Oliver, Frances E.	Cooper, James	30, Apr. 1840	L3
Olmsted, Eloise B.	Stettinius, John L.	22, June 1854	L3
Omstead, Martha B.	Lee, R.W.	28, Sept 1848	L3
O'Neal, Mary Anne	Longshore, Abner	4, May 1848	L3
O'Neil, Clara M.	Wright, Abram L.	12, Jan. 1854	L3
O'Neill, Julia F.	Daniels, Hector L.	26, Nov. 1846	L3
Oppenheim, Martha	Jonas, Joseph	29, Nov. 1838	L3
Oppenheimer, Lydia	Ottenheimer, Morris	21, Dec. 1837	L3
Orange, Martha	Slevin, R.D.	31, July 1851	L3
Orange, Rebecca H.	Cones, W.M.	3, Mar. 1853	L3
Ordeman, Methe	Suhr, H.W. (Rev)	12, June 1845	L3
O'Reiley, Cecelia	Christie, John	7, Jan. 1847	L3
O'Reilly, Catharine	Shepherd, M.L.	18, Jna. 1838	L3
Ormiston, Elizabeth	Lillie, John	16, Feb. 1854	L3
Ormon, Eliza	Skelton, Josiah W.	11, Aug. 1812	L3
Ormsby, Oliveretta	Wharton, Clifton	30, Aug. 1838	L3
Orr, Eliza (Mrs)	Matthews, W.	16, July 1840	L3
Orr, Lydia S.	Riddle, George W.	2, Jan. 1851	L3
Orr, Mary Jane	Polley, Charles C.	8, Oct. 1846	L3
Osborn, Ann	Rowan, Matthew B.	28, Oct. 1847	L3
Osborn, Margaret A.	McGrew, Alexander	19, Apr. 1825	L3
Osborn, Mary Ann	Jones, Samuel A.	25, Sept 1851	L3
Osburn, Mary Ann	McGrew, William C.	11, Feb. 1841	L3
Otis, Sarah H.	Ernst, A.H.	7, Oct. 1841	L3
Otsen, Margaret	Smith, Thomas	9, Mar. 1848	L3
Ottenheimer, Louisa	Griffin, John	3, Sept 1846	L3

Brides	Grooms	Date of Notice	Page
Oulton, Emily	Holenshade, John H.	12, Feb. 1857	L3
Ousley, Martha	Plummer, Aaron	9, Feb. 1854	L3
Owens, Elizabeth	Pearce, Henry	19, Aug. 1847	L3
Owens, Jane	McDonald, Isaac	31, Dec. 1840	L3
Owens, Mary Ann	Howell, Edward	16, Feb. 1837	L3
Owens, Mary Ann Jane	Myers, Elkunah	12, July 1849	L3
Owens, Sallie J.	Pearce, Henry	8, Jan. 1857	L3
Paddack, Rebecca	Haven, James L.	4, July 1850	L3
Page, Jennie Byrd	Bryan, Thomas B.	5, Dec. 1850	L3
Page, Maria C.	Brown, James	16, Dec. 1830	L4
Page, Martha	Avery, Charles L.	10, June 1847	L3
Pagget, Elizabeth (Mrs)	Howard, James P.	18, Apr. 1844	L3
Palmer, Florinda C.	Easton, George	6, June 1839	L2
Palmer, Mary	McBratney, Robert	6, Apr. 1848	L3
Palmer, Mary E.	Cooper, James	8, Nov. 1855	L3
Palmer, Mary M.	Judkins, William	9, Sept 1841	L3
Pancoast, Mary A.	Burnham, Nathan C.	3, Nov. 1842	L3
Pangburn, Martha	Tibbets, Robert	14, Mar. 1823	L3
Paris, Mary E.	Jackson, Charles J.	17, Dec. 1857	L3
Park, Elizabeth	King, James	5, Jan. 1827	L3
Park, Margaret	McKeely, James H.	5, Jan. 1854	L3
Parker, Ann	Tealen, Robert	10, Jan. 1839	L3
Parker, Elizabeth	Lindsay, John	18, Apr. 1844	L3
Parker, Elizabeth Ann	McLaughlin, Zenas K.	30, Jan. 1845	L3
Parker, Ellen	Maghee, J.H.	8, Jan. 1835	L1
Parker, Eunice	Stites, Robert	24, Aug. 1843	L3
Parker, Jennie	Hale, William B.	13, Sept 1855	L3
Parker, Julia A.	Camac, P.S.	10, Nov. 1842	L4
Parker, Lizzie	Gallespie, Philander	23, Nov. 1854	L3
Parker, Margaret L.	Moody, James E.	24, July 1851	L3
Parker, Mary	McMellen, Isaac	1, Aug. 1844	L3
Parker, Mary L.	Stewart, Benjamin M.	30, Sept 1852	L3
Parker, Priscilla	Brewster, O.S.	13, Sept 1838	L3
Parker, Susanna E.	Donaldson, Thomas	7, Sept 1837	L3
Parks, Grizella	Howes, Josiah	17, June 1852	L3
Parmely, Sylvia	Campbell, John L.	16, Jan. 1845	L3
Parmenter, Elizabeth T.	Hunt, Freeman	27, Oct. 1853	L3
Parmetar, Aurelia M.	Edwards, Samuel	26, May 1842	L3
Parms, Winnie Ann	Hill, Francis M.	9, Mar. 1854	L3
Parrott, Frances A.	Matthews, Fitch J.	4, June 1857	L3
Parrott, Josephine	Gaddis, Maxwell P.	17, May 1849	L3
Parry, Sarah R.	John, E.D.	11, Mar. 1841	L3
Parson, Eliza	Arthur, William, Jr.	14, Apr. 1820	L3
Parson, Elizabeth A.	Latta, Alexander B.	28, Oct. 1847	L3
Parsons, Harriet	Brooke, Reston S.	5, Apr. 1825	L3
Parsons, Mary E.	Robson, William H.	23, Apr. 1857	L3
Parsons, Olivia Jane	McCormick, Edward	9, May 1850	L3
Partridge, Sarah P.	Spoffard, A.R.	23, Sept 1852	L3
Parvin, Ruth H.	Mulford, John P.	4, Jan. 1838	L3
Patterson, Amanda	Sellers, Norris	9, Feb. 1854	L3
Patterson, Anna R.	Earhart, J.S.	24, Mar. 1853	L3
Patterson, Eleanor K.	Ells, John	21, July 1842	L3
Patterson, Eliza	White, Joseph (Rev)	10, Nov. 1842	L4

Brides	Grooms	Date of Notice	Page
Patterson, Isabella	Ware, Thomas	2, Feb. 1854	L3
Patterson, Jane	Butler, Thomas S.	2, Dec. 1841	L3
Patterson, Lizzie S.	Smith, Joseph	10, May 1855	L3
Patterson, Margaret	Venable, Samuel (Dr)	19, May 1807	L3
Patterson, Mary	Johnston, J.W.	4, Nov. 1841	L3
Patterson, Sallie E.	Posey, Oliver	5, Nov. 1857	L3
Patterson, Sarah N.	Whicher, William C.	21, Nov. 1844	L3
Patton, Matilda L.	Conklin, I.C.	17, Mar. 1853	L3
Patton, Philinda	Gabriel, Edwin T.	10, Jan. 1839	L3
Payne, Amanda G.	Curd, Thomas H.	19, May 1853	L3
Payne, Eddie A.	Chiles, Hamlet W.	25, Feb. 1847	L3
Payne, Penelope V.	Hopple, Matthew	2, Aug. 1855	L3
Payne, Permelia	Webb, John G.	31, Oct. 1844	L3
Peabody, Mary	Howe, Robert	27, May 1852	L3
Peabody, Sarah	Butler, Selar	30, Jan. 1851	L3
Pearce, Amelia J.	Guthrie, Benjamin F.	26, Oct. 1848	L3
Pearce, Jane	Thomas, D.	9, Mar. 1854	L3
Pearce, Mary	Kirby, Thomas	17, Nov. 1842	L6
Peaslee, Rebecca Ann	McAllaster, Henry	16, Feb. 1854	L3
Peck, Adeline A.	Wilson, Benjamin R.	1, Nov. 1849	L3
Peck, Amanda	Wilson, Edward J.	23, Sept 1847	L3
Peck, Delia	Fuller, John W.	30, Sept 1847	L3
Peck, Emily P.	Stout, Nathaniel R.	6, May 1847	L3
Peck, Harriet J.	Hannaford, John W.	27, Aug. 1857	L3
Peck, Mary G.	Partridge, Charles A	27, May 1852	L3
Peers, Sarah	Averel, Edward	8, Oct. 1840	L3
Peirce, Priscilla	Mode, William	9, Mar. 1854	L3
Pence, Sarah Jane	Stebbens, Uriah	9, Mar. 1854	L3
Pendleton, Anna H.	Schenck, Noah Hunt	20, Nov. 1850	L3
Pendleton, Martha E.	Dandridge, Alexander	11, May 1843	L3
Pendleton, Susan L.	Bowler, Robert B.	27, Oct. 1842	L3
Pendry, Susan B.	Goepper, Leopold	23, Dec. 1852	L3
Pennell, Emma	Sutherland, Robert	28, June 1855	L3
Pennington, Elizabet	Stout, Henry D.	13, Feb. 1845	L3
Pennington, Francis	Comly, James D.	27, Sept 1849	L3
Penton, Rebecca Jane	Dare, Clement	20, Feb. 1845	L3
Perkey, Harriet	Elliott, William	19, Oct. 1843	L3
Perkins, Elizabeth	Little, Benjamin	29, Dec. 1812	L3
Perkins, Harriet M.	Sewell, John W.	9, Sept 1852	L3
Perrine, Sarah	Stevens, E.	7, Oct. 1841	L3
Perry, Ann D. (Mrs)	Burroughs, Thomas N.	27, Aug. 1846	L3
Perry, Betsey	Bechtle, Henry C.	19, Feb. 1816	L3
Perry, Caroline	Buckner, Thomas	8, July 1820	L3
Perry, Catharine	Ferguson, Addison M.	6, Feb. 1824	L3
Perry, Elizabeth C.	Wayne, Henry	2, Nov. 1854	L3
Perry, Hetty A.	Sanxy, Theodore	2, June 1842	L3
Perry, Jemima C.	Ruffner, Henry	15, May 1851	L3
Perry, Margaret J.	Rockey, Henry	30, Jan. 1851	L3
Perry, Martha	Medaris, John (Dr)	8, Mar. 1849	L3
Perry, Martha H.	Hollister, Edward	22, Feb. 1849	L3
Perry, Mary Ann	Wise, John T. (Dr)	25, Nov. 1852	L3
Perry, Mary B.	Hoadly, George	21, Aug. 1851	L3
Perry, Mary C.	Hopkins, John (Rev)	26, Nov. 1840	L3
Perry, Virginia	Davis, James Ward	4, Oct. 1849	L3

Brides	Grooms	Date of Notice	Page
Pest, Ann	Howden, Robert	9, Nov. 1854	L3
Peters, Anna Maria	Ramsey, C. Sample	16, Sept 1841	L3
Pettit, Maria	Dumass, Benjamin	15, Oct. 1819	L3
Pettit, Mary A.	Johnston, Joseph M.	8, Jan. 1846	L3
Peyton, Harriet Jane	Wade, John M.	22, Aug. 1844	L3
Phares, Nancy	Hyter, Abraham	5, June 1816	L3
Phares, Naomi	Looker, Benjamin F.	5, June 1816	L3
Philbeck, Eliza	Pullan, Joseph	5, Aug. 1847	L3
Philips, Sarah	McCarty, Wm. (Rev)	28, July 1806	L3
Philipson, Rosa A.	Mayer, Adolph A.	9, Nov. 1848	L3
Phillips, Belle	Stewart, Ephiram	5, July 1855	L3
Phillips, Frances	Tompkins, Garretson	13, Aug. 1857	L3
Phillips, Jane	Hadley, Milton E.	6, Apr. 1854	L3
Phillips, Mary A.	Guelich, Lewis	21, Oct. 1852	L3
Phillips, Sarah Ann	Anderson, Samuel	10, Nov. 1821	L3
Philpot, Anna	Edwards, John M.	4, July 1844	L3
Philpot, Elizabeth	Coolidge, William	11, May 1843	L3
Phinney, Mary L.	Stone, James S.	21, June 1838	L3
Phipps, E.M.	Gillet, P.G.	11, May 1854	L3
Piatt, Arabella S.	McCullough, William	19, May 1826	L3
Piatt, Carrie C.	Jenkins, Thomas C.	20, Nov. 1856	L3
Piatt, Catharine S.	Lodge, Laban	13, May 1823	L3
Piatt, H.J.	Runkle, Ralph	23, Jan. 1830	L2
Piatt, Hannah A.	Piatt, Abraham S.	26, Nov. 1840	L3
Piatt, Juliet E.	Shumaker, Michael	25, July 1850	L3
Piatt, Nancy	Hamilton, Milton	21, Feb. 1850	L3
Pickering, Emeline M	Miller, Samuel	23, May 1839	L3
Pickering, Lucinda	Copelan, Harvey	16, Feb. 1854	L3
Pickering, Maria	Mustin, C.C.L.	9, Aug. 1855	L3
Picket, Cordelia	Austen, David	14, Nov. 1844	L3
Picket, Sarah Jane	James, Joseph	11, Sept 1845	L3
Pienier, Eliza	Duffield, J.J.	26, May 1836	L3
Pierce, Eunice	Wheelock, Daniel W.	3, Nov. 1817	L3
Pierce, Sally Ann	Worthington, Lewis	12, Oct. 1837	L4
Pierson, Clara	Howe, F.S. (Rev)	28, Mar. 1844	L3
Pierson, Mary Ann	DeWitt, G.V.H.	21, May 1819	L3
Pierson, Mary R.	Harrison, Livingston	26, Oct. 1822	L3
Pigman, Caroline F.	Purdy, John E.	20, Apr. 1854	L3
Pike, Clarissa B.	Harrison, J.C.S.	5, Oct. 1819	L3
Pike, Lucy A.	Develin, James	27, Nov. 1856	L3
Pile, Josephine S.	Hawes, Dan	22, Oct. 1846	L3
Pine, Matilda M.	Embick, Michael D.	27, Jan. 1842	L3
Pinkstun, Mary Ann	McDowell, Robert V.	10, Dec. 1857	L3
Pinney, Emeliza E.	Fee, William M.	9, Oct. 1851	L3
Pitcher, Laura	O'Donnell, Hugh	12, Oct. 1837	L4
Pittick, Mariamar C.	Louderback, Jacob P.	23, Feb. 1843	L3
Place, Lucy A.	Aubery, William A.	5, Mar. 1840	L3
Plasket, Mary Jemima	Pragoff, William	12, Sept 1833	L1
Plate, Louisa M.	Allen, Fernian	16, Feb. 1854	L3
Platt, Mary K.	Youmans, M.G.	19, Mar. 1857	L3
Pleasants, Frances	Febiger, George L.	8, Nov. 1855	L3
Plummer, Mary B.	Spahr, Benjamin	9, Jan. 1845	L3
Pocock, Julia Ann	Kinsey, David	9, Feb. 1843	L3
Pocock, Temperance	Kinsey, Edward	28, Jan. 1841	L3

Brides	Grooms	Date of Notice	Page
Pogue, Lida J.	Gartzell, Henry C.	3, Nov. 1853	L3
Poignand, Eliza	Weissinger, George W	30, Sept 1847	L3
Poineer, Adeline	Merrill, Robert, Jr.	18, July 1826	L3
Poinier, Cornelia S.	Biggs, H.W. (Rev)	25, Aug. 1853	L3
Poinier, Jane	Smith, James M.	22, May 1845	L3
Pointer, Mary Ann	Knies, John K.	1, July 1820	L3
Pollard, Mary Eliza	Williams, Cyrus M.	19, Aug. 1852	L3
Pollard, Sarah T.D.	Clarke, R.W.	26, Jan. 1843	L3
Pollock, Rebecca S.	Henning, John	20, Nov. 1856	L3
Pomeroy, Mary Russel	Irwin, Thomas	14, Jan. 1836	L1
Pool, Amanda (Mrs)	Campbell, Thomas	9, Feb. 1854	L3
Poor, Anne	Behne, Theodore D.	17, Aug. 1854	L3
Pope, Margaret	Baldwin, O.W.	18, Jan. 1855	L3
Porter, Abby H.	Stedman, George T.	20, Feb. 1845	L3
Porter, Mary Elizabeth	Leitch, William	12, Mar. 1846	L3
Porter, Mary Jane	Lemon, Randall	11, Feb. 1847	L3
Postlethwait, Anne M	Worthington, James T	26, Sept 1850	L3
Potter, Adeline E.	Peck, Charles A.	17, Mar. 1842	L3
Potter, Ann Jane	Scudder, Sidney	18, Feb. 1847	L3
Potter, Harriet A.	Boal, Isaac A.	11, May 1854	L3
Pottinger, Mary Ann	Duval, John	7, Feb. 1856	L3
Pouder, Elizabeth	Collier, William E.	22, May 1851	L3
Powell, Amelia	Doolittle, Henry	27, May 1852	L3
Powell, Lizzie	Cox, Jerome	17, Apr. 1851	L3
Powell, Mary Ann	Pruden, Andrew	26, Aug. 1841	L3
Powers, Frances	Massalski, Joseph	7, July 1836	L4
Powers, Lydia S.	Morris, William R.	13, May 1823	L3
Powlon, Rosanna	Elder, James	2, May 1844	L3
Pratt, Betsey	Broadwell, John	14, Apr. 1817	L3
Preble, Henrietta	Beall, A.W.	16, Feb. 1854	L3
Preston, Mary Ann	Francis, Thomas	31, Aug. 1843	L3
Preston, Mary Ann E.	Smith, Chester	12, Apr. 1849	L3
Price, Anna Eliza	Moore, Robert M.	4, May 1843	L3
Price, Clementine A.	Wilkins, S.C.	10, Feb. 1848	L3
Price, Elizabeth	Cooper, Jonas	29, Dec. 1821	L3
Price, Harriet	Logan, David O.	26, Jan. 1854	L3
Price, Harriet	Rose, Timothy	25, Mar. 1818	L3
Price, Margaret S.	Gano, Daniel, Jr.	13, Apr. 1848	L3
Price, Martha W.	Gebhart, Isaac	12, Jan. 1854	L3
Price, Mary	Goodman, John S.	9, Oct. 1851	L3
Price, Mary	Sheldon, J.A.	5, Oct. 1848	L3
Price, Mary A.	McDuffie, J.T.	14, July 1853	L3
Price, S.J.	Howe, Hammond	13, Sept 1838	L3
Prickett, Matilda A.	Dodds, Preston C.	16, Feb. 1854	L3
Priest, Sarah Maria	Well, William F.	16, Mar. 1854	L3
Protsman, Annie	Temple, Charles W.	1, Nov. 1855	L3
Prouty, Ann Janette	Hervey, Thomas	4, Jan. 1844	L3
Pugh, Leah	Marshall, Vincent C.	22, July 1820	L3
Pugh, Mary A.	Hart, Samuel	10, June 1841	L3
Pullan, Eliza	Stephens, Isaac	16, May 1839	L3
Punshon, Jane	Owen, John	9, May 1839	L3
Punshon, Mary E.	Ramsay, William E.	9, Sept 1847	L3
Punshon, Rachel	Thistlewaite, James	16, Feb. 1837	L3
Purcell, Harriet	Johnson, Alexander B	25, Dec. 1845	L3

Brides	Grooms	Date of Notice	Page
Purlier, Elizabeth	Philip, Bernhard	11, Sept 1845	L3
Purlier, Pauline	Borgman, Charles H.	29, Nov. 1855	L3
Putnam, Levina	Dill, Joseph	1, Oct. 1824	L3
Quinton, Ella A.	Morgan, Samuel J.	25, Sept 1856	L5
Quinton, Sarah Ann	Wayne, Charles	29, May 1828	L1
Raguet, Lillie	Preston, A.J.	19, Jan. 1854	L3
Raines, Vashti N.	Pike, John W.	30, Mar. 1854	L3
Ramsay, Hannah	Stevens, Elijah	12, Mar. 1829	L2
Ramsdale, Juliann	Jordan, Daniel B.	10, May 1832	L3
Ramsdale, Mary	Daniels, Archer D.	7, Dec. 1843	L3
Ramsey, Eliza (Mrs)	Taliaferro, W.T.(Dr)	27, Apr. 1843	L3
Ramsey, Margaret E.	Lawrence, William	5, Aug. 1847	L3
Ramsey, Mary	Raper, Holley	14, Mar. 1844	L3
Ramsey, Sarah L.	Irwin, William	23, Aug. 1838	L3
Rand, Emeline	Florer, Robert C.	21, Feb. 1839	L3
Randle, Mary	Hixson, James	14, Mar. 1844	L3
Randolph, Harriet W.	White, Albert S.	9, Feb. 1843	L3
Rands, Katharine	Black, Reuben	25, June 1846	L3
Raper, Margaret	Cartrite, William	16, Feb. 1854	L3
Raphael, Adelaide	Haskins, Charles	1, July 1847	L3
Rappalee, Mary Ann	Badger, William	15, Oct. 1846	L3
Rarns, Mary	Elstner, John	14, Mar. 1823	L3
Ratliffe, Nancy (Mrs)	Dunnington, Alex.	2, Mar. 1854	L3
Rauch, P.B. (Mrs)	Hiester, J.P. (Dr)	1, Aug. 1844	L3
Raxter, Eliza	Baldwin, John W.	22, Oct. 1846	L3
Ray, Ann W.	Healy, Jesse	17, Oct. 1844	L3
Ray, Anna	Holt, George H.	15, Apr. 1852	L3
Ray, Catharine W.	Bruce, Isaac	7, Nov. 1844	L3
Rayl, Polly	Crowell, Martin	25, Apr. 1810	L3
Raymond, Cora O.	Layton, James M.	9, Jan. 1851	L3
Raymond, Harriet R.	Fosdick, Sylvester L	19, May 1821	L3
Rayner, Helen M.	Aldrich, Edwin R.	26, Aug. 1852	L3
Read, Martha A. (Mrs)	Worthington, James T	11, Dec. 1856	L3
Read, Mattie L.	Woodworth, George	30, Oct. 1856	L5
Reakirt, Anna Maria	Thompson, Moses F.	24, Feb. 1853	L3
Reakirt, Arabella C.	Donaldson, William	26, Mar. 1857	L3
Rechie, Mary	Lovie, Henri	15, Sept 1853	L3
Reck, Emma L.	Bryarby, Charles W.	10, Apr. 1845	L3
Redhead, Jane	Froome, Samuel	10, Dec. 1840	L3
Redhead, Martha Ann	Sherlock, Thomas	1, Apr. 1847	L3
Redman, Anna Lizzie	Howell, H. Scott	26, Oct. 1854	L3
Reed, Angeline F.	Thorp, David W.	6, Nov. 1845	L3
Reed, Eliza M.	Bright, Ethelbert B.	28, Mar. 1839	L3
Reed, Elizabeth	VanCamp, John	30, Oct. 1856	L5
Reed, Margaret A.	DeSerisy, Louis	4, Sept 1845	L3
Reed, Mary Ann	Tyler, George	13, Apr. 1854	L3
Reed, Sarah A.	Stratton, Samuel S.	11, May 1854	L3
Reeder, Caroline A.	Follin, Augustus	16, Sept 1847	L3
Reeder, Caroline B.	Donahou, John W.	1, Mar. 1849	L3
Reeder, Charlotte M.	Boyd, Charles	15, Apr. 1852	L3
Reeder, Mary S.	McAlister, William R	6, Mar. 1845	L3
Reeder, Phebe W.	Schenck, William R.	7, Sept 1822	L3

Brides	Grooms	Date of Notice	Page
Rees, Ann	Jones, Cadwalader	29, Oct. 1846	L3
Rees, Mollie M.	Mullen, James	5, Nov. 1857	L3
Reese, Mary Jane	Paris, Peter	1, July 1847	L3
Reeves, Ellen T.	Brown, William H.	10, Nov. 1842	L4
Reeves, Mary	Miller, Henry B.	10, June 1841	L3
Regor, Prudence A.	Moore, T.S.	10, Dec. 1840	L3
Reid, Agness	Key, William J.	28, Dec. 1843	L3
Reid, Anna Maria	Bosson, Joseph	18, Nov. 1823	L3
Reid, Isabella M.	Williams, William B.	14, May 1857	L3
Reilly, Mary Ann	Irwin, A.R. (Capt)	17, Dec. 1846	L3
Reily, Jane	Campbell, Lewis D.	14, Jan. 1836	L2
Remlinger, Mary	Wiseman, Thomas	17, Feb. 1848	L3
Renard, Elizabeth	Renout, Charles E.	17, July 1851	L3
Rennick, Allisonia	Todd, James M.	3, June 1847	L3
Renshaw, Geraldine F	Wilson, Charles	15, Apr. 1852	L3
Renshaw, Mary S.	Cist, L.J.	27, May 1847	L3
Replogle, Sarah Ann	Reid, Henry	9, Mar. 1854	L3
Resor, Elizabeth	Wilson, Joseph	30, Mar. 1824	L2
Resor, Gertrude C.	Shays, Charles M.	29, Oct. 1857	L3
Revill, Amelia	Teal, Samuel R.	12, July 1827	L1
Rex, Anna S.	Winters, John	22, July 1816	L2
Rex, Maria C.	Bruner, Moses	22, July 1816	L2
Reynolds, Clara J.	Duble, John A.	12, Aug. 1847	L3
Reynolds, Cornelia	Allen, Joseph H.	9, July 1857	L3
Reynolds, Elizabeth	Bonner, David	24, Mar. 1806	L3
Reynolds, Elizabeth	Perry, Benjamin P.	4, July 1850	L3
Reynolds, Lydia B.	Phipps, William R.	5, June 1851	L3
Reynolds, Mary L.	Coleman, John	12, Feb. 1857	L3
Reynolds, Rebecca	Harrison, George	14, Jan. 1820	L3
Reynolds, Sarah	Fisher, William L.	27, Dec. 1814	L3
Rhoades, Mary E.	Bushnell, A.L.	4, Sept 1851	L3
Rhoades, Mary Jane	Brew, Thomas	30, Oct. 1851	L3
Rice, Eliza A.	Matson, William D.	23, Nov. 1837	L3
Rice, Frances P.	Nichols, John D.	2, Sept 1831	L2
Rice, Lucy	Smith, F.	11, May 1822	L3
Rice, Susan C.	Smith, S.W.	8, Sept 1842	L3
Rich, Caroline (Mrs)	Dunn, Samuel	22, Jan. 1852	L3
Rich, Eliza L.	Crawford, Henry B.	23, Feb. 1854	L3
Richards, Elizabeth A.	Gilbert, A.W.	25, May 1848	L3
Richards, Mary E.	Garrison, D.L.	10, May 1855	L3
Richards, Mary W.	Rawson, Joseph	6, Dec. 1838	L3
Richardson, Abigail	Adams, William	8, May 1811	L3
Richardson, Anna J.	MacDonald, Alexander	30, Dec. 1852	L3
Richardson, Elizabeth C.	Shattuck, William B.	30, May 1850	L3
Richardson, Elizabeth F.	Saunders, William	24, Nov. 1812	L3
Richardson, Isabella	Tibbits, Samuel	23, Oct. 1845	L3
Richardson, Laura M.	Jocelyn, Augustus	22, Dec. 1831	L2
Richardson, Louisa M.	Dilworth, Joseph	17, Jan. 1850	L3
Richardson, Rebecca	Judy, George H.	2, Feb. 1854	L3
Richardson, Rosetta	Gotchell, Alfred	19, Mar. 1857	L3
Richey, Belle	Morrison, James	20, Apr. 1854	L3
Richey, Frances B.	Burr, Edward M.	26, Aug. 1852	L3
Ricker, Leontine C.	Lakin, John S.	8, Apr. 1852	L3
Riddle, Eliza Jane	Roll, Edward C.	15, Jan. 1846	L3

Brides	Grooms	Date of Notice	Page
Riddle, Lucinda	Mufford, Howell	6, June 1844	L3
Riester, Mary	Baumann, John	22, June 1854	L3
Riggle, Sarah Jane	Buchanan, Robert	13, May 1847	L3
Riley, Amanda	Stewart, Samuel M.	9, May 1844	L3
Riley, Sarah A.	Hull, D.P.	27, May 1847	L3
Risinger, Sarah W.	Edwards, Edwin	27, May 1847	L3
Ritter, Lina	Zimmerman, John	12, July 1855	L3
Rives, Anna	Longworth, Joseph	27, May 1841	L3
Rives, Margaret	King, Rufus	25, May 1843	L3
Roads, Elizabeth H.	Swan, John M.	5, Nov. 1846	L3
Roberts, Lucy B.	Cox, Rudolph	11, Oct. 1838	L3
Roberts, Margaret	Carter, James H.	6, Jan. 1848	L3
Robertsn, Mary H.	Whitton, John Burns	23, May 1839	L3
Robertson, Jane	Heron, John	14, June 1849	L3
Robertson, Louisa	Allen, James G.	15, June 1854	L3
Robeson, Margaret	Bunnel, Benjamin	10, Nov. 1821	L3
Robinson, Ann Eliza	Lawson, L.M. (Dr)	17, Aug. 1848	L3
Robinson, Elizabeth	McClain, Edward A.	8, Jan. 1846	L3
Robinson, Elizabeth (Mrs)	Hillerman, William J	8, Mar. 1849	L3
Robinson, Ellen	Conner, Thomas H.(Dr	8, May 1845	L3
Robinson, Isabella	Gardener, Lafayette	30, Oct. 1851	L3
Robinson, Louisa J.	Edminster, James C.	6, Apr. 1854	L3
Robinson, Margaret B	Hann, George W.	16, Sept 1847	L3
Robinson, Martha A.	Barker, Emery B.	19, Dec. 1844	L3
Robinson, Mary Ann	Marsh, Richard	9, Mar. 1854	L3
Robinsn, Mary Ellen	Glidden, D.A.	24, Aug. 1848	L3
Robinson, Sarah F.	Palmer, George F.	30, Oct. 1856	L5
Rockey, Catharine O.	Pendry, John L.	17, June 1847	L3
Rockwood, Amanda J.	Lape, Jacob S.	1, Jan. 1852	L3
Rodes, Belle	McDowell, J.H.	6, Jan. 1853	L3
Roe, Sallie A.	Evans, Owen	24, Dec. 1846	L3
Rogers, Ann Eliza	Deeds, Isaac W.	9, May 1818	L3
Rogers, Elizabeth	Wayman, Henry W.	31, Apr. 1845	L3
Rogers, Fanny	Markland, Benjamin	22, Mar. 1814	L3
Rogers, Isabella	Kinsey, Abram G.	23, Oct. 1856	L5
Rogers, Julia M.	Chittenden, Edward F	18, Feb. 1836	L3
Rogers, Mary Elizabeth	Meline, James F.	3, Sept 1846	L3
Rogers, Semor A.	Lane, Andrew	24, Sept 1840	L3
Rolef, Mary E.	Cottam, Richard	9, May 1844	L3
Rollin, Mary A.	Garwood, Nicholas	17, June 1847	L3
Rose, Isabel	Shaddinger, Anderson	20, Aug. 1846	L3
Rose, Pamela	Dodson, Edward	30, Dec. 1806	L3
Rose, Parmelia D.	Oakley, Lester	15, Feb. 1844	L3
Roseboom, Martha R.	Simpkinson, Charles	31, Dec. 1857	L3
Ross, Charlotte	Nathorst, John	18, Apr. 1844	L3
Ross, Elizabeth	Kitchell, Wickliff	26, Feb. 1812	L3
Ross, Ellen Luella	Powell, W.S.	26, Jan. 1843	L3
Ross, Esther	Cory, Jonathan L.	21, Apr. 1820	L3
Ross, Frances Ellen	Downing, Hollis	9, Mar. 1854	L3
Ross, Lydia	Warren, Cyrus M.	20, Sept 1849	L3
Ross, Margaret (Mrs)	Heaver, William	25, Feb. 1847	L3
Ross, Mary Ann C.	Lyan, Andrew Madison	16, Nov. 1848	L3
Ross, Nancy	English, Benajah	1, June 1819	L3
Ross, Susannah	Billings, Charles F.	25, Feb. 1841	L3

Brides	Grooms	Date of Notice	Page
Rosyell, Louisa E.	Armstrong, James S.	1, July 1847	L3
Rowland, Mildred (Mrs)	Mackay, John	31, May 1855	L3
Ruckle, Catharine C.	Strickler, John	18, Aug. 1842	L3
Rudor, C.L.	Allen, John (Dr)	12, Nov. 1846	L3
Ruff, Ann Maria	Rodiffer, Joseph	28, Jan. 1841	L3
Ruffin, Eliza	Oliver, William (Capt)	26, Apr. 1814	L3
Ruffin, Frances	Hopkins, William H.	26, Apr. 1814	L3
Ruffin, Mary	Rockey, Henry	11, Nov. 1820	L3
Ruffner, Eliza Ann	Dransfield, Henry F.	11, May 1848	L3
Ruffner, Minerva J.	Wilson, Jesse P.	2, Mar. 1848	L3
Rush, Harriet E.	Brockenbrough, John	24, Feb. 1853	L3
Russell, Adeline	Crosley, Henry	7, Feb. 1850	L3
Russell, Angeline	Faran, James J.	2, Apr. 1840	L3
Russell, Eliza	Bradford, Daniel	17, Mar. 1807	L3
Russell, Eliza	Robertson, William	4, Oct. 1849	L3
Russell, Emeline V.	Shipley, John P.	12, Oct. 1848	L3
Russell, Helen M.	Holmes, Charles S.	20, Oct. 1853	L3
Russell, Mary	Butler, James J.	25, July 1850	L3
Russell, Mary E.	Hughart, John	10, Nov. 1853	L3
Russell, Mary Jane	Newhall, Charles H.	25, Mar. 1852	L3
Russell, Minerva	Davis, Werter R.(Rev	18, May 1843	L3
Russell, Sarah Jane	Lovell, Oliver S.	19, Jan. 1843	L3
Russell, Sarah V.	Ewing, James H	25, Apr. 1844	L3
Russell, Theodosia G	Armstrong, John H.	30, Mar. 1849	L3
Ruter, Amanda S.	Dufour, Oliver	12, May 1842	L3
Rutgers, Cornelia	Butler, James J.	2, Jan. 1845	L3
Ruth, Emily H.	Collins, Isaac C.	5, Feb. 1852	L3
Rutherford, Mary J.	Adams, Christopher T	10, Mar. 1853	L3
Rutherford, Sarah J.	Talbott, Isaiah L.	7, Jan. 1847	L3
Rutherford, Virginia	Shaw, John A.	28, May 1846	L3
Rutledge, Lucy Jane	Clason, Lewis W.	28, Oct. 1847	L3
Ryan, Julia	Emerson, Edwin S.	17, Apr. 1851	L3
Ryder, Caroline	White, Isaac H.	17, Aug. 1848	L3
Ryder, Margaret	Butler, James Oliver	26, Jan. 1843	L3
Ryland, Caroline	Thompson, R.E.	6, Sept 1849	L3
Ryland, Louisa	Keckler, Adolphus T.	28, July 1853	L3
Ryland, Mary S.	Russell, John H.W.	7, Dec. 1848	L3
Sackett, Jane Ann	Pearce, Christopher	22, Oct. 1840	L3
Saffin, Susan L.	Hart, William	24, Oct. 1850	L3
Salvin, Elizabeth T.	Harris, Daniel	2, Sept 1852	L3
Sampson, Belle	Lennan, D.B.	8, Mar. 1855	L3
Sampson, E.O.	Hoyt, J.W.	7, Dec. 1854	L3
Sampson, Martha	Stephens, Elihu	3, Oct. 1844	L3
Sampson, Mary	Farquhar, William P.	10, Sept 1835	L3
Sanders, Emily F.	Foster, J.G.	20, Mar. 1851	L3
Sanders, Julia E.	Comly, Richard N.	16, May 1833	L4
Sanderson, Frances	Baldwin, Edwin J.	9, Mar. 1854	L3
Sandford, Antoinette	Sanders, Alford	14, Apr. 1842	L3
Sandford, J.	Johnson, Campbell	3, Feb. 1824	L3
Sanxay, Charlotte	Calhoun, James	5, Sept 1844	L3
Sare, Mary Ann	Yates, Charles J.	14, Mar. 1844	L3
Sargent, Mary	Smith, Winthrop B.	13, Nov. 1834	L2
Sargent, Selina B.	Clark, Augustus	14, Mar. 1839	L3

Brides	Grooms	Date of Notice	Page
Satcher, Marian	Patmore, John	9, Sept 1847	L3
Saunders, Martha (Mrs)	Matthews, Joseph M.	16, Feb. 1854	L3
Savill, Ellen	Bennington, Samuel	13, Sept 1849	L3
Sawain, M. Louise	Foster, A.M.	27, Nov. 1851	L3
Sawtell, Lydia Jane	Woolley, Lell H.	14, Apr. 1853	L3
Sawyier, Mary A.	Hotchkiss, Henry O.	3, June 1841	L3
Saxton, Harriet S.	Finch, Joel	4, July 1844	L3
Sayre, Ann	Glenn, James	20, May 1820	L3
Sayre, Ann	Ledman, Samuel F.	18, Oct. 1838	L3
Sayre, Margaret	Sharpless, Thomas	27, Nov. 1822	L3
Sayre, Polly	Heckewelder, Thomas	27, Feb. 1811	L3
Schaffer, Catharine	Herzog, William	5, Nov. 1846	L3
Schatzman, Julia A.	Curtis, Herschel C.	29, Jan. 1846	L3
Scheidler, (Mrs)	Runge, William	1, Aug. 1850	L3
Schell, Hannah F.	Cox, R.S.	3, Feb. 1855	L3
Schenck, Jeannette A	Craighead, Samuel	10, Feb. 1853	L3
Schenck, Lucy H.	Burrows, Joseph H.	29, Aug. 1844	L3
Schenck, Mary B.	Butler, Charles	13, Feb. 1845	L3
Schenck, Mary Eliza	Denise, Denise	5, Oct. 1843	L3
Schenck, Phebe W.	Schenck, John N.C.	12, Oct. 1843	L3
Schillinger, Philomena	Sigerson, John	3, Nov. 1836	L3
Schillinger, Priscilla	Armstrong, Arthur E.	2, Nov. 1837	L4
Schnetz, Anna A.	Hickman, E.R.	20, Aug. 1857	L3
Schooley, Augusta	Tillotson, Edward R.	5, Dec. 1844	L3
Schooley, Mary	Burnet, William	22, Oct. 1857	L3
Schooley, Rebecca R.	Pepper, James H.	7, Nov. 1844	L3
Schruke, Sophia	Secrist, John M.	20, Nov. 1850	L3
Schulze, Adelaid	McCormick, Benjamin	10, Sept 1857	L3
Schwartz, Charlotte	Hafer, Henry	30, Jan. 1824	L2
Scixas, Rachael A.	Jonas, Joseph	23, Dec. 1823	L3
Scofield, Emeline	Stoton, Eli	13, Nov. 1845	L3
Scogin, Polly	Demoss, Peter	25, Apr. 1810	L3
Scott, Ann	Reed, Daniel	12, Feb. 1805	L3
Scott, Annie	Burgess, George H.	25, Sept 1856	L5
Scott, Catharine	Carbert, Thomas (Rev)	2, Oct. 1845	L3
Scott, Eliza	McLane, Henry	19, June 1851	L3
Scott, Henrietta E.	Cleveland, George P.	27, Nov. 1834	L2
Scott, Jane	Eaton, John	6, Jan. 1848	L3
Scott, Jane A.	Mitchell, William	6, Apr. 1848	L3
Scott, Lizzie	Lord, Russell E.	8, Feb. 1849	L3
Scott, Susan C.	Withers, Rolla M.	4, May 1848	L3
Scowdon, Sarah Ann	Kernes, Thomas	31, Dec. 1835	L3
Scribner, Sarah B.	Osburn, Stephen	21, Oct. 1847	L3
Scudder, Sarah L.	Hand, George R.	28, Jan. 1841	L3
Scull, Letitia	Niles, William B.	1, Dec. 1853	L3
Seaman, Mary Ann (Mrs)	Fordney, Beates	16, Oct. 1845	L3
Sedam, Eliza	Reed, Joseph	28, Jan. 1847	L3
Sedam, Mary Jane	Smith, William B.	2, Oct. 1851	L3
Sedam, Melinda	Symmes, Henry	17, Sept 1846	L3
See, Julia H.	Malone, H.B.	1, Dec. 1853	L3
Seely, Eliza	Antsim, Cyrus	6, Feb. 1851	L3
Seever, Anna	Robinson, Webster	8, Oct. 1857	L3
Sefton, Elizabeth N.	Adams, John Q.	13, Apr. 1854	L3
Seiter, Mary Louisa	Price, Rees B.	22, Jan. 1857	L3

Brides	Grooms	Date of Notice	Page
Sellman, Harriet Key	Nelson, Herron (Dr)	31, Dec. 1857	L3
Semple, Anna G.	Cook, Theodore	2, Oct. 1856	L5
Sennett, Helen M.	Trusdale, Charles	26, July 1849	L3
Severns, Rebecca	Collord, W.A.	15, Oct. 1846	L3
Seybold, Isabella	Wilson, John S.	2, Mar. 1854	L3
Seymour, C. Jane	Hall, Mitchell	6, June 1850	L3
Seymour, Emila	White, William E.	3, Mar. 1821	L3
Seymour, Jane	Wolf, Michael	4, June 1824	L3
Seymour, S. Emily	Tolle, W.B.	13, Nov. 1850	L3
Seymour, Sarah	Moonert, Augustus	14, Sept 1848	L3
Shackelton, Eliza P.	Meeker, Moses	6, Apr. 1837	L3
Shafor, Catharine	Lefferson, James B.	4, Oct. 1849	L3
Shak, Mary S.	Brooks, Thomas B.	13, Aug. 1857	L3
Shane, Araminta E.	Williamson, Alex. W.	21, Oct. 1847	L3
Shane, Mary Jane	Rogers, John W.	22, Apr. 1847	L3
Shannon, Isabella	Cline, John	17, Aug. 1813	L3
Sharp, Jennie	Thayer, William H.	8, Nov. 1855	L3
Sharp, Mary A.	McGibbens, David	21, Oct. 1847	L3
Sharp, S. Caroline	Fowler, John	26, Aug. 1847	L3
Sharpe, Fannie H.	Bradley, Lewis A.	6, July 1854	L3
Sharpless, Susan	Shawley, Lewis	21, May 1829	L3
Shaw, Ellen	Cole, John F.	23, Feb. 1854	L3
Shaw, Margaret S.	Freeman, W.D.	9, Aug. 1855	L3
Shaw, Martha E.	Palmer, William E.	22, Oct. 1857	L3
Shaw, Sarah	Hungarford, Richard	6, Mar. 1811	L3
Shaw, Zoe	Logan, C.A. (Dr)	13, Apr. 1854	L3
Shays, Frances C.	Lockwood, Daniel	8, June 1837	L2
Shays, Sallie C.	White, Julian	5, July 1855	L3
Shears, Jane	McTiernan, James	2, Oct. 1851	L3
Sheeler, Kate	Rowland, George E.	7, June 1849	L3
Shelby, Letitia	Todd, Charles S.	1, July 1816	L3
Sheldon, Rebecca A.	Lawder, John B.	26, May 1842	L3
Shellman, Rachael	Weymouth, J.H.	30, Mar. 1854	L3
Shelton, Amanda C.	Alden, George W.(Dr)	27, May 1847	L3
Shepherd, Mary P.C.	Harding, Lyman	12, Jan. 1837	L3
Shephert, Nancy	Mount, Robert M.	19, Jan. 1843	L3
Sheppard, Ella V.	Lewis, B.F.	13, Nov. 1856	L3
Shepperd, Mary E.	Foster, J.G.	20, Sept 1855	L3
Sherwin, Charlotte	Cathcart, David	4, Feb. 1818	L2
Shields, Julia M.	Newcomb, John M.	29, Jan. 1846	L3
Shields, Sarah A.M.	Fagaly, Lewis C.	17, May 1855	L3
Shingledecker, Jem.	Driver, James S.	17, Aug. 1848	L3
Shingledecker, Mary	Driver, Lucien	11, Apr. 1844	L3
Shipley, Elizabeth C	Taylor, James	31, Oct. 1844	L3
Shipman, Julia E.	Goodman, Timothy S.	19, Oct. 1848	L3
Shipman, Tryphene	Williams, Cornelius	8, Sept 1806	L3
Shoemaker, Elizabeth R.	Taylor, A.M.	14, Sept 1848	L3
Shoenberger, Elizabeth	Lytle, Edward H.	4, Oct. 1838	L3
Short, M.E.	Harshberger, Jacob	26, Jan. 1854	L3
Shoup, Emma	VanTuyl, Abram	9, Mar. 1854	L3
Shoyer, Mary Jane	Fine, John	14, Oct. 1847	L3
Shreve, Mary	Pierce, Joseph(Capt)	7, July 1831	L3
Shuff, Margaret	Long, George W.	2, Mar. 1854	L3
Shultz, Mary B.	O'Connell, Daniel A.	11, Aug. 1853	L3

Brides	Grooms	Date of Notice	Page
Shwebel, Eliza	Schuster, Paul	18, Sept 1851	L3
Sibley, Caroline	Evans, William L.	10, Apr. 1851	L3
Siebenthal, Anna (Mrs)	Daughlade, John L.A.	20, Feb. 1824	L3
Silsbee, Mary	Allen, Charles Henry	3, Apr. 1851	L3
Silsbee, Mary	Bennett, D.V.	25, May 1843	L3
Silver, Margaret M.	Rowse, John B.	25, Dec. 1845	L3
Simmons, Sallie A.	Dial, William C.(Dr)	22, Nov. 1855	L3
Simms, Honora A.	Schoolfield, John Q.	1, Jan. 1846	L3
Simns, Esther Ann	Hargan, James	31, Oct. 1850	L3
Simpson, Elizabeth	Keckley, William Hy.	13, Feb. 1845	L3
Simpson, Genett	Pike, Samuel T.	22, Feb. 1855	L3
Simpson, Mary	Brackenridge, Wm.	23, Nov. 1843	L3
Simpson, Nancy	Pomroy, Caleb M.	16, Oct. 1834	L1
Singer, Catharine	Gaskill, John C.	2, Jan. 1845	L3
Singer, Mary Jane	Bassford, Thomas	28, Jan. 1841	L3
Singer, Sallie A.	Sprigman, J.A.	24, May 1855	L3
Sinks, Belle	Parrott, George	12, Nov. 1857	L3
Sissbee, Anna	Resor, Jacob	23, Oct. 1845	L3
Sisson, Grace	Henrie, Arthur	25, Sept 1811	L3
Sisson, Mary	Gardner, Richard	4, Aug. 1817	L3
Skaats, Catharine E.	Angevine, Charles	20, Nov. 1845	L3
Skiff, Ruby S.	Seymour, Henry F.	5, Oct. 1843	L3
Skillman, Sarah E.	Morris, J.F.	21, June 1855	L3
Slack, Hannah (Mrs)	Wilson, Nathan	16, Mar. 1854	L3
Slack, M. Josephine	Talasfero, Charles W	12, Dec. 1839	L3
Slack, Rebecca (Mrs)	Hickox, Hiram S.	1, Apr. 1852	L3
Slaughter, Sarah	Center, Hartzill H.	22, Feb. 1849	L3
Slayback, Elizabeth	Sanford, D.W.C.	1, Feb. 1849	L3
Slayback, Hannah W.	Frizzell, Hugh W.	20, July 1854	L3
Slevin, Maria L.	Quinn, J.J. (Dr)	8, July 1852	L3
Slocum, Elizabeth F.	Ogborn, W. Elwood	11, June 1846	L3
Sloop, Elizabeth	Waterhouse, Josiah	9, Feb. 1822	L3
Smart, Mary W.	Godden, Edward	23, May 1844	L3
Smith, Agnes A.	Armstrong, John W.	27, Sept 1838	L3
Smith, Alice	Winston, A.V.	18, Jan. 1855	L3
Smith, Amelia	Platt, William H.	10, May 1855	L3
Smith, Ann B.	Morgan, Hugh	26, May 1842	L3
Smith, Ann F.	Dill, William J.	10, Jan. 1850	L3
Smith, Anna R.	Kirkland, John A.	26, Apr. 1855	L3
Smith, Caroline	Clement, William H.	11, Sept 1851	L3
Smith, Caroline A.	Febriger, George L.	12, Apr. 1849	L3
Smith, Carrie B.	Godley, George H.	24, Dec. 1857	L3
Smith, Catharine	Spooner, William L.	5, Nov. 1840	L2
Smith, Catharine	Pickens, James S.	27, Aug. 1857	L3
Smith, Catharine	Resin, Samuel	10, May 1855	L3
Smith, Clarissa	Huston, James H.	5, Jan. 1809	L3
Smith, Edith C. (Mrs)	Simonton, Richard	12, Dec. 1844	L3
Smith, Eliza	Sterling, Samuel G.	22, Dec. 1842	L3
Smith, Eliza (Mrs)	Wright, John F.(Rev)	12, Feb. 1846	L3
Smith, Eliza Ann	Latta, Finley	25, Mar. 1841	L3
Smith, Eliza B.	Rhodes, Thomas F.	11, July 1839	L3
Smith, Elizabeth	Brown, Richard F.	30, July 1840	L3
Smith, Emily	Roe, Daniel	7, Nov. 1821	L3
Smith, Eve	Underwood, John	26, May 1842	L3

Brides	Grooms	Date of Notice	Page
Smith, Fanny O.	Moore, John M.	20, Apr. 1848	L3
Smith, Frances	Brown, P.Y.	26, June 1851	L3
Smith, Frances M.	Todd, John P.	23, Nov. 1837	L3
Smith, H.C.	Wilson, J.W.	27, May 1847	L3
Smith, Hannah	Morris, Lorenzo D.	22, June 1843	L3
Smith, Harriet	Harp, David	28, Oct. 1847	L3
Smith, Henrietta S.	Mason, Edwin	16, Sept 1852	L3
Smith, J. Loue	Hawthorne, Lee Roy	3, Jan. 1856	L3
Smith, Jerusha	Stephens, Benjamin R	23, Jan. 1851	L3
Smith, Julia S.	Winston, John P.	7, Sept 1837	L3
Smith, Kate	Morgan, George W.	21, Sept 1854	L3
Smith, Kate C.	French, J.H.	22, Sept 1853	L3
Smith, Lizzy G.	Morgan, Edward S.	3, June 1847	L3
Smith, Louisa	Pierce, James	20, Apr. 1848	L3
Smith, Lucy A.	Haile, Andrew J.	19, May 1842	L3
Smith, Lucy Ann	Young, George H.	23, Oct. 1834	L2
Smith, Lydia	Russel, Jonathan	28, Apr. 1817	L3
Smith, Margaret J.	Butler, E.S.	25, Feb. 1847	L3
Smith, Maria	Coulson, Edward	31, Dec. 1846	L3
Smith, Marion G.	Whetstone, Richard A	6, May 1847	L3
Smith, Martha	Moss, Lewis	8, Feb. 1849	L3
Smith, Martha M.	Green, John W.	24, Feb. 1848	L3
Smith, Mary	Garrett, E.J.	26, May 1842	L3
Smith, Mary A.	Corbin, James B.	15, Sept 1853	L3
Smith, Mary Ann	Simms, Robert E.	17, Feb. 1848	L3
Smith, Mary Ann	Thompson, Samuel G.	25, Mar. 1847	L3
Smith, Mary Ann	Walker, James	18, July 1850	L3
Smith, Mary Ann	Sellman, Carberry J.	27, Oct. 1831	L4
Smith, Mary E.	Wright, John R.	12, June 1851	L3
Smith, Mary Eliza	Franklin, William	16, Sept 1841	L3
Smith, Mary F.	Prentiss, Charles S.	26, Jan. 1854	L3
Smith, Mary J.	Sargent, Edward	9, Oct. 1845	L3
Smith, Mary Jane	Irwin, William	18, Jan. 1832	L4
Smith, Mary Jane N.	Head, James Edward	29, July 1847	L3
Smith, Mary Rebecca	Duncan, Lucius C.	28, Sept 1854	L3
Smith, Mary Rebecca	Mead, John	5, Oct. 1843	L3
Smith, Nancy Jane	Potter, Thaddeus	9, Feb. 1854	L3
Smith, Peggy	Brown, James	29, May 1811	L3
Smith, Phebe Jane	Weaver, Israel	25, Sept 1845	L3
Smith, Rebecca	Neff, Ambrose W.	29, Aug. 1850	L3
Smith, Rebecca F.	Taylor, Charles A.	15, Oct. 1857	L3
Smith, Rosa M.	Donnel, W.S.H.	12, Jan. 1854	L3
Smith, S.M.	Holliday, Joseph	27, May 1847	L3
Smith, Sarah	Armstrong, James	14, Apr. 1820	L3
Smith, Sarah	Shepherd, Stephen	7, Oct. 1841	L3
Smith, Sarah B.	Mercer, Lucius	26, Jan. 1854	L3
Smith, Sarah H.	Geisendorff, Conrad	18, Jan. 1855	L3
Smith, Sarah Jane	Agin, Burroughs	10, Aug. 1848	L3
Smith, Sarah Y.	Estep, Thomas	10, Feb. 1842	L3
Smith, Sophia	VanDusen, J.	15, May 1845	L3
Smith, Susan E.	Crawford, John	9, Oct. 1851	L3
Smith, Susan M.	Goshing, Samuel M.	9, Nov. 1848	L3
Smith, Susanna	Snedicher, Isaac	30, Aug. 1855	L3
Smith, Thomasina C.	Montgomery, Henry J.	16, Sept 1852	L3

Brides	Grooms	Date of Notice	Page
Snider, Calista	Weaver, Phillip	10, May 1855	L3
Snively, Cordelia	Vinnedge, Isaac H.	23, Feb. 1854	L3
Snowden, Nancy	Murphey, A.J.	12, Jan. 1854	L3
Snyder, Anne L.	Brotherton, James H.	16, Mar. 1849	L3
Snyder, Lizzie	Laue, C.M.	7, May 1857	L3
Snyder, Margaret	Moylich, Frank	16, Feb. 1854	L3
Sommerville, Mary	Ellis, Thomas	31, July 1851	L3
Sones, Rebecca	Matthews, Jesse	16, Feb. 1854	L3
Soule, Martha S.	Conwell, Ira (Dr)	6, Apr. 1843	L3
South, Amanda	Harvey, James M.	27, Feb. 1851	L3
Southgate, Ada	Arthur, W.E.	15, Nov. 1855	L3
Southgate, Maria J.	Haws, J.M. (Capt)	5, Feb. 1857	L3
Southgate, Martha C.	Walker, Samuel J.	6, Sept 1849	L3
Soward, Elizabeth	Marshall, N.T. (Dr)	7, May 1846	L3
Soward, Maria C.	McCarty, John	29, May 1845	L3
Spalding, Caroline C	Harrington, James S.	18, Feb. 1847	L3
Spalding, Jane (Mrs)	Marshall, Robert	16, Mar. 1848	L3
Spangler, Lucy V.	McKay, Jacob F.	9, Feb. 1854	L3
Spedden, Blanche	Lumsden, F. Af.	19, Jan. 1843	L3
Speer, Caroline M.	Stephens, Jacob	17, Nov. 1836	L3
Spencer, Dorothy	Rance, Elijah (Rev)	19, Jan. 1854	L3
Spencer, E.M.	Williamson, James T.	11, Jan. 1855	L3
Spencer, Maria F.	Schultz, William J.	16, June 1842	L3
Spencer, Mary Elizabeth	Morton, Aaron Gano	21, Dec. 1843	L3
Spencer, Rhoda	Baldwin, James H.	20, May 1847	L3
Spillard, Elizabeth	Willets, Lindley M.	19, Nov. 1857	L3
Spinks, Elizabeth J.	Mapes, Joel M.	25, Nov. 1847	L3
Spinning, E.L.	McAlpin, George W.	11, July 1850	L3
Spinning, Frances M.	Walker, William H.	2, June 1836	L1
Spinning, Hannah	Argo, Ebenezer	1, Nov. 1849	L3
Spinning, Sarah Ann	Bradbury, Cornelius	24, Nov. 1821	L2
Spinning, Sarah E.	Wiltsee, William P.	26, Jan. 1854	L3
Spooner, Lucy J.	Drake, William	27, Sept 1855	L3
Sprague, Maria B.	Gregory, Uriah	29, Nov. 1849	L3
Sprigman, Augusta C.	Valleau, C.M.	27, May 1841	L3
Sprigman, M. Theresa	Pigman, William P.	12, Jan. 1854	L3
Springer, Elizabeth (Mrs)	Spofford, Jacob F.	5, Nov. 1846	L3
St.Clair, Margaret	Harrison, Henry	30, Sept 1841	L3
St.Clair, Margaret B	Tapscott, George W.	21, July 1836	L2
St.Clair, Nancy M.	Newkirk, Matthew	9, Mar. 1837	L3
Stackhouse, Susanna	Morrell, Daniel J.	20, Feb. 1845	L3
Stacy, Mary Elizabeth	French, William H.	1, Nov. 1849	L3
Stafford, Mary E.	Blakely, Zerah	24, July 1851	L3
Stake, Mary	Steman, Jacob	20, Apr. 1819	L3
Stall, Emma	North, Peter	18, Mar. 1847	L3
Stanbery, Charlotte	Holliday, Nathan	22, Oct. 1840	L3
Stanbery, Clara	Neff, George W.	10, Jan. 1856	L3
Stanbery, Frances	Impey, Robert	22, Oct. 1840	L3
Stanford, Sarah Jane	March, George P.	5, Oct. 1848	L3
Stanislaus, Catharine	Embich, Michael D.	22, Feb. 1855	L3
Stanley, Emma	Kirkup, Joseph	2, Jan. 1851	L3
Stapley, Ann	Hutton, John	6, July 1843	L3
Stapley, Elizabeth	Harberson, Robert W.	2, May 1844	L3
Starbuck, Deborah	Dodson, William B.	9, Dec. 1825	L3

Brides	Grooms	Date of Notice	Page
Starr, Elizabeth	Ward, L.B.	26, July 1849	L3
Starr, Mary	Barnes, John C.	16, Mar. 1849	L3
Statenfield, Elizabeth	Miller, Henry F.	9, Sept 1852	L3
Stauffer, Josephine	Oates, John	3, Jan. 1856	L3
Stearnes, Bulah Ann	Gilman, William	6, Mar. 1845	L3
Steedman, Alvena P.	Keelor, Alexis	15, Oct. 1857	L3
Steele, Lydia Ann	Golding, Robert J.	5, Nov. 1846	L3
Steinkamp, Elizabeth	Liebern, John N.	30, Jan. 1845	L3
Stephens, Hannah	Potts, William Henry	2, Feb. 1837	L4
Stephens, Mary Ann	Davenport, Cyrus	15, July 1847	L3
Stephens, Mary M.	Wright, David W.	10, Apr. 1851	L3
Stephenson, Lucy	Peebles, William S.	4, Nov. 1841	L3
Stephenson, Matilda	Robertson, Alexander	7, June 1855	L3
Stephenson, Nancy	Jones, Richard	23, Mar. 1854	L3
Sterling, Charlotte	Lawrence, Albert G.	29, June 1848	L3
Sterling, Elizabeth	Pindell, Daniel	21, Oct. 1841	L3
Sterling, Julia C.	Thomson, William	27, Apr. 1843	L3
Sterling, Mary Ann	McKay, Ralph	28, Jan. 1841	L3
Sterns, Fanny L.	Taylor, John C.	3, Apr. 1851	L3
Sterret, Jane E.	Wallace, Robert	10, June 1816	L3
Sterrett, M. Eunice	Keys, R.W.	21, May 1846	L3
Sterrett, Mary Jane	Lawson, George	6, July 1854	L3
Sterritt, Sallie J.	Elstner, Joseph	23, Dec. 1852	L3
Stevens, Alvira Jane	Markland, Simeon	18, Mar. 1847	L3
Stevens, Angelina A.	Frost, George W.	13, Jan. 1853	L3
Stevens, E.A.	Dunham, Joseph C.	6, Apr. 1848	L3
Stevens, Elizabeth	Priley, William	25, May 1848	L3
Stevens, Ellen	Rankin, William	10, June 1841	L3
Stevens, Jane M.	Scott, John L.	21, Oct. 1841	L3
Stevens, Sarah	Maloney, Daniel	31, Dec. 1840	L3
Stevenson, Jane	Kirker, Thomas, Jr.	27, Dec. 1832	L3
Stevenson, Mary C.	Marshall, Samuel (Dr)	25, May 1854	L3
Stevenson, Mollie	Budd, W.G.	2, Feb. 1854	L3
Stewart, Anastasia L	Meade, Nathaniel B.	12, Oct. 1848	L3
Stewart, Ann J.	Means, Thomas	17, Feb. 1848	L3
Stewart, Clarinda V.	Palmerton, Homer	15, May 1828	L3
Stewart, Cornelia A.	Bogert, Isaac	13, Jan. 1853	L3
Stewart, Elizabeth	Brochamp, Henry	13, Mar. 1856	L3
Stewart, Ella F.	Pugh, William H.	10, Apr. 1856	L3
Stewart, Hannah	Frazier, A.S.	26, Dec. 1844	L3
Stewart, Hannah	Gano, Gazzam	28, July 1853	L3
Stewart, Jane T.	Green, John K.	11, Nov. 1841	L3
Stewart, Laura	Jones, Charles	29, Sept 1842	L3
Stewart, Nancy	Burogyne, Horatio	28, Apr. 1821	L2
Stewart, Phebe (Mrs)	Stoops, Stephen M.	23, Mar. 1854	L3
Stewart, Sarah	Starling, Samuel	9, Mar. 1854	L3
Stewart, Susan V.	Jackson, Joseph	18, Apr. 1850	L3
Stibb, Mary Jane	Gilmore, James	21, July 1842	L3
Stibbs, Sarah Ann	Crosby, Joshua E.	9, June 1836	L3
Stickney, Charlotte	Wilmans, Henry	31, Dec. 1840	L3
Stillwell, Eliza	Cary, S.F. (Gen)	7, June 1849	L3
Stillwell, Sarah (Mrs)	Anderson, James	13, Apr. 1854	L3
Stinton, Mary E.	Dewey, James W.	26, Jan. 1854	L3
Stites, Pheby	Eckert, Daniel	31, Aug. 1822	L3

Brides	Grooms	Date of Notice	Page
Stockdale, Elizabeth	Lamothe, Bernard (Dr)	15, Apr. 1847	L3
Stockum, Harriet J.	Little, Joseph B.	31, Apr. 1845	L3
Stockwell, Elizabeth B.	Green, William N.	26, Nov. 1840	L3
Stoddard, Amelia N.	Larimore, Robert	18, Sept 1851	L3
Stoddart, Clarissa	Gooch, Henry	3, June 1841	L3
Stokes, Emma	Carter, E. Henry	19, Dec. 1844	L3
Stone, Amelia C.	Chisman, Edward T.	29, Oct. 1846	L3
Stone, Annes	Greene, Williard L.	18, Sept 1845	L3
Stone, Dollie M.	Macready, Robert	20, Sept 1855	L3
Stone, Eunice Ann	Gould, John	7, Oct. 1847	L3
Stone, Lucy	Blackwell, Henry B.	10, May 1855	L3
Stone, Mary Elizabeth	Lynn, John B.	3, Feb. 1848	L3
Stone, Melissa B.	Northrop, William W.	16, Nov. 1843	L3
Stonemats, Sarah	Higby, James B.	17, Feb. 1848	L3
Stonemitz, Debby	Kyler, George	14, Dec. 1807	L3
Storch, Josephine	Ballauf, William	17, June 1847	L3
Storer, Sophia	Gano, Aaron G.	25, July 1844	L3
Storms, Rody	Thomson, John C.	30, Nov. 1854	L3
Storrs, Sarah W.	Whitney, Rodney	30, Apr. 1857	L3
Story, Sally (Mrs)	Whitford, Foster	22, Apr. 1847	L3
Stout, Esther A.	VonPhul, Henry	6, Apr. 1843	L3
Stout, Harriet	Jonte, Robert	22, Sept 1853	L3
Stout, Louisa	Clough, John P.	27, Apr. 1854	L3
Stout, Margaret Elizabeth	Corwine, David M.	24, Aug. 1848	L3
Stoy, Susan	Phillipson, Simon	12, Mar. 1808	L3
Strader, Mollie F.	Woolley, Charles W.	27, Nov. 1856	L3
Strahan, Catharine A	Stephens, John M.	7, Aug. 1845	L3
Strait, Laura Burton	Hollister, G.B.	14, Aug. 1851	L3
Strange, Rhoda Ellen	Servis, John P.	23, Feb. 1854	L3
Stratton, Catharine	Foster, William S.	15, Sept 1853	L3
Stratton, Mary P.	Webb, Henry	11, Nov. 1847	L3
Straub, Mary C.	Peebles, Joseph R.	29, Feb. 1844	L3
Strawbridge, Jane	McCane, John	8, Apr. 1812	L3
Streeter, Julia Ann	Walden, Baltzer, C.	1, Nov. 1838	L3
Strickland, Mary Ada	Skiles, Thomas H.	14, May 1857	L3
Strickle, Maria E.	Bickham, William D.	10, Jan. 1856	L3
Stroman, Sarah A.	Holmes, James H.	10, Nov. 1853	L3
Stuart, Jane M.	Webber, George H.	30, Mar. 1849	L3
Stuart, Lilly	Whitecross, William	8, Jan. 1857	L3
Stuart, Mary	Harris, William	3, Mar. 1842	L3
Stumps, Jane	Elyea, John	1, Mar. 1838	L3
Sturgis, Martha E.	Brown, Elnathan W.	30, Nov. 1843	L3
Suiter, Ellen	Briggs, William H.	24, Feb. 1842	L3
Suiter, Mary	Campbell, (Capt)	24, Feb. 1842	L3
Sullivan, Mary	Holcomb, Asa	1, Apr. 1816	L3
Sullivan, Sallie Y.	Robbins, Charles E.	6, Apr. 1854	L3
Sullivant, Jane M.	Neil, Robert E.	8, June 1843	L3
Summons, Mary	Armstrong, Robert G.	2, Dec. 1847	L3
Sumwalt, Martha (Mrs)	Irwin, Archibald	13, Nov. 1850	L3
Sutherland, Elizabeth	Warner, James H.	11, Nov. 1847	L3
Suydam, Ann Eliza	Collett, William R.	22, Aug. 1833	L1
Suydant, Lydia (Mrs)	Lawrence, Robert	29, Jan. 1829	L1
Swager, Elizabeth	Ernest, Jacob	14, June 1849	L3
Swain, Elizabeth B.	Turpin, John W.	9, Mar. 1854	L3

Brides	Grooms	Date of Notice	Page
Swallow, Elizabeth	Coffeen, Zeloma	8, Jan. 1857	L3
Swan, Helen A.	Cole, Jacob F.	11, July 1850	L3
Swan, Jane	Parsens, George M.	2, Nov. 1843	L3
Swan, Lucie G.	Hardy, John C. (Dr)	15, Jan. 1852	L3
Swan, Sarah	Whiting, Augustus	2, Nov. 1843	L3
Swarmstedt, Sarah A.	Wolff, Charles H.	23, Oct. 1845	L3
Swearingen, Ellen	Grant, John H.	21, Nov. 1844	L3
Sweet, Martha	McClure, Alexander	26, July 1838	L3
Sweetland, Eliza	Cox, Edward	30, July 1857	L3
Sweitzer, Caroline	Roof, Joseph A.(Rev)	16, Nov. 1854	L3
Swenny, Eliza Jane	Horass, Fintin	2, July 1846	L3
Swift, Eliza	L'Hommedieu, Samuel	27, June 1826	L3
Swift, Lucy	Cunningham, E.W.	27, Sept 1838	L3
Swing, Priscilla	Collins, Amos	26, Mar. 1819	L3
Swinson, Margaret C.	Hillhouse, James	16, Jan. 1845	L3
Symmes, (Miss)	Moore, Hugh	2, Dec. 1805	L3
Symmes, Elizabeth	Haven, Langdon H.	4, Dec. 1845	L3
Symmes, Elizabeth (Mrs)	Graham, Thomas	5, Oct. 1819	L3
Symmes, Louisiana	Taylor, James W.	2, Aug. 1832	L3
Symmes, Mary S.	Colburn, Charles L.	5, Aug. 1847	L3
Symmonds, Esther E.	Phillips, William	22, Sept 1842	L3
Symonds, Charlotte	Townsend, Oliver	22, Nov. 1849	L3
Symsor, Christiana	Holmes, Ezekiel B.	20, Nov. 1845	L3
Tagart, Jane Mary	Prestley, James (Rev)	7, May 1846	L3
Tait, Eliza	Childs, William E.	8, June 1837	L1
Tait, Jane	Russell, Henry W.	9, Sept 1841	L3
Tait, Lizzie A.	Woods, William W.	26, Apr. 1855	L3
Tait, Mary	Jones, Thomas C.	26, May 1836	L3
Talbert, Elizabeth	Arnet, Mahlon	9, Mar. 1854	L3
Talbert, Rebecca W.	Bodley, Anthony P.	26, Jan. 1827	L3
Talbert, Sophia	Gwynne, David (Major)	13, Feb. 1845	L3
Talbott, Hester Ann	Stillman, O.D.	19, July 1838	L3
Tapley, Caroline M.	Carey, George	27, July 1848	L3
Tappan, Eliza R.	Marvin, John P.	13, Feb. 1845	L3
Tatem, Catharine	Miles, Reason S.	4, Mar. 1847	L3
Taylor, A.E.	Hunter, William	16, Mar. 1854	L3
Taylor, Ann	Tibbatts, John W.	7, Jan. 1825	L3
Taylor, Anna	Thomas, Daniel G.	27, Dec. 1849	L3
Taylor, Caroline	Dickson, James M.	12, Nov. 1846	L3
Taylor, Cornelia	Brigham, Lucius A.	3, Oct. 1850	L3
Taylor, Eliza Jane	Crary, Georgy	5, Sept 1844	L3
Taylor, Elizabeth (Mrs)	Collins, Edmund	11, Aug. 1842	L3
Taylor, Hannah D.	Shipley, Murray	29, May 1851	L3
Taylor, Jane	Bennett, Daniel R.	3, Feb. 1855	L3
Taylor, Jane	Penny, George	8, Jan. 1857	L3
Taylor, Louisa	Levassor, Armond P.	16, Jan. 1845	L3
Taylor, Lydia S.	Wright, William S.	19, Sept 1844	L3
Taylor, Martha A.	Lape, William H.	24, June 1847	L3
Taylor, Mary	Walker, Lewis S.	18, Nov. 1841	L3
Taylor, Mary Ann	Hill, James	8, May 1845	L3
Taylor, Mary Ann	Lilley, John	12, Apr. 1849	L3
Taylor, Mary C.	Reed, Edwin O.	23, Dec. 1847	L3
Taylor, Mary Elizabeth	Bliss, William W.	21, Dec. 1848	L3

Brides	Grooms	Date of Notice	Page
Taylor, Mary Jane	Patrick, Holmes C.	30, Oct. 1851	L3
Taylor, Mary L.	Carter, Samuel R.	4, Jan. 1855	L3
Taylor, Naomi	Speck, Adolphus C.	16, Feb. 1854	L3
Taylor, Parthena	Wrenn, Allen S.	22, May 1845	L3
Taylor, Polly T.	McKinney, John (Col)	24, Mar. 1817	L3
Taylor, Sarah K.	Miller, Emanuel J.	20, June 1839	L3
Taylor, Susan P.	Weller, John B.	10, Apr. 1845	L3
Teirnan, Margaret	Jones, Morris	12, Aug. 1841	L3
Templeton, Margaret	Caldwell, John D.	23, Oct. 1845	L3
Templeton, Nancy	Livingston, James	27, Oct. 1812	L3
Tendell, Charlotte	Hastings, John L.	30, Jan. 1845	L3
Tennent, Sallie	Adams, Charles	15, Nov. 1855	L3
Terry, Margaret	Kemper, Charles H.	9, Sept 1847	L3
Terry, Sarah	Moore, George W.	10, Feb. 1826	L3
Tess, Rebecca	Paine, Daniel	8, Nov. 1814	L3
Tewers, Leah (Mrs)	Anderson, Andrew	9, Oct. 1834	L2
Thacker, Patty	Huser, John	16, Sept 1816	L3
Tharp, Polly	Flake, Aaron	24, Oct. 1810	L3
Thatcher, Julia Ann	Haven, Charles H.	9, Apr. 1846	L3
Thesing, Marie E.	Becker, C.F.	30, Dec. 1847	L3
Thew, Caroline A.	Wright, N.	21, Apr. 1820	L3
Thew, Mary B.	Perry, Samuel	19, Aug. 1816	L3
Thomas, Adaline E.	Knox, James H.	10, Dec. 1840	L3
Thomas, Ann	Baymiller, Jacob	27, Dec. 1809	L3
Thomas, Belle	Corwine, Samuel L.	3, Aug. 1854	L3
Thomas, Cecilia A.	Brown, William (Dr)	21, July 1853	L3
Thomas, Eliza	LeCain, Fred G.	12, Mar. 1857	L3
Thomas, Ellen B.	Neff, William C.	23, Feb. 1854	L3
Thomas, Emily	Coles, Abraham	20, June 1839	L3
Thomas, Frances Ann	Watt, James	16, June 1836	L3
Thomas, Frances Mary	Rowe, Stanhope S.	12, Aug. 1841	L3
Thomas, Jane	Abbott, John C.	11, Apr. 1844	L3
Thomas, Martha M.	Grow, William S.	2, Dec. 1847	L3
Thomas, Mary	Mollen, Joseph	3, Apr. 1811	L3
Thomas, Mary Ann	Stout, Jesse D.	30, Nov. 1848	L3
Thomas, Rebecca Ann	Baner, Jonathan J.	21, Sept 1837	L3
Thomas, Ruth	Leeka, Philip	12, Jan. 1854	L3
Thomas, S.E.	Colburn, W.T.	20, Feb. 1845	L3
Thomason, Adelaide	Talbot, Isham	28, Apr. 1817	L3
Thompson, Agnes	Anderson, Richard C.	28, June 1855	L3
Thompson, Amelia L.	Watts, William	26, Dec. 1844	L3
Thompson, Ann	Johns, James C.	14, Apr. 1842	L3
Thompson, Ann Louise	Begraun, T.A.	13, Apr. 1848	L3
Thompson, Annie H.	Andrews, R.D.	21, Dec. 1854	L3
Thompson, Eliza	VanValkenburgh, Hy.	15, June 1854	L3
Thompson, Eliza M.	Wicker, Lawrence S.	2, Oct. 1828	L3
Thompson, Emma F.	Bechtel, William	9, June 1853	L3
Thompson, Hannah	Williams, William	19, June 1845	L3
Thompson, Jane M.	Craig, William S.	2, Apr. 1829	L2
Thompson, Lizzie	Odlin, Woodbridge	30, Mar. 1854	L3
Thompson, M.W.R.	Daviess, William	31, Oct. 1839	L3
Thompson, Margaret	Cones, William M.	11, Dec. 1845	L3
Thompson, Sarah	Minett, Julius C.	20, July 1837	L3
Thompson, Sarah E.	Jones, Rufus A.	26, Oct. 1848	L3

Brides	Grooms	Date of Notice	Page
Thomson, Nannie H.	Farnsworth, Thomas R	17, June 1852	L3
Thorn, Mary	Collord, James	10, Aug. 1819	L3
Thornton, Elvira	Mills, James R.	22, July 1852	L3
Thornton, Elvira	Whittemore, N.M.	19, Nov. 1824	L3
Thornton, Jinny	Logan, Thomas A.	19, May 1853	L3
Thornton, Mary (Mrs)	Terrell, William G.	20, Nov. 1850	L3
Thorp, Margaret	Woodworth, W.L.	30, Jan. 1840	L3
Thruston, M.L. (Mrs)	Lowe, John G.	18, May 1843	L3
Thurman, N.E.	Miller, William	18, Jan. 1855	L3
Thurston, Mary	Kelso, Charles A.	16, Feb. 1854	L3
Tiebout, Esther Y.	Adams, A.H.	15, Oct. 1846	L3
Tiebout, Mary (Mrs)	Baily, John	28, July 1836	L3
Tift, Delia Annie	Peebles, William S.	17, June 1852	L3
Tift, Laura Rebecca	Disney, T. Bishop	8, Nov. 1855	L3
Tiley, Amelia Ann	Fosdick, William	16, Sept 1841	L3
Tiley, Emma	Thorp, John T.	14, July 1836	L3
Tilley, Josephine	Maurer, F.	17, Oct. 1850	L3
Tillinghast, Anna	Breedley, Edwin R.	27, Sept 1849	L3
Tilton, Mary	Davis, Joshua	5, Sept 1850	L3
Tilton, Mary	Davis, Joshua	12, Sept 1850	L3
Tincher, Caroline	Palmer, Charles L.	20, June 1850	L3
Tindall, Eliza Ann	Lovejoy, Thatcher	7, May 1819	L3
Tinker, Elizabeth	Talbott, W.H.	30, Mar. 1848	L3
Todd, Abbie	Simpson, George B.F.	20, Dec. 1855	L3
Todd, Ann D.	Thompson, James	22, Nov. 1849	L3
Todd, Caroline	Peck, A.F.	6, Oct. 1842	L3
Todd, Caroline F.	Ross, Robert D.	21, Sept 1848	L3
Todd, Margaret	Kellogg, Charles H.	11, Nov. 1847	L3
Todd, Mary L.	Fairman, L. (Dr)	12, Mar. 1824	L2
Tolar, Charlotte C.	Hastings, Lanford W.	22, Feb. 1849	L3
Tolbert, Ruth	Benson, Abraham	16, Feb. 1854	L3
Torrence, Eliza Jane	Handy, Robert D.	24, Apr. 1851	L3
Torrence, Mary P.	Harrison, W.H.	3, July 1845	L3
Torrence, Rebecca	McNutt, James	12, Dec. 1810	L2
Torrey, Louise M.	Taft, Alphonso	5, Jan. 1854	L3
Tosso, Adele	Spining, F.A.	16, Jan. 1851	L3
Totten, Susan M.	Telford, Charles L.	24, Nov. 1842	L6
Toufly, Rosalie (Mrs)	Brachmann, Henry	1, Aug. 1833	L3
Townsend, Caroline	Johnson, G. Brainerd	15, June 1843	L3
Traber, Mary Ann	Sproul, Hasht	27, June 1839	L3
Treece, Mary A.	Henderson, Joseph	2, Feb. 1854	L3
Tressel, Sarah Mary	Myer, Lewis Henry (Rev)	12, Aug. 1823	L3
Trousdale, Hannah	Hatfield, George	13, Sept 1849	L3
Trout, Susan	English, Samuel	15, Apr. 1812	L3
Truesdale, Mary L.	Fuller, George S.	23, Oct. 1856	L5
Trumbull, Louisa J.	Lea, Henry	11, Sept 1845	L3
Tucker, Hattie D.	Bush, O.N.	13, July 1854	L3
Tucker, Lizzie C.	Moses, Simpson P.	19, July 1849	L3
Tudor, Ann C.	Hopple, Jacob	4, Jan. 1844	L3
Tudor, Elizabeth	Wells, Oliver, Sen.	27, June 1826	L3
Tudor, Mary Elizabeth A.	Shotwell, George H.	17, Nov. 1836	L3
Tumy, Caroline M.	Bruce, Benjamin	29, Jan. 1846	L3
Tunis, Caroline	Greene, Caleb	15, Oct. 1840	L3
Tunis, Emeline	Tarrant, Larkin M.	24, Jan. 1826	L3

Brides	Grooms	Date of Notice	Page
Tunis, Susan	Landis, Henry	24, Mar. 1817	L3
Turner, Ann	Hull, James M.	19, Mar. 1846	L3
Turner, Ann	Snedaker, Samuel B.	14, Aug. 1845	L3
Turner, Ann Maria	Burdsal, Stephen W.	25, Feb. 1836	L3
Turner, Edith	Lindsay, Samuel	29, July 1847	L3
Turner, Elizabeth A.	Chalmers, Horatio S.	30, Sept 1825	L3
Turner, Emily J.	McDougal, Addison B.	25, Jan. 1844	L3
Turner, O.	Bateman, James W.	2, Dec. 1847	L3
Turner, Rebecca	McCracken, Robert B.	8, June 1843	L3
Turpin, Mary F.	Wilshire, Samuel	9, Jan. 1851	L3
Turpin, Nancy C. (Mrs)	Sherlock, Thomas	30, Sept 1852	L3
Tuttle, Caroline W.	Blackly, Joseph W.	19, Oct. 1822	L3
Tuttle, Elizabeth A.	Robinson, Charles D.	3, Sept 1846	L3
Tylor, Lizzie H.	Collier, D.	24, Jan. 1856	L3
Tyner, Louisiana	Hazzard, John F.	3, Mar. 1853	L3
Tyner, Missouri	Guiteau, John Wilson	22, Jan. 1857	L3
Umpheries, Annie E.	Potter, Courtland W.	9, Feb. 1854	L3
Upham, Harriet H.	Walker, John S.	8, June 1848	L3
Upjohn, Mary Ann	Carr, Francis	3, Aug. 1822	L3
Urno, Mary	Cary, John	19, Jan. 1854	L3
Utz, Isabella	Moore, Arthur	13, Aug. 1857	L3
Valentine, Elizabeth	Hamlen, Shephard (Dr)	20, Nov. 1850	L3
Valentine, Phebe P.	Clark, John E.	24, Jan. 1856	L3
VanAmringe, Eliza J.	Stoddart, David	23, Feb. 1854	L3
Vanausdol, Emily	Gould, Levi G.	25, Jan. 1855	L3
Vanausdol, Mary R.	Jeffries, John C.	21, Apr. 1842	L3
Vanausdol, Naomi R.	Scott, David B.	27, Oct. 1853	L3
Vanausdoll, Caroline	Compton, William A.	28, Dec. 1837	L3
Vance, Mary	Hight, George W.	26, Aug. 1816	L3
VanderPool, Adareen	Hunt, Ralph P.	24, Mar. 1826	L3
VandeWater, Maria	Guthrie, M.W.	2, June 1853	L3
VanDuston, Isabella	Dopp, Solomon	3, Feb. 1848	L3
VanDuzen, Elizabeth	Hill, Edward H.	25, Mar. 1841	L3
VanDyke, Ellen	Stewart, K.F.	8, June 1848	L3
VanDyke, Fidelia R.	Hasluck, D.S.	9, June 1842	L3
VanDyke, Jane Carol.	Tweed, J.P.	20, Oct. 1836	L2
Vandyke, L.C.	Andrews, A.H.	5, Sept 1850	L3
VanHamm, Sarah	Graham, William A.	3, June 1847	L3
Vanhorn, Jane (Mrs)	Vanausdol, Garret	9, Feb. 1854	L3
VanMetre, Mary	Tharp, Jacob	4, July 1844	L3
Vannoy, Sarah	Hopkins, James	9, Feb. 1854	L3
Vantrees, Catharine	Smith, Joseph	19, May 1807	L3
VanZandt, Laura C.	Garesche, Alexander	10, May 1849	L3
VanZant, Martha (Mrs)	Gibson, Stephen	22, Mar. 1855	L3
Vater, Elizabeth M.	Longley, Elias	20, May 1847	L3
Veatch, Ann Maria	Butterfield, Algeron	28, Dec. 1843	L3
Venable, Hannah	Wills, William	6, Apr. 1854	L3
Vickers, Emeline J.	Craig, J.W.	30, Mar. 1854	L3
Vincent, Hannah M.	Hall, Dudley	22, Nov. 1855	L3
Vinton, Pamela W.	Lawrence, H.K.	1, Feb. 1849	L3
Vogelbach, Gertrude	Beitch, Marcus	18, May 1854	L3
Volander, Frances	Green, Samuel F.	17, Jan. 1850	L3

Brides	Grooms	Date of Notice	Page
Voorhis, Maggie	Hoster, Joseph C.	13, Sept 1855	L3
Vorhis, H.L.	Baxter, J. Watson (Dr)	18, Dec. 1845	L3
Vose, Mary R.	Rice, William P.	10, Jan. 1839	L3
Wade, Harriet	White, John F. (Dr)	10, Apr. 1845	L3
Wade, Mary	Oliver, David (Dr)	26, Feb. 1816	L3
Wade, Sarah	Bedinger, B.F. (Dr)	1, July 1820	L3
Wade, Susan A.L.	Guy, Alexander	31, Mar. 1830	L3
Waggoner, Mattie A.	Hood, D. Burr	3, Feb. 1855	L3
Wainwright, Jerusha	Augur, James S.	29, Oct. 1846	L3
Wainwright, Ruth	Smith, Spencer	3, June 1841	L3
Wakefield, Margaret	Dennis, Jacob J.	17, Oct. 1850	L3
Wakefield, Mary E.	Herrick, Hiram N.	16, Feb. 1854	L3
Wakelam, Anna M.	Collins, John C.	1, Dec. 1853	L3
Waldo, Fannie W.	Ross, John L.	7, Sept 1848	L3
Walker, Amelia Ann	Luckey, John S.	9, May 1839	L3
Walker, Ann Mary	Bryson, Ambrose M.	28, Jan. 1841	L3
Walker, Annie M.	Holmes, R.S. (Dr)	24, Oct. 1850	L3
Walker, Caroline S.	Blair, McLean J.	19, Apr. 1845	L3
Walker, Georgina	Crawford, Andrew	7, Sept 1848	L3
Walker, Hannah E.	Emerson, Allison	15, June 1848	L3
Walker, Margaret	McCorkle, John	27, Dec. 1814	L3
Walker, Margaret	Stannus, Richard G.	30, Dec. 1847	L3
Walker, Martha A.	Tschudy, James H.	22, Apr. 1852	L3
Walker, Mary	Medary, William	26, Nov. 1819	L3
Walker, Rebecca	Gardner, James	8, Jan. 1857	L3
Wall, Elizabeth	Lamont, Roger	30, Mar. 1843	L3
Wall, Lizzie R.	Kennedy, Samuel	27, Apr. 1854	L3
Wallace, Henrietta H	Tod, Samuel	15, Sept 1818	L3
Wallace, Lucy	Neff, William Howard	28, Nov. 1850	L3
Wallace, Margaret	Brookenshire, James	1, Aug. 1844	L3
Wallace, Martha N.	Kovatz, Augusta (Lt)	25, Nov. 1852	L3
Wallace, Mary	Perry, Samuel	11, Oct. 1809	L3
Wallace, Mary	Shillito, John	26, May 1836	L3
Wallace, Phebe F.	Webb, William H.	6, July 1837	L1
Wallace, Sarah E.	Hawekotte, Henry	13, Nov. 1856	L3
Waller, Ruth	Strange, John (Rev)	8, Sept 1812	L2
Walls, Emily	VanDeventer, P.L.	5, Dec. 1844	L3
Walsh, Martha	Clark, John	28, Aug. 1845	L3
Walters, Sallie A.	Driesbach,	11, May 1854	L3
Walton, Elizabeth	Goode, John F.	9, Feb. 1854	L3
Walton, Lydia H.	Coleman, Andrew (Rev)	3, Oct. 1844	L3
Wampole, Isabella	Lynch, Augustine	9, Apr. 1840	L3
Ward, Anna E.	Abbott, C.S.	17, May 1855	L3
Ward, Frances M.	Mitchell, Micajah B.	7, May 1846	L3
Ward, Gerogia E.	Allen, Robert E.	8, Nov. 1855	L3
Ward, Harriet	Riley, Shepherd G.	12, Aug. 1847	L3
Ward, Julia M.	Gard, Benjamin M.	10, Dec. 1857	L3
Ward, Margaret A.	Dunsmore, Joseph	9, Feb. 1854	L3
Ward, Mary	Moore, W.H.	11, Mar. 1815	L3
Ward, Mary (Mrs)	Beatty, John	15, Oct. 1846	L3
Ward, Mary L.	Walker, George W.	25, Mar. 1841	L3
Wardle, Susan F.	Hannaford, Roger	3, Jan. 1856	L3
Wardour, Mary A.	Rannells, Charles S.	26, May 1842	L3

Brides	Grooms	Date of Notice	Page
Ware, Abigail	Foote, Andrew R.	21, Sept 1837	L3
Ware, Abigail	Warren, George	24, Aug. 1819	L3
Ware, Anna Maria	Morrell, A.	10, Dec. 1840	L3
Warner, Anna S.	Atkins, Richard L.	3, Sept 1857	L3
Warren, Elizabeth A.	Townsend, Louis	9, Dec. 1852	L3
Wartman, Elizabeth (Mrs)	Lusk, Thomas	22, Nov. 1838	L3
Washburn, Harriet J.	Prince, Joseph W.	31, May 1849	L3
Washington, Marion W	McKenzie, J.M. (Dr)	18, May 1854	L3
Washington, Virginia	Todd, Alexander	29, Sept 1853	L3
Waterman, Julia	Stanley, William	24, Mar. 1807	L3
Waterman, Louisa C.	Wood, L.	14, Dec. 1854	L3
Waterman, Susan B.	Noel, Henry A.	4, July 1844	L3
Waters, Phebe (Mrs)	Reddish, Thomas	1, Feb. 1825	L3
Watkins, Jane	Bainsell, John	28, Mar. 1839	L3
Watkins, Lydia	Sprague, Andrew W.	24, Feb. 1842	L3
Watkins, Mary	Stevenson, Joseph D.	13, Nov. 1850	L3
Watson, Caroline	Smith, William R.	27, Dec. 1838	L3
Watson, Julia	Southgate, Richard H	4, Jan. 1844	L3
Watts, Letitia G.	Rives, Landon (Dr)	7, Feb. 1850	L3
Watts, Virginia	Hogan, David	21, Nov. 1833	L3
Wattson, Ann Delia	Downer, William	20, May 1841	L3
Wayne, Elizabeth	Wayne, Edward S.	26, Feb. 1846	L3
Wayne, Mary	Woods, William H.	1, Mar. 1855	L3
Weatherby, Amelia F.	Andress, Charles O.	12, Feb. 1852	L3
Weatherby, Mary G.	Schwartze, F.W.	15, Apr. 1847	L3
Weatherby, Rosalinda	Bagley, William A.	27, Sept 1855	L3
Weaver, Josephine A.	Ray, Daniel G.	17, May 1855	L3
Webb, Kate H.	West, Albert	26, Dec. 1850	L3
Webb, Lucy W.	Hays, R.B.	6, Jan. 1853	L3
Webber, Harriet	Whipple, Sumner	23, Dec. 1820	L3
Webster, Nancy	Starbuck, Calvin W.	9, Jan. 1845	L3
Weed, Sophia B.	Claflin, George D.	7, Sept 1854	L3
Weeks, Rebecca	Pawson, Thomas	11, Nov. 1847	L3
Weeks, Susan Ann	Winchell, George D.	6, May 1847	L3
Weer, Esther Ann	Orr, Robert M.	18, July 1844	L3
Weibling, Clarissa C	Gosling, George	6, Mar. 1845	L3
Weirick, Sallie H.	Dart, George L.	20, Apr. 1848	L3
Wells, Aurelia	Holden, R.A.	29, Sept 1836	L4
Wells, Rebecca	Hackley, James M.	5, May 1817	L3
Wells, Sue	Keely, George W.	21, Mar. 1850	L3
Welton, Margaret	King, J. Willard	27, Jan. 1848	L3
Werner, Ellen Agnes	Gordon, Goerge (Col)	16, June 1836	L3
Werstelle, Corinne D	Renck, J.M.	1, Oct. 1857	L3
West, Elizabeth C.	Brown, Sidney B.	30, Mar. 1848	L3
West, Mary	Thornton, Joseph	23, Dec. 1825	L3
Western, Charlotte E	Aydelote, John H.	18, Sept 1851	L3
Westlake, Susan	Hopper, Morris	22, Mar. 1838	L3
Weston, Emma	Richards, Charles A.	8, Sept 1853	L3
Wever, Catharine W.	Collins, William O.	30, Nov. 1843	L3
Whann, Mary V.D.	Williams, Miles	14, Feb. 1850	L3
Wharton, Marianne	Gillett, G.W. (Rev)	8, June 1848	L3
Wharton, Mary E.	Washington, George	19, Oct. 1837	L3
Wheeland, Elvira	Sweeny, John	9, Jan. 1845	L3
Wheeler, Cornelia D.	Lewis, John Loyd	11, Jan. 1844	L3

Brides	Grooms	Date of Notice	Page
Wheeler, Emily	Buchanan, Charles M.	18, June 1857	L3
Wheeler, Harriet Ann	Swafford, James	10, Jan. 1823	L3
Wheeler, Mary Jane	Pierce, Thomas B.	9, Oct. 1845	L3
Wheeler, Rhoda	Ferris, Abraham	29, Sept 1807	L3
Wheelright, Mary (Mrs)	Keating, John	28, Apr. 1826	L3
Wherritt, Sallie	Worden, William	23, Mar. 1854	L3
Whetstone, Caroline	Rhakirt, Charles C.	10, June 1852	L3
Whetstone, Hannah E.	Huey, George J.	22, Oct. 1840	L3
Whetstone, Julia M.	Hopkins, Lewis C.	6, Feb. 1851	L3
Whetstone, Mary	Haines, Amos	10, Aug. 1813	L3
Whetstone, Ruth	Hicks, James	5, Jan. 1809	L3
Whipple, Hannah	Silsbee, Samuel (Dr)	8, July 1841	L3
Whipple, Harriet E.	Scovill, Amon L.	29, Dec. 1842	L3
Whipple, Martha L.	Neave, Charley	18, Dec. 1851	L3
Whipple, Mary	Sanxay, Frederick	18, Mar. 1818	L3
Whipple, Sarah H.	Wells, Horace	22, Mar. 1822	L3
Whistler, Louisa A.	Helm, C.J. (Major)	22, June 1854	L3
Whitcomb, Esther A.	Maynard, John F.	9, Feb. 1854	L3
White, Adaline	Brett, William	28, Aug. 1845	L3
White, Catharine L.	Johnson, James A.	17, Feb. 1848	L3
White, Charlotte (Mrs)	Eliott, William J.	19, Sept 1850	L3
White, Elemina	Griffith, A.R.	2, Aug. 1855	L3
White, Eliza M.	Andrews, R.H.	6, Jan. 1853	L3
White, Elizabeth E.	Hall, Henry E.	12, Jan. 1854	L3
White, Elvira	Davisson, Thomas	12, Nov. 1846	L3
White, Frances	Applegate, Benjamin	12, Aug. 1847	L3
White, Harriet S.	Woodruff, Edward	25, Dec. 1845	L3
White, Jean M.	Ladd, William H.	5, Aug. 1847	L3
White, Louisa C.	Carter, J. Hamilton	13, Sept 1849	L3
White, Margaret Ann	Fox, James	2, Oct. 1856	L5
White, Maria	Lowell, James R.	9, Jan. 1845	L3
White, Wealthy Ann	Stevens, Hiram E.	18, July 1844	L3
Whitehead, Eliza F.	Jones, William C.	9, Apr. 1840	L3
Whitehead, Maria	Lowry, George W.	23, Mar. 1848	L3
Whitehead, Mary Jane	Mitchell, J.W.	13, Jan. 1848	L3
Whitehouse, Sarah	Bailey, William	16, Jan. 1851	L3
Whiteman, Louisa	Carson, William (Dr)	19, Oct. 1854	L3
Whiterow, Mary P.	McLain, Josiah	24, Feb. 1848	L3
Whitesides, Mary	Terwilliger, Nathaniel	28, July 1807	L3
Whitman, Jane S.	Buel, Lucius C.	20, Mar. 1851	L3
Whitney, Abby	Hoffman, Jacob	23, Sept 1841	L3
Whitney, Elizabeth (Mrs)	Thomas, Robert	20, May 1847	L3
Whitney, Harriet	Carnes, Peter	31, Mar. 1842	L3
Whitney, M.J.	Morrison, D. Wallis	19, Nov. 1857	L3
Whitney, Myra C. (Mrs)	Gaines, E.P. (Gen)	16, May 1839	L3
Whittaker, Anna	Nichols, Luther	9, July 1846	L3
Whittaker, Caroline	Morse, Increase	6, June 1850	L3
Whittelsey, Ann (Mrs)	Mills, Thornton (Rev)	2, Nov. 1854	L3
Wiggins, Adeline	Breese, William G.	9, July 1840	L3
Wiggins, Emma Louisa	Skinner, Ralston	9, July 1857	L3
Wiggins, Virinda	Banks, Frederick (Dr)	29, May 1845	L3
Wilcox, Mary Louisa	Allen, William	17, July 1845	L3
Wilders, Loretta	Maddux, Lewis	2, Mar. 1854	L3
Wilkeson, Julia (Mrs)	Foote, T.M. (Dr)	19, June 1851	L3

Brides	Grooms	Date of Notice	Page
Wilkins, Frances M.	Wilshire, William	31, Aug. 1843	L3
Wilkinson, Amanda	Jones, George W.	20, Dec. 1838	L3
Willett, Sarah A.	Clark, James A.	27, Feb. 1845	L3
Willey, Mary	Willey, Harrison	9, May 1810	L3
Williams, Anna	Barnhart, Daniel	15, Sept 1842	L3
Williams, Anne S.	Beman, I.C.	20, Sept 1838	L3
Williams, Catharine	Harter, L.F.	12, July 1849	L3
Williams, Charlotte	Keith, Isaac	28, Jan. 1847	L3
Williams, Charlotte	Stephens, Estep	28, Aug. 1851	L3
Williams, Eliza Jane	Sherman, Charles T.	11, Feb. 1841	L3
Williams, Eliza Jane	Widney, Steven	9, Jan. 1845	L3
Williams, Elizabeth	Perry, A.F.	23, Mar. 1843	L3
Williams, Elizabeth (Mrs)	West, Samuel	9, June 1853	L3
Williams, Euretta F.	Swift, John	16, Apr. 1857	L3
Williams, Fanny E.	Homans, Benjamin	24, Aug. 1854	L3
Williams, Hannah M.	Stone, B.T.	20, Sept 1838	L3
Williams, Laura Jane	Innis, Robert B.	17, Jan. 1850	L3
Williams, Margaret	Conclin, Caleb	9, Mar. 1824	L3
Williams, Margaret R	Rinsford, Thomas C.	2, Jan. 1845	L3
Williams, Martha	Forshey, C.C.	7, Sept 1843	L3
Williams, Mary	Applegate, John W.	20, July 1848	L3
Williams, Mary (Mrs)	Field, Henry S.	11, Dec. 1851	L3
Williams, Mary Ann	Atlee, S. Yorke	6, May 1841	L3
Williams, Mary Ann E.	Miller, Halsey B.	24, Dec. 1846	L3
Williams, Mary B.	Olds, C.N.	16, Sept 1852	L3
Williams, Sarah	Thomas, Terrill	4, June 1857	L3
Williamson, Emily	Creagh, Job	29, Nov. 1849	L3
Williamson, Frances	Huntington, Spencer	7, Dec. 1848	L3
Williamson, Harriet	Gregg, Stephen	15, Apr. 1812	L3
Williamson, Lydia H.	Richards, Channing	16, Mar. 1837	L3
Williamson, Margaret	Moore, Joseph A.	30, Dec. 1847	L3
Williamson, Mary Ann	Turner, Samuel C.	20, Feb. 1845	L3
Williamson, Mary J.	Broadwell, Charles G	9, May 1844	L3
Williamson, Orphia E	Fisher, Homer	15, Jan. 1857	L3
Willis, Martha Ann	Piatt, John H.	27, July 1813	L3
Willis, Susan	Armstrong, John	28, Dec. 1807	L3
Willson, Mary Jane	Hubbell, William T.	16, Oct. 1851	L3
Wilmot, Jennie T.	Blaghly, J. Warren	18, Dec. 1856	L3
Wilmuth, Mary Jane	Bacon, Isaac W.	25, Feb. 1847	L3
Wilshire, Elizabeth	Gano, Howell	20, Apr. 1848	L3
Wilshire, M.A.	Chester, J.H.	28, Feb. 1856	L3
Wilshire, Sallie	Moore, John M.	15, June 1854	L3
Wilson, Catharine	Barr, Baldwin	7, Jan. 1847	L3
Wilson, Isabel	Carlisle, John	15, Nov. 1855	L3
Wilson, Isabella	Borrowman, Thomas	14, Jan. 1847	L3
Wilson, Jane (Mrs)	Bryant, William	3, Feb. 1848	L3
Wilson, Louisa A.	Knight, James D.	5, Nov. 1840	L2
Wilson, Margaret A.	Brown, James D.	28, Oct. 1852	L3
Wilson, Margaret Ann	Bailey, William	18, July 1844	L3
Wilson, Margaretta	Starlin, Israel	11, Dec. 1811	L3
Wilson, Margaretta E	Johnston, Samuel	6, Dec. 1820	L3
Wilson, Maria	Simonton, William	9, Sept 1816	L3
Wilson, Maria Louisa	Perin, Lyman	19, Apr. 1849	L3
Wilson, Mary	Cist, Francis J.	20, Nov. 1856	L3

Brides	Grooms	Date of Notice	Page
Wilson, Mary E.	Betts, Morgan L.	20, July 1854	L3
Wilson, Mary J.	Coolidge, William H.	17, Apr. 1851	L3
Wilson, Matilda E.	Barwise, Edward K.	8, Apr. 1847	L3
Wilson, Rebecca	Hawpe, George(Major)	21, Nov. 1844	L3
Wilson, Sarah Ann	Flinn, Jesse	22, Apr. 1847	L3
Wilson, Sophronia Z.	Eppley, James B.	24, Nov. 1853	L3
Wiltberger, Susan (Mrs)	Decker, Josiah	18, May 1822	L3
Wiltsee, Rachel S.	Turner, Samuel	14, Mar. 1844	L3
Winans, Mary	Kline, Benneville	31, Dec. 1857	L3
Wing, Sarah H.	Ross, Thomas	6, Apr. 1848	L3
Winn, Sophia	Bates, William M.	3, Mar. 1842	L3
Winnie, Lizzie	Bradley, Orlando	9, Nov. 1854	L3
Winston, Mary	Rust, William B.	23, Sept 1852	L3
Winston, Mary E.	Blair, A.P.	8, Jan. 1835	L1
Winston, Mary L.	Ricks, Nathaniel W.	5, Mar. 1846	L3
Winston, Sarah Ann	Manzies, Samuel G.	8, Jan. 1835	L1
Winston, Sibella	Stevenson, John W.	29, June 1843	L3
Winter, Eliza	Karrmann, William	27, Nov. 1845	L3
Winter, Maria	Russell, John	13, Nov. 1845	L3
Winterbottom, Jane A	Bradbury, V.C.	10, Nov. 1853	L3
Winton, Jane M.	Hoskeir, Isaac A.	19, Oct. 1843	L3
Wise, Anna Maria	Richards, Joseph(Dr)	20, July 1854	L3
Wise, Margaret Jane	Allen, Louis A.	24, Mar. 1853	L3
Wishart, Margaretta	Carter, G.W.	31, Mar. 1842	L3
Wiswell, Isabella	Walker, John	31, July 1845	L3
Witherup, Anna C.	Swift, Charles	10, Sept 1857	L3
Witmer, Sarah A.	Mayhew, E.C.	22, Jan. 1857	L3
Wolf, Adeline	Lubenstein, Isaac	31, Oct. 1844	L3
Wolf, Christiana	Halverstaty, William	30, Mar. 1854	L3
Wolfe, Eveline H.	Talbert, Aaron S.	5, Nov. 1846	L3
Wood, Abbey C.	Cogy, Joseph (Dr)	1, July 1820	L3
Wood, Catharine	Dayton, Eli (Dr)	21, Feb. 1839	L3
Wood, Eliza	Morgan, Isaac	17, Nov. 1817	L3
Wood, Eliza Jane	Thorp, John F. (Dr)	19, Oct. 1843	L3
Wood, Ellen	Work, Frank	5, Mar. 1857	L3
Wood, Ellen P.	Walker, Timothy	19, Mar. 1840	L3
Wood, Frances P.	Childs, John R.	11, Sept 1845	L3
Wood, Harriet S.	Ogden, E.H.	13, July 1848	L3
Wood, Julia E.	Ogden, Henry S.	23, Jan. 1851	L3
Wood, Loretta	Merwin, George B.	9, Aug. 1838	L3
Wood, Maria P.	Schenck, Aaron L.	3, Aug. 1822	L3
Wood, Mary A.	Weatherby, Charles S	29, Nov. 1855	L3
Wood, Mary E.	Burdsal, James S.	16, May 1850	L3
Wood, Mary E.	Veatch, Charles W.	15, Sept 1853	L3
Wood, Mary Eliza	Pierce, James	2, Mar. 1843	L3
Wood, Matilda B.	LaBoiteaux, Andrew	13, Dec. 1855	L3
Wood, Olive H.	James, U.P.	13, May 1847	L3
Wood, Phebe M.	Smith, J. Freeman	28, Aug. 1845	L3
Wood, Susan M.	Thayer, Henry	23, Apr. 1840	L3
Woodbridge, Ellen	Creighton, W.H.	8, June 1843	L3
Woodring, Sarah M.	Wysong, Henry M.	19, Jan. 1854	L3
Woodrow, Sarah Elizabeth	Campbell, Hiram	9, May 1844	L3
Woodruff, Catharine	Parker, William	8, Nov. 1838	L3
Woodruff, Eliza	Rutter, William	10, Feb. 1842	L3

Brides	Grooms	Date of Notice	Page
Woodruff, Jinne D.	Allen, T.C.	10, June 1852	L3
Woodruff, M. Louisa	Marsh, Alanson	23, May 1839	L3
Woodruff, Mary Ann	Walton, George	25, Feb. 1847	L3
Woodruff, Phoebe	Cones, Joseph	13, May 1852	L3
Woodruff, Rozella	Hill, F.D. (Dr)	22, June 1854	L3
Woods, Ellen	Adae, Charles F.	17, Mar. 1842	L3
Woods, Martha J.	Hammond, Robert H.	23, Feb. 1854	L3
Woods, Mary	Falconer, Cyrus (Dr)	17, Oct. 1839	L3
Woodward, Elizabeth	Sexton, Charles	19, July 1855	L3
Woodward, Lucia Anna	Coleman, John W.	30, Oct. 1834	L1
Wooley, Julia Ann	Pritchett, Jeremiah	15, Apr. 1852	L3
Woolley, Caroline	Smith, Samuel W.	10, Apr. 1845	L3
Woolley, M.	White, Peter A.	27, Nov. 1856	L3
Woolsen, Emm C.	Carter, T. Jarvis	29, May 1851	L3
Worchester, Lucy	Tranter, James	3, May 1849	L3
Worley, Margarety E.	Spinning, William	31, May 1849	L3
Worrick, Lizzie	Bishop, William T.	24, May 1855	L3
Worthington, Margaret	Mansfield, Edward D.	9, May 1839	L3
Worthington, Mary T.	Macomb, David B.	1, Apr. 1816	L3
Worthington, Sarah A	King, Edward	20, May 1816	L3
Wright, Amelia	Badgley, William	22, Mar. 1814	L3
Wright, Anna	Kiloh, John	4, Sept 1851	L3
Wright, Anna Rebecca	Bradbury, George W.	26, Oct. 1843	L3
Wright, Eliza B.	Lord, Henry C.	1, July 1852	L3
Wright, Eliza S.	Guiou, Benjamin	11, May 1843	L3
Wright, Elizabeth	Shaw, John	12, Apr. 1814	L3
Wright, Hannah	Andress, Charles O.	29, June 1848	L3
Wright, Jane Isabell	Strobridge, H.	9, Oct. 1845	L3
Wright, Lucy	Sanders, David A.	16, Aug. 1838	L3
Wright, Martha Ann	Roe, John J. (Capt)	31, Aug. 1837	L3
Wright, Martha E.	Morris, Robert H.	7, Apr. 1853	L3
Wright, Mary	Miner, John L.	2, Nov. 1837	L3
Wright, Mary Jane	Higgins, William H.	24, Dec. 1857	L3
Wright, Mary M.	Haire, E.	10, June 1852	L3
Wright, Mary T.	Curwen, Maskell E.	24, May 1855	L3
Wright, Mary W.	Lowe, George W.	6, Nov. 1845	L3
Wright, Rebecca	Lathrop, Martin D.	18, Feb. 1815	L3
Wright, Sarah Jane	Campbell, Edwin R.	24, May 1849	L3
Wright, Sophia	Hunter, William	23, Apr. 1846	L3
Wright, Susan Emily	Moore, J.C.S. (Dr)	19, June 1851	L3
Wunder, Eliza J.	Beresford, Samuel	8, Nov. 1855	L3
Wunder, Susan D.	Cassatt, John W.	24, Dec. 1857	L3
Wylier, Anna C.	Simmons, L.C.	23, Oct. 1856	L5
Yeatman, Anna Maria	Anderson, W.C.	25, May 1837	L2
Yeatman, Caroline	Ward, William M.	7, June 1849	L3
Yeatman, Elizabeth	Morgan, Henry	11, May 1843	L3
Yeatman, Julia	Barker, Thomas C.	3, May 1814	L3
Yeatman, Sarah Jane	Merriweather, N.	26, Dec. 1839	L3
Yeatman, Sarah Lucy	Norris, Charles C.	18, Apr. 1839	L3
Yeo, Jane	Stanley, Thomas	10, May 1855	L3
Yocum, Elizabeth	Page, Andrew Jackson	3, Oct. 1844	L3
Young, Caroline	Woodruff, John S.	8, Nov. 1849	L3
Young, Cynthia Ann	Betts, Smith	3, Feb. 1848	L3

Brides	Grooms	Date of Notice	Page
Young, Elizabeth R.	Copelen, George W.	4, July 1850	L3
Young, Honor (Mrs)	Deaven, Thomas	12, Nov. 1829	L3
Young, Margaret	Betts, Joseph W.	8, Nov. 1855	L3
Young, Mollie T.	Baker, M.A.	4, Jan. 1855	L3
Young, Nancy (Mrs)	Copelen, Isaac C.	5, Sept 1850	L3
Zebold, Mary E.	Heferman, Thomas N.	14, Oct. 1852	L3
Zesline, Sarah (Mrs)	Borden, Samuel	16, July 1819	L3
Zimmerman, Catharine	Seybold, Emanuel F.	10, June 1847	L3

Name	Type of Notice	Date of Notice	Page
Abbot, James	Land payment notice	7, Nov. 1810	L3
Abbott, Joseph	Horse found	20, Oct. 1817	L3
Abbott, Joseph J.	Letter at P.O.	1, Jan. 1812	L3
Abbott, William	Debt relief	21, May 1829	L4
Abel, James	Horse found	26, Jan. 1819	L3
Able, James	Horse found	12, June 1815	L3
Abraham, Joseph	Debt relief	17, Nov. 1842	L5
Abrahams, William M.	Escaped convict	12, June 1828	L3
Abrams, Mary E.	Guardian	9, Apr. 1857	L3
Ackley, Clarissa	Guardian	30, Jan. 1840	L3
Ackley, Emily	Guardian	30, Jan. 1840	L3
Ackley, John	Debt relief	1, Aug. 1833	L3
Adams, Abram	Horse found	25, Dec. 1811	L1
Adams, Alexander	Debtor	16, Feb. 1819	L3
Adams, Alexander	Debt relief	9, June 1831	L3
Adams, John M.	Debt relief	1, Aug. 1833	L3
Adams, Luther C.	Debt relief	1, Aug. 1833	L3
Adams, Peter	Runaway	21, July 1817	L3
Akres, Benjamin L.	Debt relief	17, Oct. 1839	L3
Aldridge, Annias	Horse found	20, Nov. 1815	L4
Aldridge, Erasmus	Horse found	24, July 1811	L1
Alexander, James	Horse found	11, Apr. 1810	L2
Alexander, John S.	Debt relief	5, Feb. 1835	L3
Alfred, Burrel	Debt relief	9, June 1831	L3
Allan, William & Isabella	Divorce/Abandonment	25, July 1821	L3
Allbough, Zachariah	Rev. War Veteran	13, Aug. 1854	L3
Allen, Ethan	Debt relief	1, Aug. 1833	L3
Allen, Israel	Horse found	12, Aug. 1816	L3
Allen, Israel & Hannah	Divorce/Abandonment	30, Oct. 1815	L3
Allen, John	Horse lost	14, Sept 1813	L1
Allen, John	Horse found	18, Mar. 1812	L2
Allen, Nerum	Debt relief	1, Aug. 1833	L3
Allen, Thomas	Debt relief	9, Oct. 1828	L3
Alley, Amos	Debt relief	18, Aug. 1826	L3
Allison, Alexander	Deserter	29, Mar. 1814	L1
Alsop, George	Debt relief	1, Aug. 1833	L3
Alter, Frederick	Letter at P.O.	1, Jan. 1812	L3
Alves, Alexander	Guardian	7, Feb. 1856	L3
Alves, Henry	Guardian	7, Feb. 1856	L3
Alves, Jane	Guardian	7, Feb. 1856	L3
Alves, John	Guardian	7, Feb. 1856	L3
Alves, John	Guardian	5, Feb. 1857	L3
Ames, James	Debt relief	11, Nov. 1825	L3
Anderson, Adam	Debt relief	4, Aug. 1831	L4
Anderson, James	Debt relief	9, Oct. 1828	L3
Anderson, James D.	Debt relief	24, July 1828	L1
Anderson, John	Debt relief	24, July 1828	L1
Anderson, John	Horse found	26, Aug. 1816	L3
Anderson, John	Debt relief	9, Oct. 1828	L3
Anderson, John H.	Horse found	2, Dec. 1825	L3
Anderson, John H.	Debt relief	5, Feb. 1835	L3
Anderson, William	Debt relief	5, Feb. 1835	L3
Andrew, John H.	Debt relief	8, June 1827	L4
Andrews, Abijah & Hannah	Divorce/Abandonment	1, Sept 1818	L3

Name	Type of Notice	Date of Notice	Page
Andrews, Henry	Letter at P.O.	1, Jan. 1812	L3
Antrim, James	Horse found	27, May 1812	L2
Apger, Minerd	Horse found	2, Sept 1825	L2
Applegate, Israel	Horse found	31, Jan. 1810	L2
Applegate, Jarris	Horse found	14, Oct. 1820	L3
Archard, Joshua	Horse found	12, Feb. 1812	L2
Armstrong, John	Debt relief	24, July 1828	L1
Armstrong, John	Horse found	26, Aug. 1820	L2
Armstrong, John	Debt relief	21, May 1829	L4
Armstrong, Robert	Debt relief	17, Oct. 1839	L3
Armstrong, Walter	Horse found	9, Jan. 1811	L1
Armstrong, Walter	Letter at P.O.	1, Jan. 1812	L3
Arney, Frederick	Deserter	9, June 1817	L4
Arnold, Joseph G.	Guardian	7, May 1857	L3
Arnold, Montgomery (Mrs)	Birth of son	8, Mar. 1849	L3
Arnold, Richard B.	Guardian	7, May 1857	L3
Arnold, Samuel J.	Guardian	7, May 1857	L3
Arnold, Sarah C.	Guardian	7, May 1857	L3
Arnold, William G.	Guardian	7, May 1857	L3
Arthur, James	Rev. War Veteran	13, Aug. 1854	L3
Arthur, Thomas	Debt relief	17, Oct. 1839	L3
Atherton, Aaron	Horse found	14, July 1817	L3
Atherton, David	Horse found	24, Apr. 1811	L2
Atherton, David	Horse found	2, Dec. 1825	L3
Atherton, David	Horse found	21, June 1820	L4
Atkins, Abijah	Horse found	19, Oct. 1813	L1
Atkins, Silas & Phebe	Divorce/Abandonment	11, Feb. 1836	L4
Auter, Rudolph	Horse found	16, Feb. 1819	L3
Auter, Thomas	Land payment notice	7, Nov. 1810	L3
Auter, Thomas	Letter at P.O.	1, Jan. 1812	L3
Averal, Bela	Horse found	30, June 1817	L3
Avery, Emily	Guardian	7, May 1840	L3
Avery, Emily	Guardian	13, Apr. 1848	L3
Avery, Francis	Guardian	13, Apr. 1848	L3
Avery, Francis	Guardian	10, Jan. 1856	L3
Avery, Simeon H.	Horse lost	27, Nov. 1815	L3
Aydelott, Thomas	Horse found	27, Apr. 1813	L1
Aydelotte, Ann	Guardian	4, Sept 1856	L5
Aydelotte, Elizabeth	Guardian	4, Sept 1856	L5
Aydelotte, Emeline	Guardian	4, Sept 1856	L5
Aydelotte, Matilda	Guardian	4, Sept 1856	L5
Aydelotte, Rebecca	Guardian	4, Sept 1856	L5
Aydelotte, Rebecca Ann	Guardian	7, May 1857	L3
Ayres, Henry	Horse found	2, Oct. 1811	L3
Ayres, John	Letter at P.O.	1, Jan. 1812	L3
Ayres, Martin W.	Debt relief	1, Aug. 1833	L3
Ayres, Richard	Horse found	19, May 1817	L3
Babcock, (widow)	Horse found	16, June 1817	L3
Babcock, Gideon	Horse found	12, Feb. 1812	L2
Babock, Susanna	Runaway	22, Dec. 1817	L4
Bacon, Elijah	Debt relief	8, June 1827	L4
Bagley, William A.	Debt relief	23, June 1842	L3
Bailey, Robert	Horse found	1, Aug. 1810	L1

Name	Type of Notice	Date of Notice	Page
Bainbridge, Edmund & Hannah	Divorce/Abandonment	3, Apr. 1822	L4
Baird, Joseph	Horse found	26, Sept 1810	L3
Baldwin, Edward	Land payment notice	7, Nov. 1810	L3
Baldwin, John	Horse found	27, June 1810	L2
Baldwin, John	Horse found	5, July 1814	L2
Baldwin, John	Horse found	12, Mar. 1819	L3
Baldwin, Lewis W.	Debt relief	17, Oct. 1839	L3
Baldwin, Samuel	Debt relief	1, Aug. 1833	L3
Baldwin, William	Debt relief	4, Aug. 1831	L4
Ball, Abner	Horse found	9, Jan. 1811	L1
Balsel, John	Horse found	16, Jan. 1815	L3
Banfill, Enoch	Horse found	25, Aug. 1812	L1
Banham, James H.	Horse found	22, Nov. 1827	L3
Banks, William S.	Guardian	16, Oct. 1856	L6
Banks, William T.	Guardian	7, June 1855	L3
Baraes, James H.	Debt relief	1, Aug. 1833	L3
Barber, Elihu C.	Debt relief	1, Aug. 1833	L3
Barber, Nathaniel	Letter at P.O.	1, Jan. 1812	L3
Barkalow, John J.	Debt relief	24, July 1828	L1
Barker, John	Deserter from army	15, Dec. 1812	L3
Barlow, John	Debt relief	1, Aug. 1833	L3
Barmore, Stephen	Debt relief	9, Feb. 1827	L3
Barney, Daniel F.	Horse found	10, Oct. 1810	L3
Barnhart, Speck & Elizabeth	Divorce/Abandonment	3, Feb. 1806	L4
Barr, Robert	Debt relief	1, Aug. 1833	L3
Barr, Robert	Debt relief	5, Feb. 1835	L3
Barrett, John	Horse found	5, Dec. 1810	L3
Barry, Caroline H.	Guardian	7, May 1857	L3
Barry, Thomas H.	Guardian	7, May 1857	L3
Barry, W.D.	Guardian	7, May 1857	L3
Bartleson, Andrew	Deserter from army	20, Oct. 1812	L3
Bartlet, Samuel	Horse found	7, July 1817	L3
Bartlett, Charles	Guardian	3, Sept 1840	L3
Barton, James	Debt relief	9, Feb. 1827	L3
Barton, James	Debt relief	9, Oct. 1828	L3
Batchelder, George	Convict	5, Feb. 1846	L3
Baum, David C.	Guardian	14, Feb. 1839	L3
Baum, Eleanor	Guardian	14, Feb. 1839	L3
Baum, Kershner	Guardian	14, Feb. 1839	L3
Baum, Mary P.	Guardian	14, Feb. 1839	L3
Bauman, John & Magdalena	Divorce/Abandonment	28, Aug. 1851	L3
Baxter, Archibald	Debt relief	17, Oct. 1839	L3
Baxter, James	Horse found	19, Jan. 1813	L3
Baxter, John	Guardian	9, Aug. 1838	L3
Baxter, John	Guardian	3, Sept 1840	L3
Baxter, John M.	Guardian	7, June 1855	L3
Baxter, Thomas	Letter at P.O.	1, Jan. 1812	L3
Bay, James	Land payment due	22, Nov. 1809	L4
Bayles, Jesse	Debt relief	5, Feb. 1835	L3
Bayless, Elias	Debt relief	4, Aug. 1831	L4
Beach, Ebenezer N.	Debt relief	17, Oct. 1839	L3
Beadles, Abraham H.	Debt relief	11, Nov. 1825	L3
Beadman, George	Debt relief	9, Oct. 1828	L3
Beal, Isaac	Land payment notice	7, Nov. 1810	L3

Name	Type of Notice	Date of Notice	Page
Bearpark, Henry	Debt relief	11, Nov. 1825	L3
Beatson, Patrick & Eleanor	Divorce/Abandonment	7, Mar. 1839	L4
Beckelhimer, Jonathan	Horse found	9, June 1812	L3
Beckwith, Francis	Debt relief	11, Nov. 1825	L3
Beckwith, Travis	Debt relief	21, May 1829	L4
Beddo, Thomas	Rev. War Veteran	13, Aug. 1854	L3
Beebe, David	Horse found	19, Oct. 1813	L3
Beeler, Samuel	Land payment notice	7, Nov. 1810	L3
Belcher, Loring	Land payment due	22, Nov. 1809	L4
Belew, Leonard	Deserter	8, Feb. 1814	L3
Bell, Adam	Debt relief	1, Aug. 1833	L3
Bell, Fountain	Debt relief	4, Aug. 1831	L4
Bell, Jane (Miss)	Letter at P.O.	1, Jan. 1812	L3
Bell, John	Horse found	8, June 1813	L3
Bell, John	Horse found	23, Sept 1820	L3
Bell, Peter	Horse found	15, July 1816	L3
Benbridge, Henry	Debtor	31, Mar. 1820	L3
Benefield, Robert	Horse found	8, Sept 1831	L3
Benham, Richard	Horse found	13, July 1813	L3
Benjamin, Hannah (Mrs)	Debt relief	14, July 1842	L3
Bennet, Aaron & Elizabeth	Divorce/Abandonment	30, Dec. 1816	L3
Bennet, Archibald & Patsey	Divorce/Abandonment	16, Aug. 1814	L3
Bennet, Titus	Land payment due	22, Nov. 1809	L4
Bennett, Samuel	Horse found	20, June 1810	L3
Benson, Caleb	Debt relief	28, Jan. 1830	L3
Benson, Daniel	Debt relief	1, Aug. 1833	L3
Benson, Henry	Debt relief	24, July 1828	L1
Benson, Mathew	Debtor	15, Dec. 1817	L3
Benson, Matthew	Debtor	25, Feb. 1818	L3
Bergen, Simpson & Catharine	Divorce/Abandonment	21, Feb. 1839	L3
Berry, Benjamin	Reported runaway	21, Sept 1812	L3
Best, Samuel	Vattier court case	28, Apr. 1807	L3
Betts, Andrew	Guardian	3, Dec. 1840	L3
Betts, John	Guardian	3, Dec. 1840	L3
Betts, William	Vattier court case	28, Apr. 1807	L3
Betts, William & Susan	Divorce/Abandonment	19, July 1820	L3
Beumer, Henry	Guardian	8, Oct. 1857	L3
Beur, John	Letter at P.O.	1, Jan. 1812	L3
Beverlin, John	Horse found	9, Nov. 1813	L2
Bickham, Ella	Guardian	30, Mar. 1848	L4
Biddle, Bouldin	Horse found	5, May 1817	L3
Biggs, Aaron	Land payment notice	7, Nov. 1810	L3
Biggs, Dorrington	Guardian	9, Aug. 1838	L3
Billmyer, John	Debt relief	1, Aug. 1833	L3
Bills, Elizabeth	Letter at P.O.	1, Jan. 1812	L3
Binefield, Robert	Horse found	25, Aug. 1817	L3
Binett, Joshua	Letter at P.O.	1, Jan. 1812	L3
Birdcell, Warren & Anna	Divorce/Abandonment	20, Apr. 1822	L4
Birdsall, Samuel B.	Debt relief	14, July 1842	L3
Bishop, David W.	Deserter from army	20, Oct. 1812	L3
Bishop, Thomas	Letter at P.O.	1, Jan. 1812	L3
Bittle, Ezekiel	Horse found	27, Apr. 1824	L4
Black, David	Horse found	27, Nov. 1811	L3
Black, David	Horse found	8, June 1819	L3

Name	Type of Notice	Date of Notice	Page
Blacksmith, William Cooper	Name change notice	4, Dec. 1811	L2
Blair, John	Inquiry	21, Feb. 1828	L3
Blanchard, Joshua	Debt relief	9, June 1831	L3
Block, David P. & Maria L.	Divorce/Abandonment	23, Dec. 1847	L3
Bloom, Anthony & Emily	Divorce/Abandonment	5, Sept 1844	L3
Bloom, Christian & Elizabeth	Divorce/Abandonment	3, Sept 1857	L3
Blue, John & Abigail	Divorce/Abandonment	18, Nov. 1820	L3
Blue, Samuel	Horse found	27, Nov. 1811	L3
Bogar, Jacob	Debt relief	9, Oct. 1828	L3
Bolcer, Henry	Horse found	15, Aug. 1810	L2
Boles, John	Horse found	22, Apr. 1816	L3
Bolser, Alexander	Guardian	7, June 1855	L3
Bolser, Benjamin	Guardian	7, June 1855	L3
Bolser, Catharine	Guardian	7, June 1855	L3
Bolser, George	Guardian	7, June 1855	L3
Bolser, John	Guardian	7, June 1855	L3
Bolser, Samuel	Guardian	7, June 1855	L3
Bolser, Sarah	Guardian	7, June 1855	L3
Bolser, Susan	Guardian	7, June 1855	L3
Bonner, David	Letter at P.O.	1, Jan. 1812	L3
Bons, James S.	Debt relief	23, June 1842	L3
Bonta, Abraham	Land payment notice	7, Nov. 1810	L3
Bonta, Peter	Land payment due	22, Nov. 1809	L4
Boomershine, Henry	Land payment due	22, Nov. 1809	L4
Boon, Daniel	Land payment notice	7, Nov. 1810	L3
Boon, Thomas	Horse found	22, Jan. 1812	L3
Boothby, James	Debt relief	21, May 1829	L4
Bornand, H. J. & Mary	Divorce/Abandonment	6, Nov. 1811	L4
Boston, Israel & Matilda	Divorce/Abandonment	20, Oct. 1853	L3
Boura, Samuel	Letter at P.O.	1, Jan. 1812	L3
Bowman, Christopher	Deserter	15, Feb. 1813	L2
Bowman, Richard	Horse found	5, June 1815	L3
Boyce, Robert P. & Celia	Divorce/Abandonment	4, Apr. 1820	L1
Boyd, Allen	Debt relief	14, July 1842	L3
Bracken, Hugh	Vattier court case	28, Apr. 1807	L3
Bradbury, Cornelius S.	Guardian	8, Jan. 1857	L3
Bradley, John	Letter at P.O.	1, Jan. 1812	L3
Brall, William	Hughes High School	2, Feb. 1854	L3
Branch, John H.	Debt relief	17, Nov. 1842	L5
Brand, Jonathan C.	Notice	22, May 1828	L3
Brandon, Andrew	Deserter	18, Jan. 1814	L1
Brannon, Andrew & Sally	Divorce/Abandonment	6, Nov. 1811	L3
Brant, Isaac	Debt relief	9, Feb. 1827	L3
Brant, James D.	Debt relief	9, June 1831	L3
Branton, Thomas	Debt relief	1, Aug. 1833	L3
Breedling, James	Debt relief	14, July 1807	L2
Brewin, Edward	Horse found	7, Feb. 1828	L3
Brewster, Samuel	Land payment notice	7, Nov. 1810	L3
Brian, Isaac	Horse found	24, Nov. 1821	L3
Brick, John	Horse found	27, Nov. 1815	L3
Bridgford, William	Horse found	27, Oct. 1812	L2
Brigadier, Samuel	Debt relief	5, Feb. 1835	L3
Brigham, Moses W.	Debt relief	9, June 1831	L3
Brisben, Robert	Horse found	23, June 1817	L3

Name	Type of Notice	Date of Notice	Page
Brisbin, Robert	Horse found	29, Sept 1826	L3
Britt, Clark	Debt relief	9, Oct. 1828	L3
Britton, Benjamin	Convict	5, Feb. 1846	L3
Britton, Charles	Vattier court case	28, Apr. 1807	L3
Broadberry, David	Land payment due	22, Nov. 1809	L4
Broadwell, Cyrus	Debt relief	17, Nov. 1842	L5
Broadwell, Lineus	Guardian	14, Feb. 1839	L3
Broadwell, Samuel	Guardian	14, Feb. 1839	L3
Brodrick, William	Horse found	5, Jan. 1813	L3
Brooks, Amelia A.	Guardian	3, May 1855	L3
Brooks, Eri Yolney	Debt relief	14, July 1842	L3
Brooks, James & Deney	Divorce/Abandonment	10, Mar. 1821	L3
Brooks, John	Letter at P.O.	1, Jan. 1812	L3
Brooks, John	Debtor	13, Jan. 1824	L3
Brooks, John & Prudence	Divorce/Abandonment	27, May 1818	L3
Brotherton, Abel	Debt relief	18, Aug. 1826	L3
Broughhead, Christopher	Horse found	7, June 1825	L3
Brown, Augustus C.	Debt relief	14, July 1842	L3
Brown, Augustus J.	Debt relief	17, Nov. 1842	L5
Brown, Benjamin	Convict	5, Feb. 1846	L3
Brown, Cythia A.	Guardian	9, Aug. 1855	L3
Brown, Eliza	Guardian	9, Aug. 1855	L3
Brown, Ephraim	Horse found	7, July 1826	L3
Brown, Ethan A.	Letter at P.O.	1, Jan. 1812	L3
Brown, Jacob	Horse found	16, June 1812	L3
Brown, Jacob Michael & Mary	Divorce/Abandonment	23, June 1812	L3
Brown, James	Horse found	25, May 1813	L1
Brown, John	Debt relief	21, May 1829	L4
Brown, Joshua	Debt relief	24, Mar. 1807	L3
Brown, Michael & Mary	Divorce/Abandonment	28, Aug. 1815	L3
Brown, Nelson	Horse found	27, May 1816	L3
Brown, Oscar	Debt relief	9, June 1831	L3
Brown, Richard	Horse found	31, Jan. 1810	L4
Brown, Richard	Land payment due	22, Nov. 1809	L4
Brown, Robert	Cow found	23, Jan. 1824	L3
Brown, Robert	Horse found	2, Feb. 1832	L3
Brown, Samuel	Letter at P.O.	1, Jan. 1812	L3
Brown, Samuel	Horse found	1, Sept 1817	L3
Brown, Servillian	Debt relief	1, Aug. 1833	L3
Brown, Warren H.	Debt relief	17, Nov. 1842	L5
Brown, Zachariah	Debt relief	28, Jan. 1830	L3
Bruce, William	Horse lost	29, July 1823	L3
Bruce, William	Land payment due	22, Nov. 1809	L4
Brueck, Paul	Guardian	6, Sept 1855	L3
Bruen, Jabez & Rebecca	Divorce/Abandonment	30, Oct. 1811	L2
Bruin, Isaac	Horse found	3, July 1815	L3
Brunson, James C.	Debtor	1, Dec. 1821	L2
Brunton, James & Elizabeth	Divorce/Abandonment	1, Sept 1806	L2
Brunton, James & Nancy	Divorce/Abandonment	23, Sept 1806	L2
Bryant, David	Debt relief	24, July 1828	L1
Buchanan, James & Mary	Divorce/Abandonment	27, Jan. 1807	L3
Buchanan, John	Horse found	29, Nov. 1811	L3
Buell, Leonard	Debt relief	14, July 1842	L3
Bull, Aaron D.	Debt relief	9, June 1831	L3

Name	Type of Notice	Date of Notice	Page
Bull, Amasa	Debt relief	9, June 1831	L3
Bullman, Jonathan	Deserter	6, Sept 1814	L4
Bunnell, Daniel	Horse found	14, July 1817	L3
Burch, Daniel	Horse found	3, Oct. 1810	L3
Burch, Henry	Horse found	22, Jan. 1812	L3
Burgess, John	Horse lost	3, June 1816	L1
Burgin, Thomas	Debt relief	1, Aug. 1833	L3
Burk, Eliza	Debt relief	9, Oct. 1828	L3
Burk, Ulich	Horse found	22, Feb. 1814	L3
Burnham, John	Debt relief	11, Nov. 1825	L3
Burnham, John	Debt relief	1, Aug. 1833	L3
Burns, Charles	Guardian	6, Mar. 1856	L3
Burns, Charles	Guardian	5, Feb. 1857	L3
Burns, James	Horse found	16, Jan. 1815	L4
Burns, Lawrence	Horse found	5, Sept 1810	L2
Burns, Michael	Land payment notice	7, Nov. 1810	L3
Burns, Theodocia	Guardian	6, Mar. 1856	L3
Burns, Theodosia	Guardian	8, Oct. 1857	L3
Burris, John	Horse found	8, June 1819	L3
Burris, Joseph	Horse found	5, Jan. 1813	L3
Burritt, Daniel	Debt relief	14, July 1842	L3
Burt, Thomas W.	Debt relief	11, Nov. 1825	L3
Burton, Isaac	Letter at P.O.	1, Jan. 1812	L3
Bush, Preston	Debt relief	9, June 1831	L3
Bush, Stephen	Debt relief	1, Aug. 1833	L3
Bussey, Thomas	Debt relief	24, July 1828	L1
Butler, David	Debt relief	4, Aug. 1831	L4
Butler, Lemuel	Debt relief	14, July 1842	L3
Butler, Peterson	Debt relief	24, July 1828	L1
Butler, Polly	Letter at P.O.	1, Jan. 1812	L3
Butler, Robert W.	Debt relief	23, June 1842	L3
Butler, Thomas S.	Debt relief	23, June 1842	L3
Butler, Walter	Horse found	23, Oct. 1815	L3
Buzatt, Christiana	Guardian	7, Feb. 1856	L3
Buzatt, Mary Jane	Guardian	7, Feb. 1856	L3
Buzatt, Sylvester	Guardian	7, Feb. 1856	L3
Byers, Abraham	Horse found	15, Apr. 1812	L3
Byers, Georg	Horse found	14, Dec. 1813	L1
Byers, John	Horse found	4, June 1817	L3
Byers, William	Debt relief	9, Oct. 1828	L3
Byram, John	Horse found	5, June 1811	L1
Byram, Samuel & Maria	Divorce/Abandonment	26, Jan. 1843	L3
Byrne, James	Hughes High School	2, Feb. 1854	L3
Byrne, James W.	Debt relief	18, Aug. 1826	L3
Byrns, Laurence	Horse found	10, Apr. 1811	L4
Cabell, John M.	Debt relief	1, Aug. 1833	L3
Cain, Richard	Horse found	30, June 1817	L3
Caldwell, James	Land payment notice	7, Nov. 1810	L3
Caldwell, Joseph	Land payment notice	7, Nov. 1810	L3
Caldwell, Robert	Horse found	26, Dec. 1810	L3
Caldwell, Robert	Horse lost	18, Aug. 1812	L3
Calson, Jane	Runaway apprentice	15, Aug. 1823	L3
Cameron, John	Horse found	9, Nov. 1813	L1

Name	Type of Notice	Date of Notice	Page
Campbell, Delilah	Guardian	8, Nov. 1832	L4
Campbell, Henry	Debt relief	9, Feb. 1827	L3
Campbell, Nelly	Guardian	8, Nov. 1832	L4
Campbell, Richard	Horse found	26, Mar. 1819	L3
Canary, Thomas	Deserter	28, June 1814	L3
Cannon, Isaac	Horse found	4, Apr. 1810	L3
Cannon, Robert K.	Debt relief	4, June 1819	L3
Cannon, Robert K.	Debt relief	11, Nov. 1825	L3
Capp, Henry B.	Debt relief	18, Aug. 1826	L3
Capp, Jacob G.	Debt relief	9, Oct. 1828	L3
Carahan, William	Horse found	2, Feb. 1813	L2
Card, Aaron	Horse found	6, July 1813	L2
Carpenter, Daniel H.	Guardian	5, Feb. 1857	L3
Carpenter, John B.	Horse found	25, May 1813	L1
Carpenter, Joseph	Fire at his stable	11, Apr. 1810	L3
Carpenter, Joseph	Letter at P.O.	1, Jan. 1812	L3
Carpenter, Moses	Horse found	27, July 1819	l3
Carr, Samuel	Debt relief	24, July 1828	L1
Carroll, Edward	Runaway apprentice	14, June 1814	L3
Carroll, William	Debt relief	24, July 1828	L1
Carson, William	Debt relief	24, July 1828	L1
Carson, William	Debt relief	1, Aug. 1833	L3
Carson, William J.	Horse found	20, Nov. 1814	L2
Carson, William J.	Horse found	12, Feb. 1816	L3
Carson, William J.	Debt relief	18, Aug. 1826	L3
Carter, Freeman	Land payment due	22, Nov. 1809	L4
Carter, John	Runaway apprentice	26, Feb. 1816	L1
Carter, Reuben	Pension	23, Oct. 1828	L3
Carter, Robert	Letter at P.O.	1, Jan. 1812	L3
Carter, Thomas	Horse lost	8, July 1816	L1
Case, Jacob	Horse found	15, Dec. 1818	L3
Case, Lewis H.	Horse found	30, June 1821	L3
Cashaday, Thomas	Horse found	14, Feb. 1810	L3
Casteel, Robert	Horse found	31, Jan. 1810	L4
Caster, William	Horse found	27, May 1812	L2
Castle, Roswell	Debt relief	18, Aug. 1826	L3
Casto, Jonathan	Deserter	24, Aug. 1813	L2
Castor, Conrad	Land payment due	22, Nov. 1809	L4
Cattelin, James	Debt relief	9, Oct. 1828	L3
Catterlin, William	Horse found	6, June 1810	L1
Cave, John S.	Debt relief	4, Aug. 1831	L4
Cavender, Samuel	Land payment due	22, Nov. 1809	L4
Chamberlain, Lewis	Debt relief	9, June 1831	L3
Chambers, Benjamin	Land payment due	22, Nov. 1809	L4
Chambers, John	Debt relief	17, Oct. 1839	L3
Chambers, Joseph	Horse found	19, Oct. 1813	L2
Champion, Samuel	Horse found	1, Nov. 1814	L1
Champion, Samuel	Horse found	29, May 1815	L3
Chanay, Richard	Deserter from army	17, Nov. 1812	L3
Chance, John	Horse found	10, Mar. 1817	L4
Chapin, Roswell	Debt relief	9, Feb. 1827	L3
Chapman, Archable	Letter at P.O.	1, Jan. 1812	L3
Charles, John	Horse found	19, Feb. 1812	L3
Charles, Nehemiah	Letter at P.O.	1, Jan. 1812	L3

Name	Type of Notice	Date of Notice	Page
Chase, Reason	Debt relief	5, Feb. 1835	L3
Chedal, John	Letter at P.O.	1, Jan. 1812	L3
Cheek, George	Horse found	7, Aug. 1811	L4
Cheesman, Uriah	Cow found	4, Feb. 1818	L3
Cheever, Ariel G.	Debt relief	23, June 1842	L3
Cheever, Charles S.	Debt relief	23, June 1842	L3
Chess, James	Letter at P.O.	1, Jan. 1812	L3
Choate, Robert W. & Ann	Divorce/Abandonment	29, Aug. 1844	L3
Christman, Adam	Guardian	8, Nov. 1838	L3
Christman, Elias	Horse found	4, Mar. 1816	L3
Clark, Alanthus	Debt relief	17, Oct. 1839	L3
Clark, Ambrose	Horse found	10, July 1811	L1
Clark, Ichabod & Phebe	Divorce/Abandonment	27, Apr. 1813	L1
Clark, Jacob	Letter at P.O.	1, Jan. 1812	L3
Clark, James	Horse found	2, Oct. 1815	L2
Clark, James	Horse found	13, May 1816	L2
Clark, Jeremiah	Horse found	12, Aug. 1816	I3
Clark, Jeremiah	Horse found	23, Mar. 1819	L3
Clark, John	Cow lost	29, Aug. 1821	L2
Clark, John	Land payment due	22, Nov. 1809	L4
Clark, Joseph M.	Debt relief	1, Aug. 1833	L3
Clark, William	Deserter from army	1, Dec. 1812	L3
Clark, William	Letter at P.O.	1, Jan. 1812	L3
Clark, William	Horse found	23, Feb. 1813	L3
Clark, William	Horse found	19, May 1831	L3
Clarke, Houton	Horse found	18, Mar. 1812	L2
Claypool, Solomon	Horse found	19, Feb. 1812	L3
Clayton, Andrew B.	Debt relief	1, Aug. 1833	L3
Clayton, John B.	Debt relief	1, Aug. 1833	L3
Cleaveland, Milton & Sarah	Divorce/Abandonment	13, Jan. 1842	L3
Clem, George	Horse found	8, Jan. 1812	L3
Clem, John	Horse found	15, Mar. 1814	L3
Clendening, John	Letter at P.O.	1, Jan. 1812	L3
Cleveland, George P.	Debt relief	5, Feb. 1835	L3
Clifton, Simon	Debt relief	4, Aug. 1831	L4
Clizbe, Ira	Letter at P.O.	1, Jan. 1812	L3
Cobb, Mary E.	Guardian	7, June 1855	L3
Cobb, Pollock W.	Guardian	7, June 1855	L3
Cobner, Thomas & Ann	Divorce/Abandonment	17, June 1825	L4
Coburn, James	Debt relief	9, June 1831	L3
Cochern, John	Deserter	18, Jan. 1814	L1
Cochran, John	Horse found	13, Oct. 1812	L2
Coddington, Lewis	Guardian	8, Nov. 1855	L3
Colam, Thomas	Debt relief	21, May 1829	L4
Colburn, John	Debt relief	4, Aug. 1831	L4
Colby, Isaac	Horse found	29, Dec. 1812	L2
Coleman, Charles	Letter at P.O.	1, Jan. 1812	L3
Coleman, George M.	Debt relief	18, Aug. 1826	L3
Colgin, Isaac F & Elizabeth	Divorce/Abandonment	4, Mar. 1841	L3
Collier, Jane (Mrs)	Letter at P.O.	1, Jan. 1812	L3
Collins, Edward	Debt relief	5, Feb. 1835	L3
Collins, John	Horse found	14, Feb. 1810	L2
Colloway, John	Horse found	29, Jan. 1812	L2
Colver, Samuel	Land payment notice	7, Nov. 1810	L3

Name	Type of Notice	Date of Notice	Page
Colyer, Robert	Debt relief	17, Oct. 1839	L3
Comelin, Charles	Debt relief	24, July 1828	L1
Comelin, Hanna	Debt relief	24, July 1828	L1
Compton, William	Horse found	19, June 1811	L3
Conaway, James	Land payment due	22, Nov. 1809	L4
Cone, Charles	Horse found	27, May 1816	L3
Cone, Charles, Jr.	Debt relief	9, Feb. 1827	L3
Congar, Moses	Horse found	15, Jan. 1812	L3
Conklin, Abner	Debt relief	28, Jan. 1830	L3
Conklin, Stephen	Horse found	24, Nov. 1817	L3
Conkling, Pierson	Horse found	8, May 1815	L2
Connel, Benjamin	Debt relief	4, Aug. 1831	L4
Conner, Daniel	Land payment notice	7, Nov. 1810	L3
Conner, William O.	Debt relief	9, June 1831	L3
Connover, John	Letter at P.O.	1, Jan. 1812	L3
Cook, Absalom	Horse found	4, May 1813	L4
Cook, Charles	Horse found	3, Oct. 1810	L3
Cook, George	Horse found	18, June 1819	L3
Cook, Jacob C.	Land payment notice	7, Nov. 1810	L3
Cook, Jesse W.	Debt relief	23, June 1842	L3
Cook, Peter	Debt relief	24, July 1828	L1
Cook, Peter	Debt relief	8, June 1827	L4
Cook, Rudolph	Deserter	18, Jan. 1814	L1
Cook, Timothy	Debt relief	9, June 1831	L3
Cooley, Isaac	Deserter	29, June 1813	L3
Coolidge, Maria	Hughes High School	2, Feb. 1854	L3
Cooper, Daniel C.	Land payment due	22, Nov. 1809	L4
Cooper, Jesse	Guardian	14, Feb. 1839	L3
Cooper, Joseph	Land payment notice	7, Nov. 1810	L3
Cooper, Thomas	Horse found	8, Dec. 1817	L3
Cooper, Thomas	Guardian	14, Feb. 1839	L3
Cooper, William	Name change notice	4, Dec. 1811	L2
Cooper, William	Letter at P.O.	1, Jan. 1812	L3
Cooper, William	Horse found	9, Mar. 1813	L3
Cooper, William	Land payment due	22, Nov. 1809	L4
Copeland, Hiram	Debt relief	9, Oct. 1828	L3
Copes, William & Frances	Divorce/Abandonment	15, May 1815	L3
Corvin, Sylvester	Runaway apprentice	3, Nov. 1812	L2
Cosby, Thomas	Horse found	15, June 1827	L3
Cotlen, Jacob & Mary Ann	Divorce/Abandonment	22, Feb. 1838	L3
Couey, Joseph & Winefred	Divorce/Abandonment	19, Dec. 1823	L3
Coulson, Samuel	Letter at P.O.	1, Jan. 1812	L3
Coulter, John C. & Polly	Divorce/Abandonment	21, Sept 1813	L3
Covington, Edward	Horse found	15, Jan. 1812	L3
Cowgh, Daniel & Elizabeth	Divorce/Abandonment	31, Aug. 1813	L2
Cowhick, Thomas	Land payment notice	7, Nov. 1810	L3
Cox, George	Land payment notice	7, Nov. 1810	L3
Cox, John	Debt relief	28, Jan. 1830	L3
Cox, John	Debt relief	9, June 1831	L3
Cox, Joseph	Letter at P.O.	1, Jan. 1812	L3
Cox, Joseph P.	Horse lost	22, June 1813	l3
Cox, Joseph P.	Debt relief	9, Feb. 1827	L3
Craft, Joseph F.	Debt relief	23, June 1842	L3
Craig, George	Land payment due	22, Nov. 1809	L4

Name	Type of Notice	Date of Notice	Page
Craig, Samuel H.	Horse found	24, Nov. 1817	L3
Craigg, James	Debt relief	1, Aug. 1833	L3
Crail, John & Sally	Divorce/Abandonment	13, June 1810	L3
Crain, David	Horse found	12, June 1815	L3
Cramer, John	Horse found	14, July 1812	L1
Crandall, Ira	Debt relief	17, Nov. 1842	L5
Crane, Caleb, Jr.	Horse found	3, July 1815	L3
Crane, John S.	Debt relief	9, June 1831	L3
Crane, Jonas	Horse found	14, Mar. 1810	L2
Crane, William	Deserter from army	6, Oct. 1812	L1
Crary, Benjamin	Debt relief	28, Jan. 1830	L3
Crary, William	Debt relief	18, Aug. 1826	L3
Crawford, Wilson	Convict	5, Feb. 1846	L3
Creain, Andrew L.	Debt relief	17, Oct. 1839	L3
Creain, Jeremiah	Debt relief	1, Aug. 1833	L3
Credlebaugh, Andrew	Horse lost	8, June 1813	L2
Crisman, Felix	Debtor	16, Nov. 1819	L2
Crist, Jemima	Guardian	6, Sept 1855	L3
Crist, Letitia	Guardian	6, Sept 1855	L3
Crist, Lydia	Guardian	6, Sept 1855	L3
Crist, Peter	Horse found	6, July 1813	L1
Crist, Peter	Horse found	29, July 1820	L3
Critenton, Marshall J.	Debt relief	5, Feb. 1835	L3
Crneal, Thomas D.	Letter at P.O.	1, Jan. 1812	L3
Crockett, David B.	Debt relief	17, Nov. 1842	L5
Crook, James	Letter at P.O.	1, Jan. 1812	L3
Crooks, Samuel	Horse found	25, Sept 1812	L2
Crosby, Alice J.	Guardian	5, July 1855	L3
Crosby, Isaac	Debt relief	28, Jan. 1830	L3
Crosley, William M.	Horse found	29, Sept 1826	L3
Cross, Abraham	Missing boy	6, Aug. 1846	L1
Crossley, Josiah	Horse found	23, June 1817	L3
Crosson, James	Horse lost	17, Nov. 1812	L3
Crow, Matthias	Land payment notice	7, Nov. 1810	L3
Crowder, John	Horse stolen	16, June 1817	L4
Crowel, John	Horse found	25, Dec. 1811	L1
Crume, Moses (Rev)	Letter at P.O.	1, Jan. 1812	L3
Cullum, William T.	Horse found	6, Dec. 1814	L1
Cullum, William T.	Vattier court case	28, Apr. 1807	L3
Cully, Phebe	Letter at P.O.	1, Jan. 1812	L3
Cummins, Robert	Horse found	6, June 1810	L3
Cummins, Samuel	Debt relief	1, Aug. 1833	L3
Cumpton, William	Horse found	7, Sept 1813	L2
Cunning, Patrick	Horse found	25, Sept 1815	L2
Cunning, Patrick	Debt relief	11, Nov. 1825	L3
Cunning, Patrick	Horse found	27, Sept 1814	L4
Cunningham, Joseph	Debt relief	11, Nov. 1825	L3
Curch, Helan	Debt relief	17, Oct. 1839	L3
Currie, Robert	Horse found	1, Jan. 1812	L4
Curry, William	Land payment notice	7, Nov. 1810	L3
Custard, William	Land payment notice	7, Nov. 1810	L3
Cutter, Norman	Debt relief	17, Nov. 1842	L5
Dakins, James	Debt relief	1, Aug. 1833	L3

Name	Type of Notice	Date of Notice	Page
Dale, Daniel	Debt relief	28, Jan. 1830	L3
Dandy, Job	Debt relief	1, Aug. 1833	L3
Danford, Hallis	Debt relief	28, Jan. 1830	L3
Daniels, Azariah	Guardian	3, May 1855	L3
Daniels, Henry	Debt relief	9, June 1831	L3
Dansany, Henrietta	Insane	10, Mar. 1853	L3
Darby, Henry	Horse found	13, July 1819	L3
Darby, Levi, Jr.	Debt relief	9, Oct. 1828	L3
Darby, Levy	Debt relief	1, Aug. 1833	L3
Davidson, James	Deserter	18, Jan. 1814	L1
Davidson, W.	Debt relief	4, Aug. 1831	L4
Davies, John	Letter at P.O.	1, Jan. 1812	L3
Davies, Samuel W.	Debt relief	17, Nov. 1842	L5
Davis, Charlotte	Horse found	17, June 1816	L3
Davis, Cornelius	Debt relief	18, Aug. 1826	L3
Davis, Hiram & Phebe	Divorce/Abandonment	4, Nov. 1847	L3
Davis, James Handy	Lost child	25, May 1837	L3
Davis, Jesse	Horse found	15, Aug. 1810	L2
Davis, John	Horse found	14, Sept 1813	L1
Davis, Joseph F.	Debt relief	21, May 1829	L4
Davis, Joshua	Horse found	28, Dec. 1819	L3
Davis, Layton	Debt relief	9, Feb. 1827	L3
Davis, Nathan	Horse found	7, July 1812	L2
Davis, Rachel	Guardian	10, Dec. 1857	L3
Davis, Reuben	Horse found	25, Dec. 1815	L3
Davis, Samuel	Horse found	7, Dec. 1813	L3
Davis, William	Debt relief	1, Aug. 1833	L3
Davison, Archibald	Horse found	3, July 1815	L3
Davison, Thomas	Horse found	25, Jan. 1813	L3
Dawson, Matthias	Letter at P.O.	1, Jan. 1812	L3
Day, Abigail	Guardian	21, Sept 1837	L4
Day, Jane	Guardian	21, Sept 1837	L4
Day, John & Lavina	Divorce/Abandonment	13, Dec. 1825	L3
Day, Rosanna	Guardian	21, Sept 1837	L4
Day, W.L.	Guardian	21, Sept 1837	L4
Day, William	Horse found	26, May 1817	L3
Dayton, Jonathan	Land payment notice	7, Nov. 1810	L3
Dearmond, Alexander	Land payment due	22, Nov. 1809	L4
Decker, Catherine	Guardian	5, Feb. 1857	L3
Decker, Elizabeth	Guardian	5, Feb. 1857	L3
Decker, Mary	Guardian	5, Feb. 1857	L3
Decourcy, William	Horse found	2, Oct. 1815	L2
Deen, Levi	Horse found	17, July 1815	L4
Dellrymple, James	Letter at P.O.	1, Jan. 1812	L3
Demoss, William	Horse found	20, June 1810	L1
Denham, James	Horse found	3, Oct. 1810	L3
Denham, John	Horse found	14, Apr. 1817	L4
Denham, Obed	Horse found	14, Nov. 1810	L3
Denning, James	Horse found	15, Aug. 1810	L2
Dennis, Benjamin	Debt relief	14, July 1842	L3
Denny, William	Deserter	8, Feb. 1814	L3
Depew, William	Debt relief	18, Aug. 1826	L3
Depew, William C.	Debt relief	8, June 1827	L4
Deroy, John	Horse found	14, Feb. 1810	L3

Name	Type of Notice	Date of Notice	Page
Detrick, Henry	Run away apprentice	9, June 1812	L3
Dewar, Henry A.	Debt relief	17, Oct. 1839	L3
Dewit, Zachaeus P.	Letter at P.O.	1, Jan. 1812	L3
Dewitt, Andrew	Debt relief	9, Oct. 1828	L3
DeYoung, Samuel J.	Debt relief	28, Jan. 1830	L3
Dial, John	Horse found	1, Jan. 1812	L4
Dicker, James	Horse found	21, Feb. 1810	L3
Dickerson, Aaron	Lost child	21, Jan. 1820	L1
Dickey, Adam	Land payment notice	7, Nov. 1810	L3
Diel, Frederick & Maria	Divorce/Abandonment	18, Nov. 1841	L3
Dietrich, Barbara	Guardian	8, Nov. 1855	L3
Dietrich, Catharine	Guardian	8, Nov. 1855	L3
Digbay, William & Catherine	Divorce/Abandonment	9, June 1806	L2
Dilahunt, Louisa	Convict	5, Feb. 1846	L3
Dillman, Henry	Guardian	9, July 1857	L3
Dillman, John	Guardian	9, July 1857	L3
Dillman, Mary	Guardian	9, July 1857	L3
Dillman, William	Guardian	9, July 1857	L3
Dillon, Samuel	Land payment notice	7, Nov. 1810	L3
Dixon, John	Runaway apprentice	25, Feb. 1815	L3
Dobbens, Rachel	Horse found	21, Dec. 1813	L1
Dockery, James	Deserter	6, July 1813	L1
Dodds, Joseph	Land payment notice	7, Nov. 1810	L3
Dodson, Julia Ann	Guardian	9, July 1857	L3
Dodsworth, Edward	Guardian	6, Aug. 1857	L3
Dodsworth, Edward	Guardian	14, Aug. 1856	L6
Dodsworth, Ralph	Guardian	6, Aug. 1857	L3
Dodsworth, Ralph	Guardian	14, Aug. 1856	L6
Donnel, Jonathan	Land payment notice	7, Nov. 1810	L3
Donnell, John	Letter at P.O.	1, Jan. 1812	L3
Donnelly, William	Debt relief	11, Nov. 1825	L3
Doolittle, James	Debt relief	17, Oct. 1839	L3
Doran, James & Elizabeth	Divorce/Abandonment	13, Feb. 1840	L3
Doty, Sering	Letter at P.O.	1, Jan. 1812	L3
Doughty, Richard	Horse found	27, Feb. 1811	L2
Douglass, Joseph	Horse found	25, Apr. 1810	L3
Douglass, Thomas	Debt relief	1, Aug. 1833	L3
Dowden, Clemenchous	Horse lost	27, Nov. 1815	L4
Downard, Thomas & Mary Ann	Divorce/Abandonment	27, Nov. 1856	L3
Downing, J.	Debt relief	24, July 1828	L1
Dowty, Zachariah	Runaway apprentice	15, Apr. 1812	L3
Drake, Daniel	Debt relief	11, Nov. 1825	L3
Drake, Jesse	Inquiry	3, Nov. 1817	L1
Drake, Lewis	Land payment notice	7, Nov. 1810	L3
Drake, Narcissa	Inquiry	3, Nov. 1817	L1
Drake, Sarah (Mrs)	Letter at P.O.	1, Jan. 1812	L3
Drew, Catharine M.	Guardian	20, Oct. 1826	L3
Drew, Hanson	Debt relief	17, Oct. 1839	L3
Dripple, George	Debt relief	1, Aug. 1833	L3
Driver, H.	Debt relief	1, Aug. 1833	L3
Ducks, George	Deserter	22, Feb. 1814	L1
Duff, Thomas	Deserter	8, Feb. 1814	L3
Dugan, Robert	Runaway apprentice	22, Jan. 1816	L3
Dugan, Samuel & Rebeccah	Divorce/Abandonment	23, Mar. 1813	L3

Name	Type of Notice	Date of Notice	Page
Dugan, Thomas	Letter at P.O.	1, Jan. 1812	L3
Dumass, Benjamin	Debt relief	1, Aug. 1833	L3
Dunbar, Melzer	Guardian	8, Nov. 1832	L4
Dunbar, Roxana	Guardian	8, Nov. 1832	L4
Dunbar, Tomzen	Guardian	8, Nov. 1832	L4
Duncan, George	Letter at P.O.	1, Jan. 1812	L3
Duncan, John	Convict	5, Feb. 1846	L3
Duncan, William	Runaway apprentice	22, Apr. 1818	L3
Dunlap, Agnes	Guardian	22, Mar. 1838	L3
Dunlap, R.E.	Guardian	22, Mar. 1838	L3
Dunlavy, Francis (Judge)	Vattier court case	28, Apr. 1807	L3
Dunmire, Peter	Debt relief	18, Aug. 1826	L3
Dunn, James	Horse found	23, Feb. 1813	L3
Dunn, John C.	Guardian	19, Dec. 1826	L3
Dunn, Robert J.	Debt relief	9, June 1831	L3
Dunn, Samuel W.	Guardian	19, Dec. 1826	L3
Dunseth, John	Debtor	11, Feb. 1818	L3
Durham, Aquilla, Jr.	Debt relief	17, Nov. 1842	L5
Durham, Benjamin	Debt relief	8, June 1827	L4
Durrell, James	Debt relief	21, May 1829	L4
Dutton, George H.	Runaway son	30, Jan. 1840	L3
Duval, John	Debt relief	23, June 1842	L3
Dyer, George & Polly	Divorce/Abandonment	22, May 1815	L3
Eachret, John & Jemima	Divorce/Abandonment	7, Feb. 1810	L4
Eacret, Samuel & Jemima	Divorce/Abandonment	10, May 1814	L1
Eagen, John	Letter at P.O.	1, Jan. 1812	L3
Earhart, George	Letter at P.O.	1, Jan. 1812	L3
Earhart, Samuel	Letter at P.O.	1, Jan. 1812	L3
Eastling, William W. & Ann	Divorce/Abandonment	23, Feb. 1837	L4
Eaton, Joseph	Deserter	6, July 1813	L1
Eavins, James	Horse found	17, Nov. 1812	L1
Eberhart, Adam	Horse found	7, Dec. 1813	L3
Eckels, George	Guardian	9, July 1857	L3
Eckles, Sarah	Guardian	4, Sept 1856	L5
Eddy, William & Julia Ann	Divorce/Abandonment	18, Nov. 1841	L3
Edes, James	Land payment notice	7, Nov. 1810	L3
Edgell, Alexander	Debt relief	17, Nov. 1842	L5
Edmands, Horace S.	Debt relief	5, Feb. 1835	L3
Edmeston, Ada	Guardian	14, Feb. 1839	L3
Edmeston, William	Guardian	14, Feb. 1839	L3
Edmonds, Benjamin & Hannah	Divorce/Abandonment	10, Apr. 1851	L3
Edmonds, Lemuel	Cow found	9, Jan. 1824	L3
Edmonson, William	Debt relief	1, Aug. 1833	L3
Edwards, Elijah	Horse found	25, Feb. 1818	L3
Edwards, Elijah	Debt relief	18, Aug. 1826	L3
Edwards, Isaac	Horse found	25, May 1813	L1
Edwards, Isaac	Horse found	14, June 1814	L1
Edwards, Isaac	Horse found	6, Dec. 1814	L1
Edwards, Isaac	Horse found	27, June 1810	L2
Edwards, Jacob	Debt relief	9, June 1831	L3
Edwards, Jesse	Rev. War Veteran	13, Aug. 1854	L3
Edwards, Job	Horse found	26, Jan. 1819	L3
Edwards, Joseph	Horse found	16, Nov. 1822	L2

Name	Type of Notice	Date of Notice	Page
Edwards, Joshua	Horse found	19, June 1811	L3
Edwards, Thomas	Horse found	18, July 1810	L2
Elder, John & Elizabeth	Divorce/Abandonment	20, June 1839	L3
Eldred, Hiram	Debt relief	1, Aug. 1833	L3
Elkins, Stephen H.	Horse found	23, Mar. 1813	L3
Elliott, John	Horse found	11, Apr. 1810	L2
Ellis, Henry	Guardian	9, July 1857	L3
Ellis, James S.	Debt relief	17, Nov. 1842	L5
Ellis, John	Land payment notice	7, Nov. 1810	L3
Ellis, M.J.	Guardian	7, Feb. 1856	L3
Ellis, William	Land payment notice	7, Nov. 1810	L3
Ellison, Andrew	Letter at P.O.	1, Jan. 1812	L3
Emmerson, John	Horse found	9, Nov. 1813	L2
Emmitt, John	Horse found	15, Dec. 1818	L3
Engles, Fred	Guardian	16, Oct. 1856	L6
Engles, Oliver	Debt relief	17, Oct. 1839	L3
English, John W.	Horse found	23, June 1817	L3
English, Oliver	Debt relief	17, Oct. 1839	L3
Enoch, Abner	Horse found	8, Jan. 1812	L4
Enyart, David	Horse found	9, Nov. 1813	L2
Ernest, John	Horse found	25, Dec. 1815	L1
Eshelby, James	Debt relief	17, Nov. 1842	L5
Etherton, Reuben	Deserter from army	3, Nov. 1812	L3
Eulass, Jacob	Land payment notice	7, Nov. 1810	L3
Evalt, William	Horse found	31, Oct. 1810	L3
Evans, Albert	Guardian	10, Sept 1857	L3
Evans, Albert	Guardian	4, Sept 1856	L5
Evans, Albert M.	Guardian	9, Aug. 1855	L3
Evans, Arthur	Guardian	9, Aug. 1855	L3
Evans, Arthur	Guardian	10, Sept 1857	L3
Evans, Arthur	Guardian	4, Sept 1856	L5
Evans, Henry B.	Debt relief	14, July 1842	L3
Evans, Walter	Horse found	24, Jan. 1810	L4
Evans, William	Guardian	10, Sept 1857	L3
Evans, William	Guardian	4, Sept 1856	L5
Evans, William H.	Guardian	9, Aug. 1855	L3
Evatt, William	Horse found	20, June 1810	L1
Everett, Erastus	Debt relief	4, Aug. 1831	L4
Ewing, James	Debtor	16, Feb. 1819	L3
Ewing, Sarah S.	Guardian	8, Jan. 1857	L3
Ewing, William Mitchell	Runaway apprentice	14, Sept 1813	L1
Eyre, Thomas	Debt relief	1, Aug. 1833	L3
Fagan, John M.	Guardian	6, Dec. 1855	L3
Fagan, Sarah	Guardian	6, Dec. 1855	L3
Fagan, Susan A.	Guardian	6, Dec. 1855	L3
Faire, William	Letter at P.O.	1, Jan. 1812	L3
Falk, John B.	Debt relief	4, Aug. 1831	L4
Fancher, William	Horse found	14, July 1812	L3
Fantroy, James B.	Debt relief	24, July 1828	L1
Fares, Isaac	Horse found	20, June 1810	L3
Farmen, Michael	Letter at P.O.	1, Jan. 1812	L3
Farmer, James	Runaway apprentice	3, May 1814	L5
Farrell, Thomas	Convict	5, Feb. 1846	L3

Name	Type of Notice	Date of Notice	Page
Farrow, John	Debt relief	17, Oct. 1839	L3
Fasset, John B.	Debt relief	4, Aug. 1831	L4
Faulkner, Jacob	Horse found	14, July 1817	L3
Fauver, John	Horse found	22, July 1816	L3
Fay, Cutting	Debt relief	9, Feb. 1827	L3
Feltner, James	Escaped convict	12, June 1828	L3
Felton, James	Deserter	22, Feb. 1814	L1
Ferguson, John	Horse found	20, Nov. 1828	L3
Ferlong, Water	Debt relief	1, Aug. 1833	L3
Ferree, Abraham	Horse found	22, Apr. 1812	L4
Ferring, Gilbert	Horse found	5, Jan. 1818	L3
Ferris, Abraham	Horse lost	3, June 1816	L1
Ferris, Andrew	Horse found	28, Jan. 1818	L3
Ferris, John	Horse found	20, Dec. 1814	L3
Ferris, John	Horse found	12, Feb. 1816	L3
Ferris, John J.	Horse found	4, Dec. 1822	L4
Ferris, Joseph	Horse lost	3, July 1815	L3
Ferris, Solomon & Letice	Divorce/Abandonment	6, May 1816	L3
Ferry, Jesse	Convict	5, Feb. 1846	L3
Fields, Anthony	Debt relief	4, Aug. 1831	L4
Fields, Jesse	Horse found	28, Aug. 1811	L3
Findlay, James	Land payment due	22, Nov. 1809	L4
Finkbine, Tobias	Debt relief	28, Jan. 1830	L3
Finley, Robert W.	Letter at P.O.	1, Jan. 1812	L3
Fishburn, Samuel	Debt relief	1, Aug. 1833	L3
Fitch, Justus	Inquiry	24, Feb. 1817	L3
Fitsgerald, James	Debt relief	8, June 1827	L4
Fittor, Thomas	Debt relief	24, July 1828	L1
Fitzpatrick, James	Horse found	14, Feb. 1810	L3
Fix, John	Land payment notice	7, Nov. 1810	L3
Flack, Moses	Debt relief	17, Nov. 1842	L5
Flagg, Jacob J.	Horse lost	21, Sept 1819	L3
Fleming, Daniel M.	Letter at P.O.	1, Jan. 1812	L3
Fleming, Joseph	Land payment notice	7, Nov. 1810	L3
Flinn, Jacob	Horse found	5, July 1814	L2
Flint, John	Letter at P.O.	1, Jan. 1812	L3
Flomerfelt, Peter	Horse found	21, Apr. 1820	L3
Flowers, William	Deserter	6, July 1813	L1
Fogg, Jeremiah P.	Debt relief	17, Oct. 1839	L3
Foly, Isaac	Horse found	19, Oct. 1819	L3
Ford, Hobart	Debt relief	17, Nov. 1842	L5
Forman, Jonathan	Letter at P.O.	1, Jan. 1812	L3
Forsyth, John	Horse found	21, Sept 1812	L3
Fosdick, Thomas R.	Debt relief	18, Aug. 1826	L3
Foster, James	Escaped convict	12, June 1828	L3
Foster, Luke (Judge)	Vattier court case	28, Apr. 1807	L3
Foster, Peter	Debt relief	9, Feb. 1827	L3
Foster, Samuel	Debt relief	24, July 1828	L1
Foster, William P.	Debt relief	4, Aug. 1831	L4
Fothergill, George W.	Letter at P.O.	1, Jan. 1812	L3
Foulke, Thomas D.	Debt relief	21, May 1829	L4
Fouts, David	Land payment notice	7, Nov. 1810	L3
Fowble, Jacob	Debtor	18, Oct. 1820	L3
Fox, Charles	Letter at P.O.	1, Jan. 1812	L3

Name	Type of Notice	Date of Notice	Page
Fox, Stephen	Horse found	7, July 1817	L3
Fox, Stephen	Rev. Soldier Pens.	28, Apr. 1820	L3
Francisco, James	Debt relief	17, Oct. 1839	L3
Frane, William (Capt)	Letter at P.O.	1, Jan. 1812	L3
Fraser, Alexander	Deserter from army	27, May 1812	L3
Frashier, George	Debt relief	4, Aug. 1831	L4
Frazee, Jonas	Rev. War Veteran	13, Aug. 1854	L3
Frazee, Moses	Horse found	20, Mar. 1811	L1
Frazee, Thomas	Vattier court case	28, Apr. 1807	L3
Frazer, Jacob	Debt relief	1, Aug. 1833	L3
Frazer, Joseph	Debt relief	1, Aug. 1833	L3
Frazey, Samuel	Horse found	17, Nov. 1817	L3
Fream, Robert	Debt relief	1, Aug. 1833	L3
Freeborn, Jacob	Debt relief	8, June 1827	L4
Freeman, John	Horse found	19, Feb. 1812	L3
Freeman, John	Letter at P.O.	1, Jan. 1812	L3
French, Maynard	Debt relief	23, June 1842	L3
French, Ralph	Land payment notice	7, Nov. 1810	L3
French, Robert & Elizabeth	Divorce/Abandonment	10, May 1825	L1
Friend, Charles H.	Debt relief	5, Feb. 1835	L3
Fuller, J.M. & Julia Ann	Divorce/Abandonment	26, July 1855	L3
Fuller, John	Horse found	21, Feb. 1810	L3
Fuller, John, Jr.	Debt relief	17, Nov. 1842	L5
Furman, Thomas & Sally	Divorce/Abandonment	30, Oct. 1811	L2
Gaggin, Thomas	Horse found	5, July 1814	L3
Gallaspey, John	Deserter	24, Aug. 1813	L2
Galloway, William	Deserter	10, May 1814	L3
Gallycan, Thomas	Horse found	23, Jan. 1811	L1
Gano, Aaron G.	Debt relief	14, July 1842	L3
Gano, Laura	Guardian	8, Jan. 1857	L3
Garard, Jonathan	Horse found	5, Oct. 1813	L2
Gard, Aaron	Horse found	10, Aug. 1813	L3
Gard, Moses	Letter at P.O.	1, Jan. 1812	L3
Gardiner, Henry	Debt relief	18, Aug. 1826	L3
Gardner, Alexander	Horse found	4, Jan. 1832	L3
Gardner, Alexander L.	Guardian	16, Oct. 1856	L6
Gardner, Fred August Abel	Guardian	16, Oct. 1856	L6
Garey, William	Letter at P.O.	1, Jan. 1812	L3
Garman, William	Runaway apprentice	15, Aug. 1810	L3
Garret, Samuel & Jemima	Divorce/Abandonment	17, Jan. 1810	L2
Garret, William	Horse found	14, July 1812	L1
Garrish, Francis B.	Debt relief	4, Aug. 1831	L4
Garrison, Jacob	Letter at P.O.	1, Jan. 1812	L3
Garrison, Jonathan	Horse found	31, Jan. 1810	L2
Garver, David	Deserter	7, July 1817	L4
Gassaway, Henry	Debt relief	1, Aug. 1833	L3
Gassaway, Henry C.	Debt relief	14, July 1842	L3
Gay, Joseph	Horse found	6, July 1813	L1
Gayland, Horace	Debt relief	18, Aug. 1826	L3
Geer, Harris & Mariah	Divorce/Abandonment	25, July 1844	L3
Gelespy, Joshua W.	Guardian	5, Sept 1839	L3
George, William	Debt relief	21, May 1829	L4
Gerard, Eli	Horse stolen	15, Sept 1812	L2

Name	Type of Notice	Date of Notice	Page
Gerrit, William	Horse found	11, Apr. 1810	L2
Gess, Solomon	Letter at P.O.	1, Jan. 1812	L3
Gibbs, John	Horse found	7, July 1817	L3
Gibbs, Justus	Horse found	25, Aug. 1817	L3
Gibbs, Justus	Horse found	2, Sept 1820	L3
Gibson, Charles	Debt relief	4, Aug. 1831	L4
Gibson, Justus	Horse found	7, June 1814	L4
Gilbert, Richard	Horse stolen	5, May 1821	L3
Gilbreath, William	Horse found	6, June 1810	L3
Giles, David B. & Lydia H.	Divorce/Abandonment	13, Feb. 1824	L4
Gill, Robert, Jr.	Letter at P.O.	1, Jan. 1812	L3
Gillespie, George	Land payment notice	7, Nov. 1810	L3
Gilman, Benjamin Ives	Debt relief	21, May 1829	L4
Gilman, James S.	Debt relief	9, Feb. 1827	L3
Gilmon, Daniel	Letter at P.O.	1, Jan. 1812	L3
Gilmore, Malvina	Guardian	5, Nov. 1857	L3
Ginn, Thomas	Debt relief	18, Aug. 1826	L3
Ginn, Thomas	Debt relief	4, Aug. 1831	L4
Glancy, John	Horse found	27, Dec. 1822	L2
Glasco, John	Debt relief	5, Feb. 1835	L3
Glass, James	Horse found	11, Dec. 1815	L3
Glenn, Alfred	Debt relief	5, Feb. 1835	L3
Glenn, H.	Horse found	23, Dec. 1825	L3
Glidewell, Mastin	Letter at P.O.	1, Jan. 1812	L3
Glover, Elias, Esq.	Letter at P.O.	1, Jan. 1812	L3
Gold, John	Debt relief	9, Feb. 1827	L3
Golding, Aaron	Debt relief	28, Jan. 1830	L3
Golding, Stephen	Horse found	22, May 1811	L2
Goodin, Daniel	Runaway apprentice	19, Oct. 1813	L2
Gordon, Lewis W.	Debt relief	24, July 1828	L1
Gordon, Robert M.	Debt relief	9, Oct. 1828	L3
Gordon, Robert M.	Debt relief	21, May 1829	L4
Gorigh, Bailey	Horse found	20, June 1810	L1
Goshorn, Nicholas	Debt relief	23, June 1842	L3
Goudy, Edward	Debt relief	9, June 1831	L3
Goudy, Hamill	Debt relief	18, Aug. 1826	L3
Goudy, Richard	Guardian	7, Dec. 1837	L3
Gough, Jesse	Land payment notice	7, Nov. 1810	L3
Gould, Thomas	Letter at P.O.	1, Jan. 1812	L3
Gove, Amos	Debt relief	14, July 1842	L3
Grady, Richmond	Runaway apprentice	21, Dec. 1813	L1
Graf, Andrew	Guardian	6, Mar. 1856	L3
Graf, Lawrence	Guardian	6, Mar. 1856	L3
Graf, Nicholas	Guardian	6, Mar. 1856	L3
Graham, Robert C. & Mary	Divorce/Abandonment	28, Jan. 1836	L3
Graham, Thomas D.	Cow lost	17, July 1815	L4
Grant, Josiah	Debt relief	14, July 1842	L3
Gray, David	Horse found	28, Feb. 1810	L3
Gray, John	Horse found	4, Dec. 1811	L3
Gray, Moses	Runaway apprentice	28, Nov. 1810	L3
Gray, Peale	Inquiry	8, July 1820	L3
Gray, Richard	Land payment notice	7, Nov. 1810	L3
Gray, Robert & Letitia	Divorce/Abandonment	2, Feb. 1843	L3
Gray, Samuel	Horse found	12, Feb. 1812	L4

Name	Type of Notice	Date of Notice	Page
Gray, William	Horse found	15, Sept 1812	L2
Green, Elihue	Debt relief	17, Nov. 1842	L5
Green, George W.	Debt relief	24, July 1828	L1
Green, John	Debt relief	1, Aug. 1833	L3
Green, John	Debt relief	1, Aug. 1833	L3
Green, Mercy	Cow found	3, Oct. 1810	L4
Green, Silas	Horse found	5, June 1815	L3
Green, William C.	Letter at P.O.	1, Jan. 1812	L3
Greene, Oliver	Debt relief	4, Aug. 1831	L4
Greene, Timothy	Land payment notice	7, Nov. 1810	L3
Greer, James	Horse found	13, Oct. 1812	L2
Greer, William	Debt relief	23, June 1842	L3
Gregg, James	Letter at P.O.	1, Jan. 1812	L3
Gregg, Samuel	Land payment due	22, Nov. 1809	L4
Gregory, Jonathan	Horse found	14, Feb. 1810	L3
Gregory, Piatt	Debt relief	1, Aug. 1833	L3
Griffin, James	Debt relief	9, Feb. 1827	L3
Griffith, William & Martha	Divorce/Abandonment	21, July 1807	L3
Griffiths, John	Horse found	21, Sept 1813	L3
Griggs, Caleb	Deserter	18, Jan. 1814	L1
Griggs, Elijah	Runaway apprentice	12, July 1814	L3
Griggs, Samuel	Runaway apprentice	12, July 1814	L3
Grimkemeyer, Bernard	Guardian	14, Aug. 1856	L6
Grimkemeyer, Joseph	Guardian	14, Aug. 1856	L6
Grissman, David	Land payment notice	7, Nov. 1810	L3
Griswold, Urijah	Horse found	8, Apr. 1816	L4
Grooms, John	Debt relief	9, Feb. 1827	L3
Grow, Aeson	Debt relief	1, Aug. 1833	L3
Grubb, William D.	Debt relief	1, Aug. 1833	L3
Guest, Hannah	Horse found	25, Sept 1811	L4
Guibert, Henry	Debt relief	1, Aug. 1833	L3
Guiney, Andrew A.D. & Elizabeth	Divorce/Abandonment	13, Jan. 1831	L3
Gunkle, Frederika	Guardian	7, June 1855	L3
Gunter, David	Deserter	6, July 1813	L1
Gunyan, Daniel	Horse found	23, Feb. 1813	L3
Gwilym, William	Horse found	25, Mar. 1812	L3
Gwilynn, Morgan	Horse found	30, Jan. 1811	L3
Gwinnup, George	Horse found	20, Sept 1814	L3
Gynn, Joel	Debt relief	5, Feb. 1835	L3
Hackelman, Jacob & Catharine	Divorce/Abandonment	30, Apr. 1808	L3
Hacket, Isaac	Debt relief	1, Aug. 1833	L3
Hackinger, Clara	Inquiry	20, Sept 1827	L3
Haeffer, Joel & Mary	Divorce/Abandonment	6, Apr. 1822	L3
Hageman, George	Guardian	14, Feb. 1839	L3
Hageman, Jonathan	Guardian	14, Feb. 1839	L3
Hageman, Sarah A.	Guardian	14, Feb. 1839	L3
Hageman, Simon	Guardian	14, Feb. 1839	L3
Hageman, Squire	Guardian	14, Feb. 1839	L3
Haggerty, John H.	Debt relief	9, June 1831	L3
Hahn, Henry	Debt relief	4, Aug. 1831	L4
Hahn, Samuel	Horse found	29, Aug. 1810	L1
Haine, Thomas	Horse found	2, June 1812	L1
Hains, Amos	Horse found	4, Aug. 1812	L2

Name	Type of Notice	Date of Notice	Page
Hales, Charles	Cow lost	6, Nov. 1815	L3
Haliday, John	Horse found	11, Jan. 1814	L1
Hall, Elbridge G.	Debt relief	17, Nov. 1842	L5
Hall, Gershom	Escaped	8, July 1820	L3
Hall, Henry P.	Debt relief	1, Aug. 1833	L3
Hall, Jeremiah	Letter at P.O.	1, Jan. 1812	L3
Hall, Richard	Horse found	24, Jan. 1810	L4
Hallan, Charles	Debt relief	1, Aug. 1833	L3
Halstead, Peter	Horse found	19, May 1817	L3
Hamel, Thomas	Horse found	24, Nov. 1818	L3
Hamer, William	Land payment due	22, Nov. 1809	L4
Hamilton, Alexander D.	Horse found	29, May 1811	L4
Hamilton, George & Jane	Divorce/Abandonment	20, Apr. 1822	L4
Hampton, Thomas	Debt relief	24, July 1828	L1
Hanbey, William	Letter at P.O.	1, Jan. 1812	L3
Hancock, Daniel	Letter at P.O.	1, Jan. 1812	L3
Hancock, Michael	Letter at P.O.	1, Jan. 1812	L3
Hand, Furman	Horse found	21, Jan. 1820	L3
Hand, Furman & Mary	Divorce/Abandonment	15, July 1820	L3
Handcock, John	Horse found	4, Apr. 1810	L2
Hanes, Abraham	Horse found	27, Apr. 1813	L1
Hanford, Henry	Letter at P.O.	1, Jan. 1812	L3
Hangerford, Richard	Horse found	9, June 1817	L4
Hankins, Richard	Letter at P.O.	1, Jan. 1812	L3
Hanley, John & Sophia	Divorce/Abandonment	9, Dec. 1820	L3
Hanley, Nehemiah	Horse found	29, May 1815	L3
Hann, Jacob	Debt relief	24, July 1828	L1
Hannah, Joseph	Horse found	11, Mar. 1815	L2
Hannah, Joseph (Capt)	Letter at P.O.	1, Jan. 1812	L3
Hansel, John & Jane	Divorce/Abandonment	9, Feb. 1832	L3
Hanson, James	Runaway apprentice	24, May 1814	L1
Harbaugh, David	Horse found	31, July 1815	L3
Harbert, Josiah	Horse found	21, Aug. 1811	L3
Harcourt, William	Horse found	17, Aug. 1813	L2
Hardie, Patrick	Debt relief	5, Feb. 1835	L3
Harding, Robert	Land payment notice	7, Nov. 1810	L3
Hargan, Peter & Sarah	Divorce/Abandonment	27, Mar. 1845	L3
Harker, Daniel & Mary	Divorce/Abandonment	22, Apr. 1823	L3
Harlow, William	Letter at P.O.	1, Jan. 1812	L3
Harman, John	Horse found	26, Aug. 1812	L1
Harmann, Christina	Guardian	16, Oct. 1856	L6
Harmann, Lewis B.	Guardian	16, Oct. 1856	L6
Harper, John M.	Guardian	22, June 1837	L3
Harper, Mathew	Guardian	22, June 1837	L3
Harrell, James	Land payment notice	7, Nov. 1810	L3
Harrell, John	Land payment notice	7, Nov. 1810	L3
Harrington, Anthony H.	Debt relief	24, July 1828	L1
Harris, Benjamin	Horse found	14, July 1812	L1
Harris, Frederick & Maria S	Divorce/Abandonment	11, Apr. 1850	L3
Harris, Isaiah	Horse lost	21, Apr. 1817	L4
Harris, James	Debt relief	9, Feb. 1827	L3
Harris, John D.	Debt relief	14, July 1842	L3
Harris, Jones	Land payment notice	7, Nov. 1810	L3
Harris, Mark	Letter at P.O.	1, Jan. 1812	L3

Name	Type of Notice	Date of Notice	Page
Harris, Silas	Horse found	24, Jan. 1810	L4
Harrison, William H.	Town laid out	9, June 1817	L3
Harrold, Jonathan & Betsey	Divorce/Abandonment	29, Jan. 1829	L3
Harsh, Conrad	Horse found	19, May 1817	L3
Hart, Elizabeth	Guardian	10, Dec. 1857	L3
Hart, Henry L.	Debt relief	17, Oct. 1839	L3
Hart, Isabella	Guardian	10, Dec. 1857	L3
Hart, John L.	Guardian	10, Dec. 1857	L3
Hart, William F.	Guardian	10, Dec. 1857	L3
Hartpence, James	Letter at P.O.	1, Jan. 1812	L3
Hartwell, George H.	Debt relief	17, Nov. 1842	L5
Haskins, Joseph J.	Debt relief	5, Feb. 1835	L3
Haskins, Joseph J.	Debt relief	17, Nov. 1842	L5
Hastings, Charles F.	Debt relief	9, June 1831	L3
Hastings, Charles F.	Debt relief	1, Aug. 1833	L3
Hastings, Nathan	Debt relief	14, July 1842	L3
Hatch, Harlan	Debt relief	21, May 1829	L4
Hatfield, Nathan	Horse found	12, June 1815	L3
Hatfield, William	Land payment notice	7, Nov. 1810	L3
Hathaway, Henry	Horse found	3, Nov. 1812	L4
Hathaway, William	Debt relief	28, Jan. 1830	L3
Hauser, Daniel	Guardian	5, Mar. 1857	L3
Hauser, Stephen	Guardian	5, Mar. 1857	L3
Haw, Ebenezer	Horse found	23, May 1810	L4
Hawkins, Caroline M.	Guardian	5, Sept 1839	L3
Hawkins, George	Guardian	5, Sept 1839	L3
Hawkins, James C.	Debt relief	1, Aug. 1833	L3
Hawkins, John	Land payment notice	7, Nov. 1810	L3
Hawkins, Lorenzo D.	Debt relief	1, Aug. 1833	L3
Hawkins, Louisa Ann	Guardian	5, Sept 1839	L3
Hawkins, Richard	Horse found	8, June 1813	L3
Hawkins, Richard J.	Guardian	5, Mar. 1857	L3
Hawkins, Samuel	Land payment notice	7, Nov. 1810	L3
Hawks, Thomas B.	Debt relief	1, Aug. 1833	L3
Hayden, Steven	Horse found	11, Mar. 1812	L4
Hearden, George & Sarah	Divorce/Abandonment	24, Feb. 1817	L4
Hearley, Henry	Inquiry	15, Feb. 1825	L4
Hearn, George	Swindler	16, July 1819	I3
Heath, John	Debt relief	28, Jan. 1830	L3
Heath, William	Letter at P.O.	1, Jan. 1812	L3
Heaton, Jonah & Margaret	Divorce/Abandonment	31, Mar. 1806	L3
Hedges, Ezra C.	Debt relief	28, Jan. 1830	L3
Heidelbach, Bertha	Guardian	5, Feb. 1857	L3
Heidelbach, Savina	Guardian	5, Feb. 1857	L3
Heiderhoff, Albert	Insane	21, Aug. 1851	L4
Heighway, Samuel	Land payment due	22, Nov. 1809	L4
Heim, Daniel & Rebecca Jane	Divorce/Abandonment	25, Jan. 1855	L3
Heistand, Jacob	Inquiry	13, Oct. 1817	L1
Hellinger, Casper	Debt relief	23, June 1842	L3
Henderson, Frederick	Debt relief	1, Aug. 1833	L3
Henderson, John	Horse found	31, Jan. 1810	L4
Henderson, Joseph	Horse found	30, Jan. 1811	L3
Henderson, Joseph	Horse found	11, Sept 1811	L4
Hendricks, James P. & Catharine	Divorce/Abandonment	12, Mar. 1840	L4

Name	Type of Notice	Date of Notice	Page
Hendrickson, Richard	Letter at P.O.	1, Jan. 1812	L3
Herrington, A.H.	Debt relief	18, Aug. 1826	L3
Hett, Elizabeth	Guardian	8, Jan. 1857	L3
Hett, Magdalena	Guardian	8, Jan. 1857	L3
Hetzel, Mary	Guardian	5, July 1855	L3
Hewit, John	Debt relief	24, Mar. 1807	L3
Hewson, John & Anne Elizabeth	Divorce/Abandonment	2, Mar. 1837	L3
Hibbs, Eson	Letter at P.O.	1, Jan. 1812	L3
Hickman, Aaron	Debt relief	11, Nov. 1825	L3
Higgins, Jonathan	Horse found	22, Apr. 1812	L3
Highland, Andrew	Horse found	11, Dec. 1815	L3
Hildreth, George	Horse found	29, Sept 1818	L3
Hill, Andrew	Horse found	18, Aug. 1812	L1
Hill, Frederick S.	Debt relief	17, Oct. 1839	L3
Hill, George	Deserter	21, Apr. 1817	L4
Hill, John	Horse found	16, June 1812	L3
Hillyer, Charles & Catharine	Divorce/Abandonment	20, Sept 1855	L3
Hinckle, Sampson	Debt relief	5, Feb. 1835	L3
Hindes, James	Horse lost	4, Dec. 1811	L2
Hinman, Ebenezer	Debt relief	17, Nov. 1842	L5
Hinsey, William	Horse found	13, Oct. 1812	L2
Hixson, Richard	Horse found	5, June 1811	L3
Hobbs, William H.	Guardian	6, Aug. 1857	L3
Hobson, Joseph & Adelaide	Divorce/Abandonment	20, Sept 1849	L3
Hodgson, Henry	Debt relief	1, Aug. 1833	L3
Hodgson, Isaac	Debtor	16, Feb. 1819	L3
Hodgson, Richard	Debtor	16, Feb. 1819	L3
Hoffman, George W.	Guardian	21, Sept 1837	L4
Hoffman, John	Guardian	21, Sept 1837	L4
Hoffman, Sarah Ann	Guardian	21, Sept 1837	L4
Hogan, William	Deserter	14, June 1814	L1
Hohnholz, Henry & Elizabeth	Divorce/Abandonment	6, Feb. 1840	L3
Hole, Walter	Horse found	10, Mar. 1817	L4
Holland, Zachariah	Horse found	14, Jan. 1818	L3
Hollenbeck, Alfred	Guardian	4, June 1857	L3
Hollenbeck, August	Guardian	4, June 1857	L3
Hollenbeck, Henry	Guardian	4, June 1857	L3
Hollenbeck, William	Guardian	4, June 1857	L3
Hollenbeke, Alfred	Guardian	8, Nov. 1855	L3
Hollenbeke, August	Guardian	8, Nov. 1855	L3
Hollenbeke, Henry	Guardian	8, Nov. 1855	L3
Hollenbeke, William	Guardian	8, Nov. 1855	L3
Hollenshade, John	Debt relief	9, Oct. 1828	L3
Holley, Daniel S.	Debt relief	17, Oct. 1839	L3
Holley, Robert C. & Nancy	Divorce/Abandonment	5, July 1849	L3
Hollingshade, John	Debt relief	9, Feb. 1827	L3
Holms, Daniel	Horse found	15, Aug. 1810	L2
Holt, William H.	Letter at P.O.	1, Jan. 1812	L3
Homer, John	Debt relief	9, June 1831	L3
Hood, Andrew	Land payment due	22, Nov. 1809	L4
Hood, George	Guardian	9, Apr. 1857	L3
Hood, William	Horse found	20, Sept 1814	L1
Hoover, William	Debt relief	5, Feb. 1835	L3
Hope, David C.	Deserter	21, Dec. 1813	L1

Name	Type of Notice	Date of Notice	Page
Hopkins, Benjamin W.	Debt relief	5, Feb. 1835	L3
Hopkins, Edward	Guardian	4, Sept 1856	L5
Hopkins, Henry E.	Debt relief	24, July 1828	L1
Hopkins, Noah J.	Debt relief	28, Jan. 1830	L3
Horn, John	Guardian	5, Mar. 1857	L3
Horn, Samuel	Debt relief	17, Nov. 1842	L5
Horne, Finton & Eliza Jane	Divorce/Abandonment	27, Jan. 1853	L3
Horner, Benjamin	Horse found	1, May 1811	L3
Horney, William, Jr.	Debt relief	9, June 1831	L3
Horton, Henry V.	Debt relief	17, Nov. 1842	L5
Hosbrock, Archibald	Debt relief	1, Aug. 1833	L3
Hotchkiss, Ann	Guardian	5, Mar. 1857	L3
Hotchkiss, David	Horse found	21, June 1820	L3
Hotchkiss, Isabella	Guardian	5, Mar. 1857	L3
Hotchkiss, Vail	Guardian	5, Mar. 1857	L3
Howard, Benjamin	Horse found	25, Feb. 1818	L3
Howard, Benjamin	Horse found	9, June 1817	L4
Howard, Edwin D.	Debt relief	24, July 1828	L1
Howard, George	Horse found	1, Jan. 1812	L4
Howell, Seely J.	Debt relief	23, June 1842	L3
Hoyt, William	Debt relief	17, Nov. 1842	L5
Hubbard, Kearby	Horse found	8, Jan. 1812	L4
Hubbard, Kirby	Horse found	22, June 1819	L3
Hubbard, Kirby	Horse found	9, June 1817	L4
Hudson, Jacob	Letter at P.O.	1, Jan. 1812	L3
Huff, William	Debt relief	22, Aug. 1810	L2
Hughbanks, William	Deserter	15, Feb. 1813	L2
Hughes, Isaac	Deserter from army	20, Oct. 1812	L3
Hughes, John	Horse found	20, Feb. 1811	L1
Hughes, Nathaniel	Horse found	23, Oct. 1811	L4
Hull, John	Debt relief	24, July 1828	L1
Hull, John W.	Debt relief	17, Nov. 1842	L5
Hulon, Joel & Ann	Divorce/Abandonment	7, Feb. 1839	L4
Hulse, E.	Horse lost	22, Aug. 1827	L3
Humes, John	Horse found	9, Jan. 1811	L1
Hummer, John	Horse found	15, Dec. 1812	L3
Humphrey, William	Letter at P.O.	1, Jan. 1812	L3
Hungerford, Warren & Jane	Divorce/Abandonment	24, Mar. 1817	L3
Hunt, Joshua & Mary	Divorce/Abandonment	3, Nov. 1821	L3
Hunter, John	Letter at P.O.	1, Jan. 1812	L3
Hunter, John	Horse found	7, Apr. 1817	L3
Huntriss, Joseph	Debt relief	1, Aug. 1833	L3
Hurdus, George	Debt relief	9, Feb. 1827	L3
Huse, John	Debt relief	4, Aug. 1831	L4
Huston, Tennant	Horse found	21, Jan. 1818	L3
Hutchinson, Abigail	Guardian	9, Aug. 1838	L3
Hutchinson, Amos	Guardian	9, Aug. 1838	L3
Hutchinson, George M.	Debt relief	1, Aug. 1833	L3
Hutchinson, John	Deserter	8, Feb. 1814	L3
Hutchinson, Nancy	Guardian	9, Aug. 1838	L3
Hutchinson, Naomi	Guardian	9, Aug. 1838	L3
Hutchinson, Naomi	Guardian	7, May 1840	L3
Hutson, Daniel	Letter at P.O.	1, Jan. 1812	L3
Hyatt, Squire & Sally	Divorce/Abandonment	8, Feb. 1838	L3

Name	Type of Notice	Date of Notice	Page
Hyde, Ephraim	Horse stolen	22, July 1816	L3
Iddings, Lewis & Eliza Ann	Divorce/Abandonment	16, Feb. 1837	L4
Immell, Jacob & Elizabeth	Divorce/Abandonment	31, Dec. 1857	L3
Ingersoll, Henry	Debt relief	9, June 1831	L3
Ingersoll, James	Horse found	9, June 1817	L4
Ingersoll, William S.	Debt relief	17, Nov. 1842	L5
Ingersull, Daniel & Catharine	Divorce/Abandonment	27, Sept 1814	L1
Ingursall, Daniel	Letter at P.O.	1, Jan. 1812	L3
Ingursall, Enoch	Letter at P.O.	1, Jan. 1812	L3
Ireland, Aaron	Horse found	29, Jan. 1812	L2
Ireland, Aaron	Horse found	25, Sept 1812	L2
Ireland, James	Horse found	1, Nov. 1814	L1
Irish, Henry	Debt relief	24, July 1828	L1
Irwin, Alexander & Eleanor	Divorce/Abandonment	8, Feb. 1814	L3
Irwin, Archibald	Debt relief	17, Nov. 1842	L5
Irwin, John, Jr.	Debt relief	24, Mar. 1807	L3
Irwin, Mary	Guardian	22, Mar. 1838	L3
Irwin, Morton	Land payment notice	7, Nov. 1810	L3
Irwin, William	Horse found	11, Mar. 1812	L3
Irwin, William	Convict	5, Feb. 1846	L3
Irwind, James	Letter at P.O.	1, Jan. 1812	L3
Isacs, Gabriel & Sarah	Divorce/Abandonment	27, Oct. 1836	L3
Israel, Isaac	Debt relief	1, Aug. 1833	L3
Israel, Isam	Horse found	14, July 1812	L1
Ives, Henry	Debt relief	14, July 1842	L3
Jacklin, Isaac	Missing child	14, July 1821	L3
Jackson, (Major)	Letter at P.O.	1, Jan. 1812	L3
Jackson, Alban	Horse found	23, June 1817	L3
Jackson, Alice	Guardian	10, Apr. 1856	L3
Jackson, Andrew J.	Guardian	10, Apr. 1856	L3
Jackson, Anna M.	Guardian	10, Apr. 1856	L3
Jackson, Anson W.	Debt relief	21, May 1829	L4
Jackson, Edward	Horse found	5, Jan. 1813	L3
Jackson, Elizabeth M.	Guardian	10, Apr. 1856	L3
Jackson, John	Deserter	29, Mar. 1814	L1
Jackson, Martha M.	Guardian	10, Apr. 1856	L3
Jackson, Robert	Debt relief	18, Aug. 1826	L3
Jackson, Sarah	Guardian	10, Apr. 1856	L3
Jackson, Thomas & Flora	Divorce/Abandonment	7, Apr. 1806	L3
Jackson, William	Debt relief	17, Nov. 1842	L5
Jacobs, John, Jr. & Rebecca	Divorce/Abandonment	11, Sept 1811	L1
James, David S.	Debt relief	23, June 1842	L3
James, Davis S.	Debt relief	17, Nov. 1842	L5
James, Samuel	Guardian	5, Sept 1839	L3
James, Thomas	Guardian	5, Sept 1839	L3
Janes, Joseph & Mary	Divorce/Abandonment	30, July 1805	L4
Jay, Stephen	Land payment notice	7, Nov. 1810	L3
Jefferson, William	Horse found	27, May 1812	L2
Jenkins, Frances J.	Guardian	6, Aug. 1857	L3
Jenkins, Solomon	Debt relief	9, Feb. 1827	L3
Jenks, Scott	Horse found	23, Oct. 1828	L3
Jessop, Furman	Guardian	5, Sept 1839	L3

Name	Type of Notice	Date of Notice	Page
Jessup, John	Cattle found	31, Aug. 1813	l3
Jocelyn, Luther B.	Debt relief	1, Aug. 1833	L3
John, James	Land payment due	22, Nov. 1809	L4
Johnson, Albert	Guardian	4, June 1857	L3
Johnson, Helen	Guardian	4, June 1857	L3
Johnson, James	Land payment notice	7, Nov. 1810	L3
Johnson, John	Horse found	22, Apr. 1812	L3
Johnson, John & Elizabeth	Divorce/Abandonment	10, May 1855	L3
Johnson, John & Nancy	Divorce/Abandonment	3, Mar. 1831	L4
Johnson, Margaret	Guardian	4, June 1857	L3
Johnson, Mary	Guardian	4, June 1857	L3
Johnson, Mathias	Debt relief	11, Nov. 1825	L3
Johnson, Nicholas	Debt relief	17, Oct. 1839	L3
Johnson, Stephen	Debt relief	1, Aug. 1833	L3
Johnson, Stephen	Horse found	13, Oct. 1817	L4
Johnson, Wilford	Horse found	29, May 1815	L3
Johnston, Alexander & Eliza	Divorce/Abandonment	30, Jan. 1840	L3
Johnston, James	Land payment due	22, Nov. 1809	L4
Johnston, Walter	Horse found	16, Sept 1816	L3
Joice, Absalom	Letter at P.O.	1, Jan. 1812	L3
Jones, Absalom	Horse found	16, Aug. 1814	L3
Jones, Andrew	Letter at P.O.	1, Jan. 1812	L3
Jones, Anna	Guardian	3, Sept 1840	L3
Jones, C.H.	Guardian	3, Sept 1840	L3
Jones, Catharine	Guardian	3, Sept 1840	L3
Jones, Daniel	Horse found	10, Aug. 1813	L2
Jones, Enoch	Horse found	14, Mar. 1810	L2
Jones, Evan	Horse found	25, May 1813	L1
Jones, George	Horse found	27, Oct. 1812	L2
Jones, Henry	Horse found	22, July 1825	L3
Jones, J.L.	Guardian	3, Sept 1840	L3
Jones, James	Horse found	6, Dec. 1814	L1
Jones, James	Horse found	27, Apr. 1813	L2
Jones, James	Horse found	11, Feb. 1818	L3
Jones, James	Debt relief	9, Feb. 1827	L3
Jones, James	Debt relief	4, Aug. 1831	L4
Jones, Joel	Horse found	22, Dec. 1831	L3
Jones, John	Letter at P.O.	1, Jan. 1812	L3
Jones, John & Martha	Divorce/Abandonment	4, July 1844	L3
Jones, John T.	Horse found	8, July 1816	L3
Jones, John W.	Horse found	12, Feb. 1816	L3
Jones, Jonas & Nancy	Divorce/Abandonment	18, May 1822	L3
Jones, Joseph	Debt relief	1, Aug. 1833	L3
Jones, Mahlon	Guardian	3, Sept 1840	L3
Jones, Mary	Guardian	3, Sept 1840	L3
Jones, Mathias	Guardian	3, Sept 1840	L3
Jones, Michael	Letter at P.O.	1, Jan. 1812	L3
Jones, R.E.	Guardian	3, Sept 1840	L3
Jones, Reuben	Horse found	3, June 1818	L3
Jones, Richard	Guardian	3, Sept 1840	L3
Jones, Thomas	Letter at P.O.	1, Jan. 1812	L3
Jones, Thomas	Guardian	3, Sept 1840	L3
Jones, W.A.	Guardian	3, Sept 1840	L3
Jones, Willard T.	Debt relief	17, Nov. 1842	L5

Name	Type of Notice	Date of Notice	Page
Jordan, Daniel B.	Debt relief	1, Aug. 1833	L3
Jordon, Daniel B.	Debt relief	23, June 1842	L3
Joseph, Judah G.	Debt relief	14, July 1842	L3
Justice, Martin	Horse found	5, July 1814	L3
Kalapsza, John & Klara	Divorce/Abandonment	30, Aug. 1855	L3
Kate, Ebenezer & Susan	Divorce/Abandonment	21, Jan. 1836	L4
Kauffman, Frances	Guardian	10, Dec. 1857	L3
Kauffman, Henry	Guardian	10, Dec. 1857	L3
Kauffman, Jacob	Guardian	10, Dec. 1857	L3
Kauffman, Joseph	Guardian	10, Dec. 1857	L3
Kauffman, Magdalena	Guardian	10, Dec. 1857	L3
Kauffmann, John	Guardian	10, Dec. 1857	L3
Keal, Benjamin & Ann	Divorce/Abandonment	14, Aug. 1822	L3
Kearns, Peter & Anne	Divorce/Abandonment	26, Aug. 1812	L1
Keating, George	Debt relief	11, Nov. 1825	L3
Keating, Nicholas	Letter at P.O.	1, Jan. 1812	L3
Keiser, Coleman & Elizabeth	Divorce/Abandonment	16, June 1853	L3
Kelley, Alexander	Horse found	7, Aug. 1811	L2
Kelley, Henry	Deserter from army	10, Nov. 1812	L2
Kellogg, Charles F.	Debt relief	23, June 1842	L3
Kellogg, Ethel	Land payment notice	7, Nov. 1810	L3
Kelly, Alexander	Horse found	11, Aug. 1817	L3
Kelly, James	Deserter	24, Aug. 1813	L2
Kelly, James	Inquiry - 7 yrs old	14, July 1853	L3
Kelly, Jane	Inquiry - 9 yrs old	14, July 1853	L3
Kelly, John	Deserter	10, May 1814	L3
Kelly, Matthew	Debt relief	23, June 1842	L3
Kelly, Oliver	Cow lost	16, Sept 1816	L3
Kelpin, Thomas	Debt relief	1, Aug. 1833	L3
Kemp, Francis	Debt relief	17, Oct. 1839	L3
Kemp, Jacob	Horse found	20, Feb. 1811	L4
Kemper, Caleb	Notice	29, Mar. 1832	L4
Kemper, Charles A.	Notice	29, Mar. 1832	L4
Kemper, David R.	Notice	29, Mar. 1832	L4
Kemper, Edward	Vattier court case	28, Apr. 1807	L3
Kemper, Edward Y. & Joanna	Divorce/Abandonment	13, Feb. 1827	L3
Kemper, Elnathan	Notice	29, Mar. 1832	L4
Kemper, Frederick A.	Notice	29, Mar. 1832	L4
Kemper, Presley	Horse found	19, Aug. 1825	L3
Kemper, Presley	Horse found	31, Jan. 1821	L4
Kendall, Benjamin S.	Debt relief	1, Aug. 1833	L3
Kendall, Charles A.	Guardian	14, Aug. 1856	L6
Kendall, Edwin W.	Guardian	14, Aug. 1856	L6
Kendall, Ellen F.	Guardian	14, Aug. 1856	L6
Kendall, George M.	Debt relief	23, June 1842	L3
Kendall, Martha S.	Guardian	14, Aug. 1856	L6
Kennann, John & Mary	Divorce/Abandonment	24, May 1809	L3
Kennedy, Francis	Horse found	4, Mar. 1816	L3
Kennedy, James	Horse found	14, July 1812	L1
Kepner, ---- & ----	Divorce/Abandonment	13, Nov. 1850	L3
Kerr, Joseph	Debt relief	17, Oct. 1839	L3
Kerr, Thomas	Horse found	21, Feb. 1810	L2
Kessinger, Teter	Land payment notice	7, Nov. 1810	L3

Name	Type of Notice	Date of Notice	Page
Ketchum, Robert	Horse found	7, June 1825	L3
Kethber, Joseph	Horse found	12, Feb. 1812	L2
Kethler, Joseph	Horse found	4, Aug. 1812	L2
Keyes, Thomas	Debt relief	14, July 1842	L3
Kibbe, Benjamin P.	Debt relief	24, July 1828	L1
Kidd, John	Letter at P.O.	1, Jan. 1812	L3
Kidder, Samuel	Deserter	6, Sept 1814	L4
Kiger, Jacob	Horse found	21, July 1812	L3
Kiger, Peter	Horse found	27, Jan. 1817	L3
Kilbarber, Barbara	Inquiry	15, Feb. 1825	L4
Kilgore, Ezekiel	Horse found	1, Nov. 1814	L1
Kimball, Cyrus	Debt relief	17, Nov. 1842	L5
Kincaid, James	Horse found	17, Apr. 1828	L3
King, Edward A.	Debt relief	5, Feb. 1835	L3
King, Isaac	Debt relief	8, June 1827	L4
King, John	Debt relief	21, May 1829	L4
Kingrey, Joseph	Horse found	5, June 1811	L3
Kingsberry, Henry L.	Horse found	10, July 1811	L1
Kingsbey, Henry L.	Letter at P.O.	1, Jan. 1812	L3
Kirby, James D. & Hannah	Divorce/Abandonment	30, Sept 1820	L3
Kirchner, Catharine	Guardian	4, Sept 1856	L5
Kirchner, Elizabeth	Guardian	4, Sept 1856	L5
Kirchner, Jacob	Guardian	4, Sept 1856	L5
Kirchner, Margaret	Guardian	4, Sept 1856	L5
Kirk, D. Kilgour	Debt relief	9, Oct. 1828	L3
Kirk, George H. & Mary Ann	Divorce/Abandonment	26, Jan. 1843	L3
Kirkpatrick, Alexander	Land payment notice	7, Nov. 1810	L3
Kirkpatrick, William	Land payment notice	7, Nov. 1810	L3
Kister, George	Horse found	28, Aug. 1811	L3
Kitchel, Mary	Horse found	27, Feb. 1811	L1
Kitts, John & Susan	Divorce/Abandonment	16, June 1806	L2
Kitts, John & Susanna	Divorce/Abandonment	7, May 1808	L4
Klien, Catharine	Guardian	10, Dec. 1857	L3
Klien, Louisa	Guardian	10, Dec. 1857	L3
Knapp, Jacob	Guardian	10, Dec. 1857	L3
Knawlton, Sidney A.	Debt relief	18, Aug. 1826	L3
Knicely, Abraham	Horse stolen	15, Feb. 1825	L3
Knicely, Peter	Horse found	25, May 1813	L1
Knight, John	Horse found	14, Nov. 1810	L3
Knot, Joseph	Horse found	16, June 1812	L3
Knott, Joseph	Horse found	6, July 1813	L1
Koon, Luke	Debt relief	21, May 1829	L4
Korte, Elizabeth	Guardian	10, Sept 1857	L3
Korte, Francis	Guardian	10, Sept 1857	L3
Korte, John	Guardian	10, Sept 1857	L3
Kramer, Simon	Debt relief	14, July 1842	L3
Krutz, Charles F.	Letter at P.O.	1, Jan. 1812	L3
Kunse, George	Land payment notice	7, Nov. 1810	L3
Kunse, Jacob	Land payment notice	7, Nov. 1810	L3
Kyte, John	Deserter	18, Jan. 1814	L1
Kyzer, Jacob	Horse found	18, July 1810	L2
Laboyteaux, John G. & Phoebe	Divorce/Abandonment	26, May 1817	L3
Laboyteaux, Peter	Horse found	30, May 1810	L2

Name	Type of Notice	Date of Notice	Page
Lacey, Henry	Horse found	19, Oct. 1813	L1
Lacy, Thomas	Horse found	13, Aug. 1827	L3
Lafferty, Patrick	Land payment notice	7, Nov. 1810	L3
Lake, John T.	Deserter	22, June 1813	L1
Lamb, Alexander	Debt relief	5, Feb. 1835	L3
Lambert, Amos	Horse found	1, Jan. 1812	L4
Lamphier, Joseph	Debt relief	1, Aug. 1833	L3
Landon, William & Barbara	Divorce/Abandonment	28, Aug. 1815	L3
Lane, Conrad	Guardian	14, Aug. 1856	L6
Lane, Samuel	Horse found	9, Nov. 1813	L2
Lang, John	Horse found	24, Nov. 1812	L3
Langdon, Jackson	Guardian	14, Feb. 1839	L3
Langdon, John C.	Guardian	14, Feb. 1839	L3
Langdon, Joseph	Guardian	14, Feb. 1839	L3
Langdon, Mary Jane	Guardian	14, Feb. 1839	L3
Langley, John	Runaway apprentice	25, Jan. 1814	L1
Lapp, Caroline	Guardian	7, June 1855	L3
Lapp, Helena	Guardian	7, June 1855	L3
Lapp, Victoria	Guardian	7, June 1855	L3
Larabee, Anson	Horse found	9, June 1817	L3
Larowe, John	Letter at P.O.	1, Jan. 1812	L3
Larrison, George	Horse found	21, Sept 1813	L3
Larue, Francis	Debt relief	1, Aug. 1833	L3
Larue, Franklin	Debt relief	18, Aug. 1826	L3
Latham, David	Debtor	10, Feb. 1821	L3
Latimore, Samuel	Letter at P.O.	1, Jan. 1812	L3
Law, Michael	Debt relief	5, Feb. 1835	L3
Lawrence, Calvin & Eve	Divorce/Abandonment	12, July 1809	L3
Lawrence, Edward	Runaway apprentice	8, July 1823	L2
Lawrence, James	Debt relief	18, Aug. 1826	L3
Lawrence, Lorenzo	Debt relief	21, May 1829	L4
Lawton, David & Eliza	Divorce/Abandonment	14, Aug. 1856	L8
Layton, Pallatiah	Horse found	10, May 1820	L3
Leaming, Christopher	Debt relief	8, June 1827	L4
Learned, Lyman	Letter at P.O.	1, Jan. 1812	L3
Ledlie, William	Runaway apprentice	10, Feb. 1817	L3
Lee, David	Horse found	17, May 1814	L3
Lee, David & Anne	Divorce/Abandonment	22, Sept 1836	L3
Lee, Eliazer & Margaret	Divorce/Abandonment	3, Aug. 1813	L3
Lee, Joseph	Letter at P.O.	1, Jan. 1812	L3
Lee, Stephen	Letter at P.O.	1, Jan. 1812	L3
Leese, Robert	Horse found	29, Aug. 1810	L5
Leet, Abraham	Land payment due	22, Nov. 1809	L4
Lefferson, James	Guardian	8, Nov. 1832	L4
Lefferson, Mary	Guardian	8, Nov. 1832	L4
Lefferson, William	Guardian	8, Nov. 1832	L4
Leffler, David	Debt relief	9, Oct. 1828	L3
Legg, Charles	Land payment notice	7, Nov. 1810	L3
Legit, Simeon	Guardian	3, May 1855	L3
Legit, Thomas	Guardian	3, May 1855	L3
Leland, George	Deserter	9, June 1817	L4
Lemy, John J.	Debt relief	1, Aug. 1833	L3
Lenning, James	Runaway apprentice	2, Mar. 1813	L2
Leobold, John	Letter at P.O.	1, Jan. 1812	L3

Name	Type of Notice	Date of Notice	Page
Leser, Henrietta	Guardian	9, Aug. 1855	L3
Leser, Henrietta	Guardian	6, Aug. 1857	L3
Leser, William	Guardian	9, Aug. 1855	L3
Leser, William	Guardian	6, Aug. 1857	L3
Letch, Richard	Horse found	2, Dec. 1816	L3
Levitt, O.S.	Debt relief	17, Oct. 1839	L3
Lewis, Albert	Debt relief	23, June 1842	L3
Lewis, Benjamin	Debt relief	24, July 1828	L1
Lewis, Chancey S.	Debt relief	5, Feb. 1835	L3
Lewis, Israel	Debt relief	28, Jan. 1830	L3
Lewis, Timothy	Debt relief	28, Jan. 1830	L3
Lewis, William & Susan	Divorce/Abandonment	22, Feb. 1825	L3
L'Hommedieu, Richard F.	Guardian	9, Apr. 1829	L3
Lincoln, Lemuel R.	Debt relief	1, Aug. 1833	L3
Lindsay, William	Horse found	11, Dec. 1811	L4
Lindsey, David	Convict	5, Feb. 1846	L3
Lindsly, William	Horse found	17, July 1811	L3
Little, George D.	Debt relief	1, Aug. 1833	L3
Little, Norman	Letter at P.O.	1, Jan. 1812	L3
Little, Robert A.	Debt relief	17, Nov. 1842	L5
Littleton, Thomas	Horse found	23, June 1817	L3
Lockwood, Isaac M.	Debt relief	21, May 1829	L4
Lodge, Benjamin F.	Debt relief	5, Feb. 1835	L3
Lofland, William	Deserter	22, Feb. 1814	L1
Lofland, William	Letter at P.O.	1, Jan. 1812	L3
Logan, Anthony	Land payment notice	7, Nov. 1810	L3
Logan, S.C.	Guardian	4, June 1857	L3
Long, Frederick	Letter at P.O.	1, Jan. 1812	L3
Long, John	Horse found	5, June 1811	L3
Long, Mary	Horse found	15, Feb. 1814	L3
Long, Thomas	Debt relief	17, Nov. 1842	L5
Longshore, George W.	Debt relief	11, Nov. 1825	L3
Longworth, Nicholas	50th anniversary	31, Dec. 1857	L1
Loring, Daniel B.	Letter at P.O.	1, Jan. 1812	L3
Lothrap, Isaac	Horse found	1, Dec. 1817	L3
Low, Almira Ann	Guardian	22, Mar. 1838	L3
Loy, Barbara	Land payment notice	7, Nov. 1810	L3
Lucas, Benjamin	Horse found	30, June 1817	L3
Lucas, Benjamin	Horse found	11, Jan. 1820	L3
Lucas, David	Debt relief	24, Feb. 1807	L1
Lucas, Isaac D.	Debtor	12, June 1822	L3
Lucas, Jane P. & Mary	Divorce/Abandonment	16, Dec. 1841	L3
Lucian, Jane C.	Guardian	19, Dec. 1826	L3
Ludlow, Israel	Guardian	25, Aug. 1817	L4
Ludlow, James C.	Guardian	25, Aug. 1817	L4
Ludlow, Sarah	Letter at P.O.	1, Jan. 1812	L3
Ludlow, Sarah Bella	Guardian	25, Aug. 1817	L4
Ludlow, William D.	Horse found	16, Jan. 1815	L4
Ludlum, James M.	Debt relief	9, June 1831	L3
Lynn, John	Debt relief	9, June 1831	L3
Lyon, James	Horse found	3, July 1815	L3
Lyon, Oliver & Sarah	Divorce/Abandonment	2, Mar. 1837	L3
Lyon, William J.	Debt relief	5, Feb. 1835	L3
Lyons, Robert	Letter at P.O.	1, Jan. 1812	L3

Name	Type of Notice	Date of Notice	Page
Lyons, William	Letter at P.O.	1, Jan. 1812	L3
Mach, William	Escaped convict	12, June 1828	L3
Mack, Isaac	Guardian	14, Aug. 1856	L6
Madder, A.M.	Guardian	4, June 1857	L3
Madder, Agatha	Guardian	4, June 1857	L3
Madder, Berthold	Guardian	4, June 1857	L3
Madder, Civilus	Guardian	4, June 1857	L3
Madder, Elizabeth	Guardian	4, June 1857	L3
Madder, Felix	Guardian	4, June 1857	L3
Madder, Josepha B.	Guardian	4, June 1857	L3
Madder, Robert	Guardian	4, June 1857	L3
Madison, Joab	Debt relief	24, July 1828	L1
Magee, William W.	Debt relief	9, Feb. 1827	L3
Magonigal, Philip	Deserter from army	6, Oct. 1812	L1
Magreth, Michael	Debt relief	9, June 1831	L3
Mahew, Rufus D.	Debt relief	17, Nov. 1842	L5
Mains, Philip	Horse found	2, June 1812	L2
Manley, Paul & Amelia	Divorce/Abandonment	24, Aug. 1843	L3
Mann, Alexander & Phebe	Divorce/Abandonment	19, July 1849	L3
Mann, Isaac	Debt relief	14, July 1842	L3
Mann, Morris B.	Debt relief	14, July 1842	L3
Mantville, James	Debt relief	9, June 1831	L3
Markel, William N.	Debt relief	9, June 1831	L3
Markland, Joshua	Debt relief	24, July 1828	L1
Markland, Matthew	Letter at P.O.	1, Jan. 1812	L3
Marks, Henry H.	Debt relief	9, June 1831	L3
Markward, Charles	Debt relief	9, Feb. 1827	L3
Marsh, Benjamin	Deserter	26, Apr. 1814	L3
Marsh, Calvin	Horse found	13, May 1820	L3
Marsh, David	Letter at P.O.	1, Jan. 1812	L3
Marsh, Elikim	Letter at P.O.	1, Jan. 1812	L3
Marsh, George W.	Convict	5, Feb. 1846	L3
Marshall, John	Deserter	24, May 1814	L3
Marshall, John	Debt relief	9, June 1831	L3
Marshall, William	Horse found	3, Nov. 1812	L1
Martin, Abraham	Horse found	1, Sept 1812	L2
Martin, Frances D.	Guardian	21, Sept 1837	L4
Martin, Francis D.	Guardian	9, Aug. 1838	L3
Martin, Francis D.	Guardian	8, Nov. 1832	L4
Martin, G.W.	Guardian	21, Sept 1837	L4
Martin, George W.	Guardian	8, Nov. 1832	L4
Martin, Henry	Debt relief	5, Feb. 1835	L3
Martin, Jacob O.	Guardian	8, Nov. 1832	L4
Martin, Jacob O.	Guardian	21, Sept 1837	L4
Martin, James H.	Debt relief	9, June 1831	L3
Martin, James, Jr.	Debt relief	18, Aug. 1826	L3
Martin, Josiah	Debt relief	8, June 1827	L4
Martin, Mathias	Horse found	6, Oct. 1812	L1
Martin, Mathias	Horse found	20, Oct. 1812	L4
Martin, Oliver	Horse stolen	14, Sept 1819	L3
Martindale, John	Horse found	3, Aug. 1813	L3
Martz, Conrad	Letter at P.O.	1, Jan. 1812	L3
Mason, Benjamin	Vattier court case	28, Apr. 1807	L3

Name	Type of Notice	Date of Notice	Page
Masters, Perry	Horse found	28, June 1827	L3
Masters, William & Frances	Divorce/Abandonment	16, Aug. 1838	L4
Mastin, Thomas	Deserter from army	3, Nov. 1812	L3
Mathers, Catherine	Guardian	14, Aug. 1856	L6
Mathers, George	Horse found	24, Nov. 1817	L3
Mathers, James	Guardian	14, Aug. 1856	L6
Mathers, William	Guardian	14, Aug. 1856	L6
Mathews, John M.	Debt relief	1, Aug. 1833	L3
Matson, Hezekiah	Debt relief	9, June 1831	L3
Matson, James	Horse found	25, Apr. 1810	L2
Matson, John	Horse found	7, Dec. 1819	L3
Matt, George	Guardian	4, June 1857	L3
Matt, Joseph	Guardian	4, June 1857	L3
Matteer, Michael & Phoebe A	Divorce/Abandonment	11, Mar. 1847	L3
Matthews, Jonathan	Debtor	20, Mar. 1827	L3
Matthews, William T.	Guardian	4, Sept 1856	L5
Mayhood, Thomas	Convict	5, Feb. 1846	L3
McAdams, William	Horse found	7, Sept 1813	L2
McAllister, Isaac T.	Horse found	23, June 1817	L3
McAllister, John	Convict	5, Feb. 1846	L3
McArthur, Daniel	Debt relief	21, May 1829	L4
McBride, James	Deserter	6, July 1813	L1
McCain, Jesse & Christena	Divorce/Abandonment	21, Nov. 1839	L3
McCain, William	Debt relief	1, Aug. 1833	L3
McCammon, Thomas	Debt relief	9, Feb. 1827	L3
McCann, Emory & Marinda	Divorce/Abandonment	13, Mar. 1856	L3
McCann, Francis	Debt relief	28, Jan. 1830	L3
McCartey, Henry	Horse found	16, Aug. 1814	L3
McCarty, Benjamin	Land payment notice	7, Nov. 1810	L3
McCarty, Benjamin	Letter at P.O.	1, Jan. 1812	L3
McCauly, Henry	Horse found	23, Aug. 1814	L1
McChesney, Robert	Debt relief	14, July 1842	L3
McClain, Aaron	Horse found	1, Sept 1812	L2
McClean, William	Horse found	27, Oct. 1817	L4
McCleave, William & Mary	Divorce/Abandonment	3, Oct. 1810	L3
McClelland, Thomas	Deserter from army	27, May 1812	L3
McCling, John	Letter at P.O.	1, Jan. 1812	L3
McClure, Samuel	Horse found	22, June 1813	L3
McConnell, Robert	Land payment notice	7, Nov. 1810	L3
McCorkle, John	Lot for Sale	24, Nov. 1817	L3
McCormick, Chaplein	Debt relief	1, Aug. 1833	L3
McCormick, Chapline	Debt relief	8, June 1827	L4
McCormick, Francis	Horse lost	12, Aug. 1816	L3
McCormick, Mary Ann	Guardian	8, Nov. 1832	L4
McCoy, James	Land payment due	22, Nov. 1809	L4
McCoy, Theodore & Amelia	Divorce/Abandonment	7, June 1855	L3
McCoy, William	Debt relief	9, Feb. 1827	L3
McCracken, James	Guardian	5, Nov. 1857	L3
McCullock, John	Deserter	29, June 1813	L3
McCullough, Thomas	Land payment notice	7, Nov. 1810	L3
McDade, Jeremiah	Deserter	6, July 1813	L1
McDaniels, Moses	Horse found	7, Dec. 1819	L3
McDevell, Charles	Debt relief	9, Oct. 1828	L3
McDonald, Daniel	Horse found	29, Jan. 1812	L2

Name	Type of Notice	Date of Notice	Page
McDonald, James	Letter at P.O.	1, Jan. 1812	L3
McDougal, Hugh	Guardian	10, Jan. 1856	L3
McDowel, John	Horse found	18, Nov. 1816	L3
McFarland, William (Judge)	Vattier court case	28, Apr. 1807	L3
McFeely, John & Mary Ann	Divorce/Abandonment	26, Feb. 1829	L2
McFeely, Thomas	Letter at P.O.	1, Jan. 1812	L3
McGee, Bernard & Catharine	Divorce/Abandonment	28, Aug. 1851	L3
McGilery, Alexander	Letter at P.O.	1, Jan. 1812	L3
McGlaughlin, William	Horse found	21, July 1817	L3
McGrew, Robert	Letter at P.O.	1, Jan. 1812	L3
McGuire, Ebenezer G.	Debt relief	23, June 1842	L3
McGuire, Isaac	Debt relief	1, Aug. 1833	L3
McGuire, John	Debt relief	9, Feb. 1827	L3
McGuire, Thomas	Debt relief	23, June 1842	L3
McHenry, Dennis	Debt relief	17, Nov. 1842	L5
McIntire, William	Letter at P.O.	1, Jan. 1812	L3
McJannet, Andrew	Debt relief	17, Oct. 1839	L3
McJunkins, Hugh	Debt relief	9, Feb. 1827	L3
McKane, Jesse & Christeen	Divorce/Abandonment	28, Mar. 1826	L3
McKee, David D.	Debt relief	24, July 1828	L1
Mckee, John	Horse lost	14, July 1812	L1
McKee, Samuel	Horse found	9, Aug. 1814	L3
McKinley, John	Horse found	27, Jan. 1817	L3
McKinney, John	Land payment notice	7, Nov. 1810	L3
McKinney, Thomas	Land payment notice	7, Nov. 1810	L3
McKown, Thomas	Debt relief	9, Oct. 1828	L3
McLean, Elizabeth L.	Guardian	13, Feb. 1840	L3
McLean, James	Debt relief	8, June 1827	L4
McLean, Mary Jane	Guardian	10, Dec. 1857	L3
McLein, James	Letter at P.O.	1, Jan. 1812	L3
McLennans, Bernard	Guardian	7, June 1855	L3
Mcmahan, Andrew & Hannah	Divorce/Abandonment	24, Aug. 1854	L3
McMahan, James	Debt relief	4, Aug. 1831	L4
McMaken, John	Horse found	27, Mar. 1811	L3
McManus, Charles	Debt relief	9, May 1810	L3
McMeker, Patrick & Polly	Divorce/Abandonment	5, Nov. 1805	L3
McMillan, (widow)	Horse found	12, Feb. 1816	L3
McMillen, Archibald	Deserter	7, July 1817	L2
McMillen, William T.	Debt relief	17, Nov. 1842	L5
McMullen, Archibald	Horse found	5, June 1811	L3
McMullen, John & Martha	Divorce/Abandonment	21, Feb. 1856	L3
McNeaill, Archibald	Debt relief	21, May 1829	L4
McNeal, Charles B. & Catharine	Divorce/Abandonment	11, Feb. 1836	L3
McNeely, G.	Land payment notice	7, Nov. 1810	L3
McNeely, James	Land payment notice	7, Nov. 1810	L3
McNichol, Peter	Vattier court case	28, Apr. 1807	L3
McNutt, Alexander	Horse found	16, Jan. 1811	L3
McNutt, James	Horse found	10, Nov. 1812	L2
McPherin, William	Debt relief	9, Feb. 1827	L3
McPherrin, William	Horse found	23, Nov. 1819	L3
McQueen, Uriah	Horse found	20, Nov. 1814	L2
Mead, Eliza P.	Guardian	10, Sept 1857	L3
Mead, Emma W.	Guardian	10, Sept 1857	L3
Mears, Isaac	Runaway apprentice	10, May 1814	L1

Name	Type of Notice	Date of Notice	Page
Medill, Thomas	Horse found	19, Jan. 1813	L2
Meeker, Daniel S.	Debt relief	23, June 1842	L3
Meeks, Samuel	Horse found	29, July 1816	L3
Megrue, Paul	Horse found	15, June 1813	L2
Melony, Nathaniel	Debt relief	9, June 1831	L3
Melott, Peter	Horse found	11, Mar. 1812	L3
Mendenhall, Aaron	Horse found	14, July 1812	L1
Menken, Solomon	Debt relief	14, July 1842	L3
Merril, Benjamin	Letter at P.O.	1, Jan. 1812	L3
Merritt, Isaac	Horse found	7, Aug. 1811	L2
Merritt, James	Debt relief	9, June 1831	L3
Merritt, John H.	Debt relief	28, Jan. 1830	L3
Merritt, Thomas	Debt relief	28, Jan. 1830	L3
Messenger, Oliver	Letter at P.O.	1, Jan. 1812	L3
Messer, Solomon	Runaway apprentice	12, Feb. 1816	L1
Messer, Solomon	Runaway apprentice	25, Mar. 1815	L3
Messer, William & Frances	Divorce/Abandonment	8, Mar. 1849	L3
Mewhiney, James	Horse found	10, Aug. 1813	L3
Meyer, Benjamin	Guardian	9, Apr. 1857	L3
Milbis, Nathan	Debt relief	8, June 1827	L4
Miles, Israel W.	Guardian	9, Aug. 1855	L3
Miles, Israel W.	Guardian	10, Sept 1857	L3
Miles, J.W.P.	Guardian	9, Aug. 1855	L3
Miles, Louisa	Guardian	9, Aug. 1855	L3
Miles, Louisa J.	Guardian	10, Sept 1857	L3
Miles, William	Letter at P.O.	1, Jan. 1812	L3
Miles, William P.	Guardian	10, Sept 1857	L3
Miley, Abraham	Letter at P.O.	1, Jan. 1812	L3
Millard, Henry & Rebecca	Divorce/Abandonment	16, Feb. 1827	L3
Miller, Andrew	Inquiry	4, June 1817	L3
Miller, Arthur St.Clair	Horse found	1, Jan. 1816	L3
Miller, Christian & Elizabeth	Divorce/Abandonment	12, Sept 1850	L3
Miller, Daniel	Letter at P.O.	1, Jan. 1812	L3
Miller, Edward M.	Guardian	5, Mar. 1857	L3
Miller, Ezra	Debt relief	28, Jan. 1830	L3
Miller, George & Betsey	Divorce/Abandonment	19, Apr. 1814	L3
Miller, Henry	Debt relief	9, June 1831	L3
Miller, I.B.	Horse found	11, Dec. 1815	L3
Miller, I.B.	Horse found	24, Jan. 1810	L4
Miller, Jacob	Letter at P.O.	1, Jan. 1812	L3
Miller, Jacob & Susan	Divorce/Abandonment	8, Apr. 1812	L1
Miller, James	Land payment notice	7, Nov. 1810	L3
Miller, John	Debt relief	9, Feb. 1827	L3
Miller, Maria M.	Guardian	5, Mar. 1857	L3
Miller, Parsons G.	Guardian	5, Mar. 1857	L3
Miller, Robert	Land payment notice	7, Nov. 1810	L3
Miller, Thomas	Land payment notice	7, Nov. 1810	L3
Miller, William	Horse found	9, Jan. 1811	L1
Miller, William	Horse found	14, Mar. 1810	L2
Miller, William	Horse found	14, Sept 1813	L3
Mills, Abner	Horse found	5, Jan. 1818	L3
Mills, Abner	Horse found	28, July 1821	L3
Mills, Elijah	Horse found	23, Jan. 1811	L3
Mills, Isaac	Debt relief	28, Jan. 1830	L3

Name	Type of Notice	Date of Notice	Page
Minor, Eli W.	Debt relief	18, Aug. 1826	L3
Minshall, Thomas	Debt relief	1, Aug. 1833	L3
Minton, Jacob	Debt relief	26, Mar. 1808	L4
Minton, John	Letter at P.O.	1, Jan. 1812	L3
Minton, Matthew	Letter at P.O.	1, Jan. 1812	L3
Mitchel, Alexander	Horse found	1, Aug. 1810	L1
Mitchel, William	Horse found	20, Feb. 1811	L1
Mitchel, William	Horse found	20, Oct. 1812	L3
Mitchell, Cornelius	Debt relief	21, May 1829	L4
Mitchell, Samuel	Land payment notice	7, Nov. 1810	L3
Mitchell, William	Horse found	13, July 1813	L3
Mizner, Charles	Horse found	5, Sept 1810	L2
Mochring, Raphael	Hughes High School	2, Feb. 1854	L3
Mollson, Nicholas	Letter at P.O.	1, Jan. 1812	L3
Mollson, Sarah (Miss)	Letter at P.O.	1, Jan. 1812	L3
Mollson, Thomas	Letter at P.O.	1, Jan. 1812	L3
Monly, William & Martha	Divorce/Abandonment	9, July 1857	L3
Monroe, James B.	Debt relief	5, Feb. 1835	L3
Monsarrant, David P.	Debt relief	5, Feb. 1835	L3
Montfort, John	Horse found	24, Nov. 1817	L3
Montgomery, David	Horse found	27, Oct. 1812	L2
Montgomery, James	Debt relief	1, Aug. 1833	L3
Moody, Nathaniel	Horse found	30, May 1821	L2
Moor, Augustus	Deserter	18, Jan. 1814	L1
Moor, Samuel	Deserter from army	10, Nov. 1812	L2
Moore, Adam	Letter at P.O.	1, Jan. 1812	L3
Moore, Amos	Debt relief	23, June 1842	L3
Moore, Charles	Horse found	20, June 1810	L3
Moore, Cornelius	Letter at P.O.	1, Jan. 1812	L3
Moore, Eliza Ann	Guardian	13, Feb. 1840	L3
Moore, Frances	Guardian	6, Sept 1855	L3
Moore, Francis	Guardian	16, Oct. 1856	L6
Moore, Frederick W.	Guardian	6, Sept 1855	L3
Moore, Frederick W.	Guardian	16, Oct. 1856	L6
Moore, George	Debt relief	1, Aug. 1833	L3
Moore, George	Debt relief	5, Feb. 1835	L3
Moore, Georgiana	Guardian	6, Sept 1855	L3
Moore, Georgiana	Guardian	16, Oct. 1856	L6
Moore, James	Letter at P.O.	1, Jan. 1812	L3
Moore, Jane	Guardian	10, Dec. 1857	L3
Moore, John	Land payment notice	7, Nov. 1810	L3
Moore, Joseph	Letter at P.O.	1, Jan. 1812	L3
Moore, Joseph	Horse found	18, Jan. 1814	L3
Moore, Margaret	Guardian	6, Sept 1855	L3
Moore, Margaret	Guardian	16, Oct. 1856	L6
Moore, Mary Jane	Guardian	13, Feb. 1840	L3
Moore, Robert	Debt relief	8, June 1827	L4
Moore, Robert V.	Guardian	13, Feb. 1840	L3
Moore, Samuel	Horse found	25, May 1813	L1
Moore, Samuel	Horse found	30, May 1810	L2
Moore, Samuel	Horse found	28, Nov. 1810	L3
Moore, Samuel	Horse found	25, Feb. 1815	L3
Moore, Sarah E.	Guardian	6, Aug. 1857	L3
Moore, Stephen M.	Debt relief	23, June 1842	L3

Name	Type of Notice	Date of Notice	Page
Moore, Thomas Jefferson	Guardian	21, Nov. 1839	L3
Moore, William	Deserter	21, Dec. 1813	L1
More, Samuel	Horse found	3, Aug. 1813	L2
More, Samuel	Horse found	15, Apr. 1815	L3
Moredock, William	Deserter from army	29, Dec. 1812	L2
Morehead, James	Debt relief	17, Oct. 1839	L3
Moreman, Thomas	Horse found	8, Dec. 1812	L3
Moreton, Henry	Horse found	11, Feb. 1815	L3
Morgan, Hugh	Guardian	4, Sept 1856	L5
Morgan, Joel T.	Debt relief	1, Aug. 1833	L3
Morgan, John	Guardian	4, Sept 1856	L5
Morgan, Mary Ann	Guardian	4, Sept 1856	L5
Morgan, Richard	Horse found	1, Sept 1812	L2
Morres, John	Horse found	27, May 1812	L2
Morris, David	Deserter	7, July 1817	L2
Morris, James C.	Horse found	4, Sept 1815	L3
Morris, John	Horse found	15, Aug. 1810	L3
Morris, John	Horse found	11, Aug. 1812	L3
Morris, Lewis	Escaped	8, July 1820	L3
Morris, Robert	Horse found	27, Apr. 1813	L2
Morris, Thomas	Deserter from army	17, Nov. 1812	L3
Morrison, Ephraim	Land payment notice	7, Nov. 1810	L3
Morrison, Hugh	Horse found	4, July 1810	L1
Morrison, Isaac	Horse found	10, Aug. 1819	L3
Morrison, Moses	Letter at P.O.	1, Jan. 1812	L3
Morrison, William	Horse found	21, June 1814	L3
Morrison, William C.	Horse found	23, June 1817	L3
Morrow, James	Debt relief	18, Aug. 1826	L3
Morrow, Joseph	Debt relief	21, May 1829	L4
Morton, Henry	Guardian	9, Aug. 1838	L3
Morton, James T.	Horse found	3, Oct. 1810	L3
Mosebach, Morris & Barbary	Divorce/Abandonment	21, June 1855	L3
Moseberger, Barbara	Guardian	8, Oct. 1857	L3
Moseberger, Elizabeth	Guardian	8, Oct. 1857	L3
Moseberger, John G.	Guardian	8, Oct. 1857	L3
Moseberger, Mary	Guardian	8, Oct. 1857	L3
Moses, Edward	Guardian	3, May 1855	L3
Mott, John E.	Insane	20, Nov. 1851	L4
Mott, Jonathan	Debt relief	9, Feb. 1827	L3
Mott, Jonathan & Susan	Divorce/Abandonment	5, July 1820	L3
Mounce, William	Horse found	19, May 1817	L3
Moyer, George	Land payment notice	7, Nov. 1810	L3
Mulally, Richard	Debt relief	1, Aug. 1833	L3
Mulkins, John	Horse found	6, July 1813	L2
Mull, Elizabeth	Guardian	18, Apr. 1839	L3
Mull, Jacob	Guardian	18, Apr. 1839	L3
Mull, James	Guardian	18, Apr. 1839	L3
Mull, Martha	Guardian	18, Apr. 1839	L3
Mull, Susan	Guardian	18, Apr. 1839	L3
Mullen, James	Deserter from army	20, Oct. 1812	L3
Munro, Josiah	Horse found	29, Aug. 1810	L1
Munson, Roderick	Horse found	1, Nov. 1827	L4
Munson, Sylvanus	Horse found	12, Feb. 1816	L3
Muntz, William	Horse found	6, Oct. 1812	L1

Name	Type of Notice	Date of Notice	Page
Murdock, Catharine J.	Guardian	5, Sept 1839	L3
Murdock, James	Horse found	21, June 1814	L3
Murdock, John	Deserter	19, Jan. 1813	L3
Murdock, Thomas	Guardian	5, Sept 1839	L3
Mure, John	Horse found	6, Oct. 1812	L1
Myer, Henry	Land payment due	22, Nov. 1809	L4
Myers, Andrew	Horse found	12, Aug. 1825	L3
Myers, Elizabeth	Inquiry	26, Aug. 1847	L3
Myers, Jesse & Elizabeth	Divorce/Abandonment	5, Feb. 1852	L3
Myers, Jonathan	Horse found	19, Feb. 1816	L3
Myers, Matilda	Inquiry	26, Aug. 1847	L3
Myers, William	Inquiry	26, Aug. 1847	L3
Myrick, Seth	Letter at P.O.	1, Jan. 1812	L3
Myrick, Thomas	Letter at P.O.	1, Jan. 1812	L3
Naglee, Henry Augustus	Debt relief	23, June 1842	L3
Neal, Henry O.	Debt relief	1, Aug. 1833	L3
Nesbit, James Irwin	Land payment notice	7, Nov. 1810	L3
Nesbit, James J.	Land payment due	22, Nov. 1809	L4
Nesbit, William	Land payment notice	7, Nov. 1810	L3
Nesbit, William	Land payment due	22, Nov. 1809	L4
Nesmith, James	Debt relief	8, June 1827	L4
Nevers, Benjamin M.	Debt relief	23, June 1842	L3
Newel, John & Rachel	Divorce/Abandonment	21, Otc. 1806	L1
Newell, Martin S.	Guardian	16, Oct. 1856	L6
Newell, Rezin	Debt relief	18, Aug. 1826	L3
Newell, William S.	Guardian	16, Oct. 1856	L6
Newkirk, Jefferson	Debt relief	1, Aug. 1833	L3
Newman, John	Horse found	27, Nov. 1815	L3
Newman, Samuel	Debt relief	23, June 1842	L3
Nichols, Charles	Deserter	10, Mar. 1817	L4
Nichols, Thomas	Land payment notice	7, Nov. 1810	L3
Nickle, William	Letter at P.O.	1, Jan. 1812	L3
Niles, Valentine H.	Debt relief	28, Jan. 1830	L3
Noe, Ezra	Debt relief	24, July 1828	L1
Noe, Ezra	Debt relief	8, June 1827	L4
Nonest, Isaac	Horse found	22, June 1813	L4
Norris, John	Land payment due	22, Nov. 1809	L4
North, Christopher & Sarah	Divorce/Abandonment	19, Jan. 1843	L3
Nott, John C.	Debt relief	5, Feb. 1835	L3
Noyes, Charles C.	Guardian	10, Apr. 1856	L3
Noyes, George	Guardian	10, Apr. 1856	L3
Noyes, Keturah	Guardian	10, Apr. 1856	L3
Nugen, Thomas	Letter at P.O.	1, Jan. 1812	L3
Nugent, William	Horse found	6, June 1810	L3
Nutt, Adam (heirs of)	Guardian	7, Dec. 1837	L3
Nutting, William H.	Debt relief	1, Aug. 1833	L3
Oak, William	Horse found	2, Sept 1816	L3
Oalman, Samuel	Horse found	26, Apr. 1814	L2
O'Bryon, Edward D.	Debt relief	1, Aug. 1833	L3
Odell, John	Debt relief	21, May 1829	L4
Oden, David	Debt relief	1, Aug. 1833	L3
Ogden, Daniel	Horse found	6, Dec. 1814	L1

Name	Type of Notice	Date of Notice	Page
Ogden, Daniel	Horse found	12, Jan. 1813	L3
Ogden, James S.	Debt relief	17, Nov. 1842	L5
Ogden, Jonathan	Guardian	8, Jan. 1857	L3
Ogle, William	Horse found	15, Jan. 1812	L3
O'Harron, Jonathan & Mary	Divorce/Abandonment	7, Dec. 1837	L3
O'Harrow, Jonathan & Mary	Divorce/Abandonment	4, Jan. 1838	L4
Olden, John D.	Debtor	11, Feb. 1818	L3
Oliphant, James	Debt relief	18, Aug. 1826	L3
Oliver, William	Cow lost	14, Nov. 1821	L3
O'Neal, Henry & Mary Ann	Divorce/Abandonment	22, Aug. 1844	L3
Oppenheimer, Emanuel	Debt relief	1, Aug. 1833	L3
Oppenheimer, Emanuel	Debt relief	5, Feb. 1835	L3
Oppenheimer, Hezekiah	Debt relief	1, Aug. 1833	L3
O'Reilly, John	Debt relief	4, Aug. 1831	L4
Ormsby, Mary L.	Hughes High School	2, Feb. 1854	L3
Orr, John	Debt relief	9, Feb. 1827	L3
Orr, Thomas J.	Debt relief	14, July 1842	L3
Osborn, Caleb	Horse found	19, Feb. 1812	L3
Oscar, Julius	Guardian	8, Jan. 1857	L3
Osgood, Nathaniel	Horse found	24, May 1814	L3
Ott, Clemens	Guardian	5, Feb. 1857	L3
Ott, George	Guardian	5, Feb. 1857	L3
Ott, Jacob	Guardian	5, Feb. 1857	L3
Ott, Mary	Guardian	5, Feb. 1857	L3
Ott, Otho	Guardian	4, June 1857	L3
Owen, Allison	Debt relief	23, June 1842	L3
Owings, John	Debt relief	15, Sept 1807	L1
Pace, Robert	Debt relief	21, May 1829	L4
Page, John	Horse lost	21, Apr. 1817	L4
Paine, Stephen	Horse found	8, Jan. 1812	L4
Painter, Benjamin	Debt relief	9, Oct. 1828	L3
Palmer, Henry	Debt relief	8, June 1827	L4
Palmer, Henry E. & Mary E.	Divorce/Abandonment	24, Dec. 1857	L3
Palmer, James H.	Debt relief	28, Jan. 1830	L3
Palmer, James H.	Debt relief	4, Aug. 1831	L4
Palmer, Layton & Elizabeth	Divorce/Abandonment	10, Aug. 1813	L3
Palmer, Thomas	Letter at P.O.	1, Jan. 1812	L3
Palmer, Thomas	Debt relief	14, July 1842	L3
Palmer, Thomas & Nancy H.	Divorce/Abandonment	1, Jan. 1812	L2
Park, Isaac	Horse found	14, Jan. 1825	L3
Parke, Samuel	Horse found	5, Jan. 1813	L3
Parker, Francis & Elizabeth	Divorce/Abandonment	19, Feb. 1829	L3
Parker, Gideon	Runaway apprentice	9, June 1817	L4
Parker, Jacob	Horse found	27, May 1812	L2
Parker, Jacob	Horse found	5, July 1814	L2
Parker, Jacob	Horse found	18, Jan. 1814	L3
Parker, James	Horse found	11, Mar. 1816	L3
Parker, John	Debt relief	28, Jan. 1830	L3
Parks, Joseph	Letter at P.O.	1, Jan. 1812	L3
Parr, James A. & Catharine	Divorce/Abandonment	28, Nov. 1844	L3
Parsons, William	Debt relief	21, May 1829	L4
Parvin, Enoch	Letter at P.O.	1, Jan. 1812	L3
Patey, Joshua	Letter at P.O.	1, Jan. 1812	L3

Name	Type of Notice	Date of Notice	Page
Patterson, R.	Horse lost	11, May 1813	L3
Patterson, Robert	Land payment due	22, Nov. 1809	L4
Patterson, William	Debt relief	28, Jan. 1830	L3
Patton, John	Horse found	25, Jan. 1813	L3
Pearce, William H.	Debt relief	21, May 1829	L4
Pearson, Elijah	Debt relief	18, Aug. 1826	L3
Pearson, John	Horse lost	26, Oct. 1813	L3
Pease, Martin	Horse found	24, Nov. 1817	L3
Peelman, Christopher	Horse found	8, July 1816	L3
Pegg, John	Town laid out	10, June 1816	L1
Pegy, Daniel	Horse found	4, Dec. 1828	L3
Peirce, Thomas	Debt relief	8, June 1827	L4
Pelsor, Absolom & Margaret	Divorce/Abandonment	1, Feb. 1838	L3
Pendilton, James	Letter at P.O.	1, Jan. 1812	L3
Perin, Samuel	Horse found	22, May 1811	L3
Perkins, Charles E.	Guardian	6, Mar. 1856	L3
Perkins, Edward C.	Guardian	6, Mar. 1856	L3
Perkins, Henry H.	Guardian	6, Mar. 1856	L3
Perkins, James H.	Guardian	6, Mar. 1856	L3
Perkins, Stith	Debt relief	4, Aug. 1831	L4
Perrin, John	Letter at P.O.	1, Jan. 1812	L3
Perry, John	Letter at P.O.	1, Jan. 1812	L3
Perry, John	Debt relief	17, Oct. 1839	L3
Perry, Samuel R.	Debt relief	28, Jan. 1830	L3
Perry, William	Debt relief	5, Feb. 1835	L3
Perry, William B.	Debt relief	9, Feb. 1827	L3
Perry, William B.	Debt relief	9, June 1831	L3
Peters, Andrew	Horse found	11, May 1813	L3
Peters, Jacob & Mary	Divorce/Abandonment	8, Apr. 1830	L4
Peters, John	Debt relief	1, Aug. 1833	L3
Peters, S. Andrew	Horse found	4, June 1817	L3
Petrimoulx, Johan Baptist	Debt relief	24, Feb. 1807	L1
Pettigrue, Thomas	Runaway apprentice	21, Dec. 1813	L1
Pettit, Elizabeth	Runaway apprentice	6, Jan. 1824	L2
Pew, Gilbert	Letter at P.O.	1, Jan. 1812	L3
Pfisterer, William	Guardian	9, Aug. 1855	L3
Phares, Samuel	Letter at P.O.	1, Jan. 1812	L3
Phelps, Greenberry	Debt relief	21, May 1829	L4
Phennegar, Solomon	Debt relief	1, Aug. 1833	L3
Pherris, Joseph	Deserter	21, Dec. 1813	L1
Philips, Thomas	Debt relief	9, Feb. 1827	L3
Phillips, Charles C.	Guardian	9, Apr. 1857	L3
Phillips, Daniel	Deserter	27, Jan. 1817	L3
Phillips, Joseph	Debt relief	9, June 1831	L3
Phillips, Ralph	Letter at P.O.	1, Jan. 1812	L3
Phillips, William F.	Guardian	9, Apr. 1857	L3
Piatt, James A.	Letter at P.O.	1, Jan. 1812	L3
Picket, Edwin Hyatt	Debt relief	23, June 1842	L3
Pierce, James	Letter at P.O.	1, Jan. 1812	L3
Pierce, Nathaniel	Letter at P.O.	1, Jan. 1812	L3
Pierce, William Liegh	Letter at P.O.	1, Jan. 1812	L3
Pierson, Abraham	Horse found	6, Nov. 1815	L3
Pierson, Abraham	Horse found	4, May 1819	L3
Pierson, John	Guardian	9, Apr. 1857	L3

Name	Type of Notice	Date of Notice	Page
Pierson, Jonathan	Horse found	20, June 1810	L1
Pierson, Mary Jane	Guardian	10, Apr. 1856	L3
Pierson, Mary L.	Guardian	4, June 1857	L3
Pierson, Pitney	Guardian	8, Jan. 1857	L3
Pine, Abram	Guardian	6, Dec. 1855	L3
Pine, George	Guardian	6, Dec. 1855	L3
Pine, Isaac	Guardian	6, Dec. 1855	L3
Pine, Lazarus	Guardian	6, Dec. 1855	L3
Pinkstun, Willis	Debt relief	4, Aug. 1831	L4
Pitts, James C.	Debt relief	1, Aug. 1833	L3
Platt, Nathan	Letter at P.O.	1, Jan. 1812	L3
Plough, John	Horse found	10, Mar. 1817	L4
Plumbigh, Thomas	Inquiry	4, Nov. 1825	L3
Plummer, Edwin F.	Guardian	6, Mar. 1856	L3
Plummer, Enoch	Letter at P.O.	1, Jan. 1812	L3
Plummer, Hiram	Guardian	6, Mar. 1856	L3
Plummer, Rosaline	Guardian	6, Mar. 1856	L3
Plummer, William H.	Guardian	6, Mar. 1856	L3
Pollard, Anna M.	Guardian	6, Dec. 1855	L3
Pollard, Laura T.	Guardian	6, Dec. 1855	L3
Pollard, Mary	Guardian	6, Dec. 1855	L3
Pollock, Ezekiel	Horse found	8, July 1820	L2
Pollock, Guy	Horse found	1, July 1816	L3
Pollock, John	Horse found	27, May 1812	L2
Pollock, John	Horse found	13, Oct. 1812	L4
Pollok, John	Horse found	3, July 1811	L3
Pomeroy, James	Convict	5, Feb. 1846	L3
Pool, Stephen	Debt relief	1, Aug. 1833	L3
Poor, David J.	Horse found	8, June 1813	L3
Popenoe, James	Land payment notice	7, Nov. 1810	L3
Porter, Elias	Horse found	20, June 1810	L3
Porter, Elias	Horse found	4, Jan. 1814	L3
Porter, George	Debt relief	1, Aug. 1833	L3
Porter, George	Debt relief	23, June 1842	L3
Porter, James	Deserter	24, May 1814	L3
Porter, James	Horse stolen	21, May 1819	L3
Posey, Armsted	Horse found	12, Feb. 1816	L3
Pottenger, Thomas	Horse found	15, June 1813	L2
Potter, Stephen	Letter at P.O.	1, Jan. 1812	L3
Pottinger, Robert	Land payment due	22, Nov. 1809	L4
Pottinger, Samuel	Horse found	8, June 1819	L3
Potts, Joseph	Debt relief	1, Aug. 1833	L3
Potts, William	Debt relief	1, Aug. 1833	L3
Powell, William	Land payment notice	7, Nov. 1810	L3
Power, James	Debt relief	17, Oct. 1839	L3
Powers, Edward	Debt relief	8, June 1827	L4
Powers, Hiram A. & Juliana	Divorce/Abandonment	2, Jan. 1840	L3
Powers, Joseph	Horse lost	9, June 1812	L3
Powers, Thomas	Horse found	20, Apr. 1813	L1
Powsey, Zeffiniah	Letter at P.O.	1, Jan. 1812	L3
Price, Christian & Nancy	Divorce/Abandonment	7, July 1812	L2
Price, Henry	Land payment notice	7, Nov. 1810	L3
Price, Henry	Debt relief	14, July 1842	L3
Price, John	Horse found	20, Feb. 1811	L1

Name	Type of Notice	Date of Notice	Page
Price, John	Horse found	9, May 1810	L4
Price, John W. & Lucretia	Divorce/Abandonment	26, Oct. 1822	L3
Price, Maria L.	Guardian	7, June 1855	L3
Price, Rees	Horse found	18, July 1810	L3
Price, W.W.	Guardian	7, June 1855	L3
Pricket, Josiah	Horse found	20, Apr. 1813	L1
Pricket, Josiah	Horse found	3, Nov. 1812	L2
Priors, Andrew	Guardian	22, June 1837	L3
Priors, John	Guardian	22, June 1837	L3
Priors, William	Guardian	22, June 1837	L3
Probus, Alexander & Nancy	Divorce/Abandonment	18, Aug. 1806	L1
Probus, Henry	Deserter	29, Mar. 1814	L1
Profeten, Thorton	Debt relief	1, Aug. 1833	L3
Proud, Samuel	Debt relief	1, Aug. 1833	L3
Prudden, Ebenezer	Cow found	31, Oct. 1810	L3
Pruden, Isaac	Horse found	13, June 1823	L2
Prutsman, John	Horse found	9, Nov. 1813	L2
Pugh, Henry	Hughes High School	2, Feb. 1854	L3
Pyle, Jesse	Horse found	29, Aug. 1810	L1
Quail, Robert	Debt relief	9, Feb. 1827	L3
Quamby, Frederick	Guardian	10, Apr. 1856	L3
Quamby, John W.	Guardian	10, Apr. 1856	L3
Quantrill, Jesse D.	Debt relief	5, Feb. 1835	L3
Quick, Cornelius	Land payment notice	7, Nov. 1810	L3
Quigley, Samuel H.	Debt relief	1, Aug. 1833	L3
Quinan, Thomas H.	Debt relief	5, Feb. 1835	L3
Quire, Rament	Horse found	22, Nov. 1820	L3
Raco, Mary Ann	Guardian	6, Sept 1855	L3
Rambo, Thomas	Debt relief	9, Oct. 1828	L3
Ramsay, Thomas	Vattier court case	28, Apr. 1807	L3
Ramsden, James	Inquiry	30, Sept 1820	L3
Ramsey, Tobias	Debt relief	1, Aug. 1833	L3
Ramsey, William	Horse found	28, Nov. 1810	L3
Randles, John	Deserter	28, June 1814	L3
Rank, Amos	Debt relief	1, Aug. 1833	L3
Raper, Martha	Guardian	8, Oct. 1857	L3
Raper, Mary A.	Guardian	8, Oct. 1857	L3
Raymond, Edward H.	Debt relief	24, July 1828	L1
Read, David	Letter at P.O.	1, Jan. 1812	L3
Ready, William L.	Guardian	6, Aug. 1857	L3
Reddick, Joseph	Horse found	30, Jan. 1811	L4
Reddick, Richard	Horse found	16, Nov. 1813	L3
Reddish, Sarah	Guardian	20, Apr. 1837	L3
Reddish, Stephen	Guardian	20, Apr. 1837	L3
Redenbaugh, Adam	Deserter from army	1, Dec. 1812	L3
Redick, Williiam	Horse found	7, July 1812	L2
Reed, Daniel & Anna	Divorce/Abandonment	11, Aug. 1807	L3
Reed, James	Horse found	5, Feb. 1812	L3
Reeder, Jesse & Mary	Divorce/Abandonment	4, Aug. 1821	L3
Reese, Henry	Horse found	18, July 1810	L3
Reeve, William	Letter at P.O.	1, Jan. 1812	L3
Rehfuss, Emilie	Guardian	10, Sept 1857	L3

Name	Type of Notice	Date of Notice	Page
Rehfuss, Emilie	Guardian	16, Oct. 1856	L6
Rehfuss, Evahard L.	Guardian	16, Oct. 1856	L6
Rehfuss, Lewis	Guardian	10, Sept 1857	L3
Rehfuss, Otto	Guardian	10, Sept 1857	L3
Rehfuss, Otto	Guardian	16, Oct. 1856	L6
Rehfuss, Pauline	Guardian	10, Sept 1857	L3
Rehfuss, Pauline L.	Guardian	16, Oct. 1856	L6
Reichert, Anthony	Land payment notice	7, Nov. 1810	L3
Reilly, John O.	Debt relief	9, June 1831	L3
Renick, Robert	Land payment notice	7, Nov. 1810	L3
Rennett, Samuel	Horse found	24, Nov. 1817	L3
Replogol, Daniel	Horse found	22, Dec. 1812	L3
Resa, Jacob	Horse found	4, Aug. 1812	L2
Resor, Charles O.	Guardian	5, July 1855	L3
Resor, Cora E.	Guardian	5, July 1855	L3
Resor, Margaret	Guardian	5, July 1855	L3
Resor, Reuben P.	Guardian	5, July 1855	L3
Reynolds, Albert	Debt relief	14, July 1842	L3
Reynolds, Elizabeth	Hughes High School	2, Feb. 1854	L3
Rice, Euclid & Harriet	Divorce/Abandonment	13, Sept 1855	L3
Rice, John R.	Debt relief	5, Feb. 1835	L3
Rich, Thomas	Horse found	23, Feb. 1813	L3
Rich, Thomas	Horse found	24, Jan. 1810	L4
Richards, Hiram E.	Horse found	20, Oct. 1817	L3
Richardson, Abraham	Land payment notice	7, Nov. 1810	L3
Richardson, Aseaneth (Mrs)	Letter at P.O.	1, Jan. 1812	L3
Richardson, John	Debt relief	1, Aug. 1833	L3
Richardson, John	Debt relief	21, May 1829	L4
Richardson, Malachia	Letter at P.O.	1, Jan. 1812	L3
Richardson, Robert	Horse lost	15, May 1811	L3
Richey, John	Letter at P.O.	1, Jan. 1812	L3
Richey, Robert	Debt relief	28, Jan. 1830	L3
Riddle, Augustus W.	Guardian	9, Aug. 1855	L3
Riddle, Joseph	Guardian	9, Aug. 1855	L3
Riddle, Mary Elizabeth	Guardian	9, Aug. 1855	L3
Ridenour, Jacob	Debt relief	14, July 1842	L3
Rieden, William	Letter at P.O.	1, Jan. 1812	L3
Rigdon, Ezekiel	Letter at P.O.	1, Jan. 1812	L3
Riker, Samuel	Land payment due	22, Nov. 1809	L4
Rino, Presley	Horse found	3, Apr. 1811	L2
Ripley, John	Debt relief	1, Aug. 1833	L3
Ripley, William J.	Guardian	8, Oct. 1857	L3
Risingsun, Henry & Frances	Divorce/Abandonment	9, June 1817	L3
Risk, Charlotte Chambers	Letter at P.O.	1, Jan. 1812	L3
Risk, David (Rev)	Letter at P.O.	1, Jan. 1812	L3
Ritchey, John	Land payment notice	7, Nov. 1810	L3
Rittenhouse, John L.	Horse found	2, Aug. 1820	L3
Robb, Alexander & Barbara	Divorce/Abandonment	6, Apr. 1809	L3
Robbins, David	Horse found	23, Oct. 1811	L3
Robbins, David	Horse found	16, June 1812	L3
Roberson, Isaac	Horse found	18, Oct. 1814	L3
Roberts, Charles	Letter at P.O.	1, Jan. 1812	L3
Roberts, Enoch	Letter at P.O.	1, Jan. 1812	L3
Roberts, George T.	Guardian	16, Oct. 1856	L6

Name	Type of Notice	Date of Notice	Page
Roberts, Noah	Letter at P.O.	1, Jan. 1812	L3
Roberts, W.J.	Guardian	16, Oct. 1856	L6
Robertson, Isaac & Mary	Divorce/Abandonment	13, Dec. 1814	L3
Robertson, Martha Ann	Guardian	21, Sept 1837	L4
Robins, Augustus	Debt relief	1, Aug. 1833	L3
Robinson, Charles	Horse found	20, June 1810	L1
Robinson, Edward	Horse found	22, Aug. 1827	L2
Robinson, Ellen	Guardian	19, Dec. 1826	L3
Robinson, John	Horse found	7, Aug. 1811	L3
Robinson, John	Horse found	24, Nov. 1812	L3
Robinson, Robert	Horse found	17, Mar. 1817	L3
Rock, Felix	Land payment notice	7, Nov. 1810	L3
Rockenfield, Isaac A.	Guardian	9, Aug. 1838	L3
Rodgers, Joseph	Letter at P.O.	1, Jan. 1812	L3
Rogers, William C.	Debt relief	28, Jan. 1830	L3
Rohman, Anthony & Rosannah	Divorce/Abandonment	28, Dec. 1837	L3
Rohrbacker, Mary	Guardian	7, May 1857	L3
Rohrbacker, Peter	Guardian	7, May 1857	L3
Rohrbacker, Philip	Guardian	7, May 1857	L3
Roll, James	Debt relief	9, Oct. 1828	L3
Roosa, Jacob	Horse found	25, May 1813	L1
Roose, Jacob	Horse found	21, Nov. 1811	L2
Rosa, Esek H.	Debt relief	23, June 1842	L3
Rose, Charles	Convict	5, Feb. 1846	L3
Rose, James J.	Debt relief	17, Oct. 1839	L3
Rose, John	Debt relief	11, Nov. 1825	L3
Rose, John	Horse found	5, Jan. 1815	L4
Rose, Nathan D.	Debt relief	17, Oct. 1839	L3
Rose, William & Jemima	Divorce/Abandonment	11, Feb. 1808	L3
Ross, B. Rennel Aaron	Letter at P.O.	1, Jan. 1812	L3
Ross, Benjamin	Land payment notice	7, Nov. 1810	L3
Ross, Benjamin L.	Horse lost	3, June 1816	L1
Ross, Daniel	Debt relief	9, Oct. 1828	L3
Ross, Daniel & Phebe	Divorce/Abandonment	5, Mar. 1829	L3
Ross, John	Horse found	14, Feb. 1810	L3
Ross, John	Land payment notice	7, Nov. 1810	L3
Ross, John	Horse found	16, June 1812	L3
Ross, Robert	Letter at P.O.	1, Jan. 1812	L3
Ross, Stephen	Horse found	13, Dec. 1814	L1
Ross, Stephen	Horse found	3, Nov. 1812	L2
Ross, Thomas	Horse found	26, May 1817	L3
Ross, William	Debt relief	1, Aug. 1833	L3
Rouderbush, Daniel	Horse found	27, July 1813	L1
Rovsa, Sarah	Guardian	5, July 1855	L3
Royse, Vere	Horse found	26, Apr. 1814	L2
Rude, Abner	Letter at P.O.	1, Jan. 1812	L3
Rude, Zeldah	Horse found	20, June 1810	L3
Rue, Benjamin	Debt relief	24, July 1828	L1
Ruffin, William	Horse found	2, Mar. 1813	L3
Ruffin, William W.	Debt relief	21, May 1829	L4
Rule, Thomas	Debt relief	5, Feb. 1835	L3
Rump, Johanna	Guardian	9, Apr. 1857	L3
Runyan, John	Horse found	14, Feb. 1810	L3
Runyen, Isaac	Horse found	4, Nov. 1816	L3

Name	Type of Notice	Date of Notice	Page
Rush, John	Deserter	8, Feb. 1814	L3
Russell, Jeremiah	Debt relief	5, Feb. 1835	L3
Russell, John Brooks	Debt relief	23, June 1842	L3
Ruthery, George	Debt relief	1, Aug. 1833	L3
Ryan, Jacob	Deserter	24, Aug. 1813	L2
Rybolt, Elizabeth	Guardian	4, June 1857	L3
Rybolt, Harriet	Guardian	4, June 1857	L3
Rybolt, John J.	Guardian	4, June 1857	L3
Rybolt, Michael G.	Guardian	4, June 1857	L3
Rybolt, Rachael E.	Guardian	4, June 1857	L3
Ryder, William	Debt relief	18, Aug. 1826	L3
Ryder, William	Debt relief	28, Jan. 1830	L3
Ryder, William	Debt relief	21, May 1829	L4
Salyers, John	Debt relief	18, Aug. 1826	L3
Sample, John	Land payment notice	7, Nov. 1810	L3
Sampson, John	Guardian	7, May 1840	L3
Sampson, Step.	Guardian	7, Dec. 1837	L3
Sanders, David A.	Debt relief	23, June 1842	L3
Sanders, William	Horse found	2, Feb. 1813	L2
Sands, Daniel	Deserter	21, Dec. 1813	L1
Sargent, Culbertson	Guardian	7, May 1840	L3
Sargent, Mary	Guardian	30, Jan. 1840	L3
Sargent, Mary	Guardian	7, May 1840	L3
Sarver, Henry	Debt relief	11, Nov. 1825	L3
Satchell, Caroline	Guardian - minor	3, May 1855	L3
Satchell, Charles	Guardian	3, May 1855	L3
Satchell, Elizabeth	Guardian - minor	3, May 1855	L3
Sauerbeck, George & Juliana	Divorce/Abandonment	2, Apr. 1857	L3
Saunders, Robert	Convict	5, Feb. 1846	L3
Saxton, Joseph C.	Debt relief	1, Aug. 1833	L3
Sayre, Hezekiah	Horse found	27, May 1818	L3
Sayres, Daniel	Runaway apprentice	24, July 1828	L3
Sayrles, Elijah	Horse found	17, Feb. 1817	L1
Scantling, Edward	Debt relief	28, Jan. 1830	L3
Scantling, Edward	Debt relief	8, June 1827	L4
Scheid, Ann Maria	Guardian	8, Oct. 1857	L3
Scheid, Henry	Guardian	8, Oct. 1857	L3
Scheid, Maria	Guardian	8, Oct. 1857	L3
Scheid, Philip	Guardian	8, Oct. 1857	L3
Schenck, Louisa	Convict	5, Feb. 1846	L3
Schenck, O.	Land payment notice	7, Nov. 1810	L3
Schenck, Obadiah	Horse found	5, June 1811	L3
Schenck, William C.	Land payment notice	7, Nov. 1810	L3
Scheper, Elizabeth	Guardian	14, Aug. 1856	L6
Schilling, Lewis	Letter at P.O.	1, Jan. 1812	L3
Schleigh, Charles	Debt relief	5, Feb. 1835	L3
Schmidt, Ann	Guardian	5, Feb. 1857	L3
Schmidt, Christina	Guardian	5, Feb. 1857	L3
Schmidt, Joseph	Guardian	5, Feb. 1857	L3
Schmidt, Maria	Guardian	5, Feb. 1857	L3
Schmitt, Christian	Guardian	10, Jan. 1856	L3
Schnauber, Ann M.	Guardian	9, July 1857	L3
Schnauber, Margaretta	Guardian	10, Apr. 1856	L3

Name	Type of Notice	Date of Notice	Page
Schooley, John	Horse found	1, Sept 1818	L3
Schroder, Bertus	Guardian	9, Apr. 1857	L3
Schroder, John	Guardian	9, Apr. 1857	L3
Schroder, Lawrence	Guardian	9, Apr. 1857	L3
Schroder, Leo	Guardian	9, Apr. 1857	L3
Schroder, Mary	Guardian	9, Apr. 1857	L3
Schroder, Philomena	Guardian	9, Apr. 1857	L3
Schroder, Richard	Guardian	9, Apr. 1857	L3
Schug, Mary	Guardian	5, Feb. 1857	L3
Schug, Peter	Guardian	5, Feb. 1857	L3
Schultz, Caroline	Guardian	6, Mar. 1856	L3
Schulz, Cecilia	Guardian	9, July 1857	L3
Schwaers, Henry & Margaret	Divorce/Abandonment	24, Oct. 1850	L3
Schwegman, Mary	Guardian	10, Sept 1857	L3
Schwegman, Thomas	Guardian	10, Sept 1857	L3
Scissil, John	Guardian	18, Apr. 1839	L3
Scissil, Thomas	Guardian	18, Apr. 1839	L3
Scogin, Elisha	Horse found	19, Oct. 1813	L2
Scott, Daniel	Debt relief	24, July 1828	L1
Scott, Andrew	Horse found	12, Feb. 1812	L3
Scott, Elliott	Debt relief	9, June 1831	L3
Scott, Henry C.	Deserter	4, Aug. 1817	L4
Scott, James M.	Debt relief	1, Aug. 1833	L3
Scott, John	Letter at P.O.	1, Jan. 1812	L3
Scott, William	Horse found	17, June 1816	L3
Scott, William	Horse found	24, Nov. 1817	L3
Scott, William	Deserter	21, Apr. 1817	L4
Scott, William & Eva	Divorce/Abandonment	11, Feb. 1836	L3
Scovel, Benjamin	Horse found	19, Feb. 1812	L3
Scribner, Joel	Letter at P.O.	1, Jan. 1812	L3
Seager, George	Debtor	16, Feb. 1819	L3
Seaman, Joshua & Mary	Divorce/Abandonment	30, Jan. 1840	L3
Seamon, John	Horse found	2, Oct. 1811	L3
Seamons, John	Vattier court case	28, Apr. 1807	L3
Sears, Benjamin	Horse found	11, Sept 1811	L4
Sears, Samuel	Horse found	11, Sept 1811	L4
Seayrs, Benjamin B.	Horse found	1, Nov. 1814	L1
Sebring, James	Debt relief	28, Jan. 1830	L3
Sebring, John H.	Debt relief	28, Jan. 1830	L3
Sedam, Cornelius R.	Letter at P.O.	1, Jan. 1812	L3
Sedam, Cornelius R.	Horse found	25, Feb. 1815	L3
Sedam, Matthew	Guardian	3, Feb. 1826	L3
See, Peter	Debt relief	18, Aug. 1826	L3
Selars, George Escol	Debt relief	23, June 1842	L3
Sellars, Charles	Debt relief	23, June 1842	L3
Selmon, Peter	Horse found	21, Dec. 1813	L1
Seward, Andrew G.	Guardian	8, Nov. 1832	L4
Seward, George W.	Guardian	26, Sept 1826	L3
Seward, George W.	Guardian	8, Nov. 1832	L4
Seward, J. Lawrence	Hughes High School	2, Feb. 1854	L3
Seward, Jackson	Guardian	26, Sept 1826	L3
Seward, John	Debt relief	11, Nov. 1825	L3
Seward, Louisa	Guardian	8, Nov. 1832	L4
Seward, Reuben	Debt relief	21, May 1829	L4

Name	Type of Notice	Date of Notice	Page
Sexton, Joseph	Letter at P.O.	1, Jan. 1812	L3
Shaeffer, Thomas G.	Debt relief	23, June 1842	L3
Shaffer, George	Letter at P.O.	1, Jan. 1812	L3
Shanks, Michael	Land payment due	22, Nov. 1809	L4
Sharp, Matthias	Horse found	4, Jan. 1814	L4
Shavor, George	Horse found	22, Dec. 1812	L3
Shaw, Elijah	Horse found	9, June 1817	L2
Shaw, Isaiah	Horse found	1, June 1813	L2
Shaw, John	Letter at P.O.	1, Jan. 1812	L3
Shaw, William M.	Debt relief	4, Aug. 1831	L4
Sheetz, Michael	Letter at P.O.	1, Jan. 1812	L3
Sheik, Andrew	Letter at P.O.	1, Jan. 1812	L3
Shell, Philip	Letter at P.O.	1, Jan. 1812	L3
Shemard, Thomas	Deserter	19, Oct. 1813	L1
Shenkle, Henry	Horse found	22, Apr. 1812	L3
Shepherd, Solomon	Deserter	18, Jan. 1814	L1
Sheppard, Enoch	Debt relief	24, July 1828	L1
Sherer, David	Horse found	25, Jan. 1813	L3
Sherwood, John	Debt relief	5, Feb. 1835	L3
Shields, Thomas	Horse found	20, June 1810	L3
Shinkle, Jacob	Horse found	15, Dec. 1812	L3
Shipley, Joseph	Debt relief	17, Oct. 1839	L3
Shitaker, Michael	Horse found	17, July 1811	L3
Short, James	Debt relief	5, Feb. 1835	L3
Short, John I.	Debt relief	1, Aug. 1833	L3
Short, Peyton	Land payment due	22, Nov. 1809	L4
Short, Thomas	Debt relief	9, Feb. 1827	L3
Short, William	Debt relief	21, May 1829	L4
Shryock, Daniel	Land payment notice	7, Nov. 1810	L3
Shuey, Adam	Land payment notice	7, Nov. 1810	L3
Shuey, Martin	Horse found	14, Nov. 1810	L2
Shultz, Henry	Runaway apprentice	7, Dec. 1813	L4
Shuman, Jacob	Letter at P.O.	1, Jan. 1812	L3
Shumard, John	Debt relief	1, Aug. 1833	L3
Sibley, Stephen	Horse found	24, Nov. 1817	L3
Siegmund, Jacob & Mary	Divorce/Abandonment	8, Apr. 1818	L4
Silvers, James (Judge)	Vattier court case	28, Apr. 1807	L3
Silvers, John	Horse found	1, Dec. 1812	L4
Simpson, Alexander	Letter at P.O.	1, Jan. 1812	L3
Simpson, Samuel	Deserter from army	13, Oct. 1812	L2
Simpson, Samuel	Debt relief	5, Feb. 1835	L3
Sims, Hannah	Slave information	30, June 1853	L3
Sinard, William	Horse found	18, Aug. 1812	L2
Sinks, Jacob	Land payment due	22, Nov. 1809	L4
Sizer, Samuel & Mariam	Divorce/Abandonment	27, Feb. 1827	L1
Skalinger, Daniel	Letter at P.O.	1, Jan. 1812	L3
Skillman, Benjamin	Horse found	24, Nov. 1818	L3
Skillman, Eliza Ann	Guardian	14, Feb. 1839	L3
Skillman, Maria	Guardian	14, Feb. 1839	L3
Skillman, Mary	Guardian	14, Feb. 1839	L3
Slayback, Solomon	Horse found	12, Feb. 1812	L3
Sled, Joshua & Winny	Divorce/Abandonment	1, Sept 1806	L3
Sleeth, Robert P.	Debt relief	23, June 1842	L3
Sloan, David	Letter at P.O.	1, Jan. 1812	L3

Name	Type of Notice	Date of Notice	Page
Sloan, William	Horse found	4, Mar. 1815	L1
Sloane, James	Debt relief	21, May 1829	L4
Smalley, Andrew	Horse found	6, Sept 1820	L3
Smally, Daniel	Deserter	6, Sept 1814	L4
Smiley, John	Land payment notice	7, Nov. 1810	L3
Smith, Burrows	Debtor	18, Nov. 1820	L4
Smith, Charles	Horse found	28, Aug. 1811	L3
Smith, Charles J.W.	Debt relief	14, July 1842	L3
Smith, Constantine	Letter at P.O.	1, Jan. 1812	L3
Smith, Edward C.	Guardian	6, Mar. 1856	L3
Smith, Edward C.H.	Guardian	9, July 1857	L3
Smith, Edward G.	Debt relief	1, Aug. 1833	L3
Smith, Elias	Debt relief	1, Aug. 1833	L3
Smith, Elinor	Letter at P.O.	1, Jan. 1812	L3
Smith, Eliza	Letter at P.O.	1, Jan. 1812	L3
Smith, Eliza	Lost child	15, July 1820	L4
Smith, Emma Ann	Guardian	6, Mar. 1856	L3
Smith, Emma Ann	Guardian	10, Sept 1857	L3
Smith, Ephraim	Runaway apprentice	28, Oct. 1820	L3
Smith, Francis	Deserter	18, Jan. 1814	L1
Smith, Frederick & Elizabeth	Divorce/Abandonment	20, Mar. 1856	L3
Smith, George W.	Debt relief	2, June 1807	L2
Smith, Green H.	Debt relief	24, July 1828	L1
Smith, Henry	Rev. War Veteran	13, Aug. 1854	L3
Smith, Hezekiah	Horse found	1, June 1813	L2
Smith, Jacob	Horse found	23, Mar. 1819	L3
Smith, James	Horse found	7, Dec. 1819	L3
Smith, James	Debt relief	21, May 1829	L4
Smith, James F.	Debt relief	1, Aug. 1833	L3
Smith, Jeremiah	Horse found	15, May 1811	L3
Smith, Jerry	Debt relief	21, May 1829	L4
Smith, John	Guardian	6, Sept 1855	L3
Smith, Joseph	Horse found	22, Jan. 1812	L3
Smith, Joseph	Guardian	6, Sept 1855	L3
Smith, Julia S.	Guardian	10, Apr. 1856	L3
Smith, Mary	Letter at P.O.	1, Jan. 1812	L3
Smith, Nathaniel G.	Debt relief	9, Oct. 1828	L3
Smith, Orion F.	Debt relief	4, Aug. 1831	L4
Smith, Robert	Runaway apprentice	3, Jan. 1816	L1
Smith, Roswell W.	Deserter	6, Sept 1814	L4
Smith, Samuel	Debt relief	9, Oct. 1828	L3
Smith, Samuel	Debt relief	5, Feb. 1835	L3
Smith, William	Debt relief	1, Aug. 1833	L3
Smith, William R.	Guardian	10, Apr. 1856	L3
Snider, William	Horse found	14, June 1814	L1
Snively, John	Convict	5, Feb. 1846	L3
Snow, Sally	Run away apprentice	21, Sept 1812	L4
Snyder, John	Debt relief	9, Feb. 1827	L3
Sorter, Absolom	Guardian	9, Aug. 1855	L3
Sorter, Arthur	Guardian	9, Aug. 1855	L3
Southgate, Richard H.	Debt relief	14, July 1842	L3
Sparks, Ann	Letter at P.O.	1, Jan. 1812	L3
Sparks, John	Deserter	13, Jan. 1817	L3
Sparks, Kesiah	Guardian	22, June 1837	L3

Name	Type of Notice	Date of Notice	Page
Sparks, Martha	Guardian	22, June 1837	L3
Sparks, Martha	Guardian	5, Sept 1839	L3
Sparks, William	Horse found	25, May 1813	L1
Speaker, Betsey	Letter at P.O.	1, Jan. 1812	L3
Speaker, John	Horse found	26, Dec. 1810	L3
Spears, William & Mary Ann	Divorce/Abandonment	19, Feb. 1846	L3
Speer, William & Mary Ann	Divorce/Abandonment	3, July 1815	L3
Spelger, Francis J.	Guardian	5, Feb. 1857	L3
Spencer, Ezra	Debt relief	30, Aug. 1809	L2
Spencer, Ezra	Horse found	21, Aug. 1811	L3
Spencer, Ezra (Rev)	Letter at P.O.	1, Jan. 1812	L3
Spencer, Henry E.	Debt relief	14, July 1842	L3
Spencer, Samuel	Horse lost	4, Sept 1815	L1
Sperry, Truman	Debt relief	1, Aug. 1833	L3
Spiller, Jacob	Land payment notice	7, Nov. 1810	L3
St.Clair, Arthur, Jr.	Vattier court case	28, Apr. 1807	L3
St.Clair, Belfore	Guardian	3, Nov. 1831	L4
St.Clair, Francis	Guardian	11, July 1833	L3
St.Clair, Hester	Guardian	11, July 1833	L3
St.Clair, Jane	Guardian	11, July 1833	L3
St.Clair, Juliette	Guardian	11, July 1833	L3
St.Clair, Laura	Guardian	3, Nov. 1831	L4
St.Clair, Nancy	Guardian	11, July 1833	L3
St.Clair, Rebecca	Guardian	11, July 1833	L3
Stailey, Samuel	Debt relief	17, Nov. 1842	L5
Staley, Jacob	Debt relief	1, Aug. 1833	L3
Staley, John L.	Debt relief	1, Aug. 1833	L3
Stall, Edward	Guardian	8, Nov. 1832	L4
Stall, Frances	Guardian	8, Nov. 1832	L4
Stall, Lewis	Guardian	14, Feb. 1839	L3
Stallo, John M.	Guardian	14, Feb. 1839	L3
Stallo, Mary Ann	Guardian	14, Feb. 1839	L3
Stallo, Theodore	Guardian	14, Feb. 1839	L3
Stallo, Theresea	Guardian	14, Feb. 1839	L3
Stanberry, John S.	Debt relief	17, Nov. 1842	L5
Stanford, Hira	Debt relief	9, Feb. 1827	L3
Stanislaus, Cornelius G.	Guardian	10, Apr. 1856	L3
Stanley, Benjamin	Hughes High School	2, Feb. 1854	L3
Starling, Sarah	Horse found	5, June 1815	L3
Starr, Orange B.	Debt relief	4, Aug. 1831	L4
Stars, John	Debtor	27, Nov. 1822	L3
Statelare, George	Letter at P.O.	1, Jan. 1812	L3
Steel, William	Land payment notice	7, Nov. 1810	L3
Steinman, Frederick & Mary	Divorce/Abandonment	28, Aug. 1845	L3
Stephen, John	Debt relief	17, Oct. 1839	L3
Stephen, Richard	Land payment notice	7, Nov. 1810	L3
Stephens, Ann	Guardian	8, Nov. 1832	L4
Stephens, Benjamin M.	Horse found	20, Oct. 1812	L2
Stephens, Ellis	Debt relief	9, June 1831	L3
Stephens, Francis	Letter at P.O.	1, Jan. 1812	L3
Stephens, James	Debt relief	24, July 1828	L1
Stephens, John	Guardian	8, Nov. 1832	L4
Stephens, Joseph	Debt relief	5, Feb. 1835	L3
Stevens, Amos	Horse found	7, Oct. 1816	L1

Name	Type of Notice	Date of Notice	Page
Stevens, Ann	Guardian	9, Aug. 1838	L3
Stevens, Henry	Debt relief	14, July 1842	L3
Stevens, John	Guardian	9, Aug. 1838	L3
Stevens, Richard	Debt relief	18, Aug. 1826	L3
Stevens, Richard	Debt relief	28, Jan. 1830	L3
Stevenson, Stephen	Letter at P.O.	1, Jan. 1812	L3
Steward, Jacob	Letter at P.O.	1, Jan. 1812	L3
Stewart, Alexander	Debt relief	9, June 1831	L3
Stewart, David	Horse found	16, Dec. 1816	L4
Stewart, John	Land payment due	22, Nov. 1809	L4
Stewart, Joseph	Debt relief	9, Oct. 1828	L3
Stewart, Margaret	Guardian	7, Feb. 1856	L3
Stewart, Samuel	Debt relief	9, June 1831	L3
Stewart, Thomas	Horse found	22, Dec. 1812	L3
Stewart, William	Horse found	4, Jan. 1814	L4
Stites, Hezekiah	Horse found	9, Aug. 1814	L3
Stitt, William	Horse found	14, July 1812	L3
Stockton, Jesse	Horse found	26, July 1814	L3
Stokes, James	Escaped convict	12, June 1828	L3
Stokes, Thomas	Deserter	24, Aug. 1813	L2
Stoncifter, John & Ann	Divorce/Abandonment	20, Nov. 1814	L2
Stone, E.	Cow found	26, Dec. 1821	L3
Stone, Ethan	Fire at his stable	25, Apr. 1810	L3
Stone, Leonidas	Guardian	10, Dec. 1857	L3
Stout, Abraham	Horse found	29, Dec. 1812	L2
Stowe, Michael	Horse found	7, Aug. 1811	L4
Stowe, William	Horse found	1, Jan. 1812	L4
Strattion, Si	Convict	5, Feb. 1846	L3
Straught, Aaron D.	Horse found	17, Nov. 1812	L2
Streif, Frederick J.	Guardian	4, June 1857	L3
Strom, Michael	Horse found	16, Aug. 1814	L3
Strome, Michael	Horse found	26, Sept 1810	L3
Stuart, James	Horse found	4, July 1810	L3
Stuart, William	Deserter	18, Jan. 1814	L1
Stubbe, Maria	Guardian	6, Aug. 1857	L3
Stubbs, Thomas & Phoebe	Divorce/Abandonment	4, Dec. 1828	L3
Sulivant, Henry	Letter at P.O.	1, Jan. 1812	L3
Sullivan, George	Letter at P.O.	1, Jan. 1812	L3
Sullivan, Henry	Horse found	25, Sept 1815	L2
Sullivan, Henry	Debt relief	8, June 1827	L4
Summons, J. & ----	Divorce/Abandonment	13, Nov. 1850	L3
Sunderland, Francis	Horse found	11, Apr. 1810	L2
Sutton, Benjamin	Horse found	11, Mar. 1816	L3
Sutton, Stephen	Horse found	15, Jan. 1816	L1
Sutton, Tingley	Debt relief	28, Jan. 1830	L3
Swails, Isaac & Charlotte	Divorce/Abandonment	14, July 1817	L3
Swails, William	Notice	28, July 1817	L3
Swank, Jacob	Horse found	8, Dec. 1812	L4
Swartz, John	Debt relief	17, Oct. 1839	L3
Swift, Thomas	Horse found	3, Aug. 1813	L3
Swinehart, Adam	Land payment due	22, Nov. 1809	L4
Sykes, John M.	Debt relief	23, June 1842	L3
Symmes, Jeremiah	Land payment notice	7, Nov. 1810	L3
Symmes, John Cleves	Horse lost	28, May 1819	L3

Name	Type of Notice	Date of Notice	Page
Symmes, Timothy	Horse found	27, May 1816	L3
Taber, Ann J.	Guardian	7, Feb. 1856	L3
Talbert, Benjamin	Debt relief	9, Oct. 1828	L3
Talbot, Samuel	Debt relief	1, Aug. 1833	L3
Talbott, George	Horse lost	27, Nov. 1815	L4
Tarrant, Asebion	Debt relief	28, Jan. 1830	L3
Tatman, John	Horse stolen	22, June 1822	L3
Tatspaugh, Robert	Debt relief	18, Aug. 1826	L3
Tatspaw, Margaret	Debt relief	21, May 1829	L4
Taulman, Peter J.	Debt relief	17, Nov. 1842	L5
Taylor, Amanda	Guardian	7, Feb. 1856	L3
Taylor, Isaac N.	Debt relief	14, July 1842	L3
Taylor, Jacob	Horse found	7, June 1814	L4
Taylor, James	Land payment notice	7, Nov. 1810	L3
Taylor, John	Horse found	15, Jan. 1812	L3
Taylor, John	Horse found	8, Feb. 1820	L3
Taylor, John	Convict	5, Feb. 1846	L3
Taylor, John G.	Guardian	7, Feb. 1856	L2
Taylor, Lucinus J.	Debt relief	18, Aug. 1826	L3
Taylor, Robert	Horse found	27, Oct. 1812	L2
Taylor, Robert	Horse found	28, Feb. 1810	L3
Taylor, Sarah	Guardian	7, Feb. 1856	L3
Taylor, William	Guardian	7, Feb. 1856	L3
Tedroe, Isaac	Debt relief	1, Aug. 1833	L3
Templeton, John, Esq.	Letter at P.O.	1, Jan. 1812	L3
Terry, Mary E.	Guardian	8, Jan. 1857	L3
Terry, Robert	Horse found	14, Jan. 1818	L3
Terwilleger, Matthew	Horse found	14, Feb. 1823	L3
Tharp, James	Land payment due	22, Nov. 1809	L4
Tharp, John	Land payment due	22, Nov. 1809	L4
Thistlewaite, Thomas	Hughes High School	2, Feb. 1854	L3
Thomas, Abel J.	Debt relief	14, July 1842	L3
Thomas, Abraham	Land payment notice	7, Nov. 1810	L3
Thomas, Arthur	Land payment due	22, Nov. 1809	L4
Thomas, Christiana	Guardian	7, May 1840	L3
Thomas, Elizabeth	Guardian	7, May 1840	L3
Thomas, Ellen	Guardian	7, May 1840	L3
Thomas, George	Horse found	29, Dec. 1817	L2
Thomas, George	Horse found	11, July 1810	L3
Thomas, George	Horse found	23, Aug. 1814	L3
Thomas, J.	Debt relief	24, July 1828	L1
Thomas, John	Horse found	14, Feb. 1810	L3
Thomas, Josephine	Guardian	7, May 1840	L3
Thomas, Mary Ann	Guardian	7, May 1840	L3
Thomas, Pleasant	Debt relief	21, May 1829	L4
Thomas, Richard	Letter at P.O.	1, Jan. 1812	L3
Thomas, William	Horse found	31, July 1815	L3
Thomas, William	Horse found	8, Feb. 1820	L3
Thomas, William & Delilah	Divorce/Abandonment	12, July 1809	L3
Thompson, Agnes	Guardian	9, Apr. 1857	L3
Thompson, Charles & Elizabeth	Divorce/Abandonment	2, Jan. 1840	L3
Thompson, Cornelius	Debt relief	5, Feb. 1835	L3
Thompson, George	Horse found	30, May 1810	L2

Name	Type of Notice	Date of Notice	Page
Thompson, Goble	Debt relief	1, Aug. 1833	L3
Thompson, James	Horse found	21, Mar. 1810	L3
Thompson, James	Land payment notice	7, Nov. 1810	L3
Thompson, James	Horse found	19, Jan. 1813	L3
Thompson, James	Guardian	9, Apr. 1857	L3
Thompson, James B.	Debt relief	1, Aug. 1833	L3
Thompson, Jesse G.L.	Guardian	10, Jan. 1856	L3
Thompson, John	Debt relief	9, Feb. 1827	L3
Thompson, John	Debt relief	1, Aug. 1833	L3
Thompson, John	Guardian	9, Apr. 1857	L3
Thompson, John & Elizabeth	Divorce/Abandonment	14, July 1807	L2
Thompson, Levi	Guardian	9, July 1857	L3
Thompson, Mary Jane	Guardian	9, Apr. 1857	L3
Thompson, Morris	Hughes High School	2, Feb. 1854	L3
Thompson, Philip C.	Debt relief	5, Feb. 1835	L3
Thompson, Robert	Horse found	3, June 1816	L3
Thompson, Samuel	Horse found	6, May 1816	L3
Thompson, Thomas	Land payment notice	7, Nov. 1810	L3
Thompson, Thomas	Letter at P.O.	1, Jan. 1812	L3
Thompson, William	Horse found	5, July 1814	L2
Thompson, William	Horse found	15, Dec. 1818	L3
Thorn, Samuel	Letter at P.O.	1, Jan. 1812	L3
Thornton, George	Escaped convict	12, June 1828	L3
Thorp, Henry	Debt relief	5, Feb. 1835	L3
Thorp, Mark W.	Debt relief	28, Jan. 1830	L3
Thorp, Nathan	Horse found	3, Mar. 1820	L3
Thrasher, Joseph	Runaway apprentice	9, Sept 1816	L3
Throckmorton, Phillip	Debt relief	1, Aug. 1833	L3
Thurman, Narcissa	Inquiry	3, Nov. 1817	L1
Thurston, David	Debt relief	8, June 1827	L4
Tibles, John	Deserter	9, June 1817	L4
Tietfort, Abraham	Horse found	26, Dec. 1810	L3
Tillotson, Joseph	Horse found	15, Dec. 1817	L4
Tilton, Thomas	Debt relief	11, Nov. 1825	L3
Tindel, Robert A.	Debt relief	9, Feb. 1827	L3
Tolen, William	Horse found	13, Oct. 1812	L2
Tomkins, James	Debt relief	1, Aug. 1833	L3
Tomlinson, Louisa J.	Guardian	10, Dec. 1857	L3
Tomlinson, Sarah L.	Guardian	10, Dec. 1857	L3
Tompkins, James	Debt relief	23, June 1842	L3
Toole, James	Inquiry	10, May 1822	L4
Torrence, John S. & Phebe	Divorce/Abandonment	2, Apr. 1805	L2
Torrence, Samuel	Horse found	4, Jan. 1814	L3
Torrons, Samuel	Horse found	17, June 1816	L3
Townsend, John	Horse found	3, Aug. 1819	L3
Townsend, Samuel	Letter at P.O.	1, Jan. 1812	L3
Townsley, Robert	Horse found	9, Jan. 1811	L1
Townsley, Robert	Horse found	20, June 1810	L3
Townsley, William	Horse found	27, June 1810	L2
Tracy, Ann Maria	Guardian	25, Jan. 1838	L3
Tracy, Oliver P.	Guardian	25, Jan. 1838	L3
Trisler, Michael & Rachael	Divorce/Abandonment	27, Mar. 1845	L3
Trucks, John P.	Debt relief	17, Oct. 1839	L3
Trumbul, Jacob	Letter at P.O.	1, Jan. 1812	L3

Name	Type of Notice	Date of Notice	Page
Tubs, Cyrus	Horse found	9, Aug. 1814	L1
Tucker, Alfred	Guardian	16, Oct. 1856	L6
Tucker, Alfred W.	Guardian	5, Mar. 1857	L3
Tucker, Ephraim & Hannah	Divorce/Abandonment	7, Sept 1813	L2
Tucker, Martha A.	Guardian	16, Oct. 1856	L6
Tucker, Stephen	Horse found	28, Feb. 1810	L3
Tunstall, John O.	Deserter from army	3, Nov. 1812	L3
Tussey, William & Louisa	Divorce/Abandonment	24, Mar. 1853	L3
Tutin, Elizabeth	Guardian	6, Mar. 1856	L3
Tuttle, Turell	Debt relief	1, Aug. 1833	L3
Tuttle, William (Capt)	Letter at P.O.	1, Jan. 1812	L3
Twitchel, John	Debt relief	28, Jan. 1830	L3
Unterreiner, Amelia	Guardian	14, Aug. 1856	L6
Unterreiner, Caroline	Guardian	14, Aug. 1856	L6
Unterreiner, Elizabeth	Guardian	14, Aug. 1856	L6
Unterreiner, Paul	Guardian	14, Aug. 1856	L6
Upinghouse, Henry	Letter at P.O.	1, Jan. 1812	L3
Uppenhausen, Frederick	Run away child	7, July 1812	L2
Uppenhausen, Hendrick	Notice	7, July 1812	L2
Vail, Isaa	Horse found	23, June 1817	L3
Vail, Moses	Land payment notice	7, Nov. 1810	L3
Valentine, James	Guardian	16, Oct. 1856	L6
Valentine, Louise	Guardian	16, Oct. 1856	L6
VanCamp, Abraham	Debt relief	17, Oct. 1839	L3
VanCamp, Moses	Land payment due	22, Nov. 1809	L4
Vance, Alexander, Sen.	Debt relief	17, Nov. 1842	L5
Vandevort, Jonah	Vattier court case	28, Apr. 1807	L3
Vandike, Henry	Horse found	14, Oct. 1820	L3
VanDike, John	Runaway apprentice	25, Feb. 1815	L3
VanDoren, J. Livingston	Debt relief	23, June 1842	L3
Vandyke, Andrew E.	Debtor	19, May 1821	L3
VanEaton, Isaac	Horse found	24, Apr. 1811	L2
Vanhorn, John	Debt relief	24, July 1828	L1
Vanhorne, Joseph	Letter at P.O.	1, Jan. 1812	L3
VanMeter, Henry	Horse found	10, July 1811	L1
VanMiddlesworth, Tunis	Horse found	2, June 1831	L3
VanSandt, Nancy A.	Guardian	3, May 1855	L3
VanSickle, Andrew	Horse found	27, Sept 1814	L3
Vansickle, Henry L.	Guardian	10, Apr. 1856	L3
Vantilburgh, John	Horse found	31, Jan. 1810	L4
Vanzandt, Sabrean	Guardian	10, Dec. 1857	L3
Vattier, Charles	Vattier court case	28, Apr. 1807	L3
Vattorne, Isaac, Jr.	Letter at P.O.	1, Jan. 1812	L3
Veal, Peter	Horse found	2, Sept 1816	L3
Venetain, Isaac	Letter at P.O.	1, Jan. 1812	L3
Vincent, Joshua	Horse found	31, Jan. 1823	L3
Vincin, Antonelis	Horse found	6, June 1810	L3
Vinton, Lemuel	Debt relief	1, Aug. 1833	L3
Voorhees, Balinda	Guardian	22, June 1837	L3
Voorhees, Jacob	Horse found	7, Aug. 1811	L2
Voorhees, Jacob	Guardian	22, June 1837	L3
Voorhees, William	Guardian	22, June 1837	L3

Name	Type of Notice	Date of Notice	Page
Vorhees, Mary Ann	Guardian	5, Sept 1839	L3
Vorhees, Ralph	Guardian	5, Sept 1839	L3
Vorris, John J.	Debt relief	4, Aug. 1831	L4
Wadley, Thomas	Horse found	14, July 1817	L3
Waggoner, Benjamin	Debt relief	1, Aug. 1833	L3
Waggoner, George	Debt relief	24, July 1828	L1
Walburn, John	Horse found	27, Nov. 1811	L3
Walden, John	Runaway apprentice	14, Aug. 1811	L4
Waldron, Hannah	Guardian	26, Apr. 1832	L3
Walker, Alexander & Tabitha	Divorce/Abandonment	5, Feb. 1812	L3
Walker, Caroline O.	Guardian	5, Feb. 1857	L3
Walker, Christopher	Horse lost	27, Oct. 1817	L3
Walker, David	Letter at P.O.	1, Jan. 1812	L3
Walker, David	Deserter	29, June 1813	L3
Walker, James	Horse found	25, May 1813	L1
Walker, James	Horse found	2, May 1810	L3
Walker, Joseph	Cow lost	2, July 1819	L3
Walker, Peter B.	Guardian	4, June 1857	L3
Walker, Robert	Debt relief	11, Nov. 1825	L3
Walker, Wesley B.	Guardian	4, June 1857	L3
Walker, William	Debt relief	1, Aug. 1833	L3
Wallace, George T.	Debt relief	9, June 1831	L3
Wallace, Matthew G. (Rev)	Letter at P.O.	1, Jan. 1812	L3
Wallace, Robert	Horse found	16, July 1819	L1
Wallace, Thomas	Horse found	11, Dec. 1811	L4
Wallace, William	Letter at P.O.	1, Jan. 1812	L3
Walton, Nathan	Debt relief	5, Feb. 1835	L3
Walton, Wade H.	Debt relief	1, Aug. 1833	L3
Walton, Wade H.	Debt relief	1, Aug. 1833	L3
Ward, Amos & Elizabeth	Divorce/Abandonment	19, Aug. 1816	L3
Ward, Nathan	Deserter	6, Sept 1814	L4
Ward, Richard	Deserter	6, Sept 1814	L4
Ward, Samuel	Deserter from army	10, Nov. 1812	L2
Ward, Squire	Horse found	5, July 1814	L3
Ward, Thomas	Debt relief	9, Oct. 1828	L3
Ward, William	Land payment notice	7, Nov. 1810	L3
Ware, Peter	Debt relief	5, Feb. 1835	L3
Waren, Reuben	Debtor	20, Sept 1827	L3
Warnam, John	Deserter from army	27, May 1812	L3
Warren, John	Debt relief	11, Nov. 1825	L3
Washburn, Alvan	Debt relief	9, Oct. 1828	L3
Washburn, Jabez	Debt relief	9, Oct. 1828	L3
Wassell, John	Deserter	24, Nov. 1817	L3
Waters, Samuel	Debt relief	17, Oct. 1839	L3
Watson, Archibald	Inquiry	26, July 1827	L3
Watson, David & Agness	Divorce/Abandonment	12, Mar. 1819	L3
Watson, Hezekiah A.	Debt relief	1, Aug. 1833	L3
Watson, John	Debt relief	24, July 1828	L1
Watson, Zedekiah	Horse found	8, Dec. 1812	L1
Way, Joshua & Eliza	Divorce/Abandonment	20, Apr. 1822	L3
Wayland, Hannah	Letter at P.O.	1, Jan. 1812	L3
Weatherby, Danforth	Horse found	23, Oct. 1811	L4
Weaver, Daniel	Debt relief	5, Feb. 1835	L3

Name	Type of Notice	Date of Notice	Page
Weaver, Jacob	Debt relief	18, Aug. 1826	L3
Webb, George	Debt relief	9, Feb. 1827	L3
Webb, John	Debt relief	1, Aug. 1833	L3
Webb, Phebe Ann	Guardian	3, Sept 1840	L3
Webber, Ann	Guardian	7, May 1840	L3
Webber, Ann M.	Guardian	18, Apr. 1839	L3
Webber, Benjamin	Guardian	18, Apr. 1839	L3
Webber, Benjamin	Guardian	7, May 1840	L3
Webber, Julia	Guardian	18, Apr. 1839	L3
Webber, Julia	Guardian	7, May 1840	L3
Webber, Mary L.	Guardian	18, Apr. 1839	L3
Weber, D. & Catharine	Divorce/Abandonment	28, Aug. 1822	L3
Webster, Isaac H. & Nancy	Divorce/Abandonment	17, Nov. 1836	L3
Weingartner, Adeline	Guardian	5, Feb. 1857	L3
Weingartner, Louisa	Guardian	5, Feb. 1857	L3
Weingartner, Pius	Guardian	5, Feb. 1857	L3
Weingartner, Theodore	Guardian	5, Feb. 1857	L3
Weise, Joseph	Guardian	6, Aug. 1857	L3
Weise, Mary	Guardian	6, Aug. 1857	L3
Welch, Benjamin & Alley	Divorce/Abandonment	16, June 1807	L3
Welch, William	Horse found	28, Aug. 1811	L3
Welden, Elias	Debt relief	17, Oct. 1839	L3
Welden, John C.	Debt relief	17, Oct. 1839	L3
Wellar, James M.	Debt relief	1, Aug. 1833	L3
Wellman, F.H.	Guardian	16, Oct. 1856	L6
Wellman, Frederick	Guardian	16, Oct. 1856	L6
Wells, John	Horse found	26, May 1817	L3
Wells, John & Rachel	Divorce/Abandonment	16, Jan. 1815	L3
Wells, Levi	Horse found	17, Nov. 1817	L3
West, Daniel S.	Debt relief	14, July 1842	L3
West, Franklin	Horse lost	30, June 1817	L3
West, Samuel	Horse lost	23, Mar. 1819	L1
Westbrook, Abraham	Debt relief	22, Aug. 1810	L2
Westcott, John	Debt relief	28, Jan. 1830	L3
Westendorf, Ann	Guardian	6, Dec. 1855	L3
Westendorf, Henry	Guardian	6, Dec. 1855	L3
Westendorf, Joseph	Guardian	6, Dec. 1855	L3
Westendorf, Mary	Guardian	6, Dec. 1855	L3
Westfall, George	Horse found	14, Mar. 1810	L2
Weston, Edmond	Letter at P.O.	1, Jan. 1812	L3
Wetherby, Danforth	Horse found	29, July 1816	L3
Wheeler, Elnathan	Letter at P.O.	1, Jan. 1812	L3
Wheeler, George	Debt relief	18, Aug. 1826	L3
Wheeler, Jacob	Robbed	28, Jan. 1820	L4
Wheeler, Zadoc	Horse found	7, Apr. 1817	L3
Whetstone, Reuben	Letter at P.O.	1, Jan. 1812	L3
Whitaker, John	Horse found	22, Dec. 1812	L3
Whitaker, Margaret	Horse found	10, Aug. 1813	L3
Whitaker, William	Debt relief	14, July 1842	L3
White, Amos	Deserter	18, Jan. 1814	L1
White, David	Horse found	24, Jan. 1810	L4
White, George W.	Debt relief	9, June 1831	L3
White, Jacob	Letter at P.O.	1, Jan. 1812	L3
White, John	Letter at P.O.	1, Jan. 1812	L3

Name	Type of Notice	Date of Notice	Page
White, John A.	Letter at P.O.	1, Jan. 1812	L3
White, John L.	Letter at P.O.	1, Jan. 1812	L3
White, Moses A.	Debt relief	14, July 1842	L3
White, Moses D.	Debt relief	11, Nov. 1825	L3
White, Providence	Horse found	8, July 1820	L2
White, Thomas	Horse found	21, June 1814	L3
Whitefitt, James	Horse found	7, Nov. 1810	L1
Whiteman, Isaac	Horse found	15, Feb. 1814	L3
Whitemore, William & Sarah	Divorce/Abandonment	3, Nov. 1817	L3
Whitmore, Julius	Debt relief	18, Aug. 1826	L3
Whorton, John	Horse found	23, Jan. 1811	L1
Wiatt, Carey	Debtor	11, Feb. 1820	L3
Wiatt, Cary	Debt relief	11, Nov. 1825	L3
Wildey, William D.	Guardian	10, Dec. 1857	L3
Wile, Henry	Letter at P.O.	1, Jan. 1812	L3
Wile, Michael	Horse found	8, Nov. 1814	L1
Wiley, William	Runaway apprentice	21, Jan. 1818	L3
Wilkinson, Anguis	Letter at P.O.	1, Jan. 1812	L3
Wilkinson, Leah	Letter at P.O.	1, Jan. 1812	L3
Wilkinson, William	Debt relief	28, Jan. 1830	L3
Willard, Henry & Rebecca	Divorce/Abandonment	13, Feb. 1827	L3
Willey, Israel	Horse found	20, Feb. 1811	L3
Willey, William	Runaway apprentice	29, Jan. 1816	L3
Williams, Ann L.	Guardian	6, Aug. 1857	L3
Williams, B.T.	Guardian	10, Jan. 1856	L3
Williams, Catharine	Guardian	9, Aug. 1838	L3
Williams, Catharine	Guardian	3, Sept 1840	L3
Williams, Catharine J.	Guardian	7, June 1855	L3
Williams, Charles	Guardian	9, July 1857	L3
Williams, Columbus	Guardian	19, Dec. 1826	L3
Williams, David G.	Debt relief	14, July 1842	L3
Williams, Elmore	Land payment due	22, Nov. 1809	L4
Williams, Euretta	Guardian	9, Aug. 1838	L3
Williams, Euretta	Guardian	3, Sept 1840	L3
Williams, F.B.	Guardian	9, Aug. 1838	L3
Williams, Francis B.	Guardian	3, Sept 1840	L3
Williams, Jacob	Land payment due	22, Nov. 1809	L4
Williams, Jasper	Hughes High School	2, Feb. 1854	L3
Williams, Jesse	Debt relief	1, Aug. 1833	L3
Williams, John	Debt relief	24, July 1828	L1
Williams, John	Debt relief	1, Aug. 1833	L3
Williams, John & Anna	Divorce/Abandonment	7, July 1806	L3
Williams, John & Anna	Divorce/Abandonment	21, July 1807	L3
Williams, Joshua	Vattier court case	28, Apr. 1807	L3
Williams, Levi	Debt relief	9, June 1831	L3
Williams, Michael	Debt relief	5, Feb. 1835	L3
Williams, Pliny Bliss	Guardian	8, Oct. 1857	L3
Williams, Remembrance	Horse found	7, Aug. 1811	L4
Williams, Richard & Christine	Divorce/Abandonment	8, Sept 1817	L3
Williams, William & Catharine	Divorce/Abandonment	11, Feb. 1836	L4
Williamson, Abraham	Debt relief	4, Aug. 1831	L4
Williamson, Stephen	Horse found	9, June 1817	L4
Willis, Alexander F.	Debt relief	1, Aug. 1833	L3
Willis, Charles	Debt relief	9, Oct. 1828	L3

Name	Type of Notice	Date of Notice	Page
Willis, William	Horse lost	8, July 1816	L1
Wilson, Adam	Convict	5, Feb. 1846	L3
Wilson, Arthur	Letter at P.O.	1, Jan. 1812	L3
Wilson, Ebenezer & Elizabeth	Divorce/Abandonment	24, Feb. 1817	L4
Wilson, Elizabeth	Letter at P.O.	1, Jan. 1812	L3
Wilson, Henry	Hughes High School	2, Feb. 1854	L3
Wilson, James	Deserter	9, June 1817	L2
Wilson, James	Land payment notice	7, Nov. 1810	L3
Wilson, James	Letter at P.O.	1, Jan. 1812	L3
Wilson, John	Cow found	18, July 1810	L2
Wilson, John	Horse found	18, Mar. 1812	L2
Wilson, John	Horse found	18, Aug. 1812	L2
Wilson, John	Horse found	16, June 1812	L3
Wilson, John	Horse lost	15, Dec. 1812	L3
Wilson, John H.	Debt relief	14, July 1842	L3
Wilson, Mary Ann	Guardian	3, May 1855	L3
Wilson, Samuel	Horse found	5, July 1814	L1
Wilson, Sarah	Guardian	13, Feb. 1840	L3
Wilson, Sarah A.	Guardian	3, Sept 1840	L3
Wilson, Sarah Ann	Guardian	9, Aug. 1838	L3
Wilson, William	Land payment notice	7, Nov. 1810	L3
Wilson, William	Guardian	13, Feb. 1840	L3
Wilson, William	Debt relief	4, Aug. 1831	L4
Winslow, Job	Debt relief	9, June 1831	L3
Winston, John P.	Debt relief	14, July 1842	L3
Winters, Amos	Horse found	15, Dec. 1818	L3
Winters, James	Deserter	29, Mar. 1814	L1
Winters, John	Deserter	29, Mar. 1814	L1
Winters, John	Debt relief	17, Nov. 1842	L5
Winters, Joseph	Debt relief	9, June 1831	L3
Winton, Banks	Debt relief	28, Jan. 1830	L3
Winton, Banks	Horse found	25, Jan. 1814	L4
Winton, Elijah & Mealy	Divorce/Abandonment	6, Oct. 1818	L3
Wise, Henry	Horse found	25, Dec. 1811	L1
Wiseman, Margaret Jane	Guardian	23, Nov. 1837	L3
Witham, Gideon	Horse found	7, Sept 1813	L2
Witham, Nathaniel	Horse found	12, June 1811	L1
Withrow, John	Horse found	18, Dec. 1811	L3
Witman, Samuel	Debt relief	1, Aug. 1833	L3
Witt, Orange	Debt relief	21, May 1829	L4
Witter, Samuel	Horse found	12, Dec. 1810	L3
Wohlfry, Michael	Horse found	24, Aug. 1813	L3
Wolf, Barbara	Guardian	4, Sept 1856	L5
Wolf, Elizabeth	Guardian	4, Sept 1856	L5
Wolf, John	Guardian	4, Sept 1856	L5
Wolverton, Charles	Horse found	4, Apr. 1810	L2
Womble, John	Inquiry	21, Feb. 1828	L3
Wood, Harriet	Guardian	22, June 1837	L3
Wood, Harriet	Guardian	18, Apr. 1839	L3
Wood, James E.	Swindler	7, Feb. 1828	L1
Wood, Joseph	Horse found	28, Nov. 1810	L3
Wood, William (Rev)	Letter at P.O.	1, Jan. 1812	L3
Wood, William R.	Guardian	10, Jan. 1856	L3
Woodbury, Phineas C.	Guardian	6, Sept 1855	L3

Name	Type of Notice	Date of Notice	Page
Woodrow, David T.	Debt relief	23, June 1842	L3
Woodruff, Dennis	Letter at P.O.	1, Jan. 1812	L3
Woodruff, Hezekiah	Guardian	10, Apr. 1856	L3
Woodruff, Hezekiah	Guardian	7, May 1857	L3
Woodruff, Israel	Horse found	7, Nov. 1810	L2
Woodruff, Mary S.	Guardian	10, Apr. 1856	L3
Woodruff, Mary S.	Guardian	7, May 1857	L3
Woodruff, Nathaniel	Horse found	21, Dec. 1813	L1
Woodruff, Nathaniel	Debt relief	18, Aug. 1826	L3
Woodruff, Seth	Debt relief	9, Feb. 1827	L3
Woodruff, Truman	Debt relief	14, July 1842	L3
Woodruffe, John Allen	Inquiry	27, Apr. 1848	L3
Woods, Allen	Horse found	22, Apr. 1812	L4
Woods, Samuel	Horse found	2, June 1812	L2
Woodward, William	Letter at P.O.	1, Jan. 1812	L3
Woodward, William H.	Debt relief	21, May 1829	L4
Woodworth, Daniel	Horse found	5, June 1811	L1
Woodworth, Daniel	Horse found	14, Mar. 1810	L2
Woody, Adam	Debt relief	1, Aug. 1833	L3
Wooley, Eveline	Guardian	7, Feb. 1856	L3
Wooley, Eveline	Guardian	5, Mar. 1857	L3
Wooley, George	Guardian	7, Feb. 1856	L3
Wooley, George	Guardian	5, Mar. 1857	L3
Wooley, Jane	Guardian	7, Feb. 1856	L3
Wooley, Jane	Guardian	5, Mar. 1857	L3
Wooley, William D.	Guardian	7, Feb. 1856	L3
Wooley, William D.	Guardian	5, Mar. 1857	L3
Woolly, Asht	Debt relief	24, July 1828	L1
Woolverton, Daniel	Horse found	9, June 1812	L3
Works, Joseph	Deserter	18, Oct. 1814	L3
Wormsley, William	Horse found	20, Oct. 1817	L3
Wright, Crafts J.	Debt relief	17, Nov. 1842	L5
Wright, Daniel S.	Debt relief	9, June 1831	L3
Wright, John	Letter at P.O.	1, Jan. 1812	L3
Wright, Loyd	Debt relief	1, Aug. 1833	L3
Wright, Maria	Letter at P.O.	1, Jan. 1812	L3
Wright, Sylvanus	Debt relief	23, June 1842	L3
Wright, William C. & Anna J	Divorce/Abandonment	22, Jan. 1857	L3
Wunder, Daniel S.	Debt relief	23, June 1842	L3
Wyatt, Joseph	Debt relief	11, Nov. 1825	L3
Wynkly, Joseph	Letter at P.O.	1, Jan. 1812	L3
Yeakele, Michael	Horse found	8, Jan. 1812	L3
Yeatman, William T.	Debt relief	17, Nov. 1842	L5
Yost, James W.	Debt relief	4, Aug. 1831	L4
Youart, Samuel	Horse lost	15, May 1811	L3
Young, Alexander	Horse found	15, Sept 1812	L2
Young, George	Debt relief	1, Aug. 1833	L3
Young, Nathaniel	Runaway apprentice	27, May 1818	L3
Young, Samuel	Letter at P.O.	1, Jan. 1812	L3
Young, Silas	Debt relief	1, Aug. 1833	L3
Yount, Henry	Land payment notice	7, Nov. 1810	L3
Youtsey, Peter	Land payment due	22, Nov. 1809	L4